ENCYCLOPEDIA OF
FEMINIST THEORIES

ENCYCLOPEDIA OF FEMINIST THEORIES

Edited by
Lorraine Code

London and New York

First published 2000
by Routledge
11 New Fetter Lane, London EC4P 4EE

Simultaneously published in the USA and Canada
by Routledge
29 West 35th Street, New York, NY 10001

Routledge is an imprint of the Taylor & Francis Group

© 2000 Routledge

Typeset in Sabon by Taylor & Francis Books Ltd
Printed and bound in Great Britain by TJ International Ltd, Padstow,
Cornwall

British Library Cataloguing in Publication Data
A catalogue record for this book is available from the British Library

Library of Congress Cataloging in Publication Data
Encyclopedia of feminist theories / edited by Lorraine Code.
p. cm.
Includes bibliographical references and index.
1. Feminist theory – Encyclopedias. I. Code, Lorraine.
HQ1190.E63 2000
305.42'03–dc21   99-087342

ISBN 0–415–13274–6

Contents

Editorial Board

General editor

Lorraine Code
York University, Canada

Consultant editors

Lynda Birke
University of Warwick, UK

Sarah Franklin
University of Lancaster, UK

Judith Grant
University of Southern California, USA

Regina Graycar
University of Sydney, Australia

Penny Harvey
University of Manchester, UK

Stanlie James
University of Wisconsin-Madison, USA

Ruth-Ellen Joeres
University of Minnesota, USA

Linda Lopez McAlister
University of South Florida, USA

Pat Mellencamp
University of Wisconsin-Madison, USA

Chandra Mohanty
Hamilton College, USA

Beverley Skeggs
University of Lancaster, UK

List of Contributors

Sharon McIrvin Abu-Laban
University of Alberta, Canada

Yasmeen Abu-Laban
University of Alberta, Canada

Alison Adam
UMIST, UK

Sara Ahmed
Lancaster University, UK

Julie M. Albright
University of Southern California, Los Angeles, USA

Linda Martín Alcoff
Syracuse University, USA

M. Jacqui Alexander
Connecticut College, USA

Lynne Alice
Massey University, New Zealand

Linda Anderson
University of Newcastle upon Tyne, UK

Lucie Armitt
University of Wales, Bangor, UK

Allison Assiter
University of Luton, UK

Margaret Atherton
University of Wisconsin-Milwaukee, USA

Alison Bailey
Illinois State University, USA

Mieke Bal
University of Amsterdam, Netherlands

Bat-Ami Bar On
SUNY at Binghampton, USA

Karen Barad
Mount Holyoke College, MA, USA

Drucilla K. Barker
Hollins University, Roanoke, USA

Suzanne Barnard
Duquesne University, USA

Margaret Beetham
Manchester Metropolitan University, UK

Shannon Bell
York University, Canada

Susan Best
University of Technology, Sydney, Australia

Davina Bhandar
York University, Canada

Lynda Birke
Llangollen, Wales, UK

Anne Bloom
Trial Lawyers for Public Justice, USA

Susan Bordo
University of Kentucky, USA

Peta Bowden
Murdoch University, Australia

Gloria Bowles
Berkeley, CA, USA

Marilyn J. Boxer
San Francisco State University, USA

Patricia Bradshaw
York University, Canada

Rose Brewer
University of Minneapolis, USA

Janine Brodie
University of Alberta, Canada

Somer Brodribb
University of Victoria, Canada

Sue Broomhall
University of Western Australia, Australia

Heloise Brown
University of York, UK

Erica Burman
Manchester Metropolitican University, UK

Sandra Burt
University of Waterloo, Canada

Leone Burton
University of Birmingham, UK

Heather Campbell
York University, Canada

Marie Campbell
University of Victoria, Canada

Katie Cannon
Temple University, USA

Claudia Card
University of Wisconsin-Madison, USA

Cynthia Carter
Cardiff University, UK

Virginia Cawagas
University of Alberta, Canada

Satinder K. Chohan
London, UK

Donna M. Chovanec
Edmonton, Canada

Carol P. Christ
Lesbos, Greece

Lorraine Code
York University, Canada

Eileen M. Condon
Northampton, USA

Nancy Cook
York University, Canada

Diana H. Coole
Queen Mary & Westfield College, University of London, UK

Brenda J. Cossman
University of Toronto, Canada

Patricia Crawford
University of Western Australia, Australia

Julia Creet
York University, Canada

Natalie Dandekar
Maryland, USA

Cynthia Daniels
Rutgers University, USA

Udita Das
Jawaharlal Nehru University, India

Victoria Davion
University of Georgia, USA

Kathy Davis
Universiteit Utrecht, Netherlands

Julie Dennis-Hlad
Long Beach, CA, USA

Penelope Deutscher
Australian National University, Australia

Monique Deveaux
Cambridge, MA, USA

Beverley Diamond
York University, Canada

Eva Dobozy
Murdoch University, Australia

Annette Dula
University of Colorado, Boulder, USA

Jacqueline Dumas
Orlando Books Ltd., Canada

Susan Ehrlich
York University, Canada

Patricia M. Evans
York University, Canada

Laila Farah
Southern Illinois University, USA

Susan A. Farrell
Kingsborough Community College, CUNY, USA

Kathy Ferguson
University of Hawaii, USA

Susanna F. Ferlito
University of Minnesota, Twin Cities, USA

Robyn Ferrell
Macquarie University, Australia

Gloria Filax
Alberta, Canada

Sue Fisher
Wesleyan University, USA

Marie Fleming
University of Western Ontario, Canada

Louise Forsyth
University of Saskatchewan, Canada

Sarah Franklin
Lancaster University, UK

Amanda Frisken
SUNY at Stony Brook, USA

Marilyn Frye
Michigan State University, USA

Christina Gabriel
York University, Canada

Ann Garry
California State University, USA

Sara Goering
California State University, USA

Jennifer Gore
University of Newcastle, Australia

Judith Grant
University of Southern California, USA

Breda Gray
Lancaster University, UK

Reg Graycar
University of Sydney, Australia

Joyce Green
University of Regina, Canada

Pauline Greenhill
University of Winnipeg, Canada

Roberta Guerrina
Nottingham Trent University, UK

Margaret Morganroth Gullette
Brandeis University, USA

Michael Hames-Garcia
W Lafayette, IN, USA

Meira Hanson
Hebrew University, Israel

Lois Harder
University of Alberta, Canada

Zainab Haruna
Memorial University of Newfoundland, Canada

Susan Hekman
University of Texas at Arlington, USA

Lisa Heldke
Gustavas Adolphus College, MN, USA

Marsha Henry
University of Warwick, UK

Sarah Lucia Hoagland
Northeastern Illinois University, USA

Jane C. Hood
University of New Mexico, USA

Isabel Hoving
University of Amsterdam, Netherlands

Lynette Hunter
University of Leeds, UK

Suzanne M. Jaeger
York University, Canada

Dawn Jakubowski
Iowa State University, USA

Stanlie M. James
University of Wisconsin-Madison, USA

M.A. James-Guerrero
San Francisco, CA, USA

Morny Joy
University of Calgary, Canada

Rosemary A. Joyce
University of California, Berkeley, USA

Lara Karaian
York University, Canada

Catherine Keller
Drew University, USA

Jennifer Kelly
Alberta, Canada

Tessa Kelly
Norfolk, UK

Sarah Kember
Goldsmiths College, UK

Rosanne Kennedy
Australian National University, Australia

Celia Kitzinger
Loughborough University, UK

Christine Koggel
Bryn Mawr College, USA

Monica Konrad
Goldsmiths College, University of London, UK

Carolyn Korsmeyer
SUNY at Buffalo, USA

Julia Krane
McGill University, Canada

Susan Kress
Skidmore College, NY, USA

Sonia Kruks
Oberlin College, OH, USA

Petra Kuppers
Manchester Metropolitan University, UK

Kathleen S. Kurtz
Syracuse University, USA

Molly Ladd-Taylor
York University, Canada

Susan Laird
University of Oklahoma, USA

Estella Lauter
University of Wisconsin/Oshkosh, USA

Mary Jeanne Larrabee
DePaul University, USA

Lizzetta LeFalle-Collins
Oakland, CA, USA

Nancy Lewis
Toronto, Canada

Ngaire Lewis
University of Western Australia, Australia

Antje Lindenmeyer
University of Warwick, UK

Jane Long
University of Western Australia, Australia

Judith Lorber
City University of New York, USA

Susanne Luhmann
York Unversity, Canada

Fiona MacCool
Toronto, Canada

Amie A. Macdonald
City University of New York, USA

Kathleen Mack
Flinders University of South Australia, Australia

Nancy Mandell
York University, Canada

Jeanne Marecek
Swarthmore College, PA, USA

Jane Roland Martin
Cambridge, MA, USA

Joan Mason-Grant
King's College/University of Western Ontario, Canada

Cynthia Mathieson
Mount Saint Vincent University, Canada

Jessica Maynard
University of Wales, Bangor, UK

Harriette Pipes McAdoo
Michigan State University, USA

Susan McClary
University of California at Los Angeles, USA

Linda McDowell
London School of Economics, UK

Bonnie McElhinny
University of Toronto, Canada

Patrick McGann
George Washington University, USA

Kathryn McPherson
York University, Canada

Brinda J. Mehta
Mills College, CA, USA

Kate Mehuron
Eastern Michigan University, USA

Lynn Meskell
Columbia University, USA

Angelica Michelis
Manchester Metropolitan University, UK

Angela Miles
Ontario Institute for Studies in Education, Canada

Jenni Millbank
University of Sydney, Australia

Patricia H. Miller
University of Florida, USA

Haideh Moghissi
York University, Canada

Julianne Momirov
Brock University, Canada

Sharon Murphy
University College Cork, Ireland

Nima Naghibi
University of Alberta, Canada

Kate Nash
Goldsmith's College, University of London, UK

Eva Neumaier-Darugary
University of Alberta, Canada

M. Macha Nightmare
San Rafael, CA, USA

Jean Noble
York University, Canada

Brenda O'Neill
University of Manitoba, Canada

Philomina Okeke
University of Alberta, Canada

Frances Oldale
University of Stirling, Scotland

Collette Oseen
Athabasca University, Alberta, Canada

Michelle K. Owen
University of Toronto, Canada

Laura Parisi
Hollins University, Roanoke, USA

Ilya Parkins
York University, Canada

Kathryn Payne
Toronto, Ontario, Canada

Linda Peake
York University, Canada

Lynne Pearce
Lancaster University, UK

Alan Petersen
Murdoch University, Australia

Elizabeth Philipose
St. Thomas University, Canada

Judith Plaskow
Manhattan College, USA

Val Plumwood
Braidwood, NSW, Australia

Susan L. Prentice
University of Manitoba, Canada

Leslie W. Rabine
University of California, Irvine, USA

Kate Reed
University of Southampton, UK

Sandra Rein
University of Alberta, Canada

Yolanda Retter
Encino, CA, USA

Katherine Rhoades
University of Wisconsin-Eau Claire, USA

Amy Richlin
University of Southern California, USA

Celia Roberts
Sydney, Australia

Karin I. Roberts
University of Washington, USA

Phyllis Rooney
Oakland University, MI, USA

Hilary Rose
City University, London, UK

Kaz Ross
University of Melbourne, Australia

Sue Rosser
Georgia Institute of Technology, Atlanta, GA, USA

Amy Rossiter
York University, Canada

Lori Rowlett
University of Wsconsin-Eau Claire, USA

Lisa Rundle
York University, Canada

Trish Salah
York University, Canada

Catriona Sandilands
York University, Canada

Elizabeth Schüssler Fiorenza
Harvard University, USA

Lynne Segal
Birkbeck College, University of London, UK

Amy Seham
Gustavus Adolphus College, MN, USA

Anne Seller
University of Kent, UK

Jessica J. Senehi
Nova Southeastern University, FL, USA

Charlene Y. Senn
University of Windsor, Canada

Mary Lyndon Shanley
Vassar College, USA

Susan Sherwin
Dalhousie University, Canada

Margrit Shildrick
Staffordshire University, UK

Laurie Shrage
California State Polytechnic University, USA

Margaret A. Simons
Southern Illinois University Edwardsville, USA

Beverley Skeggs
Lancaster University, UK

Jennifer Smith
University of Western Australia, Australia

Malinda S. Smith
Athabasca University, Alberta, Canada

Denise L. Spitzer
University of Alberta, Canada

Judith Squires
University of Bristol, UK

Domna C. Stanton
University of Michigan, USA

Lynne Star
Massey University, New Zealand

Chelsea Starr
University of California, Irvine, USA

Filomena Chioma Steady
University of Wisconsin-Madison, USA

Gail Stenstad
East Tennessee State University, USA

Natalie Stoljar
Monash University, Australia

Cheryl Suzack
University of Alberta, Canada

Jill Mattuck Tarule
University of Vermont, USA

Mariam Thalos
SUNY at Buffalo, USA

Deborah Thom
University of Cambridge, UK

Janet Thumim
University of Bristol, UK

Toh Swee-Hin
University of Alberta, Canada

Rosemarie Tong
The University of North Carolina at Charlotte, NC, USA

Fran Tonkiss
Goldsmiths College, University of London, UK

Nahid Toubia
Research, Action and Information Network for Bodily Integrity of Women, NY, USA

Joyce Trebilcot
Washington University, USA

Nancy Tuana
University of Oregon, USA

Eva Turner
Middlesex University, UK

Mariana Valverde
University of Toronto, Canada

Kamala Visweswaran
University of Texas at Austin, USA

Hilary Wainwright
University of Manchester, UK

Kamala Visweswaran
University of Texas at Austin, USA

Ruth Wallach
University of Southern California, Los Angeles, USA

Wendy Waring
Macquarie University, Australia

Randi R. Warne
Mount St. Vincent University, Canada

Eva Warth
Universiteit Utrecht, Netherlands

Anne Waters
Albuquerque, New Mexico, USA

Chris Weedon
Cardiff University, UK

Gloria Wekker
Universiteit of Utrecht, Netherlands

Kwok Wei Leng
University of Melbourne, Australia

Susan Wendell
Simon Fraser University, Canada

Susan Wennemyr
Yale University, USA

David Wicks
Saint Mary's University, Canada

Shelley Wilcox
University of Colorado at Boulder, USA

Abby Wilkerson
George Washington University, USA

Sue Wilkinson
Loughborough University, UK

Deborah Wills
Mount Allison University, Canada

Alex Wilson
Somerville, MA, USA

Elizabeth A. Wilson
University of Sydney, Australia

Amy Wink
Stephen F. Austin State University, USA

Tamsin Wolff
New York, USA

Yoke-Sum Wong
University of Alberta, Canada

Joanne Wright
University of New Brunswick, Canada

George Yancy
McAnulty Fellow at Duquesne University, USA

Katherine K. Young
McGill University, Canada

Melvina Johnson Young
University of Wisconsin-Madison, USA

Naomi Zack
SUNY at Albany, USA

Marysia Zalewski
Queen's-Belfast, UK

Heather Zwicker
University of Alberta, Canada

Introduction

Defining and classifying

Producing an *Encyclopedia of Feminist Theories* is a challenging project, for the scope and diversity of feminism(s) are wide, their manifestations disparate, complex and changing. Yet the very idea of an encyclopedia assumes a possibility of order and a degree of constancy: of clear, neatly delineated representations of discrete subject matters. Thus to select and fix a terminology that could adequately represent so vitally evolving a set of theories and theorists smacks of that same old authoritarian imposition of mastery and control that feminists of the second wave have worked to resist. Nor can such taxonomies and classifications presume neutrality or innocence, for like all taxonomies they select, and in so doing they exclude. Both inclusions and exclusions speak of hierarchies in an area of theory and practice that has sought to dismantle hierarchies for the violence they enact.

Strikingly, for example, in *Beloved*, Toni Morrison describes a dispute between a white man and a slave over whether the slave's killing and eating a hog counted as theft or, as the slave claimed, as 'improving the Master's property'. 'Clever', Morrison writes, 'but schoolteacher beat him anyway to show him that definitions belong to the definers – not the defined'.[1] The comment points to some of the tensions in which a definitional project such as this one is inextricably caught, as the hitherto defined become definers and authoritative interpreters, while resisting the imperialism and the violence that other defining and interpreting practices have enacted. Should the claim about *women's* position among 'the defined' require further evidence, consider this: the young son of an anti-feminist once challenged

me to guess how many words the *Encyclopedia Brittanica* uses to define 'horse'. 'Thirty-eight', he declared. 'And to define 'woman'? Four', he gleefully announced, 'the female of man'. Despite the fact that his citation appears to be inaccurate, the scenario where this exchange must have been rehearsed, and the support it gives to anti-feminist comments he must have heard, show something of the everyday assumptions of power that attach to encyclopedic definitions.

In similar vein, remarking on the esteem accorded the *Oxford English Dictionary* as a repository of correct usage; noting that standard English embodies relations of power as it speaks in the voice of the cultured, white, urban, heterosexual, European, adult man, muting or drowning out the voices of all the 'Others', Jean-Jacques Lecercle reads the *Dictionary*'s authoritarian position as

> a symptom of anxiety, the anxiety that the oppressed may speak in their turn, that questions may be returned rather than obediently answered, that the possession of linguistic capital may no longer guarantee academic and social success, that women may forget that silence is golden, and Harlem blacks claim their own dialect for a full-fledged version of English.[2]

Throughout feminism's so-called 'second wave', feminist dictionary- and encyclopedia-makers have been doing just that: forgetting that silence is golden, breaking it to affirm innovative and subversive meanings that interrogate the self-certainty and contest the territorial claims of hitherto 'definitive' works. Thus in the Introduction to their 1985 *Feminist Dictionary*, Cheris Kramerae and Paula Treichler remind their readers that 'Whatever their intentions ... dictionaries have functioned as linguistic legislators which perpetuate the stereotypes and prejudices of their writers and editors, who are almost exclusively male'. Fully cognizant of the 'sociopolitical aspects of dictionary-making',[3] their aims are to produce a volume that respects women's self-defining activities, resists the exclusionary moves on which standard dictionaries rely, and puts into circulation the provocative linguistic innovations and interrogations that feminist movements have produced. This *Encyclopedia* endeavours to continue along the path that the *Feminist Dictionary* has opened.

Feminists are wary of classifications/taxonomies, then, not merely as bearers of dogma – of rigidity – but for the judgements of relative worth, the hierarchical ordering powers, the self-certainty of an assumed right to determine the centre and the margins that their makers have consistently, if implicitly, arrogated to themselves. Nowhere is the arrogance of that arrogating more apparent than in an assumption – born of logical positivism and the disinterested, dislocated theories of knowledge it underwrites – that classifications and the reference books, dictionaries, and encyclopedias that assemble them for public 'use' amount merely to neutral, objective recordings of self-announcing data. An assumption pervades both the public imagination and many academic imaginations that classificatory systems would be precisely as they are regardless of who had compiled them or of the circumstances of their production. (The persistence of this belief is apparent in the fact that, in the mid-1990s, it was necessary to make an extensive argument to a national research council that this encyclopedia-making project counted as a worthy candidate for *research* funding – that it would be more than a gathering together of ready-mades.) What amounts to an 'invisible hand' view of dictionary/encyclopedia-making confers upon the products of enterprises such as this an impersonal status that masks their quite specific human provenance. Conservatively considered, the dictionary, and derivatively the encyclopedia and the reference book still, at the beginning of the twenty-first century, count as loci of allegedly disinterested definitional authority, recordings of word usage, meanings, and nuance that offer Archimedean starting points for analysis, disputation, and agreement. Thus a work that announces its political

commitments in its title – an Encyclopedia of Feminist Theories – appears to be oxymoronic in its very conception. Its editors and contributors have therefore to announce their political commitments proudly, to show that politically committed inquiry can generate valuable, responsible scholarly work. These are commitments that the contributors to this project have sought to honour.

There is, according to Michel Foucault, 'no natural taxonomy.'[4] Indeed, Foucault is one of the most provocative and prolific contributors to twentieth-century debates over classification and taxonomy. He demonstrates, especially in his genealogical works, that it would be nothing short of naive to assume that systems of classification evolve silently and impersonally from the world's imprinting itself upon neutral minds, as classical and some modern empiricists have believed. Neither 'everyday' categorizers nor dictionary- and encyclopedia-makers merely 'read' the world and the textual evidence around them. Taxonomies and classificatory schemes are made, not found; and the principles of their making are traceable through interlocking grids of judgements about what counts as knowledge-worthy, issued from socio-historical positions of epistemic (intellectual) authority: classificatory systems sustain and reinforce social-political power structures; they perpetuate hegemonic patterns of expertise and authority.

Stereotypes are the secular version of classifications that take on an undue authority and are intransigent in the face of attempts to gainsay them. Crude devices though they are, they pose as the deliverances of empirical observation to claim an objective accuracy that amounts, instead, to the flimsiness of hasty generalization and illegitimate reductivism. Yet their crudity does not prevent their exerting a stubborn power over the subject matters they claim to encapsulate: they are peculiarly elastic in adjusting to accommodate even the self-consciously resistant, transgressive, creative activities of people they claim to know. Thus women, blacks, Jews, aborigines, the poor, the old and the infirm strive to escape one stereotype only to find themselves slotted into another equally constraining and coercive one. For reasons such as these, both in the everyday world and in the academy, issues of classification, taxonomy, naming and labelling remain crucial in feminisms and other postcolonial theories engaged in developing a politics of difference that neither aggregates women and other 'Others' coercively, nor dissolves commonalities to the extent of undoing the possibility of affirming strategic identities for political ends.[5]

Feminist challenges to entrenched ideas about the 'naturalness' of categories and taxonomies and the impersonal, quasi-biblical status of reference works have long been voiced beneath the dominant refrain. In *Three Guineas*, for example, Virginia Woolf describes the 'militarist beast' as 'making distinctions not merely between the sexes, but between the races', cautioning her readers that 'he is dictating how you shall live'.[6] Donna Haraway's 1990s challenge picks up this thread, in the idiom of a period when the contests are more audible. She writes: 'bodies as objects of knowledge are material-semiotic generative nodes. Their *boundaries* ... are drawn by mapping practices; "objects" do not pre-exist as such'.[7] Yet in feminist theory, neither the artefactuality of categories, following Foucault, nor the emergence of object-boundaries from contingent mapping processes, following Haraway, amount to makings out of whole cloth: constructedness here carries no anti-realist implications. This point is crucial to feminist and other silence-breaking taxonomic projects committed to demonstrating the real-world provenance and effects of their theories and the concrete realities at which theory-generating and -generated practices have to direct their transformative aims. Such well-known and politically effective linguistic innovations as 'sexism', 'sexual harrassment', 'colonising', 'androcentrism', 'patriarchy' could have claimed no purchase had there been no acts and practices 'out there' to be named, however disputatious the namings have been. The point, then, cannot be to dismiss classifications as inherently bad. Yet neither can even the most transgressive, subversive of category makings claim once-and-for-all accuracy: many of the best feminist definitions carry no definitive or universal import. They are, literally, *working* definitions, interpretations put to work, perhaps paradoxically, in recognition both of their potential effectiveness and of their volatility. Such definitions advance feminist theory and practice as they reframe and

regenerate some of the most vital political debates in the academy and beyond. Yet their boundaries are constantly being made and remade as the objects they map move differently into focus. They have to be remade, revised, abandoned when they cease, in practice, to generate workable, politically viable effects. The global definition of 'sisterhood' that inspired early feminists of the second wave is one fairly neat example of workability giving way to its own ephemerality when the damage of its globalizing claims gained acknowledgement, yet still worthy of celebration for what it made possible.

Refusing any suggestion that silence could be golden, the feminisms of the twentieth century – both early and late – are born out of processes of naming practices and problems that hitherto 'had no name',[8] claiming the power to label and the space to put labels into circulation, voicing and seeking 'choral support' for revisioned understandings of women's diverse experiences and oppressions. In their early, most visionary moments these namings and claimings seemed to promise fulfillment of 'the dream of a common language'[9] infused, for a time, with an ideal of sisterhood and solidarity. Now, at the beginning of the twenty-first century, the chorus is less likely to sing in unison: multivocality, even dissonance will be its tone, heteroglossia within the glossary. Feminist projects of dictionary- and encyclopedia-making are located within the maze of affirmations and contradictions that these revisionings and refusals produce, as they contest the power to name of the most visible – powerful – namers and (a more difficult task) work to loosen the grasp of the 'invisible hand' that holds taxonomy-making to an illusory ideal of neutral objectivity.

For scholarly work informed by challenges such as these to the hegemonic status of taxonomies, producing an encyclopedia of feminist theories, then, cannot pose as a mere exercise in recording and sorting. It requires a critical filtering of diverse and often mutually contradictory theories, ideas, and biographies through a structural grid that cannot fail to leave its mark on the product. Hence it invokes complex responsibilities – in Haraway's words – 'for difference in material-semiotic fields of meaning'[10] neither conserving difference, merely tolerating it, nor dismissing it as aberrant; but negotiating within and through it. The project cannot pretend to be anything other than a time- and place-bound event whose conceptual apparatus and the rhetorical spaces it enters and creates would have been quite different even ten years earlier, and whose pertinence twenty or thirty years from the moment of its appearance may be discernible only to the archivists. Yet the exercise would have no point were it disingenuously to demur from claiming 'knowledgeability' for the entries that gain entry onto its pages, testifying to women's agency as namers and as theory- and politics-makers throughout the second wave. The knowledge that informs it and the processes of selection that have acknowledged it *as* knowledge require simultaneous celebration and interrogation. Nor could it be a one-woman project, despite the politics of publishing that names one woman as its General Editor, advised by and in consultation with contributors, editorial consultants, and editorial assistants. Nor, although the volume will inevitably bear the marks of its maker(s), can acknowledging its locatedness devolve into excuses for evading the 'realist' requirements that such a work has equally – and multiply – to observe.

As a philosopher who works in epistemology (theory of knowledge), *this* editor must introduce a thought, here, about the epistemological status of such a work as this. Encyclopedias and reference books as knowledge-making and -circulating projects gained a curious ascendency in the late twentieth century. Their proliferation has a straightforward economic, market explanation: libraries and institutions continue to buy them in an age of diminishing financial resources: reference budgets are among the last to go in any self-respecting institution, where an up-to-date collection counts as public testimony to the aptness of that self-respect. But there is another way of reading this reference-production phenomenon epistemologically that is not, I think, entirely fanciful. In an age of fragmentation and instability when foundationalism has crumbled and an exaggerated threat of relativism permeates the most commonly-told epistemic cautionary tales,[11] dictionaries, encyclopedias and works of reference offer the security of solid ramparts, retaining walls to check the spread of chaos and confusion with their established factuality. They remain a locus of putative objectivity in a discursive situation that, at

the same time, grants unprecedented space to revalorizing first-personal narrative, autobiography and biography, also evidenced in proliferating publications whose market successes are equally noteworthy in a society disenchanted with its erstwhile universals. These experiential tellings claim a certain immunity to critique, in a discursive climate infused with the demands of the politics of difference, for respectful readings that refuse the colonizing moves that would claim to know better than an experiencer does her/himself. The tyrannies of objectivism and experientialism face one another still in these radically different kinds of text, to play out their drama on a different terrain, should either side be so bold as to claim interpretive immunity.

Feminist encyclopedia-making is caught, then, in a pull of tensions – *productive*, not paralysing tensions – within which it has to take 'a symptomatic stance toward its own discourse'.[12] It endeavours to devise principles of inclusion to defy the 'centricities' and 'solipsisms' (e.g. androcentricity, white solipsism, middle class centricity) that came under challenge in the late twentieth century; to develop experientially and theoretically sensitive taxonomies that do not merely replicate the structures of the everyday and the academic world that feminist theorists and activists are interrogating. Such projects work, then, in a space between acknowledging the imperialism of classifications and categories, and acknowledging the value to feminists diversely situated within inquiry and activism – and to new generations of feminists – of assembling the theoretical tools that this generation has forged and maintained in good working order. Definitions and readings that the project puts into circulation are as addressive as they are reportative, for none claims exclusive territoriality. The multiplicity of voices sets dialogues and deliberations in motion in ongoing, multiple conversations. For although they enact standards of meaning and reading that claim autoritative status, however 'interim', there is little danger that these texts can claim monologic authority, so long as they engage with the voices of other texts like themselves in these expanding, shifting rhetorical spaces. The very fact of many voices checks embryonic pretensions to mastery in the interrogations and negotiations that open up.

Together and singly, these texts are well placed to destabilize sedimented meanings and theories, to offer innovative ways of reading and seeing.

Feminist theories: a historical sketch

Writing of the origins of the 'second wave', British feminist Juliet Mitchell characterizes feminism as 'an ideological offspring of certain economic and social conditions. Its radicalism reflects the fact that it comes to prominence at points of critical change and envisages it with an imagination that goes beyond it.'[13] Second-wave feminism in the west, which came into being – albeit variously across geographical and other locations – with the radical student protest movements, and the United States civil-rights movement, in the 1960s, is an active, politically engaged project that has been instrumental in effecting wide-spread social-political changes. Feminism is likewise a theoretical project committed to producing critical-constructive analyses of systemic power structures, theoretical presuppositions, social practices, and institutions that oppress and marginalise women, and to effecting social transformation. Mitchell's observation emphasizes the tight connections between feminist practice which works 'down on the ground' to transform material and social conditions, and feminist theory, which is respectful of and responsible to the practices that are its sources and that it informs. In a reciprocal process, feminist theory is modified by what proves effective in practice, and practice is shaped by theory.[14]

In the early years of the second wave – roughly during the late 1960s and the 1970s – white western feminist theorists saw it as their principal task to develop critical analyses of the structural features of patriarchal societies in consequence of which women and men, generally speaking, live markedly different lives from one another structurally, materially, experientially. Feminists concentrated on how these experiences were/are differentiated along sex-gender lines, initially looking less closely at how they differ along lines drawn by class, race, sexuality, age, ability, ethnicity, religion. The governing idea was that in patriarchal societies men occupy positions of greater power than women, and claim readier access to what counts as valuable. In consequence of these

asymmetries, feminists demonstrated, men (i.e. affluent white men) in such societies have license to shape and control many aspects of women's lives. Feminist theorists have interrogated this uneven distribution of power and privilege, as they have (latterly) examined how women's oppression intersects with and is shaped by racial, class, religious, homophobic, ageist, and numerous other forms of oppression.

The starting point of feminist theory, both then and now, is in women's lives: in their widely diverse experiences and situations. Theory occupies a central place in feminist movements, for experiences do not speak for themselves: for this reason consciousness-raising has been a vital component of feminist practice since the beginning of the second wave. Women have had to learn from one other how to see and name their experiences; how to recognize and evaluate their commonalities and differences. Theory – and consciousness-raising – remain fundamental to feminisms' self-critical projects of revising early assumptions of female sameness (sisterhood), of defining and redefining central issues, and enacting new transformative strategies in response to evolving, and often regressive, social-political, circumstances.

In those early days, Marilyn Frye produced a provocative image to represent the miniscule oppressive structures of women's everyday lives in (western) societies.[15] She notes that a close examination of a single wire of a bird cage makes it difficult to see the other wires or to understand why the bird would not just fly around that wire and be free. A separate inspection of each wire of the cage would prompt the same question: why would such a flimsy barrier constrain the bird? Only by examining the entire structure – the interconnected, mutually enforcing system of barriers – can one see why the bird is trapped. Likewise, feminists have to understand how separate and often seemingly trivial oppressive practices reinforce one another: how patriarchy is constructed out of practices which, considered one by one, might seem neither significant nor oppressive. Together, they form an intractable structure.

During the more than thirty years since the beginning of the second wave, feminist theories have departed radically from early attempts to represent women as a caste, class, or homogeneous group. No feminist at the beginning of the twenty-first century would speak of a single, essential 'women's experience', for race, class, sexuality, ethnicity, religion, age and ability are just a few of the myriad differences between/among women that have become focal points for analysis. Thus feminists have moved to develop theoretical tools for examining points of convergence and divergence in women's lives; for acknowledging the boundaries of commonality and specificity, while recognizing that there is no pure, untainted, unmediated, or generic experience.[16]

Despite this increasingly nuanced fine-tuning that feminisms at the beginning of the twenty-first century have achieved, Adrienne Rich's early (second wave) observations capture recognitions that are still salient. Rich notes that women in the industrialized western world grow to womanhood in circumstances where it is assumed that

> women are a subgroup, that 'man's world' is the real world, that patriarchy is equivalent to culture and culture to patriarchy, ... that generalizations about 'man', 'humankind', 'children', 'blacks', 'parents', 'the working class' hold true for women, mothers, daughters, sisters, wet-nurses, infant girls, and can include them with no more than a glancing reference here and there, usually to some specialized function like breast-feeding.[17]

Counteracting these assumptions, achieving the justice for 'women, mothers, daughters, sisters' that they thwart, are ongoing tasks that animate the contributions to this volume, as to feminist theory everywhere.

The ideas and practices that feminists seek to displace are ancient in origin, deeply entrenched in the history of western thought. In a passage with whose substance Rich's claims are markedly continuous, Aristotle (384–322 BCE) writes:

> the male is by nature superior, and the female inferior; and the one rules, and the other is ruled; this principle, of necessity, extends to all mankind. Where there is such a difference as that between soul and body, or between men and animals..., the lower sort are by nature

slaves, and it is better for them as for all inferiors that they should be under the rule of a master.[18]

For Aristotle, neither women, children, nor slaves can be citizens. Because only citizens can participate in the political life of the Greek city state, women are denied such participation, as are children and slaves. Since virtue, in which the best human qualities are realized, is achievable only through political participation, it too is inaccessible to women (and slaves and children).

Many of the presuppositions that have underpinned women's disadvantaged social positions in the western world have their roots in this ancient history. The claim that a woman's nature and all of her possibilities are consequent upon her biology – her reproductive biology – is one of the most ancient and persistent of these ideas, long invoked to justify social arrangements that keep woman 'in her place'. Aristotle's is only the best-known ancient formulation of a *biological determinism* that feminists are persistently required to counter. Claims that women are incapable (physically, intellectually, emotionally) of holding certain jobs, or that placing children in day care is a violation of a mother's natural role are latter-day versions of this ancient theme.

Variations on Aristotle's ideas infuse canonical western theories of human nature from classical times to the eighteenth century. Yet it was not inevitable for him to develop the functionalist, biological determinism he did, for in his time there were theories in circulation that might have generated quite different conceptions of women and of female/male relations. Aristotle evidently resisted an innovative proposal developed by his teacher, Plato (427–347 BCE). In the *Republic*, Plato's teacher, Socrates, describes an ideal society in which every citizen will perform the function appropriate to his or her 'natural' capacities. Merchants, craftspeople, and tradespeople will be trained in skills required for their occupations; future soldiers will be educated to be suitably courageous, yet neither rash nor cowardly; members of the ruling, guardian class will be trained in music, the arts, gymnastics, athletics, mathematics and the highest arts of reason, to maintain harmony within the state and govern it wisely.

Remarkably, male and female guardians will be educated exactly alike. According to Socrates,

> there is no pursuit of the administrators of a state that belongs to a woman because she is a woman or to a man because he is a man. But the natural capacities are distributed alike among both creatures, and women naturally have a share in all pursuits and men in all – yet for all the woman is weaker than the man.[19]

He thus explicitly denies that there are natural female traits, biological or psychological, that would exclude women from ruling. So that child-rearing will not interfere with these women's education and activities, Socrates recommends that children, born as a result of cohabitation in brief marriage festivals, 'will be taken over by the officials appointed for this, men or women or both'[20] and raised communally.

Thus Plato advances a radically innovative proposal for how women might live in a 'man's world'. Yet his proposal that women participate equally in men's activities and pursuits, devised and elaborated to bring out the best in masculine nature, still implies that women could become guardians only by becoming just like men. Modern variations on this theme, where women enter professions on the (often implicit) condition that their femaleness will not 'make a difference', are only too familiar.

However, it is Aristotelian conceptions of women's nature that infuse western theory up to the eighteenth century, offering a rationale for the 'naturalness' of patriarchal social arrangements. Although women were by no means silent as thinkers and activists during these intervening centuries, only in consequence of feminist scholarly endeavour are their works and deeds becoming known: few of them achieved canonical status.[21] Indeed, it is not until the development of liberalism in the eighteenth century that the first sustained challenges to biological determinism are articulated in western thought.

The liberal political theories developed in Britain and France in the eighteenth and nineteenth centuries, together with the social and economic upheavals generated by the Industrial Revolution, began slowly to undermine the belief that women's biologically determined place is in the home, prompting a dawning recognition that women's social inferiority might be consequent upon their lack of education and opportunity, not a product of 'nature'. In the eighteenth century, too, liberal thinking began to displace beliefs that political authority was inherited, and that rulers, by natural right, stood in benevolent patriarchal relations to their subjects. In an age when people had unquestioningly accepted that members of lower social orders should submit to the greater wisdom of their natural superiors and rulers, these were startlingly innovative ideas.

Arguments to the effect that all members of a society are free and equally participating individuals prompted early feminists to contend that women, too, should be equal. Feminists still had to demonstrate the limits of the new ideals of equality, for not all of the early liberals were feminists, nor were they united in rejecting biological determinism. But it was within this climate of social-political change, and to take issue with beliefs about female natural inferiority, that Mary Wollstonecraft wrote her *Vindication of the Rights of Woman* (1792). She argues that if women had the same education and opportunities as men, they would be men's equals in every respect. Only their inferior education makes them appear merely emotional, lacking in rationality; they are not so by nature. Wollstonecraft attributes women's disadvantaged social situation to their circumscribed intellectual opportunities in a patriarchal society, arguing that women who are trained to occupy themselves with trivial tasks cannot but appear feebleminded and deficient in reason. Her *Vindication* is intended to refute Jean-Jacques Rousseau (1712–78) who, in *Emile*, advocates an education for young men designed to develop their reason to its fullest potential, training them to tame nature and understand its secrets. Women, by contrast, would be educated to complement men, adorn their lives, raise their children, and obey them. Their sexual passions must be controlled to free men from enslavement to female sensuality. Like Aristotle, Rousseau is a firm defender of biological determinism. It is small wonder that Wollstonecraft sought to challenge the substance of his much-touted egalitarianism.

Nineteenth-century liberal theorists, such as

John Stuart Mill in *The Subjection of Women* (1869), began to connect the issues of education and equal rights for women to their claims to qualify for the franchise. Yet even Mill believes that educated women who have gained the vote will be likely to choose a domestic life. The class-specificity of his position is apparent in his view that these educated women will be better able to share in their husbands' intellectual pursuits and to raise their children intelligently: he is convinced that society will thus benefit if women gain the educational opportunities available to men. Harriet Taylor Mill (1807–58) proposes radical changes to patriarchal marriage, arguing that a divorced woman should retain guardianship of and take financial responsibility for her children.[22] Her proposals were intended to ensure that women not be tied into unworkable marriages for fear of being unable to provide for, and retain custody of their children. She believes that if women are not to barter their persons for bread, they must be educated, and permitted to enter any occupation they choose. Variations on many of these liberal themes still occupy a place on feminist agendas at the beginning of the twenty-first century.

Equally important nineteenth-century sources of present-day feminisms are Marxist analyses of the modes of production and social relations that accompanied the Industrial Revolution and the rise of capitalism. Neither Marxists nor socialists believe that biology can explain social inequality and the oppression of one group of people by another. Economic factors, and connections between class oppression and women's oppression are focal issues for marxist feminists. Thus Karl Marx (1818–83) shows that culture and society are rooted in material, economic conditions, and people are, fundamentally, social creatures, shaped by material and social circumstances. For Marx, human nature cannot adequately be investigated in abstraction from historical circumstances; in particular, from the specific social organization of material productivity. Under capitalism, the ruling class (the bourgeoisie) own the means of production, and purchase the labour of the working class (the proletariat). Members of each class participate in similar productive activities and live in social-material circumstances that shape their physical development, health, interests, and consciousness.

The bourgeoisie determine the development and circulation of knowledge and values, generating perceptions of human nature and social reality distorted through their own point of view so as to make the status quo seem 'natural'. Members of the proletariat who accept these arrangements as 'natural' live in a state of 'false consciousness' that prevents their perceiving their own class interests. Constantly engaged in alienated labour, Marx believes members of the working class have no sense of themselves as participators in the work that occupies most of their waking hours, or as agents of social change.

In *The Origin of The Family, Private Property and the State* (1884) Frederick Engels develops a more sustained analysis of women's oppression under capitalism. In the nuclear family of capitalist society, Engels sees a microcosmic mirroring of the larger, macroscopic social structure, with the husband occupying the position of the bourgeoisie, and the wife that of the proletariat. He proposes that women refuse to remain confined within private domestic labour by entering the public world of productive work, and that domestic labour and child care become public, collective responsibilities. In short, for Marxist theorists, women are oppressed under capitalism because of a sexual division of labour that serves the interests of men directly, and serves the interests of capitalism indirectly, through serving the interests of men. Women are responsible for child-raising, cooking, attending to the mundane family needs, and caring for the sick and the aged, leaving men to devote themselves to productivity in the public world of waged labour. And capitalist society need not pay for the reproduction of the labour power upon which it depends.

Early socialist feminists disagreed about whether 'the woman question' would be solved in the revolutionary changes that socialists were advocating. German activist Rosa Luxemburg saw women's oppression as one of the miseries of capitalist society that would disappear after the revolution; Clara Zetkin believed that women's issues had to be addressed separately, to acknowledge women's dual oppression by capitalism and patriarchy. Zetkin helped to found the International Socialist Women's Congress, and in 1910, she declared March 8th as International Women's Day, to commemorate a 1909 strike by female garment workers in New York, protesting overcrowded, poorly ventilated, dangerous working conditions and low pay. Analogously, Russian feminist Alexandra Kollontai campaigned for a bureau in the Russian Social Democratic Labour party to address women's issues. Kollontai and Zetkin insisted that patriarchy exerts an oppression all its own.

A third source of second-wave feminisms is in analyses of sexuality and psychosexual development initiated by Havelock Ellis (1859–1939) and Sigmund Freud (1856–1939) in the late nineteenth–early twentieth centuries. Because he believed unequivocally that 'anatomy is destiny',[23] evincing no doubt that psychosexual development is biologically determined, second-wave feminists were initially critical of Freud and of psychoanalysis as designed to keep women quiet, passive, and in their place – especially sexually. The well-adjusted woman, in Freudian terms, learned to acquiesce to passive dependence in a heterosexual marriage, schooling herself to please her husband. Sexual maturity was her goal, evidenced in the ability to achieve vaginal orgasm, to recognize male supremacy, and to be content with her situation. Thus Kate Millett argues that Freudian theory convinced 'the dispossessed that the circumstances of their deprivation are organic, therefore unalterable.'[24] It may therefore seem odd to claim Freud as an inspiration for present-day feminists. But psychoanalytic theory, especially since the late 1970s, has been a fertile area of feminist discussion. Critical engagement with Freudian theory has opened up debates about sexuality, desire, primary process, and creativity: the private, disorderly, and non-rational aspects of women's lives. These debates have generated analyses of the social implications of sexuality and desire, the relations between repression and social organization, and the interplay between individual psychic formation and the production and maintenance of the social order that are still central feminist issues at the beginning of the twenty-first century.

One of Freud's most articulate pre-second wave feminist critics is Simone de Beauvoir, whose observation, 'one is not born, but rather becomes a woman,'[25] is germane to subsequent analyses of patriarchally constituted psychological and sexual femininity. Equally influential is Beauvoir's characterization of women as 'the second sex,' so designated by virtue of their creation as Other, with reference to a male norm. Responding to Jean-Paul Sartre's claim that conscious beings are distinguished from material things in their capacity for self-definition, for transcending their materiality, Beauvoir maintains that this capacity belongs to men but not to women: hence women are Other. *The Second Sex* offers a remarkable account of the social construction of femininity on the basis of biological determinism, covering such previously unmentionable topics as puberty, menstruation, sexual intercourse, childbearing. That so much could be written about the phenomenological meaning of women's lives in a male-defined world astonished Beauvoir's early readers. Their astonishment attests to the pathbreaking character of her work.

Feminist theory could not have developed as it has since the 1960s had the ground not been prepared by the intellectual and social developments outlined here. Even feminists who have taken issue with these lines of thought have found critical inspiration in them. Nor was all quiet in the feminist world between the early growth of liberalism and socialism, and the feminist resurgence of the 1960s. First-wave feminist activism in campaigning for the suffrage attests to the falsity of any such suggestion; as do the concerted activities of cultural feminists and social reform feminists at the end of the nineteenth and the beginning of the twentieth centuries. But my purpose here has been to trace some strands in earlier feminist theory as a prelude to the entries in this volume which discuss present-day feminisms in their many guises; to offer a broad, schematic mapping of the territory on which late-twentieth-century feminisms are enacted.

Coverage and contributors

This *Encyclopedia*, like all such works, is selective in its coverage and, in consequence, undoubtedly commits sins both of commission and omission. While it is impossible to account for all of them, or to claim pardon for the most egregious ones, some account of the principles of selection may be informative in explaining the choices we have made in producing it.

The aims of the project, as we defined them at the outset, were to produce a resource for students and teachers across the academic disciplines – both those already involved in feminist studies, and those interested in learning about this area of inquiry – and to produce a volume accessible in its language and conceptual framing to scholars and activists elsewhere. Its most innovative features are its cross-disciplinary scope; and the inclusion of mini-biographies of feminist theorists, designed to introduce readers to some of the makers of feminist theory, and to acknowledge the specifically located crafting processes that make feminist knowledge possible. Our principal theoretical tasks have been: (1) to develop a useful yet sensitive taxonomy which does not merely replicate the structures of the academy and the intellectual world that feminist theorists and activists have interrogated; (2) to produce biographies of feminist theorists that do not just name these thinkers and their works, but locate them within a framework of wider discussion; (3) to devise principles of inclusion that defy the 'centricities' mentioned above, that have come under challenge in the postcolonial thinking of the late-twentieth century.

The process has been long, complex, interactive and rewarding even through its inevitable frustrations. To set it in motion, a graduate research assistant searched through 'state of the art' feminist and women's studies periodicals, journals, course descriptions and textbooks across the standard and evolving academic disciplines and interdisciplinary areas of theoretical inquiry. From this search we generated a vast, initially unwieldy list, which we pared down and refined, with help from our consulting editors, to arrive at the headword list with which we launched the project. The initial list has undergone many refinements and modifications as the project has proceeded, as contributors and editors have noted gaps, or suggested omissions. The project's growth and development through the production process attest to the commitment of our contributors to producing a volume that is as true as it can be to the current state of feminist theory and practice.

The volume concentrates on second-wave feminist theory as it has developed since the 1960s, and primarily if not exclusively in the English-speaking world. Thus it contains little historical material, nor does it deal extensively with feminist theories initially written in languages other than English. The principal exception is French feminist theory which, although it does not receive comprehensive treatment here, is the subject of several entries written to acknowledge the resources that many English-speaking feminists have found in French theory. The decisions that the focus should be thus are the broadest decisions that have determined the shape and content of the volume. They are prompted by considerations of length and manageability more than by judgements of the value of English-language feminism in contrast with French-, German-, Spanish- or Italian-language feminism, to name just some of the other possibilities.

Given that feminist theory has infiltrated most if not all of the established academic disciplines and fields of inquiry/research in the English-speaking world, many of the volume's longest entries address the state of feminist inquiry in those disciplines. Deciding to distribute the focus in this way has indeed, almost in spite of ourselves, required us to respect and address the entrenched academic disciplinary 'divisions' that have structured, and continue to structure, academic research. Yet these entries show how feminist inquiry has challenged the most basic assumptions of the standard disciplines, from the language they take for granted to their generic assumptions about 'man', 'world', 'society', 'citizenship', 'work', and 'justice', to name only a few. Thus in its substance the volume presents a radical challenge to the presuppositions that hold the structures of the academy in place. Equally significant among the longest entries are those that address and explain feminisms themselves: entries on areas of inquiry that were unheard of in the academic world prior to 1960. Feminism itself, feminist film theory, feminist epistemology, the body, gender, feminist history, queer theory, women's studies, black feminism, chicana feminism, feminist theology: these are just some of the entries whose very headwords testify to the mark that feminist theory and practice have made on the shape and content of academic curricula.

The biographical entries attest to the crafting of

theories out of the lives and situations of their authors, thus working to dissolve the opposed rigidities of experientialism-objectivism, and to affirm that these theories are woman-made. Producing these biographies is at once challenging and risky: it does appear to participate in a great (wo)man practice whose counterpart, the 'great man' approach to historical scholarship, has been the focus of serious feminist critique. We recognize this problem, and cannot construct the process otherwise, except to say that the process of honouring theory-makers, many of whom have literally made certain ways of thinking and doing possible, also claims a place in feminist processes. The impression such entries convey, to the effect that the women named have made theory alone and by their own efforts is, however, difficult to dispel except by appealing to the larger, deeper underlying principle of feminist practice, captured initially in conscious-raising, and perpetuated in the best feminist conferences, class-rooms, journals, discussion groups, and cooperatives, which reminds us always of the communal nature of inquiry and practice, even as some names stand out for their specific contributions.

The list of feminists whose biographies appear here is inevitably incomplete. There will be as many incomprehensible omissions as there may appear to be whimsical inclusions. For this we apologize, and explain the process. We were permitted sixty biographies in total, from across disciplinary and interdisciplinary areas of inquiry. Initially, we asked each of ten consulting editors to name six theorists who must, without question, appear on this list. The response was instructive: the most creative approach took our question to a graduate women's studies class, and offered us the results of a lengthy – and evidently productive – discussion: an example of feminist inquiry at its best. As with the subject headword list, this list has gone through numerous additions and omissions throughout the years during which the volume has been in process. We think the final selection is a good one, whatever its imperfections, and invite our readers to join us in thanking our contributors.

Notes

1 Toni Morrison, *Beloved*, New York: Knopf, 1988, p. 190.
2 Jean-Jacques Lecercle, *The Violence of Language*, London: Routledge, 1990, p. 50.
3 Cheris Kramarae and Paula Treichler, eds, *A Feminist Dictionary*, London: Pandora Press, 1985, pp. 8, 3.
4 Michel Foucault, *The Archaeology of Knowledge*, trans. A.M. Sheridan Smith, New York: Pantheon Books, 1972, p. 70.
5 See in this connection Denise Riley, *'Am I That Name?' Feminism and the Category of Women in History*, Minneapolis: University of Minnesota Press, 1988.
6 Virginia Woolf, *Three Guineas*, New York: Harcourt, Brace, Jovanovich, 1938, p. 102.
7 Donna Haraway, '"Situated Knowledges": The Science Question in Feminism and the Privilege of Partial Perspective', in Donna J. Haraway, *Simians, Cyborgs, and Women: The Reinvention of Nature*, New York: Routledge, 1991, p. 201.
8 'The problem that has no name' is a phrase attributed to Simone de Beauvoir in *The Second Sex* (trans. 1952), and Betty Friedan in *The Feminine Mystique* (1963). See Kramarae and Treichler, *A Feminist Dictionary*, p. 358.
9 The phrase borrows the title of Adrienne Rich's book *The Dream of a Common Language: Poems 1974–1977*, New York: W.W. Norton, 1978.
10 'Situated Knowledges', p. 195.
11 See in this regard my essay 'Must a Feminist Be a Relativist After All?' in Lorraine Code, *Rhetorical Spaces: Essays on (Gendered) Locations*, New York: Routledge, 1995.
12 The phrase is due to Donna Pryzbylowicz in 'Toward a Feminist Cultural Critique: Hegemony and Modes of Social Division', *Cultural Critique* 14, 1989–90, p. 260.
13 Juliet Mitchell, 'Reflections on Twenty Years of Feminism,' in Juliet Mitchell and Ann Oakley, eds, *What is Feminism?*, New York: Pantheon Books, 1986, p. 48.
14 In this section I am drawing material from my 'Feminist Theory', in Sandra Burt, Lorraine Code and Lindsay Dorney, eds, *Changing*

Patterns: Women in Canada, (2nd edn) Toronto: McClelland and Stewart, 1993.

15 Marilyn Frye, *The Politics of Reality: Essays in Feminist Theory*, Trumansburg, NY: The Crossing Press, 1983, 4–5.

16 See Joan Scott, 'Experience', in Judith Butler and Joan W. Scott, eds, *Feminists Theorize the Political*, London: Routledge, 1992.

17 From Adrienne Rich's remarks at the Columbia University Seminar on Women and Society, 1976. Quoted by Hester Eisenstein in her *Contemporary Feminist Thought*, London: Allen and Unwin, 1984, p. 74.

18 Aristotle, *Politics*, Benjamin Jowett, trans., in Richard McKeon, ed., *The Basic Works of Aristotle*, New York: Random House, 1941, 1254b.

19 Plato, *Republic*, trans. Paul Shorey, in Edith Hamilton and Huntington Cairns, eds, *The Collected Dialogues of Plato*, Princeton, NJ: Princeton University Press, 1961, 455 d–e.

20 Ibid., 460b.

21 See in this regard Linda Lopez McAlister, ed., *Hypatia's Daughters: Fifteen Hundred Years of Women Philosophers*, Bloomington: Indiana University Press, 1996, which includes valuable bibliographical references; and Mary Ellen Waithe, *A History of Women Philosophers*, vols 1–4 (1987–95), Dordecht and Bostan: Kluwer Academic Publishers.

22 Harriet Taylor Mill, 'Early Essays on Marriage and Divorce', (1832) by John Stuart Mill and Harriet Taylor Mill, in Alice Rossi, ed., (1974) *Essays on Sex Equality*, Chicago: University of Chicago Press.

23 Sigmund Freud, *Sexuality and the Psychology of Love*, ed., Phillip Reiff. New York: Collier Books, 1963, p. 181.

24 Kate Millett, *Sexual Politics*, New York: Avon Books, 1971, p. 187.

25 Simone de Beauvoir, *The Second Sex* (1949), trans. H.M. Parshley. New York: Knopf, 1952, p. 301.

Acknowledgements

This volume could not have reached completion without the support and assistance of many people. Fiona Cairns at Routledge first suggested the project and persuaded me of its viability. I cannot thank her enough for her continued support and good-humoured encouragement throughout the inevitable stages and crises of its production. It has been a privilege to know her and work with her. In the Routledge Reference Section, able assistance throughout the process of developing this volume has come from Samantha Parkinson, Ben Swift, Mina-Gera Price, and in the final stages, Stephanie Rogers. Thanks to Tarquin Acevedo for his fine handling of the intricate production process, and to Kristina Wischenkamper for her skilled and good-humoured copy editing. The board of consultant editors provided much-needed advice; friends and colleagues too numerous to mention offered ongoing assistance and encouragement. One friend, though, deserves special mention – Genevieve (Jenny) Lloyd – for it was she who convinced me that 'it would be a good thing to have done'.

I am grateful to two former MA students in Philosophy at York University: Heather Chisholm, who compiled the initial word list, and Melisse Willems, who set up and maintained a sophisticated data base during the later stages of the work. To my exceptional editorial assistant, Fiona MacCool, my deepest thanks for assistance and wisdom that have gone well beyond the call of duty, and for her friendship that has made the work so rewarding. Without her it would not have been possible to complete the project. Nor, on a more personal level, could I have managed without Murray Code's technological assistance and consistent moral support. My thanks, also, to all of the feminist theorists whose entries appear in the volume, who have been so friendly and cooperative in working with our demanding and sometimes chaotic editorial process, and have given helpful advice beyond the limits of the terms of their obligations as contributors.

A three-year Major Research Grant from the Social Sciences and Humanities Research Council of Canada (SSHRC) made it possible to hire the editorial and research assistants who have worked on the project, to purchase the necessary equipment and meet the other inevitable expenses of such an undertaking. A Walter Gordon Memorial Fellowship from York University provided the teaching release time that I needed in 1997–8, when work on the project was especially demanding. My thanks to both organizations for their part in making this endeavour manageable.

Lorraine Code
Toronto, Canada,
June 2000

A

administrative studies

Administrative studies, sometimes called business administration or organisational studies, is the academic discipline concerned with the character-istics and functioning of formal organisations. The roots of this discipline are twofold, reflecting a divide within the field between study of the behaviour of individuals in organisational contexts (for example social and industrial-organisational psychology), or of organisations themselves within industries (for example sociology and industrial economics). The foundations of the discipline are firmly grounded in realist ontologies and positivis-tic epistemologies. Gibson Burrell and Gareth Morgan (1979) trace the history of sociological research traditions in administrative studies, show-ing that the dominant framework represents a perspective firmly rooted in the sociology of regulation, and approaches its subject from an objectivist point of view. These roots, which strongly influence the discipline today, are manifest in concerns for explaining the status quo – the ways in which the social order is maintained through commitment, consensus, cohesion, social integra-tion and need satisfaction. The dominant dis-courses of inquiry are therefore characterised by essentially rational, objective explanations of social phenomena from a highly pragmatic orientation, rooted in the tradition of sociological positivism.

Marta Calás and Linda Smircich (1996) identify the important intersection of feminist concerns and organisational issues, arguing that feminist theories are not solely about women, rather about the relationship between women and men, grounded in the cultural and social constructions that create ideas about appropriate **gender roles**. Using feminist theories as conceptual lenses can therefore focus on the concerns of many 'others', not only women, who otherwise would be passed over or marginalised by dominant organisational practices and discourses.

Historically, organisational research has been largely oblivious to issues of gender, assuming either that organisational arrangements impact men and women equally, or that only the experiences of men matter since they occupy the majority of important jobs in formal organisations. It is becoming increasingly accepted, at least by a growing body of organisational researchers, that the study of organisation itself is sexist in general, either neglecting issues of gender and **sexuality** completely, or treating them as variables that can be manipulated and/or controlled. The contribu-tions of gender-based perspectives on administra-tive studies thus include revealing the ways in which organisations, through cultural, processual and structural mechanisms, create and perpetuate discriminatory practices and behaviours. Joan Acker (1990) illustrates how the concept of a 'job' itself assumes a gendered structure based on the ways in which organisations socialise their mem-bers to adopt particular gender identities, and consequently creates organisational practices that conform to sex-biased values. Divisions of labour along gender lines, the construction of symbols and images that reinforce these divisions, and the processes that help produce gendered components of **identity** all suggest that jobs assume a particular gendered organisation of social life, despite the presentation of jobs and organisations as gender neutral. This fundamental gendered substructure of organisations is not only difficult to observe, but it also institutionalises the marginalisation of abilities, perspectives and behaviours in a manner that frequently denigrates and excludes women.

Two texts examine the study of organisation specifically from a gendered perspective. First, *Gendering Organizational Analysis* challenges the implicit characterisation of the worker as a genderless agent in organisational research. Because most workers were men at the time the field of administrative studies was developing as an academic discipline, it was commonly believed that gender did not play much of a role. This text addresses the legacy of this belief by showing that it matters very much who the subject is who occupies a 'job', and that there are implications for having a work force that is not entirely male, which stands in opposition to traditional 'gender neutral' (but implicitly androcentric) ways in which studies of organisation are portrayed. This has led to considerable errors in interpreting how organisations operate, and how organisational arrangements affect men and women as gendered subjects (for example the persistence of the male advantage, occupational inequality, sex segregation and wage gaps). Second, *The Sexuality of Organization* is a critical feminist text on the pervasiveness and power of sexuality in the ongoing production and reproduction of organisations and organisational life, and the neglect of sexuality within the study of gender, the study of organisations, and the management of organisational forms. Although the concepts of sexuality and gender are conceptually distinct, they are also closely related. Sexuality, the social expression or social relations of physical bodily desires, is a phenomenon that administrative studies has had difficulty with, if not a fear of handling, resulting in an absence of understanding of the types of sexuality and sexual practices that have become established within organisations, and consequently reproduce themselves.

Despite increased attention to gendered aspects of organisation, feminist approaches to organisation remain marginal because androcentrism remains dominant in organisational discourses. Feminist perspectives, however, identify new organisational and/or social foci (for example, experiences of oppression under **patriarchy** and capitalism, psychosexual development and class relations), any of which create the position from which the impact of institutionalised organisational discourses can be examined. Feminist organisational research builds upon the specific ideologies and assumptions that typify different schools of feminist thought, searching for causes and/or consequences of taken-for-granted practices, beliefs and attitudes that create and perpetuate systems of relative advantage and disadvantage. Feminist pedagogy builds on the growing body of feminist organisational theory and research, creating the sites in which hegemonic discourse can be dislodged (see **hegemony**), revealing alternative ways of thinking, feeling and acting that challenge conventional ideas about jobs, organisations, rights and responsibilities.

See also: androcentrism; class analysis, UK; class analysis, US; epistemology, feminist; gender; objectivity; ontology; positivism; sexism

References and further reading

Acker, J. (1990) 'Hierarchies, Jobs, Bodies: A Theory of Gendered Organizations', *Gender and Society* 4, 2: 139–58.

Burrell, G. and Morgan, G. (1979) *Sociological Paradigms and Organizational Analysis*, Portsmouth, NH: Heinemann.

Calás, M.B. and Smircich, L. (1996) 'From The Woman's Point of View: Feminist Approaches to Organization Studies', in S.R. Clegg, C. Hardy and W.R. Nord (eds) *Handbook of Organization Studies*, Thousand Oaks, CA: Sage.

Hearn, J., Sheppard, D.L., Tancred-Sheriff, P. and Burrell, G. (eds) (1989) *The Sexuality of Organization*, London: Sage.

Mills, A.J. and Tancred, P. (eds) (1992) *Gendering Organizational Analysis*, Newbury Park, CA: Sage.

DAVID WICKS AND PATRICIA BRADSHAW

adolescent girls and feminism

Feminist developmental psychologists began to question the male-centred and defined assumptions that underlie Freudian-based theories in the late 1970s.

In 1982, Carol **Gilligan**, working in the field of psychology, focused on how girls develop their identities. Her book, *In A Different Voice*, shows that adolescent girls tend to be shy and withdrawn despite being assertive and vocal in earlier girlhood. She explains the change as a reaction to social and cultural pressures to conform to gender stereotypes.

Like Gilligan, Sandra Bem challenges male-centred theories of adolescent psychological development. Bem emphasises the gender lens through which girls learn to interpret the world and its expectations of them (1993). These theories challenge the essentialist position that girls are different from boys because of their biology, and show the cultural basis for the development of gender differences in adolescence.

Based on an earlier AAUW report, Peggy Orenstein's *Schoolgirls* (1994) shows how adolescent girls' lives, self-images, and chances for success are shaped by their experiences in school, the gendered practices of the institution of education itself, its expectations of girls, and their interactions with teachers and other students. Using participant observation and interviews, Orenstein reveals how race and class intertwine with the girls' experiences to produce different self-esteem levels, identities, and expectations. Sadker and Sadker (1994) look at twenty years of research on education to show how girls are rendered invisible in schools. Taken together, feminist research in adolescent socialisation, and girls' experiences in education draw attention to theoretical concepts of voice, invisibility, and silencing.

During the 1990s, central issues were body images, eating disorders, media images, culture participation, sexuality and self-esteem. Mary Pipher's *Reviving Ophelia: Saving the Selves of Adolescent Girls* (1994) shows the harm cultural messages produce for girls' self-esteem and ways of living in society. Angela McRobbie's *Feminism and Youth Culture* (1991) shows how girls' participation in youth culture has been left out of sociological research. Also in the 1990s, feminist theory was taken up by girls themselves, through the grassroots Riot Grrrl feminist movement. Associated with **third-wave feminism**, Riot Grrrl make adolescent girls' standpoints central.

See also: essentialism; girl-child, the

References and further reading

Bem, S. (1993) *The Lenses of Gender: Transforming the Debate on Sexual Inequality*, New Haven: Yale University Press.

McRobbie, A. (1991) *Feminism and Youth Culture: From Jackie to Just Seventeen*, Basingstoke: Macmillan Education.

Orenstein, P (1994) *Schoolgirls: Young Women, Self-Esteem and the Confidence Gap*, New York: Doubleday.

Pipher, M. (1994) *Reviving Ophelia: Saving the Selves of Adolescent Girls*, New York: Putnam.

Sadker, M.P. and Sadker, D.M. (1994) *Teachers, School and Society*, New York and London: McGraw-Hill, 3rd edn.

Smith, B, (ed.) (1983) *Home Girls: A Black Feminist Anthology*, New York: Kitchen Table Women of Color Press.

Thorne, B. (1993) *Gender Play: Girls and Boys in School*, New Brunswick, NJ: Rutgers University Press.

CHELSEA STARR

adversary method

'Adversary method' is Janice Moulton's label for a method of philosophical debate modelled on oppositional confrontations, and shaped by a belief that truth will triumph against even the strongest opponents. The object is to discredit the most extreme opposition, showing that one's own position can withstand even such assaults. Moulton criticises the method's focus on arguments isolated from lives and contexts. She associates it with the aggression and competitiveness that are constitutive of stereotypical white western middle-class masculinity. Connections between aggressiveness and masculinity are commonplace, and contentious, for feminists; but Moulton's naming such activity a paradigm of philosophy, which purports to transcend 'the commonplace', reinforces claims about philosophy's androcentricity to expose an interweaving of power and interests behind its disinterested demeanour.

See also: androcentrism

References and further reading

Moulton, J. (1983) 'A Paradigm of Philosophy: The Adversary Method', in S. Harding and M. Hintikka (eds) *Discovering Reality*, Dordrecht: Reidel.

LORRAINE CODE

advertising, women in

Images of women have been used in advertising for over 150 years. It was the feminists in the early 1960s who first looked at the portrayal of women in advertisements and brought the whole question of their effect on social thinking into public consciousness and political perspective. The literature as well as direct action (defacing of adverts) drew attention to the discrepancies between the portrayals in advertisements and the real lives of women. In the 1970s feminists criticised advertisements for portraying stereotypical images of women, effectively accusing advertising and the media of producing not only misleading but, in the words of Kathy Myers (1986), 'dangerously subversive images of women'. Studies document that both sexes were shown as stereotypes; men as working outside the homes and involved in the purchase of more expensive goods and services, women as being inactive and fulfilling decorative roles. Some thought that the portrayal of women in advertising had always been used as a political tool to keep women in their place. Feminists attempted to decode the social meaning of advertisements and to interpret the personal emotions or sexual behaviour of women in them. They pointed out that the adoption of the subliminal norms portrayed was seen as conducive to the purchase of the goods advertised. By the early 1980s the movement became politicised and affected both the pornographic and the advertising industries.

Though the washing powder television advertisements of the 1990s seem to have remained the same, many advertisers responded to feminist demands and acknowledged the changing images and roles of women in society. One of the major effects of the feminist movement, however, was the championing of more exaggerated and stronger **masculinity** in the commercial press. Men began to create their own gender-specific advertisements and the advertising industry has developed new ways of portraying women as sexual objects.

In the 1990s the interest of the feminist movement in the power of advertising seems to have subsided. New and powerful technological products have entered the markets. Though particularly computer technology has affected most areas of our lives, it is controlled and purchased by men. Little research of the 1990s deals with the images of women used in the advertising of technology. The evidence suggests that women are still being used as decorative objects not capable of handling the technology. If it is the case that information is **power**, then the distribution of the tools of information processing (i.e. computers) will influence the distribution of power. If women are being excluded from gaining access to computers, then they may also be excluded from gaining access to power.

The globalisation of communications over the Internet and the development of electronic commerce has brought new possibilities of advertising goods and services. While the research hotly debates the meaning of gender in this apparently genderless space, the commercial aspects of the Internet are perceived to be predominantly male. Sixty-eight per cent of all buyers on the Internet in the first half of 1998 were reported to be men, though a serious study of advertising on the Internet from the gender point of view is not known.

See also: feminism; gender

References and further reading

Courtney, A. and Whipple, T. (1984) *Sex Stereotyping in Advertising*, Lexington, MA: Lexington Books.
Myers, K. (1986) *Under-Stains: The Sense and Seduction of Advertising*, London: Comedia Publishing Group.
Williamson, J. (1981) *Decoding Advertisements, Ideology*

and Meaning in Advertising, London: Marion Boyars.

EVA TURNER

aesthetics, feminist

Aesthetics and philosophy of art refer to the branch of philosophy that investigates the nature of the arts, creativity, beauty, and interpretation. Feminist perspectives in aesthetics have drawn upon the work not only of philosophers but also historians of the arts, literary theorists, musicologists, and film theorists. What used to be seen as timeless concepts and universal values in aesthetics have been challenged by feminists, who argue that notions such as fine art, creative genius, and aesthetic appreciation are framed with bias as to **gender**. Though traditionally regarded as gender neutral, these concepts covertly select the activities of men for attention, ignore the creative work of women, and classify women as passive objects of appreciation.

One of the first questions that prompted feminist inquiry was why there have been so few esteemed female practitioners in most fields of art. In her 1971 essay, 'Why Are There No Great Women Artists?', art historian Linda **Nochlin** detailed the systematic exclusion of women from artistic training in the Euro-American tradition. She also posited that this exclusion might indicate a bias in the very concept of art itself. This bias has been pursued by theorists who have examined the concept of fine art in terms of the social values that framed this idea. The separation of 'art' from 'craft', for example, relegates to the latter inferior category activities and objects pursued for domestic, practical use. Since many women throughout history have been occupied in domestic work, their efforts go unnoticed because they are filtered out by the concept of 'art'. The notion of artistic genius similarly has excluded recognition of women. A term of praise, particularly in the romantic period, 'genius' has been used historically almost exclusively to describe male composers, writers, and painters. Christine Battersby (1989) has discovered how 'feminine' reproductive images were appropriated to describe artistic genius but detached from women themselves, thus rejecting female

creativity as the work of genius. To correct such biases, feminist scholars have not only discovered women who have contributed to the standard fine arts, but they have also broadened their research to include areas such as domestic craft and literary genres to which women were major contributors such as **diaries** and letters.

If women have been absent in great numbers from the ranks of recognised artists, they seem to have an undue presence, usually without their clothes on, among the subjects depicted in painting and sculpture. The combination of male painter and female nude subject, who serves both as Muse and model, led feminists to question the traditional claim that aesthetic attention is 'disinterested'. Philosophers have long singled out disinterestedness as the distinguishing characteristic of aesthetic value, marking it off from interested values such as economic, moral, scientific, or personal advantage. Perhaps pure form may be appreciated free from interest, but could all those nude models really be painted for the purpose of being looked at disinterestedly? By whom? Such questions developed into feminist theories of perception that collectively have come to be known as theories of 'the **gaze**'. These analyses reject the assumption that perception is gender neutral and has no reference to the 'subject position' of the person who is looking. Rather, feminists contend, perception is subtly filled with power or its absence: whether the perceiver occupies an empowered position (such as that of a male of a dominant social class) or the margins of social notice.

Theories of the gaze often employ terms of psychoanalytic theory (see **psychoanalysis**), positing that the pleasure gained from vision has its genesis in the formation of gender identity in infancy and childhood. These theories have been provocative and controversial, for not only are the tools of psychoanalysis contested among feminists, but the ability of the imagination to transcend one's actual subject position complicates determination of how a viewer appreciates a work of art. What is uncontested, however, is the idea that looking and appreciating are highly inflected with social values, and that these include gender as well as variables of class and ethnic or national identity.

Theorists and practitioners draw upon each other's work to reveal and combat the exclusion of women from recognition in contemporary art circles. The Guerilla Girls, for example, are a group of practising artists who, wearing their signature gorilla masks, leaflet art venues and expose discriminatory practices that have governed the world of art. Feminist artists often incorporate explicit political messages into their art, drawing the ire of critics who believe they have violated the proper boundaries of aesthetic value. Some artists have developed styles that employ symbolism from women's bodies, and many shun conventional media such as paint and canvas and use materials such as embroidery, fabric, or even foods to draw attention to the creative traditions of women that are excluded from standard concepts of high art.

Such efforts have raised the question of whether there is a 'feminine aesthetic', that is, a recognizable style that is more associated with women artists than with men. While there are advocates of this idea who see such traits as cooperation and blurred boundaries of the self as distinctive values discoverable in women's art, the notion of a feminine aesthetic faces both the difficulty of empirical test and the criticism that it trades on what are nothing more than stereotyped and incorrect generalisations about what is 'feminine'. The debate over this issue is replicated in many areas of philosophy as feminist theoretical perspectives are deepened and pursued.

See also: African American art history; censorship; deconstruction, feminist; film theory, feminist; interpretation; lesbian litera-ture; literary theory, feminist; literature, images of women in; mass media; musicology, feminist; pornography; psychoanalytic feminist literary theory; women's writing

References and further reading

Battersby, C. (1989) *Gender and Genius*, Bloomington, IN: Indiana University Press.

Brand, P.Z. and Korsmeyer, C. (eds) (1995) *Feminism and Tradition in Aesthetics*, University Park: Pennsylvania State University Press.

Felski, R. (1989) *Beyond Feminist Aesthetics*, Cambridge, MA: Harvard University Press.

Hein, H. and Korsmeyer, C. (eds) (1993) *Aesthetics in Feminist Perspective*, Bloomington, IN: Indiana University Press.

Nochlin, L. (1988) *Women, Art, and Power and Other Essays*, New York: Harper and Row.

Pollock, G. (1988) *Vision and Difference*, London: Routledge.

Wolff, J. (1990) *Feminine Sentences: Essays on Women and Culture*, Cambridge, MA: Polity Press.

CAROLYN KORSMEYER

affidamento/entrustment

Advocated in the 1980s by the Milan Women's Bookstore Collective the term affidamento designates a social alliance between two women of different age and/or status. Predicated on a theory of sexual **difference**, affidamento seeks to establish a female frame of reference where the transmission of knowledge and authority and the exchange of mutual valorisation and trust between women is enabled through existing disparities and power differentials between them. Affidamento celebrates the figure of the symbolic mother theorised by Luisa Muraro as ensuring symbolic mediation between women. The notion of disparity is embedded in the term affidamento which in Italian legal terms refers to custody – a meaning lost in the word entrustment. Controversy over this practice focuses on its diadic hierarchical structure, its potential stifling of the less empowered woman, and its challenge to an egalitarian ethos.

References and further reading

Milan Women's Bookstore Collective (1987) *Sexual Difference: A Theory of Social-Symbolic Practice*, trans. from the Italian by P. Cicogna and T. de Lauretis, Bloomington, IN: Indiana University Press, 1990.

SUSANNA F. FERLITO

affirmative action

Affirmative action refers to a range of mechanisms – legislated or voluntary – designed to address **systemic discrimination** experienced by members of groups, such as women and people of colour. Such initiatives are broadly directed toward increasing the participation and status of disadvantaged groups in the labour force and/or may encompass reforms that seek to increase representation of particular groups within public bodies and educational institutions (Bacchi 1996: 15). In contrast to complaint based anti-discrimination provisions, which address issues of discrimination after the fact, affirmative action is considered proactive.

Affirmative action rests on a category based – 'women', 'blacks' – approach to equality. Feminists have analysed the problematic nature of a legal model that tends to simplify complex intersecting social relations by emphasizing one characteristic of difference over another. They have also pointed out that categories are constructed, by those with power, within particular contexts. And, they implicitly reference a dominant group norm (Iyer 1993: 182–94).

Affirmative action is being virulently attacked by neo-conservatives who are attempting to dismantle initiatives. The 1995 University of California decision to prohibit the use of race-based affirmative action in admissions is viewed as a key victory for opponents. The debate has focused on what measures of 'preferential' treatment are acceptable as opposed to what factors account for the exclusion of women and other groups from positions of power (Bacchi 1996: 34). Measures have been characterised by opponents as 'reverse racism', 'unfair' and denying merit. This characterisation is based on an assumption that many feminists have vigorously challenged, namely that every individual should be treated exactly the *same* as every other individual. It thus denies the social and historical context in which groups have been excluded or treated inequitably. Moreover, it neglects the ways in which public policy and organisational practices incorporate gendered and racialised assumptions that reproduce systemic inequality.

At the heart of the debate is the question of what measures are 'just'. This controversy is an example of the application of a 'distributive paradigm of justice' which emphasises the allocation of material goods (Young 1990: 15–38). Within these terms, racial and gender justice become defined in terms of how jobs and tasks are distributed among individuals and groups. Yet feminists are also concerned with social constructions of women's work. Jobs and occupations may be associated with masculine or feminine characteristics. And, 'this is not itself a distributive issue' (Young 1990: 23).

See also: categories and dichotomies

References and further reading

Bacchi, C. (1996) *The Politics of Affirmative Action*, London: Sage.
Iyer, N. (1993) 'Categorical Denials: Equality Rights and the Shaping of Social Identity', *Queen's Law Journal* 19: 179–207.
Young, I. (1990) *Justice and the Politics of Difference*, New Jersey: Princeton.

CHRISTINA GABRIEL

African American art history

Racism has affected all aspects of African American life. That some black artists have been embraced by the wider art world does not ignore the reality that most black artists' accomplishments have been ignored due to a lack of gallery representation, critical reviews and offers of museum exhibitions. The reality is that the market place plays a critical role in the careers of artists and for black artists their parallel artistic lives are separate and unequal. This will continue to be the case in a society where institutionalised racism is so entrenched that it is not only acceptable and condoned, but also unrecognised by those who are the perpetrators.

Before they came to the USA, art was an integrated part of life for most Africans. Historically, many African slaves came to the USA with skills and knowledge of an artistic past and, as a form of resistance, they integrated African designs into their lives and material culture in the USA. They were allowed to create functional crafts which could be of use on the plantations. As artisans, men carved furniture, worked with iron and did silversmithing and women practised needlework, although there is evidence that older men also did some of the needlecrafts like patch-work quilting.

Even before the end of slavery there were free men and at least one freewoman of colour who were active professional painters. Joshua Johnston, Edward M. Banister, Robert S. Duncanson, Jules Lion, and Grafton Tyler Brown concentrated primarily on landscape and other scenes. Working as early as 1833, educator Sarah Mapps Douglass was an ardent abolitionist and feminist and her surviving works are the earliest known paintings by an African American woman. After the Emancipation Proclamation, 1863 (freeing all slaves in territories held by Confederates), Mary Edmonia Lewis became the earliest African American sculptor and, more significantly, her 1867 *Forever Free* focused on the liberation of slaves. While other professional black artists avoided the black figure Lewis, as had Douglass, undertook it directly, depicting not just the freed man, but also a freed woman. Although very similar to Douglass's kneeling slave of 1833, Lewis's freedwoman's kneeling position next to the freedman has been viewed by some late twentieth-century art historians as problematising her free status.

In the first two decades of the twentieth century, the Industrial Revolution changed the face of northern cities with factories and with the arrival of hundreds of black migrants from the southern states. Northern black intellectuals focused on the migrants, making them the subjects of their music, literature and visual arts, especially during what is known as the Harlem Renaissance of the late 1920s. The recognition of an African American culture heightened a sense of racial identity and solidarity among blacks.

The Harlem Renaissance and New Negro movements selectively promoted African American artists from New York and major northern centres like Chicago, Detroit, Washington, DC and the San Francisco Bay Area. As African American men were just gaining recognition, there were a few women who persisted to develop careers in the visual arts, such as August Savage, Elizabeth Prophet and Selma Burke. Even more importantly,

many black women who could not practice art supported it through organizing exhibitions or art shows in their homes, as well as providing opportunities through art education and patronage for black artists.

In the following decades, with a few exceptions such as Lois Mailou Jones and Elizabeth Catlett, black women artists made little impact on the art world, and remained in the background until the black nationalist movement in the 1960s and 1970s. Revolutionary-minded African Americans producing art with overt and urgent political messages dominated that era. Faith Ringgold was one of the most visually outspoken women artists with her painting *Die Nigger* as was Betye Saar with her multi-media assemblages *Liberation of Aunt Jemima* and *Sambo's Banjo*. Ringgold vividly showed bloodletting in the streets, while Saar questioned whether blacks were going to dance to whites' tune as Sambo did, or fight. She also armed the ever-familiar Aunt Jemima mammy figure with a rifle and inserted a Black Power fist at her foot, further empowering the domestic icon. Creating a precedent for other women, black women artists began to exhibit as frequently as black men and by the 1980s and 1990s women artists such as Adrian Piper, Lorna Simpson, Alison Saar (Betye Saar's daughter), Carrie Mae Weems, and Kara Walker dominated the black postmodernist art scene. Black women artists have become increasingly vocal, not just about race but also about their identities and sexual sensibilities. Surely, feminism and woman-centred studies have benefited these women, both by articulating their aesthetics and through patronage. Yet sexual politics as a factor in the reception of some artists' works over others cannot be ignored. For example, the sexual exploits that run rampant in Walker's works have given rise to a following, mainly white and often men, who encourage candid and often fantasised narratives on intimate even (for many black folks) taboo themes and situations of black women's sexual behaviour. Causing a storm of controversy within black communities, this type of imagery has engendered debates on censorship, manipulation of black artists by a powerful white art world and a manipulation of white men by black women artists. Yet Walker's work has found support among feminists, black and white.

The presence of the black figure in American art by black as well as white artists has always been politically motivated and thus many African American artists continue to be centred on the black figure even if only in abstract conceptualisations. It is a subject that eluded their control in the slavery and reconstruction eras, but one with abundant complexities and histories. Because African Americans are continually marginalised in American society, each era offers opportunities for self-redefinition as black women and men expand their identities.

See also: African feminism; race

References and further reading

Buick, K.P. (1995)'The Ideal Works of Edmonia Lewis, Invoking and Inverting Autobiography', *American Art* 9, (2) (Summer): 9.

Collins, P.H. (1991) *Black Feminist Thought: Knowledge, Consciousness and the Politics of Empowerment*, New York: Routledge.

Patton, S. (1998) *African American Art* (Oxford History of Art), New York: Oxford University Press.

Suttleworth, C. (ed.) (1996) *Three Generations of African American Women Sculptors: A Study in Paradox*, Philadelphia, PA: The Afro-American Historical and Cultural Museum.

LIZZETTA LEFALLE-COLLINS

African American families

African American families, adults, and children can be fully understood only in relation to the interaction of social class (see **class analysis**), culture, ethnicity, and **race**. The 1960s and 1970s were times of hope, while the 1980s and 1990s were periods of despair. The twenty-first century will be a time of consolidating our gains and moving forward to reach our interpretation of feminist goals.

African Americans are about one-eighth of the American population, and will be one in seven within twenty years. There is a growing diversity within the African American community: diverse socio-economic groups; religious groupings; and life styles. The diversity will go beyond just race to a greater examination of gender-related theories.

The historical subordination of and devaluation of African American families is substantially different from all other immigrant groups in the USA. The American enslavement experience brought loss of control and violent uprootings. These brutal experiences have shaped the ideological forces of the strengths and weaknesses of modern day families. The African/Caribbean continuities have contributed to the strengths that have enabled families to cope with adversities. Among the cultural legacies that are African derived, and have been altered in the USA, are the oral traditions, spirituality, rhythmic movements of expression, and communalism.

Family structure

The active roles of women, along with men, have often been misinterpreted by social scientists as being matriarchal. The typical family organisation was often at odds with the wider community that held to the more nuclear family forms. Children were often closer to the women's fictive and blood kin relatives. Because of culture and poverty, the extended families and their support systems have been cited as one of the major survival systems. Even when families are no longer in poverty, these patterns of strong connections continue.

Bumpass has stated that African American children have only a 1 in 5 chance of growing up with two parents until the age of 16, with fewer resources than with two married parents.

Poverty is present for 65 per cent of single mother/child units, but only 18 per cent of married couples. The imbalance of the sex ratio is a major problem, and lack of eligible men is unacknowledged by those who are in positions of formulating national social policies. Even if all men married, there would still be many women who would be left without mates. Most important is the growing disparity of black and white incomes that are the result of economic restructuring, discrimination, and impoverishment and lead to greater exploitation of women.

See also: family, the

References and further reading

Ingrassia, M. (1993) 'A World Without Fathers: The Struggle to Save the Black Family', *Newsweek*, 16–29, August 30 (special report).

McAdoo, H.P. (1997) *Black Families*, Thousand Oaks, CA: Sage, 3rd edn.

Sudarkasa, N. (1993) 'Female-Headed African American Households: Some Neglected Dimensions', in H.P. McAdoo, (ed.) *Family Ethnicity: Strength in Diversity*, Newbury Park, CA: Sage, 81–9.

HARRIETTE PIPES McADOO

African feminism

African feminism operates within a global political economy in which **sexism** cannot be isolated from the larger political and economic forces responsible for the exploitation and **oppression** of both men and women. The result is a form of feminism that is transformative in human and social terms rather than in personal and sexist terms. It is activist and shaped by responses to foreign domination, racist ideologies and gender-based discrimination. It has relevance for societies on the African continent and in the African diaspora.

Studies of African women have contributed to the development of a significant body of anthropological theory and feminist revisionist analyses in many academic disciplines. African historiography represented women as active political and economic actors prior to and even during the colonial era. The complexity of African social systems has challenged many approaches inspired by dichotomous models, including the **public/private** debate, the **nature/culture** debate and the tendency to explain social change through evolutionary paradigms. Feminists of all persuasions have welcomed the presence of relatively egalitarian gatherer/hunter societies and matrilineal systems in Africa as a challenge to the myth of universal male dominance. The flexibility of gender systems in some African societies, particularly among the Igbo of southeastern Nigeria, has added new dimensions to the discourse on gender asymmetry as a social construct which is subject to change.

British functionalism/structuralism which flourished between 1920 and 1970 focuses on a wide array of subjects dealing with **kinship** and marriage systems implicitly revealing the important position of women in maintaining the corporate structure of these groups. A number of these studies were conducted during the colonial period, but colonialism as a subject of study was either ignored or considered as a given. Reactions from some feminist scholars, neo-Marxists and dependency theorists who analyse the extent to which Africa's underdevelopment is a result of its historical and current exploitation by Europe and the west in general, have emphasised the negative impact of colonialism on women.

For much of the nineteenth and twentieth centuries, the African continent was dominated by external powers in ways that have profoundly influenced social structures, gender relations and alliances. A large number of women's movements and associations in Africa have their origins in anti-colonial and nationalist struggles. They increased their strength by establishing coalitions with political movements, trade unions and youth leagues, many of which were committed to ending colonial rule, apartheid and neo-colonialism. There are many examples of studies and novels about women protesting against colonial rule throughout Africa, the most famous being the 1929 Igbo Women's War in Nigeria. Today, most women's groups continue to emphasise women's rights within larger socio-political contexts of democratic change, economic development and social justice.

By historical and demographic extension, African feminism has relevance for women of African heritage in the African diaspora, including north and south America, the Caribbean and Europe, who have also been exposed to oppressive forces of domination. This domination is manifested primarily through slavery, institutional racism and internal colonialism in addition to sexism (see **slavery in the USA**). African feminism results in multiple consciousness based not just on gender but also on race, socio-economic status and historical realities. African feminism represents reaction to an inclusive and compounded form of oppression which makes the majority of black women among the most oppressed women of the world. On the other hand African feminism has enabled them to develop survival skills, strength, resourcefulness and power through alliances with others. Lack of guaranteed male support has increased their capacity for self-reliance.

From the perspective of African feminism, patriarchal systems within a global political economy are hierarchically ordered. Men as well as women in well financed and politically dominant patriarchal systems can exercise absolute power over subjected groups. Within Africa, the patriarchal impact can be modified by male loss of status and land to a foreign power. A number of internal contradictions can also dilute excessive patriarchal rigidities. Among the Luo of Kenya, for example, the paradox of male dominance on the one hand tends to conflict with the social significance of women as mothers and food producers on the other. Among the patrilineal Zulu the priesthood is reserved for women. Women's influential interest groups tend to be prevalent in patrilineal societies and many African women writers have demonstrated the strength and resilience inherent in African feminism when confronted by the challenges of patriarchal rigidities.

African women have traditionally performed important social, economic and political roles including executive positions as chiefs, queens and leaders in government. Parallel institutions representing female and male social worlds have enabled African women to achieve a measure of independence and **autonomy** while cooperating with men and having the power to impose sanctions on them. Secret societies like the Sande (female) and Poro (male) in west Africa are examples of this. Female political decision is inherent in representative institutions such as the Iyalode (Yoruba) and Omu (Igbo) in Nigeria. Gender-based and collective acts intended to ridicule, shame, boycott and pressure someone or groups of the opposite sex are frequently used in times of violation of cultural norms and rules but also to release tension between men and women. For example, these acts can result in a man being pressured to meet his obligations to his family, or to stop abusing his wife and in a woman to refrain from nagging her husband. Nature is an integral part of culture and not in opposition to it. Women's fertility is valued and often associated with fertility

of the land. The centrality of children and multiple mothering systems provided by the extended family reduce the isolation characteristic of the privatised western nuclear family.

African feminism faces enormous challenges which go beyond conventional international feminist concerns, although many aspects of the articulated international feminist agenda are shared. These include women's role in production and in maintaining households, their lack of access to productive resources, access to **education**, **health** and social services, **violence** against women, rape, sexual harassment, forced or economically coerced **prostitution**, gender-based discrimination in employment and exposure to injurious cultural practices. In addition, the majority of African women struggle daily against poverty and malnutrition produced by destructive international and national policies which include structural adjustment programmes, the debt burden, reverse resource flows, globalisation of production and markets, armed conflict and political instability.

The feminist agenda for African women is comprehensive, holistic, urgent and human-centred. It relates directly to questions of human survival and well-being. The social and economic development of nations and the **welfare** and rights of all people are central to its quest for full gender equality (see **equality and difference**). Many women's groups in Africa demonstrate a feminism that is also self-critical, challenging antiquated customs and cultural practices maintained by religious laws and customary practices and, ironically, by women themselves. At the same time they are also striving to preserve the many positive and relevant traditional customs which recognise their social, economic and political importance and contribute to their self-reliance, resourcefulness and empowerment.

References and further reading

Adadiume, I. (1987) *Male Daughters, Female Husbands: Gender and Sex in an African Society*, London: Zed Books.

Bay, E. and Hafkin, N. (eds) (1976) *Women in Africa*, Stanford, CA: Stanford University Press.

Lebeuf, A. (1963) 'The Role of Women in the

Political Organization of African Societies', in D. Paulme (ed.) *Women of Tropical Africa*, Berkeley, CA: University of California Press.

Khasiani, S.A. and Njiro, E.I. (eds) (1993) *The Women's Movement in Kenya*, Nairobi: Association of African Women for Research and Development (AAWORD).

Steady, F.C. (ed.) (1981) *The Black Woman Cross-Culturally*, Cambridge, MA: Schenkman Books.

Sudarkasa, N. (1973) *Where Women Work: A Study of Yoruba Women in the Market Place and in the Home*, Ann Arbor, MI: Museum of Anthropology, University of Michigan.

Terborg-Penn, R. *et al.* (eds) (1987) *Women of Africa and the African Diaspora: An Interdisciplinary Perspective*, Washington: Howard University Press.

FILOMENA CHIOMA STEADY

Afrocentric analysis

Afrocentricity is a theory of social change which builds on négritude, the black power movement and black cultural nationalism. It places Africa and the diaspora at the centre of analysis. Molefe Asante suggests 'Afrocentricity is a perspective which allows Africans to be subjects of historical experiences rather than objects on the fringe of Europe' (1987). Afrocentric historiography challenges the Eurocentric preoccupation with Greece; however, in turn, it valorises Egypt.

Afrocentric views on social relationships tend to be culturally conservative. Black nuclear families are considered authentic. Black lesbian and gay relations are deemed unnatural, dangerous to the black family (see **African American families**), and a cultural imposition of western civilisation and white slave society. For Asante, homosexuality is not an 'Afrocentric way of life', rather a sickness or a 'racial death wish'. Some black feminists criticise Afrocentricism as an ahistorical and masculinist romanticisation of pre-diaspora history which enables a black macho and essentialist view of 'race', gender, sexuality and family. Others interpret Afrocentricity as a standpoint that affirms the black gendered self across time and space.

See also: black consciousness; black feminism(s); standpoint theory

References and further reading

Asante, M.A. (1987) *The Afrocentric Idea*, Philadelphia, PA: Temple University Press.

Collins, P.H. (1998) *Fighting Words: Black Women and the Search for Justice*, Minneapolis, MI: University of Minnesota Press.

MALINDA S. SMITH

age studies and gender

Feminist age studies is a nascent movement toward integrating 'age' into theory-building as well as into research, politics, and practice – not only as a variable, but on a par with **gender**, class, **race/**ethnicity, sexual orientation, religion, disability, and place. A critical cultural studies, its purview includes all ages of life, considered relationally; the institutions of the *life course* as differentiated for different subject positions; and intergenerational relations, in history and now. Age becomes another indispensable tool for reconceptualizing narrative, embodiment, socioeconomic organisation, age ideology, epistemological bias, interpersonal relations, and the development of selfhood. Age studies analyse power issues around age and devise emancipatory interventions.

Age studies' founding tenet – even old age is 'not solely a biological but also a cultural fact' – is exhaustively documented in the critical half of Simone de Beauvoir's *omnium gatherum*, *The Coming of Age* (1972: 13). **Beauvoir** focuses on the puzzle that men, although they dominate society, have condemned most of their own old to 'poverty, decrepitude, wretchedness, and despair' in so many historical periods and cultures (2). She isolates diverse sources of ageism: class – destroying 'the solidarity between workers and the unproductive old', 'the hatred of parents [sic] bred by patriarchal harshness' (3, 46), revolutionary or unstable regimes, technological change, consumerism, the cult of youth, the decline of cyclical religions, and the inability of younger adults to imagine their own future as elders.

Feminist gerontology has concentrated on justifying and performing analyses of gendered difference, and considering and valuing 'old women' within depersonalised, androcentric disciplines.

This necessary and heroic perspective, 'ageing and women', has also developed through engagements with multiculturalism, feminist men's studies, midlife studies, and poststructuralism (see **poststructuralism/postmodernism**).

Age studies is also called into being by fear that age is becoming an overriding category-slicer and constructor of subjectivities, a trend generating (in the USA) new stages like 'the midlife' and 'syndromes' like the 'empty nest', named 'cohorts' like 'Generation X' and 'the Boomers', and a master biography of decline starting at midlife. When 'age' predominates, the effects are to subordinate the politics of gender and other differences, reify stage theory, and justify age discrimination, generation gaps (e.g. the construction of **third-wave feminism** while older feminists are still alive and active), and intergenerational wars (e.g. over social security).

Feminist age studies provides a basis for theory and resistance by firmly re-placing old age – and other ages – within the continuum of particularised life courses. 'Ageing' in this conjunctural approach emphasises being aged-by-culture. Contexts include: early gendered socialisation into a culture's age ideology; cumulative biosocial effects (such as the damage from environmental racism or caretaker stress), historical conditions that affect cohorts diversely at different chronological ages (such as economic depressions, new divorce laws or remarriage customs); cultural signals that the 'entrance' into the next age-class of the not-young is occurring (such as menopause or Viagra discourse, the glass ceiling of age, or tropes that associate elders with childish dependency).

The political-economy perspective on the life course, for example, argues that women's (and some men's) excessive poverty in old age is mainly 'a consequence of the lifelong effects of gender, racial, and socioeconomic stratification ... the institutional arrangements and processes of the family ... the labour market and the state', in the words of Terry Arendell and Carroll Estes (1991: 209). Looking at their various 'longitudinal' materials, scholars in many fields (psychologists, literary critics, historians, psychoanalysts) challenge traditional notions of decline and static rigidity over the later lives of women. They have found creativity; new psychodynamic conflicts; cognitive,

ethical, and psychological development (including desired transformations in gender identity and increased autonomy, assertiveness, and political activism).

Many theorists emphasise the narrativising the life course beyond youth genres. In *Remembered Lives*, anthropologist Barbara Myerhoff listens to poor, elderly Jewish immigrant women in California, and invents a genre to highlight their activist agency and their unstated values. Asking why these women are better than men at being old, the Grace Paley of ethnographers answered by looking diachronically at the way the women had been considered 'custodians of the mundane realm' in their earlier shtetl (small Jewish town) lives – good preparation for the time when '*the* full-time role for both sexes' becomes the expression (1992: 200, 212). Male later-life supremacy, familiarly known as the 'double standard of ageing', is also problematised in Margaret Morganroth Gullette's speculations, in *Declining to Decline* (1997), that postindustrial capitalism cares less than before about protecting patriarchal midlife privilege, and that the commerce in ageing needs male consumers too to buy anti-ageing products.

Life story-telling can be reparative, as tellers become conscious of how they were socialised into age lore, starting in childhood. Women and men can learn to recognise period and cohort pressures on them, the psychostructural constraints on ageing-into-the-middle-years and beyond, as well as discursive incitements to internalise decline and live according to standard biographical scripts. If these people can simultaneously hold fast to their own multiple linked stories of identities reinterpreted over time, Gullette envisions the emergence of a new genre: self-reflexive and critical 'age autobiography'.

Feminists also theorise intergenerational attachments, usually between women, as a resistance to ageism as well as to heterosexism and capitalist alienation. Some of this work builds on Audre **Lorde**'s insight that generation gaps can be 'an important social tool for a repressive society', operationalised through 'historical amnesia' (1984: 116–7). Literary and psychoanalytic theorist Kathleen Woodward (1999), critiquing the rigid separation of parent/child generations constructed by Oedipal theory, revitalises the bonds between grandmother and granddaughter, and among female lineages and 'fictive kin'. Observing traditional female age-hierarchies, anthropologists Judith K. Brown and Virginia Kerns (1992) find that ageing-into-the-midlife may increase women's power, albeit through the oppression of younger women.

'Gerontophobia' names the belief that however thoroughly ageism can be deconstructed, it has an essential, ahistorical component of horror. Although feminists know that 'an expulsion' is typically *followed* rather than preceded by a 'repulsion' (as Iris Marion Young notes), gerontophobia lingers, supported as Woodward demonstrates in *Aging and Its Discontents* (1991), by Freud, Proust and other high-culture fictions. She counterposes phantasms of the 'immobile', 'fragmenting' or 'empty' body of old age with alternatives to the 'youthful structure of the look' such as visualisations of self-accepting bodies and theory that ends 'the repression of ageing'.

Age studies, named only in 1993, is undertheorised. Its practitioners need a heightened sense of unity, to sharpen debate. Theorists not recognizing age as a category of diversity and oppression might ask what impedes them. How old is their implied subject? Does she ever age? Noticing that diverse theorists are youthfully busy 'double-crossing' and 'defying' **phallogocentrism**, causing 'trouble', being 'unruly', 'messing up' margins and centre, can we spot another reason why they do not confer on 'older' women, despite their being multiply Othered, either transgressive chic or compelling abjectness?

See also: class analysis, UK; class analysis, US; disability, women and; heterosexism, heteronormativity; menopause (medical); political economy, feminist

References and further reading

Arber, S. and Ginn, J. (1995) *Connecting Gender and Ageing*, Buckingham: Open University Press. (See also J. McMullin on 'Theorizing age and gender relations' pp. 30–41.)

Arendell, T. and Estes, C.L. (1991) 'Older Women in the Post-Reagan Era', in M. Minkler and C.L. Estes (eds) *Critical Perspectives on Aging*, Amityville, NY: Baywood.

Beauvoir, S. de (1972) *The Coming of Age*, trans. P. O'Brian, New York: Norton.

Bell, N. (1997) 'What Setting Limits May Mean: A Feminist Critique of Daniel Callahan's *Setting Limits*', in M. Pearsall (ed.) *The Other Within Us*, Boulder, CO: Westview.

Guillemard, A-M. (1996) 'Equity Between Generations in Aging Societies', in T.K. Hareven (ed.) *Aging and Generational Relations*, Hawthorne, NY: Aldine de Gruyter.

Gullette, M.M. (1997) *Declining to Decline: Cultural Combat and the Politics of the Midlife*, Charlottesville, VA: University Press of Virginia.

—— (1999) 'Age Studies as Cultural Studies', in T.R. Cole, R. Ray, and R. Kastenbaum (eds) *Handbook of the Humanities and Aging*, New York: Springer.

Hockey, J. and James, A. (1993) *Growing Up and Growing Old*, London: Sage Publications.

Kerns, V. and Brown, J.K. (1992) *In Her Prime*, Urbana, IL: University of Illinois Press.

Laws, G. (1995) 'Understanding Ageism: Lessons from Feminism and Postmodernism', *The Gerontologist*, 35, 1.

Lorde, A. (1984) *Sister Outsider*, Trumansburg, NY: Crossing Press.

Myerhoff, B. *et al.* (1992) *Remembered Lives: The Work of Ritual, Storytelling, and Growing Older*, ed. M. Kaminsky, Ann Arbor, MI: University of Michigan Press.

Ray, R.E. (2000) *Beyond Nostalgia: Aging and Life-Story Writing*, Charlottesville, VA: University Press of Virginia.

Squier, S.M. (1994) *Babes in Bottles*, New Brunswick, NJ: Rutgers University Press.

Woodward, K. (1991) *Aging and Its Discontents. Freud and Other Fictions*, Bloomington, IN: Indiana University Press.

MARGARET MORGANROTH GULLETTE

agency

The notion of agency is both a facet of and a deliberate corrective to the more traditional philosophical topic of action. In Anglo-American philosophy, action is usually discussed in terms of the possibility of free will, the nature of rationality and motivation, and the capacities of persons; the social and political contexts in which action takes place are often overlooked. By contrast, agency is concerned with the social conditions for and requirements of action, as well as with the internal and external barriers to action. As such, agency is a subject of central importance for feminist theorists and activists seeking to identify the causes of women's subordination and oppression, and possibilities for their self-realisation and freedom.

Contemporary discussions of agency in philosophy and political thought can be traced to developments in social theory during the 1980s and 1990s. In particular, Michel Foucault's writings on the nature and effect of social power and relations of power; material, cultural and discursive practices, including 'disciplinary' practices of the modern state; and the 'technologies of the self' in the constitution of modern subjects have been important for feminist discussions of subjectivity, **oppression**, and agency. Feminist thinkers such as Jana Sawicki and Sandra Bartky have employed Foucault's thought to explore the ways in which modern states shape women's identities both as specific socio-historical subjects and as self-disciplining, feminine subjects through social practices and discourses.

The issue of agency has come to the fore in recent debates between feminists sympathetic to postmodernism and psychoanalytic theory, and feminists critical of postmodernism. Judith **Butler** argues in her highly influential *Gender Trouble* that identities are discursively produced through gender 'performances'; her controversial suggestion that the very notion of 'woman' is overly essentialist has generated the criticism that without this category we cannot name and work to transform sex-based oppressions. Seyla **Benhabib** and Nancy Fraser question the usefulness of deconstructionist thought for feminism (especially the work of Jacques Derrida), and disagree with postmodernists' suggestions that feminists should dispense with Enlightenment conceptions of **autonomy**, rationality, truth, and the idea of a unified subject. Postmodern feminists counter that deconstructive approaches do not efface the possibility of agency or social change, but merely offer a more accurate, and radical, picture of the contingency and instability of social identities and relations.

See also: deconstruction, feminist; post-structuralism/postmodernism; self, the

References and further reading

Bartky, S. (1990) *Femininity and Domination: Studies in the Phenomenology of Oppression*, New York and London: Routledge.

Benhabib, S., Butler, J., Cornell, D. and Fraser, N. (eds) (1995) *Feminist Contentions: A Philosophical Exchange*, New York and London: Routledge.

Butler, J. (1990) *Gender Trouble. Feminism and the Subversion of Identity*, New York and London: Routledge.

Foucault, M. (1978) *The History of Sexuality*, vol. 1, trans. R. Hurley, New York: Pantheon.

MONIQUE DEVEAUX

agential realism

Agential realism is a theory of knowledge and reality whose fundamental premise is that reality consists of *phenomena* that are reconstituted in *intra-action* with the interventions of knowers. 'Intra-action' signifies a dynamic involving the inseparability of the objects and agencies of intervention (as opposed to interactions which reinscribe the contested dichotomy). Agential realism accounts for both the contingency and efficacy of knowledge. It provides an understanding of the interactions between human and nonhuman, material and discursive, and natural and cultural factors in the production of knowledge. One of its basic aims is to move considerations of epistemic practices beyond the traditional realism versus **social constructionism** debates.

Agential realism provides an embodied understanding of **objectivity** and calls for accountability for the intra-active constitution of 'subjects' and 'objects'. It builds upon the insight that observations do not provide a window onto an observation-independent reality; rather, the interventions of observers form an integral part of what observations reveal. The intra-active entanglement of the 'agencies of observation' and the 'objects of observation' is called a phenomenon. Objective properties refer to phenomena, not to abstract 'objects'. For example, ultrasound technologies do not reveal an observation-independent entity with inherent properties, rather the sonogram records properties of the intra-action of 'the foetus' as iteratively constituted through various practices and the apparatuses of observations. Agential realism offers an analysis of the constitution of the foetus as a human subject, including issues of responsibility for those constituting practices. At the same time, agential realism recognises the **agency** of both the objects and subjects of knowledge (e.g. the fact that the foetus 'kicks back').

In its reformulation of agency and its analysis of the productive, constraining, and exclusionary nature of practices (including their crucial role in the materialisation of the **body**), agential realism goes beyond performativity theories (see **Butler, Judith**) by providing a framework for taking account of the discursive *and* material nature of social practices. In particular, it provides a way to incorporate important material constraints and conditions into analyses while recognising the role that *material-discursive* practices play in making these factors intelligible. And it understands the dynamics of power in terms of intra-actions, thereby providing an alternative to **essentialism** versus constructionism, agency versus structure, and idealism versus materialism debates in feminist theory. Intra-actions entail a nondeterministic causality and enlarge the possibilities for agency beyond liberal and poststructuralist conceptions (see **poststructuralism/postmodernism**).

See also: philosophy of science; situated knowledges

References and further reading

Barad, K. (1998) 'Agential Realism', in M. Biagioli (ed.) *The Science Studies Reader*, New York: Routledge.

—— (1998) 'Getting Real', *Differences: A Journal of Feminist Cultural Studies* 10 (2): 87–126.
—— (1996) 'Meeting the Universe Halfway', in L.H. Nelson and J. Nelson (eds) *Feminism, Science, and the Philosophy of Science*, Dordrecht: Kluwer.

KAREN BARAD

AIDS, women and

Federally funded research, preventive education, and media representations about the HIV pandemic have been controversial topics for feminists since the federal recognition of the US HIV epidemic in the 1980s. AIDS (acquired immune deficiency syndrome) is a cluster of opportunistic infections incurred by the compromised human immune system caused by HIV (human immunodeficiency virus). HIV is contagious through the exchange of body fluids: semen, vaginal secretions, and blood. HIV transmission quickly became politicised due to exclusionary and stereotypical categories initially coined by the Centres for Disease Control (CDC) to refer to socially marginalised groups adversely affected by the epidemic. Feminist medical researcher Gena Corea (1992) chronicles that by 1981, the CDC had identified the new syndrome; yet the National Institute of Health did not begin to fund research on this syndrome until the mid-1980s. Until 1992, gynecological symptoms associated with HIV infection were excluded by the CDC's list of opportunistic diseases correlated with this syndrome. This exclusion caused the clinical misrecognition of many women's AIDS-related deaths and contributed to the pre-1993 paucity of federal funding for research on HIV-infected women.

Feminist philosopher Linda Singer (1993) argues that in the 1980s, homophobic media and public policy discourses about AIDS encouraged panic about homosexuality and colluded with the neoconservative backlash signified by 'family values' campaigns against women's reproductive rights. In opposition to the neoconservative backlash, feminists initiated coalitional efforts with male AIDS activists to persuade federal research agencies to adopt more egalitarian procedures, humane methods, and clinical research trials that are inclusive of women and people of colour. They continue to try to persuade local school boards to adopt preventive education strategies that include information about women's reproductive and sexual health care, and to persuade public health officials to redress race and gender inequities in public health policies and institutional health care. Feminists have succeeded in persuading the CDC to revise the definition of AIDS to include cervical cancer and other opportunistic diseases typically associated with women, and to expand the CDC's standards of care and prevention. Gena Corea describes the feminist **cultural politics** of AIDS activism that demands inclusion and equity for women and people of colour.

Feminist participation in AIDS activism dovetails with the broader feminist agenda of addressing the neoconservative backlash against the civil rights movement by the US federal government and the courts in the 1980s and 1990s. Political theorist Zillah Eisenstein (1994) shows the debilitating effect of neoconservatism on policy makers' efforts to remedy the disproportionately high HIV transmission rates and AIDS lethality rates in communities of people of colour and in socioeconomically disadvantaged groups. Feminist theory will continue to challenge the interlocking structures of **oppression** experienced by marginalised groups, and to critique the homophobic, sexist, and racist assumptions that may subvert coalitional efforts to prevent HIV transmission in specific communities.

See also: homophobia; oppression

References and further reading

Corea, G. (1992) *The Invisible Epidemic*, New York: Harper Collins.
Eisenstein, Z. (1994) *The Color of Gender*, Berkeley, CA: University of California Press.
Singer, L. (1993) *Erotic Welfare*, New York: Routledge.

KATE MEHURON

alterity

Used to characterise being different, otherness, alterity is a term of art in postcolonial feminist discourse, especially in discussions of *cultural alterity*.

It refers to the imperialism and silencing consequent upon representing (usually non-white) cultures as subordinate to dominant cultures, viewing them through the power structures, and requiring them to legitimate themselves in the language and value systems of the dominant. Issues about the limits of cross-cultural communication when compromise and translation go only one way – from subordinate to dominant – are constitutive of postcolonial commitments to refusing recolonisation. It becomes incumbent on the dominant to cease arrogating to themselves the right to translate alterity without remainder into 'their own' language, practices, and values. For many feminists male/female relations map these dominant/subordinate relations structurally, and in the imperatives they generate.

See also: Other, the

References and further reading

Schutte, O. (1998) 'Cultural Alterity', *Hypatia* 13 (2).

LORRAINE CODE

Amorós, Cèlia

Cèlia Amorós has laid the groundwork in the Spanish-speaking world for a feminist critique of patriarchal genealogy and of postmodern approaches to the concept of the feminine (see **patriarchy**; **poststructuralism/postmodernism**). Amorós has carried her philosophical inquiry into the political realm by advocating the emancipation of humankind through the total emancipation of women.

Cèlia Amorós teaches philosophy at the Universidad Complutense in Madrid where she is also the director of the Instituto de Investigaciones Feministas through which she coordinates a series of seminars entitled 'Feminismo e Ilustración' (Feminism and the Enlightenment). From 1987 to 1991, Amorós headed the interdisciplinary research project 'Mujer y poder' (Women and Power) of the Instituto de Filosofía of the Consejo Superior de Investigación Científica. She is little known in the English-speaking world, but is highly regarded in feminist circles in Spain and Mexico.

In much of her work, Amorós examines the philosophy of the enlightenment with its gendered definition of knowledge and rationality, and builds a case for a new feminist philosophy of 'clear, distinct, and universal ideas'. Writing on the relationship between Cartesianism and feminism, Amorós examines the works of Poulain de la Barre, particularly his rational arguments against prejudice towards women (see **Cartesianism, feminist critiques of**). Amorós reconstructs the relationship of feminism to the enlightenment and argues for placing the woman, not the man, as the norm for the 'generic human' in philosophical and political thought.

In *Feminismo: igualdad y diferencia* (1994), Amorós studies the distinction between the **public/private** spheres and how it defines gender assignments. She favours 'feminism of equality' founded on the enlightenment principle of universal typology over 'feminism of difference', and brings the two systems together to define feminism as a social movement located within the context of other emancipatory struggles.

Hacia una crítica de la razón patriarcal (1985) is Amorós's first and most important book. In it, she advocates 'feminism of suspicion' in examining the feminist movements' reactions to patriarchal reason. Amorós discusses 'feminism of equality', 'feminism of difference', and '**radical feminism**', and proposes that feminist ethical inquiry act as a bridge between the liberation of women and other social and political liberation movements. Like many Spanish and Latin American feminists, Amorós emphasises the role of feminist movements in reshaping political processes and institutions.

See also: equality/difference; ethics, feminist

Selected writings

Amorós, C. (1985) *Hacia una crítica de la razón patriarcal*, Barcelona: Ed. Anthropos.
—— (1994) *Feminismo: igualdad y diferencia*, Mexico, DF: Universidad Nacional Autónoma de México.

RUTH WALLACH

analogical method

The analogical method or argument from analogy uses points of similarity between objects, practices or events to infer other similarities between them. Analogies are strengthened when similarities are confirmed, discredited by discoveries of disanalogy. Some early second-wave feminists relied on analogies with racism to understand sexism; analogies with the position of the proletariat under capitalism to theorise the position of women under patriarchy. Despite their heuristic value, non-white and working class feminists have protested against the crude understandings of racism and classism on which these analogies were based. Similarly, feminist archaeologists have disputed readings of ancient sites that rely on analogical interpretation to conclude that ancient societies were patriarchally ordered just as modern western societies are. Yet for many feminist scholars the intelligent interpretive possibilities analogy offers prompt them to continue working to develop a viable analogical method.

References and further reading

Wylie A. (1985) 'The Reaction Against Analogy', *Advances in Archaeological Method and Theory*, 8.

LORRAINE CODE

anarchist feminism

Anarchist feminism refers to the inspiration feminists have gained from the concept of anarchy (from the Greek, literally, non-rule).

The foremother of anarchist feminism is Emma Goldman (1869–1940). In her over two decades of notoriety preceding deportation to Russia in the Red Scare of 1919, she had become famous as a union organiser, an advocate of contraception, and an opponent of the traditional family. For Goldman, political ideas were pointless unless they were acted on; she was arrested numerous times for speaking out and advocating such action. As an anarchist, she knew that men and women are oppressed by authoritarian social structures, but she also saw that women are oppressed specifically as women. The convergence of feminist concerns with anarchism meant that no mere reform of hierarchical institutions would be adequate to the task of allowing women to live full lives. Thus, she spoke out against women's suffrage because she saw it as merely a way to gain women's cooperation in the maintenance of an essentially unchanged structure. Goldman was remarkable for her time in that she was able to draw on theory without being entrapped by it; while inspired by communism and anarchism, she insisted that their application be flexible and adaptable, resisting any impulse toward rigidity, uniformity, or **essentialism**.

Throughout the 1980s, feminist theory-building came under scrutiny by philosophers who were concerned that feminist theory would do what male-dominated theorising had been doing: exclude the voices and experiences of women in all their complexity and diversity. Feminists of differing classes, races, and cultures began to question the ability and right of well-educated white women to speak for all women (see **class analysis**; **race**). This questioning resonated with criticism of essentialist presuppositions about 'woman'. Postmodern thinkers such as Luce **Irigaray** sketched strategies which would enable feminists to realise the dangers of traditional philosophical methods of theorising, and to depart creatively and constructively from the limitations of those methods and their goals. Gail Stenstad proposed the strategy of anarchic thinking, 'atheoretical, rule-less thinking which is bound neither to some ideal of truth or reality nor tied to a guiding first principle or ultimate referent' (Stenstad 1988: 96). Anarchic thinking moves by way of persistent questioning, heeding multiplicity and ambiguity without demanding resolution, being alert for strangeness within the familiar and presupposed, and resisting closure and finality.

Anarchic thinking has been criticised for seeming to undermine the validity of claims about the reality of oppression, and for failing to provide a theoretical basis for political action. However, the rigid either/or dichotomy between objectivism and relativism within which this criticism emerges has itself been severely shaken by the work of feminist epistemologists (see **objectivity**; **epistemology, feminist**). The primary value of anarchist feminism is that, in freeing thinkers from the demand for

commitment to and defence of a theory, it broadens the possibilities for feminist thinking and strategic action. Anarchist feminism gives a green light to actions on behalf of women, whether or not those acting together agree on a theory, or have a theory.

References and further reading

Irigaray, L. (1985) *This Sex Which Is Not One*, trans. C. Porter, Ithaca, NY: Cornell University Press.
Shulman, A.K. (ed.) (1983) *Red Emma Speaks: An Emma Goldman Reader*, New York: Schocken Books.
Stenstad, G. (1988) 'Anarchic Thinking', *Hypatia* 3 (2): 87–100.

GAIL STENSTAD

ancient world, women and the

The study of ancient women grew out of the second-wave feminist project of making women visible in history and documenting the long duration of patriarchy. Feminist work began in the early 1970s in Classics, paralleling work done in **religious studies** on ancient Jewish and Christian women. Work bridging areas and cultures is still rare due to disciplinary distances and language gaps (classicists are trained in Latin and Greek but not in the dozens of other ancient languages). Influenced by work on feminist literary theory, work in the 1970s focused on images of women in texts as well as on recovering information on the lives of real women. Both projects were hampered by the lack of first-person material from ancient women, but feminist scholarship has hugely expanded the database. For all periods, archaeology remains an important, sometimes the sole, source.

The term 'ancient world' here refers to Greek and Roman pagan cultures from before 1700 BCE to about 500 CE, but also to contemporary and earlier cultures in the Near East, Egypt (see Robins 1993), Ethiopia, North Africa, Armenia, and Persia, to the Iron Age cultures of western Europe, and to Jewish and Christian cultures of the ancient Mediterranean. For an overview of the ancient world that includes the Americas, Africa, and Asia, see Vivante 1999.

Women in Greece before *c*.700 BCE are known primarily through the Homeric texts; Sappho, the best-known Greek woman writer, wrote on the island of Lesbos in the late seventh century BCE. The athletic, sex-segregated world of Spartan women in this period is known through fragmentary texts and later histories; vase paintings from the sixth–fourth centuries BCE illustrate life in city-states. Classical Athens, comparatively well-documented by court-room speeches as well as canonical literature, tends to stand for 'Greece', a mistake to be avoided; the fifth-century law code from Gortyn, in Crete, shows a less male-dominated culture. Further women writers are extant from the Hellenistic period (fourth century BCE onward), along with papyri from Egypt preserving evidence of women's daily lives, continuing into the period of Roman domination.

A great deal more evidence survives of Roman women's lives from the Republic (510–31 BCE) through the Empire (31 BCE–313 CE) to the Byzantine period, though from pagan women writers only a few poems remain (first century CE). Like the Greek city-states, Rome was imperialist and slave-owning, and citizen women were involved in both projects. Feminists have studied Roman women as owners of property, workers (especially slaves and freed slaves), politicos, speakers; women's sexuality, bodies, family relations, experience of domestic and public space; gynaecology; the use of women as sign in texts and art. The amount of evidence increases greatly in late antiquity, as Christianity opened up opportunities previously unavailable to women (travel, monasticism, sainthood).

See also: biblical studies, feminist; classics, feminism and the; literary theory, feminist

References and further reading

Brooten, B.J. (1996) *Love Between Women: Early Christian Responses to Female Homoeroticism*, Chicago, IL: University of Chicago Press.

Fantham, E., Foley, H.P., Kampen, N.B., Pomeroy, B., and Shapiro, H.A. (1994) *Women in the Classical World*, New York: Oxford University Press.

Kraemer, R.S. (1988) *Maenads, Martyrs, Matrons, Monastics: A Sourcebook on Women's Religions in the Greco-Roman World*, Philadelphia, PA: Fortress Press.

Lefkowitz, M.R., and Fant, M.B. (1992) *Women's Life in Greece and Rome: A Source Book in Translation*, Baltimore: The Johns Hopkins University Press, 2nd edn.

Robins, G. (1993) *Women in Ancient Egypt*, Cambridge, MA: Harvard University Press.

Vivante, B. (ed.) (1999) *Women's Roles in Ancient Civilizations*, Westport, CT: Greenwood Publishing Group.

AMY RICHLIN

androcentrism

Androcentrism (Greek, *andro*/male) refers to entrenched practices that base theory and practice on men's experiences masquerading as 'human' experiences and counting as unquestioned sources of knowledge 'in general'. Androcentrism permeates ideals of reason and rationality defined by exclusions of the 'feminine'; research that is based on allegedly 'standard' male situations or studying only male subjects; normative standards that are achievable principally in circumstances available to men. In such inquiry, women's experiences and concerns are simply invisible. Psychological and/or medical research that presents as universally valid conclusions reached from studies of male subjects offer one example. Nor do such studies routinely investigate an appropriately heterogeneous male sample: they are often as white-centred, age-centred, and affluence-centred as they are androcentred.

Feminists interrogate the presumptions that sustain androcentrism by examining the location of inquiry within socio-political-economic *and* gendered structures, and uncovering the exclusions and suppressions of its governing ideology.

LORRAINE CODE

androgyny

Androgyny (Greek *andro*/male, *gyn*/female) derives from Jungian psychology, according to which individuation requires people to know and 'own' unconscious, contradictory aspects of their psyche: a woman her animus (her masculine aspect), a man his anima (his feminine aspect). Translated into feminist theory of the early 1970s, androgyny seemed to allow that people are, essentially, neither female nor male, but human. It granted women permission to reject the softer, feminine mould to express their assertive (masculine) 'side' and men permission to reject the rigid, masculine mould to express their caring (feminine) 'side'. Androgyny did not deny biological differences: androgynous people would still be androgynous men and androgynous women. But 'masculine' and 'feminine' would become descriptive terms, stripped of their mutually exclusive, dichotomous connotations.

As a psychological and literary ideal that united masculine and feminine natures in one person, androgyny appealed to American feminists in the 1970s as a regulative concept to promote freedom from the tyrannies of sex-stereotyping with their hierarchical social expectations. Two of its principal spokeswomen were psychologist Sandra Bem, whose research tested for androgynous traits in girls and boys, women and men; and literary theorist Carolyn **Heilbrun**, who believed that androgyny could escape the constraints of the imperatives that had produced distorting ideals of personality development for both sexes, and social arrangements of gendered inequality.

Despite its apparent appeal, androgyny was short-lived as a feminist ideal. Among reasons for its demise was a recognition of its dependence upon essentialised, stereotyped 'masculine' and 'feminine' traits that were integrated, uncontested, into the androgynous being. Often androgyny was interpreted asymmetrically, to emphasise encompassing traditionally admirable male traits within female personalities, or of 'allowing' men to express feelings. (Ideal) androgynous men thus seemed quite different from androgynous women, despite the promised merging of all possible characteristics. Some feminists also objected to the structure of the word itself, where the masculine 'half' comes first, declaring it illusory to imagine that emancipatory goals could be achieved by combining the archetypal masculine and the archetypal feminine into a whole, meant to be adequate to the spectrum of human possibilities. Increasing emphasis in the 1980s and 1990s on the social production of sex/gender differences, together with acknowledgement of the crude inadequacy of the masculine and feminine stereotypes that remained intact in their amalgmation into an androgynous 'whole' have resulted in the virtual disappearance of androgyny from feminist theory.

See also: essentialism; gender

References and further reading

Bem, S. (1987) 'Gender Schema Theory and Child Development', in M.R. Walsh (ed.) *The Psychology of Women: Ongoing Debates*, London: Thames and Hudson.

Heilbrun, C. (1973) *Toward a Recognition of Androgyny*, New York: Harper and Row.

Singer, J. (1976) *Androgyny: Toward a New Theory of Sexuality*, New York: Doubleday.

LORRAINE CODE

anthropology

Anthropology is distinguished by its combination of a fine-grained, qualitative, descriptive field methodology (**ethnography**) and **cross-cultural analysis** (ethnology). While not a necessary feature of late twentieth-century anthropology, historically another distinguishing characteristic has been a focus on non-western peoples as objects of study. In Great Britain and Europe, ethnography and ethnology constitute the discipline. In the Americas, anthropology also encompasses archaeology and biological or physical anthropology, including primatology (see **archaeology, feminism in**; **biology**; **primatology**).

Anthropology's contributions to feminist analysis have generally been grounded in ethnographies. Some ethnographic studies have undermined the assumption of universals of women's experience. Anthropology has generated sustained theoretical debates about the nature and significance of such universals, particularly the division of labour by sex; distinct **public/private** spheres; male **dominance**; and the categorical symbolic association of **nature/culture** with dichotomous sex/gender identities. Feminist anthropology has participated in feminist critiques of the methodology of **science**, and in the development of experimental forms of writing to convey women's experiences, including life histories, biographies and autobiographies, and fictions. The most significant contribution that anthropology has made to feminist thought is undoubtedly the development of a social concept of sex/gender systems.

Kamala Visweswaran (1997) uses changing concepts of **gender** within anthropology to divide the history of feminist ethnography into four periods. Until 1920, gender was equated with biological sex, and **biological essentialism** justified fixed divisions of labour along lines of sex. Following the development of first-wave feminism, beginning in the 1920s with the work of scholars such as Margaret Mead (Visweswaran 1997: 601–2), sex and gender were analytically distinguished, and considerable attention was paid to the social construction of gender. Nonetheless, the focus of feminist ethnography during this period was on women, conceived of as a unitary subject. In the 1960s and 1970s, as second-wave feminist activism emerged, a new generation of feminist anthropologists devoted considerable effort to the formal definition of sex/gender systems in which the facts of biology were the basis of culturally-specific gender systems (see **first-wave/ second-wave feminism**). Critiques of the universality of 'woman' emerged within anthropology in the 1980s and 1990s as part of broader discussions of neglected aspects of **difference**, inspired by cultural studies, postcolonialism, and gay and lesbian studies. This latest phase of feminist ethnography has confronted many issues raised by third-wave feminist activism.

Henrietta **Moore** argues that universal male dominance and a division of society into domestic and public spheres, associated respectively with women and men, are embedded assumptions of anthropological **kinship** theory, also critiqued by Collier and Yanagisako (1987). Similarly, Micaela di Leonardo (1991) argues that from 1920 to 1970, anthropological analyses of social organisation and kinship assumed the existence of universal male dominance and a normative male viewpoint. Di Leonardo characterises the anthropology of this period, which includes the ethnographic contribu-

tions to sex and gender studies of Margaret Mead, as 'pre-feminist'.

Explicitly feminist anthropology emerged in the 1970s with the publication of two significant collections of essays. Edited by Rayna Rapp Reiter, *Toward an Anthropology of Women* provided the site for Gayle **Rubin**'s explication of the sex/gender system. This construction carried forward Margaret Mead's definition of gender as only loosely constrained by biological sex, and thus subject to many different social forms. It also incorporated the persistent anthropological assumption, present from the late nineteenth century on, that sex was a necessary and biologically given ground for gender. Thus, while other societies might construct maleness and femaleness differently, they would always construct them as linked, dichotomous categories determined by sex (see **dichotomies**).

In *Women, Culture and Society*, Rosaldo and Lamphere (1974) provide a venue for a set of arguments that present universal male domination of women as founded on specific cultural classifications which follow universal structural principles, and women's position in society as universally tainted by close association with a domestic sphere. Sherry **Ortner** in her famous essay 'Is Female to Male as Nature is to Culture?' (67–87) argues that cross-culturally women's biological role in **reproduction** has led to their structural association with nature, balanced by an equation of men with culture. Women's close association with the domestic sphere reinforces their categorical symbolic position, since the domestic sphere is the origin of challenges to social order. Michelle Rosaldo, in the same volume (17–42), further explicates the presumed universal nature and origins of the domestic/public dichotomy.

With these two central propositions established in the feminist anthropology of the 1970s, the basis for the universal domination of women by men is explicated. The public sphere, which is exclusively the domain of men, is where society was constituted, institutionally through politics, and symbolically as the opposite of nature. This notion that men everywhere were dominant over women was not new in the anthropology of the 1970s. Visweswaran (1997: 596, 600–1) identifies Elsie Clews Parsons as establishing the idea of women's experience of universal **patriarchy** as the coherent ground for cross-cultural analysis in the early twentieth century. But the feminist anthropology of the 1970s takes asymmetric relations of power as the justification for regarding all women, cross-culturally, as inhabiting identical subject positions, even though anthropology might otherwise demonstrate stark differences between women in different cultures.

The propositions that women inhabit a domestic sphere and are excluded from a public sphere, that this dichotomy reflects a symbolic association of women with nature because of the biological facts of reproduction, and that men exercise universal dominance justified by their symbolic association with culture and order, and institutionally enabled by their control of the public sphere, while framed by feminist anthropologists, are in fact congruent with the dominant symbolic **structuralism** and functionalist analysis of social organisation that had been developed in anthropology between 1920 and 1970, as Moore (1988) notes. Once clearly articulated, these ideas were subject to intense debate by feminist anthropologists in an influential series of edited volumes. One strand of debate questions the identification of male dominance by pointing to the presence within societies of multiple arenas of distinction, and documenting shifting hierarchies among men and women. Other critiques present analyses of cultures in which men and women were not symbolically associated with culture and nature. Some of these studies begin to problematise the assumption that woman, and, although seldom explicit, man, are unitary categories. The domestic/public dichotomy is repeatedly challenged. These varied critiques are perhaps most cogently illustrated in the work of Marilyn **Strathern** (1987; 1988). By the end of the 1980s, few feminist anthropologists could argue for the real universality of the **dichotomies** men/culture/public/dominant versus women/nature/domestic/subordinate.

Challenges to the unitary nature of 'woman' as a subject emerge from these feminist anthropological debates, but they also are seen in anthropology during the 1980s and 1990s as a result of critiques of ethnography from postcolonial studies and gay and lesbian studies. Third-wave feminist critique, particularly Indigenous feminist theory and First Nation feminism, directly challenges feminist anthropology's assertion of a unified female subject (see **third-wave feminism**; **Indigenist feminism**; **First Nations and women**). Di Leonardo (1991) argues that under these pressures, anthropology, and feminist anthropology in particular, have begun to reconceptualise their subject of study as gender difference, rather than gender **identity**. Feminist anthropologists question the biological essentialism of the sex/gender dichotomy.

Late twentieth-century anthropology witnesses the growth of a body of explicitly feminist ethnography, often biographical and experimental in form. Such ethnographic experiments reflect, even if indirectly, feminist **standpoint theory**. They place in sharp relief contradictions in the position feminist ethnographers assume in speaking as women and for (other) women. Visweswaran (1997) argues that experiments with the form of ethnographies are not exclusively products of postmodernism in anthropology (see **poststructuralism/postmodernism**). She notes the use of **autobiography**, fiction, and other narrative forms in the ethnography of the period between 1920 and 1960. She draws particular attention to the fact that feminist ethnographies written between 1960 and 1980, under the influence of second-wave feminism, are notable for their narrative and reflexive questioning of identification between female ethnographer and female ethnographic subjects.

Di Leonardo (1991) characterises feminist anthropology in the 1990s as sharing five main assumptions. It rejects social evolutionism, particularly the idea that different contemporary peoples can be used as proxies for past stages of human development. It emphasises historical context, often a context of colonialism. It problematises apparently stable categories, exemplified by the realisation (following Foucault) that diverse forms of sexuality have specific histories. Late twentieth-century feminist anthropology builds on this insight to question the terms of debate about human universals, and is committed to resist essentialising. Feminist anthropology assumes that gender is inextricably linked to, or embedded in, other institutions and discourses, and does not assume that gender has a primary or overarching status. As a result, feminist anthropologists study the simultaneous construction of **race**, gender, sexuality, age, ethnicity and class. Feminist anthropology in the 1990s transformed the question of male domination into one of the existence and nature of social stratification, without assuming the form it might take, and without assuming that social stratification is stable. Finally, di Leonardo suggests that late-twentieth-century feminist anthropology, in common with other anthropologies, is concerned with a reflexive and critical awareness of the 'social location' of the ethnographer and the ethnographic subject.

See also: ethnomethodology; matriarchy; narrative, feminist uses of; positioning/positionality; Spivak, Gayatri

References and further reading

Collier, J.F. and Yanagisako, S. (eds) (1987) *Gender and Kinship: Essays Toward a Unified Analysis*, Stanford, CA: Stanford University Press.

di Leonardo, M. (1991) 'Gender, Culture and Political Economy: Feminist Anthropology in Historical Perspective', in M. di Leonardo (ed.) *Gender at the Crossroads of Knowledge: Feminist Anthropology in the Postmodern Era*, Berkeley, CA: University of California Press.

MacCormack, C. and Strathern, M. (eds) (1980) *Nature, Culture and Gender*, Cambridge: Cambridge University Press.

Moore, H.L. (1988) *Feminism and Anthropology*, Minneapolis, MI: University of Minnesota Press.

Ortner, S. and Whitehead, H. (eds) (1981) *Sexual Meanings: The Cultural Construction of Gender and Sexuality*, Cambridge: Cambridge University Press.

Reiter, R. (ed.) (1975) *Toward an Anthropology of Women*, New York: Monthly Review Press.

Rosaldo, M.Z. and Lamphere, L. (eds) (1974) *Woman, Culture and Society*, Stanford, CA: Stanford University Press.

Rubin, G. (1975) 'The Traffic in Women: Notes on a "Political Economy" of Sex', in R. Rapp Reiter (ed.) *Toward an Anthropology of Women*, New York: Monthly Review Press.

Strathern, M. (ed.) (1987) *Dealing with Inequality: Analysing Gender Relations in Melanesia and Beyond*, Cambridge: Cambridge University Press.

—— (1988) *The Gender of the Gift*, Berkeley, CA: University of California Press.

Visweswaran, K. (1997) 'Histories of Feminist Ethnography', *Annual Reviews in Anthropology* 26: 591–621.

ROSEMARY A. JOYCE

anti-militarism, feminist

Feminist anti-militarism claims that militarism and the interests of women are deeply antithetical. This is often expressed as the argument that as mothers women will nurture life rather than risk it. Thus suffragettes argued that if women were admitted to politics, war would end. This view has obvious flaws: for example, it implies an essentialist view of women's nature, it denies obvious examples of aggressive and war-like women. It has subsequently been refined and sophisticated, basing it more on women's socialisation and experience than their biology, but remains open to the charge of making false generalisations about women's nature. Women are not necessarily anti-militarist, but increasingly sophisticated analysis suggests that feminists must be.

Women are not only required to service the military, in such roles as prostitutes, stenographers, munitions workers and suppliers of the next generation of soldiers; they are needed also as icons of vulnerability which motivate young men to fight in order to protect. Thus militarism requires gender inequality despite the claim that equality of opportunity exists in the modern military. At best, women soldiers can never be more than tokens as the functions listed above continue to be required. However, this analysis suggests contradictions in the demands that the military makes on women, and in those contradictions lies the space for resistance. For example, as technological developments erode the home/battle front distinction, military elites can no longer rely upon a traditionally gendered politics of 'man-power', nor can they give it up. Women are increasingly likely to become aware of these contradictions, and the opportunities to protest them. Further, the ideology of militarism is closely linked to unrealizable ideals of masculinity. Boys are taught to be men by suppressing such emotions as compassion, and by proving themselves in acts of aggression and dominance. Some feminists (e.g. Nancy **Hartsock**) have argued that these values are closely linked to a refusal to accept mortal embodiment so that, paradoxically, deaths are multiplied in the pursuit of abstract historical immortality. Most have acknowledged that militarism will only be routed if structures of masculinity are transformed. Thus Virginia Woolf showed the continuity between competitiveness, dominance and exclusivity of the church, university and state with the military. All these institutions treat life as a struggle in which survival and ultimately honour are achieved by aggressively dominating others. She argues that because of their marginalised position women are able to see this, and should work together to produce different forms of social and political cooperation.

In the 1980s, women opposed to the nuclear arms race developed this theory through practice. They renounced hierarchy, refused the coercion of majoritarian politics and developed consensual and imaginative models of political activism which demonstrate how women can enter the public sphere on their terms: pro-active, consensual, non-competitive and respectful of feelings. The attempt to develop non-militaristic organisations to contain the nuclear threat thus contributes to feminist theories and models of politics, just as feminist insights radically influence the direction of the peace movement, and the insights gained are as likely to be found in critiques of **economic globalisation** as in discussions of **nationalism and gender**.

See also: military metaphors

References and further reading

Enloe, C. (1983) *Does Khaki Become You?* London: Pluto Press.

Harris, A. and King, Y. (1989) *Rocking the Ship of State*, Boulder, CO: Westview Press.

Woolf, V. (1938) *Three Guineas*, London: Hogarth Press.

ANNE SELLER

Anzaldúa, Gloria (b. 1942)

Gloria Anzaldúa describes herself as a 'chicana tejana feminist-dyke-patlache poet, fiction writer, and cultural theorist' (1987) and as a 'Third World lesbian feminist with Marxist and mystical leanings' (1981). Anzaldúa writes about people of the borderlands, particularly the Mestiza (mixed-race Latina), who slip between cultures, religions, ethnicities, sexual norms and geographic locales. In much of her writing she describes, often through autobiographical narrative, the socioeconomic, political and spiritual **oppression** of women of colour, particularly the Chicanas.

Anzaldúa identifies herself as a threshold person who defies rigid classification of **identity**, who is not entirely inside nor outside a community, and who crosses the borders between different cultures. In her important 1987 book, *Borderlands / La Frontera: The New Mestiza*, she calls for Mestiza consciousness to reshape a world which suffers from Anglo-American tyranny over the Mexicanos, from men's oppression of women, and from Catholic submersion of Aztec spirituality. In this book, she writes in a language of the borderlands – a mixture of English, Spanish, North Mexican dialect, Tex-Mex, and Nahuatl, and blurs conventional forms of discourse by combining **autobiography**, **history**, poetry and myth.

As an editor and writer, Anzaldúa has been instrumental in publishing the philosophical, political, and creative writings of women of colour. In *This Bridge Called My Back: Writings by Radical Women of Color* and in *Making Face, Making Soul / Haciendo Caras*, she published prose, poetry, personal narrative and political analysis from African American, Asian American, Latina, and Native American women. In her autobiography, *La Prieta* (in Anzaldúa and Moraga 1981), she describes the oppression of indigenous cultures, as well as **homophobia** and oppression of women within the Chicano culture.

While Anzaldúa writes and teaches about the oppression of the borderlands by the dominant white culture and criticises white feminists for assuming that they speak for all women, she also galvanises Third World women and lesbians of colour to build a new world, Mundo Zurdo (left-handed world), which necessitates 'a going deep into the self and an expanding out into the world, a simultaneous recreation of the self and a reconstruction of society' (1981).

Anzaldúa has been criticised for mixing genres and lacking theoretical rigour in her writing, for her spirituality, strong identification as a lesbian of colour, and for her criticism of Anglo-American feminism. She has broad support, however, for speaking the people's language, and for introducing the concept of the borderlands into feminist and literary analysis.

See also: Chicana feminism; lesbian literature

Selected writings

Anzaldúa, G. (ed) (1990) *Making Face, Making Soul / Haciendo Caras: Creative and Critical Perspectives by Feminists of Color*, San Francisco: Aunt Lute Foundation Books.

Anzaldúa, G. and Moraga, C. (eds) (1981) *This Bridge Called My Back: Writings by Radical Women of Color*, Watertown, MA: Persephone Press.

—— (1987) *Borderlands / La Frontera: The New Mestiza*, San Francisco: Spinsters / Aunt Lute.

RUTH WALLACH

archaeology, feminism in

In the 1980s feminist archaeology emerged within the framework of a postprocessual archaeology, with its explicit focus on **heteroglossia**, pluralism and subjectivity. It became *de rigeur* to critique the construction of knowledge within the field, especially those studies which claimed scientific **objectivity**. The first major paper appeared in 1984 (Conkey and Spector) – late in comparison with other social sciences – and had little substantive impact until the 1990s, when the validity of feminist perspectives gained widespread recognition. Reasons for this initial reluctance have been posited as the earlier positivist, hypothetico-deductive trends in processual archaeology, particularly in its American guise (see **positivism**). The first volume devoted to gender and informed by feminist theory appeared as late as 1991 (Gero and Conkey) and was influenced by long-standing feminist contributions in **anthropology**.

Extensive studies that have highlighted equity issues both in academic and non-academic archaeologies have underscored a glaring bias in regard to education, employment, publication, and academic seniority. The inherent sexism involved with conducting fieldwork, central to both archaeology and anthropology, has been another central issue. Remedying this is a flood of volumes dedicated to eminent women of the past, many of whom were far from feminist in their own politics (e.g. Kathleen Kenyon, Harriet Boyd Hawes). Feminist contributions then moved toward revisionist histories, recasting women as active agents, creating their own social realities and resisting domination in the process. This process is particularly visible in prehistoric scenarios which had tacitly promoted a history of 'mankind', characterised by 'man the hunter' and similar stone-age mentalities. Subsequently, a feminist reading has reinstated the presence and participation of women in prehistory. Other essentialist narratives have focused upon archaeological practice: the archaeologist as explorer, hero and invariably male. Balancing the scales to reveal women's presence and volition in the past was a necessary disciplinary step, as was combating androcentric viewpoints and language (see **androcentrism**).

In fact there has been a misleading conflation of feminist approaches to archaeology, identifying **gender** and studying women in antiquity. Given that the vast majority of relevant publications have emanated from female practitioners, this is hardly surprising. However, one can be a feminist without investigating gender issues and vice versa. Yet gender archaeology has become synonymous with studies of women. Debates over sex and gender still rage, often without cognisance of recent feminist theorising in related fields. Salient topics of analysis in archaeology tend to revolve around philosophy (inspired by the critique of science), writing and narrative, iconography, household production, the **body**, concepts of the **Goddess** and social relations. Feminist-inspired archaeology opens up new arenas in a rapidly developing social archaeology (see Claassen and Joyce 1997). But as feminists themselves have noted, their contribution to archaeology is not necessarily a methodological or technological breakthrough, but rather an interpretative one.

Interestingly, when archaeology finally embraced feminism it turned to first- and second-wave feminisms and it often remains locked in the practice of 'finding women'. As such it continues to be an additive and remedial strategy. The famous maxim 'add women and stir' continues to define the field, despite archaeology's self-proclaimed assertion that it has moved on. Generally, there has been a reticence to adopt the findings of theorists who are sometimes referred to as third-wave feminists (e.g. **Butler**, Grosz, **Lauretis**, **Spivak**) who acknowledge the additional subjectivities of age, class, ethnicity, sexual orientation. Concomitantly, there has been little application of masculinist or **queer theory** – although British archaeologists have been noticeably more amenable to third-wave feminism (e.g. Meskell 1996 and 1999; Moore and Scott 1997).

The major impact of feminism in archaeology has been felt in America, Britain, northern Europe and Australia. Two distinct schools have emerged, centred in the UK and USA. American feminists have rallied around a circle of prominent, senior scholars who fuelled the initial movement, and work primarily on prehistoric material. British feminists are more varied in theoretical approach and areas of study, from prehistory to Medieval periods (Gilchrist 1994), and have yet to consolidate politically. Generally, there is little overlap between feminist approaches to prehistoric data (often relying on analogy and ethnography) and later historical studies (with the benefit of textual and contextual information). Moreover, insights gleaned from feminist developments in Mediterranean, Near Eastern and Egyptian archaeologies, as well as classics, have made little impact in theoretical archaeology *per se*.

The future success of feminist-inspired analyses will rely on an increasing consolidation of rigorous theory and suitable material data conducive to such nuanced social readings. A major and lasting contribution of feminist theorising is the promotion of wider studies of gender and **sexuality**, and the constitution of the subject and undoubtedly a more wide-ranging social archaeology. Its impact extends beyond heuristics, since it can provide significant temporal and cultural dimensionality to current debates – debates over the social construction of sex categories, sexuality, individual subject posi-

tions, issues of **difference** as well as the myriad variability of female experience (Meskell 1999). At present there is a burgeoning corpus devoted to feminist-inspired analyses of sex/gender, sexuality, embodiment, social relations, and issues of identity in archaeology, drawing upon the rich suite of ancient data at our disposal. Archaeology's intrinsic value for feminism lies in offering a horizon of possibilities through its study of socio-cultural variability and exploration of multiple realities in the past.

See also: ancient world, women and the

References and further reading

Claassen, C. and Joyce, R.A. (eds) (1997) *Women in Prehistory: North America and Mesoamerica*, Philadelphia, PA: University of Pennsylvania Press.

Conkey, M.W. and Spector, J.D. (1984) 'Archaeology and the Study of Gender', in M.B. Schiffer (ed.) *Advances in Archaeological Method and Theory*, 7: 1–38.

Gero, J.M. and Conkey, M.W. (eds) (1991) *Engendering Archaeology: Women and Prehistory*, Oxford: Blackwell.

Gilchrist, R. (1994) *Gender and Material Culture: The Archaeology of Religious Women*, London: Routledge.

Meskell, L.M. (1996) 'The Somatisation of Archaeology: Institutions, Discourses, Corporeality', *Norwegian Archaeological Review*, 29, 1: 1–16.

—— (1999) *Archaeologies of Social Life: Age, Sex, Class etc. in Ancient Egypt*, Oxford: Blackwell.

Moore, J. and Scott, E. (eds) (1997) *Invisible People and Processes: Writing Gender and Childhood into European Archaeology*, London: Leicester University Press.

LYNN MESKELL

art, feminist issues in

Individual *artists* have raised feminist issues across the verbal, visual and performing media of the arts for many decades, even centuries. Since the 1970s, *critics* and *theorists* have addressed feminist concerns as they arise in the arts: achieving parity with men in the canons of art, revaluing women's work in scorned artistic genres, affirming differences among women artists and audiences of varied cultural backgrounds, bringing about change in social practices or beliefs through art. While some feminists have sought equal opportunities for artists in galleries or concert halls, others have decoded the images assigned to women in various media, and proposed alternatives. Still others have worked to recover women composers, performers, writers and visual artists who were lost from history, or to revalue arts such as quilt-making and domestic novels that had been relegated to craft or popular culture. Still others have dug beneath these problems of omission to find their roots and branches in cultural systems. The arts have served as sites of and stimuli for feminist thought despite the fact that art has been defined since the eighteenth century as separate from other modes of knowledge and social interaction – indeed, as useless, suitable only for the limited purpose of aesthetic contemplation.

Artists have raised issues, sometimes without intending to be part of a feminist discourse, by focusing attention on figures, characters, sounds, voices, gestures, movements, feelings, predicaments, or stories that had not been understood previously from the perspectives of women. Such works, performances, events have posed important questions for feminist critics and theorists. These questions, among others, have concerned the woman artist's agency in systems that define women as **Other**; the difficulty of changing stereotypes and myths in accepted systems of representation or of recording new knowledge, say, of women's sexual preferences and expressions in those systems; the possibilities and limits of dialogue among women; the feeling of being in a **body** that has been appropriated by a culture for purposes other than its own. Amelia Jones's *Sexual Politics* shows how one complex visual work, Judy Chicago's *Dinner Party* (1979), has provoked both artists and critics to take up such issues for more than two decades.

Although some members of the art world still believe that art exists only to give aesthetic pleasure that has no ethical or political relevance, most feminist critics and theorists understand the arts as decidedly useful – sometimes for perpetuating the wishes of a powerful elite, as in the history of the nude in painting and sculpture, others for effecting

changes in perception or belief, as in the African American spiritual. Thus feminists have been particularly interested in art criticism or theory that seems to intervene successfully in cultural practices, thereby *constructing* what we call reality rather than merely reflecting it.

At least two vexing questions have persisted since the 1970s. For whom can any artist speak; in what sense is she able to represent any other person or experience besides her own? Having given up the romantic idea of the artist as (male) genius who is able to present a universal insight, feminist theorists generally agree that there can be no such thing as a *female* point of view in the arts that transcends historical, material or cultural factors. The possibility remains, however, that a perspective can be feminine or feminist. The term *feminine*, once synonymous with weakness in the arts, has come through Julia Kristeva's work to mean all that is culturally subversive. A European exhibit organised in the mid-1990s by M. Catherine de Zegher, however, expresses the hope that art can reveal heretofore invisible elements that will reconstitute the feminine in culture. Although few doubt that art can express *feminist* consciousness, the meaning of that term remains uncertain, along with the right to claim it. Does an artist have to espouse a recognised feminist **identity**, for example, in order for her (or his?) work to have a feminist impact?

This question about what constitutes a feminist identity reveals another one concerning the possibility of meaningful relationship between **feminism** and art. For those who still see art through the lens of Enlightenment thought as separate from all political action, the term *feminist art* is an oxymoron; art can be either feminist or aesthetic but not both, and in this view feminists are simply anti-aesthetic. Others who are troubled by specific political positions use the term feminist negatively. Just as artists used to shrug off the term 'woman' as second class ('I'm not a woman, I'm an artist'), they now refuse the label 'feminist', ironically rejecting the body of work that has expanded public consciousness of the term 'artist' to include women.

If the antidote to both of these persistent problems within feminist thought is more flexible theories of both feminism and aesthetics that respond to changing data from the arts, the prognosis is good. Since an artist's ability to make a difference depends on others' ability to 'read' (look, listen, interpret, feel kinaesthetically), feminist critics and theorists have turned attention to these processes of reception in addition to acts of creation formalised in a text. Such studies reveal that reading is a complex act, deeply affected by the person's background and viewpoint (including gender), and inevitably enmeshed with emotion. The artist's identity is less important than the dialogue that results from 'reading' – a point that is nowhere more apparent than in the passionate African American film criticism of bell **hooks**. Thus the eighteenth-century ideal of psychical distance, on which the definition of art as separate depended, is revealed as unattainable. Feminists finally have empirical grounds, then, for healing the split between aesthetics and politics or ethics by forming a new aesthetic theory (not specific to women) that preserves distinctions between art and life without seeing them as oppositional spheres.

See also: aesthetics, feminist; African American art history; audience response; black women's literature; dance, women and; detective fiction, feminist; diary; emotions/rationality; feminist presses; gaze, the; genre theory; gynocritics; identity politics; interpretation; language, gender and power; lesbian autobiography; lesbian literature; literary theory; literature, images of women in; metaphors; musicology, feminist; narrative, feminist uses of; psychoanalytic feminist literary theory; reader response theory; romance as genre; science fiction, feminist; theatre; utopias, feminist; women's writing

References and further reading

Cvetkovich, A. (1992) *Mixed Feelings*, New Brunswick, NJ: Rutgers.

de Zegher, C.M. (ed.) (1996) *Inside the Visible*, Cambridge, MA: MIT Press.

hooks, bell (1996) *Reel to Real*, London: Routledge.

Jones, A. (ed.) (1996) *Sexual Politics: Judy Chicago's Dinner Party in Feminist Art History*, Los Angeles: University of California Press.

Krumholz, L. and Lauter, E. (1991) *Annotated Bibliography on Feminist Aesthetics in the Literary,*

Visual and Performing Arts, Madison: Women's Studies Librarian.

Mills, S. (ed.) (1994) *Gendering the Reader*, London: Harvester Wheatsheaf.

Nead, L. (1992) *The Female Nude*, London: Routledge.

Schwab, G. (1996) *The Mirror and the Killer Queen*, Bloomington, IN: Indiana University Press.

ESTELLA LAUTER

Asian feminism

The designation 'Asian' encompasses enormous geographical, demographic, social, economic, political, and cultural diversity. Mohanty's (1991) insight that women are constituted through the 'complex interactions between class, culture, religion and other ideological institutions and frameworks' suggests a need to formulate 'autonomous, geographically, historically, and culturally grounded feminist concerns and strategies'.

Nevertheless, the historical experiences of Asian societies under colonialism and imperialism, followed by nationalist struggles for independence, demonstrated parallel initiatives by women in different countries. The post-independence decades of modernisation leading into the contemporary phase of globalisation are raising signs of cross-nation solidarity. Asian feminist thinking and movements now share some common understandings and transformative strategies to challenge the continuing marginalisation of Asian people. While acknowledging that postmodern thinking has usefully deconstructed the concept of 'universal woman', Aguilar (1997) cautions that rejecting 'totalizing' grand theory can overlook the presence of predatory systems dedicated to profit maximisation and state power. Yet a final caveat to this overview of Asian feminisms and women's movements recognises the 'north' and 'south' within Asia, expressed in the economic gulf between an advanced industrial Japan and the NICs (newly industrialised countries) and the less industrialised low-income societies in the region.

Early feminism in Asia was an important force for social change in the late nineteenth and twentieth centuries (Jayawardena, 1986). Despite differences in cultural roots, women across Asia have suffered from centuries of inequities sustained by patriarchal pre-capitalist 'traditional' practices (see **patriarchy**). As anti-colonial nationalist movements grew, women's participation helped to dismantle some aspects of patriarchal inequities and marginalisation. But this did not necessarily awaken national consciousness that questioned women's subordinate roles within family and society. In the Chinese and Vietnamese context, feminist ideology was a significant part of revolutionary consciousness. Women fought beside men in the revolutionary struggles which helped to undermine traditional Confucian norms domesticating women (see **nationalism and gender**). But everyday post-revolution relationships continued to foster gender inequities as patriarchal legacies remained strong. Likewise, Aguilar criticises the Filipino progressive movement for its refusal 'to acknowledge the significance of feminist insights in the articulation of transformational politics' (1997: 310).

The limits of nationalist, anti-colonial and anti-imperialist consciousness in Asian societies in furthering feminism were played out in the decline of women's movements and groups after independence. Many such groups 'degenerated into social welfare organisations' (literacy, handicraft and home care).

Deconstructing modernisation and development

Post-independence for non-socialist Asian societies ushered in the modernisation paradigm of development based on western capitalism and fuelled by foreign aid. Rural/urban development emphasised integration into the global market system through commercialisation of agriculture, foreign investment, and flow of cheap primary resources and consumer products from south to north (see **economic globalisation**). International agencies like the International Monetary Fund strengthened their grip on southern economies burdened by the debt crisis, structural adjustment policies, and increasing rich/poor gaps.

From the 1970s, the recognition that women were being excluded from the 'benefits' of modernisation strategies catalysed the growth of women's movements. The initial efforts to integrate women in development (WID) was replaced by the more critical WAD (women and development) and GAD (gender and development) paradigms. WAD and GAD stress structural transformation of the unequal power relationships between men and women (see **gender roles**). In Asia, the expansion of women's NGOs embracing WAD and GAD analysis reflects a strengthening of feminism and movements with a regional Asian character. Grassroots women's groups and movements challenged rural and urban modernisation along similar lines. The empowerment of women to control the nature of their integration into the modernised rural sector is exemplified by organisations like SEWA (India), BRAC (Bangladesh) and PILIPINA (Philippines). These networks promote gender-equitable cooperatives, micro-credit, appropriate technology, land reforms, low-cost housing and literacy projects.

In the urban 'industrialised' sectors, the integration of Asian women into the new international division of labour has also helped to articulate Asian feminisms through workers' organising. Women provide cheap labour in foreign-dominated export processing or free trade zones. Today broader 'working-class' consciousness is fostered in a number of Asian countries. In India, SEWA shows how unorganised self-employed women labourers can develop skills in confronting problems like usury, police harassment and bureaucratic regulations. In Korea, women workers' associations have arisen due to the failure of unions to take on women's specific problems. In the Philippines, GABRIELA emerged as a coalition of women's voices challenging both patriarchal and capitalist structures of society, injecting a strong nationalist consciousness critical of northern economic and political interventions. The forces of globalisation, neoliberal agenda, and structural adjustment programmes have galvanised women's movements and feminist consciousness against top-down globalisation that benefits only a few. Asian women's groups were strongly visible at peoples' summits challenging APEC and WTO agendas.

The global economic system has stimulated a flow of migrant labour where women are pushed by poverty to work as domestic workers, nurses, and entertainers (see **work, women and**). Asian women are a major source of such migrant labour to richer Asian countries and other regions. Women's movements in both the sending and receiving countries have emerged to protect the rights of these women migrant workers.

Flowing out of women and development analysis and organising is the link between modernisation and environmental destruction (see **development theory**). Ecofeminists like Shiva (1989) acknowledge women not merely as victims of marginalisation but as voices for the just transformation of people/nature relationships and the well-being of nature (see **ecofeminism**). Many grassroots women's associations reflect ecofeminist consciousness that translates into sustainable community-building and challenges the power of agribusiness transnational corporations.

Human rights fulfilment

Asian women play a substantive role in the expansion of women's **human rights** movements worldwide. Feminist analysis and monitoring have challenged social and cultural systems that rationalise human rights violations (campaigns against sexual/domestic violence, anti-rape legislation). The continuing violation of women's human rights has strengthened feminist consciousness and organisation in the face of both traditional subservient sexual roles of women and modern channels of sexual exploitation (military bases 'R & R', sex tourism, and sex trafficking). According to Matsui (1998) the feminist movement against sex tourism opened the eyes of Japanese women to Japanese Army atrocities during the war. Korean women pointed out that while wartime sex slavery was driven by military and colonial power, current sex tourism is sustained by economic power. Women of both the north and south have joined hands to denounce the national use of rape and **sexual slavery** as a weapon of war. China's coercive policies of family planning ('one-child') illustrate the violation of women's reproductive rights, reinforcing traditional patriarchal practices, accentuating the abuse of women and girls (see **reproduction**). However, resistance among Chinese women has emerged despite repressive state sanctions.

Advocates of women's human rights in Asia argue that universality can be upheld without denying the relevance of specific cultural and social knowledge(s). This requires an interrogation of indigenous/traditional values to see how such values may sustain women's human rights (see **Indigenist feminism**).

Challenging cultural traditions

Asian feminists are challenging cultural norms and traditions that subordinate women and sustain patriarchal injustices (**dowries**, deaths, **bride/widow burning (suttee burial)**, sex-selective abortion). While religious institutions and doctrines remain difficult areas for Asian feminist consciousness, women's organising has resisted the spread of fundamentalism, demanding reinterpretations of sacred writings and greater access to leadership roles. For example, the Sisters in Islam in Malaysia educate women about the Qur'an and its relation to the human rights of women in Islam (see **Islam and feminism**). The Ecumenical Association of Third World Women Theologians has challenged the patriarchal dimension of traditional theologies through an Asian feminist theology/spirituality that critiques religion and culture while acknowledging possible liberating forces (see also **theology, feminist**). Recognising the social, political and economic contexts of injustices, a feminist Asian theology seeks reinterpretations of religious insights, not only internally but also across boundaries of inter-faith dialogue (Mananzan and Park 1990).

Liberal, radical, right-wing perspectives

In post-independent, non-socialist countries, a liberal feminist strand has usually developed with educated middle-class women's leadership over issues of equity, non-sexist education, employment opportunities, revisions in family law and improved participation in political systems (see **liberal feminism**). Women's movements have been able to increase participation of women voters and numbers of female political representatives. But despite a few women coming to power (Bhutto, Aquino, Gandhi) political systems have remained male-dominated.

Asian women have been less influenced by **radical feminism**. Feminist consciousness and organisation around **sexuality** issues (rights of gays and lesbians) has emerged mainly in Japan and the NICs. In other Asian societies, strong cultural taboos on homosexuality are barriers to the growth of such radical feminist discourses.

In the majority of cases, the rise of Asian feminisms and women's movements has tended towards the politics of emancipation and gender equity. However, as in the west, right-wing movements have also involved the active participation of women. The pull of violent communalism on women to join right-wing militant political movements has been most visible in India.

This overview highlights the importance of locating the emergence and development of Asian feminisms and women's movements within local, national, regional, and global economic, social and political structures and relationships. Certainly, distinct historical and cultural contexts need to be understood to avoid a false universalism or convergence. Nevertheless, evidence suggests many commonalities especially within the political-economic 'north' and 'south' societies of Asia. The forces of globalisation are also tying the lives of women in Asia in webs of domination and exploitation as well as solidarity in theory and practice towards the liberation of women.

See also: Jayawardena, Kumari; Shiva, Vandana

References and further reading

Aguilar, D. (1997) 'Gender, National and Colonialism: Lesson from the Philippines' in N. Visvanathan, L. Duggan, L. Nisonoff, and N. Wiegersma. (eds) *The Women and Development Reader*, Halifax: Fernwood.

Jayawardena, K. (1986) *Feminism and Nationalism in the Third World*, London: Zed Books.

Mananzan, M.J., and Park, S.A. (1990) 'Emerging Spirituality of Asian Women' in V. Fabella and M. Oduyoye (eds) *With Passion and Compassion*, New York: Orbis.

Matsui, Y. (1998) 'History Cannot Be Erased' in I. Sajor (ed.) *Common Grounds*, Quezon City: ACWHR.

Mohanty, C.T. (1991) 'Cartographies of Struggle: Third World Women and the Politics of Feminism' in C.T. Mohanty, A. Russo, and L. Torres (eds) *Third World Women and the Politics of Feminism*, Bloomington, IN: Indiana University Press.

Shiva, V. (1989) *Staying Alive*, London: Zed Books.

VIRGINIA CAWAGAS AND TOH SWEE-HIN

aspect theory of self

The aspect theory of self, developed by US feminist Ann Ferguson in the mid-1980s, rejects liberal humanist/Enlightenment conceptions of selfhood/subjectivity for which the human self is defined by consciousness and is an unchanging, coherent, transparent and unified being. This liberal self manifests characteristics that are necessary, essential to its nature, and others that are merely contingent, accidental products of circumstance. But its coherent, rational self-consciousness defines it.

Writing when feminist psychologists, anthropologists, philosophers, and radical theorists were working to explain the social perpetuation of male dominance, Ferguson articulates a theory of self and human agency complex enough to explain how change can be mobilised out of the agency of women socialised to occupy subordinate positions in a hierarchical social order. She contends that an adequate theory of the self is a prerequisite for understanding how women who have internalised a sense of their 'natural' inferiority and subordination can develop a sense of self that is sufficiently strong and powerful to combat institutional sexism.

The aspect theory avoids the excesses of the rational maximiser theory, for which people live so as to maximise their self interest; and the difference theory for which there are fundamental, constitutive male/female differences. For rational maximisers, social oppression derives from external constraints that systemically prevent women, non-white people, or otherwise 'disadvantaged' groups from achieving their goals. To minimise oppression and frustration, it is rational for the oppressed to adjust their goals and expectations within what these systemic barriers allow. For some difference theorists, biological determinism explains male/female differences; for others, differences are the products of a sexual division of labour which produces and justifies social arrangements. Both theories are essentialist and static, albeit differently.

The aspect theory, Ferguson suggests, escapes the dichotomies inherent in these views. This a self with many aspects that develops in a process in which specific individual priorities and broader social constraints work with and against each other to promote and limit (interim) achievements of self-identity. It avoids subjection to those of its attributes judged 'more authentic' as it develops in social practices that require and encourage diverse realisations of selfhood. Thus it escapes subjection to 'women's roles', 'men's roles' and to behavioural expectations that follow the dictates of femininity or masculinity. Empowered in these new capacities, it is equipped to require and work for transformations in a social order built upon the essentialist assumptions that it contests. It is in many respects a precursor of more explicitly embodied postmodern conceptions of subjectivity.

References and further reading

Ferguson, A. (1987) 'A Feminist Aspect Theory of the Self', in M. Hanen and K. Nielson, (eds) *Science, Morality and Feminist Theory*, Calgary: University of Calgary Press.

LORRAINE CODE

audience response

From the 1930s to the 1970s, investigations of the audience were dominated by the social-scientific paradigm of mass communication studies with its focus on empiricist/positivist methodologies (see **empiricism**; **positivism**). If female audiences are included in these surveys, gender is conceived as an essentialist category, as one variable among others. During the 1970s, this disciplinary mono-poly was challenged by explorations of (mass) culture consumption in the humanities in the context of **reader response theory** in literary studies and the institutionalisation of film and television studies. During the 1980s, British cultural studies began to challenge film and television studies' focus on the textual construction of ideologically positioned subjectivities by reconcep-tualising the viewer as a historically and socially situated subject, who actively produces meanings by negotiating the discourses of the media text with those of the (sub)culture s/he is part of. (Thus, as one audience study demonstrated, black female viewers may experience *The Color Purple* positively by focusing on its strong female characters, in contrast to black male spectators' rejection of the film due to its racial stereotyping.) The centrality of the text thus makes way for a more open, dispersed and non-linear field of research in which film and television are studied at the intersection of a range of discourses that circulate through a culture, a shift which leads to reception studies which emphasise the viewing context. The appeal of the culturalist paradigm to feminist criticism is threefold. Not only do they share the political concern of a neo-Marxist conceptualisation of culture as a site of struggle for power, but the **agency** attributed to social subjects and the emphasis on difference and historical specificity offers a welcome rejection of mass communication's ideology of scientism and a departure from the determinism, pessimism and universalism of feminist film criticism of the 1970s. While culturalist investigations of film audiences began to appear in the 1990s, television scholars of the 1980s had already embraced cultural studies' methodological plurality (sociological, ethno-graphic and historical) in studies on gendered television audiences which investigate how women watch television, how they interpret it and/or how the context of domesticity relates to these modes of reception. In an effort to authenticate female pleasure and low-status genres, these studies centre mainly on 'feminine' television forms such as soap operas and examine the particular pleasures these programmes offer to female viewers. Other studies demonstrate how women's television consumption is embedded in the sexual politics of the living room and gendered notions of leisure. In contrast to social scientific research, these studies are informed by a constructivist notion of identity and therefore emphasise the way in which televi-sion constructs, rather than presupposes, social categories such as gender.

See also: cultural theory/cultural studies, feminist; film theory, feminist

References and further reading

Ang, I. (1985) *Watching Dallas*, London: Methuen.
Morley, D. (1986) *Family Television*, London: Comedia.

EVA WARTH

autobiography

Autobiography is the literary term which refers to a
writer's account of his or her own life. Autobiography thus names a distinct literary genre but the
extent to which this genre can be kept separate
from the adjacent genres of memoirs and journals,
or biography which is also a form of life-writing
which, like autobiography, lays claim to a factual
basis, has been questioned by feminist critics.
Definitions of genre are historical and ideological
and, in the case of autobiography, bound up with
notions of a transcendent unified subject which
excludes heterogeneity and difference. The canonical autobiographical texts – by Saint Augustine
and Rousseau for example – could be said to
establish models for both the subject and the genre
which have prevented the recognition of women's
different texts. The study of women's autobiography has therefore required questioning generic and
theoretical boundaries as well as recognising the
range and importance of women's autobiographical writing. Women's autobiography spans different
eras, cultures and literary modes and forms a rich
and diverse field; feminist critics, however, have
also pointed to the ways **women's writing** has
been viewed as transgressive in relation to a form
which assumes a masculine subject. According to
Domna Stanton, women's autobiography drama-
tises women's 'alterity and non-presence' even as it
strives to assert the woman's status as subject within
discourse (Stanton 1987). Critical approaches to
women's autobiography, therefore, have tended
either to emphasise the range of subjectivities or
subject positions employed by women in autobiography, arguing against any general category of the
subject, or to demonstrate women's different
relation with the tradition of autobiography as
they negotiate through concealment, apology,
parody or fiction, with a narrative from which
they are debarred.

The development of interest in women's autobiography has also extended beyond the literary
and has provided the impetus for questioning
disciplinary as well as generic boundaries. Within
the social sciences, there has been a demand for
'self-reflexivity' and acknowledgment of a self
which is situated within a particular lived history,
as against the traditional assumption that the self of
the theorist was objective, and, therefore, a-
gendered. For feminist historians, women's autobiographies provide not just source material about
lives which have traditionally been overlooked but
ways of thinking about subjectivity and its forms
and representations within historical accounts.
Autobiography has also supported radical developments within teaching, providing a means for
women to employ their own autobiographcal
accounts as sources of knowledge and recognise
themselves as subjects within their own worlds. The
use of autobiography in the classroom can be a
means of crossing not only subject disciplines but
the divide between author and reader and theory
and practice as well. Autobiography has played an
important part, too, in feminist recognitions of the
heterogeneity of women's lives and the differences
among women which can get lost in theoretical
generalisations; in its engagement with a particular
point of view, autobiography can provide a more
complex view of Woman than simply the Other of
man, seeing her instead as the product of distinct
histories, marked by the complicated crossings of
gender, ethnicity, **race** and class (see **class
analysis, UK; class analysis, US**).

Autobiography has been the site of important
debates within feminism about the relation of
theory to practice and the challenge of the specific
to any theoretical framing; it has therefore offered
one of the most important feminist challenges to
postmodernist theory (see **poststructuralism/
postmodernism**). At the same time, it has also
provided a reading of the 'fictional' or 'literary' as
components within the representation of subjectivity and warned against the dangers of collapsing
the textual into too simple or direct a notion of
'experience'. Julia Swindells has argued how nineteenth-century women autobiographers turned to
fiction, the genre where women were most visible,
to provide a model for their own self-representa-
tions as situated Others. It becomes necessary,

therefore, to read their autobiographies in terms of conflicting genres and the gaps between the literary and the material (Swindells 1985). Acording to Leigh Gilmore, the 'truth' of autobiography has less to do with the text's presumed accuracy than the way it 'fits' cultural discourses of truth and **identity** (Gilmore 1994). For Reginia Gagnier, the key methodological perspective should be 'the pragmatics of self-representation', what an auto-biography does rather than its experiential base (Gagnier 1991). Shari Benstock has offered important poststructuralist psychoanalytic readings of autobiography, seeing women as situated as Other within the symbolic system (see **psychoanalysis**; **psychoanalytic feminist literary theory**). According to this reading women cannot simply make their stories present; they can only be read through attention to what is missing or not yet. Virginia Woolf provides an important example in the way she questions both the status of the self and the written in the very act of writing (Benstock (ed.) 1988). Bella Brodski and Celeste Schenck, on the other hand, have perceived a danger in too much attention being paid to the textual and the constructed nature of identity in the way it elides the notion of the 'bios', the lived element in autobiography. To do so, they argue, is to ignore 'the crucial referentiality of class, race and sexual orientation'. It is to lose the possibility of addressing the subject as also a social subject and to deny agency for women (Brodski and Schenk 1988: 13). Feminist critics have stressed, therefore, that there are serious political questions to be asked in relation to how autobiography is thought about and theorised.

References and further reading

Benstock, S. (ed.) (1988) *The Private Self: Theory and Practice of Women's Autobiographical Writing*, London: Routledge.

Brodski, B. and Schenck, C. (eds) (1988) *Life/Lines: Theorizing Women's Autobiography*, Ithaca, NY and London: Cornell University Press.

Broughton, T.L. and Anderson, L. (eds) (1997) *Women's Lives/Women's Times*, Albany, NY: State University of New York Press.

Gagnier, R. (1991) *Subjectivities: A History of Self-Representation in Britain 1832–1920*, New York and Oxford: Oxford University Press.

Gilmore, L. (1994) *Autobiographics: Feminist Theory of Women's Self-Representation*, Ithaca, NY and London: Cornell University Press.

Smith, S. and Watson, J. (eds) (1992) *De/Colonizing the Subject: The Politics of Gender in Women's Autobiography*, Minneapolis, MI: University of Minnesota Press.

Stanton, D.C. (ed.) (1987) *The Female Autograph: Theory and Practice of Autobiography from the Tenth to the Twentieth Century*, Chicago, IL: University of Chicago Press.

Swindells, J. (1985) *Victorian Writing and Working Women*, Cambridge, MA: Polity Press.

LINDA ANDERSON

autogynography

Autogynography is a term coined by Domna Stanton in *The Female Autograph* (1987) to highlight (and counter) the canonical identification of **autobiography** with men's writing. Moreover, 'gyno' raises the possibility that female self-narrations may be different from those of men, but opposes both the androcentric trope that women can only write about the self and (premature) feminist claims of thematic and stylistic differences, such as relatedness, detailedness or dailiness, which essentialise women's 'life experience'. By effacing 'bio', *autogynography* also questions generic assertions about the referential reality of autobiography and its representation of a whole life. Thus, *autogynography* undermines the notion that autobiography is a discrete genre, and promotes consideration of other modes of self-writing, including **diaries**, letters, memoirs and testimonials.

See also: essentialism

References and further reading

Stanton, D.C. (ed.) (1987) *The Female Autograph: Theory and Practice of Autobiography from the Tenth to the Twentieth Century*, Chicago, IL: University of Chicago Press.

DOMNA C. STANTON

autonomy

Autonomy (Greek *auto*/self, *nomos*/rule) comes into western philosophy from Immanuel Kant (1724–1804). Contrasting with *heteronomy* (governance by the rule or law of others), autonomy was inspirational in the French and American revolutions, where it promised freedom from the arbitrary power of religious and aristocratic rule. Autonomy celebrates a morality of individual self-rule, a politics of self-definition, and an epistemology of knowledge achieved by reason alone (see **epistemology, feminist**). Mary Wollstonecraft's *Vindication of the Rights of Women* (1792) argues for women's autonomy; and present-day feminists advocate autonomy as freedom for women *from* patriarchal oppression and *to* realise their 'own' powers.

Yet autonomy is a contested ideal for late-twentieth-century feminists, many of whom claim that the Enlightenment ideal of 'autonomous man' could only be realised by affluent heterosexual men whose wives manage the necessities of everyday life (see **heterosexuality**). White western child-raising practices nurture boys to become autonomous men, while they nurture in girls a caring connectedness that will contain them within the (private) world of self-sacrificing nurturance that enables (public) men to realise their autonomy. Furthermore, autonomy in its associations with liberal **individualism** has evolved into an ideal of a radically self-contained, atomistic, unified self, maximally defended against connections that threaten self-sufficiency: an ideal inimical to many women. Yet despite its self-centred connotations, autonomy still counts as an achievement that is as essential to the well-being of the marginalised as to the creation of a just society. Women, blacks, refugees from totalitarianism, the poor, the disabled often rightly name autonomy as their overarching goal.

Medicine is an instructive example. Since the 1960s patient-autonomy activists have challenged the profession's paternalistic practices that render patients passive, denying their autonomous agency; insisting that the doctor – like father – knows best. They have argued, often successfully, for interactive health care, including access to information that enables patients to participate in their own treatment. Medicine's long history of infantalising women gives feminists a special stake in these arguments.

Working within these tensions, feminists committed to autonomy's emancipatory promise attempt to erase its connections with excessively individualistic practices along with its ideals of a transparent and unified self, and its exaggerated rationalism. They preserve the mutual concern and cooperation that are overriding values for many women and other Others in articulating a relational autonomy that affirms the embodied and socially embedded nature of selves out of which responsibilities and commitments are enacted.

References and further reading

Code, L. (2000) 'The Perversion of Autonomy and the Subjection of Women', in C. Mackenzie and N. Stoljar (eds) *Relational Autonomy*, New York: Oxford University Press.

Grimshaw, J. (1988) 'Autonomy and Identity in Feminist Thinking', in M. Griffiths and M. Whitford (eds) *Feminist Perspectives in Philosophy*, London: Macmillan.

LORRAINE CODE

B

backlash

The term backlash refers generally to a perceived conservative or right-wing reaction to social changes or progressive ideas. Susan Faludi (b. 1959), who has most recently popularised the term, uses 'backlash' to refer to an anti-feminist counter-attack in retaliation for the achievements of the women's movement of the 1960s and 1970s, in areas like political and media representation of women, employment, health, educational opportunities and the environment. Faludi argues there has been a significant 'counter-assault on women's rights' since the 1980s that directly targets and attempts to undermine the achievements of the women's movement (Faludi 1992: 12). Her distinctive use of 'backlash' is to emphasise that it is often the specific achievements of feminism that are highlighted by opponents as being detrimental to women. She examines aspects of popular culture and focuses upon how feminism has been blamed by critics for a range of social ills facing women: increasing rates of depression to inadequate capacity for personal savings; teenage suicides and eating disorders; increases in female poverty and a flourishing male fascination for slasher movies. Faludi attributes such negative images of feminism, not only to anti-feminist opposition but more subtly to a reluctance on the part of many women to say they are feminist: 'Saying one is "not a feminist" (even while supporting quietly every item of the feminist platform) seems the most prudent, self-protective strategy' (1992: 58).

Faludi maintains that struggles for women's rights have progressed through four eras, each marked by a backlash: 'A struggle for women's rights gained force in the mid-nineteenth century, the early 1900s, the early 1940s and the early 1970s. In each case, the struggle yielded to backlash' (1992: 68). Contemporary backlash takes particular forms. For example, the myth that women's infertility greatly increases after the age of thirty; that women's standards of living deteriorate with their choice to divorce; that tertiary education diminishes women's chances to marry; and that declining mental health is an outcome of increased opportunities to prioritise careers above childbearing.

Faludi has been criticised for over-emphasising commonalities between feminists in the USA and UK and generalising that feminists everywhere share basic objectives against the universal subordination of women. Sylvia Walby (1993: 79) questions whether backlash against women takes the same form historically and culturally. Walby argues that the recognition of differences between women suggests that an emphasis on shared experiences may distort the social significance of female diversity, and that feminist-assisted strategies for change impact differently on various groups of women. Faludi agrees with Walby that not to examine commonalities 'underplays the significance of what can be learnt from the experiences of women in different times and cultures'.

'Backlash' has been used by feminists before Faludi to denote conservative responses to struggles for women's equality in the workplace and in legal and political structures. Carol Smart's 1989 book on the legal status of women and Cynthia

Cockburn's 1991 study of 'men's resistance to sex equality in organizations' are examples of empirically based research about 'backlash' where feminism is alleged to have provided a basis for social changes that *disadvantage* women. Martha Fineman's and Martha T. McCluskey's collection (1997) explores negative images of feminism in the media while Ann Oakley's and Juliet Mitchell's (1997) book explores common myths around what 'second-wave' feminists have or have not achieved.

The term 'backlash' is also sometimes linked to 'postfeminism'. 'Postfeminism' was coined in the period between the achievement of women's suffrage in the USA and the rise of 'second-wave' feminism during the 1960s. It denoted the successful outcome of struggles by women for the right to vote, to hold public office and to occupy many more personal spheres. In the late 1980s and 1990s, 'postfeminism' acquired new currency, which is often hostile and directed towards individual feminists. It is the belief that the 1970s struggle for 'women's rights' has achieved all that it was reasonable to expect to achieve, and that the 'excesses' of feminist lobbying have been 'exposed' as a passé anti-male fad. Despite many feminists maintaining that such a use of 'postfeminism' is a backlash reaction that rejects the on-going struggles of women for basic needs and rights, 'postfeminism' is also used in a variety of more positive ways in academic cultural studies. Both the popular *and* academic responses imply that 'postfeminism' may also operate as an imperative towards defining and containing certain forms of liberal feminist thinking. 'Postfeminism' is also used to denote the privileged positions of women who claim psychological freedom from subordination, maintaining that feminism has never and could never be relevant to them. The term is used to critique feminism's complicity in modernist thinking, specifically to note feminism's appropriation of analyses by 'Third World women', Indigenous women and 'women of colour'. For some the question posed by popular uses of 'postfeminism' is whether it usefully corrects the limitations of feminist analyses of women's lives and highlights those aspects of feminisms that must change to remain effective in a postmodern era. Arguably, 'postfeminism' adds little to feminist encounters with postmodern challenges to identity, community and politics, but provides a timely caution about the complex intersections of definition and location.

References and further reading

Alice, L. (1995) 'What is Postfeminism? Or – Having it both ways', *Feminism/Postmodernism/ Postfeminism, Working papers in Women's Studies*, no. 1, Massey University, New Zealand.

Cockburn, C. (1991) *In the Way of Women: Men's Resistance to Sex Equality in Organizations*, Basingstoke: Macmillan.

Faludi, S. (1991) *Backlash: The Undeclared War Against American Women*, New York: Crown.

Fineman, M. and McCluskey, M.T. (eds) (1997) *Feminism, Media, and the Law*, New York: Oxford University Press.

Oakley, A. and Mitchell, J. (1997) *Who's Afraid of Feminism?: Seeing Through the Backlash*, New York: New Press.

Smart, C. (1989) *Feminism and the Power of Law*, London and New York: Routledge.

Walby, S. (1993) 'Backlash in Historical Context', in M. Kennedy, C. Lubelska and V. Walsh (eds) *Making Connections, Women's Studies, Women's Movements, Women's Lives*, London: Taylor and Francis.

LYNNE ALICE

beauty (the feminine beauty system)

From the practices of foot-binding in ancient China to chemical face peeling and collagen-inflated lips in Southern California, women have been prepared to go to great lengths to meet the cultural ideals of feminine beauty. Although the aesthetic ideals of feminine shape and countenance have varied greatly from culture to culture and shifted dramatically over the years, the underlying assumption always seems to be that beauty is worth time, money, pain, and sometimes even life itself.

Feminists have tended to cast a critical eye on women's involvement in the 'beauty system'. The 'beauty system' includes women's countless everyday rituals of **body** improvement like make-up and dieting as well as the cosmetic and fashion industry, medical technologies like **cosmetic surgery**, and the media and advertising businesses with their deployment of idealised images of femininity (see **advertising, women in**). Feminists have shown how the practices and discourses of beauty are integral both to the production and regulation of femininity and to asymmetrical relations of power between the sexes and among women. Symbolically, Woman as sex is placed upon a pedestal as the incarnation of physical beauty, while most ordinary women are rendered 'drab, ugly, loathsome, or fearful bodies' (Young 1990). The beauty system creates hierarchies among women as women of colour are bombarded with messages linking beauty to whiteness and, more generally, to eurocentric superiority (see **eurocentrism**).

Originally, feminists described beauty in terms of suffering and oppression. Women were presented as the victims of beauty norms and the ideology of feminine inferiority which these norms sustain. The beauty system was compared to the 'military industrial complex' and decried as a major articulation of capitalist **patriarchy** (Bartky 1990).

In recent years, feminist discourse on beauty as **oppression** has begun to make way for postmodern perspectives which treat beauty in terms of cultural discourses (see **poststructuralism/ postmodernism**). Following Foucault, the focus shifts to the multiplicity of meanings which are inscribed upon the female **body** and to the insidious and pervasive workings of disciplinary power through routine beauty practices and regimes.

While the postmodern turn in feminist discourse on beauty theoretically opens possibilities for thinking about beauty practices in new ways – for example, fashion as a site for creativity, subversion or even empowerment – feminist scholarship continues to focus primarily on the repressive features of beauty and how beauty practices control or discipline women.

See also: cosmetic surgery; eating disorders

References and further reading

Bartky, S. (1990) *Femininity and Domination: Studies in the Phenomenology of Oppression*, New York: Routledge.

MacCannell, D. and MacCannell, J.F. (1987) 'The Beauty System', in N. Armstrong and L. Tennenhouse (eds) *The Ideology of Conduct*, New York: Methuen.

Young, I. (1990) *Justice and the Politics of Difference*, Princeton, NJ: Princeton University Press.

KATHY DAVIS

Beauvoir, Simone de (1908–86)

Simone de Beauvoir was a French existentialist philosopher, writer, and author of the feminist classic, *The Second Sex* (1949). Once considered Sartre's philosophical follower, scholars have differentiated Beauvoir from Sartre and, using posthumous manuscripts, identified her philosophical originality. Her 1927 diary, written while studying philosophy at the Sorbonne two years before meeting Sartre, shows early philosophical influences: Bergson, Nietzsche, Schopenhauer, Baruzi, and Leibniz, the subject of her graduate thesis. Existential themes in the diary include the anguished experience of nothingness and the temptations of self-deception. Beauvoir affirms the value of emotionality and embodiment in philosophy, defines a methodology for doing philosophy through literature, and establishes the theme of her philosophical work: the opposition of self and other that results when the desire for self-realisation collides with the desire for domination and fusion with the other.

Beauvoir's philosophical work on this problem of the other leads to murder in her 1943 novel, *She Came to Stay*. In *Ethics of Ambiguity* (1946) and other writings of her 'moral period', during the Second World War, Beauvoir subordinates the demands of self to an ethics of generosity and solidarity. Beauvoir returns to the problem of the other in *The Second Sex*, where she situates the ethical problems of personal relationships within the historical context of women's oppression as **Other**. Contrasting the situation of women with those of blacks, Jews, and the proletariat, Beauvoir draws on a critique of Freudian psychoanalysis and Marxist economic analysis to lay the theoretical foundations of a radical **feminism**, arguing that the only authentic moral action is women's collective struggle for their own liberation.

In years that followed, Beauvoir wrote memoirs, novels, articles on the Algerian War, and an essay on old age. Hers was an international voice condemning women's oppression throughout the 1950s and 1960s, and an activist voice in the 1970s. Vintges (1996) argues that Beauvoir's stylisation of herself as an intellectual woman in her multi-volume autobiography is her most important contribution to ethics, providing practical guidelines in the art of living for young women struggling to reconcile freedom and love.

See also: dutiful daughters; French feminism; second sex

Selected writings

Beauvoir, S. (1943) *She Came to Stay*, trans. Y. Moyse and R. Senhouser, Cleveland: World Publishing Co., 1954.
—— (1946) *Ethics of Ambiguity*, trans. B. Frechtman, Secaucus, NJ: Citadel Press.
—— (1949) *The Second Sex*, trans. H.M. Parshley, New York: Knopf, 1952.

References and further reading

Bergoffen, D. (1997) *The Philosophy of Simone de Beauvoir*, Albany, NY: State University of New York Press.
Simons, M. (ed) (1995) *Feminist Interpretations of Simone de Beauvoir*, University Park: Penn State University Press.
Vintges, K. (1996) *Philosophy as Passion*, trans. A. Lavelle, Bloomington, IN: Indiana University Press.

MARGARET A. SIMONS

becoming woman

We owe the concept 'becoming woman' to Simone de **Beauvoir**. She begins the second volume of *The Second Sex* (1949) with the now much-cited phrase, 'one is not born a woman: one becomes one'. Second-wave Anglophone feminists have most commonly construed this statement to mean that being 'a woman', or being 'feminine', is not a natural attribute. Having a female-sexed biological body does not automatically make one a woman; rather one becomes a woman through a process of initiation into a socially constituted identity. In short, sex (anatomical differences between women and men) and **gender** are not synonymous.

Although Beauvoir did not use the term gender, the distinction between sex and gender is implied in her observation that 'every female human being is not necessarily a woman' ([1949] 1989: xix). Beauvoir sets out to describe what she calls 'the lived experience' of becoming a woman. She begins with those early childhood experiences through which girls learn to feel that they are inferior to boys, and continues through accounts of sexual initiation, marriage, **motherhood** to reveal how women acquire a sense of inferiority to men and frequently come to accept their situation of **oppression** rather than assert freedom.

However, the phrase 'becoming woman' is open to further interpretations, which later feminists have explored. The verb 'to become' is ambiguous, being both passive and active in its implications. Passively construed, it may imply that one is *made* a woman by forces beyond one's control: women are forced to comply with norms of femininity that are not of their choosing. It may also be read to imply that social constructions, social pressures, or else what feminists influenced by Foucault have called 'disciplinary practices' (e.g. Ramazanoglu 1993), have the effect of constituting some persons as 'women' without their being consciously aware of that process.

However, construed in a more active sense, 'becoming woman' can imply a volitional engagement in the creation of one's gender identity. Beauvoir herself suggests that women are often complicit in their oppression, choosing to assume 'feminine' characteristics because there are benefits – such as male protection – associated with them or because the costs of resisting are high. More recently Butler (1990) has suggested that 'becoming woman' can also be construed as an on-going 'performance' in which – albeit under duress – female gender is produced and sustained over time by the repetition of certain styles of action that signify femininity.

See also: gender roles

References and further reading

Beauvoir, S. de ([1949] 1989) *The Second Sex*, trans. H.M. Parshley, New York: Vintage Books.

Butler, J. (1990) *Gender Trouble: Feminism and the Subversion of Identity*, New York and London: Routledge.

Ramazanoglu, C. (ed.) (1993) *Up Against Foucault: Explorations of some Tensions between Foucault and Feminism*, London and New York: Routledge.

SONIA KRUKS

Benhabib, Seyla (b. 1950)

Seyla Benhabib's commitment to moral and political universalism and to a reconstruction of critical theory gives her a unique place in contemporary feminism. Like feminists generally, she rejects the illusion of a self-legislating reason, the fiction of the disembodied subject, and the dream of a context-independent standpoint. However, unlike many, she does not conclude that universalism has to be dismantled.

Drawing constructively on the work of Jürgen Habermas, and taking serious notice of the 'different voice' thematised by Carol **Gilligan**, Benhabib argues for an 'interactive universalism' that gives moral and political weight to the concreteness of everyday communication. Of particular significance for feminism is her reformulation of **public/private** in terms of two conceptions of self/other relations: the standpoint of the 'generalised other' and that of the 'concrete other'. To take the standpoint of the generalised other is to view every individual as a rational being with entitlements to the same rights and duties we claim for ourselves. Taking the standpoint of the concrete other means seeing every rational being as an individual with a concrete history, particular identity, and specific needs and aspirations. According to Benhabib, moral deliberation belongs to both types of interaction: generalised others are subject to moral categories of right, obligation, and entitlement, whereas concrete others are connected through moral categories of responsibility, bonding,

and sharing. In ascribing a moral dimension to the interactions of concrete others, Benhabib seeks to correct for a 'legislative' universalism that relegates women to the sphere of the private and the irrational. In her reconstructed critical theory, women are rational and moral beings, and women's activities are brought directly into the moral and political spheres. Themes of concreteness and interaction also emerge in Benhabib's study of Hannah Arendt, especially in discussions of the narrative elements of action and the intersubjective aspects of judgement.

Benhabib argues against bringing the aesthetic into feminist politics and takes a sceptical view of postmodernism. She herself is criticised for being insufficiently critical of modernity and for retaining a predisposition to foundationalism that undermines her espousal of a contextual and historical reason.

See also: critical theory, feminism and; modernity, feminist critique of; poststructuralism/postmodernism

Selected writings

Benhabib, S. (1992) *Situating the Self: Gender, Community and Postmodernism in Contemporary Ethics*, New York: Routledge.

—— (1996) *The Reluctant Modernism of Hannah Arendt*, London: Sage.

Benhabib, S., Butler, J., Cornell, D. and Fraser, N. (1995) *Feminist Contentions: A Philosophical Exchange*, New York: Routledge.

MARIE FLEMING

bias, observational

Observational bias suggests that observations are informed, even contaminated, by the beliefs, prejudices, and background assumptions of the observer(s). Feminist empiricists thus propose that the task is to displace such biases as **sexism**, racism, or **androcentrism**: a goal they regard as achievable by ever stricter adherence to scientific method, which will cleanse the final product – the knowledge – of bias. Empiricists such as Helen Longino, by contrast, argue that background assumptions necessarily shape projects of inquiry, so that the task is to examine and critique those assumptions, to chart their effects. Longino's contrastive examples of inquiry conducted from diverse assumptions, demonstrate the radically different conceptions of reality they yield. Other feminist epistemologists contend still more strongly that absolute, bias-free **objectivity** is impossible. They argue that working with the concept of bias as someone's 'possession' obscures from view the social conditions that shape and constrain knowing as process and as product.

See also: empiricism; epistemology, feminist

References and further reading

Longino, H. (1990) *Science as Social Knowledge*, Princeton, NJ: Princeton University Press.

LORRAINE CODE

biblical studies, feminist

Feminist biblical studies, which in a very short time has developed into a vibrant field of scholarship, is best defined as theory, art and praxis of interpretation in the interest of wo/men. (This writing indicates the ambiguity of the term.) Its object of research is the bible both as Scripture and as a classic of western culture. Although feminist biblical inquiry is still marginal, its research nevertheless has fructified all areas of biblical studies.

Feminist interpretation engages two seemingly contradictory insights. The bible is written in kyriocentric (i.e. lord/master/father/husband-elite male) language, originated in the patri-kyriarchal cultures of antiquity, and has functioned to inculcate misogynist mindsets and oppressive values. The bible also has functioned to inspire and authorise wo/men in their struggles against dehumanising oppression. Feminist biblical interpretation serves simultaneously as a resource for wo/men's religious and cultural victimisation and for their agency and empowerment.

While wo/men always have interpreted the Scriptures, feminist biblical studies is a newcomer in theology and religious studies. Only in the context of the wo/men's movements of the nine-

teenth and twentieth centuries have feminists begun to explore the possibilities of a critical hermeneutics that takes the institutional silencing of wo/men in biblical religions and the cultural impact of biblical texts on wo/men into account. In the nineteenth century, Elizabeth Cady Stanton initiated the project of the *Woman's Bible* because she was convinced that no area of society could be reformed without reforming all areas of it.

Since religion and the bible play a significant role in wo/men's oppression and liberation, feminists cannot afford to neglect it. Instead, they must both reclaim the authority of wo/men as subjects of interpretation and reconceptualise the act of interpretation as a moment in the struggle for liberation. A critical feminist interpretation is distinct from other forms such as the literary and historical study *about* wo/men, the defence of scriptural injunctions *against* wo/men, or the tracing out of gender constructs inscribed in biblical texts and interpretations.

Popular and academic biblical interpretations *by women*, the reading of the bible *as a woman* or its interpretation in terms of *gender* are not simply identical with a critical feminist hermeneutics which is a practice of rhetorical inquiry that aims at a critical historical and religious consciousness. Whereas hermeneutics seeks to understand the *meaning* of texts, rhetorics attends to the effects biblical discourses produce, how they produce them, and for whom they are produced. Feminist rhetorics moves beyond 'mere hermeneutics' to a complex process of critical analysis. It seeks to overcome the theoretical binaries (see **binaries/ bipolarity**) between sense and meaning, explanation and understanding, distanciation and empathy, reading 'behind' and 'in front of' the text, interpretation and application, realism and imagination.

Interpretations of the bible by wo/men are *not* feminist simply because they are readings of wo/men. Insofar as conservative interpretations do not employ a critical analysis of wo/men's sociopolitical and cultural-religious subordination and second class citizenship, they tend to read kyriocentric biblical texts as authorisation for cultural and religious femininity and subordination. By insisting that not all biblical readings *of wo/men or about wo/men* are feminist, one does not deny agency and respect to individual wo/men who engage in such readings.

Although a critical feminist hermeneutics is well aware of the postmodern debates on 'woman', 'difference', and 'master narratives', it nevertheless insists on a systemic analytic that employs the categories of domination and subordination. It utilises not just the analytic of gender but engages in an analysis of the multiplicative structures of domination inscribed in and advocated by kyrio-centric texts. It does not begin by placing the bible at the centre of its attention but instead focuses on the struggles of wo/men at the bottom of the patri-kyriarchal pyramid of domination because their struggles reveal the fulcrum of oppression threatening all wo/men.

Feminist hermeneutics therefore insists on a critical reflection of experience and social location as its starting point. A rich array of readings by wo/men from different social and religious locations has challenged the fundamental assumptions of white Euro-American, predominantly Christian biblical scholarship. They have elucidated not only that the bible has different meanings in different cultural contexts but also is constituted differently in various religious contexts.

The hermeneutical process of a critical interpretation for liberation entails at least seven strategies of inquiry: reflection on experience and social location, systemic analysis of structures of domination, suspicion, reconstruction, evaluation, imagination, and transformation. These strategies are not simply independent steps of inquiry or methodological rules, but hermeneutical practices that interact with each other in feminist interpretations of biblical or any other cultural texts. These strategies have as their *reference point* both the language-systems, ideological frameworks, and socio-political-religious locations of contemporary readers and the linguistic systems and socio-historical locations of biblical texts and their effective histories.

A feminist hermeneutics that understands interpretation as a cultural-religious practice of resistance and transformation utilises not only historical-literary, and ideology-critical evaluative methods of rhetorical analysis. It also employs methods of storytelling, bibliodrama, dance, and ritual for creating a 'different' religious imagina-tion. Its critical hermeneutical processes are not limited to biblical texts. They can be equally applied to extra-canonical sources and other classics of religion and culture.

Insofar as feminist biblical studies participates as an academic discipline in the methodological debates that have occupied biblical scholars in the past decades, it is in danger of reproducing them. Although it eschews value-neutrality and positivist objectivity, it nevertheless is subject to the pressures of producing standard scientific knowledge accept-able to malestream scholarship. Finally, even though it clearly has been conceptualised as an interdisci-plinary field of study, feminist biblical inquiry is in danger of remaining within the boundaries of traditional disciplines that dictate scholarly educa-tion and research interests. Navigating between the Scylla of marginalisation and the Charybdis of co-optation feminist biblical scholarship nevertheless has made significant contributions to biblical studies and most importantly has empowered wo/men for reading the bible differently.

References and further reading

Bach, A. (ed.) (1999) *Women in the Hebrew Bible*, New York: Routledge.

Cannon, K.G. and Schüssler Fiorenza, E. (eds) (1987) *Interpretation for Liberation*, Semeia 47, Atlanta: Scholars Press.

Kwok, Pui-lan (1995) *Discovering the Bible in the Non-Biblical World*, Maryknoll: Orbis.

Kwok, Pui-Lan and Schüssler Fiorenza, E. (eds) (1998) *Women's Sacred Scriptures*, Concilium, Maryknoll: Orbis.

Russell, L.M. (ed.) (1985) *Feminist Interpretation of the Bible*, Philadelphia, PA: Westminster Press.

Schüssler Fiorenza, E. (ed.) (1993/94) *Searching the Scriptures*, 2 vols, New York: Crossroad.

—— (1997) *Sharing Her Word*, Boston: Beacon Press.

Suskin Ostriker, A. (1993) *Feminist Revision of the Bible*, Oxford: Blackwell.

Washington, H.C., Lochrie Graham, S. and Thimmes, P. (eds) (1999) *Escaping Eden. New Feminist Perspectives on the Bible*, New York: New York University Press.

ELISABETH SCHÜSSLER FIORENZA

binaries/bipolarity

Binary oppositions, and bipolarity, refer to a practice that runs through western thought of arranging conceptual/theoretical systems in opposed, contrasting pairs. The idea is that *good*, for example, can be understood only in contrast with *bad*, *light* by contrast with *dark*. Characterising these contrasts as *bipolar* represents the opposed terms as radically separate from one another, not as points on a continuum. This arrangement might appear to be a perfectly neutral way of classifying attributes of the world, both physical and human. But feminist critiques contest the neutrality, showing that the pairs mark not merely descriptive but also evaluative contrasts, which are enlisted to condemn one 'side' while promoting and celebrating the other. The male/female polarity is no exception.

See also: dichotomies

References and further reading

Lovibond, S. (1994) 'An Ancient Theory of Gender', in L. Archer, S. Fischler and M. Wyke (eds) *Women in Ancient Societies*, New York: Routledge.

LORRAINE CODE

bioethics

Bioethics is the study of ethical problems and policies arising in the sphere of biology, especially those involving questions of (human) health and health care. Feminists bring to the field recognition of the relevance of gender and power as important dimensions of analysis. Feminist contributions include (1) revisiting traditional issues from the perspective of feminist ethics, (2) expanding the agenda to include topics and perspectives largely ignored by non-feminist theorists, and (3) challenging the terms, presuppositions, or fundamental methods of the field.

(1)   Feminists have been prominent in several central areas, most notably in discussions of **reproduction**. Issues such as abortion, use of new reproductive technologies, so-called surrogacy (contractual pregnancy) arrangements, and genetic testing have all attracted significant feminist debate. Most non-feminist bioethicists tend to focus on the well-being of foetuses or to offer impartial utility measures for all those affected by a policy; they ignore the differential effects of reproductive policies on women. In contrast, feminists tend to emphasise the unique roles women play in human reproduction while challenging illegitimate essentialist and naturalising assumptions; they evaluate the distinct impact of medical and legal reproductive policies on women's health and social status.

Feminists have also entered into discussions about the ethics of research involving human beings, demanding safeguards against the exploitation of members of oppressed and devalued groups in hazardous research. At the same time, they have challenged the injustice of systematically excluding women from participation in promising clinical trials (such as the large scale MRFIT heart health study), because exclusion results in inadequate knowledge about women's specific health needs and, thereby, leads to inferior health care for women.

Feminist interventions include discussions of euthanasia and physician-assisted deaths (where the vulnerability and devaluing of the oppressed must be considered), consideration of policies regarding HIV infection and AIDS (where attention must be paid to the different ways in which women are affected by the disease and by associated social policies), and determination of fair allocations of health-care resources (within a health-care system heavily dependent on the unpaid and underpaid labour of women). (See **AIDS, women and**).

(2)   Feminists have also expanded the agenda and perspective of bioethics. Some include environmental questions, for example, the concerns of **ecofeminism**. Others explore the ethical dimensions of the ways in which medicine has played a role in the social construction of the **body** and of our understanding of what is male and what is female. Most feminists understand that bioethics, like ethics, is an inherently political domain requiring explicit discussion of biopolitics. Raising ethical questions regarding medicine's response to such gendered practices as **eating disorders** and **cosmetic surgery** and its normative and inter-

ventionist role in matters of **sexuality** are further examples of feminism's redefining of bioethics.

Some feminists have proposed that bioethics should address the 'small' issues as well as the grand ones. As Virginia Warren argues (Holmes and Purdy 1992: 32–45), bioethics must concern itself with 'housekeeping issues' as well as 'crisis issues'. It needs, for example, to consider the ways in which power is concentrated in the hands of a privileged elite while most of the labour is carried out by members of disadvantaged groups. Such disproportionate distributions of labour become more visible as the bioethics community is enlarged to include more women and minority members, and as it reflects on the perspectives not only of physicians, but also of other sorts of health-care workers and of patients and their families. For example, some feminists with disabilities have demanded the inclusion of issues surrounding disability and chronic illness in bioethical discussions (see **disability, women and**).

In addition, feminists have insisted that bioethical discussions not be restricted to analysis of abstract patient/physician relations in isolation, but that they acknowledge that individuals belong to social groups which may significantly influence the ways others relate to them. The gender, as well as the race, class, disability status, age, ethnicity, and sexuality of a patient may play a major role in the treatment she receives. (Such factors may also affect patients' trust in the health professionals who care for them and the willingness of third parties to act on some caregivers' recommendations.)

(3) Feminist work has gone yet deeper in its engagement with bioethics, challenging some of the fundamental methods and terms of the discussion. Many feminists have demanded a shift from the dominant principles-based or 'ethics of justice' approach to an approach based in an **ethic of care**. Indeed, some practitioners – most notably nurses and volunteer caregivers (family and friends) – find that an ethic of care is essential to capture their sense of responsibility in the provision of health services. Many feminists have expressed scepticism about reliance on deduction from a set of abstract principles (the leading bioethics methodology).

Various feminists have proposed rejecting or refashioning two of the central ethical concepts used in bioethics, justice and **autonomy**. In the former, some recommend moving from a distributive paradigm to an ideal of social justice. In the latter, feminists have proposed shifting from a traditional individualist, liberal sense of autonomy to a more social, politically complicated notion of relational autonomy.

Finally, feminist bioethics is characterised by its determination to look at patterns within health care systems: how health and illness are understood, what problems are deemed worthy of intervention, where responsibility for care is assigned, how the 'important' ethical issues are identified and framed. Feminists ask how power and privilege shape these considerations and how alternative constructions might help to redistribute power more fairly in society.

See also: ethics, feminist

References and further reading

Dula, A. and Goring, S. (eds) (1994) *It Just Ain't Fair: The Ethics of Health Care for African Americans*, Westport, CT: Praeger.

Holmes, H.B. and Purdy, L.M. (eds) (1992) *Feminist Perspectives in Medical Ethics*, Bloomington, IN: Indiana University Press.

Mahowald, M. (1993) *Women and Children in Health Care: An Unequal Majority*, New York: Oxford University Press.

Purdy, L. (1996) *Reproducing Persons: Issues in Feminist Bioethics*, Ithaca, NY: Cornell University Press.

Sherwin, S. (1992) *No Longer Patient: Feminist Ethics and Health Care*, Philadelphia, PA: Temple University Press.

Wolf, S.M. (ed.) (1996) *Feminism and Bioethics: Beyond Reproduction*, New York: Oxford University Press.

SUSAN SHERWIN

biography

Feminist biographers as well as feminist theorists of biography have to contend with the fact that biography has a tradition that assigns a marginal status to women. Since the beginnings of biographical theory in the nineteenth century, biographies have been seen as the life stories of great men who are exceptional in their achievements and at the same time representative of the spirit of their age. Feminist scholars and biographers have challenged this tradition and insisted that women should be subjects of biographies; and on their own merits, not because of their relationship to a famous man. However, there is a danger that feminist biographers will create a heroine who is modelled on the heroes of traditional biographies: an isolated subject who resembles, in Liz Stanley's words, 'a Gulliver among Lilliputians' (1992: 9).

Another strategy that contests the androcentric tradition of biography is the claim that feminist biography is a genre that is fundamentally different from traditional biography. Feminist critics have argued that this difference shows itself in the subject matter feminist biographers include: for example child abuse, or lesbian sexuality. This subject matter challenges the assumption that it is excellence in public life that makes a person worthy of a biography. For feminist biographers, a 'life' worth describing is more than the sum of public achievements; moreover, the biography can reveal the political relevance of the supposedly private life of the biography's subject. The other key assumptions of traditional biography, as feminist critics have pointed out, are the subject's individuality and the biographer's presumed impartiality which serves to hide his involvement in shaping the narrated life. Thus, feminist biographers should discard the ideal of impartial detachment and become involved with the life they are researching. In this sense, all biography must become auto/biography: the biographer acknowledges that her own personal history, and the process of research, influences the way in which the biography is written. The inclusion of the biographer's life reveals the perspective she writes from, and the contingency of the biography as only one possible version. For Liz Stanley (1992) this contingency, together with an 'anti-spotlight stance' that recognises the subject's social context, is the defining principle of feminist biography. Good examples for 'contingent' auto/biographies are Germaine Greer's *Daddy We Hardly Knew You* (1989) and Carolyn Steedman's *Landscape For A Good Woman* (1986). In both the author describes a search for the truth about her father/mother that does not end with her discovering the truth, but includes

gaining personal and social insights (see Stanley 1992).

See also: androcentrism; autobiography

References and further reading

Frank, K. (1997) 'Auto/Biography: Writing the Lives of Women', *Auto/Biography* 1997: 2.
Stanley, L. (1992) *The Auto/Biographical I*, Manchester and New York: Manchester University Press.
Wagner-Martin, L. (1994) *Telling Women's Lives*, New Brunswick, NJ: Rutgers University Press.

ANTJE LINDENMEYER

biological essentialism

Biological essentialism is a specific form of **essentialism** that conveys the idea that the essence of a person is rooted in their **biology**; that is, that their personality and characteristics are caused by something internal to the body (such as hormones or genes). An alternative term is biological determinism, meaning that biology determines, or causes, the traits concerned. One example is the claim that women are naturally maternal because of their hormones.

In addition to feminist critiques of essentialism in general, feminist biologists (such as Lynda **Birke**, Ruth **Bleier**, Anne **Fausto-Sterling**, Ruth **Hubbard** and Sue **Rosser**) have criticised biological essentialism for three reasons. First, it denies external, cultural influence, and posits biological causes as the root of who we are, i.e. biologically essentialist ideas ignore the sociocultural production of gender. Second, it oversimplifies scientific accounts of how biological bodies work; it ignores, for example, the influence of environment on the body (hormones can be affected by stress, lifestyle and so on). Third, it is usually generalised to describe specific groups of people; thus, differences associated with **gender**, **sexuality** or **race** may be attributed to biological bases.

Feminist critics have noted how biologically essentialist ideas typically support the status quo – examples include the idea that male aggression or domination depends upon male hormones, or that women's biology, or the biology of black people, makes them less suitable for certain jobs. So in general, biological essentialism is antifeminist and racist.

Occasionally, feminist writers have used a form of biological essentialism to argue for women's superiority in certain traits (such as nurturance). This position is often attributed to radical feminist theorists, although the evidence that **radical feminism** is biologically essentialist is scant and the claim is contested.

See also: Darwin, feminist critique of

References and further reading

Fausto-Sterling, A. (1992) *Myths of Gender: Biological Theories about Women and Men*, New York: Basic Books.

Hubbard, R. (1990) *The Politics of Women's Biology*, New Brunswick, NJ: Rutgers University Press.

Rosser, S. (1992) *Feminism and Biology*, New York: Twayne.

LYNDA BIRKE

biology

The term 'biology', from the Greek *bios*, or life, means the study of living things. It is also used to mean the various ways that an organism works – as in 'human biology', or 'the biology of flowering plants'.

The word has been in circulation for only two centuries; before that, the study of living things was classified under 'natural philosophy' (which included the physical sciences), natural history, or medicine. 'Biology' today includes many, overlapping subdivisions, from the study of whole ecosystems, to the study of tiny molecules; its subdivisions have, however, changed during the twentieth century. Earlier, it was dominated by zoology and botany, the study of specific kinds of organism. Now, the major subdivisions reflect different approaches to studying life, such as genetics and evolution, physiology, or molecular genetics. Each of these asks different kinds of questions about how life works.

Biology is particularly relevant to feminism, and

has influenced feminist thought, in four ways. First, women involved in self-help **health** groups have engaged with ideas about the body and how it works; one example is the Boston Women's Health Collective's *Our Bodies, Ourselves* (1976). Second, feminists have always opposed ideas that stereotypes of **gender** and **sexuality** are fixed and unchangeable; such ideas underlie **biological essentialism**. Third, the concerns of biology are deeply entwined with the concerns of environmentalists. So, ecofeminists and feminists working for animal rights have interests in biology (see Gaard 1993). And fourth, the practices of biotechnology have many social implications, especially in genetic engineering. Vandana **Shiva** has pointed out, for example, how introducing genetically engineered crops into agricultural systems of developing countries impacts upon indigenous knowledge and farming practices.

Biological essentialism is often used by antifeminists to define 'women's place'. The assumption underlying such claims is that, because of her underlying biology, a woman is more suited to some roles (such as childcare) than others. Biological arguments have been used similarly regarding sexuality and **race**. Among the areas of biology that particularly serve these claims are genetics and evolution, **endocrinology** (see Oudshoorn 1994), and brain lateralisation theories. An example of genetic determinism is the claim that there is a 'gay gene', which is responsible for all the complex behaviour and lifestyle of being gay or lesbian. Similarly, the so-called sex hormones might be said to be the cause of gender differences in endocrinological explanations.

We inherit genes from our parents; they are made of the molecule biologists call DNA (deoxyribonucleic acid), and are organised into chromosomes. Genes provide information, contained in the DNA; this might tell our cells to make a particular protein for example, or it might 'switch off' other genes. Scientists have now developed techniques for moving genes around – between one organism and another, for example – in genetic engineering. They are also identifying the function of many genes, including those involved in genetic diseases.

The claims about genes and behaviour have met feminist criticism, for several reasons (see **biological essentialism**). Biological explanations are often reductionist – that is, they reduce complex phenomena to simple internal causes (such as genes or hormones). This involves what Ruth **Hubbard** has called context-stripping, ignoring all other possible contributory factors. One example of this is the claim that male aggression is caused by levels of male hormones. This claim omits sociocultural reasons for aggression, and attributes it solely or largely to molecules inside an individual's body. The solution to social problems must then be found in biological 'fixes', aimed at the individual, such as drugs.

Relatedly, feminists are opposed to the reductionism of modern medicine: bodies become assemblies of parts (see **body, the**). One consequence is that illness comes to be seen as disease of a specific body part, and treated accordingly. Feminist health work largely opposes this approach, insisting on understanding illness as disease of the whole person in their environment.

Feminist opposition to reductionism is also problematic, however, in its insistence on the social construction of gender; biological influences are thus easily omitted altogether. But denying the body and its functions (its biology) ignores the experiences of many women in, for instance, menstrual pain (see **menstruation, PMS, medical**), or childbirth. Recent work on theorising the body goes some way toward redressing this omission (see Birke 1999).

One response to the dichotomy of social gender versus biological body comes from feminist biologists, who have tried to move beyond simple divisions of nature versus nurture (see **nature/culture**). They have done so by developing ideas in biology of biological processes as transformative, rather than fixed. That is, they insist that the environment (nurture) is always in interaction with the organism's biology (nature). This interaction is not, however, merely a case of adding nurture onto nature. We cannot say that one is more fixed or fundamental than the other – rather, both can be changed in the interaction. This kind of approach avoids reductionism, by insisting on complexity. Thus, we might say that, if hormones affect who we are, then they are also affected by who we are and how we live. And as these factors interact, we are changed. Genes, similarly, do not work in isolation, but are constantly interacting with their environments within a cell.

One example of this kind of thinking comes from the work of Donna **Haraway** (1991), and Emily Martin (1994), on the immune system. Both these writers have explored how our immune systems (the body's defences) must constantly respond to the external world; they are thus always changing and adapting. Another comes from thinking about how embryos develop; embryos are not simply unfolding from a genetic 'plan', but are actively engaged in influencing their own environments. For human embryos, that environment is normally the mother's uterus. So, by emphasising the active role of the embryo, we can challenge the idea that organisms (including human beings) are merely products of genes.

Thinking about biology as transformation thus opposes genetic determinism. Feminist biologists usually reject the idea that specific genes might cause, say, homosexuality (see Fausto-Sterling 1992). Rather, they argue that genes can affect one another, and are themselves influenced by their environments (in the cell for example). So, how any one gene acts will be subject to many other effects; it is, moreover, a big step from the molecules of the cell to complex behaviour such as that involved in homosexuality. If genetic influences are involved at all, they argue, then the effects are complex and poorly understood. Evolution, similarly, can be rethought (see **Darwin, feminist critique of**); thus, rather than organisms being seen as 'fitter' or 'less fit', we might see them as actively engaging in altering their environment, shaping it to their own needs.

Donna Haraway's work emphasises biology as a discourse that developed in the west. As such, it is a discourse that names nature and makes universal claims about what other species (and human beings) are. For that reason, it is important that feminists engage with scientific literature and challenge its assumptions by writing different accounts, she argues. Feminist work on biology as transformation is one example.

Biology is also important to **ecofeminism**, and feminists working for animal rights. In the case of ecofeminism, the work of ecologists may supply important information about damage to global ecosystems, and thence to women's work in, for example, agriculture. Yet, at the same time, feminists work to challenge **science**, for it seems both to cause and to offer solutions to environmental crises. Overlapping with these issues are connections between feminism and animal rights, explored particularly by Carol Adams (1994), and Marti Kheel (1995). Biology is relevant to these issues most strongly through its laboratory practice and use of living animals, as well as in the ways that biologists describe animals and nature (see Birke and Hubbard 1995).

Another major area of importance to feminism is **biotechnology**. Although biotechnology – in the sense of human manipulation of living organisms – has been practised for centuries, it is the new developments in gene mapping and genetic engineering that most concern feminists. A particular issue is the question of 'ownership' of genes, and whether patents can be granted on organisms created in the laboratory. Genetic engineering includes many techniques, but fundamentally involves cutting up DNA and resplicing it in a new sequence – rather like editing a cassette tape. This means that DNA can be taken from one organism and inserted into another; potentially, the DNA itself, or the resulting organism, could be counted as a new invention and be subject to a patent claim.

Globally, the implications for women are many, Vandana Shiva (1988) has argued. Genetically engineered plant crops may oust indigenously grown crops, with potentially disastrous results. Relying on one such crop may damage the local environmental balance, and could be economically disastrous if the crop fails. Women, moreover, stand to lose most given the importance of their role in subsistence agriculture.

Apart from the probability of direct effects on women, the introduction of genetically engineered crops is also reductionist. It assumes that alteration of one or two genes will have only the effects predicted by the scientists. Some organisations, such as Third World Network (based in Penang, Malaysia) are opposed to this, and insist on an interactive model (see above). Introducing genetically engineered organisms, they argue, could have unpredicted and disastrous consequences because we cannot know how the introduced gene will affect other parts of the organism or its environment. (See also the Rural Advancement Foundation; Forest Networking.)

However, there are problems with uncritically opposing genetic engineering, argues Donna Haraway (1997). Some of the opposition rests on hostility to the idea of crossing species boundaries (to create hybrid organisms). But we should beware of valorising purity, Haraway points out, because it has often been the root of highly discriminatory claims and practices – racism, for example. Rather, we should welcome boundary crossings and view hybrid organisms as our kin.

What unites these different relationships of feminist theory and biology is a concern to criticise reductionism and essentialism, which have generally operated in the interests of only a tiny minority of the world's people. But criticising must not mean rejecting: biology, as Donna Haraway reminds us, is far too important to be ignored by feminist theorists.

Feminist biologists, for example, are also united by a concern to understand biology differently; rather than accepting reductionist explanations, feminist critics have described ways in which biology might itself be seen as more complex and interactive. This concern draws upon many ideas that are well developed in the practice of biology itself, but are often much less well known than the reductionist concepts. Thus, feminist critiques of Darwinism include discussion of the evolution of cooperation, rather than competition.

See also: homosexuality, bio-medical pathologisation of

References and further reading

Adams, C. (1994) *Neither Man nor Beast: Feminism and the Defence of Animals*, New York: Continuum.

Birke, L. (1999) *Feminism and the Biological Body*, Edinburgh: Edinburgh University Press.

Birke, L. and Hubbard, R. (eds) (1995) *Reinventing Biology: Respect for Life and the Creation of Knowledge*, Bloomington, IN: Indiana University Press.

Fausto-Sterling, A. (1992) *Myths of Gender: Biological Theories about Women and Men*, New York: Basic Books.

Forest Networking
    http://forests.org (campaigns for biodiversity and protection for rural communities)

Gaard, G. (ed.) (1993) *Ecofeminism: Women, Animals,*

Nature, Philadelphia, PA: Temple University Press.

Haraway, D. (1991) *Simians, Cyborgs and Women*, London: Free Association Books.

—— (1997) *Modest_Witness@Second_Millennium: Female-Man$^{©}$_Meets_OncoMouse^{TM}*, London: Routledge.

Hubbard, R. (1990) *The Politics of Women's Biology*, New Brunswick, NJ: Rutgers University Press.

Kheel, M. (1995) 'Licence to Kill: An Ecofeminist Critique of Hunters' Discourse', in C. Adams and J. Donovan (eds) *Animals and Women*, Durham, NC: Duke University Press.

Martin, E. (1994) *Flexible Bodies: Tracking Immunity in American Culture from the Days of Polio to the Days of AIDS*, Boston: Beacon Press.

Oudshoorn, N. (1994) *Beyond the Natural Body: An Archeology of Sex Hormones*, London: Routledge.

Rural Advancement Foundation International http://www.rafi.org (opposes genetic modification)

Shiva, V. (1988) *Staying Alive: Women, Ecology and Development*, London: Zed Books.

LYNDA BIRKE

biopolitics

Michel Foucault uses 'biopolitics' to refer to the restructuring of life, labour and language productive of the modern subject. Within feminism, it refers to the political dimensions of the biological, both as an authoritative scientific discourse, and in other cultural domains, such as popular culture or health care. From evolutionary and genetic models of sex difference to racial classification systems, feminists have criticised the use of biology to legitimate inequalities. 'Biopolitics' describes the social consequences of biological knowledge in which the characteristics of life and living systems have traditionally been depicted through a masculinist, colonial and Eurocentric frame, as part of a male-dominated professional culture. From early modern definitions of women's reproductive capacity as monstrous and pathological, to contemporary forms of genetic determinism and evolutionary psychology, biopolitics describes the reproduction of inequality based on explanations of the innate,

the natural, and the inherited as they figure within larger social systems of regulation and surveillance.

References and further reading

Hubbard, R. (1992) *The Politics of Women's Biology*, New Brunswick, NJ: Rutgers University Press.

SARAH FRANKLIN

biotechnology

Much attention has been focused within the feminist critique of science generally, and of biology in particular, on the Cartesian legacy of defining nature in mechanistic terms, as a subordinate and feminised domain to be controlled, deciphered and managed by science (see **Cartesianism, feminist critiques of**). Biotechnology describes intervention into living systems with the aim of exploiting their capacities, and often redesigning them for the purpose of extracting surplus value and profit. The mechanisation, or technologisation, of living systems reached an apotheosis of sophistication and breadth in the twentieth century in large part due to rapid developments within the life sciences, and in particular within biogenetics. Both human reproduction and the reproductive systems of plants, animals and micro-organisms have become the tools available through molecular genetics. For feminists such as Vandana **Shiva**, Donna **Haraway**, Ruth **Hubbard** or Hilary **Rose**, the re-engineering of life itself has a distinctly gendered character, and reflects the overprivileging of a narrow and exclusive set of interests and knowledge practices.

Examples of biotechnology can be drawn from many branches of science and industry, from agriculture (genetically-modified seeds), to medicine (assisted conception technologies) to zoology (the cloning of higher mammals). Feminist analysis of phenomena such as *in vitro* fertilisation (IVF) or transgenic animals points to the cultural specificity of the forms of classifying and defining living systems necessary for such 'advances' to be conceived of in the first place. In turn, the partial perspective necessary to envisage living systems as forms of capital or manufacturing is argued to be both historical and political. Biotechnology is both a descriptive term for what anthropologist Marilyn **Strathern** (1992) has called the 'enterprizing-up' of nature, and a description of the forms of hybridity – between animals and machines, nature and culture, biology and society – necessary to such mergers.

Disagreements arise as to the patriarchal character of biotechnologies and their applications. For example, feminists remain divided on the topic of reproductive technology, with some claiming procedures such as IVF are unavoidably complicit with patriarchal definitions of women and reproduction, while others support a guarded acceptance of such techniques. Other feminists argue that the politics of biotechnology defy simple for-or-against positions and demand more radical and innovative ways of thinking to articulate the politics at stake. Another feminist tradition looks to biotechnology as a form of liberation, in an attitude linking 1970s radicals such as Shulamith **Firestone** to 1990s cyberfeminists.

The politics of biotechnology poses one of the major challenges for feminist theory in the twenty-first century. Long attentive to the politics of **biology** and **reproduction**, the unique legacy of critical feminist thought devoted to the biological sciences will be of particular relevance as the process of evolution comes increasingly under human control. As reproduction and heredity become ever more technologically mediated there are continuing consequences for definitions of **gender**, much as gendered perspectives will shape the direction of new biotechnologies in the decades to come.

See also: mechanistic model, critiques of

References and further reading

Shiva, V. (1989) *Staying Alive: Women, Ecology and Development*, London, Zed Books.
Stratherm, M. (1992) *Reproducing the Future: Anthropology, Kinship and the New Reproductive Technologies*, Manchester: Manchester University Press.

SARAH FRANKLIN

biphobia

Biphobia refers to the fear of **bisexuality**. The concept is similar to those of **homophobia** and lesbophobia. It is a psuedo-psychological term referring to a fear of intimacy and closeness to people who do not identify as monosexual (see **monosexuality**). It is often manifest as a fear of difference – homophobia in the heterosexual community or heterophobia (fear of **heterosexuality**) in the homosexual community. Biphobia presumes two, and only two, sexes, that these sexes are stable and that male and female persons are absolutely different. Biphobic slurs imply that attractions to both sexes are inferior to hetero- or homosexuality, pathological or deviant. Biphobic thinking often associates bisexuality with promiscuity, contamination (i.e. bisexual people as vectors of disease) and disloyalty (to heterosexual or homosexual communities).

References and further reading

The Bisexual Anthology Collective (1995) *Plural Desires: Writing Bisexual Women's Realities*, Toronto: Sister Vision, Black Woman and Woman of Colour Press.

KATHRYN PAYNE

Birke, Lynda (b. 1948)

Lynda Birke is best known for her work on women and **science**. She has published widely in the fields of animal biology, women's studies and science studies, criticising both the representation and limited participation of women in science. Birke studied **biology** at the University of Sussex (UK) in the late 1960s and 1970s where she became actively involved in the Women's Liberation Movement and the radical science movement. In the late 1970s she formed the Brighton Women and Science Group from which the collaborative work *Alice Through the Microscope* (1980) emerged. In 1986 she set up a group called Women for Science for Women based in London. Since then, she has been involved in promoting women-friendly science in Britain and abroad. She has also fostered an exchange of ideas with American feminists working in feminism and science.

Although Birke originally trained in science and has continued to publish and teach in this field, she has also participated in debates on women's **health** and reproductive technologies, and examined the relationship between feminism, animals and science. She has challenged scientific discourses, especially medical, which depict menstruation and pregnancy as illnesses, contesting scientific readings of the female body as weak, fragile and 'diseased'. Her studies of new reproductive technologies reveal that science, medicine and technology can be both beneficial and hazardous to women's health (1990). More recently she has addressed the use of gendered and anthropomorphic stereotypes to describe animal behaviour (1994). By unpacking the **nature/culture** dichotomy, she has provided feminists with the material to examine the way in which both human beings and non-humans are 'othered' in biological discourses. More generally, her work has contested positivist science and reductionist biology (see **positivism**).

By criticising scientific paradigms, Birke has provided opportunities to rethink scientific knowledge-making (1995). In doing so, she has advocated better science communication, encouraging public understanding of science. Lynda Birke has been one of the few scholars to write about feminism and animals, making her work a significant contribution to feminist critiques of science.

See also: biology; menstruation, anthropological; positivism

Selected writings

Birke, L. (1994) *Feminism, Animals and Science: the Naming of the Shrew*, London: Open University Press.

Birke, L., Himmelweit, S. and Vines, G. (1990) *Tomorrow's Child: Reproductive Technologies in the Nineties*, London: Virago.

Birke, L. and Hubbard, R. (eds) (1995) *Reinventing*

Biology: Respect for Life and the Creation of Knowledge, Bloomington, IN: Indiana University Press.

MARSHA HENRY

bisexuality

Bisexuality is generally understood to refer to sexual desires that are not limited to one gender. The question of whether bisexuality exists, or can be a viable sexual **identity**, has been an issue in western feminism since the 1970s. **Lesbian feminism** has been criticised for its failure to include bisexuality in its analyses. Bisexual women are framed by lesbian feminist discourse as confused, fence-sitting and unwilling to give up the privileges of heterosexuality (see **privilege**). It was only in the 1980s – encouraged by other critiques of lesbian feminism, queer politics and a rising focus on **diversity** – that large numbers of bisexuals began to claim their identity proudly. Their doing so has enabled the creation of a bisexual movement, (particularly in America and Britain), bisexual books and theories. Bisexual politics seeks to break down the **dichotomies** of heterosexual and homosexual, male and female, and challenge heteronormative monogamous relationship models (see **heterosexism, heteronormativity**).

See also: biphobia; homosexuality; lesbianism; Millet, Kate; monosexuality

References and further reading

Hutchins, L. and Kaahumanu, L. (1991) *Bi Any Other Name: Bisexual People Speak Out*, Boston: Alyson Publications.

KATHRYN PAYNE

black female sexuality

Century-old stereotypes severely impact the sexuality of modern black women. There is no single ideal notion of black sexuality or womanhood because experiences are too diverse and are complicated by a history of slavery, racism and **sexism** (see also **slavery in the USA**). Those black women who exert wilful behaviour when it comes to their own sexuality are viewed as acting outrageous, irresponsible, too grown or 'womanish' as Alice **Walker** has defined the term in *In Search of Our Mother's Gardens* (1984). Depending on the context, being womanish can be a curse or compliment.

In *Stolen Women* (1997) Gail Wyatt asserts that the overriding stereotype of a black women is that she is out of control sexually, regardless of the circumstances or her appearance and that it is assumed that she is for sale for some price. Wyatt places black women's position on the slave auction block at the heart of problems of sexual behaviour and conduct since that period. She further asserts that black women will remain victims of slavery and stolen women, captives of their own unexamined sexual experiences, altered by strangers, if they only define their sexuality in the eyes of others.

During slavery, feigning submission and happiness, not being allowed to discuss sexual abuse by their masters because of the threat of a beating, and attempting to maintain a degree of dignity in spite of abuse had their effects on how black women were defined sexually.

For men, emancipation called for regaining control over one's family (woman companion and children), which usually meant that they controlled and directed the lives of their wives and daughters. As with most everything else following the slavery era, upwardly mobile blacks became very conservative in all aspects of their family lives. They sought to redefine the black person in the eyes of white society and for themselves. Sexual conservatism was primarily to dispel the image of blacks as heathens and black women as sexually permissive. Black women who did not conjure up images of 'mammy', described as an obese, domesticated, asexual house-slave/servant with unsurpassed wisdom and compassion, were often viewed as sexually permissive, a vestige from the slavery experience in the USA.

The polar opposite of the mammy's romanticised image is that of the equally romanticised and much thinner, long haired, lighter skinned mulatto. She became a tragic object of desire for many whites during slavery and reconstruction and continued to be desired by them as well as black men long into the twentieth century. More recently, the not-so tragic well-dressed executive black woman and the young girls who dress in baggy, masculine clothing share the perception of being unfeminine, hard, masculine and rejecting femininity for toughness, for making it alone, without a man. Wyatt's landmark study on black women's sexuality highlights the degree to which black women have believed, internalised and accepted the stereotypes that have been constructed for them because they have not explored any viable alternatives to those stereotypes.

Black women's sexuality has further been politicised due to the feminist movement that aims to eliminate sexist oppression. Yet, many black women in general have moved away from active participation in the movement because they cannot support a feminist ideology that for them has become too dogmatic and absolutist. In *Feminist Theory from Margin to Center* (1984), bell **hooks** asserts that **heterosexuality** does not negate a woman's participation in the political movement of feminism and feminists must not impose restrictions on or condemn the preferred sexual preference of anyone. The black feminist movement provides avenues for exploration of black sexuality, a subject that often remains taboo for the average black woman given the history of equating black women, worldwide, with promiscuity.

Yet, younger black adolescent women who participate in the hip-hop culture and those who are afro-centric are more self-conscious in the outward display of their **sexuality**. While the women of hip-hop use their sexuality to empower themselves, the afro-centric women view their sexuality as a natural part of life. The take charge attitude in hip-hop became associated with Queen Latifa, who promoted empowerment of women through her song lyrics and videos. Her success has spawned a series of black female performers who have turned men's sexism in on itself. Because black women's sexuality has been shrouded in secrecy and privacy, public displays of sexuality in music videos have created outrage among many black women (and men) who were trying to dispel the perception of permissiveness.

An older generation of both genders views such public displays as harmful to blacks, feeling that they feed into unfair stereotypical representations of blacks by whites. According to Wyatt's study, most black women have led very conservative sex lives, not deviating from established norms and decorum sanctioned by the culture as a whole. This conduct is in part connected to the concept that a man does not want a sexually assertive and controlling woman as a wife. Yet, a new generation of black women are examining their sexuality and welcome unconfined sexual fantasies as liberating, feeling that sexual conservatism, for whatever reason, has limited their self-definition. In the past, 'womanish', indeed, was levelled at young girls who were viewed as 'too grown' or worldly, but currently, for many women, the act of being 'womanish' with respect to taking charge of one's own sexuality is a cherished attribute and not a condemnation.

References and further reading

hooks, b. (1984) *Feminist Theory from Margin to Center*, Boston: South End Press.

Walker, A. (1984) *In Search of Our Mother's Gardens*, New York: Harcourt Brace.

Wyatt, G.E. (1997) *Stolen Women, Reclaiming Our Sexuality, Taking Back Our Lives*, New York: John Wiley and Sons, Inc.

LIZZETTA LEFALLE-COLLINS

black feminism(s)

Contemporary black feminism(s) in the USA has its origins in African American women's historical encounters with enslavement, emancipation, seg-regation and patriarchy, and is rooted in traditions of intellectual, social and political activism. Although nineteenth-century women such as Maria W. Stewart, Sojourner Truth and Harriet Tubman would not have used the term black feminist to describe themselves they were ever cognisant of the deleterious impact of racism, sexism and poverty, and sought redress to such problems through crafting a variety of responses. By the 1890s black women's tradition of visionary pragmatism and collective activism – confronting and defining problems and devising ameliorative strategies – was flourishing in local clubs and national black women's organisations. Founded in 1896 the National Association of Coloured Women (NACW) served as an umbrella organisation for the emergent praxis of black club women's political activism and intellectual vision. Under the leadership of Mary Church Terrell NACW became an authoritative unifying voice in defence of black women. Encouraging self reliance in its membership, NACW worked to improve the socioeconomic conditions of black women, children and men. To repudiate the prevalent negative images and stereotypes of black women and to develop their own positive self definitions, a dynamic interrelationship of critique and challenge was forged by such women as Terrell, Anna Julia Cooper and Ida B. Wells to address the forms of oppression they were encountering within their communities and the broader society.

The recently rediscovered text *A Voice from the South* (1892) by educator Anna Julia Cooper has been recognised as one of the original texts of the black feminist movement. Employing allegory, autobiography and history, it addresses such issues as race, gender and education, but it was deemed insignificant and excluded from black intellectual history because it was by a woman about women. Cooper criticised the (white) women's movement and its leaders including Susan B. Anthony and Anna B. Shaw for racism, elitism and provincialism, and was the first to take exception to the use of the phrase 'the black man' to refer to all black people. She argued that the true measure of racial progress for both men and women resided in the status of the black woman and was thus evident only whenever and wherever the black woman could quietly and with dignity enter without violence, suing or special patronage.

Ida B. Wells, suffragette, anti-racist worker and a founder of the NAACP, was another significant early contributor to the emergent black feminist praxis of intellectual inquiry and political activism. Today she is perhaps most respected and remembered for her anti-lynching work which incorporated a sophisticated integrated analysis of race and gender. As she engaged in the dangerous enterprise of gathering information on over 700 lynchings occurring in the later part of the nineteenth century, she revealed the existence of interracial liaisons that should not have been, but often were, defined as rape by black men of white women. She also explicated the racist-sexist connection between the existence of rampant sexual assaults on black women by white men and the construction of the threat of black male rape. Such topics were incendiary and writing about them within the context of lynching resulted in the burning of her newspaper office in Memphis and her banishment from the south. At the same time, some black men were disturbed by her efforts because they felt such work was better left to a man. Undaunted she continued to wage her anti-lynching campaign both in the USA and in England.

Despite the stalwart efforts of these nineteenth- and early-twentieth-century black feminists, black women continue to struggle with such familiar issues as racism, segregation, mob violence, poverty and sexism. Building on tradition new activists, who also did not necessarily identify themselves as feminists, including Mary McLeod Bethune and Amy Jacques Garvey, became involved in local, national and even international politics focusing on issues of concern to black women, men and children.

Founder of Bethune Cookman Institute, President of NACW, and founder of the National Council of Negro Women (NCNW), in 1936 Mary McLeod Bethune was appointed Director of the Division of Negro Affairs in the National Youth Administration which provided her with unprecedented access to Eleanor Roosevelt. She arranged a historic meeting between the First Lady and a group of black women who lobbied for the establishment of policies that would be beneficial in terms of both race and gender, and for appointments to positions that had not previously been held by blacks in federal bureaus. Amy Jacques Garvey, wife of Marcus Garvey, was active in her own right in the Universal Negro Improvement Association (UNIA). Employing a radical feminist and black nationalist political perspective in her capacity as editor of the women's page of the *Negro World*, the UNIA newspaper, Garvey articulated the interrelationships of problems encountered by coloured women around the world. In their own unique ways both Garvey and Bethune were upholding black women's critical tradition of analysis, strategising and confrontation.

Although black women's feminist activism seemed dormant in the period from the 1920s through the 1960s, their continued opposition to injustice and inequality was demonstrated through their work in clubs, churches, sororities, the NAACP and Urban League. Contemporary black feminism(s) is a product of the tradition of women's oppositional agency in which victims resist subjugation and claim their subjectivity through mobilising and strategising to effect change within their own lives and the lives of their families and communities.

Toni Cade's anthology *The Black Woman* (1970) signals the beginning of the contemporary black feminist movement. This landmark collection of black women's poetry, essays and short stories grew out of what Cade describes as her impatience with the dearth of feminist literature by and about black women including the lack of viable Afro-American women's magazines, and her impatience with white women's liberation groups. Other groundbreaking texts of the 1970s include Toni Morrison's first novel *The Bluest Eye*, Audre Lorde's *Cables to Rage*, Shirley Chisolm's autobiography *Unbought and Unbossed*, sociologist Joyce Ladner's urban ethnography on young black girls *Tomorrow's Tomorrow* (1972), Ntozake Shange's choreopoem *For Colored Girls Who Have Considered Suicide/When the Rainbow is Enuf* (1975), Mary Helen Washington's anthology of short fiction by black women *Black-Eyed Susan*, Alice Walker's civil rights novel *Meridian* (1976) and Michelle Wallace's *Black Macho and the Myth of the Superwoman* (1978), a controversial critique of black male sexism and the rampant misogyny in black liberation struggles.

Founded in 1973 by Margaret Sloan, its first and only president, Florence Kennedy and Eleanor Holmes Norton, the National Black Feminist Organization (NBFO) was the first explicitly black feminist organisation in the USA committed to the eradication of sexism and racism. The NBFO objectives included providing a forum for black women who were distressed by the racism they were encountering in the women's movement, raising the consciousness of all black women particularly the poor and working class, and encouraging black women to develop all their talents and creativity through assuming leadership roles in their communities. Much like their predecessors, NBFO also pledged to redefine black womanhood in new and positive terms. Attended by some 400 women, the first regional conference of NBFO was held in New York City at the Cathedral of St. John the Divine Nov. 30–Dec. 2, 1973. Ten chapters were quickly established, but by 1979 due to inadequate funding, the lack of strong organised leadership and its inability to be everything to everybody the organisation became defunct.

In 1974 the Boston Chapter of NBFO broke away to form the anti-capitalist socialist revolutionary **Combahee River Collective**. In existence for six years the collective focused on issues of sexuality and economic development and was deeply engaged in intellectual political activism within the Boston community. Barbara Smith, Beverly Smith and Demita Frazier drafted 'A Black Feminist Statement' which eloquently articulates their conceptualisation of multiple oppression, advocates the eradication of homophobia, and insists that the critical role of lesbians in the development of black feminism be acknowledged.

Black feminist literature flourished during the 1980s as black women intellectuals carved out spaces across the disciplines in the academy through their writing and teaching. Some (but certainly not all) of the important texts of this period include Gloria T. Hull, Patricia Bell Scott, and Barbara Smith's foundational text *All the Women are White, All the Men are Black, But Some of Us Are Brave: Black Women's Studies* (1992) which is devoted to legitimising Black Women's Studies as a serious area of intellectual inquiry. In 1981 bell **hooks**'s *Ain't I A Woman?* appeared, Angela Davis's *Women, Race and Class* and *The Black Woman Cross Culturally* edited by Filomina Chioma Steady appeared followed in 1983 by *Home Girls: A Black Feminist Anthology* edited by Barbara Smith, Alice Walker's collection of essays *In Search of Our Mother's Garden* (1983), Paula Giddings's *When and Where I Enter: The Impact of Black Women on Race and Sex in America* (1984) and Audre Lorde's *Sister Outsider* (1984).

The 1990s were characterised by the continued production of a wide range of literature including Patricia Hill Collin's *Black Feminist Thought: Knowledge, Consciousness and the Politics of Empowerment* (1990), Stanlie M. James and Abena P.A. Busia, editors of *Theorizing Black Feminisms: The Visionary Pragmatism of Black Women* (1993), *Words of Fire: An Anthology of African American Feminist Thought* (1995) edited by Beverly Guy Sheftall and *Critical Race Feminism* (1996) edited by Adrian Wing, by two important conferences and a grassroots media project. Robin Kilson and Evelyn Hammonds convened the national conference 'Black Women in the Academy: Defending our Name, 1894–1994' January 13–15, at M.I.T. Two thousand women listened to keynote addresses by Angela Davis, Lani Guinier and Johnnetta Cole: women who had been forced to defend their own names in very public venues; while other less famous but equally concerned and committed women shared their work within the conference format. From June 15–18, 1995 approximately 1080 black women participated in the conference 'African American Women and the Law: Extending our Power Reclaiming our Communities' organised by Barbara Arnwine, director of the Lawyers' Committee for Civil Rights Under Law. After this conference Arnwine led a delegation of black women to the UN Word Conference in Beijing where they worked to insure that the Platform of Action would include the concerns of black women. Elsa Barkley Brown, Barbara Ransby, and Deborah King mobilised 1603 black women to draft a statement 'African American Women in Defence of Ourselves' supporting Anita Hill, which appeared in the New York Times 17 November, 1991 and in half a dozen black newspapers across the country. The legacy of visionary pragmatism, oppositional agency and collective activism will continue to inspire black women and to inform black feminist social, political and intellectual activism in the twenty-first century.

STANLIE M. JAMES

black feminist consciousness

Black feminist consciousness, in the (primarily) English-speaking diaspora, assumes that black women's lived experiences produce specific understandings of their raced, gendered and classed positions in white/racialised society. Such consciousness is expressed in the symbols, norms, and ideological forms black women create to give meaning to their lives – an '"outsider within" stance that stimulates a special perspective' that is different from the perspectives of those who are not both black and female (see Collins 1990).

Identification of a black feminist consciousness evolved in relation to the changing economic, social and political locations of black women. In the USA, recognition of black feminist consciousness is located historically within the African American community, however in Britain, its theorisation comes after the Second World War and relates to a political understanding of black as a recognition of common experiences rather than origins. Seen as empowering, as well as essentialist and reductionist in terms of definition, black feminist consciousness has emerged in relation to and differentiation from two main 'waves' of feminism as well as the male-centred 1960s American Black Power movement. Thus first-wave feminism's (1860–1920) willingness to present white women's suffrage as a means to retain white supremacy, and second-wave (1960–80) mainstream liberal feminism's failure to recognise black women's differing understandings of patriarchy, reproduction, and work highlight the differing states of consciousness. Exposure to literature and poetry produced by women of the diaspora further reinforces consciousness of these differences, thus enabling black feminists to recognise similar raced experiences with black men, while at the same time allowing critique of patriarchal relations.

Identity politics and **standpoint theory** have seemed to answer the problem of essentialism. However, such a position from which only the authentic insider can speak of a group's oppression is open to critique as a mechanism of renewed exclusion and domination.

Implicit within conceptions of black feminist consciousness is the assumption that such consciousness will be 'critical', leading to action and social transformation. Such a postulation is problematic because not all women who are located similarly in racialised structures will have the same response – class, religion, sexuality and culture are also important (see **Lorde, Audre**; **hooks, bell**). Thus, theorisation of a black feminist consciousness can fail to problematise the post-colonial location of Third World black women. Further, black feminist consciousness can conflate thinking with being, giving rise to a theoretical unity that can be uncritically celebrated, but can also draw charges of essentialism. To avoid the latter some black feminists have come to view an exclusionary response to domination as 'strategic' – an acknowledgement of the dangerousness of something we cannot do without (see Spivak 1993).

See also: black feminism(s); epistemology, black feminist

References and further reading

Collins, P.H. (1990) *Black Feminist Thought: Knowledge, Consciousness and Empowerment*, Cambridge: Unwin and Hyman.

Spivak, G. (1993) *Outside in the Teaching Machine*, New York: Routledge.

JENNIFER KELLY

black women's health

Improving women's health was one goal of the 1970s feminist movement. White middle class women in the USA achieved this goal through advocacy, grass roots, and feminist networks. However the movement had little effect on the health of women of colour because their specific concerns, experiences, and voices were largely ignored. US white feminists focused on what they considered to be the shared health needs of all women, for example, home births, right to abortion, the doctor/patient relationship. They focused on different treatment between the sexes, rather than inequities based on race and class.

African American women have been health activists in the black community since the early twentieth century. Despite their expertise, the voices of black women were excluded from the white feminist health movement. As white women generalised and essentialised their particular health experiences as those of all women (ignoring the intersection of race, class, and gender), black women continued to organise around their health needs and those of their larger communities. For example, the National Black Women's Health Project, founded by Billye Avery, addresses the different health perspectives, experiences, and social situations of black women.

Responding to critiques of African American scholars and feminists like Audre Lourde, bell hooks, Evelyn Hammonds, Paula Giddings, Dorothy Roberts, and Angela Davis, white feminists have tried to be more inclusive in advocating for policies that improve the health of all women. Nevertheless, the health of women of colour continues to lag significantly behind that of white women.

For almost all health conditions, African American women are worse off. Black women are 50 per cent more likely to be hypertensive than white women and 44 per cent are obese, compared to 24 per cent of white women. In the USA, blacks make up 55 per cent of AIDS cases; and the diabetes rate is twice that of white women.

Black women are 4 times more likely than white women to die from complications surrounding childbirth. For white women breast cancer mortality has decreased; for black women it has increased. Twice as many African American women die from strokes and cancers of the cervix and uterus. Death rates for heart disease are 50 per cent higher, and occupational injuries are 30–50 per cent higher in black women. Because of this increased sickness, as well as unequal access to health care, black women live an average of 6 years fewer than white women.

Society offers various explanations. For some, a renewed interest in genes explains the disparities. According to them, blacks are genetically more susceptible to certain conditions, for instance obesity, breast cancer, low infant birth weight, and diabetes – all conditions that disproportionately affect women of colour. In this explanation, race and health are perceived solely as biological constructs rather than also as social ones.

A second popular explanation for the high incidence of sickness and death is that African American women lead irresponsible lives: African American women eat too much, do not exercise enough, worry too much; rely too much on alternative care providers; have too much sex with the wrong kind of men. The poor health of African American women, then, is seen as a consequence of genetic inferiority and personal irresponsibility. These explanations have limited validity. Some genetic diseases are more prevalent in some ethnic groups. And some people do live irresponsibly, but irresponsibility is neither race- nor gender-specific. These explanations mask the real cause of

disparities: low-paying jobs, poor education, substandard housing, environmental degradation, and lack of adequate access to health care.

Racism as an explanation is finally gaining some credence outside the black community. Evidence is accumulating – even in mainstream media and journals like the *New England Journal of Medicine* – that race and racism play a significant role in resource allocation, access to care, and physicians' referrals. For example, pregnant black women receive different information from physicians than white women. White women are more likely to be screened, diagnosed, and treated for cholesterol; elderly white women receive more mammograms, hip replacements, and flu shots than do black women.

During the 1990s in the USA, several federal initiatives have emerged, aimed at improving women's health. But until recently these initiatives have been colour-blind. The 1993 Revitalization Act mandates the inclusion of women and minorities in federally-funded research. In January 1997, the Office of Women's Health established the Minority Women's Health Initiative. And in a February 1998 radio address, President Clinton challenged the nation to eliminate ethnic and racial disparities in infant mortality, cancer screening and management, cardiovascular disease, diabetes, HIV infection, and child and adult immunisations – all conditions that directly contribute to the poor health of women of colour.

These initiatives are praiseworthy; however, their reliance on the biomedical model of health ignores social conditions that devastate the health and lives of poor women and women of colour. Initiatives rooted in the biomedical model must be complemented with social and economic policies that target the situations of poor women and women of colour.

Feminists' achievements have substantially improved the health of middle-class women. Unfortunately, the feminist movement has not effected substantial improvements in health, education, and welfare for poorer and darker sisters. The historical and current experiences of black women – slavery, rape, forced sterilisations, inadequate housing, medical abuse, racism in the health care system and in society at large – have been of minimal importance to white feminists.

A reconstruction and reconceptualisation of

feminism and health concerns appears to be in the making. Although white feminists today are more aware of the diverse needs, attitudes, and perspectives of different groups of women, a chasm still exists. The concerns of women of colour are still marginalised; racism and sexism are still rampant; and feminism still needs to be more inclusive. At the beginning of the twenty-first century, feminism and feminist health movements must more aggressively advocate for social, economic, and health policies that improve health, living, and working conditions, with a focus on ethnic and minority women's needs. Such a restructuring must respect and build on the different perspectives, concerns, and attitudes of different groups of women, but at the same time not lose sight of our commonalties. Otherwise the health gap between middle class white women and poor women and women of colour will continue to widen.

References and further reading

Dula, A. and Goring, S. (eds) (1994) *It Just Ain't Fair: The Ethics of Health Care for African Americans*, Westport, CT: Praeger.

ANNETTE DULA

black women's history in the USA

In pre-colonial Africa, African women had more economic independence, autonomy and political power than their European and American counterparts. African women were expected to grow or buy food for their families, a practice that continued during and after slavery. In the Americas slave women were further empowered by the practice of shared community property.

In her 1851 address 'Ain't I A Woman?' Sojourner Truth articulated the mutual dependence of **race** and **gender**, connecting women's rights with black people's freedom. In *Frederick Douglass on Women's Rights* (1976), P.S. Foner writes that Truth found an ally in the black abolitionist Frederick Douglass, who had become an early supporter of the women's movement. Douglass was committed to exposing the **oppression** of

women because he suffered oppression himself in a society dominated by white men. Following emancipation in 1867, Sojourner Truth spoke out about disparities between men and women, declaring that emancipation left slavery partly destroyed but not entirely. She encouraged black women to fight for equal status with men. In 1892, an outspoken Ida B. Wells began a long crusade against lynching and published *A Red Record, Tabulated Statistics and Alleged Causes of Lynching in the United States*. Anna Julia Cooper published a volume of essays entitled *A Voice from the South: By a Black Woman of the South* (1892) about the challenges and opportunities facing black women in a white capitalist society.

At the 1904 National Negro Business League convention, Fannie Barrier Williams spoke of women as 'silent partners' who were always concealed from the public eye. She said it was wives who stood between successful businessmen and their bankruptcy. Because so many women were initially in the work force as 'silent partners', supplementing their husband's incomes, it became easier for women to move into a dominant place within the workforce and to become their households' sole supporters. By the 1920s, black women shared responsibility with their husbands in business as they had in labour; in 1929 they showed the highest rate of employment of any racial group.

Black women as labourers and domestics were often stereotyped along colour lines with the darkest women portrayed as labourers and as asexual. In popular culture, skin colour was also used to define the psychological and moral character of black women, especially in the case of the mulatto mistress or black mammy who lovingly cared for her white family. One of the most outrageous examples of racial stereotyping was in D.W. Griffiths' 1915 film, *Birth of a Nation* where he attributed psychological characteristics to black women based on physiognomy. Although these physical and psychological characterisations were grossly over-simplified, they had a lasting effect on the American consciousness.

In the 1920s, on the surface, the Harlem Renaissance seemed to be the great race leveller for black cultural expression, attempting to debunk stereotypical portrayals of black people. Yet further investigation reveals broad social factors and patterns of intra-race and gender exclusion that were in dangerously close agreement with some of the Griffiths stereotypes.

W.E.B. Du Bois, a sociologist, black activist and historian introduced the concept of a double-consciousness (one black and one white) among blacks in his classic 1903 work, *Souls of Black Folk.* Among his predictions was that skin colour would be a significant issue in the twentieth century for African Americans. To challenge discrimination within black communities between lighter and darker skinned blacks, artists and writers focused on darker skinned blacks in portraying Harlem's inhabitants fostering (at least in literature and art) a pride and consciousness of difference from whites. They also explored the lives of working class blacks as the 'salt of the earth' who, for black intellectuals, exemplified the reality of black life. Between 1931–43, anthropologist Zora Neale Hurston's field work in rural black communities and published works such as *Moses, Man of the Mountain, Mules and Men* and *Their Eyes Were Watching God* focused keenly on African American folk practices.

The civil rights movement of the mid-1950s to the late 1960s, though dominated by men, opened the doors for more participation by women. Rosa Parks's resistance to moving to the back of a bus in Montgomery, Alabama so a white man could take her seat launched a firestorm of activism. This action energised and empowered other women to boycott merchants, to march, to sit in at lunch counters and go to jail. Lesser-known Ella Baker encouraged a resistant Martin Luther King Jr. to take the southern Christian Leadership conference (SCLC) to ordinary people. These women were radical thinkers who also rebelled against the notion that only men could lead the freedom fight. Baker for instance, as Joanne Grant writes in *Ella Baker: Freedom Bound*, was a strong believer in organising people to formulate their own questions, define their own problems, and to find their own solutions. To this end, she pushed the concept of group-centred leadership rather than a leadership-centred SCLC. By the early 1970s the former Freedom Rider, Fannie Lou Hammer, had alienated many of her supporters by her radicalism toward land redistribution and her stance against the Vietnam War.

Hammer's radicalism was echoed by a younger and more militant group of political activists that included Angela Davis and Elaine Cleaver who increasingly challenged a Black Panther Party dominated by men. Their rise as activists echoed what Du Bois saw as a twentieth-century challenge for African Americans, namely skin colour. Alice **Walker**'s informal survey during the 1970s suggests that most militant black power leaders of the century (including Marcus Garvey) had lighter-skinned mates, like Davis and Cleaver. She suggests that Malcom X, because he married a darker skinned woman, gained the support of black women in general. While radical black female voices have had a levelling effect on the black cultural playing field, for Alice Walker it is not just the gender struggle, in culture and labour, but the more insider 'colourism' struggle of the different hues of black people, that will be a major burden for black folks in the twenty-first century.

References and further reading

Bogle, D. (1994) *Toms, Coons, Mulattoes, Mammies, and Bucks: An Interpretive History of Blacks in American Films*, New York: Continuum International Publishing Group.

Foner, P.S. (ed.) (1976) *Frederick Douglass on Women's Rights, Contributions in Afro-American and African Studies*, Number 25, Westport and London: Greenwood Press.

Grant, J. (1999) *Ella Baker: Freedom Bound*, New York: John Wiley.

Robertson, C. (1996) 'Africa into the Americas? Slavery and Women, in Family, and the Gender Division of Labor' in D.B. Gaspar and D.C. Hine (eds) *More Than Chattel, Black Women and Slavery in the Americas*, Bloomington and Indianapolis: Indiana University Press.

LIZZETTA LEFALLE-COLLINS

black women's literature

In this entry black women's literature is taken to mean the literature written by black women in Africa and its diaspora. Whether in the fiction, poetry or drama genres, and whether in Africa, the

UK, the Caribbean or North America, black women's literature is of significance for feminist theory because it focuses mainly on issues from women's perspectives and experiences such as sexism, gender relationships, marriage, politics, education, and employment. Also, the literature portrays black women's quest for emancipation from sexism and male dominance. Black women writers are united in exploring feminist issues but they seem to assume varying feminist standpoints. Unlike African American women writers like Alice Walker and Tony Morrison of the USA, some black women writers in Africa such as the late Folra Nwapa, Zaynab Alkali and Efua Sutherland reveal through their writings and interviews that they prefer to be regarded as women writers not feminists. Only a representative sample of black women writers and themes of black women's literature are discussed here.

Various forms of sexism are treated in black women's literature, as understood and experienced by black women. Sexism, in this context, is the discrimination against, and prejudicial stereotyping of the social role of women, on the grounds of sex. Sexism might differ for black women from the sexism experienced by white women. In the USA, for example, black women experience sexism because of their colour and gender. Because polygamy is illegal in North America, white women do not experience this form of sexism as their women counterparts in Africa do. Also, unlike divorced white women, divorced black women, especially in Africa, receive little or no divorce settlements.

In the black family domain there is, relatively, a strong influence of **patriarchy** and male **dominance** whereby the family is mostly male-headed, and male children are preferred to female children because male children can maintain the patriarchal system. The stereotyping of women as being less valuable than men often results in women's displacement, whereby young women are either married away or given out to wealthy families to work as nannies or housemaids. As revealed in Buchi Emecheta's 1975 novel *Second Class Citizen*, the birth of a female child is received with disappointment because everyone expects and predicts a boy to maintain the patriarchy. Emecheta's 1976 novel *The Bride Price* presents Akunna, the central character, as a woman who is valued only because of her bride price. Efua Sutherland's play *The Marriage of Anansewa* portrays Ananse, a trickster father, trying to acquire wealth by auctioning his daughter Anansewa to wealthy chiefs. Maya Angelou's 1971 novel, *I Know Why the Caged Bird Sings*, reveals the African American female child as a target of displacement and sexual abuse within and outside her family.

In marriage and in dating situations, women are exploited and abused by the men in their lives. Ann Petry (1946) Alice **Walker** (1982) examine sexual oppression and economic exploitation of African American women outside and within the black community. Emecheta's novel *The Joys of Motherhood* challenges the notion that the joy of a married woman should depend on her ability to bear children, preferably male children. Flora Nwapa's novels *Efuru* and *One is Enough* examine the problem of childlessness in marriage and how it is regarded as a curse and a failure on the part of the woman. Zaynab Alkali's 1984 novel *The Stillborn* examines women's shattered dreams caused by abusive marriages. Maraima Bâ's novel *So Long a Letter* challenges sexism in Muslim marriages whereby Muslim men can marry additional wives without the consent of their first wife.

The wider society is influenced by the family structure. Consequently, men are firmly placed at the centre of both family and community lives, while women are marginalised and treated as second class citizens. Women's work domains are restricted to their households. Women who try to acquire high levels of western education, and to secure key positions in governments, businesses and religious organisations are ridiculed or accused of being subversive and rebellious. Petry (1946) reveals that many African American women are denied quality jobs because of their gender and their colour. Bâ (1981) questions the discrimination against women in Senegal's politics where women can vote but cannot be voted for.

Central to black women's literature are the motifs of resistance, positivism, triumph, and quests for a better life and emancipation from sexism, racism, and poverty. When in crisis, women do not just fold their arms in tears and self-pity. Alkali (1984), Bâ (1981) and Nwapa (1982; 1966; 1960) depict African women searching and finding success and happiness outside marriage, suggesting that marriage and **motherhood** are not the only keys to female happiness and fulfilment. Toni Morrison's novels *Paradise*, *Tar Baby* and *The Bluest Eye* represent African American women's quests for self-acceptance and self-identity. *Paradise* depicts women who seek refuge in the convent as escaping from abusive heterosexual relationships. Walker's novel *The Color Purple* (1982) advocates unity among African American women to enable them to achieve self-identity, empowerment and happiness. The assertive black woman's voice in Angelou's 1978 motivational Poems 'And Still I Rise' and 'Phenomenal Woman' is that of self-acceptance and triumph over racism and sexism.

Black women writers explore ideal and actual issues concerning black women using literary devices such as autobiographical form, folk narrative and powerful imagery, ambiguity and clarity. Black women's literature in Africa is postcolonial, mainly because women did not have access to western education until the 1960s. However, it explores precolonial, colonial and postcolonial life in Africa. In America, black women's literature has expanded since the time of the Civil Rights movement.

References and further reading

Angelou, M. (1978) *And Still I Rise*, New York: Random House.

Bâ, M. (1981) *So Long a Letter*, trans. M.B. Thomas, Ibadan: New Horn Press.

Morrison, T. (1970) *The Bluest Eye*, New York: Henry Holt and Co.

Otokunefor, H.C. and Nwodo, O.C. (eds) (1989) *Nigerian Female Writers: A Critical Perspective*, Lagos: Malthouse Press Limited.

Petry, A. (1946) *The Street*, Boston: Houghton Mifflin.

ZAINAB HARUNA

Bleier, Ruth (1923–88)

Ruth Bleier was one of the leading feminist biologists who worked on developing critiques of sexist assumptions in science (see **sexism**). She trained originally in medicine, at the Woman's Medical College of Pennsylvania, where she also began involvement in political activism. After practising medicine for some years, she began research in neuroanatomy, focusing particularly on the area of the brain called the hypothalamus.

Bleier moved to Madison, Wisconsin in 1967, and became actively involved in campus feminism in the early 1970s; in 1975, she became part of the new Women's Studies programme there. This move led her to question the assumptions made about gender in biological science, and in 1984 she produced her influential book *Science and Gender* – the first full-length book to look at feminist critiques of **biology**. Topics included analysis of evolutionary ideas of human origins, assumptions about hormones and behaviour, and a detailed critique of research into brain function (see **split brain theory**). Bleier was a vociferous critic of **biological essentialism** which, she insisted, served to reinforce the status quo, and to deny the possibility of social change.

Bleier was concerned not only to criticise biology for its sexist and racist assumptions, but also to ensure that women generally became aware. If more women felt ready to criticise science, then together we might be able to challenge and change it. Like Ruth **Hubbard**, she was also concerned to develop alternative ideas, and to insist on non-reductionist approaches to biology. Her introduction to her later collection, *Feminist Approaches to Science* (1986), asks how science could be different if it began to listen seriously to feminist voices. This is a theme she developed also in her concluding chapter to *Science and Gender* (1984), where she considers the possibility of a 'feminist science'. While this idea has met criticism, on the grounds that a feminist science cannot be achieved without total transformation of the rest of society, it has been an influential one; its importance is that it asks us to think beyond criticism, to what we might want science to look like, if it is better to serve human needs. As Bleier points out, this would make it much better science, not only for women but for everyone.

Selected writings

Bleier, R. (1984) *Science and Gender: A Critique of*

Biology and Its Theories on Women, Oxford: Pergamon.

—— (ed.) (1986) *Feminist Approaches to Science*, Oxford: Pergamon.

LYNDA BIRKE

body, the

In the dominant western tradition, the body has long been the unspoken of abstract theory, dismissed from consideration as the devalued term of the mind/body split that marks the post-Cartesian modernist period. It has been seen simply as a material and unchanging given, a fixed biological entity that must be transcended in order to free the mind for the intellectual pursuits of fully rational subjectivity. Not surprisingly, however, the ability to effect such transcendence has been gender marked as an attribute of men alone, such that women remain rooted within their bodies, held back by their supposedly natural biological processes and unable to exercise full rationality. In consequence, feminism has been deeply concerned with the body – either as something to be rejected in the pursuit of intellectual equality according to a masculinist standard, or as something to be reclaimed as the very essence of the female. A third, more recent alternative, largely associated with feminist postmodernism, seeks to emphasise the importance and inescapability of embodiment as a differential and fluid construct, rather than as a fixed given.

Where the body is viewed through conventional biological taxonomies, it is taken for granted that sexual difference is an inherent quality of the corporeal, and that male and female bodies may each be known universally. In terms of the historical disempowerment of women, the justificatory linking of the female to the body has been centred largely on the reproductive processes (see **reproduction, modes of**). The very fact that women are able in general to menstruate, to become pregnant and give birth, to lactate, is enough to suggest a potentially dangerous volatility, in which the body is out of control, beyond, and set against, the force of reason. In contrast to the apparent self-containment of the male body, which

may then be safely forgotten, the female body demands attention and invites regulation. The age-old relation between **hysteria** and the womb (*hystera* in Greek) is just one example of how femininity itself becomes marked by the notion of an inevitable irrationality. Women just are their bodies in a way that men are not, biologically destined to inferiority. At the same time, however, that women are seen as more wholly embodied, and hence inferior, the boundaries of that embodiment are never secure (see **embodiment/dis-embodiment**). As the processes of reproduction make clear, the body has a propensity to leak, to overflow the proper distinctions between self and other, to contaminate and engulf. Thus women themselves are, in the masculinist imagination, not simply lesser beings, but objects of fear and repulsion. The devalued body is capable of generating deep anxiety; and indeed, as Susan Wendell (1996) points out, feminists too have difficulty in accepting lack of control in conditions such as disability.

So powerful are such ideas that many feminists have been reluctant to theorise the female body, preferring instead to deny the links that have worked so efficiently in the interests of **patriarchy**, and even those contesting the determinism of **biology** have seen it in a decidedly negative light. At the beginning of the second wave of feminism, Simone de **Beauvoir** ([1949] 1952) famously likened it to 'a carnivorous swamp', and Shulamith **Firestone** (1979) looked forward with optimism to a time when the incipient advanced reproductive technologies might free woman from the 'oppressive 'natural' conditions' of procreation. Against such somatophobia which to an extent mimics the masculinist fear and rejection of the body, other feminists have responded by celebrating their bodyliness, particularly with regard to reproduction. The uniquely female capacity to give birth 'naturally' has been taken up as the centre of women's power, to be jealously guarded against the incursions of biotechnology, while more generally women are urged to take control of their own bodies in the face of the medical establishment (see *Our Bodies Ourselves*, 1976 for an early example). In addition, for many feminists, the maternal body has come to figure the claim that woman have a unique ethical sense that lays stress on caring, relationality and responsibility in contradistinction to the masculinist goods of autonomous rights and duties which equally figure the separation of body and mind, and body and body. This stress on the embodied nature of sexual difference runs two related risks: on the one hand it may uncritically universalise the male and female body, while on the other it appears to reiterate the **biological essentialism** that historically has grounded women's subordination.

The intention to take up positively the issue of female embodiment has, then, been highly controversial, and nowhere more so than in the response to the work of Luce **Irigaray**. Her project of rewriting sexual difference beyond the binary of male:female – a binary which positions the sexed body as static, ahistorical and determinate – nevertheless makes constant reference to the anatomical differences between the sexes. Her concern is to revalue the way in which femininity is inscribed on to the female form in a culture in which masculinity is in retreat from the body and where disembodiment is privileged. Irigaray (1985) places great emphasis on the multiple forms of female embodiment, the self-touching 'two lips' that characterise female morphology, and on the fluidity that marks the inherent excess of the feminine that is uncontainable within binary sexual difference. But hers is not a 'real' biology, as much as the imaginative redeployment of a contested terrain that takes on board the force of psychic investments and insists on the sexed specificity of **corporeality**. In being strongly influenced by **psychoanalysis**, Irigaray engages with a body which, though material, is never given, but always filtered through and constructed by a set of discursive strategies. As with many other contemporary feminists, and notably Liz Grosz, she is concerned with the irreducible interplay of text and physicality which posits a body always in process, never fixed or solid, and never one.

In large part, the enormous proliferation of feminist theorisations of the body has been mobilised by the response to the insights of **poststructuralism/postmodernism**, which ironically in their masculinist forms often have been accused of an indifference to materiality. With the demise of the belief in a given reality, what feminists have seized on is not simply that the body is a discursive construction, but that the notion of 'the' body is untenable. There are only multiple bodies, marked not simply by sex, but by an infinite array of differences – race, class, sexuality, age, mobility status are commonly invoked – none of which is solely determinate. Inspired by the work of theorists such as Foucault – who sees the body as a text variously inscribed by history, and most recently in the interests of capitalism – feminists have undertaken to extend that analysis to take account of patriarchy. The discursive operations that construct the useful, manipulable body – what Foucault calls the 'docile body' – have been a fertile ground for feminist understandings that make clear the links between the everyday body as it is lived, and the regime of disciplinary and regulatory practices that shape its form and behaviour. Theorists such as Susan Bordo (1993) and Sandra Bartky (1988) have been in the forefront in analysing how the processes of surveillance and self-surveillance are deeply implicated in constituting a set of normativities towards which bodies intend. The practices of diet, keep-fit, fertility control, fashion, health care procedures and so on, are all examples of disciplinary controls which literally produce the bodies that are their concern. Given the pre-eminent position of the discourse of biomedicine in such a schema, it is incumbent on feminists, and particularly those associated with the longstanding women's **health** movement, to rethink the traditional claims of medical practice to cure and care, not simply in terms of control, but also in terms of the constitution of the body.

It is, then, the forms of materialisation of the body, rather than the material itself, which is the concern of feminism. As Judith **Butler** puts it: 'there is no reference to a pure body which is not at the same time a further formation of that body' (1993: 10). Butler's notion of performativity is highly relevant here in theorising the ways in which the deployments of the body, especially in terms of gendered sexuality, are both open and constrained. The normative binaries of male/female, health/ill-health, heterosexual/homosexual and so on, that are used to characterise embodiment may be exposed in their instability – but also paradoxically confirmed – by the performativity of abject bodies. Butler's argument is at times highly abstract, but she never loses sight of the body as a lived entity, or that 'language and materiality are fully embedded in each other' (69). That move away from a purely textual analysis is even more evident in the feminist take-up of the phenomenology of Merleau-Ponty, in which the being-in-the-world of the subject is intricately and irreducibly bound up with the constitution and extension of the body. In the phenomenological tradition, the structure of the self is indivisible from its corporeal capacities, but what feminist theorists importantly add is an emphasis on the differential forms of embodiment that confound normative boundaries. The work of Iris Marion Young (1990), Ros Diprose (1994), and increasingly Liz Grosz (1994), is deeply concerned with the processes of embodied subjectivity as it evolves within temporal and spatial parameters. The contrast with the Cartesian mind/body split could not be clearer.

The body, then, has become the site of intense inquiry, not in the hope of recovering an authentic female body unburdened of patriarchal assumptions, but in the full acknowledgment of the multiple and fluid possibilities of differential embodiment. As Grosz puts it: 'the stability of the unified body image, even in the so-called normal subject, is always precarious. It cannot be simply taken for granted as an accomplished fact, for it must be continually renewed' (1994: 43–4).

References and further reading

Bartky, S.L. (1988) 'Foucault, Femininity and Patriarchal Power' in I. Diamond and L. Quinby (eds) *Feminism and Foucault*, Boston: Northeastern University Press.

Beauvoir, S. de (1949) *The Second Sex*, trans. H.M. Parshley, New York: Knopf, 1952.

Bordo, S. (1993) *Unbearable Weight: Feminism, Western Culture and the Body*, Berkeley, CA: University of California Press.

Butler, J. (1993) *Bodies that Matter: On the Discursive Limits of 'Sex'*, London: Routledge.

Diprose, R. (1994) *The Bodies of Women: Ethics, Embodiment and Sexual Difference*, London: Routledge.

Firestone, S. (1979) *The Dialectic of Sex*, London: The Women's Press.

Grosz, E. (1994) *Volatile Bodies. Towards a Corporeal Feminism*, London: Routledge.

Irigaray, L. (1985) *This Sex Which Is Not One*, Ithaca, NY: Cornell University Press.

Schildrick, M. (1997) *Leaky Bodies and Boundaries: Feminism, Postmodernism and (Bio)ethics*, London: Routledge.

Wendell, S. (1996) *The Rejected Body: Feminist Philosophical Reflections on the Disabled Body*, London: Routledge.

Young, I.M. (1990) *Throwing Like a Girl*, Bloomington, IN: Indiana University Press.

MARGRIT SHILDRICK

bonding, maternal, feminine

Feminist and psychoanalytic theorists re-examine and articulate views of feminine and maternal bonding (or attachment) in order to reconceive of ethics and sociality. Traditional philosophical and psychoanalytical discourses have rendered maternal, feminine, and woman as either passive, antisocial or absent. Consequently, the occurrence of bonding between mother and infant is based on a distorted view of maternal function.

Historically, the role attributed to maternity was confined to a natural role and opposed to culture. Freud argued that civilisation is the result of repressing unconscious, irrational drives and that women, because of their anatomy, cannot fully control and therefore cannot transcend. Kelly Oliver (1997) shows how Lacan and his followers have continued to promote theories that associate the mother with nature and the father with culture, theories that demand that proper development includes leaving the mother behind. For Lacan, the mother is associated with a realm of need and nature that is left behind as soon as the paternal agent intervenes and introduces the infant to language.

Jessica Benjamin's (1988) intersubjective analysis represents a significant alternative to Freudian human development. For Benjamin and her adherents, the mother is not associated with anti-social nature, but rather, the mother/infant relationship is the prototypical social situation. The writings of psychoanalytic thinkers – Julia Kristeva, Daniel Stern, and Luce Irigaray – along with the work of feminist theorists – Teresa Brennan, Kelly Oliver, and Cynthia Willett –

continue to articulate notions of maternity as social and provide a framework for reconceptualising ethical subjectivity based on bonds of love and attunement between caregiver and infant. Both Oliver and Willett demonstrate that the interaction between mother and infant grows out of expressions of 'nondiscursive affect attunement' which become the basis for sociality, language, and culture. According to Willett (1995), ethics develops not from the discipline of desire (depicted by Eurocentric/paternalist moralities) but from cultivating a 'social eroticism' that can find its roots in the relationship between nurturer and infant.

Revisionary theories of maternity and carework critique egoistic, antisocial conceptions of subjectivity and offer an ethical model for challenging post-Enlightenment models of the self and social relations. Intersubjective theorists are unified by the conviction that ethics requires the possibility of a relationship between different people. Maternal bonding is regarded as a source of value that can help us transform and gain a better understanding of the dynamics of our psychological and cultural relationship to difference. As our conceptions of the maternal and feminine change, so too will our ethical relationships to one another.

References and further reading

Benjamin, J. (1988) *The Bonds of Love*, New York: Pantheon.

Oliver, K. (1997) *Family Values*, New York: Routledge.

Willett, C. (1995) *Maternal Ethics and Other Slave Moralities*, New York: Routledge.

DAWN JAKUBOWSKI

bourgeois capitalism

The concept of bourgeois capitalism might rightly be said to belong to Karl Marx, whose analysis of the economic relations of the early industrial period led to both a materialist conception of history and the notion of capitalism as an historical epoch. Capitalist social and economic relations are defined by significant class divisions, particularly between the owners of capital (the bourgeoisie) and the workers (the proletariat).

For feminists, Marx's class analysis of capitalism raised three important concerns (all of which were underdeveloped by Marx himself). First, what was the place of women's productive labour (i.e. in the workforce, particularly as a reserve army of labour) under capitalism? Second, what was the place of women's so-called non-productive labour (i.e. housework and caring responsibilities) under capitalism? Finally, class analysis also led to questions about women's place within the so-called ruling or bourgeois class particularly, given that a) a woman's assigned class was generally determined by her husband's or father's class position; and, b) gender-based oppression seemed to transcend class distinctions.

SANDRA REIN

See also: class analysis, UK; class analysis, US

bride/widow burning (suttee burial)

Suttee (*sati*) burial came to prominence in feminist theory with Mary **Daly**'s 1978 text *Gyn/Ecology*, in which the self-immolation of Hindu widows on their husband's funeral pyres is analysed as violence against women which proves the universal nature of **patriarchy**. British colonial attitudes had held that *sati* was emblematic of the ill-treatment of women in 'backward' traditional societies and so used *sati* to justify colonial intervention. Feminist uses of *sati* as *symbol* have been positioned by post-colonial feminists as open to charges of neo-colonial orientalism. They have historicised the practice, reclaimed the subjectivity of the widow and challenged simplistic attempts to represent *sati* as a nationalistic or religious practice. Bride burning (kitchen/dowry death in which women are involuntarily burned by their husbands or families) is recognised as separate from *sati* and treated by feminists as murder.

See also: postcolonial feminism

References and further reading

Daly, M. (1978) *Gyn/Ecology: The Metaethics of Radical Feminism*, Boston: Beacon Press.

KAZ ROSS

Buddhism

As a religion which is not based on a concept of the divine embodied in a male anthropomorphic icon, nor dependent on a central authority invested in a male hierarchy, Buddhism harbours the potential for an inclusive religion. However, despite emphatic statements in some of the canonical texts as to the ephemeral nature of sex and gender (e.g. *Vimala-kirtinirdesha-sutra*), the social and historical reality of the various Buddhist traditions in Asia and elsewhere exhibits a significant influence of male-centred thinking which often expresses itself in blatant misogyny. Some scholars (e.g. I.B. Horner) argue that in its earliest phases Buddhism was less affected by gender bias than later on, when (so they argue) male monasticism became dominant and inscribed its own prejudice vis-à-vis woman on to the authoritative texts. Other scholars (e.g. Diana Paul) offer the opinion that, while early Buddhism exhibits gyno-phobic traits due to the dominance of monastic discipline (*vinaya*), Mahayana and particularly tantric Buddhism are more appreciative of the feminine and of women. Textual evidence can be found for both opinions. Historical studies indicate that Buddhist institutions soon came under the influence of the various monarchies and were often absorbed into court culture where only men held power and swayed influence. This situation affected the position of women in Buddhism more than any possible tendency toward theoretically buttressed misogyny.

In recent years, scholars of a feminist leaning as well as practising Buddhist women have reflected on the situation of gender as a category, significantly contributing to what Buddhism is in a social and ethical context (Jose I. Cabezon, J. Willis, A. Klein, E. Neumaier-Dargyay, R. Gross, K.L. Tsomo). A major concern is the re-installation of full ordination of Buddhist nuns (*bhikkhuni*), and some Buddhist nuns, mainly of North American or European descent, have made this the cornerstone of a women's movement in Buddhism. The line of ordination in the pre-Mahayana *vinaya* traditions (misleadingly often identified as *Theravada*) became extinct well before Buddhism reached its maximum dissemination (between the eleventh and sixteenth centuries). While in these traditions full ordination is not available, many Buddhist women seeking a spiritual life nevertheless form religious communities that afford them a life of seclusion and contemplation. These contemplative communities of women (e.g the *Dasa Sila Matavo* of Sri Lanka) often enjoy a higher esteem in the eyes of the laity than the fully ordained monks who are often seen as being too involved in politics and enjoying too many perks. However, in *vinaya* traditions of the Far East the nuns' full ordination lineage has continued. Therefore, some new movements, such as Fo Kuan Shan (originating from Taiwan), fully integrate monks, nuns, and lay men and women in their teaching, meditational practice and social services while other Buddhist movements continue to bar women from full participation.

Despite some initial attempts, a comprehensive philosophical reflection on some of the key concepts of Buddhist thought grounded in feminist theories, as well as a sociological study of the role of women in today's Buddhist movements, are still a desired goal of feminist scholarship.

References and further reading

Barnes, N.J. (1996) 'Buddhist Women and the Nuns' Order in Asia' in C.S. Queen and S.B. King (eds) *Engaged Buddhism: Buddhist Liberation Movements in Asia*, Albany, NY: State University of New York Press.

Cabezon, J.I. (ed.) (1992) *Buddhism, Sexuality and Gender*, Albany, NY: State University of New York Press.

Neumaier-Dargyay, E.K. (1995) 'Buddhist Thought from a Feminist Perspective', in M. Joy and E.K. Neumaier-Dargyay (eds) *Gender, Genre and Religion: Feminist Reflections*, Waterloo, ON: Wilfrid Laurier University Press.

EVA K. NEUMAIER

Bunch, Charlotte (b. 1942)

Charlotte Bunch, feminist activist and theorist, has had a formative theoretical and strategic influence at every stage of **feminism** in North America and globally. She believes, as do most feminist radicals, that theory is not only or even primarily made by specialist feminist theorists. When feminist movement is vibrant all feminists participate in the collective development of theory grounded in practice.

Charlotte Bunch early and clearly articulated the importance of feminism's **autonomy** from other social movements. She has contributed hugely to the development of feminism as a women-centred perspective on the whole of society rather than simply a list of women's issues – a politics which encompasses at its core, resistance to colonial, racial, class and heterosexist oppression (see **heterosexism, heteronormativity**; **oppression**). These principles enable solidarity to be built through the recognition rather than denial of differences among women. They ground international feminist networking and are central to the 'global feminism' being forged by feminists around the world. Charlotte Bunch is closely associated with 'global feminism' and is playing an important role in its development. She is, for instance, a prime mover in the international Women's Rights are Human Rights campaign which is contributing to new forms of organising among women as well as challenging the traditional concept of **human rights**. Her landmark article 'Women's Rights as Human Rights: Toward a Re-Vision of Human Rights' has been widely translated and is used around the world.

Many of Charlotte Bunch's most important, now classic, articles were originally published in *Quest: A Feminist Quarterly*, an influential movement-based journal she founded with others in 1973 to encourage debate and to support the development and dissemination of 'practical theory'. A selection of these and other articles appears in a collection of her work entitled *Passionate Politics: Feminist Theory in Action, 1968–1986* (1987), a major source on the theory and practice of feminism today. Charlotte Bunch's political writing is a model of clarity and accessibility and the book situates each of her theoretical contributions in the chronology of personal and movement development that gave rise both to the issues she addresses and the insights she offers.

See also: class analysis UK; class analysis US; diversity; lesbian feminism; race

Selected writings

Bunch, C. (1987) *Passionate Politics: Feminist Theory in Action, 1968–1986*, New York: St Martin's Press.
—— (1994) *Vienna World Conference Campaign: Demanding Accountability; The Global Campaign and Vienna Tribunal for Women's Human Rights*, New York: UNIFEM and the Centre for Women's Global Leadership.

ANGELA MILES

butch/femme

'Butch/femme' refers to *homo-sexual* but *hetero-gendered* erotic practices which emerged in post-Second World War urban working class lesbian communities in the USA. These practices were driven underground after a harsh condemnation by **lesbian feminism** in the 1970s but reappeared in the early 1980s after the acrimonious **sex wars**. Lesbian feminism, challenging the homophobia of mainstream feminism and attempting to redress the structural inequities among women, argued that butch/femme reproduced dominant/submissive power imbalances thought inherent in heterosexuality. Lesbian feminism sought to recentre lesbianism as quintessentially feminist by privileging a lesbian subject position – the woman-identified woman – which disavowed all manifestations of masculinity and femininity.

Cultural work in the mid-1980s began to reconceptualise butch/femme, arguing instead that what was being dismissed was an important erotic system as well as pre-Stonewall lesbian working-class erotic history. Joan Nestle's *A Restricted Country* (1987), restores butch/femme as embodied resistance to the sex/gender system by establishing butch/femme as lesbian gender identities which eroticise gender, not power, differences. If *sex* is biology and *gender* the culturally constructed subjectivities of masculinity and femininity mapped onto biology, then Nestle, **Rubin**, Feinberg and **Butler** began to argue that boys could be girls, and some girls, boys, regardless of biology. Butch or masculine women challenge the 'naturalness' and **biological essentialism** of the sex/gender system while lesbian and bisexual femmes trouble the necessary alignment of gender (femininity) with the overdetermined object choice (male-embodied masculinity). Butch/femme, then, is no longer an imitation of gender but a parody of heterosexuality which exposes the operations of the sex/gender system, and subsequently, all gender identities as performative effects.

Most recently, debates around butch/femme have widened to overlap with those of **transgender** and transsexuality (see **transsexuality/ gender dysphoria**). At stake in these debates are the ways in which female masculinity has erroneously become synonymous with 'lesbian' (not all female masculinities are lesbian and not all lesbians are masculine). Also at stake were definitional border wars between female-to-male transsexual (FTM) masculinity and butch masculinity where butch women may still identify as female and/or lesbian in comparison to FTM transsexual men who identify as neither lesbian nor female, but who might identify as *men* (gay, bisexual or heterosexual) instead. These debates have implications for femme women, some of whom might identify as *non-heterosexual*; as *non-lesbian* but *heterogendered* (bisexual femmes with FTMs); or as *homogendered* (femmes with femmes). Reconsiderations of butch/femme have contributed to both the development of non-dichotomous histories of sexual cultures and an increasingly complex understanding of gender, sex and sexuality.

See also: bisexuality; masculinity

References and further reading

Halberstam, J. (1998) *Female Masculinity*, Durham: Duke University Press.
Harris, L. and Crocker, E. (eds) (1997) *Femme: Feminists, Lesbians and Bad Girls*, London: Routledge.
Munt, S.R. (ed.) (1998) *Butch/Femme: Inside Lesbian Gender*, London: Cassell.

JEAN NOBLE

Butler, Judith (b. 1956)

Judith Butler's significant contributions to feminist theory are her engagement with the Foucauldian account of the body as the inscribed surface of regulatory discourses, an elaboration of gender as the performative stabilisation of sexual difference, and considerations of the exclusions inevitable to any identity category. The popularity of Butler's work indexes an increasingly philosophically-minded feminism in the Anglo-American academy.

Gender Trouble: The Subversion of Identity (1990) is one of the most widely-read and controversial critiques of 'woman' as a universal and stable subject grounding feminism. Following Michel Foucault's claim that juridical systems of power produce the subjects they ostensibly represent, Butler argues that the subject 'woman', understood to ground the feminist enterprise, is, instead, a representational product of feminism. This argument and its ethical implication – that feminism must reckon with the exclusions foundational to any prescriptive description of identity – corroborates long-standing social difference critiques of the implicit attributes of the woman *supposed* to be *the subject* of feminism ('able-bodied', white, heterosexual, middle class).

Butler is best known for her formulation of 'gender as performative', which articulates models of social life as a series of pre-scripted or ritual performances, with psychoanalytic descriptions of femininity as 'masquerade', and philosophical accounts of linguistic performativity. Employing Monique **Wittig**'s and Adrienne **Rich**'s critiques of compulsory heterosexuality, Butler describes a 'heterosexual matrix' – a hegemonic, discursive/epistemic model of gender intelligibility – through which stable relations between sex ('male', 'female'), heterosexual object choice, and gender ('masculine', feminine) are produced and maintained. Compulsory 'gender performativity' produces the naturalness of 'sex', while gay and lesbian parodies of gender, Butler argues, 'implicitly reveal the imitative structure of gender itself – as well as its contingency' (1990: 137).

Though Butler's target audience is feminist, *Gender Trouble* has been hailed as a major contribution to the nascent field of **queer theory**. Popular applications of Butler's work largely emphasise the theatrical valences of gender 'performance', valorising (queer) texts which denaturalise 'sex' (camp, drag). Her *Bodies That Matter* (1993) responds to criticisms that *Gender Trouble* evacuates the materiality and historicity of the body, leaving gender simply a matter of choice. *Bodies That Matter* underscores the constraints upon performative utterance (symbolic intelligibility, for instance), and situates gender performativity in relation to **speech act theory**.

See also: Beauvoir, Simone de; essentialism; gender; identity; psychoanalysis

Selected writings

Butler, J. (1990) *Gender Trouble*, New York: Routledge.

—— (1993) *Bodies That Matter*, New York: Routledge.

—— (1997) *The Psychic Life of Power*, Stanford, CA: Stanford University Press.

—— (1997) *Excitable Speech: A Politics of the Performative*, New York: Routledge.

JULIA CREET

C

Card, Claudia (b. 1940)

Claudia Card's philosophical development indicates a shift in focus from the perspectives of ideal legislatures and the search for universal truth, to a focus on ethical issues as they pertain to inter-personal relationships and informal practices among individuals with particular ethnic, economic, religious backgrounds and sexual orientations.

In her major work on lesbian philosophy, *Lesbian Choices* (1995), Card treats the term 'lesbian' primarily as a quality, a modifier of experiences, rather than a noun naming a social **identity**. Drawing upon Wittgenstein's concept of family resemblance and Nietzsche's genealogical method, Card maintains that lesbian qualities are related to each other through patterns of resemblance and difference, the way family members resemble each other, without sharing one essential feature. Thus, Card maintains that we can meaningfully describe a person, relationship, or **experience** as 'lesbian' without presupposing any essence of what it means to be a lesbian. This allows her to recognise that same-sex eroticism and bonding are older than the notion of a lesbian identity. Card argues that most women have had experiences that can be called 'lesbian' in one way or another. It is, in her view, a combination of moral luck (chance) and choice that determines which women in fact identify as lesbians. Thus, Card's understanding of the term 'lesbian' is loose in ways that allow for the possibility of lesbian aspects in any woman's life, regardless of her self-identification. This is a philosophically rich and obviously provocative position.

Moral luck is also central in Card's recent book, *The Unnatural Lottery* (1996). Here Card focuses on the part that luck plays in determining opportunities or impediments to people's character development. She explores the impact of behaviours of individuals and social institutions, which are often outside one's control in determining the shape one's moral development takes. Card discusses responsibility, justice and care, rape, gratitude, **gender**, sexual orientation, and **race**.

Card's work succeeds in bringing complex philosophical concepts to bear on everyday questions and controversies. Card clearly is a pioneering leader in the fields of feminist ethics and lesbian philosophy. Dealing with such topics as gays in the military and the morality of the traditional family, Card's work is not only highly sophisticated, but highly relevant.

See also: ethics, feminist; lesbian ethics

Selected writings

Card, C. (1991) (ed.) *Feminist Ethics*, Lawrence: University Press of Kansas.
—— (1995) *Lesbian Choices*, New York: Columbia University Press.
—— (1996) *The Unnatural Lottery: Character and Moral Luck*, Philadelphia, PA: Temple University Press.

VICTORIA DAVION

care, provision of

The provision of care is, by now, a familiar point of debate among feminists of different disciplines.

Carol **Gilligan** brought this debate to the forefront with her landmark book of 1982 *In a Different Voice*. Although Gilligan's work was devoted to what she called the ethic of care, it brings to light an important discussion for the provision of care.

Feminist theory long ago exposed the socially constructed version of 'woman' as caregiver and nurturer. Men (and many women) labelled these roles as 'natural' thereby implying 'unnaturalness' in some women's rejection of them. Such assumptions have been harmful to women by limiting their options as persons and therefore carving out a pre-determined destiny to be the care-giving sex, collectively.

In a patriarchal culture, social roles dictate that a woman's main responsibility is that of reproducer of the human species. Society then continues to objectify women as 'natural' care-givers. Women's desires for fulfilment in life may include or preclude motherhood; however, a gender-biased society still insists on the provision of care as the woman's responsibility. This insistence is harmful to both men and women.

For women, the assumption that they must provide the care-giving in the family leads to social expectations that restrict their options and create disapproval for pursuing goals that do not include that of care provider. For men, it assumes that they are not capable of providing care, thus supporting a vision of man that misses out on the potentially rewarding human experience of providing care to or for another.

Kuhse (1997) discusses the problems in seeing the provision of care as women's work by looking at the nursing profession. Within our current institution of medicine, nurses (mostly women) are the care-givers, while doctors (mostly men) are considered the experts. In seeing nurses' highest priority as caregiver, the provision of care comes to be more important than any other responsibility the nurse might have (to herself, hospital policy, the law). This creates ethical problems even for a profession which self-admittedly is about providing care. If a nurse's natural response and main job is supposed to be to provide care, that provision comes to be more expected by her superiors, patients, and peers than any other values or norms including her own personal and professional ethics (159).

Gilligan has been criticised for implying differences in women and men that could be harmful to feminist work. However, feminist goals include the eradication of oppression based on socially constructed views of what is natural for and about women.

See also: ethic of care; family, the; Gilligan, Carol

References and further reading

Gilligan, C. (1982) *In a Different Voice*, Cambridge, MA: Harvard University Press.

Gordon, S., Benner, P., and Noddings, N. (eds) (1996) *Caregiving: Readings in Knowledge, Practice, Ethics, and Politics*, Philadelphia, PA: University of Pennsylvania Press.

Kuhse, H. (1997) *Caring: Nurses, Women, and Ethics*, Oxford: Blackwell Publishers.

KATHLEEN S. KURTZ

Cartesianism, feminist critiques of

The Cartesianism criticised by contemporary feminists is the potent legacy from Descartes that survives in present-day philosophy. Feminists looking at this Cartesian legacy have found a transformation of the philosophical conception of the self and its relation to the world. They have focused in particular on the consequences of Cartesian dualism, the isolating of a rational self, independent of the sensual, emotional body and on an epistemological outlook that grounds knowledge of acts of a self whose first act is to know itself in isolation from other selves and from the world. Feminists have discussed the contribution of these views to the support of an ideology that privileges an autonomous rational masculinity over a relational, emotional, corporeal femininity. Cartesianism in Descartes's own day seems to have struck women somewhat differently, encouraging them to see themselves, although deficient in education, as possessing rational faculties.

MARGARET ATHERTON

case study analysis

A case study involves a single unit of analysis, for example a city or community, person, organisation, or family. Case studies may involve either the holistic analysis of a single case or the comparative study of several cases. Not to be confused with ethnographies (see **ethnography**), case studies generally rely upon many methods of data-gathering (observations, ethnographic interviews, surveys, and documents) to compile as much information as possible about 'the case'. Although no one can make statistical generalisations from a single case, scholars, feminist and otherwise, disagree about *whether or not* as well as *how* one may generalise from case studies. For example, Robert Yin and others describe a form of 'theoretical generalisation' (1998: 239) which allows one to link cases to theoretically similar phenomena. Feminist theorist, Dorothy **Smith**, however, goes a step further in *The Everyday World as Problematic* seeing cases simply as 'points of entry' (1987: 157).

References and further reading

Smith, D.E. (1987) *The Everyday World as Problematic: A Feminist Sociology,* Boston: Northeastern University Press.

Yin, R.K. (1998) 'The Abridged Version of Case Study Research', in L. Bickman and D. Rog (eds) *Handbook of Applied Social Research Methods,* Thousand Oaks, CA: Sage.

JANE C. HOOD

categories and dichotomies

All perception and thought involve and depend upon categories. There are categories of concrete things, such as Living and Non-Living, Furniture and Fruit and Chair/Table/Bed, Orange/Apple/Pear. Animal and Plant are categories; Furry and Scaly cross the category Animals. There are abstract categories, such as Cause, Democracy, ideas with criss-crossing sub-categories such as Western or Confucian, Ancient or Modern). Theories (scientific, mathematical, social) involve distinctive central categories. Physics has the categories of Time, Matter, Sub-atomic particle, Energy. Biology has the categories of Species, Endocrine. In the case of feminist theory, the **gender** categories Woman and Man are central for analysing political, social and historical situations.

The categories Woman and Man are troublesome, partly because they are also the central categories in the 'theory' of male supremacism or patriarchy (they embody ideas and beliefs that make patriarchy seem 'right' or 'natural'). As used in patriarchal thought, these categories are often dichotomous or binary; feminists have seen this as oppressive to women, and are concerned not to replicate such usage themselves.

Categories are *dichotomous* when they divide a certain domain into two groups which are mutually exclusive and exhaustive, and the two groups are seen as each other's opposites; for example, Reality being divided into Nature and Culture, where every phenomenon is classed as one or the other, and the qualities of Nature and Culture are seen as opposite.

Mutually exclusive means that no items can be in both categories; *exhaustive* means every item has to be in one category or the other. If a pair of categories is mutually exclusive and exhaustive, they must be *absolute opposites,* meaning there is no spectrum of intermediate cases between them. *Polar opposites* such as Hot and Cold are at the ends of a spectrum of intermediate cases. Strictly speaking, categories should only be called 'dichotomous' if they involve absolute opposites, but people often refer to polar opposite categories as 'dichotomous'.

A *binary* category divides the universe, or a domain, into those things which are its members, and *everything else,* presented simply as 'not this category'; for example, the category Number simply contains all numbers, and leaves everything else in the universe undifferentiated as Not-Numbers.

In some contexts, the category Man (or the category of things male or masculine) functions as a binary category, leaving women (or things female or feminine) with no specific characterisation, merely as *not-Men/not-male/not-masculine.* Man is functioning as a binary category, and women disappear into *not-Man* in all the situations where men's experience or subjectivity is taken to be what experience or subjectivity *is*, and a person has to have that experience or subjectivity, or be just off the map. If membership in the category A is thought of as the member's **identity**, then using the category A gives no corresponding or parallel identities to any of the things outside A. If the A-identity qualifies A-members for respect, dignity, privileges and so on, then such categorisation leaves all others off the map, without identity or value. This not only deprives those who are not A-members of something valuable, it masses them all together, relative to A, as having no distinctions among themselves and having no identities or names of their own; this, in turn, works against their being able to form political resistance to their exclusion and deprivation.

In other contexts, the categories Woman and Man seem to function as dichotomous, when, for instance, people think of women and men as having distinctive kinds of sexuality, work styles, or personality (e.g. relational/performance, passive/aggressive), and see these as in some sense opposites.

Some people think that mutually exclusive and exhaustive opposite genders can be equal in status (and the above definition of *dichotomous* leaves this possiblity open). They believe that the opposites can be complementary and the two categories interdependent, with neither being dominant or subordinate. But many feminists think either that this is impossible in contemporary societies, or that *dichotomy* necessarily implies hierarchy, i.e., one group being in some sense dominant or primary, the other subordinate or secondary.

If you think dichotomous categories can only be hierarchical and that genders are dichotomous categories, then you will not be able to put the idea of gender and the idea of equality together. You would think that as long as there are genders, there will be inequality – domination, oppression. So, instead of thinking the goal of feminism is gender equality (which many people do think), you might begin to think about creating a world in which there is no gender. Another option might be to think about the possibility that genders which are dichotomous (and hence, hierarchical) in patriarchal social orders might be differently constructed in a non-oppressive social order, so that they are two categories, but are not dichotomous. If practices and usage were changed so gender categories were not dichotomous, then one could

imagine an individual being both genders, or being neither, and one might imagine there being three or more gender categories.

Words have meanings by virtue of contrasts with other words, for example, *red*, by contrast with *blue*, *yellow*, *round*, *tall* …, or *car*, by contrast with *bus*, *house*, *boat*, *lawnmower* … But as these examples suggest, it does not have to be a dichotomous contrast or a binary contrast. Even a word that apparently has a dichotomously contrasting term, such as *husband* (versus *wife*), may in fact have its meaning through many non-dichotomous contrasts such as the whole array of other kin terms: *brother*, *uncle*, *mother*, *father*, *cousin*. We can recognise that categories operate by way of contrasts with and differentiation from other categories, without assuming that all categorising is dichotomous or binary, hence likely to be oppressive. Categorising is unavoidable. Categorising in ways that are oppressive is avoidable.

See also: alterity; binarism/bipolarity; dichotomies; essentialism; race

MARILYN FRYE

censorship

Censorship is 'a process that occurs over time, and it is also an outcome' (Schrader 1995). Some see it as a means of repressing ideas, impulses and feelings in unconscious and conscious ways. Others see censorship as a means to protect groups such as women and children from stronger, oppressive groups. In the context of feminism, most discussions of censorship have centred on pornography.

Robin Morgan set the terms of the debate in her 1978 book, *Going Too Far*, when she wrote: 'Pornography is the theory, rape is the practice'. In other words, pornography is extreme misogyny that authorises the sexual degradation of women and functions to keep them subordinate. Andrea Dworkin (1979) and Catharine A. MacKinnon (1987) further argue that, because it is a means and not just a metaphor for the **oppression** of women, pornography is a violation of **civil rights** and thus legally actionable sex discrimination.

MacKinnon (1987: 1–17) states that 'the social relation between the sexes is organised so that men may dominate and women must submit and this relation is sexual – in fact, sex'. Men sexualise inequality. To treat **gender** as difference rather than hierarchy is to treat gender 'as a bipolar distinction, each pole of which is defined in contrast to the other by opposed intrinsic attributes'. Pornography is 'a key means of actualizing these two dynamics in life', as it turns 'sex inequality into sexuality' and 'male dominance into the sex difference'. By packaging gendered and sexualised inequality as free speech, and thereby a right, pornography turns the 'practice of sex discrimination into a legal entitlement'. In this context, *freedom of speech* means free male access to women. Protecting pornographers, as does the US First Amendment, 'does not promote the freedom of speech of women. It *has* not done so. Pornography terrorises women into silence'.

The legal solution to pornography in Canada found its expression in February 1992 when the Supreme Court, in *Regina* v. *Butler*, upheld the lower court conviction of the owner of a video store who had been found guilty of possessing, selling and exposing obscene materials to the public view. The Court agreed that the violation of the freedom of expression guarantee in the 1982 Canadian Charter of Rights and Freedoms was justifiable as a 'reasonable limit prescribed by law' in that pornography harms women in their pursuit of equality.

For some feminists, censorship is problematic in that it exerts pressure on the expression of opinion, rather than on the opinion itself, thus removing discourse from the public realm and denying alternative visions from entering public debate. While they accept the harm analysis, agreeing that pornography reflects the power structures of the **patriarchy**, they claim the effects of legal remedy will come to inhibit women's freedom, that gay, lesbian, feminist and other marginalised groups are most likely to suffer from the potential abuse of state censorship. They argue that in the aftermath of the *Butler* decision, the power to censor has time and again been used against gay and lesbian groups, while mainstream, heterosexual pornography appears to be flourishing.

Other feminists assert that the harm element is unproven, and further assert that pornography can be sexually liberating for women, particularly in its lesbian representations and the specific communities within which these representations are produced and exchanged. Lorraine Johnson (1997: 6) writes that most censorship is ignited by 'a deep cultural anxiety over the conjunction of children and sexuality; entrenched homophobia; alarm over representations of the body (sexualised or not); anger at representations that challenge cherished belief systems; and concern about public funding of the arts …'. Thelma McCormack in her article 'If Pornography is the Theory, is Inequality the Practice?' (Johnson (ed.) 1997: 173–90) notes that pornography 'has become the excuse for censorship in a neo-conservative state that deregulates the economy and regulates morality'. Lesbian feminists have 'opened up the traditional understanding of erotic knowledge' and have contributed to 'a new discourse, an alternative to a phallocentric model of *jouissance*'. She further notes that legal strategies 'do not have an impact on the most serious form of censorship already in place, the censorship of the marketplace. It is this that silences women, not pornography'. Without economic power to produce their own cultural products and spaces, 'women's voices are not heard and they remain unempowered'. If 'pornography silences women, censorship silences them even more, as censorship "silences all"'.

In the 1994 trial of *Little Sisters Book and Art Emporium* v. *Canada*, Little Sisters offered testimony demonstrating that, in the aftermath of the *Butler* decision, Canada Customs was routinely seizing books and other items on route to gay and lesbian bookstores, thereby applying powers of censorship in a discriminatory way. Speaking against censorship, lesbian writer Jane Rule testified as follows:

> … if we were going to deal with questions of humiliation, of sexual explicitness, we would have to know that … there have always been writers who have been preoccupied with the darker sides of human experience, who are perhaps best equipped to give us insights into those very troubling and often horrifying things that go on in the world today, where in Bosnia women are routinely raped and children are molested, where in almost every case there is a sexual component which, if we do not finally come to understand in all its complexity, we are

in great danger of not knowing how to live our lives.

(Rule 1995: 6)

The debate continues: does censoring questionable materials offer protection, or does it more often silence the very groups it claims to protect?

References and further reading

Cossman, B. *et al.* (1997) *Bad Attitude/s on Trial*, Toronto: University of Toronto Press.

Dworkin, A. (1979) *Pornography*, New York: G.P. Putnam.

Fuller, J. and Blackley, S. (1996) *Restricted Entry*, Vancouver: Press Gang, 2nd edn.

Johnson, L. (ed.) (1997) *Suggestive Poses*, Toronto: Riverbank Press and Toronto Photographers Workshop.

MacKinnon, C.A. (1987) *Feminism Unmodified*, Cambridge, MA: Harvard University Press.

Morgan, R. (1978) *Going Too Far*, New York: Vintage.

Rule, J. (1995) *Detained at Customs: Jane Rule Testifies at the Little Sister's Trial*, Vancouver, BC: Lazara Press.

Schrader, A.M. (1995) *Fear of Words*, Ottawa: Canadian Library Association.

JACQUELINE DUMAS

chastity, critique of

In Christianity, chastity is an ideal state of being for all men and women, entailing elimination or control of sexual thoughts, language, and behaviour, for mystical and/or procreative purposes. Opposed to carnal lust – a diabolical vice which some medieval ecclesiastical writers deemed insatiable in women – chastity is a virtue in whose name many thousands of women were raped, tortured, and executed by male church and civil authorities in **witchcraft** trials throughout Europe and the Americas, from the medieval era through (and in some areas beyond) the Enlightenment. In *Pure Lust* (1984), philosopher Mary **Daly** attacks chastity and asceticism as misogynistic tools of **patriarchy**, offering in place of them an alternative virtue, 'pure lust', which places female sexuality not

outside but inside a life-affirming, earthly-life-oriented spirituality.

See also: Christianity and feminism; corporeality; female circumcision/female genital mutilation; womanist theology

References and further reading

Daly, M. (1984) *Pure Lust: Elemental Feminist Philosophy*, Boston: Beacon Press.

EILEEN M. CONDON

chauvinism, male

Nicolas Chauvin was a Napoleonic soldier famous for his patriotism. His name evolved into the French word *chauvinisme*, which means extreme and uncritical patriotism; the word came into English meaning extreme patriotism or uncritical belief in the absolute superiority of one's nation and culture. It carries the suggestion that the chauvinist has an exaggerated confidence in his own individual and inborn superiority to anyone not of that nation or culture. Exploiting the semantic link between *patriot* and *patriarch*, US feminists in the late 1960s coined the term *male chauvinism* as a name for a man's belief in the superiority of men and everything masculine, and in his own innate superiority, as a man, to any woman. The term carried, also, the idea of uncritical loyalty to men (male bonding). Men who exhibited these convictions and loyalties were also dubbed 'male chauvinist pigs'.

MARILYN FRYE

Chicana feminism

The feminism or pro-woman standpoint of Chicanas (women of Mexican descent, born and living in the USA, and who claim that identity) derives from the challenges of living at the 'intersection of oppressions', where issues of ethnicity, class, gender and sexual orientation, meet and often clash. In Chicana feminist thinking one finds the refrains of multiple identities that cannot be subsumed under one category, and a struggle to combine theory with **praxis** in the face of social and academic environments that demand assimilation into a dominant symbolic.

The current struggle began in the late 1960s, when Chicana activists (like women of colour involved in other social movements), were faced with a difficult truth: their male cohorts preferred, even demanded, that they play the traditional role of supportive *mujer*. Chicanas were pressured to choose between *La Raza* and their interests as women. This dilemma, caused Chicanas like Gloria **Anzaldúa** to ask: 'Which collectivity does the daughter of a dark skinned mother listen to? (1990: 377).

For Chicanas who challenged the **sexism** in both the Chicano movement and the larger ethnic culture, the focus during the 1970s began to shift from race to a bi-cognitive struggle over both **race** and **gender**. These activists were inspired by Chicanas and Mexicanas who had preceded them in other socio-political struggles (see Cotera in García 1997: 41–4).

The response to these shifts was (and still is) hostile. Resistant women within the Movement and the larger Chicano culture were variously accused of being *vendidas* ('sell-outs') and 'anti-family, anti-cultural, (and) anti-male' (Nieto Gomez in García 1997: 88). When Chicanas turned to mainstream (white) feminism for support, they faced another battle. As Ana Castillo notes, 'brown women' had to struggle 'against a prevalent condescension on the part of middle-class white women toward women …whose culture is not mainstream American' (in García 1997: 310). As a result, many Chicana activists have an ambivalent relationship with what Chela Sandoval refers to as 'hegemonic feminism' (1991: 1).

Chicana-based feminism is forged in what Sandoval calls 'consciousness in opposition' (1991: 11). Overarching issues of concern to many Chicanas include the tension between the traditional roles of *Virgen* (the good woman) v. *Malinche* (the bad woman, the whore, the betrayer); how *familia* (family) both supports and controls a woman's life; education as a tool for improving one's socio-economic position; **affirmative action**, immigration and labour laws; bilingualism, **health** and **childcare** issues.

Approaches to social change among Chicana feminists vary. Denise Segura and Beatriz Pesquera's study of Chicana feminists in higher education identifies three basic groups: 'Chicana liberal feminists', 'Chicana insurgent feminists' and 'cultural nationalist feminists' (1992: 80). These groups share some characteristics with their white feminist counterparts, while at the same time maintaining a cultural consciousness that at times stands in opposition to white feminism. It must be noted that academic Chicanas are the ones whose texts and articulations are examined for theoretical content (as in this essay), thus privileging this class over others from the same culture.

Although there is no unified Chicana theory, there are many strands of thought. Theory itself is problematic for Chicana feminists concerned with the uses and mis-uses of theory and with the gap between the community and the academy. Anzaldúa and others have called for women of colour to 'de-academise theory and to connect the community to the academy' (1990: xxvi). Whether positioned in academia or the community, Chicana feminists do agree that theory must be put to work in the service of social change.

When articulating theory, Chicana feminists, often turn to their cultural traditions and non-traditional sources, because as Anzaldúa and others have noted, for marginalised groups, 'social issues are intertwined with the narrative and poetic elements of a text, elements in which theory is embedded' (1990: xxvi). This approach results in resistant articulations that challenge established structures (white, male, cultural) as well as those 'ideological configurations that dichotomise (Chicana) experiences and exploit (Chicana) political loyalties' (Segura and Pesquera 1992: 70).

The close relationship between the personal and the collective in Chicana feminism is salient in Gloria Anzaldúa's work, wherein she argues that new theoretical and political positions are articulated in the 'Borderland worlds' of ethnic communities, academia, feminist circles and work worlds. Like other women of colour feminists in the USA, Chicana feminists reside 'between and among' subject positions and critical cultural discourses, developing and practising what Rosa Linda Fregoso (1993) calls a form of 'mestizaje and bricolage'. For bilingual Chicanas, this oppositional consciousness includes code-switching.

Marginalised cultures have always lived in the Borderlands. This standpoint is *nada nuevo* (nothing new). In an attempt to articulate how Chicanas navigate in a postmodern world, Chela Sandoval has outlined a typology of consciousness that identifies five types of ideology: 'equal rights', 'revolutionary', 'supremacist', 'separatist', and 'differential'. The last, she argues, 'permits functioning within, yet beyond the demands of dominant ideology' and 'between and among' the other ideologies (1991: 12–14).

Differential Chicana feminist practice is both an ongoing process of emic recovery on the part of the marginalised, and a critique of **hegemony** in any guise. For example, Rosa Linda Fregoso makes use of feminist critical film discourse to analyse 'the relationship of human gender to representation', but she 'retreats' when the discourse 'lodges itself in a male/female binary, thus eliding race, class and sexual subjectivities' (1993: 21–2).

In similar fashion, historian Emma Pérez makes use of **Irigaray**'s female symbolic to argue for the importance of Chicana/Latina *sitios* (sites) *y lenguas* (discourses) that are positioned outside 'masculinist, Eurocentric, colonizing institutions'. In these liberated spaces, Chicanas/Latinas can work within a 'culturally specific female symbolic' that does not seek to homogenise what are basically 'irreducible differences' (Pérez in Trujillo 1998).

The terrains of 'irreducible differences' are sites of contestation (see Anzaldúa, xxi). Hegemonic feminism argues that sexism is the underlying oppression and impetus for feminist action, while Chicana feminists argue that the complexities of Chicana lived experience call for a different analysis and response (see Sandoval 1991). For example, while many white women unequivocally support abortion rights, Chicanas also want to ensure that abortions are not used in the service of forced sterilisation (Hurtado 1998: 139).

In developing theory, Chicanas intergrate material from the forbidden zones of essentialism and **cultural feminism**. Patricia Zavella argues that the 'structure in which women's experiences are rooted becomes the primary analytical locus' (1989: 32), while Emma Pérez, following Gayatri **Spivak** and others, employs 'strategic essentialism'

as an oppositional standpoint. Pérez defines this strategy as 'practised resistance against dominant ideologies that silence and/or model marginalised groups' (Pérez, in Trujillo 1998: 88).

As women of colour articulate theory and praxis in a contentious environment, they must also contend with the appropriation and exoticising practices of the dominant culture. Gloria Anzaldúa's work on living within the actual and metaphorical 'Borderlands', and inhabiting the consciousnesss of a *Mestiza* who operates in a 'pluralistic mode', is part of the foundation of Chicana theory. Currently these concepts are singled out for referencing or footnoting in hegemonic feminist works. This practice signals yet another invasion, since the concepts are often used as analogies and 'add-ons' rather than as a central component of a new analysis. This practice is part of what Pérez (in Trujillo 1998: 93) calls 'invasionary politics', and it is a cause of division between white women and women of colour.

Less divisive is the Chicana feminist challenge to positivist research (see **positivism**). Cherrìe Moraga and Gloria Anzaldúa's 'theory in the flesh' is part of an alternative to objective, distanced research. Rather than relying on a detached look at 'the Other', it is based on the 'physical realities of our lives, our skin colour, the land or concrete we grew up on, our sexual longing, [which] all fuse to create a politic born of necessity' (1983: 23). Like its white counterpart, Chicana feminist research also challenges the objectification of research subjects and supports the process of 'intersubjectivity'.

Within Chicana feminist circles, one finds divisions based on the very 'isms' they struggle against. For example, differences between working class and privileged Chicanas create tensions, as does the issue of class and how it interfaces with gender and race (Hurtado 1998: 145). Yet, the most overt source of division between Chicanas is generated by differences over sexual orientation and lesbian identity. In the late 1970s, Chicana lesbian feminists began to articulate social change models that also challenged **homophobia**. Their efforts were not welcome. They were often left out of Chicano/a texts, and endured attacks and labels ('lesbian terrorist') from both threatened Chicano men and 'loyalist' Chicana women (see González, Pérez in Trujillo 1998).

Chicana lesbians like Gloria Anzaldúa, Cherríe Moraga, Emma Pérez, Carla Trujillo and Deena González, have been at the forefront of Chicana feminist analysis, theory and activism. What they have done is to 'complexify' Chicana analysis and theory by adding the factor of sexual identity to what González calls the 'holy trinity' of class, race and gender (in Trujillo 1998: 50). In her essay on homophobia in the Chicano community, Carla Trujillo contends that Chicana lesbians are threatening, because they 'disrupt the established order of male dominance' and raise the awareness of Chicana women regarding issues of 'independence and control' (in Garcìa 1997: 281).

Aida Hurtado notes that 'the theoretical basis of Chicana feminisms is not consensus, but contentious confrontation', and argues that 'writers must be honest about how difficult it is to relate across differences' (1998: 149). In a postmodern world, Chicana feminists continue the project of developing a differential consciousness and praxis that can both manage and supersede the torsional forces of internal and external socio-political and cultural demands.

References and further reading

Anzaldúa, G. (ed.) (1990) *Making Face, Making Soul/ Haciendo Caras*, San Francisco: Aunt Lute Foundation Books.

Fregoso, R.L. (1993) *The Bronze Screen*, Minneapolis, MI: University of Minnesota Press.

García, A. (ed.) (1997) *Chicana Feminist Thought*, New York: Routledge.

Hurtado, A. (1998) 'Sitios y Lenguas', *Hypatia* Spring: 134–61.

Moraga, C. and Anzaldúa, G. (eds) (1983) *This Bridge Called My Back*, New York: Kitchen Table Press.

Sandoval, C. (1991) 'US Third World Feminism', *Genders* Spring: 1–24.

Segura, D. and Pesquera, B. (1992) 'Beyond Indifference and Antipathy', *Aztl.n* 19, 2: 69–92.

Trujillo, C. (ed.) (1998) *Living Chicana Theory*, Berkeley, CA: Third Woman Press.

Zavella, P. (1989) 'The Problematic Relationship of Feminism and Chicana Studies', *Women's Studies* 17: 25–36.

YOLANDA RETTER

childcare

Childcare, as it has been conceptualised within western feminist thought, focuses on issues surrounding the (mis)identification of women as mothers. As a site of theorising and political struggle, childcare is impacted by predominant assumptions regarding gender roles, on-going contestation concerning the appropriate relationships among the state, the market and the family, and the equality/difference debate within feminist thought and practice. Socialist feminists have observed that although bearing children is women's domain, their care is not an inherently female occupation. Thus, in the interests of realising sexual equality, individual men, the broader community and/or the state should acknowledge a social responsibility to children and commit substantial resources to their care. By contrast, some cultural feminists are concerned that a broader sharing of responsibility for the care of children will undermine an historic source of women's power. It might be argued that, in its realisation, the latter view bears an unintended resemblance to the conservative position on 'family values' in that it reifies women's primary identity as mothers.

The simultaneity of women's increased labour force participation and the launch of second-wave feminism thrust the issue of childcare into the forefront of women's political activism. For, regardless of one's views on whether or not child rearing *should* be a non-gendered task, it is widely recognised that caring for children has, in fact, been a woman's responsibility. Childcare centres had existed prior to feminism's second wave, notably during the world wars when women were drawn into the workforce in the service of the war effort. However, these facilities were rapidly dismantled as the soldiers returned. It was unthinkable that women would continue in the role of industrial worker while their husbands attended the children. Instead, the closure of childcare facilities ensured the rebalancing of the gender order to prewar social norms.

In the period of rapid industrial growth that followed the Second World War, the child-care needs of the middle class were supported by the family wage system. White male industrial workers were paid substantial wages that facilitated the support of a family by a single income. In the moral economy, this family form, already declared superior by the bourgeoisie of the industrial revolution, became the standard. The emerging disciplines of the social sciences underscored the benefits of the nuclear family arrangement for children and popular cultural forms reflected the happy family in which father knew best and mother made sure the kids were clean and respectful. For the poor who lacked access to high-wage industrial work, and for single parents, however, the necessity for work and, hence, for childcare was an ongoing concern. The children of people in these categories were cared for in noninstitutional settings, by friends and relatives.

Although the nuclear, sole-income family is a relatively recent invention, its grip on the collective imagination is vice-like. Even as the family wage system has broken down and two incomes have become a necessity for maintaining a family's standard of living, the moral superiority of the postwar, middle-class-family model has been sustained. Further, the gender division of labour regarding children's care has also been sustained, though the receipt of income for the care of children implies some acknowledgement of the social contribution represented by women's caring work.

In the Anglo-American democracies of the UK, USA, Australia, New Zealand and Canada, the liberal presumption of the sanctity of the home and the emphasis on market provision over state provision informs child care policy and delivery. This presumption has meant substantial institutional and social resistance to publicly funded childcare. The care of children, as opposed to their education, is viewed as the responsibility of their parents. If one parent cannot forego paid employment to care for the children, that care should be sought out in the market or through affective networks. In the case of market provision, the conflation of the profit imperative and the

presumption of the moral superiority of a mother's care is reflected in low wages for childcare and domestic workers and limited programmes and resources for children. Reliance on non-institutional child minders may also raise concerns regarding programmes and resources as well as accountability. It is not surprising then, that childcare advocates in these countries list affordability, accessibility, quality, safety and accountability as their primary demands.

Of course, some state provision of childcare is available within the Anglo-American democracies. Historically, this provision was conceived as aid to the poor, with subsidies available to the most destitute. To a considerable degree, this view is still operative, though the collision of the liberal promise of equality with women's demands for inclusion has forced policy makers to view the need for childcare as further reaching. The state's response has been two-fold. First, it has supported the establishment of non-profit, regulated childcare centres. These centres have a reputation for high quality care. However, demand for their services is greater than the supply. Second, the state has used fiscal mechanisms, including subsidies and tax credits, to offset the costs of childcare. In the case of tax credits, however, the necessity of an income sufficient to benefit from a tax credit and the requirement of receipts, implying institutional care, has limited the efficacy of these measures.

In contrast to the liberalism of the Anglo-American democracies, the social democratic governments of Scandinavia have viewed childcare provision as a social entitlement, as a feature of citizenship. Even in these countries, however, the presumption that children are best cared for by their mothers is reflected in generous and lengthy maternity leave provisions and regulations that ensure women continued access to good jobs despite irregular labour-force participation. Although fathers may also avail themselves of parental leave provision, the percentage of male participation is low. State run, institutional childcare is widely available and there are fewer moral strictures regarding the use of these services. Still, although a social responsibility for the care of children is acknowledged, childcare policies in Scandinavia do little to disrupt traditional gender roles.

Feminist theorists of women's citizenship have observed that, historically, women have laid claim to their citizenship status on the basis of motherhood, whereas men have laid claim on the basis of being workers. As the welfare state has undergone crisis and restructuring, women have redefined themselves as, and have been redefined as, workers. In this milieu, the necessity for adequate childcare has intensified, though the state, as yet, has been disinclined to address this pressing need. The issues of childcare and claims-making strategies thus remain at the forefront of feminist agendas.

See also: biological essentialism; economic restructuring; ethic of care; liberal feminism; political economy; public/private; reproduction; sex equity v. sexual equality; welfare; work, women and

References and further reading

Brennan, D. (1994) *The Politics of Australian Child Care: From Philanthropy to Feminism*, Cambridge: Cambridge University Press.

Bussemaker, J. (1998) 'Rationales of Care in Contemporary Welfare States: The Case of Child Care in the Netherlands', *Social Politics: International Studies in Gender, State and Society*, 5, 1: 70–96.

Ferguson, E. (1991) 'The Child-Care Crisis: Realities of Women's Caring', in C. Baines, P. Evans and S. Neysmith (eds) *Women's Caring: Feminist Perspectives on Social Welfare*, Toronto: McClelland and Stewart.

Leira, A. (1992) *Welfare States and Working Mothers: The Scandinavian Experience*, Cambridge: Cambridge University Press.

Mahon, R. (1997) 'Child Care in Canada and Sweden: Policy and Politics', *Social Politics: International Studies in Gender, State and Society*, 4, 3: 382–418.

Orloff, A. (1993) 'Gender and the Social Rights of Citizenship', *American Sociological Review*, 58, 3: 303–29.

Randall, V. (1996) 'Feminism and Child Day Care', *Journal of Social Policy* 25, 4: 485–506.

LOIS HARDER

child development

Child development refers to the psychological, social, physical, and moral development of infants, children, and adolescents. Feminist research has focused, especially in the USA, on the differential socialisation of boys and girls (see **Chodorow, Nancy**), girls' moral systems based on connections to other people more than on issues of individual rights and objective justice (see **Gilligan, Carol**), discrimination against girls in the classroom (e.g., AAUW report), and girls' eroding self esteem during early adolescence (e.g., Gilligan). Feminist approaches identify ways in which girls' development is directed, and even hindered, by society's masculine values and privileges.

Developmental work emphasises three areas: (1) gender differences, particularly in intellectual (e.g., mathematical and spatial reasoning) and social (e.g., prosocial behaviours) abilities, (2) the acquisition of **gender roles**, as defined for women and men by the culture, and (3) children's development of concepts of **gender**, male, and female, as part of their more general conceptual development. Recent additional topics related to gender include repressed (and later sometimes recovered) memories of sexual, or other physical, abuse during childhood, images of the body during adolescence (including **eating disorders**), and adolescent **sexuality**, particularly as it pertains to self **identity**.

Developmentalists address several issues: What are children like at various points in development? Is development gradual and continuous, or stage-like? What causes development (explanations of how interactions of innate/biological and learned/social environmental events cause development)? Since the mid-1970s, child development has been integrated into the study of 'lifespan development' from conception to death.

Developmentalists have focused on gender-as-a-variable – how gender influences development. However, feminist critiques raise fundamental issues that are important for constructing both an inclusive theory of child development and feminist theories that are not limited to adult women. First, the very definition of development is biased toward male values. For example, developmentalists focus on how children separate from their mothers rather than on how children develop a self-in-connection-with-others. Another example is Piaget's notion that the endpoint of development is an autonomous, distanced individual who thinks like a scientist. Second, developmentalists focus on white, middle-class children of Euro-American ancestry, and usually assume heterosexuality. In fact, gender interacts with other moulders of **experience** such as **race**, ethnicity, social class, nationality, and sexual orientation. Third, feminists question the very notion of development as necessarily progressive. What looks like improvement from the adult (especially male) perspective may include regression (or 'dedevelopment') in other ways, as when developing romantic relationships with boys may contribute to girls' 'loss of voice' (see **Gilligan, Carol**).

See also: adolescent women and feminism; childcare; development theory; moral development

References and further reading

Burman, E. (1994) *Deconstructing Developmental Psychology*, London: Routledge.

Miller, P.H. and Scholnik, E.K. (eds) (2000) *Toward a Feminist Developmental Psychology*, New York: Routledge.

PATRICIA H. MILLER

child labour, feminist critique of

This critique takes two forms; first, it highlights the role of children's work in supporting or working alongside women – thus, measures directed at supporting children run the risk of disadvantaging women, practically and economically; second, given normative presumptions of the gendered division of labour and **public/private** divide, girls' work – as generally more likely to be un- or low-paid, home-based, and correspondingly less valued – frequently remains unnoticed. Proposals to eradicate, or regulate, child labour thus need to address *intersections* between the social categories of age and **gender**, rather than treating these as separate, as they enter into the broader economy

and value of labour. While often seen as a 'Third World' issue, this is very much a global issue.

See also: girl child, the; sustainable development

References and further reading

Nieuwenhuys, O. (1996) 'The Paradox of Child Labour and Anthropology', *Annual Review of Anthropology* 24: 237–51.

ERICA BURMAN

child sexual abuse

The sexual abuse of children and youths has been described as a problem with an extensive past but a relatively short history. It has been said to exist in almost all societies at almost all times, but only recently has it been recognised as a particular social problem in western society. In the last quarter of the twentieth century, largely resulting from feminist efforts, the silence shrouding children's experiences of sexual abuse was lifted. Whereas children's allegations were once commonly dismissed as rich fantasy or acts of maliciousness, current-day discourse reflects more willingness to listen, believe, act and prevent. Though secrecy and denial of the very existence and pervasiveness of sexual abuse still prevail, considerable strides have been made in accepting children's disclosures and in protecting them. However, the direction such developments have taken calls for continuing feminist critical analysis.

A brief sketch of the major theoretical trends for understanding sexual abuse in contemporary times begins in the 1930s with the psychoanalytic focus on girls seducing their fathers. By the 1960s, the emphasis shifted to the dysfunctional family within which sexual abuses take place. This analysis represented a radical departure from the concentration on the child's pathology to a vision of sexual abuse as one of many socially deviant behaviour patterns operating in a pathological family. Thus clinicians, predominantly men, located the aetiology in the nature of the family system, and the roles and interactions of family members. Although all family members were assumed to have established and maintained the sexual abuse, mother was

considered to be the cornerstone in the dysfunctional family; it was she who apparently consciously
or unconsciously orchestrated and sanctioned the
abuse. Put differently, theoreticians and practitioners assumed that mother knew of the abuse, set
it up through her acts or omissions, colluded, or
failed to protect her children following disclosure.

In current-day lay and professional discourse,
child sexual abuse continues to be understood in
terms of dysfunctional family dynamics. This
analysis has achieved the status of common sense
(MacLeod and Saraga 1988). As Hooper (1992)
aptly put it, we have witnessed a move from the
surveillance of sexually abused girls in the early
part of the twentieth century to scrutiny of their
mothers in the latter part. Historically, then,
women and children have been centrally embroiled
in sexual abuses perpetrated almost exclusively by
men.

Feminists have made every effort to counter
prevailing dominant explanations of child sexual
abuse by locating the issue in the broader contexts
of the social construction of masculinity, male
sexuality, and violence against women and children. Drawing on gendered analyses of child sexual
abuse, wherein most victims are women and most
abusers are men, feminists have argued that the
issue represents an exaggeration rather than a
deviance from the norm of heterosexual relations.
The eroticisation of male dominance, the sexual
objectification of women, and cultural images of
the child as seductress illuminate the connection
between the actions of some sexually abusive men
and the desires of all too many other men (Glaser
and Frosh 1993).

Though feminists have achieved success in
gaining public recognition of and response to the
problem, including social service and criminal
justice involvement for the immediate protection
of victims, efforts to redefine child sexual abuse
from family dysfunction to the social construction
of masculinity, male sexuality and male dominance
have been painstakingly slow in mainstream theory
and practice. From a feminist perspective, the
repercussions of the family dysfunction analysis are
many.

For one, this analysis divorces child sexual abuse
from the social, cultural, and political conditions
that set its stage. Two, it establishes a false

dichotomy between intra- and extra-familial child
sexual abuse through an assumption that fathers do
not abuse children outside the family. Three, the
idea that sexual abuse is only a family matter
reproduces the notion of families as safe havens for
women and children. Finally, the pathological
family analysis places sexually abusive behaviour
in the context of marital and familial interactions
which shifts the focus from offender behaviour and
full responsibility to women's demeanour and
inadequacies as wives and mothers. Ultimately,
the offender's behaviour fades from the fore and is
replaced, instead, with a focus on the ways in
which women contribute to and maintain the
sexual abuse (Krane and Davies 1995).

It is this contradiction with which feminists have
recently taken issue. In contrast to earlier conceptions of women as blameworthy for having known
or suspected, colluded or failed to patrol the abuser
or protect the child, feminist investigations have
revealed enormous variety. Briefly, researchers
have discovered that: women's knowledge of the
abuse ranges from unaware to suspicious to aware;
some mothers have been defeated, victimised, and
themselves entrapped and thus are unable to
protect; and, with adequate material conditions
and individual problem-solving and coping skills,
many women are able to take effective protective
measures. Despite empirical evidence to challenge
the legacy of mother-blame, dominant theory and
practice remain unaltered.

Where do we go from here? Further feminist
attention is required to reconceptualise child sexual
abuse from an instance of dysfunctional family to
an issue that reflects the complex, insidious and
central problems of the social construction of
masculinity and gender relations. Such attention
cannot remain in the realm of theoretical debate
but must permeate everyday practice. It is here that
the blame of women as inadequate wives or
mothers, and the attribution of responsibility for
assuring the welfare of their children, prevail.
Feminist efforts to weave into practice in child
sexual abuse deconstructions of the most basic
gender-, class-, and race-bound assumptions held
about the institution of motherhood are wanting.
In the meantime, explorations into and advocacy
around the emotional, social, and material resources needed to assist women in their protective

efforts are essential. Ultimately, a reconstruction of the problem will give rise to a reexamination of our responses to child sexual abuse which no longer hold women exclusively responsible for the care, nurture, and protection of their children.

References and further reading

Glaser, D., and Frosh, S. (1993) *Child Sexual Abuse*, Toronto: University of Toronto Press, 2nd edn.

Hooper, C. (1992) *Mothers Surviving Child Sexual Abuse*, New York: Tavistock/Routledge.

Johnson, J.T. (1992). *Mothers of Incest Survivors: Another Side of the Story.* Bloomington, IN: Indiana University Press.

Krane, J., and Davies, L. (1995) 'Mother-Blame in Child Sexual Abuse: A Look at Dominant Culture, Writings, and Practices', *Textual Studies in Canada*, 7: 21–35.

MacLeod, M., and Saraga, E. (1988) 'Challenging the Orthodoxy: Towards a Feminist Theory and Practice', *Feminist Review*, 28: 16–55.

JULIA KRANE

chilly climate

'Chilly climate' is the combined result of practices – each of which may seem relatively inconsequential when taken alone – which cumulatively marginalise women/minorities. Much like the 'ton of feathers' syndrome, a chilly climate is produced by a variety of micro-inequities such as: denying the status and authority of women and minorities through sexist comments, anecdotes or 'jokes'; excluding or impairing access to information; evaluating male and female behaviour and experience differentially; and signalling lesser importance through words, behaviours, tone or gestures which indicate that women and/or minorities do not need to be taken seriously. Chilly climate is most often used in relation to post-secondary education, but is also common in discussions of workplaces and other institutions.

References and further reading

Hall, R. and Sandler, B. (1982) *The Classroom Climate: A Chilly One for Women*, Washington, DC: Project on the Status and Education of Women, Association of American Colleges.

SUSAN L. PRENTICE

Chodorow, Nancy (b. 1944)

Nancy Julia Chodorow's *The Reproduction of Mothering* (1978) shaped American feminist thinking about female and male psycho-sexual development and women's apparently natural desires to bear and raise children as contributors to women's oppression. Chodorow introduced object-relations theory to American feminists. The theory explains self-development in terms of relationships to particular, intimate others, analysing the pleasures and ambivalences such relationships generate.

Because a woman – the mother – is the first object an infant responds to in defining a separate self, women become the objects of infantile longing and ambivalence. Attributing differences in male/female gender identity to woman-dominated parenting, Chodorow maintains that a mother treats her daughters as extensions of herself, encouraging them to identify more deeply with her than her sons will. She encourages her sons to repudiate their primary identification with her to develop the rigid ego boundaries that enable them to enter the competitive male world, while encouraging her daughters to sustain connectedness, to develop an ego whose boundaries remain permeable, open to relationships.

Rigorous separation from the mother, Chodorow contends, generates a defensive **masculinity** marked by denial of connection, denigration of whatever is feminine or associated with the mother, and celebration of detached autonomous objectivity. Women's fluid ego boundaries foster imaginative, empathic engagement with others through strong connections such as few men can achieve. Yet the negative consequence is women's marginal position in the public world, together with their tentative efforts to maintain an autonomy that can resist absorption of the self into the needs of others. Because of women's preoccupations with mothering, public power has concentrated in the hands of men, sustaining a gendered social division between love and work, emotion and reason. Thus women's mothering is thoroughly ambivalent: it yields great satisfaction and love, yet it is a fundamental source of their secondary position in (patriarchal) society, and of men's ongoing fear of women.

Chodorow is criticised for drawing global conclusions from affluent white women's lives in heterosexual nuclear families, thus glossing over differences; yet her influence in American feminist theory cannot be ignored.

See also: autonomy; motherhood; patriarchy; psychoanalysis; public/private

Selected writings

Chodorow, N. (1978) *The Reproduction of Mothering: Psychoanalysis and the Sociology of Gender*, Berkeley, CA: University of California Press.
—— (1986) 'Toward a Relational Individualism: The Mediation of Self Through Psychoanalysis', in Heller, Sosna, and Wellbery (eds) *Reconstructing Individualism*, Stanford, CA: Stanford University Press.
—— (1989) *Feminism and Psychoanalytic Theory*, New Haven: Yale University Press.

LORRAINE CODE

choice, freedom of

The concept of freedom of choice is both an instrumental and an intrinsic good: instrumental in that it is an expression of the **power** to act in a certain way, namely to choose between one or multiple possibilities including the possibility to stay indifferent in relation to a particular phenomenon. It is also of intrinsic value as an important element in women's well-being and self-fulfilment. To make this concept more informative, we will have to break it up into the two separate notions of freedom and choice; further we will have to add specifications to the notion of freedom, such as freedom *from*, for instance, freedom from constraints and freedom *to*, freedom to choose.

The issue is the contradictory space between constraints such as **oppression** and desires such as freedom and **autonomy**. When we are constrained in one way or another, our wants are denied their satisfaction, which is a disempowering and frustrating experience. It is for this reason that we believe that freedom of choice or a certain amount of autonomy, which could be termed the absence or limitation of constraints and hence of frustration and unhappiness, is a desirable condition.

In modernity, gender oppression and the undisputed inequitable distribution of power for different social groups is defined by boundaries of **gender** and/or **race** and/or class and/or age. This concept, used in a postmodern sense which goes beyond modern definitions of equality and oppression, is invoked in recent writings on the issue of female freedom of choice and what this might mean. Feminists such as Brooks (1997), Taylor (1995) and Faludi (1992) suggest that we women should be much more aware of the various relationships of power and choice and acknowledge that gender is just one of our multiple identities (see **identity**). Postfeminism challenges the hegemonic assumption that patriarchal and imperialist oppression was and still is universally experienced oppression. Postmodern positions hold that this in turn may lead to a feminism capable of granting freedom of choice to local, fragmented, and at times paradoxical female identities. It may also offer greater possibilities of awareness that each person has various freedoms of choices at various times.

Underlying these philosophical differences is the continuing debate over what school of thought most accurately describes the implications and ramifications of women's freedom of choice.

References and further reading

Brooks, A. (1997) *Postfeminism: Feminism, Cultural Theory and Cultural Forms*, London: Routledge.
Faludi, S. (1992) *Backlash: The Undeclared War Against Women*, London: Chatto and Windus.
Taylor, S. (1995) 'Skinned Alive: Toward a Postmodern Pedagogy of the Body', in P. McLaren (ed.) *Postmodernism, Postcolonialism and Pedagogy*, Albert Park: James Nicholson, 101–20.

EVA DOBOZY

Christianity and feminism

Christianity is the dominant religious tradition of the western world, a primary cultural site for the development, transmission, and maintenance of gender ideology. Consequently, it has been the subject of considerable feminist scrutiny. However, the relationship between Christianity and feminism is not wholly negative. Instead, it is part of a complex history in which women have been conceived of in contradictory and ambivalent ways.

From the outset, there have been dual discourses about women in Christianity. There are two Genesis stories, one in which Adam and Eve are created together, and another version in which Eve is made out of Adam's rib. The letters of the apostle Paul are equally mixed: Galatians 3:28 states that 'In Christ there is neither male nor female' while Ephesians 5:21–24 clearly sets up a hierarchy within which women are subordinated. Some scholars believe that the teachings and behaviour of Jesus of Nazareth were more egalitarian towards women than was common in his culture, and evidence exists to suggest that women were active and in leadership positions in the primitive church. However as Christianity institutionalised, female leadership became identified with heresy. As early as the middle of the second century CE, a typological link is set up between the sinful, sexual Eve, whose lot women share, and the pure, chaste and obedient Virgin Mary, whom women are to emulate. Discourses about women were thereafter shaped in a context which views female sexuality as dangerous and female leadership as inherently sinful and unnatural. Women were thus given two options for redemption: subordination to their husbands in marriage, or 'transcending' their sex through celibacy, as 'brides of Christ' in the religious life.

In fact, becoming a nun gave women a number of advantages, including education, healthier living conditions, adequate food, freedom to travel, and a release from the dangers of endless childbearing. Some women gained considerable power as abbesses, ruling over 'double monasteries' of women and men, exercising the same powers and privileges as bishops and noblemen on church councils and in parliaments. Medieval women's mystical experience also carried cultural power,

allowing Catherine of Siena to virtually order Pope Gregory XI to return the papal see to Rome from Avignon. At the same time, the growing European witch craze threatened women outside monastic life, and the Protestant Reformation brought its mixed blessing of abolishing the distinction between ordinary layfolk and a celibate spiritual elite in favour of a norm of married life in which childbearing was women's only means to salvation.

The rise of romanticism in the early nineteenth century recast the hierarchical 'woman as deficient' gender ideology into a more complementary dualism in which characteristics traditionally associated with women, like emotion and intuition, were positively valued. A 'separate spheres' ideology emerged which argued that women's nature – with 'the true woman' normatively understood as white and middle-class or above – gave them a mandate for moral motherhood, properly exercised within the 'sacred precincts' of the home. Because religion was now understood to be grounded in emotion rather than reason, religion and morality were seen to be especially a 'woman's sphere'. This dramatic reversal of earlier cultural patterns set the stage for women eventually claiming moral authority to speak on a range of issues, on the ground that they have a divine mandate to do so.

Slavery was one such issue. Although clearly the doctrine of separate spheres privileges white women of a particular social status, the new cultural authority implied by the location of religion and morality in 'woman's sphere' was also seized by women of colour. Mariah Stewart's powerful essays and speeches against slavery in the 1830s are firmly grounded in a Christian religious vision of justice for 'Afric's sons and daughters' as well as whites. Quakers Sarah and Angelina Grimke protested slavery on the ground that God has placed equal moral obligations on all humanity, regardless of race and that women and slaves were equally being denied their full personhood as God's creatures. Christian faith has remained a powerful force within the black community in North America, providing a site of resistance and transformation of racist structures of oppression. Currently, **womanist theology** challenges both feminist and traditional theologies to engage their racism, while articulating a compelling vision of faith and justice for human community.

Where some women have used the cultural space offered by this new cultural gender script to argue for women's full and equal humanity with men, others, like contemporary cultural feminists, have emphasised the distinctiveness of the sexes (see **cultural feminism**). Seeing all women united by a common nature, many Euro-North American women felt an obligation to share the 'privilege' of western Christian civilisation with their less advantaged sisters through missionary activities. While missionary women clearly served imperial aims through their work, they also provided women in India, China and elsewhere with education and health care which was not otherwise available. Missionary women were able to travel and lead independent lives, and participation in missions, whether at home or abroad, provided many women with organisational skills which would later prove useful in a variety of reform activities, including suffrage and temperance. As today, women's inclusion in traditional cultural forms brings with it the danger of complicity in their strategies of domination.

Feminists began to challenge the depiction of woman as sinful Eve, a view which has persisted despite the new ideology of women's special nature. Elizabeth Cady Stanton's influential 1898 publication *The Woman's Bible* offers alternative interpretations of major segments of scripture, provided by Stanton and a 'revising committee' of female preachers and scholars. Matilda Joslyn Gage's 1983 text *Woman, Church and State* is even more critical of Christianity in its extensive analysis of the development of religion from its origins in a primitive woman-ruled society, or Matriarchate. Others like Katherine Bushnell (*God's Word to Women*) believed that scriptural texts were not denigrating to women, but their translation and interpretation by men were. For Christian feminists overall, obedience to God took precedence over obedience to male human beings, the teachings of tradition notwithstanding.

Although women were denied ordination within almost every Christian denomination in the nineteenth century, revivals and holiness movements provided women with the opportunity for charismatic religious leadership and preaching, an avenue which persisted well into the twentieth century with powerful evangelical leaders like Aime Semple McPherson. However, institutionalisation of women's religious leadership through ordination to the ministry or priesthood remains to be fully accomplished. While several (though not all) Protestant denominations ordain women, the Roman Catholic church, like the Eastern Orthodox, opposes women priests. Debate on this point played a significant role in the development of feminist theology in the 1960s and 1970s (see **theology, feminist**). However, whether or not official ministerial status is available to them, the numbers of women in theological schools have increased dramatically.

Dramatic changes are in the offing as Christianity enters the twenty-first century. Women's presence in theological education has brought with it debates about human sexuality, equality, and inclusiveness, including the intentional ordination of lesbian and gay people. The shift of the majority of the world's Christians from Europe and North America to the equatorial regions and hemisphere portends further challenges, though the impact of indigenising Christian tradition within those cultures is not yet clear. The global rise of fundamentalism raises yet other concerns, as women's social and political liberties, including rights to reproductive choice, may be sharply circumscribed under theocratic regimes.

As Christianity has taken on new cultural forms, new possibilities have arisen to negotiate the contradictions inherent in its double discourse on women. Despite the misogyny of much of traditional Christianity, historically women have been able to find resources within it to advance their personal and collective goals.

References and further reading

Clark, E. and Richardson, H. (1996) *Women and Religion: The Original Sourcebook of Women in Christian Thought*, San Francisco: HarperSanFrancisco, 2nd edn.

Lindley, S.H. (1996) *'You have Stept out of your Place': A History of Women and Religion in America* Louisville: Westminster John Knox.

RANDI R. WARNE

Christian feminist ethics

Christian feminist ethics affirms women's inclusion as self-directed agents in churches and Christian commitment to promoting opportunity wherever it is denied. Advocates argue that, lacking female input, traditional theology deems male experience normative, casting women as deviant, so that Christianity perpetrates mistreatment of women. Strategies for transformation have varied with place and time.

With roots in the US suffragist movement fifty years earlier, a theological movement criticising traditional Christian ethics arose in North American universities and seminaries in the 1970s. Mary Daly termed biblical morality 'phallic', demonstrating the effects of exclusion by addressing only female students' questions after lectures. Many challenged biblical images of a male God, God-like men, and submissive women. Theologians challenged as androcentric the equation of sin with pride, as arrogance was the luxury of the dominant sex while low self esteem was a greater problem for women.

Addressing the American Academy of Religion in 1984, Rosemary Radford Ruether called for a move from criticism to reconstruction of Christian sources. Elizabeth Schüssler-Fiorenza identifies early Christian egalitarianism and cites scriptural inconsistencies that require choosing a 'canon within the canon'. While suffragettes had emphasised Genesis 1:27–8 on the simultaneous creation of the sexes, the scriptural Archimedean point of this generation was often Galatians 3:28, affirming 'neither male nor female' in Christ. Elaine Pagels documents women's inclusion in rejected circles of early Christendom. Theologians Reuther, Sallie McFague, and Carter Heyward stress the earth and human bodies as ethical priorities. The pioneers of the 1970s and 1980s thereby advocate women's ordination; **Goddess** imagery; recognition of women's experience as theologically normative; shifting from individualistic to communal theological anthropologies; redefining sin to discourage female self-effacement; opposing class bias, racism, discrimination against gays and lesbians, ecological neglect, and tolerance of nuclear weapons; and prioritising praxis over theory.

Considerable activism ensued. Decades after female theologians had chained themselves to pulpits to demand ordination, Christian women marched for gay rights, physically blocked entrances to nuclear missile sites, and encircled trees scheduled for the chain-saw. Many formed 'women-churches' to realise their ideal community while established churches debated and sometimes rejected desired reforms. '**Womanist theology**' seeks cooperation across racial and national lines to promote women's rights.

The commitment to praxis has been consummately realised in less-developed nations, where Christian feminists have fought child prostitution in Southeast Asia; female genital mutilation in parts of Africa; and **bride/widow burning (suttee burial)** in India. These feminists have promoted inclusion of women in economic development via contraceptive education, literacy, and microlending. In the 1990s westerners increasingly joined these movements through international churches and NGOs. In the Academy, a new generation demands greater methodological coherence, challenging 'feminine identity' and 'woman's experience' as stable categories, and criticising claims to **objectivity**. The challenge remains to reform ethics in academe, where power is regularly reported in senior/junior faculty relations and professor/student dynamics.

See also: hermeneutics; religious studies

References and further reading

Heyward, C. (1989) *Touching Our Strength: The Erotic as Power and the Love of God*, San Francisco: Harper and Row.

McFague, S. (1993) *The Body of God: An Ecological Theology*, Philadelphia, PA: Fortress Press.

Schüssler-Fiorenza, E. (1984) *Bread Not Stone: The Challenge of Feminist Biblical Interpretation*, Boston: Beacon Press, p. 12.

SUSAN E. WENNEMYR

citizenship

Citizenship, as an idea within western political philosophy, emerged in the classical Greek period, where Aristotle considered citizenship to be based on the active participation of an individual in the *polis*. This definition refers not to individuals, as such, but rather to a male member of the community who owns property, and can therefore take on a leadership role. Recent notions of citizenship are more closely linked to the emergence of a modern ideal arising from the revolutionary politics of the eighteenth century. During this period the meaning of citizenship shifted to assume a set of universal ideals, including, freedom, equality and liberty. Various commentators on citizenship, such as Bryan Turner (1993), have suggested that modern citizenship is constitutive both of a set of practices, (i.e. cultural, economic and symbolic), and of a set of rights and obligations defined through legal, political and social parameters. The universal ideals that act as the foundation for the rights and obligations of citizenship are understood to be protected by the membership or 'contract' entered into between the individual citizen and the political society at large. However, citizenship in western liberal democracies is also typified as a process of inclusion and exclusion of membership and as sets of entitlements or social obligations within a political or social community. As the boundaries that mark inclusion and exclusion shift through historical periods and geopolitical locations, women have confronted the paradox between abstract universal claims of 'citizenship' versus the patriarchal limitations of citizenship practices (see **patriarchy**).

Indeed, since the birth of modern political rights marked by the universal 'Declaration of the Rights of Man and The Citizen', women have struggled for full and equal political and social recognition. However, as various feminist theorists and activists have illustrated, this seemingly metaphorical relationship between Man and Citizen is actually both real and concrete in the daily practices of political and social life (Scott 1996). Throughout the development of western liberal democratic theory, the citizen has been based on the unambiguous and reified idea that individuality could only be represented by men. Hence, the abstract centrality of the male universal figure has produced concepts of citizenship where women have been denied basic political rights because of an existing patriarchal hierarchy within society.

The denial of basic citizenship rights has been central to the formation and perpetuation of women fighting for full and equal recognition in society. Generations of feminist interlocutors, from the first wave of suffragettes, who fought for full and equal citizenship rights, to contemporary engagements of identity politics, have confronted the paradox that the concept of universality, based on a male subject, has presented to them.

See also: liberal feminism; political theory; public/private

References and further reading

Lister, R. (ed.) (1997) *Citizenship: Feminist Perspectives*, New York: New York University Press.
Scott, J.W. (1996) *Only Paradoxes to Offer French Feminists and the Rights of Man*, Cambridge, MA: Harvard University Press.
Turner, B. (ed.) (1993) *Citizenship and Social Theory*, London: Sage Publications.
Young, I.M. (1990) *Justice and the Politics of Difference*, Princeton, NJ: Princeton University Press.

DAVINA BHANDAR

civil rights

While **human rights** are rights that each person has simply by virtue of being human, civil rights are those each person has by virtue of being a citizen. Civil rights are granted by a state to its citizens and are often articulated in constitutions or legislation. However, such guarantees of full **citizenship** have been and continue to be violated in practice. Thus, civil rights have come to be associated with the movements of various disenfranchised groups within particular societies to obtain the rights specified in a country's constitution but denied to some of its citizens on the basis of factors such as race, gender, and sexual orientation. Civil rights movements ground their justification for protest in claims that such discriminatory practices violate basic human rights. These claims grounded the movement that began in the 1960s to secure civil rights for African Americans just as they ground the anti-apartheid movement to secure civil rights for black Africans in South Africa. Civil rights have come to be associated with the civil rights movement in the USA and with the political rights and civil liberties enshrined in the American Constitution and Bill of Rights, but civil rights and the movements to secure them can also be conceived more broadly.

The United Nations Universal Declaration of Human Rights is generally interpreted as articulating a set of **international human rights**. It enumerates civil and political rights as well as economic, social, and cultural rights. Civil rights tend to be closely aligned with particular liberties valued in western liberal societies. Freedom to own property, freedom of thought and religion, freedom of opinion and expression, and freedom of peaceful assembly and association are examples. That political rights advance equality is evident in such political rights as equal recognition before the law and equal protection against racial, ethnic, sexual, or religious discrimination. Civil and political rights are often referred to as negative rights because they flow from the notion that the state should not interfere in the lives of its citizens. Economic, social, and cultural rights are examples of positive rights and those who defend them endorse state interference to ensure that basic human needs such as food and shelter are provided. Examples of positive rights in the UN Declaration include the right to work; the right to equal pay for equal work; the right to education; and the right to a standard of living adequate for health and well-being. The two sorts of rights are further differentiated and elucidated in two major UN treaties: the International Covenant on Civil and Political Rights and the International Covenant on Economic, Social, and Cultural Rights. The distinction between these rights is also reflected in the debate between conservative liberals in the west who defend the primacy of civil and political rights and non-westerners and those on the left who argue that civil and political rights have meaning for all citizens only when economic and social rights are secured. Social movements in different parts of the world that have come into being demanding civil and political rights are often transformed by the discovery that more than the elimination of legal and formal barriers is needed to achieve equality. This transformation is reflected in the American civil

rights movement and women's movements more generally.

The civil rights movement developed in the late 1950s as a campaign for the legal enforcement of rights guaranteed to American blacks as citizens under the US constitution. Its goal was integration – the inclusion of blacks in American institutions. Its tactics included boycotts, sit-ins, and marches to protest against racial separation in places such as schools, public transportation, parks, and restaurants. Even under great provocation, the movement tried to adhere to the principles of civil disobedience and non-violence espoused by its leader, Dr Martin Luther King Jr. The movement achieved successes such as the Civil Rights Act of 1964 and the Voting Rights Act of 1965, but became increasingly disunited by the mid-1960s with the growth of more militant black power organisations. These groups took the strategies of integration in securing civil and political rights to be insufficient for removing inequalities in wealth, for example, and they emphasised the importance of economic, social, and cultural rights. These new goals reflected a growing critique of capitalism and fed into other movements that surfaced in the 1960s including anti-war protests as well as the organised protests of other racial/ethnic minorities and of the women's movement in the late 1960s.

While the women's movement emulated the civil rights movement in some respects, the two struggles were not united. Black women tended to view the women's movement as working to improve conditions for white middle-class women and argued that sensitivity to issues of race and class was lacking. Only later were African American women openly critical of the male chauvinism encountered in the civil rights and black power movements (see **chauvinism, male**). One of the important contributions of black feminism is the analysis it has provided of the intersections of race, gender, and class (see **black feminism(s)**).

Feminists have become increasingly critical of the strategy of integration, that women ought to strive for what men have by way of rights. They have also provided valuable critiques of the ways in which the very language and concept of rights reflects male experience and norms. Such critiques need not be viewed as a rejection of rights; rather they call for reconceiving rights by taking account of the social and political contexts within which various rights get their meaning. Such reconceptions challenge prevalent ideas about rights as fixed and universal, including the idea that civil and political rights are about acquiring liberties and achieving equal participation in a public sphere. The Argentine Mothers of the Plaza de Mayo, protesting the disappearance of children during the military junta of 1976–83, comprise one example of women working to expand the conception of civil and political rights.

References and further reading

Blumberg, R. (1991) *Civil Rights: The 1960s Freedom Struggle*, New York: Twayne Publishers.

Bouvard, M. (1996)*Women Reshaping Human Rights*, Wilmington: SR Books.

CHRISTINE KOGGEL

Cixous, Hélène (b. 1937)

Known as one of the leading exponents of '**French feminism**' in the 1970s, Hélène Cixous deeply influenced feminist theory through her concept of *écriture féminine* and her passionate critique of **phallogocentrism**. A contemporary of poststructuralist theorists who posited the inseparability of social and linguistic structures, Cixous sought to transform patriarchal social structure by exiting from phallocentric structures of language (see **posstructuralism/postmodernism**; **patriarchy**).

In *La Jeune Née* (*The Newly Born Woman*), she defines phallogocentrism with reference to the paternal law organizsng thought according to hierarchical, bi-polar oppositions (see **binaries/bipolarity**). For her, the most crucial of these are man/woman, masculine/feminine, active/passive, Father/Mother, **nature/culture**, reason/emotion, Logos/Pathos, original/derived, primary/secondary, centre/margin. A metaphoric chain connects these dualities, identifying man with activity, the Logos, the origin, and the centre. According to Cixous, every western philosophy identifies woman with passivity and casts her aside as secondary and marginal. As master signifier of this linguistic system, the paternal phallus centres language around the Logos. This latter, as operative principle of the system, makes its gendered hierarchical dualisms appear natural, necessary, essential and unchangeable. Thus, for Cixous **logocentrism** is by necessity also phallocentrism.

In *The Newly Born Woman*, as well as in her 1975 essay 'The Laugh of the Medusa' ('Le Rire de la Méduse'), Cixous engages in a critical dialogue with the psychoanalytic theories of Jacques Lacan (see **psychoanalyis**; **psychoanalytic feminist literary theory**). She attacks the law that makes woman represent the lack brought about by symbolic castration. Influenced by Jacques Derrida and his philosophy of deconstruction, Cixous proposes a practice of writing – *écriture féminine* – that dismantles the essentialised dualisms and destabilises the meanings of their terms. Through a poetic language that makes the meanings of words undccidable, *écriture féminine* performs *différance*, making the reader feel the bi-sexual, erotic drives of the feminine body and the relation to the repressed mother through the rhythms and ambiguities of the text (see **bisexuality**).

Cixous practices this writing in her many poetic publications. She has also published critical works on James Joyce and Clarice Lispector, as well as several plays. Born in Algeria of multi-ethnic Jewish parents, Cixous is Professor of English Literature at the University of Paris VIII, and founding Director of the *Centre de recherches en études féminines*.

Selected writings

Cixous, H. and Clément, C. (1975) *La Jeune Née*, Paris: Union Générale des Éditions; trans. Betsy Wing as *The Newly Born Woman*, Minneapolis, MI: University of Minnesota Press, 1986.

—— (1976) 'The Laugh of the Medusa', trans. K. Cohen and P. Cohen. *Signs* I (Summer): 875–99.

LESLIE W. RABINE

class analysis, UK

Questions of class have been important for feminist theory in the United Kingdom in three ways: in attempts to analyse women's class locations; in terms of the relationship between class and gender inequalities; and in respect of class differences between women. The links between class and gender present complex problems for feminist theory, and have shaped women's political interests in contradictory and potentially divisive ways.

Class analysis within the UK has been heavily influenced by Marxist thought (see **Marxism**). In Marxist terms, an individual's class is determined by their relationship to the means of production. Such a model is based on the male bourgeois or worker; women's class positions are given by their relation to men within the family. This perspective has also been common in non-Marxist approaches to class, which have taken the (usually male) head of household's occupational class as representative of their family's class as a whole. This practice obscures the fact that working women can occupy different occupational classes from their male partners, and in a larger sense assumes a patriarchal family structure where men provide for and represent the interests of women and children (see **patriarchy**).

Both Marxist and mainstream perspectives have difficulty accounting for women's distinctive patterns of work (see **work, women and**). Since the early nineteenth century, women have tended to work outside the sphere of industrial production with which Marxist theory has been chiefly concerned – in services, trade and agriculture; in 'intermediate' class positions as shopkeepers, craftswomen, teachers or governesses; or as domestic servants within the 'private' space of the home. At the same time, much of women's working-time is expended on unpaid domestic labour and care within the family (see also **Oakley, Ann**).

Some feminist theorists and sociologists have suggested that women constitute a distinct social class. In the 1970s, materialist feminists brought together a radical feminist view of sex-class with an analysis of social class, arguing that marriage formed a 'labour contract' between men and women (see **radical feminism**). Women's **oppression** in this sense was organised around a patriarchal mode of exploitation and domestic modes of production (see Barrett 1988; and **production, modes of**). Similarly, some sociologists saw women's occupational roles – particularly as full-time housewives – as configuring a separate social class.

Such an account does not fit with increased labour force participation by women, nor address the complexity of women's dual role (or **double burden**) in waged labour and domestic labour. Other sociological accounts have examined how class and gender inequalities are interrelated, and how gender discrimination shapes labour markets. Pay disparities, for example, have tended to be greater between men and women at the lower end of the occupational scale, while protective legislation covering women's work, and a male-dominated labour movement, have historically divided the rights and conditions of male and female workers.

Social and occupational changes after the mid-twentieth century saw increasing levels of female employment, particularly with the entrance of middle-class women into the labour force. The 'feminisation' of the UK workforce has constituted a key challenge to conventional forms of class analysis, given the concentration of women's work in services, clerical work, and the public sectors of health, education and welfare. In this sense, women's employment patterns are central to a shift away from industrial production and towards service industries in the UK economy after the 1960s, and to attempts to reconstruct theories of class around these new occupational structures.

Women's complex relationships to work and class have had important implications for questions of political agency. Apart from establishing divisions within the labour movement between male and female workers, women's differing class locations have presented problems for feminist politics. In nineteenth-century Britain, the fact that certain women were isolated in middle-class homes in which they had no productive function and where servants performed the domestic labour, while many others worked for a wage, meant that bourgeois and working women lacked common political interests. Bourgeois women's struggles tended to centre on issues of political and **civil rights**, concerning the vote, property, education, divorce, custody of children, and contraception. Working women meanwhile struggled for a shorter working day, better pay and working conditions, and trade union rights.

The gradual winning of legal equality, together with bourgeois women's entrance into the workforce over the twentieth century, has produced a changing set of issues for feminists in the UK. Different kinds of division have emerged between, for example, campaigns to enhance women's access to the professions or for the involvement of greater numbers of women within government, and those which focus on women's poverty, such as the fight for a minimum wage. Neoliberal programmes to cut back welfare spending after 1979 clearly mark out the interests of women who are dependent on state benefits – such as single mothers, pensioners, carers and unemployed women – from those of women in paid employment or whose partners are in paid employment.

Class has been crucial to the manner in which issues of **difference** have entered feminist theory in the UK, marking divisions both between women's experiences, and between feminist political priorities. In this context Ramazanoglu (1989) argues for the relevance of a concept of contradiction to the analysis of women's class positions. Women have variable and sometimes conflicting standpoints in relation to logics of class and gender that run across the boundaries of work and family. Perhaps most critically, feminist perspectives on class highlight the issue of some women's power and privilege in respect of others, putting into question the notion that women's shared interests take primacy over the differences between them.

See also: bourgeois capitalism; domesticity, cult of; industrialisation; public/private; socialism and feminism

References and further reading

Barrett, M. (1988) *Women's Oppression Today: The Marxist/Feminist Encounter*, London: Verso.
Crompton, R. and Mann, M. (eds) (1986) *Gender and Stratification*, Cambridge, MA: Polity Press.
Ramazanoglu, C. (1989) *Feminism and the Contradictions of Oppression*, London: Routledge.

FRAN TONKISS

class analysis, US

In Marxist theory, class is a central concept in identifying systems of **oppression** and in providing the way to overthrow such systems (see **Marxism**). Social change in the USA is largely viewed as change within the existing system rather than revolutionary change. Mainstream second-wave feminism is largely **liberal feminism**, concerned with improving women's status in society, rather than with *transforming* society. The American cultural preoccupation with individualism, meritocracy, and anti-Communism has made Marxist analyses of *classes* of people less common than in Europe.

Most Americans perceive themselves to live in a classless society where everyone except the homeless and millionaires are 'middle class'. This perception presents a challenge to feminists who try to explain the relationship of social class to women's subordinate position in society. Using Marxist theory as a starting point, feminist theorists first focused on the origins and reproduction of sexual inequality in capitalist society and/or its relationship to **patriarchy**.

In the 1980s and early 1990s poststructuralist and postmodern theorists began to look beyond Marx to see class as a cultural and symbolic construction that reproduces itself in the emerging symbolic economy, though some tried to show that discourse and symbolism also had economic origins and consequences (see **poststructuralism/ postmodernism**). Class became less central in this type of work.

Feminists of colour and lesbian feminists have looked at how class intersects with **race**, **gender**, and **sexuality** to construct knowledge and social life. At the end of the 1990s, class was one of several variables that intertwined in a complex system of interrelationships, and theorists moved away from 'grand theory' in favour of specific substantive analyses (see **black feminism(s)**; **Asian feminism**; **lesbian feminism**).

Second-wave feminists were influenced by Marxist theories of class conflict that posit two classes: the owning class (bourgeois) and the workers' class (proletariat). The classes have different economic interests, and the struggle between them eventually leads to revolution and social equality. Kate **Millet**'s *Sexual Politics* (1970) suggests that the concept of class does not make sense for feminism because it pits women of different classes against one another. In addition, women are not identified explicitly within Marxist theory as having a 'class position' except through association with their husbands.

In 1974, Karen Sacks reinterpreted Engels to characterise women's domestic exploitation as part of the economy. Heidi Hartmann (1976) tried to reinterpret traditional Marxism to include women. Marxist and socialist feminists like Christine Delphy theorised women as a 'sex class', gendered by society into inferior social positions (see **socialism and feminism**).

Class is central to theories that see sexism as a result of capitalism; gender is central to theories that see capitalism and sexism as the result of **patriarchy**. Unable to find a way out of the conundrum of which came first, theorists stopped asking where sexism came from and started asking how it was being reproduced (see **heterosexism, heteronormativity**). Nancy **Hartsock**, Michelle Rosaldo, Nancy Sokoloff, and Sylvia Walby began to look at the **public/private** split, dual labour markets, and male gatekeeping as mechanisms that reproduce both patriarchy and capitalism through complex social mechanisms.

Feminists of colour have insisted that sexism cannot be understood apart from racism and classism. In 1981, bell **hooks** published *Ain't I a Woman?*, challenging white middle-class feminists to include class and race in their analyses of gender inequality. Women of colour are oppressed simultaneously under three interlocking systems of oppression: race, class, and gender. Ending sexism or eliminating social class inequality will not necessarily end racism (see Collins 1991).

Standpoint theories gained popularity in the 1980s and 1990s, allowing researchers to look at how social class intersected with other inequalities like gender, race, and sexuality (see **standpoint theory**). Chicana and other feminists of colour continued to theorise about their class, gender, and racial position using fragmentation as a metaphor for the complicated borderland between identities that women of colour inhabited (see Andalzúa 1987.) See also **Chicana feminism**.)

Lesbian feminists point out that heterosexism and sexuality must also be a part of a theory of women's oppression. *Out of the Class Closet* (Penelope (ed.) 1994) is an important work linking lesbian feminism and class experience in the USA. Sexuality became another factor in multiple and overlapping systems of status, **privilege**, and access to resources that define women's relative positions in a hierarchy of privilege.

Theoretical interest in identity construction and subjectivities, rather than class analysis, drives examinations of how gender, class, race, and sexuality are socially constructed and continually negotiated. The 1992 collection *Feminists Theorize the Political*, edited by Butler and Scott, covers such postmodern concerns as the importance of discourse in constructing social class inequality.

As postmodern theorists moved away from class and towards identity as a way of talking about women's experience in the early 1990s, bridge works appeared that attempt to re-establish the materialist basis for postmodern **social constructionism** (e.g. Hennessey 1993). Postmodern **discourse analysis** in its strong form tends to elide class as an analytical category in favour of cultural and symbolic forces of diffuse and hegemonic power (see **hegemony**; **power**).

By the end of the 1990s, grand theories like Marxism largely had been abandoned in favour of using class as one of several variables that intertwine to produce a woman's experience in society's institutions. The focus on difference rather than commonality is reinforced by multiculturalism in feminist theory and by individualism in American culture. Class, rather than being the origin category in the reproduction of social inequality, and target for feminist action, had become one of an array of variables.

References and further reading

Anzaldúa, G. (1987) *Borderlands/La Frontera: The New Mestiza*, San Francisco: Spinsters/Aunt Lute.

Butler, J. and Scott, J.W. (eds) (1992) *Feminists Theorize the Political*, New York and London: Routledge.

Collins, P.H. (1991) *Black Feminist Thought: Knowledge,*

Consciousness, and the Politics of Empowerment, New York and London: Routledge.

Hartmann, H. (1981) 'The Unhappy Marriage of Marxism and Feminism', in P. Sargent (ed.) *Women and Revolution*, Boston, MA: South End Press.

Hennessy, R. (1993) *Materialist Feminism and the Politics of Discourse*, New York and London: Routledge.

Millet, K. (1970) *Sexual Politics*, New York: Doubleday.

Penelope, J. (ed.) (1994) *Out of the Class Closet: Lesbians Speak*, Freedom, CA: Crossing Press.

CHELSEA STARR

classics, feminism and the

'Classics' is an area study, delimited by Greek and Latin languages and cultures from before 1700 BCE to about 500 CE, but covering law, philosophy, religion, art, archaeology, history, and literature, and the skills needed to access them (reading manuscripts, inscriptions, papyri, coins, and material remains in general); unsurprisingly, empiricist in its assumptions. Graduate training in Classics thus has excluded critical theory, which, like feminist professors, in the late 1990s was still available in only a few programmes: a problem for the spread of feminism in Classics.

Feminist classicists therefore find themselves caught between a historically male and conservative field and an increasingly presentist feminism. Work began in the 1970s, as did feminist history and literary theory generally, with attempts to recover women's lived reality alongside analysis of images of women in literature – work carried from the outset by the journals *Helios* and *Arethusa* (see **history, feminist**; **literary theory, feminist**). Lack of sources by women produced intensive thought on how to write the history of muted groups and on sex and gender as cultural systems; the value of a transhistorical perspective for understanding histories of women, sexuality, and the body was taken as axiomatic. The all-male classical landscape was transformed by research on women and the ancient world (see **ancient world, women and**); the literary canon was

shaken as the shortage of ancient women writers pushed feminists to analyse texts as an element in ideological constructions of gender, to privilege previously obscure texts, and to deprivilege texts altogether. The search for slave and colonised women, for gender subcultures, and for race/gender intersections (led by Shelley Haley) challenged old top-down and centripetal models. Theoretical reflection in the mid-1980s, led by Phyllis Culham, Judith Hallett, and Marilyn Skinner, demystified the subject position of the researcher and problematised the idea of 'Classics'.

Work in the 1990s was characterised by efforts to reach out to a general feminist/theory audience, complicated by conflicts between feminists and Foucauldians, by a decline of interest in premodern times, and by postmodernist distrust of transhistorical theoretical models. Meanwhile, the 1990s saw outbreaks of feminism in art history, after pioneering work by Natalie Boymel Kampen and Eva Keuls in the 1980s; and in archaeology (see S. Brown in Rabinowitz and Richlin 1993). Feminism in Classics overlaps with the membership of the Women's Classical Caucus, a group formed in North America in 1972 to change both the content of Classics and the rules governing the profession (see McManus 1997: 35–45).

References and further reading

McManus, B.F. (1997) *Classics and Feminism: Gendering the Classics*, New York: Twayne Publishers.

Rabinowitz, N.S., and Richlin, A. (eds) (1993) *Feminist Theory and the Classics*, New York: Routledge.

AMY RICHLIN

Code, Lorraine

Lorraine Code's work in epistemology has been at the forefront of feminist critiques of prevailing assumptions concerning the **objectivity**, **impartiality** and universality of knowledge in mainstream Anglo-American philosophy. Her focus on questions concerning the everyday lives and practices of knowledge claimants – their motivations and aspirations, their socio-political standing and ideological biases – has highlighted the ways in which knowledge claims are inevitably inflected by the subjective, partial and local practices in which they are confirmed and refuted. Code's work also shows how knowledge-making practices are collective endeavours, and centrally involve knowing and responding appropriately to other people. As a result, knowledge is a matter of ethics as well as epistemology (see also **fact/value dictinction**).

Institutionalised disciplines producing knowledge under the auspices of mainstream epistemology and philosophy are marred by their failure to take account of the influence of socio-political relations on the internal cognitive capacities of knowers, and on the external authority and legitimacy accorded to their products. Standard and easy cases of knowledge, for example, knowledge of cups on tables and cats on mats – what Code calls knowledge of medium-sized material objects – for which there is relative unity of cognitive perspectives, give rise to mistaken ideals of objectivity, value-neutrality and rational **autonomy**. In the perplexing but pervasive hard cases for which no such unity obtains – for example, determining the credibility of expertise and testimony – these ideals are called up by socially dominant institutions in ways that mask the specificity and contestedness of the perspectives promoted in their names.

Attention to hard cases, Code argues, brings to light the intrinsically collective nature of knowledge-making practices, and the important and exemplary role that knowing other people plays within these practices. Such a focus foregrounds the inherent contingency, subjectivity and tentativeness of knowledge while maintaining its cogency. Once these dimensions are acknowledged a key task for epistemology is to understand the mutually implicative and complexly interwoven relations that connect flesh-and-blood, engaged and socially-formed knowers with each other, the knowledge they produce, and the socio-political and natural environments in which they participate. Code is currently exploring the insights of ecological thinking for this project.

See also: androcentricism; dispassionate investigation; empiricism; epistemology, feminist

Selected writings

Code, L. (1991) *What Can She Know? Feminist Theory and the Construction of Knowledge*, Ithaca, NY: Cornell University Press.
—— (1995) *Rhetorical Spaces: Essays on (Gendered) Locations*, New York: Routledge.
—— (1996) 'What is Natural About Epistemology Naturalized?', *American Philosophical Quarterly*, 33, 1: 1–22.

PETA BOWDEN

collaboration/collaborative research

A recurrent theme in feminist scholarship refers either to projects that are jointly pursued by two or more scholars or to strategies that actively engage research participants in designing, implementing, and evaluating research about their lives. Collaboration encourages shared decision-making, prizes cooperative initiatives, strives for egalitarian interactions, values multiple perspectives, and attempts to mediate power imbalances between the researcher and the researched. It extends from a conviction that feminist research for and about women is most effectively accomplished when women join forces with each other to form communal rather than hierarchical models for scholarship.

See also: egalitarianism; hierarchical models of decision making; qualitative research

References and further reading

Reinharz, S. (1992) *Feminist Methods in Social Research*, New York: Oxford University Press.

KATHERINE RHOADES

collaborative learning

Collaborative learning is a pedagogy emphasising the social context of classrooms as a site for constructing knowledge. Power is more evenly distributed between teacher and students based on the assumption that knowledge is a consensual process conducted in a learners' or peer community. Although this approach is not often identified as a specifically feminist classroom practice, feminist pedagogical concerns with **power**, authority, voice, positionality and dialogue (Maher and Tetreault 1994; Tarule 1996) align with and advance theory about collaborative learning practice. The reverse is not the case: non-feminist theorists do not integrate these new ideas into their work.

See also: pedagogy, feminist; positioning/ positionality

References and further reading

Maher, F. and Tetreault, M. (1994) *Inside Feminist Classrooms*, New York, Basic Books.
Tarule, J.M. (1996) 'Voices in Dialogue', in N. Goldberger, J.M. Tarule, B. Clinchy, and M. Belenky (eds) *Knowledge, Difference, and Power*, New York: Basic Books.

JILL MATTUCK TARULE

collectivity as action, as process

The formation of feminist small groups, or collectives in the 1960s, was a reaction against the over-structured, hierarchical organisation of society in general and of male-dominated leftist groups in particular. Building a movement on a foundation of small collectives was intended to create a revolutionary culture consistent with a feminist new society. For radical feminists, *what* feminists wanted to achieve was inextricably bound up with *how* feminists organised (see **radical feminism**). In their view, hierarchical structures of group organising and decision making could not lead to the formation of an egalitarian and participatory society. What was needed was the creation of an alternative participatory mass movement organised around loose affinity groups. Large bureaucratised organisations, such as the National Organization of Women (NOW), were seen as reproducing inequality and elitism through a hierarchical power structure which relied on conservative rules for meeting procedures and the election of office bearers. For radical feminists such as Ti-Grace Atkinson, who resigned from NOW in

1968, such structures were perpetuating the oppression of women. In contrast, building feminist organisational structures such as collectives would ensure that there was no build-up of power by an elite. Tasks would be rotated, there would be no leaders, no hierarchy and no committees. Each woman would participate equally in decision making and attention would be paid not only to achieving the aims of the group but also to how decisions were made and to group processes. Essentially, the power of cooperation and mutual trust would effect social and personal change. Fundamental to this process was **consciousness raising**. Some collectives were open to all, including men, while others were closed to new members in order to achieve continuity and trust.

Collectives as structure and collectivity as a method of organising were considered to be morally superior to 'male' hierarchical organisational structures. However critics maintain that the emphasis on process politics led to the internal workings of the group taking precedence over achieving objectives. Jo Freeman, in her influential 1970 essay 'The Tyranny of Structurelessness', maintains that the suspicion of structure leads to the formation of collectives as informal groups where, contrary to the theory of collectivity, friendship groups and networks ensure that some women remain disenfranchised. In her view unstructured collectives are only useful as consciousness-raising groups not as the basic unit of feminist political organisation.

While there has been a marked shift away from collectivity since the mid 1980s, the idea that organisational structures are not politically neutral is still salient.

References and further reading

Freeman, J. (1984) 'The Tyranny of Structurelessness' in *Untying the Knot*, London: Dark Star.

KAZ ROSS

Collins, Patricia Hill (b. 1948)

With the publication of *Black Feminist Thought: Knowledge, Consciousness, and the Politics of Empowerment*

(Routledge, 1990) Patricia Hill Collins emerged as the leading theorist of black feminism in the USA. Since its publication, *Black Feminist Thought* has become possibly the most significant theoretical work on black feminism to date. A sociologist by training, Patricia Hill Collins fundamentally challenges and retheorises sociological knowledge by placing black women at the centre of the discipline. Indeed, many of the ideas developed in *Black Feminist Thought* were prefigured in a 1986 *Social Problems* article titled, 'Learning from the Outsider Within: The Sociological Significance of Black Feminist Thought'. Three key themes are explored in this piece: 1) black women's self-definition and self valuation; 2) the interlocking nature of oppressions; and 3) the importance of African American women's culture. These ideas are explored in the context of a sociology that historically had rendered black women invisible, except as problem or pathology. Collins compellingly argues for a transformed sociology deeply informed by black women's knowing.

Nevertheless, it is *Black Feminist Thought* which excites the feminist imagination. In that work she asks a foundational question, 'What is black feminism?' There is no essentialised answer to this, but it does open the door for interrogating the knowledge production of African American women. The idea that black women create knowledge is a heretical notion in western thought. The idea of black women's knowledge creation, grounded in black women's lived experiences, is the central contention of *Black Feminist Thought*. That black women have created an independent, yet subjugated, self-defined standpoint rooted in experience is its fundamental premise.

Patricia Hill Collins has also co-edited with Margaret Anderson *Race, Class, and Gender: An Anthology*. A second book, *Fighting Words: Black Women and the Search for Justice* was published in 1998. In that work Collins moves somewhat beyond the themes of black feminist thought, looking at the politics behind black women's representation. How black women are constructed in the public eye is not accidental, asserts Collins. Indeed, there is a politics of containment afoot, and breaking silence, giving voice, around black women's invisibility may not be enough. The crucial question is whether a 'fighting words'

stance is enough. The answer, of course, is probably not, especially if disconnected from the everyday struggles of black people. Possibility lies here with a black feminism deployed in a way that connects it to the African American struggle for freedom, argues Collins.

ROSE M. BREWER

Combahee River Collective

In 1977, intent on establishing black women's presence in contemporary feminist movements, the Combahee River Collective articulated specifically black feminist issues and politics in 'A Black Feminist Statement'. Collective members affirmed the simultaneity and intersectionality of racism, sexism, heterosexism and class exploitation as systems of domination in black women's lives. Begun as the Boston chapter of the National Black Feminist Organization in 1974, the Collective represented one of the first successful second-wave feminist mobilisations of black women. Though the organisation existed for only six years, the Combahee River Collective was critical to the growth of black feminist theory and black women's studies in academia and to reshaping feminist discourse in the USA.

Veterans of the Civil Rights, Black Power and Women's Liberation movements, Collective members asserted that singular issue movements for the eradication of either racial or gender oppression had forced them to define themselves and their concerns in ways that fractured black women's identities, experiences and spirits.

In Civil Rights and the more stridently androcentric Black Power movement, black activists besieged by white resistance and violence accused the black women who voiced concerns about sexism of detracting attention from the primary goal of racial equality.

In the feminist movement, black women became frustrated with the position of white liberal and cultural feminists that sexism constituted the dominant oppressive force in women's lives. Even socialist feminists did not undertake a racial analysis. Generally, white feminists did not have a critical understanding of racism, particularly their own. At best, they treated racism as a lesser analogue of sexism or a form of class oppression. At worst, they did not consider the impact of race in women's lives at all.

Because Collective members reasoned that the most profound and radical politics came directly out of their own identities, they used their experiences as black, female, mostly poor, lesbian and heterosexual to forge an identity politics which addressed their own specific oppressions. The Collective's conceptualisation of identity and oppression as increasingly complex allowed a discussion of power relations among feminist women. Even though all women were oppressed as a group, women could and did oppress other women: white women oppressed women of colour; wealthy women oppressed poor women; heterosexual women oppressed lesbian women.

Two germinal volumes of black feminist theory emerged from the praxis of the Combahee River Collective and reshaped Women's Studies in American Universities: *Home Girls: A Black Feminist Anthology* (1983); and *All the Women are White, All the Blacks are Men, But Some of Us are Brave* (1982).

MELVINA JOHNSON YOUNG

commensurability/ incommensurability

Thomas Kuhn introduced the concept of the incommensurability of scientific theories in 1962, arguing that, as science evolves, competing 'paradigms' could be incapable of translation because concepts and concerns from one theory lack adequate counterparts in the other. The incommensurability thesis entails a rejection of the received view that scientific progress is cumulative and based solely on logical concerns. Kuhn reveals that standards of evidence are not pretheoretic, but are linked to the beliefs and practices of a particular scientific community. This realisation that selection and justification of scientific theories is an inextricable combination of objective and subjective factors made credible the concern that androcentric or sexist biases held by scientists could affect the evolution of theories and standards of evidence in **science** (see also **objectivity**; **an-**

drocentrism; **heterosexism, heteronormativity**). Investigation of this concern has become a central focus of feminist science studies.

References and further reading

Fausto-Sterling, A. (1985) *Myths of Gender*, New York: Basic Books.

NANCY TUANA

commodification

In developing his analysis of capitalism, Karl Marx formulated what is generally known as the Principle of Commodification. Put most simply, commodification is the process by which the exchange-value of an object is determined as distinct from the use-value of that object; for example, an object, such as labour, is valuable in the capitalist economy only because it can be exchanged, or sold. Commodification reduces all social interaction to a form of market exchange. In the instance of labour, capitalism successfully reduces the exchange-value of labour (through low wages and worker exploitation) while increasing the exchange-value of commodities.

Marxist feminists initially took up the question of commodification in consideration of the 'value' of domestic labour, the so-called 'wages for housework debate'. Today, commodification figures more in feminist discussions surrounding the decline of the welfare state and the role of women as privatised care-givers in the face of reduced government participation in areas of health care, **childcare**, or elder care.

SANDRA REIN

communication theory

From the mid-twentieth century, *communication theories* developed to provide models to map the operation of human communication as processes in which messages are encoded and transmitted from a sender to a receiver through a particular channel with certain effects ('transmission model'). Such theories were primarily created by media and marketing professionals seeking to understand and maximise the impact of communication messages on audiences (communication as persuasion) (see McQuail 1994).

Feminist *communication theories* based on transmission models have tended to presuppose that communication processes operate in a linear fashion (sender–message–receiver) transmitting to audiences particular (patriarchal) messages about gender. Thus, one of the main functions of the **mass media** is to contribute to the social control of women. Because most of the sources of media messages are men, it is in their continuing interest to shape media content so as to legitimate and reproduce patriarchal privilege (see **patriarchy**; **privilege**). Media content is therefore thought to reflect a male 'world view'. The media's portrayal and legitimisation of this 'world view' encourages audiences to accept and conform to traditional gender roles.

Utilising such theories, feminist researchers have criticised the media for their portrayal of women, arguing that images tend to reinforce traditional sex-role stereotypes which inhibit women's advancement in society. Significantly, however, gender issues remain largely peripheral to most communication research where they tend to be regarded as belonging to a distinct area of study instead of being part of the 'mainstream'.

Research examining media images of women has been challenged for assuming that stereotypical portrayals of gender are a direct result of the sexism of media owners and producers who intentionally or unintentionally seek to oppress women. It has also been criticised for maintaining that it is possible to reflect accurately the 'true nature' of gender. Critical feminist *communication theories* propose that **gender** is best understood as 'a set of overlapping and sometimes contradictory cultural descriptions and prescriptions referring to sexual difference' (van Zoonen 1994: 40). Transmission models tend to accept that the media can directly and accurately reflect social reality whereas critical approaches propose that the mass media contributes to the social construction of 'reality'. The idea that audiences simply accept and conform to stereotypical gender roles portrayed in the media is also questioned. Underlying this claim is the presumption that audiences receive media

messages exactly as media producers intended, thus ignoring the social and cultural contexts within which media audiences negotiate the meanings of media texts.

See also: advertising, women in; audience response; pornography; positivism; television

References and further reading

Creedon, P.J. (ed.) (1993) *Women in Mass Communication*, Newbury Park: Sage, 2nd edn.
McQuail, D. (1994) *Mass Communication Theory*, London: Sage.
Rakow, L. (ed.) (1992) *Women Making Meaning: New Directions in Communication*, New York and London: Routledge.
van Zoonen, L. (1994) *Feminist Media Studies*, London: Sage.

CYNTHIA CARTER

communism, women and

Communism is an emancipatory discourse, a transformative theory of class relations which achieved most in revolutionary Russia, but there changed into a model of the woman citizen's subordination to the state. The theory of women's position was based upon two spheres, production and reproduction. Women belong to two collectives, the family and the workplace.

The two major expositions of communist principles, Marx's *Communist Manifesto* and Engels's *The Origins of the Family, Private Property and the State* posit two spheres, production and reproduction, equally important in reproducing human society. Marx and Engels reject the idea of the family as natural, outside social change, arguing that it is a major site of social power, closely tied to relationships of production, and that sexuality and emotional attitudes are formed by economic forces. Communists following Marx and Engels wished to make change by organising people in the political party, based on the revolutionary potential of the organised working class, whose power is based upon production, thus women are important insofar as they are productive workers, without separate or special interests. August

Bebel's 1878 *Women Under Socialism* proposes women's entry into the workforce and attacks persistent inequality within the family. Clara Zetkin organised women within German Social Democracy on the assumption that women would transform their lives by entering industrial labour. Contradictions within the communist project between the interests of the working class and of women have remained both theoretically and organisationally problematic, denying women independent organisation.

The 1917 Bolshevik Central Committee's Soviet constitution introduced substantial change, outlined by Alexandra Kollontai, Minister for Welfare, in *Society and Motherhood* (1916) and *Communism and the Family* (1918), arguing that women's subordination at work mirrors domestic slavery and limits the emancipatory potential of sexuality (seen only as heterosexuality) by women's treatment as property in marriage, and undermines maternal love by seeing the child as property. Law could transform sex and family. The new government made some legislative change. Divorce and marriage were both equalised and made easier; abortion and birth control were legalised; prostitution designated parasitism; equal opportunity in education and employment proclaimed. Kollontai went further, arguing for policies to remove women's double burden by socialising housework and replacing the idea of children as private familial property with that of children as a communal responsibility, carried out in collective housing. This 'abolition' of the family was based on the theory that individuals could choose how to live and love without constraints of property or the need for support for dependents. The *Zhenotdel* women's organisation was designed to transmit reform ideas to the female population.

The ideal of a new society based on free love, collective parenthood and equality failed. Civil war, the priority given to industrialisation and public discontent over unequal effects of divorce, multiplying and neglected orphans and female emancipation stigmatised as heedless promiscuity limited innovation. The state denied women's distinct interests and independent organisation, abolishing the *Zhenotdel* in 1930. The 1936 family code outlawed abortion and limited divorce. Other communist states followed Stalinism, encouraging

workforce participation but neither attacking the **double burden** of housework and paid employment nor making special arrangements for female political representation. In China, state interests in production, population size and docility overrode ideas of female emancipation; party and state were seen as identical.

DEBORAH THOM

communitarianism, women and

Communitarianism, as the name suggests, places the community rather than the individual at the centre of analysis. The core thesis that an individual is shaped in a community forms a significant strand in **philosophy** from Plato and Aristotle to Hegel, but communitarianism has re-emerged in political thought as a challenge to liberal theory. Communitarian thinkers reject a liberal individualist conception of people as atomistic and freely choosing beings in favour of a conception of people as shaped by attachments and community values (see **individualism**). Because it has not been systematised into a theory in the way that liberalism or **Marxism** have and because communitarians tend to have the label ascribed to them rather than identify themselves as such, communitarianism has been a largely critical position rather than a distinctive **political theory**. However, the communitarian critique has resulted in positive contributions to metaphysical inquiries into the **self** and to moral and political questions about human flourishing.

As developed by feminists, an **ethic of care** centred on our responsibilities to others in the context of concrete relationships also supports a conception of selves as embedded in communities. Feminists and communitarians part company, however, in their analyses of the implications of the embedded self for moral and political theory. Michael Sandel, Alasdair MacIntyre, Charles Taylor, and Michael Walzer argue that people flourish when the common values and goals of a community serve as guides to the conduct of its members (see Avineri and De-Shalit 1992). Feminist theorists such as Marilyn Friedman and Seyla

Benhabib have criticised this model of social relations.

People may be *shaped* by the communities they are born into, but the notion that they are *fully constituted* by them is belied by the way that members of actual communities question and revise the practices and values of their communities. The model of a cohesive community of like-minded members with a shared identity of practices and values is unrealistic; disagreement and a plurality of values characterise most communities. More seriously, communitarianism cannot serve as an adequate base for normative theory. Using cohesiveness and the values that *do* exist as a model for what *should* exist risks excluding those who are disadvantaged and rules out the assessment of unjust community practices and values.

Without institutions of justice, conflicts in a 'cohesive community' would be settled by reference to 'common' ends or goals, ones that risk ignoring the perspectives of some members. Feminist theorists aim to expose community norms and practices that perpetuate oppressive relationships (see **oppression**). Communitarian complacency about the moral values held in communities, its disregard for differences within communities, and its obliviousness to relations of **power** and oppression make it a poor ally for feminism.

References and further reading

Avineri and De-Shalit. (eds) (1992) *Communitarianism and Individualism*, Oxford: Oxford University Press.

Friedman, M. (1989) 'Feminism and Modern Friendship', *Ethics* 99.

CHRISTINE KOGGEL

complementarity

Complementarity is the concept of **gender** systems with balanced **dichotomies** of male and female that, while distinct, are not ranked. It achieved popular currency through the writing of Riane Eisler, who presents complementarity as at the heart of original **matriarchy** in *The Chalice and the Blade*. It has also been employed in **ethno-**graphy of societies, such as the Hopi and Aymara, with an **ideology** of bounded domains of authority for men and women, without inherent male **dominance**. Complementarity has been criticised for problematic assumptions of **essentialism** of male and female natures, and for heterosexism (see **heterosexism, heteronormativity**). It may project into the past an ahistoric concept of a **public/private** division, and perpetuate the equivalence of **nature/culture** with female and male. Used critically, the concept can draw attention to non-oppositional ways of representing gender, which may be particularly characteristic of indigenous societies of the Americas and Oceania.

References and further reading

Eisler, R. (1987) *The Chalice and the Blade*, San Francisco: Harper and Row.

ROSEMARY A. JOYCE

computer science

Gender and technology is a relatively new and evolving field of study, as feminist theorists and researchers attempt to keep up with the rapid pace of technological development. Feminists scholars point to a long tradition in western philosophical thought of associating men with technology and rationality, and women with nature and emotionality, which has problematised women's relationship with technology. Feminists have taken one of two approaches to changing this problematic relationship: either focusing on changing the gendered occupational culture of computing, or re-envisioning the masculine cultural images tied to computing and technology. Both approaches view technology as potentially empowering for women.

Those who advocate changing the gendered occupational culture of computing view as problematic the declining number of women pursuing computer-technology-related education: called the 'pipeline effect', it means that the higher up the academic pipeline one goes, the fewer the computer science degrees earned by women. Since 1986, men have been five times more likely than women to earn a master's degree in the computer sciences. Though women represent a minority in computer science, many have made important contributions to the field: the word 'computer' itself originally referred to women programmers who worked on the first programmable computer, the ENIAC, used to calculate ballistics trajectories in the USA during the Second World War. Other women have also made important contributions to computer science, such as Grace Murray Hopper, who developed the first compiler and the COBOL computer language. Lastly, some studies suggest that up to 70 per cent of workers who work from home, or 'telecommute' (also called 'telework'), are women, with most saying they do so to accommodate family. The benefits of being at home with the children are weighed against conflating the public and private sphere, where women's additional work may actually be exacerbated.

A second approach to changing the connection of women to computing has focused on the socially constructed masculine image of technology. Donna Haraway (1991) sees technology as potentially empowering for women, and uses the cyborg as a metaphor for that power, the cyborg being a melding of human and machine. Others have argued that computer-mediated communication is potentially 'freeing', since traditional markers such as race, class and gender are not immediately apparent in a computer-mediated environment, allowing 'gender-bending', or the blurring of the boundaries of gender by people assuming the identity of someone of the opposite sex. These arguments have been criticised by some as being overly utopian.

References and further reading

Haraway, D. (1991) 'A Cyborg Manifesto: Science, Technology and Socialist-Feminism in the Late Twentieth Century', in *Simians, Cyborgs and Women*, New York: Routledge.

Wajcman, J. (1995) 'Feminist Theories of Technology', in *Handbook of Science and Technology Studies*, Thousand Oaks, CA: Sage.

JULIE M. ALBRIGHT

consciousness-raising

Consciousness-raising (CR) is a method for developing feminist theory and political action from the sharing of personal experiences. The term 'consciousness-raising' was first used in a feminist context in 1969 by Redstockings, radical women in New York City angry about their treatment by men in the **civil rights** and anti-war movements. These women met in small groups, taking turns telling their experiences about a selected topic – sex roles, housework, relationships between women, money. Their purpose was to analyse structures of male domination on the basis of their stories and to carry out political actions implied by the analyses.

In CR, a woman is likely to discover that she is not alone – other women have experiences and feelings similar to her own – and also that the personal is political – women's troubles are not the result of our own inadequacies but of systems of male supremacy. CR has inspired women to make profound changes in work, sexuality, religion, politics, and personal style. It has also given birth to ongoing feminist institutions such as shelters, lobbying organisations, and academic programmes.

Problems CR groups struggle with include avoiding domination by one or a few members; resisting the tendency to discuss only the lives of individual women without moving to theory or collective action; connecting with other groups and so being actively part of larger liberation movements. Also, because CR was developed primarily by educated white women, it has tended to rely on a polite, middle-class style of expression; women not practised in this way of talking may be ignored or ostracised.

The most serious challenge for CR groups is that because the groups are small, many women's experiences are not included in the data on which the theories are based. For example, among heterosexual women, CR on the topic of sex is not likely to lead to an analysis authentic to the experiences of lesbian, bisexual, asexual, or queer women. In a group that does not include many ethnicities, classes, abilities, ages, and the like, the breadth of the theories that can be developed from the groups' experiences is limited.

Ways around these difficulties include restricting the number of women from a dominant group (e.g. white women) who speak during some meetings; forming or join groups with women of different backgrounds; introducing material from books and other sources outside the group. The evolving process of CR (although often without this name, especially after the 1970s) continues to be central to feminism.

See also: epistemology, feminist; experience; identity politics; methodology, feminist; narrative, feminist uses of

References and further reading

Sarachild, K. (1975) 'Consciousness-Raising: A Radical Weapon', in Redstockings, *Feminist Revolution*, New York: Redstockings.
Stanley, L. and Wise, S. (1993) 'Feminist Consciousness', in *Breaking Out Again: Feminist Ontology and Epistemology*, New York: Routledge.

JOYCE TREBILCOT

consensual models of decision making

Consensual models of decision making were adopted by sections of the feminist movement (particularly **radical feminism**) in the early 1970s in order to produce more participatory and egalitarian decisions. Consensus is a process of decision making without voting which relies on discussion and persuasion, thus stressing the co-operative development of an agreement between all group members. Consensual models of decision making aim to equalise power within groups, while promoting personal and social change through the common ownership of ideas and through mutual trust and the valuing of feelings Although consensus as a decision-making model was later criticised as a slow process which stifles differences by imposing uniformity and was subsequently abandoned by many groups, the notion of non-hierarchical inclusive decision making remains a strong influence on feminist organising.

See also: collectivity; consciousness-raising

KAZ ROSS

consent, establishment of

Early feminist analyses of rape criticise the prevailing legal standards of sexual consent for wrongly imputing consent to rape victims. Courts frequently have been prepared to admit irrelevant information, such as a plaintiff's sexual history, her clothing and demeanour at the time of the alleged rape, and her relationship with the accused, as evidence that their sexual relations were consensual. The evidentiary criteria for consent reflect a male-biased understanding of what it is for women to give their sexual consent, which in practice subjects rape victims to a second violation by the **criminal justice system**, implies that women are in a constant state of sexual consent unless they are explicitly or even forcefully resisting, and suggests that women cannot be taken at their word. These feminist criticisms have led to desirable changes in standards for sexual consent: **rape shield laws**, for instance, narrow the range of admissible evidence concerning plaintiffs' sexual histories.

Some feminist legal scholars, however, contend that narrowing the evidentiary criteria for consent is insufficient; the evidentiary criteria for *non*consent must also be broadened. In *Real Rape*, Susan Estrich criticises the propensity of courts to admit only physical resistance to force as evidence of nonconsent on the grounds that it permits passive but unwilling submission to sexual activity to be seen as consensual participation, and essentially precludes women from establishing their nonconsent in date rape trials. This influential critique has given rise to additional reforms, such as Antioch College's 'Sexual Offense Policy', in which the absence of verbal consent supplants physical resistance to force as the primary criterion for sexual nonconsent.

Radical feminists, such as Catharine **Mac-Kinnon** and Carol **Pateman**, reject the liberal focus on legal reform, arguing that even if legal standards of sexual consent were changed so as to reflect women's understandings of what it is to give or withhold consent, women's consent to certain institutions, however it is given, cannot be genuine under conditions of **patriarchy**. What appears to be women's genuine consent to heterosexual sex and relationships is spurious since the beliefs and desires that give rise to such consent have been shaped by a male dominated and heterosexist society. Ironically, radical feminists have been criticised for reinscribing a problem identified in earlier feminist critiques: the claim that women's consent to heterosexual sex and relationships cannot be genuine implies that women cannot be taken at their word. Whereas earlier feminists criticise legal standards of consent for suggesting that women cannot say 'no', the radical feminist critique implies that women can never say 'yes'.

See also: child sexual abuse; lesbian jurisprudence; liberal feminism; radical feminism

References and further reading

Estrich, S. (1987) *Real Rape: How the Legal System Victimizes Women who Say No*, Cambridge, MA: Harvard University Press.

MacKinnon, C. (1989) *Toward a Feminist Theory of the State*, Cambridge, MA: Harvard University Press.

Pateman, C. (1989) *The Disorder of Women: Democracy, Feminism, and Political Theory*, Cambridge: Cambridge University Press.

SHELLEY WILCOX

context of discovery v. context of justification

The distinction between the context of discovery (the social, economic, and political situations in which theories are generated) and the context of justification (how theories are tested) in science was a central doctrine of logical positivist philosophy of **science**. Only the context of justification was deemed epistemically significant, since any bias caused in the context of discovery was supposedly removed by rigorous testing. Feminist science

studies theorists have argued that the context of discovery is epistemically relevant in that it shapes the selection and definition of problems for research. Feminists have also called to attention the ways in which the social arrangements of science, in particular the awarding of cognitive authority and the division of cognitive labour within science, can have a bearing on the nature of theorising and justification in science.

See also: fact/value distinction; naturalistic method/naturalised epistemology

Further reading

Nelson, L.H. (1990) *Who Knows: From Quine to a Feminist Empiricism*, Philadelphia, PA: Temple University Press.

NANCY TUANA

contextualism

Contextualism is a view for which interpretation, knowing, and understanding always occur within some framework, circumstances or social relations: within a tradition and/or the practices of a way of life, that shape the knowledge itself. This thought may seem unremarkable to anyone who considers how people usually go about knowing the world around them. But in positivist-empiricist theories of knowledge, and in the scientific and social scientific practices that these theories inform, contextualism is not much in favour. The ideals of objectivity and universality central to such theories yield the assumption that contextualising knowledge-production detracts, necessarily, from the purity and value-neutrality of objective knowledge, universally valid across human circumstances. Introducing context only muddies and confuses the clarity that scientific method promises, as it investigates its objects/ subjects of study in controlled, replicable observation conditions. Because it considers specificities that are irrelevant to knowledge properly so-called, contextualism risks a pernicious situational relativism. The implication is that if all facts are relative to context, then no facts are properly objective.

Feminists, with other post-colonial and post-modern theorists, have contested the atomistic view that knowledge worthy of the name is possible in investigations that isolate subjects/objects from their circumstances. Feminists and anti-racists have shown how universalist theories of human nature or of masculinity and femininity, to take the most obvious examples, have coercive, oppressive effects precisely because they fail to address the 'contextual' factors that produce human diversity across temporal and geographical-cultural locations. Only by studying human beings in the contexts of their lives, the argument goes, is it possible to know them well.

Yet many theorists are critical of contextualism because of the near-impossibility of separating 'text' from 'context'. Putting the context outside the subject of study, depicting the subject as interacting *with* a (fixed) context obscures the relations between the two, their reciprocal effects and mediations, out of which subjectivity and situation are continually produced and reproduced. It generates an assumption that the context (situation, location) is in order as it stands, thus undervaluing the agency of subjects who intervene in, and alter, their circumstances. It is hard to believe that context is merely a given when the context – the society, culture, specific living situation – is itself a patriarchal, sexist, racist, homophobic, ageist, site open to political intervention. 'Contextualizing' sexual assault, for example, to a legal context that is already saturated with sexist assumptions, will not produce adequate transformative analyses. Thus many feminists propose multi-layered analyses that take practices, activities, social structures, as interacting, interwoven parts of a more complex whole which requires investigation across those of its strata that pertain to the purposes of a specific inquiry.

LORRAINE CODE

corporeality

Corporeality is the study of the body and things to do with the body, how it is perceived and represented, its meaning and interpretation. Concerns over corporeality have been central to contemporary feminist theory as women have historically been associated with the body which is viewed as subordinate to men's association with the life of the mind.

Feminist studies of corporeality challenge the notion that women's relationships to their bodies and roles associated with bodies are immutable. But some feminists are uncomfortable with postmodern interpretations which, in denying anything outside the text, apparently deny the validity of women's lived, embodied experiences. We have yet to discover how far communication in the virtual worlds of cyberspace may allow us to step beyond the corporeal.

See also: body, the; cyberspace, women in; embodiment/disembodiment; nature/culture

References and further reading

Gatens, M. (1996) *Imaginary Bodies: Ethics, Power and Corporeality*, London and New York: Routledge

ALISON ADAM

cosmetic surgery

Cosmetic surgery belongs to the growing arsenal of techniques and technologies for body improvement and beautification which are part of the cultural landscape of late modernity. Women are, both numerically and ideologically, the primary recipients of cosmetic surgery. In the USA alone, more than a million women every year have their wrinkles smoothed out, their thighs, stomachs or buttocks 'suctioned' or 'tucked' and their breasts 'enhanced'.

Cosmetic surgery is not only popular; it is also painful and dangerous, with serious side-effects ranging from disfiguring scars to wandering silicone breast implants to, in some cases, death. For feminists, cosmetic surgery is also problematic for ideological reasons. It is viewed as a particularly dramatic expression of the feminine beauty system which reproduces discourses of feminine inferiority (see **beauty (the feminine beauty system)**). Women's bodies are defined as too fat, too old, too flat-chested, or too 'ethnic'. Cosmetic surgery is regarded as a mainstay of the subordination of women. It belongs to the disciplinary **power** practices which fuel the illusion that women can gain control over their lives by improving their appearance, thereby channelling their energies into an impossible search for the perfect body.

The feminist critique of cosmetic surgery addresses three issues. The first concerns the necessity of situating cosmetic surgery in the *culture* which makes it both readily available and culturally acceptable as solution to women's problems with their appearance. Susan Bordo's (1993) analysis of western culture with its dualistic conception of body and mind, its obsession with control and the makeability of the body, and its tendency to define women through their bodies is a case in point.

The second issue concerns the necessity of taking women's *experience* with their bodies and their reasons for having cosmetic surgery seriously. Cosmetic surgery is not simply an expression of the cultural constraints of the feminine beauty system. For some women, it is perceived as a way to alleviate unbearable suffering and reappropriate formerly hated bodies (Davis 1995).

The third issue concerns the necessity of situating cosmetic surgery in an *ethical* framework. Cosmetic surgery belongs to the biotechnological interventions which inevitably raise ethical questions concerning the desirability of altering the human body, the distribution of medical resources, the nature of informed consent and choice, as well as what constitutes welfare and a just measure of pain. These issues require a feminist perspective which introduces notions of difference and social inequality.

See also: beauty (the feminine beauty system); biotechnology; bioethics; body, the

References and further reading

Bordo, S. (1993) *Unbearable Weight: Feminism, Western Culture, and the Body*, Berkeley, CA: University of California Press.
Davis, K. (1995) *Reshaping the Female Body: The Dilemma of Cosmetic Surgery*, New York and London: Routledge.
Wolf, N. (1991) *The Beauty Myth*, New York: William Morrow and Company, Inc.

KATHY DAVIS

courtly love tradition

The term 'courtly love' was first used by Gaston Paris in 1883 to describe the adulterous love between Lancelot and Guinevere in Chrétien de Troyes's *Le Chevalier de la charette*. 'Courtly love' denotes a codified form of love believed to have originated among the Occitan troubadours, where the subservient lover worships, serves and suffers for his elevated lady as if she were his feudal lord, and in so doing is himself ennobled. This development has been linked to contemporary society and seen as fantasy literature, allowing younger brothers access to women and status – unavailable to them legitimately – through adulterous means. Originally seen as empowering for women, feminist critics have seen the misogynistic impulses of the system, which limits the **agency** of women by banishing them to the pedestal, where as 'ladies' they are differentiated from 'women' who retain the undesirable charactersitics associated with femininity throughout the middle ages (see **misogyny**). Silent and chaste, the lady is denied both desire and a voice with which to communicate it. Courtly love is seen to be the basis of western romantic love as we know it today.

See also: literature, images of women in

References and further reading

Boase, R. (c. 1977) *The Origin and Meaning of Courtly Love: A Critical Study of European Scholarship*, Manchester: Manchester University Press.

JENNIFER SMITH

craniometry, biology of

Craniometry is the study or measurement of the head. Craniometry was prevalent during the middle of the nineteenth century; scientists attempted to measure various features of the head and/or the brain, believing that intelligence is linked to brain size. As women's brains tend to be, on average, somewhat smaller than men's, the scientists concluded women must be less intelligent. Similar arguments were made about brain size and **race**. These conclusions ignore the relationship between brain size and body size – smaller bodies house smaller brains.

Scientists also measured head shape, and attributed particular characteristics to particularly well-developed 'bumps'. This process led them to illustrate the head shapes that a man should look for in, for example, a good wife. Reading the shape of the skull (a practice called phrenology) thus supports sexist and racist ideas, as phrenologists claim that 'typical' African skulls or 'typical' women's skulls indicate lesser intelligence.

See also: biology; intelligence studies, gender, bias in

References and further reading

Harrington, A. (1987) *Medicine, Mind and the Double Brain*, New Jersey: Princeton University Press.

LYNDA BIRKE

criminal justice system

Many different stories could be told about gender and criminal justice. The story that has the most significance for feminist theory, however, concerns the project to eliminate discrimination against women from the law itself and from enforcement systems. This project has repeatedly run into the dilemmas of 'equality versus difference' explored by feminist legal and political philosophy.

Since the emergence of modern women's movements in the late nineteenth century, the gender bias of both the criminal law itself and the workings of the justice system has been a key focus of activity. The draconian enforcement of the English Contagious Diseases Acts of the 1880s against prostitutes and other working-class women, for example, was a major factor in the formation of the British suffrage movement.

Until recently, across common-law jurisdictions there were many offences that were thought to be inherently gendered: only women could be prostitutes, only men could be rapists, and so forth. In the present day, most English-speaking states have moved to make the laws themselves gender-neutral, as a result of the general shift away from rigid gender separations. Just as it is no longer legal to

advertise for a man or a woman to fill a particular job, even for jobs which are almost universally performed by one gender only, the criminal law too has generally shifted toward eliminating gender-specific statutes and rules. England tends to lag behind in this, since there are still crimes (such as 'buggery') that can only be committed by one sex/gender; but the general international trend is toward de-gendering the text of all criminal statutes, even those, like the sexual assault or rape laws, that do not easily lend themselves to gender neutrality.

In addition, some jurisdictions have attempted to eliminate not only the textual bias of the statutes but even the gendered effects produced by apparently neutral, 'normal' procedural rules. Canada's 'rape shield' laws, for example, are on the face of it about the rules of evidence in criminal trials, not about sex or gender, but their purpose is to prevent victims of sexual assault/rape from being broadly questioned about their past sexual history. Given that the vast majority of victim witnesses in sexual assault trials are women, changing the rules to protect the witness has in this case the effect of protecting women from the traditional humiliating 'fishing expeditions' of zealous defence counsel.

Rape shield laws can be upheld by constitutional courts because, while they have come under suspicion of feminist favour for protecting women, they can be justified as being concerned to protect victims, and victims are increasingly influential in criminal justice proceedings. Other areas of criminal justice, however, present greater difficulties for feminists who do not want to go back to the days of gender-specific laws but who are wary of some of the practical consequences of de-gendering laws regulating areas of social life that are still highly gendered.

A notorious example of the problems involved in de-gendering criminal laws and procedures is that of domestic assault laws and policies. Feminists have demanded and to some extent obtained greater police and prosecutorial efforts against the crime that they usually call 'wife assault' or 'woman abuse' (to stress its gendered character). But in some cases, when police officers have been told to charge any spouse if there is evidence of physical or psychological abuse, husbands and boyfriends have alleged that 'she hit me too', and police officers have responded by charging the women as well as the men. Police and prosecutors argue that one can't have one law for men and one for women, and that so-called 'mandatory charging' policies apply to the rather abstract, non-gendered category of 'spouse', not to men and women.

Gender neutrality has also had contradictory effects in other areas of criminal justice. Women prisoners, for instance, have in some cases used the gender equality argument to obtain access to the sort of training and vocational programmes that are available to male prisoners, succeeding against the correctional institutions' arguments that female prisoner populations are just too small to warrant programmes. But at the same time, given the increasing harshness of sentences currently being imposed in many English-speaking countries, particularly in the USA but elsewhere as well, it is not clear that 'equality with male prisoners' is a desirable goal for feminist reformers to pursue.

Therefore, although feminist lawyers and activists have succeeded to a very great extent in removing some of the most glaring features of masculine bias from criminal statutes and from some of the relevant institutions – at the same time that women police officers and women prosecutors have become a common sight in most of the English-speaking world – nevertheless new challenges have developed. Gender neutrality has not proven itself to be always favourable to the interest of women victims or to those of women charged with offences.

Consequently, some feminist legal thinkers – most famously the US law professor, Catharine MacKinnon – have advocated the development of post-liberal strategies that do not pursue or presuppose gender equality and that substantively recognise women's subordination. Such strategies have not met with much practical success, since the common-law tradition is built on the presumption that individuals appear before the law as formally equal individuals. In some jurisdictions, systemic discrimination (i.e. a structural oppression that is not necessarily caused by individual, intentional prejudice) has been legally recognised, and has given rise to some novel legal remedies. But this has affected the civil law, particularly family and employment law, more than the criminal law.

One reason for the relative dearth of post-liberal feminist legal strategies in the criminal law field is that while powerful women's groups have managed to obtain innovative policies affecting divorced housewives, unionised female employees, and other large groups of women (e.g. pay equity and affirmative action), few women, relatively, come before the criminal courts, and those who do are largely marginalised even by feminists. Women convicted of prostitution and drug-related offences, who constitute a very large percentage of convicted women, continue to be largely ignored even by feminist law reform organisations, and it is only when this marginalisation is overcome that innovative policies will develop.

MARIANA VALVERDE

critical race theory

Critical race theory emerged in response to the end of the American **civil rights** movement in the early 1970s (see Delgado 1995). This theoretical development occurred in response to the stagnation of social movements of the 1960s and sought to examine the perpetuation of the deeply racialised and stratified society of the USA. Engaging with key legal texts and issues, critical race theory has sought to question how and why the perpetuation of deep racism continues through political, social and legal systems. Utilising critical epistemological strategies, such as, treating the law as a narrative formation, **standpoint theory** and subjective experience, critical race theory seeks to render the often abstract and universal objectivist epistemological framework of legal studies into one grounded in the social and material.

Feminist interventions in critical race theory have been crucial in shaping and developing a legal discourse that recognises the intersectionality of race, class and gender formations. Through the 1970s and 1980s this theoretical approach made major contributions to North American feminist theory and politics. This critical perspective illustrates the racial bias and underlying **eurocentrism** that is pervasive in western feminist discourses. Kimberle Crenshaw, Patricia **Williams** and Angela Harris, among a host of eminent legal feminist scholars, discuss the need for a multilayered critical approach to understand and disarm the operation of discrimination in the study of legal cases. For example, Kimberle Crenshaw (1989) argues that the location of the black woman in America is unrepresentable in legal and political discourses, since sex discrimination terms do not take into account the racialised experience of black women and anti-racial discrimination cases are understood through a patriarchal lens. In this sense critical race theory has been used as a framework to establish the various ways in which legal definitions of discrimination fail to acknowledge the double or triple bind that is experienced through multiple sites of discrimination.

An important strategy of critical race theorists has been the employment of narrative formations in relation to the study of law. The use of narration, for example through story-telling, is a technique which disturbs the naturalised conception of law as being founded on an objective or universalist system that transcends the social and material relations of the everyday. This strategy is particularly compelling in critical interrogations of the Anita Hill and Clarence Thomas case of sexual harassment in 1991 (see Morrison 1992). This theoretical perspective allows for a discursive analysis of the formation of various racialised and gendered subjectivities that are being re-called and re-invented.

See also: black feminism(s); discrimination and the law; epistemology, black feminist; race

References and further reading

Crenshaw, K. (1989) 'Demarginalizing the Inter-section of Race and Sex: A Black Feminist Critique of Antidiscrimination Doctrine, Feminist Theory, and Antiracist Politics', *Chicago Legal Forum* 139–67.

Delgado, R. (ed.) (1995) *Critical Race Theory: The Cutting Edge*, Philadelphia, PA: Temple University Press.

Morrison, T. (ed.) (1992) *Race-ing Justice, En-gendering Power: Essays on Anita Hill, Clarence Thomas and the Construction of Social Reality*, New York: Pantheon Books.

DAVINA BHANDAR

critical theory, feminism and

Feminism's relation to critical theory is a contested site of theory and practice that generates new understandings of modernity and new types of social and political critique.

Critical theory, sometimes called the Frankfurt School, began in Germany in the 1930s as an interdisciplinary, action-oriented approach to social analysis that attempted to integrate Marxian economic and social theory with Freudian psychoanalysis. The school's optimism regarding fundamental change, even of reason itself, was severely tested by the emergence of fascism and persecution of the Jews (see **fascism, women and**). Well-known critical theorists Max Horkheimer and Theodor Adorno, in exile in the USA, sought explanations for the terror by placing fascism in a deeper context of domination and oppression and by investigating the 'unreason' of Enlightenment reason. Today, in the influential work of Jürgen Habermas, critical theory develops a more positive conception of reason and expresses its commitment to Marx through a theory of communicative action grounded in theories of language (see **language, gender and power**).

Like Habermas, feminists working in critical theory reject the 'value free' approach of positivist research and aim at a theory with 'practical intent' (see **positivism**). In general, they share his scepticism of totalising theories of reason, which he asserts against Horkheimer and Adorno, and for the most part do not join those feminists who understand reason as inherently male- and western-centred. However, feminist critical theorists also dispute key aspects of Habermas's project, which are androcentric and still too dependent on western ideals (see **androcentrism**), and in this context they introduce into critical theory a range of radical and transformative theoretical strategies.

Within critical theory, feminists address problems involving **identity**, exclusion, **history**, **power**, and culture. Sometimes they draw on alternative conceptual frameworks developed, for example, by Carol **Gilligan**, Julia **Kristeva**, and Jessica Benjamin, or by Michel Foucault or Jacques Derrida. As in critical theory generally, there are differing perspectives and lively debates on methodology and politics, but the main area of contention among feminists is the value of universalist thinking. Seyla **Benhabib** (1992) argues for a 'historically self-conscious universalism' that includes feminist reconceptualisation of important (Habermasian and modernist) concepts, such as **autonomy**, **impartiality**, and the 'moral point of view'. Iris Marion Young supports a postmodernist reinterpretation of the links between justice, identity, and **difference**. Nancy Fraser advocates a neo-pragmatist approach combining elements of critical theory with elements of poststructuralism (see **poststructuralism/postmodernism**). Feminist critical theorists all agree, however, that social criticism has to move between history and practice, culture and society, present needs and future emancipation.

See also: internal colonisation; modernity, feminist critiques of

References and further reading

Benhabib, S. (1992) *Situating the Self: Gender, Community and Postmodernism in Contemporary Ethics*, New York: Routledge.

Fleming, M. (1997) *Emancipation and Illusion: Rationality and Gender in Habermas's Theory of Modernity*, University Park: Pennsylvania State University Press.

Fraser, N. (1989) *Unruly Practices: Power, Discourse and Gender in Contemporary Social Theory*, Minneapolis, MI: University of Minnesota Press.

Meehan, J. (ed.) (1995) *Feminists Read Habermas: Gendering the Subject of Discourse*, New York: Routledge.

Young, I.M. (1990) *Justice and the Politics of Difference*, Princeton, NJ: Princeton University Press.

MARIE FLEMING

crone, symbolism of the

The crone is woman in the post-menopausal phase of life. She is sometimes called hag, from the word for sacred, because traditionally the older woman is the repository of sacred knowledge. She is the wise woman who possesses the powers of healing, divination and clairvoyance, all associated with the dark of the moon and the dark time of year.

The new moon symbolises the maiden. The full moon is the fruitful mother. The crone represents death and destruction to make way for regeneration. In pre-Christian Europe, the time between Samhain (Halloween) and winter solstice belonged to the crone. She is often depicted as hideous, with a harvest scythe or scissors to cut the thread of fate when life is complete. Because people fear her connection to the mysteries of life and death, the older woman is often despised. However, many women are reclaiming the crone as a symbol of empowerment.

See also: menopause (medical)

LORI ROWLETT

cross-cultural analysis

Cross-cultural analysis involves exploring and evaluating concepts and practices from a culture other than one's own, using tools from one's own culture. Placing cultures in dialogue with each other reveals aspects of each culture that are invisible when each is considered on its own. Examples of cross-cultural analysis include North American feminist critiques of African practices of **female circumcision/female genital mutilation**, and Latin American critiques of North American agribusinesses' exploitation of the genetic heritage of the southern hemisphere.

Ideally, feminists undertake cross-cultural analysis in ways that do not presume the superiority of one culture, or falsely universalise the experiences of some women. In reality, the practice is fraught with challenge, due to the legacies of racism, imperialism and colonialism under which all cultural exchange labours.

Challenges arise, for example, when analysis goes on across the divide between First World and Third World women. Here, the goals of promoting women's liberation while simultaneously respecting women's autonomy and self-determination sometimes conflict. For a First World feminist, this may require acknowledging that, in the context of colonisation, respect for Third World women's autonomy and self definition trumps the desire to 'reveal' to them their own oppression. For a Third World feminist, it may mean determining how to give voice to her critique of a culture that has subordinated and infantilised her own, thereby making her unintelligible. For example, theorists from the southern hemisphere have had to try to make intelligible the fact that Andean women growing potatoes do genetic research, just as do North American biotechnology firms. If such firms' work is patentable, so too ought to be the work of Andean farmers.

Cross-cultural analysis goes on not only between First World and Third World cultures; Third World feminists explore and evaluate other Third World cultures as well. In doing so, they may acknowledge influences of imperialist powers, but do not place them at the centre of their analyses.

This description of cross-cultural analysis implies that a person's membership in particular cultures is never ambiguous and never in dispute. However, persons are often simultaneously members of several different cultures, and their membership in some of those cultures might be contested. Thus, 'cross-cultural analysis' may go on within the life and thought of an individual feminist, as she interrogates and reconciles the different beliefs and practices under which she functions.

See also: Afrocentric analysis; cultural imperialism; Spivak, Gayatri

References and further reading

Lugones, M. and Spelman, V. (1983) 'Have We Got a Theory for You!' *Women's Studies International Forum* 6: 573–81.

Mohanty, C., Russo, A. and Torres, L. (1991) *Third World Women and the Politics of Feminism*, Bloomington, IN: Indiana University Press.

Trinh T. Minh-ha (1989) *Woman, Native, Other*, Bloomington, IN: Indiana University Press.

LISA M. HELDKE

cross-dressing

There are many traditions of cross-dressing across cultures and art forms, with historical figures such as Joan of Arc informing the construction of cross-

dressed characters in fiction and art while, in turn, legends and images have inspired many to deploy the possibilities of cross-dressing in reality. Cross-dressing has been a staple of theatre. On the Shakespearean stage, where boys played all female roles including those such as Viola in *Twelfth Night*, who disguises herself as a boy, cross-dressing functions to destabilise categories of sex, gender and sexuality and their conventional alliances. Consequently, cross-dressing has played a key role in the construction of gay and lesbian identities. The English sexologist Edward Carpenter studied the role of cross-dressing in ancient religious rituals as a means of signalling divinity, an otherness from oneself. To related effect, cross-dressing continues in festivals, from sports events to Mardi Gras, as a temporary freedom from the constraints of gendered identity.

See also: gender; sexuality

References and further reading

Carpenter, E. (1914) *Intermediate Types Among Primitive Folk*, London: George Allen and Unwin.

ELIZABETH McMAHON

cultural imperialism

Postcolonial theory seeks to show how imperialism involves the cultural realm of meanings and representations (see **postcolonial feminism**). Imperialism normally conjures up associations with intrusion, exploitation and conquest. The term 'cultural imperialism' hence suggests that imperialism also involves cultural conquest, or conquest *through* culture. Imperialism involves the violent destruction of indigenous or native cultural traditions and the introduction of the cultural formations of the invading nation. As a result, resistance to imperialism often takes place through culture; through re-claiming 'lost' cultural traditions or through re-writing the narrative of empire itself.

Cultural imperialism also renders the imperial culture the reference point for meaning. It involves the process whereby 'the colony' is constituted as part of the invading nation's imaginary as well as actual **geography**. Through writing, painting, naming and mapping the colonised space, the imperial nation discursively appropriates that space. As Nicholas Thomas writes in the introduction to *Colonialism's Culture*:

> Colonialism has always, equally importantly and deeply, been a cultural process; its discoveries and trespasses are imagined and energised through signs, metaphors and narratives; even what would seem its purest moments of profit and violence have been mediated and enflamed by structures of meaning

(Thomas 1994: 2)

Cultural imperialism also involves a process of self-othering whereby the colonised others are constituted as the imaginary 'outside' of culture itself. For example, writings on Aboriginal people in Australian exploration discourse relegated Aboriginal people to pre-history and to nature. Through this relegation, the colonisers become the subjects or agents of cultural history.

Culture itself becomes a site of struggle in imperialism. For example, in nineteenth-century India the conflicts over the practice of widow burning or *sati* involved a collision between the imperial narrative of social mission ('we must save Indian women from such a barbaric cultural practice') and the nationalist narrative (where sati became celebrated as a sign of tradition). Feminists have pointed out how women's bodies became the site over which validity of empire itself was contested. This claim suggests that any understanding of the role of culture in imperialism must attend to the intersection between gender and race in cultural formations.

Western feminism has been complicit in forms of cultural imperialism. For example, Chandra Mohanty (1991) discusses how feminist attempts to account for the universality of gender oppression have led to the production of the category of the 'Third World woman' within feminist analysis. Here, the 'Third World woman' is interpreted in terms of a western understanding of gender oppression: the representation of her as a victim of a universal patriarchy positions the western feminist subject as an authority, while taking the west as a reference point for understanding different forms of power relations. A feminist concern with cultural imperialism should

hence not only involve an outward gaze, but also an inward reflection on feminism's own histories of theorising, researching and acting on the world.

References and further reading

Mohanty, C. (1991) 'Under Western Eyes: Feminist Scholarship and Colonial Discourses', in C. Mohanty, A. Russo and L. Torres (eds) *Third World Women and the Politics of Feminism*, Bloomington and Indianapolis: Indiana University Press.

Thomas, N. (1994) *Colonialism's Culture: Anthropology, Travel and Government*, Cambridge, MA: Polity Press.

SARA AHMED

cultural feminism

Cultural feminism is an approach to feminist thinking and action which claims that either by nature and/or through nurture, women have developed what society refers to as 'feminine' or 'female' characteristics. This set of characteristics, say cultural feminists, is to be compared and contrasted with the set of 'masculine' or 'male' characteristics which men have developed, also through nature and/or nurture. Cultural feminists fault western thought for its tendency to privilege 'male' ways of being, thinking, and doing over 'female' ones. Specifically, they argue that the traits typically associated with men – 'independence, autonomy, intellect, will, wariness, hierarchy, domination, culture, transcendence, product, asceticism, war and death' (Jaggar 1992: 364) – are no better, and perhaps worse, than the traits typically associated with women – 'interdependence, community, connection, sharing, emotion, body, trust, absence of hierarchy, nature, immanence, process, joy, peace and life' (Jaggar 1992: 364).

As cultural feminists see it, an entity known as the autonomous self, generally pictured as biological male and intent on maximising his self-interest, pervades western philosophical and theological thought. This autonomous, separate self at times fears annihilation by others. The interests of separate individuals collide and then conflict ensues. At other times, the autonomous self's separation has caused him to feel alienation from others. He has not been able to find friends to ease his loneliness. In sum, separation, whether it results in annihilation or alienation, whether it is experienced as freedom or isolation, seems to be man's tragic origin (West 1988: 6).

Cultural feminists reject this separation thesis and, with it, so-called male **ontology**. In its stead they offer a connection thesis, stressing that women are linked to all of human life, 'both materially, through pregnancy, intercourse, and breast-feeding, and existentially, through the moral and practical life' (West 1988: 10). Importantly, despite their common acknowledgment of the connection thesis, cultural feminists disagree with each other about the effects 'being connected to others' has on women's lives.

One group of cultural feminists stresses the positive side of the connection thesis, praising women's capacities for sharing, giving, nurturing, empathising, and connecting. In their estimation, women value their relationships with others above everything else in life, viewing separation from others as the quintessential harm. The fact that they menstruate, gestate, and lactate gives women a unique perspective on the meaning of human connection. For women, connection is not about separate individuals signing social contracts, but about life as most people experience it on a daily basis – within kinship groups in which they have involuntary membership.

Cultural feminists who emphasise this positive side of the connection thesis include Carol **Gilligan**, Nel Noddings, Sara Ruddick, Virginia Held, and Caroline Whitbeck. Gilligan and Noddings are best known for maintaining that, at least in western society, women tend to espouse an **ethic of care** which stresses relationships and responsibilities, whereas men tend to espouse an ethics of justice which stresses rules and rights. Gilligan rejects accounts of moral development such as Lawrence Kohlberg's in which he claims that moral development is a six-stage, universal, invariant, and hierarchical process; she insists this model is 'male-biased' and reflects men's, but not women's, typical moral experiences. Gilligan offers an account of moral development that more adequately reflects the way in which women develop morally. She claims women vacillate between stressing first their own interests and then others' interests before they realise that truly morally-developed persons weave their own and others' interests together. Agreeing with Gilligan, Noddings develops a relational ethics which puts emphasis on the role of feelings in ethics. For her, caring is more than being benevolently disposed toward humankind in general; it is about being concerned with the specific people who occupy one's emotional space.

Related to these respective ethics of care are the maternal ethics of Ruddick, Held, and Whitbeck. They maintain that a moral paradigm built upon transactions between equally informed and equally powerful adults cannot adequately guide the bulk of our human relationships which, after all, are mostly between unequals. Were ethics really gender neutral, it would not favour paradigms like the contract model, which speak more to men's traditional experience in the public world than to women's and children's experiences in the private world. Rather, it would place equal value on the kind of moral paradigm which guides our relationships with ageing parents, ailing siblings, distraught friends, and young children. The world would, according to maternal thinkers, be a better place were the public as well as the private world guided by the lessons taught through observing an ideal mother/child relationship.

As mentioned above, not all cultural feminists are enthusiastic about women's connectedness. Those who emphasise the negative side of connectedness claim that, all too often, women's connections – particularly experiences of heterosexual intercourse and pregnancy – set women up for exploitation and violation, including **pornography**, **prostitution**, sexual harassment, rape, woman-battering, forced contraception, sterilisation, abortion, or imposed pregnancy. Women do not fear either annihilation by or alienation from the other, as much as they dread occupation by the other – the uninvited penis, the unwanted foetus.

Cultural feminists who emphasise this negative side of the connection thesis include Mary **Daly**, Janice Raymond, Andrea **Dworkin**, and Sarah

Lucia **Hoagland**. Daly is particularly suspicious of a woman's culture or ethics built on values such as care. She sees care as a coping mechanism or defensive strategy which women use in a patriarchal world structured to work against their best interests and limit their freedom. Women 'care' because unless they care they will be pronounced 'bad' (i.e., selfish) by patriarchal society. Women 'mother' because they have to, a point which Hoagland reinforces when she explains that men have decided a woman's function is mothering, for mothering maintains the social structure which best serves men's interests.

Although connection and caring have negative as well as positive aspects, cultural feminists on both sides agree that in a non-patriarchal world it would be safe for all human beings to care for each other and delight in their connections with each other.

References and further reading

Daly, M. (1984) *Pure Lust*, Boston: Beacon Press.

Held, V. (1989) 'Feminism and Moral Theory' in E. Kitty and D. Meyers (eds) *Women and Moral Theory*, Savage, MD: Rowman and Littlefield.

Hoagland, S.L. (1991) 'Some Thoughts about Caring', in C. Card (ed.) *Feminist Ethics*, Lawrence, K.S: University of Kansas Press.

Jaggar, A. (1992) 'Feminist Ethics', in L. Becker (ed.) *Encyclopedia of Ethics*, New York: Garland.

Noddings, N. (1984) *Caring: A Feminist Approach to Ethics and Moral Education*, Berkeley, CA: University of California Press.

Raymond, J. (1986) *A Passion for Friends*, Boston: Beacon Press.

Ruddick, S. (1989) *Maternal Thinking: Towards a Politics of Peace*, Boston, MA: Beacon Press.

West, R. (1988) 'Jurisprudence and Gender', *University of Chicago Law Review*, 55, 1.

Whitbeck, C. (1984) 'The Maternal Instinct', in J. Trebilcot (ed.) *Mothering: Essays in Feminist Theory*, Totowa, NJ: Rowman and Allanheld.

ROSEMARIE TONG

cultural identities

An emphasis on cultural identities suggests that subjects are positioned in multiple and contradictory ways. The multiplicity of cultural identities is simultaneous: our experience of identities overlaps to produce a subject position which is contingent. Culture involves processes of identification whereby we assume certain identities over others. The determination of cultural identities demonstrates the relationship between culture and power: certain identities become normalised precisely through the delegitimisation of others.

In his essay, 'Cultural Identity and Diaspora', Stuart Hall distinguishes between two models of cultural identity. The first model defines cultural identity 'in terms of one shared culture', where the experience of one culture provides the self with its true nature or essence. Here, culture and identity are understood as 'stable, unchanging and continuous frames of reference or meaning' (Hall 1990: 223). The second model sees cultural identity also as coming from somewhere, as having a history or specific modality, but sees that history as discontinuous and fractured. Here, culture is not a seamless whole, but a multiple and contradictory space in which differences are internal and constitutive. It is this second model which shifts us from a model of cultural identity *per se*, towards a model of cultural identities.

For feminism, one of the significant influences on the shift from notions of an identity to identities has been black feminism (see **black feminism(s)**). If identity is understood as that which makes something identical to itself (sameness), then defining 'women' as an identity assumes that there is something identical about all women's experiences. Black feminists have argued that what was assumed to provide the identity 'women' was actually drawn from the experiences of white women, such that black women become the other against which 'women' is defined. Audre Lorde argues this point powerfully 'as white women ignore built-in privilege of whiteness and define *woman* in terms of their own experience alone, then woman of colour become "other", the outsider whose experience and tradition is too "alien" to comprehend' (Lorde 1984: 117).

One of the effects of this critique of ethnocentrism in white feminist theory is the recognition that 'women' or indeed 'gender' cannot be isolated as categories. That is, cultural identities are multiple and simultaneous: our sense of self is dependent on the interlocking of these identities. Identities are not additive: it is not a question of race + class + gender. Rather, cultural identities are transformative such that our experiences of each identity affect the other.

The black feminist critique also suggests an alternative understanding of the relationship between identity and **difference**. In one model, identity exists as such due to its exclusion of difference (women have a shared identity due to their difference from what is not-women). But an emphasis on cultural identities may suggest that difference is internal rather than external to identity. There is difference, then, within the category of women and not just outside this category. Cultural identities involve a complex interplay between identity and difference.

Here, identity is not seen as something that belongs to an individual, that marks out our individual uniqueness (as self-presence). An emphasis on cultural identities suggests instead that culture involves *processes* of identification, where being designated as having an identity (such as male or female) produces that identity. Judith Butler, for example, defines gender as involving processes of identification whereby we 'assume' a sexual identity. As she makes clear, identification does not involve a single act or event, but rather it involves the citing of social norms which are regulatory (Butler 1993: 3). By identifying as 'female', for example, we must cite the varying laws or social scripts which define norms of 'female-ness': so identification approximates fantasies of female-ness and, in doing so, prohibits other possibilities.

To speak then of processes of identification rather than identity as self-presence is not to assume that we simply then have the power to change our identities. Rather, identifications take place at a cultural level and involve processes of fixation whereby some meanings are assigned over others. So, working-class-ness, for example, may not be an identity as such which belongs to a subject, but involves a process of identification which has material effects: being identified, or identifying, as working class tells you where you can and cannot go, how you should and should not behave, and so on. However, the effects of such identification may not always be fully determined in advance. Identifications, to the extent that they involve citing a cultural norm, open out the potential for that norm to be repeated with a difference.

An emphasis on the multiple nature of cultural identities hence opens out new possibilities for theorising transformation. If identities are not fixed in nature, but rather constituted through cultural processes, then identities can be transformed. Identities are moving rather than static. However, it is important that we do not forgo an analysis of how identities may be fixed and the means by which relations of power are reproduced. While we might want to argue that gendered identities are unstable, we also need to account for how those identities stabilise. After all, the difficulty of achieving feminist social reform demonstrates the degree to which ideas about identity are fixed within culture. So, although cultural identities are unstable and not fully determined, they also involve fixation, however partially and temporarily.

It is also important to recognise that cultural identities are not equivalent. If culture is a conflictual space in which different identities co-exist, then those differences also represent hierarchies where some identities are more powerful than others. Culture itself is not one space but an overlapping of different spaces which themselves have a different relation to power and capital. Consider, for example, how heterosexuality constitutes mainstream culture such that it becomes a norm: and how lesbian and gay cultural spaces are de-legitimated and policed through this normalisation. Cultural identities involve a contingent positioning of subjects in relation to these conflictual and overlapping spaces. This position means that one's relation to power and legitimisation is often contradictory.

References and further reading

Butler, J. (1993) *Bodies that Matter: On the Discursive Limits of 'Sex'*, London and New York: Routledge.

Hall, S. (1990) 'Cultural Identity and Diaspora' in

J. Rutherford (ed.) *Identity: Community, Culture, Difference*, London: Lawrence and Wishart, pp. 222–37.

Lorde, A. (1984) *Sister Outsider.* New York: The Crossing Press.

SARA AHMED

cultural methodologies

The term cultural methodologies is generally used to refer to **qualitative methodologies** (various forms of textual analysis, audience research) employed by cultural studies researchers. Cultural studies research 'treats culture and systems of meaning in connection with questions of power and politics' (Alasuutari 1995: 2) and makes use of a range of theories and methods which are both pragmatic and politically strategic to each study. Consequently, the concept *bricolage* (the reordering and recontextualisation of cultural objects to create new meanings or new discourses) is sometimes used to describe cultural methodologies. Cultural studies research aims to offer new intellectual insights into the social or discursive construction of 'reality' (or realities) rather than seeking to be 'theoretically correct' by proving the existence of an objective 'truth'. Some critics, however, have suggested that some forms of cultural studies research have resulted in a form of 'cultural populism'. The argument is that cultural studies researchers have tended to focus narrowly on the analysis of popular consuming practices, using audience research methods, tending to turn away from using 'critical forms of depth explanation that were concerned with the material conditions of cultural production, such as the political economy of culture' (McGuigan 1997: 139).

Similar concerns have been raised concerning feminist cultural studies research, although it should be noted that critical feminist scholarship seems to have taken different political forms in the USA from those in the UK. In the USA, primarily influenced by poststructuralist theories, feminist cultural scholarship has employed a range of textual methodologies to examine how cultural representations, particularly those found in a range of women's media genres such as women's

magazines, soap operas, romance fiction, and melodrama, construct and naturalise certain preferred definitions of femininity. Implicit in some of this work has been the assumption that audiences consume popular cultural forms in ways which often resist such preferred definitions (Radway's romance readers using these texts as a form of 'escape' from domesticity (Radway 1987)). Feminist opposition in the USA to this emphasis in much of cultural studies research primarily comes from radicals (such as Andrea **Dworkin** and Catharine **MacKinnon**) who argue for the recognition of women's shared experiences of patriarchal oppression thus challenging the poststructuralist view that 'woman' is the product of particular historical and discursive practices rather than a description of an essentialist subjectivity.

In the UK, feminist cultural studies analysis has been strongly influenced by a socialist tradition where there has been an influence not only on the effect of gender but also of class and race, amongst other forms of cultural identity. Economic considerations have formed a vital part of feminist research in the form of investigations into the ways in which economic inequalities, as well as those of gender, 'race', and sexuality contribute to women's experiences of subordination. Although feminist poststructuralist cultural research has assumed a position of theoretical dominance since the mid 1980s in humanities research in the UK, economic concerns remain central to its conceptual projects. However, the 'economic' has been reconceptualised as discourse conditioning experiences of gender rather than as determinant. Yet, as McRobbie (1997: 171–2) observes, the theoretical dominance of poststructuralist, textual research has resulted in a shift in emphasis away from feminist cultural research which examines the history and cultures of working-class girls and women and their negotiations with the institutions, forms and practices of the dominant (white, male and middle class) culture. That said, since the late 1980s, there has been a renewed interest in audience research (the 'ethnographic turn') in cultural studies. However, this has tended to result in studies which have been less concerned with the socio-economic (macro) context within which girls and women engage with cultural forms and more centrally concerned with the micro-politics of everyday, domestic life. Investigations by feminists have examined such areas as the gendered use of media technologies in the household, women's use of romance fiction as part of an individual strategy for coping with the demands of family life, how soap operas are used by women in the workplace as a way of sharing their experiences of personal life, and how women's magazines construct feminine discourses through which readers negotiate the meanings of contemporary womanhood.

McRobbie (1997) argues that feminist cultural studies researchers have become so concerned with exploring the politics of meaning, utilising qualitative *cultural methodologies* to deconstruct discourses of femininity or the micro-politics of everyday life that they have tended to neglect intervening in political discussions 'armed with data, facts and figures and "empirical results" necessary for participating in public debates' (1997: 170). Thus, she urges feminists to 'return [...] to the empirical, the ethnographic and the experiential, and to use these tools to explore the social and cultural practices and new subjectivities which have come into being alongside and in relation to what has been happening in the theoretical world of anti-essentialism, psychoanalysis and poststructuralism' (1997: 186).

See also: advertising, women in; audience response; cultural feminism; cultural identities; cultural politics; cultural theory/cultural studies, feminist; empiricism; methodology, feminist television

References and further reading

Alasuutari, P. (1995) *Researching Culture*, London: Sage.

Brown, M.E. (ed.) (1990) *Television and Women's Culture: The Politics of the Popular*, London: Sage.

Franklin, S., Lury, C. and Stacey, J. (eds) (1991) *Off-Centre: Feminism and Cultural Studies*, London and New York: Harper Collins Academic.

McGuigan, J. (1997) 'Cultural Populism Revisited', in M. Ferguson and P. Golding (eds), *Cultural Studies in Question*, London: Sage, pp. 138–54.

McRobbie, A. (1997) 'The Es and the Anti-Es: New Questions for Feminism and Cultural Studies', in M. Ferguson and P. Golding (eds),

Cultural Studies in Question, London: Sage, pp. 170–86.

Radway, J. (1987) *Reading the Romance: Women, Patriarchy and Popular Literature*, London: Verso.

van Zoonen, L. (1994) *Feminist Media Studies*, London: Sage.

CYNTHIA CARTER

cultural politics

Cultural politics is a term which refers to the ongoing struggle over meanings and values in society. It encompasses language (see **language, gender and power**), images, discourses, the means of cultural production and distribution, and the mechanisms of evaluating culture (see Jordan and Weedon 1995). In the process of cultural political struggle, specific groups with particular interests attempt to define the meaning of what is natural, true, good and desirable, as well as what is not. Cultural politics mobilise cultural processes and practices to fix meaning in order to legitimate particular social relations which are often those of inequality between classes, genders, sexual orientations, racial and ethnic groups (see **class analysis, UK; class analysis, US; gender; race; sexuality**). Cultural politics also encompass the struggle to transform these relations. Cultural politics determine the hegemonic meanings of social practices and the groups and individuals who have the power to define these meanings (see **hegemony**). Cultural politics also play a central role in the constitution of subjectivity and **identity**.

Cultural politics have always been an important dimension of feminist theory and struggle. Early examples of this include the demands of liberal feminists, like Mary Wollstonecraft, from the eighteenth century onwards for access to an education which would equip women to participate in the public sphere and the professions rather than limit them to socially defined 'feminine' pursuits (see **liberal feminism**). Examples from second-wave feminism include much publicised events such as the demonstrations at the Miss World competitions in the early years of second-wave feminism, attacks on sex shops, pro-abortion

campaigns, peace camps and environmental protests (Morgan 1993). Other cultural political
struggles have attracted much less media attention
but have made steady inroads into publishing,
education, the visual and performing arts.

Political struggle over meaning is central to
feminist cultural politics. Feminism contests the
ways in which biological and anatomical differences
between the sexes have been defined in patriarchal
societies. These definitions have political and social
implications for woman. Most types of feminism see
femininity and **masculinity** as culturally constructed rather than naturally given. Yet even
radical feminists, who are often concerned to
identify the true nature of woman and femininity,
see them as distorted by patriarchal culture and
patriarchal social relations (see **radical feminism; patriarchy**). Thus radical feminist cultural
politics have often been concerned with the
expression of women's non-patriarchal culture. In
fictional texts, the visual arts, and criticism, radical
feminist ideas have encouraged writers, artists and
critics to explore female **sexuality, motherhood**
and lesbian identity. Such works often search for a
truly female language and aesthetics (see **aesthetics, feminist**).

Culture itself is a plural and contested category.
It is used in many different ways which range from
broadly anthropological views of culture as the way
of life of a particular community to definitions
which see it as referring to a select body of literary
and artistic texts which constitute both national and
international cultural canons (see Williams 1976:
76–82). In feminist theory and practice culture
tends to be understood as all the signifying processes
and practices which constitute and reproduce
meanings and individual and collective subjectivity.
These include popular cultural forms and practices
as well as 'high' culture. The concept of cultural
politics is relevant to all definitions of culture which
involve norms of selectivity and value. For example,
'Culture', understood as a selective body of literary
and artistic texts, has often been thought to embody
universal truths and values and to express a fixed
and recognisable human nature. As such, high
culture has traditionally been thought to transcend
politics. Feminists have challenged this assumption
pointing to the political nature of cultural canons
and the many interests excluded from them. A key

objective in feminist cultural politics is to gain
access to the means of cultural production and
distribution and to the institutions which define
what is valuable culture.

The undervaluing and invisibility of women's
cultural production and history have been central
focuses of feminist cultural politics. At the heart of all
cultural politics is the question of whose culture
counts. Second-wave feminism has identified the
established cultural traditions in the west as androcentric and almost exclusively white. One of the most
important dimensions of feminist cultural politics –
whether black, white or of colour – has been the
recovery of women's lost history and culture.

A further aspect of feminist cultural politics has
involved the critique of patriarchal constructions of
gender. A classic example of this is Kate **Millet**'s
Sexual Politics (1970/77). Moving on from critique,
many feminists have sought to explore women's
experience which has been marginalised in much
mainstream culture. They have asked whether
women have languages and modes of expression
that are different from men's and how women can
use existing language to resist patriarchal forms of
subjectivity. Particular groups of women have
sought to identify the specificity of their own
culture, for example, Afrocentric feminism has
looked for the African roots of black women's
culture (see also Collins 1990). Feminists have also
attempted to produce new works which depict
women in non-patriarchal ways. This has given rise
to feminist film, art and publishing initiatives (see
Brunsdon 1986; Parker and Pollock 1987; Jordan
and Weedon 1995).

For feminists, culture is a key site of political
struggles and resistance to patriarchy. Successful
resistance to domination is necessarily rooted in
culture and experience. The struggle for social
equality has included attempts to transform the
nature of the educational system, to shift the
pattern of control in the national media, to rewrite
history and to change women and men (see
equality and difference).

Subjectivity – understood as encompassing
rational, emotional and unconscious dimensions
of the self – is at the heart of cultural politics.
Cultural struggles involve powerful emotions.
Feminists seek to transform emotions such as those
that are integral to **sexism** and racism. They also

address women's sense of self under patriarchy. Like other forms of **consciousness-raising**, cultural practices such as the visual arts, literature, film and history writing can offer the possibility of new forms of identity in which 'female', 'black', 'lesbian' or 'working class', gain new and positive meanings. Identities are an important dimension of cultural struggle since the forms of subjectivity which we inhabit play a crucial part in determining whether we accept or contest existing **power** relations. For women the construction of new and resistant identities is a key dimension of a wider political struggle to transform society.

Cultural politics remains a central focus of feminist activity in the arts, **education**, the media and publishing. Yet it is also an important dimension of campaigns and struggles in all areas of social life where meanings matter.

See also: ancient world, women in; Cixous, Hélène; classics, feminism and the

References and further reading

Brunsdon, C. (ed.) (1986) *Films for Women*, London: BFI Publishing.

Collins, P.H. (1990) *Black Feminist Thought*, Boston, London, Sydney and Wellington: Unwin Hyman.

Jordan, G. and Weedon, C. (1995) *Cultural Politics: Class, Gender, Race and the Postmodern World*, Oxford: Blackwell.

Millet, K. (1977) *Sexual Politics*, London: Virago.

Morgan, R. (1993) *The Word of a Woman: Selected Prose 1968–1992*, London: Virago.

Parker, R. and Pollock, G. (1987) *Framing Feminism: Art and the Women's Movement, 1970–1985*, London: Pandora Press.

Williams, R. (1976) *Keywords*, London: Fontana.

CHRIS WEEDON

cultural theory/cultural studies, feminist

Within feminism there are many different definitions of the cultural and many types of feminist cultural theorists. Feminist cultural theory should not be confused with **cultural feminism**. It has a very different history, different objects of analysis and different politics. Feminist cultural theorists do not believe that there are essentialist cultural differences between women and men (see **essentialism**). Feminist cultural theory developed from a critique of and engagement with emerging Cultural Studies in the 1970s and 1980s, crucially forming the shape which Cultural Studies now takes in its many permutations (see Franklin *et al.* 1991; Brunsdon 1996).

Drawing on a range of disciplinary areas and generating its own theoretical spaces, feminist cultural theory is not confined by disciplinary boundaries. Nor is theory used for its own sake; theorising has to have a political purpose. So, for example, science as an area of investigation is studied as a cultural formation to understand how certain forms of knowledge and power relations appear as 'truth'. In this investigation attention is drawn to how science operates as an authorising discourse, giving power and prestige to those who hold certain ideas and enabling other ideas to be discredited. The interrogation of the concept of **objectivity** is central to understanding how **science** comes to represent the interests of certain privileged groups (see also **epistemology, feminist**). In the movement across traditional disciplinary boundaries transformations can occur in which concepts are resignified and come to take on new meanings. This forging of a space outside traditional boundaries has meant that many feminists have often not been acknowledged from within their disciplinary areas: Meghan Morris's introduction to the *Pirate's Fiancée* shows the enormous amount of work produced by feminists on postmodernism before it became fashionable (see **poststructuralism/postmodernism**). Yet all this work is rarely acknowledged by those who claim a central role in postmodern theorising, who do not bother to read feminist work. Feminist cultural theory acknowledges work that has no traditional home and it forges new areas of inquiry by asking different and non-traditional questions of culture. Who people read and cite is a central political activity in generating disciplinary boundaries and claims to legitimate knowledge. The naming of feminist cultural theory is an example of this citational practice. It is an attempt to generate a new space where questions which were previously unthinkable can be asked. In this way, it keeps pushing at the boundaries of what we already know in the hope of finding new ways of knowing and thinking.

Culture, logically, is always the central object of analysis. Culture may be defined in many ways and investigated through different forms. The traditional definition of culture as something that only the privileged can own is challenged and culture is seen as the participation of all groups in social relations. Culture is often broken down into its constituent parts: the study of cultural processes can involve examining **reproduction**, governmentality, subjective constructions, spacialisation, identification, to name but a few. The study of cultural products investigates sites of representation such as advertising, film, music and television. Cultural objects, such as clothing, furniture, records and magazines are investigated for their significance and symbolic relevance and the study of cultural meanings involves analysis of how we interpret and understand products and processes. Often these analyses are informed by different theoretical and political positions, so some feminists may focus on discourse whilst others may focus on materiality. Others bring together different forms of analysis in new and novel ways (see Donna **Haraway** and Anne **McClintock**). The study of representations has been central to a great deal of the work produced by feminist cultural theorists because representations are the means by which culture comes to be known and forms of knowledge packaged and distributed.

Cultural Studies emerged out of disenchantment with the possibilities of change that were offered by the more traditional analysis of **Marxism** and structuralism based on economic reductionism. Theorists turned from the French structuralist, Althusser, to the Italian Marxist, Gramsci, and later to French poststructuralist, Foucault, to try to understand how culture is reproduced, how power operates and is lived by people through the production of their own subjectivity and how change is possible. What has been called a 'turn to the cultural' marks culture out as a site where change may occur in which culture is not always subservient to, dependent on and determined by the economic.

This concern in Cultural Studies with locating change, however, often neglects to include gender in its analysis. As Brunsdon (1996) notes, the interruption of **gender** into cultural studies was a deeply disturbing but significant act. It disturbed the actual theoretical frameworks that were completely taken for granted. For instance, structuralism (a major theoretical framework which influenced many variants of feminist theory) was based on a model developed by Lévi-Strauss in which the exchange of women was considered to be the founding cultural moment, thus ensuring that any cultural analysis within this tradition continually reproduces women and men as essentially different (Franklin et al. 1991).

This movement of attention away from the economic and into the cultural has produced different sites for analysis such as: the shift from the state to the subject; from the economy to identity. Although the cultural is taken as the central site for analysis, many feminist cultural theorists explore different ways of materialising cultural moments. They take into account the material production of life and social institutions (such as the labour market, education, science and knowledge systems). Others examine how particular forms of cultural knowledge (such as literature, **anthropology** and medicine) are generated through what Haraway (1991) describes as a 'material-semiotic system'. Some feminist cultural theorists, however, do not take the material or institutional into account, leading to confusion over what actually is meant by the cultural and how it is different from any other formation. There are also problems in separating out the cultural from the social. This is particularly problematic for the analysis of representations which become collapsed into social relations. Social relations are far more complex than just representations: the distance between the sign and the referent is lost and all forms of differentiation are relativised.

A distinctive feature of feminist cultural theory is the attention paid to the categories that we use on a daily basis to make sense of different forms of social organisation. Categories, concepts and classifications have the power to constitute both objects of study and how people live these categories. Therefore, theory is always interrogated for how it positions and is used by the people to whom it applies. Feminist cultural theorists are interested in theorising rather than in theory as an end in itself. The term cultural itself is an example: culture has always had a specific gendered, raced and classed meaning (see **gender**; **race**; **class analysis, UK**; **class analysis, US**). Historically, culture was seen to be a property which could only be owned by white western bourgeois men. The rest, the mass, were classed, raced and gendered as others not worthy of culture. Culture itself was also raced: minority groups have often been essentialised through culture, that is, their differences have been explained precisely because they occupy a different cultural position that is not equally valued. Femininity was central to how definitions of popular culture came into existence. The popular was equated with the less valued, potentially vulgar, feminine whilst high culture was associated with highly valued discerning bourgeois **masculinity**. Cultural distinctions are usually coded markers predicated on sexual, race, class and gender divisions.

Categorical analysis generated by feminist cultural theorists has led to an understanding of how specific terms have come into practice (see Riley (1987) on 'woman'; Butler (1993) on 'gender' and Spivak (1990) and McClintock (1995) on 'race' and class). This work has led to a hesitancy over using any term which assumes universal homogeneity. For some theorists this has meant a rethink of the politics which claimed to speak for all women generated in academia. This rethinking has led to a more nuanced understanding of the differences between women. However, rather than abandon the concepts for their universal pretensions, Butler (1992) argues that if we presuppose that categories designate an undesignatable field of differences, one that cannot be totalised or summarised by a descriptive identity category, then terms become a site of openness and re-signification.

Another feature of feminist cultural theory is the attention it pays to the construction of knowledge and how the methodology that is used by theorists is constitutive of the knowledge that is produced (see **methodology, feminist**). For instance, the use of **discourse analysis** produces a different political attention and theoretical explanation to analysis which uses **oral history** or **Marxism** (see Skeggs 1995).

So feminist cultural theory is always developing, always theorising and always contextual. It is formed through the politics of citation, the objects of its analysis, the methodology and politics to which it subscribes. It turns to the cultural for the promise of change but does not forget how the cultural itself is being continually constituted.

See also: Butler, Judith; Spivak, Gayatri

References and further reading

Brunsdon, C. (1996) 'A Thief in the Night: Stories of Feminism in the 1970s at CCCS'; in D. Morley and K.H. Chen (eds) *Stuart Hall: Critical Dialogues in Cultural Studies*, London: Routledge, pp. 276–87.

Butler, J. (1992) 'Contingent Foundations: Feminism and the Question of "Postmodernism"', in J. Butler and J. Scott (eds) *Feminists Theorize the Political*, London: Routledge, pp. 3–22.

—— (1993) *Bodies that Matter: On the Discursive Limits of 'Sex'*, London: Routledge.

Franklin, S., Lury, C. and Stacey, J. (eds) (1991) *Off Centre: Feminism and Cultural Studies*, London: Hutchinson.

Haraway, D. (1991) *Simians, Cyborgs, and Women: The Reinvention of Nature*, London: Free Association Books.

McClintock, A. (1995) *Imperial Leather: Race, Gender and Sexuality in the Colonial Context*, London: Routledge.

Morris, M. (1989) *The Pirate's Fiancée*, London: Verso.

Riley, D. (1987) 'Does a Sex have a History? "Women" and Feminism' *New Formations* 1: 35–45.

Skeggs, B. (ed.) (1995) *Feminist Cultural Theory: Process and Production*, Manchester: Manchester University Press.

Spivak, G.C. (1990) *The Post-Colonial Critic: Interviews, Strategies, Dialogues*, ed. Sarah Harassym, London: Routledge.

BEVERLEY SKEGGS

cyberspace, women in

In the debate over the relationship between women and cyberspace, the main issues include access, **identity** and feminist intervention. Cyberspace is a term coined by William Gibson, author of the science fiction novel *Neuromancer* (1986). It refers to the interactive and immersive environment of information and communication technologies such as virtual reality and the internet. Cyberspace is widely regarded as a new frontier forged by NASA and the US military but neither owned nor centrally regulated. Attempts to govern cyberspace have generally failed and consequently it has been idealised as a potentially democratic space which offers equal access to all.

This utopian view has been criticised for being technologically deterministic and for failing to recognise that cyberspace, like any other social space, is structured by **gender**, racial and economic divisions which restrict access and limit individual freedom (see **utopias, feminist**; **race**). Laura Miller (1995) argues that the frontier metaphor of cyberspace reproduces the negative gender roles which are embedded in the traditional narratives of American westerns. Women users of the internet have reported incidents of intimidation, sexual harrassment and even virtual rape which would seem to undermine the assumption that because cyberspace is 'bodiless' it is also, therefore, genderless.

Although cyberspace is not free from the constraints of social reality, it does offer women an alternative space in which to experiment with their identities. Multiple user domains (MUDs) are virtual communities populated by fictional characters. Here, women can create and perform any number of roles and need not be restricted to either a feminine or masculine gender identity. Experimentation does not preclude discrimination, but the opportunity to invent and inhabit multiple identities in cyberspace may have ramifications for women's real lives and open up possibilities for self-transformation.

Cyberfeminism is the branch of feminist theory and practice which is concerned with the impact of cyberspace and technological change in general on women. It also seeks to use technology in order to combat patriarchal capitalism and change women's lives for the better. Activists such as VNS matrix intervene by producing computer games and other cybercultural forms while theorists such as **Haraway** and Braidotti construct complex parodic figures like the **cyborg** and nomadic subject which challenge conventional identities and human/machine relationships. Cyberfeminism continues to develop in line with the pace of technological change and it makes a significant contribution to contemporary feminist theory.

References and further reading

Braidotti, R. (1994) *Nomadic Subjects: Embodiment and Sexual Difference in Contemporary Feminist Theory*, New York: Columbia University Press.
—— (1996) 'Cyberfeminism with a Difference', *New Formations*, 29.
Miller, L. (1995) 'Women and Children First: Gender and the Settling of the Electronic Frontier', in J. Brook and I.A. Boal (eds) *Resisting the Virtual Life*, San Francisco: City Lights.
Turkle, S. (1997) *Life on the Screen*, London: Phoenix.

SARAH KEMBER

cyborg

The figure of the cyborg was introduced into feminist theory by Donna **Haraway**, in her highly influential and widely reprinted article 'A Cyborg Manifesto' (1985). Associated with both a critical perspective on the foundational categories of western secular humanism, and the radicalism of feminist myth-making, the cyborg concept has since become a major locus of debate, particularly within science studies. This figure is now widely used to denote the hybridities interconnecting human beings with the technological systems that shape human worlds, identities, and futures. It has been criticised by some as contributing to an over-estimation, or celebration, of the power of science and technology in contemporary society. More commonly, the cyborg is used as a metaphorical device to draw attention to the complex imbrications through which human beings are positioned within, and embody, a world profoundly shaped by the possibilities and contaminations of techno-scientific systems.

References and further reading

Haraway, D. (1991) '"A Cyborg Manifesto"': Science, Technology and Socialist Feminism in the Late Twentieth Century' in *Simians, Cyborgs and Women: The Reinvention of Nature*, New York: Routledge.

SARAH FRANKLIN

cyborg feminism

Cyborg feminism seeks to transform the subordinate relationship between women and technology. Cyborgs (cybernetic organisms) are hybrids of organisms and machines or separate organic systems (see **hybridity**). They were developed in the military as technologically augmented pilots and became central material and mythical figures in the late twentieth century.

Donna **Haraway**'s influential 1991 text *Simians, Cyborgs and Women* is critical of the cyborg as a tool of patriarchal capitalism where it represents **power**, profit and the domination of others (see **patriarchy**; **dominance**). In her manifesto, she redefines the cyborg with reference to socialist-feminism (see **socialism and feminism**) where it stands for a celebration of **difference** and women's desire to build affinities with human, animal and machinic others. Haraway's cyborg challenges traditional western social and scientific structures of power and knowledge. It undermines dualisms such as nature/culture, self/other by incorporating multiple identities and marginalised standpoints.

See also: biotechnology; Cartesianism, feminist critiques of; cyberspace, women in; feminism; situated knowledges; utopias, feminist

References and further reading

Haraway, D. (1991) *Simians, Cyborgs and Women*, New York: Routledge.

SARAH KEMBER

D

Daly, Mary (b. 1928)

Mary Daly is a unique and lyrical feminist theorist who has recreated herself several times. One of the first strong voices in feminist theology in the 1960s, she left the Catholic Church, became a radical feminist, and wrote several influential books in feminist theory (see **theology, feminist**; **radical feminism**). Her most original contribution is arguably found in her foundational recasting of language. By newly capitalising words, and re-defining and revaluing misogynist meanings (see **misogyny**), Daly has created a rich language for women to rename themselves, their circumstances, and the world.

Daly's 1968 critique of the Catholic Church, *The Church and the Second Sex*, invited the Church to transcend its 'archaic heritage', and asked men and women to work together in partnership to transcend sexual differentiation. Five years later her radical *Beyond God the Father* called for the complete 'castration' of phallic language and religion, arguing 'if God is male, then the male is God'. Her shift from a single-nature view of humanity, in which differences between women and men are ontologically insignificant, and the hierarchical, dual-nature view of her later work, is striking. *Gyn/Ecology* daringly defines men as necrophilic, destructive, and gynocidal, hating women because they possess the biophilic (life-loving) energy men lack. Daly is relentless in her depiction of the destruction that global phallocratic culture has wreaked on women. Lesbian **separatism** is hence women's only reasonable option.

In *Gyn/Ecology* and *Pure Lust* Daly offers both a new language and a new **metaphysics** to women who are seeking to free themselves from the 'mindbinding' of **patriarchy**. For Daly, the logic of **radical feminism** is a spiralling spiritual journey in which women come to know and experience their true Selves. This state of be-ing is not temporally bound, nor can it be contained within the linear framework of conventional logic. Instead it connects to a transcendental reality which is rooted in the Earth and its elements. Women who choose biophilic be-ing are connected with animals and the natural world, a matrix with immense spiritual energy. Women's struggles are thus cast in terms of a cosmic spiritual battle in which biophilic energies are aligned against the destructive power of phallic culture. Daly does not speculate on the origins of this dualism, and offers no remedy for men's redemption or transformation. Her **essentialism** has also been criticised as insensitive to racial differences. Nevertheless her work remains a provocative account of the techniques by which women are constrained.

See also: lesbian feminism; ontology

Selected writings

Daly, M. (1973) *Beyond God the Father: Toward a Philosophy of Women's Liberation*, Boston: Beacon Press.
—— (1975) *The Church and the Second Sex*, New York: Harper and Row.
—— (1978) *Gyn/Ecology: The Metaethics of Radical Feminism*, Boston: Beacon Press.

—— (1984) *Pure Lust: Elemental Feminist Philosophy*, Boston: Beacon Press.

—— (1987) *Websters' First New Intergalactic Wickedary of the English Language*, Boston: Beacon Press.

RANDI R. WARNE

dance, women and

Just as feminist literary theory focuses on the internalisation of cultural values and the discursive construction of the female body, so too in dance theory, critical concern is directed towards both the sexual politics implicit in various dance practices, and the productive nature of the act of interpreting the meaning of particular dances. Poststructuralist anthropology, ethnology, phenomenology and deconstruction have served as theoretical tools for rethinking the social and cultural meanings, interpretations and history of dance (see **poststructuralism/postmodernism**; **anthropology**; **deconstruction, feminist**).

Among the basic feminist issues are: the role, status and representation of women in the history and practice of western art-dance forms, such as ballet, modern and postmodern dance. In some respects, the evolution of theatre dance in western culture from its social status as morally suspect to its present cultural value as an art form is a history parallel with women's struggle for power in society. At the practical level, women dancers have fought to be recognised as artists in their own right, to be seen as persons with creative powers and not merely as objects for the male gaze. They have striven to represent themselves, to choreograph and perform with artistic authority, to be directors and producers, and to be respected as more than tools for predominantly male choreographers and artistic directors.

This history of struggle is manifest, for example, in the progress of European classical ballet from its exclusion in the traditional catalogue of fine arts to its present status as an art form on par with poetry, music, painting and sculpture. During the Romantic period of the eighteenth and nineteenth centuries, except for the more famous ballerinas such as Marie Taglioni and Anna Pavlova, the social status of theatre dancers was ambiguous.

Ballets were popular, but because a career in the theatre offered lower-class 'working girls' one of few available alternatives to either low-paid drudgery or marriage and child-rearing, and because these 'dancing girls' had reputations for being promiscuous bohemians, a certain moral disdain for dancers was harboured by the upper classes. More respect for dancers' artistic stature has come with changes in society's sexual mores as well as the increasing technical and expressive demands of classical ballet.

Similarly, many of the early-twentieth-century modern dancers whose careers began in show dancing and vaudeville went on to achieve artistic eminence within their invention of modern dance as an art form. Both modern and postmodern dance continue their legacy of rebellion against the oppression of women indigenous to classical ballet, for example, its standards of feminine perfection epitomised by the ballerina and achieved by severe dieting regimes, physically disabling training and a restricted scope of creative authority.

References and further reading

Banes, S. (1998) *Dancing Women*, London: Routledge.

Desmond, J.C. (ed.) (1997) *Meaning in Motion*, London: Duke University Press.

SUZANNE JAEGER

Darwin, feminist critique of

Darwin developed his theory of evolution in the mid-nineteenth century. It was controversial because it conflicted with ideas that God created different species. Key concepts were: (i) species evolved by natural selection, and (ii) members of one sex compete for the other's attention – sexual selection. These ideas met feminist criticism; nineteenth-century writer Antoinette Blackwell, among others, criticised male bias in Darwin's work.

Natural selection means that some individuals have characteristics allowing them to survive better, and so produce more offspring; others without the characteristic will die. However, some saw this difference as meaning competition: Darwin's contemporary, Herbert Spencer, described natural selection as 'survival of the fittest', which he saw in human society.

Modern feminist critiques focus on the idea of competition, and continued sexist assumptions. Evelyn Fox **Keller**, for example, has noted how evolution often becomes a 'fight for survival', or 'struggle for existence' (1992). Such rhetoric serves capitalism, and denies the importance of cooperative behaviour in evolution, notes Keller. Concepts of 'fitness' also serve racism and **eugenics**, as some people are described as more fit than others.

Analysis of sexism in evolutionary theory has focused on recent sociobiology – the study of animal societies and evolution; this theory became particularly controversial when applied to human societies. Ruth **Hubbard** has looked at sexism in Darwin's writing, particularly regarding sexual selection – ideas of eagerly promiscuous men, competing for coy, submissive women.

These stereotypes persist. But now it is genes that are emphasised, rather than individuals – hence the notion of 'selfish genes'. Ruth **Bleier** analyses sexism in sociobiology – for example, the idea that men are more promiscuous because they 'invest' less in each sperm than women do in larger eggs. To spread genes around, it pays men to fertilise many women, or even to rape. But women invest more in each egg, so it pays them to invest more in the care of offspring. Some sociobiologists, Bleier argues, use this theory to explain conventional gender roles; women stay home and raise children.

Anne **Fausto-Sterling** has noted problems of using contentious terms like rape or homosexuality to describe animal behaviour. Sociobiologists, she notes, have trouble explaining homosexuality, given assumptions about reproductive fitness.

However, feminist primatologists, such as Sarah Blaffer Hrdy, have developed sociobiological ideas for feminist purposes, arguing that female primates are often rather sexually assertive and promiscuous; Hrdy suggests this gives evolutionary advantages to women – they can, for instance, actively choose between men to produce the 'best' offspring (see **primatology**). So, Darwinian ideas about evolution can also fit with more progressive politics, such as feminism (see Masters 1995).

See also: biological essentialism; eugenics

References and further reading

Haraway, D. (1989) *Primate Visions: Gender, Race and Nature in the World of Modern Science*, London: Routledge.
Hrdy, S.B. (1986) 'Empathy, Polyandry and the Myth of the Coy Female', in R. Bleier (ed.) *Feminist Approaches to Science*, Oxford: Pergamon.
Keller, E.F. (1992) *Secrets of Life, Secrets of Death*, London: Routledge.
Masters, J. (1995) 'rEvolutionary Theory: Reinventing our Origin Myths', in L.Birke and R. Hubbard (ed.) *Reinventing Biology: Respect for Life and the Creation of Knowledge*, Bloomington, IN: Indiana University Press.

LYNDA BIRKE

data collection, bias in

Bias in data collection concerns what information is sought, from whom and under what circumstances. No research is objective, rather, methodology, ideology and power must all be considered when researching. Kirby and McKenna claim that certain methods of data collection have been sanctioned by the status quo as the 'proper means of producing knowledge that will be recognised as legitimate' (1989: 63). Due to this bias, certain methods of data collection are underdeveloped and certain information has remained unresearched and undocumented. Common causes of bias in research include: assumptions and ethnocentric attitude of the researcher, selective omissions of certain groups from the data collection process (gender, race, class, ethnicity, sexual orientation and age), and power imbalances between parties. Bias can also take place in the design of the study, implementation of data collection and interpretation of results. The collection of data in research from the margins seeks to address some of these imbalances.

References and further reading

Kirby, S. and McKenna, K. (1989) *Experience,*

Research, Social Change: Methods from the Margins, Toronto: Garamond Press.

LARA KARAIAN AND NANCY MANDELL

Davis, Angela Yvonne (b. 1944)

Angela Davis is a renowned philosopher teaching in the Department of History of Consciousness at the University of California, Santa Cruz. At UCLA as early as 1969, Davis was teaching black philosophy, encouraging students to compare Hegel's *Phenomenology* with Frederick Douglass's master–slave experiences. Davis gained national and international attention when she was fired from her teaching position because of her membership in the Communist Party USA. She then began work on prisoners' rights, particularly for the Soledad Brothers. Reinstated in her job, she received death threats. In 1970, she purchased two guns which Jonathan Jackson, younger brother of Soledad Brother George Jackson, appropriated. He took a judge, a district attorney, and several jurors hostage, demanding a public hearing for the Soledad Brothers. When police fired haphazardly, the judge and Jonathan were killed. The guns having been registered in her name, Davis was unjustly linked to the killings, placed on the FBI's Ten-Most-Wanted list and charged with murder, kidnapping, and conspiracy. Retreating underground, she was eventually caught. Acting as her own counsel, Davis was acquitted in 1972.

Davis understands theory and praxis as dialectically linked. With Herbert Marcuse, Davis rejects theory as abstract, ahistorical and decontextual. Synthesising theory, community and critical coalition politics is key to revolutionary change. As a teenager, Davis engaged in demonstrations with the children of prominent thinkers (e.g., Herbert Aptheker) in the Communist Party. In 1968, she joined the Communist Party USA, and participated in the Che-Lumumba Club, and also joined the Black Panther Party for Self-Defense. Davis says, 'The theme of my work, of my life, has been the attempt to use whatever knowledge, skills and wisdom I may have acquired to advance emancipatory theory and practice' (Yancy 1998).

Davis's philosophical and political corpus involves an intersectionist analysis of **race**, class, **gender**, sex and economic **hegemony**. Her work emphasises 'the reappearance of, and recognition for, the contributions of the intersections of Marxist, anti-racist, and feminist praxes and radical female activists' (James 1998). Davis analyses feminism within an international context, the rape and commodification of women's bodies during slavery as a site of white terrorism, transnational capitalism as a destabliser of black communities, **homophobia**, and women's **health** as physical, psychological, emotional and spiritual. In 'Afro Images: Politics, Fashion, and Nostalgia' (1994), she addresses the de-politicisation of Black politico-cultural objectivations. In *Blues Legacies and Black Feminism* (1998), Davis examines how the performances of Gertrude 'Ma' Rainey, Bessie Smith, and Billie Holiday illuminate 'the politics of gender and **sexuality** in working-class black communities' as sites of black feminist attitudes.

See also: African American families; black female sexuality; black feminism(s); slavery in the USA

Selected writings

Davis, A. (1981) *Women, Culture and Politics*, New York: Random House.
—— (1998) *Blues Legacies and Black Feminism*, New York: Pantheon Books.

References and further reading

James, J. (ed.) (1998) *The Angela Davis Reader*, Oxford: Blackwell.
Yancy, G. (ed) (1998) *African-American Philosophers, 17 Conversations*, New York: Routledge.

GEORGE YANCY

Davis, Natalie Zemon (b. 1927)

Natalie Zemon Davis is a pioneering scholar of the cultural construction of **gender** in early modern Europe. Her historical career began with detailed archival study of France, and the Lyons region in particular, and has since extended to neighbouring regions of Europe in the sixteenth through eighteenth centuries. Davis's work explores the cultural meanings of social practices, highlighting their role in the maintenance of hierarchies that have kept women, peasants and working people in their proper places. At the same time, Davis stresses the **agency** of the historical actors whose lives she chronicles, as they manœuvre within, and adapt, their particular cultural frameworks.

Davis employs an interdisciplinary method, borrowing insights from **anthropology** and literary theory, to give voice to the silent in history. Her anthropological eye for festival and ritual enriches our understanding of the lives of early modern women, artisans and peasants, too easily erased by scholarship that relies on written sources alone. By reconstructing customs, and exploring contradictions evident in textual sources, Davis presents worlds of prohibitions and possibilities that are sensitive to ethnic, **gender**, and regional diversity. Her literary eye likewise complicates standard readings of archival documents. By looking at her sources as narrations as well as records of events, Davis explodes the notion of **objectivity** in historical documents, which are in themselves stories of a kind, and vary in form and content depending upon the teller.

As historian and storyteller, Davis illuminates a vexing quandary of historical inquiry. Davis's recovery of the historian's role as storyteller has left her open to criticism for her own interpretations. In fact, Davis quite openly engages the problem of interpretation in her work, insisting on a scrupulous attention to detail, exhaustive archival evidence, and a rigorous interdisciplinary analysis. That the traditional American Historical Association elected Davis, a left-wing, Jewish woman, to be President of the organisation in 1987, making her only the second woman President in the history of the organisation, is testimony to the acceptance by the discipline of the power and potential of her historical method.

See also: cultural studies/cultural theory; history; literary theory, feminist; public/private

Selected writings

Davis, N.Z. (1975) *Society and Culture in Early Modern France: Eight Essays*, Stanford, CA: Stanford University Press.
—— (1987) *Fiction in the Archives: Pardon Tales and their Tellers in Sixteenth-Century France*, Stanford, CA: Stanford University Press.
—— (1995) *Women on the Margins: Three Seventeenth-Century Lives*, Cambridge, MA: Harvard University Press.

AMANDA FRISKEN

deconstruction, feminist

The relationship between feminism and deconstruction has always been difficult; according to Diane Elam (1994), the 'and' between feminism and deconstruction is not an unproblematic link. Deconstruction, as developed by Jacques Derrida, provides a critique of binary oppositions: two terms, for example 'man' and 'woman', are defined as oppositional, but one term is defined as primary and self-sufficient, the other as secondary and supplementary. What this definition hides is that the supposedly dominant term is constructed in relation to its opposition, so that 'man' is defined as 'non-woman'. Derrida links this pattern with Lacanian psychoanalysis: the (male) subject defines itself by cutting itself off from the Other represented by the mother, and entering the realm of the Law of the Father. From this point of departure, Derrida explores the use of Woman as a metaphor (especially for Truth) within western philosophical tradition (see **metaphors**). However, a 'text', that is, any system that produces meaning within language, always produces meanings that are unintentional. Thus, Woman can never be fully contained within the philosophical tradition, but always exceeds and disrupts it. Feminist philosophers have used this model, in Drucilla Cornell's words, 'to 'describe' the referent Woman as it has been played with on the historical stage and as it has trapped, oppressed, and subordinated actual women' (1991: 82). Feminist deconstruction exposes sexual difference as arbitrary and analyses the ways in which it operates to uphold a system of representation in which Woman, and women, are subordinated. However, because all identities are discursively constructed, it is not possible to claim a 'true' femininity obliterated by the patriarchal metaphor of Woman: feminist deconstruction is by definition anti-essentialist (see **essentialism**). The only way out of Woman's subordination is to subvert the binary oppositions it is based on. Cornell (1991) explores yet another possibility for the feminist alliance with deconstruction: to develop a feminist ethics that does not prescribe equality of men and women within the confines of androcentric society without having to rely on an essentialist feminine ethics of mothering or caring. Using Derrida's formulation of justice as 'owed to the Other', she constructs a dialectic relationship between utopian justice and descriptive law. Women, especially women lawyers, must work within the law and address its injustice towards women, without losing sight of a justice that is beyond the system of law, and thus can never become law, or be defined once and for all.

See also: ethics, feminist; poststructuralism/ postmodernism; psychoanalysis

References and further reading

Cornell, D. (1991) *Beyond Accommodation*, New York and London: Routledge.
Elam, D. (1994) *Feminism and Deconstruction*, London and New York: Routledge.
Feder, E., Rawlinson, M. and Zakin, E. (eds) (1997) *Derrida and Feminism*, New York and London: Routledge.

ANTJE LINDENMEYER

deep ecology

Deep ecology is a male-dominated school of thought aimed at bringing about a major paradigm shift in the perceptions, values and lifestyles of industrialised societies, as a necessary precondition for creating an ecologically sustainable society. The term originates in a distinction made by Norwegian philosopher Arne Naess (1973), between 'shallow' anthropocentric and technocratic environmental movement, which emphasises mainly resource depletion and the health of people in the developed world, and a 'deep' movement aimed at long-range change.

Renowned for the centrality of wilderness protection to its philosophy and related campaigns, deep ecology has been criticised by ecofeminists and social ecologists for focusing on a critique of anthropocentrism while neglecting an analysis of hierarchies among human beings; and for the regressive implications of deriving guides for human practice from nature (particularly in its population policy).

References and further reading

Naess, A. (1973) 'The Shallow and the Deep, Long-Range Ecology Movement: A Summary', *Inquiry* 16: 95–100.
Sessions, G. (ed.) (1995) *Deep Ecology for the 21st Century*, Boston: Shambhala Publications.

MEIRA HANSON

dependency

'Dependency', is a neo-liberal term used to problematise low-income people's 'reliance' on the state. Political and popular media discourses have constructed the 'problem' of dependency, to demonise a wide range of people including welfare mothers, the disabled, immigrants and refugees.

This fear and hatred of dependency is critiqued by such feminist theorists as Nancy Fraser and Linda Gordon, who argue that this fear grows out of the masculinist-capitalist view that the normal human condition is independence and that dependence is deviant. For a culture that devalues and relegates responsibilities of caring onto women's shoulders, the fear and loathing of dependency is constructed along intersections of race, class and gender in that care providers of those pathologised as 'dependent', are predominantly working class, immigrant, First Nation and women of colour. Able-ism, racism and gender discrimination also intertwine when we examine the extent to which non-white peoples, women and persons with disabilities share a long tradition of exclusion from western ideals of rational autonomy and disembodiment.

See also: autonomy; care, provision of; disability, women and

References and further reading

Fraser, N. and Gordon, L. (1994) 'Dependency Demystified: Inscriptions of Power in a Keyword of the Welfare State', *Social Politics* 1, 1: 94: 4–31.

FIONA MacCOOL

depression

Depression is a term in modern psychology and psychiatry which refers to 'pathologically' persistent and intense sadness, hopelessness, and worthlessness, combined with loss of interest in previously pleasurable activities. Depression is a gendered psychopathology, as women in most industrialised nations are twice as likely to be diagnosed with depression men. While this differential is often attributed to innate sex differences, feminists generally understand women's higher rates of depression to result from social inequality, gender stereotypes, and effects of traditional **gender role** socialisation: these factors operate both within the context of clinical diagnosis and in society at large. Within clinical contexts, women may be diagnosed with depression more often because they are more likely than men to seek treatment, to verbalise dysphoric feelings, and to be perceived by mental health professionals as depressed. Feminists also underscore the negative effects of historically persistent differences in men's and women's economic and social opportunities (e.g., employment level, income potential, and social status) on women's perceptions of themselves and their responses to social situations.

The emphasis on depression as an effect of social inequality is a legacy of American feminisms of the 1960s and 1970s. Since the mid-1970s, American and French psychoanalytic feminists have turned a more narrowly focused lens on the western, heterosexual family to understand effects of gender role socialisation on the psychosocial and emotional development of girls. For example, Nancy **Chodorow** and Dorothy **Dinnerstein** claim that the division of labour in traditional western parenting roles renders the developmental processes of separation and identity formation more complicated for girls than for boys. Although their accounts diverge from those of French psychoanalytic feminists Julia **Kristeva** and Luce **Irigaray** at crucial junctures, all four highlight ways in which the simultaneous pressures placed on girls to identify with and separate from their mothers make it more difficult for them to individuate and mourn the loss of the mother as primary attachment figure; the cultural devaluation of stereotyped femininity also negatively impacts on the process of girls' identity formation. Although many psychoanalytic feminists underscore the positive potential of a less rigidly autonomous and more relational identity, they also emphasise the risk for depression this poses for women in cultures where independence and autonomy are highly valued.

Feminist philosophers and historians have focused on the broader cultural, historical and political contexts within which depression as a clinical diagnosis emerged and is maintained. They mark the transition from valorisation of melancholic traits in ancient, medieval, and early classical periods to their increasing pathologisation in the late Classical period; this shift is understood to result from a devaluing of the 'romantic self' of pre-modernity and optimism about progress through rationality and mechanisation in modernist science and industrialised culture. 'Othered' aspects of modern culture – including experiences of hopelessness, powerlessness, mourning and loss – have since been systematically projected onto women and members of other marginalised groups, and are often internalised by them. Within this framework, both the greater incidence of depression in women and the widespread use of antidepressants to 'treat' women in late modern and postmodern culture can be seen as functions of dominant cultural emphases on technological mechanism, productivity, and efficiency.

References and further reading

Kristeva, J. (1989) *Black Sun: Depression and Melancholia*, trans. L. Roudiez, New York: Columbia University Press.

SUZANNE BARNARD

detective fiction, women's

Given the generic properties traditionally associated with both 'golden age' and 'hard-boiled' detective formulas – on the one hand, a faith in the ability of the transcendent intellect to solve mysteries by logical deduction, and on the other, a reliance on vigilante morality ('[w]hen in doubt', said Raymond Chandler, 'have a man come in a door with a gun in his hand') – women's detective fiction might seem to pose some ideological contradictions. The whodunits of the 1920s and 1930s, best exemplified in John Dickson Carr's meticulously plotted 'locked-room' puzzles, seem to endorse narrative closure, the expulsion of the 'deviant' and a restoration of the social status quo: generally, the triumph of liberal individualist patriarchy. And while the hardboiled school did partly interrogate such epistemological complacencies (see **epistemology, feminist**), female characters invariably figured as symptomatic of a decadent urban culture, victims, hustlers, *femmes fatales* – the objects of investigation rather than investigators themselves. Women writers, however, have often succeeded in at once working within and transgressing the boundaries of the genre, exploiting narrative conventions to undermine gender and sexual norms.

Anna Katharine Green's *The Leavenworth Case* (1878) is customarily cited as the first detective novel by a woman, though it is the later work of Agatha Christie and Dorothy L. Sayers that established the genre as one suited to both feminine and feminist critiques of patriarchal institutions. Sayers's *Gaudy Night* (1936), in addressing the prejudices encountered by Oxford women academics, extends the formula beyond merely mechanical concerns, while *The Murder of Roger Ackroyd* (1926), Christie's celebrated experiment in which narrator is both murderer and local doctor, subverts textual and social authority. In introducing resourceful female detectives like Miss Marple and Harriet Vane who applied the particularities of female experience to detective work, Christie and Sayers provided models for writers such as P.D. James (*An Unsuitable Job for a Woman*, 1972) and Amanda Cross (otherwise known as the literary critic Carolyn **Heilbrun**), whose *Death in A Tenured Position* (1984), again playing on the closed com-

munity of academe, reflects the 1970s conflict between liberal and radical feminisms. Parodic elements integral to the genre have also lent themselves to feminist recastings of the tough-guy idiom, in the 1980s in the work of Mary Wings. *She Came Too Late* (1986) features a lesbian private eye, Emma Victor, who, though sharing her male predecessors' propensity for wisecracking and world-weariness, also presents an insight into the instabilities of gender identity.

See also: lesbian literature

References and further reading

Carr, H. (ed.) (1989) *From My Guy to Sci-Fi: Genre and Women's Writing in the Postmodern World*, London: Pandora Press.
Craig, P. and Cadogan, M. (1986) *The Lady Investigates: Women Detectives and Spies in Fiction*, Oxford: Oxford University Press.
Munt, S. (1994) *Murder by the Book: Feminism and the Crime Novel*, London and New York: Routledge.

JESSICA MAYNARD

development theory

Development theories address the development of girls and women across their many dimensions (e.g., psychological, social, physical, economic, political, and educational). They show both how social constructions of **gender** limit the development of women and how feminist work can empower women and further their development.

Two influential North American feminist developmental theories have been Nancy Chodorow's object relations theory and Carol Gilligan's moral theory. **Chodorow** argues that social definitions of **gender roles** lead to different socialisation experiences for boys and girls. Mothers encourage sons to separate from them, but allow daughters to remain connected. **Gilligan** broadened previous accounts of **moral development**, which were focused on individual rights and universal concepts of justice, to include accounts based on one's connections to, and responsibilities for caring for, others. Such feminist theories challenge theories that use male development as the norm, show that women do not measure up to men, and ignore the experiences and values of girls and women (see **experience**).

Other development theories address certain issues about gender. According to social learning theory, observing same-sexed adults and peers, along with the reinforcement of so-called 'gender appropriate' behaviours and nonreinforcement or punishment of 'gender inappropriate' behaviours, contributes to the development of gender roles and other gender differences in behaviour, knowledge, values, and beliefs. In contrast, other theories focus on biological influences such as hormones or the evolution of species-specific behaviours in men and women. Another category, cognitive developmental theories, emphasises contributions of children's developing thinking to concepts of gender, cognitive differences between female and male children, and the understanding of gender roles. Surprisingly, cultural-contextual or Vygotskian approaches, though compatible with many feminist theories, rarely have been integrated with such theories.

Some feminist developmental theories focus on development during adulthood. Jean Baker **Miller** and Judith Jordan emphasise personal growth through relationships with others, which contrast with masculine views of an ideal self as autonomous and disconnected. An influential book on 'women's ways of knowing' (Belenky *et al.* 1986) traces the development of connections, women's voices, and self. Feminists critique the work on child and adult development that takes a white, middle class, heterosexual perspective.

'Development theory' sometimes is used to refer to the development of an 'underdeveloped country' (from the perspective of the industrialised west/ north). Postcolonial feminist theories argue that 'progress' introduced by richer nations often excludes, and takes power and resources away from, women (e.g., their role in agriculture), makes their life more difficult (e.g., by having to travel further from home to find water), or dedevelops the nation in other ways (see **postcolonial feminism**).

See also: adolescent women and feminism; child development

References and further reading

Belenky, M.F., Clinchy, B.M., Goldberger, N.R., and Tarule, J.M. (1986) *Women's Ways of Knowing*, New York: Basic Books.

Jordan, J. (1991) 'Empathy and Self Boundaries' in J.V. Jordan, A.G. Kaplan, J.B. Miller, I.P. Stiver and J.L. Surrey (eds) *Women's Growth in Connection: Writings from the Stone Center*, New York: Guildford Press, pp. 67–80.

Rosser, S.V. and Miller, P.H. (2000) 'Feminist Theories: Implications for Developmental Psychology', in P.H. Miller and E.K. Scholnick (eds) *Toward a Feminist Developmental Psychology*, New York: Routledge.

PATRICIA H. MILLER

diaries

The diary, or journal, plays an important role in feminist recovery of women's voices. Loosely defined, a diary is a written daily record, composed privately by one individual; however, diaries may also consist of entries made irregularly over a lifetime, or during a particular period in a person's life (such as a travel diary). Diaries may be written by more than one writer, often a mother and daughter, or sisters, or friends. Some diaries may also be composed for an intended audience, such as family or friends, or 'posterity', and therefore are not strictly private documents as we often consider them during the twentieth century. As an important record providing critical insight into women's lived **experience**, diaries have contributed evidence to the historical study of women's lives previously ignored in patriarchal historical and literary study (see **patriarchy**). In addition, diaries have proved invaluable to researchers examining women's **autobiography** and life-writing. As a form of autobiography, diaries have provided many 'ordinary' women with the opportunity to compose an autobiography, which is usually reserved for more publicly significant persons. While the composition of a diary relies on its creator's economic status and literacy, these texts offer many women more public voices than previously assumed. Though generally considered private, or secret, in a twentieth-century context, scholars explored the functions and audiences for diaries during different historical periods.

Recognised by early autobiography scholars as a preliminary form of autobiography and a text which pays close attention to self-examination, the diary's ability to reveal the true **self**, or the real image of its writer, has been the focus of many early critical studies. Diaries of famous writers, such as Virginia Woolf, were seen as valuable tools to pin down the 'actual' or real self and accurate **identity** of the writer in question. These personal documents also provide important historical and biographical facts pertaining to the author, or the particular period of its composition, such as the American Civil War. With the questions posed by postmodern critics concerning the stability of identity, diaries are seen less as purveyors of 'true' identity, than as texts which reveal the 'process of being in a particular world' (Blodgett 1988: 7), the struggle for self-understanding, and the transitory nature of cultural identity (see **cultural identities**).

Since diary-keeping has often been seen as a feminine practice, increasingly so in the late-nineteenth and twentieth centuries, diaries have provided insights into women's gendered experiences and the process of enculturation. Diary-keeping has been viewed as more suited to the private, emotional, domestic activities of women than published, and public, autobiographies (see **public/private**). Additionally, it can be argued that diary-keeping trains women for an introspective life, thus reinforcing cultural ideas of femininity as concerned more with emotions and personal relationships. Scholars have suggested that the diary form is well-suited to serve as the most common form of women's autobiography due to the fragmentary and multidimensional nature of women's lives. However, other scholars have argued that the diary is not a fragmented form or lesser autobiography, but rather a genre requiring specific study of its varied characteristics and narrative complexity. Rather than view the diary (and women's lives) as fragmented, scholars suggest that the components of a completed diary must be examined to understand the text as a whole.

Rebecca Hogan (1991) suggests the seemingly disparate entries can be viewed as a form of parataxis and thus understood not as fragmentary writings but as individual writing moments linked together in the diary form. Additionally, scholars have focused on the diary as a suitable place for women to explore and assert an identity unacceptable in more public avenues of autobiography, which demand adherence to culturally prescribed feminine norms. Thus, the diary has provided women with the opportunity to create and compose a self, serving as a means of creative **agency** for women limited by confining cultural **ideology**.

The self-reflexive nature of the diary has also led to critical self-reflexivity and the examination of the role of critic as reader. In reading a personal and private text, diary scholars have elaborated on the autobiographical nature of critical study and the personal impact of these texts. This personal/autobiographical critical approach has provided feminist scholars with opportunities to re-examine the critical authority and elaborate on the personal aspects of feminist inquiry.

Diaries also reflect cultural conditions of **race**, class, and **gender**. While the diary is a more accessible autobiographical form, its creation does require economic and educational advantages not available to all women. Very few diaries written by nineteenth-century African American and immigrant women exist. The preponderance of diary literature available is composed by middle-class white women. Despite this limitation, diaries still provide invaluable insight into women's lives, contributing to the feminist *œuvre* on women's autobiography. Critical to the recovery of women's voices, the diary can illuminate biographical and historical studies, as well as contribute to discussion of textual production, agency, self-construction, and identity.

See also: autobiography; diaries as historical sources; narrative; oral history; women's writing

References and further reading

Benstock, S. (ed.) (1988) *The Private Self*, Chapel Hill: University of North Carolina Press.

Blodgett, H. (1988) *Centuries of Female Days*, New Brunswick, NJ: Rutgers University Press.

Bunkers, S. and Huff, C. (eds) (1996) *Inscribing the Daily,* Amherst: University of Massachusetts Press.

Franz, C.E., and Stewart, A.J. (eds) (1994) *Women Creating Lives*, Boulder, CO: Westview Press.

Hoffman, L. and Culley, M. (eds) (1985) *Women's Personal Narratives*, New York: Modern Language Association of America.

Hogan, R. (1991) 'Engendered Autobiographies: The Diary as Feminine Form', *Prose Studies* 14, 2: 95–107.

Personal Narratives Group (1989) *Interpreting Women's Lives*, Bloomington, IN: Indiana University Press.

AMY L. WINK

diaries, as historical sources

Although diaries and personal journals are frequently used in conventional historical research, this genre of primary evidence has been particularly important to feminist scholars. Historians of women, often frustrated by the abundance of source material written about women but not by women, rely on diaries to hear women's own 'voices', to gain access to women's own thoughts and feelings. Analyses of women's personal journals have revealed that in the midst of social or economic upheaval, the daily and seasonal rhythms of **reproduction**, **childcare**, and domestic work might well persist, or even be strengthened. Women's diaries suggest that historical events such as **industrialisation** or the American Revolution did not always constitute a sudden or discernible turning point, leading some historians to conclude that traditional historical periodisation or causation may not be appropriate to understand the lives of women in the past.

KATHRYN McPHERSON

dichotomies

A dichotomy is a conceptual division into two mutually exclusive kinds: male is radically distinct from female, reason from emotion. Nancy Jay traces the gendered significance of dichotomous thinking to Aristotelian logic, where everything must be A or Not-A; A and Not-A exhaust all possible characteristics. Continuity or overlap between them is logically impossible, for Not-A is the privation or absence of A. In the principal dichotomies constitutive of western philosophy – mind/body; objective/subjective; reason/emotion; universal/particular; active/passive – the terms are hierarchically ordered with the first representing the positive, valued attribute, the second, the negative, devalued one. Feminists have demonstrated parallels with the male/female and **public/private** dichotomies to show how dichotomous thinking functions to denigrate everything aligned with the female, containing it within private, controlled social spaces.

See also: binaries/bipolarity

References and further reading

Jay, N. (1981) 'Gender and Dichotomy', *Feminist Studies*, 1.

LORRAINE CODE

difference

Difference as a concept appears in early texts of the second wave to signify women's difference from men (see **first-wave/second-wave feminism**). Here, difference claims a speaking position for women in the face of male privilege. Difference in this usage is therefore related to women's common **identity**.

Current use of the concept, however, shifts emphasis away from identity towards irreconcilable differences *within* the grouping called 'women'. Difference in this sense draws attention to **power** differentials occluded in difference as identity: differentials along the axes of **race**, ethnicity, culture, class, sexual orientation, age and ability, for instance. And so the current use of difference additionally marks a vital, self-critical turn in feminist theory: through difference, feminist thinking is forced to reassess some of its most foundational premises.

See also: cultural identities; diversity; equality/
difference; essentialism; identity politics;
poststructuralism/postmodernism

References and further reading

Crosby, C. (1992) 'Dealing with Differences', in J.
Butler and J.W. Scott (eds) *Feminists Theorize the
Political*, New York: Routledge.

Gordon, L. (1991) 'On "Difference"', *Genders*,
no.10: 91–111.

Trinh, T. Minh-ha (1989) '"Difference": A Special
Third World Women's Issue', in *Woman, Native,
Other*, Bloomington and Indianapolis: Indiana
University Press.

KWOK WEI LENG

Dinnerstein, Dorothy

Dinnerstein's best known book (1976) attempts to
explain the origins of the sexual division of labour
as both a product of the relations of human beings
to nature and the implications of social relations
between the sexes. She argues that the sexual
division of labour reflects assumptions about
female and male biology which link female roles
to childbearing and mothering and male roles to
history-making. Dinnerstein is concerned about
the potential of the sexual division of labour to
shape destructive gender relationships. She maintains that the extent of responsibility for children
borne by women threatens to destroy all forms of
life, not just families, because it perpetuates sex-
based inequalities. She stresses that mother/child
relationships are foundational in the development
of any society and an important 'force' in history.
The mother provides children with their first
contact with life and the environment, with
emotions and first social experiences. Dinnerstein
maintains that an individual's development of
rationality and sexuality is built upon these mostly
unconscious experiences. The human need to
balance mastery and creativity with responsibility
originates within the mother/child relationship,
which sets up a disproportionate association of
women with child-rearing so that women become
positioned in society to serve the needs of others.

Men's repression of their infantile relationships and
emotions shapes their tendency to treat women as
separate and different and produces relationships
of dependence between the sexes.

Dinnerstein stresses the need for dual parenting to change male psyches for the better to help
shape culture more equitably. Women's subordination and social inequalities cannot be remedied
until child-rearing practices are more inclusive of
men. Her work on the implications for social
power relations of the volatile development of the
individual psyche also have enabled an analysis of
the impact of childrearing on the development of
gender identity. Both Dinnerstein and **Chodorow**, whose ideas are often compared, view
biology and gender as produced interactively
within social relations. Yet both theorists have
been criticised as paying insufficient attention to
the specific political and economic contexts of
childrearing and the shifts in understandings and
practices over time and between cultures. Dinnerstein's work goes some way to developing a
social psychology but although it recognises the
impact of the unconscious on social behaviours
and institutions it also maintains a somewhat
deterministic view of biology that disables an
adequate explanation of personality and agency
within the family and in other forms of social
relations.

Selected writings

Dinnerstein, D. (1976) *The Mermaid and the Minotaur:
Sexual Arrangements and Human Malaise*, New York:
Harper and Row.

LYNNE ALICE

disability, women and

Women with disabilities have brought attention to
gender differences in the experience of disability
and developed feminist analyses of the social
construction of disability. They have contributed
to feminist theory of the **body** by analysing their
different relationships to both feminine and
feminist body ideals and by arguing that the
suffering body is underrepresented in feminist

thought. They have also demonstrated that the experiences and interests of people with disabilities and those who care for people with disabilities are vitally relevant to such feminist philosophical concerns as developing an **ethic of care** and to feminist discussions of abortion, euthanasia, and **health** care.

Researchers working on disability have, as Michelle Fine and Adrienne Asch put it, 'focused on disability as a unitary concept and have taken it to be not merely the "master" status but apparently the exclusive status for disabled people' (1988: 3). One consequence is that gender differences in the experience of disability were only brought to light in the mid-1980s, primarily in the writings of women with disabilities (see, for example, Browne, Connors and Stern 1985). We now know that living with similar disabilities is different for women and men, and different for women of different races, classes, sexual identities, ages and ethnicities (see **race**; **identity**). Moreover, we know that living with disabilities is different for women with different disabilities, for example, paraplegia and blindness, and different for women whose disabilities are readily apparent compared to those whose disabilities can be hidden or overlooked. It is therefore important not to assume that women with disabilities identify with all others who have disabilities or share a single perspective on disability (or anything else), or that having a disability is the most important aspect of a woman's identity or social position. It is various aspects of their treatment by their societies that women with disabilities are most likely to have in common. These include: verbal, medical and physical abuse; neglect of the most basic educational needs; sexual abuse and exploitation; denial of reproductive rights; enforced poverty; harassment by public and private sector bureaucracies; job discrimination; segregation in schools, housing and workshops; inaccessibility of buildings, transportation and other public facilities; social isolation due to people's prejudice and ignorant fear; erasure as a sexual being; and many more subtle manifestations of disability-phobia, experienced as daily stress and wounds to self-esteem. As in every oppressed group, not everyone has experienced all aspects of the **oppression**, but the pattern of oppression produces overlapping patterns of experience among group members. This overlap, combined with the awareness that many things have happened to them because they are identified by others as members of the group, has motivated women of diverse experiences to adopt the identity, 'women with disabilities', to re-define what being a woman with a disability means, and to work together for their common welfare. It has also led them to recognise that their experiences give women with disabilities different perspectives on the world from those available to disabled men and non-disabled people.

The social construction of disability

Disability activists and some scholars of disability began in the 1970s to analyse disability as socially constructed (Zola 1982), challenging both the popular view of disability as a personal tragedy and the medical model of disability prevalent in the literature of rehabilitation. In the 1980s, feminist scholars (Fine and Asch 1988) began applying feminist analyses of the social construction of femaleness to their thinking about disability; virtually all feminist theorists of disability argue or imply that it is socially constructed. Although they differ as to how much emphasis they place on social and biological factors respectively (see **biology**), these analysts agree that social responses to biological **difference** construct disability, determining both its nature and severity.

On this analysis, not only do social factors affect people's health and functioning, but social arrangements make a person's biological condition more or less relevant to any situation. Disability is created by social conditions that cause or fail to prevent damage to people's bodies; for example, global injustice makes malnutrition and inadequate treatment of curable diseases major causes of disability in poor countries (Boylan 1991: 18–24). But disability is also constructed socially by such factors as expectations of performance, the pace of life, the physical and social organisation of societies to fit a young, non-disabled, 'ideally' shaped, healthy adult male paradigm citizen, failure or unwillingness to create ability among citizens who do not fit the paradigm, and cultural representations, failures of representation, and prejudices.

The concept of 'the **Other**' is useful for understanding the social treatment of people with disabilities. Making people 'the Other' involves grouping them together as the objects of our experience instead of regarding them as subjects of experience with whom we might identify, and seeing them primarily as symbolic of something else – usually, but not always, something we reject and fear. To the non-disabled, people with disabilities symbolise, among other things, imperfection, failure to control the body, and everyone's vulnerability to weakness, pain and death. Their 'Otherness' contributes to the social exclusion of people with disabilities, allows many cultures to ignore their subjectivity, and makes people with disabilities vulnerable to psychological, physical, economic and sexual abuse. In opposing this 'Otherness', disability activists tend to regard disability more neutrally as a form of difference from what is considered usual or paradigmatic in a society; their perspective leaves open the possibility that having a disability is as good as or even better than being non-disabled.

Disability and feminist theory of the body

Feminists with disabilities have pointed out that the social construction of femininity through idealisation, objectification, and demands for control of the female body is particularly damaging to the self-image and social value of women with disabilities, many of whom have bodies that are defined by their cultures as unacceptable and unattractive (Driedger and Gray 1992). Because they cannot aspire to meeting ideals of femininity, many women with disabilities have a different, more critical, relationship to them than women who can hope to approximate their cultures' ideals through their own efforts. Bonnie Klein (1992) draws attention to feminist body ideals of strength and energy which contribute to excluding women with disabilities from feminist movements.

Susan Wendell (1996) argues that feminist theory has failed to confront the suffering body. Much feminist writing of the 1970s and 1980s expresses the implicit belief that if women can only create social justice and overcome our cultural alienation from our bodies, our bodily experience will be mostly pleasant and rewarding. Other poststructuralist and postmodernist feminist analyses (see **poststructuralism/postmodernism**) offer a concept of the body which is limited only by the imagination and ignores bodily experience altogether. By neglecting the experience of bodily suffering, feminist theory has overlooked a strong reason for wanting to transcend the body, underestimated the subjective appeal of mind/body dualisms, and failed to offer an adequate alternative conception of the relationship of consciousness to the body.

Disability and feminist ethics

In feminist philosophical discussions of an **ethic of care**, the paradigm caring situation is usually a non-disabled adult caring for non-disabled children. Yet many children who need care have disabilities, and Barbara Hillyer (1993) describes how providing care for children with disabilities is significantly different from providing care for non-disabled children. Moreover, many people who give care also need it. Jenny Morris (1991) points out that people with disabilities who need care are also parents providing care to children and friends and relatives providing care to others with disabilities. This means that an adequate ethic of care must address the diverse needs of caregivers and the possibilities of reciprocal care.

In addition, many people who need care are adults with disabilities. Whereas the vast majority of children are not ready or competent to make a lot of decisions about their lives, most adults with disabilities are both competent and eager to make most of the decisions about their lives. Anita Silvers (1995) argues that an institutionalised ethic of care, unlike an ethic of equality, obliges adults with disabilities to present themselves as incompetent and needy by placing them in the social role of dependent recipients of care. Clearly, an adequate ethic of care must deal with the problems that arise for the receiver of care and the caregiver when both are competent adults and yet one needs more physical help than the other. It must also address the more ambiguous, complex relationships where one person's competence is partial, intermittent or deteriorating (e.g., when one person has mental disabilities).

'The widespread assumption that disabled

people's lives are not worth living' (Morris 1991:12) lies at the heart of much theorising about abortion, euthanasia, and health care, putting the welfare and security, and the social acceptance, of people with disabilities in jeopardy. On the other hand, people with disabilities who have extensive experiences of medical treatment and its limitations do not necessarily support an ethic of life at any cost, or a reduction of individuals' rights to choose death. While wanting to increase disabled people's choices and control of their lives, disability activists are concerned that individual 'choices' (such as those to abort a potentially disabled foetus, to die by assisted suicide, or to undergo or refuse a treatment) can quickly become social imperatives, especially when combined with such powerful social prejudices as fear of disability. Any feminist **bioethics** which includes the perspectives of women with disabilities must consider which positions on abortion, euthanasia and health care are compatible with valuing and protecting the lives of people with disabilities.

References and further reading

Boylan, E. (1991) *Women and Disability*, London and New Jersey: Zed Books.

Browne, S.E., Connors, D. and Stern, N. (eds) (1985) *With The Power of Each Breath: A Disabled Women's Anthology*, San Francisco: Cleis Press.

Driedger, D. and Gray, S. (eds) (1992) *Imprinting Our Image: An International Anthology by Women with Disabilities*, Canada: Gynergy Books.

Fine, M. and Asch, A. (eds) (1988) *Women with Disabilities: Essays in Psychology, Culture and Politics*, Philadelphia, PA: Temple University Press.

Hillyer, B. (1993) *Feminism and Disability*, Norman and London: University of Oklahoma Press.

Klein, B.S. (1992) "We Are Who You Are': Feminism and Disability', *Ms.* III, 3: 70–4.

Morris, J. (1991) *Pride Against Prejudice: Transforming Attitudes to Disability*, Philadelphia, PA: New Society Publishers.

Silvers, A. (1995) 'Reconciling Equality to Difference: Caring (F)or Justice For People With Disabilities', *Hypatia* 10 (1): 30–55.

Wendell, S. (1996) *The Rejected Body: Feminist Philosophical Reflections on Disability*, New York and London: Routledge.

Zola, I.K. (1982) *Missing Pieces: A Chronicle of Living with a Disability*, Philadelphia, PA: Temple University Press.

SUSAN WENDELL

discourse analysis

Discourse analysis has been characterised as one of the most vast and least-defined areas of linguistics (Schiffrin 1994), in part, because definitions of discourse vary according to one's theory of language (see **language, gender and power**). Indeed, two influential definitions of discourse within linguistics – discourse as a unit of language larger than the sentence versus discourse as language embedded in social interaction – have their origins in formalist versus functional theories of language, respectively. For feminist linguists, both formalist and functional definitions of discourse have been useful in broadening our conception of sexist linguistic representations beyond single words and expressions, and in turning our attention to the way meanings are negotiated and modified in actual social interactions.

Feminists have attempted to challenge the absolute **hegemony** of male-defined meanings and grammar by introducing nonsexist and feminist linguistic innovations into English. Most attempts at linguistic reform have focused on codified instances of sexist language, that is, on those aspects of English, or any other language, that are in some sense intrinsic to its grammatical and lexical structure. For example, by replacing masculine generics (e.g., *he, man*) with neutral generics (e.g., singular *they, he/she*, generic *she*) advocates of nonsexist language reform are challenging the claim implicit in the use of masculine generics that men are the typical case of humanity and women, a deviation from this norm. Another instance of feminist linguistic resistance is the coining of new terms to express women's perceptions and experiences, phenomena previously unexpressed in a language encoding a male worldview. Thus, innovative terms such as *sexism* and *sexual harassment* are significant because, as Gloria **Steinem** has remarked, 'A few years ago, they were just called life' (1983: 149).

While nonsexist and feminist linguistic innovations are commonplace in our culture, their intended meanings are routinely modified and reconstructed in actual language use, i.e., discourse. That is, simply introducing nonsexist terms or terms with feminist-influenced meanings into a language says nothing about how such terms will be used once they circulate within the wider speech community, especially given the sexist and androcentric values that pervade this larger community (see **sexism; androcentrism**). Because linguistic forms depend for their full interpretation on social context, including mutually accessible cultural knowledge, the question of whose beliefs and values inform this cultural knowledge is crucial to understanding how meanings are socially constructed. Sally McConnell-Ginet (1989) argues that the cultural knowledge forming the background for the interpretation of linguistic utterances is not neutral but rather has been contributed to disproportionately by dominant groups. Thus, the utterance 'You think like a woman' functions as an insult in most contexts in our culture, not because all listeners adhere to the proposition that women have questionable intellectual abilities, but rather because listeners are aware that such a proposition is part of a set of mutually accessible (dominant) cultural beliefs. Likewise, Muriel Schulz (1975) traces the semantic derogation of terms designating women in English, demonstrating that words such as *mistress* and *spinster*, originally positive or neutral in interpretation, have taken on negative meanings in a way that has been unparalleled for words designating men (e.g., *master*, *bachelor*). The point here is that the process whereby linguistic forms are invested with sense or meaning in discourse is a socially-conditioned one often involving sexist (and racist) beliefs and values, e.g., that being single is an undesirable state for women.

By claiming that meanings are socially constructed and constituted in discourse, McConnell-Ginet is also saying that challenges to dominant groups' meanings are possible in the context of speech communities that endorse alternative mean-

ings. Because meanings are authorised or codified through the social support of speech communities, alternative linguistic communities have the potential to authorise non-sexist, non-racist and non-homophobic meanings. Consider the case of lesbian and gay communities reclaiming terms such as *dyke* and *queer* and investing these terms with in-group positive associations. Indeed, feminist versions of discourse analysis consider the complex processes by which sexist and androcentric meanings are both reproduced and challenged in discourse.

See also: backlash; context-=ualism; interpretation; language, gender and power

References and further reading

McConnell-Ginet, S. (1989) 'The Sexual (Re)Production of Meaning', in F. Frank and P. Treichler (eds) *Language, Gender and Professional Writing*, New York: Modern Language Association.

Schiffrin, D. (1994). *Approaches to Discourse*, Oxford: Blackwell.

Schulz, M. (1975) 'The Semantic Derogation of Women', in B. Thorne and N. Henley (eds) *Language and Sex: Difference and Dominance*, Rowley, MA: Newbury House.

Steinem, G. (1983) *Outrageous Acts and Everday Rebellions*, New York: Holt, Rinehart and Winston.

SUSAN EHRLICH

discrimination and the law

Discrimination refers to unequal or differential treatment. Generally, discrimination is illegal only when there is no reasonable basis for the discriminatory conduct. For many years, most discrimination on the basis of sex was considered 'reasonable' and was therefore not illegal. In the USA, for example, it was not until the early 1970s that the US Supreme Court found sexually discriminatory laws to be illegal. Prior to that time, discrimination on the basis of sex was considered a 'reasonable' means of maintaining the traditional roles of men and women.

In the 1970s, the US Supreme Court found that the Equal Protection Clause of the Fourteenth Amendment of the United States Constitution bars discrimination on the basis of sex in most instances (see *Reed* v. *Reed*, 1971). Discrimination on the basis of sex is still permissible, however, where there are substantial and reasonable grounds for different treatment (see, e.g., *Craig* v. *Boren*, 1976). Also in the 1970s, a number of states adopted Equal Rights Amendments to their Constitutions, which explicitly bar discrimination on the basis of sex. An attempt to adopt an Equal Rights Amendment to the US Constitution failed, however, in 1982.

Other US laws prohibiting discrimination on the basis of sex include Title VII of the 1964 Civil Rights Act and Title IX of the Education Amendments of 1972 (barring sex discrimination in employment and education, respectively). Generally, these laws have been interpreted to prohibit both intentional discrimination and conduct that has a discriminatory impact on women. Sexual harassment has also been interpreted to be a form of sex discrimination that is prohibited by these laws and court decisions.

Similar protections are provided in other countries and by international law. The European Convention on Human Rights, for example, prohibits discrimination on the basis of sex, as does The Universal Declaration of Human Rights. Very few of these statutes and rulings, however, provide protection against discrimination on the basis of sexual orientation.

Feminist theorists have played an important role in shaping discrimination law, most notably in the debate over when and whether it should be legally permissible to treat women differently from men. Many feminists, such as Nancy **Chodorow**, argue that discrimination based on relevant differences between the sexes is appropriate. Others, such as Judith **Butler**, argue that the notion of sex-based differences is itself a socially constructed and discriminatory assumption. These different arguments give rise, in turn, to different conclusions about when and whether laws should, if ever, discriminate on the basis of sex.

See also: affirmative action; civil rights; equality/difference; feminist legal theory; lesbian jurisprudence

References and further reading

Higgins, T.E. (1995) 'By Reason of Their Sex: Feminist Theory, Postmodernism, and Justice', *Cornell Law Review*, 80: 1536–94.

MacKinnon, C.A. (1987) *Feminism Unmodified: Discourses on Life and Law*, Cambridge, MA: Harvard University Press.

Rhode, D. (1989) *Justice and Gender: Sex Discrimination and the Law*, Cambridge, MA: Harvard University Press.

ANNE BLOOM

dispassionate investigation

Dispassionate investigation is inquiry – usually scientific or social scientific – which is maximally objective. The inquirer scrupulously erases emotion, interest, personal investment from the investigative processes and products, to ensure objective neutrality cleansed of subjective contaminations. The idea is that emotions – passions – are beyond rational control, and would compromise the claim of research to the status of knowledge; that the quality of investigations is diminished if the inquirer has a stake in their outcome. Many feminists and other Others argue, however, that the mask of disinterestedness merely conceals how interests of the powerful drive and legitimate knowledge-making projects that preserve the status quo. Feminists have sought to expose the underlying passions that inform every theoretical commitment, including feminism itself, arguing for a self-scrutinising requirement as part of every project of inquiry.

See also: objectivity

References and further reading

Ferrell, R. (1996) *Passion in Theory*, London: Routledge.

LORRAINE CODE

diversity

The term diversity is used to refer to differences between women arising from biological and social factors, such as ethnicity, educational opportunities, health status, age and cultural location. Robin Morgan has commented that:

> Feminism itself dares to assume that, beneath all our (chosen or forced) diversity, we are in fact much the same – yet the *ways* in which we are similar are not for any woman or group of women to specify, but all of us, collectively, to explore and define – a multiplicity of feminisms. In other words, our experience as female human beings in patriarchy may be the same, but our experiences of that experience differ.
>
> (Morgan 1991)

Unlike the term **difference**, which has recently gained a more specialised usage in feminist writing, 'diversity' generally conveys an acceptance of what Sheila Ruth (1995) has called the 'different similarities' of women's lives and feminist perspectives.

References and further reading

Morgan, R. (1991) 'Feminist Diplomacy', *Ms.*, May/June: 1.

Ruth, S. (1995) *Issues in Feminism: An Introduction to Women's Studies*, Mountain View, CA: Mayfield Publishing Company.

LYNNE ALICE

divine feminine

Images of the divine feminine, the Great **Goddess**, Giver, Taker, and Renewer of Life, Earth Mother, Queen of Heaven, Mother of Compassion are found in almost all religions. Athena, Aphrodite, Istar, Inanna, Kwan Yin, Kali, Durga, Oshun, White Buffalo Woman, Corn Woman, Old Spider Woman, Ezili, Coatlicue: her names are as diverse as the people who invoke her. Only the aggressively monotheistic faiths, Judaism, Christianity, Islam, prohibited images of the female God. And they were not entirely successful. The ancient Hebrews were castigated by their prophets for continually returning to female divinities. Some believe that devotees of Mary and the female saints are worshipping the divine feminine. Others contend that Jews honour her as Shekinah and the Sabbath Bride. It has even been suggested that Jesus viewed himself as the prophet of Sophia, the divine feminine personifed as Wisdom. Carl Jung argues that the suppression of the divine feminine has led to the over-rationalisation of modern societies, causing psychic and spiritual illness. His follower Erich Neumann catalogued images of the divine feminine in *The Great Mother* (1955). From a feminist standpoint, Jungian studies of the feminine are flawed by Jung's theory that the feminine is the unconscious, the dark, and the chaotic, while the masculine is the conscious, the light, and the rational. The feminist movement has a strong spiritual feminist component (see **spiritual feminism**). Matilda Joslyn Gage and Elizabeth Cady Stanton in the nineteenth century were followed by Mary **Daly**, Ntozake Shange, Merlin Stone, and many others in the twentieth who argued that when God is male, the male is God. In both the widely popular Goddess movement (see **Goddess; witchcraft**) and in feminist reform movements in Christianity and Judaism, western women and men are beginning again to pray to God She, God the Mother, and Goddess (see **Christianity and feminism**; **Judaism and feminism**). Proponents of the divine feminine argue that 'She' allows women to see that they are created in the divine image and thus promotes women's psychic and spiritual, social and political liberation. For many, images of the divine as Gaia or Earth offer important symbolic support for the ethics of **ecofeminism**. Nonwhite feminists have called attention to the many images of the divine feminine in Native American, Asian, African, and Pacific cultures. Some fear that focus on the divine feminine perpetuates stereotypes that associate women exclusively with the body and nature. Others argue that the divine feminine includes the body and the mind, the conscious and the unconscious, the light and the dark, the rational and the non-rational, nature and culture.

See also: earth/Gaia/Mother Earth

References and further reading

Christ, C.P. (1997) *Rebirth of the Goddess: Finding Meaning in Feminist Spirituality*, New York: Addison.

Olson, C. (ed.) (1983) *The Book of the Goddess: Past and Present*, New York: Crossroad.

CAROL P. CHRIST

Doane, Mary Ann

Mary Ann Doane, a leading feminist film critic, is known for her groundbreaking work on the female spectator, and on modernity, time and technology. 'Film and the Masquerade: Theorizing the Female Spectator' (1991), originally published in 1982, contributes to theories of female spectatorship – the central issue in feminist film theory in the 1980s (see **film theory, feminist**). Whereas Laura **Mulvey** had famously theorised the conditions of the male **gaze** in classic Hollywood cinema, Doane analyses the position of the female spectator and her desire in relation to the 'woman's picture' – a subtype of Hollywood melodrama that centred on a female protagonist and assumed a female audience. In response to the unacceptable alternatives available to the female spectator – narcissistically over-identifying with the image or uncomfortably adopting the masculine position to objectify the onscreen woman – she draws on Joan Riviere's concept of femininity as masquerade. Albeit a limited strategy, by wearing femininity as a mask, the female spectator can create enough distance between herself and the image to resist being drawn into cinema's often masochistic scenarios of femininity. In *The Desire to Desire* (1987), she analyses female subjectivity and spectatorship in women's films of the 1940s, showing how they repetitiously inscribe scenarios that prohibit or punish woman's looking. Feminist psychoanalytic theories of spectatorship, including Doane's, were criticised in the late 1980s for treating the 'female spectator' as a homogeneous category. In response, Doane and Janet Bergstrom observe that differences between approaches to the female spectator 'cannot be flattened out', since they stem from conflicting 'epistemological premises and theories of subjectivity'. Whereas the concept of the unconscious is central to psychoanalysis, it is irrelevant to ethnography (1989: 12).

Although Doane works within the psychoanalytic tradition, she does not treat psychoanalysis as a 'true discourse' that can explain cinema. Rather, she traces coincidences between psychoanalytic and cinematic discourse: both purport to be about the feminine, which they repress. In 'Dark Continents: Epistemologies of Racial and Sexual Difference in Psychoanalysis and the Cinema' (in *Femmes Fatales*, 1991), she examines inter-connections between the representation of the white woman and the black woman in psychoanalytic and cinematic discourse. She shows how racial difference has continually been sexualised, and considers whether psychoanalysis can be useful in analysing this construction, or is simply complicit in it. In her 1990s work on cinema, modernity and time, Doane explores the implications of new technologies – photography and cinema at the end of the nineteenth century, and information technologies at the end of the twentieth century – for conceptualisations of sexual difference and assumptions about the body.

Selected writings

Doane, M.A. (1991) 'Film and the Masquerade: Theorizing the Female Spectator' in *Femmes Fatales: Feminism, Film Theory, Psychoanalysis*, New York: Routledge.

—— (1997) 'Technology and Sexual Difference: Apocalyptic Scenarios at Two "Fins-de-siècle"', *Differences*, 9 (2).

Doane, M.A. and Bergstrom, J. (1989) *Camera Obscura* 20 21 (May–September), special issue: 'The Spectatrix'.

ROSANNE KENNEDY

domesticity, cult of

The notion of the home as both incubator of a sound character and haven from the outside world became part of middle-class culture in Europe and the USA by the late eighteenth century. Mid-Victorian domestic ideology assigned middle-class husbands the roles of provider, disciplinarian, and educational director while reserving the roles of nurturer-mother and household manager to the wife, often depicted as an 'angel-mother' upon whose bosom the weary husband might rest his head (Tosh 1991). As the family home became the focus for personal life, demands for home-based gentility (comfortable, attractive, and clean homes, fine cuisine, and healthy, well-behaved children) increased. However, among the slowly growing nineteenth-century urban professional class, this kind of genteel domesticity was possible only to the extent that the husband's income allowed hiring servants to free the wife from household production so that she could devote her energies instead to **motherhood**, homemaking, and the production of gentility.

Although the *cult of domesticity* has its origins in Victorian culture, domesticity as a central value reappears in the interwar years, subsides during the Second World War, and returns with a vengeance (particularly in the USA) in the 1950s. As household technology gradually replaced paid domestic help, and men's real incomes rose, growing numbers of working-class as well as middle-class women were able to partake of postwar domesticity. As Palmer (1989) notes, between 1920 and 1945 middle-class housewives transitioned from 'ladies' directing their paid household workers to wives serving their families with the help of African American, Hispanic and Japanese domestic workers.

Both the root causes and the actual practice of domesticity vary greatly across time periods, regions, and social classes. In the early nineteenth century, the rise of domesticity accompanies the development of an urban middle class, the male career, and the demise of 'putting out' systems whereby children were sent to other families as apprentices or servants. Although the doctrine of separate spheres specified that men belonged in the public and women in the private spheres (see **public/private**), historians such as Elizabeth Pleck point out that middle-class men worked in or near their homes while women's duties brought them often into the public sphere. The doctrine of separate spheres, therefore, existed primarily as an ideology barring women from most occupations while protecting men from household work. It is only during the postwar years that the briefcase-carrying husband-commuter married to suburban-

housewife-shopper-chauffeur becomes the model household type in North America.

See also: work, women and

References and further reading

Palmer, P. (1989) *Domesticity and Dirt: Housewives and Domestic Servants in the United States, 1920–1945*, Philadelphia, PA: Temple University Press.

Pleck, E. (1976) 'Two Worlds in One: Work and Family', *Journal of Social History* 10: 178–95.

Tosh, J. (1991) 'Domesticity and Manliness in the Victorian Middle Class: The Family of Edward White Benson', in M. Roper and J. Tosh (eds) *Manful Assertions: Masculinities in Britain since 1800*, London: Routledge.

JANE HOOD

dominance

Feminists have been introducing conceptual innovations into socio-political theory. Among these is the understanding of men's and women's relationships as oppressive, and of gender **oppression** as the unjustifiable dominance by men and the respective subordination of women. Prior to feminism, gender dominance/subordination was seen as appropriate and acceptable. But, inspired by the revolutions of the eighteenth and nineteenth centuries and struggles for the abolition of slavery, feminists like Mary Wollstonecraft, Harriet Taylor and John Stuart Mill, and members of the women's suffrage movements began to challenge the subordination of women to men.

During the late 1960s and early 1970s, second-wave radical, socialist, and lesbian feminists (see **lesbian feminism**), such as Shulamith **Firestone**, Kate **Millet**, Juliet **Mitchell**, and Charlotte **Bunch**, drawing critically on the existentialism of Simone de **Beauvoir**, Freudian conceptions of repression, current analyses of capitalism, racism, imperialism, and more generally of socio-political **power**, argued against discourses that naturalise the hierarchical relationship between men and women and the myriad social practices of privileging men and discriminating against women (see **privilege**). They asserted that the dominance/subordination relationship between men and women must be thought of systemically, redeployed the term '**patriarchy**' and interjected new expressions like 'sex/gender system' to refer to the totality of the structured relationships of gender dominance/subordination.

Because they claimed for the system of gender dominance/subordination both antiquity and universality and at times even said that it was the model for other forms of dominance/subordination, they have been criticised, particularly by feminists of colour, like Angela **Davis** and bell **hooks** for establishing a priority among oppressions. This claim also elides some women's dominance with respect to other women and some men as a function of women's membership in different classes or of being socio-culturally positioned as racially/ethnically superior. Feminists of colour, such as María **Lugones** and Kimberlé Crenshaw, and their allies, for example, Elizabeth Spelman, assert that instead of thinking about systems of dominance/subordination as discrete and isolated, they need to be conceived of as intersecting or interlocking.

Ecofeminists have added a dimension to feminist understandings of dominance/subordination by showing that there are interesting parallels and connections between the portrayal of men's relationships to women and to nature (see **ecofeminism**). Similar connections have been made by postcolonial feminist theorists showing that the representation of women, the colonised, and nature construct them all as needing and being quasi-capable of being tamed by men from colonising groups (see **postcolonial feminism**). Another addition to feminist theories of dominance/subordination has resulted from the influences of poststructuralism (see **poststructuralism/postmodernism**). These have also complicated feminist theorisations of the possibility of resistance to gender subordination.

References and further reading

Nicholson, L. (ed.) (1997) *The Second Wave: A Reader in Feminist Theory*, New York: Routledge.

BAT-AMI BAR ON

double burden

Double burden refers to the dual oppression experienced by women who are both paid workers and unpaid homemakers, wives and mothers in the household. The term emerged in feminist theory in the late 1970s, as the structure of the paid labour force was radically changed by high numbers of working women (including married women, white women, and mothers). Implicitly, the concept assumes that the primary site of a woman's oppression is the private sphere, and that this oppression doubles if and when she also participates in the public sphere of employment. The term has been criticised for its assumption of whiteness, since racialised women bear a double burden which compounds to a triple burden when they participate in employment. Others have critiqued its heterosexist assumption that all women are oppressed by their sexual relationship to a male head of family (see **heterosexism, heteronormativity**).

See also: public/private; socialism and feminism; work, women and

SUSAN L. PRENTICE

dowries

Based on Indian (primarily Hindu and Sikh) rituals of exchange, dowries involve the transferral of material wealth and objects from natal to conjugal households in largely hypergamous marriages (between equal or superior castes). While fulfilling sacred parent/daughter obligations, dowries also function as potentially prestige-enhancing symbols for the bride and natal family. Indirect dowries ('buying a bride') conversely involve dowry payments from the bridegroom's family to a poorer family.

India's 1961 Dowry Prohibition Act and later legislation have failed to regulate dowry practice, female infanticide, suttee and other dowry-related deaths. As modernising forces intensify existing pressures for families to fulfil the material expectations of receiving conjugal households, dowries continue to highlight the complex interaction among **agency**, **gender**, ritual distributions of

power and property within destabilised **kinship** structures.

See also: bride/widow burning (suttee burial); Hinduism

References and further reading

Minturn, L. (1993) *Sita's Daughters: Coming Out of Purdah*, Oxford: Oxford University Press.

SATINDER KAUR CHOHAN

dual systems theory

Dual systems theory is a strand of feminist theory, also known as socialist feminism, that synthesises the Marxist analysis of capitalism and the radical feminist theorisation of patriarchy to demonstrate the importance of both social systems in the structuring of gender relations (see **socialism and feminism**; **Marxism**; **radical feminism**). Some dual systems theorists disagree about the specific articulation of **patriarchy** and capitalism. For example, some argue that there has been a fusion of capitalism and patriarchy into a single capitalist-patriarchy, while others conceptualise these structures as mutually independent, yet interactive, systems of gender oppression.

Dual systems theory enables feminists to theorise the exploitation of women's paid and unpaid labour, as well as their cultural, legal and political oppressions (see **work, women and**). It has been critiqued for its predominantly monolithic and ahistorical conceptualisations of capitalism and patriarchy, and its general lack of attention to how other oppressive structures, such as **sexuality**, **violence**, racialisation and imperialism, contribute to contemporary gender inequalities.

NANCY COOK

dutiful daughters

The phrase 'dutiful daughters' enters English-language feminism from the (1987) translation of volume one of Simone de **Beauvoir**'s autobiography, *Memoirs of a Dutiful Daughter* (*Mémoires d'une jeune fille rangée*, 1958). Rooted in the socially restrictive imperatives within which a girl was to become a woman in 1920s bourgeois France, it is emblematic of the constraints that shape growing up female in white western societies. To be a member of the first generation of European women educated in all-male institutions, as Beauvoir was, entailed defying the law of the father. Some commentators read Beauvoir's relationship with Jean-Paul Sartre as a reenactment of dutiful daughterhood in a philosophical project of 'theoretical-loving admiration' dedicated to a new father (in Michèle Le Doeuff's phrase). **Le Doeuff** notes that Beauvoir rejected this interpretation.

See also: Beauvoir, Simone de

References and further reading

Le Doeuff, M. (1991) *Hipparchia's Choice*, trans. T. Selous, Oxford: Blackwell.

LORRAINE CODE

Dworkin, Andrea (b. 1946)

Andrea Dworkin is amongst the most maligned feminists of the late twentieth century. Yet as we move into the twenty-first century she remains a fierce and passionate warrior in her fight against 'male power, violence and the war against women' (see **sex wars, the**). Sources of aversion towards her are multiple and murky. One may wonder about the depth of animosity directed towards a woman who writes assertively about the abuses done to women and the arrogance of male power, especially when she is so frequently represented as the quintessential antithesis of what western patriarchal man imagines woman should be. Dworkin is not pretty, she is fat and she refuses to shut up.

Her work on **pornography**, **sexuality**, and **misogyny** has attracted most attention. Her book on pornography goes to the root of the word. Pornography does not mean 'writing about sex' but is instead about the 'graphic depiction of the lowest whores' (1989: 200). She places pornography at the centre of male domination and female subordination, arguing that pornography acts as 'a kind of nerve centre of sexual abuse'. Because Dworkin believes pornography actually harms all women, she (with Catharine **MacKinnon**) attempted to use the law to get pornography recognised as a violation of women's civil and human rights (see **censorship**). Passed twice in Minneapolis and Indianapolis, this law was ultimately defeated by the US Supreme Court.

Through her other major works, non-fiction writing, and public speaking activities, Dworkin exposes violent inequalities in the institutions and practices of **heterosexuality**, aiming to obliterate male power and 'tear down the hierarchies of sex and race and class'. Her ambitious aims and apparently essentialist, universalising and exclusionary foundations seem anachronistic to contemporary feminists. Indeed, some of her most zealous critics have been other feminists.

No doubt many feminist criticisms about Dworkin's work have validity. She can seem to deny women's agency with regard to defining what sex is, as well as conflating representation with reality. Nevertheless, these points cannot invalidate the passion, power and energy of Dworkin's work and her commitment to speak about untenable and often invisible abuses towards women. Her work serves as a reminder that saying things and getting them 'wrong' is not the main problem. Not being allowed to say them at all, is.

Selected writings

Dworkin, A. (1987) *Intercourse*, London: Arrow Books.
—— (1989) *Pornography: Men Possessing Women*, New York: Plume.

—— (1997) *Life and Death: Unapologetic Writings on the Continuing War Against Women*, London: Virago.

MARYSIA ZALEWSKI

dystopias

A dystopia projects in fictional form a vision of an impending evil world, avoidable only through intense social resistance. Its dialectical counterpart is the utopia, the dream of the good society (see **science fiction, feminist**; **utopias, feminist**). However from Thomas More's sixteenthth-century *Utopia* onwards, the utopias of men have all too commonly been women's dystopias.

Twentieth-century anglophone feminists used dystopias to warn women of impending and deeply gendered political dangers. Thus in 1937 Katherine Burdekin depicted a post-Nazi society, while in 1986 Margaret Atwood depicted a post-nuclear-holocaust society. A key image is of the master of the house raping the 'handmaid', lying passively between his infertile wife's legs, as only conception guarantees survival.

The actual millennial horror of genocide and mass rape as a weapon of war was beyond our worst nightmares.

References and further reading

Atwood, M. (1986) *The Handmaid's Tale*, London: Cape.
Burdekin, K. (1937) *Swastika Night*, London: Lawrence and Wishart, 1985.

HILARY ROSE

E

earth/Gaia/Mother Earth

Earth may have been the first divinity to be worshipped by most peoples of the world. For those not separated from nature by urban technology, earth (which included sky and water) appeared to be the literal source of all life, human and nonhuman. In many gathering and hunting and early agricultural societies, Earth was personified as Mother, giving life from her body. According to Hesiod (*c*.700 BCE) Gaia (the Greek word for earth) was the most ancient divinity.

Indo-European myth and theory elevates the Sky Father over Earth Mother, negatively identifying the feminine, earth, and matter with unconsciousness, chaos, danger, death, and darkness. J. Lovelock and L. Margulis proposed the 'Gaia hypothesis', which views the earth as a self-regulating system. 'Gaia consciousness' connotes respect for the web of life. Contemporary Goddess worshippers, witches, neo-pagans, and ecofeminists view earth as sacred.

See also: ecofeminism; Goddess; pagan religion, feminist; witchcraft

References and further reading

Gimbutas, M. (1989) *The Language of the Goddess*, San Francisco: Harper.
Lovelock, J.E. (1982) Gaia: *A New Look at Life on Earth*, Oxford: Oxford University Press.

CAROL P. CHRIST

eating disorders

From a feminist theory perspective, three facts about eating disorders are striking. First, as significant social phenomena eating disorders are new. Instances have been documented, infrequently, throughout history, but it is not until the second half of the nineteenth century that something like a minor epidemic of anorexia nervosa is first described in medical accounts. Second, anorexia, bulimia and compulsive eating are predominantly problems of girls and women. Third, during the 1980s and 1990s the incidence of eating disorders dramatically escalated and apparently 'spread', with increases noted globally, among men, and among ethnicities (e.g., African Americans) previously – and inaccurately – thought to be immune. (It is unclear, however, how many such cases have previously been ignored because patients were ashamed to report them or because therapists failed to perceive them in groups that did not fit their clinical expectations.)

Before we explore these facts, we first need to ask: What is an eating disorder? This question is the tip of an iceberg that, when chiselled at, exposes provocative issues concerning medicine, **gender**, and culture (see **cultural politics**). To begin with, what counts as a medical disorder depends not only on scientific knowledge but also on social beliefs. Behaviours regarded as signs of mental disease in one culture may be may viewed as signs of moral failure in others. Today, self-starvation (anorexia nervosa), bingeing and purging (bulimia), compulsive over-eating, and even compulsive exercising are likely to be to be viewed as the province of medical professionals, to be treated through self-help manuals, psychotherapy, or drugs. But in Europe in the sixteenth century, if a young woman steadfastly refused to eat it was likely to be interpreted as evidence of spiritual zeal, and possibly miraculous (Brumberg 1988). Behaviours and attitudes involving food, perhaps because desire and self-gratification are at issue, are still frequently seen in moral terms. Compulsive overeating, for example, is often – and inaccurately – viewed as a failure of will power. But during the twentieth century, eating problems increasingly became the domain of medical science, psychiatry, and psychology.

Ideas about eating disorders have undergone many changes. Anorexia nervosa is a striking example. Initially, anorexia was defined (in 1870, by William Gull) as a disturbance of appetite; it was believed that anorexics had no *desire* for food. In the 1950s, the prominence of psychoanalysis shifted emphasis to fears about eating as 'oral' anxieties with symbolic significance – of pregnancy, for example. In the 1970s, largely through the important insights of Hilde Bruch (1973; 1979), the 'relentless pursuit of thinness' became key. From this crucial shift followed a host of psychological explanations and syndromes: 'Body Images Distortion Syndrome', 'pathological fear of fat', extreme perfectionism, dysfunctional dynamics within upwardly mobile families, and so on. These conceptualisations have left their stamp on popular stereotypes: many people today still picture the anorexic as a pampered little princess ('the best little girl in the world', as a psychiatrist's best-seller tagged her [Levonkron 1981]) with nothing better to do than look in the mirror and imagine herself fat. Recent work detailing how eating disorders may often be a response to sexual abuse, ethnic and racial prejudice and exclusion, and even poverty (Thompson 1994) is slowly changing these perceptions.

It is instructive to look at the conceptualisation of anorexia in historical context. It did not take a stretch of the imagination for Victorian physicians to perceive wasting women as without appetite; the symptom was on a continuum with dominant notions of femininity. In the 'return to domesticity' of the post-war 1950s (see **domesticity, cult of**), physicians readily interpreted women's problems as a struggle with resuming our 'natural' destiny as wives and mothers. During the ensuing commercial boom, adolescents came into their own as the first teenage consumers, with their own specially targeted teen idols, clothing fads, magazines, and products. 'Becoming a woman' now revolved around emulating the airbrushed images presented in magazines and movies. In this context, it was inevitable that the conceptualisation of eating disorders would begin to focus on issues specific to adolescence and the developing culture of all-consuming images.

And gender? It is only with the emergence in the 1980s of specifically feminist perspectives (Orbach, Chernin, Bordo, Bloom) that attention begins to be paid to the importance of sexual abuse, gender ideology (e.g. women should feed others, not themselves,) gendered images (e.g. of the cool, hyperslim superwoman,) and new social demands on women (e.g., that girls compete successfully with men while 'never letting them forget they're men'). New research has revealed, too, how distressingly common obsessive dieting, bingeing, compulsive exercising, purging and laxative abuse are among girls and women (not only those who suffer from full-blown anorexia or bulimia). It begins to seem that when it comes to attitudes and behaviours concerning food, weight, and body-image it is difficult to draw a neat division between the pathological and the normal. What is *normal* in our culture may itself involve extremely *disordered* behaviours and attitudes.

One study asked ten- and eleven-year-old boys and girls to rank drawings of children with various physical handicaps: drawings of fat children elicited the greatest disapproval and discomfort, over pictures of children with facial disfigurements and missing hands. At any given time, 85 per cent of American women are dieting – and diets are now known to be a chief culprit in the proliferation of anorexia, bulimia, and compulsive eating. Our cultural notions of the body beautiful, too, are clearly disorder-producing, and growing more so (see **beauty (the feminine beauty system)**). Those in the fashion trade admit that models have been getting thinner since 1993, when Kate Moss first re-popularised the waif look. Consumer-culture thrives on spreading its tentacles across race, class, and gender; the models advertising K-Mart outfits are now as fashionably emaciated as those modeling for *Vogue*. The main contender against the reign of such images is a muscular aesthetic that *looks* more life-affirming but is no less punishing in its demands on bodies. (There is growing evidence of rampant eating disorders among female gymnasts and athletes.)

This is not to say, however, that eating disorders are only about images. Rather, the imagery we idealise is itself expressive of cultural values (Bordo 1993). The body, with its insistent needs and unconquerable vulnerabilities, has always been a flashpoint for anxieties about control and order, arguably especially acute in our own time. For those who are starving from poverty or disease, the thin body may symbolise death. In a culture geared toward over-consumption, on the other hand, slenderness symbolises self-discipline and self-control, a tantalising ideal when so much around us encourages us to binge! Fashion's boyish but passive waifs may also reflect long-standing ambivalence toward women's desires and hungers, and new anxieties as well. Eating disorders began to escalate at a certain historical conjunction, where traditional ideas about femininity collided with new roles and liberties for women (see **gender roles**). Young women today, more seemingly 'free' and claiming greater public space than ever before, are also beset by contradictory demands and tremendous pressures to succeed in both the traditionally male *and* traditionally female worlds. Images of cool and contained – and seemingly desireless – androgynes speak to them about how to stay safe, avoid hurt, 'get it together'(Bordo 1997).

Clearly, *cultural* nutrients are what is causing eating disorders to thrive and extend their domain. Recognising this does not make anorexia, bulimia, and compulsive eating less physiologically dangerous or less disruptive of individual lives. Nor does it follow that everyone who goes on a diet or worries about getting fat will develop an eating disorder. *All* human disorders are extremely complex ecologies, which are best understood in terms of the interplay of multiple systemic factors: physiological, economic, historical, psychological, and cultural. Biochemistry plays a significant role in *turning* a diet into an eating disorder. But biochemistry is not responsible for the cultural diet-mania that is putting more and more people at risk from eating disorders every day. Family pressures may encourage the development of anorexia. But appearance-conscious or food-controlling families do not exist in a cultural vacuum. Neither do 'peer pressure', 'perfectionism', 'body image distortion', and 'fear of fat'. These behaviours, values, and attitudes are not universal; they have flourished in a certain cultural context. In a very important sense, then, anorexia, bulimia and compulsive overeating are cultural disorders.

References and further reading

Bloom, C., Gitter, A., Gutwill, S., Kogel, L. and Zaphiropoulos, L. (1994) *Eating Problems: A Feminist Psychoanalytic Treatment Model*, New York: Basic Books.

Bordo, S. (1993) *Unbearable Weight: Feminism, Western Culture, and the Body*, Berkeley, CA: University of California Press.

—— (1997) *Twilight Zones: The Hidden Life of Cultural Images from Plato to OJ*, Berkeley, CA: University of California Press.

Bruch, H. (1973) *Eating Disorders: Obesity, Anorexia Nervosa, and the Person Within*, New York: Basic Books.

—— (1979) *The Golden Cage: The Enigma of Anorexia Nervosa*, New York: Vintage.

Brumberg, J.J. (1988) *Fasting Girls: The Emergence of Anorexia as a Modern Disease*, Cambridge, MA: Harvard University Press.

Chernin, K. (1981) *The Obsession: Reflections on the Tyranny of Slenderness*, New York: Harper and Row.

Levonkron, S. (1981) *The Best Little Girl in the World*, New York: Warner Books.

Orbach, S. (1985) *Hunger Strike: The Anorectic's Struggle as a Metaphor for Our Age*, New York: Norton.

Thompson, B. (1994) *A Hunger So Wide and So Deep*, Minneapolis, MI: University of Minnesota Press.

SUSAN BORDO

ecofeminism

Ecofeminism, which is often stereotyped in the singular terms of Goddess-worshipping or the earth mother image, is actually a highly diverse position.

As Karen Warren notes, 'Ecological feminism has its roots in the wide variety of feminisms'. 'What makes ecofeminism distinct is its insistence that nonhuman nature . . . and the domination of nature are feminist issues' (Warren 1997). Ecofeminist cultural issues have close links to activism, and include animal and ecological defence, peace, and ecospirituality; global capitalism is contested by socialist, anti-colonial, materialist and critical developmental ecofeminisms. Ecofeminisms have some claim to be the most inclusive forms of feminism, recognising in the treatment of nature and animals a greater variety and depth of **oppression** than other feminist positions. Thus ecofeminisms are important sites for testing and theorising new connections between oppressions, but their inclusiveness can also magnify problems and conflicts around intersection areas.

Ecofeminism aims to have feminism and ecology mutually inform one another, developing a feminism that is ecological and an ecology that is feminist (King 1989). Ecological feminism challenges us to understand the contribution of **gender** to the forms of culture and economic rationality that bring contemporary societies into ecological danger zones. These appear at the cultural level, among others; ecofeminist historical scholars Rosemary Ruether (1975) and Carolyn Merchant (1980) established major conceptual connections between women and nature in western culture (see **nature/culture**). As Karen Warren puts it, nature has been feminised and women naturalised, so that understanding these connections is necessary to understanding their respective oppressions. Ecofeminisms challenge feminism to rethink both the concept of woman and that of the human in ecological terms, and to theorise women's inclusion in humanity in ways respectful of nonhuman difference and sensitive to human continuity with nonhuman nature. Since western culture has long denied this continuity and defined the human as mind or reason (coded male) in opposition to the **body** (coded female and animal), it moves feminism beyond the liberal feminist strategy of seeking equality within this masculinist model of the human to questioning the model itself (see **equality and difference; liberal feminism**). Joint rethinking of these linked categories of women, humanity, reason and nature is necessary.

Feminist environmental philosophy applies insights from feminist philosophy to the problems of environmental philosophy. It critiques masculinist foundations for environmental philosophy, challenging dualism or binarism in human/nature relationships and in the history of western thought and culture. Warren (1990), Plumwood 1993, Merchant (1996), and Cuomo (1998) develop for non-human life, alternative feminist foundations stressing care, communicative and mutualistic ethics, while Cuomo develops an Aristotelean ethic of flourishing which crosses the boundary between human and nonhuman ethical concerns. Plumwood reconceives the nonhuman in anti-mechanist terms that provide a richer intentional concept of embodiment, argues for the applicability to nonhumans of concepts of othering, recognition and justice, and stresses methodological openness towards the nonhuman envisaged as potentially active agent, narrative subject and communicative other. Plumwood develops logical parallels between **androcentrism**, **eurocentrism** and anthropocentrism, and argues that western culture's historical phases of 'progress' can be understood as phases of colonisation of the various forms of 'nature' by 'reason' (1993).

Feminist theology was initially a major site for the development of ecofeminism. Early authors such as Ruether and Daly drew on divergent political ideals, Ruether on communitarian socialism (see **communitarianism, women and**) opposing all oppressions including the nonhuman, Daly on a **radical feminism** which privileges masculinity and patriarchal culture as causal factors (see **patriarchy**). This split persists in later ecofeminisms. The ecofeminism of the 1970s and 1980s critiqued dualised conceptions of spirit as transcendent male deity and developed alternative ecofeminist spiritualities of embodiment and immanence (Spretnak 1991). Later ecofeminism emphasised social, socialist and anti-colonial approaches. Despite some convergence, opposition appears in conflicts around the animal ecofeminism developed from the late 1980s. Carol Adams's work on the sexual politics of meat shows how sexism and meat-consumption are interwoven in some parts of contemporary western societies. However, limitations of context for this interweaving are inadequately registered, leaving a universalist construction of masculinity and meat eating. Adams (1994) shows the continuing methodological influence of radical feminism in her universalising account of women's relationship to predation and stress on masculinity as creating an oppressive construction of animals in reductive terms as 'meat'. In advocacy for a universalised veganism which will reconstruct as non-predator the masculinised human, a vegan model of human life is seen as corresponding to 'women's gathering'. But there is a big methodological difference between rejecting predation in universalist terms and rejecting what particular social contexts have made of predation. Economic rationalist reductive and self-maximising re-constructions of the predation relationship in the abuses of factory farming would be at least a major focus of socialist ecofeminism.

Ecofeminism is often accused of **essentialism**, Sturgeon argues, damaging forms of essentialism that are not inevitably present in ecofeminism. The adoption of universalising concepts of woman can register strategic or ethical stances of solidarity rather than essentialist claims about women's nature (Sturgeon 1997). This becomes dangerous and culturally hegemonic mainly when radical feminist methodologies falsely universalise the experience and perspectives of privileged women, especially racially and economically privileged women, and obscure those of other women (Adams 1993). For example, from an anti-capitalist and anti-colonial ecofeminist perspective, the unqualified assumptions that 'women' do not hunt, that female-led 'gathering' societies were vegan or plant-based, and that hunting is strongly masculinist (Adams 1994: 107; Collard 1988), presuppose a modern western urban life, along with a gendered dualism of foraging activities which denies and disappears the gender-mixed forms of hunting and gathering encountered in many societies – Australian Aboriginal societies where women routinely hunt smaller animals, for instance. The radical feminist proclivity to universalise and decontextualise 'woman' and to privilege explanations focused on masculinity means neglect both of ethnic and cultural difference and of capitalist forms of economic rationality behind contemporary animal debasement. This hegemonic methodology plus the assumption of a gendered hunting/gathering dualism ensures that hunting is

the main focus of attention in radical ecofeminist literature, although economic maximisation in factory farming accounts for the vast majority of animal deaths and extreme suffering. The outcome is problematic for activism because the careful contextualisations required for opposition to hunting are neglected, while strategies of opposition to economic abuse in factory farming are de-emphasised (Adams 1993: 203). The deployment of universalised and decontextualised concepts of 'woman' thus yields hegemonic conflicts with ecofeminist ideals opposing all forms of oppression. The idea that opposition to oppression can be thought of as additive, and that ecofeminism can be extended as a singular generalised opposition to oppression in all its forms, must be reconsidered in the light of such essentialist conflicts. Ecofeminist ethics have stressed contextualisation (Warren 1990), so ecofeminism can either try to develop a contextualising route out of these dilemmas, or envisage itself in more plural terms as a cluster or family of related positions.

For socialist ecofeminisms the category of reproduction associated with women's labour is interpreted in solidaristic terms as including the human and nonhuman ecological conditions that support production, the privileged male-coded category defined in opposition to reproduction (Merchant 1980). Recent developments in socialist ecofeminisms include ecofeminist neo-Marxism or 'materialist' ecofeminisms based on analysis of the sex/gender division of labour around human embodiment. Mellor argues that 'to the extent that human societies are biologically sexed and/or socially gendered, men and women stand in a different relation to the natural world'. (1997: 2). Capitalism's production of gender and other kinds of subordination through these spheres of labour and consequent blindspots about how processes of (material) production depend on reproduction are crystallised in forms of production that simultaneously assume and disavow ecology, the body and **reproduction** and that are now in crisis. Despite an effort to break with old economic reductionist Marxist meanings of materialism, Mellor's materialism is not entirely free of tendencies to dismiss cultural factors in explanation or to treat them as secondary to economic ones.

Anti-colonial and ecosocialist ecofeminisms are combined in analyses of western capitalism as the colonisation of society and nature by a colonising and enclosing form of development or reason (Mies and Shiva 1993; Plumwood 1993). The dual connection of women and other subordinated groups with nature and male elites with reason is the key to the fundamental colonising problematic of western culture. The resulting sets of interwoven reason/nature dualisms support multiple interlocking oppressions and colonising movements, including racism through its assimilation of patriarchal colonising groups to reason and non-western and indigenous peoples to nature as the primitive. They also support capitalism as a distorted form of reason which maximises the throughput of nature to generate wealth without allowing for its renewal, thus assuming but simultaneously denying its ecological base (Mies and Shiva 1993; Plumwood 1993). Mies and Shiva blend anti-colonial and anti-capitalist positions by analysing capitalism as imposing the hegemony of a western development model based on the master subject White Man which is eurocentric, androcentric, and anthropocentric. Anti-colonial forms of ecofeminism to date provide the most convincing and detailed account of how environmental crises and nonhuman forms of oppression are linked to human oppression. The distortion of rationality through the dualistic construction associated with domination is the foundation of the distorted western concept of development and progress, or 'maldevelopment', as Shiva calls it. Shiva's and Mies's powerfully articulated anti-colonial and ecosocialist ecofeminism which identifies the problem as white capitalist patriarchy may ultimately need to be envisaged in more integrated and open-ended terms than as a list of some leading contemporary oppressions. Nevertheless this analysis is particularly relevant to the current attempt by capitalist economic rationalism in the form of agribusiness corporations to enclose the commons represented by genetic and biological reproduction, by promoting for example the Terminator (a genetic engineering technology for agriculture which inserts a gene that renders treated seeds sterile, but which has the potential to escape and replicate in wild plant populations). As perhaps the leading critical discipline for understanding this potential threat to all global life,

ecofeminisms provide some of the most important, courageous and deeply subversive perspectives on the world today.

See also: Shiva, Vandana

References and further reading

Adams, C.J. (1993) 'The Feminist Traffic in Animals' in G. Gaard (ed.) *Ecofeminism : Women, Animals and Nature*, Philadelphia, Temple University Press, pp. 195–218.

—— (1994) *Neither Man nor Beast*, New York: Continuum.

Collard, A. (1988) *Rape of the Wild : Man's Violence Against Animals and the Earth*, Bloomington, IN: Indiana University Press.

Cuomo, C. (1998) *Feminism and Ecological Communities*, London: Routledge.

Daly, M. (1978) *Gyn/Ecology: The Metaethics of Radical Feminism*, London: The Women's Press.

King, Y. (1989) 'The Ecology of Feminism and the Feminism of Ecology' in J. Plant (ed.) *Healing the Wounds*, Philadelphia, PA: New Society Publishers, pp. 18–28.

Mellor, M. (1997) *Feminism and Ecology*, Cambridge, MA: Polity Press.

Merchant, C. (1980) *The Death of Nature*, London: Wildwood House.

—— (1996) *Earthcare: Women and the Environment*, London: Routledge.

Mies, M. and Shiva, V. (1993) *Ecofeminism*, London: Zed Books.

Plumwood, V. (1993) *Feminism and the Mastery of Nature*, London: Routledge.

Ruether, R. (1975) *New Woman, New Earth*, Minneapolis, MI: Seabury.

Spretnak, C. (1991) *States of Grace*, New York: Harper Collins.

Sturgeon, N. (1997) *Ecofeminist Natures*, London: Routledge.

Warren, K.J. (1990) 'The Power and Promise of Ecological Feminism', *Environmental Ethics* 12 (2), 121–46.

—— (1997) *Ecofeminism*, Indianapolis: Indiana University Press.

VAL PLUMWOOD

economic globalisation

Economic globalisation refers to transformations in the world economy that result from improvements in electronic communication and transportation. It is a market-driven and multidimensional process characterised by rapidly expanding markets that transcend national boundaries and are increasingly independent of geographical distance. Nearly instantaneous electronic communication has facilitated the mobility of financial capital and the emergence of transnational corporations. Transnationals are able to relocate their low-skill production operations in areas characterised by low-wages and business-friendly political regimes. Two significant changes occur as a result of economic globalisation: changes in the international division of labour and a decrease in the power of states to regulate and tax market activities. These changes have been accompanied by a neo-liberal rhetoric that champions free markets and free trade, and rationalises the dismantling of protective labour legislation, health and safety standards, and welfare services.

Economic globalisation challenges the ability of individuals to exercise effective decision making through democratic processes. The mobility of transnational capital has increased competition among regions, countries and workers to attract and retain businesses, and this has undermined the power of labour unions and weakened the regulatory powers of the state. (It has not, however, diminished the power of the state to act in ways that facilitate the interests of business.) Multi-national trade agreements such as those implemented by the World Trade Organization (WTO) and regional trade agreements such as the North American Free Trade Agreement (NAFTA) weaken the ability of the state to rectify and alleviate gender inequality because they establish laws that are outside the domain of the democratic legislative process. For example, NAFTA has a series of clauses that require that private corporations be compensated for any losses that result from initiating new public programmes, including those in **health** and **welfare** services. The additional expense associated with compensation effectively prevents establishing new public programmes such as subsidised day care (Cohen 1995). Similarly free trade agreements place serious limits on the abilities of states to enact protective environmental legislation.

Much of the developing world is constrained by heavy debt obligations to international financial institutions. Meeting these obligations has entailed the imposition of structural adjustment programmes (SAPs) that require cuts in public spending on health, welfare and food subsidies. Feminist scholars have noted that SAPs affect women and men differently. Women make up a disproportionate share of the world's poor (70 per cent) and bear the double burden of unpaid household work and low-wage market work. Consequently women rely on the public sector to redistribute income and provide public health and welfare services, and when these programmes are cut, women's unpaid work increases (Elson 1992).

All of these developments underpin the need for states to remain flexible and competitive in order to reap the financial gains from globalisation. This flexibility and competitiveness largely depends on an international sexual division and feminisation of labour. Women are undervalued in both the public and private spheres because of their identification as housewives, rather than as workers (Mies 1999). When women work outside the home they are often segregated into low-wage occupations and, on average, are paid less than men. Capitalism depends on a certain amount of low-wage-paying labour and unpaid reproductive labour to keep it functioning. In this way, the relegation of women to the private sphere helps keep capitalism's costs low and the ideology surrounding women's work provides a justification for this strategy. The end result is limited economic opportunity for women, since in the capitalist system of profits and capital accumulation their labour takes the form of underpaid or unpaid labour.

Peterson and Runyan (1999) argue that women workers are in high demand in both the service sector and light industry (such as technology), two of the fastest growing occupations in the post-industrial era. Women are sought for these jobs because of the stereotypical perception that they are more dexterous than men (i.e. 'nimble fingers') as well as more compliant and passive. These occupations are low paying, non-unionised and weakly regulated with regard to health and safety requirements. Low pay is due in part to the devaluation of women's labour and in part due to the assumption that their wages are used for 'extras' rather than to support themselves and their families. The state is complicit in perpetuating this sexism because of its need to stay competitive in global markets (see **work, women and**).

The domestic and informal sectors of labour are also heavily feminised and tied to the processes of economic globalisation. Due to cuts in social welfare benefits, many women in developing countries have migrated (often-times unwillingly) to other countries to work as maids, prostitutes (see **sexual slavery**), cleaners and nannies. Another type of informal sector feminised labour is 'home-work' in which women work as subcontracted labourers in their homes for transnational corporations looking to cut costs. This outsourced labour, such as sewing and lace and rug making, is also underpaid due to the work's location in the home, rather than in the formal work sector. Moreover, it brings no benefits and offers no workplace amenities.

Globalisation exacerbates economic, social and political inequalities in ways that are deeply gendered. Increasingly, feminist scholars, activists and policy-makers in the developing world are challenging women in the north to build effective international alliances with women in the south to expose and rectify the injustices generated by global capitalism.

See also: economic restructuring

References and further reading

Elson, D. (1992) 'From Survival Strategies to Transformation Strategies: Women's Needs and Structural Adjustment', in L. Benería and S. Feldman, (eds) *Unequal Burden: Economic Crises, Persistent Poverty and Women's Work*, Boulder, CO: Westview Press.

Enloe, C. (1990) *Bananas, Beaches and Bases: Making Feminist Sense of International Politics*, Berkeley, CA: University of California Press.

Griffen, M.G. (1995) 'Macho Economics: Canadian Women Confront Free Trade', *Dollar and Sense*, November/December.

Kofman, E. and Youngs, G. (eds) (1996) *Globaliza-tion: Theory and Practice*, London: Pinter Publishers.

Mies, M. (1999) *Patriarchy and Accumulation on a World Scale*, London: Zed Books, 2nd edn.

Peterson, V.S. and Runyan, A.S. (1999) *Global Gender Issues*, Boulder, CO: Westview Press, 2nd edn.

DRUCILLA K. BARKER AND LAURA PARISI

economic restructuring

Economic restructuring refers to wide-ranging processes of change arising from transformations in the global economy. These processes are often characterised as gender neutral. Feminist interventions in restructuring policies and debates have sought to demonstrate how **gender** relations are central to understanding current dimensions of these changes.

Restructuring is frequently presented as a necessary response to **economic globalisation** (Bakker 1996: 3). Developments such as the internationalisation of production, rapid technological change and the increasing casualisation of work signal profound changes in the international economy. In an effort to address the consequences of such change, states have pursued a variety of adjustment strategies. In the north, many countries have embraced neo-liberal prescriptions that emphasise trade liberalisation, cutbacks in government spending, and state deregulation and privatisation. Similarly, many countries in the south have had to adopt structural adjustment policies (SAPs) as a provision for securing loans from multilateral lending institutions. These policies often demand similar measures such as export-oriented production, reductions in food and agriculture subsidies and in public sector expenditure, and currency devaluation. Countries in both the north and south have been affected by economic restructuring although particular expressions of the process have varied within and among national economies. However, all these processes have been underwritten by the exigency to be more competitive in a rapidly changing and increasingly inter-dependent global economy (Cagatay *et al.* 1995: 1834).

Feminists have emphasised how structural adjustment and restructuring policies are developed and implemented without consideration of unequal social relations between different groups of men and women. The very terms associated with restructuring – competitiveness, efficiency, productivity – are conceptualised and presented as apparently gender neutral (Elson 1992; Bakker 1994). This discourse, however, 'masks an underlying male bias' and economic models of restructuring neglect to consider social **reproduction** and women's unpaid labour within that domain (Elson 1992: 34). For example, current neo-liberal attempts to reform and/or cut back the public sector neglect to consider the impact of shifting costs on the reproductive sphere. As feminist economist Diane Elson writes, 'this is equivalent to assuming that there is an unlimited supply of unpaid female labour, able to compensate for any adverse changes resulting from macro-economic policy' (1994: 42).

Relatedly, feminists have focused on the increasing feminisation of work within current rounds of economic change. Women, in both the north and the south, have been increasingly drawn into the realm of paid work. However their participation in the labour market is structured by both the ideological construction of less-valued 'feminine' skills and the sexual division of labour (McDowell 1991: 406). Greater numbers of women can be found in flexible insecure employment. Simultaneously, labour market standards have deteriorated as a result of both explicit and implicit deregulation. In explicit deregulation, previous regulations are 'eroded or abandoned through legislative means'; while implicit deregulation refers to a process whereby regulations are rendered less effective through either a failure to implement them or through poor enforcement (Standing 1989: 1077). Feminists have argued that gender relations are a central element of processes of restructuring (McDowell 1991; Bakker 1994).

Feminist analysis also suggests that the overall consequences of restructuring on gender divisions are unclear, and feminists themselves do not agree on the extent to which economic change has benefited or adversely affected women (see McDowell 1991). While many women workers have been drawn into insecure and low paid work, restructur-

ing has also created significant opportunities for others. This latter group may be able to use these gains to purchase domestic labour and reduce their disadvantage vis-à-vis men in the labour market. However, they will still remain responsible for the management of the household (Elson 1992: 37–8). Additionally, recent trends in industrialised countries suggest 'a convergence of male and female labour market experiences within what are increasingly polarised labour markets' (Bakker 1996: 8). Nevertheless, processes of economic change are creating new divisions between and among men and women that underscore the necessity for gender-based research that is sensitive to social relations of class and race.

Gendered readings of economic restructuring have forced a reconsideration of feminist political strategies as processes of restructuring and globalisation have profoundly shifted the terrain of struggles. The internationalisation of production, for example, may provide possibilities for workers to forge transnational solidarity links (Elson 1992: 29). Similarly, Linda McDowell points out that changes in national labour markets which place men and women in similarly situated low paid jobs may also force a reconsideration of future political strategies (1991: 411). Diane Elson has argued that processes of economic change speak to the imperative of developing strategies to 'influence the terms of restructuring' to effect not only production but also social relations (1992: 29).

See also: work, women and

References and further reading

Bakker, I. (1994) 'Introduction: Engendering Macroeconomic Policy Reform in the Era of Global Restructuring and Adjustment', in I. Bakker (ed.) *The Strategic Silence*, London: Zed Books.

—— (1996) 'The Gendered Foundations of Restructuring in Canada', in I. Bakker (ed.) *Rethinking Restructuring*, Toronto: University of Toronto Press.

Cagatay, N., Elson, D. and Grown, L. (1995) 'Introduction: Gender, Adjustment and Macroeconomics', *World Development* 23, 11: 1827–36.

Elson, D. (1992) 'From Survival Strategies to Transformation Strategies', in L. Beneria and S. Feldman (eds), *Unequal Burden. Economic Crisis, Persistent Poverty and Women's Work*, Boulder, CO: Westview Press.

—— (1994) 'Micro, Meso, Macro: Gender and Economic Analysis in the Context of Policy Reform', in I. Bakker (ed.) *The Strategic Silence*, London: Zed Books.

McDowell, L. (1991) 'Life Without Father and Ford: The New Gender Order of Post-Fordism', *Transactions of the Institute of British Geographers* (New Series) 16: 400–19.

Standing, G. (1989) 'Global Feminization through Flexible Labour', *World Development* 17, 7: 1077–95.

CHRISTINA GABRIEL

economics

Economics is a mode of inquiry that seeks to understand how societies organise their material existence – production, distribution and consumption. Feminist economics deconstructs the dimensions of **gender**, **race**, ethnicity and class embedded in contemporary economic theory, and constructs new theoretical approaches and empirical methodologies that incorporate feminist insights. The notion that gender is the basis for a division of labour between productive and reproductive labour is central to this project. Productive activities are what we normally think of as paid work or market work; reproductive activities include housework, raising children, and the physical and emotional care of others. In most societies, reproductive labour is considered women's work (see **work, women and**). Fundamental to feminist economics is an analysis of the implications of this social stratification, and its intersections with other stratifiers such as ethnicity and class.

Although there is a variety of schools of economics – Marxist, institutionalist, and post-Keynesian – neoclassical economics is by far the predominant form of contemporary economic theory. Neoclassical economics is defined not by its domain of study, but rather by its method of explanation. Economic agents are rational, self-interested, and autonomous individuals who maximise their well-being subject to the constraints of income and time. As economically independent adults with no contingent responsibilities or obligations they enter into exchange relations with others only when it is in their own self interest. In the story that economists tell, individual economic decisions are coordinated through markets, and economic outcomes are simply the collective results of their choices. Feminist economists argue that adherence to this rigidly prescribed methodology seriously limits the way in which economic issues can be studied, and that these limitations bias and distort economic knowledge.

Neoclassical economists argue that economic explanations based on self-interested **individualism** and contractual exchange merit their high status in the profession because of their logical superiority and explanatory power. Diana Strassmann (1993) challenges this claim and calls attention to the role of values and power in the production of economic knowledge. She argues that economics is an interpretive community whose members are socialised not to question the primacy of these explanations nor the simplifying assumptions behind them. Julie Nelson (1996) argues that the emphasis on choice in economics is related to the Cartesian dichotomy between embodiment and rationality (see **embodiment/disembodiment**; **Cartesianism, feminist critiques of**). Making the detached *cogito* the object of study in economics means that nature, the **body**, children, and the need for human connectedness remain cut off from masculine concern. Nancy Folbre (1995) maintains that neoclassical economics cannot offer an adequate conceptualisation of caring labour – labour undertaken out of affection or a sense of responsibility for other people. Feminist economists argue that the assumption of rationality central to neoclassical theory is a profoundly gendered and incomplete account of human **agency** and that an economic theory which focuses only on the decisions of independent income earning adults will obscure the realities faced by those with unequal access to income and other economic resources. For both ethical and practical reasons, these realities are an important part of economics, and an important part of the feminist economics project.

The economics of the **family** is an important concern for feminist economists. Since the individual is the fundamental unit of analysis for neoclassical economics, the household is often treated as though it were a stable unit of cohesive interest rather than a collection of people of differing genders, ages, and access to market incomes. Feminist economists have shown that treating the household as though it were a locus of unified interest obscures and marginalises the needs and wants of women, children, the elderly, and any other people who do not have their own income or whose needs cannot be adequately met through market exchange. Moreover, it naturalises women's roles in the household as wives and mothers and reinforces the gendered division of labour – a division of labour that segregates men and women into different occupations and holds women primarily responsible for household work, even when they work outside the home as well.

Heidi Hartmann's (1981) classic marxist-feminist analysis of the family posits the family as a locus of struggle, a place where both household production (housework and child rearing) and redistribution (allocations of family income and resources) take place, and hence a place where people with different interests conflict with one another. Hartmann shows that the family is still the primary arena where men exercise their patriarchal power over women's labour. Bina Agarwal (1997) conceptualises the family as a complex web of relationships. Family dynamics contain elements of both cooperation and conflict, the outcomes of which depend on a variety of qualitative and quantitative factors such as the role of social norms in bargaining, the coexistence of self-interest and altruism, and the role of the household in wider social institutions. She argues that the success of social and economic policies depends upon a nuanced understanding of these household dynamics.

The study of women's participation in labour markets is another important area of study for feminist economics. On average, women's wages are around 30 per cent lower than men's, and labour markets are highly segregated by sex. For example, nearly all dental hygienists are women, and nearly all dentists are men. Less than 10 per cent of all skilled labourers such as carpenters and electricians are women, and only a very small percentage of **childcare** workers are men. The wage gap and sex segregation persists within occupations as well. Women are often segregated into lower paying, less prestigious specialities. Neoclassical economists hold that these labour market outcomes are determined by supply and demand and are the result of the free market process. Men's wages are higher than women's because of differences in skills and training, what economists call human capital. According to the theory, women are paid less because they invest less in human capital. This is considered a rational decision since women will be in the labour force for a shorter period because they are expected to drop out of the labour force to rear children. Thus, according to neoclassical economics, women rationally choose to remain in segregated, relatively low wage occupations.

Barbara Bergmann (1986) offers a cogent feminist alternative explanation. She carefully documents and analyses women's participation in the labour force, the wage gap, the persistence of occupational segregation, and the conflicts between housework and market work. Bergmann argues that occupational segregation by sex is the key to women's poor position in labour markets. Sex segregation, like any other system of dominance and privilege, perpetuates itself through the self-interest of its beneficiaries. Unfair and discriminatory labour market outcomes are the result of a traditional sexual division of labour institutionalised in the norms and practices of contemporary society. Teresa Amott and Julie Matthaei (1996) present a historical, marxist-feminist analysis of labour markets. They argue that there is no common experience of gender oppression among women. Rather, it is the intersections of gender, race-ethnicity and class that determine and differentiate women's work lives. Labour market hierarchies, stablised by both race-ethnicity and class, play a central role in reproducing **oppression** and inequality.

Development economics is concerned with strategies to promote economic growth and modernisation in the Third World. Many scholars now argue that rather than progress and prosperity, development has contributed to the growth of poverty, the Third World debt crisis, and environmental degradation. Women in the developing world are especially affected because they make up a disproportionate share of the world's poor and bear the double burden of unpaid household work and low-wage market work. Moreover, sex and gender biases in mainstream development policies increase women's unpaid work and worsen already oppressive and exploitative conditions. Ester Boserup's (1970) landmark study shows that development projects have often deprived women of economic opportunities and status and have been less effective than they might have been since they ignore the important economic contributions of women. Boserup's work mounts an effective critique of the effects of development on gender relations but does not question the fundamental values and assumptions embedded in the development paradigm. Lourdes Benería and Gita Sen (1981) critique the modernisation process and examine the processes of capital accumulation set in motion during the colonial period, and the effects of this process on the sexual division of labour. They argue that the problems for women are their subordinate role in the household and their participation in labour markets under gendered conditions.

Sen and Caren Grown (1990) are concerned with grounding feminist theorising in Third World realities and transforming socially constructed gender and class roles. They argue that while women constitute the majority of the poor and are the most economically and socially disadvantaged, it is their work that provides the human link in the availability of food, water, and energy sources for many parts of the world. Thus development planning should begin from the standpoint of poor women. The economic restructuring that has resulted from the Third World debt crisis has had particularly adverse effects on women. Diane Elson (1992) shows that structural adjustment programmes implicitly rely on the unpaid labour of women to alleviate the adverse effects of policies that reduce public expenditures on **health**, and **welfare**, increase food prices, and reduce the role of the government. These burdens on women are ignored because policy makers implicitly accept a consensual view of the family and disregard its role in the subordination of women.

See also: Marxist feminist literature/literary theory; political economy, feminist

References and further reading

Agarwal, B. (1997) '"Bargaining" and Gender Relations: Within and Beyond the Household', *Feminist Economics* 3 (1).

Amott, T. and Matthaei, J. (1996) *Race, Gender and Work*, Boston, South End Press.

Bergmann, B. (1986) *The Economic Emergence of Women*, New York: Basic Books.

Benería, L. and Sen, G. (1981) 'Accumulation, Reproduction, and Women's Role in Economic Development: Boserup Revisited', *Signs* 7 (2).

Boserup, E. (1970) *Women's Role in Economic Development*, New York: St Martin's Press.

Elson, D. (1992) 'From Survival Strategies to Transformation Strategies: Women's Needs and Structural Adjustment', in L. Benería and S. Feldman (eds) *Unequal Burden: Economic Crises, Persistent Poverty, and Women's Work*, Boulder, CO: Westview Press.

Folbre, N. (1995) 'The Paradox of Caring Labor', *Feminist Economics* 1 (1).

Hartmann, H. (1981) 'The Family as the Locus of Gender, Class, and Political Struggle: The Example of Housework', *Signs* 6 (3).

Nelson, J. (1996) *Feminism, Objectivity and Economics*, London and New York: Routledge.

Sen, G. and Grown, C. (1990) *Development, Crises and Alternative Visions: Third World Women's Perspectives*, New Delhi: DAWN Secretariat.

Strassmann, D. (1993) 'Not a Free Market: The Rhetoric of Disciplinary Authority in Economics', in M.A. Ferber and J.A. Nelson (eds) *Beyond Economic Man: Feminist Theory and Economics*, Chicago, IL: University of Chicago Press.

DRUCILLA K. BARKER

education

The term 'education' refers to many different things, among them: the activity of educating someone; the process a person undergoes in the course of being or becoming educated; the desired end result of that activity or process (i.e. the state of having had an education or of being an educated person); the social institution within which education as activity and process occurs; the field or discipline of inquiry that studies education in all its senses.

Until the twentieth century it was generally acknowledged that school is one educational institution among many and by no means the most important. As school's functions expanded in the 1900s while the educational role of family, church, and community decreased, education in the institutional sense came to be equated with schooling. This false equation greatly simplified the task of educational scholars by allowing them to focus their investigations on schools, but the price of simplification was high. A culture that ignores the educational contributions of family, church, community, libraries, museums, boys scouts and girl scouts, advertisers, publishers, recording companies, talk radio, television, the internet, and more will not know what its youth are learning. It will not know if its nonschool educational agents are reinforcing or undermining the school's curriculum. It will not know if one of its nonschool educational institutions is failing to perform the educational functions on which it relies.

Even as twentieth-century commentators on education were confusing the institution of education with one of its forms, they were formulating reductive definitions of it in the activity, process, and achievement senses. Portraying education as always and everywhere intentional, witting, voluntary, and requiring the giving and assessing of reasons, educational scholars defined the hoped for result as the acquisition of theoretical knowledge and intellectual understanding. Excluding from the educational realm the kind of unintended, unwitting, nonvoluntary learning that characterises the hidden curriculum of both school and society, these narrow definitions once again serve to keep educational researchers from knowing the full extent of what society's young is learning. Turning the whole of education into a highly intellectual enterprise aimed primarily at the development of mind, they neglect the roles played in education by feeling and emotion, bodily movement and physical action.

From the standpoint of feminist theory the reductionist agenda demands attention, for in addition to turning education into a mere shadow of its full bodied self, it is thoroughly androcentric. Excluding the **hidden curriculum** from the realm of education, it places the learning of **gender roles** and stereotypes, gender bias and **misogyny**, **sexism** and **androcentrism** beyond the pale, but this is the least of it. The reductive definitions of education in its activity and process senses incorporate the qualities Socrates displayed in his philosophical conversations with his male companions in the marketplace while disregarding altogether the care, concern, and nurturance that mothers across the ages have exhibited in the course of rearing their children. The definition of education in the achievement sense assumes the desirability of a liberal education based on the study of science, mathematics, history, philosophy, and the like – all fields historically associated with men – and ignores the claims of teaching, nursing, and other fields that have culturally and historically been associated with women. And into the definition of what it is to be an educated person are built rationality, self government, critical acumen, and other traits historically and culturally associated with white, middle-class men, even as the 3Cs of care, concern, and connection and all the other traits culturally associated with women are ignored.

Despite the fact that women and girls represent at least half the world's population and that the great majority of teachers at the lower levels of education are female, those who practice education in the disciplinary sense have, by definitional fiat, placed women outside the domain of education. Not surprisingly, the private home and family have also been banished from the realm.

Feminist theorists have shown that western culture has historically tended to divorce mind from body and reason from feeling and emotion; to associate both mind and reason with men and masculinity; and to devalue body and emotion while associating both with women and femininity. The reductive definitions of education testify that this dualistic thinking prevails in the educational realm. In addition, the definitions reflect a dualistic analysis of society itself, one that feminist historians have rightly called outmoded.

Where education is concerned, parents, politicians, school teachers and administrators, scholars, and just plain citizens implicitly divide social reality into two opposing worlds – that of the private home and that of work, politics, and the professions. All take for granted that the function of education is to transform children who have heretofore lived their lives in the one world into members of the other. Furthermore, all assume that the private home is a natural institution and that, accordingly, membership in it is a given rather than something one must achieve; in consequence, they think there is no need to prepare people to carry out the tasks and activities associated with it. In contrast, all perceive the world of work and politics as a human creation and membership in it as something at which one can succeed or fail; and they therefore make the business of education preparation for carrying out the tasks and activities associated with it.

None of this in itself makes education gendered, and neither does the unquestioned assumption that the world of work, politics and the professions is far more important and praiseworthy than the world of the private home. Rather, education's gendered quality is conferred by the fact that, culturally speaking, the two worlds are gender coded. Given that the one world is considered men's domain and the other is considered women's, gender becomes a basic dimension of the whole educational system: so basic that it permeates western culture's educational ideals, aims, curricula, methodologies, and organisational structures; so basic that the underlying definitions, beliefs, and practices of western education can be said to constitute an education-gender system.

Feminist research and scholarship has uncovered many elements of this education-gender system, among them: a chilly coeducational classroom climate for girls and women (see **chilly climate**), the androcentric bias of the subjects of the liberal curriculum, the sexual harassment of schoolgirls, a hidden curriculum in misogyny and anti-domesticity, the under-representation of women in the higher ranks of the professoriate. Despite the advent of women's studies programmes, it has proved extremely difficult to improve the plight of girls and women, perhaps because the offending phenomena are so often treated as separate and unrelated rather than as systemically related.

Any feminist who wants to rethink the social and political structures of this two-sex society must sooner or later acknowledge the existence of the education-gender system and seek ways to eradicate or radically transform the beliefs and practices that constitute it. For to ignore this system is not to dispense with it but to assume its continued existence.

Of contemporary feminist theorists Adrienne **Rich** and bell **hooks** have been among the most attentive to the gendered character of education. In the 1970s Rich cast new light on women's higher education. In the next decades hooks helped clarify the intersection of race and gender in higher education. But feminist theory must ultimately concern itself with the education of *both* sexes over the *whole* life span and across the *full* range of society's educational agents. It is self-defeating to seek improvement in the education of girls and women without attending to the education of boys and men, to attempt to transform higher education without effecting corresponding changes in the lower grades, and to focus exclusively on schools and universities. Regarding this last, the transformation of home and family in the last decades of the twentieth century renders the recognition that home – whether a traditional household or one with two breadwinners, a single parent, a same-sex couple – and school are as partners in the education of a nation's young extremely important. Casting doubt on home's ability to carry on single-handedly its culturally assigned educational functions and reclaiming John Dewey's insight that when home changes radically, school must undergo an equally radical change, Jane Roland **Martin** has proposed that schools be turned into moral equivalents of home. One of the many questions still to be answered is how best to bring society's other educational agents – including the media in all its forms – into a cooperative, beneficial relationship with both home and school.

The great western political and social thinkers of the past knew the importance of education, they knew that to rethink society they had also to rethink education. Plato, Rousseau, and Dewey held very different opinions about the good life and the good society, but each realised that his vision of the ideal state depended in the last analysis on an equally bold conception of education. All three understood that without a theory of education to complement their theories of politics and society, their philosophies would be hopelessly incomplete, if not fatally flawed. Mary Wollstonecraft, one of the first feminist theorists, knew this too. Although *A Vindication of the Rights of Woman* (1792) is usually read strictly as a political treatise, like Plato's *Republic* and Rousseau's *Emile* (1762), it is both. And, joining a well-developed theory of education to a feminist social vision, so is Charlotte Perkins Gilman's utopian novel *Herland* (1915). The education-gender system makes the need to rethink education in tandem with the rethinking of society and politics as pressing as it has always been.

See also: public/private

References and further reading

American Association of University Women (1992) *How Schools Shortchange Girls*, Washington DC: AAUW Educational Foundation.

Diller, A., Houston, B., Morgan, K.P. and Ayim, M. (1996) *The Gender Question in Education*, Boulder, CO: Westview Press.

hooks, b. (1994) *Teaching to Transgress*, New York: Routledge.

Martin, J.R. (1985) *Reclaiming a Conversation*, New Haven: Yale University Press.

—— (1992) *The Schoolhome*, Cambridge, MA: Harvard University Press.

—— (1994) *Changing the Educational Landscape*, New York: Routledge.

Noddings, N. (1992) *The Challenge to Care in Schools*, New York: Teachers College Press.

Rich, A. (1979) *On Lies, Secrets, and Silence*, New York: Norton.

Sandler, B.R., Silverberg, L.A. and Hall, R.M. (1996) *The Chilly Classroom Climate*, Washington, DC: National Association for Women in Education.

Titone, C. and Maloney, K. (eds) (1998) *Thinking Through Our Mothers*, Cincinnati: Merrill Education.

JANE ROLAND MARTIN

egalitarianism

Originating in classical liberal theory, egalitarianism is an ideal that fosters freedom and equality for all (see **equality and difference**). Famously articulated in the American Declaration of Independence, it affirms the rights of *man* to 'life, liberty, and the pursuit of happiness'. Liberalism declares the ultimate equality of each individual, in political institutions that must not unjustly subordinate any person(s) to any other(s). Yet feminists have shown that classical egalitarian theory rarely addresses the rights of *women* or non-white men. Historically regarded as deficient in the reason that enabled (educated, propertied, white) men to realise their autonomous freedom (see **autonomy**), women were to remain subordinate to masculine authority in their private lives, pursuing happiness within circumscribed realms where they were neither at liberty, nor men's equals. Egalitarianism is likewise contested for the class, **race**, ethnicity, ableist and homophobic exclusions it tacitly condones (see **homophobia**).

References and further reading

Wollstonecraft, M. (1792) *A Vindication of the Rights of Woman*, London: Penguin Books, 1975.

LORRAINE CODE

Eisenstein, Zillah

Zillah Eisenstein in best known for her pathbreaking contributions to socialist feminist theory, particularly her introduction of the term 'capitalist patriarchy' to the literature. In her 1978 edited book, *Capitalist Patriarchy and the Case for Socialist Feminism*, she argues that capitalist development both undermined the familial patriarchal system by further differentiating the home and work spheres and instituted new forms of gender inequality through the exploitation of women's productive labour.

In the 1980s, Eisenstein's work examined the contradictory relationship between liberalism and feminism. In *The Radical Future of Liberal Feminism*, she argues that feminism's historical demand for equality and rights is deeply indebted to the liberal conception of the independent and autonomous self. Yet liberalism is fundamentally limited as a foundation for claims for women's equality for it is founded philosophically and practically on the private servitude of women. Even mainstream liberal feminist demands for equality, therefore, have radical potential as such demands expose the patriarchal roots of liberal theory and practice. She argues that in the 'recognition of women as a sexual class lies the subversive quality of feminism... because liberalism is premised upon women's exclusion from public life on this very class basis' (1979: 6).

In *The Female Body and the Law*, Eisenstein examines the meaning of sexual difference for gender equality, arguing for decentring the white male body as the referent for policy and law. She calls for the analytic placement of the pregnant body at the centre of political theory and practice and defends a 'radical pluralism' which addresses race, class and sexual diversity without reinforcing the structural hierarchies which have helped to produce such differences. Eisenstein's early work (*The Color of Gender*, 1980 and *Hatreds: Racialized and Sexualized Conflicts in the 21st Century*, 1996) shifted to the intersection of nationalism, sexuality, race and class, providing important insights into feminist activism, political resistance and state power in the USA and Eastern Europe. She argues that nationalist ideologies rely on both racialised and sexualised cultural practices and structures which must be challenged in reconstructing democracies world-wide.

See also: capitalism; liberal feminism; Marxist feminist literature/literary theory; patriarchy; sex equity v. sexual equality; socialism and feminism; race

Selected writings

Eisenstein, Z. (ed.) (1978) *Capitalist Patriarchy and the Case for Socialist Feminism*, New York: Monthly Review Press.
—— (1979) *The Radical Future of Liberal Feminism*, New York: Longman Press.
—— (1980) *The Colour of Gender*, Berkeley, CA: University of California Press.
—— (1984) *Feminism and Sexual Equality: Crisis in Liberal America*, New York: Monthly Review Press.
—— (1988) *The Female Body and the Law*, Berkeley, CA: University of California Press.
—— (1996) *Hatreds: Racialized and Sexualized Conflicts in the 21st Century*, New York: Routledge.

CYNTHIA R DANIELS

embodiment/disembodiment

A recurrent theme in western philosophy involves the question of how far our knowledge, understanding and experience of the world belongs to a purely mental realm separate from the **body**. This is the question of embodiment. Traditional Cartesian philosophy, in splitting off and elevating the mental over the corporeal, assumes that knowledge is disembodied. However phenomenologists and feminist theorists have challenged such a view arguing, instead, that the body is crucial to an understanding of the world and that knowledge cannot be disembodied. The body has been left out in western rationalist philosophy because of the *somatophobia* surrounding women's association with the body, the backcloth against which men distance themselves in constructing the life of the mind.

See also: Cartesianism, feminist critiques of; corporeality; epistemology

References and further reading

Kirby, V. (1997) *Telling Flesh: The Substance of the Corporeal*, New York and London: Routledge.

ALISON ADAM

emotions/rationality

The traditional association of women with emotions and men with rationality has shaped the emotions/rationality dichotomy as a gender-coded one. As is the case with other gender-laden

dichotomies, feminist reflection here encompasses a range of approaches, from revaluing the 'feminine' and consequently devalued emotions to uprooting the dichotomy itself and uncovering the theoretical limitations of its uncritical adoption. The dominant traditional view of emotion as disruptive of reason is now being challenged by some philosophers, and many feminist epistemologists are arguing for enhanced conceptions of rationality and knowledge that take account of the *cognitive* role of emotions and attendant values in different contexts (Jaggar 1996). In feminist ethics, for instance, theorists argue that emotions associated with care and relationship are critical to the development of moral perception and moral deliberation, and they thus question the adequacy of moral theories that frame conceptions of moral reasoning largely in terms of the formation and application of abstract moral principles (see **ethics, feminist**).

Feminist work in psychology and in the social sciences is also critical to more nuanced understandings of emotions. Some of this work is directed toward uncovering the truths and untruths behind the stereotype that women are more emotional than men. Research shows that supposed gender differences are less apparent in the *feeling* of emotion than in the *expression* of emotion, especially where greater emotional expression is encouraged in women. The gender-coding of specific emotions is also of interest to feminists: sadness and fear are often considered more appropriate for women while anger and rage are considered more acceptable emotions for men (Geer and Shields 1996). Cross-cultural studies also reveal the extent to which emotions are socially mediated and the ways in which gender norms play a significant role in the social and individual interpretation of emotions.

These feminist reflections are important for understanding crucial aspects of women's subordination. The view that 'feminine' emotions conflict with 'manly' reason has been a powerful silencer of women. Such silencing is exacerbated in societies where women's anger is interpreted as 'irrational', that is, where it is not accorded the same kinds of reasonable justification that would normally be accorded men's anger (Lorde 1984; Spelman 1989).

References and further reading

Geer, C.G. and Shields, S.A. (1996) 'Women and Emotion: Stereotypes and the Double Bind', in J. Chrisler, C. Golden, and P. Rozee (eds) *Lectures on the Psychology of Women*, New York: McGraw-Hill.

Jaggar, A. (1996) 'Love and Knowledge: Emotion in Feminist Epistemology', in A. Garry and M. Pearsall (eds) *Women, Knowledge, and Reality: Explorations in Feminist Philosophy*, London and New York: Routledge, 2nd edn.

Lorde, A. (1984) 'The Uses of Anger: Women Responding to Racism', in A. Lorde *Sister Outsider*, Trumansburg, NY: Crossing Press.

Spelman, E. (1989) 'Anger and Insubordination', in A. Garry and M. Pearsall (eds) *Women, Knowledge, and Reality: Explorations in Feminist Philosophy*, Boston: Unwin Hyman.

PHYLLIS ROONEY

empathy

Empathy refers to affective, experiential engagement with (an)other person(s), captured in the expression 'I know just how you feel' (Code 1995). Early **consciousness-raising** produced such moments, showing feminists how affiliative empathy is fostered in women's psychosocial development in white western patriarchal societies (see **patriarchy**). Female 'connectedness' came then to be seen as a resource for transforming a depersonalised instrumental world into a less alienating place. Thus, central to Kathy Ferguson's (1984) 'feminist case against bureaucracy' is the argument that bureaucratic values inhibit practices of entering vicariously into other people's feelings: practices upon which empathic, benevolent social institutions depend. Empathy often figures as integral to an **ethic of care**; and feminist critiques of medicine deplore the absence of empathy in the care administered in scientistic medical practice (More and Milligan 1994), advocating more empathic caregiver/patient relationships.

Yet its 'feminine' associations have blocked empathy's acceptance as socially and scientifically respectable. Representing it as an emotional attunement akin to stereotypically feminine **intuition** separates empathy from knowledge, reason, and **objectivity**, confining it to the softer margins of social institutions. 'Knowing just how you feel' contrasts sharply and unfavourably with the detached, impersonal knowledge that is the received epistemological ideal, and the impartial, dispassionate action that is the dominant moral-political ideal (see **epistemology, feminist**; **impartiality**; **dispassionate investigation**).

Moreover, empathy is a double-edged phenomenon. If it is 'just naturally' female and women are 'just naturally' empathic, it does not count as a skilled achievement, but only as another instance of women doing what comes naturally. Empathic *knowing* becomes oxymoronic in conceptions of empathy as an instinctual (i.e. non-rational) female attribute; and there is no question of extending it beyond a narrow female/feminine domain. Moreover, in situations marked by differences in **power**, knowledge, and expertise 'I know just how you feel' expands easily into 'I will tell you how you feel', and 'I will be right because my greater expertise overrides your ill-informed perceptions'. Such imperialism is too familiar in western patriarchal societies where men alone (white affluent men) have claimed knowledgeable authority, while women and other Others, allegedly more dependent on intuition and feeling than on reason, have been systematically disbelieved, even about their experiences and feelings. Hence integral to responsible empathy is an empathic sensitivity to its appropriateness in certain situations, its intrusiveness – even coerciveness – in others.

References and further reading

Code, L. (1995) 'I Know Just How You Feel', in *Rhetorical Spaces: Essays on (Gendered) Locations*, New York: Routledge.

Ferguson, K. (1984) *The Feminist Case Against Bureaucracy*, Philadelphia: Temple University Press.

More, E. and Milligan, M. (eds) (1994) *The Empathic Practitioner: Essays on Empathy, Gender and Medicine*, New Brunswick, NJ: Rutgers University Press.

LORRAINE CODE

empiricism

Empiricism is a theory of knowledge, and a method, for which claims to know are developed, judged, and justified in accordance with **experience** – especially sensory experience, observation. Originating in seventeenth- and eighteenth-century British philosophy, with such philosophers as Francis Bacon, David Hume, and John Locke (and sometimes traced back to Aristotle), empiricism developed into the theory that informed most twentieth-century science and philosophy of science. Its emphasis on neutral, replicable observation and experimental verification underwrites empiricism's claim to offer the most purely objective route to knowledge of 'the external world'.

Empiricists claim that the senses give access to how things are, and that things indeed *are* in certain ways, independent of human observation. Moreover, according to strict empiricism, any competent observer in normal – or scientifically controlled – observation conditions will know reality in precisely the same way as any other. This public observability of objects in the world, together with a presumed invariance in human observational capacities, grant evidence its status as the basis of both scientific and everyday knowledge.

Perception, memory, and testimony are the recognised sources of empirical knowledge. For orthodox empiricists, evidence imprints itself upon uniformly receptive sensory apparatuses. Accumulated in memory, and communicated in testimony, it comprises an increasing store of knowledge that enables people competently to negotiate their material and social circumstances, and equips them to manipulate, predict, and control the objects in their environment. Elaborated into scientific discourse, multiples of such basic knowledge claims are the stuff of which sophisticated scientific theories and technological achievements are made.

For the system to work, empiricists have to presuppose a uniform, homogeneous 'human nature' that allows any knower to act as a substitute for any other: this is a consequence of belief in the interchangeability of knowers/observers, of the assumption that the particularities of situation and history are irrelevant to properly objective knowledge-making projects, for they will reduce the product of those projects to subjective opinion. Thus the abstract individual emerges as the knowing subject: an individual who, feminists argue, is by no means generic, or insubstantial, as the theory assumes, but is implicitly male, and shaped by *his* class (see **class analysis**), **race**, sex, and other specificities. His knowing cannot but be informed by who he is. Feminist empiricists believe, therefore, that rigorous empirical investigation of the circumstances of knowers must be incorporated into scientific and everyday judgements of knowledge, to cleanse the final products of **sexism**, **androcentrism**, racism, and other specificities.

See also: epistemology, feminist

References and further reading

Code, L. (1995) 'Taking Subjectivity Into Account', in *Rhetorical Spaces*, New York: Routledge.

Hankinson Nelson, L. (1990) *Who Knows: From Quine to a Feminist Empiricism*, Philadelphia, PA: Temple University Press.

LORRAINE CODE

endocrinology

The analysis of endocrinology, the science of hormones, is central to feminist critiques of scientific and medical views of **biology** and **gender**, and **biological essentialism**. Endocrinology has also been responsible for major medical developments in relation to women's **health** (e.g. the contraceptive pill and hormone replacement therapy) and so is important to feminist theorising of medical knowledges and practices around women's health, sexuality and the **body**.

Hormones were identified by scientists in the early twentieth century. Increasingly, endocrinologists have studied the role of these biochemical compounds, especially the sex hormones oestrogen and testosterone, in the production of biological differences between men and women. In recent decades very strong claims have been made for the role of sex hormones in the production of physical differences during foetal growth and at puberty. Along with the sex chromosomes, sex hormones are held responsible for the development of male and female reproductive systems, as well as bodily characteristics of the sexes such as hair distribution, breasts, and voice depth. Some behavioural endocrinologists also claim that sex hormones are responsible for behavioural differences between men and women. Others make claims for the role of sex hormones in the production of heterosexuality and homosexuality, although such claims are more contentious.

Feminist theorists of **science** and medicine have mounted strong critiques of endocrinological theories of biological sex differences. Arguments are made by theorists such as Anne **Fausto-Sterling** and Lynda **Birke** that much endocrinological research overestimates the role of hormones and fails to understand the complex interweaving of the biological and social in the production of both animal and human bodies and behaviours. Such investigations are important to feminist theories because they analyse this powerful area of scientific knowledge-production; because they provide excellent examples of a more general feminist approach to science; and because they provide valuable resources for feminist rethinkings of the biological/social, nature/nurture distinctions, as well as traditional understandings of the body as a passive and natural entity.

The use of hormones in medication has also provoked much feminist discussion. Issues concerning side effects of medications such as hormone replacement therapy (used after menopause), the contraceptive pill, and other contraceptives – especially in relation to cancer – are central to feminist analyses of medicine. Discourses and practices around these hormonal medications are shown to rely on and perpetuate limiting views of gender and sexual differences. Race, class and global politics are also at play in the testing and availability of such medications.

See also: menopause (medical)

References and further reading

Birke, L. (1992) 'Transforming Biology' in H. Crowley and S. Himmelweit (eds) *Knowing Women: Feminism and Knowledge*, Cambridge, MA: Polity Press, pp. 66–77.

Callahan, J.C. (1993) *Menopause*, Bloomington and Indianapolis: Indiana University Press.

Fausto-Sterling, A. (1992) *Myths of Gender*, New York: Basic Books, revised edn.

Oudshoorn, N. (1994) *Beyond the Natural Body*, London and New York: Routledge.

CELIA ROBERTS

environmental science

Environmental science is that branch of science concerned with things and processes external to the organism(s) in question, usually human beings. More commonly, the term connotes the measurement of the (usually negative) impact on the environment of human activity; it thus directs attention to very specific human/nonhuman interactions, and tends to render invisible the **power** relations (including **gender**) through which 'human activity' is organised. Typically, the field includes issues of population growth and consumption, biodiversity, resource availability and use, pollution, and atmospheric change. Like any branch of **science**, environmental science poses interesting epistemological and political questions (see **epistemology, feminist**); at the same time as it forms the basis of important green and ecofeminist claims about ecological and social damage, some of its assumptions and applications are highly problematic. Postmodern feminists suggest interesting alternatives (see **poststructuralism/postmodernism**).

In 1962, biologist and author Rachel Carson wrote *Silent Spring*. Although negative effects of pesticide use on human health and the environment were already acknowledged in scientific circles, Carson's task – to collect and make compelling a complex body of data for lay readers – was enormous. It was also highly controversial: the book's articulate condemnation of the pesticide industry and state regulatory bodies inspired numerous personal attacks on Carson. Not insignificantly, her abilities as a scientist were called into question because the writing was 'too emotional'; the text was called hysterical and Communistic (Hynes 1989). Still, *Silent Spring* became a lightning rod for environmental protest and, eventually, state response; a discourse of environmentalism based on scientific proof (as opposed to earlier versions based on preservation and aesthetics) became the standard.

Many ecofeminists rely on this discourse to make claims about women's environmental health issues, for example, about relations between environmental toxins (especially organochlorines) and serious human and nonhuman illness (especially breast cancer); it is up to environmental science to establish causation and provide credibility. Environmental science is similarly used to underline the need for alternatives to so-called malestream, environmentally destructive development; invisible pollution and ozone depletion are revealed to human perception through scientific study, to appear then as evidence of what Vandana **Shiva** calls 'mal(e)development'. Indeed, there is a contradiction in this kind of usage: environmental science is simultaneously utilised to legitimate claims of environmental degradation and condemned, as a science, as a symptom of androcentric, western thought, among the imputed causes of degradation in the first place.

Two examples are instructive: biodiversity and population. In scientific practice, the (relatively recent) term biodiversity refers simultaneously to the array of living creatures in a given area, and to their *genes*. Thus, on the one hand, feminist work on development has engaged in interesting ways with the relationship between biodiversity and cultural diversity; in response to expanding capitalist 'monoculture', the preservation, renewal or generation of women's species-knowledges and agricultural practices – alongside the actual species – ties together feminist and ecological resistances. On the other hand, preserving genetic biodiversity is often supported by pharmaceutical companies wishing to keep alive potentially profitable genetic 'resources'; subsistence cultures may be displaced from the land under the guise of protecting biodiversity, or find their ecological knowledges 'mined' for their profit potential.

While feminism has amply questioned concepts and practices of population control, environmental science has generally lent legitimacy to strategies for controlling women's fertility, in part by directing attention away from political and social questions of consumption and distribution. There is an unfortunate lack of dissent among mainstream environmental scientists on the topic of population; their view is that there are simply more people than is sustainable. Where gender issues are discussed at all, it is assumed that women's reproductive rights, desires, or needs are subordinate to questions of carrying capacity or resource availability. That women of the south are unwillingly sterilised while women of the north are strongly encouraged to give birth suggests that there is more at stake in population discourse than numbers of people; environmental science may not create this disparity, but neither does it seriously challenge it.

Throughout both of these issues, 'nature' is a strongly normative term: biodiversity is natural (and, by extension, so is cultural diversity) where as excess population (wherever the line of 'excess' gets crossed) is not. In addition, views of nature prevalent in environmental science – based on conservative concepts of system and balance and oriented toward sustainability – are seldom questioned despite their frequent overlap with (reductionist, often sexist) sociobiology. Despite these questions, and to a greater extent than in other movements, environmental scientists are considered the arbiters of the knowledge that will be considered real or important by environmental activists or policymakers – including many ecofeminists.

To challenge this view, some feminist writers have begun to highlight the social relations of environmental science, to examine closely what counts as 'nature' or 'natural' in scientific discourse, and to emphasise the importance of other knowledges of nature. Donna **Haraway** and N. Katherine Hayles, for example, have called into question the boundaries between the natural and the artificial, and between the observer and the observed, thus problematising any innocent, objec-

tive view of unspoiled nature or environmental balance. Haraway (1991) especially insists that narratives of nature are hotly contested, that gender and race are crucial dimensions of that contest, and that feminism cannot rely on 'nature' to legitimate environmental or social claims. Environmental science, in this view, becomes a non-innocent and non-reductive practice of narrative investigation.

See also: agential realism; ecofeminism; green movement, feminism and the; malestream thought

References and further reading

Carson, R. (1962) *Silent Spring*, Greenwich: Fawcett Publications.
Diamond, I. (1994) *Fertile Ground: Women, Earth, and the Limits of Control*, Boston: Beacon Press.
Haraway, D. (1991) *Simians, Cyborgs and Women: The Reinvention of Nature*, New York: Routledge.
Hayles, N.K. (1999) *How We Became Posthuman: Virtual Bodies in Cybernetics, Literature and Informatics*, Chicago, IL: University of Chicago Press.
Hynes, H.P. (1989) *The Recurring Silent Spring*, New York: Pergamon Press.
Mies, M. and Shiva, V. (1993) *Ecofeminism*, London: Zed Books.
Sachs, W. (ed.) (1993) *Global Ecology: A New Arena of Political Conflict*, London: Zed Books.

CATRIONA SANDILANDS

epistemology, black feminist

Epistemology, in philosophical terms, is strictly concerned with the study of knowledge production. The criteria for upholding claims are often couched in notions of western, scientific objectivity and rationality as the universal standard for evaluating knowledge. Black feminist epistemology refers to the nature, theory and production of knowledge grounded in the lived experiences of black women as a point of entry into the forums and constituencies where feminist knowledges are produced and evaluated. Feminist epistemology emerged, questioning the basis for an androcentric standard (see **androcentrism**), which denies women a place as knowers. Similar to men's, women's experiences and analyses, it argues, are crucial to defining our world. But feminist knowledge production in the mainstream made the experiences of middle class white women the universal basis for addressing the circumstances of all women. Given their access to the sources of and materials for knowledge production relative to other groups of women, white feminist scholars articulated experiences of oppression that ignored the voices of non-white women.

From the 1970s, black feminists in the USA and the United Kingdom such as Angela **Davis**, Audre Lorde and Filomina Steady began to voice their discontent with feminist knowledge which has failed to validate their experiences. By the late 1970s, African female scholars along with their counterparts in Asia and Latin America were adding their voice to the charges of domination and exclusion. They rejected 'the imposition of concepts, proposals for political solutions and terms of relationship' emerging from this scholarship, insisting that the dominant western tendencies in this knowledge base must give way to the untapped indigenous expertise (Amadiume 1987: 8). These critiques have made way for a burgeoning scholarship with black women's experiences at the centre. But, the emphasis on the location and authenticity of feminist writings has also given way to identity politics. The latter, at its extreme, promotes a relativist stance by black feminist scholars who consider themselves insiders to the experiences of and knowledge about black women. While many black feminists do not advocate this stance, there exists the unanimous view that feminist scholarship cannot afford 'to ignore issues of identity or to critique concern for self without posing alternative approaches' (hooks 1989).

Since the early 1990s, the strong and distinct voices of black feminist scholars have witnessed an increasing conflation with postmodern, poststructural and postcolonial feminist critiques (see **poststructuralism/postmodernism**; **postcolonial feminism**). These theoretical incursions into feminist debates, some western feminists argue, have catapulted the voices at the margin into mainstream feminist thought. Such incursions, 'sensitise us to the interconnections between knowledge claims…and power…[where] our own search for an Archimedes point may conceal and obscure our entanglement in an episteme in which truth claims may take only certain forms and not others' (Flax 1990: 48). Although a number of black feminist scholars have entered the larger feminist debate, the celebration of their works could merely serve as a diversion away from confronting the steady stream of knowledge claims and assertions the forum continues to nurture. Michelle Wallace (1989) makes the point that most contemporary critiques which claim to resurrect the voices of the marginalised only mirror the outsider's or immigrant's or nomad's sense of being in the world. Thus, feminist scholarship, informed by such critiques, constitutes itself exclusive of its target subjects. White feminist scholars' intent may be to defend the subjugated voices, even while maintaining their position as gatekeepers, defining the insider and the outsider within feminist scholarship. But it certainly matters who says what and the location from which it was said.

Black feminist epistemology faces a number of challenges. It must not only de-construct the labels imposed on black women in existing feminist literature, but must also resurrect and develop knowledge bases which place black women's experiences at the centre. At the same time, it must continue to ask questions about the origins of feminist knowledge, the locations of knowers and subjects of enquiry, the grounds for knowledge claims and their implications for the place of black women's experiences and their scholarship within the larger feminist mainstream.

See also: epistemology, feminist

References and further reading

Amadiume, I. (1987) *Male Daughters and Female Husbands: Gender and Class in an African Society*, London: Zed Books.

Collins, P.H. (1991) *Black Feminist Thought: Knowledge, Consciousness, and the Politics of Empowerment*, London: Routledge.

Davis, A. (1982) *Women, Race and Class*, New York: Women's Press.

Flax, J. (1990) 'Post Modernism and Gender Relations in Feminist Theory', in L. Nicholson (ed.) *Feminism/Postmodernism*, London: Routledge, pp. 39–62.

hooks, bell (1989) *Talking Back: Thinking Feminist, Thinking Black*, Boston: Black Women's Press.

Oyewumi, O. (1997) *The Invention of Women: Making an African Sense of Western Gender Discourses*, Minneapolis, MI: University of Minnesota Press.

Steady, F. (1987) 'The Studies of Women in Indigenous Africa and the African Diaspora', in R. Terborg-Penn, S. Harley and A. Benton-Rushing (eds) *Women in Africa and the African Diaspora*, Washington DC: Howard University Press, pp. 25–42.

Wallace, M. (1989) 'The Politics of Location: Cinema/Theory/Literature/Me', *Framework*, 36: 53.

PHILOMENA OKEKE

epistemology, feminist

Epistemology – theory of knowledge – investigates the nature and conditions of knowledge. Traditional epistemologists evaluate sources of evidence and methods of inquiry, seeking criteria for justifying beliefs and knowledge claims, and ways of refuting scepticism. Feminist epistemologists are equally concerned to analyse the nature and positioning of knowers and the (gendered) politics of knowledge.

Non-philosophers may see epistemology as an esoteric inquiry, relevant only to philosophers; yet reliable, authoritative knowledge is integral to feminist practices of developing informed analyses of social-political oppression and marginalisation, and engaging in emancipatory projects. Feminists have to *know* women's experiences and the circumstances of their lives, not superficially, but in their social-structural implications, and to explain the absence of women – as knowers and known – in public knowledge, where women still claim minimal epistemic power and authority. These activities require knowing social and discursive structures well enough to show how they sustain hierarchical distributions of power and privilege. Thus epistemology is central to feminist theory.

Epistemology and philosophy of science resisted intervention long after feminists were producing critiques of other aspects of the philosophical canon. A conviction prevailed that knowledge just is knowledge. Traditional distinctions between knowledge and 'opinion' elevate knowledge above individual experiences, assuming that facts, if factual they are, will prevail. Yet mainstream epistemologies are remarkably incapable of providing guidance for regulating the situated knowledge-producing and -evaluating that is crucial to informed feminist practice. Asking 'Whose knowledge are we talking about?', feminists insist that knowers claim responsibility for the knowledge they produce and circulate. They can no longer remain invisible behind formulas like 'it has been shown', 'science has proved'. Feminists in diverse disciplines are thus engaged, often explicitly, with epistemological questions: about research strategies, **objectivity**, evidence, discovery, justification and relativism; about methods that oppress neither women nor other marginalised, disempowered people. They are committed to taking women's experiences seriously – acknowledging differences while drawing general, even lawlike conclusions.

The standards of objectivity and value-neutrality central to an idealised picture of physical science define the epistemologies of modernity. In these theories, 'objectivity' is a disinterested approach to publicly observable subject matters, separate from knowers/observers, and making no personal claims on them; and 'value-neutral' knowers have no vested interest in the objects of knowledge, no motivation beyond 'pure' inquiry. Yet for feminists, such ideals could regulate the knowledge-making only of people capable of achieving a 'view from nowhere', of performing 'a god-trick' (following Donna **Haraway**) to escape location within specific bodily circumstances. The fact that champions of such dislocated epistemologies are usually male, white, able-bodied, heterosexual, and neither too young nor too old, attests to the androcentricity (see **androcentrism**), and the racial, cultural, historical, class, and other 'centricities' of these theories that tacitly validate affluent white male epistemic lives. In positivist-empiricist epistemologies, knowers are detached spectators and objects of knowledge are inert items in knowledge-gathering processes. Knowledge is replicable by anyone in the same circumstances and straightforwardly testable in appeals to observational data, while each knower is separately, individually accountable to the evidence. Knowers seek to know in order to manipulate, predict, and control their environment. From positivism comes the conviction that expressions of value ('sexism is wrong') have no epistemic content. Because they merely report how people feel, they have no factual significance. Feminist, anti-racist and gay-rights commitments thus count only as values: they cannot legitimately inspire, govern, or justify research; and to be a feminist is, in effect, to conduct value-laden research, which cannot be objective. Such ideologies sustain the myth of the neutral man who impartially represents everyone's interests, while women, and other Others produce only subjective, partial conclusions.

Western philosophy aligns mind/reason with maleness, body/emotion with femaleness, representing emotions as irrational and denigrating women's alleged emotionality. Indebted to Genevieve **Lloyd** (1993), feminists argue that embodiment is not incidental to but constitutive of both subjectivity and cognitive possibilities (see **embodiment/disembodiment**). It is in consequence of 'different' (from affluent white male) embodiment that people are assigned marginal epistemic status, as epistemologies that assimilate experiences to a single norm assume universal access to uniform experiences for which differences are irrelevant aberrations. Feminist analyses of differences actively contest these assimilations.

Knowing medium-sized material objects – a positivist-empiricist exemplar – does not translate well into knowing social-political power dynamics or the implications of sexual assault, nor do observational models translate into psychological knowledge of the experiential effects of systemic racism or marital rape (see **observational method (in science)**). The **fact/value distinction** blocks recognition that some alleged 'facts' – the 'harmlessness' of the Dalkon Shield or nuclear testing – are the products of power-based research. Hence feminists have, since the early 1980s, generated critiques and reconstructions of the epistemological project.

Feminists analyse the nature and situations of would-be knowers and of evidence or data, with some concentrating on evidence, others on epistemic situation. In the mid-1980s these differences

prompted Sandra **Harding** (1986) to distinguish *feminist empiricism* from *feminist standpoint theory* (see **standpoint theory**). Empiricists focus on evidence-gathering, advocating a method cleansed of androcentrism; while standpoint theorists concentrate on the historical-material positioning of women's practices and experiences.

For feminists, an empiricism committed to objective evidence-gathering and justification yet informed by feminist ideology can produce more adequate knowledge than classical empiricism, which works in ignorance of its complicity in a sex/gender system. An enhanced vision enables feminists to enlist empiricist tools to expose the **sexism**, racism, and other 'isms' that (often silently) inform knowing. In Helen Longino's social empiricism (Alcoff and Potter 1993), communities, not individuals, are knowers, whose background assumptions shape knowledge as process and product. In genetic research, Longino shows how assumption- (value-) driven differences in knowledge-production contest the possibility of value-neutrality. Yet she endorses community respect for evidence and accountable, collaborative cognitive agency. Lynn Nelson (in Alcoff and Potter 1993) develops from 'naturalised epistemology' a neo-empiricism for which communities, not individuals are the primary knowers; and knowers come to evidence through webs of belief, available for communal critique.

Because the marginalised cannot realise their emancipatory goals without understanding the intractable aspects of the world and its malleable, contestable features, they have to achieve a fit between knowledge and 'reality', even when 'reality' consists in such social artifacts as racism, oppression, or pay equity. For feminist empiricists, an empiricism alert to gender-specificity can achieve just this. Thus, according to Harding, politically-informed inquiry yields a better empiricism, based in 'strong objectivity'.

For standpoint theorists Nancy **Hartsock** (1983) and Hilary **Rose** (1983), empiricists cannot address the historical-material diversity from which people produce knowledge. Standard-setting knowledge in western societies derives from the experiences of white, middle-class, educated men, with women (like the Marxian proletariat) occupying underclass epistemic positions. As capitalism 'naturalises' the subordination of the proletariat, **patriarchy** 'naturalises' the subordination of women. And as examining material/social realities from the standpoint of the proletariat denaturalises these assumptions, so starting from women's lives denaturalises the patriarchal order. A feminist standpoint is a hard-won product of **consciousness-raising** and social-political engagement, in which the knowledge that enables the oppressed to survive under oppression becomes a resource for social transformation.

Neither empiricist nor standpoint feminism has resolved all of the issues. Even the new empiricism fails fully to address the power-saturated circumstances of diversely located knowers, or to pose interpretive questions about how evidence is discursively constituted, and whose evidence it suppresses in the process. Nor, in the absence of a unified feminism, can standpoint theory avoid obliterating differences. Its 'locatedness' offers a version of social reality as specific as any other, yet distinguished by its awareness of that specificity. But empiricism's commitment to revealing the concealed effects of gender-specificity in knowledge-production cannot be gainsaid; nor can standpoint theory's production of faithful, critical, analyses of women's experiences, with its focus on how hegemonic values (see **hegemony**) legitimate **oppression**.

In the years since empiricism and standpoint theory seemed to cover the territory, with postmodernism addressing anti-epistemological challenges to both, feminists have found these alternatives neither mutually exclusive, nor able, separately or together, to explain the sexual politics of knowledge production and circulation. Cross-fertilisations across disciplines and methods have proven more instructive than adherence to methodological orthodoxy.

Most feminists cognisant of the differences that difference makes do not, in fact, hope to achieve a unified standpoint. Patricia Hill **Collins** (1990) advocates an 'outsider-within' black feminist standpoint: an Afrocentred epistemology that shows how knowledge produced in subordinate groups fosters resistance. And María **Lugones** advocates 'world travelling and loving perception' (1989) for escaping a too-particular, self-satisfied location. Donna Haraway (1990) recasts the subject and object of knowledge as radically located and unpredictable, and knowledge-construction as learning to see – from positions discredited in dominant accounts of knowledge and reality.

Evelyn Fox **Keller**'s (1983) biography of geneticist Barbara McClintock reveals a scientist attuned to differences and engaged with her objects of study, offering evidence for a psycho-socially gender-specific style of research. Lorraine **Code** (1991; 1995) examines how power and privilege yield asymmetrically gendered standards of authority in medical knowledge, in the experiences of welfare recipients, in testimonial credibility, and in women's responses to sexist and racist challenges. Her ecological model of knowledge and subjectivity challenges the hegemony of the 'master' model that governs mainstream epistemology.

Taking women's cognitive experiences seriously enables feminists to eschew the **individualism** and universalism of mainstream theory, to examine specifically located knowing, where theory and practice are reciprocally constitutive, and knowers are diversely positioned and active within them.

See also: modernity, feminist critiques of; Other, the; patriarchy; racism

References and further reading

Alcoff, L. and Potter, E. (eds) (1993) *Feminist Epistemologies*, New York: Routledge.

Code, L. (1991) *What Can She Know? Feminist Theory and the Construction of Knowledge*, Ithaca, NY: Cornell University Press.

—— (1995) *Rhetorical Spaces: Essays on (Gendered) Locations*, New York: Routledge.

Collins, P.H. (1990) *Black Feminist Thought: Knowledge, Consciousness, and the Politics of Empowerment*, Boston: Unwin Hyman.

Haraway, D.J. (1990) 'Situated Knowledges', in Haraway, *Simians, Cyborgs and Women*, New York: Routledge.

Harding, S. (1986) *The Science Question in Feminism*, Ithaca, NY: Cornell University Press.

Hartsock, N. (1983) *Money, Sex, and Power: Toward a Feminist Historical Materialism*, Boston: Northeastern University Press.

Keller, E.F. (1983) *A Feeling for the Organism: The Life*

and Work of Barbara McClintock, New York: W.H. Freeman.

Lloyd, G. (1993) *The Man of Reason: 'Male' and 'Female' in Western Philosophy*, London: Routledge, 2nd edn.

Lugones, M. (1989) 'Playfulness, "World-Travelling" and Loving Perception', in A. Garry and M. Pearsall (eds) *Women, Knowledge and Reality*, Boston: Unwin Hyman.

Rose, H. (1983) 'Hand, Brain and Heart: A Feminist Epistemology for the Natural Sciences', *Signs*, 9 (11).

LORRAINE CODE

epistolarity

Epistolarity involves the theory and practice of epistolary fiction. Functioning on the shifting boundaries between 'real' letter writing and 'fictional' letter narrative, epistolarity designates those writing practices that create meaning through the use of letter forms. The genre's dominant themes have been personal, amorous, and/or political, its mode sentimental, satirical, ironic or didactic. Epistolarity lends itself much more to processes of expression, reflection and resistance than to those of action. The first famous woman letter writer was Sappho, who appeared as both historical figure and fictional character in Ovid's epistolary *Heroides*. Most letter writers represented in fiction have since been female. Until the eighteenth century, however, these women's epistolary voices, whether historical or fictitious, were usually appropriated by male authors and editors. The epistolary novel was a major literary form during the seventeenth and eighteenth centuries in Europe. Letter narrative was transformed in the twentieth century by creative experimentation with epistolarity and new theoretical and critical insights. For feminist writers, epistolarity has become a protean genre with limitless possibilities for borrowing and embedding extraneous subjects, languages and techniques, and for giving voice and context to those who have been silenced by hegemonic discourses (see **hegemony**).

Most seventeenth- and eighteenth-century epistolary fiction by men featured women as seduced, betrayed, solitary, cloistered and obsessed by their passion for the addressee, an unfaithful male lover. Examples include Guilleragues's *Letters of a Portuguese Nun* (1669), Marivaux's *La vie de Mariane* (1728), Richardson's *Clarissa; or, The History of a Young Lady* (1747), Rousseau's *Julie, ou la nouvelle Héloïse* (1761), Laclos's *Les liaisons dangereuses* (1782). In recent decades, many undeservedly forgotten collections of letters and letter narratives by women from the same periods have been re-published, including Graffigny's groundbreaking *Lettres d'une Péruvienne* (1747). It is now possible to see correspondence and letter narrative by women to women as challenges to compulsory **heterosexuality** and passionate commentary on society, personal relations, politics, history and culture.

Janet Gurkin Altman (1982) has made an important study of the formal and functional properties of the letter used for narrative purposes. Letter narrative has much in common with other first person narrative forms such as autobiography, journals, private letters, published correspondence, memoirs, diary and other novels (see **autobiography**; **diaries**). Unique to the letter narrative are: the presence of one or more persons engaged in the process of writing letters (intradiegetic writers) to one or more addressees (intradiegetic readers); plot without narrative voice; exchange of letters as slow-motion conversation in a series of discontinuous, unstable and polyvalent present moments; spaces for the frequently conflicted play of confidence and confidentiality; structures that proceed discontinuously, serially and dialogically, precluding definitive closure.

Some of the women writers who have worked in a significant way with letters are Héloïse, Lafayette, Sévigné, Behn, Riccoboni, Austen, Wollstonecraft, Shelley, Charlotte Brontë, Staël, Sand, Huch, Colette, Woolf, **Beauvoir**, Lessing, Atwood, **Walker**. The twentieth century favoured hybrid forms that combine epistolary with other types of fiction in challenges to conventions of closure, subjectivity, **identity**, signature, authority, **gender**, genre, **race**, class, other underlying assumptions of dominant representation systems (see also **genre theory**). One of the first radically subversive feminist works of the contemporary period was

New Portuguese Letters (Barreno, Horta and Velho da Costa 1975). As a response to Guillargues's *Letters of a Portuguese Nun*, the book continues a long tradition of women writing letters, while challenging both tenacious conventions of the genre and stereotypes of desolate women driven only by desire for absent male lovers. In *New Portuguese Letters*, the three authors produce poems, borrow textual fragments, write directly to one another, write to and from the letter-writing seventeenth-century nun, Mariana Alcoforado – who may or may not have been real. The book, accused by Portuguese authorities of obscenity, caused a scandal. It was banned and the authors imprisoned. However, international feminist protests have mounted a strong and effective protest against yet another attempt to censor, appropriate or intercept women's letters.

References and further reading

Altman, J.G. (1982) *Epistolarity: Approaches to a Form*, Columbus: Ohio State University Press.

Barreno, M.-I., Horta, M.-T. and Velho da Costa, M.-F. (1975) *New Portuguese Letters*, trans. H.R. Lane, Garden City: Doubleday.

Goldsmith, E.J. (ed.) (1990) *Writing the Female Voice: Essays on Epistolary Literature*, Boston: Northeastern University Press.

LOUISE H. FORSYTH

equality and difference

Women's equality with men has always been an aim for feminists; in fact, it may be seen as the founding principle of **feminism**. In general it has been interpreted as women possessing the same essential capacities as men such that both sexes should enjoy access to the same opportunities and activities and be valued as of equal worth. However, since the nineteenth century, if not before, feminists have also taken the view that women and men are different and that women's particular skills and attributes should be recognised as being of equal value with those of men. These two tendencies are in tension because 'equal but different' is not necessarily a feminist slogan; in fact

it has generally served to keep women subordinate where femininity and femaleness define 'a woman's place'. In second-wave feminism the issue of 'equality and difference' has come to the fore because of struggles for legal equality, in particular the problems raised by sex discrimination legislation and the 'male comparator' test. 'Equality' is seen as problematic because it reproduces a male norm, both in terms of the content of the law and its form. The ideal of **androgyny**, in which sexual differences are minimised to achieve equality, has come to be interpreted negatively, as women taking on male characteristics. 'Equality' is also linked to the representation of women, and indeed men, as a homogeneous group. Black feminists, for example, question equality as an aim, asking 'equality with whom?' (see **black feminism(s)**). As a result, from the mid-1970s there has been an increasing interest in various aspects of '**difference**'. Three main schools of feminist thought on difference may be identified, each of which has different political implications: maternalists who follow Nancy **Chodorow** and Carol **Gilligan** and for whom difference is primarily moral; poststructuralist theorists of *différance* for whom the feminine is that which is unrepresentable; and those for whom what is important is multiple differences which cut across sexual difference. The binary opposition of equality/difference is widely seen as limiting for feminism and there are various attempts to deconstruct it by contextualising it in historically specific practices and political cultures. However, the importance of equal rights to feminism and the difficulties of reconciling equality and difference seem to make it indissoluble in theory and practice, at least in the west.

Feminist theories of difference

Sex discrimination legislation in western liberal-democracies outlaws the practice of treating men and women differently in awarding benefits or positions. While it has been effective in gaining some women entry to traditionally male domains, it has not resulted in equality between the sexes: men are over-represented in better paid, high status, powerful positions while women are over-represented in poverty statistics. Feminists argue that this is because although it creates ostensibly gender-neutral access, it is actually established on a male norm. First, in terms of content, sex discrimination legislation grants gender-neutral access to institutions already constructed from a male perspective. This is evident in the notorious 'male comparator' test in which to prove discrimination a woman must show that she has been treated less favourably than a man in a comparable situation. Difficult to do given occupational segregation, it is impossible where physical differences such as pregnancy are at issue (MacKinnon 1987). It is possible to argue against this view that it is not the concept of equality as such that is at fault; what is needed is a genuinely gender-neutral standard against which discrimination should be measured. Secondly however, it is argued that the very form of legislation aimed at establishing equality between the sexes is intrinsically masculine. On this view, 'equality' is necessarily an inadequate way of dealing with the subordination of women.

This view is associated with the maternalist ethics of Carol Gilligan (1993), so called because it is based on the psychoanalytic theory of Nancy Chodorow (1978) which privileges the early relationship to the mother as crucial in psychic development. For Chodorow, women are more oriented towards relatedness while men have a more detached sense of self as a result of differing relationships to a primary carer who was a woman. According to Gilligan's women-centred moral psychology, as a result, women and men tend to think differently about moral dilemmas. While men approach them using the universal principles on which morality and law have been based in patriarchal societies, women prefer to think of what is relevant in particular situations in order to sustain relationships of care for those involved (Gilligan 1993). An 'ethics of justice' involves a masculine orientation towards abstraction and individualism: justice is achieved insofar as each detached person is treated identically according to universal principles. The feminine 'ethic of care' treats people differently according to their particular needs in a given situation and with an understanding of their necessary interdependence. Maternalists see equality as a fundamentally masculine ideal, so that to apply it to women involves nothing but a further subordination of the

feminine. Against this view it is often argued, by Catharine **MacKinnon** (1987) among others, that to celebrate the feminine in this way is only to replicate the traditional virtues of self-sacrifice instilled in women in a patriarchal society.

French feminist theorists of '*différance*', like Luce **Irigaray** and Julia **Kristeva** also take issue with the masculinism implied by the idea of equality on the grounds that it subordinates the feminine (see **French feminism**). From this perspective, however, the 'difference' espoused by maternalists remains within the masculine insofar as it essentialises a feminine identity, the subversive potential of which is precisely that it is unrepresentable in phallocentric, masculine discourse (see **essentialism**). The silenced feminine is associated with fluidity and instability, it is that which cannot be captured in the net of categories and concepts of rational thought and which continually disrupts closure. For these poststructuralist feminists the feminine is akin to Derrida's undecidable '*différance*'. For Kristeva (1977), both men and women may adopt the feminine position as artists; on this understanding, aesthetic transgression is political. For Irigaray (1993), the feminine is more closely associated with the female body, and although unrepresentable in conventional language, it should be symbolised in such a way as to allow genuine dialogue between the two sexes. Although for Irigaray this counter-symbolisation would itself be political, she is also concerned with legal rights which would facilitate such a dialogue. They are not to be seen as rights to equality, however, since this would imply a single standard rather than making space for the feminine in public life. The main problem with Irigaray's approach is that it is difficult to adopt in mainstream political life where it continually risks a biologistic interpretation.

An alternative strand of poststructuralist feminism stresses multiple differences as a way of deconstructing the male norm. Judith **Butler** (1990) is also opposed to the essentialist representation of women, arguing that what the feminist project should involve is the disruption of 'women' as an identity in order to deconstruct the male norm in practice. In particular it is necessary to overturn the heterosexual matrix in which masculine men desire feminine women and *vice versa* with a transgressive proliferation of sexed and sexual identities. The political possibilities of a feminism which does not represent women seem limited, however. Other theorists of differences, like Iris Marion Young (1990), are less opposed to the representation of 'women' as a political strategy, but argue that it is important that differences of 'race', ethnicity, sexuality, class, age and so on are not neglected in the feminist project. Young proposes democratic forms in which different voices within the category 'women' may be heard, while the 'fixing' of any identities as 'natural kinds' or essences is to be avoided.

Differences between feminists

Feminists of all theoretical orientations are concerned to deconstruct the binary opposition between equality and difference. However, as long as the law takes the form of universal principles such that differential treament is discriminatory, it is difficult to see how it can be transcended in practice. Carol Bacchi (1990) has shown how feminists are forced into arguing in terms of equality or difference as a strategic response to political culture, legal doctrine and historical circumstance. Debates over the issue vary, then, according to time and place. They are, she argues, most acute in the USA, where the lack of welfare state provision and the relative success of equal rights legislation means that feminists are continually faced with only two alternatives: joining the system on its own terms or staying outside it. As a result feminists find themselves pitted against one another in the courtroom over such issues as protective legislation, maternity rights and affirmative action. In countries like Britain, where the welfare state has recognised women's maternal responsibilities to a limited extent, feminists have not been forced into such polarised positions.

The equality/difference issue is not central to Third World feminists. Insofar as it is reasonable to generalise about such diverse movements, they tend to be linked to political liberation movements in common cause with men, against colonialism and oriented towards re-structuring the state. The identity of 'women' in this case is invariably also a class, 'racial', ethnic or religious identity so that an absolute difference from men is unthinkable, while

the issue of equality is itself part of a broader liberation struggle. The question of 'difference' arises mainly in relation to differences between women, both within the 'imagined community' of Third World feminists and between women of colour and the white women who dominate feminism in the west. Although conflicts sometimes seem intractable, debates turn on how to construct commonalities and alliances across differences in order to mobilise against gender oppression and economic exploitation in a global context (Mohanty *et al.* 1991).

See also: categories and dichotomies; citizenship; discrimination and the law; liberal feminism

References and further reading

Bacchi, C. (1990) *Same Difference: Feminism and Sexual Difference*, Sydney: Allen and Unwin.

Butler, J. (1990) *Gender Trouble: Feminism and the Subversion of Identity*, New York: Routledge.

Chodorow, N. (1978) *The Reproduction of Mothering: Psychoanalysis and the Sociology if Gender*, California: University of California Press.

Gilligan, C. (1993) *In a Different Voice: Psychological Theory and Women's Development*, Cambridge, MA: Harvard University Press, 2nd edn.

Irigaray, L. (1993) *Je, Tu, Nous: Toward a Culture of Difference*, New York: Routledge.

Kristeva, J. (1977) *About Chinese Women*, trans. A. Burrows, New York: Marion Boyars.

MacKinnon, C. (1987) *Feminism Unmodified: Discourses on Life and Law*, Cambridge, MA: Harvard University Press.

Mohanty, C., Russo, A., and Torres, L. (1991) *Third World Women and the Politics of Feminism* Bloomington and Indianapolis: Indiana University Press.

Young, I.M. (1990) *Justice and the Politics of Difference*, Princeton, NJ: Princeton University Press.

KATE NASH

erotica, feminist

The erotic is broader than **sexuality**: it is a biopolitical space for authenticising different ways of being human (see **biopolitics**). The erotic is a site of freedom, joy, pleasure, desire; a site of **jouissance**. The erotic, however, is constructed in historical relations of **power**; feminist erotica has developed in a context of **gender** inequality. Feminist erotica is premised on female **autonomy** and active female desire; woman as an active subject who can give and receive pleasure.

In feminism there are two dominant and contradictory positions on feminist erotica: the radical feminist and the postmodern feminist (see **radical feminism**; **poststructuralism/postmodernism**). The radical feminist position is that female sexual **agency** and thus a feminist erotica is an impossibility in a heterosexual patriarchal social system, that all actions and representations are cooptable by heteropatriarchy (see **patriarchy**; **heteropatriarchy**). The postmodern feminist position contends that female desire, female agency, female pleasure and feminist sexual practices and representations comprise a lived politics of subversion that destablises the dominant system and constructs a space of autonomy.

Women situated away from the centre of the dominant heterosexual reality have since the 1980s been producing feminist erotica. This production has two intellectual sources – the North American **sex wars** which divided feminists over the line between **pornography** and erotica, leading female artists, writers, photographers and filmmakers to begin making 'authentic' female erotica; and, Luce **Irigaray**'s influential claim that the way for women to undermine and destablise the phallic libidinal economy and to find our own feminine feminine (as opposed to the phallic feminine) is to engage in autoerotic practice and lesbian practice.

Three main sites of feminist erotic production are lesbian sexual representation including lesbian sadomasochism (s/m), autoeroticism (masturbation and female ejaculation), and prostitute performance art. Lesbian sexual representations, in such magazines as *On Our Backs*, *Bad Attitude*, *Quim*, *Wicked Women*, the writings of such feminist erotographers as Pat Califia, Joan Nestle, Susie Bright and Carol Queen, the films of Blush Production, the photos of Della Grace depict sex between women who **privilege** and engage in sex with one other; the images are produced and consumed in a lesbian context. Lesbian s/m representations 'inscribe codes specific to lesbian s/m practice: role playing, the exchange of power, confession, attention to rules and restrictions, staged sexual scenes, costume, drama and ritual'. (Cossman *et al.* 1997: 159) Autoerotic practice presented in workshops, books and films, such as Betty Dodson's masturbation workshop/book/film *Sex For One. The Joy of Self-Loving* and Blush Production's film *How to Female Ejaculate* teach women the art of self-pleasure and orgasm; female ejaculation repositions the female sexual body as powerful, active, autonomous with the capacity for a sexual fluid discharge through the urethra. The prostitute performance art of Annie Sprinkle, Scarlot Harlot, Veronica Vera, reclaims the prostitute body as a female erotic body in which the dichotomy between the sacred and profane historically dividing women into good girls/bad girls is exposed as a phallogocentric convention (Bell 1994: 142). (See **prostitution**; **dichotomies**; **phallogocentrism**.)

References and further reading

Bell, S. (1994) *Reading, Writing and Rewriting the Prostitute Body*, Bloomington, IN: Indiana University Press.

Cossman, B., Bell, S., Gotell, L. and Ross, B. (1997) *Bad Attitude/s on Trial: Pornography, Feminism, and the Butler Decision*, Toronto: University of Toronto Press.

SHANNON BELL

essentialism

The term 'essentialism' refers primarily to certain metaphysical positions – for example, that woman's nature is biologically determined – though it also has political and rhetorical uses within feminist theory. Essentialism is often identified with a perspective that privileges a white, middle-class, heterosexual conception of womanness and excludes women of colour and women of different classes or sexualities from the political category 'woman' (see **heterosexuality**). Because feminists typically reject both essentialism and its political connotations, the term 'essentialist' has come to be associated with outmoded and incorrect conceptions of womanness and sometimes operates rhetorically as an expression of disapproval.

Two forms of essentialism should be distinguished. The first, called *universalism* or *generic essentialism*, says that members of the group 'woman' have the same nature and thus there is a single universal womanness that all share. The second, called *individual essentialism*, says that each individual's womanness is part of *her particular* essence or nature in the form of a biological or otherwise 'natural' property of her or of a necessary – or essential – property of her. In principle, these forms of essentialism are distinct. It does not follow from universalism that womanness is part of each individual woman's essence because for example womanness could be an accidental, non-essential, property of her. And it does not follow from individual essentialism that womanness is a universal because each individual woman could instantiate a *particular* womanness, similar to, yet distinct from, that of every other woman. However, in practice many conceptions of essentialism comprise both universalism and individual essentialism, as, for example, Aristotelian essentialism.

Feminists have rejected universalism by arguing that a person's womanness is the product of a unique interplay of the different features of her situation – her **race**, class, culture, **sexuality**, **experience** and **gender** role – and hence it is not a universal. If this is true, the question arises of whether women constitute a genuine political category, and if not how feminism can operate as a political movement. Feminists have also rejected individual essentialism by arguing that since gender is socially constructed, womanness cannot be a fixed biological, natural, or necessary part of the natures of individuals who are women. In postmodernist critiques of essentialism, the two forms of essentialism are rejected simultaneously (see **poststructuralism/postmodernism**). The postmodernist position against individual essentialism, namely that subjects are unstable or fragmented, is understood as *ipso facto* opening up the possibility of differences between subjects and hence as incompatible with universalism of any sort.

See also: biological essentialism; difference; diversity; identity; identity politics

References and further reading

Schor, N. and Weed, E. (eds) (1994) *The Essential Difference*, Bloomington and Indianapolis: Indiana University Press.

Stoljar, N. (1995) 'Essence, Identity and the Concept of Woman', *Philosophical Topics* 23, 2: 261–94.

Witt, C. (1995) 'Anti-Essentialism in Feminist Theory', *Philosophical Topics* 23, 2: 321–44.

NATALIE STOLJAR

ethic of care

The term 'ethic of care' was taken up in feminist thought following the publication of psychologist Carol **Gilligan**'s work (1982) on **moral development**. Gilligan used the term to refer to a cluster of themes that she claimed distinguish the moral perspective of many women from the moral perspective of justice more commonly expressed by men. Among the characteristics associated with an ethic of care are a concern with care and responsiveness in relationships, an emphasis on attachments and the prevention of harm, and a context-sensitive style of deliberation that resists formulations of moral problems in terms of abstract principles.

The resonance of the ethic of care with the values and concerns endorsed by many women in their caring roles in patriarchal societies has led to the view that the ethic may provide the key to a much needed transformation of conventional masculine conceptions of moral life (see **masculinity**). A leading proponent of this position is educationalist. Nel Noddings (1984), who argues that the feminine receptivity, relatedness and responsivity of caring lies at the basis of truly ethical action. Strengthened by the force of women's biological and social engagement in **motherhood**, popular conceptions of this position have tended to identify the ethic of care as one of the central insights of feminist thought.

Many feminists, however, are far more cautious about the liberatory potential of the ethic of care. Its strong ties with stereotypes of feminine nurturance, emotionality and self-sacrifice have brought allegations that the ethic of care may be little more than the romanticised symptoms of social powerlessness. Its links with female biology and the caring roles of white, middle-class, western women have brought charges that it is an illegitimate naturalisation and reduction of the rich variety of different women's different ethical possiblities. Its connections with the practices of personal and informal relationships have been seen as intrinsic limits to the application of the ethic in the larger realm of impersonal and formal relations. Accordingly much contemporary philosophical work on the ethic of care is concerned to show how the care perspective is interwined with self-empowerment, the recognition of difference and/or norms of justice, impartiality and equality.

These cautions and reconsiderations notwithstanding, the emphasis of the ethic on giving voice to previously silenced concerns for the value of attachments among persons and responsiveness to the needs of others has inspired renewed interest in, and understanding of, the social, political, and psychological importance of caring relations, and the potential for their revaluation.

See also: cultural feminism; ethics, feminist

References and further reading

Gilligan, C. (1982) *In a Different Voice: Psychological Theory and Women's Development*, Cambridge, MA: Harvard University Press.

Held, V. (eds) (1995) *Justice and Care: Essential Readings in Feminist Ethics*, Boulder, CO: Westview Press.

Noddings, N. (1984) *Caring: A Feminine Approach to Ethics and Moral Education*, Berkeley, CA: University of California Press.

PETA BOWDEN

ethics, feminist

Ethics seeks wisdom in the conduct of life, traditionally in three areas. Axiology (value theory) explores the good/bad distinction as applied to possible objects of desire. Theory of right explores the right/wrong distinction as applied to actions, choices, policies. Character ethics examines virtues, vices, responsibility, bases of praise and blame and of judgements of good and evil as applied to persons, motives, character traits. Historically, influential ethical theories have attended to one or other of these areas and perhaps secondarily to another, rather than addressing all three. In principle, feminist ethics might take up any of these areas. In practice, most feminist ethics focuses on character and responsibility. Yet a significant body of feminist ethics literature also addresses issues of justice in the theory of right, and there is disagreement among theorists about the importance of justice for feminist ethics.

Three things basically distinguish feminist ethical theorising. First, its motivation comes from contexts of female **oppression**. Second, it centres the data of female lives as starting points for philosophical reflection. Third, it seeks ways to nourish female vitality, resist oppression, overcome past oppression, facilitate healthy bonding, and develop sound relations with larger environments.

Yet feminist ethics is not simply about women and girls but about the conduct of life as problematised by female experience in oppressive environments and oppressive relations. It envisions better alternatives, better relations, and social transformations. Thus it overlaps feminist politics. Beginning with an issues focus – from women's legal disabilities in the eighteenth, nineteenth and early twentieth centuries to abortion and **affirmative action** in the 1960s and 1970s – it moved in the 1980s and 1990s to more wide-ranging, pluralistic, multi-levelled theorising. It includes global as well as intimate concerns.

Although certain themes are widely associated with feminist ethics – antipathy to hierarchies and dualisms, preference for circles, suspicion of competition and aggression – feminist ethics is not a body of doctrines or a unified theory or world-view. It is a family of approaches to ethics growing out of overlapping histories and motivations. This naturally gives it potential for great diversity. It includes reflexive criticism as well as adventurous work in new hypothesis construction and critical analysis of antifeminist work.

African American playwright Lorraine Hansberry wrote in 1957 to *The Ladder*, a lesbian magazine, that women should take on ethical questions produced by a male dominated culture (Card 1991). Simone de **Beauvoir** was already doing it in France before it was called 'feminist ethics'. In the USA the second wave of feminist politics of the late 1960s and 1970s became a major influence on feminist ethics. In 1978 Mary **Daly** subtitled her treatise *Gyn/Ecology: The Meta-Ethics of Radical Feminism*. After Carol **Gilligan** published her research on patterns of ethical thinking in women's psychological development, the term 'feminist ethics' was widely applied to feminist analyses and appraisals of that research.

Appreciating women's oppression creates a tension for feminist ethics. On one hand, as women's lives have been treated disrespectfully in patriarchal philosophical literatures, a profound feminist commitment has been to listen to women's voices respectfully wherever they are heard. On the other hand, the damage of oppression can show itself in the judgement, perceptions, and emotional responses of women who embody patriarchally constructed femininities (see **patriarchy**). An example is the misplaced gratitude and corresponding sense of obligation women may feel toward men who are simply less abusive than they might be. The challenges are to distinguish women's special insights from the peculiar damage to which women are liable under patriarchies and to avoid the pitfalls of either glorifying women's experience or treating women simply as victims.

There are many traditions of feminist ethics. Some theorists focus on specific areas of activity, such as paid or unpaid labour, **education**, healing, spirituality, **sexuality**, **friendship**, self-defence, or law (see **feminist legal theory**). Some, in traditions of applied ethics, apply classical texts and principles to new questions. Others use their findings in specific areas of activity to advance new theorising. Historically-oriented theorists, such as Elizabeth Spelman and Annette Baier, turn a critical eye to classical texts, such as those of Plato, Aristotle, and Descartes, either explicitly discussing women or taking only men's lives as paradigms of humanity. Other theorists reclaim historically buried defences of women, such as those of Mary Wollstonecraft, Margaret Fuller, Frederick Douglass or John Stuart Mill. Some identify historical positions friendly to feminist concerns, as Annette Baier does with David Hume and Lynne Tirrell does with themes in Nietzsche.

Others, wishing to start over, advance new theories, explore new paradigms, and analyse concepts such as bitterness that have not received past philosophical attention. A major tradition in this vein is feminist care ethics, which revalues, analyses, and develops the idea of caring as a fundamental ethical activity. Its paradigms of caring are relationships historically central to many women's lives: mother/child relationships, passionate female friendships, nursing and educational relationships, lesbian bonding. Care ethics addresses relationships with particular others, not just others in general (see **ethic of care**). It values emotional responsiveness and takes seriously material needs. Its focus on selves allies it with character ethics, in contrast with modern teleological traditions that focus on the consequences of actions and deontological traditions that focus on obligations and rights.

Yet, care ethics is not always feminist. Patriarchal traditions praise women for service to men, children, the community, God and encourage women to bond emotionally to men who have power over them. Such service and bonding are popularly identified as caring. Women's voices in patriarchy may simply endorse both, disregarding conditions underlying the relationships and attachments. Thus care ethics can be traditionally feminine, rather than critically feminist. Consequently, important questions for any care ethic are whether it valorises the subordination of women as servants or glorifies women's martyrdom (or can easily be used to do either). Care ethics that takes historical mothering as a paradigm is especially vulnerable in these respects.

Still, if feminist ethics centres female experience as starting points for theorising, it can scarcely ignore mothering. Some theorists seek special wisdom in mothering ideals if not practices. Sara Ruddick, mindful of the dangers of endorsing servitude or glorifying martyrdom, argues for extending 'maternal thinking' from home to international relations. Her 'maternal thinking' at its best embodies 'attentive love' (a term borrowed from Iris Murdoch who got it from Simone Weil), which is central to mothering's defining tasks: preserving the child's life, fostering her growth, and making her acceptable to a wider society than her family. Sara Ruddick envisions a nonviolent world where peace is an enduring outcome of virtues of maternal thinking rather than a precarious outcome of adversarially oriented conflict resolutions.

Sarah Lucia **Hoagland**'s lesbian ethics offers an alternative to the mothering model of care. Her paradigms are relationships of lesbians in community with each other. She rejects the mother/child paradigm because of its lack of reciprocity. Like Sara Ruddick, she seeks modes of conflict resolution that centre attentive love, which she calls 'attending', as alternatives to the social-control orientation dominating modern moral and political philosophy. Both Sara Ruddick's and Sarah Lucia Hoagland's approaches are friendly to ecofeminism, which has criticised what Karen Warren calls 'the logic of domination' and explores parallels between the obsessions with control characterising oppressions of women and of other animals and the natural environment.

Advocates of feminist care ethics disagree about the values of justice, rights, impartiality, law, and institutions, all of which invoke what Seyla **Benhabib** calls the 'generalised other' (as opposed to the 'concrete other' of particular relationships). Nel Noddings finds justice a poor substitute for caring and Sarah Lucia Hoagland finds it not a useful concept, whereas Virginia Held finds justice indispensable but also that it needs to be supplemented by care.

Disagreement about justice may stem from care ethics' preoccupation with character and motivation. Justice is defined in part independently of anyone's motivations (for example, in terms of the shares of benefits and burdens among members of a community). A common view is that caring is a remedy for violence. Yet if violence is also definable in part independently of anyone's motivations, some such concept as justice may be required to address it (or even identify it) adequately. Thus, some theorists call for a feminist, anti-racist theory of justice, starting from paradigms of injustice. African American legal scholar Patricia **Williams** finds the possibility of claiming rights 'deliciously empowering'. Marxian political philosopher Iris Young calls for a theory of justice centred on decision making, divisions of labour, and culture. Justice is also central to much feminist biomedical ethics.

Argentinian-born philosopher María **Lugones**, of Gaucho and European ancestry, centres cultural pluralism and offers the concept of 'world-travelling', which facilitates both justice and care, as a way for women of culturally diverse backgrounds to develop the understanding necessary to resist oppression together. World-travelling is a wilful exercise of an ability acquired spontaneously by members of a marginalised group to shift perceptually and emotionally from a construction of life where one feels 'at home' although others are outsiders to other constructions of life where former outsiders are now at home and one is oneself an outsider. Not an armchair exercise, it requires real interaction. She finds world-travel an antidote to privilege-induced arrogance, which blocks both justice and love. She advocates doing it, however, only with an attitude of non-competitive playfulness, an openness to finding oneself sometimes foolish or inept. Thus, taking women seriously may require laughter, even (perhaps especially) at oneself.

See also: bioethics; black feminism(s); bonding, maternal, feminine; care, provision of; ecofeminism; emotions/rationality; friendship; lesbian ethics

References and further reading

Card, C. (ed.) (1991) *Feminist Ethics*, Lawrence, KS: University Press of Kansas.
—— (1999) *On Feminist Ethics and Politics*, Lawrence, KS: University of Kansas Press.
Cuomo, C.J. (1997) *Feminism and Ecological Communities: An Ethic of Flourishing*, New York: Routledge.
Gilligan, C. (1982) *In a Different Voice: Psychological Theory and Women's Development*, Cambridge, MA: Harvard University Press.
Guy-Sheftall, B. (ed.) (1995) *Words of Fire: An Anthology of African-American Feminist Thought*, New York: The New Press.
Hoagland, S.L. (1988) *Lesbian Ethics: Toward New Value*, Palo Alto, CA: Institute of Lesbian Studies.

Lugones, M. (1987) 'Playfulness, "World-Travelling", and Loving Perception', *Hypatia* 2 (2): 1–19.

Noddings, N. (1984) *Caring: A Feminine Approach to Ethics and Moral Education*, Berkeley, CA: University of California Press.

Ruddick, S. (1989) *Maternal Thinking: Toward a Politics of Peace*, Boston: Beacon Press.

Sherwin, S. (1992) *No Longer Patient: Feminist Ethics and Health Care*, Philadelphia, PA: Temple University Press.

Young, I. (1990) *Justice and the Politics of Difference*, Princeton, NJ: Princeton University Press.

CLAUDIA CARD

ethics of linguistics (Kristeva)

The question of ethics is one of the main themes in Julia Kristeva's major work on linguistics, *Revolution in Poetic Language*, and the subject of two articles: 'The System and the Speaking Subject' and 'The Ethics of Linguistics'. Her interest in the ethical imperative arises from a reconsideration of the human subject as the main focus of linguistic study, and thus is also a critique of structuralist and poststructuralist approaches to the field of language. By drawing on the theoretical work of Marx, Nietzsche, Hegel, Jakobson and, above all, on Freudian **psychoanalysis**, Kristeva develops a theory of language as a heterogeneous process brought about by the dynamic relationship that occurs when the drive-governed semiotic (chora) disrupts the symbolic order that seeks to confine it. The product of this relationship between the semiotic and the symbolic is what she calls the subject in process/on trial; and it is precisely this instability and precariousness of subjectivity which becomes the locus of an ethics that is not one of repression, but of innovation and renewal. This concept of ethics is thus directed against those views of ethics based on order and stability generated by coercion and submission to the law. By linking the revolutionary force of the semiotic dimension of language with questions of ethics, Kristeva argues for the necessity of a social code which is able to accomodate the transgressive nature of psychic life (founded on the death drive

and Eros) in the social space. Such a code would offer possibilities of accounting for violence, aggression and also pleasure and **jouissance**. By formulating the ethical imperative as one of struggle rather than of observation of laws, Kristeva establishes an essential link between ethics and negativity.

The reinsertion of subjectivity in the field of linguistics is for Kristeva also a reintroduction of the social and political domain as that which is structured and produced by language. By conceptualising the semiotic as charged by negative and positive, creative and destructive drives, as productive of the subject in process but itself unrepresentable, she links it to the feminine/maternal body. The pre-symbolic mother is thus manifested as the materiality of the symbolic: as rhythm, gesture, word-play; in short, as that which is excluded from the communicative function of language but present as its disruption and innovation, as its ethical function. Thus, the linguistics of ethics becomes in Kristeva's work also an ethics of **motherhood**. However, formulated as an ethics of negativity it can neither be defined as marginality nor conformity to the law.

See also: ethics, feminist; ethics of linguistics (Kristeva); feminist literary theory

References and further reading

Kristeva, J. (1980) 'The Ethics of Linguistics', trans. T. Gora *et al.*, in *Desire in Language*, Oxford: Blackwell.

—— (1984) *Revolution in Poetic Language*, trans. M. Waller, New York: Columbia University Press.

—— (1986) 'The System and the Speaking Subject', in T. Moi (ed.) *The Kristeva Reader*, Oxford: Blackwell.

ANGELICA MICHELIS

ethnic cleansing

The highly contested, euphemistic and politicised phrase 'ethnic cleansing' entered popular discourse after 1991 to describe the policies of the Serbian nationalist wars in Bosnia to found and occupy 'Greater Serbia'. Defined by the United Nations

(UN) to refer mainly to Bosnian Serb aggression against Muslims and Croatians in Bosnia-Herzegovina (BiH), ethnic cleansing includes these legal parameters: the forcible means of implementing an *intentional nationalist policy* that was *coordinated and financed* by Serb officials *in conjunction with* the Federated Republic of Yugoslavia and its army (JNA). While the UN attributes violence to all sides in BiH and recognises Croatian nationalist violence as 'ordinary' nationalism with elements of ethnic cleansing, ethnic cleansing most often designates violent measures to eliminate or dramatically reduce Muslim and Croat populations that were within Serb-held territory ('extreme' nationalism). Choosing the language of ethnic cleansing instead of genocide is controversial, seen to be a political move made by both Serb nationalists and the US government to soften the conceptual impact of Serb nationalist violence and diminish an international impetus to intervene on behalf of victimised populations (see **language, gender and power**).

While the historical incidence of rape and sexual **violence** in war has been widely documented by feminists, the UN distinguishes between the 'opportunistic' rape of women in war and rape as a tool of ethnic cleansing. The majority of documented violence against women in Bosnia was committed by Bosnian Serb nationalists against Bosnian Muslim and Bosnian Croat women as part of a systematic scheme of terror. Women were targeted as the moral property of men and as the embodiment of culture, community and the nation. Serbian soldiers forcibly impregnated women and held them captive until they could not safely seek abortions, to force them to reproduce 'Serbians'. Women were tortured in order to demoralise the men who were fighting against Serb nationalists. The systematic rape and sexual assault of women occurred throughout the wars, in homes, refugee camps, detention camps designated for forced pregnancies, and camps designated to provide soldiers with sexual services. Because UN institutions both disregard opportunistic sexual violence and focus on extreme nationalism, the analysis of violence against women in war and the concomitant proposals for remedy are limited to those acts which demonstrably contribute to ethnic cleansing. In this way, they do not account for the violence inflicted against women in war regardless of their ethnic classification nor for the targeting of women *as women*, of which there are numerous examples. Thus the responses for peace reproduce the warmakers' characterisation of women's bodies as tools of the nation.

See also: international tribunal of crimes against women; nationalism and gender

References and further reading

Askin, K.D. (1997) *War Crimes Against Women*, The Hague: Kluwer Academic Press.

Stiglmayer, A. (ed.) (1994) *Mass Rape*, Lincoln: University of Nebraska Press.

ELIZABETH PHILIPOSE

ethnography

Ethnography, or the writing of culture, was for many years thought restricted to the discipline of **anthropology**, and limited to the form of the classic monograph, in which the constituent elements of a culture – its politics, religion, economy and social structure – were discussed in discrete chapters. This conception was challenged by a series of debates about the nature of ethnographic authority and experimental writing reflected in the 1986 edited collection, *Writing Culture*. Inspired by literary criticism and postmodern theory, the book had a controversial reception in anthropology. Yet, because of it, ethnography is now better understood as a series of (often overlapping) genres: expository essay, diary (see **diaries**), novel, memoir, short story, life history, testimonio, self-reflexive narrative, biography and **autobiography**. Although women particularly in the American (or Boasian) tradition had, since the late nineteenth century, been writing ethnographies in modes distinct from what came to be canonised as the classical ethnographic monograph, the contributions of writers like Elsie Clews Parsons, Ella Deloria, Zora Neale Hurston, or Ruth Landes to debates on self-reflexivity in the discipline were not recognised until the 1990s (Behar and Gordon 1995).

At the same time that feminist anthropologists questioned why ethnographies written by women were not judged to be classic ethnographies, and were therefore absent from the canon, feminists in other disciplines turned to ethnography for what they thought would be a less intrusive, and thus more feminist research methodology (see **methodology, feminist**). However, Judith Stacey (1988) concludes that the ethnographic medium, because of its reliance upon **participant observation** to establish intimacy or rapport between researcher and informant, actually has more potential to betray feminist principles of trust and collaboration in making those intimacies public.

The question of what constitutes feminist ethnography has thus evolved along two parallel lines. On the one hand it necessitates different strategies of reading, so that older works which utilise more polyphonic or novelistic devices might both be understood as feminist, and incorporated into the canon as exemplars of unique forms of writing. On the other hand, feminist ethnography has been understood to entail different processes of research and writing which would enact non-exploitative strategies of address between author, subject and audience – in other words, writing by women, for women, about women. Some critics have argued, however, that such assumptions rely upon forms of gender **essentialism** or feminist universalism which are increasingly under scrutiny. Ironically, perhaps because 'feminist ethnography' emerged in relation to the 'Writing Culture' critique of anthropological representation, there has been more discussion of its form and genre than of the meaning of the term 'feminist' in feminist ethnography.

References and further reading

Behar, R. and Gordon, D. (eds) (1995) *Women Writing Culture*, Berkeley, CA: University of California Press.

Clifford, J. and Marcus, G. (eds) (1986) *Writing Culture*, Berkeley, CA: University of California Press.

Stacey, J. (1988) 'Can There Be A Feminist Ethnography?', *Women's Studies International Forum* 11 (1): 21–7.

KAMALA VISWESWARAN

ethnomethodology

Coined by Harold Garfinkel in the 1950s, ethnomethodology originally referred to the use of everyday knowledge by social actors. Garfinkel sought to understand how people make sense of interactions, how they exhibit **agency**, create coherence and reproduce the social order in daily existence. Ethnomethodology elevates the importance of common-sense knowledge and the contextual basis of meaning – generally by concentrating on decision-making and the practice and reproduction of social reality.

Ethnomethodology is predicated on reflexivity, the act of simultaneously articulating and creating interactions, and indexicality, the notion that the meaning of symbolic forms is in part contextual. As social actors, people make sense of interactions in ways that appear 'rational' and common-sensical through shared agreement with others. Through practice that re-creates and reinforces social reality, people order their world and re-invent the social structure on a daily basis.

Eschewing methods such as interviewing, ethnomethodologists often focus their attention on commonplace situations for investigation and may utilise conversational analysis, ethnographic methods such as **participant observation**, or empirical information such as video or tape recordings to collect research data. Experimental methods have also been employed that involve breaching social rules in order to interrogate their use in reproducing reality.

Ethnomethodological theory has been used as an analytical tool in studies of social action, intersubjectivity and the social construction of knowledge. Ethnomethodology is often linked with phenomenology and its notion that social action is a product of the practice of social actors and not the result of abstract social forces; however, some assert that ethnomethodology ignores the questions of experience and life-world that characterise the phenomenological approach. Mary Rogers (1983) has challenged ethnomethodology's relationship to symbolic interactionism, suggesting that while the former focuses on common-sense interactions and the structures they re-create, symbolic interactionism attends to meaning as a self-evident feature of social life. The slipperiness of the subject may be due to divisions within ethnomethodology between positivist approaches and more critical efforts which seek to undermine the self-evidence of social life.

Feminist critiques of ethnomethodology contend that it engages in problematising the subject without making theoretical contributions. Moreover, the focus on the observation of interaction lends itself to an objectivism that disregards the social and political past and present context and tends to reify social exchange. Ethnomethodologists, such as Garfinkel (1967), have been criticised for failing to reflect on the common-sense understandings of **gender** and their own relationship to the gendered subject.

See also: sociology

References and further reading

Bologh, R. (1992) 'The Promise and Failure of Ethnomethodology from a Feminist Perspective', *Gender and Society* 6, 2: 199–206.

Garfinkel, H. (1967) *Studies in Ethnomethodology*, Englewood Cliffs, NJ: Prentice Hall.

Rogers, M. (1983) *Sociology, Ethnomethodology, and Experience*, Cambridge: Cambridge University Press.

DENISE L. SPITZER

eugenics

Eugenics is a branch of study which is concerned with the genetic 'improvement' of human populations by the systematic eradication of genetic characteristics which are deemed dysfunctional (or 'dysgenic'), and the simultaneous promotion of 'preferred' genetic profiles. Eugenic language regarding the health of populations, gene pools, and the 'breeding stock' of particular societies draws heavily upon discourses of **biology**, heredity and animal husbandry, lending a patina of scientific **objectivity** and distance to its projects. Clearly, however, the politics of **race**, **gender**, class, and intellectual and physical ability have all been central to the history of eugenics, and varying hierarchies of social value have crucially informed definitions of what constitute 'desirable' genetic

traits. Further, women's bodies and reproductive experiences (particularly those of indigenous and poor women) have always been centrally implicated in the politics and practices of eugenics, and the area has elicited diverse responses from feminists (see **body, the**; **reproduction**).

Francis Galton in late-nineteenth-century England coined the term 'eugenics', and originated the broader school of thought which was popularised in the first half of the twentieth century. The process and meanings of human reproduction have never been determined by 'nature', but have been always situated within specific cultural, political and social parameters. The eugenicist twist on population management, however, was a specific interest in evolutionary theories, and a belief that social progress could be secured using systematic 'scientific principles'. Adherence to eugenicist approaches to combat population 'degeneration' – particularly 'racial degeneration' – crossed conventional political boundaries. Eugenicist thought found a home at times in racist, nationalist, imperialist, social liberal, and feminist politics alike. The association of eugenic thought with Nazi extermination and compulsory sterilisation programmes in the period 1933 to 1945 in Europe is frequently highlighted: less well known, perhaps, is the association between eugenic thought and policies in liberal democratic societies such as the USA and Australia, which underpinned state-sanctioned sterilisation programmes, the prohibition of 'miscegenation' (racial 'interbreeding'), and the forcible removal of children from 'undesirable' families both before and well after 1945.

Historically, some (white, middle-class) feminists embraced eugenicist principles, seeing them as a means, variously, of 'strengthening the nation', advancing their sectional political interests over other groups campaigning for enfranchisement, or ameliorating conditions for reproductively 'overburdened' poor women. More recently, some feminists have argued that a newer form of organised eugenics is effectively being practised through the spread of commercialised genetic engineering and screening, and lucrative reproductive technologies such as *in vitro* fertilisation (IVF). The task of addressing the issues raised by such practices, within a feminist politics and ethics, is ongoing (see **ethics, feminist**).

See also: ethnic cleansing

References and further reading

Bland, L. (1995) *Banishing the Beast: English Feminism and Sexual Morality 1885–1914*, Harmondsworth: Penguin.

Kevles, D. (1985) *In the Name of Eugenics*, Cambridge, MA: Harvard University Press.

JANE LONG

eurocentrism

Eurocentrism depicts the inherent belief that European culture, knowledge and society is superior, and therefore establishes the normative standard from which to adjudicate all other cultures and groups. Ella Shohat and Robert Stam suggest that eurocentric discourse first emerged as a 'discursive rationale for colonialism' (1994: 2). It is a term derived from critiques of universal forms of epistemology which indicate that all knowledge is produced from or located in European Enlightenment (see **epistemology, feminist**). Furthermore, eurocentric thought also presumes the existence of a universal transcendent subject that underlines the notion of a western European *cogito*. Since the appearance of Edward Said's seminal work titled, *Orientalism* (1979), which reveals the underpinnings of a process of racialisation and otherness endemic to the production of knowledge, eurocentric concepts or imaginations of the world have been subjected to criticism.

Although eurocentrism connotes a pure, authentic, and somewhat homogenous understanding of a transcendental Europe, the actual discursive formation of eurocentrism is highly conflictual and multifarious. In order to undo or confront eurocentric formations, it has become a challenge not to duplicate or simply mimic the same chauvinistic attempts to recover authentic or essentialised subjects. That is to say, critiques of eurocentrism, have the tendency to replace or invoke a host of other ethnocentric positions. This ethnocentrism has become commonplace in debates regarding multiculturalism, identity politics and political correctness. A critical strategy that has been employed in non-essentialist positions is to invoke the hybridisation or transcultural relationship that exists between and through the production of cultures (see **hybridity**).

Feminist scholars engaged in postcolonial and anti-racist positions have critically examined the formation of the concept of eurocentrism in order to question the implicit quality of the absent referent of the European male/female subject within the formation of modernity (see **postcolonial feminism**). Rather than simply postulating an alternative essentialist category, feminist scholars critical of eurocentrism have articulated multicultural, cross-cultural and transnational modes of investigation. The critique of eurocentrism resonates strongly within western feminist scholarship, as the very definitions of 'Third World' and 'First World' woman, 'woman of colour' and the subaltern have become critical sites of struggle and redefinition.

See also: McClintock, Anne; Spivak, Gayatri; Trinh T. Minh-ha

References and further reading

Mohanty, C. (1991) 'Under Western Eyes: Feminist Scholarship and Colonial Discourses', in C. Mohanty, A. Russo and L. Torres (eds) *Third World Women and the Politics of Feminism*, Indiana: Indiana University Press.

Said, E. (1979) *Orientalism*, New York: Vintage Books.

Shohat, E. and Stam, R. (1994) *Unthinking Eurocentrism: Multiculturalism and the Media*, London: Routledge.

DAVINA BHANDAR

existentialism

Existentialism is a twentieth-century movement growing out of the convergence of ideas from Edmund Husserl, founder of phenomenology; Søren Kierkegaard, the father of existentialism; and Friedrich Nietzsche. The movement emphasises aspects of human life devalued in many European philosophies, in particular that of G.W.F. Hegel.

Kierkegaard sought a reemergence of the individual from its status as mere cog in the machines of State, Church, and History, and posited the value of choices that could not be rendered rational. Kierkegaard found the individual's existence defined by a leap of faith responding to a call from God; later existentialists say all choice is a leap into an abyss. Nietzsche described a way to be an individual: someone not subject to the crowd, its tastes and beliefs, who was to follow a rigorous path of self-development, based in part on recognising the death of God; some existentialists see the path to authenticity as most valuable and similarly rigorous. Husserl developed phenomenology, which describes lived experiences and structures of consciousness as constitutive of the self, social relationships, and life-worlds (see **life-world**). Most existentialists use parts of this descriptive method.

Existentialism takes in a broad sweep of philosophers: **Beauvoir**, Martin Buber, Martin Heidegger, Gabriel Marcel, Maurice Merleau-Ponty, José Ortega y Gasset, Jean-Paul Sartre, and others. The themes of free choice and its correlative responsibility, of experiences ranging from the dread/anxiety of facing freedom and death to the ambiguities of interpersonal life and its ethical demands, run through their works. Sartre asserts the limitations of rational systems in many decisions, saying that the leap of choice creates value for individuals. Sartre also describes the body as marker for the glances and determinations of the **Other**, an aspect of facticity that exceeds body's 'objective' definition and necessarily leads to conflict. Beauvoir analyses ways in which women and their bodies are culturally constituted; she offers those who would be ethical a way to embrace the ambiguity of freedom as the greatest value, so great that a choice of freedom for all others is necessitated.

More recently, in a echo of Beauvoir's denunciation of racism and sexism as ways of 'othering' others, of making them objects defined by our definitions and thus disallowing their freedom, Lewis Gordon (1994) uses Sartre's notion of self-deception to describe racist societies, drawing upon the black Caribbean thinker, Frantz Fanon (*Peau noire, masques blancs*, 1952), who was influenced in France by the existentialists (see Beauvoir

1963). In the recent *Existence in Black* (Lewis 1997), black philosophers take up the name existentialist: Paget Henry discusses black Afro-Caribbean and African existentialist philosophies, Clarence Sholé Johnson sees existentialism in Cornel West's thought, and Patricia Huntington discusses **race** and gender.

References and further reading

Beauvoir, Simone de (1963) *La Force des Choses*, trans. R. Howard as *The Force of Circumstance*, Harmondsworth: Penguin, 1981.

Gordon, L. (1994) *Bad Faith and Antiblack Racism*, Atlantic Highlands, NJ: Humanities Press.

—— (ed) (1997) *Existence in Black: An Anthology of Black Existential Philosophy*, New York: Routledge.

MARY JEANNE LARRABEE

existentialist feminism

Existentialist feminists draw inspiration from existentialists including Beauvoir, Merleau-Ponty, and Sartre: they see women's and men's lives as concretely situated and emphasise concepts like freedom, interpersonal relations, and experience of lived body. They value the capacity for radical change, but recognise – with Sartre and Beauvoir – that various factors limit it, such as self-deception, the Other's construction of us, and anxiety raised by change and self-responsibility. Many of them, dedicated to articulating and undermining socially imposed gender roles, and culturally constructed discourses that 'write' us, criticise not only the sexist limitations of earlier existentialists but also those poststructuralist feminists (deconstructionist, postmodernist, francocentric and French feminists) who deny the individual subject and her freedom.

Simone de **Beauvoir** is considered by some as the first existentialist feminist, given *Le Deuxième Sexe* (1949). At the beginning (1960s–70s) of the French women's movement, some portrayed her as an 'old' feminist and their work as 'new feminism', so that existentialist work soon dropped out of the title French feminist. But the 1980s–90s saw a diversity of feminisms developed globally and in France, including a reclamation of Beauvoir's feminism, in particular by Margaret Simons. Recent writers proclaim the uniqueness of Beauvoir's existentialism, refuting claims of essentialism and misogyny others find in her writings.

Existentialist feminists have charged other existentialist writers with sexism: Margery Collins and Christine Pierce fault Sartre's limited anti-essentialism for sexist views, despite his stand against social prejudices; Hazel Barnes refutes the charge of sexism. Maryellen MacGuigan criticises Ortega's views on women's inferiority, Juliá Marías's idea of sexuate condition, and Frederick Buyendijk's narrative of women's experience.

The essay collection, *The Thinking Muse* (Allen and Young 1989), provides a rich illustration of different approaches taken by existentialist feminists. Jo-Ann Pilardi describes female eroticism in Beauvoir's writings, and Eléanor Kuykendall discusses the place of action therein. Iris Marion Young examines girls' experiences of their bodies, Jeffner Allen questions patriarchal existentialism but values its emphases on self-reflection and radical change, while Judith Butler provides a critique of the sexual ideology in Merleau-Ponty's method. Julien Murphy compares the **gaze**/Look in Sartre and Adrienne **Rich**.

Work in the 1990s continued to extend existentialist methods and concepts to gender and race studies: Nancy Potter (1995) aligns women incest survivors' experiences with the notion of dread/anxiety, Janice McLane (1996) uses Merleau-Ponty's concept of flesh to describe self-mutilation, and Shannon Sullivan (1997) criticises Merleau-Ponty's 'anonymous' body. Linda Bell (1993) moves Sartre's notion of authenticity into feminist ethics (see **ethics, feminist**). T. Deneane Sharpley-Whiting (1998) uses Fanon's analyses of racist and colonialised subjectivities to discuss feminism. The work of existentialist feminism, including those using phenomenological techniques, continues studying ways in which some women experience their lives as existed, not as theorised.

References and further reading

Allen, J. and Young, I. (1989) *The Thinking Muse: Feminism and Modern French Philosophy*, Bloomington, IN: Indiana University Press.

Barnes, H. (1990) 'Sartre and Sexism', *Philosophy and Literature*, 340–7.

Bell, L. (1993) *Rethinking Ethics in the Midst of Violence*, Lanham, MD: Rowan and Littlefield.

Collins, M. and Pierce, C. (1973) 'Holes and Slime: Sexism in Sartre's Psychoanalysis', *Philosophical Forum (Boston)*, 5: 112–27.

MacGuigan, M. (1973) 'Is Woman a Question?' *International Philosophical Quarterly* 13: 485–505.

McLane, J. (1996) 'The Voice of the Skin', *Hypatia* 11 (4): 107–18.

Potter, N. (1995) The Severed Head and Existential Dread', *Hypatia* 10 (2): 69–92.

Sharpley-Whiting, T.D. (1998) *Frantz Fanon: Conflicts and Feminisms*, Lanham, MD: Rowan and Littlefield.

Simons, M. (1981) 'Beauvoir and Sartre: A Question of Influence', *Eros* 3: 25–42.

—— (1999) *Beauvoir and* The Second Sex*: Feminism, Race and the Origin of Existentialism*, Lanham, MD: Rowman and Littlefield.

MARY JEANNE LARRABEE

experience

The term 'experience' was first emphasised by feminist activists and in early feminist consciousness-raising groups. It is most likely to have entered feminist theory via these radical feminist groups. The feminist usage is derived from the tendency of radical groups of that period to employ crude and sometimes incorrect versions of Marxist theory. Marx had argued that the proletariat saw the world under a condition of 'false consciousness' insofar as it accepted the point of view of the bourgeoisie. Early feminists reasoned by analogy that women saw the world from the male point of view. Like the proletariat who mistook bourgeois opinion for truth, women also mistook the biased, male perspective for truth and reality. The process of consciousness-raising was a way for women to share their experiences and to reinterpret them from a female, and ultimately a feminist, perspective. 'Experience' is linked to the idea that the 'personal is political' in that the female experience occurred in the realm of the private or personal (e.g. in the home, the kitchen, the bedroom). Both imply that political action would have to take a new form and could no longer be limited to passing just laws.

'Experience' quickly became one of the core concepts of feminist theory, and formed the basis for feminist epistemology. 'Since sex, class was' as Shulamith Firestone wrote in 1993 (11), 'so deep as to be invisible', all institutions, theories and political perspectives, indeed, reality itself, it was argued, were reality and truth only as told from the male perspective. In order to get at a more 'objective' truth; that is, at a truth that incorporated the full range of human perspectives, women's point of view had to be represented. Thus feminists began to speak of 'women's experiences', or sometimes even of 'women's experience'. The latter implies that there is a connection among all women and a commonly shared experience of womanhood. In the 1980s some feminist theorists talked about mothering as a universal female experience. In so doing, they were responding to problems in feminist theory created by the predominance of the term 'experience'. That is, a universal female experience suggests that the category is transhistorical. Yet, clearly, women's experiences vary across time and culture. What, then, could function as a universal grounding for the category 'Woman'? In order to avoid essentialism and to account for female differences, the grounding would have to be materialism. That is, it would have to be rooted in materiality and practice rather than merely in abstract idealism. Yet, it would have to be an experience that truly was common to all women in some sense. To feminists like Adrienne **Rich**, Sara Ruddick, Joyce Trebilcot, Carol **Gilligan**, Nancy **Chodorow** and others, motherhood seemed just such a universal female practice. Other feminists (myself included) denied, sometimes vehemently, that this was the case.

Another candidate for 'universal female experience' was sexuality. The principal theorists advancing this argument were (and are) Andrea **Dworkin** and Catharine **MacKinnon**. The claim here is that male sexuality invariably combines violence with sexual enjoyment. Thus, women's universal experience of sex under patriarchy (even when they are lesbians) is primarily one of victimisation and disempowerment. This line of argument is connected to the so-called 'sexuality debates' of the 1980s which pitted anti-pornography feminists like Dworkin and MacKinnon against so-called 'pro-sex' feminists like Gayle **Rubin** and Ellen Willis.

The term, 'women's experiences', on the other hand, acknowledges that experience varies from woman to woman but still implies that the differences, when tallied, can and should be united under the term 'woman'. Both seem to say that women's ways of knowing are fundamentally different from those of men and that, therefore, feminist theory needs to be grounded in its own feminist epistemology. This epistemology would necessarily be grounded in the female experience.

In feminist theory, the single most important and sustained attempt at developing a feminist epistemology based on women's experience is feminist **standpoint theory** which, in early incarnations, used Marxism in a way very similar to the one described above. The use of 'experience' in feminist theory has been criticised by continental philosophers along with many others because it tends to invent, essentialise and reify the female experience. In so doing the category 'Woman' remains an abstract and essentialised category.

References and further reading

Firestone, S. (1993) *Dialectic of Sex: The Case for Feminist Revolution*, New York: Quill.

Grant, J. (1993) *Fundamental Feminism: Contesting the Core Concepts of Feminist Theory*, New York and London; Routledge.

Rubin, G. 'Misguided, Dangerous and Wrong: An Analysis of Anti-Pornography Politics' in A. Assiter and A. Carol (eds) *Bad Girls and Dirty Pictures: The Challenge to Reclaim Feminism*, London: Pluto, pp. 18–40.

Ruddick, S. (1989) *Maternal Thinking: Towards a Politics of Peace*, Boston, MA: Beacon Press.

Scott, Joan W. (1992) '"Experience"' in J. Butler and J.W. Scott (eds) *Feminists Theorize the Political*, New York: Routledge.

Trebilcot, J. (ed.) (1984) *Mothering: Essays in Feminist Theory*, New Jersey: Rowman and Allanheld.

Willis, E. (1994) *No More Nice Girls: Countercultural Essays*, Connecticut: Wesleyan University Press.

JUDITH GRANT

F

fact/value distinction

The fact/value distinction originates in the positivistic contention that facts are products of neutral, disinterested observation performed in controlled conditions such as laboratory experiments. These conditions ensure replicability (i.e. the same observations are available to every normal observer in identical conditions); and **objectivity** (i.e. none of the observer's biases or values will influence the knowledge produced). Facts are 'value neutral'.

The distinction hangs on the belief that values which are inherently subjective, infused with the idiosyncrasies, commitments, and passions of the would-be knower, block the very possibility of knowledge. Statements of fact that are verifiable in observation – 'the cat is on the mat' – comprise the only meaningful knowledge claims. Statements of value – '**homophobia** is oppressive', 'Alice Neal is a fine painter' – neither derive from nor are testable in controlled observation: they merely convey personal preferences. Because they are not verifiable by the observational criterion which distinguishes meaningful from meaningless claims, they are neither true nor false, but meaningless. Ethical, political, aesthetic, and religious claims fall into this category, for orthodox positivists. Derivatively, denigrations of qualitative research by contrast with quantitative research appeal to this same standard.

Feminists have shown that behind this mask of objectivity and value-neutrality are complex power structures of vested interest, dominance, and subordination. These are the structures that legitimate certain kinds of knowledge, especially those modelled on the knowledge (ideally) achieved in physical science; and confer authority upon those knowers who are best able to claim the neutral detachment that produces objectivity. Thus assumptions about 'human nature' work in concert with the fact/value distinction, fostering the belief that only a small segment of the population – male, usually white, propertied, well educated, heterosexual, and reasonably young (see **heterosexuality**) – are capable of the dispassionate, value-neutral distance that yields epistemic authority (see **dipassionate investigation**). The irony of claiming that value-neutrality can be the product of these heavily value-laden requirements informs feminist, and other post-Enlightenment critique.

By virtue of its feminist commitments, feminist inquiry is explicitly value-laden all the way down. It is neither apolitical nor neutral. Yet one of its most positive contributions is in its demonstrations, across its academic and activist projects, that self-confessedly value-laden inquiry can yield well warranted conclusions. Indeed, precisely because of its enhanced sensitivity to the values concealed behind the mask of disinterestedness, feminist inquiry often achieves a 'stronger' objectivity than allegedly value-neutral inquiry. Ongoing critical-constructive debates, within feminism and with its critics, show that feminists are well equipped to counter any accusation that avowed value-ladenness must precipitate a descent into 'mere' subjectivism.

See also: observational method (in science)

References and further reading

Harding, S. (1991) *Whose Science? Whose Knowledge?*,

Ithaca, NY: Cornell University Press (see especially chapter 6, '"Strong Objectivity" and Socially Situated Knowledge').

LORRAINE CODE

fairy tales and feminism

Feminist approaches to the interpretation of fairy tales have been instrumental in revealing the form's potential for renegotiating and transforming categories of gender. Early feminist work on fairy tales begins with critiques of the negative gender stereotypes offered by the best known printed versions of these tales. Simone de **Beauvoir** and Betty **Friedan**, for instance, argue that as a socialising force fairy tales are effective in curtailing the desires of young girls, teaching them the damaging 'virtues' of self-effacement and sexual restraint. If the zenith of the female protagonist's ambition in stories such as *Cinderella* is to be rescued by and married to the hero/prince, then this ambition fosters fallacious hopes of a 'happy ever after' ending in generations of young women readers, discouraging them from thinking for themselves.

In the 1970s there is a shift away from criticisms of the passive female stereotype, however, as many women writers begin to offer alternative versions of fairy tales featuring enterprising heroines, and to rework fairy tale plots and motifs in their novels. Feminists also draw attention to lesser known international fairy tales which contain women who display a liberating resilience to patriarchal constrictions. Rosemary Minard's collection *Womenfolk and Fairy Tales* provides good examples of such tales. Some feminist scholars begin to reappraise the submissive protagonist, looking at instances of her inner resourcefulness.

Bruno Bettelheim's influential book on fairy tales, *The Uses of Enchantment*, has come under insistent attack from feminists, for Bettelheim can only conceive of female sexuality within the final frame of wife and motherhood, implying that a girl's deepest desire is to exist as the object rather than as a subject of desire. His characterisation of the fairy tale as a vehicle for the expression of

universal human problems overlooks problems of gender and also goes against the historical grain of fairy tales, which have frequently been adopted by women in order to plot escape from imposed limits. Marina Warner's and Jack Zipes's works in particular provide insights into the ways in which the diversity and subversiveness of the oral tradition was quashed. Both scholars explore the ways in which fairy tales from this rich tradition were subsumed into the educational literature of the nursery. Warner has been particularly important in drawing attention to the major part played by women in the dissemination of folk and fairy tales.

See also: heroines

References and further reading

Bettelheim, B. (1991) *The Uses of Enchantment: The Meaning and Importance of Fairy Tales*, London: Penguin Books.
Carter, A. (1977) *The Bloody Chamber*, London: Virago.
Minard, R. (1975) *Womenfolk and Fairy Tales*, Boston: Houghton and Mifflin.
Warner, M. (1995) *From the Beast to the Blonde: On Fairy Tales and Their Tellers*, London: Vintage.
Zipes, J. (1993) *The Trials and Tribulations of Little Red Riding Hood: Versions of the Tale in a Socio-Cultural Context*, New York: Routledge.

TESSA KELLY

family, the

The family is an abstraction infused with symbolism and controversy that has led politicians, academics and moralists to focus on its meanings and future. In traditional usage, 'family' commonly refers to a group of two or more people united by 'blood' (genetics), marriage or adoption, who share a common residence, economic responsibilities, regulation of sexual expression and possibly the raising of children. In practice this definition and most others are exclusionary, reflect hegemonic interests (see **hegemony**) and are contestable.

From the late nineteenth to mid-twentieth century, anthropologists and sociologists searched for universal family properties and an all-encompassing definition. The dominant functionalist approach emphasised the normativity in industrialised societies of the nuclear family (of parents and progeny) and gender-role specialisation. Research, particularly after 1970, challenges these views, documenting that family structures vary, e.g., by time, place, class, race and ethnicity. Common references to 'the' family mislead because, in the singular, the concept implies a monolithic, stable entity, a social ideal inconsistent with the reality of heterogeneity.

Various feminisms tend to address the institution of the family in differing ways. Typically, liberal feminism emphasises family impediments to gender equality, e.g., socialisation, reproduction, childcare and domestic labour. Radical feminism sees family as the embodiment of **patriarchy**, imposing heterosexism (see **heterosexism, heteronormativity**) and **sexism**. Cultural feminism often acknowledges family tyrannies, proposing changes that reflect women's culture. Socialist/Marxist feminism views families as economic units that, linked with patriarchy, benefit the capitalist system. Postmodern feminism targets the biases and implications of family as a coded, socially constructed category. Standpoint and anti-racist feminisms are more likely to focus on families as sources of strength and contradiction in relation to larger forces of social oppression.

Overall, feminist challenges decentre many malestream views of family by substantiating that power and oppression can operate within families, particularly along lines of gender and age; that family members can experience the same event differently; that any monolithic vision of the family ignores the significance of class, culture, ethnicity and race, age, gender and sexual orientation; that glorified characterisations of family harmony in times past are unsubstantiated; and that families need to be understood within a larger social/economic historic context.

More work is needed to theorise enduring patterns of intimacy and reciprocity in ways that attend to feminist theoretical perspectives, the range of criticisms regarding scholarly conceptualisations of family, and the increasing opportunity for designing chosen families. New theorising needs to incorporate the diversities of race, ethnicity, age,

class, gender, sexualities, and culture, allow for advances in biotechnology, telecommunication and genetics, and be responsive to our human genius for 'familial' innovation.

See also: African American families; kinship

References and further reading

Nelson, H.L. (ed.) (1997) *Feminism and Families*, New York: Routledge.

SHARON McIRVIN ABU-LABAN

family law

Family law was for many centuries based on the notion that the family was a natural association of husband, wife, and their biological children, with men and women by nature fit for different tasks and responsibilities. The husband was the head-of-household, having authority to decide such matters as the family's residence, the education and religion of children, and the disposition of family income. The common law doctrine of spousal unity or 'coverture' subsumed a wife's legal personality into her husband's, preventing her from holding property or making contracts in her own name.

In the course of the nineteenth century, grounds for divorce, often previously confined to a wife's adultery, expanded to include a husband's infidelity, desertion and cruelty. Married women's property statutes gave wives the right to keep their earnings. In the USA, slaves were not allowed to marry or have custody of their children. The enactment of the post-Civil War Amendments to the Constitution gave legal protection to black families.

Marriage law reform, like women's suffrage, encouraged women's independence; some scholars see these changes as part of the general shift in law from 'status' to contract. In the twentieth century, reformers struck down laws prohibiting marriage between people of different races; legalised contraception and abortion; and criminalised domestic violence. Children gained greater recognition when laws prohibited child labour and made education compulsory.

Greater legal autonomy for family members has

not, however, eliminated the social and economic forces that preserve both male dominance and greater economic resources for white than for non-white families. Occupational segregation ('men's' and 'women's' jobs) and higher wages for male occupations have kept many women economically dependent on men. In the late twentieth century declining real wages for many workers made two incomes necessary to support a family. Poor people, especially single mothers, who were unable to support their children on wages alone turned to **welfare**.

At the end of the twentieth century, legal recognition of gay and lesbian marriages, and the rights of gays and lesbians to become parents through adoption or assisted procreation were sharply contested. For same-sex and heterosexual couples alike, the use of **biotechnology** in **reproduction** raised questions about the respective rights of genetic and social parents. Such controversies promise to continue the reshaping of family law.

See also: African American families; ethic of care; lesbian juris-prudence; motherhood

References and further reading

Davis, P.C. (1997) *Neglected Stories*, New York: Hill and Wang.

Fineman, M.A. (1991) *The Illusion of Equality*, Chicago, IL: University of Chicago Press.

Shanley, M.L. (1989) *Feminism, Marriage and the Law in Victorian England*, Princeton, NJ: Princeton University Press.

MARY LYNDON SHANLEY

fascism, women and

'Fascism' and 'women' are not monolithic categories. It is helpful to approach them as part of political continua, making arguments for specific cases and policies. Nazi Germany, 1936–45, and Mussolini's Italy, 1922–45, have generated feminist research addressing the positioning of women. However these examples scarcely circumscribe 'fascism'. Numerous twenty-first-century dictatorships, single-party governments, political subgroups

and 'democratic' policies worldwide may be counted on the fascist continuum.

Fascist regimes tend to inferiorise women, smash free trade unions, feminist and other liberationist organisations, practice censorship, eugenics and terror, centralising power in the name of nationalism and/or the cult of the virile male leader. In fascist Italy and Germany, women's treatment and responses varied by cultural heritage, politics, social class, religion, age, relationship to men (or not), sexualities, and whether they chose to collaborate or resist, to what degrees and at what historical junctures. Acts of omission, including refusing to speak up or assist those in danger, and overlooking atrocities, are increasingly considered as culpable as collaboration, succouring criminals, and ruling elite membership. Koonz (1987) argues that a majority of German women were complicit with the Third Reich. The careers of female resisters and artists present instructive counterpoints (Pickering-Iazzi 1995).

Both regimes developed from conditions in the 1920s when men were struggling with the conflicting demands of modernity, requiring the skills and talents of *all* people, against their drive to reimpose patriarchal authority in the face of threatening gender role anomalies wrought by women's achievements under feminisms, homosexual liberation and socialisms. Masculine insecurity was intensified by the trauma of the First World War and the economic depression of the late 1920s and 1930s.

As an expression of these tensions, the reworking of national imaginaries and policies concerning women's 'proper' enterprises assumed monumental importance for fascist ideologues and policy-makers. Local rhetorics of 'traditionalism' founded on linked discourses of biologistic gender, race, and bodily 'purity' were increasingly expressed in eugenicist and xenophobic terror. The torture, rape and murder of millions of 'deviant' and 'degenerate' Jewish, intellectual, leftist, lesbian and gypsy women and girls under the Third Reich is the better-known side of ostensibly benign organisations and policies, sometimes devised and administered by women, that pressed women by turn either into employment and training, or into childrearing and volunteerism, as self-sacrificing servants of the male/fatherland, under rubrics like 'strong' roles for 'The New Woman'.

See also: biological essentialism; ethnic cleansing; Judaism and feminism; lesbian history; nationalism and gender; patriarchy; race

References and further reading

de Grazia, V. (1992) *How Fascism Ruled Women: Italy 1922–1945*, Berkeley, CA: University of California Press.

Koonz, C. (1987) *Mothers in the Fatherland: Women, the Family and Nazi Politics*, London: Jonathan Cape.

Pickering-Iazzi, R. (ed.) (1995) *Mothers of Invention: Women, Italian Fascism and Culture*, Minneapolis, MI: University of Minnesota Press.

LYNNE STAR

Fausto-Sterling, Anne (b. 1944)

Anne Fausto-Sterling is one of the early feminist biologists to criticise mainstream scientific theories of **gender** differences. In the mid-1960s Fausto-Sterling studied zoology at the University of Wisconsin (USA), later in the decade, developmental genetics at Brown University (USA), and upon completing her Ph.D., published in both women's studies and **biology**. Like many other feminists, she exposes the shortcomings of any science which purports to be objective, neutral and above social relations (see **objectivity**).

Fausto-Sterling's landmark book *Myths of Gender* (1985) reveals the inadequacies of biological theories of sex differences. In this book she deconstructs claims made by biologists and sociobiologists who explain gender differences by way of genetics; she challenges the assumption that genes are the *sole* cause of behavioural differences between the sexes and examines what is meant by genetically determined behaviour. In particular, she argues that biological claims of male 'superiority' oversimplify science because they reduce our understanding of human beings to one cause, underestimating the impact of the environment on social development. Her critiques of reductionist biology have extended to racial IQ testing and the search for a homosexual gene. Fausto-Sterling's

analysis of the search for genetic answers exposes further the way in which science often attempts to justify social prejudices with scientific explanations.

Fausto-Sterling has been equally critical of scientific discourses which contribute to a deterministic and reductionist reading of **race**. As with gender, she argues that biological constructions of race are embedded in the politics of race relations. By examining the **biological essentialism** in scientific theory, she reveals how science is historically connected to, and implicated in, colonialism. In her work concerning 'Hottentot' women, she argues that nineteenth-century concepts of black women's sexuality and bodies as 'animal-like' (and therefore inferior to non-European races) provided scientific justification for imperialist expansion.

Fausto-Sterling is one of the few feminists to look at the connections between race, gender and science. She continues to contribute to feminist critiques of science, expose the limits of science and challenge its paradigmatic nature.

See also: women's studies: autonomy v. mainstreaming

Selected writings

Fausto-Sterling, A. (1985) *Myths of Gender*, New York: Harper Collins.

—— (1989) 'Life in the XY Corral', *Women's Studies International Forum* 12, 3: 319–31.

—— (1995) 'Gender, Race and Nation: The Comparative Anatomy of "Hottentot" Women in Europe 1815–1817', in J. Terry and J. Urla (eds) *Deviant Bodies*, Bloomington, IN: Indiana University Press, pp 19–48.

MARSHA HENRY

female circumcision/female genital mutilation

Female Circumcision (FC) or Female Genital Mutilation (FGM) is the cutting of parts of the external genitals of girls as a rites of passage to womanhood. An estimated 100–130 million girls and women in the world have undergone this ritual. It is practiced mostly in 28 African countries and among minorities in Asia. In the 1990s many African refugee and immigrant women moved to Europe, North America and Australia carrying with them the culture of the practice and its consequences. Those countries, together with several African countries, have passed laws prohibiting the practice in the past decade.

FC/FGM is a cultural practice and not a religious requirement. It is practised by some Muslims, Christians of various denominations, the Ethiopian Jews and followers of indigenous African religions. Commonly, girls undergo circumcision between the ages of four and twelve years, some before marriage and some as early as the first two years of life. In societies where FC/FGM is part of a larger initiation ritual, urbanisation and economic pressures have reduced the initiation to genital cutting.

According to the World Health Organization there are four types of FGM:

Type I: Excision of the prepuce with or without excision of part or all of the clitoris (mostly clitoridectomy).

Type II: Excision of the prepuce and clitoris together with partial or total excision of the labia minora.

Type III: Excision of part or all of the external genitalia and stitching/narrowing of the vaginal opening (infibulation).

Type IV: Rare and unclassified types.

FC/FGM can cause many physical complications and may have lasting sexual and psychological effects depending on individual constitution, the circumcision experience and the socialising process.

While the practice was first problematised by outsiders, the growing African women's movement is becoming vocal against the practice. The Inter African Committee (IAC) was started in 1984 and today has affiliates in over 24 countries. Other organisations dealing with issues of health and human rights are including FC/FGM within their mandate defining it as a violation of women's health and sexual rights.

Because of the severity of this form of control of women's sexuality and because it occurs primarily in black Africa it has ignited many racial and cultural conflicts. The handling of some western feminists of the practice as a 'barbaric ritual' of more inferior cultures drives many Africans to defend their cultures regardless of whether they approve or disapprove of the practice. The paucity of exposure of indigenous Africans' efforts to stop this practice by a biased western media feeds into existing patronising and racist attitudes. Increased collaboration and networking between women's organisations in Africa and the international women's movements is overcoming past rifts between African and western feminists. Progressive African women welcome all support and collaboration given in a spirit of equality and justice.

NAHID TOUBIA

feminism

Feminism may be understood as *theory* – systems of concepts, propositions and analysis that describe and explain women's situations and experiences and support recommendations about how to improve them. Such theory is distinguished from non-feminist thinking about women or gender by its general respect for women's own perspectives and authority, and its persistent attention to the workings of power structures which privilege men. Feminism may also be understood as a kind of *social movement*, one that may generate and be aided by theory. Both are concerned with women's flourishing – women controlling adequate resources, of all sorts, to live well.

Employing the first sense, one must immediately say that there are many feminisms – many feminist theories. One might assume that if these 'isms' can all be called by a single name, they must have some common elements which could be specified in an encyclopedia entry, and that if there are no such common elements then this name, *feminism*, must be meaningless. In fact, the diversity of these theories is impressive, and it does not seem to be possible to state any principle, doctrine, method or vision common to them all. Strangely enough, in the final years of the twentieth century and the opening years of the twenty-first century some feminist theorists would conclude that there cannot be any entry at this point in the encyclopedia. But it is not necessary to state any doctrines shared by all feminisms, or try to find terms that have the same meanings in all feminisms. One can speak from within one feminism and, from there, note some of the dimensions along which various feminisms differ from each other.

Human beings generally live in social groups. Social groups are not homogeneous, but are structured by webs of relations among individuals which give meaning to words, symbols, images and actions. Such webs construct and maintain **power**, resources, obligations and expectations, and distribute them in all dimensions through the social fabric, maintaining criss-crossing and interacting roles, statuses, identities (e.g. farmer, mother, legislator, priest and so on). And they produce a fault line between women and men – they allocate distinctive packages of meanings, powers and entitlements to people in rough correlation with some idea of bodies' reproductive functions. For instance, there is some degree of division of 'women's work' from 'men's work' in most cultures (both material work and ritual or cultural work) and corresponding differences in expectations and rewards. In most human societies, this distribution yields a broad asymmetrical pattern privileging men and subordinating women: social power and control of resources are concentrated on the male side of the fault line; and most men are entitled to something like an owner/property relation to one or more women, while most women do not have parallel general entitlements with respect to a man or men, especially within their own class/race/ethnic group.

The preceding paragraph is composed in the terms and assumptions of one feminism. But some such systematic asymmetries, widespread across cultures and history, are recognised and interpreted by various feminisms. They may be referred to as **gender** inequality, male dominance, **sexism**, **patriarchy**, phallocracy, the oppression of women, the suppression of women, sex discrimination, sex oppression, heterosexualism, hierarchical sex–gender system, systemic misogyny, the construction of women as an exploited class, patriarchy as a global religion, male supremacism. Differences of terminology are important, for different terms are embedded in different ways of grasping what is going on and different experiences of living in such

systems. Different terminologies, different conceptions of this asymmetry, also are tied in with different understandings of the relations between it and constructions of race, economic classes, national identities, sex and sexuality, colonialism, and with different philosophical and ideological frameworks (such as liberalism, postcolonial theory, psychoanalytic theory, existentialism, postmodernism and so on). However named and interpreted, such asymmetry is presented by feminisms as something not to be taken for granted and accepted, nor accommodated as inevitable or unchangeable, but as something to be critiqued and changed by ways and means which are conceived in the terms and frameworks provided by various feminisms. Recommendations, grounded in different interpretations of the asymmetries and envisaging different 'better worlds', include revising the distribution of resources and power to women and men, changing the nature and ways of exercising social power, reconstructing what it means to be a woman or a man, adding more genders and introducing choice of gender identity, abolition of any social distinctions related to any coding of differences among bodies.

In the second sense of the word, feminism is a kind of social/historical phenomenon. Where enduring social arrangements are oppressive to women, there are also enduring tendencies among women to resistance, rebellion, and creative alternative world-making. At some times and places this tendency intensifies and forms into a relatively coherent, explicit, conscious and collective organisation of attention and effort, into a 'movement' – a pattern of acts and happenings that is recognisable in its context as a force oriented to critiquing and substantially changing those social arrangements. Such historical passages, such movements, are instances of feminism.

Feminism, in this 'movement' sense, may come into being, generate historic change, and subside or become diffuse again over time. As a relatively structured and identifiable social phenomenon it has occurred at various levels and locations in many different cultures and eras and has had effects that extend through the fabric of a culture or sub-culture long after its period of intense energy and identity as a social movement. For instance, the nineteenth- and early-twentieth-century feminist movement in North America opened secondary and higher education to women – a change which endured and immensely affected those cultures long after that movement subsided as an intensely-organised and well-defined political force.

Feminism, both theory and political action, is plural, mixed, and moving. Late twentieth-century feminism is rich with the constant blending and borrowing of themes and ideas among different theories and theorists. No one need feel that she has to choose or identify with one feminism to the exclusion of all others.

See also: anarchist feminism; black feminism(s); class analysis UK; class analysis US; lesbian feminism; liberal feminism; race; radical feminism

MARILYN FRYE

feminist presses

At the beginning of the twenty-first century, bookstore shelves crowded with women's texts or publishers' catalogues comprised exclusively of women authors seem unremarkable. Yet it was not long ago that publishers argued that there was no market for books by women, about women. The first *Women's Media List* (Allen 1974: 40–1), counted fewer than ten feminist presses. Thirteen years later, there were over 100 (Allen 1987) – from Naiad Press which publishes popular lesbian detective novels or gynergy books whose focus is experimental poetry and prose to larger diverse presses like Virago or The Women's Press (UK). These second-wave feminist publishers distinguish themselves from preceding ventures by their scale and their legitimacy. They have paved the way for university presses and mass market publishers which produce work by women, and legitimised the efforts of smaller political or literary presses which support **women's writing**.

The emphasis in the 1960s and 1970s on women speaking for themselves and controlling or creating the means to do so resulted in a blossoming of presses and periodicals, libraries and archives, book stores and women's centres. It also produced a variety of women-only practices in feminist publishing. Many feminist publishers insisted that books about women should be authored by women; some also took this principle further – to the creation, production and dissemination of women's works, to encourage not only women writers, but editors, designers, printers, distributors, and critics as well.

Two ideas are important here. One presupposes that the establishment of alternative media will allow a woman to speak directly from her own experience without the taint of patriarchal oppression (see **patriarchy**; **oppression**); it hopes for new and true meanings heard genuinely by a new community of women. The other signals a commitment to sharing skills and to developing analysis collectively through the involvement of women in all stages of the development and production of feminist texts (see also **collectivity as action, as process**). This emphasis on skill building was crucial in feminist publishing; it enabled women to bypass a publishing hierarchy and information complex historically dominated by men, and to work differently: to level the distinctions which separate authors and editors from typesetters or designers.

In the early days of feminist publishing, the principle that even production work – design, typesetting, printing, and binding – should be done by women led to the establishment of women's production services. As some of these services like typesetting (particularly before the advent of desktop publishing) required a considerable outlay of capital, few remained in the 1990s. Nevertheless, some all-women printers and typesetters, like Press Gang in Vancouver, Canada, still operate. Distribution was one of the major stumbling blocks to feminist publishing; here women have made small local efforts and ambitious national ones. Volunteers run mobile women's libraries to rural and isolated communities not served by a women's or even chain bookstores. There are women-run national distributors (such as *Frauenbuchvertrieb* in Germany) and several women's bookstores in many countries.

While feminist publishing accounts for a wide variety of political practices and choices (from collective to corporate control; from subscription sales to state funding to co-operative ownership); some allegiance to the principle of **autonomy** was common. Even the 'mass market' women's presses

– Virago, Pandora, The Women's Press (UK) – publish only women, and rely in part on feminist practice for their organisational structure, while at the same time operating according to the corporate designs of **mass media**.

Generally, a woman simply recounting her experience has no ready-made guarantee of finding a feminist publisher: for the most part, her manuscript must also reconstruct that experience in a way informed by feminist politics. Feminist presses were dedicated both to increasing the publishing resources available to women and to disseminating feminist views. Yet such economic and structural considerations were often coupled with a belief in a woman's 'true voice', that only a woman could speak of the **experience** of being a woman. Underlying the construction of feminist presses in the 1970s and 1980s were the theoretical tenets of **identity** politics. The arrival of men in feminism (see **femmenism (men in feminism)**) coincided with questions from **queer theory** about sexual identity, and critiques by women of colour of the racist assumptions underlying aspects of the women's movement. Falling through the cracks of the identity of 'black' and 'woman', black women found themselves without publishing options, as neither black presses nor women's presses sought out their work. The furore in the late 1980s over the discovery of a Virago Press author who turned out to be a white male Anglican parson masquerading as a shy, retiring East Indian woman writer illustrates this crisis. Can a man write in a woman's voice? Is feminism's Woman straight, white and middle-class? The theoretical foundations of feminist presses were challenged.

Responses to these crises were several: publishers like The Women's Press (Canada) changed the composition of their list, actively seeking out manuscripts from women of colour, working-class women, and others. Kitchen Table Press in the USA; SisterVision Press in Canada; Sheba Press in England were set up to publish work that was not being published by other black and women's presses, ironically relying on principles of autonomy and identity to do so. Other presses moved to more issues-based criteria for their list, using affiliation rather than identity as the principle by which they chose new works.

We might imagine that women-only principles have cloistered feminist publishing in a self-sufficient enclave, functioning on a different footing from the 'mainstream' market. Second-wave feminist publishing is not, however, the product of a homogeneous community. It is broadly based, self-consciously political, telecommunicatively linked, both suspicious of and ambiguously linked to corporate capital. And with the advent of 'cybergrrls' publishing on 'The Web', it is likely to become even more diverse and dispersed.

See also: gynocritics; hermeneutics; separatism

References and further reading

Allen, M. (ed.) (1974) 'Index/Directory' *Media Report to Women* 33–51.
—— (1987) 'Index/Directory' *Media Report to Women* 29–33.

WENDY WARING

feminist legal theory

Feminist legal theory or feminist jurisprudence has had a profound effect on legal scholarship over the last few decades. Since feminist legal scholarship began to appear in the law journals, feminist jurisprudence has grown exponentially. Almost every major law journal has devoted at least one symposium issue to this theme, specialist journals have proliferated, and a number of law schools have established specialist chairs in feminist legal theory, or 'women and the law'.

Feminist legal theory differs from other strands of legal theory in a number of significant ways. First, it has grown out of a political concern for the ways in which law may be implicated in women's subordination, and therefore has always related theory to practice. In addition, unlike other strands or developments in legal theory, it has drawn broadly on a range of related theoretical developments in law at the same time as it has contributed to their development. For example, feminist legal theory has some common threads with critical legal theory, and more recently with narrative scholarship and critical race scholarship, or what is more broadly starting to be called 'outsider jurispru-dence'.

Feminist legal theory has also drawn broadly on general feminist critiques of mainstream western scholarship. For example, a central focus of feminist legal theory is on epistemology and legal method, echoing feminism's concern with critiques of knowledge formation (see **epistemology, feminist**). Law is particularly amenable to such critiques, as it relies so heavily on notions such as reasonableness, **objectivity** and neutrality. But as Catharine **MacKinnon** has so persuasively de-monstrated, liberal legalism, or mainstream (male-stream) legal theory hides its partiality behind its purported 'point-of-viewlessness'.

Consistent with feminism's focus on epistemol-ogy and methodology, feminist legal theory has tried to find new ways to allow the voices of diverse groups of women to be heard in legal discourses. One of the more recent developments, mentioned above, is the growth of feminist narrative scholar-ship in law and with it, storytelling as a form of legal method.

While feminist jurisprudence is generally seen as relevant to areas of law where women are most visible (such as sexual assault and family law), more recent scholarship has shown that it has profound implications for many areas of law not readily identified as 'women's issues'. For example, feminists have made key contributions to issues such as contract law, corporations law, as well as tort law (the law of injuries), evidence and many others. Not only have women been 'added and stirred', but by introducing an understanding of the gendered nature of legal relations, the 'hidden gender' of law has been revealed and the ways in which assumptions about **gender** have informed the development of a variety of legal doctrines have been increasingly articulated. In addition, feminist legal theory has revealed much about the gendered nature of legal decision making, through examination of the gendered dimensions of credibility and the assumption that both lawyering and judging are the appropriate domain of white men.

There are a number of particular issues that feminist legal theory has played a significant role in reconceptualising. Perhaps most important of these is the meaning of 'equality'. Feminist jurisprudence

has profoundly influenced the ways in which the concept of equality is understood in a broad range of legal concepts. Until the mid-1980s, feminists concerned about the subordination of women were locked within a dualistic framework of arguing either that women were the same as men or different from men. For example, the issue of how to treat pregnancy in the workplace divided feminists, some of whom wanted pregnant women treated without reference to their pregnancy, while others argued for 'special treatment' for pregnant women. In her groundbreaking work, Catharine MacKinnon has explained that both these ap-proaches are really only one side of the same approach: an approach that she describes as the 'differences' approach. What they have in common is that men are presumed to be the standard against which women are judged: women are either the same *as men*, or different *from men*, but what this approach does not question or challenge is maleness as the referent. In this way of conceptualising women's inequality, men retain the privilege of being considered the standard or benchmark from which women's sameness or difference is measured. MacKinnon reconceptua-lises inequality as an issue of power, hierarchy and subordination. Difference, she argues, in *Feminism Unmodified*, (1987) is itself not the determinant – after all, men are as different from women as women are from men. What is significant is the way in which those differences have been accorded social power. So in order to approach an equality question, the issue is not the similarities between women and men, but rather the ways in which those differences and similarities have been used to disadvantage women. This approach, the disad-vantage or subordination approach, has found favour with a number of constitutional courts, most notably the Supreme Court of Canada (SCC) and the Constitutional Court of South Africa.

Another very important theme in feminist legal theory has been to take feminism's general concern with the **public/private** distinction and show how that is experienced in the legal sphere through law's failure to regulate those aspects of women's lives that have been constructed as 'private' and hence not the law's concern. An obvious example here is domestic violence, or woman battering in the home, which has for too long not been treated as the criminal behaviour that it is. While more recently, postmodern critiques have led to a reconsideration of the shifting boundaries between public and private, nonetheless, at a normative level, the public/private distinction still maintains a powerful position within legal theory.

In common with feminist theory in other disciplines, feminist legal theory has been the subject of challenge by women of colour for its essentialist focus on white women as the measure of all women. Of course, that challenge to the 'benchmark woman' of feminism has not come just from women of colour. Similar concerns have been raised by lesbians, by women with disabilities, and by other 'outsider' women. One particular form that the focus on **essentialism**, and the need to move beyond it, has taken in feminist legal scholarship, is the increasing attention paid to intersectionality. Broadly speaking, the term inter-sectionality was coined by American Professor Kimberlé Crenshaw in an article demonstrating the inability of legal discourses to comprehend the ways in which identities (in the context she discusses, **race** and **gender**) can intersect so as to particularise the way someone experiences the world. The doctrinal example Crenshaw chooses to illustrate this is discrimination law. Through a careful analysis of a series of cases involving African American women, she graphically demonstrates how they lost discrimination cases because courts found it impossible to say of them that they were victims of race discrimination (ie. white people/ women would not be treated that way) or sex discrimination (men – white or African American – would not be treated that way). Her point is that the law, as presently structured, is unable to comprehend a situation where a woman is discriminated against because of the intersection of her race and sex. A similar study of Canadian Human Rights cases undertaken by Professor Nitya Iyer reaches the same conclusion.

It was suggested earlier that feminist jurisprudence is a form of legal theory particularly implicated in practice. So, for example, there has been considerable engagement by legal feminists in law reform activities, and, in North America, in litigation as a feminist strategy. In Canada in particular, the coming into effect of the Canadian Charter of Rights and Freedoms led to the establishment of the Women's Legal Education and Action fund (LEAF) which has played a significant role by intervening in litigation that has particular implications for women. This became particularly controversial following LEAF's intervention in a case involving obscenity when the SCC in *R* v. *Butler* (1992) adopted LEAF's proposed harm-based approach to **pornography**. Following this, a number of lesbian and gay bookshops were the subject of raids and prosecutions, leading to considerable questioning within the feminist com-munities as to which women LEAF represents, and about whether it is possible for any particular group to articulate a 'women's' position. More broadly, there remain real questions about law's amenability to non-essentialist feminist critiques informed by postmodern insights, given law's adherence to a method that reifies what have been called 'truth' claims. Carol Smart (1989), for example, has suggested that law should be 'decentred'. But as MacKinnon once argued, '[l]aw is not everything…but it is not nothing either' (1987: 116). While law plays such a powerful role in regulating the lives of women, feminists will continue to engage with it, but the form of that engagement has grown and become more complex as the sophistication and diversifica-tion of feminist legal theory continues to develop.

See also: malestream thought

References and further reading

Crenshaw, K. (1989) 'Demarginalising the Inter-section of Race and Sex: A Black Feminist Critique of Antidiscrimination Doctrine, Fem-inist Theory and Antiracist Politics', *University of Chicago Legal Forum* 139.

Iyer, N. (1996) 'Disappearing Women: Racial Minority Women in Human Rights Cases', in S. Rodgers and C. Andrew (eds) *Women and the Canadian State*, Montreal: McGill-Queens Uni-versity Press.

MacKinnon, C. (1987) *Feminism Unmodified: Dis-courses on Life and Law*, Cambridge, MA: Harvard University Press.

Smart, C. (1989) *Feminism and the Power of Law*, London and New York: Routledge.

REG GRAYCAR

feminisation of poverty

The issue of the 'feminisation of poverty' focuses attention on the gendered dimensions of women's poverty. The phrase is attributed to a 1978 article by Diana Pearce who used it to capture the paradox that lone-mother households represent an increasing proportion of the poor, despite the apparent advances women have made in the labour market. Up until this time, the problems of poverty were viewed in relation to men and the labour market (the 'working poor') and the elderly, although the prominent profile of women in this latter group was ignored.

A feminisation of poverty perspective locates explanations for women's economic vulnerability in the gendered division of labour in which women are held primarily responsible for domestic work while men are identified as the principal bread-winners. Women's household responsibilities may place constraints on their ability to participate in the labour market, but the combined influences of familistic ideology and the material conditions of capitalism help to ensure that women's paid work is undervalued. Welfare states reinforce the distinctions between 'breadwinner' and 'dependent'. Women, because of labour market disadvantage, are less likely to make claims as workers, and more likely to claim through their status as mothers, and therefore, have to rely on very low levels of income provided by welfare benefits. The feminisation of poverty, then, emerges from the interconnections among women's disadvantaged position in the family, the labour market and the state.

Although the idea of the feminisation of poverty was extremely important in focusing attention on the gendered dimensions of women's poverty, it has been used less frequently in recent years. In emphasising the economic disadvantage that women, as women, share, it tends to underplay the significant role of race and class in differentiating both the causes and the extent of women's poverty. The feminisation of poverty phrase is also critiqued for its assumption of the deterioration in women's economic conditions. This assumption implies that women's poverty is a recent phenomenon, whereas poor women have always out-numbered poor men. Women's poverty, however, has become more visible with the growth in the numbers of lone mothers. The economic disadvantage of many women continues to be hidden through household and family 'counts' which wrongly assume that all members share the non-poverty income equally.

See also: care, provision of; double burden; economics; gender roles; welfare; work, woman and

References and further reading

Glendinning, C. and Millar, J. (eds) (1992) *Women and Poverty in Britain: the 1990s*, New York: Harvester Wheatsheaf.

Goldberg, G. and Kremen, E. (eds) (1990) *The Feminization of Poverty: Only in America?*, New York: Praeger.

Pearce, D. (1978) 'The Feminization of Poverty: Women, Work and Welfare', *Urban and Social Change Review*, 2: 28–36.

PATRICIA M. EVANS

femmenism (men in feminism)

The term 'Men in Feminism' was introduced in a ground-breaking anthology edited by Alice Jardine and Paul Smith (1987) and refers to the rethinking of masculinity by male academics who have begun to absorb aspects of feminist politics and theory into their thinking, sometimes to the extent that they proclaim themselves feminists. While some of these male feminists have limited themselves to an admission of the complicity of men in perpetuating **patriarchy** and beg women to understand that not all men are oppressors, others explore what it means to be a man and the practices and discourses which shape **masculinity** in various social, cultural and historical contexts. At its best, 'femmenism' situates the study of masculinity in a **gender/power** framework, linking it to relations of power between men and women as well as among men.

References and further reading

Jardine, A. and Smith, P. (eds) (1987) *Men in Feminism*, New York and London: Routledge.

KATHY DAVIS

fetishism, female

The term 'female fetishism' was first used by Naomi Schor in her essay 'Female Fetishism: the Case of George Sand' published in 1985. Here, Schor embarks on the theoretical act of 'perversion theft', for Freudian psychoanalysis maintained that fetishism was an exclusively male perversion. The girl may respond to the castration of the mother by disavowing her own castration but does not, according to Freud, disavow the castration of the mother, which is the basis for fetishism's characteristic duplicity: the simultaneous affirmation and denial of the maternal phallus. Feminist theorists have taken issue with this construction to identify and examine ways in which women do enact fetishistic investments, as in dress, and to analyse relationships between psychoanalytic fetishism and commodity fetishism of Marxist theory. Elizabeth Grosz has examined operations of disavowal in the construction of the feminine subject to suggest ways in which lesbianism could be seen as a form of female fetishism.

References and further reading

Grosz, E. (1995) 'Lesbian Feminism?' in her *Space, Time and Perversion: The Polotics of Bodies*, Sydney: Allen and Unwin.

Schor, N. (1985) 'Female Fetishism: The Case of George Sand' in *The Female Body in Western Culture* (ed.) Susan Robin Suleiman, Cambridge MA: Harvard University Press, pp. 363–72.

ELIZABETH McMAHON

film theory, feminist

Feminist film theory emerged in the wake of the second-wave women's movement. Before film studies became an academic field, women's film festivals were an important forum for political activism and discussion of women and film. Like feminist literary theory and feminist art history, feminist film theory began, in the early 1970s, with a critique of images of women in film. Unlike its sister fields, however, feminist film theory was quickly dominated by **psychoanalysis** and semiotics, an approach advocated by journals such as *Screen*, *m/f*, and *Camera Obscura*. British feminists, in particular, considered film – a sophisticated representational system that produced fantasy and incited desire – to be ripe for psychoanalytic readings. (By contrast, **psychoanalytic feminist literary theory** was not developed until the 1980s.) In the 1980s, many feminists contributed to the psychoanalytic tradition, expanding, challenging and rethinking its premises. Others argued that psychoanalysis, with its emphasis on sexual difference, marginalised issues such as history, race, female and lesbian spectatorship, and women's pleasure. By the 1990s, feminist film critics, like feminists in other fields, were developing new approaches grounded in **queer theory**, cultural studies, and theories of **race** and ethnicity, to explore issues of marginality and **difference** in cinema.

In the early 1970s, feminists mobilised against stereotypical, male-oriented images of women in advertising, art, literature and film. They evaluated images as positive or negative, depending on whether they reflected the lives and experiences of real women. Molly Haskell's *From Reverence to Rape: The Treatment of Women in the Movies* (1973) and Marjorie Rosen's *Popcorn Venus: Women, Movies and the American Dream* (1973) adopted this approach, condemning Hollywood for its limited portrayals of woman. Criticising 'images of women' for retaining a realist framework, British feminists such as Griselda **Pollock** advocated a semiotic approach, which viewed 'woman' as the product of sign systems. The first feminists to apply semiotics and psychoanalysis to cinema, Pam Cook and Claire Johnston, analysed the meaning of 'woman' in films by Raoul Walsh. They argued that although his films apparently offered positive images, in fact, 'woman' functioned as a sign in a system of exchange controlled by men, and was defined negatively in terms of masculine desire and fantasy, rather than on her own terms (Cook and Johnston 1990: 20). They advocated denaturalising cinematic images of woman by examining the way contradictory codes and absences structure the film text, and tracing 'its relationship to ... symbolic castration' (26). In adopting a semiotic rather than realist approach, Johnston and Cook laid the groundwork for further analyses of the production of sexual difference in cinema – one of the most widely addressed issues in feminist film criticism.

In another first, Laura **Mulvey** used psychoanalysis to theorise the relationship between cinematic images of woman and male visual pleasure. In 'Visual Pleasure and Narrative Cinema', originally published in *Screen* in 1975, Mulvey argues that in classic Hollywood cinema, an active/male and passive/female dichotomy controls both narrative structure and looking relations. The male character advances the plot, while the female character functions as an erotic object for the male characters and the male spectator (Mulvey 1988: 62). The male spectator identifies with 'his screen surrogate, so that the power of the male protagonist as he controls events coincides with the active power of the erotic look, both giving a satisfying sense of omnipotence' (63). Although an object of pleasure, the woman poses a threat: her lack of a penis unconsciously reminds the male spectator of his own potential castration. Mulvey argues that cinema developed two strategies – voyeurism and fetishism – to allay male castration anxiety and reinforce scopophilic pleasure. She calls for the development of an alternative cinema that denies scopophilic pleasure, which she exemplifies in *Riddles of the Sphinx* (1977), a film she made with Peter Wollen.

Influencing a generation of film scholars, Mulvey's theory of the male **gaze** initiated a new field – feminist theories of spectatorship. Responding to criticism that she has ignored the female spectator, Mulvey analyses *Duel in the Sun*, a Hollywood melodrama with a female protagonist aimed at a female audience (Mulvey 1989). She argues that the female spectator has two choices, neither of them satisfactory: she can masochistically identify with the woman on the screen, as the object of the male gaze, or, like a transvestite, she can assume the male gaze and objectify the woman – which she finds uncomfortable. Also considering melodrama, Mary Ann **Doane** (1991) advances an equally pessimistic thesis: that Hollywood cinema repetitiously plays out scenarios which punish or deny women's looking. Arguing that the female spectator lacks the necessary distance from the image to resist being drawn into film's often masochistic scenarios of femininity, she suggests that Joan Riviere's theory of femininity as mas-

querade may provide a limited solution to the problem of over-identification with the image. Gaylin Studlar's *In the Realm of Pleasure* (1988) draws on Deleuze's theory of masochism to theorise a position for the female spectator. She argues that cinema evokes the female spectator's desire to return to pre-Oedipal unity with the mother, and that the woman can identify with and take pleasure in the figure of the femme fatale. In *The Acoustic Mirror* (1988), Kaja Silverman departs from the focus on the gaze, using psychoanalysis to examine how cinematic conventions of voice contribute to the production of sexual difference.

Towards the end of the 1980s, numerous feminists began criticising psychoanalytic theories of spectatorship. B. Ruby Rich (1998) argues that psychoanalytic critics place too much emphasis on the textual construction of meaning, ignoring the active role of spectators. The spectator's role in producing meaning received considerable attention in the 1980s and 1990s, partly by theorists of lesbian spectatorship. Teresa de **Lauretis** (1995) argues that Sheila McLaughlin's film, *She Must Be Seeing Things*, articulates 'fantasy, masquerade, and voyeurism in lesbian terms', and 'constructs a lesbian subject as the subject of its fantasy...' (76). She cautions, however, that this lesbian subject-position 'is not necessarily accessible to all viewers... because the film's fantasy may... not be their own' (76). Two collections published in 1988 – *Female Spectators* and *The Female Gaze* – introduce approaches grounded in cultural and media studies, as a means of addressing the female spectator as a social subject who brings a lived identity and history to film viewing. The debate on theories of the female spectator came to a head in a special issue of *Camera Obscura* (Bergstrom and Doane (eds) 1989).

Another issue that catalysed feminist film critics early on, and that parallels developments in feminist literary theory and art history, is the question of women filmmakers as producers of meaning. Feminist film critics had convincingly argued that male cinema represents woman as a sign of male fantasy and desire, but never as a subject. Asking whether women filmmakers had succeeded in representing women in non-phallocentric terms, Claire Johnston analyses films by Dorothy Arzner, a Hollywood director from the 1930s and 1940s. Arguing that Arzner's films are progressive but still work within the dominant patriarchal ideology of Hollywood, Johnston (1988) calls for feminist directors to produce a counter-cinema, which would differ from conventional cinema in form and content. The narrative flow would be ruptured and the process of the film's production would be exposed for interrogation. In the 1970s, feminists analysed experimental films by women directors, neglecting both popular women's films and feminist films that used conventional forms. In the late 1980s, however, critics began to address films that had a wider audience appeal. Jane Gaines argues that the 'correct pleasure' of avant garde cinema was not available to all viewers, and that popular films such as *Flashdance*, which uses conventional narrative, provide pleasure for women viewers and are consequently important vehicles for social change (Gaines 1990a). In the second edition of *Women's Pictures* (1994), Annette Kuhn concedes that feminism might creatively function within the mainstream cinematic apparatus, citing Sally Potter's *Orlando* as exemplary. In *And the Mirror Cracked* (1998), Anneke Smelik considers narrative films by women directors from the 1970s and 1980s, which represent female subjectivity and address female spectators who are seeking new forms of visual and narrative pleasure.

Perhaps because feminist criticism was dominated by psychoanalysis and Hollywood had practised a system of apartheid that denied opportunities to black filmmakers, questions of race were addressed later in feminist film criticism than in other fields. Gaines (1990b) was one of the first to criticise psychoanalytic feminists for their exclusive focus on sexual difference, to the exclusion of differences of race and class. In *Black Looks* (1992), bell hooks admonishes feminist film critics to acknowledge that intersecting axes of race and class, as well as gender, structure women's experience. In the late 1990s, questions of sexual preference, racial identification, imperialism and globalism were still among the most compelling for feminist theorists, (as evidenced in E. Ann Kaplan's *Looking for the Other: Feminism, Film, and the Imperial Gaze* (New York: Routledge, 1997)). Two anthologies – *Multiple Voices in Feminist Film Criticism* (1994) and *Redirecting the Gaze: Gender, Theory, and Cinema in the Third World* (1998) – expanded the field by drawing in previously marginalised films and theoretical perspectives. In *Deviant Eyes, Deviant Bodies* (1996), Chris Straayer draws on queer theory to interrogate the heterosexist presumption that underpins much of feminist film theory. Another recent trend concerns writing the history of feminist film criticism. B. Ruby Rich's *Chick Flicks* (1998), an autobiographical history of feminist film criticism, and the second edition of E. Ann Kaplan's *Women in Film Noir* (1998) contextualise and reassess film criticism of the 1970s and 1980s. Feminist film critics have, at various moments, lamented that the field is 'in crisis'. While every field has its impasses and blockages, feminist film theory has achieved spectacular success in the academy, and has transformed the study of film. A cornerstone of film studies, feminist film theory is a powerful testament to the role that feminist approaches have played in transforming knowledge.

See also: literary theory, feminist; literature, images of women in

References and further reading

Bergstrom, J. and Doane, M. (eds) (1989) 'The Spectatrix' (special issue), *Camera Obscura*, 20–21.

Carson, D., Dittmar, L., and Welsch, J. (eds) (1994) *Multiple Voices in Feminist Film Criticism*, Minneapolis, MI: University of Minnesota Press.

Cook, P. and Johnston, C. (1990) 'The Place of Woman in the Cinema of Raoul Walsh', in P. Erens (ed.) *Issues in Feminist Film Criticism*, Bloomington, IN: Indiana University Press.

Doane, M. (1991) 'Film and the Masquerade: Theorizing the Female Spectator', in *Femmes Fatales*, New York: Routledge.

Gaines, J. (1990a) 'Women and Representation: Can We Enjoy Alternative Pleasure?' in P. Erens (ed.) *Issues in Feminist Film Criticism*, Bloomington, IN: Indiana University Press.

—— (1990b) 'White Privilege and Looking Relations: Race and Gender in Feminist Film Theory' in P. Erens (ed.) *Issues in Feminist Film Criticism*, Bloomington, IN: Indiana University Press.

Johnston, C. (1988) 'Dorothy Arzner: Critical Strategies', in C. Penley (ed.) *Feminism and Film Theory*, New York: Routledge.

Lauretis, T. de (1995) 'On the Subject of Fantasy' in L. Pietropaolo and A. Testaferri (eds) *Feminisms in the Cinema*, Bloomington, IN: Indiana University Press.

Mulvey, L. (1988) 'Visual Pleasure and Narrative Cinema', in C. Penley (ed.) *Feminism and Film Theory*, New York: Routledge.

—— (1989) 'Afterthoughts on "Visual Pleasure and Narrative Cinema", inspired by King Vidor's *Duel in the Sun*', in *Visual and Other Pleasures*, Bloomington, IN: Indiana University Press.

Rich, B. R. (1998) *Chick Flicks: Theories and Memories of the Feminist Film Movement*, Durham, NC: Duke University Press.

ROSANNE KENNEDY

Firestone, Shulamith (b. 1945)

A Canadian radical feminist, Shulamith Firestone was born in 1945 and studied at the Art Institute of Chicago. Her earliest published work, from the period when she was involved in anti-Vietnam protests and women's liberation includes *Notes from the First Year* (1968). She edited *Red Stockings*, a radical feminist journal in 1969. Firestone is probably most noted for her book *The Dialectic of Sex* (1970). In it she develops an explanation of the oppression and subordination of women. She builds upon the Marxist concept of 'materialism' to argue that women's oppression originates from the nature and function of female biology and is not simply a result of social and economic positioning. Firestone comments that the unique capacity of women to reproduce shapes the way that the gender division of labour within patriarchal social systems becomes regarded as 'normal'. Firestone argues that this is an implicitly sexist process in which biological characteristics become the basis for justifying a 'sexual class system'. Her controversial solution is that women must seek to control the means of **reproduction**, that this would constitute a feminist revolution.

Firestone maintains that female and male equality is impossible, unless women gain control of their reproduction. She believes that scientific advances in medicine have liberatory potential and that women may be able to reproduce by cloning or artificial wombs. Firestone's assumption is that sexual equality must be based upon sex differences becoming irrelevant, in favour of a more androgynous and therefore classless society. Her theory of social subordination is comprehensive – she also insists that children's liberation would and must occur alongside women's gaining control of reproduction. As a result the structure of families will no longer be constrained by patriarchal assumptions and social regulation and the end of the traditional nuclear family will become possible. Firestone believes that sexism and racism are integrally linked forms of oppression and she argues that both would be vanquished with the end of female inequality. Firestone's ideas are still influential and controversial.

There are three main criticisms of her theory of oppression, first that locating the origins of women's subordination in women's biological nature possibly 'essentialises' woman as well as undermining the possibility of significantly changing social circumstances. Secondly, science and technology do not in themselves necessarily present a means of liberation for women, since they have often been mobilised to oppress or accentuate female social inequalities. Finally, Firestone's work has been criticised as insufficiently recognising differences in women's and men's access to and use of technology.

Selected writings

Firestone, S. (1968) *Notes from the First Year*,
—— (1970) *The Dialectic of Sex*, London: The Women's Press.

LYNNE ALICE

First Nations and women

First Nations is a contemporary term of historical and political significance that has been appropriated by Canadian Aboriginal communities to designate a group of people with a shared language, culture, and history who identify with each other as belonging to a common political entity. The term reconceptualises the misnomer

'Indian' used historically in legislation and statistics, and indicates the continuing socio-legal status of Aboriginal peoples under Canadian law as the signatories of treaties and land claim settlements, and as bands under the *Indian Act*. The term is a political appellation distinct from the designations 'Métis' and 'Inuit' that does not replace individual, culturally-specific tribal names (e.g. Mi'kmaq, Dene). Contemporary First Nations issues include land claims, self-government, sovereignty, recognition of treaty rights, recognition of cultural diversity and renewal, and enhancement of educational and economic opportunities. First Nations women's issues intersect with those of First Nations communities on two levels: at the formal level of negotiating for the reinstatement of native women and men who were voluntarily and involuntarily disenfranchised through government legislation; and at the practical level of calling for a reconstruction of Aboriginal family life through the combined efforts of native women and men.

Indian Act and Bill C-31

The colonial government's formulation of a distinct legal status for Aboriginal peoples in the *Indian Act* of 1869 represents the most trenchant example of legalised sexual discrimination against First Nations women. Although fundamentally discriminatory in nature and formulated without the consent of native peoples, the *Indian Act* stipulates in subsection 12(1)(b) that Indian women marrying 'any other than an Indian' lost their status and treaty rights such that they could no longer own property on the reserve, were prevented from inheriting property on the reserve, were refused participation in band affairs, had their children unrecognised as Indian and denied access to the cultural and social amenities of the Indian community, and could be prevented from returning to live on the reserve even if they were in dire need, very ill, widowed, divorced, or separated (Green 1985: 82, 94). The discriminatory nature of the *Indian Act* of 1869 builds on existing legislation formulated in the assimilationist policies of the Act of 1857 which stipulates that Indian women married to Indian men who were voluntarily or involuntarily enfranchised were automatically enfranchised along with their minor-age children.

These provisions consolidate the patriarchal notion that native women are primarily the property of first their fathers and then their husbands, and establishes the criteria for determining Indian status through the patrilineal line of descent (see **patriarchy**).

The passage of Bill C-31 in 1985 to amend the status and band membership provisions of the *Indian Act* positioned First Nations women at the centre of conflict between band councils and the federal government over the issue of band membership. Although Bill C-31 restored status to those who had lost it under subsection 12(1)(b), reinstated first-generation children of restored persons, and abolished the concepts of enfranchisement, the Bill separates the determination of membership between the jurisdiction of native bands and the control of the federal government thus exacerbating the problems of self-determination and treaty rights within native communities. First Nations women reinstated under Bill C-31, who had been the subjects of racist discrimination by the federal government under the *Indian Act*, now found themselves and their families the targets of sexist discrimination by band members who resented yet another intrusion on band authority by the federal government. The problem of reinstatement remains a cultural and social issue within native communities in spite of the passage of Bill C-31, as some bands choose to ignore the legislation. It also raises the question of the validity of a *Charter of Rights and Freedoms* that guarantees the rights of all persons to enjoy their culture in their community when that guarantee is not also embodied in material resources. For First Nations women caught in the nexus of contemporary forms of racism and sexism the question remains a significant one.

Reconstructing First Nations communities

First Nations women express concerns for themselves and for their families that have less to do with a commitment to gender parity in the dominant society than with reconstructing their historically-fractured roles within their communities. The issues they prioritise for effecting change toward a future vision of themselves as self-governing, self-determining peoples include 'the *Indian Act* and Bill

C-31 amendments; health and social services that are culturally appropriate, with a priority focus on healing; the vulnerability of women and children to violence; and accountability and fairness in self-government' (Royal Commission on Aboriginal Peoples 21). Since an important aim of First Nations self-government is to avoid the imposition of Canadian norms and institutions, and because the common vision of First Nations women entails the values of kindness, honesty, sharing, and respect, the question emerges for feminist theory of how to represent the concerns of First Nations women while remaining attentive to their demands for new forms of political community and holism that reflect their diverse situations.

See also: discrimination and the law

References and further reading

Canadian House of Commons (1983) *Indian Self-Government in Canada: Report of the Special Committee*, Ottawa: published under the authority of the Speaker of the House of Commons by the Queen's Printer for Canada.

Canadian House of Commons' Royal Commission on Aboriginal Peoples (1996) *Perspectives and Realities*, vol. 4, Canada: Minister of Supply and Services.

Dickason, O.P. (1992) *Canada's First Nations: A History of the Founding Peoples from Earliest Times*. Toronto, Oxford, New York: Oxford University Press.

Green, J. (1985) 'Sexual Equality and Indian Government: An Analysis of Bill C-31 Amendments to the Indian Act', *Native Studies Review* 1 (2): 81–95.

Turpel, M.E. (1993) 'Patriarchy and Paternalism: The Legacy of the Canadian State for First Nations Women', *Canadian Journal of Women and the Law* 6: 174–92.

Voyageur, C.J. (1996) 'Contemporary Indian Women', in D.A. Long and O.P. Dickason (eds) *Visions of the Heart: Canadian Aboriginal Issues*, Canada: Harcourt Brace.

CHERYL SUZACK

first person(s)

The term first person refers to the experiencing self or I who, for example, speaks the utterance 'I think that's unfair!'. In our everyday lives we are all first persons, each with our own embodied, located and personally lived perspective upon the world. While we may share many aspects of our lives with others, as first persons we each possess a subjective individuality that is uniquely ours. This subjective individuality however, leaves us awkwardly positioned in anglophone epistemologies (see **epistemology, feminist**) that presuppose first person subjective activities to be radically private, and require knowledge to be impersonal, publicly accessible and objective (see **objectivity**). Within such epistemologies, as first persons we are considered too enmeshed in our own unseen and possibly mistaken subjective understandings to know reliably. While I am the one living my life, I am deemed inadequately situated to know my own life objectively or to know the real conditions that may lead my life into fulfilment or frustration. Knowledge of such real conditions is considered attainable only through authorised avenues of objective knowing from which all but the socially privileged were, until recently, historically excluded. And yet, as a particular first person I may find that my lived understanding of myself jars with how I am authoritatively known by others. This experience is familiar to many women who as first persons have found their concrete self-understandings affronted by knowledge that, for example, objectively knows women to be naturally deficent in rationality and moral maturity. Feminism's concern with first persons is part of its broader concern to combat exclusionary practices of knowing that perpetuate inequalities against first persons and groups of first persons by denying them a legitimate say in public determinations of what can be known of them.

Recognised incongruities between women's lived understandings of themselves and knowledge suspiciously attuned to **patriarchy** have motivated feminist critiques of **androcentrism** and dominant conceptions of 'who' can know best. Attempts to counter the capacity of objective knowledge to misrepresent actual people have led feminists to explore modes of knowing that may emerge among first persons within concrete discursive contexts such as **friendship**, story-telling, and **gossip**. Attending to the ability of first persons to know for themselves is not however a defence of first person incorrigibility with respect to self-knowledge or lived experience, as feminist theory also critiques the notion of the authoritative 'I' that is transparent to itself and capable of knowing alone its own subjective states and experiences. Awareness of the opacity of selves and the ambiguities of experience have led such critiques to emphasise a key role for collaborative interpretation in attaining non-imperialistic knowledge of selves, others and experience.

See also: Cartesianism, feminist critiques of; narrative, feminist uses of; public/private

References and further readings

Campbell, S. (1997) *Interpreting the Personal*, Ithaca and London: Cornell University Press.
Code, L. (1995) *Rhetorical Spaces*, New York and London: Routledge.

SHARON MURPHY

first-wave/second-wave feminism

A long tradition of writers and thinkers has criticised the position of women in western societies, but not until the nineteenth century did that critique inspire a mass movement. Between approximately 1880 and 1920, and beginning again in the 1960s, questions of women's social, economic and political rights generated substantial popular support and public discussion, initially in Europe, North America, Australia and New Zealand and then, in the twentieth century, on all continents. Although the term **feminism** did not come into popular use until the 1910s, commentators since have termed the two movements 'first-' and 'second-wave' feminism, likening the ebb and flow of the movements' mass appeal to that of a cresting wave.

The origins of nineteenth-century feminism lie in the changes that transformed western societies in the early part of the twentieth century. Foremost was **industrialisation** which undermined household production and established a hierarchy between the male-dominated public sphere and the female-dominated private one (see **public/ private**). At the same time, liberal-democratic ideologies, socialism, evangelical Protestant Christianity, and social reform movements, especially abolitionism and temperance, propelled a wide spectrum of women to challenge their exclusion from the public realm. The relative importance of each factor depended on the specific national or even regional circumstances: as historian Christine Bolt has observed, the story of first-wave feminism 'is one of national distinctiveness within an international cause' (1993: 5).

The fledging women's rights movement that emerged in the 1850s through 1870s advocated a single sexual standard for men and women, (primarily within marriage), dress reform, equal property and other legal rights, and higher education for women, especially in professions such as medicine and law. With the movement's dramatic growth after 1880, concerns over the conditions and wages of working-class women gained prominence, as did a revitalised interest in temperance and a new commitment to social purity – protecting women from sexual 'vice'. In the process, feminism became allied with myriad other social reform movements.

As the goals of the women's movement diversified, so too did its ideological underpinnings. Liberal ideals of political and educational equality, along with socialist principles of redistributing economic wealth, remained influential, but by the end of the nineteenth century, the rhetoric of maternalism was being deployed with increasing frequency. Maternal, also called domestic or social, feminism celebrated women's superior morality as the justification for female participation in public affairs and for improved state services for mothers and children. Although some non-European women used similar rhetoric, maternalism often relied upon racialised images and arguments to marshal support and to legitimate white women's special 'civilising' role in reform and missionary work.

By 1900, ideological differences were overshadowed by the growing agreement amongst activists that success on key legal, educational and economic issues could not be gained without greater political leverage, and thus the vote emerged as a unifying objective for feminists of all persuasions and in many nations. Suffrage societies and other women's organisations campaigned vigorously for political enfranchisement. Enthusiasm over early victories such as in New Zealand (1893) soon gave way after bitter defeats elsewhere. While most feminists used speeches, petitions and the press to gain public attention, British militants or 'suffragettes' took more radical action, committing arson, planting bombs and, when arrested, launching hunger strikes. The First World War era witnessed some important suffrage victories, such as in the new Soviet Union (1917) and the USA (1920), but the drives for enfranchisement had drained the movement of its vitality. Despite sustained feminist activism internationally, by the 1920s the momentum of the 'first wave' had passed.

A comparable groundswell of mass support for women's rights emerged in the 1960s. Inspired by influential texts such as Simone de **Beauvoir**'s *The Second Sex* (1949, trans. English 1952), and her powerful claim that 'one is not born a woman, one becomes one', feminists began articulating the cultural and social forces that perpetuated the subordination of women. In North America, Betty **Friedan**'s 1963 publication *The Feminine Mystique* captured the frustrations of many educated, middle-class women who were disillusioned with the isolation of suburban domestic life. Many other women developed a critique of male domination when their contributions to radical movements, like the New Left, **civil rights**, national liberation or student movements, were devalued or ignored. Advocates of women's liberation insisted that their personal struggles stemmed from social, not individual, problems, thereby popularising the phrase 'the personal is political' and fostering grassroots **consciousness-raising** groups.

Like its predecessor, second-wave feminism was characterised by diverse goals and political perspectives, but it differed from the first wave in several important ways. Most prominent was the late-twentieth-century demand for greater sexual freedom for women, outside conventional heterosexual relationships and within lesbian ones. Legalised birth control and abortion; legal reform

for victims of domestic violence, sexual harassment, sexual violence and rape; liberalised divorce laws; rights for lesbian mothers; and improved medical services especially in obstetrics and gynaecology were all key elements of women's campaigns to control their own bodies. Equal pay for equal work and access to non-traditional areas of employment remained important economic goals, but second-wave feminists also sought recognition for work conventionally done by women, calling for 'equal pay for work of equal value'. 'Wages for housework' campaigns, demands for state-supported day care, and the more general insistence that men should share housework and childcare duties all served to reassess women's traditional responsibility for the domestic sphere. In contrast to the international consensus around questions like suffrage that had shaped the first wave of feminism, late-twentieth-century feminist movements in Africa, the Middle East, the Caribbean, South America and Asia challenged the priorities and analyses of their western counterparts; questions of imperialism, religion and cultural difference all demanded new answers. As a complement to social activism, academic feminists created a new area of scholarship: the establishment of women's studies programmes is the result of, and has resulted in, important new theoretical positions, ranging from psychoanalytic feminism to postcolonial analyses.

Throughout the second wave, socialist-feminists pursued analyses of class-based differences among women, but by the 1980s organisations of non-western, visible minority, immigrant, refugee and aboriginal women complicated and diversified feminist notions of a female condition. At the same time, academic feminists informed by postmodernist and literary theory challenged the belief that women are united by biological sex and asserted that the 'category of women' is neither natural nor essential, but socially constructed. Differences, rather than commonalties, were emphasised, prompting some, but by no means all, commentators of the 1990s to claim that the second wave of feminism is over and that the 'postfeminist' age or third wave(s) of feminism has begun.

As historians have debated the nature and impact of nineteenth- and twentieth-century feminisms, many have become dissatisfied with the wave analogy. They note that although the 'woman question' garnered much less media and popular attention in the 1920s through 1950s, women involved in socialism, communism, the peace movement, as well as suffrage societies across the globe, continued to work towards improving the position of women. The concept of a wave thus masks the substantial feminist activism occurring before and after the ostensible 'crest', but also infers an inevitability of feminism's ascent and decline. For these reasons, the wave metaphor, while a convenient shorthand to compare the two movements, is used with caution.

See also: communism, women and; socialism and feminism; third-wave feminism; women's studies (history and development of); women's studies: autonomy v. mainstreaming; work, women and

References and further reading

Bolt, C (1993) *The Women's Movements in the United States and Britain from the 1790s to the 1920s*, Amherst: University of Massachusetts Press.

Daley, C. and Nolan, M. (eds) (1994) *Suffrage and Beyond: International Feminist Perspectives*, Auckland: Auckland University Press.

Jayawardena, K. (ed.) (1986) *Feminism and Nationalism in the Third World*, London: Zed Books.

Le Gates, M. (1996) *Making Waves: A History of Feminism in Western Society*, Toronto: Copp Clark.

Mohanty, C.T., Russo, A. and Torres, L. (eds) (1991) *Third World Women and the Politics of Feminism*, Bloomington, IN: Indiana University Press.

KATHRYN McPHERSON

Flax, Jane

Jane Flax writes from the unique position of political theorist, activist and practising psychotherapist. Her work, revolving around issues of gender, justice, knowledge, power and subjectivity, reflects these multiple levels of engagement. Flax employs object relations theory to develop a conception of feminine subjectivity, explore the dynamics of mother/daughter relations, and draw attention to conflicts among women. Flax's work is most notable for putting into conversation with each other three dominant strains of theorising in the contemporary west: **psychoanalysis**, **feminism** and postmodernism (see **poststructuralism/postmodernism**). In particular, Flax's book, *Thinking Fragments* (1990), assesses the possibilities and limitations of these three modes of thinking.

Flax's encounters with psychoanalysis are motivated by a suspicion of the Kantian (derived from Immanuel Kant) subject of pure reason, a model of the self that, she argues, is a thin, unsatisfying and masculine model of subjectivity. Freudian psychoanalytic theory offers a richer model of subjectivity, but one with its own limitations, primarily the separation of the inner life of the unconscious from the outer world of social relations, and its bias towards masculine subject formation. In contrast, Flax argues that D.W. Winnicott's object relations theory offers an understanding of intersubjectivity in which the inner self resides and develops in relation to the outer world.

Flax is joined in her efforts to develop feminine subjectivity with object relations theory by feminists Nancy **Chodorow**, Dorothy **Dinnerstein**, and Carol **Gilligan**. Feminist revisions of object relations theory locate differences in masculine and feminine subject formation in parenting practices dominated by women. Sons achieve adulthood by separating from their mother, while daughters remain connected, thus achieving relationally structured identities. Preferring the model of subjectivity offered by object relations theory, Flax argues that uncritical valorisation of women's connectedness and emphasis on the mother's centrality to subject formation obscure the difficulties and ambivalence of mother/daughter relations.

Similarly, Flax's work also emphasises differences among women, drawing attention to the mutually constitutive nature of **race** and **gender**. Flax challenges feminist theory, (for example Susan Moller **Okin**'s feminist theory of justice) that addresses the category of gender to the exclusion of issues of race.

Flax criticises feminist and postmodern scholarship that offer successor projects even as they critique and unravel the humanistic projects of the Enlightenment. In contrast, Flax carefully avoids replicating the Enlightenment projects she critiques, surfacing dissonance instead of striving for coherence, and exploring ambivalence instead of seeking resolution.

See also: philosophy; political theory

Selected writings

Flax, J. (1990) *Thinking Fragments*, Berkeley, CA: University of California Press.
—— (1993) *Disputed Subjects*, New York: Routledge.
—— (1995) 'Race/Gender and the Ethics of Difference', *Political Theory*, 23, 3: 500–10.

KARIN ROBERTS

folklore

Feminist folkloristics understands **gender** as a fundamentally sociocultural construct. It recovers and (re)evaluates women scholars' and researchers' hitherto un(der)paid, un(der)valued labour, but also their often distinctive **praxis**; examines women's traditional and popular cultural productions as commentaries upon their lives and opportunities to envision alternatives to convention; and explores how not only culture but also scholarship is metaphorically and metonymically represented as gendered. Margaret Mills suggests that such investigations are inherently theoretical; 'we … are *always already* speaking 'theory' – somebody's theory, theory in the everyday – and it's our job to sort out *whose* theory' (1993: 174). Feminist folklore theory involves multiplicity in (sub)textual meanings and social locations, analyses that come from the **body** as well as the intellect, and an appreciation for women's ways of knowing.

Women folklorists have been stereotyped in **malestream thought** as atheoretical collectors and popularisers of traditional culture, but feminist scholarship reclaims and critiques their often groundbreaking accomplishments. Nineteenth- and early twentieth-century academic folklore scholarship, teaching, and research were literally male-dominated. Yet women with little or no academic training, minimal financial and institutional support, and domestic duties, pursued lifelong careers researching a variety of genres,

from folktale and folksong to belief and practice. Their collections were consulted by their academic male contemporaries, who nevertheless failed to acknowledge this work's inherent values and aesthetics. A few women gained recognition, often more for their unconventional personal lives than for their research. Many succeeded primarily by ventriloquising standard scholarship, and by separating their academic and other writing. Those who resisted such practices were marginalised, as was Zora Neale Hurston, now celebrated for her innovative linking of viewpoints from, and blurring of boundaries between, **anthropology**, folklore, literature, **oral history**, and **autobiography**. These women's inquiries were theoretically founded in a rejection of their contemporaries' scientific rationalism and **positivism** in favour of a profound respect for **local knowledges**.

In addition, scores of women have long gathered their **family** and community traditions as historians, newspaper columnists, and domestic archivists of personal and local documents. Such works provide models for feminist praxis; radical subtexts can be discovered in these women's deeply personal connections with their research, lack of separation between **self** and subject, and consciousness of their own positions and effects as researchers and writers. Often their studies show an inherently political sensibility around issues such as gender, class, race/ethnicity, and religion, absent in the purported **objectivity** of non/anti-feminist theorising's obsession with the identification, historic-geographic tracing, and evaluation of texts.

Traditional male folkloristics values genres and contexts dominated by men. Feminist folkloristics reclaims and recognises women's lives and experiences, their creativity, expressiveness, and communicative acumen. It examines women-associated genres like quilting or **gossip**, and women's appropriation of men's cultural forms by preaching from the pulpit or dressing as men, for example (see also **cross dressing**). It also (re)interprets traditional ballads, **fairy tales**, and other traditions, to expose the heterosexism, **misogyny**, **sexism**, and other patriarchal biases of previous analysis, and to provide (re)visions of these texts. Women-centred forms, like the 'kernel story', an indexical commentary on or reference to a longer commonly-understood narrative often employed in **consciousness-raising** groups (see Farrer 1975), provide links between **feminism** and women's texts. The gynocentric evaluation of these and others dismissed by the malestream as 'minor genres' has meant recognising their analytical, resistant, and spiritual value for women.

Finally, feminist folklore theory aims to move women's experiences from the margin to the centre of cultural production by developing the links implicating folklore and women's studies, particularly in considering the significance, meaning, and resistant power of women's everyday culture. Joan Radner and Susan Lanser's programmatic work on feminist coding (Radner 1993) suggests that women's dominated and marginalised social locations necessitate the deployment of multivalent, covert expressions of subversive ideas. Thus, women's oral performances, material creations, and even day-to-day routines simultaneously communicate a variety of messages to different segments of their audiences. Irish women's keening covers the truth-telling about violence and abuse in the texts of their mourning laments; the humorous gift of a 'scandalous Sunbonnet Sue' quilt is also a diatribe against the constrictions of women's required, gendered roles; a woman burning the family dinner may be dismissed as incompetent, or recognised for her expression of disgust with domestic labour. Whether deliberate or latent, the equivocation in coding avoids risk from those who find feminist assertions disturbing; the performer can deny feminist intentions. In their everyday lives, women are skilled practitioners of the techniques of appropriation, juxtaposition, distraction, indirection, trivialisation, and incompetence, and consequently are analysts and theorists of their own experiences. Thus feminist folklore theory represents women's practices as resistant as well as acquiescent, contingent as well as contextual.

Feminist folklore most often embraces a 'low theory' perspective; it maintains close dialogue between researchers and their subjects of study as knowers. Its theorising is usually firmly grounded in particular texts and contexts. Its transformative models have developed in part through exchanges across disciplines and beyond academic boundaries. Practices of collaboration between research-

ers impel the literal recognition of multiple voices, and edited collections predominate over single authored works. Such studies critically link folklorists' activities – **ethnography** as well as analysis – to **hegemony** in the contexts of all women's labours, but also to **cultural politics** and feminism, particularly as alternatives to **oppression**.

See also: collaboration/collaborative research; language, gender and power

References and further reading

Farrer, C.R. (ed.) (1975) *Women and Folklore: Images and Genres*, Prospect Heights, IL: Waveland Press.

Greenhill, P. and Tye, D. (eds) (1997) *Undisciplined Women: Tradition and Culture in Canada*, Montreal: McGill-Queen's University Press.

Hollis, S.T., Pershing, L. and Young, M.J. (eds) (1993) *Feminist Theory and the Study of Folklore*, Urbana, IL: University of Illinois Press.

Jordan, R.A. and Kalcik, S.J. (eds) (1985) *Women's Folklore, Women's Culture*, Philadelphia, PA: University of Pennsylvania Press.

Mills, M. (1993) 'Feminist Theory and the Study of Folklore: A Twenty Year Trajectory', *Western Folklore* 52, 2–4: 173–92.

Radner, J.N. (ed.) (1993) *Feminist Messages: Coding in Women's Folk Culture*, Urbana, IL: University of Illinois Press.

PAULINE GREENHILL

form/matter distinction

The form/matter distinction derives from a set of metaphysical principles in Ancient Greek philosophy that divide the world, descriptively and evaluatively, into pairs of opposites. The first term – form – is more highly valued than the second – matter. Form is intelligible, determinate, rational structure; matter the underlying, inchoate 'stuff'. The form/matter distinction maps the male/female distinction: not only is maleness aligned with determinate form and femaleness with unruly matter, but these alignments take on a definitive aspect in Aristotelian reproductive **biology**. Aristotle maintains that women contribute only unformed material to the future child whereas men contribute the shaping, individuating form. These distinctions inform a persistent sexual division in western European social and political thought that consistently associates men – and form – with rational, knowing mind; women – and matter – with the non-rational, disorderly body.

See also: binaries/bipolarity; dichotomies

References and further reading

Lloyd, G. (1993) *The Man of Reason: 'Male' and 'Female' in Western Philosophy*, London: Routledge.

LORRAINE CODE

French feminism

French feminism refers to a diverse and influential body of thought that, while heterogenous, has in common several themes and areas of investigation. Its stance tends to be idealist rather than materialist; informed by a suspicion of any intellectual mode that assumes the existence of an essential or empirical external reality, it posits instead a reality that is constructed and contingent. Concerned with the deep structures of language, in which it locates both women's **oppression** and potential for freedom and dissent, French feminism directs its inquiry away from the historical and material conditions of women and towards the textual, representational, linguistic, and discursive (see **language, gender and power**). Those theorists most closely identified with French feminism, Hélène **Cixous**, Luce **Irigaray**, Julia **Kristeva**, and Monique **Wittig**, deploy in different ways a strategic revaluation of the feminine; they emphasise the reclamation of the **body**, discounted by **patriarchy** as inferior to the mind, as a way of resisting and recasting patriarchal thought and challenging the post-Enlightenment domination of reason. Using a writing style that is distinctively lyrical, disjunctive, impassioned, and deeply subjective, these writers oppose both western patriarchal thought and **liberal feminism**, on the ground that the latter leaves unchallenged the binary oppositions – between

male and female, mind and body, order and disorder, light and darkness, reason and emotion – upon which the former depends (see **binaries/bipolarity**).

French feminists argue that the Anglo-American tradition of feminist scholarship, with its emphasis on broadening the canon to include unrepresented women writers, on recovering the silenced, overlooked or forgotten places of women in history and literature, and on documenting the exclusion of women from access to means of production, is misdirected (see **production, modes of**). Such disregarded literary texts, they suggest, are too deeply embedded in patriarchal language and therefore in patriarchal ideology to be truly emancipatory; the work of their recovery therefore indirectly supports patriarchy's fundamental identification of 'woman' as other from and inferior to the normative, standard-setting 'man'. French feminism, in contrast, identifies itself with and attempts to value and reclaim the 'Other' side of the binary division, privileging the 'feminine' and previously denigrated qualities of unreason, fluidity, formlessness, darkness and, especially, **body**. To undo and de-stabilise these binaries, and to unsettle the power relations between them, is one of French feminism's chief projects.

The product of a European tradition which maintains that ideas are inherently political and that the intellectual's role is therefore revolutionary, French feminism has evolved in part from poststructuralist thought (see **poststructuralism/postmodernism**), especially its defining and revolutionary challenge to the 'metaphysics of presence', the belief that meaning is present in a verifiable reality and enacts a straightforward relationship with that reality. This belief, structuring western humanist thought, is critiqued by poststructuralism's dissolution of absolute principles and its figuration of a reality that is fluid and ambivalent, a process of construction marked by ambiguity and absence rather than the presence of anchoring, monolithic, eternal truths.

Poststructuralist theorists such as philosopher Jacques Derrida and psychoanalyst Jacques Lacan, themselves writing in response to such earlier thinkers as Karl Marx, Friedrich Nietzsche, Sigmund Freud, and Ferdinand de Saussure, established concepts that French feminists have critiqued, exploited, and extended for their own use. Derrida's idea of **logocentrism**, for example, offers a reading of western philosophy as inextricably imbricated in unitary principles, exclusive of **difference**, and detrimental to otherness; these 'violent unities' must therefore be exploded through a deconstructive textual practice. Irigaray and Cixous similarly question the authority of patriarchal language as expressing the exclusion of the feminine. In *The Newly Born Woman*, Cixous adds a pointed analysis of gender to Derrida's notion, observing the 'solidarity' between 'logocentrism and **phallocentrism**', while in *This Sex Which Is Not One* Irigaray celebrates the radically random, incoherent, and contiguous discourse which she identifies as feminine and able to defeat the linear 'logic of reason'. In order to sidestep what they see as the fundamentally patriarchal order of language, Cixous and Irigaray deliberately cultivate a non-phallogocentric discourse, subverting the patriarchal logic of order, mastery, authority and sequentiality.

A similar concern for language and discourse is found in French feminist theory responding to the work of Jacques Lacan. For Lacan, the speaking subject exists only in language, which composes and dismantles gender identities. Like culture and politics, language exists in the realm of law and order, which Lacan refers to as the 'symbolic'. The symbolic, a zone of loss and alienation, is entered through acceptance of phallic law, which involves a repression of desired unity with the mother; the female child, whose lack of a penis ensures that she enters the symbolic only tentatively, is doubly alienated. Taking up Lacan's ideas of the Law of the Father as defining the symbolic, Kristeva argues that this law can be subverted by a return to what she calls the 'semiotic', a pre-Oedipal, pre-linguistic space in which the maternal and infant body exist in an undifferentiated state of utopian wholeness and plurality.

For French feminists, the oppressively phallogocentric language that has exiled woman must be rejected and replaced by a language situated in and drawing its vocabulary from the female body, an *écriture féminine* that is fundamentally and essentially feminine. Wittig privileges the lesbian body, rather than the heterosexual body, as the site of meaning, arguing that it is patriarchy's true Other. For Cixous, although she argues for the **bisexuality** of all women and disputes fixed oppositions of male and female, the trope for this kind of writing is still profoundly biological, connected to the 'white ink' of maternal breast milk. Irigaray, too, uses the physical image of 'two lips' touching and speaking together as a metaphor for **women's writing**. Even Kristeva, who rejects the possibility of an intrinsically feminine writing because of her insistence that all identity is fluid, unstable, and in process rather than fixed, associates the liberatory and fruitfully disruptive potential of the semiotic with the trope of the maternal body. This association can be seen as part of French feminism's larger enterprise of revaluing the body as the site of *jouissance* and the maternal for its connection to writing and creativity, a significant break from Simone de **Beauvoir**'s earlier assertion, in *The Second Sex*, that motherhood is oppressive.

The reclamation of **motherhood** is just one way in which French feminism has been extremely influential, if in complex ways, in feminist scholarship as a whole. Although received with mixed feelings, it has reinvigorated Anglo-American feminism by complicating the ideas of history, culture, and identity upon which such scholarship had relied; by demanding that the language feminists speak be closely examined; and, not least, by generating an often heated dialogue between those who found French feminism's intervention into feminist practice deeply problematic and those who welcomed it. While proponents of French feminism's poststructuralist tenets see its fluid and indeterminate subject as freeing, and jouissance as an endlessly pure form of resistance able to oppose patriarchy while remaining uncontaminated by it, others distrust these ideas as essentialist and their advocates as intellectually elitist (see **essentialism**). While much contested, French feminism continues to be the catalyst for fertile debate.

See also: essentialism; 'immanence', woman as; phallogocentrism

References and further reading

Beauvoir, S. de (1949) *The Second Sex*, trans. H.M. Parshley, New York: Knopf, 1952.

Cixous, H. and Clément, C. (1975) *The Newly Born Woman*, trans. B. Wing, Minneapolis, MI: University of Minnesota Press, 1986.

Irigaray, L. (1985) *This Sex Which is Not One*, trans. C. Porter and C. Burke, Ithaca, NY: Cornell University Press.

Kristeva, J. (1980) *Desire in Language: A Semiotic Approach to Literature and Art*, trans. T. Gora, New York: Columbia University Press.

Marks, E. and de Courtivron, E. (eds) (1980) *New French Feminisms*, Brighton: Harvester.

Moi, T. (1987) *French Feminist Thought*, Cambridge: Blackwell.

Wittig, M. (1980) 'The Straight Mind', *Feminist Issues* 1.

DEBORAH WILLS

Friedan, Betty (b. 1921)

An American feminist activist and writer, perhaps best known as a founder of NOW, National Women's Political Caucus, and NARAL, Friedan was born in 1921, graduated from Smith College in 1942 and later studied at Berkeley. She began writing for women's magazines in the 1950s after several years of contributing to the trade union journal *UE News*. Friedan's *The Feminine Mystique* (1963) is generally regarded as a liberal feminist classic. She has also written a retrospective on the women's movement in the 1960s and 1970s titled *It Changed My Life: Writings on the Women's Movement* (1976) and two books *The Second Stage* and *The Fountain of Age*, which discuss changing issues in feminist activism around women's rights. In 1997 Friedan published *Beyond Gender: The New Politics of Work and Family* which considers the employment situations of women in the USA, including the downsizing of organisations; the displacement of workers and the implications of manpower policies.

In *The Feminine Mystique* Friedan argues that women are constantly caught up in the mystique of traditional female social roles, which are ultimately unsatisfying. She coined the phrase 'the problem that has no name' to emphasise the extent to which subordination of (middle-class, white, heterosexual) women as a sex class becomes normalised. Friedan's solution for women's emotional enslave-ment to being mother and wife is to promote the view that women become educated and work outside the home: 'The assumption of your own identity, equality, and even political power does not mean you stop needing to love, and be loved by, a man, or that you stop caring for your own kids' (1963: 380).

The Feminine Mystique has been criticised as not addressing wider issues of how women might fulfil multiple roles without structural changes to family and workplace practices. Her later book *The Second Stage* goes some way to exploring these subjects, but also criticises the feminist movement as depicting men negatively and denying 'that core of women's personhood that is fulfilled through love, nurture, home' (1981: 27). Her thinking has arguably moved from a liberal feminist agenda, which advocates equality between the sexes, to promoting in the 1980s gender specific laws and a humanist recognition of differences between the sexes.

Friedan has been a high profile feminist speaker for three decades and has also written for publications such as *McCall's*, *Harper's*, *The New York Times*, *The New Republic*, and *The New Yorker*. In 1975, Friedan was named Humanist of the Year by the American Humanist Association and received an honorary Doctorate of Humane letters from Smith College. She has been a Visiting Distinguished Professor at the University of Southern California, New York University, and George Mason University; an Adjunct Scholar at the Wilson International Centre for Scholars at the Smithsonian; and the Distinguished Professor of Social Evolution at Mount Vernon College.

Selected writings

Friedan, B. (1963) *The Feminine Mystique*, New York: Norton.

—— (1976) *It Changed My Life: Writings on the Women's Movement*, New York: Random House.

—— (1997) *Beyond Gender: The New Politics of Work and Family*, Baltimore: Johns Hopkins University Press.

LYNNE ALICE

friendship

Feminist studies of friendship have been less politicised than those of a related concept, sisterhood, and have frequently been confined to discrete literary, psychoanalytic, historical and sociological studies. While mainstream research on friendship has emphasised the individual, affective means by which friendship may be recognised, feminist theory has attempted to reinterpret this work and to demonstrate that friendship continues to be subordinated to those other social relationships – family ties, motherhood, and romantic or sexual relationships – in which women are involved. Although feminism has attempted to challenge this subordination, it has done so mainly through the concept of sisterhood, which reasserts familial imagery as closer to and more substantial than the ties of friendship.

In addition to the politicised terminology of sisterhood, some feminist theories have appropriated friendship as part of a focus upon sexuality and woman-to-woman relationships. Radical feminists such as Adrienne **Rich** and Janice Raymond have argued that women have an innate ability to bond with other women (see **radical feminism**). Raymond has specifically criticised 'feminist philosophies' for romanticising friendships between women, arguing that this process gives rise to feelings of betrayal and disaffection which produce hostility among women towards feminism and female friendship (1986: 20). She suggests the need for a distinction between passionate commitment to female friendship, and unrealistic expectations based upon sentimentality or essentialism.

Where friendship has been examined as a separate issue from a sexual continuum, it has been characterised by two distinct explanations, the psychosexual and the socio-cultural. The psychosexual standpoint, typified by Nancy **Chodorow**, focuses upon the argument that the process of mothering reproduces heterosexual women who have emotional needs for other women. These friendships foster individual development by providing opportunities for greater discovery of the self. Rich (1976) produced a similar theory from a radical feminist perspective, arguing that by constructing motherhood as a social institution and attempting to restrict it to the context of the nuclear family, patriarchal society aims to prevent close emotional bonds between women. Social and cultural approaches have been more diverse, and tend to focus upon the regionally and historically specific contexts which give rise to different forms of friendship (Smith-Rosenberg 1975; O'Connor 1992). Pat O'Connor has argued that a realistic approach is needed within feminist theory which takes account of power dynamics and recognises the existence of conflicting feelings such as commitment and obligation, guilt and loyalty – in short, all the issues which feminist theory has considered with respect to family life, but not in relation to women's friendships.

See also: bonding, maternal, feminine; family; kinship; motherhood

References and further reading

O'Connor, P. (1992) *Friendships Between Women: A Critical Review*, New York: Guilford Press.

Raymond, J. (1986) *A Passion for Friends: Toward a Philosophy of Female Affection*, London: Women's Press.

Rich, A. (1976) *Of Woman Born: Motherhood as Experience and Institution*, New York: Norton.

Smith-Rosenberg, C. (1975) 'The Female World of Love and Ritual: Relations Between Women in Nineteenth-Century America', *Signs* 1, 1: 1–30.

HELOISE BROWN

frigidity

Frigidity is a concept utilised in nineteenth- and twentieth-century psychology to explain women's apparent inability – physical or psychological – to accommodate or participate in heterosexual intercourse, or to derive pleasure from this or other heterosexual activities. It stands in some contrast to 'impotence' in men – an inability to perform. Frigidity's connotation of 'coldness' is pejorative, assuming the perspective of another as temperature-taker – whether doctor, husband, or psychiatrist. In *Human Sexual Inadequacy* (1970) Masters and Johnson substituted the term 'orgastic dysfunction' which covers intermittent and situational absences of orgasm. 'Frigidity' persisted into 1970s popular and clinical psychology, in books geared to guide women toward heterosexual fulfillment, which in Freudian terms consisted of achieving the dubious 'vaginal orgasm' through heterosexual intercourse – as opposed to other varieties of experience with other forms of sexual stimulation.

See also: lesbian feminism; sexuality; therapy, feminist

References and further reading

Masters, W.H. and Johnson, V.E. (1970) *Human Sexual Inadequacy*, Boston: Little, Brown.

EILEEN M. CONDON

Frye, Marilyn (b. 1941)

Marilyn Frye's 1983 collection *The Politics of Reality* defines the radical feminist view that the **oppression** of women can be explained by the institution of compulsory **heterosexuality**, and that women's liberation lies in a radical reconstruction of **sexuality**. Frye's analyses of **sexism**, **oppression**, coercion, and lesbian **separatism** explain how phallocratic reality excludes all women, and especially lesbians, from the process of creating human meaning. However, this phallocratic erasure of women's thought creates the conditions whereby lesbians gain epistemic privilege, access to the 'unusual knowing' (1983: 154) necessary to challenge and ultimately to transform patriarchal hegemony.

Frye argues that under **patriarchy** women are systematically oppressed, not as individuals but as members of a sex class. A network of interrelated forces and barriers restricts women's choices (see **choice, freedom of**). Social conventions compel women to act feminine and men to act masculine; this sex-marking behaviour is inherently sexist since it makes sex relevant in order to divide human beings into subordinates and dominators. Men perceive women arrogantly, leading women to abandon the formulation and pursuit of their own interests, and to dedicate themselves to assisting men to accomplish their goals. Paradoxically, phallocratic reality depends for its existence on this systematic subjugation of women.

The reality that defines all women as heterosexual makes lesbian existence logically impossible, but offers lesbians the opportunity to dislodge the power structures that guarantee men's unconditional access to women. By separating from reality, lesbians claim the authority to redefine sexualities and reality. Women liberate themselves by focusing on each other, and on women's power to make meaning.

Frye is criticised for presuming that heterosexuality is central to the oppression of all women, and that lesbianism is therefore the foundation of women's liberation. This radical feminist analysis is potentially alienating to any women for whom intimate relationships with men are culturally, emotionally, and/or economically important. However, her 1996 essay 'The Necessity of Differences' is indicative of Frye's theoretical shift towards a multicultural feminist perspective that aims to preserve the category of *woman*, while embracing differences (in race, class, nationality, sexuality, religion, and so on) among women, and thereby avoiding the **essentialism** and **white privilege** (**race privilege**) that characterises much of radical feminist theory.

See also: epistemology, feminist; radical feminism

Selected writings

Frye, M. (1983) *The Politics of Reality: Essays in Feminist Theory*, Trumansburg, NY: The Crossing Press.
—— (1992) *Willful Virgin: Essays in Feminism*, Freedom: The Crossing Press.
—— (1996) 'The Necessity of Differences: Constructing a Positive Category of Women', *Signs* 21, 4: 991–1010.

AMIE A. MACDONALD

functionalism v. interactionism

Structural functionalism and symbolic interactionism are two antithetical sociological theories. Functionalists study large-scale social structures and institutions, their functions, and their constraints on social actors. For example, gender relations are conceptualised in terms of sex roles where husbands play the instrumental role and wives the expressive one within the family (see **gender roles**).

Symbolic interactionism was constructed in reaction to functionalism's focus on the causal relationship between social roles, norms, values, and structures and human behaviour. Interactionists argue that functionalism ignores the importance of social actors in creating, maintaining, and changing the social system. They emphasise that individual behaviour is not determined by external constraints, but is rather an outcome of people endowing social forces with meaning. Structural functionalists counter this emphasis on human agency by arguing that human behaviour is never free from the social structures and institutions within which it occurs.

NANCY COOK

G

gaze, the

The gaze is a term that derives from **psychoanalysis** and, in particular, from the account of vision offered by the French psychoanalytic theorist Jacques Lacan. For Lacanian theory the crucial point is the fact that the gaze is not reducible to human vision. The gaze precedes and makes possible human vision but remains itself elusive and indefinable: it is on the side of objects rather than viewing subjects, others rather than selves, and it subjugates the subject rather than offering visual mastery. In sum, Lacan presents the gaze as an external force that shapes the subject. The term is used in this Lacanian sense by feminist theorists such as Kaja Silverman, Bracha Lichtenberg Ettinger, and Joan Copjec.

In feminist theory the term is also used much more loosely as a synonym for the act of looking, and most particularly the act of viewing cultural products such as films, advertising, and the visual arts. Feminists contend that these cultural products generally presuppose (or naturalise) a masculine viewpoint and hence a masculine gaze. In other words, the gaze is largely, if not exclusively, a masculine property or phenomenon and thus implicated in the production and maintenance of gendered social positions. Laura **Mulvey** discusses these gender positions in her classic essay of 1975, 'Visual Pleasure and Narrative Cinema'. Her pithy phrase 'woman as image, man as bearer of the look' demonstrates how the polarisation of the sexes is refracted through vision and visuality.

In this article, Mulvey identifies two common kinds of viewing pleasure – identification and objectification – both of which presume, or conform to this asymmetrical relation between the sexes. Women, she argues, are usually objectified by mainstream realist cinema; visual pleasure here derives from voyeuristically looking at the woman-as-spectacle. Men, on the other hand, are the active figures with whom one should narcissistically identify.

This identification of the gaze with masculinity has generated much further discussion in both art history and film theory. A central question, pursued by theorists such as Mary Ann **Doane**, is how to think about the female gaze. Are women spectators obliged to either assume a masochistic identification with the masculine viewpoint, or to accept their role as objects of that gaze? Doane uses the idea of femininity as a masquerade to disrupt this untenable dichotomy. Other lines of inquiry have pursued the diversification of the gaze by looking at such issues as the queer spectator, the black gaze and so forth.

References and further reading

Copjec, J. (1994) 'The Orthopsychic Subject: Film Theory and the Reception of Lacan', *Read My Desire: Lacan against the Historicists*, Cambridge, MA: MIT Press, pp. 15–38.

Doane, M.A. (1987) 'Film and the Masquerade: Theorising the Female Spectator', *Screen* 23, 3–4: 77–87.

Lichtenberg Ettinger, B. (1995) *The Matrixial Gaze*, Leeds: Feminist Arts and Histories Network.

Mulvey, L. (1975) 'Visual Pleasure and Narrative Cinema', *Screen* 16, 3: 6–18.

Silverman, K. (1996) *The Threshold of the Visible World*, London: Routledge.

SUSAN BEST

gender

Gender, according to the *Concise Oxford Dictionary*, refers primarily to the grammatical classification of nouns. The usage of the term in regard to a person's sex occurs only in colloquial discourse. What this definition omits is the significance of gender – social roles based on biological sex – to western feminist thought. The distinction between sex, binarised physical anatomy, and gender, the cultural interpretation and expression of the sexed **body**, has marked second-wave feminisms (see **first-wave/second-wave feminism**). In other words, feminists have revealed the category 'woman' as a social construction premised upon the female body (see **social constructionism**). This shift which signals that biology is not, in fact, destiny, served as a catalyst for women's liberation. In a postmodern landscape, however, gender has become an increasingly problematic and contested site (see **posstructuralism/postmodernism**).

The Aristotelian view that women are naturally inferior to men, and thus destined to fulfil different and unequal roles, is embedded in western philosophy. At the onset of second-wave feminism, even more than today, a newborn's sexual anatomy, situated in a network of class, race, and sexuality, demarcated a narrow set of possibilities. White middle-class boys were expected to grow up to be successful breadwinners, while white middle-class girls were meant to be wives and mothers. If these women did work outside the home, it was in a suitably 'feminine' field such as education or health, jobs which they would leave when they married. By contrast, women of colour have long been employed, and often exploited, as domestics, caring for white people's families. Less privileged white women have also worked in middle-class homes, or performed manual labour in the workforce (see **work, women and**).

The modern feminist usage of gender, as distinct from sex, is most clearly articulated by Simone de **Beauvoir** when she asserts that 'One is not born, but rather becomes, a woman' (267) in her 1949 treatise *The Second Sex*. However, it is important to note that Beauvoir herself did not use the terms 'sex' and 'gender'. In the French language, gender translates as *genre*, a grammatical term, whereas *sexe* can mean sex, gender, or sexuality. Beauvoir, who has been hailed as the 'grandmother of feminism', set out to determine the limits to women's freedom, and how these obstacles might be overcome. She concludes that it is not biological, psychological, or economic factors which shape 'this creature, intermediate between male and eunuch, which is prescribed feminine' ([1949] 1989: 267). Rather, 'woman' is socially constructed as the **Other**. Women's inferiority is not natural, according to Beauvoir's ontological explanation, although the division between people is often disguised as such (see **ontology**). This hierarchical binarism is a patriarchal invention designed to promote male authority: 'Thus humanity is male and man defines woman not in herself but as relative to him.... He is the Subject, he is the Absolute – she is the Other' ([1949] 1989: xxii). So not only is woman a social construct, but woman is also a less valuable category than man. Women rarely strive to become subjects, Beauvoir maintains, because they are bound economically and psychologically to their oppressors.

Although Beauvoir's analysis of woman's place in society is considered revolutionary by many feminists, it is important to note that her ideas have not been universally embraced. Cultural feminists, maternal feminists, and some radical feminists prefer to retain a close connection between biological sex and social roles (see **cultural feminism**; **radical feminism**). Women, they argue, are special, or even superior, because of their unique physical features and their capacity to bear and nurture children. Iris Marion Young, for example, unfavourably contrasts what she perceives as Beauvoir's 'humanism' with 'gynocentrism', or a feminine perspective. According to Young, Beauvoir's theorisation of gender has had the effect of erasing gender difference and devaluing femininity.

In a related vein, feminist standpoint theorists seek to reclaim women's experience by positing a special female perspective (see **standpoint theory**). Nancy **Hartsock**, writing from a Marxist framework, asserts that women have a unique and advantageous view of the world because they are not part of the ruling structure. This type of theorizing, as black feminist **hooks** points out, rests problematically upon the assumption of a shared and essentialised gender (see **biological essentialism**). From her race-critical perspective, hooks troubles the classification 'woman' on the grounds that not all women are marginalised in the same way or to the same degree. White middle-class heterosexual women, for instance, are sometimes the oppressors of, or benefit from the oppression of, 'other Others'. Hence gender, as Elizabeth Spelman proffers, has the potential to obscure all other identities by seeking priority over social locations such as race and class.

Judith **Butler** maintains that the ramifications of Beauvoir's deconstruction of gender are even more far-reaching than has been hitherto presumed. Not only does the separation of sex and gender loosen the restrictions on social roles, but this extrication insinuates the existence of distinct sorts of beings (i.e., 'female' and 'woman'). The implication is that a certain 'sex' does not necessitate a certain 'gender,' although there are powerful social constraints. Thus those beings categorised as female need not aspire to, or need not be the only ones to aspire to, 'womanhood'. Girls can become 'women' or 'men', or something else entirely. Likewise boys have the possibility of becoming 'men' or 'women', or something else entirely. For Monique **Wittig**, lesbians are not women, and their existence highlights the artificiality of the categories 'woman' and 'women' (see **lesbian feminism**).

Implicit in the notion of gender as socially constructed is the idea that sex is a solid, 'natural' base. Thus, being a woman is infinitely more complicated than being female, due to the unstable quality of the process. As Butler puts it: 'to be a gender ... is to be engaged in an ongoing field of cultural possibilities' (1986: 36). Although potentially empowering, she notes that the formulation of gender as a project proves problematic in at least two ways. First, it presupposes a doer behind the deed and rests upon a starting point, namely the sexed body, outside the social world. Second, this conception of **agency** sounds much like existentialist, unfettered freedom of choice for the unfet-

tered individual. Yet Butler holds that Beauvoir's use of the verb 'become' ultimately reveals itself as ambiguous, for we are culturally constructed and we construct ourselves. Gender hence emerges simultaneously as a project in which choice is involved and a strategy for survival.

Paradoxically, the sexed and the gendered body are ultimately indistinguishable. Indeed, as Butler puts it, 'we never know our sex outside of its expression as gender. Lived or experienced "sex" is always already gendered' (1986: 39). Beauvoir's analysis both disassociates gender and sex and reveals sex as a gendered category. Gender is posited as an active process, more a verb than a noun. As human beings we perform our gender every day, under great duress, and rarely do we reflect on this process:

> Because there is neither an 'essence' that gender expresses or externalises nor an objective ideal to which gender aspires, and because gender is not a fact, the various acts of gender create the idea of gender, and without those acts, there would be no gender at all. Gender is, thus, a construction that regularly conceals its genesis.
>
> (Butler 1990: 140)

Hence gender emerges as performative, rather than expressive, with the acts themselves constituting the illusion of the very identity they were once thought to reveal. This is significant, for if our acts create our gender and thus our sex (albeit in a framework of rarefied social norms), can we not then re-create our gender through our acts? Trans(gressively) gendered activist Kate Bornstein, a self-defined 'gender outlaw', strives to do precisely this. In her case: 'the body becomes a choice, a mode of enacting and reenacting received gender norms which surface as so many styles of the flesh' (Butler 1986: 48).

Camp, cross-dressing, **butch/femme** personae, and so on, all parody gender and expose it as fundamentally 'unnatural.' The mimicking of gender norms exposes the relationship of homosexuality to **heterosexuality** not as 'copy to origin' but rather as 'copy to copy'. Thus gender cannot be said to be true or false, nor does it properly belong to any particular type of body. From this perspective there is little difference between a biological 'female' who goes through her daily beauty rituals, and the preparatory activities of a drag queen. Drag, according to Butler, reveals that 'gender is a kind of imitation for which there is no original' (Butler 1991: 21). In this case then, is it possible, or indeed desirable, for gender to be used as a basis for feminist collective action?

The need to endorse and disavow 'women' simultaneously is the conundrum which underpins modern-day feminisms. The problem is that although gender categories have proven to be politically useful, they also have inherently limiting effects. Rather than search for a common identity from which to act, Butler suggests that feminists consider the extent to which this quest has precluded a more radical inquiry. Only by retaining 'women' as a 'field of differences' will movement be possible (Butler 1992: 16). Joan **Scott** acknowledges that the revisioning of women's experience as anti-foundational has been charged with denying the subject agency and precluding political action. She however argues that only by historicising, and hence 'denaturalizing', concepts such as gender will questions pertaining to difference and subjectivity be opened up for critical scrutiny (1992: 34).

See also: homosexuality, bio-medical pathologisation of

References and further reading

Beauvoir, S. de (1949) *The Second Sex*, trans. H.M. Parshley, introd. D. Bair, New York: Vintage Books, 1989.

Bornstein, K. (1994) *Gender Outlaw: On Men, Women and the Rest of Us*, New York and London: Routledge.

Butler, J. (1986) 'Sex and Gender in Simone de Beauvoir's *Second Sex*', *Yale French Studies, Simone de Beauvoir: Witness to a Century* 72: 35–50.

—— (1990) *Gender Trouble: Feminism and the Subversion of Identity*, New York: Routledge.

—— (1991) 'Imitation and Gender Insubordination', in D. Fuss (ed.) *Inside/Out: Lesbian Theories, Gay Theories*, New York: Routledge, pp. 13–31.

—— (1992) 'Contingent Foundations', in J. Butler and J. Scott (eds.) *Feminists Theorize the Political*, New York and London: Routledge, pp. 3–21.

hooks, b. (1984) *Feminist Theory: From Margin to Centre*, Boston: South End Press.

Scott, J. (1992) 'Experience', in J. Butler and J. Scott (eds.) *Feminists Theorize the Political*, New York and London: Routledge, pp. 22–40.

Spelman, E. (1988) *Inessential Woman: Problems of Exclusion in Feminist Thought*, Boston: Beacon Press.

Wittig, M. (1981) 'One is Not Born a Woman', *Feminist Issues* 1, 2: 47–54.

MICHELLE K. OWEN

gender gap, the

Much of the activism of first-wave feminists in western countries was directed to winning voting rights for women. Women now vote in the elections held in these countries at about the same rate as men. But with the exception of the Nordic countries, women's participation in political life at decision-making levels has not matched their electoral turnout. In spite of some affirmative action measures in Britain and Canada, for example, women are fewer than 25 per cent, and most commonly are about 10 per cent, of elected representatives. Furthermore, similar electoral participation rates have masked gender differences in policy and partisan preferences.

In 1980 such opinion differences resulted in 8 per cent fewer women than men supporting Ronald Reagan in the American presidential election, although there was no gender difference in voter turnout. The term gender gap was created by Betsy Dunn of the Democratic National Committee to describe this vote spread, and it was part of her effort to generate support for the Equal Rights Amendment to the American Constitution. The term gender gap has been popular among American pollsters and journalists, who use it to describe what they consider to be significant gender policy preference or voting differences. Its use has generated debates among feminists about the meaning and measurement of opinion differences, in view of pollsters' reliance on empirical research methods grounded in positivist assumptions of causality, validity and reliability (see **positivism**). The term was most useful as a tool for publicising women's increased levels of political participation in the USA in the 1980s. Women's voting turnout had been significantly lower than men's until the 1950s, and the media's attraction to gender gaps as news items contributed to growing awareness among researchers and the public that women were increasingly taking part in voting and voting-related activities. However, political analysts have been much less successful in convincing policy-makers that gender differences in voting patterns are associated with clear policy preferences.

Feminist interest in women's electoral participation is based on several claims, including the possibilities that women as voters will force governments to be sympathetic to women's concerns, and that women as legislators will be more consensual and constituency-responsive. In addition, since the early 1970s feminist activists and researchers increasingly have challenged the notion (most popular in the US) that political participation is restricted to election-related activities. They have argued that the personal is political, and have shown that political participation extends beyond voting to activities such as community and interest group involvement.

See also: empiricism; qualitative/quantitative methods

References and further reading

Mueller, C.M. (ed.) (1988) *The Politics of the Gender Gap: The Social Construction of Political Influence*, Newbury Park, CA: Sage.

Phillips, A. (1991) *Engendering Democracy*, Cambridge, MA: Polity Press.

SANDRA BURT

gender roles

Relying on a distinction between sex (as a natural attribute) and **gender** (as a system of social meaning ascribed to physical difference), 'gender roles' refers to social practices associated with masculinity or femininity – what an earlier generation termed 'sex roles'. The term is useful for challenging discrimination which is not specifically sex-based; for example, feminists use the concept to demand that employed women (see **work, women and**) need both maternity leave (which is sex-based) and provisions to manage their on going responsibilities to children and family members (based on their gender roles). Nevertheless, 'gender roles' suffers from the same problems that bedevil all role theory: it is prescriptive; roles are conceived of as static and unchanging; it assumes that the person voluntarily and freely plays her part; and also naively implies that individualistic change is all that is required for a person to switch roles.

See also: liberal feminism; sociology; systemic discrimination

SUSAN L. PRENTICE

gender scepticism

It is virtually a law of intellectual and political transformation that ground-breaking ideas are first presented in broad strokes. Once those bold, new ideas have been absorbed, the next generation of thinkers can turn to the complexities, nuances, exceptions, exclusions that raise scepticism about any too-general formulation, law, or category. Feminist theory is a case in point.

The first critical writings and political agendas to emerge in both the 'first' and 'second' waves of modern feminism (see **first-wave/second-wave feminism**) drew their energy from a belief in shared experience and common cause. Whether agitating for the vote or reproductive choice, feminists assumed that they were working toward ideals which would benefit all women, and felt no need to qualify or elaborate when they used terms such as 'woman' or 'women'. Ultimately, however, a more sceptical attitude toward undifferentiated **gender** categories was to emerge within both movements.

These waves of 'gender scepticism' (a term coined by Bordo, 1989) have some commonalties, but also key differences. The scepticism that emerged in the 1920s and 1930s was largely focused on recognising the 'individuality' of each woman, and on disputing nineteenth-century notions about moral and psychological differences between men and women (Cott 1987). This has been a strain, too, of contemporary feminism. But two other elements of contemporary gender scepticism are unique to late twentieth-century culture.

The first is the 'politics of difference': the call for feminist theory and politics to more adequately represent the range of women's experiences and not covertly assume a white, middle-class, heterosexual subject as the norm. This call emerged first from the strong, specific criticisms of African American feminists, but soon became a more general operating principle of feminist theory.

The emerging postmodern strain in feminism has reinforced these critiques (see **poststructuralism/postmodernism**). Postmodern theorists emphasise the inadequacy of all universals, and advocate what might be called a 'theoretics of heterogeneity', in which ideas, history, texts are always more multiple in their meanings than they appear on the surface. Postmodernists are especially critical of the tendency to reduce the heterogeneity of things to simple oppositions, or dualisms – 'man' and 'woman' being one example.

The 'gender sceptical' strain in contemporary feminist theory thus insists on historical, racial, sexual, and class specificity, with gender considered an inseparable strand among many. Such an approach has added a welcome range and complexity to feminist theory, while sometimes being too doctrinaire in condemning and proscribing generality.

Some degree of generality seems necessary to thought itself, since the range of 'particulars' one might consider is endless. It is important to note, too, that feminist scepticism owes its very emergence to the gains – both theoretical and practical – made by the 'generalities' of earlier generations. The activists of the first wave brought about the social changes that it made it *possible* for professional women in the 1920s to claim their 'individuality' alongside men. Second-wave theorists of gender difference challenged the assumption that 'human equals male', opening the door for other 'differences' to stake their claims to representation.

Women are indeed highly diverse, but may nonetheless share certain 'common differences' from men in their cultures. Exploring these commonalties – while remaining alert to the dangers of generalisation – remains an important feminist project.

References and further reading

Bordo, S. (1989) 'Feminism, Postmodernism and Gender Scepticism', in L. Nicholson (ed.) *Feminism/Postmodernism*, London: Routledge; revised in Bordo, S. (1993) *Unbearable Weight; Feminism, Western Culture, and the Body*, Berkeley, CA: University of California Press.

Cott, N. (1987) *The Grounding of Modern Feminism*, New Haven: Yale University Press.

SUSAN BORDO

genealogy

Genealogy inquires into how things come to be; it denaturalises established understandings by giving them a history. Genealogy (Greek *genea*/race or stock and *logos*/word) comes to feminism primarily through Nietzsche, who criticises efforts to ground knowledge in a secure foundation of history, science, nature or god, and instead advocates a historicised, situated perspectivism. Feminist genealogy is often in conversation with hermeneutic arguments grounding feminism in a standpoint or experience that is considered fundamental to women's lives (see **hermeneutics**). Claims to fundamentals are problematic for genealogical thinkers, who see unstable categories and incomplete histories in all of our accounts of things. The struggle to find a way to continue talking productively about women, while still calling the category of 'women' into question, animates much feminist genealogy.

Genealogists take the world to be a place of flux and discord in which language is never fully capable of apprehending life. Suspicious of confident distinctions between appearances and reality, or surface and depth, genealogists view claims to reality as yet another level of appearance and take the surfaces of things as significant sites of meaning rather than as covers for the real thing. Following Foucault, genealogists problematise identity by viewing subjectivity as the outcome, rather than the source, of modernity's disciplinary practices.

Believing that there is always more to being than knowing, genealogists are suspicious of grand narratives, fearing that life's animating heterogeneity is erased in efforts to theorise it. Yet genealogists also try to understand the world, and use language to do so; thus they inhabit the paradox of using language to investigate language's limits.

Genealogically inclined feminists employ deconstructive linguistic strategies to break up the categories of analysis that have enabled **patriarchy** and compulsory **heterosexuality** to operate (see **deconstruction, feminist**). Judith **Butler** argues that gender categories reflect layers of performativity in which historically constructed signs of gender are repeated and sedimented into familiar corporeal practices. Butler claims that gender performances can be subverted, resisted, performed against the grain in ways that disrupt conventional power arrangements. Donna **Haraway** writes against the dream of a pure foundation for feminist knowledge and in favour of a disorderly multiplicity of perspectives. Her image of the **cyborg** represents hybridity that disrupts conventional borders between women and men, human and animal, human and machine. **Trinh T. Minh-ha** uses language disruptively to interrupt the drive toward mastery often inherent in the power to name. Genealogical thinking provides resources for feminists trying to think critically about prevailing forms of power without reproducing those forms in the guise of liberation.

References and further reading

Butler, J. (1993) *Bodies That Matter*, New York: Routledge.
Haraway, D. (1991) *Simians, Cyborgs, and Women*, New York: Routledge.
Trinh T. Minh-ha (1991) *When the Moon Waxes Red*, New York: Routledge.

KATHY E. FERGUSON

generality v. specificity

The generality-versus-specificity issue is significant for feminists because of an assumption that theory,

almost by definition, must achieve generality by establishing over-arching, law-like conclusions. Feminists, particularly in the social sciences and humanities, have shown that general conclusions consistently filter out specificities of **gender**, **race**, class (see **class analysis**), ethnicity, age, ability, **sexuality**: the differences that make a difference to theory's effects in shaping and controlling people's lives. Whereas traditional theorists fear that concentration on specificity blocks the way to viable, comprehensive conclusions, feminists and other Others argue that only by concentrating on the divergences that varied specificities produce can theorists bridge a theory/practice divide that renders many theoretical generalities irrelevant to the specificities of concrete experiences.

References and further reading

Benhabib, S. (1987) 'The Generalized and the Concrete Other', in S. Benhabib and D. Cornell (eds) *Feminism As Critique*, Minneapolis, MI: University of Minnesota Press.

LORRAINE CODE

genre theory

Genre theory has proved useful to the work of feminist theorists who are interested in addressing the devaluation of cultural production by and for women.

'Genre' refers to a body of works that share important characteristics such as iconography, central themes, or structures that allow audiences to engage with them. Film scholars have used the term to move away from a preoccupation with the auteur, the power of the single, artistic voice, and to point instead to the diversity of productions and receptions of cultural texts.

Traditional cultural criticism has often devalued women's cultural consumption and output. Critics arguing about high versus low art have assigned women's novels, films or other cultural products an inferior place on the grounds of being formulaic, domestic, derivative or lacking a strong artistic vision. Thus, they have seen women's material as governed by women's particularity, in opposition to male material which they have seen as being ungendered and universal.

At various times in history, preachers, teachers and other instructors saw romance, gothic novels, soap operas and melodrama as mindless junk and escapism, 'poisoning' the minds of women. These criticisms portray women consumers as weak and passive, in need of protection and guidance, since they depict women as too easily programmed into obedience and acceptance by unsuitable sources.

Feminist genre theorists point to the assumptions underlying these value assignments. Tania Modleski (1982) argues that critiques are misplaced when aimed at the 'mindless consumer' – she wants them directed at social forces which create the contradictions that women need to resolve through their consumption of the generic material.

But feminist genre theorists have quickly moved away from any scenario casting women as victims, and instead emphasise the productive nature of their pleasures. Janice Radway (1987) investigates the symbolic community which springs out of shared pleasure of reading romance novels, and the productive readings and re-engagements with patriarchy, and other theorists draw similar conclusions in their work on *Star Trek* or other fiction texts. In these accounts, the reader becomes an active participant in the exchange – a move towards a vision of a text as part of a larger cultural field, open to appropriation.

Following Ian Ang (1985), many critics stress the need for genre theorists to see themselves as consumers of popular culture, and to break down categories between analysts and 'the field'.

In all of these accounts, theorists have moved away from the single, authored text, to an investigation on the level of genre. They show the complexities of the interactions that shape consumption.

See also: romance as genre; television

References and further reading

Ang, I. (1985) *Watching Dallas*, London: Methuen.
Modleski, T. (1982) *Loving with a Vengeance*, Hamden, CT: Archon Books.
Radway, J. (1987) *Reading the Romance*, London: Verso.

PETRA KUPPERS

geography

Geography – once a rather dreary subject, all capes and bays, maps and products – has in these postmodern, reflexive times, when positionality and situatedness, borderland and margins, standpoint and difference, are key words among feminist theorists, suddenly found itself in the forefront of contemporary debates in the social sciences and humanities (McDowell 1996; Pollock 1996). A combination of material and theoretical shifts has brought to prominence the concept of location: a place to speak from, a place to claim in a world in which mobility and displacement are increasingly common experiences, as well as the reconceptualisation of 'real' places as fluid and relational networks rather than bounded spaces.

It is common to define geography as a discipline not in terms of substantive subject material but rather as a synthetic point of view addressing both difference and particularity, the causes and consequences of uneven development and the patterns of flows and movement discernible over space, linking places with real and symbolic meanings for their inhabitants and outsiders that differentiate them from elsewhere. It is now axiomatic that spatial relations affect and reflect social relations (albeit less well reflected in the practices of many of the social sciences) and that location makes a difference to the constitution of gendered subjectivities and identities. Thus the terms space (flows or relations) and place (locations) are what define geography. To these two terms must be added a third: that of scale. A geographical imagination spans the spatial scale from the body to the globe and feminist inquiries focus not solely on the small-scale or the local – the **body**, the home and the community – but also on the region and the nation, indeed the world in its entirety. What holds together this ambitious agenda is the idea of connections: the links between places at a range of spatial scales that produce the particularity of any single place. Thus in a world in which millions of women are wrenched out of place, driven away from their homelands by wars or by famine, by economic hardship or household changes, by global capital flows, **economic restructuring** and structural adjustment programmes, and are forced to recreate their place in the borderlands of other nations, a range of social processes and events at different spatial scales combine to reshape the links between their identity and their location. The results often challenge conventional geographic divisions. As Mohanty (1991) notes, 'Third World women', defined by their common political interests, are as likely to live in the 'First' as the 'Third' world.

Global flows of labour and capital in combination with the development of new technologies for overcoming the friction of distance and permitting an instantaneous transfer of information and capital have resulted in space/time compression (Harvey 1989), even, according to some, the end of geography in the sense of marked differences between places. With the growing dominance of capitalist social relations at the global scale and the **hegemony** of western culture, it seems that everywhere is increasingly similar, and that the 'non-places' or 'spaces of flows' (Castells 1996) of global capital – airports, stock exchanges, the internet – have replaced fundamental attachments to place and territory on which **cultural identities** were based and which gave us our sense of belonging. While some postmodern theorists celebrate and others rue this apparent deterritorialisation, the counter claims are androcentric and ethnocentric (see **androcentrism**). Money, **power** and knowledge are needed to escape the bounds of place, yet many women without these assets might approve of reducing the ties that bind them in place. But as feminist critics have pointed out, through a range of examples at different spatial scales, from the ethnic nationalism of the former Yugoslavia to the barrios of the world's poorest cities, the poor, and paradoxically even the mobile among them, remain trapped in place, in the least desirable spaces of exclusion in cities and nations, where daily life is spatially bounded, but affected by large-scale forces and spatial flows beyond local control. The significance of place has not declined, although it has been retheorised to combine local and global processes.

Feminists have also retheorised concepts of place and location in metaphorical, as well as material, ways. The redefinition of notions such as borderlands and margins has become an important part of the broader challenge to the inherent spatiality of western enlightenment theory, in which the distinction of mind from the body, reason from emotion, the public sphere from the private arena, placed men on one side, and relegated 'Woman', as **Other**, to the other side (see **emotions/rationality**; **public/private**). Thus all that was 'naturally' female and feminine was located inside, in private, at the smallest spatial scale and so taken for granted and untheorised. The long struggle to unseat these divisions and spatial associations is well known. More interesting and potentially disruptive for feminism as a theory and a political practice has been the recognition of difference and in this the importance of location as a place to speak from. The internationalism of Virginia Woolf's much-quoted claim that 'as a woman I have no country. As a woman I want no country. As a woman my country is the whole world' was challenged by the development of what Rich in 1986 termed the politics of location. Such a politics is not necessarily divisive but may lead instead to alliances between women in different locations and speaking positions. This politics marks welcome progress in the displacement of the singular and universal view from 'nowhere' in phallogocentric knowledge claims (see **phallogocentrism**). Feminism too is not a universal perspective. Position and location – geographies – matter in the constitution of subjectivity and identity, in theory construction, in the making and marking of the body, in customs and practices and in political struggles against oppression. The place from which we speak affects the claims we make and recognising difference strengthens these claims. As hooks (1990) insists, the margins are a place of radical openness from which the singular view of phallogocentrism may be undermined and superseded.

References and further reading

Castells, M. (1996) *The Rise of the Network Society*, Oxford: Blackwell.

Harvey, D. (1989) *The Condition of Postmodernity*, Oxford: Blackwell.

hooks, b. (1990) *Yearning*, Boston: South End Press.

McDowell, L. (1996) 'Spatialising Feminism', in N. Duncan (ed.) *Bodyspace*, London: Routledge, pp. 28–44.

Mohanty, C.T. (1991) 'Cartographies of Struggle', in C.T. Mohanty *et al.* (eds) *Third World Women and the Politics of Feminism*, Bloomington, IN: Indiana University Press, pp. 1–47.

Pollock, G. (1996) *Generations and Geographies in the Visual Arts*, London: Routledge.

Rich, A. (1986) *The Politics of Location in Blood, Bread and Poetry*, New York: W.W. Norton.

LINDA McDOWELL

Gilligan, Carol (b. 1936)

Published in 1982, Carol Gilligan's landmark book *In a Different Voice* set in motion a series of debates, especially in North American feminist theory, the effects of which are still in evidence at the beginning of the twenty-first century. Gilligan, now Professor of Gender Studies in the Harvard Graduate School of Education, had been measuring children's moral maturity using Lawrence Kohlberg's scale of moral development. Unable to explain why girls appeared consistently to achieve lower scores on the Kohlberg test, Gilligan made the apparently simple but in fact revolutionary move of asking whether the test might be at fault, not girls' inborn incapacity to achieve moral maturity.

According to the Kohlberg scale, moral maturity demonstrates a growth away from obedience to particular, authority-derived moral rules. It culminates in a capacity for autonomous reasoning according to abstract moral principles. Noting that such reasoning tended to be nurtured in the socialisation practices within which boys are raised, Gilligan determined that girls' moral reasoning tended to follow more contextualised, situationally specific lines. In studies of girls' approaches to academic learning, to decisions about whether to have an abortion, and to Kohlberg's well-known 'Heinz dilemma', she discerned the 'different voice' that has become the hallmark of her challenge to Kohlbergian stage theory. This voice speaks for and from an '**ethic of care**' that Gilligan counterposes to the 'ethic of justice' which, she contends, typifies received moral theory in the western world. Although it is in this voice that Gilligan's female subjects speak, she contends that its gendered specificity is more a matter of contingency than of necessity: each mode of ethical thought is available to men and women alike.

Feminist legal theorists, epistemologists, literary theorists, theorists of education have drawn, whether critically or constructively, on Gilligan's work: many who disagree with her do so within the terms of a debate she has made possible. Yet critiques of Gilligan's work are wide-ranging: they centre on the taken-for-granted liberalism of her position, its whiteness, its derivation from interviews with privileged subjects, its tacit heteronormativity. Partly responding to these criticisms, Gilligan's more recent work has directed its attention to questions of embodiment and cultural location as these bear upon psychological development.

Selected writings

Gilligan, C. (1982) *In a Different Voice*, Cambridge, MA: Harvard University Press.

—— (1996) 'The Centrality of Relationship in Human Development', in G. Noam and K. Fisher, *Development and Vulnerability in Close Relationships*, Mahwah, NJ: Erlbaum.

LORRAINE CODE

girl-child, the

The girl-child is the designation used in international instruments to recognise the special needs of girl children. Although many international **human rights** treaties declare protection from sex discrimination for both adults and children (defined by the Convention on the Rights of the Child as 'every human being under eighteen, unless national laws recognise the age of majority earlier'), the 'girl-child' designation recognises that girls, because of their sex, often experience discrimination in ways that boys do not. In many countries, fewer girls than boys reach adulthood because of early childhood discrimination. The 1995 Fourth

World Conference on Women's Platform for Action (Section L) is the first international instrument to specifically document discrimination against girl-children and to develop a strategy to meet girls' needs and protect their rights in education, health, marriage, motherhood, citizenship, sexuality, and violence.

References and further reading

Fourth World Conference on Women, Platform for Action: http://www.un.org/womenwatch/daw/beijing/platform

LAURA PARISI

glass ceiling

In 1987 Ann Morrison identified the glass ceiling as the invisible barrier that has kept, and continues to keep, women and minorities out of top management jobs in large commercial organisations. Slower career advancement is caused primarily by women's inability to gain the support of mentors.

The glass ceiling is a barrier that applies to women as a group who are kept from advancing as quickly or as high in the organisation as their male counterparts because they are women. This barrier refers to invisible obstacles to career advancement, yet ones that are systemic or perceived in organisational practices (e.g. tradition, compatibility with those in senior positions, and stereotypes). Even women who successfully break through the glass ceiling can encounter glass walls that continue to separate them from top executive level.

References and further reading

Morrison, A. (1987) *Breaking the Glass Ceiling*, Reading, MA: Addison Wesley.

PATRICIA BRADSHAW AND DAVID WICKS

Goddess

The meaning of the Goddess in historic and prehistoric times was a matter of intense scholarly debate throughout the nineteenth and twentieth centuries. Numerous female images such as the ample-bodied Goddess of Willendorf have survived from upper paleolithic (*c.*32,000–10,000 BCE) and neolithic (*c.*6500–3500 BCE) periods. For some scholars these images point to a widespread religion of the Great Goddess in prehistoric times, while for others they are relatively unimportant 'fertility figurines' associated with agricultural production and human reproduction. A widespread popular Goddess movement (**divine feminine**) holds not only that Goddesses once were widely worshipped, but also that the demotion, demonisation, and eventual suppression of Goddesses in the west was one of the ways patriarchal control of women was ensured. The matriarchal hypothesis which asserts that an earlier Goddess-worshipping and female-dominated society preceded later patriarchal God-worshipping societies was first proposed by J.J. Bachofen in the nineteenth century and was widely accepted by classicists and by theorists as diverse as Engels and Jung. Current theories in classics and archaeology reject the matriarchal hypothesis and dismiss the idea of a religion of the Goddess.

A number of feminist scholars in religion and archaeology propose a new Goddess hypothesis. They argue that Goddess was understood to be the Giver, Taker, and Renewer of life, and correlate the prominence of Goddesses in neolithic cultures with high status for women as the likely inventors of agriculture, weaving, and pottery. Archaeologist Marija Gimbutas distinguishes peaceful, artistic, sedentary, agricultural, matrifocal Goddess cultures of neolithic 'Old Europe' (see **matrifocality**) from later 'Indo-European' cultures which were warlike, horse-riding, aggressive, patriarchal, and worshipped the shining gods of the sky. Unlike her predecessors, Gimbutas proposes that the earlier cultures of Old Europe were in many ways superior to those that followed. Avoiding the controversial matriarchal hypothesis, she argues that in 'matrifocal' societies women share power with men. According to Gimbutas, the familiar Goddesses of classical Greek mythology, such as Athena and Aphrodite, and their counterparts in other Indo-European (including Hindu) mythologies, are truncated versions of earlier more powerful Goddesses.

Scholarly consensus about the Goddess is not likely to be achieved soon, as normative ideas about women's roles, the place of religion in society, the inevitability of patriarchy, the alleged superiority of classical Greek and modern cultures, and the possibility of understanding non-literary cultures are embedded (but not often acknowledged) in the debates.

References and further reading

Baring, A. and Cashford, J. (1991) *The Myth of the Goddess: Evolution of an Image*, London, Viking.

Gimbutas, M. (1989) *The Language of the Goddess*, San Francisco: Harper.

Goodison, L. and Morris, C. (eds) (1998) *Ancient Goddesses: The Myths and the Evidence*, Madison: University of Wisconsin Press; London: British Museum Press.

Preston, J.J. (ed.) (1982) *Mother Worship: Theme and Variations*, Chapel Hill, University of North Carolina Press.

CAROL P. CHRIST

Gordon, Linda (b. 1940)

Linda Gordon, a US feminist historian, has influenced a generation of feminist historians and activists through her research on birth control, family violence, and welfare. With other socialist-feminist historians in the 1970s, she integrated class and race issues into early women's **history** scholarship. Stressing the richness and diversity of the feminist political tradition in the USA, Gordon advances a broad definition of feminism: as a critique of male supremacy which assumes that it can be changed. Thus she argues that 'feminist' advocates of birth control ranged from conservative proponents of **eugenics** and sexual purity to socialist and feminist sex radicals, while 'feminist' **welfare** activists included white maternalists and African American club women who had very different ideas about family life.

Gordon also expands the meaning of 'political' by illuminating the ways in which the mass of women have been involved in political activity in their daily lives. She was among the first to define women's efforts on behalf of 'voluntary motherhood' and birth control as political, and to see family **violence** as political, in the sense that it is rooted in family **power** struggles and affected by historical changes in power relations of **gender**, class and age (see **class analysis, UK**; class analysis, US; **age studies and gender**).

Rejecting the concept of gender as acculturated **difference** between men and women because that conception obscures power, Gordon describes a gender power system in which women's subordination is embedded, contested and renegotiated. Power, in Gordon's view, is never complete; there is always resistance as well as domination, **agency** as well as social control. Battered women are not mere victims but sometimes 'heroes of their own lives', and their efforts on their own behalf are political as well as individual. The pressure clients exerted on social workers influenced how social problems were defined and contributed to the creation of the 'welfare state'.

Although Gordon insists on the historically shifting meanings of words and concepts like welfare, **dependency**, and birth control, she maintains a distinction between representation and experience. In a debate with poststructuralist historian Joan **Scott**, she characterises discourse as coexisting and interacting with material relations of class, race and gender.

See also: history, feminist

Selected writings

Gordon, L. (1988) *Heroes of Their Own Lives*, New York: Viking.

—— (1990) *Woman's Body, Woman's Right*, New York: Penguin, 2nd edn.

—— (1994) *Pitied But Not Entitled*, New York: Free Press.

MOLLY LADD-TAYLOR

gossip

Gossip is private, everyday, intimate talk in which people reveal themselves in talking about others, constructing a communal narrative. It is informal discourse that deals with personal matters specific to individual lives; talk often directed to no specific purpose or end. It repeats and circulates information usually heard from someone else or seen where it was not meant to be noticed. In a climate of trust people gossip to think aloud about themselves and one another, to work through extraordinary events, to know one another better and to establish community. In a climate of distrust, gossip is often malicious, playing with reputations, circulating truths better concealed or half-truths elevated to the status of truth.

Traditionally, gossip has a bad name because of its common representation as a trivial part of women's lives that contrasts with allegedly more serious male practices of 'discussion'. Such dismissals ignore gossip's function as a means of achieving solidarity. They demean its political power, and erase its potential as a resource for the subordinated and as a source of knowledge properly so-called, in which co-gossips, together, negotiate emancipatory understandings and meanings. Malicious gossip is a powerful weapon of personal and political harm: it plants the seeds of destruction. It can make and unmake lives and reputations, undermine settled beliefs. It manipulates and creates power structures within groups; fragments community as readily as it cements it. Yet gossip can also be enlisted powerfully and systematically both in small, close communities and in wider social-political practice, where it can instigate searches for information integral to knowledge and action.

Feminists proclaim the value of gossip as an underground, subversive way of communicating unorthodox perceptions of the social world. As with many practices dubbed 'feminine' it originates in, and perpetuates, the constraints attendant upon being female in a male world, even as it works, often anecdotally, to contest and caricature the self-certainties of that world.

Gossip (Code 1995) is unruly in the literal sense that it obeys no rules: it is unpredictable, attentive to the unexpected, the surprising, the aberrant. It is located, situated discourse, attuned to the location, the historical moment, and the circumstances that generate it. It is subtly informative, yet neither stable nor fixed. Yet gossip is not indifferent to truth: indeed its commitment to ferreting out truths often thought best concealed can be relentless, for its effectiveness as an emancipatory tool for exposing injustice and oppression depends on its accuracy.

See also: discourse analysis

References and further reading

Code, L. (1995) 'Gossip, or In Praise of Chaos', in *Rhetorical Spaces*, New York: Routledge.
Jones, D. (1980) 'Gossip: Notes on Women's Oral Culture', *Women's Studies International Quarterly*, 3.
Spacks, P. (1985) *Gossip*, New York: Knopf.

LORRAINE CODE

green movement, feminism and the

A heterogeneous collection of environmental concerns, politics, and ideologies, the green movement is a difficult terrain for feminism. While women led the earliest – and remain among the most vocal – grassroots green activists, and while environmental concerns infuse some creative ecofeminist thought (see **ecofeminism**), most mainstream **environmental science**, politics and thought continues to ignore and marginalise feminist issues. In addition, issues of **essentialism** plague attempts to draw direct connections between women's and nature's 'liberation'.

One of the earliest struggles of the modern green movement was initiated by Lois Gibbs at Love Canal (New York, 1978). In response to concerns about the health of local children, Gibbs transformed a once-woman fact-finding mission into international recognition of the dangers (especially to disadvantaged communities) of industrial toxic waste dumping. Not a feminist before her activism, Gibbs became convinced that knowledge from women's everyday activities of care was crucial to environmentalism. Similar insights, extended to include nonhierarchical and nonviolent tactics, informed the feminist antimilitarism of Greenham Common and the ecofeminist Women's Pentagon Actions of 1980 and 1981 (see **anti-militarism, feminist**). Petra Kelly, an influential member of the [then] West German Green Party, was elected to the Bundestag in 1985; her writings reveal that feminist concerns and visions had an influence on green politics even outside specifically women's organizing.

Perhaps more than other social movements, however, the green movement has been characterised by a strong shift toward the mainstream; in the corporate co-optation and state bureaucratisation of environmentalism, and even in the politics of most formal green parties, feminist concerns are isolated and marginalised. 'Shallow' green understandings of environmental issues as scientific or technological problems are quite consistent with gendered capitalist social relations; western women are thus included in calls for green consumption, but global feminism is not likewise included in international environmental policymaking. Even in 'deep' ecological circles, there is a powerful assumption that feminist issues need to be put on hold until the environmental 'crisis' is addressed.

In many 'left' and grassroots green circles that insist on the articulation of environmental with social analyses, however, feminist voices are more prominent. Working-class women and women of colour remain at the forefront of antitoxics politics, and women's health concerns (e.g., breast cancer) catalyse struggles over industrial processes. Some ecofeminists (e.g., Vandana **Shiva**) even argue that, in addition to requiring feminist analyses of the social causes of environmental degradation, the green movement should base its sociopolitical vision on women's subsistence practices. Such assertions, while provocative, may essentialise and reify particular gendered practices of/in nature.

See also: deep ecology

References and further reading

Kelly, P. (1994) *Thinking Green! Essays on Environmentalism, Feminism and Nonviolence*, Berkeley, CA: Parallax.

Seager, J. (1993) *Earth Follies: Coming to Feminist Terms with the Global Environmental Crisis*, New York: Routledge.

CATRIONA SANDILANDS

Greer, Germaine (b. 1939)

In her varied career as academic, literary critic, art historian, social activist, journalist and broadcaster, Australian feminist Germaine Greer has been particularly concerned with ways in which patriarchal modes of thinking inhibit women's **autonomy** and productivity. In *The Obstacle Race* (1979), for example, she analyses the forces that have traditionally inhibited women's success as artists. Her work in literary history, including the anthology *Kissing the Rod* (1989) and the Stump Cross editions of Aphra Behn (1989) and Katherine Philips (1992), has primarily involved making readily accessible the work of women poets of the seventeenth century. Her most important contributions, however, have been in the areas of social and **cultural feminism**. *The Female Eunuch*, published in 1970, is widely credited with galvanising the Women's Liberation Movement in Britain. Like much of her journalism of the 1970s and 1980s it energetically addresses the **misogyny** which is fundamental to **patriarchy**. Greer argues that the social conditioning which shapes **gender roles** and relations, and which is expressed in all forms of social and political discourse from law to marriage to rape to romance, inscribes women as socially, sexually and intellectually passive and weak. To achieve autonomy, women must learn to accept their bodies and their **sexuality**, and take individual control of their own emancipation. This necessarily includes refusal to participate in oppressive social institutions such as marriage or to accept the expectations of the patriarchal social code.

In recent years, Greer has been charged with contributing to the **backlash** of the 1980s and 1990s by abandoning her early militancy and retreating into biological determinism: *Sex and Destiny* (1984), for example, glorifies motherhood and indicts the developed world for urging the use of birth control in developing countries; *Daddy, We Hardly Knew You* (1989) has been criticised for demonising Greer's mother in an attempt to come to terms with her father's perceived distance and passivity; and *Slip-shod Sibyls* (1995) suggests that women poets have themselves been largely to blame for their lack of public acknowledgement. Still, the central theme of her work, that women must take responsibility for their own liberation, is clearly articulated in these later works, and her importance in the development of the second wave of feminism is indisputable.

See also: adolescent women and feminism; art, feminist issues in; chauvinism, male

Selected writings

Greer, G. (1970) *The Female Eunuch*, London: Granada Publishing.
—— (1986) *The Madwoman's Underclothes: Essays and Occasional Writings*, London: Pan Books.
—— (1992) *The Change: Women, Ageing, and the Menopause*, New York: A.A. Knopf.

HEATHER CAMPBELL

gynaecology, history of

Feminist scholars take a critical view of gynaecology, which the *Oxford English Dictionary* defines as that branch of medical science which treats the functions and diseases peculiar to women. In particular, feminist historians have challenged the traditional history of gynaecology which has been told as a story of the triumph of male medical practitioners whose discoveries have improved women's lives. Medical historians describe the practice of gynaecology as involving skill in a range of medical specialisms, including surgery, and, according to the *Encyclopaedia Britannica* of 1971, 'in dealing with minor psychiatric problems which commonly arise among gynaecological patients'.

Women have always been involved in **health** and healing, particularly in providing assistance to each other in reproductive matters (see **reproduction**). In medieval and early modern Europe, women were responsible for gynaecological knowledge; experience and information were shared in the female community. Many women disliked allowing men to examine their bodies. Midwives, licensed by the church for their moral characters rather than their gynaecological skills, assisted in child-birth and provided expert witness for the courts in matters gynaecological. Recent studies by feminist historians (see **history, feminist**) have shown that in the sixteenth and seventeenth centuries, midwives usually trained through an informal system of apprenticeship, learning from other midwives. Midwives' practice could usually extend to women's health generally. Furthermore, unlicensed female medical practitioners advertised their services for a female clientèle in large cities such as London. By the later seventeenth century, women's expert knowledge in gynaecology was being challenged by men. The aristocracy led the way in preference for a male *accoucheur*. During the eighteenth century, the increasingly confident medical practitioners in England and in France challenged the basis of women's knowledge. They emphasised the importance of professional training, usually at universities which were, at that period, closed to women. Increasingly, during the eighteenth century, men claimed to be the experts on women's bodies. Doctors' views of the female body as unstable encouraged them to associate women with **hysteria** and madness (see **madness, feminisation of**).

During the eighteenth and nineteenth centuries, the claims made by **science** to knowledge were shared by the men who practised gynaecology. Despite challenges from women as both midwives and patients, doctors increased their control over women. Medical intervention and hospitalisation increased during the nineteenth and twentieth centuries. Some women doctors have offered alternative ideas about child-birth, but governments in western Europe have generally supported the more conservative claims of the medical practitioners.

References and further reading

Marland, H. (ed.) (1993) *The Art of Midwifery. Early Modern Midwives in Europe*, London: Routledge.
Moscucci, O. (1990) *The Science of Women: Gynaecology and Gender in England*, Cambridge: Cambridge University Press.

PATRICIA CRAWFORD

gynaecology, medical

Gynaecology is a medical specialisation focusing on the physiology of the female **body** and reproductive health. Merging with obstetrics in the 1920s at a time when both fields were consolidating their economic and epistemic primacy over **midwifery** and other healing practices, gynaecology situated itself as the dominant authority on women's **health** from puberty to post-menopause. Reinforced by scientific and medical institutions whose interlinking research and practice created an atmosphere of authoritative knowledge, gynaecology expanded the medicalisation of women's bodies, particularly in the area of childbirth. By laying claim to scientific authority, gyneacologists were presumed to 'know' women's bodies.

Through the 1940s as pharmaceutical companies and research facilities highlighted the significance of hormones, gynaecologists played an important role in providing the link between research product (hormone therapies) and the target market (women) and in promulgating common notions of the body as hormonally-mediated. Gynaecologists were later conferred with the authority to determine biological sex and assign sex categories in the event of ambiguous or intersex identification. Their decisions were often conflated with efforts to reinforce traditional **gender roles**.

In the 1970s–80s, works such as Diana Scully's *Men Who Control Women's Health* articulated male bias in medical practice by focusing on the education and enculturation of gynaecologists. Gynaecological interventions such as episiotemies, ceasarean sections, hysterectomies and hormone replacement therapy for menopausal women were regarded as elements of social control and as means to assert patriarchal values by privileging procedures that enhanced women's roles as mother, caregiver and heterosexual mate or in the case of hysterectomy, discarded organs that were deemed to have served their primary function (see **menopause**; **patriarchy**; **heterosexuality**).

In her efforts to reclaim language from its phallocentric usage, Mary **Daly** assigned the term gynaecology to the practice of patriarchal professions that oversaw the diseases and surveillance of women's bodies. Emphasising the iatrogenic nature of gynaecology and its symbolic penetration of women, she invented the term gyn/ecology to refer to a woman-centred relational claim to the universe.

The publication of Boston Women's Health Collective's *Our Bodies, Ourselves* in 1976 was a watershed in the women's health movement, spurred on by women's dissatisfaction with gynaecology. The movement proffered a feminist critique of gynaecology and male visions of the body, and fostered a movement towards self-help and women-centred care.

In the 1990s, the feminist critique of gynaecology was closely linked with critiques of **science**, efforts to decentre expert knowledge, the deconstruction of ideas of a sexually-dichotomised body and the political economy of health.

See also: endocrinology; gynaecology, history of; menstruation, anthropological; menstruation, PMS, medical; reproduction

References and further reading

Oudshoorn, N. (1994) *Beyond the Natural Body*, London: Routledge.
Scully, D. (1980) *Men Who Control Women's Health*, Boston: Houghton Mifflin Company.
Sherwin, S. (ed.) (1998) *The Politics of Women's Health*, Philadelphia, PA: Temple University Press.

DENISE L. SPITZER

gynephobia

Gynephobia is a term coined by Adrienne **Rich** to refer to male fear and hatred of woman bonding. In her essay, 'Disloyal to Civilization', Rich confronts existing schisms between women: black and white, lesbian and heterosexual. She suggests that all women have a self-defining relationship with each other, elsewhere theorised as the **lesbian continuum**. But gynephobia diverts energies away from these connections, expressing itself in racist and heterosexist language. For Rich, women must end this false consciousness and become disloyal to civilisation (white capitalist **patriarchy**).

Rich's ideas can be criticised in the light of recent thinking on **difference**. For in asserting women's common difference from men, Rich's **cultural feminism** tends to erase irreducible differences within the category of women.

References and further reading

Rich, A. (1979) 'Disloyal to Civilization: Feminism, Racism, Gynephobia', in *On Lies, Secrets, and Silence: Selected Prose 1966–1978*, New York: W.W. Norton.

KWOK WEI LENG

gynocritics

Coined by Elaine **Showalter**, 'gynocritics' signifies the study of women writers. Focusing on history, genres, styles, themes, and structures of writing by women, it emphasises the importance of female perspectives, bringing women writers into the canon and analysis in terms of **gender roles**. Developing alongside female aesthetics, gynocritics

sought to interpret elements of authentic female experience in **women's writing**, often in opposition to unreliable and sexist male representations of female experience. Gynocritics has developed in many theoretical directions but shares a 'second-wave approach' to literary criticism (see **first-wave/second-wave feminism**). The first-wave critique, known as feminist reading, analysed the **misogyny** in books by men. Some see gynocritics' popularity within feminist literary criticism as short-lived. Others argue it offers a political agenda enabling **praxis** through which silenced voices become heard.

See also: aesthetics, feminist; feminism; literary theory, feminist

References and further reading

Showalter, E. (ed.) (1986) *The New Feminist Criticism: Essays on Women, Literature and Theory*, London: Virago.

KATE REED

Haraway, Donna

Donna Haraway's writings have been instrumental to a wide range of feminist debates about gender, race, nature and science, as well as to numerous questions of method and epistemology. Her first major publication, *Crystals, Fabrics and Fields: Metaphors of Organicism in Twentieth-Century Development Biology* (1976), was based on her doctoral thesis concerning the role of specific metaphors and analogies in the work of three early-twentieth-century embryologists. A two-part article in *Signs* in 1978 marked her extension of an interest in science as a cultural system into the feminist analysis of biopolitics. A prolific writer with a strikingly original voice, Haraway's major study of primatology, *Primate Visions: Gender, Race and Nature in the World of Modern Science*, became an instant classic when it was published in 1989. It has been followed by a collection of essays, *Simians, Cyborgs and Women: The Reinvention of Nature* (1991), and *Modest_Witness@ Second_Millienium.FemaleMan$^{©}$_Meets_OncoMouse^{TM}* (1997).

Following her best-known article, 'A Manifesto for Cyborgs: Science, Technology and Socialist Feminism in the 1980s', Haraway has become a leading theorist of the embodied and lively connections uniting human beings, animals, machines and the systems of knowledge and meaning through which they exist and are known. One of the most important concepts throughout Haraway's work is that of 'material-semiotic production' which, like the figure of the cyborg, describes the inextricability of meaning systems from the material worlds and bodies they structure, and are

structured by. This inextricability is most evident in how Haraway defines the cultural politics, or stakes, of identities and embodiment as 'world-making consequences'. Always for Haraway there is a politics of emergence and survival at stake in questions of whose worlds are authored into being, how, for whom, and at what cost to others. She is a prominent theorist of the ways in which forms of inequality work in and through one another, and she has extended this principle to include both animals and machines to an unprecedented degree.

Haraway is acutely attentive to the politics of knowledge production, and is well known for her concept of 'situated knowledges', by which she proposes an ethics of the knowing subject, and its limits. Her distinctive and excessive writing style comprises an essential, and controversial, aspect of her work, through which she has become increasingly autobiographical, and with which she seeks always to convey the specific density of the lives, bodies, selves and connections she describes with unforgettable passion and force.

Selected writings

Haraway, D. (1978a) 'Animal Sociology and a Natural Economy of the Body Politic, Part I: A Political Physiology of Dominance' *Signs* 4 (1): 21–36.

—— (1978b) 'Animal Sociology and a Natural Economy of the Body Politic, Part II: The Past is a Contested Zone: Human Nature and Theories of Production and Reproduction in Primate Behaviour Studies' *Signs* 4 (1): 37–60.

—— (1985) 'Manifesto for Cyborgs: Science,

Technology and Socialist Feminism in the 1980s' *Socialist Review* 80: 65–108.
—— (1989) *Primate Visions: Gender, Race and Nature in the World of Modern Science*, New York: Routledge.

SARAH FRANKLIN

Harding, Sandra G. (b. 1935)

Sandra Harding argues that starting thought from women's lives and the analyses of social life that they produce makes possible more accurate and comprehensive scientific and philosophical accounts, and can provide valuable resources for democratic social relations. Harding's work was important, first, in defining feminist epistemology and philosophy of science, and, later, in pursuing issues in these fields in multicultural and post-colonial contexts.

Her 1983 co-edited anthology, *Discovering Reality: Feminist Perspectives on Epistemology, Metaphysics, Methodology, and Philosophy of Science*, shows how feminist analyses are relevant even to the most abstract and 'value-neutral' knowledge projects – how they are selected, organised, and philosophically legitimated. Beginning in *The Science Question in Feminism* Harding conceptualises in influential, if controversial, ways the diverse array of feminist approaches to sciences and theories of knowledge. She argues for the importance of feminist standpoint epistemologies (see **standpoint theory**), which social theorists such as Nancy **Hartsock**, Hilary **Rose**, and Dorothy **Smith** were also developing, as a complement to feminist empiricist approaches (see **empiricism**). She points also to the significance of poststructuralist challenges to these epistemologies (see **poststructuralism/postmodernism**), and, later, to the ways in which elements of each approach are incorporated into the others. Her analysis of the importance of understanding **gender** as a structural and analytical category has also proved influential.

Harding's critics include some poststructuralists – who find her excessively faithful to Enlightenment philosophies or unwilling to face the deep incompatibility between standpoint theory and poststructuralism; and some empiricist philosophers – who accuse her of abandoning philosophy

for sociology of knowledge. Nevertheless, standpoint epistemology is influential as a research methodology and philosophy of science in many social science disciplines. It is valued because it brings to bear on fundamental research assumptions dissatisfactions with the sexist and andro-centric outcomes of research projects, and because it provides philosophical tools helpful to those concerned with political consequences of intellectual frameworks.

Is Science Multicultural? Postcolonialisms, Feminisms, and Epistemologies takes a standpoint outside the dominant conceptual frameworks in the west to examine the eurocentrism and androcentrism of standard histories and philosophies of science. Harding explains the epistemological consequences of European imperialism and colonialism and of contemporary Third World development concepts. She develops further here her accounts of 'strong **objectivity**', of the scientific and political dysfunctionality of universality claims for scientific knowledge, and of the ways to obtain more accurate and democratic models of knowers and knowledge-systems.

See also: epistemology, feminist

Selected writings

Harding, S.G. (1986) *The Science Question in Feminism*, Ithaca, NY: Cornell University Press.
—— (1991) *Whose Science? Whose Knowledge?*, Ithaca, NY: Cornell University Press.
—— (1998) *Is Science Multicultural?*, Bloomington, IN: Indiana University Press.

ANN GARRY

Hartsock, Nancy (b. 1943)

The publication of *Money, Sex and Power: Toward a Feminist Historical Materialism* (1983) by Nancy Hartsock was the definitive statement of feminist **Marxism** in the USA. Hartsock adapts Marx's theory of the standpoint of the proletariat in capitalist society to the position of women in patriarchal society. Marx had argued that the oppression of the proletariat allowed them to achieve an understanding of the underlying truth of social relations under capitalism; Hartsock argues that the oppression of women in patriarchal society provides them with a true understanding of patriarchy. Hartsock's goal is to define a distinctive theory of **power** for women. The realisation of this goal is the 'feminist standpoint' (see **standpoint theory**). Women in western capitalist societies are primarily concerned with the material reality of human lives: **reproduction**; the care and nurture of infants, the sick and the elderly; attending to daily bodily needs. Awakened consciousness of this material condition of women, Hartsock argues, allows them to achieve a feminist standpoint: an understanding of social reality that exposes the partiality and perversity of the ruling class of men. Specifically, the feminist standpoint allows women to identify the 'abstract **masculinity**' of ruling class men as a false universal and a distortion of social reality. Hartsock defines 'abstract masculinity', the basis of western **science** and logic, as the removal from the real, material world. It is at the same time the most highly valorised quality in western thought and defined in exclusively masculine terms.

As the question of differences among women came to the forefront in the 1980s, Hartsock adapted feminist standpoint theory by arguing that although women are not a monolithic group, that is, although they occupy different material situations in society, the ruling class (or 'centre') remains monolithic. At least in western societies, the ruling class has been and continues to be made up exclusively of white, upper-class men of property. It follows that despite the diversity of women the oppression and bias of the ruling class can still be exposed through the achievement of the feminist standpoint.

Hartsock's concern to develop a distinctively feminist theory of power has led her to strongly oppose the influence of **poststructuralism/ postmodernism** in feminist theory. Specifically, she has asserted that the poststructuralist theory of power advanced by Michel Foucault fails to provide an adequate theory of power for women. Postmodern/poststructuralist theories, she asserts, do not provide the systemic understanding of the world necessary for a feminist critique. She also rejects poststructuralism/postmodernism on the ground that it erases the concept of the subject just as women are beginning to define themselves as subjects.

See also: socialism and feminism

Selected writings

Hartsock, N. (1983) *Money, Sex, and Power: Toward a Feminist Historical Materialism*, New York: Longman.

—— (1990) 'Foucault on Power: A Theory for Women?', in L. Nicholson (ed.) *Feminism/Postmodernism*, New York: Routledge.

—— (1998) *Feminist Standpoint Revisited and Other Essays*, Boulder, CO: Westview.

SUSAN HEKMAN

health

Historically, medicine and **gender** have been inextricably interwoven and characterised by an ongoing struggle. For generations women were the predominant healers in the domestic economy and community. However from the witch hunts of the late fifteenth and early sixteenth centuries forward, there has been a consistent effort to unseat them. The arguments have changed but the struggle to suppress women healers and to disease women's normal bodily processes has remained remarkably consistent. Although these struggles often took place in a medical lexicon, at a deeper level they were about **power** and **privilege**. Given this history it is not surprising that health care has been a central concern in both waves of the women's movement, providing the grounds for political action and intellectual debate.

Ehrenreich and English (1972) document how the witch hunts in Europe united male university-trained physicians with male church leaders in a struggle for power and control. With church support, university-trained doctors became the only legitimate healers. They gained economic control as well as social and institutional powers, including the power to define health and illness and to delineate cultural assumptions about women. But women lost. Healing performed by women became a crime punishable by death, largely eliminating women healers, the real skills they provided and their voices in ideological struggles over the meaning of gender differences.

Although struggles in the USA lacked the violence of the witch hunts, the outcome was much the same. By the nineteenth century white men of the upper classes, using ties to other powerful men in foundations and government, were successful in making a university education the basis for a medical licence (Starr 1982). Since people of colour, lower class people, and women usually did not have access to a university education, they were denied a medical licence. These changes, like those occurring earlier, had a major impact on women, especially those from the lower classes and those of colour.

However at this time neither a medical license nor **race**, class and gender privilege ensured the capacity to cure. No one yet had a clear idea about how the physical body functioned (Stevens 1966). There was no medical science and technology as the western world now understands them. While two years of medical education were required for a degree, training lasted for only three or four months a year, the second year usually repeated the material of the first and the curriculum consisted of Latin as well as natural and experimental philosophy (Starr 1982). The lack of both medical knowledge and empirical skill produced an array of bizarre and dangerous treatments, leaving the door open for a variety of health care practitioners, including midwives, to continue practising, especially among urban poor immigrant populations and in rural areas (see **midwifery**). Although these practitioners might also lack an ability to cure, they usually had empirical skills and medical knowledge acquired through apprenticeship and their treatments were far less invasive and dangerous than those provided by the 'regular' doctors of this time.

This opening was soon narrowed (Reissman 1983). In the absence of superior skill, doctors had to convince the public that they had something to offer. Childbirth was a central arena in this struggle. If doctors could capture the childbirth market, especially the childbirths of well-to-do women, they would have a gateway to the families of those who could pay for care and from there to larger healing markets. To do so, doctors argued that a normal pregnancy was the exception not the rule, birth should be medically managed instead of allowed to proceed naturally and women should be sedated and freed from pain rather than being active participants in a natural, albeit difficult, process. Even without superior skills and often with poorer outcomes than midwives, doctors were still able to redefine birth as a pathological condition in need of medical management. With both technology and drugs under doctors' control, women's access to the health care market was further limited, their definitional power more muted and their choices increasingly structured.

This struggle for economic control and social and institutional power, when combined with the role that women's reproductive capacity played in the medical market, placed women at special risk. Ehrenreich and English (1973) argue that early on the diagnosis and treatment of women was structured by the belief that uterus and brain compete for energy. While lower class, and by implication non-white, women could both work for wages and reproduce, in upper class women education and the concomitant development of the brain were believed to atrophy the uterus. To accomplish their primary function, **reproduction**, these women were encouraged to give up their education and concentrate their energy on their wombs. In addition from the mid-nineteenth to the mid-twentieth century the medical profession took a pivotal role in both the decision to deny women contraception and abortions and later to legalise them again (Gordon 1977). In each case, they had a major role in delineating dominant cultural assumptions about women.

While feminist scholars agree that medicine and gender have a long and embattled history in which women healers were suppressed and women's bodies diseased, they disagree about how to analyse this relationship, what politics are involved and what practices could be most effectively employed. During the second wave of feminist scholarship these divisions were first expressed in terms of liberal, radical and Marxist feminism. Later socialist and postmodern feminism joined the discussion as did some attempts to bridge these categorical distinctions.

Fee (1983) lays out these early distinctions. In describing gendered inequities for providers and consumers of health care, liberal feminist scholarship first suggested that while women were primarily nurses, men dominated in the higher-status more lucrative medical profession (see **liberal feminism**). Today when many more women are entering the medical profession, men still dominate. Moreover the male bias first described in the practice of medicine – the contempt for women, their bodies and their minds – is still being documented today. The solution also remains the same: equal opportunity for women to enter the upper reaches of the job market and equal treatment once they get there. Here plurality politics is called for.

Radical feminist scholarship argues that medicine is just another institution which conforms to the pattern of the patriarchal family – doctor/father, nurse/mother, patient/child (see **radical feminism**). To resist this pattern, women need to uncover the truth about their oppression. **Consciousness-raising** uncovers the values which contain them and alternative institutions, often run cooperatively, support different values. Here the solution and the politics are separatist.

In marxist-feminist scholarship women's disadvantaged position as providers and consumers of health care is seen as useful to capitalism. Unpaid domestic labour in the family serves capitalism by maintaining and reproducing the labour force while providing a potential reserve army of women workers (see **reserve army of labour**). It also establishes a rationale to pay women less, dividing the labour force by gender while increasing profit margins. In addition these capitalist interests shape the way medicine diseases women's bodies, how biological functions such as reproduction are diagnosed and treated and how legislation, for example on contraception and abortion, is passed. Here women's victimisation is ended through political action which links the liberation of women to the rejection of capitalism and its replacement by democratic socialism.

Radical and Marxist scholarship are united in their rejection of liberal analyses. However, they disagree about whether gender or class is the primary oppression reflected in and reinforced by the inequities women experience in the health care system as well as about potential solutions and appropriate politics. For Marxists neither changing values nor having separate institutions is enough.

Economic structures have to change. To end this dispute socialist feminist scholars unite radical and Marxist concerns under one broader rubric which includes gender and class as well as economic structures, values and institutions (Jaggar 1983). However, by maintaining a commitment to **patriarchy** and capitalism, these scholars also leave intact the potential for women's victimisation.

Fisher (1995) reviews the postmodern feminist response and attempts to bridge the new distinctions they create. At its heart this response has a very different understanding of power. It does not flow in a top-down fashion from specific locations in the structural arrangements of society – capitalistic and/or patriarchal arrangements – and therefore is neither solely prohibitive nor repressive. It circulates in a local, continuous and productive manner and functions through numerous micropractices. If it is everywhere and in everyone, oppression and resistance can no longer be oppositional categories. Instead power is linked to and accompanied by resistance.

With power no longer held by one group, women are not passive victims of economic domination or patriarchal oppression. They are actively engaged in a politics of everyday life. Power and resistance are produced and dismantled in these mundane social practices, especially those occurring in institutional sites. Medicine is one such site. In it men and women struggle for institutional dominance while doctors and women patients do battle over definitions of health and illness and delineation of gendered and professional ideologies. These struggles disrupt the assumption that women, as a universal group, are objects of oppression and instead display how the category woman and notions of the body are constructed socially and discursively in relationship to other categories, and cross-cut by similarities and differences (see **difference**).

Postmodern feminist scholarship supplies a valuable critique and an expanded understanding of power, resistance and the production of meaning; however, some argue that it provides no way to consider how struggles might be coordinated and what kinds of change might be accomplished. Both Marxist and radical feminism do this by directing us to the social and historical conditions in which action and meaning, power and resistance are produced and deployed. Just as socialist feminism integrated two seemingly disparate positions, today some feminist scholars are moving toward an approach which integrates agency and conflict as well as the construction and deconstruction of cultural meanings and social action (see also Donna **Haraway** and Sandra **Harding**).

References and further reading

Ehrenreich, B. and English, D. (1972) *Witches, Midwives and Nurses: A History of Women Healers*, New York: Feminist Press.
—— (1973) *Complaints and Disorders: The Sexual Politics of Illness*, New York: Feminist Press.
Fee, E. (1983) 'Women and Health Care: A Comparison of Theories', in E. Fee (ed.) *Women and Health: The Politics of Sex in Medicine*, New York: Baywood Publishing Company.
Fisher, S. (1995) *Nursing Wounds: Nurse Practitioners, Doctors, Women Patients and the Negotiation of Meaning*, New Jersey: Rutgers University Press.
Gordon, L. (1977) *Woman's Body, Woman's Right: A History of Birth Control in America*, New York: Penguin Books.
Jaggar, A.M. (1983) *Feminist Politics and Human Nature*, New York: Rowman and Allanheld.
Reissman, C.K. (1983) 'Women and Medicalization', *Social Policy*, 14: 3–18.
Starr, P. (1982) *Social Transformation of American Medicine*, New York: Basic Books.
Stevens, R. (1966) *American Medicine in the Public Interest*, Hartford: Yale University Press.

SUE FISHER

hegemony

A concept derived from the work of Antonio Gramsci (1971), hegemony refers to a form of dominance which legitimates and secures the position of the ruling class based on the consent of those ruled. This form of dominance does not require coercion through the use of naked force but is constructed and sustained largely through ideological means which represent the interests of the ruling class as universally fair, and in the best interests of the society at large.

Although Gramsci did not specifically refer to any gender issue, and in fact concentrated his discussion of women within domestic and sexual activity vis-à-vis the economic realm, hegemony has become an important tool for feminist analyses of patriarchy.

For feminists, the question of women's collusion in what can be seen as an unequal or exploitative relationship is interlinked with the ideology of a ruling sex in both the public and the private spheres: why do women acquiesce to patriarchal practices, and how are these practices cultivated and reproduced? A landmark text by Michèle Barrett (1980) proposes that psychoanalytic theory could shed tremendous insight into the material conditions in which female consciousness is formed. She also argues that women's passivity is constructed and it is through various ideological apparatuses, i.e. schools, churches, the family, that gender roles are structured and maintained. While Barrett's materialist theory of gender ideology has been criticised for her failure to identify biological, specific socio-historical, and geographical locations, her work raises crucial questions regarding arguments pertaining to cultural contexts.

The feminist movement too has been criticised for its own hegemonic stand in ignoring the inherent class/status, race/ethnic (even nationalist) and sex/gender differences among women. Criticisms directed at simplistic dichotomies such as public/private, man/woman have turned feminist studies to acknowledge more complex socio-cultural realities which constitute gender identities and relations.

The development and popularity of feminist cultural studies has lately problematised hegemony particularly within poststructuralist and postmodernist theories. Understood usually within Marxist ideas of false consciousness and class struggle, hegemony has been criticised as being reductionist since it presupposes a social reality that offers a universally true condition for all women. The popularity of discourse analysis especially within Michel Foucault's power/knowledge axis has prompted the re-examining of how women manage their worlds, and what constitutes them as acting subjects. A seemingly passive stand has little to do with a dominant and exploitative patriarchal ideology, and more with a position of negotiation and resistance.

While hegemony offers an important analytical tool to interrogate the workings of gender ideology, it is ultimately an abstraction which provides generalised explanations to the specificities of women's lives.

See also: contextualism; cultural identities; cultural theory/cultural studies, feminist; difference; discourse analysis; ideology; Marxism; patriarchy; positionality; poststructualism/postmodernism; power; psychoanalysis

References and further reading

Barrett, M. (1980) *Women's Oppression Today*, London: Verso.

Gramsci, A. (1971) *Selection from the Prison Notebooks of Antonio Gramsci*, ed. and trans. Q. Hoare and G. Nowell-Smith. New York: International Publishers.

Pryzybylowicz, D. (1990) 'Towards a Feminist Cultural Criticism: Hegemony and Modes of Social Division', *Cultural Critique* No. 14 Winter 1989–1990: 259–301.

YOKE-SUM WONG

Heilbrun, Carolyn G. (b. 1926)

Carolyn G. Heilbrun urges that women develop strong, autonomous selves, not bound by the marriage-centred 'romance plot' but motivated by the achievement-centred 'quest plot' (see **autonomy**). Such a plot demands a revised notion of marriage (based on **friendship** not lust), of female friendship (based on collaboration not competition), and of ageing (to be embraced not feared).

As critic, Heilbrun's first important book was *Toward a Recognition of Androgyny* (1973), in which she introduces the notion of **androgyny** as a solution to the problem of socially constructed **gender** roles. Accused of basing her ideas on literary abstractions rather than on social realities, and of perpetuating rather than erasing gender stereotypes, Heilbrun then wrote *Reinventing Womanhood* (1979), a more pragmatic account of the ways women might imitate male achievement patterns

while resisting cooptation as 'token women'. Heilbrun's most influential book is *Writing a Woman's Life* (1988), which convincingly argues that biographies of women should be structured in accordance with a recognition of what elements make achievement possible. Heilbrun distills her theory in a biography of Gloria **Steinem** (1995), but her admiring account of Steinem's public activism and her failure to tease out the complexities of Steinem's private life have produced a cool critical reception. Heilbrun's autobiographical *The Last Gift of Time* (1997) captures key experiences of Heilbrun's seventh decade.

Under the pseudonym Amanda Cross, Heilbrun revived the feminist detective novel, inspiring a new wave of contemporary feminist crime writers, with her urbane, independent protagonist, Kate Fansler, amateur sleuth and professor of literature at a prestigious New York City university (see **detective fiction, women's**). What characterises this popular series are the intertextual literary allusions and the transformations of Fansler, who becomes increasingly feminist in her negotiation of the culture wars and her battles against the crimes of patriarchal academic institutions (see **patriarchy**).

Some critics complain that Carolyn Heilbrun focuses on privileged white women, that she urges an uncritical adoption of male models of action, and that her work is insufficiently theoretical. Nevertheless, one of the few members of her generation to be influenced by feminism, Heilbrun provides an important record of her own feminist evolution, exhorts women to claim public power, and reaches a wide audience through her lucid, accessible prose.

Selected writings

Cross, A. (1981) *Death in a Tenured Position*, New York: Dutton.

Heilbrun, G. (1988) *Writing a Woman's Life*, New York: Norton.

References and further reading

Kress, S. (1997) *Carolyn G. Heilbrun, Feminist in a*

Tenured Position, Charlottesville, VA: University Press of Virginia.

SUSAN KRESS

hemisphere specialisation studies

The cerebral cortex is the outer area of the brain associated with higher cognitive functions. It is anatomically divided into a right and left hemisphere. Hemisphere specialisation studies investigate how the hemispheres may differ. Post-mortem studies investigate differences in structure, and studies of the live brain investigate differences in function using positron emission technology (PET) and magnetic resonance imaging (MRI). The left hemisphere is associated with language, and the right with visuospatial processing and emotion. However, these complex processes involve component tasks, some of which are localised in the opposite hemisphere.

Some live-brain studies of men and women performing the same specific tasks have indicated brain activity in both hemispheres for women, and brain activity more lateralised in one hemisphere for men. This, along with a few structural findings, suggests women may have more inter-hemispheric connectivity. Or, women and men may have been socialised to perform the tasks in different ways.

See also: split brain theory

References and further reading

Blum, D. (1997) *Sex on the Brain*, New York: Viking.

JESSICA SENEHI

hermeneutics

Hermeneutics is a theory of interpretion of texts or events. Hermeneutics (Greek *hermeneutikos*/interpreting, from Hermes/messenger of the gods) was originally developed around biblical disciplines, but has come to mean historical and cultural rather than strictly theological inquiry. Sometimes hermeneutic inquiry has aimed at recapturing the correct meaning of a text, and sometimes at establishing the precise intent of an author.

Feminist theory has been strongly influenced by the hermeneutic approach of Karl Marx, Sigmund Freud, Jürgen Habermas, and others. They employ a hermeneutics of suspicion, tearing away misleading appearances in order to reveal the underlying reality that has been distorted but not destroyed by the disguises that cover it. Hermeneuticists generally assume that there is a truth that can be discovered by proper inquiry, that knowing can at least to some extent apprehend being. A fully developed hermeneutic seeks a 'big picture' of the world, one that fully represents and accounts for its subject. Hermeneutic inquiry is generally subject-centred, relying on the clarified self-understanding of individuals or groups to penetrate the ideological masks that cloud knowledge: for example, workers utilising a Marxist hermeneutic can penetrate the free market ideology masking capitalism's oppressive class relations. Hermeneutic inquiry often searches for the origins of knowledge practices, and relies on conceptual unities such as the proletariat, women, or the west in order to compare them with the bourgeoise, men, or the Third World. Hermeneutic inquiry often finds the resources for imagining a better society in the experiences and perspectives of the oppressed.

Feminist standpoint theory inherits much of its analytic energies from hermeneutics. Nancy **Hartsock** uses a hermeneutics of suspicion to go beyond the surface of social relations and reveal the real practices of power beneath them. Nancy Fraser also connects political economy to gender analysis, analysing the production of cultural hegemonies (see **hegemony**) and the possibilities for emancipatory social change. Seyla **Benhabib** draws resources from Habermas to inquire into feminist reconstructions of public space. The power of feminist hermeneutics is partly in its ability to constitute 'women' as a more or less unified category of analysis, and to critique patriarchy in the name of women's point of view. Feminist hermeneutics also offers positive visions of a more liberated society that can anchor movements for social change. Many feminists are searching for connections between the political vision provided by feminist hermeneutics and genealogical attention to the limits of our categories.

References and further reading

Benhabib, S. (1995) *Feminist Contentions*, New York: Routledge.

Fraser, N. (1997) *Justice Interruptus*, New York: Routledge.

Hartsock, N. (1983) *Money, Sex and Power*, New York: Longman.

KATHY E. FERGUSON

heroines

Feminist critics have instigated an exhilarating demythologising process which has worked to reveal the gender bias of the heroic narrative and the way in which negative representations of women are necessary to the successful functioning of patriarchal culture. It is through their inter-rogatory practices that feminists have opened up a space for the reappraisal and reinvention of the heroine. The constant denigration of women and of the feminine divine would initially appear to negate the possibility of strong, autonomous heroines. Patriarchal mythology focuses most prominently on heroes, whilst female experience is generally silenced, yet ironically, the hero's tale is told as if it were universally representative of human experience. Moreover, damaging feminine archetypes deriving from myth find their way with monotonous regularity into male-authored texts. Unsurprisingly, the heroine's fate in such works frequently remains one of rape, madness or death. Largely due to feminist critiques and creativity, however, these negative heroines are being dis-placed by bolder, more wilful, role models.

Perhaps the most interesting heroines to emerge in feminist works thus far are those that may be termed grotesque heroines, heroines who have the power to actually break up the existing order. This is a case of feminism confronting patriarchy with female monstrosity on its own terms. In this way, the grotesque female archetype/form becomes a source of power and regeneration, heralding the birth of new (sexual) identities beyond the limiting binary oppositions which sustain western metaphy-sical thought. Medusa, for instance, who in patriarchal mythology has embodied men's deepest fears of women, is re-presented in Hélène **Cix-**

ous's famous feminist essay 'The Laugh of the Medusa', as a liberated and liberating heroine. Cixous's Medusa is a utopian image of the return of the repressed who is not deadly but beautiful. She is a realisation of female power and suppressed desire, a joyous figure who celebrates a moment of becoming, and whose laugh signals new possibi-lities as it undoes past restraints.

See also: divine feminine; fairy tales; Goddess; narrative, feminist uses of; Other, the and feminism

References and further reading

Carter, A. (1993) *Wayward Girls and Wicked Women*, London: Virago.

Cixous, H. (1981) 'The Laugh of the Medusa', in E. Marks and I. de Courtivron (eds) *New French Feminisms*, London: Harvester Wheatsheaf.

Powers, M.A. (1991) *The Heroine in Western Literature*, North Carolina: McFarland.

Russo, M. (1994) *The Female Grotesque: Risk, Excess and Modernity*, London: Routledge.

TESSA KELLY

heteroglossia

Heteroglossia (Mikaïl Bakhtin) is the multiplicity of discursive strands, each with their own social provenance, in any linguistic utterance, specifically the novel. This view breaks with the monolithic, monological equation one speaker/one utterance, which defines dialogue as taking turns speaking without considering power relations and more diffuse voices.

Instead, Bakhtin proposes that words have a memory. The context that has accrued to any discursive unit – word, sentence, plot, tone – sticks to it when it is recycled in another context. Hence, sterotypes, opinions, disparaging meanings cannot be disavowed by claiming 'I didn't mean it that way'. Even a high-literary novel or film featuring a male/female relationship based on the idealisation of the one and the condescendence of the other, cannot prevent the Cinderella-plot from resonating with its own.

Distinguishing among Bakhtin's plethora of

terms and concepts offers a guideline for a feminist and anti-racist analysis of texts and artifacts.

Heterogeneity, heterodox, heteroglossia: three related terms that Bakhtin and his followers use, all coined with the Greek root *hetero-*, meaning 'other'. Heterogeneity has 'genus', kind: different kinds, different in kind. Heterodoxy has -doxa: common opinion; hence: deviating from standard assumptions: ideological diversity. Heteroglossia has glossia: language. The social modality of discourse is to be involved in, and composed of, a variety (hetero-) of discourses (glossia).

Bakhtinian cultural analysts today interested in feminist and postcolonial analysis like to use the idea of the 'migration' of concepts implied in Bakhtin's philosophy. The term now refers to the global postcolonial condition of contemporary societies. This reference teaches us what to avoid in and what to expect of concepts. The notion of 'internal exile' helps transform our tendency to 'apply' concepts like tools provided by a master-discourse or -discipline, making room for what is cast aside even within the artifact.

The pair dialogue/dialogism expresses the difference between Bakhtinian and structuralist views of language. The formal, technical condition of turn-taking speech (dialogue) only reflects the more general condition of social speech (dialogism). Dialogism is the use of speech that results in polyphony.

Polyphony refers to a plurality (poly-) of voices (phony): as a consequence of the inherent dialogism of speech, the reader 'hears' many voices within a single utterance. Heteroglossia is the social aspect of the phenomenon of which dialogism is the linguistic aspect. The term refers to group-bound speech and establishes a relation between the use of language and relations of power.

References and further reading

Bakhtin, M. (1981) *The Dialogic Imagination*, edited by Michael Holquist, trans. Caryl Emerson and Michael Holquist, Austin, Texas: Texas University Press.
Hirschkop, Ken and David Shepherd (eds) (1989)

Bakhtin and Cultural Theory, Manchester and New York: Manchester University Press.

MIEKE BAL

heteropatriarchy

Heteropatriarchy ensures male right of access to women. Women's relations – personal, professional, social, economic – are defined by the ideology that woman is for man. Heteropatriarchy is men dominating and de-skilling women in any of a number of forms, from outright attack to paternalistic care, and women devaluing (of necessity) female bonding. Hetereopatriarchy normalises the dominance of one person and the subordination of another. Carol **Pateman** argues that social contract establishes men's political right over women and orderly access by men to women's bodies.

The logic of heteropatriarchy includes the invisibility of lesbians, the construction and tolerance of dominant male violence together with intolerance of female violence against abusers, blaming the 'feminine' victim, and targeting a group of men as predators against whom dominant men can 'protect' chosen women, most notably in peace-time USA, black men.

See also: heterosexism, heteronormativity; sexism

References and further reading

Pateman, C. (1988) *The Sexual Contract*, Stanford, CA: Stanford University Press.

SARAH LUCIA HOAGLAND

heterosexism, heteronormativity

Heterosexism is discrimination against lesbians and gays. A father raping his daughter or a man killing his wife are legally tolerated in ways men having sex with men and women loving women are not. Understanding heterosexism involves understanding how women are defined in terms of men or not at all, how lesbians and gays are scapegoated as perverts.

In 1975 the Dutch lesbian feminist Purple September staff named heteronormativity an instrument perpetuating power. Both lesbian feminists and queer theorists address the compulsory nature of heterosexuality (see **lesbian feminism; queer theory**). However, 1990s queer theorists focused on transgression and deviance while lesbian feminists focused on structural analysis. The difference: lesbian feminists regard a heterosexual man buying a prostitute as normative heterosexuality, queer theorists could regard it as transgressive/progressive.

See also: heteropatriarchy; homophobia

References and further reading

Rich, A. (1980) 'Compulsory Hetereosexuality and Lesbian Existence', *Signs* 5 (4).
Schutte, O. (1997) 'Critique of Normative Heterosexuality', *Hypatia* 12 (1).

SARAH LUCIA HOAGLAND

heterosexuality

Few topics have aroused such passionate contention as that of 'heterosexuality'. Yet, '**sexuality**' only makes its appearance in the *Oxford English Dictionary* after 1800, and the notion of sexual types of people, the 'homosexual', and the 'heterosexual', make their appearance even later – at the close of the nineteenth century. This is also the time of the 'first-wave' of organised feminism and, interacting with it, the rise of sexology and psychoanalysis. Many first-wave feminists saw men's sexual behaviour with women as a scourge on womanhood, spreading disease and degradation. Others argued for women's sexual rights and pleasures. Second-wave feminists, emerging at the close of the 1960s, would prove no less divided. At first, like Germaine **Greer**, they embraced notions of sexual liberation, and fought for women's sexual autonomy, rejecting the comprehensively androcentric language and sexist practices of their day (see **androcentrism**). They wanted to construct new definitions of 'the

sex act' unfettered by notions of male activity and female passivity. Soon, however, some feminists criticising dominant notions of heterosexuality began to focus upon the political significance of what they saw as the erasure of lesbian consciousness in women's experience. In an influential essay in 1980, Adrienne **Rich** introduced the notion of 'compulsory heterosexuality', described as a key institution for undermining the 'woman-identified' consciousness necessary for building 'female power'. Simultaneously, feminists were highlighting the prevalence of rape and men's routine sexual harassment of women while, like Susan Brownmiller, beginning to target male sexuality as the overriding cause of women's oppression. From the close of the 1970s one forceful strand of radical feminism, spearheaded by Andrea **Dworkin** and Catharine **MacKinnon** (equating the traditional patriarchal symbolic with the experiential dynamics of sexuality), declared genital heterosexuality an encounter in which women are ineluctably positioned as colonised and subordinated. Other feminists (see Segal 1994), while deconstructing normative conceptions of heterosexuality, and the symbolic equations securing 'masculinity' and 'femininity' to sexual 'activity' and 'passivity', rejected the misleading reductionism in such equations. Gender hierarchy, they argue, does not reduce to sexuality; nor does sexual experience simply mirror normative gender codings. Through appropriations of Foucault, and the emergence of 'queer theory', some feminists, like Judith **Butler**, argue that we should be working to disrupt and resignify the symbolic and material effects of these oppressive equations binding gender to sexuality, which encourage (though far from secure) phallocentric codes of normative heterosexuality, alongside the cultural repudiation of homosexuality. This would allow feminists the space, once again, to develop a radical sexual politics which stresses the importance of women's sexual agency.

References and further reading

Butler, J. (1990) *Gender Trouble*, London: Routledge.
Segal, L. (1994) *Straight Sex: Rethinking Heterosexuality and The Politics of Pleasure*, London: Virago.

LYNNE SEGAL

hidden curriculum

A hidden curriculum consists of the learned, although not openly intended, outcomes or byproducts of schools or nonschool settings. No special subject matter need characterise these outcomes, nor are the outcomes restricted to one kind of learning. They can be worldviews, character traits, cognitive states, emotions, attitudes, values. They can be important, trivial, praiseworthy, abhorrent. It is often assumed that hidden curricula are everywhere the same. Since, however, a hidden curriculum is always of some setting, at some time, and belonging to some person or group of people, empirical research is needed to determine what, if any, variation exists across settings, time, and populations.

In general, a hidden curriculum is not something one just finds. One must hunt for it. This is what feminist researchers began doing in the early 1970s. Their studies of social practices and examinations of school readers, math books, history texts, and the like unearthed the hidden curriculum of school and society in **gender** role stereotypes and **sexism**. The subsequent discovery of a chilly coeducational classroom climate for girls and women added vital details to our knowledge of the gendered hidden curriculum of both higher and lower **education** (see **chilly climate**). And research on the sexual harassment of girls and women at all levels of schooling has since uncovered a hidden curriculum in misogyny. Because the liberal curriculum's content derives from the disciplines of knowledge, feminist discoveries about the **androcentrism** of those scholarly fields are also discoveries about higher education's gendered hidden curriculum. Indeed, because women have culturally and historically been assigned primary responsibility for child-rearing and the other occupations associated with domestic environments, the neglect and devaluation of women's lives, experiences, and works teaches lessons not only in gender bias but in a full-blown anti-domesticity.

The importance to feminist theories of both the concept of a hidden curriculum and research into the gendered hidden curriculum of school and society can scarcely be exaggerated. How can feminist dreams of a better world be achieved when school and society are bearers of a hidden curriculum in gender-bias, anti-domesticity, and misogyny? Hidden curricula are notoriously difficult to eradicate. One task facing feminist theories is to integrate research on hidden curricula into their respective frameworks. Another is to decide what to do with the gendered hidden curriculum of school and society now that feminist scholars have found it.

References and further reading

Frazier, N. and Sadker, M. (1973) *Sexism in School and Society*, New York: Harper and Row.

Martin, J.R. (1994) *Changing the Educational Landscape*, New York: Routledge, chapter 8.

—— (2000) *Coming of Age in Academe*, New York: Routledge.

Sandler, B.R., Silverberg, L.A. and Hall, R.M. (1996) *The Chilly Classroom Climate*, Washington, DC: National Association for Women in Education.

JANE ROLAND MARTIN

hierarchical models of decision making

Since feminism is simultaneously political theory and political practice, questions of how to organise and make decisions are critical. Hierarchy is central to patriarchy: top-down authority, chain of command, separation of manual and mental labour, inequalities of power and reward, and formal systems of record keeping are organisational strategies perpetuating male dominance, class inequality and **white privilege (race privilege)**. Hierarchy is so familiar within modern life that it is readily naturalised; feminists politicise hierarchy by telling its history and exploring alternatives. Feminists seek organisational models that are egalitarian, participatory and integrated, more based on the image of the web than the pyramid. Yet feminists have also acknowledged that working within established institutions often requires accomodating hierarchy. The tension between democratic and hierarchical processes of decision making continues to trouble feminists because we live both inside and outside established institutions.

References and further reading

Feree, M. and P. Martin (eds) (1995) *Feminist Organizations*, Philadelphia, PA: Temple University Press.

KATHY E. FERGUSON

Hinduism

Hinduism has affected women's lives by officially legitimating only one norm – that of the 'good' wife (which implies **motherhood**). The restrictions created by this norm have led to both exceptions and reforms. Traditional Hindu wives have used their power (*śakti*; *śrī*) – both natural (the ability to generate life) and cultural (the ability to increase power through yogic-like vows) – to regulate the reproductive and intergenerational cycles at the heart of the life process (see **reproduction**); to provide prosperity, a better rebirth, or heaven for themselves and others; and to maintain the kingdom and cosmos. In the past, kings understood their own power (*ksatra*) in connection with dominion, wealth, prosperity, good fortune, and splendour as nothing other than *śrī* with its invisible aspects of vigour, greatness, auspiciousness, truth, life, longevity, and immortality and its visible manifestations as milk, food, progeny, water and cattle. Women's righteous use of their power is *strī-dharma*; their *dharma*, in turn, contributes to an ordered universe (*rta*).

After the sixth century BCE, the bodies of some men had become marginalised due to urbanisation (which meant that size and strength were no longer important) leading to fear or jealousy of women's nature and culture even as they tapped its plenitude for their own benefit. They tried to compensate culturally for their marginalisation by the following: (1) viewing women's menstrual blood as impure (representing a dead, and therefore polluting, foetus); (2) transforming the religious spheres of sacrifice and Vedic education – which had once been cooperative activities – into ones almost exclusively masculine; (3) demeaning wi-dows as inauspicious women (who had not generated enough good karma through their vows, causing their husbands to die prematurely) and consigning them to an austere life within the extended family; (4) conversely, acknowledging as auspicious the nature of women who raised their husbands from death to win heaven for them both through the additional power generated by their self-immolation (widow burning; suttee), thereby encouraging these acts; (5) reserving for themselves *saṃnyāsa* (renunciation of marriage and wandering alone) and claiming that it was the only way to achieve salvation (*mokṣa*) in this life (though few would try); (6) ensuring that daughters, wives, and mothers were economically dependent on them by not allowing them to work for pay and by not giving them inheritance; (7) relegating women to the private realm (which sometimes took the form of seclusion) and keeping the public one for themselves; (8) demanding dowries from the bride's family, which contributed to son-preference and bride burning; (9) allowing widowers but not widows to remarry; (10) instituting child marriage to ensure the chastity of potential wives; and (11) permitting men to marry more than one wife, even lower-caste women, but not allowing women to do the same thing. With these developments, women's lives became structured by the oppositions of auspiciousness (*śubha*) and inauspiciousness (*aśubha*) – symbolised by the presence or absence respectively of a dot on the forehead – as well as pure (*śauca*) and impure (*aśauca*). In times of stress (such as periods of foreign rule), the negative pole was exploited to create extreme male **dominance**, a cultural antidote to men's loss of political power (in addition to their loss of physical relevance). Both the creation and the exploitation of the negative pole constitute Hinduism's version of 'patriarchy'.

Reforms of these customs escalated during the colonial period. But in times of both reaction and reform, Hindu women themselves have quietly maintained their vows and have taken pride in their identity. Mahatma Gandhi derived many of his strategies for nonviolence, to end British rule, from their unassuming spiritual power. This linked nationalism to gender (see **nationalism and gender**). After Indian independence in 1947, Hindu women increasingly asserted themselves in the world beyond the home, thanks to education, work, and law reform. But even before this, there had been independent Hindu women whose lives were not confined or even defined by family ideology – working tribal, low-caste and 'outcaste' women; courtesans (*veśyas*); literary figures (*gaṇikas*); military heroines and queens (*vīrāganās*); devotional saints (*bhaktas*); temple dancers (*devadāsīs*), ascetics (*yoginīs*); and spiritual-sexual adepts (*tāntrikas*). It is striking that despite insistence on domestic norms in Hindu society, the roles of these exceptional women, though theoretically illegitimate, have nevertheless been eulogised after the fact. In this way, the rule and the exception both have found their place in the **diversity** of Hinduism.

See also: bride/widow burning (suttee burial); chastity, critique of

References and further reading

Altekar, A.S. (1978) *The Position of Women in Hindu Civilisation from Prehistoric Times to the Present Day*, Delhi: Motilal Banarsidass.

Gupta, A.R. (1976) *Women in Hindu Society: A Study of Tradition and Transition*, New Delhi: Jyotsna Prakashan.

Hejib, A. and Young, K.K. (1988) 'Sati, Widowhood and Yoga' in A. Sharma (ed.) *Sati: Historical and Phenomenological Essays*, Delhi: Motilal Banarsidass.

Jacobson, D. and Wadley, S.S. (1977) *Women in India: Two Perspectives*, New Delhi: Manohar.

Leslie, I.J. (1989) *The Perfect Wife: The Orthodox Hindu Woman According to the Stridharmapaddhati of Tryambakayajvan*, Delhi: Oxford University Press.

Narayanan, V. (1999) 'Brimming with Bhakti, Embodiments of Shakti: Devotees, Deities, Performers, Reformers, and Other Women of Power in the Hindu Tradition' in A. Sharma and K.K. Young (eds) *Feminism and World Religions*, Albany, NY: State University of New York Press.

Shastri, S.R. (1969) *Women in the Vedic Age*, Bombay: Bharatiya vidya Bhavan.

Tharu, S.J. and Lalilta, K. (eds) (1991) *Women Writing in India: 600 BC to the Present*, New York: Feminist Press at the City University of New York.

Young, K.K. (1987) 'Women in Hinduism' in Arvind Sharma (ed.) *Women in World Religions*, Albany, NY: State University of New York Press.

—— (1993) 'Women in Hinduism' in A. Sharma (ed.) *Today's Woman in World Religions*, Albany, NY: State University of New York Press.

KATHERINE K. YOUNG

history

The writing of history is a political act. By their choice of subject and the evidence examined, historians construct an account of the past which seeks to explain what they understand to be important in the present. What the historian considers to be 'the past' involves selection and choice, and therefore is always implicitly, and sometimes explicitly, contested. For feminist historians (see **history, feminist**), the absence of women has been central to their critique of the narratives which have been constructed to obscure the position of women and to justify the inequalities which women experience in societies today. **Gender** is a central category of explanation deployed in feminist historical scholarship, and constitutes one of the major differences between it, and what has been called malestream history (see **malestream thought**). Apart from feminist history, there are many varieties of historical scholarship reflecting the major intellectual influences of the times at which they were written. The writing of history by and about women has occurred within, against and beyond this broader, complex historiographical framework.

In the nineteenth century, historians believed that they should write of the 'great men' whose deeds had shaped the past. They sought to equate their work with that of the scientists, and argued that they were simply examining the evidence and recounting the story 'as it really was'. The claims to **objectivity** and scientific standards of truth were enunciated by the German historian Leopold von Ranke and the school of historical **positivism** in the nineteenth century. Their scholarly monographs worked to privilege perspectives of the powerful, the visible, the articulate and the literate in history, whose lives were abundantly documented in verifiable evidence. Positivists eschewed notions of historical causation, insisting that the historian's role was not to pass judgement. The early historical profession was composed almost exclusively of white, middle-class men whose selections of 'facts' and definition of history clearly bore the hallmarks of their own position within the patriarchal west (see **patriarchy**). Their public profession of 'legitimate' history as value-free severely undermined the development of history as a critical and self-reflexive discipline. The positivist tradition has been so influential that some historians, even at the end of the twentieth century, still have difficulty with the notion that their interpretations are subjective.

History writing over the past century has developed in many directions, with historians adopting different frameworks of explanation and historical causation.

The *Annales* school which developed in France in the early twentieth century rejected positivist narrative history and focused instead on 'total history'. Led by Lucien Febvre and Marc Bloch, *Annales* historians investigated landscape, climate, family structure, *mentalités*, and economic trends. Through their research about multiple interrelationships between these factors, they sought to explain the patterns and conjunctures of the past. Historian Susan Stuard among others has critiqued their androcentric bias (see **androcentrism**): *Annales* history was skewed towards male activities. *Annalistes'* research about women was usually interpreted through the trope of domesticity (see **domesticity, cult of**), while gender remained under-interrogated as a socially constructed category. Although some *Annales* historians were fascinated with lives of individual women, such as Joan of Arc and Marguerite of Navarre, the biographies they wrote were highly conventional.

Marxist historians seek to explain the past through the dynamic of class struggle. Power obtains for those who own the means of production. Thus in the period before about 1500, the feudal power of the landlords was dominant. During the period 1500–1800, the feudal order and the old monarchies were overturned by middle classes who had developed their wealth during the process of **industrialisation**. Under modern industrial capitalism, the middle class owns the means of production while the working class has nothing but it's labour. Some Marxist histories have usefully focused on the politics, culture and experiences of the working class, and, influenced by Marxist feminism, have debated the significance of domestic labour within production. However, a limitation of many Marxist perspectives, identified by Joan **Scott** and others, has been a tendency to devalue the role of **reproduction**, as well as production, in the construction and maintenance of capitalism. Moreover, women's position in the class structure has often been viewed as deriving from their fathers or husbands.

Psychohistory has offered very different approaches to the causes and course of historical change. Some psychohistorians have concentrated on psychoanalytic explanations of prominent individuals, such as Martin Luther or Mahatma Gandhi. Others have focused on explaining collective mentalities, and investigated how children were socialised in particular societies. Their answers have varied according to the different bodies of psychoanalytic theories being employed, including, although by no means limited to, Freudian psychoanalytic models. Most psychohistorians have posited crucial links between childhood, and both individual and collective psyche throughout history. Other historians have been sceptical about the application of psychoanalytic concepts, some arguing that those frameworks assume an ahistorical, universal psychoanalytic theory, particularly in studies of the mass psychology of fascism (see **fascism, women and**), and in histories of childhood.

With the expansion of social history from the 1960s in particular, several new methodologies were developed. Some of these appeared to hold promise in that they involved more specific and overt recognition of women, but that recognition at times has remained at the level of simple description, rather than enabling more critical historical analysis. Historical demography, for example, is the study of the details about birth, marriages and deaths in the past, usually termed fertility and mortality. Historical demographers have not on the whole adopted a feminist perspective to interrogate the contemporary meanings and implications of the categories used (such as the category 'bastard' for the 'illegitimate' child in Europe well into the twentieth century). Further, because demographers' methodology depends upon parish records, the male surname is used to trace and define the family. More positively, historical demography does enable the comparison of fertility and mortality over time. Demographers have calculated intervals between births, important both to some women's life experiences and to the history of population growth.

Some historians have also engaged in partial borrowings and perspectives from other disciplines. Ethnohistory, for example, has a methodology strongly influenced by cultural anthropologists such as Clifford Geertz (see **anthropology**). Geertz argues that by a technique of 'thick description' of events, the cultural life of a society, and its systems of shared meaning, can be uncovered. The methodology has been used particularly for the history of societies where the only written sources have been generated by observers from other cultures, as for example, by missionaries in the Pacific. In some cases, observation of the 'ethnographic present' of the society which interests historians may be used to supplement the written records. Forms of anthropological observation again, however, have been critiqued for their androcentricity. Nevertheless, feminist ethnographic historians, like other historians aware of gender, have aimed to more subtly interrogate the evidence about the actions of people in the past for its revelations about shared culture.

In many societies, the bulk of surviving records have been created by those with power. In an attempt to find evidence about the lives of ordinary people, historians have embarked on oral interviews. **Oral history** methodologies create source material which may in turn be interrogated as is any other source: who created the material, and for what purpose? An emphasis upon the spoken rather than written word, and the 'evidence of experience', have both been useful approaches when adapted to a feminist historical methodology.

From the 1980s, some historians have adopted the tools or perspectives of poststructuralism in historical analysis (see **poststructuralism/postmodernism**). Poststructuralism posits the centrality of language in creating social meaning, and is concerned with the ways in which power and knowledge are circulated and contested within discourse. Conventionally, Michel Foucault is cited

as the theorist who has been most influential in bringing poststructuralism to the attention of historians, although clearly his work developed in a much broader context in which feminists and other scholars were posing similar questions about the direction and status of historical knowledge. Poststructuralist approaches within history are hotly contested. Some argue that a focus on discourse (see **discourse analysis**) obscures material relations, and that the assumption of a discursively constructed subject erases historical agency. Others claim that poststructuralism is so at odds with existing methodologies and approaches that its wide adoption must lead to the end of history 'as we know it'. Alternatively, postmodernist (see **poststructuralism/postmodernism**) views, that traditional disciplinary and epistemological boundaries have worked consistently to exclude historically marginalised groups, have been taken up more positively by a number of historians, working with poststructuralism to destabilise the parameters of more traditional history.

Against a complex background then, feminist history has developed and diversified from the late 1960s to the present. Mounting a significant challenge to the hegemonic character of much historical writing (see **hegemony**), feminist historians have revisited traditional historical sources with a view to tracing the gendered assumptions operating about the shape of societies, and have utilised methodologies which more effectively explore the histories of hitherto marginalised groups. Focus on gender and **sexuality** in history as well, has led concurrently to the growth of **lesbian history** which has sought to redress the erasure of lesbian experience from the historical record. The relationship of lesbian historiography to other areas of history of women and sexualities has generated important debate, problematising the normative heterosexual frameworks employed within some feminist historical projects, and challenging any too uncritical subsumption of lesbian history and its specific concerns within broader gay or **queer theory**.

While critics may argue that feminist history is subjective and has a political agenda, feminist historians would reply that history has never been objective. Historian Pieter Geyl declares that 'All history is an argument without end': with more feminists contributing to historical scholarship, so the terms of that argument have shifted to illuminate the landscapes of gender, sexualities, **difference** and **power** in past and present.

References and further reading

Duberman, M., Vicinus, M. and Chauncey, G. (1991) *Hidden from History: Reclaiming the Gay and Lesbian Past*, Harmondsworth: Penguin.

Gay, P. (1985) *Freud for Historians*, Oxford: Oxford University Press.

Jenkins, K. (1991) *Rethinking History*, London: Routledge.

Scott, J. (1996) *Feminism and History*, Oxford: Oxford University Press.

Stuard, S.M. (1987) 'A New Dimension: Medieval Women in French Historiography', in Stuard (ed.) *Women in Medieval History and Historiography*, Philadelphia, PA: University of Pennsylvania Press.

PATRICIA CRAWFORD AND JANE LONG

history, feminist

Feminist history developed with the late 1960s feminist movement. Substantial gains have been made in writing the history of women, and in challenging the hegemonic masculinist traditional academic history (see **hegemony**).

The whole tradition of historical writing has been criticised by feminist historians who see the writing of history as a political act which has served to consistently obscure, deny and ignore the presence of women. History has been seen as a patriarchal story (see **patriarchy**), a powerful element contributing to the continuing silencing and **oppression** of women. In response to some historians who have argued that history can be scientific, based on facts, feminists have questioned the possibility of **objectivity** and emphasised the subjectivity of the historian.

Since the 1970s, there has been a huge upsurge of interest in research and teaching about women in the past, although there were earlier historians of women. Natalie Zemon **Davis**, one of the foremost in the recent development of the writing of women's history, has identified different strands in earlier work. The first she termed a history of women worthies, stories of women to be praised or blamed, to be admired and emulated or despised and avoided. Many books took the form of celebrations of individual women: queens, warriors, and other heroines. Some historians sought to make women visible in the past, and concentrated on recovering documents and sources about their lives. Such history was sometimes of the 'add-women-and-stir' variety, simply slotting women into the existing phallocentric accounts and leaving the basic categories of historical analysis unchallenged. Many early critics of academic and popular history in the 1970s pointed to the absence of women in historical accounts, thereby seeking to delegitimate the assumptions on which the writing of history had been based for so long. They argued that they way in which the past has been periodised, for example, was focused on men. 'The Renaissance', for example, was a term widely used to describe the cultural activity in learning and the arts of the fourteenth and fifteenth centuries in western Europe. Since the only women ever discussed within this genre of Renaissance history were by definition exceptional, Joan **Kelly** argued that the conventional accounts obscured the history of women. She posed a question which became famous: did women have a Renaissance? The delegitimisation of existing histories and recovering evidence about women in the past can still be valid feminist historical projects.

Initially, many critics argued that there were no source materials for a history of women, because most records from earlier times had been written and preserved by men. These claims were demonstrated to be false, as feminist historians found archival sources which had been ignored, and developed techniques of reading the male sources 'against the grain' so that they might illuminate the ways in which difference of sex structured social life in the past.

Other feminist historians celebrated the 'different nature' of women, and wrote histories of women's bodies, maternity, and work, ignoring the conventional historical issues. Marxist feminists sought to explain the economic subordination of women, but found that Marxist theory did not easily accommodate issues of gender.

Feminist history and the international women's movement were closely allied in the 1970s, but in the 1980s, many feminist scholars became more involved in academic debates. Feminist history increased in sophistication, but lost some links with the broader social movement. By the 1980s, some feminist historians endeavoured to rethink the past more holistically. In 1986, Joan **Scott** published an important article arguing that gender was a useful category of historical anaylsis. 'Woman', she argued, was a discursively constructed being.

Subsequently, in line with other post-colonial and postmodernist shifts in western thought, the whole category 'woman' was brought into question, leading to important debates about women's **agency** (see also **postcolonial feminism**). Women of colour rejected the idea of some common identity between women which did not ackowledge difference. Bell **hooks**' famous publication, *Ain't I a Woman Too?* challenged the exclusivity of many feminist platforms. From a different perspective, indigenous women have argued that their histories have been ignored by white women. They deny the utility of gender as an organising principle for historical writing claiming that colonisation and imperialism were more significant. Feminist historians have sought to rethink their categories of analysis to make **race** central as well as class (see **class analysis**). Many would argue that there is no universal class or race or gendered experience, and that the challenge is to integrate these and other experiences into a compelling analysis while retaining a critical purchase on the significant themes.

In the 1990s, feminist historians returned to an interest in the **body**, discussing the connections between body, psyche, and sexual **difference**. Lyndal Roper argued against overemphasis on the cultural construction of subjectivity. Discursive construction of sexual difference, she argues, is too limited. Nor does the notion of gender as socially constructed help us to understand historical change. Some elements of the body and psyche in the past are not so different as we have thought.

Feminist historians have had varying degrees of success in different areas of historical enquiry and in the institutions in which they work. While most historians would now acknowledge that gender has some historical significance, not all are interested in feminist history. Fot this reason, Judith Allen argues that we should turn our backs on the discipline of **history** as one which is predicated on the exclusion of women.

While feminist historians have written a huge body of lively and exciting history, some conventional history continues to ignore all questions of gender. So long as feminist history focused on issues related to women's bodies, political historians felt able to disregard it. However, recent feminist work in the area of political history may force a reappraisal of the nature of politics, just as the problematisation of masculinity may enable wider discussion of the mutability of gender identities.

For feminists seeking knowledge about the past, questions and debates continue. In the early twenty-first century, the question of difference between women is politically as well as analytically challenging. While many historians insist upon the discursive construction of 'woman', others are convinced that historians must write histories that take account of bodies.

How gender, class, and race are related in a way that can explain historical change is the current major challenge.

See also: Marxism; patriarchy; poststructuralism/postmodernism

References and further reading

Allen, J. (1986) 'Evidence and Silence: Feminism and the Limits of History', in C. Pateman and E. Gross (eds) *Feminist Challenges: Social and Political Theory*, Sydney: Allen and Unwin.

Davis, N. (1996) '"Women's history in transition": The European Case', in J. Scott (ed.) *Feminism and History*, Oxford: Oxford University Press.

hooks, b. (1981) *Ain't I A Woman: Black women and feminism*, Boston, MA: South End Press.

Kelly, J. (1988) *Women, History, and Theory: The Essays of Joan Kelly*, Chicago, IL: University of Chicago Press.

Roper, L. (1994) *Oedipus and the Devil: Witchcraft, sexuality and religion in early modern Europe*, London: Routledge.

Scott, J.W. (1986) *Gender and the Politics of History*, New York: Columbia University Press.

PATRICIA CRAWFORD AND JANE LONG

Hoagland, Sarah Lucia (b. 1945)

Lesbian feminist philosopher Sarah Lucia Hoagland, in her pioneering book, *Lesbian Ethics* (1988), writes that lesbians can have moral agency – make real moral choices – even while living in heterosexualist cultures where men control women. Her concept of agency under oppression provides a guide for lesbian resistance and creativity.

A main focus of *Lesbian Ethics* is on separating from conceptual frameworks of heterosexualism, including the idea that ethics means rules and principles. Modern Anglo-European ethical systems, the author believes, undermine lesbian agency by coercing consensus and creating false community. She advocates instead the development of 'autokoenony' – a sense of self as neither autonomous nor controlled by others but as one among many, as one who is neither dependent nor independent but interdependent. Lesbians creating this kind of community come from many cultures and so have possibilities of understanding our differences with one another in ways distinct from those of Anglo-European culture.

Lesbian Ethics challenges traditional values such as the split between reason and emotion and the idea that power over others is worth having. The author recommends attending one another instead of seeking power over others: a lesbian who attends to another can act as a 'reality check' in a world in which women's perceptions are ridiculed and denied. *Lesbian Ethics* also sets aside duty and obligation in favour of caring, and connecting in favour of making ourselves intelligible to one another. Through such interactions, lesbians can avoid horizontal hostility and more effectively resist oppression.

Lesbian Ethics has inspired ongoing discussions among lesbians and feminists. Topics include whether the account of separating from heterosexualist communities applies to lesbians of colour as well as to white lesbians; whether the ideas of the book are useful only for lesbians interacting with lesbians or more broadly; and whether lesbians need ethics at all.

In addition to her work as a theorist and as a teacher at Northeastern Illinois University in Chicago, Sarah Lucia Hoagland is an active participant in lesbian, feminist, and philosophical gatherings, including women's festivals, the Institute of Lesbian Studies, and the Society for Women in Philosophy.

See also: agency; ethics, feminist; lesbian ethics; lesbian feminism; separatism

Selected writings

Hoagland, S.L. (1988) *Lesbian Ethics: Toward New Value*, Palo Alto, CA: Institute of Lesbian Studies.
—— (1992) 'Why *Lesbian* Ethics?' in *Hypatia* 7 (4): 195–206.
Hoagland, S.L. and Penelope, J. (eds) (1988) *For Lesbians Only: A Separatist Anthology*, London: Onlywomen Press.

JOYCE TREBILCOT

homophobia

Some people respond to lesbians and gay men, and the image or thought of same-sex sexual contact, with a horror and dread – responses like people have to objects of phobia such as spiders or snakes, or to *taboo* objects they believe have powers to harm or contaminate them. *Homophobia* refers to this kind of response to homosexual desire, acts, or persons. It is also used more generally to refer to discrimination against lesbians and gays, and to intolerant, hateful, hostile or other hurtful acts and attitudes. Feminists have suggested that mainstream definitions of **gender** define 'real men' and 'real women' as heterosexual, and that homophobia is produced by these norms and also works to enforce them. Anti-feminists tap into homophobia, identifying feminist women and pro-feminist men as dykes and faggots.

See also: heterosexism, heteronormativity; lesbian feminism

References and further reading

Pharr, S. (1997) *Homophobia: A Weapon of Sexism*, Little Rock, AR: The Women's Project.

MARILYN FRYE

homosexuality, bio-medical pathologisation of

Although same-sex relationships have long been documented in many societies, the bio-medical term 'homosexuality' is a relatively recent invention, gaining popularity only from the late nineteenth century. The first use of the term 'homosexuality' (in 1868) is credited to Karl Maria Benkert (1824–82), a German-Hungarian writer who sought to remove legal barriers against those engaging in same-sex behaviour. Carl Westphal (1833–90) and Richard von Krafft-Ebing (1840–1902) are early figures who sought medical-scientific explanations for same-sex desires and laid the groundwork for the **pathologisation** of homosexuality.

Interest in the history of the medicalisation of homosexuality gained momentum after the publication in 1976 of Michel Foucault's first volume of the *History of Sexuality*. In this book, Foucault highlights the significance of a shift in the 'technology of power' for how western peoples came to view sex and **sexuality**, and the move away from the confessional to the research laboratories and clinics, where sexuality became the object of scientific investigation. According to Foucault, the work of the nineteenth-century sexologists marks the birth of the modern homosexual as an identity and homosexuality as a pathology. The development of the gay rights movement in the aftermath of the Stonewall riots of 1969 fuelled new historical studies into the history of homosexuality as part of the effort to counter the growing pathologisation of homosexual bodies and behaviours and to assert the legitimacy of a sexual identity that is chosen rather than imposed as a medical label of deviance.

One of the strongest arguments against the medicalisation of homosexuality is that it reinforces heterosexism and intolerance of sexual difference

(see **heterosexism, heteronormativity**). Homosexuality challenges social constructions of sex/**gender**, where boys and girls learn to become men and women through attaining opposite and distinct traits based on sex. The dominant heterosexist assumption is that 'opposite sexes' are naturally attracted to each other, much like other aspects of the physical world, e.g. magnetic fields. This assumption has underpinned many efforts to identify and treat 'sexually maladjusted' persons – to bring their gender into alignment with their sex – and thus help to prevent the spread of sexual deviance throughout the population (for example the Sex Variants study conducted in the USA between 1935 and 1941). **Sexism** is evident in disparaging descriptions of homosexuals. Male homosexuals are portrayed as 'effeminate' men and female homosexuals as masculine women. The behaviours of gay men and gay women have been pathologised to different degrees: the former have been punished as a crime (sodomy) in many jurisdictions, whereas the latter have been treated as symptoms of **frigidity**.

References and further reading

Bland, L. and Doan, L. (1998a) *Sexology is Culture: Labelling Bodies and Desires*, Cambridge, MA: Polity Press.
—— (1998b) *Sexology Uncensored: The Documents of Sexual Science*, Cambridge, MA: Polity Press.
Bulloch, V.L. (1994) *Science in the Bedroom: A History of Sex Research*, New York: Basic Books.
Foucault, M. (1980) *The History of Sexuality. Volume One: An Introduction*, New York: Vintage Books.
LeVay, S. (1996) *Queer Science: The Use and Abuse of Research into Homosexuality*, Cambridge, MA: The MIT Press.

ALAN PETERSEN

hooks, bell (b. 1952)

Born in Hopkinsville, Kentucky, Gloria Jean Watkins, the daughter of a domestic worker and a janitor grew up in a family of six children within the supportive environment of a black community which was coping with the disruptive influences of desegregation struggles. Although as a child Gloria Jean was encouraged to recite and write poetry, she later came to realise that familial and community patriarchal and racial traditions were inhibiting her ability and opportunities to express herself orally and in writing. Seeking escape from such restrictions, she sought autonomy through the tradition of acquiring an education. Watkins received a B.A. degree from Stanford University in 1973, an M.A. from the University of Wisconsin in 1976, and in 1983 she attained a Ph.D. from the University of California at Santa Cruz. Gloria Jean Watkins has chosen to develop her voice through writing and speaking under the uncapitalised pseudonym bell hooks. The adoption of her great grandmother's name signifies her reclamation of her grandmother's legacy of a quick wit, a sharp tongue, wilful defiance, courage and outspokenness, and serves as a strategy of empowerment.

Feminist, theorist, writer, cultural critic, self-described artist, and 'seeker on the path', bell hooks has chiselled a space in the margins of the academy for transcendent speech and interdisciplinary scholarship. In a voice that effectively combines standard English, limited academic jargon, and the vernacular of the street, hooks is engaged in the monumental task of challenging all forms of domination, exploitation and oppression while creatively envisioning tangible beloved communities. Relying upon her insurgent intellect and appropriating her own life experiences, she has developed and effectively employed a strategy of being publicly private in her writing in order to challenge what she terms 'white supremacist patriarchal domination'.

Unable to find work that accurately portrayed the impact of the multiple and complex forms of oppression upon the lives of black women, she began writing her first book at the age of 19. Six years later when it was finally completed she had difficulty in finding a publisher willing to accept a text that challenged the historical and contemporary constructions of gender and race from a black woman/feminist perspective. When it was finally published in 1981 by South End Press, *Ain't I A Woman: Black Women and Feminism* forced publishers to recognise the existence of a relatively untapped market for books by and about black women. Her commitment to the development of feminist analysis

and theory that reflects and incorporates wide ranging human experiences has informed her numerous contributions to journals and anthologies.

A prolific writer who has authored many collections of essays and poems that grapple with the complexities and nuances of oppression, survival and agency, hooks has focused on producing feminist theory from a black woman's perspective and applying it to such subjects as film reviews, teaching and public speaking in *Feminist Theory: From Margin to Center* (1984) and *Talking Back: Thinking Feminist, Thinking Black* (1989). She has authored a self help book for black women *Sisters of the Yam: Black Women and Self Recovery* (1993), has engaged in an intellectual conversation with Cornel West in *Breaking Bread: Insurgent Black Intellectuals* (1991) and written two innovative autobiographies *Bone Black* (1996) and *Wounds of Passion: A Writing Life* (1997). Characterised by Cornel West as a 'truth teller', hooks's unorthodox, interdisciplinary, polemical scholarship written in accessible language has achieved only grudging acceptance within the academy even as it has touched the hearts and minds of many who exist in the margins of both the academy and the society.

STANLIE M. JAMES

Hubbard, Ruth (b. 1924)

Ruth Hubbard is well known for her work in feminist critiques of **biology**. Born in Austria, she and her family moved to the USA in 1938; she went to Radcliffe College (for women) and began graduate work in medicine. But she then took up biology, and began research on how vision works. Long involved in political protest, she became part of feminist groups in the late 1960s.

Ruth Hubbard's feminist critiques began with teaching courses on women and biology at Harvard. This led to one of the first collections on feminism and **science**, *Women Look at Biology Looking at Women* (1979); Hubbard's own contribution to that collection focused on feminist critiques of Darwin.

Among her best-known works are *The Politics of Women's Biology* (1990) and (with her son) *Exploding the Gene Myth* (1993). Hubbard has long been a fierce critic of reductionist biology, especially around recent developments in genetics and **biotechnology**, and an advocate of greater accountability of scientists to the public. She is, for example, actively involved with the Boston-based Council for Responsible Genetics and has worked to oppose research in recombinant DNA (the basis for genetic engineering).

More recently, Hubbard has worked also on human relationships to animals, especially in the context of science; this interest led to the collection (with Lynda **Birke**) *Reinventing Biology* (1995).

Hubbard was one of the first feminist scientists openly to criticise the assumptions and practice of biology from within. Her work is particularly important to feminism, because she covers a wide range of issues relevant to women and women's **health**, and explains the science too. Hubbard's work always assumes that science is made, and is part of a social process; inevitably, that process reflects the concerns of the wider society. Thus, it is generally white, western men who make the science, and women's contributions to knowledge are downplayed.

Social inequalities are similarly reflected in the content of science; although supposedly objective, biological theory tends to represent stereotypical images of gender. It is also largely reductionist, tending towards simple, biological explanations of complex events; feminist biologists like Ruth Hubbard are deeply critical of reductionism, especially applied to human behaviour. Hubbard has, for example, been very outspoken in the media about the claim that scientists have found 'gay genes'. Reductionism, moreover, ignores complexity both inside an organism (genes affecting each other, for instance) and between inside and outside (environments affecting how, say, hormones work); Hubbard insists instead on a view of internal biology that sees it as inseparable from external environments – both affect each other.

Ruth Hubbard's work has been extremely important: not only has it ensured that feminists confront the ideology and practice of science, but it has also insisted that scientists begin to listen to feminists.

See also: Darwin, feminist critique of

Selected writings

Hubbard, R. (1990) *The Politics of Women's Biology*, New Brunswick, NJ: Rutgers University Press.

Hubbard, R. and Birke, L. (eds) (1995) *Respect for Life and the Creation of Knowledge*, Bloomington, IN: Indiana University Press.

Hubbard, R. and Wald, E. (1993) *Exploding the Gene Myth*, Boston: Beacon Press.

LYNDA BIRKE

human rights

Human rights are moral imperatives. Rights holders are entitled to a range of freedoms. Even claiming these freedoms is a transformative act, affirming one's moral value as a rights holder. According to social contract theory people initially belong to a pre-political natural order. There all individuals' rights are unenforceable and insecure. To remedy these defects individuals rationally agree to institute political systems safeguarding their most important rights through legal entitlements. Oddly, this agreement eventuates in a system where some men possess politically protected entitlements. In theory, these men protect their dependents, women and children. Universal human rights filter through institutions that guarantee a limited number of politically protected human rights to a limited number of men only.

At first feminists responded by seeking the same rights as privileged men. Thus Mary Wollstonecraft argued against Jean Jacques Rousseau that women should be able to claim the same rights his philosophy demanded only for men. During the struggle for suffrage, the right to vote was likewise claimed as a human right and as an expression of equality for women. Eventually, feminists recognised that the concept of human rights makes an awkward tool for advancing feminist goals. First and most importantly, the model of social contractors is in important respects detrimental to women's lives and circumstances. Second, human rights may be incoherent. Third, human rights are unstable guides. Fourth, human rights are indeterminate. Fifth, human rights may reinforce the power of the state, not the people.

Taking these in turn. The model implicit in

social contract theory idealises a picture of individual men engaged in autonomous independent self-realisation while sheltering behind the protective fence provided by human rights. Women find gender-limited self-realisation in the separate sphere of the private realm (see **public/private**). This picture promotes falsifications that serve women badly. Men and women are inter-dependent, on each other and their environment. Yet this picture suggests men are independent agents, while women are dependent upon men. This picture promotes the validation of separate sphere assumptions. Important rights for women, including the right to control reproductive choice, have no place in the list of rights privileging men. Moreover when, as too frequently occurs, freedom promised by the right to privacy impairs women's right to security in the home, rights theory fails women.

Consider the way rights today function to maintain separate spheres valorising differently-gendered values, as shown by the dilemma of a woman seeking to break away from a domestic abuser. If she seeks protection, intrusively 'protective' state bureaucracies may substitute **oppression** by the state for oppression by a husband. Keeping the state out leaves the woman in an oppressive domestic relationship. For many, the point at which a battered woman actually leaves her abuser marks a period when she (and her parents and children as well) are at great risk of being killed by him. To stay seems only to postpone the day on which the batterer escalates the **violence** to the point where she dies. Yet, if a battered woman ultimately kills her abuser while he sleeps, constructing a self defence justification runs up against great difficulties because the right to self defence is not formulated appropriately for women in long term relationships (French, *et al.* 1998). To the extent that women and men are socialised to have different values, women are more generally oriented toward care and responsibility. The **autonomy** model of human rights falsifies the nature of her dilemmas and raises questions about the extent to which a feminist **ethic of care** is morally compatible with seeking to advance women's causes through the pursuit of human rights protections.

Feminist critics of human rights question whether expanding traditionally conceived human rights to include women will prove ultimately incompatible with feminist goals. Maternity leave proposals, for example, become mired in questions of what it means to be similarly situated persons. This questioning legitimates the debate whether a man who is nauseous with a hangover and misses work is similarly situated with a woman who has morning sickness. It overlooks the disparate effect of a 'no leave' policy for men as a group and women as a group. Nor, as L. Finley makes clear, can obfuscation be replaced by clarity if one concentrates on equality of outcome. Like equality of opportunity this doctrine is built upon a conception of isolated autonomy, 'defined as the realisation of self-fulfillment guided by the ultimate authority of self-judgement without interference from others'. To achieve equal autonomy requires 'an irreducible and universal aspect of humanity' which ultimately 'means removing individuals from their context and connection . . .' (Finley in Weisberg 1993).

Reliance on human rights likewise betrays feminists with reference to a woman's right to control her own **sexuality** since rights theory is inadequate to the problem of conceptualising sexuality. From the perspective of rights theory, the problem of sexuality is one of where social controls should end and sexual freedom should begin. As Frances Olsen sees it, the important issue for feminism is not where to draw this rights-oriented line, but rather to discuss the substance and meaning we give to sexuality. Feminists who might otherwise engage in

> the project of challenging the dominant definition of sexuality come to perceive themselves as opposing one another. Feminists on one side accuse those on the other of being anti-sex. The other side accuses those on the first of contributing to their own oppression through 'false consciousness'.
>
> (Olsen 1993)

Equality for women requires awareness that the law operates on gendered subjects, whose desires and values are often socially constructed (see **social constructionism**). While the concept of rights remains based on the value of non-interference with abstract individuals, the concept of affirmative rights, for example to reasonable maternity leave, remains a distrusted anomaly. Rights to non-interference fail to serve women's interests when women confront domestic abuse. Concentrating on rights harmfully distracts feminists from the task of re-conceptualising that ultimately interdependent realm of sexuality.

Is the realm of rights itself coherent? The realm claimed for human rights is constantly expanding. In addition to negative protections in the United States Bill of Rights, individuals also claim education, welfare and other positive enablements as human rights (Held 1998). Group-based rights include claims to a homeland and language (Turpel 1997). Cultural traditions are represented as generating rights claims contrary to those of other cultures. The Universal Declaration of Human Rights puts forward a list of rights as 'a common standard of achievement for all peoples and all nations' and suggests measures to secure 'their universal and effective recognition and observance'. Such a laundry list raises troubling questions about theoretical coherence.

Does protecting important yet contradictory human needs of independence and community solidarity, through protecting the exercise of abstract rights (such as free speech), issue in protection of the free speech of pornographers? Or does it just issue in instability?

Human rights are also unstable. Rights theory claims that everyone enjoys the same rights while acknowledging that special rights may be necessary to remove the effects of past exclusion or deprivation of rights or to address some special characteristics of certain groups. But rights theory offers no answer to the question: when are attributions of difference acceptable; when are they false? In the USA today such questions are too often answered only by judicial opinion, leaving human rights theory vague and unstable in this important respect.

In addition to instability, human rights are indeterminate. No particular outcome is logically compelled when rights arguments are applied to a given set of facts. Thus legal decisions may frequently uphold the rights of the privileged against those with fewer resources, material and psychological, for exercising their rights.

To the extent that human rights are moral claims ratified through legal instruments with states as signatories, movements intent upon achieving human rights are encouraged 'to substitute rights-consciousness for self-understanding. In doing so, they allow the state to reinterpret their radical social goals in terms of rights and affirm that social power resides in the state, not the people' (Weisberg 1993).

Nevertheless, feminists continue to work within the human rights tradition for nothing else we know provides the same benefits. Caregiving has too often consigned women to community under the control of their fathers, in-laws, husbands, and even work-place colleagues who sexualise work interactions. A woman struggling for a room of her own may cherish the isolating effect of rights (Olsen 1993). As Patricia Williams puts it:

> The goal is to find a political mechanism that can confront the *denial* of need. The argument that rights are disutile, even harmful, trivialises this aspect of black experience specifically, as well as that of any person or group whose vulnerability has been truly protected by rights.
> (Williams 1991)

Feminists working to use rights in the law argue for appropriate changes such as the need to see multiple categories. Then, for example, women of colour will no longer fall between categories that presume all the women are white, and all the blacks are men (Crenshaw 1989). They seek to reinterpret equality so that unlike cases are treated in proportion to their differences, making difference 'costless'. Then apparently gender-neutral schemes with differential impact on men and women can be coherently understood as discriminatory (Smith 1995 and Littleton 1989). Feminist jurisprudence clarifies ways in which rape law has held women to the standard of a 'reasonable person' who 'is a real man' (Estrich 1987). Such clarification leads to a reasonable woman standard for these laws.

Finally, although human rights hold an important place in moral discourse as a weighty element in the domain of law and economics, feminists know these are not the only domains within which people live their lives. Held promotes 'employing different moral approaches for different domains, while retaining the force of rights claims where appropriate' (Held 1988).

References and further reading

Estrich, S. (1987) *Real Rape*, Cambridge, MA: Harvard University Press.

French, S.G., Teays, W. and Purdy, L.M. (eds) (1998) *Violence Against Women: Philosophical Perspectives*, Ithaca, NY: Cornell University Press.

Held, V. (1998) 'Feminism and Moral Theory' in E.F. Kittay and D. Meyers (eds) *Women and Moral Theory* Savage: Rowman and Littlefield.

—— (1987) 'Rights' in A. Jaggar and I.M. Young, (eds)*A Companion to Feminist Philosophy*, Malden: Blackwell Publishers.

Olsen, F. (1993) 'Statutory Rape: A Feminist Critique of Rights Analysis' *63 Texas Law Review*, 387.

Turpel, M.E. (1997) 'Aboriginal Peoples and the Canadian Charter' in Soifer, E. (ed.) *Ethical Issues, Perspectives for Canadians*, Peterborough: Broadview Press.

Weisberg, D.K. (ed.) (1993) *Feminist Legal Theory: Foundations*, Philadelphia, PA: Temple University Press.

Williams, P.J. (1991) *The Alchemy of Race and Rights*, Cambridge, MA: Harvard University Press.

NATALIE DANDEKAR

hybridity

Popularised within postcolonial theory by Homi Bhabha, hybridity must not be confused with difference even though the concepts are inter-related. Hybridity specifically addresses the binary experience of coloniser/colonised relations in which displacement of authority is engendered through a series of mimetic identifications with the coloniser by the colonised. The conjunction of two cultures produces a hybridised cultural identity that is neither fully indigenous nor exogenous. This cultural location is described by Bhabha as a 'third space of ambivalence'. Hybridity has since been prominently featured in globalisation debates pertaining to western influences in 'Third World' societies and emergent immigrant cultures in the west. The concept is relevant to identity and cultural politics in feminist scholarship and is evident (although not exclusively discussed) in the work of Asian-American/Asian scholars such as Trinh T. Minh-Ha who examines the slipperiness of her own cultural identity which constantly negotiates the east and the west.

See also: cultural theory/cultural studies, feminist; difference; identity politics; Other, the; postcolonial feminism; Trinh T. Minh-ha

References and further reading

Bhabha, H. (1994) *The Location of Culture*, London and New York: Routledge.

YOKE-SUM WONG

hysteria

Hysteria has been a subject of interest to feminist theories in relation to two issues: as the casting of woman as other and inferior, and as a strategic means to remobilise feminine language.

Hysteria refers to a physical condition described by various medical and psychoanalytic scholars predominantly in the nineteenth century. The condition which took its name from the imagined site of the disorder (*hysteron*, Greek: uterus) could include fits, temporary paralysis and mood swings. The symptoms were traced back to the physical and psychological condition of women. The French clinician Charcot made a systematic study of hysterical women, producing numerous photographs. His collection has been linked to a visual study of woman as 'other', charting and mapping her difference to the male norm.

Sigmund Freud wrote on hysterical women to introduce the concept that a specific memory blocks the movement of limbs, and that a reactivation of that memory can remove the symptom: the basis of the talking cure. Writers such as Carrol Smith-Rosenberg have addressed this reading and showed how the immobility of hysteria is not an unconscious effect of a singular, private experience, but a social protest against conflicting demands on women. Smith-Rosenberg thus sees hysteria as a bodily acting out of the restrictions and repressions at work on a woman's identity, magnified and thrown back at the repressor. But this 'acting out' or literalisation of discourse is not a liberating experience or political act: in the immobility of her legs a woman is restructured into her public invisibility, confined to the sick room.

Elaine Showalter acknowledges this ambiguity of hysteria in her work. She shows how the symptoms of hysteria act out the specific, historical image of femininity. This work links hysteria to the sexual politics of illness. In the theory of illness, issues of normativity and difference structure gender politics and the imaging of one gender by the dominant one.

Theorists such as Hélène **Cixous** and Catherine Clément have reappropriated the hysteric as rhetorical figure, destabilising and ridiculing the dominant discourse:

> Those wonderful hysterics, who subjected Freud to so many voluptuous moments too shameful to mention, bombarding his mosaic statue/law of Moses with their carnal, passionate body-words, haunting him with their inaudible thundering denunciations, were more than just naked … they were dazzling.
>
> (Clément and Cixous 1986: 95)

Cixous recasts the helplessness of the single woman in the grip of a debilitating fit into a protesting force of physical femininity.

See also: psychoanalysis

References and further reading

Clément, C. and Cixous, H. (1986) *The Newly Born Woman*, trans. B. Wing, Minneapolis, MI: University of Minnesota Press.

Showalter, E. (1985) *The Female Malady*, New York: Pantheon.

Smith-Rosenberg, C. (1985) *Disorderly Conduct*, New York: Knopf.

PETRA KUPPERS

I

identity

Identity is an important concept in feminist theory and in the social sciences more generally. Many debates within feminism have centred on the question of the **essentialism** of identity, and on the prospects of developing an **identity politics** that avoids the worst excesses of essentialism. Recent trends in social thought, particularly the turn towards **poststructuralism/postmodernism**, have led to a radical re-appraisal of 'identity' along with other core feminist concepts such as 'women' and '**experience**'.

Originally developed in the social sciences in the 1950s, theories of identity have tended to involve either psychological reductionism or sociological reductionism. In the first view, identity is conceived as a fixed and stable characteristic of the person. It reflects the notion that one can know who someone really *is*. In the second view, identity is seen as acquired through socialisation or the internalisation of imposed social roles. According to the 'acquired' definition, identity is not so deeply inscribed in the psyche of the individual, and so there is scope for transforming identity (Gleason 1983). Feminist theory has involved many attempts to mediate between these two contending positions. For example, feminist **psychoanalysis** has posited a complex interaction between 'intra-psychic' processes and social expectations. However, these two conceptions have continued to dominate thinking about identity and have influenced the development of identity politics, whereby one bases one's politics on a sense of personal identity – as female, as Jewish, as black, and so on.

According to the prevailing 'additive' model of identity, one's identity is simply a composite of various natural and socially constructed attributes. Thus, one is defined as an African American woman, a lesbian feminist, a white Anglo-Saxon man, and so on. The problem with this model, critics note, is that no matter how exhaustive the descriptions, there will always be exclusions and disjunctures between identity labels and personal experiences. Some of the harshest critiques of identity as a category of knowledge and politics have been offered by those who have been most marginalised and excluded by this labelling process. Women of colour, Third World women and lesbians have criticised western academic feminism for the assumption of commonality of 'women's' experiences and the use of theoretical categories which implicitly exclude those who are not European, white and heterosexual. Women of colour, for instance, have drawn attention to the influence of racism on their lives, and to the impossibility of choosing between their commitment to feminism and the struggle with their men for racial justice (McKay 1993). The growing critique of essentialism in the social sciences and beyond has led to a re-appraisal of traditional conceptions of identity, and debates about the prospects of developing a re-conceptualised or 'post-identity' politics. Postmodern and poststructuralist theorists have drawn attention to the dangers of 'fixing' identities through labelling and denying the fluidity of **gender**, **race**, and sexual self-identifications.

An important figure in feminist debates about the essentialism of identity, or the politics of naming practices, is Diana Fuss (1989). In Fuss's view, in identity politics the tendency has been to assume a causal relationship between identity and politics, with the former determining the latter. Thus, there is expectation that one will 'claim' or 'discover' their 'true' identity before they elaborate their personal politics. The political is often reduced to the personal, with the implication that the political activity is limited to self-discovery and personal transformation. Fuss sees a need to challenge the reduction of the political to the personal in reassessing and repoliticising identity politics. Drawing on Derrida's deconstruction of essence and Lacan's theory of the constitution of the subject in language, Fuss argues for a shift away from the focus on the identity of things in themselves towards an analysis of *identity statements*. Under the influence of postmodernism and post-structuralism, feminists such as Fuss have emphasised the fictitious character of identity and the ways in which identity categories such as 'gender', 'sex', 'race' and 'sexuality' operate as normative ideals to regulate the self and social relations. This theoretical turn is reflected in growing **gender scepticism** within feminism – that is, scepticism about the use of gender as an analytic category – and in the greater attention devoted by scholars to the question of **difference**.

Queer theory represents an important post-structural influence on thinking about identity and about gender-based identity politics in particular. According to queer theorists, identities are always multiple and there is literally an infinite number of ways in which the components of identity can combine. Furthermore, any specific identity construction is arbitrary, unstable, and exclusionary. The contributions of Eve Sedgwick, Teresa de **Lauretis** and Judith **Butler** represent a new wave of anti-essentialist thinking which is concerned with exposing the limitations of identity and the implicit heterosexism in many academic disciplines and strategies of identity movements (see **heterosexism, heteronormativity**). While the deconstructivist impulse within social theory has led to some disenchantment with identity politics, others see possibilities for a more contingent, strategic use of identity for pursuing political goals. The concept of 'strategic essentialism' proposed by some feminists, women of colour, anti-racist scholars and queer scholars suggests that identity labels can be strategically employed according to perceived situational advantage, political gain, and conceptual utility, and indeed must be used this way if one is to protect and advance social rights in a context of **backlash** against the gains of feminists and virtually all minority groups.

See also: identity politics

References and further reading

Appiah, K.A. and Gates, H.L (1995) *Identities*, Chicago, IL: University of Chicago Press.

Fuss, D. (1989) *Essentially Speaking: Feminism, Nature and Difference*, New York: Routledge.

Gleason, P. (1983) 'Identifying Identity: A Semantic History', *Journal of American History* 69, 4: 910–31.

McKay, N.Y. (1993) 'Acknowledging Differences: Can Women Find Unity Through Diversity?', in S.M. James and A.P.A. Busia (eds) *Theorizing Black Feminisms: The Visionary Pragmatism of Black Women*, London: Routledge.

Seidman, S. (ed.) (1996) *Queer Theory/Sociology*, Cambridge, MA: Blackwell.

Young, I.M. (1990) *Justice and the Politics of Difference*, Princeton, NJ: Princeton University Press.

ALAN PETERSEN

identity politics

'Identity politics' has become a lightning rod of political contestation even while its precise definition and practical implications are nowhere agreed upon. Most generally, the term simply means that identity is relevant to one's politics. It may also imply that political organisations should be based on **identity**. In the 1970s, the **Combahee River Collective** declared in 'A Black Feminist Statement' (1977) that black women need to rely principally on other black women for their liberation – that no other group besides themselves would be as consistent and committed to winning their freedom. This claim presupposes that one's politics are at least partially determined by one's social identity, a claim rooted in Marx's view that one's ideas and beliefs are related to one's material conditions.

Identity politics is also associated with 'the politics of recognition' or political struggles organised against the vilification of specific identities – for example, Chicanos, women, lesbians. Identity-based political movements developed in the second half of the twentieth century as cross-class efforts to fight bigotry and remake dominant cultural representations, and in this sense multi-culturalism is the current heir of these movements.

Neither feminist theory nor feminist politics have uniformly supported identity politics. Opposition can be grouped into two categories. First, both leftists and liberals have been concerned that identity politics undercuts the possibility of creating a progressive political majority by emphasising difference or by diverting attention and energies from class-based organising. Second, the concept of a coherent or unified identity itself is said to be an illusion based on dubious modernist assumptions. In reality, identity is imposed on a fluid and open-ended subjectivity and it aids in making subjects of the state more susceptible to dominant ideologies and disciplinary techniques. The attachment to identity is a pathological attachment to victimisation rather than a move toward freedom. Identity-based political movements thus foreclose future options that might radically alter the conceptions of and practices around race, gender, and sexuality. Liberation must include the possibility of liberating one *from* identity rather than reifying those identities that have been produced under conditions of domination.

Despite these critiques, identity politics persists in varied forms. Its proponents argue that it need not be either essentialist about identity nor lead to separatist politics. Political worries about movements that emphasise differences are argued to be themselves based on modernist assumptions that all citizens must be fundamentally the same to claim equal rights. It is only where justice requires sameness that cultural, racial or sexual identity cannot be accorded political significance without endangering progress. Moreover, although identities are dynamic, they are nonetheless a fundamental aspect of present social reality. Identity politics is simply the attempt to reveal that social identity makes a political difference that needs always to be taken into account.

See also: essentialism

LINDA MARTÍN ALCOFF

ideology

'Ideology', in classical **Marxism**, is more sophisticated than in its now-popular connections with fanaticism, mystification and disregard for truth. As Michèle Barrett shows, Marxists are by no means in agreement about whether ideology necessarily deludes or distorts, or is opposed to knowledge. A Marxist-informed critical analysis of the relations of production in capitalist societies provides a way of understanding the social effects of economic production relations, out of which social hierarchies and incommensurable subjectivities derive. These relations generate a hegemonic social consciousness that manifests itself as much in everyday beliefs about the 'naturalness' of an asymmetrical social order as in dominant philosophies and religions (see **hegemony**). Marxist feminists have shown that ideology critique can be a powerful tool for feminist analysis if it is elaborated to address structural inequalities of **gender**, **race**, and ethnicity as well as those of class (see **class analysis**).

References and further reading

Barrett, M. (1991) *The Politics of Truth*, Stanford, CA; Stanford University Press.

LORRAINE CODE

'immanence', woman as

The term 'woman as immanence' is employed by the existentialist philosopher Simone de Beauvoir in her 1949 feminist classic *The Second Sex* to describe women's situation in a world where men have defined themselves as the human norm and ideal. Men achieve transcendence by reaching beyond themselves in projects of self-realisation. In contrast, women are defined by men as Other, marked as different, permanently subordinated to and overshadowed by male subjectivity. In a world so ordered women are enmeshed in the material, local, familial, biological, and relational. They lack an authentic subject position from which to act freely and to choose projects of self-realisation which expand into an indefinitely open future. Defined and constrained by their position as Other, women are 'doomed to immanence'.

See also: existentialism

References and further reading

Beauvoir, S. de (1949) *The Second Sex*, trans. H.M. Parshley, New York: Knopf, 1952.

RANDI R. WARNE

impartiality

To be impartial one must not be motivated by private considerations. One must not do for one person what one would not do for anyone else in a similar situation. The commitment to impartiality rests on a fundamental commitment to the equality of all human beings and to the universality of moral reasoning. The stance of detachment that produces impartiality is attained by abstracting from the particularities of context, feeling and body. John Rawls has put forward the most influential articulation of justice as impartiality in recent years. Feminist theorists have challenged the ideal of impartiality in three ways: first, by arguing that impartiality has inappropriately been applied only to the public realm, leaving the operation of the private realm and the family unaddressed. Susan Moller **Okin** (1989) argues that the neglect of the family in theories of justice ought to be rectified by extending the requirement of impartiality to the private sphere. The second critique, largely at odds with the first, challenges the dominance, rather than the delimitation, of the impartial point of view. Drawing on the work of Carol **Gilligan** many feminists argue that impartiality is a specific form of moral reasoning, rather than moral reasoning per se. It corresponds poorly to relations characteristic of family and personal life, which require engagement rather than detachment. These theorists call for recognition of the importance of an 'ethic of care' as well as an 'ethic of justice'. The third critique is that impartiality denies difference in that

the aspiration toward universality reduces differences to unity. Iris Young (1990) argues that the ideal of impartiality generates a dichotomy between universality and particularity that masks the particular perspectives of dominant groups and marginalises people associated with the body and feeling, notably women. However, in contrast to the other two forms of feminist critique that valorise impartiality and particularity respectively, this perspective would undermine the pertinence of the dichotomy itself. Some theorists, who wish to synthesise impartial with contextual forms of moral reasoning, adopt a model of discourse ethics as a means to subvert the distinction between the two. Notably, Seyla **Benhabib** (1992) suggests that discourse ethics, properly formulated, can mediate between the standpoint of the generalised and the concrete other: between impartial and partial forms of moral reasoning. Many, more postmodern, feminists remain sceptical that this Habermassian mode of securing impartiality via the ideal speech situation is open to such modification. Those drawing on a more Foucauldian framework, such as Judith **Butler**, criticise the attempt to exclude bodily and aesthetic aspects of human existence from public discourse and emphasise the contingent and power-laden nature of discursive regimes.

See also: political theory; situated knowledges; veil of ignorance

References and further reading

Benhabib, S. (1992) *Situating the Self*, Cambridge, MA: Polity Press.
Okin, S.M. (1989) *Gender, Justice and the Family*, New York: Basic Books.
Rawls, J. (1971) *A Theory of Justice*, Cambridge, MA: Harvard University Press.
Young, I. (1990) *Justice and the Politics of Difference*, Princeton, NJ: Princeton University Press.

JUDITH SQUIRES

Indigenist feminism

Indigenist feminism is a **political theory** and praxis that seeks to eliminate the global oppression of women. It embraces an Indigenist political

infrastructure situating traditional Indigenist women's values in the nucleus of diverse women's
liberation movement theories. Indigenism is a
political theory for descendants of land-based
economic cultures in struggle to maintain a way
of life. Indigenists struggle against a cultural
imperialism of using military might and a global
capitalist economy, to overrun the land base of
antecedent cultures. In the Americas, many traditional indigenous cultural networks retain powerful
family and community positions for women in all
phases of culture generation (e.g. as kinship
sustainers, cultural keepers, and economic providers). Feminism is a political theory and praxis
focused on acquiring or maintaining equal gender
status. Maintaining traditional Indigenist equality
of status, self-determination and sovereignty is an
Indigenist feminist endeavour. If this activity is the
progenitor of EuroAmerican feminism then the
contemporary marginal feminist paradigm (see
paradigms) for Indigenist thought is overturned,
engendering the praxis of Indigenist feminism to be
situated at the centre of American feminism.

Nativism and Indigenism

Many Indigenist women are engaged in two
parallel gender activities: nativism, which maintains traditional local cultural values, kinship,
biodiversity, and ways of being; and Indigenism,
which counters global environmental and economic genocide. Indigenist women engage land
based struggles of regional native politics, and
ecological struggles of global and international
politics. Both politics emanate from generations of
cultural value. The nativist paradigm engenders
traditional nativist epistemology taught for the next
seven generations. The Indigenist paradigm engenders Indigenist epistemology of an interdependent global biodiversity. Global Indigenism
envelops nativism, and thus many American
Indian women are native-Indigenists.

Womanism

American Indian sovereign nations have long
recognised women's power, strength, beauty and
intellect. Women's traditional roles as life givers
and kinship keepers maintain teachings that last for

seven generations. These two roles typify womanist
community values and suggest a womanist epistemology. From this standpoint it is a native woman's
sacred obligation to uphold Indigenist womanist
values.

Feminism

In the Americas, one method (among others)
western Europe used to subordinate indigenous
populations was imposing a legal system. Sexism,
racism, and classism were so integrated into the
language and culture of the legal paradigm brought
to the Americas that neither women, people of
colour, nor the poor were seen as government stake
holders. This legal context is the vessel of political
struggle for many American feminists. During early
settlement in the Americas, many native women
taught land survival values and skills to many
EuroAmerican women. By the eighteenth century
mixed blood women were participating in the
building of nationhood, and women were demanding legal rights. Abigail Adams wrote to her
husband John Adams at the Constitutional Convention in Pennsylvania, warning him that denying
women equal rights to men in the new government, would foment a revolution lasting until these
rights were bestowed.

American Indian values of personal autonomy,
equality, and freedom were mirrored by the
eighteenth-century colonist's demand for freedom
and autonomy from the English monarchy. However, in shifting these concepts from an indigenous
context (egalitarian), to a European context
(exclusionary), legal inequalities of the European
empires persisted. The nineteenth-century judicial
system, although outlawing slavery, buttressed a
racism, sexism, and classism put in place by that
Constitutional Convention. In the twentieth century, a legal sex, but not race equality, was to be the
prize for early white feminists. The result was a
right to human dignity and worth for white
women, yet a more deeply entrenched racial
subordination for all people of colour.

Gender relations

Traditional gender networks remain active in many
communities and nations. Women maintain gender

equality roles in sovereign nations by acting in autonomous and self-determining ways that focus on holding and keeping equality on a land base for all genders, and all nations. Maintaining this right to be recognised by all as self-determining autonomous nations is necessary to maintain women's traditional values, ways of being, and to maintain equality for all women and all genders.

Women's power, and stories about gender in indigenous America, must be situated in their cultural context to be adequately understood (see **situated knowledges**). For example, native women exclude themselves, during menses, from some community rituals. Because women are recognised as inherently powerful during menses, this inherent power has the potential to unbalance an energy cycle. A person without this contextual knowledge might interpret the exclusion as an oppression, rather than an acting out of the meaning of the profound powers exclusive to women.

Marginal feminism

Indigenist women do not bring to American feminist theory an epistemological standpoint of an outsider (see **standpoint theory**). An Indigenist perspective assesses mainstream American feminism to be unknowingly dispersed, by roots of Indigenist womanism. The same climate of indigenous values that spawned American feminist values remains at the nucleus of most feminist theory. An Indigenist feminist position holds that non-Indigenist cultures brought severe gender inequities to the Americas, imposing them on indigenous people. If Indigenist feminists appear marginal to non-Indigenist feminists, it is because the standpoint of most non-Indigenist feminists is ethnocentric and self located, rather than historic and community situated. An Indigenist feminist stance is to keep all communities within her **gaze**.

Indigenist feminists understand political issues like rape, suicide, and **depression**, to be powerful terrorist tools of global colonisation and repression. An indigenous infrastructure of rape analysis reflects victimisation based upon gender categories as they merge with **race**, class, ageing, disability, and ethnic categories (see also **class analysis, UK**; **class analysis, US**; **disability, women and**).

American Indian feminists live the reality that the heart of a nation is not gone until its women lie on the ground. Indigenous women bear a responsibility and duty to lead amidst value conflicts, and carry the privilege of holding and keeping traditional respect for women, as leaders amidst sovereignty struggles. Indigenist and Native American feminism, as seen by a eurocentric vision, was peripheral, and at the margins of feminist thought. Today Indigenist feminism is an axis, positioned at the centre of American feminist thought. Indigenist feminism as the core spirit of American feminism joins a Fourth World feminism. In paving the way for seventh generation women, one millennium invitation is to landscape a just global terrain of resource allocation and balance.

Fourth World feminism

Twentieth-century political freedoms in South Africa were won by coalitions of African Indigenist womanists, EuroAfrican feminists, African American womanists, and American feminists and womanists. Some feminists of the 1970s, 1980s, and 1990s joined with indigenous people to strengthen global environmental struggles. Valuing a woman's right to challenge authority in New Zealand and Australia, Indigenist women ally with feminists of many nations, in an Indigenist Movement against colonial hegemonic **power** of the New Zealand and Australian national governments (see also **hegemony**). America's Indigenist women, in struggle against continued forms of colonisation, align with Fourth World feminists.

Aggregate issues of Forth-World survival include government and corporate environmental racism and machiavellian retention of land base, genetic biopiracy and human genocide, disgraceful confiscation of economic resources and pillage of culture vultures, obstruction of sovereignty and abduction and murder of political prisoners, unjust economic competition and sabotage of culturally appropriate education, media, and technology, religious proselytisation and invasion of sacred spirituality.

In the Americas, whether in Canada among First Nations women, the USA among Native American women, or in South America among women in guerrilla warfare operations, Indigenist women are frequently on the forefront of political encounters for global survival.

A Forth-World feminism would enable an axis of biodiversity and ecological harmony to breathe, help the kernel of self-determination and autonomy grow a full field of equally sized corn, and help coalitions of economic integrity and global accountability strengthen what reckless colonisation has weakened.

Indigenist feminism

Many womanist and feminist values are similar to Indigenist values. Paula Gunn Allen, in identifying some red roots of **radical feminism** on the American continent, claims that many American radical feminist perspectives are rooted in America's Indigenist cultures. To take American women's collective cognitive experience and values seriously is to participate in an American Indian tradition; it is to value women's lives. It is also to locate feminist experience and value in an historical continuum of the indigenous cultures of the Americas. Thus, American feminist theory generates out of Indigenist women's experience in the Americas (Indigenist womanism) as it encounters EuroAmerican women's experience (radical feminism) in the Americas. Moreover, radical feminist theory is radical precisely because of those red roots. The strength of American feminism partly mirrors the strength of generations of Indigenous women's thought, actions, and communal roles that maintained an extensive autonomy for women in the Americas. To harvest Indigenist feminism is to identify and distinguish roots of a radical strain in feminism that honours a tradition of autonomy and self-determination for all including a sovereign women's nation.

Indigenist feminists locate a political turf for American feminists. Indigenous-knowledge-based systems of Native women's political struggles nourish complex epistemologies, belief systems, and social systems not yet highlighted by feminist thought. The metaphysics of these systems go unexamined, while the metaphysics of dominant cultures place Indigenist feminists in a most radical epistemological struggle.

See also: class analysis UK; class analysis US; gender; sexuality

References and further reading

Beck, P.V., Walters, A.L. and Francisco N. (1996) *The Sacred: Ways of Knowledge, Sources of Life*, Tsaile: Navajo Community College.

Churchill, W. (1996) *From A Native Son: Selected Essays on Indigenism, 1985–1995*, Boston: South End.

Cook-Lynn, E. (1996) *Why I Can't Read Wallace Stegner and Other Essays: A Tribal Voice*, Madison: University of Wisconsin.

Ewen, A. (ed.) (1994) *Voice of Indigenous Peoples: Native People Address the United Nations*, Santa Fe: Clear Light.

Grinde, D.A. and Johansen, B.E. (eds) (1995) *Ecocide of Native America: Environmental Destruction of Indian Lands and Peoples*, Santa Fe: Clear Light.

Jaimes, M.A. (ed.) (1992) *The State of Native America: Genocide, Colonization, and Resistance*, Boston: South End.

Klein, L.F. and Ackerman, L.A. (eds) (1995) *Women and Power in Native North America*, Norman: University of Oklahoma.

Shoemaker, N. (ed.) (1995) *Negotiators of Change: Historical Perspectives on Native American Women*, New York: Routledge.

Verble, S. (ed.) (1981) *Words of Today's American Indian Women: Ohoyo Makachi*, Wichita Falls: Ohoyo Resource Centre.

Wub-E-Ke-Niew (1995) *We Have The Right To Exist: A Translation of Aboriginal Indigenous Thought*, New York: Black Thistle.

ANNE SCHULHERR WATERS

individualism

In post-Enlightenment philosophy and **political theory** of the liberal and the German romantic traditions, individualism is the view that human beings are separate, distinct 'atomistic' units who are not 'naturally' social, but for whom sociality compromises their autonomous self-sufficiency. Often elaborated as *abstract* individualism, for which every individual is interchangeable with every other, as knower or moral-political agent, the 'individuals' it presupposes are rarely individu*ated*. In moral-political theories and epistemologies that endorse individualistic assumptions (see **epistemology, feminist**), if individuals were individuated according to their specificities and differences, egalitarian theories and practices would no longer be viable. According to the principle of **impartiality** on which egalitarianism depends, social policies and actions must benefit and constrain everyone equally. Each individual counts as one and no more than one recipient of benefits; and special disadvantages, oppressions, loyalties, and affiliations are morally-politically irrelevant. In epistemology, individualism informs the belief that every observer in 'normal' observations will perceive and know the world in precisely the same way. Each knower is equivalent to every other; any knower could stand in for any other. Ideal **objectivity** enshrines these assumptions. Similarly, from a moral point of view, every actor, every benefactor of a moral action, every deliberator, is interchangeable with every other, equally able to act impartially and claim impartial treatment. Honouring universal, impartial principles, properly moral action will override differences in favour of universal, underlying sameness. There is no room for loyalty, or special interests or treatment in consequence of sex, race, ability, age, prosperity, or need.

Around individualism, social policies of self-reliance are constructed: policies according to which each individual's circumstances (poverty, illiteracy, single parenthood, unemployment) are products of choice, and would be different if other choices were made. Thus, for example, individualism represents welfare recipients as morally accountable for failing to achieve what an equal opportunity society allows every individual to do. Neo-conservative populist movements of the 1990s, attacking the politics of the **welfare** state, traded on these assumptions. The idea that a society has responsibilities to its oppressed and disadvantaged members finds no place in such analyses.

Individualism has been an issue for feminists especially since the beginning of the second wave, as feminists have shown that individualistic theory masks the very differences in whose name sexist, racist, ageist, and other analogous oppressions and marginalisations justify themselves. Despite their maintained anonymity and interchangeability, individuals who are placeholders in moral-political-epistemological theory are implicitly male, living in circumstances that enable them to take advantage of 'equal' opportunities. The expectations that individualistic theory engenders and sustains make it impossible for women to escape oppression and underclass status unless they have the means of being just like (educated, white) men.

See also: communitarianism, women and

LORRAINE CODE

industrialisation

Industrialisation involves the widespread development of industrial and technological modes of production. Feminist scholars argue that the processes of industrialisation and its usual concomitants – consumerism, urbanisation and industrial time discipline – cannot be understood without reference to the social hierarchies operating where industrialisation occurs. The process is often characterised by more deeply entrenched sexual divisions of labour within production, and historically has entailed a more distinct spatial separation of home and workplace, trends which contribute to the construction of gendered **public/private** spheres. Widespread industrialisation in late-eighteenth- and nineteenth-century England, for example, saw factory employment taken up by some women, but the vast majority remained concentrated in 'low-skilled', low-paid, non-industrial occupations such as domestic service. Early economic models of industrialisation obscure its variable impacts by gender, region and culture, and the process remains an important focus of concern and critique within contemporary feminist development studies.

See also: public/private; work, women and

JANE LONG

instrumentality

Instrumentality refers to values, forms of rationality, and modes of relationship within which something is valued only for its use as a means to a further end, in contrast to being valued as an end in itself, or itself or for its own sake. (The latter is sometimes identified with intrinsic or inherent value, but depending on interpretation, this is open to contest.) For example, when women are defined or valued just as mothers, carers or servicers of others (men or children) who are taken to be of primary value, or when altruism as self-sacrifice is treated as the ideal for women's lives and egoism for men's, women are treated instrumentally. Strong forms of instrumentalism not only override and subsume the used party's goals or projects in favour of the user's, but may also justify this practice by conceptualising the used party as passive or deficient in agency of their own.

VAL PLUMWOOD

intelligence studies, gender bias in

Attempts to prove sex differences in intelligence have included comparative analyses of skull size, language comprehension, and mathematics proficiency; however, these studies have been widely discounted due to biased methodologies. Intelligence tests can be manipulated through wording and context such that girls are at a disadvantage relative to boys. Gender gaps on such tests are then attributed to natural sex differences, rather than to the structure of the tests. On standardised math tests, girls often score lower than the boys they outperform in classwork. Some studies suggest that standardised tests favour speed, efficiency and risk-taking over sustained reasoning and attention to detail, and these factors, rather than intelligence differences, account for the gender gap. Intelligence differences have also been claimed for race and class, with similar shortcomings.

See also: craniometry, biology of; Fausto-Sterling, Anne; Gilligan, Carol

References and further reading

Mensh, E. and Mensh, H. (1991) *The IQ Mythology:*
Class, Race, Gender and Inequality, Carbondale, IL: Southern Illinois University Press.

SARA GOERING

internal colonisation

Critical theory contrasts two types of rationality: the instrumental (or systems) rationality of economic exchange and bureaucratic regulation and the communicative rationality of intersubjectivity, dialogue, and consensus. Ideally, there is balanced development between the two rationalities, but in modernity, instrumental rationality becomes dominant and invades or 'colonises' private and public spheres of life normally dependent on communicative rationality. Critical theory resists this colonisation, but advises only limited use of legal-bureaucratic remedies because it associates such remedies with instrumental rationality. Feminist analysis complicates the picture by showing that critical theory's reluctance to support legal-bureaucratic intervention into patriarchal family institutions (see **patriarchy**) can be traced to its idealised, outdated, androcentric view of family. In rejecting critical theory's **androcentrism**, feminists strive for a new, gender-inclusive communicative rationality.

See also: critical theory, feminism and

References and further reading

Fraser, N. (1995) 'What's Critical about Critical Theory?', in J. Meehan (ed.) *Feminists Read Habermas*, New York: Routledge.

MARIE FLEMING

international human rights

International human rights are moral-legal claims. Individuals are guaranteed a range of freedoms through two principal types of documents: covenants between nations and reports issued by non-governmental human rights organisations.

Women's international human rights find important expression in CEDAW, the Convention on the Elimination of All Forms of Discrimination Against Women. Article 3 of CEDAW guarantees to women the 'full enjoyment of human rights and fundamental freedoms on a basis of equality with men'. Women's rights to reproductive health are specifically affirmed in two later documents: first, in the programme of action adopted by 184 UN member states at the 1994 International Conference on Population and Development in Cairo and again in the Platform for action adopted by 187 UN member states at the 1995 Fourth World Conference on Women in Beijing.

Discussions at Beijing articulated the human rights of women to include rights to decide freely on matters related to their sexuality. Sexual and reproductive health, free of coercion, discrimination and violence, opportunities and gainful employment are all crucial to empowering women to protect rights to reproductive health and ultimately, reproductive choice. Yet, this range of freedoms that has to be guaranteed to women still relies upon the assumption that states are appropriate agents to protect women's rights. Evidence too easily demonstrates that states frequently protect those who oppress women. The Non-Governmental Organizations Forum (1995) held a global tribunal on women's human rights. Testimonies on violence against women repeatedly implicated state organisations or, in the case of civil war, organisations supported by one or another claimant to state power. Algerian women described 'detention camps operated by Muslim fundamentalists in which Algerian women and girls are enslaved and coerced into temporary marriages, raped, tortured and forced to become pregnant in the name of religion'. Elsewhere, a young girl raped by her father or mother's boyfriend may be 'protectively' institutionalised in a centre for juvenile delinquents. Young women lured to foreign countries on the pretext of a job may find themselves imprisoned, forced into prostitution, and even forced to have an abortion to end any pregnancy. Poor minority women of Myanmar suffer what may be the cruellest practice of all – sexually enslaved in a foreign brothel and forced into unprotected sex, they are sent back 'home' if they develop AIDS (see **AIDS, women and**). Since they and their families are told that these young women have a contagious fever, they

are then sent to live alone in huts set out in the rice fields, to die in tragic isolation.

Moreover, politically active women of India's lowest caste organised to end their **oppression** have suffered human rights abuses at the hands of the police. A woman from the USA was hospitalised for depression at age fourteen. Instead of treating her depression, hospital authorities treated her for 'gender identity disorder' and sought to force her to behave in a more 'feminine' manner (Roche 1996). Genital mutilation of girls, performed as a circumcision rite necessary to 'traditional' respectability, also challenges the extent to which protection of women's bodily integrity can occur in a state system established upon patriarchal traditions (see **patriarchy**).

Where states offer institutional protections to those oppressing women, respect for state sovereignty may mean respect for a systematically sanctioned oppression of women. The instances cited above reinforce this suspicion. Moreover this inherent problem is exacerbated at the international level since covenants between nations, including the United Nations Charter, the Universal Declaration of Human Rights and the UN Refugee Convention 'empower states to act against states, not individuals or groups to act for themselves' (MacKinnon 1994). The two programmes protecting women's reproductive rights both lack mechanisms for holding governments legally accountable (Cook and Fathalla 1997). Moreover, most Non-Governmental Organizations (NGOs) follow the pattern set by the International Red Cross, respecting states as the sovereign actors in the arena of international human rights. These institutional barriers to the effective practice of women's rights lend credibility to **MacKinnon**'s charge – 'each state's lack of protection of women's human rights is internationally protected and that is called protecting state sovereignty' (MacKinnon 1994).

However, to become aware of the problem can be a first step toward effecting change. In 1998, Radhika Coomaraswamy, special reporter on **violence** against women for the UN Human Rights Commission called for a protocol on the elimination of violence against women so that CEDAW might inquire from all signatory governments what their procedures are. She called for national plans of action to eradicate violence against women, with mechanisms to deal with incest, domestic violence, rape and sexual harassment, and stringent measures to stop sex trafficking. Seeking concrete steps to sensitise the criminal justice system, she also proposed media campaigns to raise awareness and national plans of action for developing effective partnership between police and NGOs working in the field.

It is also important for feminists that women become acknowledged agents capable of claiming their own international human rights. Going beyond Ms Coomaraswamy's suggestions, women need to be able to seek asylum from gender-specific violations. Means for controlling rogue states like Myanmar are also necessary for women's international human rights to serve women in response to the reality of women's own lives.

See also: female circumcision/female genital mutilation

References and further reading

Cook, R. and Fathalla, M.F. (1997) 'Advancing Reproductive Rights: The Cairo Programme and the Beijing Platform', *Women's International Network News*, 23 (Spring).

MacKinnon, C. (1994) 'Rape, Genocide and Women's Human Rights', *Harvard Women's Law Journal*, 17.

O'Neill, O. (1993) 'Justice, Gender and International Boundaries', in Nussbaum, M.C. and Sen, A. *The Quality of Life*, Oxford: Clarendon Press.

Roche, S.E. (1996) 'Messages from the NGO Forum on Women, Beijing, 1995', *Affilia: Journal of Women and Social Work*, 11 (4).

NATALIE DANDEKAR

international relations

International relations is a paradigmatically male dominated subject. The academic discipline is overwhelmingly male and the conventional practices of international relations are typically associated with men. War is still regarded as the core topic of international relations. The discipline itself originated in 1919, instigated by the carnage of the First World War, inspiring the laudable aim to understand wars in an attempt to prevent them. This concern with war leads international-relations scholars to be pre-occupied with power, security, international structures, and relations between states especially in the realms of foreign policy and military strategy. A concurrent underlying theme of international relations is a desire to achieve order and stability on a global scale.

Feminism, in all its manifestations, with its questions about women, domestic/personal politics and interest in disrupting the traditional (see **patriarchy**) order seems inherently incompatible with international relations. It is perhaps not surprising that there is such resistance to feminist intrusions into international relations as they appear to be 'politically at odds with one another' (Whitworth 1994: ix).

The formal introduction of feminist scholarship into international relations can be dated to the late 1980s, particularly with the publication of Cynthia Enloe's book, *Bananas, Beaches and Bases* in 1989 and the conference on 'Women and International Relations' held at the London School of Economics in May 1988. Since then, feminists have approached the gendering of the discipline in several simultaneous ways, all perhaps inspired by Enloe's question, 'where are the women?'

One of these is the classic 'add women and stir' approach, influenced by liberal feminist theory and politics (see **liberal feminism**). In the 'real world' of international politics, this is a logical move, especially in the context of western liberal democracies apparently committed to equal rights. A brief look around the world's senior politicians and diplomats, combat soldiers or military commanders reveals the scarcity of women. However, the ontological move of 'adding women' reveals something initially paradoxical; that women are already in international relations. This does not simply mean some women are in traditionally powerful international roles; but rather that traditional (and therefore invisible) women's activities ensure the international system works smoothly and efficiently.

Examples are the work done by diplomatic wives and military prostitutes. Feminist methods of questioning the personal and the domestic ensure that analysis moves beyond revealing the paucity of women diplomats, but inquire how the demands of heterosexual femininity impact upon the agency of diplomats' wives. From the initial question, 'where are the women?', feminists open up new areas to study in international relations including: the sexual politics of **prostitution** and domestic service, the international sex trade, tourism, and the activities of mothers.

A second approach, evolving from the liberal-inspired one, is more concerned with epistemology (see **epistemology, feminist**). This has at least two strands; one linked with **radical feminism** and standpoint feminism (see **standpoint theory**); the second influenced by postmodernism and cultural studies (see **cultural theory/cultural studies, feminist**). The radical feminist focus on the lives and experiences of women and the standpoint feminists' interest in the gendered construction of knowledge encourages some feminists to investigate how we understand traditional topics in international relations. Security, for example, is conventionally understood as militarily defending the state from attack. Feminists studying women's lives ask if this idea about security is a 'male' one, shot through with the typically masculinist belief that power concerns control rather than empowerment (Tickner 1992). If women defined security, the important issues might be different because women are more likely to be attacked by men they know, rather than strangers from other states.

Such views about 'typical women's lives' or 'women's ways of knowing' are attacked for their essentialist, stereotypical and universalising views about women (see **essentialism**). Nevertheless, they open up new ways of thinking about the gendered nature of international relations, first by showing how women's activities are made invisible on the international scene and second by alerting us to the idea that **gender** may be structuring how we think in the international context.

Take, for example, the language used by nuclear strategists. Carol Cohn's work shows that gender acts as a 'pre-emptive deterrent to thought' (1993: 232). Emotions and values associated with femininity unconsciously rule out consideration of them in matters paradigmatically associated with men and masculinity. Extending this kind of analysis to

popular culture, other feminist scholars analyse films to assess how states are popularly inscribed and reinscribed as strong and manly. Rambo's famous line 'do we get to win this time?' might be understood as one way in which the USA attempted to re-masculinise and re-militarise itself after its 'humiliating' defeat in Vietnam (see **nationalism and gender**).

Conventional international relations scholars have difficulty understanding that feminist work goes beyond a desire to be included onto the traditional agenda (Sylvester 1994: 134). Tracing the resistance to anything but domesticated feminism reveals a pattern of incredulity towards political analyses which insists on the relevance of women's lives and the power of gendered imaginations to construct both international relations – and, crucially in this most adversarial of disciplines – the construction of the 'other'.

As in many other disciplines, in international relations, 'feminists have made the academy itself a site of feminist politics' (Clough 1994: 2). Since the early days of 'adding women', contemporary conventional international relations is finding it harder to imagine, in the words of Cynthia Enloe, that relations between states can be understood as resembling a 'superman comic strip' and instead has to come to terms with a global reality that is more akin to a Jackson Pollock painting.

References and further reading

Clough, P.T. (1994) *Feminist Thought*, Oxford: Blackwell.

Cohn, C. (1993) 'Wars, Wimps, and Women', in M. Cooke and A. Woollacott (eds) *Gendering War Talk*, Princeton, NJ: Princeton University Press, pp. 227–48.

Enloe, C. (1989) *Bananas, Beaches and Bases*, London: Pandora.

Jeffords, S. (1989) *The Remasculinization of America*, Bloomington, IN: Indiana University Press.

Sylvester, C. (1994), *Feminist Theory and International Relations in a Postmodern Era*, Cambridge: Cambridge University Press.

Tickner, J.A. (1992) *Gender and International Relations*, New York: Columbia University Press.

Whitworth, S. (1994) *Feminism and International Relations*, London: Macmillan Press.

MARYSIA ZALEWSKI

international tribunal of crimes against women

The United Nations established tribunals to name, investigate and punish those responsible for war crimes committed in Rwanda (1994) and the former Yugoslavia (1993). Both tribunals acknowledge rape, forced prostitution, forced pregnancy and sexual enslavement as violations of basic women's rights, instruments of genocide, violations of the laws of war and crimes against humanity. Both tribunals acknowledge sexual abuse as a serious crime of torture. Moreover, rules concerning rape put the burden of proof on the defendant.

Thus far gender parity seems elusive. Three women serve on the two tribunals. All five appellate judges are men. Yet the prosecutors, Richard Goldstone, of South Africa and then Canadian judge Louise Arbour have effectively prosecuted gender-based crimes.

This represents a profound shift in the theory of international law. Now civil war crimes against women can be seen truly as international crimes against humanity.

NATALIE DANDEKAR

interpretation

In ordinary language, interpretation (Latin *interpretari*: to explain, expound) refers to any effort to explain things. In feminist theory, interpretation has come to mean a particular kind of explanation, one rooted in a hermeneutic inquiry (see **hermeneutics**). Interpretion seeks to penetrate misleading surfaces to the underlying reality behind them, to articulate a unified theory that can comprehend the totality of its subject matter. Interpretation is often contrasted to **genealogy**, a way of thinking that is suspicious of the stable appearance/reality distinction relied upon by interpretive thinkers. Many feminists are trying to bring interpretive and genealogical analyses together, combining the critical energies entailed in deconstructing analytical categories with the political vision required to push them forward.

References and further reading

Ferguson, K. (1993) *The Man Question*, San Francisco: University of California Press.

KATHY E. FERGUSON

intersexuality

Intersexuality is the clinical designation for the condition popularly termed hermaphroditism. Roughly one in one hundred births demonstrates anomaly in sex differentiation and approximately one in two thousand is sufficiently anomalous to make categorisation of an infant as male or female problematic. Since the 1950s, medical practitioners have attempted to 'manage' intersexuality – customarily through extreme surgical intervention intended to render intersex infants' genitalia unambiguously female or male in appearance.

In the1990s intersexuals began challenging the medicalisation of intersexuality, protesting medical and social insistence upon binary, biological, sexual difference and drawing public attention to the devastating consequences of inscribing sexual dimorphism on intersex bodies. Some intersex activists have made common cause with transsexual and **transgender** activists; indeed some intersexuals self-identify as transgender.

See also: Fausto-Sterling, Anne; gender; transgender; transsexuality/gender dysphoria

References and further reading

Chase, C. (1998) 'Hermaphrodites with Attitude', GLQ: *A Journal of Lesbian and Gay Studies*, 4 (2).

TRISH SALAH

intuition

Intuition (Latin, *intuere*: to look at), in western philosophy, is direct, unmediated knowledge achieved by a sort of mental vision: by the purest, surest activity of reason. Historically, intuition was seen as a particularly reliable route to knowledge, uncluttered by the messiness of concrete detail. Yet feminist theorists note a curious reversal in its valuation. 'Women's intuition' counts less as evidence of superior rationality or knowledgeability than as confirmation of women's deficiency in reason. Represented as radically subjective, closer to having a 'hunch', to 'feeling it in your bones', intuition's sensitivity is trivialised in claims that women are *reduced to* reliance on intuition, whereas men are *capable of* proficiency in reason. Thus stereotypes of the feminine, private woman receive confirmation from beliefs that women are 'naturally' intuitive and therefore properly left in charge of monitoring emotional climates. The strength and skill of intelligent intuition disappears in such denigrations.

LORRAINE CODE

Irigaray, Luce (b. 1932)

Born in Belgium, Luce Irigaray is a philosopher and practising analyst who works in Paris. A former member of the Freudian School, Irigaray was expelled from Lacan's charmed circle after the publication of *Speculum of the Other Woman* in 1974. It has been suggested that Lacan disapproved of Irigaray's feminist critique of psychoanalysis.

In the Anglo-American context, Irigaray's early major works were first translated in 1985. Because of their particular reliance upon **psychoanalysis** and philosophy, these texts ensured Irigaray's reception as a major figure of **French feminism**. *Speculum*, for example, uses the technique of symptomatic reading to read Freud against himself. When Freud says that the girl is a little man, or when he confines female sexuality within phallomorphic parameters as nothing to be seen, he speaks volumes about an indifference to sexual difference, a desire for symmetry. Irigaray coins the term 'specula(risa)tion' to capture this economy and extends her method (back) to philosophers like Plato.

To interrupt the hom(m)osexual exchange of the philosophers (where *homme* = man) Irigaray takes

what is circumscribed by masculine discourse – female sexuality – as heterogeneous. Challenging Lacan, Irigaray replaces his flat mirror with the concave mirror of the speculum, used non-conventionally. This way, femininity is no longer measured by the One Sex; nor is it 'seen' in the manner of gynaecology. Instead, female sexuality 'speaks' a proximity and multiplicity (*parler femme*) – a 'form' expressed by the two lips of *This Sex Which is Not One* (1985).

Some regard this work as a valorisation of pre-Oedipal female sexuality, dismissing Irigaray as hopelessly essentialist in the context of **essentialism** versus anti-essentialism. Others emphasise the figurative and non-referential possibilities of the two lips, particularly for a 'vulvomorphic' or 'lipeccentric' deconstruction of **phallogocentrism** (see also **deconstruction, feminist**). Irigaray herself has more recently promoted the idea that women need to imagine their own relation to the maternal, a genealogy thus far appropriated by men. Here, the two lips figure with the idea of a 'female transcendental' as strategies for jamming masculine theoretical appropriations of origin stories and the symbolic exile/dereliction of women. This way, Irigaray's subsequent work tends to resist the essentialist readings that have been given to her.

Selected writings

Irigaray, L. (1985) *Speculum of the Other Woman*, trans. G.C. Gill, Ithaca, NY: Cornell University Press.
—— (1985) *This Sex Which is not One*, trans. C. Porter with Carolyn Burke, Ithaca, NY: Cornell University Press.
—— (1993) *An Ethics of Sexual Difference*, trans. C. Burke and G.C. Gill, Ithaca, NY: Cornell University Press.

References and further reading

Chanter, T. (1995) *Ethics of Eros: Irigaray's Rewriting of the Philosophers*, New York: Routledge.
Whitford, M. (ed.) (1991) *The Irigaray Reader*, Oxford: Basil Blackwell.

KWOK WEI LENG

Islam and feminism

Political and ideological mobilisation around women's rights in Islam has been a reality in the Middle East since the early nineteenth century. Male secular reformers like Fathali Akhundzadeh and Mirza Aghakhan-e Kermani in Iran, and Islamist modernisers, Namik Kemal and Ahmed Mithat Efendi in Turkey and Qasim Amin in Egypt, denounced *Shari'a* (Islamic codes of law) and *Hijab* (dress code for women) in an attempt to modernise women's status; Muslim jurists like Cevdet Pasha in Ottoman Turkey and Muhammad Abduh in Egypt sought to reinterpret Islamic family law. To reform-minded men, women's education, enlightenment and emancipation would benefit society: women would become better mothers, better wives.

Early female reformers were sharper and more gender-focused (see **gender**). Ghorat-ul-Ain and Bibi Khanoum (early and late 1800s Iran), Fatma Aliya Hanim (late 1800s Turkey) and Nazira Zin al-Din (1920s Lebanon) criticised misogynist interpretations of the Qur'an and the male-serving fabrication of *Hadith* (sayings on religion and daily life attributed to the Prophet), attacking the veil, sex segregation and gender-based restrictions imposed on Muslim women (see **misogyny**).

If feminism, at its core, is a political project advocating equal rights and women's access to public life, then it has always been crucial in Islamic societies. Historically, participation in national liberation movements created gender consciousness among Middle Eastern and North African women. Beginning in the 1900s women organised autonomous groups (in Iran, beginning in 1905; Turkey, 1908; Egypt, 1920s). Left and liberal nationalist women were at the forefront of these activities, promoting also the organisational and ideological goals of the socialist and nationalist movements.

Postcolonial nation-building and modernisation in the 1960s–70s, except in Saudi Arabia and the Gulf States, relaxed sex-segregation and encouraged women's workplace participation but disrupted independent feminist activity. 'State feminism' emerged. Following the west-inspired agenda of the modernising states, self-consciously catering to patriarchal values (see **patriarchy**), feminism lost its early progressive character and mobilizing power.

The new wave of Islamic revivalism, instigated by the 1979 Revolution in Iran, the outright suppression of women's legal rights and personal freedoms by Islamic states in Iran, Sudan and Afghanistan, and the brutal treatment of secular women by Islamists in Algeria, straining further civic and personal liberties, have provoked a new era of gender activism. Women-centred activities in the region, perhaps the most vibrant, energetic, and politically engaged in the world, today encompass both conservative Islamist as well as secular, liberal and socialist women. Suitably toned down and indigenised, feminism seems to accommodate a broad range of advocates, including women committed to *Shari'a* such as Zaynab-al-Ghazali and Safinaz Kazim (Egypt), Monireh Gorji and Zahra Rahnevard (Iran) and Nagwa Kamal Farid and Hikmat Sid-Ahmed (Sudan). Some are close to Islamic regimes, oppose the cultural influence of feminism and secular western values, but advocate an enlargement of women's public space. Today's feminism also includes Muslim women activists who see an Islamic framework as the only legitimate terrain for advocating women's rights, but who also draw with much ingenuity from secular feminist ideas to demand gender equity in the family, access to education, work, and political power and an end to sexual exploitation and gender-violence.

Following in the footsteps of women's rights pioneers a century ago, this latter group of women blame gender inequity on factors outside Islam's legal, cultural and political traditions. They believe that Islam has given rights to women but that Muslim men have arrogated to themselves the task of prejudicially interpreting the Qur'an and *Hadith* and of defining the position of women. Their ideology, home-grown, culturally-grounded, is increasingly embraced by feminist academics in North America and Europe (Leila Ahmed, Yvonne Haddad, Mai Yamani, Parvin Paidar, Afsaneh Najmabadi) who apparently see Islamic feminism as the most effective framework for advocating women's rights in the region. They advise feminists in the west to 'listen to the "other", even when that voice speaks from beneath a veil' (Sabbagh 1996). Other scholars like Fatima **Mernissi** (1987) and

Rifat Hassan (1992) also use apparent inconsistencies among Islamic texts to suggest a more women-friendly, gender-equitable interpretation against jurists and traditionalists who, in the name of Islamic order, derive gender asymmetry and female domesticity from the same texts.

Finally, there are secular feminist individuals, organisations and publications in Tunisia, Morocco, Egypt, Algeria, Pakistan, Bangladesh, along with a multitude of Palestinian and Iranian women, who, under the most hostile conditions, struggle for legal and personal autonomy, in opposition to an equity-negating Islamist project which claims Islamic solutions to all social and cultural problems. Their regional and international coalitions and networks such as the Association for the Solidarity of Arab Women and Women Living Under Muslim Law speak eloquently of the rise of a new wave of feminism in the region. By connecting gender equity to the drive for democracy and national autonomy these women inspire struggle for progressive change, long overdue in Islamic societies (Kandiyoti 1995). Theoretically, their most powerful message is that both the Islamist project and western modernisation have failed women. Hence, women need to develop a new discourse and 'begin a more fruitful discussion of the changing lives of women of different classes, of different ethnic groups, and of different regions' (Hatem 1993).

References and further reading

Hassan, R. (1992) 'Muslim Women and Post-Patriarchal Islam', in P.M. Cooey, W.R. Eakin and J.B. McDaniel (eds) *After Patriarchy: Feminist Transformations of the World Religions*, Maryknoll, NY: ORBIS Books.

Hatem, M. (1993) 'Toward the Development of Post-Islamist and Post-nationalist Feminist Discourses in The Middle East', in J. Tucker (ed.) *Arab Women: Old Boundaries: New Frontiers*, Bloomington and Indianapolis: Indiana University Press.

Kandiyoti, D. (1995) 'Reflections on the Politics of Gender in Muslim Societies: From Nairobi to Beijing', in M. Afkhami (ed.) *Faith and Freedom: Women's Human Rights in the Muslim World*, Syracuse: Syracuse University Press.

Paidar, P. (1995) *Women and the Political Process in Twentieth-Century Iran*, Cambridge: Cambridge University Press.

Sabbagh, S. (ed.) (1996) *Arab Women: Between Defiance and Restraint*, New York: Olive Branch Press.

HAIDEH MOGHISSI

J

Jaggar, Alison (b. 1942)

Alison Jaggar is best known for her book *Feminist Politics and Human Nature* (1983) in which she turns a critical eye on feminist theories of the early 1980s. She distinguishes four distinct political theories, **liberal feminism**, traditional **Marxism**, **radical feminism**, and socialist feminism (see **socialism and feminism**), which she classifies in relation to their conceptions of human nature and their prescriptions for promoting gender equality. She advocates socialist feminism because it recognises knowledge and human nature as sociohistorical constructs and focuses on the special standpoint of women. Women's historically subordinate social and class position offers them a 'more reliable and less distorted' (1983: 370) view of how society is constructed than that of more privileged individuals in society. Socialist feminists reject the view that biology is destiny, and thus argue that women's traditional role as caregivers is not inherent to women's nature.

Jaggar rejects liberal feminism due to its emphasis on **individualism**, which cannot account for the intricate social web of relations most women exist in, and its reliance on the unattainable standpoint of pure **objectivity**. Liberal feminism's goal of gender equality is a valuable one, but it is unlikely to be attained through simple legal measures (e.g. non-discrimination law) without a more serious critique of the existing social organisation (e.g., less focus on individualism, rejection of capitalism).

Jaggar argues that traditional Marxism tends to overemphasise the role of class in assessing oppression, and consequently leaves room for patriarchal influences in the ideal society. By de-emphasising gender and race inequalities, traditional Marxists do not adequately account for the double- or triple-jeopardy faced by working class women, especially women of colour. Marxist theory does, however, rightly emphasise the historical nature of knowledge and the role of capitalism in widespread oppression.

Finally, Jaggar rejects radical feminist theory because of its focus on the evils of patriarchy to the exclusion of the role of capitalism and class in creating and maintaining women's unequal status. Radical feminists demonise men to such an extent that feminist coalitions between women and men are nearly impossible.

Jaggar has been critiqued for setting up this taxonomy in a way that falsely separates 'feminisms' as distinct camps and suggests an evolutionary theoretical path from liberal to radical to Marxist to socialist.

Selected writings

Jaggar, A. (1983) *Feminist Politics and Human Nature*, Totowa, NJ: Rowman and Littlefield.

SARA GOERING

Jayawardena, Kumari

Kumari Jayawardena is a leading feminist and civil rights activist from Sri Lanka whose critical writings in English and her native Singhalese have raised the international visibility of South Asian feminisms. She received her secondary education in Sri Lanka before obtaining her Ph.D. from the London School of Economics. Until 1985, she was an Associate Professor of Political Science at the University of Colombo, Sri Lanka. She currently teaches Women's Studies at Colombo University while doing research at the Social Scientists' Association.

Jayawardena's feminist politics expose the complexities of Third World women's subordination within the triple bind created by male-centred imperialist, nationalist and religious revivalist discourses. Her work demonstrates how all three discourses are based on an exclusionary model of bourgeois **heterosexuality** that promotes a hierarchy of discrimination along gender and class lines. She claims that because men have always dictated the terms of national and colonial policy, women have been located outside citizenship by being denied equitable agency in national history. Instead, they have been reduced to symbols of male mythological readings that have situated them as concepts or abstractions concretised in glorified images of Mother Nation or glorified ideals of Virtue, Purity and Sacrifice. She asserts that colonialism and nationalism sustain an implicit power structure in which men are active subjects of nation building while women are marginalised through fetishised imagery and confined to religiously-sanctified motherhood (see **nationalism and gender**).

Jayawardena's work also highlights the active role played by Third World women in resisting repressive structures by arguing that feminism was not exported to the Third World by western liberalism. She chronicles the historical and idelogical changes that have impacted women's lives like education and socio-economic enhancement, to document the history of indigenous feminisms in Third World locations (see **Indigenist feminism**).

Her most recent scholarship de-essentialises the category of British colonial women by showing that not all colonial women were affluent members of the *Raj*. She describes the presence of certain independent women who spoke with 'a different voice' to openly undermine the Christianised colonial mindset by adopting Eastern traditions. These transgressions represented the first semblance of coalition building between these 'different' white women and their Asian sisters in their common struggle against gendered colonialism and nationalist oppression.

It is inconceivable to study **postcolonial feminism** without considering the significant contributions of Kumari Jayawardena.

Selected writings

Jayawardena, K. (1985) *Feminism amd Nationalism in The Third World*, London: Zed Press.
—— (1995) *The White Woman's Other Burden*, London: Routledge.

BRINDA J. MEHTA

Johnston, Claire (1940–87)

As a pioneering 1970s British feminist cine-theorist alongside Laura **Mulvey** and Pam Cook, Claire Johnston amalgamated structuralist, semiotic and Lacanian psychoanalytic influences in her textual (rather than sociological) analysis of film. Her edited anthology *Notes on Women's Cinema* (1973) foregrounds the debate around feminist film theory and practice, Johnston's own essay 'Women's Cinema as Counter-Cinema' establishing the deconstructive basis for a revolutionary feminist 'counter-cinema' seeking to interrogate and disrupt the textual and ideological operations of dominant film practice.

Johnston identifies women as signs within the patriarchal and bourgeois structures of a male-dominated cinema (see **patriarchy**). As a discourse controlled by and communicated between men constructing women as mythic objects of male fantasy, Johnston declares that '... despite the enormous emphasis placed on woman as spectacle in the cinema, woman as woman is largely absent' (1973: 23). By releasing women's desires and collective fantasies, a feminist counter-cinema would alter the means of signification and directly challenge constructions of 'femininity' and **sexuality** in mainstream cinema.

Criticising Hollywood realism for its representations of women as 'other' and 'non-male', Johnston also dismisses early 1970s feminist cinema vérité films for their exclusively political and content-based perspectives. Instead, Johnston envisions a counter-cinema which deploys both entertainment and politics as tools in oppositional spaces located within avant-garde as well as mainstream cinema. She explores the work of classic Hollywood directors Dorothy Arzner (1920s–1940s) and Ida Lupino (1930s–1940s), positing their strategic subversions of the classic realist film text as incipient moments in a feminist counter-cinema.

Johnston herself acknowledged the initial criticisms of ahistoricality and delimiting textuality ensconced in the workings of her chosen methodologies (see **methodology, feminist**). Indeed, some feminists remain critical of the shaping Freudian and Lacanian phallocentrisms and inherent failure to consider broader political and historical factors of psychoanalytic film criticism. Grappling with the patriarchal underpinnings of cinematic and related discourses, Johnston nevertheless has created a foundational cine-feminist understanding of female desire, sexual and cultural **difference**, spectatorship and film history within both a dominant and feminist counter-cinema.

See also: film criticism, feminist; psychoanalysis; structuralism

Selected writings

Johnston, C. (1973) 'Women's Cinema as Counter Cinema', in C. Johnston (ed.) *Notes on Women's Cinema*, London: Society for Education in Film and Television.
—— (ed.) (1975) *Dorothy Arzner: Towards A Feminist Cinema*, London: British Film Institute.
—— (1980) 'The Subject of Feminist Film Theory/ Practice', *Screen*, 21 (2).

SATINDER KAUR CHOHAN

jouissance

The concept of *jouissance* is strictly untranslateable from the French, conveying in its meaning both an excess of pleasure – what we might in English call bliss or ecstasy – and a surplus or profit taken in other ways. The concept is undeniably sexual, being the word used for orgasmic pleasure, and it is in this foremost sense that Lacan deploys the notion in his Encore seminars to capture the notion that there is a part of the feminine which, by its very nature as the negation of the masculine, exceeds a 'phallic economy' (the nature of words being the nature of things, Lacan says).

His seductive gesture has been taken up by French feminists Luce **Irigaray**, Hélène **Cixous** and Julia **Kristeva**, who exploit the excessive character of the figure in a variety of strategies to imagine the place of woman beyond **phallogocentrism**.

See also: French feminism; psychoanalytic feminist literary theory; psychoanalysis

ROBYN FERRELL

Judaism and feminism

Jewish feminism, like the feminist movement as a whole (see also **feminism**), takes a number of different forms with distinct agendas and goals. Some Jewish feminists have focused on gaining equal access for women to all the roles and responsibilities of Jewish religious life, from full synagogue participation and leadership, to complete access to Jewish learning, to rabbinic ordination. Others want to move beyond what they see as participation in a patriarchal tradition (see **patriarchy**) to transform Jewish practice and Jewish self-understanding.

Jewish feminism emerged in the late 1960s and early 1970s as a movement for equal rights. The earliest Jewish feminist writings focused on the disadvantages of women under Jewish law: the exclusion of women from a minyan (the quorum of ten required for a full synagogue service); the prohibitions on women leading prayer, being called to the Torah, or serving as witnesses; women's exemption from study, and, in family law, the inability of women to initiate divorce. Together, these restrictions reflect and reinscribe the notion that men are normative Jews, while women are '**Other**'. Jewish feminists contend that women are full Jews and full persons with the same spiritual needs and aspirations as men. To deny them access to study and public prayer is both to deprive them of their spiritual heritage, and to impoverish Judaism by dismissing the skills and insights of half the Jewish people.

As a theoretical perspective, this equal access position applies the insights of **liberal feminism** to Judaism. In demanding equality in school and synagogue, Jewish feminists essentially are demanding equal citizenship as Jews. For Orthodox feminists, who have to deal with a traditional worldview that uses the rhetoric of **complementarity** to mask women's subordination, articulating an equal rights position remains a theoretical challenge. For nonOrthodox feminists, whose denominational bodies recognise and support the equality of women, the challenge lies in making equality a reality in particular institutions.

Other Jewish feminists are critical of an equal rights model, however, because, in their view, it strives for access to a tradition that women had little hand in creating. From this second perspective, women's Talmud study, ordination, and leadership in the synagogue, while necessary as foundations, simply expose the contradictions between women's full participation and the content of tradition. Women may study halakha (Jewish law), for example, only to discover that women's perspectives are absent both from legal rulings and from the very way questions are framed. Women may lead prayer only to realise that the God they are praying to is never imaged as female. From this feminist transformational viewpoint, full equality for women in Judaism would necessarily involve a radical reworking of thought and practice, rather than simply admission to the rights and responsibilities of Jewish religious life.

Feminists interested in the transformation of Judaism draw on many aspects of feminist theory and raise many significant theoretical questions.

What understanding of feminism underlies the transformational model? Is Judaism essentially patriarchal? How radically can one change a tradition before it becomes something else? Insofar as feminists are interested in incorporating women's voices into Jewish tradition, how can they acknowledge the **diversity** of women's experience and resist defining it in essentialist ways? (See **essentialism**.)

Feminists are posing these questions in relation to many dimensions of Judaism. They are reclaiming women's history, for instance, through historiography and creative midrash (a traditional Jewish exegetical technique). Jewish feminist scholars are examining traditional sources through new lenses, lifting up issues of women's participation and leadership often downplayed or obscured by normative texts. By juxtaposing nonconventional evidence – for example, archeological and inscriptional materials concerning women's roles – with normative sources, they are coming to understand the ways in which such sources are often ideological constructions rather than accurate guides to historical reality. At the same time, feminsts are using midrash to ask new questions of biblical narratives, filling in silences in biblical texts with new stories framed from feminist perspectives.

Another area in which Jewish feminists are transforming tradition is that of ritual. One of the earliest feminist innovations was the creation of naming ceremonies for girls that sought to welcome daughters into the covenant with the same sense of celebration normally reserved for a boy's brit milah (covenant of circumcision). This and other areas of ritual innovation raise important theoretical questions about how one conceptualises the central events in women's lives. Many feminist rituals mark central female biological turning points ignored by Jewish tradition – childbirth, weaning, menopause, and so on. But some Jewish feminists are critical of this focus as reinforcing the identification of women with their biology. Other new rituals, therefore, celebrate a range of moments in women's lives – from ordination, to coming out as a lesbian, to becoming a vegetarian, to moving to a new city.

Ritual innovation spills over into the larger area of liturgical change, and here Jewish feminist work has centred particularly on the issue of God-language. Questioning the effects on women of imagining God as a male, dominating Other, feminists have proposed a host of alternative images. Some have written prayers referring to God as 'She' and giving Her female and feminine characteristics. Others have reclaimed Shekhinah, the feminine aspect of God in the Jewish mystical tradition, as their name for the sacred. Still others have composed new liturgies using natural and gender-neutral imagery. Jewish experiments in this area have gained from dialogue with **Christian** and **Goddess** feminism.

These are just some of the areas in which Jewish feminists are seeking to transform Judaism. In rethinking notions of community and family, criticising and reconstructing Jewish approaches to **sexuality** and **heterosexuality**, reflecting on the nature of Jewish law and role of law in Judaism, Jewish feminism intersects with and contributes to many areas of feminist theory.

References and further reading

Adler, R. (1998) *Engendering Judaism: An Inclusive Theology and Ethics*, Philadelphia, PA: The Jewish Publication Society.

Greenberg, B. (1981) *On Women and Judaism: A View from Tradition*, Philadelphia, PA: Jewish Publication Society.

Heschel, S. (ed.) (1983) *On Being a Jewish Feminist*, New York: Schocken Books.

Levine, E.R. (1991) *A Ceremonies Sampler: New Rites, Celebrations, and Observances of Jewish Women*, San Diego: The Women's Institute for Continuing Jewish Education.

Plaskow, J. (1990) *Standing Again at Sinai: Judaism from a Feminist Perspective*, San Francisco: Harper Collins.

JUDITH PLASKOW

K

Keller, Evelyn Fox (b. 1936)

Evelyn Fox Keller's historical and philosophical analyses of **gender** and **science** have been foundational to the development of Anglo-American feminist critiques of science. Keller's advocacy for a gender-free science, her psychoanalytic critique of scientific objectivity and her concern with the effects of language and metaphoricity in scientific knowledges have been particularly influential on feminist and social analyses of the natural sciences.

Keller has argued for the establishment of a 'gender-free', rather than feminine or feminist, science. This gender-free scientific methodology is best exemplified in *A Feeling for the Organism*, Keller's biography of the Nobel laureate and cytogeneticist Barbara McClintock. McClintock describes her relation to genetic material as 'a feeling for the organism' that is based on 'listening' to what her object of study has to say to her. Keller argues that this dialogic methodology demonstrates a deep emotional connection to the objects of science that is independent of the gender of the observer. It is the division of this emotional labour from intellectual labour that marks many scientific pursuits as masculine and objective.

Keller turns to object relations theories to analyse the gendered nature of **objectivity**. Traditional conceptions of scientific objectivity reflect a characteristically masculine notion of **autonomy**. Scientific objectivity is the cognitive counterpart of a psychological detachment that is preferentially cultivated in boys and men. However, rather than argue against the possibility of objectivity because it is essentially masculine, Keller contends that scientific objectivity can be reclaimed through a more social and interpersonal understanding of autonomy.

The constitutive effect of language on scientific knowledges and practices has been Keller's other major critical concern. Keller has demonstrated how metaphor (e.g., the biological figuration of fertilisation as a relation between a passive egg and active sperm, or the genetic figuration of development as a relation between passive cytoplasm and active nucleus) has been a powerful guide of scientific models and methods. Keller has occasionally drawn on postmodern theories to support her analysis of scientific metaphor, but her relation to these theories is ambivalent and she stops short of advocating a radical linguistic constructivism.

See also: science; science, philosophy of

Selected writings

Keller, E.F. (1983) *A Feeling for the Organism: The Life and Work of Barbara McClintock*, San Francisco: W.H. Freeman.
—— (1985) *Reflections on Gender and Science*, New Haven: Yale University Press.
—— (1995) *Refiguring Life: Metaphors of Twentieth-*

Century Biology, New York: Columbia University Press.

ELIZABETH A. WILSON

Kelly, Joan (1928–82)

The essays of Joan Kelly have been instrumental in feminist revisionist history by recognising sex/ **gender** as a category of analysis (see **history**; **history, feminist**). Before her early death in 1982, Kelly fostered an approach to historical study based on the 'vantage point' of women; that is, analysing the experiences, and from the perspective, of women. Kelly's marxist-feminist approach insisted on the interplay of sex, class and **race** in the formation and diversity of social relations (see also **Marxism**; **class analysis, UK**; **class analysis, US**).

In her 1976 article 'The Social Relation of the Sexes' Kelly reviews women's experiences to problematise historical periodisation and western historians' categories of social analysis, and to suggest new theories of social change. She argues that periodisation based on the concept of progression and change in history is not experienced uniformly by all people living at that time and shows that in many accepted periods of progressive social change, women's status has tended to be significantly restricted. This view is highlighted in her influential 1977 article 'Did Women have a Renaissance?' where she concludes that the European Renaissance saw a relative lack of improvement in economic, political and cultural conditions for a significant proportion of women. Kelly maintains however that periodisation markers could be a valuable analytic tool in relational studies, comparing women and men's experiences of perceived historical advances.

Marxist-feminism led Kelly to postulate that through history, sexual inequalities have been bound to control of property, wealth and labour. She observes that in societies where familial activities coincide with the public domain, women's status has been higher than in those where the domestic and public spheres are clearly delineated. The relation of the **public/private** realms, Kelly concludes, has meant that reviewing the organisation of modes of production could help us understand the domestic order with which women have been associated most strongly through history (see **production, modes of**). Kelly argues that an integrated view of class and sex relations is necessary in historical study. She develops this idea in her 1979 article 'The Doubled Vision of Feminist Theory' where she suggests that sex, class and race oppositions need to be taken into account. A perspective that unifies economic and sexual based realities will raise awareness of how the sex/ gender and productive relation systems operate simultaneously both in the past and present. For Kelly, a unified social theory will situate historical subjects in a new social and political position that allows historians to recognise the effects and pervasiveness of **patriarchy** through history.

Selected writings

Kelly, J. (1984) *Women, Theory and History: The Essays of Joan Kelly*, Chicago, IL: University of Chicago Press.

SUSAN BROOMHALL

kinship

In **anthropology**, kinship has traditionally referred to consanguine (biological) and affinal (marriage) ties that give meaning to marriage and **reproduction** through the formation of descent lines and social relations. Early works on the anthropology of women were subsumed under kinship studies and situated women in the domestic sphere. Through the 1970s–1980s, anthropologists challenged the assumption that women as a category are naturally linked to kinship and its referents – **gender**, reproduction and biological descent. Kinship is no longer a 'natural fact', but an analytic tool or symbolic experience that is culturally, economically and historically constituted. The advent of **biotechnology** has created a call to re-cast kinship in light of reproductive technologies and the undermining of 'natural' facts of reproduction.

See also: Haraway, Donna; nature/culture; Rubin, Gayle

References and further reading

Tsing, A.L. and Yanagisako, S. (1983) 'Feminism and Kinship Theory', *Current Anthropology* 24, 4: 511–16.

DENISE L. SPITZER

Kofman, Sarah (1934–94)

Contemporary French philosopher Sarah Kofman realised a major corpus of more than twenty works. Drawing on psychoanalytic, deconstructive and Nietzschean approaches, she analyses representations of women and femininity in the history of philosophy (see **psychoanalysis**; **deconstruction, feminist**). Her publications also include studies in Ancient Greek philosophy and essays on literary figures such as Diderot, Hoffman, Blanchot and Nerval. Autobiographical writing (notably *Rue Ordener, rue Labat*) evokes Kofman's experience as a Jewish survivor of the French occupation, her childhood loss of her father and the betrayal of her mother, and the complex relationship of this biography to her philosophical production (see also **autobiography**).

Kofman's work challenges the myth that rationality is a domain divorced from the passions, desires, identification and unconscious drives. She claims that her feminism is manifest in her analyses of the role of sexual identification, gender and sexuality in the works of the great male philosophers of history. These analyses incorporate an innovative methodology, in which Kofman refers a philosophical writing to the author's biography not to explain the writing, but to demonstrate that the author's 'art' and their 'art of living' can be interpreted as interrelated 'text'.

Kofman's work can be compared usefully with that of Luce **Irigaray**. Both analyse the presence and role of **phallogocentrism** in the history of philosophy. Both have offered substantial critiques of Plato, Kant, Hegel, Nietzsche and Freud from this perspective. Both draw on deconstructive and psychoanalytic approaches. Although their work concurs as diagnostic criticism of phallogocentrism, Kofman lacks the 'generative' aspect of Irigaray's project. She does not attempt to introduce positive concepts of sexual identity or to offer a new conceptual basis for relations between the sexes. For some, this is a limitation of Kofman's work, while others appreciate her resistance to **identity politics**. Working at the borders of autobiography, biography and the history of philosophy, Kofman analyses the unstable, conflicting sexual identifications of the great historical and contemporary philosophers. Simultaneously, she emphasises the unstable identity of the feminist deconstructive critic who engages in this project, avowing a critic's inevitable debt to the philosophers who serve as the object of critique.

Selected writings

Kofman, S. (1985) *The Enigma of Woman: Woman in Freud's Writings*, trans. C. Porter, Ithaca, NY: Cornell University Press.
—— (1996) *Rue Ordener, rue Labat*, trans. A. Smock, Lincoln and London: University of Nebraska Press.

References and further reading

Deutscher, P. and Oliver, K. (eds) (1999) *Enigmas: Essays on Sarah Kofman*, Ithaca, NY: Cornell University Press.

PENELOPE DEUTSCHER

Kristeva, Julia (b. 1941)

Julia Kristeva is a linguist, cultural theorist and practising analyst. Born in Bulgaria, Kristeva began her career in Paris where she paid particular attention to the **corporeality** of the signifying process – a dimension absent in structuralist accounts prominent in the sixties. Kristeva's work was then introduced to Anglo-American feminists in the seventies and eighties, most notably through translations of major early works. Since then, Kristeva has earned the reputation as a major figure of **French feminism**, especially in her use of **psychoanalysis** to understand subjectivity.

Following Lacan, Kristeva suggests that the subject is constituted by the acquisition of language (read: articulated network of differences). Language intervenes into an imaginary state of fusion marking subject and object, self from (m)other. Language is consequently defined as a paternal third, the *nom-du-père* that smashes dyadic (mis)-identifications, symbolically castrates the subject and places each subject as a differentiated and sexually different self in the Symbolic order (with femininity as the condition of lack). But Kristeva offers an important revision to this model. Recognizing that the *nom-du-père* leaves much to be explained, Kristeva investigates the pre-subject who enters the symbolic universe. For in Kristeva's writings, the maternal space is not only the smooth mirroring of primary narcissism: it is, additionally, full of tensions, stases and pleasures as maternal regulations order primitive oral and anal drives. These processes come to have meaning for the subject, a *semiotic* meaning that collects in what is called the *chora*. And as a challenge to Lacan, Kristeva insists that the semiotic *chora* remains heterogeneous to the signifying process to put each subject in process/on trial.

Kristeva's recent work introduces terms like 'abjection' and 'primary identification' to the earlier concept of the *chora*. Of appeal to feminists are the implications that might be drawn from Kristeva's work as a whole. Kristeva herself calls for an ethics that would attend to the violence of separation in symbolic differentiation. Could it be that the maternal semiotic, with its material drives and regulations, holds the key to such ethics (her/ethics)? Less optimistically, feminists have criticised Kristeva for relying upon the **phallogocentrism** of Lacan and for her ambivalence towards feminism.

References and further reading

Mitchell, R. (ed.) (1996) *Julia Kristeva: Interviews*, Guberman, NY: Columbia University Press.

Moi, T. (ed.) (1986) *The Kristeva Reader*, Oxford: Basil Blackwell.

Oliver, K. (1993) *Reading Kristeva: Unraveling the Double Bind*, Bloomington, IN: Indiana University Press.

—— (ed.) (1997) *The Portable Kristeva*, New York: Columbia University Press.

KWOK WEI LENG

L

language, gender and power

Feminist linguists generally assume that language is not a neutral and transparent means of representing social realities, but rather one that is inextricably implicated in the socio-political systems and institutions in which it functions. Like other social institutions and practices, linguistic systems serve the interests of some groups – dominant groups – better than others. Thus, it is perhaps not surprising that feminist theorists have long been interested in language as both a reflection of gender relations and ideologies (see **ideology**), and as an important resource drawn upon in the social construction and enactment of **gender**.

The assumptions informing early research in feminist linguistics (in the 1970s and 1980s) took 'difference' between men's and women's linguistic behaviour as axiomatic and as the starting point for empirical investigations. At least two types of explanations were offered for the male/female linguistic differences catalogued in this research. The first type of explanation, characterised as the **dominance** approach, sees male dominance as operative in the everday verbal interactions of women and men, thus giving rise to linguistic reflexes of subordination and dominance. Don Zimmerman and Candace West (1983), for example, document a widely publicised (and exaggerated) finding, namely that in cross-sex conversations men interrupt women more than women interrupt men. An earlier version of the 'dominance' approach can be found in Robin Lakoff's (1975) *Language and Women's Place* (a book that launched over two decades of scholarly work

in this area) in which Lakoff presents aspects of women's speech that she claims are manifestations of women's subordinate status. Lakoff argues that women show a preference for linguistic forms that signal tentativeness and lack of authority, such as rising intonation in declarative statements, tag questions, and expressions that mitigate the truth of propositions.

The second type of explanation arising from early research, characterised as the difference approach, suggests that women and men learn different communicative styles based on the segregated same-sex peer groups they play in as children (see Maltz and Borker 1982; Tannen 1990). Lacking a systematic analysis of the **power** differential between women and men, this framework has been the subject of much criticism to the extent that it views cross-sex miscommunication as the somewhat benign and innocent result of different socialisation patterns.

Whether within the 'dominance' or 'difference' framework, many of the claims about gender-differentiated language that emerged from studies in the 1970s and 1980s have since been challenged on both empirical and political grounds. The idea that women and men do not constitute internally-homogeneous groups is one that pervades much contemporary feminist scholarship. Indeed, many early findings of linguistic sex differences were overgeneralised to all women and men based on limited populations (white, North American and middle-class) engaged in situationally-specific contexts, cross-sex conversations, where some have argued gender is probably maximally salient.

Other scholars have questioned the political

utility of research questions that presuppose a female/male dichotomy. Nancy Henley and Cheris Kramarae (1991) argue, for example, that focusing on differences rather than similarities between women and men functions to exaggerate and reinforce gender polarities and abstracts gender away from the specificities of its social context. Likewise, Deborah Cameron (1992) warns that merely paying attention to sex differences only strengthens the salience of a polarity that ultimately may not serve the interests of women.

The shift away from overarching generalisations about women's and men's language has been characterised by Penelope Eckert and Sally McConnell-Ginet as 'thinking practically and looking locally'. In this influential article, Penelope Eckert and Sally McConnell-Ginet (1992) recommend that the interaction between language and gender be examined in the everyday social practices of particular local communities (what they term 'communities of practice') because they claim: (1) gender is not always easily separated from other aspects of social identity and relations; (2) gender will not always have the same meaning across communities; and (3) the linguistic manifestations of gender will also vary across communities. As Elinor Ochs has argued, there are few features of language that 'directly and exclusively index gender' (1992: 340). Because a linguistic form, such as silence or interruptions, can have different meanings and effects across situational, institutional and cultural contexts, it becomes difficult to generalise about gender-differentiated aspects of language such as 'women's silence' or 'women's silencing'. Recognising the dynamic and contextual nature of linguistic meanings, then, calls into question earlier research that simply 'read off' gender identities from linguistic forms.

Much work in feminist linguistics has also abandoned categorical and fixed notions of gender identities in favour of more constructivist and dynamic ones. Rather than viewing gender as a set of attributes residing permanently within an individual, more recent conceptions of gender characterise it as something individuals do as opposed to something individuals are or have. Under this account, language is one important means by which gender (an ongoing social process) is enacted or constituted. And, while dynamic approaches to gender allow for the possibility of individuals actively reproducing and/or resisting linguistic practices involved in normative constructions of gender, Susan Gal (1991: 197) makes the important point that a society's institutions: 'are far from neutral arenas: they are structured along gender lines, to lend authority not only to reigning classes and ethnic groups but specifically to men's linguistic practices'.

See also: discourse analysis; essentialism; ethics of linguistics (Kristeva); power; sexism

References and further reading

Cameron, D. (1992) *Feminism and Linguistic Theory*, New York: St. Martin's Press, 2nd edn.

Eckert, P. and McConnell-Ginet, S. (1992) 'Think Practically and Look Locally: Language and Gender as Community-based Practice', *Annual Review of Anthropology* 21: 461–90.

Gal, S. (1991) 'Between Speech and Silence: The Problematics of Research on Language and Gender', in M. di Leonardo (ed.) *Gender at the Crossroads of Knowledge*, Berkeley, CA: University of California Press.

Henley, N. and Kramarae, C. (1991) 'Gender, Power and Miscommunication', in N. Coupland, H. Giles, and J. Wiemann (eds) *Miscommunication and Problematic Talk*, Newbury Park, CA: Sage.

Maltz, D. and Borker, R. (1982) 'A Cultural Approach to Male–Female Miscommunication', in J. Gumperz (ed.) *Language and Social Identity*, Cambridge: Cambridge University Press.

Ochs, E. (1992) 'Indexing Gender', in A. Duranti and C. Goodwin (eds) *Rethinking Context: Language as an Interactive Phenomenon*, Cambridge: Cambridge University Press.

Tannen, D. (1990) *You Just Don't Understand*, New York: Ballantine Books.

West, C., and Zimmerman, D. (1983) 'Small Insults: A Study of Interruptions in Cross-sex Conversations Between Unacquainted Persons', in B. Thorne, C. Kramarae, and N. Henley (eds) *Language, Gender and Society*, Rowley, MA: Newbury House.

SUSAN EHRLICH

Latin American feminism

It is hardly possible to define a single feminism in a region of over twenty countries with diverse histories and identities. For this reason, women in Latin America prefer the plural term 'feminisms'. Despite vast differences, the countries stretching from Mexico to the Southern Cone share the tragedy of Spanish, Portuguese or French conquest and colonisation succeeded by the new imperialism of **economic globalisation**, often advanced by military dictatorships. Latin America's exploitation on the world stage for over 500 years has left a legacy of debt and dictatorships, poverty and underdevelopment. It is well known that women are disproportionately affected by **economic restructuring**. Although there is a history of **oppression**, there is also resistance and dissent with a vibrant history of political, revolutionary, and social movements in the region.

Latin American feminisms emerge from this historico-political backdrop and consequently, despite some early commonalities with western feminism, fundamentally unique features have developed in the region. Particularly evident is an inclusive approach distinguished by a broad-based outreach orientation and collective demand for social justice. Economic and political repression have spawned a proliferation of women's activism throughout the region since the 1970s. **Human rights** groups and grassroots organisations exist alongside feminist groups that are often associated with the political left. While there is some debate in the region about which of these are feminist activities, there is little doubt that, by transforming the private spheres of pain and survival into public issues, masses of women have become rapidly politicised and the Latin American feminist agenda has been challenged to embody the concerns of the popular classes.

Feminist consciousness develops

In some ways, the development of feminisms in Latin America parallels that of western feminism. As in the west, the 'first-wave' feminist struggle for educational access for women and girls gained momentum in the late nineteenth and early twentieth century (see **first-wave/second-wave feminism**). Subsequently, female teachers in the new middle classes were a vital force in suffrage movements that fundamentally challenged the notion of citizenship. In Latin American countries, women achieved the vote mid-century across a thirty year span (1929–61). Among the early feminists, two of the better known are Chilean winner of the Nobel Prize for Literature, Gabriela Mistral, and Argentinean Victoria Ocampo.

Woman poets, novelists and journalists such as Alfonsina Storni (Argentina), Clarice Lispector (Brazil), and Julieta Campos (Cuba, Mexico) have played a significant role in contesting and reforming identities. Likewise, radio and press have a long and rich history in the region. For example, *Mujer/fempress* is a monthly journal with articles representing the entire region. *Mujer y sociedad* is a Peruvian example of a monthly supplement for women that is carried in a daily paper.

Feminisms in Latin America are generally less oriented to liberation of the individual than to liberation of the society from imperialism and underdevelopment. During the twentieth century, women worked alongside men in revolutionary struggles. Women revolutionaries believe that a socialist revolution is a prerequisite for the development of the women's movement while at the same time admitting that women do not have equality within the movement (see **equality and difference**). Women who attempt to incorporate feminist views are often accused of dividing the class struggle or of capitulating to the imperialism of First World feminism. Moreover, it is well documented that women's issues related to the 'double-day' or abuse, for instance, have never been fully addressed within revolutionary movements.

As elsewhere, Latin American feminisms have been challenged to confront classed and raced definitions of women's realities and to incorporate instead the reality of intersecting oppressions. This struggle offers significant insights for feminists in other places.

The movement transforms

Feminist theorists identify a distinctive 'second wave' of feminisms (post-1970) that emerged as a consequence of brutally repressive military regimes in combination with the crippling economic model imposed on the region. 'Contemporary feminisms in Latin America were therefore born as intrinsically oppositional movements … instrumental in shaping a Latin American feminist praxis distinct from that of feminist movements elsewhere' (Sternbach *et al*. 1995: 244). Three broad categories of women's political activity are evident during this period: feminist activities, human rights groups and *movimientos de mujeres* (grassroots women's organisations).

Women in the Left have been at the vanguard of the feminist front. These women are often educated and politicised women disillusioned with the immobility of the Left in addressing women's issues. They introduce a distinctly gendered analysis in relationship to the prevailing economic and political regimes. A most influential feminist critique is an analysis of state repression as the ultimate expression of **patriarchy**. 'Whereas male analysts stressed the cultural or economic determinants … feminists argued that such politics are also rooted in the authoritarian foundations of patriarchal relations in the so-called private sphere' (Sternbach *et al*. 1995: 244–5).

Feminist practice in Latin America is historically linked to grassroots organising and service provision in poorer neighbourhoods. Such outreach activities include legal assistance and support to victims of torture and other abused women. Working from basic needs, feminists are often instrumental in lobbying for legal reforms.

Human rights groups were the first to organise opposition to the dictatorships. Formed by women searching for their 'disappeared' loved ones, these groups brought international attention to the oppressive treatment of the citizenry. Well-known among these is *Las Madres de la Plaza de Mayo* in Argentina who march in front of the presidential palace with pictures of their missing relatives. In El Salvador, the *CoMadres* risk their own lives to publish photographs of those tortured or killed.

Collectively termed the *movimientos de mujeres*, there is a vast and loose network of grassroots women throughout Latin America. These women are the force behind popular subsistence and survival-oriented initiatives in urban, poor and working class neighbourhoods. Responding largely to the effect of structural adjustment policies,

women organise both to demand basic services and to provide them. Collective kitchens, wherein family groups gather together to feed their families communally, are a widespread strategy. Other examples are popular health centres, land invasions and defence committees. Organisations for particular groups of women also emerge, for example, the CONAVIGUA Widows of Guatemala are indigenous rural women and the Haitian Women's Solidarity represents market sellers.

Determining which of these activities are considered feminist is the source of some debate. Regional conferences have been forums for the expression of this tension as the veteran feminists are challenged to make theoretical space for the vast numbers of women in the *movimientos de mujeres*, and women formerly averse to feminism begin to reclaim the label. While some organisations and women openly identify themselves as feminist, many actively avoid the term. There is widespread representation of feminists as divisive and anti-male and the movement as imported and imperialist. Moreover, some distinguish theoretically between 'feminine' activities that emerge from and support women's traditional roles and 'feminist' activities that actively question women's place in society.

Such a dichotomy has been challenged by many who claim that even when the term is renounced, feminist engagement is evident. Jelin (1990) contends that 'the various types and planes of actions converge in social reality, thus obviating the analytical need to differentiate between women's participation, women's organisations and feminist movements' (184). Indeed, Latin American women's movements may be the quintessential expression of feminist consciousness – transforming traditionally private spaces into profoundly public domains. In the process of fighting for survival and justice, many women newly apprehend themselves as political subjects and redefine what counts as political.

In Latin America, a politics of *conscientización* has developed…. The fusion of a radical critique of economic, political, and social injustice with a gendered analysis has resulted in a syncretic understanding that has transformed both feminism and the politics of social change in Latin

America. It has also deeply influenced the global women's movement.

(Miller 1995: 205)

Implications for global feminism

Latin American feminists' **praxis** offers insights for understanding and contextualizing multiple and intersecting oppressions and proposes useful strategies for feminists around the world. Characteristic examples are: learning how women become political subjects/actors (Jaquette 1989); the genesis of social movements (Jelin 1990); the process of **consciousness-raising** (Radcliffe and Westwood 1993); and mobilizing broad-based masses of women (Sternbach et al. 1995). Jelin's (1990) analysis that women respond politically and publicly during 'critical' moments has potential implications for feminists everywhere who confront the gendered impact of economic and political policies.

Miller (1995) identifies another predominant feature of Latin American feminisms: 'Bringing international attention to an issue was a political strategy that Latin American feminists helped to pioneer, and it was one that would serve them well over time' (194). Human rights abuses were widely publicised, for example, by Chilean artisans who smuggled out tapestries, and by Rigoberta Menchú, an indigenous peasant woman who won the 1992 Nobel Peace Prize for focusing international attention on widespread persecution of indigenous Guatemalans.

In another international effort, Latin American feminists have converged at congresses around the hemisphere: for example, the International Congress of Women (1910), the First Interamerican Congress of Women (1947) and, since 1981, biannual region-wide conferences called *Encuentros*. Sternbach et al. (1995) trace the history of the first five *Encuentros* which grew from 200 to 2,500 participants in nine years. The International Day Against Violence Against Women was inaugurated by Latin American feminists at an *Encuentro* in Mexico in 1987 and is now commemorated globally.

See also: communism, women and; inter-

national human rights; public/private; socialism and feminism

References and further reading

Alvarez, S. (1990) *Engendering Democracy in Brazil*, Princeton, NJ: Princeton University Press.

Andreas, C. (1985) *When Women Rebel: The Rise of Popular Feminism in Peru*, Westport: Lawrence Hill and Company.

Collinson, H. (ed.) (1990) *Women and Revolution in Nicaragua*, London: Zed Books.

Jaquette, J.S. (ed.) (1989) *The Women's Movement in Latin America*, Boston: Unwin Hyman.

Jelin, E. (ed.) (1990) *Women and Social Change in Latin America*, trans. J.A. Zammit and M. Thomson, London: Zed Books/UNRISD.

Menchú, R. (1984) *I, Rigoberto Menchú: An Indian Woman in Guatemala*, London: Verso.

Miller, F. (1995) 'Latin American Women and the Search for Social, Political, and Economic Transformation', in S. Halebsky and R.L. Harris (eds) *Capital, Power and Inequality in Latin America*, Boulder, CO: Westview.

Nash, J. and Safa, H.I. (eds) (1980) *Sex and Class in Latin America*, New York: Begin.

Radcliffe, S.A. and Westwood, S. (1993) *Viva: Women and Popular Protest in Latin America*, London: Routledge.

Sternbach, N.S., Navarro-Aranguren, M., Chuchryk, P., and Alvarez, S.E. (1995) 'Feminisms in Latin America: From Bogotá to San Bernardo', in B. Laslett, J. Brenner and Y. Arat (eds) *Rethinking the Political*, Chicago, IL: University of Chicago Press.

DONNA MAUREEN CHOVANEC

Lauretis, Teresa de

Working at the intersection of feminist film theory, critical theory and **queer theory**, Teresa de Lauretis is widely known for her nuanced analyses of the relationships among representation, gender, and subjectivity in film, literature and theoretical discourse. In the 1980s, she published two groundbreaking books in which she draws on semiotics, **psychoanalysis** and Michel Foucault's work to address fundamental issues in feminist theory. In *Alice Doesn't* (1984), she urges feminists to theorise the concept of experience. This intervention was timely, given the importance of 'experience' in feminist theory. In 'Semiotics and Experience' (the final chapter of *Alice Doesn't*), she introduces Charles Pierce's semiotic account of 'habit' as a means of linking subjectivity to life practices. In *Technologies of Gender*, she argues that the concept of sexual difference was limiting feminist theory's ability to explore the construction of female subjectivity across multiple axes of difference, including race, class and sexuality. Drawing on Foucault's work on sexuality, and Althusser's account of ideology, she elaborates a model of gender as both product and process. Gender, she argues, is a product of technologies such as cinema, and discourses including feminist theory. By responding to and embodying representations and discourses of femininity, women participate in the process of making gender a lived ideology.

In the late 1980s, de Lauretis turned her attention to lesbian subjectivity and sexuality. Despite criticism that she had urged feminists to abandon a psychoanalytic account of subjectivity in favour of a Foucauldian approach, her most profound engagement with psychoanalysis occurs in *The Practice of Love* (1994). Noting that 'lesbian scholarship hasn't had much use for psychoanalsyis', she advocates a psychoanalytic framework on the grounds that lesbian identities 'are not only grounded in the sphere of the sexual, but actually constituted in relation to a sexual difference from socially dominant, institutionalised, heterosexual forms' (xii). Forging links between queer theory and psychoanalysis, she draws on Freud's writings to elaborate a model of perverse desire, 'where perverse means not pathological but rather non-heterosexual nor non-normatively heterosexual' (xiii). Reading texts such as Radclyffe Hall's *The Well of Loneliness*, she demonstrates how this model can account for representations of lesbianism in literature, film and everyday life.

See also: critical theory, feminism and; film theory, feminist; Mulvey, Laura; narrative, feminist uses of

Selected writings

Lauretis, T. de (1984) *Alice Doesn't: Feminism, Semiotics, Cinema*, Bloomington, IN: Indiana University Press.
—— (1987) *Technologies of Gender: Essays on Theory, Film and Fiction*, Bloomington, IN: Indiana University Press.
—— (1994) *The Practice of Love: Lesbian Sexuality and Perverse Desire*, Bloomington, IN: Indiana University Press.

ROSANNE KENNEDY

Le Doeuff, Michèle

Contemporary French philosopher Michèle Le Doeuff is best known in France as a specialist in Renaissance English philosophy, particularly the work of Bacon. She became widely known to Anglophone readers, however, through her feminist writing. Her inclusion in Elisabeth Grosz's *Sexual Subversions: Three French Feminists* demonstrates the diversity of French feminist thinking (see **French feminism**). In contrast to other figures deemed 'French feminist' (**Cixous**, **Kristeva** and **Irigaray**) Le Doeuff is wary of affirmations of feminine specificity, sexual difference or *écriture féminine*.

In *The Philosophical Imaginary*, Le Doeuff analyses such figures as More, Descartes, Rousseau and Kant. Though seen as mere ornament in the history of philosophy, she argues that metaphor and imagery have often concealed blind spots in a philosopher's argument. The work includes a feminist analysis of the figure of women in the history of philosophy. Representations of women as intellectually limited (or as philosophy's '**Other**') constitute a further blind spot in the history of philosophy, sustaining the prestige of the male philosopher.

Hipparchia's Choice is notable for its innovative methodology, which arises from Le Doeuff's view that philosophical thought is not self-contained from contemporary life, nor from the gender politics of the thinker. She interweaves her analyses of philosophers with autobiographical fragments from her own life as a woman philosopher, student and teacher (see **autobiography**). Discussing limitations in the work of Sartre and **Beauvoir** she integrates biographical discussion of the relationship between the couple, interpreting their philosophy in tandem with their letters and **diaries**. She interweaves discussion of the history of philosophy with discussion of everyday feminist issues (such as laws and mores covering contraception, abortion, postcolonialism and equal opportunity in France). The work is often cited as one of the most important and original in Beauvoir studies.

Over two decades Le Doeuff has been an acute critic of contemporary laws, institutional and public policy concerning women. She demonstrates that apparently progressive, 'women friendly' measures on the part of public institutions should always be subjected to closer analysis: often, they indirectly reconsolidate male bias.

Selected writings

Le Doeuff, M. (1989) *The Philosophical Imaginary*, trans. C. Gordon. London: Athlone Press.
—— (1991) *Hipparchias's Choice: An Essay Concerning Women, Philosophy, etc.*, trans. T. Selous, Oxford, UK and Cambridge, MA: Blackwell.

References and further reading

Deutscher, M. (ed.). (1999) *The Philosophy of Michèle Le Doeuff*, Atlantic Highlands, NJ: Humanities Press.

PENELOPE DEUTSCHER

Lerner, Gerder

Women's historian Gerda Lerner has insisted from the outset of her career upon the centrality of women's experiences to the writing of **history**. Widely credited with developing the theoretical foundations of a heterogeneous women's history, Lerner challenges historians to grapple with the overlapping categories of **race**, ethnicity, class and **gender**. From the publication of her first college textbook, *The Woman in American History* (1971), to her most recent collection of essays, *Why History Matters* (1997), Lerner's work actively seeks out new methodologies and bodies of sources to reveal the voices of women in history. Her two collections of primary documents, *Black Women in White America* (1972), and *The Female Experience in American History* (1977), exemplify her early desire to ensure that the multiplicity of voices in America's past should not be silenced by women's historians.

Lerner argues that women experience a unique kind of discrimination. Unlike those marginalised on the basis of race and class differences, women live in intimate association with the higher ranking group, namely, men. Insistence upon the **agency** of women thus embedded in patriarchal societies, and a quest for an empowering theory for women within debates over the historical construction of **patriarchy**, forces Lerner to depart from a strict historical method. Her two-volume synthesis, *Women and History*, traces broad themes in a global women's history, in a bold narrative redefinition of a 'usable past' that encompasses the **diversity** of human experience. Critics complain that this project disregards, in its sheer breadth of coverage, the specific historical, social, and national contexts in which women have functioned throughout history. However, the work represents a pioneering attempt to incorporate the rich historiographic insights of women's history into the broad swathe of historical narrative.

Why History Matters returns to the problem of **difference** both as actively constructed and as historical artifact, as well as the ways in which it is used to justify unequal distributions of power. Lerner continues to direct women's historians toward what she calls a more 'holistic' definition and understanding of the intertwining categories of race, ethnicity, class, and gender.

See also: class analysis UK; class analysis US; ethnicity; history

Selected writings

Lerner, G. (1979) *The Majority Finds Its Past: Placing Women in History*, New York: Oxford University Press.
—— (1986) *The Creation of Patriarchy*, New York: Oxford University Press.

—— (1997) *Why History Matters: Life and Thought*, New York: Oxford University Press.

AMANDA FRISKEN

lesbian autobiography

Much lesbian writing since the 1970s has been overtly autobiographical, particularly in the mode of the 'coming out' story, a combination of the confessional and the political manifesto, which speaks to the need for visibility and affirmation for lesbians. But lesbian autobiography presents more of a theoretical conundrum than a concept or genre which can be easily described. The idea of mimetic representation is complicated on several fronts given that both terms, 'lesbian' and 'autobiography', are complex concepts in their own right.

Biddy Martin's excellent essay 'Lesbian Identity and Autobiographical Difference[s]' (1988) argues that the combination of these terms:

> brings out the most conventional interpretation in each, for the *lesbian* in front of autobiography reinforces conventional assumptions of transparency of autobiographical writing. And the *autobiography* that follows *lesbian* suggests that sexual identity not only modifies but essentially defines a life, providing it with predictable content and an identity possessing continuity and universality.
>
> (Martin 1988: 78)

Suspect are texts which explicitly write themselves into a mode of 'truth' evoked by the adage, 'the personal is political', and the command to 'come-out', giving voice to an almost infinite collection of instructive, cathartic, and reassuring 'personal narratives', which tend to rewrite the lives of their authors in the light of contemporary political demands. Texts that stand out are self-conscious about their historiographic investment, for example, Gloria **Anzaldúa**'s multilingual, pan cultural New Mestiza in *Border/Lands*, *La Frontera*, and Minnie Bruce Pratt's concretisation of her personal history in relation to geographical, demographic and architectural sites (1984).

Combinations of lesbian and autobiography which slide towards 'autobiographical fictions or fictive autobiographies' (Zimmerman 1984) are often intentionally confusing in genre, as if neither fiction nor autobiography are sufficient categories for the telling of unconventional lives. Signal in this regard are Audre **Lorde**'s *Zami* (1982), a 'biomythography'; Virginia Woolf's *Orlando* (1928), a 'biography'; Gertrude Stein's *Autobiography of Alice B. Toklas* (1933); and Leslie Feinberg's, *Stone Butch Blues* (1993). This last book, like its predecessor, Radclyffe Hall's *The Well of Loneliness* (1928), a product of social realism, verges on undoing the category of lesbian in favour of another set of genders, both blurring and delimiting the boundaries of 'lesbian autobiography'.

References and further reading

Martin, B. (1988) 'Lesbian Identity and Autobiographical Difference[s]', in B. Brodzki and C. Schenck (eds) *Life/Lines: Theorizing Women's Autobiography*, Ithaca, NY: Cornell University Press.

Pratt, M.B. (1984) 'Identity: Skin Blood Heart', in Bulkin, Pratt and Smith (eds) *Yours In Struggle*, New York: Firebrand Books.

Zimmerman, B. (1984) 'The Politics of Transliteration: Lesbian Personal Narratives', *Signs*, 9, 4: 663–82.

JULIA CREET

lesbian continuum

A term coined by Adrienne **Rich** (1980), the concept of a 'lesbian continuum' counters overly narrow descriptions of lesbianism operative in feminist discussions during the 1970s. Rich construes the parameters of lesbian existence to encompass the broad 'continuum' of female erotic behaviour, from suckling a female child to female friendships, from genital eroticism to political solidarity between women. Rich's redefinition of the erotic in 'female terms', 'as that which is unconfined to any single part of the body or solely to the body itself', supports scholarly efforts to reclaim (uncover) lesbian texts made inaccessible by the normative heterosexual presumption structuring existing literary and historical scholarship. As well, and crucially, it makes 'lesbian', feminist. However, critics of Rich's continuum have argued that it effaces historical, political, and sexual specificities of lesbian identity.

References and further reading

Rich, A. (1980) 'Compulsory Heterosexuality and Lesbian Existence', *Signs*, 5, 4: 631–60.

JULIA CREET

lesbian ethics

An ethics of resistance and creation, lesbian ethics is a liberatory conceptual journey which emerges within the context of oppression. It is not rules of right behaviour, injunctions of duty, or delineations of character – not an application of these values to lesbian lives. Its major contributions for feminist theory include reconceptualising agency and community/difference.

In *Women and Honor* Adrienne **Rich** raises questions about the ways women use lying against each other unselfconsciously or as a weapon. Mary **Daly** exposes ways patriarchal value structures our thinking about good and evil, beginning with Eve. The good woman under heteropatriarchy is self-sacrificial; she who chooses herself is selfish. Sarah Lucia **Hoagland** argues that among lesbians, agency is creative, not sacrificial. The selfish/self-sacrifice dichotomy stems from the imperialist edict that everything is ours so when we have to choose, we lose. Among lesbians, however, what exists has been created by lesbians. Where we focus attention, put our energy, there we create meaning.

Since lesbians come from every culture and class, community holds new value. In hetero-patriarchy difference is a threat. Challenging white women's ignoring of racism, Audre **Lorde** reconceptualises difference. Resting not with dualism but working toward pluralism, she argues that without investigating the contexts of our lives, we will not recognise why we resist, nor how we are indoctrinated and perpetuate oppression, nor how we create alternatives.

Gloria **Anzaldúa** develops the concept of *la mestiza*, the border dweller. People living in the borderlands, the place between cultures where reside those who inhabit both but fit nowhere, become adept at switching modes. In the borderlands the Other has its own identity separate from the narcissism of the norm; and those exist who exceed dualism, who are neither norm nor Other. *La mestiza* breaks down the subject/object duality to create new ways of relating, for lesbian desire is relational.

Claudia **Card** explores hostile and objectifying attending: not racism, but incest, lesbian battering, stalking. She suggests difficulties may be alleviated by friendlier background institutions supporting female friendship, formalising boundaries, even roles.

María **Lugones** focuses on failure of love, as whites fail to identify with people of colour. Playful world-travel, instead, involves going to the world of another without destroying it and finding oneself another person there, understanding ourselves in their eyes. She looks to the state between structures and boundaries where habitual thinking fails.

Sarah Lucia Hoagland pursues liberatory possibility through lesbian communities, not riveted on the agendas of the fathers, which lesbians of all cultures construct.

See also: lesbian feminism

References and further reading

Card, C. (1995) *Lesbian Choices*, New York: Columbia.
Hoagland, S.L. (1988) *Lesbian Ethics*, Chicago, IL: Institute of Lesbian Studies.
Rich, A. (1977) *Women and Honor*, Pittsburgh: Motherroot.

SARAH LUCIA HOAGLAND

lesbian feminism

Lesbian feminism has been grassroots and working class everywhere it emerged. This entry concerns US emergence.

Lesbian feminism emerged in reaction to male dominance in the New Left and Gay movements as well as homophobia in the feminist movement. In 1969 in California, Judy Grahn mimeographed and distributed *The Common Woman Poems*. Spreading like wildfire when there was no women's distribution network, the poems became a focal point for women. Shortly she, Wendy Cadden and others formed Lesbian/feminism. Simultaneously Rita Mae Brown and others left the newly formed Gay Movement after the 1969 Stonewall riot. And after the NOW (National Organization of Women) purge of lesbians, Martha Shelley, Sydney Abbot, Barbara Love and others formed the New York Radicalesbians, publishing 'Woman-Identified Woman' in 1970 which begins: 'What is a lesbian? A lesbian is the rage of all women condensed to the point of explosion'. Meanwhile in Chicago, Michal Brody and others formed the Women's Caucus of Gay Liberation, again because of male dominance, and soon, while feminism was turning its back on lesbians, lesbians began developing theories of feminism which led in 1971 to the formation of the Lavender Woman collective and newspaper, Family of Women Band, and numerous other lesbian feminist organisations. In 1971 Charlotte Bunch, Coletta Reid, Joan Biren (JEB), Ginny Berson and others formed *The Furies* separatist collective and newspaper in Washington DC, dedicated to lesbian-feminist political analysis and ideology (see **separatism**). In 1972 Diana Press, Olivia Records, *Quest*, and Women in Distribution were formed as women's economic and cultural institutions that could employ women and affect culture. By 1975 the Michigan Womyn's Music Festival began. And so the sparks ignited.

Central to the contagion was the rejection of women's male-identification. While those forming lesbian feminism, particularly on the US west coast, were deeply involved in anti-racist, anti-Vietnam war, anti-rape, anti-classist, and animal rights work, they chose to continue political work in a woman-centred contextualised space. In heteropatriarchy, woman is for man and exists only in relation to man. A heavily working-class movement initially, lesbian feminism focused on women, not on men or on men's ideas of women, embracing woman bonding and woman-centred values. Central to this possibility was the political nature of lesbianism. Jill Johnston coined the slogan 'feminism is the complaint, lesbianism is the solution', which evolved

into 'feminism is the theory, lesbianism is the practice', and Rita Mae Brown coined the slogan: 'an army of lovers cannot fail'. And so women loving women burst forth as active resistance to the limitations and oppressions of the female role in society. There is something about being a lesbian that serves as a base to reorient ourselves and challenge assumptions of the dominant frame.

Lesbian feminism exists in sharp contrast to dominant gay politics of assimilation and acceptance. Lesbian feminist analysis refuses the defensive, instead analysing and critiquing institutions such as family, motherhood, marriage, indeed heterosexuality, as cornerstones of male supremacy. Lesbian feminism is an emotional, sexual, political, and economic commitment to women as a political entity leading to power for women. One major instance of the personal is political, lesbian feminism literally embodies putting women first in male-supremacist society.

Lesbian feminism also signals a major shift from earlier lesbian practice: lesbian sexual and emotional love became overt, not coded as Gertrude Stein perfected. What NOW women wanted not to see was lesbians holding hands. From the beginning lesbians explored sexuality. Soon lesbian sex practices came under analysis in light of ongoing critiques of the dominance/subordinate relationship of heterosexuality. Butch/femme roles were critiqued as mimicking the man/woman relationship. In the process, pre-feminist and pre-gay liberationist lesbians were dismissed until Joan Nestle launched a counter critique arguing that lesbian feminists were not recognising the nature of the resistance older lesbians practised: being overtly sexual and two women on the street. Debates about lesbian sexuality continue, but the basic uncoded affirmation and celebration of lesbians' right to love continues unabated.

Unabashedly choosing women, lesbians are labelled manhaters, and lesbian feminists address this head on: certainly many lesbians hate men, but so do many straight women. The equation of 'lesbian' with 'manhater', for example, is interesting since a lesbian is one who withdraws her intimate energy from men while manhating involves significant expenditure of energy. So how can one equate withdrawal with attack? A withdrawal is an attack when what is withdrawn is essential to the survival of those it is withdrawn from. When society regards lesbians as manhaters, it means society believes men cannot survive without women's attention.

By 1979, lesbian feminists of colour and Jewish lesbian feminists were articulating different problems, insisting white women directly consider **race**. While lesbian feminists emerged from other political activism, and while there developed in the first decade awareness that one's race and class affect what one sees and understands, a major shift was about to begin in lesbian understanding of **difference**. Lesbian feminists analysing institutions of female oppression were failing to acknowledge other oppressions and how lesbians can perpetuate them. Embarking on a process of understanding how one can be both oppressed and oppressor, lesbian feminism began complicating understandings of identity and subjectivity. The resulting theoretical re-conceptualisations of difference have been as beneficial to US and Canadian lesbian feminism as the initial woman-identification. Ultimately we have discovered that difference is not a threat (as white heteropatriarchy prescribes), it is essential to lesbian survival.

The most resounding re-theorising of difference began with Audre **Lorde** challenging white women's ignoring of racism. While recognising that in much of western European history, difference between us has meant that one of us must be inferior, she nevertheless finds the concept of difference the source of possibility for new value. Audre Lorde does not accept difference as constructed by white men in power. Her insight is to rest not with dualism, but to work toward pluralism. Basically, she argues that the **Other** is created by *ignoring* difference(s): to deny difference between two of us in the name of love is to abandon the relationship. Seeking unity in sameness because in heterosexuality difference means hierarchy and dominance, and perpetuating a romantic myth that to be truly connected we can't in any way be separate, lesbians had resisted looking at differences among us. But believing a relationship can only accommodate ways we are alike forces each to leave parts of herself outside it. The separation that falls outside relationship involves risks that lovers, friends, and collective

members choose not to take. What lesbian feminism discovered is that separateness or difference need not undermine the relationship, instead it can be an integral part of the relationship, expanding desire to learning and making connections across borders.

Cherríe Moraga and Gloria Anzaldúa's anthology, *This Bridge Called My Back*, continued the work. Radical women of colour, many lesbian, began giving voice to radically distinct experiences, constructing theory, at times through storytelling. One theme concerns having learned to live with contradictions, especially the contradiction of the pressure to fit into a dominant white culture while realizing that success would lead to self-annihilation. Another concerns how white women use race privilege at the expense of women of colour, for example using something a woman of colour has said when it supports the white woman's theory, but otherwise ignoring the work of women of colour. A third is that one could be both oppressor and a victim.

Gloria Anzaldúa develops the concept of *la mestiza*, the border dweller. In the borderlands, the place between cultures where reside those who inhabit both but fit nowhere, one becomes adept at switching modes: the queer, the half-breed, *la mestiza*. By straddling two or more cultures and being caught where beliefs are not constructed and there are no definitions, she experiences a loss of meaning and sense of agency, entering a state of intimate terror. Once here, by calling on Coatlicue who devours terror, and finding the strength of the resistor who refuses to accept outside authority, *la mestiza* can create a new consciousness and develop new abilities. María Lugones argues that she must give up all pretense to safety; for the borders that supposedly keep undesirable ideas out are our entrenched habits and patterns of behaviour. *La mestiza* makes herself vulnerable to foreign ways of seeing and thinking, strengthening her tolerance for ambiguity and her flexibility, because rigidity means death. The work of *la mestiza* is to break down the subject/object duality and create new ways of relating to each other for, as Gloria Anzaldúa argues, our desire is relational.

Focus on women or lesbians is a choice lesbian feminists make. And so woman-identification expands in depth and complexity. Lesbian feminists were seeking to separate from dominant, male-identified ideologies and practices. Because in a white-identified culture whiteness is not seen as culture but as reality, it took affirmations of difference to bring to consciousness ways one nevertheless is enculturated in one's access to sense-making. Without seeing women and lesbians in specific contexts, we do not recognise various ways we resist nor understand various manifestations of oppression nor how we are indoctrinated in ways we have not suspected and perpetuate oppression, and we will not understand how we create alternatives. The work of lesbian feminism in the USA and Canada and comparable movements of radical lesbians in European countries over nearly three decades has been a difficult, charged, and incredible journey of women identifying women.

Monika Reinfelder has edited a new book reporting on lesbian feminism in South and Southeast Asia, Southern Africa, and South and Central America.

We are everywhere.

See also: feminism; heterosexism, heteronormativity; patriarchy

References and further reading

Anzaldúa, G. (1987) *Borderlands*, San Francisco: Spinsters/Aunt Lute.

Beck, E.T. (1982) *Nice Jewish Girls*, Boston: Beacon Press, 1989.

Brody, M. (1985) *Are We There Yet?*, Iowa City: Aunt Lute.

Bulkin, E. *et al.* (1984) *Yours in Struggle*, Ithaca, NY: Firebrand.

Frye, M. (1983) *The Politics of Reality*, Trumansburg, NY: Crossing Press.

Grahn, J. (1978) *The Work of a Common Woman*, New York: St Martin's Press.

Lorde, A. (1984) *Sister Outsider*, Trumansburg, NY: Crossing Press.

Moraga, C. and Anzaldúa, G. (eds) (1981) *This Bridge Called My Back*, New York: Kitchen Table.

Myron, N. and Bunch, C. (1975) *Lesbianism and the Women's Movement*, Baltimore: Diana Press.

Penelope, J. and Valentine, S. (eds) (1993) *Lesbian Culture*, Freedom, CA: Crossing Press.

Reinfelder, M. (1996) *Amazon to Zami*, London: Cassell Press.

Smith, B. (1983) *Home Girls*, New York: Kitchen Table.

SARAH LUCIA HOAGLAND

lesbian health

Lesbian health is the physical, psychological, social, cultural and spiritual well-being of women who identify as lesbian or bisexual. Prior to the 1970s, the notion of lesbian health was non-existent, restricted to a disease model that pathologised homosexuality (see **homosexuality, bio-medical pathologisation of**). The emergence of feminism created a discourse in which **sexuality** was a major concern. The construct of lesbian health uses this discourse and also that of the women's health movement. Both claim that women's health care and research have been marginalised in the medical model. Feminist scholars have argued that scientific paradigms are inadequate to address women's experiences of health care. The emergence of a community who identify as lesbian has magnified the inability of the medical model to conceptualise lesbian health and has challenged the notion that a cohesive set of objectives comprise the women's health movement.

A coherent body of knowledge about lesbian health does not exist. As an invisible and marginalised group, lesbians are inaccessible to the research community. There are no illnesses unique to lesbians, yet their experiences of health care differ from those of heterosexual women. The empirical literature suggests that lesbian clients are a vulnerable group. The quality of their health care and accessibility to services are often compromised. In this way, they may be like other minority groups. For feminists, it is significant that heterosexism is at the root of lesbians' oppression in the health care system. The major barrier is the deeply held heterosexist bias/homophobia of health care providers (physicians, nurses, social workers, therapists) (see **heterosexism, heteronormativity**; **homophobia**). Lesbian and bisexual women are hesitant to disclose – to come out – to their providers for fear that the care they receive will be negatively affected and that labelling will have a long term impact on their health care interactions. Reasons why lesbians fail to seek traditional (allopathic) care include this fear, their actual experiences of discrimination, and/or a desire for a more holistic approach.

The dominant ideology of medical discourse sustains a situation where lesbian health concerns may go unnoticed in the provider/client interaction. When providers make false assumptions, they are apt to provide inappropriate information about birth control, cancer screening, substance abuse, lesbian battering, conception, and parenting issues. It is probable that lesbians are less likely to be screened for breast and cervical cancer. The prevalence of sexually transmitted diseases is low among lesbians. However, there is a concern that lesbians have been slow to adopt safe sex practices because of lack of readily available, accurate information from health care providers. The assumption that lesbians engage exclusively in non-risky safe sex restricted to women is a particularly dangerous myth precluding proper HIV/AIDS prevention education.

Feminist theory and methodology are in a pivotal position to critique the oppressive structure inherent in a health care system that supports the discrimination of lesbian, bisexual and gay clients.

See also: health

References and further reading

Eliason, M.J. (1996) *Institutional Barriers to Health Care for Lesbian, Gay, and Bisexual Persons*, New York: NLN Press.

Kitzinger, C. (1987) *The Social Construction of Lesbianism*, London: Sage.

Stern, P. N. (ed.) (1993) *Lesbian Health: What are the Issues?*, Washington, DC: Taylor and Francis.

CYNTHIA MATHIESON

lesbian history

Lesbian history is faced with two problems which it shares with other minority identity projects. Historians have to excavate voices silenced by dominant history. They also have to identify themselves against images which lesbians did not create themselves. A need for a history is strong, as described by Joan Nestle:

> We need to know that we are not accidental, that our culture has grown and changed with the currents of time ... that we have the story of a people to tell.
>
> (Nestle 1988: 110)

But this story has to distance itself from the creation of a unified, strong, easily recognisable storyline of the 'the lesbian' as defined against the heterosexual world. It has to evolve into a more complex narrative where a diversity of voices is presented.

The writing of a history is thus already situated in the discourses it is writing against. It needs to present facts politically, since power is always at stake: a pure, factual history does not exist.

Until the 1960s, lesbian visibility in the mainstream mainly existed in isolated fictional stories, or in discourse about 'the lesbian'. Many early lesbian stories centre on the singular experience of a lesbian woman, who sees herself as different from everybody else, and tries to find an identity within that difference. A group identity of 'lesbian', a recognition of the other desire as shared experience of the world, is rarely found within early coming-out and self-quest narratives. The other form of visibility of the lesbian woman in popular discourse again centres on her difference: characters such as the Baroness in the film *Pandora's Box* (Pabst 1928) create the lesbian as the tragic, lonely and hopeless counterfoil to the heterosexual norm. This kind of visibility in literature and film was complemented by a growing awareness of 'the problem' in medicalised discourse. To understand why a cloak of silence surrounded the fact that lesbian women have always managed to create fulfilling lives together, it is necessary to acknowledge the militancy with which the dominant policed itself. Laws against homosexual relationships, the negation of female desire in any form, the general invisibility of women's culture: all worked towards silence and isolation. Any attempt to create a counter-history is thus faced with an inscription of the lesbian as alone, singular and different.

The situation changed with the advent of women's liberation. The 1960s and 1970s saw struggles to shape an identity for woman outside patriarchal narratives, and to recognise the importance of women as agents of culture. Although the movement aimed most visibly at the situation of the heterosexual white woman's position vis-à-vis her male partner, the general impetus broadened possibilities for all women to come together and create affirmative visions of their lives. This included the beginnings of oral history projects and other reclamations of the experience of lesbian women through the ages. The difficulties of finding a political voice, a voice which could talk back to the mainstream, have expressed themselves in the struggle to 'fix' the right kind of lesbian historical writing. As part of this process, some lesbians have rejected butch/femme identities as politically unsound and disavowed the political efficacy of an earlier lesbian subculture which did not address its oppressors. Others such as Mary **Daly** prescribed lesbianism as a public political act, where the love of women was the tool to bring down patriarchy.

During the 1970s, women were able to make their life experiences more visible in the mainstream, and anthologies acknowledging the existence of the 'lesbian' as a widespread, varied and fulfilling identity started to appear. Lesbian history writing was now faced with the problem of how to shape lesbian experience. Should historians edit and create positive images of women considered desirable in the heterosexual mainstream, or should they acknowledge the wide experiences of lesbian women who might think of their race, age or disability as far more determining of their identity than their sexuality?

In the 1980s and 1990s images, narratives and visible experiences started to proliferate. But this avalanche of writing still shows the problems of history: most women who have spoken out are white, middle-class and educated, and had thereby been given the opportunity of self-expression. Women's studies courses started to appear in universities, writing groups for women became commonplace, and lesbian self-help groups appeared. These courses re-write dominant history and make explicit invisible desires and identities.

But now that women's voices had become established as part of syllabi, it became important to balance the diversity of experience, and include experiences of different minority groups. Thinkers such as Audre **Lorde** have brought consciousness of these issues to white feminism.

Another issue that started to interest lesbian historians was that a proliferation of counter-culture did not necessarily challenge the narratives of dominant history: counter-culture is easily relegated to the margins. Artists interested in creating a history of lesbian women include filmmakers Barbara Hammer, Greta Schiller and Cheryl Dunye. In documentary films, the genre of history creation itself is examined: the relationship between visual evidence and narrative, the way that dominant history has silenced lesbian desire by focusing on 'publicised' facts. Powerful fiction films address the desiring gaze of the lesbian woman searching for traces of lesbian history embodied in the desirable woman.

Projects such as **oral history** workshops and the creation of lesbian archives have provided lesbian history with sophisticated methodologies and a new sensitivity to the diversity of lesbian experience. Yet contemporary culture recycles practices regardless of their origins and has appropriated 'lesbian chic'. In such a post-identity-politics world, lesbian archives and evidence of an ongoing lesbian culture can provide a sense of connection and grounding in a world which is still characterised by homophobia as well as lesbian pride.

See also: history, feminist

References and further readings

Faderman, L. (1980) *Surpassing the Love of Men: Friendship and Love Between Women from the Renaissance to the Present*, London: Junction Books.

Hall Carpenter Archives Lesbian Oral History Group (1989) *Inventing Ourselves: Lesbian Life Stories*, London: Routledge.

Lorde, A. (1984): *Sister Outsider*, Trumansburg, NY: Crossing Press.

Nestle, J. (1988) *A Restricted Country*, London: Sheba.

PETRA KUPPERS

lesbian jurisprudence

The often overlapping experience of lesbians and gay men in legal arenas has meant that much lesbian scholarship, even when centring women or conscious of women's specific experience, has also extended to cover issues relevant to gay men. Likewise some of the discrimination which lesbians experience is a direct result of gender-based **oppression**, and overlaps considerably with that of other women. In early writing and activism, this has sometimes been expressed as a dualistic choice – a humanistic civil rights discourse along with gay men, or as part of feminist approach along with other non-lesbian feminists. This division has never been satisfactory as, apart from overlooking many other important sites of oppression such as class and race, it offers a false dichotomy of theory and de-centred lesbian experience.

The idea of a specifically lesbian jurisprudence is most closely associated with American lawyer and law teacher, Ruthann Robson who, in the early 1990s writes in her wide-ranging book, *Lesbian (Out)Law*, 'I insist on a *lesbian* legal theory, meaning a theory that is inclusively and specifically lesbian' although she immediately recognises that 'As lesbians we are hardly unified in our approaches to either theory or law'. Robson's conception of lesbian jurisprudence is that a lesbian standpoint need not always be understood as an 'exception'; it can be centrally located and provide insights beyond itself.

The concept of lesbian jurisprudence has been criticised as necessarily essentialist, as an attempt at 'grand theory' reducing lesbians to an essential or unitary group (see **essentialism**). The aim and challenge of lesbian jurisprudence has been to fashion a legal theory which centres and responds to the real needs and experiences of lesbians while recognising that such experience is extraordinarily diverse. However, whether lesbian legal theory is seen as a distinctive strand of jurisprudence or not, much of it continues to speak to, and intersect with, other strands of thought and political movements – notably feminist jurisprudence, critical legal studies and queer scholarship.

A distinctive element of lesbian legal theory has been its pragmatism and direction towards practical change: as Robson has said, 'The most important criticism of theory, it seems to me, is that it is useless'. In terms of focus, much early lesbian legal work and writing centred on child custody disputes involving lesbian mothers, as this was the area where most public battles were (and indeed continue to be) fought. In the 1980s this work extended to cover issues of concern to lesbians in all legal arenas, concentrating on issues such as pornography and censorship, violence, employment discrimination, immigration and relationship recognition. Despite the increasing breadth of coverage, lesbian legal writers have maintained a particular emphasis on issues regarding family. In recent years a volume of this work across Canada, the UK, Australia and the USA has built up which interrogates the **ideology** of motherhood and the family, exploring how such ideas underpin legal discrimination against lesbians, and lesbian relationships in particular.

See also: lesbian feminism; lesbian jurisprudence, sex wars, the

References and further reading

Herman, D. (1990) 'Are We Family? Lesbian Rights and Women's Liberation', *Osgoode Hall Law Journal*, 28, 4: 789–815.

Herman, D. and Stychin C. (eds) (1995) *Legal Inversions: Lesbians, Gay Men, and the Politics of Law*, Philadelphia, PA: Temple University Press.

Robson, R. (1992) *Lesbian (Out)Law: Survival Under the Rule of Law*, NY: Firebrand Books.

JENNI MILLBANK

lesbian literature

The most comprehensive historical study of lesbian literature remains the first one ever written: Jeannette H. Foster's *Sex Variant Women in Literature* (1956). For Foster 'variant' meant lesbian, bisexual, cross-dressing, transsexual women engaged in virtually any act (or thought) of innocent pleasure, Sapphic love, sexual intent, or monstrous debasement and 'literature' spanned well beyond *belles-lettres* to the case study in all its scientific and scurrilous guises.

Foster's book begins with Ruth and Sappho (600

BCE). Plato called Sappho the tenth muse and she has proven to be an enduring inspiration for writers of both sexes, with varying sympathies. One of the earliest acts of 'ventriloquism' (Harvey 1996) was Ovid's epistle 'Sappho to Phaon'. Sappho's heartbroken leap off the Luccidean cliff over the indifference of the ferryman Phaon would set a pattern of narrative for two thousand years to come, where Sapphic interests usually end badly (in Sappho's case with both a reversion to men and a bad end). Most of the lesbian figures in literature are more accurately bisexual or transgendered. Some are innocent, products of all female environments and the male imaginary. Some are licentious, some pornographic, some monstrous: 'Damned Women' in the language of Baudelaire (1857).

It is entirely impossible to cite a reasonable list of books published under this rubric in the twentieth century, so these mentions are partial in every sense. In the Romantic tradition came the *Claudine* (1900–07) series by Collete and 'Willy' (Henry Gauthier Villers). 1928 was a watershed with the publication of Virginia Woolf's *Orlando* and Radclyffe Hall's *The Well of Loneliness*. The first was a pansexual fantasy and farce, a love-letter to Vita Sackville-West, and Woolf's bestseller. The publisher of the second was put on trial; the sociological sympathy shown to the novel's protagonist Stephen Gordon was deemed immoral and obscene. The craft of these two books, the modern lightness of the first compared to the Victorian social realism of the second, attracted attention in kind. Lesbian characters were tolerable as diversions, as mannish women they were inevitably reviled. These books were part of a wave of writing on the subject of sapphists – lesbians, inverts, mannish women, the third sex, 'Bostonians' – accompanied by public discussions of sexual variation from sexology and psychoanalysis. The 'new woman', a product of sexual, economic, and political entitlement, authorised a few young women to write as they wished, famously the American expatriots in Paris: Natalie Barney, Renée Vivien (Pauline Tarn), Djuna Barnes, Gertrude Stein, and American poets, Amy Lowell, Hilda Dolittle and Edna St. Vincent Millay

Some of the most memorable lesbian figures in years between the wars were immortalised on film and stage: The German *Mädchen in Uniform*, a film of Christa Winsloe's *The Child Manuella* (1932), and Pabst's *Pandora's Box* of twenty years earlier. These kinds of expressions were suppressed by the Nazi regime of sexual purity, censorship more blatant but similar to what would occur in the USA under McCarthyism when authors like Lillian Hellman, who had penned the play 'The Children's Hour' (1942), would be blacklisted for their 'leftist politics'.

American censorship and cheap presses helped spawn an explosion of sexual material in the postwar period, and the lesbian slid from the pages of literature onto the shadowy covers of pharmacy bookracks. Many of these books have been reclaimed as gritty classics, in particular Ann Bannon's *Bebbo Brinker* series and Tereska Torrès's *Women's Barracks*. Ann Schokely created one of the first black lesbian characters of the time, notable in the sexual revolution of the late 1960s and early 1970s. From then on, the ethnographic drive of an emerging community resulted in a explosion of writing from committed presses – fictional, sociological, psychological and political – in forms as various as their content: novels, poetry, experimental prose, autobiographies, manifestos, and theory. Sappho reappeared taking mythical proportions (*Sappho was a Right-On Woman*; *Les Guérillères*) and conjectural retrospective reclaimed, following Foster, George Sand, Emily Brontë, George Eliot, Margaret Fuller and Emily Dickenson, to name a few.

Some critics, notably Bertha Harris, called for an embrace of the monstrosity of lesbian literary history, but mimetic demands have driven the body of criticism and writing since the 1970s in the direction of rereading, reclaiming, recasting. Few novels have stood out like *The Lesbian Body*, **Wittig**'s celebration of the visceral grotesque. By the early 1980s the category of 'lesbian' which had become somewhat usefully solid for a short while began to fracture in light of questions about interrelationship with other kinds of race, class and cultural locations. Audre **Lorde**, Adrienne **Rich**, Cherríe Moraga, and Gloria **Anzaldúa**, were only some of the plethora of liberatory voices, while a body of theory foregrounding the visceral quality of experience produced Hélène **Cixous**, Luce **Irigaray** and others.

By the end of the decade, popular culture began to reflect a literary coming of age with wide distribution of films based on Alice **Walker**'s *The Colour Purple*, Jeanette Winterson's *Oranges are not the Only Fruit* and Jane Rule's, *Desert of the Heart*. But once again, an unstable category was wrought asunder by the publication of Leslie Feinberg's *Stone Butch Blues*, a book which has served as a clarion call to a growing transgendered movement, a movement which once again is rewriting a history of variant women.

See also: lesbian autobiography

References and further reading

Abbot, S. and Love, B. (1972) *Sappho Was A Right-On Woman*, New York: Stein and Day.

Bannon, A. (1986) *I Am A Woman*, Tallahassee: Naiad Press.

Feinberg, L. (1993) *Stone Butch Blues*, New York: Firebrand Books.

Foster, J. (1956) *Sex Variant Women in Literature*, Tallahassee: Naiad Press.

Hall, R. [1928] (1965) *The Well Of Loneliness*, London: Virago.

Harvey, E. (1996) 'Ventriloquizing Sappho, or The Lesbian Muse', in E. Greene (ed.) *Re-Reading Sappho*, Berkeley, CA: University of California Press.

Hellman, L. (1942) 'The Children's Hour', in *Plays*, New York: Random.

Jay, K. and Glasgow, J. (eds) (1990) *Lesbian Texts and Contexts*, New York: New York University Press.

Moraga, C. and Anzaldúa, G. (eds) (1983) *This Bridge Called My Back*, New York: Kitchen Table/Women of Colour Press.

Woolf, V. [1928](1956) *Orlando*, New York: Harcourt Brace.

JULIA CREET

liberal feminism

Liberal feminism advocates equal rights for women. It was most prominently advocated in the nineteenth century by John Stuart Mill in *The Subjection of Women*. The dominant form of **feminism** in the nineteenth and early twentieth centuries, for second-wave feminists it has primarily been an object of criticism. This is despite the fact that most gains by the women's movement in the west have been made in terms of liberal rights. Socialist feminists have criticised the empty formalism of rights which do not enable women to achieve substantive equality, and the way the **public/private** distinction central to liberalism obscures women's subordination in the domestic sphere, ruling it outside legitimate intervention (see also **socialism and feminism**). Other feminists have argued against the 'malestream' assumptions of liberalism, with particular reference to the supposedly gender-neutral individual. However, alongside this critique there is also a feminist revision of liberalism, which argues that it is not *necessarily* hostile to feminist claims, even if liberal arguments have generally been used to support the *status quo*.

Mill's (1869) statement of liberal feminism was enormously influential in the first-wave feminist movement. From the initial premise that men and women have essentially the same capacity for reason and therefore self-determination, he argues that women should not be excluded from exercising that capacity in professional work and political life by being confined to the domestic sphere under the direction of their husbands. They should have equal rights with men to education and access to training and work, to the representation of their political interests by means of the vote, and to personal autonomy with rights over property, divorce and so on. However, he does not attack the sexual division of labour as such; on the contrary, he supposes that only exceptional women would choose to compete in the workplace and that most would be principally wives and mothers, dependent on husbands who would support them and their children in the home. The liberal acceptance of socio-economic relations which contribute to the inequality of the sexes is the basis of more radical feminist criticisms of liberal feminism.

The second-wave feminist critique of liberalism

There were self-identified liberal feminists in the twentieth century, notably the influential National Organization of Women (NOW) in the USA, of which Betty **Friedan** was a founding member. However, the approach has been largely rejected by feminist theorists and the term has been more readily used to discredit political rivals. First, it is argued that not only are formal, legal rights insufficient to liberate women, they even contribute to women's subordination. Liberal rights treat like individuals alike. This treatment is inadequate insofar as women and men are not alike. They are, at the very least, differently positioned as a result of the historical construction of the sexual division of labour. Women, for example, find it hard to compete in the labour market on the same terms as men, even where they formally have equal rights to do so, while they remain the primary carers in the home. Equal rights in law are seen as doing nothing to address social and economic inequalities. Furthermore, they mystify existing inequalities by creating the appearance of a meritocracy in which each individual succeeds or fails according to their own merits, while in fact women are disadvantaged relative to men.

Second, it is argued that the distinction between public and private fundamental to liberalism obscures and mystifies women's oppression in the home. For liberals, state intervention is only legitimate in the public sphere; individual rights to privacy *against* the state are crucial. Private and domestic spheres need not be seen as synonymous, but in practice they have been treated as the same since the seventeenth century. Critics of liberal feminism see this division as an intrinsic feature of liberalism: it divides society into the political and non-political, reinforcing the idea that relations between the sexes are 'natural' and therefore outside the law in a self-perpetuating system of oppression. Furthermore what is non-intervention from a liberal perspective is intervention for feminists. The refusal to treat domestic violence seriously, for example, defines the limits of the state regulation of marriage and the legal status of a wife as subordinate.

Third, according to the critique of liberalism as masculinist, liberal feminism is a contradiction in terms. Liberalism cannot be extended to include women's rights on an equal basis with men because the supposedly gender-neutral individual is actually a man. It is notable, for example, that it is very difficult to find a formulation for maternity leave which recognises pregnancy as a stage of life, rather than a gender-neutral illness. On different occasions it has been ruled that discrimination on the grounds of pregnancy is not discrimination at all because *similarly affected men* would be subject to the same treatment, or that it may be considered discrimination in comparison with the way in which a sick or disabled man should be treated. Feminists like Carol **Pateman** (1989) and Seyla **Benhabib** (1987) have argued that such difficulties arise because the universal form of liberal rights means that the individual in the public sphere must leave embodiment and everything that differentiates 'it' from any other particular individual behind in the private sphere. It is an abstraction from actual differences between real, concrete persons. In practice, however, since it is impossible to conceive of individuals without attributes at all, legal rights pick out male attributes which are then passed off as gender-neutral. Furthermore, the abstract disembodied individual is seen as independent of any social ties, fully-formed and self-sufficient. This condition is only possible insofar as liberalism ignores and obscures the relations of reproduction with which women have traditionally been concerned.

Feminist revisions of liberalism

There is also, however, a feminist revision of liberalism growing alongside the more prominent critique. This revision began in the early 1980s with Zillah Eisenstein's *The Radical Future of Liberal Feminism*. Eisenstein (1981), a socialist feminist, sees all feminism as rooted in liberalism insofar as it aims to liberate women to be autonomous. However, she argues that liberal feminism goes beyond abstract individualism insofar as it is concerned with women who have been excluded from liberal rights *as a group*. Eisenstein sees liberal feminism as developing its radical potential in the campaigns of NOW for abortion rights and childcare since they link demands for equal rights with an implicit theory of women's social and economic position. She believes that liberal feminism has the potential to liberate women from capitalist **patriarchy** since demands for equal rights for women could undermine the public/private distinction on which the liberal state is premised.

Similar suggestions have been made from other perspectives concerning the radical potential of liberal feminism. From a poststructuralist perspective, Kate Nash (1998) has deconstructed liberalism, showing how liberals have used 'women' both to refer to individuals who are 'like men', autonomous and gender-neutral, and also feminine figures, 'naturally' caring and subordinate to men in the domestic sphere (see also **poststructuralism/postmodernism; deconstruction, feminist**). Nash argues that feminist movements have had some success historically using both the 'official' and the 'unofficial' figure of women in liberalism, influencing the creation of the welfare state and gaining some group rights for women. Susan **Okin** (1989) builds on John Rawls's theory of liberalism as justice. She argues that, although it has neglected inequalities between the sexes in the past, once they are problematised, it is intrinsic to liberalism that it should address women's subordination in the private sphere as well as ensuring equal opportunities in public life.

Some feminists continue to see the idea of a private sphere of non-intervention as unintelligible given our necessary interdependence as social beings. Others see it as mystificatory since desires and interests are socially constructed rather than individually given. However, in general, there is now greater sympathy among feminists towards liberal concerns for individual privacy. In part this change follows the abuses of state power evident in the totalitarian regimes of Eastern Europe. It is also the case that progressive rulings for women have been based on rights to privacy, notably the right to abortion in the USA. Although the difficulties of accepting this ruling have exercised feminists greatly, it does suggest that the liberal distinction between public and private need not be identical to that between public and domestic; it may be drawn, as in this case, between the individual and society. Furthermore, it has been argued that women are particularly in need of rights to privacy within the home, notably by Virginia Woolf in *A Room of One's Own*.

A more radical revision of the liberal public/private distinction is that of Anne Phillips (1991). She argues that feminists need to reconsider the popular slogan 'the personal is political'. Politics in the public sphere is qualitatively different from activities that take place in private since, ideally, it requires us to negotiate issues across different perspectives, particularly in a multicultural society, in order to take common concerns into account. As Phillips sees it, women need representation as a group in democratic procedures because this is where the most important political decisions should be made. As a civic republican, she aims to revive politics, subordinated in liberalism to economic and social freedom. The implication is that if women were genuinely involved in political decision-making the liberal distinction between public and private, although not abolished, would look very different.

See also: equality and difference; human rights; Marxism; reproduction; socialism and feminism; veil of ignorance; welfare; work, women and

References and further reading

Benhabib, S. (1987) 'The Generalized and the Concrete Other', in S. Benhabib and D. Cornell (eds) *Feminism as Critique*, Minneapolis, MI: University of Minnesota Press.

Eisenstein, Z. (1981) *The Radical Future of Liberal Feminism*, New York: Longman.

Mill, J.S. (1959/1869) *On Liberty* with *The Subjection of Women*, in S. Collini (ed.), Cambridge: Cambridge University Press.

Nash, K. (1998) *Universal Difference: Feminism and the Liberal Undecidability of 'Women'*, London: Macmillan.

Okin, S.M. (1989) *Justice, Gender and the Family*, New York: Basic Books.

Pateman, C. (1989) *The Disorder of Women*, Cambridge, MA: Polity Press.

Phillips, A. (1991) *Engendering Democracy*, Cambridge, MA: Polity Press.

KATE NASH

life-world

'Life-world' gained prominence through conceptualisations by Edmund Husserl and Maurice Merleau-Ponty. Husserl described horizon and world (horizon of all horizons) in *Ideas I* (1913) and finalised them in his *Crisis* idea of life-world

(1938). Subjectivity constitutes and is affected by its surroundings, seen as variously physical, spiritual, personal, ideational. The subject lives at the centre of these surroundings bounded by horizons that taken together are 'the world'. Thus life-world is an individual's world(s) of life with a complexity of meanings (cognitive and noncognitive) or is the world of a group where individuals share meanings from common experiences – for example, under-standings of 'physical' surroundings (the 'world' of natural **science** is one such understanding). Merleau-Ponty extended Husserl's analyses to the mutual constitutivity of self and world, through a dynamic interplay called 'flesh'. These ideas prefigure feminist postmodernists' claims that persons and bodies are discursively constructed and underlie some existentialist feminisms (see **poststructuralism/postmodernism; existentialist feminism**).

MARY JEANNE LARRABEE

literary theory, feminist

Feminist literary theory emerged from the inter-section of two concurrent but disparate move-ments: the international women's movement of the 1960s, and the European intellectual movement known as poststructuralism (see **poststructuralism/postmodernism**). Feminist literary theory is a critical form of knowledge which analyses the role that literary forms and practices, together with the discourses of literary criticism and theory, play in perpetuating or challenging hierarchies of gender, class, race and sexuality. As a term, feminist literary theory only gained currency from the mid-1980s. Previously, feminist literary criticism was used. Traditionally, criticism refers to the practical aspect of literary study – the close reading of texts – while theory examines the philosophical and political underpinnings of interpretive and evalua-tive practices, including the construction of the category of 'literature'. Today, criticism and theory appear simultaneously in the titles of several feminist anthologies, and feminist literary theory includes both practical and theoretical approaches to literature (Showalter 1985b; Warhol and Herndl 1997).

Although feminist classics such as Virginia Woolf's *A Room of One's Own* (1928) and Simone de **Beauvoir**'s *The Second Sex* (1949) are significant precursors, feminist literary criticism began with second-wave feminism. In the 1970s, feminist approaches to literature were framed by the concept of **patriarchy** – the belief that women as a group are universally oppressed by men as a group, on the basis of sexual difference. Mary Ellmann's *Thinking About Women* (1968), Kate **Millet**'s *Sexual Politics* (1970) and Eva Figes's *Patriarchal Attitudes* (1970) were groundbreaking texts, which argued that images of women in male literature do not reflect female experience, but rather, reflects misogynist stereotypes of woman. Consequently, the literary canon should not be regarded benignly, as a collection of great texts expressing universal truths and humanistic values, but as texts that are deeply structured by social and sexual ideologies. As early as 1974, when Juliet **Mitchell** published *Psychoanalysis and Feminism*, there were healthy signs of diversity among feminist critics. In response to Millet's dismissal of Freud, Mitchell advocated psychoanalysis as a tool for feminism, paving the way for **psychoanalytic feminist literary theory**.

By the mid-1970s, feminist critics turned to **women's writing**, studying canonical authors such as Jane Austen, the Brontës, George Eliot and Virginia Woolf, and neglected writers such as Charlotte Perkins Gilman and Kate Chopin, who quickly became fixtures in an alternative female canon. In *A Literature of Their Own* (1977), Elaine **Showalter** reconstructs a tradition of women's literature, which she plots in terms of three stages – female, feminine and feminist. In another major work, *The Madwoman in the Attic* (1979), Sandra Gilbert and Susan Gubar use a psychohistorical approach to explore the anxieties that plagued women writers in the patriarchal society of the nineteenth century. They argue that the identities of 'woman' and 'writer' were diametrically opposed; consequently, women wrote in conflict with the cultural demands of femininity, and with themselves. The figure of the 'madwoman in the attic', which often appears in women's fictions, was a metaphor for a self internally divided. While these critics assume a heterosexual women writer and female culture, Adrienne **Rich** and

Audre **Lorde**, well-known poet-critics, raise the issue of lesbian writing and culture, initiating the field of lesbian literary criticism (see **lesbian literature**).

By the turn of the decade, liberal feminist critics were pressed to articulate the theoretical foundations of their practice. In 'Toward a Feminist Poetics', originally published in 1981, Showalter advocates **gynocritics** – the study of women's writing and creativity from the perspective of female experience and culture – as a theoretical basis for feminist criticism. In an influential essay published in the same year, Myra Jehlan argues that rather than focusing exclusively on female culture, and risk creating a female ghetto, feminist critics should study the links between gender, ideology and literature. Also writing in 1981, Annette Kolodny urges feminists to adopt a pluralistic approach rather than a single methodology or theory. Ultimately, however, it was strong criticism by poststructuralist and black feminist critics that forced a major reassessment of the feminist inheritance of the 1970s, and the liberal humanism that grounded it. While both groups criticise gynocriticism as essentialist, they do so for different reasons. Poststructuralists argue that by grounding feminist criticism in women's writing and culture, feminists reinforce the belief that 'woman' is an identity that pre-exists discourse, rather than a product of discourse. Black feminists criticise gynocriticism for mistakenly assuming that women share a common **identity** and experience as women, which transcends differences of culture, race, class and sexuality. In challenging the philosophical and political foundations of liberal humanist feminism, poststructuralists and black feminists, with their very different theoretical approaches and political agendas, have pushed the field in new directions, and profoundly affected the future development of feminist literary theory.

In the USA, the encounter with poststructuralism was initially mediated through **French feminism**, often by American feminists specialising in French literature. Important texts including *New French Feminisms* (1980) and *The Future of Difference* (1980) introduced feminists to the exciting but challenging work of French feminists such as psychoanalyst Luce **Irigaray**, linguist and critic Julia **Kristeva**, and writer Hélène **Cixous**.

Whereas American critics had relied upon familiar humanist concepts such as the self, experience, and authenticity, French feminists, schooled in semiotics, **psychoanalysis** and deconstruction (see **deconstruction, feminist**), analyse the construction of Woman in representation and discourse, and view literary and philosophical texts as a locus for revolutionary change. In her pithy *Sexual/Textual Politics* (1985), Toril Moi dramatically contrasts the American acceptance of the category of Woman to its deconstruction in the writings of French feminists, thereby setting the stage for heated debates on essentialism that continued well into the 1990s.

In Britain the feminist encounter with poststructuralism was initiated through film studies and the influential journal *Screen Education*. Feminist film and art critics, including Laura **Mulvey**, Elizabeth Cowie, and Griselda **Pollock**, had been concerned, since the 1970s, with the role that representation – in film, literature and art – played in the construction of Woman as sign, that is, as a product of sign systems. Following Mitchell's lead, these critics use psychoanalysis to examine the role of fantasy and desire in the construction of gender and subjectivity. Other important influences were British cultural studies and social history, both of which had strong ties with Marxism. British feminists such as Michèle Barrett have played a significant role in the development of Marxist feminist literary criticism (see **Marxist feminist literature/literary theory**).

While in Britain the category of class was central (see **class analysis, UK**), in the USA, the category of **race** dominated literary theory in the 1980s and beyond. In 1981, the first anthology of black women's writing and criticism – *This Bridge Called My Back* – launched the field of black feminist criticism. In another influential anthology, black feminists argue that white feminist criticism assumes that 'all the women are white', and black male criticism assumes that 'all the blacks are male'; both frameworks exclude the experience and social reality of black women (Hull, Bell and Smith 1982). They criticise white feminists for ignoring literature by women of colour, and insist that feminists must examine the inter-relation of gender, race, class and sexuality in women's texts. In *Black Women Novelists* (1980), Barbara **Christian** lays the groundwork for further study of black women novelists in the twentieth century. In *Reconstructing Womanhood* (1987), Hazel Carby uses the methods of cultural studies to reconstruct the history and culture of Afro-American women novelists. Gloria **Anzaldúa** (1987) explores the conflicts that face writers and critics positioned on the border between two or more cultures, thereby spurring the study of ethnicity and women's literature.

By the late 1980s, the rubric of multiple intersecting differences dominated feminist critical practice, and white feminist critics had become obsessed with **black women's literature**. Works by Toni Morrison, Alice **Walker** and Zora Neale Hurston frequently appeared on university curricula. Gayatri **Spivak**, a major postcolonial critic, brought a sophisticated encounter with poststructuralist theories to bear on issues of gender, race, class and imperialism. In a number of dazzling essays (1987), she draws on Marxism, deconstruction, and psychoanalysis to intervene in debates on French feminism, liberal feminist criticism, cultural studies and pedagogy, and to examine the ways in which feminist and progressive critical practices themselves often further an imperialist hegemony.

The fracturing of the category of 'woman' that took place in the 1980s was, in the 1990s, accompanied by other significant shifts: firstly, from 'women' to 'gender', which includes masculinity and femininity, and from heterosexuality to homosexuality. Eve Sedgwick's influential 1985 text, *Between Men*, launched the field of **queer theory**. Using a feminist deconstructive methodology to examine representations of homophobia in nineteenth-century literature (see **deconstruction, feminist**), Sedgwick argues that an analysis of representations of homophobia, when considered together with misogynist representations of woman and femininity, can provide insight into how the gender system operates. Secondly, with the widespread development of cultural studies, often housed in literature departments, feminist literary theory has expanded to include popular culture texts. In *Reading the Romance* (1984), Janice Radway uses an ethnographic approach to study women readers of romance fiction, pioneering the development of

feminist cultural studies. Arguably, feminist literary theory's greatest achievement has been to politicise and open the field of literary criticism. It has brought into question the literary canon and, as a consequence, has broadened the notion of the 'text' itself to encompass all forms of language and representation, from film and psychotherapeutic narratives to shopping centres.

See also: cultural theory/cultural studies, feminist; classics, feminism and the

References and further reading

Anzaldúa, G. (1987) *Borderlands/La Frontera: The New Mestiza*, San Francisco: Aunt Lute Books.

Hull, G., Bell, P. and Smith, B. (1982) (eds) *All the Women are White, All the Blacks are Men, But Some of Us Are Brave*, Old Westbury: Feminist Press.

Jehlen, M. (1997) 'Archimedes and the Paradox of a Feminist Criticism', in R. Warhol and D. Herndl (eds) *Feminisms*, New Brunswick, NJ: Rutgers University Press.

Kolodny, A. (1985) 'Dancing Through the Minefield', in E. Showalter (ed.) *The New Feminist Criticism*, New York: Pantheon Books.

Moraga, C. and Anzaldúa, G. (eds) (1981) *This Bridge Called My Back: Writings By Radical Women of Color*, Watertown, MA: Persephone Press.

Rich, A. (1979) *On Lies, Secrets, and Silence*, New York: Norton.

Showalter, E. (1985a) 'Towards a Feminist Poetics', in E. Showalter (ed.) *The New Feminist Criticism*, New York: Pantheon Books.

—— (ed) (1985b) *The New Feminist Criticism: Essays on Women, Literature and Theory*, New York: Pantheon Books.

Spivak, G. (1987) *In Other Worlds: Essays in Cultural Politics*, New York: Routledge.

Warhol, R.R. and Herndl, D.P. (eds) (1997) *Feminisms: An Anthology of Literary Theory and Criticism*, New Brunswick, NJ: Rutgers University Press.

ROSANNE KENNEDY

literature, images of women in

The issue of the image is particularly important for second-wave-feminist politics and academic inquiry. Kate Millet's *Sexual Politics* (1970) opened a new field of literary criticism by arguing passionately that images of women must be seen in terms of patriarchal power dynamics. Using the concept of 'literary reflection', **Millet** produces readings of male literary texts to demonstrate both the misogyny of high literature and the potential of a 'resisting reading' – though this term was made current not by Millet but by Judith Fetterley. Adrienne **Rich** argues for a feminist poetics based on what she calls 're-vision'. Throughout the 1970s feminist academics and activists took the argument about the power of images – literary, visual and mass media – as an important focus. In the academy this focus came under attack from a number of directions in the late 1970s. Elaine **Showalter** (1979) argues that critics should concentrate on 'gynocriticism', that is on women as writers rather than as readers or viewers (see **gynocritics**). This claim opened a whole new area of literary criticism focused on women writers. More direct attacks on 'images of women' criticism came from visual artists and critics, notably Griselda **Pollock** (1977). When Toril Moi in *Sexual/Textual Politics* (1985) attacks both Millet and Showalter, she is articulating a more positive feminist critical engagement with psychoanalysis, precipitated in Britain by Juliet **Mitchell**'s *Psychoanalysis and Feminism*, and influenced by French feminists Hélène **Cixous** and Julia **Kristeva** (see also **French feminism**).

The debate on literary images of women has thus become entangled with wider questions of women's relation to representation as producers and consumers of texts, and with questions of the unconscious as well as the social and political. Deborah Cameron's *Feminism and Linguistic Theory* (1985) draws together several strands of thinking which emphasise the importance of women being seen as acting in society, and how that affects visual and verbal texts. Much of the 1980s' discussion of images continued to be between those who argue that, because women think differently from men and operate with different value systems in society, what is crucial is that it is a *woman* who is the artist, writer or consumer of texts, and others who disagree, arguing that women are complicit in their own stereotyping and that such essentialist positions are based on simplistic models of subjectivity and of how images of the (female) self work. Mary Jacobus has suggested (1986) that women readers, like all readers, are positioned within an exchange that constitutes meaning, and that images acquire meaning through these processes of exchange.

Such literary theories have drawn on psychoanalytic models which have been even more central to theorising visual media, particularly film. Laura **Mulvey**'s influential essay 'Visual Pleasure and Narrative Cinema' (1975) places sexual difference at the centre of visual pleasure so that woman is always positioned as the object of the male gaze in an economy of desire which does not allow for a feminine subject who looks. The question of whether woman is always the object of the look and therefore the object of desire has become a major concern for film theorists and some feminist practitioners. In the 1990s such debates were taken up into a proliferation of other discourses. Research on other media (especially television and popular romance), audience research and critiques of this earlier feminist work as assuming a white, relatively privileged and heterosexual subject, all helped to open up the debate on how visual and verbal images work. Tania Modleski and Janice Radway, in relation to different popular media, argue that images of women in television and in romance must be understood in terms of the dailiness of women's lives. Such images, they suggest, simultaneously thrust women back into roles defined by patriarchy and also offer spaces in which to use viewing and reading for psychological and recreational needs. Jackie Stacey in her 1995 discussion of women and Hollywood stars, *Star-gazing*, argues for a complex process of viewing whereby women move in and out of positions of identification with and distance from the film stars who represent women in popular cinema. The rejection by many feminists of arguments that images of women work directly as expressions and instruments of male power has deeply divided feminists around the issue of pornographic images – both visual and verbal (see **pornography**).

It is significantly the case that black, Indian Asian and First Nations women are much more positive about the focus on images of women than white western feminists (see **First Nations and women**). Janice Acoose in *Iskwewak: Neither Indian Princesses nor Easy Squaws* (1995) points out the political necessity of writing new images for Native American women. In the west, black women, and women of colour have sometimes criticised the way psychoanalytically inflected models have been used without an awareness of power relationships other than those of sexuality and gender. bell **hooks**, in her work on black women and film, argues both that race is a crucial element in all western image-making and that black women can and do construct an oppositional gaze. While her work has been criticised as itself essentialising a black female self, there are other non-white feminist writers and activists such as Patricia Hill **Collins** and Patricia **Williams**, who stress that awareness of the power of images is a necessary element in collective understanding and struggle.

Others who speak from or for marginalised groups have made analogous arguments. Valerie **Walkerdine**, for example, argues that class is a category which needs to be brought back into our analysis of how popular culture works and in particular how it deploys images. Lesbian and queer theorists have entered into this debate from rather different positions. Making the lesbian visible, rescuing lesbian identities from historical erasure, asking 'What a Lesbian Looks Like' (British National Gay and Lesbian Survey 1992), have been important tasks for lesbian scholars and activists. The agenda of being and making visible was in the 1990s taken up into debates around the proliferation of lesbian identities and media fascination with 'lipstick lesbianism' and the 'out-ing' of soap opera and media stars, as well as clergy and other establishment figures. Still the political and academic project remains. For lesbian and queer writers the other important aspect of images of women has been the possibility of a positive female erotic gaze. Queer theorists like Elspeth Probyn seek to move the images or representation of the female body into a new kind of writing and a new way of being, one which refuses the straight-jacket of straight identities. In all these areas, work

on different cultural forms – visual, verbal, popular and high literary – has often overlapped.

The problem of stereotyping is central to this debate, and not specific to women (see **Code** 1995). Both verbal and visual texts can distance the image of woman, rendering it impersonal, general-ised and only good for third person ethics. But as the Fergusons note in *Images of Women in Literature* (1991), consciously recognised stereotypes can have their uses: they are dangerous if they encourage us to take the image for granted, but they also offer shortcuts to response upon which we may have to depend; they help us to recognise what society sees as stereotypical; they let us see women as others see them; they encourage us to think about images both in terms of changing them, and in terms of their continuity and power which reminds us of the silencing and exclusion of women. There is a paradox here that is well-caught by Kadiatu Kanneh's comment (1992), from 'Love Mourning and Metaphor', on the 'intolerable visibility of women'. But there is a further issue: people may be brutalised by the way they stereotype others, yet it always lies within their power to reverse the stereotype. Luce **Irigaray** notes in *I Love to You* (1996) that women (and men) often neglect to take images of women seriously, as valued.

Because women on the whole are not in positions of power, or even with relative access to it, they work with different knowledge and value parameters, and need different representations and ways of representing, in order to value their lives. Recent feminist theory has approached these issues by looking at representation as ideologically permitted identity, as discursive subjectivity, and as commonality. Jacqueline Rose, in *Sexuality in the Field of Vision* (1986), draws on psychoanalysis, which defines and describes the individual's rela-tion to ruling ideology as one of subjection to specific and fixed representation, to argue that no image is without the problem of inadequacy to identity. There is no unified subject, and this inadequacy is the source of desire. Negotiating desire as a field of possibility rather than lack, discourse studies has tended to deal with 'images of women' as the site of complicity in subject positions. Judith **Butler**'s work on the image as individual performance underlines this ambiva-lence (1986 and 1992), while Lynne Pearce in

Feminism and the Politics of Reading (1997) argues that this complicity means that when women deal with images of women they cannot relate their interpretations to their feelings.

A number of feminists, such as Rita Felski and Rosi Braidotti, have dealt with representation in terms of commonality rather than identification. Commonality involves valuing affect, for which images are particularly enabling. Ellen Esrock (1994) notes that although the connection between knowing and seeing has been rejected, for many individuals it is there emotionally. She defines a direct connection between image, emotion, aesthetic value and knowledge. The images and the process of producing and consuming them are culture and class specific and gender inflected. 'Woman' is not singular; each woman will have a specific situation from which to relate to representation, with more or less commonality with others. These critics argue for an affective location to value the images of women within a community that makes up a shared response of commonality, **alterity** and **difference**.

See also: narrative, feminist uses of; romance as genre

References and further reading

Betterton, R. (1989) *Looking On*, London: Pandora.

Braidotti, R. (1996) 'Cyberfeminism with a Difference', *New Formations*, 29.

Cameron, D. (1985) *Feminism and Linguistic Theory*, London: Macmillan.

Esrock, E. (1994) *The Reader's Eye*, Baltimore and London: Johns Hopkins University Press.

Felski, R. (1989) *Beyond Feminist Aesthetics*, Cambridge, MA: Harvard University Press.

hooks, b. (1992) *Race and Representation*, London: Turnaround Press.

Pollock, G. (1977) 'What's Wrong with "Images of Women"', *Screen Education*, 24.

Probyn, E. (1995) 'Queer Belongings: The Politics of Departure', in E. Grosz and E. Probyn (eds) *Sexy Bodies, The Strange Carnalities of Feminism*, London: Routledge.

Wilton, T. (1995) *Lesbian Studies, Setting an Agenda*, London: Routledge.

MARGARET BEETHAM AND LYNETTE HUNTER

Lloyd, Genevieve (b. 1941)

Genevieve Lloyd taught Philosophy at the Australian National University from 1967–87, and was Professor of Philosophy at the University of New South Wales from 1987–2000. Many eminent younger Australian feminist philosophers have studied with her. Among her numerous books, *The Man of Reason* (1993) is a landmark reference point without which feminist epistemology could not have established its claims (see **epistemology, feminist**).

Lloyd shows that, throughout the western philosophical canon, Reason is defined by contrast with and exclusion of 'feminine' values and attributes. Ancient Greek philosophers invoked a metaphysical principle to separate positive masculine from negative feminine qualities: *maleness*, limit, light, good, and square signify determinate form; *femaleness*, unlimited, dark, bad, and oblong, align with formlessness. Variations on these principles infuse philosophical and popular beliefs about the rational capacities of women and men, and inform stereotypes of femininity and masculinity now in common currency.

Reason is discursively constructed in symbols and metaphors that shape and are shaped by dominant ideals of masculinity. Its association with ideal masculinity stakes out a rational domain inaccessible, or accessible only uneasily, to people whose positionings have not fostered the characteristics of ideal masculinity. Lloyd thus traces a feminine/masculine division through the history of philosophy that unifies femininity and masculinity along lines that other postcolonial theorists contest (see **postcolonial feminism**). But this homogeneity is a consequence of her chosen domain: the texts that comprise the western philosophical canon. Hence her analysis attests, also, to the local character of hegemonic Reason (see **hegemony**), and its connections with specific, practical-political circumstances. It is an exemplary instance of local inquiry, specific to the symbolic events that have shaped malestream western philosophy – and to their 'trickle-down' social-political effects.

Lloyd's work is informed as much by literature as by canonical philosophy: her eloquent, moving *Being In Time* draws as deeply on Virginia Woolf and Marcel Proust as on such philosophers as

Bergson, Augustine, Ricoeur and Derrida. Some of her recent work focuses on how philosophical-social imaginaries work to configure enactments of selfhood, collective responsibility, citizenship, postcolonial politics, and gendered being. In two books she offers sensitive historical readings of the philosophy of Benedict de Spinoza within his time, and subtle arguments for the pertinence of his thought in enabling philosophers to rethink present day social and **political theory**. Her engagement with questions of sexual **difference** illuminates and is located within broader theoretical and social analyses.

See also: emotions/rationality

Selected writings:

Lloyd, G. (1993) *The Man of Reason: 'Male' and 'Female' in Western Philosophy*, London: Routledge, 2nd edn.
—— (1993) *Being in Time: Selves and Narrators in Philosophy and Literature*, London: Routledge.
—— (1994) *Part of Nature*, Ithaca, NY: Cornell University Press.

LORRAINE CODE

local knowledges

'Local knowledges' comes into English from the translation of Michel Foucault's 'Two Lectures' delivered in 1976. The expression contests the universality and neutrality claims of scientific-governed conceptions of knowledge which establish their **hegemony** in 'global, *totalitarian theories*'. Local knowledges by contrast are historically and situationally specific, derived in opposition to the exclusionary power exercised in the 'scientific hierarchisation of knowledges'. Although Foucault fails to address the gendered implications of local, oppositional knowledge struggles, feminists have derived from the concept of local knowledges a powerful means of articulating the struggles of women and other marginalised people to claim a voice in dominant discourses where their experiential knowledge is systemically subjugated, denied acknowledgement, dismissed as lacking in epistemic authority.

References and further reading

Foucault, M. (1980) 'Two Lectures', in *Power/ Knowledge: Selected Interviews and Other Writings*, trans. C. Gordon, L. Marshall, J. Mepham, K. Soper, New York: Pantheon Books.

LORRAINE CODE

logocentrism

The term logocentrism refers to the metaphysical assumption in western philosophy that ideas are the origin and organisational centre of all discourse, including all speech and writing. In the deconstructive critique of western metaphysics, the technical reference of the term is the presumption that there exists an order of priority among ideas, speech, and writing such that meaning has its unequivocal and determinate origin in the pre-linguistic idea. However, the concept has been used by some feminist theorists to articulate how certain entrenched ideas inappropriately and problematically structure an entire discourse or way of thinking. For example, the term **phallogocentrism** refers to the fact that, in patriarchal societies, discourse is organised with reference to the idea of maleness or **masculinity** which tacitly functions as the normative **gender**.

References and further reading

Spivak, G.C. (1974) 'Translator's Preface' in J. Derrida *Of Grammatology*, Baltimore and London: Johns Hopkins University Press.

JOAN MASON-GRANT

Lorde, Audre (1934–92)

There are few who are gifted and courageous enough to blend elegance, skill, vision, vulnerability, power and eroticism into a lifetime of intentional scrutiny. Fewer still have been able to fold it all into a visionary poetics in which the transformative capacity of the desire for beauty, the practice of truth and the struggle for social justice are its moorings. Audre Geraldine Lorde was such a person.

Born as the third and youngest daughter of a West Indian immigrant family in Harlem, New York City in 1934, with bad eyesight, resisting speech until the age of five, she came in later years to demand of things that she see them and that silence be transformed into language and action. Poetry was Lorde's consistent medium for such expression, fierce, precise and full, culminating in eleven volumes, of which *The Marvelous Arithmetics of Distance* (1993) was published posthumously. She was honoured with the distinction of Poet Laureate of New York (1991–3) and numerous other awards. Her zest for life and librarian's passion for knowledge lent a celebratory voice to her poetry, unearthing lesbian love and African heritage. The body of Lorde's work, both poetry and prose, stands at the crossroads of the poetic, the personal, the spiritual and the political, and she strikes an important unity between the themes there and those of her own life (see the biomythography *Zami, A New Spelling of My Name,* 1982). Always insistent on naming herself, 'Black, feminist, activist, poet, warrior, mother of two come here to do her work', Lorde was anchored at the intersection of three major social movements of the second half of the twentieth century: the movements for black liberation and for women's and lesbian and gay liberation.

As the lesbian mother of two interracial children and later as a partner in an interracial relationship, Lorde fashioned her understanding of difference from these experiences and brought them to bear on her political involvements and theoretical insights. In the latter years of her life, she became a staunch internationalist, advocating for sustainable development, connecting black women across USA, Europe, Australia, the Caribbean, New Zealand and South Africa. In 1985, she became a member of SISA, Sisters in Support of Sisterhood in South Africa. After a courageous struggle with breast and liver cancer for fourteen years, she died in St Croix, US Virgin Islands on November 17, 1992, at the home she shared with her partner Dr Gloria I. Joseph. She has truly become one of *Our Dead Behind Us* (1986).

Selected writings

Lorde, A. (1982) *Zami, A New Spelling of my Name,* New York: The Crossing Press.

—— (1985) *Our Dead Behind Us,* New York, London: W.W. Norton.

—— (1993) *The Marvelous Arithmetics of Distance, Poems 1987–1992,* New York, London: W.W. Norton.

M. JACQUI ALEXANDER AND GLORIA WEKKER

Lugones, María (b. 1944)

A prominent member of the Society for Women in Philosophy (SWIP) and a pioneer in the field of Latina feminism (see **Latin American feminism**), María C. Lugones has greatly furthered the development of feminism within **philosophy**. Her contributions to feminist theories of **identity**, **difference**, and **cultural imperialism** are significant. Argentine born, Lugones is influenced by the **Chicana feminism** of Gloria **Anzaldúa** and Cherríe Moraga. Her critiques of modernity and emphasis on multiplicity and difference resemble claims associated with postmodernism. Lugones, however, locates her work within Latina, radical, and lesbian feminisms and has distinguished her views from those of Judith **Butler** and Donna **Haraway** (Lugones 1994: 475). Specifically, Lugones has criticised poststructuralist feminism's dismissal of **identity politics** and the political significance of groups.

Lugones's work has been important for feminists seeking to theorise cross-cultural coalitions without minimising the political salience of group difference. Her essays address not only differences between/among women but also possibilities for achieving understanding across those differences. For example, her collaborative work with white/Anglo feminist Elizabeth Spelman examines the difficulties cultural imperialism poses to the description and **interpretation** of **experience**. It offers suggestions for doing respectful feminist theory that avoids the pitfalls of ethnocentrism.

Much of Lugones's work lies within the context of feminist **ontology** and epistemology (see **epistemology, feminist**). Her influential essay, 'Playfulness, "World"-Travelling, and Loving Perception', seeks to explain cross-cultural loving and understanding without doing violence to or erasing plurality and difference. Toward this end, Lugones explores 'world'-travelling, the difficult practice of moving among different social contexts and constructions of a society or societies. Travel between 'worlds' can help people to understand the reality of other people's experiences of oppression. Lugones therefore offers 'world'-travelling as an answer to questions of **commensurability/ incommensurability** which plague feminist standpoint epistemology. In 'Purity, Impurity, and Separation', Lugones tackles the ontological connections between domination (pure separation) and resistance (impure separation, or 'curdling'). Lugones advocates an impure separation that embraces multiplicity, after the model of *mestizaje* (racial mixing), as an alternative to the pure separation of domination, which violently fragments the multiplicity of the **self**.

See also: cultural identities; embodiment/ disembodiment; lesbian feminism; metaphysics; modernity, feminist critiques of; race; radical feminism; sexuality

Selected writings

Lugones, M. (1987) 'Playfulness, "World"-Travelling, and Loving Perception', *Hypatia* 2 (2): 3–19.
—— (1994) 'Purity, Impurity, and Separation', *Signs* 19,2: 458–79.
Lugones, M. and Spelman, E.V. (1983) 'Have We Got a Theory for You!', *Women's Studies International Forum* 6,6: 573–81.

MICHAEL HAMES-GARCÍA

MacKinnon, Catharine (b. 1946)

Catharine MacKinnon is a feminist legal theorist, activist, and professor of law at the University of Michigan. She is recognised internationally for her innovations in the area of sexual harassment legislation and for her controversial Minneapolis ordinance on **pornography**. That a hostile work environment can be understood to constitute sexual harassment, and that sexual harassment itself is considered a form of discrimination under American law, is due largely to MacKinnon's efforts.

Extending this argument, MacKinnon argues in *Only Words* (1993) that if the words and expressions that make up sexual and racial harassment are recognised as the discriminatory acts that they are, so too should the words and images in pornography be recognised as discriminatory. Against pornographers and civil libertarians who seek First Amendment protection for pornography as speech, MacKinnon claims that pornography is not a mere representation of sex, but is a sex act itself. With Andrea **Dworkin**, MacKinnon drafted an anti-pornography ordinance for the residents of Minneapolis that defined pornography as an infringement of women's civil rights. The ordinance was ultimately overturned by the US Supreme Court in 1986, but was used as the basis for the Supreme Court of Canada's 1992 Butler decision which rejected a freedom of expression defence against a criminal charge for distributing pornography.

Sexuality is, in MacKinnon's words, the linchpin of women's **oppression**; and sexuality in a male-dominated culture is about the sexualisation of dominance and submission. Deliberately provocative and explicit in its description of the sexual abuse of women, MacKinnon's writing is a rhetorically powerful articulation of radical feminist theory. Employing a standpoint epistemology, MacKinnon treats women's lived experiences as sources of knowledge, as the foundation of feminist theory. The central problem with this view, as with all standpoint theories, is determining whose experience should form the basis of knowledge. Indeed, MacKinnon is widely criticised for failing to account for lesbian sexuality and racial and class-based differences between women; and for circumscribing women's sexual agency, just as patriarchal society has done.

MacKinnon's contribution to feminist legal theory and practice, and to feminist debates on sexuality and rape, remains formative. She has also been active in the attempt to take the case of the Bosnian rape victims to the International Court of Justice.

See also: critical race theory; discrimination and the law; speech act theory; standpoint theory

Selected writings

MacKinnon, C. (1987) *Feminism Unmodified: Discourses on Life and Law*, Cambridge, MA: Harvard University Press.
—— (1989) *Toward a Feminist Theory of the State*, Cambridge, MA: Harvard University Press.
—— (1993) *Only Words*, Cambridge, MA: Harvard University Press.

JOANNE H. WRIGHT

madness, feminisation of

Representations of 'woman' have been linked to images of insanity throughout the history of western thought and culture. While influential philosophical and medical discourses have assumed a natural relation between the two, feminists understand the feminisation of madness as an historical and cultural phenomenon related to the hierarchical opposition between male and female in western systems of language and representation. For example, Luce **Irigaray**, Hélène **Cixous**, and Genevieve **Lloyd** all highlight western philosophy's use of male/female symbolism to mark subordinate relations between aspects of a dual world; within this framework, maleness is associated with 'superior' principles of form and consciousness, and femaleness with 'inferior' principles of formlessness and materiality. Applied to human nature, this symbolism links masculinity with historically-valued capacities of rationality, objectivity, and culture, while femininity is associated with devalued traits of irrationality, emotionality, and embodied sexuality. Such associations render madness and 'woman' complicit in their mutually dis-ordered rationality, corporeality, and morality.

Michel Foucault and Elaine **Showalter** have highlighted ways in which a natural rapport between women and madness is assumed in early medico-scientific and legal formulations of mental disorder. Foucault suggests that madness – previously valorised as a source of esoteric knowledge – was increasingly understood in classical medicine as both a sign and consequence of traits associated with femininity and perverse sexuality, including moral lassitude, constitutional weakness, and 'unreason'. In the late 1800s, Jean-Martin Charcot's and Sigmund Freud's work on *hysteria* (derived from the Greek word for 'uterus') established the theoretical edifice upon which early psychiatry and psychoanalysis were both constructed; although they diagnose the disorder in men, both Charcot and Freud characterise hysteria as a *symbolically* female disorder, one linked specifically to female sexuality. Showalter and other feminists have chronicled similar gender asymetry within nineteenth- and twentieth-century European, English and American psychiatry and psychology, arguing that while diagnoses, causal explanations, and treatments have changed across time, mental illness continues to be represented as a female malady.

Feminists understand the impact of these dominant assumptions as an important factor in the historical overrepresentation of women in mentally ill populations. In underscoring the additional effects of oppressive social and economic conditions on women's mental health, feminists suggest that women's madness can be seen simultaneously as a consequence of social victimisation and as a form of feminine protest. For example, many feminists have documented the 'writing' of madness as both impasse and resistance in literature by women. Women's 'madness' can thus be understood both as an effect of the denial of modes for women's self-affirmation *and* the denial of means to protest rigid and devalued gender roles, lack of economic power, and exclusion from public genres of speaking, writing, and discourse.

References and further reading

Showalter, E. (1985) *The Female Malady: Women, Madness, and English Culture, 1830–1980*, New York: Pantheon.

SUZANNE BARNARD

malestream thought

Malestream thought is an ironic expression coined by Mary **O'Brien** in *The Politics of Reproduction* (1980) to encapsulate the claim that the canonical theories and ideas that comprise the western intellectual 'mainstream' are more properly named 'malestream' theories. They are made and circulated by white men in positions of **power** and **privilege**, drawn from their experiences, and based on a tacit assumption that these particular male lives are 'normal', representative of human lives as such. With a nearly-imperceptible sleight of hand, 'malestream' theories and practices effectively exclude the ideas and experiences of women from theoretical consideration. Feminist and other critics have noted that these theories also fail to take into account the ideas, experiences, and situations of men who are neither white, nor privileged, nor powerful.

See also: androcentrism

References and further reading

O'Brien, M. (1980) *The Politics of Reproduction*, London: Routledge and Kegan Paul.

LORRAINE CODE

Martin, Jane Roland (b. 1929)

Jane Roland Martin introduced philosophy of education to feminist theorists and feminist theory to philosophers of education. More radical than the revisions of liberal curriculum and pedagogy by the Women's Studies movement, Martin's feminist critique of **education** has systemic implications for education of men and children as well as women. She theorises a **hidden curriculum** of gender embedded in the ideal of the educated person and in basic concepts of teaching, schooling, and education itself, often assumed to be gender-blind.

Martin identifies an epistemological inequality in contemporary analytic philosophy of education that excludes, distorts, and devalues women as subjects and objects of educational thought. Her *Reclaiming a Conversation: The Ideal of the Educated Woman* (1985) addresses that fault by acknowledging that mothering can be educating and proposing that historians of educational thought should question their assumptions about sources of data, methods of study, and authorship itself. While critiquing classic gender-blind and gender-bound educational ideals, it engages women's educational thought to argue for a *gender-sensitive* educational ideal, which has become the basis for much subsequent feminist work in philosophy of education, including Martin's own.

This ideal requires educators constantly to be aware of gender's workings in the lives of both sexes, where gender can make an educational difference and where it should make none. Sensitive to rather than prescriptive of gender, Martin's ideal presumes no essential traits in either sex, but constitutes an aim that both sexes should be educated in, about, and for both 'productive' (political, cultural, economic) and 'reproductive' (nurturing) processes of society. Responsive to critics, her later work on this ideal has developed more subtlety.

Martin's numerous articles demonstrate the necessity of rethinking premises and purposes of coeducation, which she undertakes in *The School-home* (1992). Re-theorizing gender-sensitivity, it critiques the epistemological fallacy that reduces curriculum to spectator knowledge and re-conceptualises school as a 'moral equivalent of home' for both 'learning to live' and learning about dominated and dominating cultures.

Martin has also contributed to feminist philosophy of **science**, and she provocatively questions some dogmas of recent feminist theory, specifically naming 'proscribed categories', 'compulsory historicism', and 'compulsory *verstehenism*'. But her signal contribution has been as a founder of contemporary feminist philosophy of education.

See also: pedagogy, feminist

Selected writings

Martin, J.R. (1994) *Changing the Educational Landscape: Philosophy, Women, and Curriculum*, New York: Routledge.
—— (1994) 'Methodological Essentialism, False Difference, and Other Dangerous Traps', *Signs*, 19, 3: 630–57
—— (1996) 'Aerial Distance, Esotericism, and Other Related Traps', *Signs*, 21, 3: 584–614.

SUSAN LAIRD

Martindale, Kathleen (1947–95)

As a teacher, scholar and activist, Kathleen Martindale was an important contributor to literary theory and criticism, lesbian culture and women's studies in Canada. In *Un/Popular Culture: Lesbian Writing After the Sex Wars* (1997), Martindale analyses contemporary lesbian literary and cultural theory by asking how lesbian-feminism became an un/popular culture, shifting from a political vanguard into a cultural neo-avant-garde.

Using the publication of Adrienne Rich's 'Compulsory Heterosexuality and Lesbian Existence' (1980) and the outbreak of the American **sex wars** as starting points, Martindale traces the emergence of lesbian postmodernism, through her 'anti-disciplinary' study of un/popular non-academic texts such as lesbian comic books, 'Dykes to Watch Out For' and 'Hothead Paisan', Joan Nestle's **butch/femme** autobiographical narrative 'A Restricted Country' (1987), contemporary lesbian fiction by Sarah Schulman and lesbian pedagogy. These texts, Martindale argues, are postmodernist rewritings and revisions of lesbian-feminist modes of cultural expression (see **lesbian feminism**).

Her analysis raises questions about how lesbians read, what they read, and what counts as lesbian theory. Examining the history of lesbian theory, Martindale interrogates the role of reading in the production of lesbian cultures asking how **sexuality** and textuality produce and are produced by each other, how the reading of texts, particularly theoretical texts, has helped to create and transform individual and collective identities such as the lesbian, the lesbian-feminist, the butch/femme couple, the sex radical, the queer, and her favourite, the theory-head. Martindale asks us to examine what is productive, seductive and destructive about theorising identity in and through texts.

Her final chapter draws on her experience as a teacher of feminist theory and gay and lesbian studies, concluding with a discussion of the status of queer pedagogy in academic institutions, interrogating what measures need to be taken to promote and safeguard its existence in what are often homophobic educational settings. Praised for its engagement with and emphasis on popular material, and the popular/unpopular binary of academic scholarship, this text is an important contribution to the burgeoning field of lesbian literary theory, and testifies to the depth of Kathleen Martindale's passionate engagement with lesbian identity and ethnography. Posthumously published, *Un/Popular Culture* is her last book.

Toward the end of her life, Martindale's life-long activism was again ignited as she began to speak out and write about the epidemic of breast cancer and the horrors particular to her experience of breast cancer as a lesbian, calling for education and action on the issue.

See also: lesbian feminism; Rich, Adrienne; poststructuralism/postmodernism

Selected writings

Godard, B. and McCallum, P. (eds) (1997) 'Passionate Ethics', *Resources for Feminist Research* 25 3: 4.
Martindale, K. (1994) 'My Lesbian Breast Cancer Story: Can I Get a Witness?' in M. Oikawa, D. Falconer and A. Dector (eds) *Resist: Essays Against a Homophobic Culture*, Toronto: Women's Press.
—— (1997) *Un/Popular Culture: Lesbian Writing After the Sex Wars*, Albany, NY: State University of New York Press.

FIONA MacCOOL

Marxism

Marxism is a theory of revolutionary transformation based upon the central contribution of labour to the creation of value and therefore is economically determinist. It is also a dual systems theory, which argues that domestic life in the sphere of reproduction is as important for women as the sphere of production.

Marxism arose from Karl Marx's and Friedrich Engels's attempts to replace Heglian idealism with a new revolutionary, materialist analysis. This analysis is based upon the labour theory of value which argues that value is created through the impact of labour upon nature, thus work is the central creative human social act. This process also creates the potential for radical change in capitalism through a theory of consciousness, which sees ideas coming from the individual members of a group, a social class, defined through the group's relationship to production. This consciousness can be helped, or articulated, by revolutionaries who bring the workers to an awareness of the power of their position since it is their labour which creates value. Once this is understood by workers who achieve revolutionary class consciousness, it leads to revolution in which the expropriators, those who control production through their control of capital, are expropriated by those who produce, once they have recognised their own interests. Thus there is no timeless human nature but a contingent social nature based upon the means of production. The *Communist Manifesto* of 1848 argues for an egalitarian polity based upon revolution in the means of production. Engels's 1888 *The Origins of the Family, Private Property and the State* posits two spheres, production and reproduction, equally important in reproducing human society; rejecting the family as natural, outside social change, arguing it is a major site of social power, closely tied to relationships of production, that sexuality is formed by economic interests and the role of property's transmission through inheritance. As a theory it thus creates two key concepts which underpin subsequent feminist analysis. One is the twin roles of production producing the material means of existence and **reproduction** producing the workers to produce; the other is the role of ideology which helps to maintain the relations of expropriation and exploitation in people's thinking about their existence. Some early versions of Marxism were deterministic, believing that society followed scientific laws which could lead inevitably through a falling rate of profit to revolution; they were also optimistic in that this transformation of society in the interests of the majority would happen soon. However, the relationship between socialism with its commitment to justice and equality and Marxism with its commitment to revolution for one group within existing society has contradicted the coming to power of the world class, which is what the working class were because upon their labour all value rested.

Feminist theorists early recognised one of the problems of this theory for explaining the position of women. Although Engels had argued for the primary importance of reproduction to maintaining social order by making it possible for society to continue, the world of reproduction is not really seen as a site of potential transformation in itself. Labour's power and unequal reward expose inequality and exploitation while reproduction demonstrates **oppression** and inequality. The theory also naturalises a division between the sexes which ignores the contribution of women to both worlds – that of labour and that of social reproduction, i.e. housekeeping and childbearing,

as well as physiological processes of pregnancy, birth and lactation.

Marx's account in *Das Capital* shows clearly the processes through which capital acts upon workers' lives at work but does not at all explain how it affects domestic life. The implications for political mobilisation and activism are clear – those who add most value to raw materials are most important in creating an uprising against capitalism. Hence women, if referred to at all by Marx, are mostly seen as either subsumed under the category worker or as inert bystanders in the revolutionary process. In Communist parties and writings this theoretical account leads to a refusal to allow women to organise separately and a rejection of welfarist strategies for amelioration in favour of workplace-based movements for revolution, and also to low levels of interest in **sexuality** although this was a subject of intense political debate in Europe and the USA in the late nineteenth century.

Marxist feminists in the inter-war period challenged these omissions and exclusions in two ways. First, through their insistence that there is a politics of reproduction and that childbearing is women's work, it suffers from the same problems of alienation and expropriation as manufacture. This theme returns in the discussion of domestic labour in the 1970s when some argue that wages alone are not the only determinant of production and that the maintenance of workers through unwaged but vital domestic labour is essential to the maintenance of and challenge to capitalism. Marxists were much involved in birth control campaigns and demands for socialised childcare as a result. Some European Marxists also challenged the Fascist separation of women into a corporation based on sex, arguing that women were not only destined for childbearing and child rearing but could contribute as citizens.

Marxism as a dynamic revolutionary theory of social relationships revived in the 1970s especially in France among university students after the upheavals of 1968–9. The idea of critique became especially important in the challenge to dominant ideologies at the time. Women's participation in radical politics led them to question their subordination within revolutionary organisations and to relate Marxist critique to their own social position. Engels and Lenin had both argued that women's full entry into production would remove sexual difference as a cause of women's exclusion from the benefits of revolutionary change but the experience of late capitalism has demonstrated that workplace participation is not enough to challenge male power. A second strand of Marxism sees the challenge to male power in the patriarchal social system of separate spheres carried to its logical conclusion in 'dual systems' theory. Here women's contribution is primary to reproduction and this should be the site of struggle. Wages for housework and rights for prostitutes and wives alike on the grounds that sex is work were put forward as the way of challenging inequality. Others argue that the placing of women with primary responsibility for childcare remains a source of political weakness because there is no symmetry between the two worlds and the two sorts of political struggle. In a society determined by two social systems – capitalism and **patriarchy** – whether both operate independently or one is dependent on the other, the theoretical and practical question of which operates and which should be prioritised at any one time remains.

A third strand of Marxism looks to ideology as the basis for women's oppression. One version, a Marxist analysis of psychoanalysis, sees that power, based on economic infrastructures, is internalised in social relationships mediated through sexual difference. In this view, psychoanalysis both maps inequality and provides the means to critique and challenge it. In the 1980s theorists used the metaphor of the 'unhappy marriage' to describe the relationship of capitalism and patriarchy, and Marxism and feminism. In particular the volume of essays edited by Lydia Sargeant (1981) using that title holds the tradition of socialist thinking about women up to scrutiny. Some contributors notice that Marxism was not only blind to sexual difference but to other differences which contribute to inequality and political divides, especially race, in debates in North America. Discussion by historians of the relation between men and women and patriarchy and capitalism have developed the metaphor of the double helix replacing a more dynamic division of men and women with constructions of gender both separate and together. Ideas of **difference** provide for a politics of

contingent alliances rather than monolithic class struggle. The unhappy marriage has ended in divorce in which as is often empirically the case one partner has lost more in the long run than the other. The creative input of feminism to Marxism has not created very much change in Marxism, which was less influential than it had been after the 1980s. North American writers have increasingly abandoned the attempt to synthesise an argument based upon both production – work – and reproduction. The centrality of both labour outside the home and economic inequality to women's subordination is rarely put forward. Ideology and attitude are considered far more effective forces in creating subordination. Catharine **MacKinnon** expresses this as the failure of Marxism, because as she argues in her *Toward a Feminist Theory of the State* (1989), Marxism cannot explain the location of female subordination in sexuality. However the role of capitalism and labour remains a matter of practical concern to feminists and the theoretical contribution of Marxism continues to provide a discourse of alienation, exploitation and materialism which means that it remains pertinent to social theory and political activities especially in less affluent parts of the world. Shulamith **Firestone** notes in *The Dialectic of Sex* that Marxism has not paid any attention to sex and using the language of dialectic, Marxist method, and socialism, class, she argues that women are a sex class. Her pun upon materialism asserts that the material experience of the body is as important in the social division of labour. MacKinnon does the same thing with her argument that 'sex is to feminism what work is to Marxism, that which is most one's own and is most taken away'. Marxism has thus remained the form of materialist, economistic arguments and the idea of alienation – but the idea of revolutionary challenge has not, in part rejected because of the masculine style of politics it represents. Critique remains a central idea of feminism, but the promotion of revolution has been by and large abandoned.

See also: political economy, feminist; production, modes of

References and further reading

Barrett, M. (1988) *Women's Oppression Today: The Marxist/Feminist Encounter*, London: Verso.

Barrett, M. and Philips, A. (eds) (1992) *Destabilizing Theory: Contemporary Feminist Debates*, Cambridge, MA: Polity.

Engels, F. [1884] (1985) *The Origins of the Family, Private Property and the State*

Kruks, S. Rapp, R. and Young, M.B. (eds) (1989) *Promissory Notes: Women in the Transition to Socialism*, New York: Monthly Review Press.

MacKinnon, C. (1989) *Toward a Feminist Theory of the State* Cambridge, MA: Harvard University Press.

Mitchell, J. (1975) *Psychoanalysis and Feminism*, Harmondsworth: Penguin.

—— (1984) *Women: The Longest Revolution*, London: Virago.

Sargent, L. (1981) *Women and Revolution: A Discussion of the Unhappy Marriage of Marxism and Feminism*, London: Pluto Press.

Young, I.M. (1990) *Throwing Like a Girl and Other Essays in Feminist Philosophy and Social Theory*, Bloomington, IN: Indiana University Press.

DEBORAH THOM

Marxist feminist literature/ literary theory

The relationship between **Marxism** and feminism is fraught with difficulty and contradiction. Questions about the usefulness of combining Marxist analysis, focused on **class analysis** and labour production, with feminist analysis have challenged theory and practice across a wide array of academic disciplines and social movements. In the context of literary criticism, particularly, the Marxist feminist encounter has had important outcomes for literary theory, although it is difficult to speak of a literary theory that is explicitly Marxist feminist.

In order to best conceptualise Marxist feminist literary theory, it is necessary to examine each of the constituent parts as they inform and interrogate each other. Marxist literary theory itself has a history that dates back to the early commentary on literature offered by both Marx and Engels. A more systematic approach to literary criticism was subsequently developed by Georgii Plenakhov and Mikhail Bakhtin. Today, well-known Marxist critic Terry Eagleton argues that Marxist criticism has historically developed through four key approaches so that Marxist criticism embodies a variety of approaches to literary criticism. These approaches can be briefly summarised as anthropological, political, ideological, and economic. The anthropological approach is associated mostly with the Second International. The key question posed by these critics focuses on the function of art within social evolution. Political Marxist criticism subsequently arose as a result of the Russian Revolution and focuses attention on the political intention of a text. Ideally, literature was to be found in the service of the revolution. Ideological Marxist criticism, largely attached to the work of the Frankfurt school, develops literary theory that examines the material conditions of history that produce literature. Finally the economic approach tends to transcend any specific historical period in the development of Marxism, and instead seeks to interrogate the modes of cultural production, including cultural institutions such as theatres and publishing houses.

Feminist criticism, like Marxist criticism, also defies simple classification. It is best to view 'feminist' as a label that attaches to what can be described as an eclectic group of literary theorists who share the common project of promoting women's liberation. In her 1986 essay, Toril Moi describes feminist criticism as a specific form of political discourse that is more than simply a concern for gender in literature. According to Moi, feminist literary criticism examines literature from within a strong commitment to struggles against patriarchy and sexism, rendering feminist criticism as more than just another interesting approach to literature, but a form of political **praxis** in and of itself.

Although Marxist and feminist literary theory have a great deal in common, actual attempts to form what could loosely be called a theoretical alliance between Marxist and feminist theory have met with limited success. In the 1930s, women Marxist writers such as Tillie Olsen initiated literary works that interweave class with gender and race. Authors such as Olsen demonstrate a strong commitment to the socialist project and to Marxist literary theory. However, as Olsen, for example, developed her literary characters she increasingly demonstrated the importance of gender and race over issues of class. The 'proletariat women' genre, generally, challenges the male-dominated political Marxist criticism of the day and demonstrates the need for social change to account for issues of gender oppression and social exclusion.

With the ferment of women's radicalism in the 1960s (as with other social movements including socialism and student radicalism), theoretical debates about the relevance of Marxist theory and feminism were initiated by writers such as Sheila Rowbotham, Juliet **Mitchell**, and later Michèle Barrett and Gayatri **Spivak**. The outcome of these debates among socialist and feminist women gave rise to attempts at a unified Marxist feminist theory that is perhaps best demonstrated by the writing of the Marxist Feminist Literary Collective. Although the Collective produced only one published piece, the act of writing as a collective proved important for literary criticism generally. As Maggie Humm notes of the work and writing that was undertaken by the Marxist Feminist Literary Collective, the focus was specifically on the nineteenth-century novel, specifically examining marriage and paterfamilias. By examining the women characters of the Brontës and Barrett Browning, the Collective interrogates the 'patriarchal ideology of Victorian life'. Importantly, the Collective asserts that feminism 'is to be found not in what characters say but in what they cannot say' (1994: 86).

By the mid-1980s, the proposed 'marriage' of Marxism and feminism had, for most theorists, been called off. However, the result of this 'critical engagement' continues to be felt among contemporary literary critics. The Marxist focus on social structures (including ideology) and modes of cultural production has ensured that literary criticism is firmly rooted in material circumstances and not exclusively focused on 'high' art; while feminism fused a new political project with literary theory and opened up critical space for the exploration of issues surrounding gender and women's social roles as represented in literature. Although the 'alliance' continues to be beneficial to various forms of literary criticism, including the burgeoning field of cultural studies, it is unlikely that a unified Marxist feminist literary theory will emerge in the future.

See also: cultural theory/cultural studies, feminist

References and further reading

Barrett, M. (1980) *Women's Oppression Today: Problems in Marxist Feminist Analysis*, London: Verso Editions.

Eagleton, T. (1998) 'Marxist Literary Theory' in S. Regan (ed.) *The Eagleton Reader*, Oxford: Blackwell, pp. 252–7.

Fairbairns, Z. (1979) *Benefits: A Novel*, London: Virago.

Humm, M. (1994) *A Reader's Guide to Contemporary Feminist Literary Criticism*, New York and London: Harvester Wheatsheaf.

Marxist Feminist Literary Collective (1978) 'Women's Writing: Jane Eyre, Shirley, Villette, Aurora Leigh' in *Ideology and Consciousness*, 1 (3): 27–48.

Moi, T. (1986) 'Feminist Literary Criticism', in A. Jefferson and D. Robey (eds) *Modern Literary Theory: A Comparative Introduction*, London: Batsford, 2nd edn.

Olsen, T. (1961) *Tell Me a Riddle: A Collection*, New York: Lippincott.

Poovey, Mary (1984). *The Proper Lady and the Woman Writer: Ideology as Style in the Works of Mary Wollstonecraft, Mary Shelley, and Jane Austen*, Chicago, IL: University of Chicago Press.

Rowbotham, S. (1973) *Women's Consciousness, Man's World*, Harmondsworth: Penguin Books.

SANDRA REIN

masculinity

Masculinity refers to the range of physical, behavioural, and attitudinal qualities that characterise what it means to be a 'man' in any given historical or cultural context. Masculinity increasingly has come under critical scrutiny largely as a result of feminist theory and activism.

First-wave feminist challenges to **patriarchy**

initially focused on issues such as women's equal access to the political arena and educational institutions. Yet entrenched assumptions about what women were and were not capable of doing and, indeed, what they ought to be allowed to do, stood in the way of these challenges. At issue were certain reigning beliefs about the nature of 'femininity'. In the 1970s, feminist scholarship and activism began to analyse and rethink **gender** more directly, focusing on the social meaning and influence of the idea of femininity itself. In such critiques, masculinity was necessarily implicated – at first implicitly then, increasingly, explicitly – as the gender norm against which femininity is both defined and diminished. Such critiques have spawned a proliferation of critical theory about masculinity.

Traditional thinking about gender is often essentialist (see **essentialism**). Many people presume that masculinity and femininity are universal and natural expressions of being male or female. However, essentialist assumptions are not confined to ordinary thinking about gender. Some theorists argue, for example, that possession of the Y chromosome, and the subsequent production of the hormone testosterone during puberty, naturally result in the normal gender expression known as masculinity. Others offer sociobiological arguments that, like males of other species, the human male is subject to the laws of natural selection; on this view, masculinity – which is presumed naturally to include sexual aggressiveness, competition and **dominance** – is simply a function of the evolutionary drive toward maximising 'inclusive fitness'. Not all essentialist arguments are biological, however. Drawing on Jungian psychology, Robert Bly (1990) maintains that masculinity is the manifestation of universal primordial archetypes such as the Wild Man and the Warrior.

In general, essentialist explanations hold that the outward, socially apparent qualities of maleness derive from certain elements inherent to the male human being. Often, such explanations do not question the universality or appropriateness of male dominance in modern society. Indeed, some appeal to essentialist theories to argue that patriarchy reflects a natural order between men and women. However, essentialists need not be apologists for male dominance and violence. For example, Bly argues that contemporary society has alienated men from their true, balanced masculine selves.

By contrast, social constructionist approaches to gender are suspicious of the presupposition that prevailing social relations and structures express a natural biological or psychological order (see **social constructionism**). Instead, masculinity and femininity are regarded as powerful social concepts that are produced, shaped, and maintained by social conventions and institutionalised practices.

Constructionist theory focuses on how the ideal of masculinity is exemplified in cultural productions, such as literature, film, and art, and in the conventions and practices of male-dominated activities, such as sports and the military. Constructionist arguments show how the predominant ideals of masculinity and femininity constitute a rigid gender binarism that is not only complementary in structure, but establishes a social and political asymmetry (see **binaries/bipolarity**). Those qualities deemed masculine – for example, independence, rationality, assertiveness, physical strength and protectiveness – place men in a relation of **power** over women, who are construed as dependent, emotional, passive, weak and in need of protection. The construction of the masculine/feminine dyad is also inherently heterosexual and therefore integral to sustaining heterosexism (see **heterosexism, heteronormativity**). Social constructionists further argue that, in patriarchal contexts, masculinity functions as the normative gender. The qualities associated with masculinity tacitly structure the key institutions of modern society, including law, science, and medicine. Feminists such as Anne **Fausto-Sterling** and Carol **Gilligan** have shown how scientific explanation has uncritically presumed the normativity of masculinity. Others have argued that the standards for such things as 'reasonable behaviour' in the law and 'merit' in the workplace reflect masculinist values.

Constructionists maintain that masculinity and femininity not only structure social relations and institutions, they also mediate the psycho-sexual development of individual persons. The development of boy-children into adults occurs under the force of social sanction; those who conform to the prevailing standards of masculinity are socially accepted, while those who do not are punished. Masculinity is unevenly exhibited in the behaviours and practices of actual men. While all persons identified as 'men' tend to benefit socially and politically, to some degree, from their inclusion in the ambit of masculinity, many (perhaps most) men do not and cannot embody the gender ideal. Indeed, while early feminist theory often implicated a monolithic and reductive notion of masculinity, theorists have come to recognise that, even as a gender ideal, masculinity is neither monolithic nor universal. It varies along lines of culture, race, and class. For example, some theorists have argued that the prevailing norm of masculinity in the west is ineluctably white, affluent and non-disabled. If this is the case, men who are dark-skinned, poor and/or disabled are systematically less able to conform to its demands and, thus, subject to greater diminishment.

Finally, masculinity does not only have to do with men. From the woman who is simply assertive, strong, and self-confident to the woman who explicitly identifies as butch, to defy the boundaries imposed by femininity is to be deemed 'masculine' (see **butch/femme**). Excursions into 'masculinity' by women would not be socially frowned upon were they not recognised to be claims on social power.

Initial feminist resistance to focusing energy on masculinity has given way to the recognition that transformation of oppressive gender relations requires critical scrutiny of the predominant ideals of masculinity no less than femininity.

See also: phallogocentrism; queer theory; transgender

References and further reading

Berger, M., Wallis, B. and Watson, S. (eds) (1995) *Constructing Masculinity*, New York and London: Routledge.

Bly, R. (1990) *Iron John*, Reading, MA: Addison-Wesley.

Clatterbaugh, K. (1997) *Contemporary Perspectives on Masculinity: Men, Women and Politics in Modern Society*, Boulder, CO: Westview Press.

Mac an Ghaill, M. (ed.) (1996) *Understanding Masculinities*, Buckingham and Philadelphia, PA: Open University Press.

Smith, P. (ed.) (1996) *Boys: Masculinities in Contemporary Culture*, Boulder, CO: Westview Press.

JOAN MASON-GRANT

mass media

The term mass media refers to large-scale, institutionalised, public forms of production, dissemination and consumption of newspapers, magazines, film, radio, and television. Processes of communication via the mass media result in the formation of a mass relationship between media producers and audiences. This relationship is primarily one-directional (from a message sender to receivers) and impersonal because most messages are created and distributed by large and centralised media institutions in locations that are situated at some distance from their audiences.

Mass communication differs from interpersonal communication in a number of significant ways. First, senders of mass media messages tend to be highly professionalised (e.g. journalists, actors) who are employed by large media institutions (e.g. national newspapers, television networks). Second, content is constructed according to standardised and routinised methods of mass production. Third, messages are products with a commercial value to be sold and bought in the marketplace. Fourth, output is the product of industrial activity shaped by the policies and by professional routines of large media organisations and the political, economic and legal structures of the societies in which they operate. Finally, because messages are consumed by large audiences, they have the potential for wide-scale social influence.

From the 1960s, feminist research has assessed how the mass media contribute to the construction of gender identity. Researchers have typically studied images of women and the effects of stereotypical portrayals on audiences. This emphasis can be partly attributed to the publication of feminist texts like American author Betty **Friedan**'s *The Feminine Mystique* (1963) which investigates the gap between the media's portrayal of post-war American suburban domesticity as the ideal against women's feelings of disillusionment, isolation and despair ('the problem with no name'). Subsequent research has tended to focus on quantitatively measuring the number of stereotypical images of women in the mainstream media to demonstrate their overwhelming predominance and how they might affect audiences' understanding of women's 'proper' roles in society. Empirical, quantitative feminist research has sometimes been criticised for a tendency to suggest that mass media content is unambiguous in its meaning and effects on audiences. Critics argue that such studies often assume that audiences passively accept stereotypical media messages and therefore unproblematically reproduce traditional forms of gender identity which are oppressive to women.

The analysis of gender **ideology** has been a central focus of critical communication studies since the 1970s making conceptual links between the operation of capitalism and its 'ideological state apparatuses', such as the mass media, and the patriarchal subordination of women. Analyses often examine the ways in which textual constructions of femininity in the media encourage female audiences to 'consent to' their subordination in patriarchal society. Drawing from Marxism, feminist researchers have analysed how human nature in capitalist society is ideologically structured by gender as well as other forms of cultural identity within the context of specific historical, social and economic conditions. Others have used insights drawn from psychoanalytic, structuralist and semiotic theories to investigate the role of the mass media in the ideological construction of gendered subjectivity. Subjectivity is constituted in language, with each person making sense of themselves within the limits and possibilities imposed by the meaning systems of a given society. Rather than seeing language as a transparent medium conveying authentic experiences (reality), language is said to construct subjectivity and 'reality'. Following this conceptual trajectory, in the 1980s Angela McRobbie (1991) analysed the visual and verbal signs of the British girls' magazine *Jackie*, concluding that it constructs heterosexual romance as an all-consuming interest of teenage girls. This emphasis is significant because it helps to construct and reinforce a gendered separation between the public

(masculine) and private (feminine) spheres of operation to which men and women are accordingly assigned. The discourses of such mass circulation magazines have tremendous potential to influence conceptions of what constitutes 'appropriate' forms of femininity because many girls and women read them regularly over the course of their lives.

Feminist engagements with **pornography** have generally emphasised how it represents a male sexual desire to objectify women and to eroticise male power and violence against women. Some feminists, such as Andrea **Dworkin** and Catharine **MacKinnon**, regard pornography as a form of sexual violence against women or a cultural expression of men's hatred of women and the product of a misogynistic society. Pornography typically represents women as ready and willing to be consumed by men, thereby reinforcing the patriarchal ideology that women are essentially objects that exist for the satisfaction of men's sexual desires. Because pornography aimed at male audiences typically portrays women's bodies in fragments, offering close-ups of sexual organs and other body parts, some feminists have argued that, as a result, women are reduced to depersonalised, submissive and powerless objects. Yet, not all feminists agree with this view. Some suggest that this radical feminist view tends to conflate representation with social reality, arguing that pornography is a representation rather than a concrete action. However, this view fails to recognise that representations are socially constructed within patriarchal societies and therefore (re)construct certain myths about women and that consumption of pornographic representations takes place within the context of patriarchal societies in which women's bodies have been widely constructed as sexualised objects. Still other feminist media researchers urge us to examine pornography as part of a continuum of patriarchal representations of women which includes, for example, 'mainstream' media forms like advertising, Hollywood cinema, music videos and women's magazines.

See also: advertising, women in; audience responses; communication theory; cultural methodologies; cultural theory/cultural studies, feminist; film criticism, feminist; objectification; pornography; television

References and further reading

Carter, C., Branston, G. and Allan, S. (eds) (1998) *News, Gender and Power*, London: Routledge.

Creedon, P. (ed.) (1993) *Women in Mass Communication*, Newbury Park: Sage, 2nd edn.

Macdonald, M. (1995) *Representing Women: Myths of Femininity in the Popular Media*, London: Arnold.

McRobbie, A. (1991) *Feminism and Youth Culture: From Jackie to Just Seventeen*, Basingstoke: Macmillan.

Rakow, L. (1992) *Women Making Meaning: New Directions in Communication*, London and New York: Routledge.

van Zoonen, L. (1994) *Feminist Media Studies*, London: Sage.

CYNTHIA CARTER

mathematics, feminist

Since mathematics is represented to the world as abstract, general, often termed a universal 'language', it may be difficult, at first sight, to see how a feminist mathematics might exist and, if it did, what form it might take. Unlike the empirical processes of **science** which have been usefully shown as able to be undertaken differently, the deductive proof processes of mathematics and the highly stylised ways in which these are presented to the mathematical community constitute the discipline in a way which may appear to be unchallengeable. However, all is not lost. Some feminist mathematicians and mathematics educators have been concerned to explore questions about women, and women's lives, that appear to impede them from doing mathematics. More importantly, they have been eager to understand how the culture of mathematics itself has been realised such that it leaves women, and other marginalised groups, feeling excluded. I agree with other feminists that feminism has both an ideological and a socio-political function. It advances beliefs and values about women and gender relations but is also concerned with social change.

The objective of change requires that some of the epistemological preconceptions about mathematics as a discipline as well as about its practices must be investigated and challenged (see **epistemology, feminist**).

How, then, might we pursue the project of construing a feminist mathematics? One way is to analyse how women are positioned in relation to the discipline. Rogers and Kaiser (1995) draw on a five-phase model beginning with Womanless mathematics (Phase One), through Women in mathematics (Phase Two), Women as a problem in mathematics (Phase Three), Women as central to mathematics (Phase Four) to Mathematics reconstructed (Phase Five). But the linearity of the model should not deceive. As they point out 'individuals may weave back and forth between and among the phases' (3). By far the greatest amount of research which has been undertaken would be characterised as lying in Phases 1–3. Many enquiries establish and try to explain the absence of women in the study and practices of mathematics or to focus on necessary pedagogical shifts which appear to encourage women to participate in mathematics (see **pedagogy, feminist**). Such studies begin in schools but extend across all educational sectors. Their focus is on the women and not on the mathematics but they are nonetheless feminist for this. As Sue Willis points out:

> School mathematics (which is most people's experience of mathematics as a body of knowledge) was traditionally, and still is, used to provide a particularly narrow form of socialisation: following directions, completing exercises rotely and automatically, doing one's own work, neatness, punctuality and so on.
>
> (Willis 1990: 200)

Not only does this use of mathematics as an instrument for social control do disservice to learners *and* to the discipline of mathematics, but also those who *are* successful at mathematics appear to have rejected such a 'narrow socialisation' (201). For women to do so often runs counter to socialised conformity which values female compliance. To explain girls' frequently observed choice of behavioural compliance in mathematics classrooms, Zelda Isaacson introduces the notions of 'coercive inducements and compulsion' (seductive rewards, such as approval, for expected behaviour) and 'double conformity' (the expectation that women will conform socially, i.e. to the expected pattern of femininity while at the same time conforming professionally i.e. to the expected, masculinist, behaviours of mathematicians) (1986: 235–9).

What kinds of mathematics might have women at its centre, engaged in its reconstruction (Phases 4 and 5 above)? Suzanne Damarin points to the need for 'a radical reorganisation of the familiar ways of thinking about and interpreting issues and studies of gender and mathematics' (1995: 242) in order that 'women as a group … might claim the rights both to learn mathematics and to have the mathematic knowledge they have constructed recognised as valuable, and acknowledged in curriculum and instruction' (254). Moving closer to an epistemological challenge to the discipline, Leone Burton proposes defining:

> Knowing in mathematics in relation to … its person- and cultural/social-relatedness, the aesthetics of mathematical thinking it invokes, its nurturing of intuition and insight, its recognition and celebration of different approaches particularly in styles of thinking and the globality of its applications.
>
> (Burton 1995: 287)

She draws attention to inclusivity, accessibility, and recognition of differences as necessary to a challenge of dualistic, objectivist and value-free assumptions which permeate mathematics (see **objectivity**). Subsequently, in a study of the epistemologies of practising research mathematicians (Burton 1999), she establishes that her model's description of *their* epistemologies is robust but, as in many studies, she observes gender differences in their reports of professional experiences. Not only does her model turn out to be a good descriptor of the epistemologies of the mathematicians interviewed, whatever their **gender**, but it also offers a bridge to those in mathematics education from the universally unsatisfactory transmissive pedagogy to learning as the practice of research. This has profound implications for the ways in which mathematics is experienced in classrooms and for what is recognised, and valued, as mathematics. The implication is that, in its creation, a feminist mathematics is person-centred, rooted in the culture where it is produced collaboratively, is intuitive, open to many different styles of construal and, consequently, of interpretation. At the present time, the creative process is hidden in the abstract, objectivist style of public presentation. Valuing the process of its derivation and, consequently, of those who have derived it, allows space for the valuing of the human, social and cultural situatedness of the product even though that product, itself, may achieve a form of 'objectivity' in its generalisability. In time, it is to be hoped, such valuing may influence the excessive abstraction and dehumanisation in the experience of the discipline. A crucial difference, here, is between developing knowing in, and of, mathematics, and recognising established mathematical knowledge. The over-valuing, indeed reification, of established mathematical knowledge has allowed the discipline to achieve a mystical status which distorts both the **experience** of learners struggling to acquire and understand it, as well as the style and structure of the subject itself. It leads to a public expectation that only mathematics which is mystifying, and presented in a stylised abstract way, is 'real'. A feminist mathematics, then, is not understood as being a female mathematics but is a mathematics which is open and accessible to all, and, as a result, influenced by, and responsive to, the many and varied voices, positions and cultures out of which it develops.

The challenge to the orthodox views of mathematics, and the orthodoxy of its practices is still in its early days. But 'contesting, subverting and destabilizing hegemonic gendered discourses is what the politics of gender is about' (Kenway and Willis 1995: 67). It is to be hoped that the experience of becoming and being a mathematician will no longer remain as biased and distorted as has been reported in the past. Furthermore, the form that mathematics has taken, objectivist, person-free, distanced from human concerns, will expand to include, recognise and value different kinds of mathematical creativity, different processes through which mathematics is explored and, consequently, a diverse range of mathematics and mathematicians.

References and further reading

Burton, L. (1995) 'Moving Towards a Feminist Epistemology of Mathematics', *Educational Studies in Mathematics*, 28: 275–91.

—— (1999) 'The Practices of Mathematicians: What Do They Tell Us About Coming to Know Mathematics?' *Educational Studies in Mathematics*, 37: 121–43.

Damarin, S. (1995) 'Gender and Mathematics from a Feminist Standpoint', in W.G. Secada, E. Fennema and L.B. Adajian (eds) *New Directions for Equity in Mathematics Education*, Cambridge: Cambridge University Press.

Fennema, E. and Leder, G. (eds) (1990) *Mathematics and Gender: Influences on Teachers and Students*, New York: Teachers' College Press.

Isaacson, Z. (1986) 'Freedom and Girls' Education: A Philosophical Discussion with Particular Reference to Mathematics', in L. Burton (ed.) *Girls Into Maths Can Go*, London: Cassell.

Jungwirth, H. (1996) 'Symbolic Interactionism and Ethnomethodology as a Theoretical Framework for the Research on Gender and Mathematics', in G. Hanna (ed.) *Towards Gender Equity in Mathematics Education: An ICMI Study*, Dordrecht: Kluwer Academic Publishers.

Kenway, J. and Willis, S. (1995) *Critical Visions*, Department of Employment, Education and Training, Canberra, Australia. (Publication No. 5607.NPQS. DEET No. 965080).

Murphy, P.G. and Gipps, C.V. (eds) *Equity in the Classroom: Towards Effective Pedagogy for Girls and Boys*, London: Falmer Press.

Rogers, P. and Kaiser, G. (1995) *Equity in Mathematics Education*, London: Falmer Press.

Willis, S. (1990) 'The Power of Mathematics: For Whom?' in J. Kenway and S. Willis (eds) *Hearts and Minds: Self-esteem and the Schooling of Girls*, Lewes, UK: Falmer Press.

LEONE BURTON

matriarchy

Early discussions on matriarchy can be traced to nineteenth-century debates by European scholars on kinship and descent in other cultures. The term was variously treated – as a myth, a system of female rule overrun by regimes of **patriarchy**; a dual and complementary system which, though distinct from patriarchy, has little or no substantial power base. Since that time, matriarchy has taken on a standard definition as female rule in a social organisation. It places women as *mothers* in positions of authority and leadership as heads of families (lineages), clans and tribes. Social descent and lines of inheritance are traced through mothers on whom are vested major decision-making powers over marriage, communal property, and relations with other social groups.

The treatment of matriarchy in western literature since the nineteenth century has generated considerable controversy. The European masculine standards defined and imposed on other cultures a world view that presumed and easily rationalised women's subordination to men. Since this world view was considered superior and universal, matriarchy and patriarchy became two irreconcilably opposed principles of social organisation. Hence, those aspects of social relations in these societies which did not fit the Eurocentric model were seen as facets of primitive and savage cultures in evolution towards a higher form (see **eurocentrism**). Engels's analysis of the capitalist state, for instance, engendered an interpretation of African social formations as a shift away from an egalitarian pre-class society to a progressive loss of female autonomy with the advent of private property. Placing Engels in the African social context, western scholars claimed that polygyny, bride wealth, female labour, among other cultural practices, sustain patriarchy.

The negative connotations inherited by matriarchy in current usage reflect its decline in status and visibility in western social discourse. For example, the high concentration of female-headed families and domestic servants in black communities evokes images of social dysfunctionality, with the 'super woman' and the big powerful 'ma'am' as symbols of female usurpation of male power and annihilation of black manhood. Similar family clusters in native reserves juxtapose images of female power with their helplessness. Both elide memories of the prominent leadership role women have played in aboriginal cultures, especially those who practise matrilineal family descent.

But, matriarchy as a form of social organisation

that empowers women has been politicised in western feminist scholarship. Feminist comparative analyses have found a more acceptable platform under an autonomy thesis which advances the feminist quest for a tradition which would reaffirm the independence and autonomy of women at any period in the past. As June Hannan points out, 'only if a woman's role could be shown to be socially constructed and rooted in a specific historical context, rather than natural and universal, could feminists hope to argue that it was open to change' (1993: 303). African women's celebrated autonomy was attractive to women in other parts of the world because of the amount of control they appeared to exercise in both the domestic and public domains. Matriarchy in this context became not only a symbol of women's empowerment as equal members of society with men, but also of male domination by a powerful female league.

Western constructs of matriarchy, especially in the African context, have invited biting critiques from African scholars who offer a more expansive conceptualisation. Beyond the successive reign of queens and female warriors in some African cultures, which fit the standard definition, critics point to women's prominence in certain aspects of contemporary social life as traces of a precolonial – dual gender – social arrangement which gave women considerable control in managing their own affairs. For instance, mothers of kings or older women in royal families exert significant influence in deciding the affairs of state. Women by virtue of their age or calling (and not necessarily as mothers) could join the council of leaders, become chief priestess and market-place leaders. This social arrangement, African critics admit, has suffered serious breaches with colonisation and capitalist expansion. The western feminist construct of a powerful female league, in particular, is seen by many African scholars such as Amadiume (1997) and Ogbomo (1997) as a straight jacket that attempts to reorder the masculine paradigm to suit its own agenda. Matriarchy as a form of social organisation, they argue, has existed in various forms, often in juxtaposition with patriarchy, harbouring elements of gender relations which may be considered contradictory because they do not invoke any western comparison. Matriarchy in

an African context does not necessarily translate into a regime of female domination. Fitted within the western straight jacket, it captures neither the dynamics of female autonomy nor the complexity of gender relations in these cultures. Thus, representing female rule and domination of men as a point of reference endorses the binary opposition to patriarchy.

While the debate on matriarchy continues, its more recent theorisation significantly advances feminist thought on the dynamics and fluidity of gender in different social contexts. The critical analysis of African social contexts in particular, provides a starting point for assessing existing female power bases on which new strategies for empowerment may be built.

See also: matrifocality

References and further reading

Amadiume, I. (1997) *Reinventing Africa: Matriarchy, Religion and Culture*, London: Zed Books.

Diop, C.A. (1989) *The Cultural Unity of Black Africa: The Domains of Matriarchy and of Patriarchy in Classical Antiquity*, London: Karnak House.

Hannan, J. (1993) 'Women, History and Protest', in D. Richardson and V. Robinson (eds) *Thinking Feminist: Key Concepts in Women's Studies*, New York: Guildford Press, pp. 303–23.

Ogbomo, O.W. (1997) *When Men and Women Mattered: A History of Gender Relations Among the Owan of Nigeria*, Rochester: University of Rochester Press.

PHILOMENA OKEKE

matrifocality

Matrifocality refers to the basis of social relations in organisations such as a family, kinship, clan, tribe, ethnic group, which designates women leaders. In matrifocal organisations women could assume leadership positions as mothers (matriarchs), daughters, sisters, wives. The basic characteristic in such an organisation is social descent. Age relative to other members of the group is a major criterion. Thus, elderly women command respect and hold decision making powers along with male counterparts. The concept of the elder in many aboriginal and African cultures, especially where the family-clan system is the norm, places many women in positions of authority not necessarily as women but as elders. Women could hold the positions of chief priestess in village shrines, market-place leaders, and community advisors. While some of the historical evidence on matrifocality remains controversial, feminist debate continues on the nature and substance of matrifocal social organisations, especially their implications for women's struggle for social emancipation. The dynamics of social relations reflected in these analyses make more visible the fluidity of and construction of gendered social relations across time and space.

See also: matriarchy

References and further reading

Amadiume, I. (1997) *Reinventing Africa: Matriarchy, Religion and Culture*, London: Zed Books.

Diop, C.A. (1989) *The Cultural Unity of Black Africa: The Domains of Matriarchy and of Patriarchy in Classical Antiquity*, London: Karnak House.

Weaver, S. (1993) 'First Nations Women and Government Policy, 1970–92: Discrimination and Conflict', in S. Burt, L. Code and L. Dorney (eds) *Changing Patterns: Women in Canada*, Toronto: McClelland and Stewart, 92–150.

PHILOMENA OKEKE

McClary, Susan (b. 1946)

Susan McClary has pioneered the move in historical musicology from a rigid belief in the transcendence and autonomy of musical texts, to a serious concern with social practices that constitute music as meaningful discourse. Feminist analysis in musicology began in the late 1980s, much later than in cognate disciplines, though the exploration of other socially constructed meanings in music was historically central in ethnomusicology. An influential work is McClary's 1991 book *Feminine Endings: Music, Gender, and Sexuality* which examines gender/ sexuality constructions in diverse repertoires: opera, symphonic music, contemporary concert composition, peformance art, and popular music. Part of McClary's success in attracting mainstream discplinary attention lies in her ability to demonstrate the operation of gendered musical codes across historical and generic boundaries.

In opera of the seventeenth to early twentieth centuries, she analyses a narrative (like Showalter's literary 'madwoman in the attic') in which women characters suffer and die when they exceed boundaries prescribed by their social milieux. She examines what she labels 'discursive promiscuity', demontrating how chromaticism and other 'threats' to tonal order are equated with the sensuality and exoticism of characters like Salomé and Carmen (the subject of her most detailed opera study to date where a feminist textual reading complements an exploration of ideologies underpinning the opera's production and reception).

Analogous gendered codes are less obvious in instrumental music where explicit verbal narratives are lacking. Here, however, McClary historicises labelling practices (e.g., the identification of cadences on 'strong' and 'weak' beats as 'masculine' and 'feminine'). She explores the teleological implications of large-scale Classic-Romantic forms, expecially sonata-allegro form in which the foreign key of the second subject (sometimes labelled 'feminine') is recapitulated and 'recontained' in the primary 'home' key. She reads the 'desire' implicit in the need for such narrative 'closure' as coercively patriarchal. Her exploration of 'resistant' works with unconventional departures from structural norms opened the way for gay and lesbian music criticism. She has explored discursive strategies of women musicians, including Janika Vandervelde, Laurie Anderson, and Madonna whose work she reads as a 'refusal of definition' – play and conscious manipulation of cultural expectations.

McClary's work develops several recurrent themes. After **Lauretis**, she regards music as a technology of the body, producing 'mediated patterns of kinetic energy, being in time, emotions, desire, pleasure' (1994: 33). Another theme concerns the ideologies of institutions controlling musical knowledge, whether the bourgeois Lutheran sphere of Bach, the social elitism of modernist composers, or musicology's responses to feminism. She has drawn fire from backlashers who reclaim the autonomy of concert music with assertions that her readings are not reflective of actual interpretive communities. Her refusal to separate the textual from the contextual, however, and her consideration of both the production and reception of musical texts has enabled an unprecedented dialogue among scholars in popular music studies, ethnomusicology, historical musicology, and related disciplines.

See also: musicology, feminist

Selected writings

McClary, S. (1991) *Feminine Endings*, Minneapolis, MI: University of Minnesota Press.
—— (1992) *Georges Bizet: Carmen* (Cambridge Opera Handbook), Cambridge: Cambridge University Press.
—— (1993) 'Reshaping a Discipline: Musicology and Feminism in the 1990s', *Feminist Studies* 19: 399–423.
—— (1994) '"Same As It Ever Was": Youth Culture and Music' in A. Roos and R. Rose (eds) *Microphone Friends: Youth Music and Youth Culture*, New York: Routledge.

BEVERLEY DIAMOND

McClintock, Anne

Anne McClintock is known for her interrogation of the term 'postcolonialism' and the proliferation of 'post' words in her article 'The Angel of Progress' (1992). She suggests that the term 'postcolonialism' is used to generalise about a range of very different circumstances and argues for maintaining a sense of historical and geopolitical distinctions. In McClintock's view, the term 'postcolonial' is organised around a binary axis of *time* (colonial/postcolonial) which she sees as less politicised than the binary axis of coloniser/colonised which is figured around *power*. This shift to a time axis runs the risk of obscuring the continuities and discontinuities of imperial power. Yet, she is also anxious to displace simplistic binaries such as coloniser/colonised, colonialism/postcolonialism, which, she

suggests, overlook the contradictory and ambiguous nature of the imperial project.

McClintock is also author of monographs on Simone de **Beauvoir** and Olive Schreiner, and her book entitled *Imperial Leather: Race, Gender and Sexuality in the Colonial Contest* was published in 1995. Throughout the book, which brings together some of her published articles with further work, McClintock suggests that imperialism cannot be understood without a theory of domestic space and its relationship to the market. She draws on feminist, postcolonial, psychoanalytic and socialist theories to examine a range of cultural forms and the dynamics of imperialism (**psychoanalyis; socialism and feminism**). McClintock also investigates the success of nationalism which, she argues, emerges from the popular collective unity created through 'the management of the mass national *commodity spectacle*' (1993: 70). Despite the Enlightenment view of nationalism as embodying progress, McClintock notes that it is experienced and transmitted through potentially more 'traditional' activities such as the ritual organisation of national flags, anthems, cuisines, as well as the organisation of collective events such as football games or military displays.

McClintock calls for a more materialist postcolonial analysis which focuses on the material specificity of conditions of colonial rule and relations between class (see **class analysis, UK; class analysis, US**), **race** and **gender**. Gender, she maintains 'is not simply a question of **sexuality**, but also a question of subdued labour and imperial plunder; race is not simply a question of skin colour but also a question of labour power, cross-hatched by gender' (5). She identifies three themes of western imperialism: transmission of white male power through control of the colonised woman; the emergence of a new global order of cultural knowledge; and the imperial project of commodity capitalism (see **commodification**). McClintock traces the shift from the scientific racism that informed and was informed by anthropological and scientific work, as well as travel writing and novels, to commodity racism at the end of the nineteenth century. Commodity racism drew on the cult of domesticity which involved the civilising of the colonised and the expansion of markets.

The two central tropes of imperialism are, according to McClintock, panoptical time and anachronistic space. When a single spectacle represents global history as if from an objective point of view, panoptical time is produced. For example, the figure of the Tree of Man which naturalises notions of a measurable, evolutionary or teleological progress in global human history produces a panoptical sense of time. Anachronistic space is that space into which those who are seen as backward, irrational or atavistic are placed. Groups such as women, the working classes, and colonised are located here because they are constructed as 'inherently out of place in the historical time of modernity'. With the advent of social Darwinism, McClintock suggests that the metaphoric figure of the evolutionary 'family' naturalised the hierarchical positioning of women, the colonised and others into 'a single narrative of the Family of Man' (44).

Although McClintock's work is an important and innovative contribution to feminist theory, some commentators argue that her use of psycho-analysis may be reductive and that inadequate attention is paid to socio-economic factors.

See also: agency; cultural imperialism; Darwin, feminist critique of; dichotomies; domesticity, cult of; modernity, feminist critiques of; nationalism and gender; postcolonial feminism

Selected writings

McClintock, A. (1992) 'The Angel of Progress: Pitfalls of the Term "Postcolonialism"', *Social Text* 32/32: 84–98.

—— (1993) 'Family Feuds: Gender, Nationalism and the Family', *Feminist Review* 44: 61–80.

—— (1995) *Imperial Leather: Race, Gender and Sexuality in the Colonial Context*, New York, London: Routledge.

BREDA GRAY

mechanistic model, critiques of

Historians of modern western thought trace the mechanistic model of nature to seventeenth-century France where, Carolyn Merchant suggests,

'mechanism arose as an antidote to intellectual uncertainty and as a new rational basis for social stability' (1980: 194). While the model developed in conjunction with a new faith in physical scientific explanation, Merchant associates it also with a quest for certainty in a world of social upheaval and religious conflict. Particularly in the philoso-phy of René Descartes (1596–1650), the view emerges of the entire universe, including all of its parts (both physical and biological) except rational consciousness, as explicable by mechanical laws. The image is of a clockwork machine whose workings can be understood, predicted, and controlled.

In *The Death of Nature* (1980), Merchant develops a sustained critique of the mechanistic model, which she holds responsible for the death that her title announces. She contends that this view displaced an older organicist view according to which the world was vital, animated, and ensouled, whereas the mechanistic universe consists in dead corpuscles, inert, and moved only by contact with other moving bodies. Unlike feminists who resist associating things animate and untamed with 'the feminine', Merchant suggests that the 'soul' of the premechanistic view is female.

Merchant attributes the appeal of mechanism, most significantly, to its development into a view of the human being as an ordered system 'of mechanical parts subject to governance by law and predictability through deductive reasoning' (214), rational master of its passions and feelings. Such a conception of human nature gave twen-tieth-century behaviourist psychology its plausibil-ity; and this same conception legitimates more global analyses and orderings of human behaviour according to statistical probabilities and condition-ing practices.

Val Plumwood's ecofeminist critique of mechan-istic thinking in *Feminism and the Mastery of Nature* resonates with Merchant's, tracing the effects of mechanistic thinking to Skinnerian behaviourism and sociobiology, both of which, she claims, treat human beings as passively determined by larger evolutionary or environmental factors. One con-sequence of this explanatory framework is to disguise or deny the political character and significance of such actions as rape (1993: 122). Plumwood connects the treatment of nature as lifeless and mechanistically governed with the rational egoism and instrumentalism that characterise liberal free enterprise societies. Such thinking legitimises treating nature as a resource for human usage, and colonising people deemed inferior in reason as instruments to serve 'more civilised' people. It perpetuates the structures of mastery that are instrumental in sustaining patriarchal oppression of women as inferior 'others'. Both Merchant and Plumwood advocate an ethical relationship to a nature that merits preservation and respect.

See also: ecofeminism

References and further reading

Merchant, C. (1980) *The Death of Nature*, New York: Harper and Row.

Plumwood, V. (1993) *Feminism and the Mastery of Nature*, London: Routledge.

LORRAINE CODE

menopause (medical)

The medical definition of menopause can be traced to developments in sex **endocrinology** research of the 1920s and 1930s, where human sexual behaviour, **sexuality** and **reproduction** were first understood as the effects of fluctuating sex hormones. In such research, oestrogen was established as a female sex hormone. And although it was noted that the female body could supply oestrogen in several forms, it was *ovarian oestrogen* that nonetheless became the quintessential female hormone. This allowed sex endocrinology research to explain many functions of female sexual and reproductive life with respect to the fluctuation of hormonal secretions in one particular site – the ovaries. This in its turn produced the medical view of menopause as the result of *diminishing ovarian production of oestrogen*. From there, it was a short step to the medical construction of menopause as a function of ovarian oestrogen 'decline'. And it was an even shorter step to the definition of menopause as a 'disease': an illness with symptoms pertaining to 'deficient' ovarian functioning and treatable through commercially prepared oestrogen replacement as 'therapy'.

This medical definition of menopause was first popularised by Dr Robert Wilson who used the media to excerpt his book, *Feminine Forever* (1966). The popularity of Wilson's book was matched only by sales in oestrogen as replacement 'therapy' for the menopause 'disease'. But the medical definition of menopause is specifically challenged by feminists who point out its link to patriarchal attitudes towards women (see **patriarchy**). According to certain feminists, the medical definition of menopause perpetuates patriarchal assumptions about women as 'the sex', the sum of her **body** (ovaries). Moreover, the medical definition of menopause – in setting up a patriarchal menopause 'industry' – reproduces the myth in patriarchal culture that women and their bodies (ovaries) would be completely unruly were it not for a medical (male) **gaze** and masculine intervention. Finally, the medical definition of menopause marks another instance of the colonisation by men of women's natural and normal biological processes and experiences (e.g. reproduction). A rejection of the medical definition of menopause and the patriarchal foundations upon which it rests, together with the creation of a separate, women-centred perspective where women can develop their *own* experiences of menopause, are therefore seen as central to a feminist politics of menopause. More recently, however, this feminist challenge to the biomedical model of menopause has itself been criticised by feminists who refuse to constitute the two positions as monolithic entities.

See also: age studies and gender; biology; biotechnology; health; ideology; menstruation, anthropological; pathologisation; menstruation, PMS, medical

References and further reading

Callahan, J.C. (ed.) (1993) *Menopause: A Midlife Passage*, Bloomington, IN: Indiana University Press.

Greer, G. (1991) *The Change*, London: Hamish Hamilton.

Komesaroff, P., Rothfield, P. and Daly, J. (eds) (1997) *Reinterpreting Menopause*, NY: Routledge.

Kwok, Wei Leng (1996) 'On Menopause and

Cyborgs: Or, Towards a Cyborg Politics of Menopause', *Body and Society*, 2 (3), pp. 33–52.

KWOK WEI LENG

menstruation, anthropological

Anthropological approaches to the study of menstruation focus on the cultural meanings different social systems ascribe to notions of human reproduction, fertility and sexuality. However, these approaches have undergone shifts in emphasis, in line with other developments in theory and social anthropology over the past half-century.

Early fieldwork from the 1940s on the belief systems and social practices underpinning menstrual symbolism in 'traditional' non-industrial societies appears in the ethnographic record – notably for parts of Africa, Papua New Guinea, and Aboriginal Australia – mainly in terms of an overriding analytic preoccupation with menstrual taboos. Several ethnographies detail a series of local prohibitions and rules for behaviour during menses which relate typically to women's handling of foodstuffs and implements, and may also concern spatial proscriptions relating to women's physical movements and to the avoidance of intercourse. Much of this work is cast in functionalist-structuralist terms, especially where a 'pollution' model of women's symbolic impurity and denigration also describes the stabilisation of the social system as a whole community. It is also important to note that these analyses, at least up until the late 1960s, are generally the products of western-trained and usually male anthropologists who depended on contact with key male informants for the best part of their fieldwork. This also explains the greater interest in this literature on men's initiation, and the lack of explicit analytical attention towards gendered procreative labour, the materiality of women's bodies and the symbolism of fertility as imputed sources of female power.

Recent ethnographic work since the 1980s, however, has addressed the theme of taboo and gender much more explicitly, drawing out subtle distinctions between multivalent and ambiguous associations both across and within given cultural contexts. Many of the contributors to Buckley and

Gottlieb's (1988) volume explore the relation between menstrual blood as 'life force' and women's creative social agency. For example, some of the case studies based on women's testimonies from rural Portugal and the local beliefs of the Beng people of the Côte d'Ivoire explore how ritual seclusion in 'menstrual huts' may have been initiated by women themselves – as expressions of sexual autonomy, or as moments of spiritual or economic empowerment. Many of the essays in this volume also suggest that more ethnographically-informed and interdisciplinary theoretical work is required as to how women themselves may perceive such 'rites of maturity' as significant social processes of achieving gender and personhood (see Lutkehaus and Roscoe 1995).

From a different perspective, another contemporary anthropologist has drawn upon selected aspects of sociobiology, palaeoanthropology and Marxist political economy to offer a structuralist-inspired *mythical* synthesis (Knight 1991: 5) of female menstruation as the instantiating origin of 'human' culture. Chris Knight argues that inter-female gender solidarity in early hunter/gatherer societies may be seen as evidence of early women's abilities to change the course of human sexual relations through a kinship structure focused around matriliny. In this account, women's collectively staged 'blood' relations are interpreted as women's revolutionary sex strike action (no meat, no sex), female ovarian synchrony and evolving ovulation concealment. Knight's analysis presents some intriguing if not unproblematic insights for further conceptual analysis. One obvious point is that it remains unclear what kind of attribution of agency and volition is invested in human behaviour described here as prototypically 'female'.

From the viewpoint of feminist anthropological theory, much of this recent work highlights how menstruation cannot be explained in universal terms as a biological given, but is always rather a cultural event experienced in different ways by individual women. It also represents part of a broader theoretical attempt to situate local understandings of bodily boundaries and gendered identities in subjective experience. In terms of directions for future anthropological and gender analysis, there is much scope here for re-thinking exactly how male initiation ritualism involving induced genital bleeding is understood in local terms to constitute transgendered variations of women's blood-making/child-rearing powers.

See also: body, the; biology; gender; reproduction; sexuality

References and further reading

Buckley, T. and Gottlieb, A. (eds) (1988) *Blood Magic: The Anthropology of Menstruation*, London/ Berkeley, CA: University of California Press.

Knight, C. (1991) *Blood Relations: Menstruation and the Origins of Culture*, New York/London: Yale University Press.

Lutkehaus, N. and Roscoe, P. (eds) (1995) *Gender Rituals: Female Initiation in Melanesia*, New York/ London: Routledge.

Sobo, E.J. (1992) '"Unclean deeds": menstrual taboos and binding "tie" in rural Jamaica', in M. Nichter (ed.) *Anthropological Approaches to the Study of Ethnomedicine*, New York: Gordon and Breach.

MONICA KONRAD

menstruation, PMS, medical

Menstruation signals the potential for physical, reproductive capability for a woman. Because it begins at puberty and ceases at menopause, menstruation serves as a visible, biological marker for the complex interaction among the brain, hormones, ovaries, and uterus occuring each month in most women from adolescence through middle age. Menstruation becomes a defining stage in the female life cycle which describes women in terms of reproductive status capability.

Although menstruation represents both a normal process in most women's lives and a biopsychosocial event, as with many aspects of women's bodies in much of western society, menstruation has become increasingly medicalised. One motivation for such medicalisation may be men's interest in controlling **reproduction**. The current medical structure in the USA segregates issues of women's reproduction, and virtually all aspects of women's health, into the specialty of obstetrics/gynaecology (see **gynaecology, medi-**

cal). Although many proponents of women's health and feminists seek to end the bifurcation by integrating women's health into all specialties and primary care, menstruation and PMS fall squarely within obstetrics/gynaecology with its focus on procreation and heterosexual activity. This specialisation remains under surgery, which contributes further to the medicalisation of menstruation and PMS and distances them within medicine from other specialties such as psychiatry, primary care, and family medicine more prone to including systems, social, and psychological interactions in their theoretical approaches to research, diagnosis, and treatments.

Feminist critiques of medicine in the USA in general, and in obstetrics/gynaecology in particular, have delineated its hierarchical and patriarchal aspects which reinforce negative images of women and their bodies and attempt to exert control over them through increasing medicalisation of these normal, natural processes. Medical models of menstruation and PMS reflect these negative images through their depiction of menstruation as failed reproduction and their attempts to control PMS and menopause through administration of synthetic hormones and drugs.

The medical model of menstruation describes day one of the cycle (in a normative 28-day model) as the first day of menstruation. At this time, the uterine lining is being sloughed off (because of failed implantation of a fertilised egg) and low levels of oestrogen and progesterone produced by the ovary circulate in the blood and are detected at the hypothalamus in the brain. In response to the low levels of the hormones, the hypothalamus begins to release gonadotropin releasing factor (Gn-RF) to which the anterior pituitary responds by producing follicle stimulating hormone (FSH). By approximately the end of menstruation (days 5–7), one or more follicles in the ovary begin to prepare to be released (ovulated) at mid-cycle and also release oestrogen and some progesterone. A few days later (8–12) during this oestrogen-dominated follicular phase, the uterine lining begins to rebuild (proliferatory phase) and the cervical mucus is thinner. In response to increasing levels of oestrogen, the hypothalamus releases Gn-RF which causes the anterior pituitary (adenohypophysis) to produce luteinising hormone (LH) and decrease some of its FSH production. In response to the surge in LH, an egg is ovulated from the ovary on day 14. The cervical mucus at this time is thin and stringy, with a crystalline alignment which facilitates sperm entry.

After the egg is released at ovulation, the follicle turns into the corpus luteum, which produces increasing amounts of progesterone and less oestrogen. Under the influence of this progesterone-dominated luteal phase (days 15–28), the cervical mucus becomes thick, dry, and hostile to sperm entry; the uterine lining thickens and enters the secretory phase where it becomes prepared to receive a fertilised egg for implantation. In the absence of fertilisation and implantation, the high levels of progesterone and the oestrogen feed back to the hypothalamus, causing it to stop its production of Gn-RF; in response to decreasing Gn-RF, the anterior pituitary cuts its production of LH and FSH, to which the corpus luteum responds by decreasing its output of progesterone and oestrogen. Falling levels of oestrogen and progesterone cause the uterine lining to be sloughed off (menstruation), signalling day 1 of the next cycle.

Following this medicalised model of menstruation, in which hormones and physiology predominate in a context of failed reproduction, loss, and sloughing off, premenstrual syndrome (PMS) is ascribed primarily to hormonal and physiological causes. Although the medical literature acknowledges that PMS constitutes a group of social, psychological, behavioural, and physiological symptoms which vary widely among women and within the same woman and that the timing and severity of the symptoms also vary, physical, rather than psychological and social reasons, are sought to explain the syndrome. For example, inadequate levels of progesterone relative to oestrogen become the underlying hypothesis to explain a number of social, psychological, and physical symptoms common to PMS ranging from breast tenderness, weight gain, irritability, and depression, as a result of water retention promoted by excessive oestrogen relative to progesterone.

Under this medical model, hormones (progesterone) and/or drugs such as bromocriptene or anti-diuretics become the cures to alleviate both physical and psychological symptoms. An extreme version of this medical model, advocated by British physician Katharina Dalton, led not only to the prescription of progesterone to counteract the excessive oestrogen in women with PMS, but in the use of PMS as a defence to have women acquitted of charges of murder. Although these essentialist theories have been used to keep women out of high paying, leadership positions under the guise that fluctuations in hormones during PMS render them incapable of making rational decisions, socialist, existentialist, or radical feminist analyses of why women might experience PMS remain outside the medical model (see **essentialism**; **socialism and feminism**; **existentialist feminism**). Little attention is paid to underpinning social, psychological factors which may underlie or exacerbate the physical symptoms; non-drug alternatives such as changes in diet (decrease in salt, caffeine, alcohol, and sugar) or increasing exercise may be accepted because they are seen as fitting the medical model (i.e. they serve as natural sources or enhancers of synthetic hormones and drugs).

Although many women who experience PMS report alleviation of symptoms by using the drugs or hormones, no drug or hormone has been shown to be effective in a double-blind study with placebos, the criterion used by those ascribing to the medical model as the appropriate test for drug effectiveness for controlling disease symptoms. This failure, coupled with questions raised by feminists and others about whether it is appropriate to give a label such as PMS or Late Luteal Phase Dysphoria (LLD) to a variable, vague group of symptoms which as many as 70 to 90 per cent of women experience, challenges the medical model as the most useful depiction of normal life cycle events for women such as menstruation and PMS.

References and further reading

Dan, A. and Lewis, L.L. (eds) (1992) *Menstrual Health in Women's Lives*, Urbana/Chicago, IL: University of Illinois Press.

Golub, S. (1992) *Periods: From Menarche to Menopause*, Newbury Park, CA: Sage.

Martin, E. (1987) *The Woman in the Body: A Cultural Analysis of Reproduction*, Boston: Beacon Press.

SUE V. ROSSER

Mernissi, Fatima (b. 1940)

Fatima Mernissi's *Beyond the Veil* (1975) introduces a **Middle Eastern feminism** based on reinterpreted Islamic texts, ideologies and the contemporary realities of Middle Eastern women as shaped by existing Moslem attitudes towards female roles and **sexuality**. In her analysis of Islamic traditions, Mernissi variously interrelates historical, mythological and folkloristic approaches with socio-political analysis, personal and spiritual testimonies. Cognisant of western thought and its sometimes glaring misinterpretations of Islam, Mernissi argues that female repression under Islam is by no means unique; Judaism and Christianity are as guilty in their repressive outlook towards women as other patriarchal religions (see **patriarchy**).

In *Beyond the Veil*, Mernissi concludes that female subjugation in Islamic societies contradicts earlier Islamic models (arising during the Prophet Muhammad's lifetime) which proclaim 'potential equality' between the sexes (see **equality and difference**). Sexual inequalities involving male supremacy derive from later socio-political interpretations when secular and institutional laws were stalwartly enforced with the sanctity of the 'shari'a' (divine law). As 'fitna' (disorder/chaos; beautiful woman), woman came to epitomise destructive sexuality. From the patriarchal family, which permitted polygamy invested female relatives with notions of male honour, the existing social order was soon directed towards containing women's subversive influence in order to protect male authority, their relationships to Allah and the Moslem Umma (community).

In *Beyond the Veil* and later works, Mernissi proceeds to examine the attendant effects of rapid modernisation, urbanisation and sexual desegregation, resulting in women's increased independence but also male frustration towards disrupted traditional roles. In *Women and Islam* (1991), she explores an Islamic feminist paradigm deriving from an historical and theological framework to reinforce notions of female **power** in Islam. Numerous other publications recover historical instances of women wielding authority in traditionally male bastions of Islamic power from politics, sainthood to erotic literature.

Widely recognised as at the forefront of Middle Eastern scholarship, Mernissi's contributions to feminism are seen to counter the racist and imperialist assumptions of some western feminists who contrast repressive Islam against an emancipatory western feminism. Mernissi's comprehensive project conversely preserves the sanctity of Islam, its feminist agenda clearly deriving not from exogenous western influences but emphatically from within the Islamic tradition itself.

See also: folklore; history; Islam and feminism; public/private; theology, feminist

Selected writings

Mernissi, F. (1975) *Beyond the Veil: Male–Female Dynamics in Modern Muslim Society*, London: Schenkman Publishing.
—— (1988) *Doing Daily Battle: Interviews With Moroccan Women*, London: The Women's Press.
—— (1991) *Women and Islam: An Historical and Theological Inquiry*, Oxford: Basil Blackwell.

SATINDER KAUR CHOHAN

metaphors

According to traditional literary definitions, metaphors are those figures of speech that communicate meaning by transposing qualities from one plane of reality to another (Jacobson and Halle 1956). A metaphor simultaneously exploits similarity and difference. In this process of interpretation, meaning is conveyed through analogy (e.g. 'mother is the pillar of a family'). It is like an abbreviated simile though similes are a weaker form of analogy for they use 'like' or 'as' in order to create meaning (e.g. 'mother is like the pillar of a family').

In the metaphor 'mother is the pillar of a family', family, the smallest unit of social structure, is being referred to as if it is a part of a physical structure and the mother within this social unit is referred to as its central figure. Without the pillars, the building is likely to be shaky and in no position to survive the vagaries of nature; by extension, it is implied that because of the mother, the members of a family withstand the ups and downs of life. There has to be enough similarity between the elements, as in this case, family/building and mother/pillar to be able to talk about them on the same plane, but there also must be enough difference for the comparison to have the necessary aspect of contrast. Literally, therefore, mother supports the members of a family and metaphorically, is the pillar, the backbone and the foundation. Through the process of metaphoric transposition, characteristics of the pillar, such as strength, endurance and support, are transposed onto the person, namely, mother. Similarly, characteristics of a building are transposed onto the family.

However, metaphors should not be perceived as a mere literary device used only for poetic or literary purpose. They also have a much more fundamental, everyday function and to that extent they are central to our thinking and communication, a fundamental means of generating meaning (Lakoff and Johnson 1980). For example, using money as a metaphor for time may also be seen as a manner of disciplining our thought process in a way that is appropriate to and part of the ideology of a work-centred capitalist society. When we say, save time, invest time or waste time, we are assuming that, like money, time can and should be saved and therefore we give it the attributes of money. In other words, we imply that any time that is not used for working productively is misspent. Such everyday metaphors are insidious, working covertly without attracting any attention to them. They invariably take the form of 'common sense' and appear as natural and universal while in fact they are always culturally produced.

See also: language, gender and power; military metaphors

References and further reading

Corradi Fiumara, G. (1994) 'The Metaphoric Function and the Question of Objectivity' in K. Lennon and M. Whitford (eds) *Knowing the Difference: Feminist Perspectives in Epistemology*, London: Routledge.

Jacobson, R. and Halle, M. (1956) *The Fundamentals of Language*, The Hague: Mouton.

Lakoff, G. and Johnson, M. (1980) *Metaphors We Live By*, Chicago, IL: University of Chicago Press.

UDITA DAS

metaphysics

Metaphysics as taught today at university is an assortment of such topics as free will, God, space and time, the mind, causality, personhood, and personal **identity**. Aristotle, to whose editors we owe the term 'metaphysics', established the field to have all actually existing beings as its objects, owing to what belongs to them purely as beings. He then proceeded to organise the objects that exist under categories, conceiving of the task as one at which one can be successful objectively, according to whether the world of beings *in fact* divides according to one's proposed lines, and not as a task at which one can succeed only by human- or culture-relative standards of assessment. While Aristotle's analysis is directed at the structure of reality, another class of analyses, which have many feminist supporters, proceeds by directing attention to the structure of thought itself. The *locus classicus* of this style of analysis is Kant's *Critique of Pure Reason* (1781).

With Kant, who inspired the likes of Ludwig Wittgenstein (on the one hand) and Rudolf Carnap (on the other, hero of **positivism**), a tradition criticising classical metaphysics as a discipline took up permanent residence. In our time it is spearheaded by such philosophers as W.V.O. Quine and Thomas Kuhn, who urge that there is no absolute or objective, or even natural, organisation of the denizens of the world, which is in the market for being discovered by interested parties. For the organisation of objects by whatever methods or instruments is a matter of convenience, and the extent to which one scheme of organisation is more convenient than another is a goal-relative affair. Thus the extent to which we may urge one scheme as more preferred is a matter of the aims we hold dear; it is not an objective, aim-independent given, which answers only to how the world is, in itself. So the scheme of organisation we choose will always be a matter also of the values we embrace, and there is no clear line of demarcation between what we value or hope to achieve, on the one hand, and the conceptual apparatus we utilise to organise what we take to be the facts of the world, on the other (see also **fact/value distinction**).

P.F. Strawson writes: 'Metaphysics has been often revisionary, and less often descriptive. Descriptive metaphysics is content to describe the actual structure of our thought about the world, revisionary metaphysics is concerned to produce a better structure' (*Individuals: An Essay in Descriptive Metaphysics*, 1959: 9). The many varieties of feminist philosophical theory and criticism, from the very beginning of the feminist movement, are located squarely within the revisionist camp, and range from minimally revisionary to radically revisionary. The minimally revisionary includes what has been called **liberal feminism**, which maintains that traditional metaphysics has misclassified women, *vis-à-vis* men, in the order of the world, that women and men belong in the same metaphysical category despite incidental physical differences (if there are any), and that therefore they deserve equal treatment within any respectable normative theory, whether moral or political. The form of liberation which minimally revisionary feminists seek is liberation from *incorrect*, and therefore oppressive, classifications of women. Radically revisionary forms of feminism, which include postmodern feminism, reject the entire enterprise of metaphysics, viewing it as a hostile form of sociopolitical engagements, in which the so-called investigator is really engaging in tactics of divide-and-conquer against the investigated – the **Other** – who is placed on a lower branch of the tree of life. The radically revisionary seek liberation from metaphysics itself.

Intermediate between these positions is something that deserves calling 'constructivism', which holds that categories, as well as the entities that belong to them, are created in the normal course of human social, economic and cultural interactions. So that, as we practice, so we are. This is a view many feminists hold regarding the **self**.

See also: deconstruction, feminist; essentialism; nature/culture; ontology; poststructuralism/ postmodernism

MARIAM THALOS

methodology, feminist

Methodology – the study of the methods and practices employed in research – investigates the gathering of evidence in the process of knowledge and theory formation. Traditional methodology, rooted in liberal-positivist epistemology, employs **empiricism**, **objectivity** and rationalism as foundational principles. Feminist methodology critiques the theoretical principles and application of traditional methodology from a variety of perspectives. Originally engaged in a search for a single method appropriate to feminist research, feminists increasingly employ a variety of methods informed by feminist values that vary with context, subject and researcher. While feminist epistemology asks 'whose knowledge are we talking about?', feminist methodology asks, 'how should we go about producing knowledge?'

Feminist methodology is grounded in a critique of positivist research methodology. Women's 'invisibility' in the selection of topics deemed worthy of research, as participants in that research, and in the knowledge and the theories developed, are longstanding critiques. Additional evidence of androcentric assumptions in the design and application of research projects, and of the over-generalisation of research findings based on male-only samples, have strengthened the call for the development of feminist research practices (see **androcentrism**). Feminist methodologists maintain a vigilant eye on mainstream research but their goal has moved beyond 'adding women on'; the motivation now lies in reformulating the philosophy underpinning that research. There is disagreement among feminists, however, over the nature of this reformulation.

To appreciate feminist critiques, a brief review of positivist research methodology is necessary. Assuming the existence of an objective reality that can be logically and rationally discovered through observation sets the requirements for the research process (see Babbie 1998). Theory development requires the construction of hypotheses and the operationalisation of concepts which are then tested against the evidence collected. Researchers are expected to remain objective and ensure that their research is not biased by personal values. The many rules and prescriptions that form the keystone of the traditional research process guard against this at every stage – theory development, research design, data collection, and analysis – to allow for the discovery of knowledge untainted by subjectivity.

Positivism assumes that knowledge exists outside the lived experiences of the objects of study. Truth is discoverable through an objective, rational review of the evidence. Researchers (i.e. the *subjects*) must achieve a professional 'scientific' distance from their research allowing them to rationally and objectively collect and evaluate data. The achievement of intersubjectivity, that is, agreement among researchers on the conclusions generated from their research, increases confidence in the validity of the generated knowledge. The *objects* of the study (i.e. those who are studied) are assumed unable to achieve a similar degree of objectivity and as such play a limited role in the research project. The *subject/object dichotomy* assumes that the researcher is better able to understand the meaning of lived experiences than those who actually live them. The collection of data from experiences is considered the means of truth discovery, rather than truth discovery itself.

Finally, the techniques employed are often linked to a desire for quantification. Quantitative methods translate experiences and observations into categories to which values are assigned for analysis. The most common method is the survey employing a series of close-ended questions administered in a formal interview. The assignment of numerical values allows for the aggregation and summarisation of data and for the use of statistical techniques to uncover causal relationships across variables. Categorisation minimises bias in the data and the statistical analysis of data is considered value-free in that values play no part in the mathematical principles guiding it.

Some feminist researchers take issue with the search for knowledge underlying this model. The assumption that an objective 'truth' can be rationally determined through empirical observation based on strict rules produces a range of critiques. The strongest variant, postmodernism, rejects a logically ordered objective reality, and instead suggests multiple constructions of experience (see **poststructuralism/postmodernism**). Feminist researchers, Liz Stanley and Sue Wise (1983) for example, argue for a methodology that validates women's subjective experiences as women by merely recounting them without imposing any alternative interpretations on them.

The majority of feminist critiques, however, identify the application of the scientific method rather than the search for an agreed upon truth as problematic: examples of highly subjective research permeated by western and androcentric values are held up as evidence. An early example is Carol **Gilligan**'s (1982) research revealing that theories of moral development were neither informed by, nor reflective of, women's experiences. This androcentrism was due to a number of factors, including the methods employed to collect data and the value judgments employed by male researchers to assess data on women. Claims of objectivity are weakened by the existence of theories based on research that neither speaks to women nor reflects their lived experiences.

Few feminist researchers are totally willing to abandon the goal of objectivity in the scientific method. Recognising that complete objectivity is unlikely, they incorporate subjective elements into their work while continuing to guard against bias. Moreover, they highlight the fact that the authority granted the scientific method increases the chances the research results can be employed to bring about political and social change. As such, it serves as an important and valuable feminist research tool. However others argue that positivist principles underlying quantitative methods, which are often generalising, are so inconsistent with feminist values that a complete shift to **qualitative methodologies** is required.

The arguments for moving away from quantitative methods are several, including the critique that they provide a simplistic and often superficial view of the topic of study, referred to by Maria Mies (1983) as 'context-stripping'. Feminist methodology often moves away from grand theorising towards the local, specific, detailed and situated explanation. The authority granted the 'hard numbers' of statistical methods, in spite of weaknesses such as sexist assumptions in the definition of variables, also renders many feminists sceptical of their use. And in line with non-feminist critiques of positivist methods, feminists argue for 'participatory research' which removes the exploitative hierarchical relationship between the researcher and the objects of study. Instead, the knower/researcher assumes a more equal relationship with the *participants* in the research undertaking, one based on cooperation, mutual respect and inter-dependence which elevates the participants' role in the production of knowledge. Thus, for example, Maria Mies's (1983) argument that 'the *view from above*, must be replaced by the *view from below*'. Feminists have also called for an elimination of hierarchical exploitative relationships within research teams themselves.

As a *reflexive methodology*, feminist methodology attempts to learn from and about the process of conducting research while producing knowledge. As such, many feminists reject the tradition of value neutrality and argue for personal engagement with research participants. Ann **Oakley**'s (1981) research on housewives, for example, concludes that a researcher must 'invest his or her own personal identity in the relationship' and indeed forge lasting friendships with research participants if at all possible. For Oakley, interviews are tools for validating women's subjective experiences as women and as people; to reduce them to a contrived and restricted set of interview questions is completely antithetical to feminist beliefs and values. Others note that feminist research is valuable if it is rendered accessible to those being studied, so that they may employ it to bring about social change. Of critical importance is the adoption of a methodology that neither restricts the voices of the researched nor demands the adoption of a distant value-neutral position. For Sandra **Harding** (1986), the introduction of subjectivity (i.e. feminist values) in research nevertheless requires a need for reflection on the degree to which those values influence it at every stage. Keeping research diaries is suggested by some as one possible method for ensuring such self-reflection.

Semi-structured interviewing has become an important element in feminist qualitative methods for its ability to record women's thoughts, beliefs and values employed in the development of feminist theory. Some additional methods include: **ethnography**, adding a period spent living among the research participants to interviewing to provide a richer and fuller understanding of their experiences; women's **oral history** on either topical, biographical or autobiographical projects; and content-analysis of cultural artifacts including **diaries** (see Reinharz 1992). Nevertheless, many feminists accept the guarded use of mainstream

quantitative methods, most notably surveying, when the information required to answer research questions necessitates it. Others advocate triangulation, the use of multiple methods including qualitative and quantitative alike, in research projects. Valuing 'inclusiveness more than orthodoxy', feminist researchers employ traditional scientific methods, modify them when necessary to suit feminist principles and purposes, rediscover methods ignored by mainstream researchers, and when necessary, develop original methods when conventional ones are found lacking (Reinharz 1992: 244).

Feminists challenge the belief that pure research, and the search for truth, are removed from and of little consequence for the perpetuation of systems of power. As such, mainstream research is criticised for perpetuating the many stereotypes and myths that serve to sustain women's dependency. Additionally, feminists argue that the value in research lies in its ability to fight women's oppression and exploitation in addition to contributing to knowledge. As Renate Duelli Klein argues, making it 'research for women' rather than 'research on women' is instrumental to achieving this goal (1983: 90).

See also: case study analysis; cross-cultural analysis; cultural methodologies; data collection, bias in; ethnomethodology; observational method; participant observation; positivism

References and further readings

Babbie, E. (1998) *The Practice of Social Research*, Scarborough, ON: ITP Nelson Canada, 8th edn.

Gilligan, C. (1982) *In a Different Voice*, Cambridge, MA: Harvard University Press.

Harding, S. (1986) *The Science Question in Feminism*, Ithaca, NY: Cornell University Press.

Jayaratne T.E. and Stewart, A.J. (1991) 'Quantitative and Qualitative Methods in the Social Sciences: Current Feminist Issues and Practical Strategies', in M.M. Fonow and J.A. Cook, *Beyond Methodology: Feminist Scholarship as Lived Research*, Bloomington, IN: Indiana University Press.

Klein, R.D. (1983) 'How To Do What We Want To

Do: Thoughts About Feminist Methodology', in G. Bowles and R.D. Klein (eds) *Theories of Women's Studies*, Boston: Routledge and Kegan Paul.

Mies, M. (1983) 'Towards a Methodology for Feminist Research', in G. Bowles and R.D. Klein (eds) *Theories of Women's Studies*, Boston: Routledge and Kegan Paul.

Oakley, A. (1981) 'Interviewing Women: A Contradiction in Terms', in H. Roberts (ed.) *Doing Feminist Research*, Boston: Routledge and Kegan Paul.

Randall, V. (1994) 'Feminism and Political Analysis', in M. Githens *et al.* (eds) *Different Roles, Different Voices*, New York: Harper Collins.

Reinharz, S. (1992) *Feminist Methods in Social Research*, New York: Oxford University Press.

Stanley, L. and Wise, S. (1983) *Breaking Out: Feminist Consciousness and Feminist Research*, London: Routledge and Kegan Paul.

BRENDA O'NEILL

Middle Eastern feminism

The Middle East is a geographical area that covers some twenty-one countries with a diversity of ethnic, linguistic, political, and religious groups. The dominant religion in these countries is Islam. Iran is the only state in the region with a predominantly Shi'ite Moslem population, while other Middle Eastern nations possess a large Sunni Moslem population. The countries in this vast area are mainly Arab states with the exception of Iran, Turkey, and Afghanistan. Thus, to posit the 'Middle East' as a broad and generalisable category is as misleading a claim as to suppose the nations of Europe or North America are reducible to one common culture or religion. By the same token, it is as difficult to proffer a category of 'Middle Eastern feminism' as it is to offer a single definition of 'western' feminism. Nevertheless, if generalisations are to be made, I would say that unlike feminist movements in the west, Middle Eastern feminist movements have been historically connected to nationalist and anti-

imperialist movements in their respective countries (see also **nationalism and gender**).

Feminist movements in the Arab Middle East

Egypt played a pioneering role in women's movements throughout the Middle East as women of all classes participated in nationalist and feminist agitation in the late-nineteenth and early-twentieth centuries. At the time of the Egyptian national revolution (1919–23), rural women, imperilling their lives, actively participated in thwarting the movement of British troops by cutting telephone wires and disrupting railway lines. During this time, upper-middle-class urban women founded a number of feminist organisations, most notably the Society for the Advancement of Woman (1908) and the Intellectual Association of Egyptian Women (1914). Hoda Sha'rawi, a prominent feminist of the 1920s and 1930s, initiated a lecture series for women at the Egyptian University in 1908. The proliferation of feminist discourses in the first three decades of the twentieth century prompted the development of two distinct schools of feminism (Ahmed 1992). The dominant school of Egyptian feminism – one espoused by the upper strata of Egyptian society – sought to emulate western feminist movements; the more marginal voices of Egyptian feminism attempted to redefine women's social roles from within an indigenous Islamic framework (see also **Islam and feminism**).

Arab women in other nations were equally militant in nationalist and feminist struggles. By 1944, they had consolidated Arab feminist activism by forming the Arab Feminist Union. Pan-Arab feminism re-emerged in the mid-1980s under the aegis of the Arab Women's Solidarity Association with Egyptian feminist Nawal el **Saadawi** as President. Pan-Arab feminists contest conservative factions aiming to rescind the legal and professional advances that women made in the late twentieth century.

Feminist movements in the non-Arab Middle East

During a period of increased national awareness in the late-nineteenth and early-twentieth centuries in Iran, a growing number of women activists inserted themselves into the Iranian political arena. The Tobacco Protests of 1890 were amongst the strongest manifestations of resistance to foreign economic domination. The protests were in response to a total monopoly awarded a British company for the production, sale, and export of Iran's tobacco crop. Urban and rural women joined forces to advocate a ban on all tobacco products. The uncompromising participation of the Shah's royal wives was an important factor in the success of the boycott. Women's participation in anti-imperialist protests enabled the mobilisation of a new group of affluent urban women activists demanding women's rights and suffrage during the Constitutional Revolution of 1905–11.

The decade following the Revolution produced a number of women's nationalist and feminist secret societies. In 1911, the Ladies of the Homeland organisation appealed to British suffragists for their help in pressuring the British government to support Iran in the face of growing Russian threats to the country's independence. The suffragists responded by confessing their own powerless status in British patriarchal society (Afary 1996).

In the 1978–9 anti-imperial revolution, Iranian women played a significant national role by protesting alongside Iranian men for the deposition of Mohamad Reza Shah. In March of 1979, one month after the revolution, Iranian women organised five consecutive days of mass feminist protests against the misogynist policies of the newly established Islamic Republic. In post-revolutionary Iran, a number of feminist journals including *Zanan* (Women) strive to place Iranian feminist concerns at the forefront of public debate.

In late-nineteenth-century Ottoman Turkey, the subject of women's education and women's role in society became the focus of much debate. As in other Middle Eastern societies, the debate about the status of women took place within the parameters of Islamic doctrine. In 1908, the first women's club, 'Red and White', was formed in Salonika. These were the colours of the Young Turk movement which was committed to the abolition of the Sultanate and to a reconceptualisation of Turkey as a 'modernised' and 'westernised' state. Other women's organisations included the 'Association for the Betterment of Women' and the 'Ottoman Association for the Defence of Women's

Rights' led by Nuriye Ulviye Mevlan who also launched the journal *Women's World*. After the establishment of the Turkish Republic in 1923, the question of women's role in Turkish society assumed centre stage but these discussions continued within the framework of Islamic principles and patriarchal nationalist ideals.

Middle Eastern feminist movements emerged in tandem with nationalist and anti-imperialist movements in their respective countries. Although they played a significant partnership role with their male counterparts in combating foreign rule, Middle Eastern women were relegated to the status of second-class citizens even after successful nationalist revolutions. Middle Eastern feminists find themselves repeatedly in the unenviable position of having to choose between their allegiance to the nation and their allegiance to feminism – a concept often misrepresented by patriarchal nationalists as a western import.

References and further reading

Afary, J. (1996) *The Iranian Constitutional Revolution, 1906–1911*, New York: Columbia University Press.

Ahmed, L. (1992) *Women and Gender in Islam*, New Haven: Yale University Press.

Badran, M. and Cooke, M. (eds) (1990) *Opening the Gates*, Bloomington, IN: Indiana University Press.

Jayawardena, K. (1986) *Feminism and Nationalism in the Third World*, London: Zed Books Ltd.

NIMA NAGHIBI

midwifery

Midwifery is the skilled and caring assistance women have provided to other women throughout pregnancy, miscarriage, abortion, and childbirth, from ancient times to the present. The Old Testament affirms the independence and age of the profession; the Book of Exodus opens with praise for midwives who disobeyed and outwitted a murderous king in order to protect the women and children they served. Midwifery exists in tension with efforts of patriarchal institutions (e.g., medieval

Christianity, western obstetrics) to control or eliminate the variety of services which constitute its practice. In *Midwives, Society and Childbirth* (1997), Marland and Rafferty demonstrate that midwives around the world have adapted and reinvented their profession in the face of modern medicine's technological and regulatory impacts on how they may assist women through complicated as well as 'normal' deliveries.

See also: gynaecology; motherhood; witchcraft

References and further reading

Marland, H. and Rafferty, A.M. (eds) (1997) *Midwives, Society and Childbirth*, New York: Routledge.

EILEEN M. CONDON

military metaphors

Metaphors are tools for understanding one kind of thing in terms of another; they highlight some dimensions of the subject and obscure others. For example, when physicians think of themselves as engaged in a war against disease they treat patients differently than when they think of themselves as therapists helping patients live well. When we describe arguments, political contests, sports events, and even love affairs in military terms such as 'attack', 'defend', 'overpower', 'conquer', or, simply, 'win' and 'lose', we approach these practices in a distinctly aggressive fashion. Some feminists have suggested supplanting these pervasive military metaphors with more peaceful, cooperative alternatives such as play, nurture, share, explore, and communicate in the hope that these alternative ways of thinking will encourage less violent ways of engaging with others.

See also: language, gender and power

References and further reading

Lakoff, G. and Johnson, M. (1980) *Metaphors We Live By*, Chicago, IL: University of Chicago Press.

SUSAN SHERWIN

Miller, Jean Baker (b. 1927)

Jean Baker Miller, MD, is best known for *Toward a New Psychology of Women* (1976), a book that produced a 'click' experience for many readers in its day. Eschewing the technical language of psychoanalysis and its preoccupation with early childhood, the slim volume offers a direct and compelling account of how subordination shapes women's identity, intimate relations, and daily experience. Even if women experience themselves as freely foregoing their needs in order to fulfil the needs of others, Miller argues, such self-denial blocks personal development and authentic living. Nonetheless, caring for others can endow women with unique capacities for perceiving the intricacies of human relationships and for appreciating the emotional dimensions of life.

Miller's subsequent work shifted toward women's psychological problems and individual psychotherapy. The Stone Centre, founded by Miller in 1981 at Wellesley College, gathered a group of women psychotherapists who pursued Miller's insights. The model they have developed, called the Self-in-Relation Model, is cast within a narrower frame than *Toward a New Psychology of Women*. It substitutes a focus on individual development and an emphasis on therapeutic processes in place of Miller's earlier attention to cultural norms and social practices. The Self-in-Relation Model, like much of the **cultural feminism** of the early 1980s, claims to describe universal womanly ways of being, celebrating womanhood and its redemptive possibilities. By the late-1990s, the model was renamed the 'Relational/Cultural Model' and it was revamped to include the perspectives of women of diverse ethnic backgrounds, sexualities, and social locations.

Many women in the counselling and psychotherapy professions have found the ideas of Jean Baker Miller and her coworkers appealing and inspiring. The Jean Baker Miller Training Institute, founded in the late 1990s, conducts an ongoing programme of seminars, workshops, courses, and public speeches aimed at practitioners. It also offers certification in the Relational/Cultural Model of therapy. Perhaps because Miller and her coworkers have chosen to reach out to practising therapists, their work is not widely known among academic feminist psychologists and other women's studies scholars and researchers.

Selected writings

Miller, J. Baker (1976) *Toward a New Psychology of Women*, Boston: Beacon Press.

Miller, J. Baker, Jordan, J.V., Kaplan, A.G., Stiver, I.P. and Surrey, J. (1991) *Women's Growth in Connection*, New York: Guilford Press.

Miller, J. Baker and Stiver, I.P. (1997) *The Healing Connection: How Women Form Relationships in Therapy and In Life*, Boston: Beacon Press.

JEANNE MARECEK

Millet, Kate (b. 1934)

Kate Millet's classic second-wave feminist text *Sexual Politics* (1970) introduced a critique of **patriarchy** based on the unequal **power** politics of **sexuality**. *Sexual Politics* provided a pioneering foundation for both contemporary Anglo-American feminist literary criticism and the women's movement. Deploying psychosocial, historical and literary methodologies, Millet rejects the prevailing ahistoricism of the New Critics to develop an emerging Images of Women criticism. Her dehierarchised readings of sexist and misogynistic representations in selected male-authored works seeks to symptomatically expose the invisible ideological and cultural underpinnings of a permanent patriarchy effecting women's **oppression**.

Millet's nascent form of **radical feminism** asserts that female oppression begins through the primary patriarchal institution of the family. Socialisation, sex-role and **gender** stereotyping establish the psychosocial blueprint of women's 'interior colonisation' in power-structured sexual relationships and by political extension, broader cultural and institutional life. Her explicit distinction between sex and gender rejects the biological basis of propagated notions of male supremacy, arguing that gender constructs of 'instrumental' **masculinity** and 'passive' femininity confine men and women to socially prescribed sex and behavioural roles.

Millet analyses the historically grounded reproduction of masculinity and femininity under patriarchy during the 1830–1930 sexual revolution and through contemporary discourses such as **psychoanalysis** and literature in the subsequent modern era counterrevolution against women's liberation.

Criticising a biologically essentialist Freudian psychoanalysis (particularly Freud's theory of penis envy), Millet proceeds to polemically deconstruct the sexual and political ideologies of **dominance** and subordination implicit in the writings of D.H. Lawrence, Henry Miller, Norman Mailer and Jean Genet, exposing for example Lawrence's phallic fiction and the misogynistic **violence** inherent in Miller's work.

Millet's text has been criticised for its totalising conceptions of patriarchy, occasionally simplistic and contradictory approaches, reductive treatment of Freudian psychoanalysis and disavowal of tangible feminist influences including that of Simone de **Beauvoir**. Despite its limitations, *Sexual Politics* initiated vigorous debate in second-wave feminist theory and criticism, enacting the personal as political through a methodological fusion continued in Millet's later political feminist work, particularly her autobiographical narratives and woman-centred fiction.

See also: biological essentialism; history; ideology; language, gender and power; literature, images of women in; misogyny; public/private; sexism

Selected writings

Millet, K. (1970) *Sexual Politics*, New York: Doubleday.

—— (1971) 'Prostitution: A Quartet for Female Voices', in V. Gornick and B.K. Moran (eds) *Woman in Sexist Society: Studies in Power and Powerlessness*, New York: Basic Books.

—— (1979) *The Basement: Meditations on a Human Sacrifice*, New York: Simon and Schuster.

SATINDER KAUR CHOHAN

misogyny

Misogyny (Greek *misein*: to hate, *gyn*: woman) is implicit or explicit male denigration and/or hatred of women, and latterly of feminism. In western thought it runs from Aristotle's lesser esteem for women's political rationality, through Augustine's belief that woman, unlike man, is not made in the image of God, to Rousseau's unease about women as merely sexual beings, and Marx's perpetuation of a view of women as dangerous beings who are too close to nature. Feminist literary scholars note the social misogyny behind the literary works of such figures as Henry Miller and Norman Mailer, and cultural theorists analyse the misogyny that objectifies women in advertising and the media, reducing them to sexual, bodily beings. Although misogyny and sexism inform one another, misogyny manifests itself in psychologically-based fear or hatred of women, sexism in **systemic discrimination**, or failure to take women into account.

See also: advertising, women in; Millet, Kate

LORRAINE CODE

Mitchell, Juliet (b. 1940)

Born in New Zealand, Juliet Mitchell is a practising analyst who works in London. In 1966, through The British New Left, Mitchell published 'Women: the Longest Revolution', an essay which examines the ideological level of women's lived reality and figures women in the socialist project. The essay additionally anticipates key preoccupations of the women's movement: production, **reproduction**, **sexuality** and the socialisation of children. It is the use of Louis Althusser's notion of **ideology**, however, which connects this essay to Mitchell's subsequent psychoanalytic writings.

Psychoanalysis and Feminism (1974) is credited for introducing Freud to a feminist audience largely unfamiliar with (or hostile to) his ideas. In her book, Mitchell mounts a strenuous defence of Freud, claiming his theories lend explanation to the ideological structure of **patriarchy**. According to Mitchell, Freud tells us exactly how the laws of human culture – which in the **anthropology** of Claude Lévi-Strauss amount to the **kinship** rules

of exogamous exchange – are acquired by each and every child. Central to Mitchell's account is the unconscious: in the unconscious lies the personal history of human history, ontogeny repeats phylogeny. Thus Freud's theory of castration (especially Jacques Lacan's reading of castration as symbolic) does not prescribe a situation but describes one, namely, the constitution of the subject in a division between the sexes according to the requirements of humanity.

Mitchell's ground-breaking book initiated further feminist engagements with **psychoanalysis**, including her own work with Jacqueline Rose. In *Feminine Sexuality* (1982), Mitchell shifts from her initial characterisation of the unconscious, losing the structuralism which had become widely criticised. In its place, Mitchell amplifies her earlier Lacanian inflection, in particular, the idea that subjectivity is assigned to the child at the moment of symbolic castration (the division between self and (m)other). Following Lacan, Mitchell notes that sexed subjectivity is simultaneously constituted through castration in a necessary yet arbitrary way (the phallus as transcendental signifier of the division). But Mitchell additionally notes that sexed subjectivity is fundamentally incomplete: this is, after all, the meaning of the unconscious. Any achievement of masculinity or femininity is thus always precarious. And with this point, feminism joins psychoanalysis as one and the same project.

Selected writings

Mitchell, J. (1974) *Psychoanalysis and Feminism*, London: Allen Lane.
—— (1984) *Women: The Longest Revolution. Essays on Feminism, Literature and Psychoanalysis*, London: Virago.
Mitchell, J. and Rose, J. (eds) (1982) *Feminine Sexuality: Jacques Lacan and the École Freudienne*, London: MacMillan.

JOANNE H. WRIGHT

modernity, feminist critiques of

Modernity is commonly associated with a set of intellectual and political traditions that developed in the west in the eighteenth century. Feminist critiques of modernity rest on a problematic basis because first-wave feminism developed alongside and as a product of modernity and its traditions. Indeed, it was only in the twentieth century that feminists provided explicit critiques of modernity. These critiques are centred on the belief that women have been excluded from the traditions and political practises of modernity.

Hence, feminists have critiqued modernity's exclusion of women by drawing attention to several theoretical processes. The primary process is the construction of false universalism. Many feminists believe that modernity has seen the development of a supposedly gender-free and universal picture of the paradigmatic 'human being' that actually transpires to be based on male-associated traits of abstract selfhood and reason. Instead of universality, feminists believe that modernity rests on a set of **dichotomies** — man/woman, reason/unreason, public/private — which associate women with the latter and lesser half of the pair and excludes them from its privileged concepts. The most important dichotomy for feminists has been the **public/private** divide. For many feminists the public in modernity has been the realm of action, politics and impartiality: processes that have been made possible by the creation of a woman-centred private sphere that takes care of everyday needs and particularity. Consequently, difference and emotion are able to be excluded from the public realm which remains committed to a unifying and dominating code of rationality. Modernity, according to feminist critiques, has perpetuated the exclusion of women in these ways because it continues to be underpinned and structured by **patriarchy** that privileges male interests and values as the norm.

Although feminist critiques of modernity have identified similar themes, not all feminists have responded in the same way. Some twentieth-century feminists such as Simone de **Beauvoir** believe that feminists should seek inclusion in modernity on equal terms with men. Whereas, feminists such as Jean Bethke Elshtain suggest that feminists can only be included in modernity if its central themes have been transformed to give equal recognition to women's specific values. In the 1980s and 1990s a third critique developed. Some

feminists looked at issues of postmodernism to suggest a more radical critique and rejection of modernity as an exhausted set of traditions. Instead, they stressed the diversity of women and the potential for disunity. However, many feminists feel that such a thorough critique of modernity threatens the possibility of a feminist project.

See also: classics, feminism and the; feminism; poststructuralism/postmodernism

References and further reading

Elshtain, J. (1992) 'The Power and Powerlessness if Women' in G. Bock and S. James (eds) *Beyond Equality and Difference: Citizenship, Feminist Politics and Female Subjectivity*, London and New York: Routledge.

Nicholson, L. (1990) *Feminism/Postmodernism*, London and New York: Routledge.

Okin, S. Moller (1992) *Women in Western Political Thought*, Princeton, NJ: Princeton University Press, 2nd edn.

FRANCES OLDALE

monosexuality

Monosexuality is a term used to describe sexual orientations that are not bisexual – i.e. both heterosexual and homosexual. It refers to sexual orientation toward one and only one of the two recognised biological sexes – male and female (Nagle 1993). Monosexuality presumes there are only two sexes, male and female, that one's sex is fixed and that there are clear and quantifiable differences between the sexes. Bisexual activists identify monosexism (the belief that monosexuality is superior to and more natural than bisexuality) in heterosexual communities, gay male communities and lesbian communities. Monosexism perpetuates the bipolar sex and gender system (see **binaries/bipolarity**). Bisexuality challenges monosexual assumptions of the fixity of sex and the degrees of sexual difference.

See also: biphobia; bisexuality; heterosexuality; homosexuality

References and further reading

Nagle, J. (1993) 'Framing Radical Bisexuality: Toward a Gender Agenda' in Tucker, N. (ed.) *Bisexual Politics: Theories, Queries and Visions*, New York: Harrington Park Press, 1995, pp. 305.

Rust, P.C. (1995) *Bisexuality and the Challenge to Lesbian Politics: Sex, Loyalty, and Revolution*, New York: New York University Press.

Tucker, N. (ed.) (1995) *Bisexual Politics: Theories, Queries and Visions*, New York: Harrington Park Press.

KATHRYN PAYNE

Moore, Henrietta (b. 1957)

Henrietta Moore is a British social anthropologist whose theoretical scholarship on gender has made a ground-breaking contribution to the development in contemporary social science of a critical cross-cultural and trans-disciplinary 'feminist anthropology'.

Though Moore has written extensively on such diverse topics as economic anthropology, nutrition, development, feminist theory, hermeneutics, psychoanalysis, and questions of method and representation in anthropology, her work remains centrally concerned with attempts to define analytically the scope of the relations (and limitations) between gender and social anthropology, both as intersecting fields of social enquiry and as conditions for effective practical action and social change. These concerns were first elaborated in the highly influential text *Feminism and Anthropology* (1988). This is a critical synthesis of cross-cultural ethnography and feminist analysis in which Moore selectively reviews material relating to regions in Africa, the Middle East, Southeast Asia, Europe and the Caribbean on such issues as property, marriage transactions, the redistribution of household resources between kin, wage labour and migration.

However, Moore's own earlier fieldwork experiences in East and Central Africa, especially amongst the Marakwet of Kenya, and her own critical reflections on voice, authorship and processes of theorisation within academia (see also **epistemology, feminist**; **positioning/posi-**

tionality) have also played a significant role in the formation and presentation of her analyses (Moore 1986/1996). Drawing on the insights of Bourdieu, Ricoeur and Foucault, her theoretical monograph on gender, space and social relations sets forth a series of spatial 'texts' to examine spatial relations as practices of gendered action between Marakwet women and men.

In subsequent work, Moore develops these themes of **power**, **agency** and social change through critical explorations of the relation between language, embodiment and resistance in the wider context of poststructuralist feminist debates on discourses of **identity**, **difference** and desire. The collection of essays entitled *A Passion For Difference* (1994) further explores the workings of discourses of gender as dominant ideologies within and across cultural systems, especially in terms which address the broader theoretical impasse of the western 'sex/gender' dichotomy (see **categories and dichotomies**). For instance, how debates about the nature of western personhood (see also **self, the**) have been filtered through this dichotomy as the defining constructs of biology and culture, leads Moore to question the referential power of the very category of 'gender' itself. On the modelling of gender as difference internal to human bodies, 'it is far from apparent', she states, 'how we should distinguish sex from gender, and, even more problematic, it is unclear what gender as a concept or category refers to' (1994: 14).

The challenge presented by Moore's work is precisely how such conceptual indeterminacy is confronted not as an intractable problem of social analysis, but rather as the very occasion for locating points at which new inter-disciplinary dialogues in and beyond the academy need to be addressed afresh.

See also: anthropology; critical theory, feminism and; cross-cultural analysis; feminism; gender; nature/culture; postcolonialist feminism; psychoanalytic feminist literary theory; Strathern, Marilyn

Selected writings

Moore, H.L. (1986) *Space, Text, and Gender: An Anthropological Study of the Marakwet*, Cambridge:

Cambridge University Press (see also 1996 edition with new preface published by The Guildford Press, New York).

—— (1988) *Feminism and Anthropology*, Cambridge, MA: Polity Press.

—— (1994) *A Passion For Difference*, Cambridge, MA: Polity Press.

—— (1994) 'Gendered Persons: Dialogues Between Anthropology and Psychoanalysis', in S. Heald and A. Deluz (eds) *Anthropology and Psychoanalysis*, London: Routledge.

—— (1996) 'The Changing Nature of Anthropological Knowledge', in H.L. Moore (ed) *The Future of Anthropological Knowledge*, London: Routledge.

Moore, H.L. (ed) (1999) *Anthropological Theory Today*, Cambridge, MA: Polity Press.

Moore, H.L., Saunders, T. and Kaare, B (eds) (1999) *Those who Play with Fire: Gender, Fertility and Transformation in Southern Africa*, London: Athlone Press.

MONICA KONRAD

moral development

Feminist interest in moral development stems from a recognition that the principles that describe and regulate 'the moral maturation process' derive from and speak to expectations of male children in patriarchal families in affluent white western societies. Moral development is charted from a situation of childhood dependence, usually upon the mother, toward ever greater independence, with an end result described and prescribed as moral autonomy. Feminist theorists such as Nancy **Chodorow** have noted, however, that maturity is conceived and nurtured differently for male and female children. Indeed, it is male children who are to strive for standard autonomous maturity, manifested in separation from the mother and self-reliant emotional independence. Girl children in the families from which the norms derive are nurtured to remain connected with the mother, and to prepare for the emotionally nurturant life of a wife and mother in a nuclear family. Thus the standard maturation process fosters development into an adulthood of capitalist heterosexual conformity that replicates and endorses essentialised male and female social positioning (see **essentialism**).

Theories that derive from the work of Jean Piaget in France and Lawrence Kohlberg in the USA view moral development as a series of stages through which a child passes from a conventional, rule-bound dependence on parents and other adults in learning right moral conduct, to a rational autonomy in which he can, as the term implies, give the law unto himself: determine, from a principled stance, the right, universally valid, rules of conduct. The masculine pronoun signals reasons for feminist interest in this topic: feminists show that standard theories are both descriptively and normatively androcentric, suited to address the experiences and patterns of conduct common to this specific group of male children.

In the USA, the landmark feminist challenge comes from Carol **Gilligan**, who proposes that girls' failure to achieve high scores on Kohlberg's scale of moral development attests to the insensitivity of the scale, not to girls' 'natural' immaturity. She demonstrates the androcentricity of orthodox theories of moral development, and the consequent silencing of women's moral voices (see **androcentrism**). Focusing as fully on class (see **class analysis**) and **race** as on **gender**, Valerie **Walkerdine** argues that Piagetian theory, far from offering the universal picture of moral maturation it claims to present, is driven by a specific agenda: that of fostering the triumph of reason over emotion, of producing 'children who would become adults without perverse pleasures'. Looking at how meanings are created in practices in which participants are concretely situated, and at how emotionality and desire are carried by the relations within practices, Walkerdine challenges Piaget's emphasis on rational mastery for the suppressions of affect that it engenders. She notes that for Piaget, the 'reasonable person' is 'in love with ideas' not bodies.

LORRAINE CODE

Morgan, Robin (b. 1941)

A feminist activist, writer, editor, and poet, Robin Morgan played a defining role in the creation and evolution of the American radical feminist movement. She compiled and edited the first comprehensive anthology of the Women's Liberation Movement, *Sisterhood is Powerful* (1970), and she has served both as a contributing editor and, from 1990–3, as editor-in-chief, of *Ms. Magazine*. As a radical feminist, Morgan posits women's oppression to be the foundational social **oppression**, the template for all others. Her **radical feminism** emerges out of her increasing disillusionment with the **sexism** of the **civil rights** and New Left movements in the late 1960s. Renouncing the male-dominated Left in her landmark polemic 'Goodbye to All That', Morgan identifies the need for an autonomous, mass-based women's movement to bring about a feminist revolution. She joined the New York Radical Women, who staged the 1968 feminist protest against the Miss America Pageant, and she was a founder of WITCH (Women's International Terrorist Conspiracy from Hell).

In the 1970s, Morgan invoked a woman-centred, **Goddess**-worshipping feminist vision, grounded in the historically-spurious belief in an ancient matriarchal tradition. This phase in her thought is connected to radical feminism's early quest for the origins of women's oppression. Nevertheless, her collected essays reveal the scope of her political activism and thinking, from the new physics and its uses for feminism to **pornography**. As a founder of Women Against Pornography in 1979, Morgan coined the controversial phrase 'Porn is the theory, rape is the practice'.

In general, radical feminism has been criticised for relying on an essentialist view of women, and for overemphasising women's common experiences. Morgan's feminism, while exhibiting these tendencies, ultimately defies easy categorisation. She has written on the challenges and necessity of feminist solidarity, and she has been critical of racism and heterosexism within and outside the women's movement (see **heterosexism, hetero-normativity**). Having published an international feminist anthology, *Sisterhood is Global*, Morgan brought an international focus to the regenerated, ad-free *Ms.* in 1990 and continues to serve as the magazine's International Editor.

See also: cultural feminism; Marxism

Selected writings

Morgan, R. (1970) *Sisterhood is Powerful: An Anthology of Writing from the Women's Liberation Movement*, New York: Vintage Books.
—— (1977) *Going Too Far: The Personal Chronicle of a Feminist*, New York: Random House.
—— (1984) *Sisterhood is Global*, Garden City, NY: Anchor Press/Doubleday.
—— (1992) *The Word of a Woman: Feminist Dispatches 1968–1992*, New York: W.W. Norton.

JOANNE H. WRIGHT

motherhood

The equation of motherhood with womanhood, as women's reproductive counterpart to men's productive labour under compulsory **heterosexuality** and capitalism, has led to divergent feminist views of women's childbearing and childcaring capacities. Whilst often seen as a key source of women's **oppression**, other (cultural) feminist accounts have attempted to reclaim women's (purported) orientation towards caring for non-biological and non-familial relationships (especially between women). While feminists attempt to counter the **essentialism** of the presumption that women can, will and want to be mothers, feminist strategies and analyses about the choices and meanings of motherhood intersect with other arenas of women's marginalisation including class (see **class analysis**), race, **sexuality** and (dis)-ability (see **disability, women and**). Given the centrality of women as mothers to mainstream theory and policy on the **family**, work (see **work, women and**), moral socialisation, and control of women's sexuality, feminist debates on motherhood reiterate in microcosm the spectrum of feminist thought.

Second-wave feminism (see **first-wave/second-wave feminism**) has disentangled the conflation of women as childbearers and childcarers structured within notions of 'maternal instinct' which, as a biological pseudoexplanation, works to warrant normative assumptions about what women can, and should, do. Not only are women thereby naturalised and essentialised as mothers, but this process also obscures how the desire to have children is neither inherent, nor specific, to women; nor are women equipped thereby with know-how to care for children. Alongside popular subscription to the maternal instinct, the prevalent cultural idealisation of motherhood as the crowning fulfilment of a woman's life (but only if she is married) is held by some feminists to account for the high rates of depression among mothers – with isolation, lack of social support and inadequate public **childcare** driving home how little women's reproductive and caring labour is really valued within modern industrialised societies.

The elision between bearing and caring for children within prevailing gendered arrangements as they map onto the **public/private** divide makes women economically dependent upon men and, by self-fulfiling prophecy, has warranted a rationalisation for women's disadvantaged place within the paid labour market – as less committed because of their current, or presumed future, childcare commitments. Economically active women predominate in low-paid, casual and part-time work because the flexibility and limited hours allow for combination with childcare (as in home-working, or child-minding) or can fit around schooltimes. Notwithstanding the cult status of motherhood within most world religions (e.g. Christianity; Warner 1976), feminists have high-lighted how having children disadvantages women socially and economically. Further double binds follow from the women/mother equation, so that women without children (child-less or child-free) are generally regarded as not quite fully female, while mothers who leave their children in the care of others are vulnerable to the charge of generating 'maternal deprivation'.

The extension of the labour of mothering from mere(!) delivery to guidance of the offspring into responsible adult citizenship makes the political and affective relationships between women and children particularly vexed, and policies for children tend either to presume equivalence, or, alternatively, absolute separation of interests between mothers and children. This has also given rise to a relative silence on the part of feminists about the role of children in feminist politics and practice (Thorne 1987). Feminists have critiqued models of **child development** for their tendencies to blame mothers for their children's current and future actions (interpreting later difficulties as due to 'maternal neglect' or 'overinvolvement'), or at best to render the labour of childcare and education invisible (Walkerdine and Lucy 1989). Less well theorised is how class, sexuality and racialised positions have structured different feminist agendas for mothers.

The centrality of the 'motherhood imperative' to the modern nuclear heterosexual family makes discussions of motherhood intersect with the oppression of lesbians, disabled women and women from nonEuropean backgrounds. While for white middle class heterosexual women the issue of choice has typically meant the choice *not* to have children (as in the abortion campaign slogan 'a woman's right to choose'), lesbians, disabled women and black women have struggled for the choice *to* have and keep their children. In many countries access to assisted reproduction, fostering, and adoption continues to be difficult for lesbians, and the price of 'coming out' has often meant losing custody of children. While the diversity of family organisation and arrangements among African and Asian peoples constitutes a major challenge for Anglo-Eurocentrically based (but presumed universal) psychological models, minority black women suffer additional stigmatisation as mothers for having children younger, and more often being single heads of households (recalling that this is also a class issue) (Phoenix 1991). Even early British feminist campaigns diverged around strategies for emancipation along class lines: over-prioritising the vote versus childcare provision (Riley 1987).

While cheap and accessible contraception in the 1960s freed western women from the fear of unwanted conception (but made them more vulnerable to coercion into unwanted sex), Shula-mith **Firestone** envisaged completely separating being a woman from bearing children. Rather than repudiating motherhood as only and entirely oppressive, other feminists, such as Adrienne **Rich**, seek to reclaim pre-patriarchal features of the bodily and social experience of motherhood, as an actual or metaphorical representation of women's creativity.

In summary, feminist analyses document (1) how the 'realities' of motherhood diverge from their dominant representation, and (2) the diversity of experiences of mothering, to (3) portray motherhood as a site of strength as well as struggle for women. Whatever the approach, motherhood is a barometer for the analysis of differences between feminists, as well as a prime site for feminist intervention.

See also: African American families; matriarchy; reproduction

References and further reading

Nakano Glenn, E., Chang, G. and Rennie Forcey, L. (eds) (1994) *Mothering*, New York: Routledge.

Phoenix, A. (1991) *Young Mothers?*, Oxford: Polity Press.

Rich, A. (1977) *Of Woman Born:* London: Virago.

Riley (1987) 'The Serious Burdens of Love? Some Questions on Child-care, Feminism and Socialism', in A. Phillips (ed.) *Feminism and Equality*, Oxford: Blackwell.

Thorne, B. (1987) 'Revisioning Women and Social Change: Where are the Children?', *Gender and Society* 1, 1: 85–109.

Walkerdine, V. and Lucy, H. (1989) *Democracy in the Kitchen*, London: Virago.

Warner, M. (1976) *Alone of All Her Sex*, London: Weidenfeld and Nicolson.

ERICA BURMAN

Mulvey, Laura (b. 1941)

Laura Mulvey is an English avant-garde film maker and theorist whose 'Visual Pleasure and Narrative Cinema' (1975) marked academic recognition of 1970s feminisms' momentous journeys into film theory. Mulvey's account of the gendered structuring of Hollywood cinema broke with the British Left by integrating psychoanalytic, Marxists and feminist theories. Afterwards, (pro)feminist film theory's task became to theorise visual pleasure as an issue of sexual difference (or not).

Mulvey raises the issue of sexual pleasure in cinema arguing, after Freud, that male fantasies about women born of Oedipal castration anxieties drive conventional narrative texts. Distinguishing 'woman as image' from 'man as bearer of the look' she reasons that in a world structured by sexual difference and an industry dominated by men, scopophilia (Freud's 'drive' to visual pleasure) appears figured as male desire to possess women. Audiences are 'interpellated' into film texts through mechanisms reproducing unconscious phallocratic pleasures. Conventions like framing, shot countershot and the synchronising of sound to bodies encourage identification with the hero/subject as he gazes on the woman/object, through the controlling 'look' of the camera. The cinematic apparatus, and men, 'look' at women in two ways: sadism-voyeurism, which punishes women, and fetishism-scopophilia, which fetishises the female body.

Feminists have observed that the theory places women in the invidious position of identifying with the sadistic-voyeuristic gaze or accepting our to-be-looked-at status. Mulvey (1981) addresses women's pleasures, revisiting Freud to suggest more fluid, cross-gender identifications. Critics like Neale, Cowie, Dyer and **hooks** have unpacked the theory's globalising, monolithic and heterosexist assumptions.

Mulvey's art criticism and films resonated with 1970s feminist praxis, searching for new ways to represent 'women', and exploring feminist aesthetics, myth, memory and change. *Riddle of the Sphinx* (1977) stimulated experiments in deconstructing the 'scopic gaze', resulting in classics like Sally Potter's *Thriller* (1977), Yvonne Rainer's *Journeys to Berlin/71* (1979), Marlene Gorris's *A Question of Silence* (1982) and Bette Gordon's *Variety* (1983).

See also: aesthetics, feminist; art, feminist issues in; film theory, feminist; patriarchy; psychoanalysis

Selected writings

Mulvey, L. (1975), 'Visual Pleasure and Narrative Cinema', *Screen* 16, 3: 6–18.

—— (1981) 'Afterthoughts on "Visual Pleasure and

Narrative Cinema"', *Framework*, 15/16/17: 12–
15. (Inspired by *Duel in the Sun*.)
—— (1982) *Frida Kahlo and Tina Modotti*, London:
Whitechapel Art Gallery. (Catalogue of exhibi-
tion organised with Peter Wollen.)

References and further reading:

Doane, M. (1982) 'Film and the Masquerade:
Theorising the Female Spectator', *Screen*, 23 (3–
4): 74–87.
Humm, M. (1997) *Feminism and Film*, Bloomington,
IN: Indiana University Press.

LYNNE STAR

musicology, feminist

For most humanities disciplines, feminist approaches constitute a branch of the broader
enterprise of criticism. Before the most recent
wave of feminism appeared on the scene in the
1970s, questions concerning the autonomy of
literature or art works – their susceptibility to
social analysis, criteria for addressing cultural
meanings – had already been raised and debated
in the context of projects focusing on class and
other issues. Consequently, when feminist interrogations began to arise, they could build on
methodological foundations that antedated their
specific emphases on gender and sexuality.

Musicology had long resisted the intrusion of
social questions into a realm admired for its
imperviousness to such concerns. Thus when
feminist criticism first appeared in musicology in
the 1980s, it introduced not only the whole set of
debates centred on gender and sexuality that had
permeated literary and film studies for over a
decade, but it also raised – as though for the first
time – questions concerning autonomy and the
possibility of dealing with signification *of any kind* in
music. The fact that these volatile issues all
appeared simultaneously in music studies accounts
for the intensity of the ensuing controversy.

The questions raised by feminist musicologists
resemble those pursued by feminists in other
disciplines. The first group concentrate on establishing an account of music history that contains

female as well as male artists. As a result of their
efforts, dozens of women musicians have come to
the attention of the music world through books,
recordings, and increased concert programming
(Bowers and Tick 1986; Sadie and Samuel 1994).
Similar projects examine women in jazz and
popular music and have altered received notions
of those traditions as well. But the addition of these
supplementary repertories has had unexpected
repercussions within music studies. If the canon
of great music has long seemed to be an objectively
constituted constellation, the high quality of some
of this rediscovered music raises questions concerning canon formation – in whose interests
canons operate, what gets included, what gets
excluded, and by means of what criteria (Citron
1993).

If feminist music historians focus their attentions
on women musicians from earlier times, feminist
ethnomusicologists incorporate questions concerning gender ideologies into their studies of music
cultures around the world (Koskoff 1989). Moreover, this ethnographic examination of gendered
divisions of labour across cultures has helped to
diminish the long-standing gap between the
western art tradition and the cultures of Others:
it sheds light not only on people in remote parts of
the globe, but also on European cultural practices
and traditions, which have long claimed exemption
from ethnographic analysis (see **ethnography**).

Despite the implications of such projects,
however, most debates concerning feminist musicology have targeted neither the rediscovery of
women composers nor cross-cultural studies (see
cross-cultural analysis). Instead, the controversies have centred on feminist interpretations of
the classical repertory. Disagreements occur, moreover, not only over what a particular work might be
said to mean, but also over whether music may be
considered a signifying medium at all.

An isolated yet highly influential work of
feminist music criticism appeared in 1988: Catherine Clément's *Opera, or the Undoing of Women*. Before
this book, scholars had not even addressed
representations of gender in the *plots* of operas,
let alone the possibility of gender-encoding in
untexted music. Accordingly, feminist music criticism begins with this volume, which introduced
into musicology the kinds of critiques long familiar

in the other humanities concerning cultural representations of women and men, masculinity and femininity.

The 1990s witnessed the development of several kinds of feminist work. Some writers bring a critical perspective to the study of classical music, often dealing in detail not only with plots or lyrics, but also with the music itself. They address, in other words, how music – its codes and basic structural procedures – participates in the production of cultural representations and predisposes listeners to certain points of view. These studies deal not only with representations of gender, but also with class, race, and exoticism – domains often mapped onto gender in operas (Kramer 1995; McClary 1991). Other scholars involved in gender studies maintain strong allegiances with the music of the canon and justify those allegiances by means of a variety of feminist theoretical strategies. The collections of feminist musicology that have appeared recently (e.g., Solie 1993) offer a spectrum of critical positions.

With the rise of feminist musicology, other areas of music research have likewise opened up to questions concerning gender. Music education, for instance, has begun to rethink philosophical premises and revise curricular planning. Perhaps most surprising, given the insular nature of their area, a number of music theorists too have started developing ways of dealing with gender.

In most humanities disciplines, the feminist research of the 1970s had already established itself before sexuality became a matter of widespread scholarly interest. But because feminism itself entered musicology late, its emergence coincided with that of **queer theory**, which has developed in tandem with feminist criticism (Brett *et al.* 1993).

When studies of gender and sexuality first began to appear, some musicologists objected that they would bring prurient concerns into the discipline. Far from diminishing or tainting the repertories they examine, however, these lines of inquiry have opened all music to crucial questions about the cultural construction of subjectivity. Put simply, feminist and queer scholars have altered the discipline of musicology fundamentally and permanently.

References and further reading

Bowers, J. and Tick, J. (eds) (1986) *Women Making Music*, Urbana, IL: University of Illinois Press.

Brett, P., Thomas, G. and Wood, E. (eds) (1993) *Queering the Pitch: Essays in Gay and Lesbian Musicology*, New York and London: Routledge.

Citron, M. (1993) *Gender and the Musical Canon*, Cambridge: Cambridge University Press.

Clément, C. (1988) *Opera, or the Undoing of Women*, Minneapolis, MI: University of Minnesota Press.

Koskoff, E. (ed.) (1989) *Women and Music in Cross-Cultural Perspective*, Urbana, IL: University of Illinois Press.

Kramer, L. (1995) *Classical Music and Postmodern Knowledge*, Berkeley and Los Angeles: University of California Press.

McClary, S. (1991) *Feminine Endings: Music, Gender, and Sexuality*, Minneapolis, MI: University of Minnesota Press.

Sadie, J.A. and Samuel, R. (1994) *The Norton/Grove Dictionary of Women Composers*, New York and London: Macmillan Press.

Solie, R. (ed.) (1993) *Musicology and Difference: Gender and Sexuality in Music Scholarship*, Berkeley and Los Angeles: University of California Press.

SUSAN McCLARY

mysticism, feminist

Mysticism, within the western Christian tradition, is an unmediated experience of the divine. Feminist mysticism is a term employed by contemporary feminist scholars in their research and reinterpretation of women mystics, many of whose lives had remained in obscurity. The records of others had often been distorted by pious hagiographers (mainly male) who wanted to make these extraordinary women conform to ecclesiastical or doctrinal standards. The period when mysticism flourished was during the Middle Ages, a time when women were excluded from universities, and the monasteries and convents, to which religious women were confined, ceased to be centres of learning. This is not to imply, however, that all mystics were uneducated. Also not all women mystics belonged to religious orders and much interest has focused on the Béguines, lay women from the low countries of Europe who, during the thirteenth and fourteenth centuries, lived communally and devoted themselves to prayer and good works. Many mystics belonged to this movement, but their independence from hierarchical Church structures was viewed as a threat by the authorities and, by the fifteenth century, they were enclosed in traditional convent institutions and subject to the supervision of male clergy. They are nonetheless claimed as prototypes of feminist activity for their attempts to lead lives that provided alternative vocations from the conventional restrictions placed on women of their time.

The feminist reclamation of women mystics takes different forms. The most renowned mystics, for example, Catherine of Siena (1347–80) and Teresa of Avila (1515–82), are often invoked as feminists because of the exceptionally strong impact of their lives and teaching. Sometimes the ecstatic behaviour of female mystics is interpreted as resistance to patriarchal domination, while others view their conduct as valiant, but irredeemably compromised.

The forms of expression of women mystics vary. Hildegard of Bingen (1098–1179) is a visionary whose theology remains orthodox, yet she was the first to formulate absolute love and the divine in feminine form. Béguines, such as Mechtild of Magdeburg (c.1207–c.1294) and Hadewijch of Antwerp (thirteenth century), both employed explicit sexual imagery to depict their quest for union with a divine lover, who was characterised as Lady Love. This search was also one that did not reject the body as sinful, but sought to include both body and soul in the experience of divine union. Marguerite Porete, who was burnt as a heretic in 1310, also spoke of the soul's journey towards merger with a feminine form of love. For Marguerite the final state, however, was dependent on the absolute negation that is part of the apophatic tradition, where God is beyond all human qualifications. In all these explorations (except Hildegard's) it is love that is regarded is superior to reason, for it is love alone that guides the mystic to the intimate form of knowing that surpasses theoretical speculation. The actual feminism of these expressions is open to debate. The argument centres on the fact that though women mystics exercised powerful spiritual influence, they did not strive to reform the ecclesiastical or social structures in ways that would enhance the position of women.

Philosophical analysis of female mysticism is limited. In her book, *Power, Gender and Christian Mysticism*, Grace Jantzen laments that contemporary philosophy of mysticism is limited to post-Enlightenment paradigms, specifically William James's emphasis on interiority and effability, which fail to do justice to the eloquent expositions of women mystics.

See also: Christianity and feminism

References and further readings

Jantzen, G. (1995) *Power, Gender and Christian Mysticism*, Cambridge: Cambridge University Press.

Zum Brunn, E. and Epiney-Burgard, G. (1989) *Women Mystics in Medieval Europe*, New York: Paragon House.

MORNY JOY

narrative, feminist uses of

Narrative (the story to be read in images, texts, music, events) has often been understood in its capacity of representation. It is increasingly analysed as a speech act too: narrative has an effect, it performs acts. For this reason the new narratives created by women writers and artists should not just be analysed as alternative forms of representation, but rather in terms of affection, intervention, and address.

Four of the many possible purposes and effects of feminist uses of narrative are focused on here, namely that they create an identity, they construct a collective history, they effectuate a cultural critique and they offer alternative epistemologies.

Identification can be said to occur through narrative: by appropriating a cultural narrative which structures one's subjectivity and desires by promising ultimate satisfaction, one positions oneself into a narrative. Since cultural authority is traditionally defined as male, women cannot easily claim full cultural and narrative subjectivity through identification with authority. They have to negotiate the restricted choice of subject positions available to them in the dominant narratives of their cultural contexts. Feminists use narrative as a means of re-imagining their own processes of identification, revising and subverting the original (Oedipal) plot. In contrast to classical psychoanalytical accounts of identification, wo-men's narratives often insist on the inevitable hybridity of identity, in which gender is always constructed in its interweaving with ethnicity, class, sexuality, age.

These multiple identities are not primarily created by describing them, but by strategies of address. Feminists and womanists in the African diaspora especially (e.g. Toni Morrison) demonstrate the effectivity of the narrative strategies of address. They revise narrative not only on the level of the story, but also on the level of the text. By varying speaker positions, by addressing a hetero-geneous audience, and by using different discourses and languages, a narrator creates a multiple, hybrid self. At the same time, by addressing it, a new, hybrid collectivity is called into existence.

In the postmodern, postcolonial age, the author-itative master narratives of history have made way for a plurality of narratives expressing different perspectives. Both individuals and communities need a past as a narrative necessary for identifica-tion. Narratives by women writers and artists reinvent a communal historical past in which women appear as agents, as much as men. Since women's histories have not been well documented (e.g. the history of working class women, and the women in the African diaspora) and since parts of their histories have been deeply traumatising, the reinvention of their history occurs through the intense blending, deconstructing and re-imagining of images, silences and narratives into a new narrative. Often myth is evoked as an essential aspect of this narrative historiography.

Feminist uses of narrative challenge the cultural categories that are also, and eminently, operative in narrative, such as time and space. Structuralist narratology has argued that the basic form of narrative consists in two elements in a simple chain: entry into a closed space, and emergence from it. This closed space is then defined as feminine (as womb, home, grave), and the travelling agent as male, as **Lauretis** points out. This gendering of narrative is rooted in a more general western cultural tradition of defining space as female, time and movement as male (see Julia **Kristeva**). In addition, space and stasis are associated with cultural and ethnic otherness, whereas movement and time are related to western modernity. From this perspective, narrative is not only gendered and racialised by virtue of the identity of its narrators, or the content of its representations, but by its very structure. When feminists use narrative to criticise these definitions of time and space, their narratives have a double effect: they transform narrative by working on its basic levels, and they articulate a cultural critique. Marlene Nourbese Philip's work, for example, criticises dominant western notions of language by re-imagining the (repressed) language of the African diaspora as a healing, maternal silence. In addition, she redefines black femininity as mobile.

In redefining cultural categories, feminist narrative can offer new theories of knowledge. As Morrison argues, narrative has always been one of the principal ways of gaining knowledge. The paradigm of narrative modes of knowing differs from the dominant paradigm in the sciences, which has been rendered as 'knowing things' (see Lorraine **Code**). Narrative, in contrast, works within the paradigm of 'knowing other people'. It produces knowledge through interaction, address, performance (Bal 1996). Since, in the twentieth century, women had little access to the privileged paradigm of knowing (dominant in the sciences), the second paradigm has been associated with femininity. Not because of this association, however, but primarily because of its effectivity in articulating both a cultural critique and a new understanding of the world, narrative has been a favoured medium for feminist cultural knowledge production (the centrality of autobiography in feminist theorising is a good example). Feminists have been active contributors to the narrative turn in the academy, using narrative as both the focus and the medium of their critical interventions. Since dominant forms of narrative are so often organised around notions of male/white agency and female/black passivity, a focus on the narrative

of gender and ethnicity implied in many scientific models and discourses can be an effective means for effectuating a (anti-racist) gender critique of science and theory (see Evelyn Fox **Keller**).

See also: literary theory, feminist; literature, images of women in; narratology; psychoanalytic feminist literary theory

References and further reading

Bal, M. (1996) 'First Person, Second Person, Same Person', in M. Bal *Double Exposures: The Subject of Cultural Analysis*, London: Routledge.

Henderson, M.G. (1990) 'Speaking in Tongues: Dialogics, Dialectics, and the Black Woman Writer's Literary Tradition', in H.L. Gates (ed.) *Reading Black, Reading Feminist*, New York: Meridian/Penguin.

Lauretis, T. de (1984) *Alice Doesn't. Feminism, Semiotics, Cinema*, Bloomington, IN: Indiana University Press.

Morrison, T. (1987) *Beloved*, New York: Alfred Knopf.

—— (1994) *The Nobel Lecture in Literature. Lecture and Speech of Acceptance*, London: Chatto and Windus.

Philip, M.N. (1991) *Looking for Livingstone: An Odyssey of Silence*, Stratford: Mercury Press.

ISABEL HOVING

narratology

Narratology examines 'narrative texts', which inform, manipulate, please, indoctrinate, arouse or repulse. They are both cultural artifacts and cultural agents. Narratology studies artifacts that 'tell a story', in whatever medium, influencing how people think and feel about what is being told. It helps to understand, analyse, and evaluate narratives and their effects. The cultural predominance of narrative makes it a privileged site to harbour ideology and to venture contestation. Such a form participates in the cultural construction and maintenance of gender. It provides insights into how cultures maintain gender-biased representations in the face of the contestation of unequal power-relations. The most productive narratology is, then, geared toward critical practice.

Narratives offer accounts of events. Their overt mission is to inform. Even if the story is fictitious or obviously a construction, its affirmative mode solicits belief, acquiescence, or identification. Understanding this de-naturalises the affirmative power of information, instead enabling debate. Once narrative is unpacked in its voices, strands, and imaginative and rhetorical components it will be less intimidating, less compellingly manipulative.

The analysis of the narrating voice affords insight into the identity of the speaker, who sometimes imperceptibly espouses the voice of a character in the story. Disentangling these voices is revealing. The narrator, a linguistic subject of utterances or a visual 'director' of a spectacle, deploys a text of a linguistic, visual or auditive texture. The narrator positions the narrative in a community that can understand and appreciate it; a specific audience.

But narrative's subjective specification is more effective when less obvious. Even recounting objective facts, the narrator's subjectivity precludes an objective account. The events and characters, the place where they evolve and the temporality that determines the narrative's rhythm 'colour' the events. A narrative's seductive subjectivity might be hostile to women. To account for that elusive subjectivity, one asks whose perspective, bias, or experience propels the narrative. Narratology calls this focalisation, its implied agent, the focaliser.

The focaliser's activity promotes identification with some figures experiencing and causing the events, the characters. Thus, one can be solicited, although never forced, to identify with an objectionable character or a painful position. In western culture, many artifacts promote identification with either male characters or female characters presented from a male perspective. Alternatively, by means of the subtleties of character depiction, emphasis, description, or the relationship of characters to their environment, otherness or **alterity** is created, so that identification with female characters or other non-mainstream figures is hampered.

Narratives manipulate by seducing readers into an identification that can be either liberating – being 'like' or 'on the side of' another – or confining – to an identity not sympathetic to one's own. Identification can take different forms. As feminist Kaja Silverman has argued, one can absorb the other in 'cannibalistic' or idiopathic identification: sympathy dissolves alterity. One can also step out of oneself, identify with the other *qua* other, in heteropathic identification. Then, one can stand at the side of someone whom mainstream culture might reject. This helps change social attitudes towards others more effectively than rational persuasion alone. The rape scene in the film *The Accused*, by not producing the spectacle that the rapists allege has enticed them, and by instead developing long-standing attention for the woman who was raped (Jody Foster), might distance viewers from their own standards so that they identify with her. Such heteropathic identification overcomes the cheap but short-lived thrill of sentimental identification with a woman 'just like me', effectively intervening in debates about the sometimes fine yet distinct line between rape, violence, and consent.

Given the abundance of gender-biased visual representations, theories of narrative must also work for visual imagery, like Barthes's *S/Z* (see **narrative, feminist uses of**). He analyses Balzac's short story 'Sarrasine' through codes which the reader allegedly activates when reading this story. *S/Z* places reading within cultural constraints.

One code concerns models of action that help readers place details in plot sequences: because we have stereotyped models of 'falling in love', or 'kidnapping', or 'undertaking a perilous mission', we organise the details we encounter as we read or look. This code accounts for the cultural stickiness of stereotypical plots (soap operas). Another code inserts cultural stereotypes, the viewer's 'background information', to make sense of the figures in the image in terms of class, gender, ethnicity, age. Here, forms of identification or the reverse have feminist implications, according to the narrative's force in promoting identification against the grain of what this code passes off as 'natural'. With the help of the symbolic code, the viewer reads details in terms of an overall theme, for example 'love', 'hostility', 'loneliness', 'theatricality', or 'masquerade'. Together, such codes produce a 'narrative', as a satisfying interpretation in which every detail has a place. This narrative is produced by the reader as a way of dealing with the (visual) text; it produces the story through the processing of a strange image into a familiar mindset. Barthes's theory helps explain the effects of narrative on the reader without imagining the latter as a helpless victim of manipulation. Understanding how the reader cooperates with the narrative to construct the interpretation and accept its affective appeal? makes critical practice less of a complaint than an assessment of what happens, and how it could be different.

The intertwining of codes produced by prior discourses relates Barthes's approach to Bakhtin's. Barthes's starts from the receiver. Bakhtin's **heteroglossia**, the cacophony of incongruous strands of cultural discourses, starts from the side of the sender or writer, or the maker of the image. This view enhances awareness that the text is not unified. The resulting need to pay attention to marginal elements, to fractured discourses, increases the understanding of women's 'voices', even in texts with predominantly male narrators or focalisers, and in texts by male authors – both their marginality and notwithstanding their cultural presence.

See also: heteroglossia

References and further reading

Bal, M. (1997) *Narratology: Introduction to the Theory of Narrative*, Toronto: University of Toronto Press.
Barthes, R. (1976) *S/Z*, trans. R. Miller, New York: Hill and Wang.
Silverman, K. (1996) *The Threshold of the Visible World*, New York: Routledge.

MIEKE BAL

nationalism and gender

Nation and gender construct and reinforce one another: successful nationalisms depend on mobilising particular gender identities, and gender takes particular forms in specific national settings. Metaphors like 'motherland' or 'fatherland' are among the most obvious gendered tropes for articulating nationalism, although abstractions like Mother Ireland, Mother India and Mother Africa perform similar ideological work by at once symbolising the idea of a nurturing (if beleaguered) homeland and at the same time, more insidiously, suggesting a restrictive gender role for women to play.

The understanding that nations delimit gender possibilities fuelled many feminist initiatives throughout the twentieth century. Suffragists and first-wave feminists in Europe and North America directed many of their demands at the nation state, insisting on full legal enfranchisement for women as equal members of a national community, rather than as adjunct wives and daughters of male citizens (see **first-wave/second-wave feminism**). Similarly, feminism developed in conjunction with nationalist independence movements in many Third World locations.

Virginia Woolf's famous dictum, 'As a woman, I have no country. As a woman I want no country. As a woman my country is the whole world', set the tone for second-wave feminism's denial of the importance of nationalism to gender. While Woolf meant her statement to mark a critical distance between feminist women and patriarchal, imperialist nationalisms, it was taken up in the service of such women's liberation concepts as global sisterhood and the universality of gender, which supposed that women could stand outside national formations.

Third-wave feminism of the late 1980s and 1990s disputes this idea. Feminists now recognise nationality, along with **race**, class (see **class analysis**), **sexuality** and ethnicity, as a significant axis of gender differentiation among women. This means not only that different nations produce different genders, but also – and more importantly – that women of different races, classes, ethnicities, and sexualities are positioned differently within the same nation. (Recently, feminist scholarship has turned its attention to the ways that nationalism constructs **masculinity** as well as femininity.) Many third-wave feminists see the state in a more nuanced way, too: as a political body that on the one hand has a history of limiting women's political liberties, but on the other hand serves as one of the only legislative bodies still capable of protecting hard-won rights from the ravages of global capitalism.

The recognition of the importance of nation to gender finds expression in debates about **citizenship**. Contemporary gender theorists understand citizenship to involve more than conventional, formal rights such as possessing a passport and having the right to vote. Instead, feminist citizenship theorists understand full participation in a national community to depend on expansive economic, social and political enfranchisement even when those forms of enfranchisement may not appear to be national in the first instance.

HEATHER ZWICKER

native women, civil rights, and sovereignty

Native people have had to contend with many issues in claiming their rights as US citizens. Their history is complicated by ambiguities in the meaning of 'dual citizenry', and the imposition of 'blood quantum' criteria for 'federal-recognition' of an individual member or tribal group. A majority of Native people who identify as American Indian have loosening ties with their tribal communities for reasons beyond their control. **Kinship** and tribal relations with those living off the reservation have been weakened. Today, only approximately 30 per cent of American Indians reside permanently on tribal reservations, while an increasing number live in major metropolitan areas. Of the 50 per cent of the Native American population who are women, an increasing number are single mothers. Moreover, Native women are still in the minority with regard to political representation and clout. They are among the most disenfranchised and dispossessed members of today's US society, in a political climate in which Native women and their family members are often treated as Third World refugees. This situation is the result of an advanced colonialist and patriarchal history which pits civil rights against sovereignty.

The American Indian Bill of Rights (1968), for example, was written and enacted for federally-recognised American Indian tribes by the Subcomittee on Constitutional Rights. US colonisation had resulted in the subordination of tribal peoples, who traditionally held collective rights that were supposed to be protected by treaty from exploitation. Approximately 400 tribes made treaties with the US government in the 1700s and 1800s. Each of these nation-to-nation agreements has been violated. The Indian Bill of Rights was needed to address this colonialist history, as a result of which *treatied* Indians were treated as second-class citizens, often residing in Third World conditions on reservations, marginalised from US society. However, the Indian Bill of Rights was a paternalistic act which eroded tribal communal and collective rights, and Native women were for the most part voiceless in the proceedings.

Thus, although the Iroquois Confederacy had influenced the founding fathers' conception of the federalist Republic, the Indian Bill of Rights did not contain an equivalent to the Second, Third, Ninth and Tenth Amendments to the US Constitution. Nor did it incorporate the Fifteenth Amendment, prohibiting discrimination in the right to vote based on race. Furthermore, the Indian Bill of Rights favoured Indian men over women, ignoring the significant role the Clan Mothers played among the Iroquois nations in their traditional intertribal governance.

Early records indicate that most if not all tribal societies were matrilineal before the European invasion. Native women held positions of authority as exemplary leaders. Under the coercion of the American colonialists, with their eurocentric subordination of women as male property, these societies changed to patrilineal and later patriarchal ways. This change has eroded Native women's matrilineal and matrifocal authority as Clan Mothers among their tribal peoples (see **matrifocality**).

Native women's loss of tribal status was often the result of marrying outside the tribe, which could threaten a Native woman's tribal membership and that of her offspring. The Indian Reorganization Act of 1934 restructured tribal governments to become part of the US federal system, eroding traditional Indian ways and collective landholdings, and making legally apparent the loss of women's rights. Tribal membership decisions were now being made by male-controlled tribal councils, who practised a form of traditional nepotism that favoured kinship clans and families.

In the 1978 US Supreme Court case, *Martinez* v.

Santa Clara Pueblo, Julia Martinez challenged the decision of the tribal council to remove her Indian status and that of her children because she had married outside the Pueblo. The family was expected to leave the community, and was denied educational, health, and housing services by the tribe. Invoking her civil rights, Martinez sued the Pueblo. However, the Court refused to interfere with the tribal sovereignty of the male-controlled Pueblo council. In this case there is a clear correlation between colonialism, racism, and sexism, evidencing a 'trickle-down patriarchy' in a Pueblo society that once adhered, in precolonialist times, to matrilineal traditions.

It should be noted that Native men are also at risk of losing their Indian status or tribal membership. However, since the tribal councils are mainly male-controlled it is more likely, generally-speaking, for Native women to lose their tribal membership as a result of marrying outside the community, as the Martinez case and others illustrate. Such circumstances also affect offspring of both genders in such cases (*Russell Means v. the Navajo Nation*, 1999).

A comparison can be made with the Canadian case involving Sandra Lovelace Sappier in which a Canadian Tobique Native woman lost her aboriginal status and rights because she married a non-Indian. When Lovelace Sappier tried to return to her community with her son, both she and her son were denied housing services. She appealed to the Canadian government, invoking her civil rights. When the government did not respond she took her case to the United Nations (UN) in the form of a human rights grievance, with the support of a local Native women's movement. In 1981, the UN directed the Canadian government to amend its Indian Act to protect aboriginal women from this kind of discrimination. This was a very different outcome from the Martinez case. However, the Tobique Reserve council decried what they saw as the interference with their tribal sovereignty.

See also: Indigenist feminism

References

Deloria, V. Jr, and Lytle, C.M. (1983) *American Indians, American Justice*, Austin, TX: University of Texas Press.

—— (1984) *The Nations Within: The Past and Future of American Indian Sovereignty*, New York: Pantheon.

Grinde, D.A. Jr. (1977) *The Iroquois and the Founding of the American Nation*, San Francisco: Indian Historian Press.

Jaimes, M.A. (ed.) (1992) *The State of Native America*, Boston, MA: South End Press.

Jaimes Guerrero, M.A. (1977) 'Civil Rights vs. Sovereignty: Native American Women in Life and Land Struggles', in C.T. Mohanty and M.J. Alexander (eds) *Feminist Genealogies, Colonial Legacies, Democratic Futures*, New York: Routledge, pp. 101–21.

Lyons, O., and Mohawk, J. (eds) (1992) *Exiled in the Land of the Free: Democracy, Indian Nations, and the US Constitution*, Santa Fe, NM: Clear Light.

Wunder, J.R. (1994) *Retained by the People: A History of American Indians and the Bill of Rights*, Oxford: Oxford University Press.

M.A. JAIMES-GUERRERO

naturalistic method/naturalised epistemology

Naturalistic method – a product of the 'naturalistic turn' of the late 1960s – reconceives the (post-positivist) epistemological project by eschewing attempts to derive a priori conditions and normative guidelines for knowledge in general. Denying the very possibility of 'knowledge in general', whose conditions could be determined merely formally, naturalists study how specific knowledge is produced by real knowers, in real (i.e. natural) cognitive activities. They derive normative principles from the conditions that make knowledge possible, in real-world practices.

Feminists, disenchanted with the experience-remote analyses of knowledge legitimated by the epistemologies of the mainstream, have looked to epistemological naturalism for ways of reconnecting theories of knowledge with everyday epistemic practices. In orthodox naturalism they have found both renewed promise, and new reasons for disenchantment.

Orthodox naturalism in North America, which

has its starting point in the philosophy of W.V.O. Quine, holds that the best and most reliable place to study 'natural' human knowing is in the activities of scientists in the laboratory. Naturalists believe that scientific psychology offers the best picture of the scope and limits of human cognitive powers: that epistemology could thus become a chapter of psychology – conceived as a natural science. For many feminists, appealing to laboratory experiments that study how people actually know, is an improvement over attempting to derive abstract, universally necessary and sufficient conditions for knowledge. Yet others take exception to the claim that knowledge-making in controlled experiments counts as 'natural'. They question whether everyday knowing can accurately be modelled in scientific experiments, where cognition is lifted out of the very conditions and circumstances that structure and enable it. The sanitised picture of knowing that emerges in laboratory experiments necessarily erases the myriad differences that, feminists have shown, are constitutive of radically different knowings in diverse circumstances. Laboratory knowing is cleansed, too, of the politics of knowledge that positions women – and other marginalised people – at a significant disadvantage with respect to epistemic authority and credibility. Hence despite its promise, many feminists have argued that both the 'scientism' of orthodox naturalism, and its conceptions of the 'natural' require critical scrutiny if the new naturalism is not to replicate the oppressions and silencings that are the legacy of standard epistemologies with the politics of knowledge they engender. Thus Lorraine Code (1996) advocates a naturalism located within such epistemic practices as medicine and law; Sabina Lovibond (1989), a naturalism that analyses the politics and value-systems operative within 'institutions of knowledge production'.

See also: epistemology, feminist; positivism; science, philosophy of

References and further reading

Code, L. (1996) 'What Is Natural About Epistemology Naturalised?', *American Philosophical Quarterly* 33 (1).

Lovibond, S. (1989) 'Feminism and Postmodernism', *New Left Review* 178.

Nelson, L.H. (1990) *Who Knows. From Quine to a Feminist Empiricism*, Philadephia: Temple University Press.

LORRAINE CODE

nature/culture

There are two important, related strands within the nature/culture dualism in relation to feminist theory. The first, broader question concerns how far individuals are products of their nature or their culture. This includes both the issue of how far characteristics and capabilities are inherited from parents, and how far certain characteristics might be common to one or other gender or one or another race. Balanced against the notion of inherited characteristics is the question of how much individuals are shaped by their cultures and traditions. This strand contains elements which have proved important in various contexts and particularly in feminist theory. Relationships to feminist theory are also apparent in the second aspect of the nature/culture dualism. Feminist writers have noted the way in which women have been universally identified with nature and men with culture and the way that this has resulted in women's secondary position.

The question of how far we inherit characteristics from ancestors versus how far our environment, cultural or otherwise, shapes us, has a long history and has been significant in debates over evolution. The problematic quality of the nature/culture debate is shown by the way that certain subordinate groups are considered to have natural characteristics often by members of a dominant group, and these characteristics are then used to explain their subordinate position. If subordination is naturalised in this way it then becomes more difficult for the subordinate group to find arguments to challenge its inferior position. Hence it is clear that the nature/culture question is a highly charged political issue. Arguments are often couched as scientific and thereby gain a measure of perceived **objectivity**. For instance, in the late-nineteenth century, the science of **eugenics** was used to argue for the natural inferiority of the poor. Such arguments re-emerged in relation to the superiority of one race over another to devastating effect in the Second World War.

As the contemporary form of these evolutionary and eugenic arguments, sociobiology claims that biology (i.e. nature) determines culture and our social arrangements. This claim reinforces 'biology as destiny' arguments. Sociobiology has been seized upon in the USA to fuel the arguments of IQ advocates in the discussion surrounding race and class, to justify cutting welfare benefits to poor, often black, women and their children. In the UK, it fitted the ideology of early Thatcherite Britain to keep women in the home and out of the labour market. Such arguments legitimate white male domination over female and black subordination, seen as rooted in biology, and therefore natural.

In terms of women's lives, the nature/culture distinction, outlined above, has been and continues to be used to naturalise women's subordinate position in most societies. Women are held to have certain natural attributes and these are almost always seen as inferior to the equivalent masculine versions. The assumption of characteristics which are seen to apply universally to women is a form of **essentialism**.

If women's characteristics put them in a less favourable position than men in the equivalent social group there is often little comment, as their natural inferiority is tacitly assumed. However, if men are cast in a less favourable light, then it often excites more interest. For instance, there is more concern over heart disease in men than in women although it also affects a high number of women. In primary or elementary education, where girls often achieve better results than boys in many western societies, it has been argued that elementary education favours girls and so should be changed so that boys can perform better. However arguments are rarely made to change university education, in a similar way, where women rather than men are disadvantaged.

The characteristics which are assumed to be part of women's nature often relate to motherhood and nurturing and so women are seen to be closer to biological concerns and to nature itself. This view brings in the second part of the nature/culture argument i.e. the identification of women

with nature and the body and men with culture and the mind.

Hilary **Rose** (1994) notes that women's association with nature and bodily matters involves them in an invisible labour of looking after bodies which leaves men free to make culture and to be involved in the life of the mind. Genevieve **Lloyd** (1984) shows that the association of women with nature and the body and men with culture and reason has contributed to the Cartesian split between mind and body and hence the association of women with the non-rational and men with the rational. The life of the mind is seen as more important than the life of the body.

A number of tensions emerge in the association of women with nature. Val Plumwood (1993) argues for the variability of the concept of nature from one culture to another. The argument that nature itself is culturally determined and is not fixed and objective turns the sociobiology argument on its head and is a challenge to the hegemony of scientific objectivity from feminism. Many feminists see nature as culturally contingent rather than the other way round. Juxtaposing nature with culture is a form of dualism, a structure which Plumwood (1993) argues is always oppressive as it involves a hierarchy within the dualistic categories. Nevertheless, some feminists, writing from an ecofeminist perspective, would like to preserve women's special relationship with nature (see **ecofeminism**). Susan Griffin (1978, 1982) argues that woman's power lies in her relationship to nature which gives her special ways of knowing the world.

See also: body, the; biological essentialism; eugenics; ecofeminism

References and further reading

Griffin, S. (1978) *Woman and Nature: The Roaring Inside Her*, New York: Harper and Row.

—— (1982) *Made from this Earth*, London: The Women's Press.

Lloyd, G. (1984) *The Man of Reason: 'Male' and 'Female' in Western Philosophy*, Minneapolis, MI: University of Minnesota Press.

Plumwood, V. (1993) *Feminism and the Mastery of Nature*, London and New York: Routledge.

Rose, H. (1994) *Love, Power and Knowledge: Towards a Feminist Transformation of the Sciences*, Cambridge, MA: Polity Press.

ALISON ADAM

neoliberalism and neoconservatism

Neoliberalism (also known as neoclassical economics) is an economic ideology that advocates an economic arena free of government regulation or restriction, including labour and environmental legislation, and free of government participation in the marketplace via public ownership; it advocates a retreat from the welfare state's publicly funded commitments to equality and social justice, and the construction of **citizenship** as consumption and economic production. Neoliberal restructuring deepens the divide between the **public/private** spheres of social existence by reducing state commitments to universal public goods. Women are affected in three primary ways. First, women have found some of the best jobs in the pink-collar ghetto in public service, and these are now being reduced (contracted out to private enterprise, or eliminated). That is, the shrinking of the state disproportionately affects women. Second, the privatisation of provision of these goods and services results in erosion of job quality for those who remain employed, as private for-profit companies pay some women less to do what public-sector employees were formerly better paid to do. Third, needs such as childcare, elder care, and early childhood education, not met by the state, and not affordable or provided through the private sector, tend to be met disproportionately by women in the home and in communities for free through 'volunteerism'.

These transformations are legitimised by rhetoric emphasising the importance of individual, familial and community self-reliance (termed 'neoliberal discourse') at the expense of community solidarity. Neoliberal practices reduce citizenship from a universal and other-regarding role with rights and duties to an economic status based on individual self-reliance and concern; and from a public political role to private consumer choice among various market alternatives.

Neoliberalism is compatible with and advances in tandem with neoconservatism, a social ideology advancing a more hierarchical, patriarchal, authoritarian and inequitable society, grounded on the patriarchal heterosexual family and on well-defined, state-supported and regulated male and female roles (see **gender roles**). It is explicitly anti-feminist and anti-egalitarian. Neoconservatism holds that social stability and moral authority inhere in the patriarchal ('traditional') family and advocates modelling other social relations on it. This ideology prefers socially activist governments to the extent that they discipline deviations from the heterosexual patriarchal family, and provide financial, cultural and policy supports for it (see **patriarchy**).

Both citizenship and state sovereignty are eroded through neoliberal ideology domestically and through the globalisation of both the ideology and the free market for capital.

These impulses are implemented through 'restructuring' of business and of government; and through multilateral trade agreements which have supra-sovereign characteristics, and are enforced through the propagandisation of citizen populations, orchestrated through the privately owned and controlled media, and through the disciplinary potential of the fluidity and hyper-reactivity of transnational investment capital on state policies.

References and further reading

Green, J. (1996) 'Resistance is Possible', *Canadian Women Studies* 16 (3).

JOYCE GREEN

Nochlin, Linda (b. 1931)

As Laura **Mulvey** gained an audience for feminist film theory, American Linda Nochlin launched feminist art history in one of the most conservative disciplines. Her landmark essays, 'Why Have There Been No Great Women Artists?' (1971) and 'Eroticism and Female Imagery in Nineteenth Century Art' (1972), were written amid the fire and enthusiasm of 1970s feminisms, creating an uproar. They were simply the most popular in an outstanding scholarly contribution that spanned realism, nineteenth- and early-twentieth-century (Modern) art, contemporary art and women artists. Reading against the grain, Nochlin raised issues about the gendered representation and reception of images of women, the myth of male artistic genius and the exclusion of women artists. Her witty photograph of a nude male model presenting a tray of bananas ('Achetez des Bananes', 1972) parodied nineteenth-century male erotic art, such as Gauguin's 'Tahitian Women with Mango Blossoms', to make the point that 'the imagery of the erotic is gender-specific and non-reversible' (1988: xiii). While controversial, such questions were central twenty later in feminist art history, now a recognised discipline.

Throughout her career Nochlin has adhered to close textual analysis, deconstructing **ideology** in gendered and classed representations of female bodies and femininity. An elegant stylist, she interprets art in socio-historical context, using memorable illustrations and a detailed eye for how oppressive social assumptions become built in as 'transparencies'. Her studies rehabilitate numerous neglected women artists like Rosa Bonheur, Emily Mary Osborne, Florine Stettheimer and Alice Neel, many of whom she analyses as 'proto-feminist' because they are highly socially conscious, notwithstanding their non-conformity to oppositional male art conventions of their day.

Despite forays into the rhetoric of **discourse analysis** (1988; 1996) her work has remained structuralist and potentially vulnerable to criticisms of **structuralism**. She tends to approach **power** exclusively as a 'power down' phenomenon, to globalise, and to assume a univocal readership (eg all middle class, white men). She concentrates on Anglo-American, European art, neglects readings available to marginalised groups, and under-theorises power and agency.

Selected writings

Nochlin, L. (1988) *Women, Art, and Power and Other Essays*, New York: Harper and Row.

—— (1994) 'Starting from Scratch (Beginnings of Feminist Art History)', *Women's Art Magazine*, 61: 6–11.

—— (1996) *The Body in Pieces: The Fragment as a Metaphor of Modernity*, New York: Thames and Hudson.

References and further reading

Gouma-Peterson, T. and Mathews, P. (1987) 'The Feminist Critique of Art History', *The Art Bulletin*, LXIX, 3: 326–57.

Harris, A.S. and Nochlin, L. (1977) *Women Artists, 1550–1950*, Los Angeles: Los Angeles County Museum of Art, New York: Knopf.

LYNNE STAR

normative v. descriptive

The normative/descriptive distinction separates inquiries designed to describe phenomena and behaviours from those committed to discerning or establishing norms, standards for action and/or evaluation. Normative and descriptive exercises are usually separated: attempts to derive norms from mere descriptions commit the sin of deriving an 'ought' from an 'is': a prescription of how things *should* be from how they are. Thus for example, demographic data (descriptions) that show women occupying the 'private' sphere turn into prescriptions about women's rightful place. Feminist analyses of this seemingly neutral distinction note that the **androcentrism** of western thought rests on a series of such derivations, with observations of male experiences and lives, and female lives under **patriarchy**, elevated to inform standards of how people generally should reason, act, know, and live. Feminists argue for situated, empirically specific descriptive inquiries, arguing that they can inform more viable, and less oppressive, norms of conduct (see **oppression**).

LORRAINE CODE

Oakley, Ann (b. 1944)

Having published over eighteen scholarly volumes, six novels, an **autobiography** and a **biography**, Ann Oakley has contributed significantly to the development of feminist social science in both theoretical and methodological arenas. Since the 1970s, Oakley and Juliet **Mitchell** have edited a series of three volumes whose goal is to position **feminism** in each ensuing decade. The publication, *Sex, Gender and Society*, in 1972, however, is one of Oakley's premier works, and is credited with introducing the notion of **gender** as a cultural construct into sociological discourse. The assertion that women's **oppression** is linked to culturally-elaborated expectations of women instead of biological difference became an important analytical concept for feminist theory.

A sociologist, Oakley has focused on the social production of **health** and on women's productive and reproductive work. Her interrogation of the label 'housewife' situates it as a gendered role that services the family and the economy and is predicated upon women's economic dependence and disregard for their own economic contribution. Housework includes the work of caring for and maintaining the health of family members and is fundamental to the economy and the informal health-care system. This burdensome labour dominates all other aspects of women's lives and can diminish women's own health status.

Oakley's work on pregnancy and childbirth locates women's reproductive labour in the web of social relations effected by **patriarchy** and capitalism. She has decried the medicalisation of childbirth, in particular the hegemonic character of biomedical knowledge and its ability to supplant women's ways of knowing. Furthermore, Oakley demands an understanding of health as a product of social and material conditions and has critiqued assumptions about the superior ability of working class women to access the buffering effects of social support.

Methodologically, Oakley combines qualitative and quantitative methods (see **qualitative methodologies**). She has eschewed notions of the objective interviewer in favour of a relationship-based approach in which the interviewer is an important instrument whose presence can influence the outcome of the exchange. Oakley has written reflexively about obtaining funding for projects that challenge methodological boundaries and invoke sentiments of engagement with the subject.

See also: sociology

Selected writings

Oakley, A. (1992) 'What is a Housewife?' in L. McDowell and R. Pringle (eds) *Defining Women: Social Institutions and Gender Divisions*, Cambridge, MA: Polity Press.
—— (1993) *Essays on Women, Medicine and Health*, Edinburgh: Edinburgh University Press.
Oakley, A. and Mitchell, J. (1997) *Who's Afraid of Feminism? Seeing Through the Backlash*, London: Hamish Hamilton.

DENISE L. SPITZER

objectification

'Objectification' was first used in 1970s analyses of film, art and popular media to explore treatments of women (frequently 'images of women') that reduce us to passive, gendered objects (to be desired, exploited and hurt) rather than presenting us as fully human subjects. Objectification theory associates patriarchal and capitalist ideologies with 'male' technologies and unconscious pleasures. Related ideas include the **gaze**, stereotyping, commodification, spectatorship, and the learning of gendered roles.

Objectifying techniques position viewers voyeuristically, overemphasising fragmented and fetishised body parts (breasts, black penises), and/or social attributes (female nurturing, lesbian sexuality). The fragment is collapsed onto a social category or individual who is then understood principally in its light. Abandoned by poststructuralists, 'objectification' is sometimes adapted to analyses of other inferiorised groups: 'the disabled'.

See also: advertising, women in; art, feminist issues in; Mulvey, Laura; Nochlin, Linda; pornography; psychoanalysis; violence

References and further reading

Kaplan, E.A. (1983) *Women and Film: Both Sides of the Camera*, New York and London: Methuen.

LYNNE STAR

objectivity

In empiricist and positivistic epistemologies, objective knowers are disinterested in and separate from objects of knowledge. Knowledge emerges from, and serves, no specific interests or agendas. Thus any knower in standard observational conditions can know in exactly the same way as any other. Objective knowledge is universally replicable and publicly verifiable.

Feminist epistemologists argue, however, that orthodox objectivity derives from and promotes the interests of knowers who generalise a rarefied conception of scientific knowing into an ideal that neither practising scientists nor lay knowers ever approximate. Thus such conceptions yield only a 'weak objectivity'. For Sandra **Harding**, **standpoint theory**, taking material, historical, and cultural diversity into account, can generate a stronger objectivity that is able to address differences in power and epistemic authority. Yet standpoint theory's critics doubt that 'taking into account' can itself be objective, or be sufficiently generalised to inform viable feminist practice. These are ongoing debates for standpoint feminism.

See also: empiricism; positivism

LORRAINE CODE

O'Brien, Mary (1926–98)

Mary O'Brien's brilliant and iconoclastic book *The Politics of Reproduction* (1981) is feminist theory about theory and the world. It transcends traditional social and **political theory**, specifically the work of Marx and Hegel, to develop a thoroughly dialectical, historical and materialist account of **reproduction** and production (see **production, modes of**). In this her work overtakes a 1980s Marxist-feminist cohort intent on production only and debates on domestic labour and surplus value. She is also critical of a **radical feminism** focused on liberation solely through sexual revolution and artificial reproduction. O'Brien challenges the sexist exclusion of birth from the philosophical canon and shows how other biological events – death, sex and eating – are given tremendous theoretical significance in theories of consciousness and history and in the works of Sartre, Freud and Marx.

Reminding Marxists of the importance of reproduction as the 'other' of production, a substructure necessary to human history, O'Brien introduces new concepts of consciousness, labour and value. Her theory of 'reproductive consciousness' contends that for women, birth mediates the separation of the individual from the species. Female reproductive consciousness is integrative, in contrast to male alienation, discontinuity and the uncertainty of paternity. Patriarchal 'potency principles' (52) such as legal rights to the appropriation of children seek to provide 'artificial modes of continuity' (55).

O'Brien was strongly critical of Simone de **Beauvoir** and Shulamith **Firestone** for accepting the male supremacist point of view on reproduction.

'Biological determinism' and 'bourgeois deviation' are common responses to O'Brien's formulation of reproductive labour and consciousness and the revision of traditional Marxist categories, but this is to overlook the social and political grounding of her analysis.

It is as much her work as a midwife in working-class Glasgow as Marxist materialism and Hegelian dialectics which informed her labour 'to give birth to a new philosophy of birth' (13). A highly regarded and engaging public speaker, O'Brien's irreverent vision and exemplary activist commitment was an inspiration to countless feminists. Her speeches and essays are collected in *Reproducing the World* (1989).

O'Brien's work retains its significance in discussions of sexual **difference**, standpoint epistemology and materialist feminisms.

See also: malestream thought; Marxism

Selected writings

O'Brien, M. (1981) *The Politics of Reproduction*, London: Routledge and Kegan Paul.
—— (1989) *Reproducing the World, Essays in Feminist Theory*, Boulder, CO: Westview Press.

References and further reading

Brodribb, S. (ed.) (1989) 'Feminist Theory: The Influence of Mary O'Brien', special issue of *Resources for Feminist Research* 19, 1.
Brodribb, S. and Miles, A. (eds) (1999) 'Remembering Mary O'Brien', special issue of *Canadian Woman Studies* 18 (4) (Winter).

SOMER BRODRIBB

observational method (in science)

It is often forgotten that at the heart of natural scientific research lie both experiment and observation, the latter entailing the observation of phenomena as they occur in nature. While there have been, and are, brilliant women experimenters, unquestionably women have excelled in the fields which demand observation, notably botany, **primatology** and cosmology. While it is tempting to suggest that the process of gendering has led women to eschew the interventive violence of the experiment, this would be too simple and too reductive.

In the eighteenth century, botany was the cultivated activity of both ladies and gentlemen, and a number of women even achieved a measure of recognition and success. This required some literary ingenuity as the Linnaean classificatory system was organised around the political minefield of sexuality and gender as Scheibinger (1993) discusses. However by the early nineteenth century, botany was made into a modern science located within the university and the women botanists were 'elbowed out' (Shteir 1996). Ironically such exclusiveness enriched the cultural world of generations of children. Thus denied recognition as a naturalist, Beatrix Potter created the stories and exquisite illustrations of Peter Rabbit and his friends.

Recently primatology has been dominated by a handful of outstanding women, including Jeanette Altmann, Jane Goodall, Sarah Hrdy and Diane Foss. This non-violent discipline fitted well with the constructions of the late twentieth century – albeit adventurous and comfortably off – both feminine and feminist women. Feminist ethologists watching animals, patiently recording and analysing their interactions have replaced highly androcentric models with new. These focus on infant care, food gathering and female sexuality. Accounts of primate nature, as the nearest species to 'us', are deeply interwoven with accounts of gendered and raced human nature, thus decentring primatology has been integral to the feminist struggle to decentre modern culture (Haraway 1989).

Lastly cosmology, where from antiquity onwards, the record (typically grudgingly) acknowledges the contribution of women to the meticulous observation of the night sky, frequently linked with their possession of 'astronomical computing skills'. Even the great Caroline Herschel herself was a sea of contradictions, subordinating herself to male relatives despite being one of finest astronomers of her age. Today cosmology has a number of highly distinguished women contributors, but despite its encounters with religion, the field has not, so far, been seen as a matter for feminist re-visioning.

See also: participant observation

References and further reading

Haraway, D. (1989) *Primate Visions: Gender, Race and Nature in the World of Modern Science*, New York: Routledge.

Shteir, A. (1996) *Cultivating Women, Cultivating Science: Flora's Daughters and Botany in England 1760 to 1860*, Baltimore: Johns Hopkins University Press.

Schiebinger, L. (1993) *Nature's Body: Sexual Politics and the Making of Modern Science*, Boston: Beacon Press.

HILARY ROSE

Okin, Susan Moller (b. 1946)

The publication of *Women in Western Political Thought* (1979) was a landmark of feminist **political theory**. Okin's work was the first book-length feminist analysis of the major political philosophies of the western tradition, thus setting the stage for subsequent discussions. Okin examines the work of Plato, Aristotle, Rousseau and John Stuart Mill. She concludes that for each of these theorists women's role is defined exclusively by her function in the patriarchal family, and, specifically, her reproductive role (see **patriarchy**; **reproduction**). She argues that this functionalist attitude toward women is an integral rather than an incidental part of these theories. From this analysis Okin concludes that since the inequality of the sexes is an inherent part of western political philosophy, women cannot simply be added to the subject matter of existing political theories, but, rather, those theories must be radically redefined.

This conclusion is the starting point of Okin's second major work, *Justice, Gender, and the Family* (1989). She begins with the assertion that women cannot be equal citizens until the relationship between the public and domestic spheres is reorganised and until public policies facilitate and

encourage the sharing of work previously assigned on the basis of sex. She rejects the approach taken by some feminist theorists that justice is a masculinist concept and hence inappropriate to feminist moral and political theory. In her book Okin surveys the major contemporary theories of justice – principally that of John Rawls, Alasdair MacIntyre and Michael Walzer – and critiques them from a feminist perspective. Focusing exclusively on the heterosexual **family**, she argues, first, that these theories ignore issues of gender and the family and, second, that the family must be part of any adequate theory of justice. Her thesis is that social justice is impossible as long as inequalities of gender persist. In the conclusion to the book, she outlines public policies that would minimise **gender** and lead to the genderless society that she envisions. Prominent among these policies are the payment of all wages to both spouses in a marriage and the division of assets after divorce to ensure an equal standard of living in both post-divorce households.

In subsequent work Okin has pursued the question of the significance of differences among women for feminist political thought and theories of justice. She argues that feminists should not be paralyzed by differences among women but, rather, seek to define the principles of a feminist theory of justice that can account for many different voices.

See also: public/private

Selected writings

Okin, S.M.(1979) *Women in Western Political Thought*, Princeton, NJ: Princeton University Press.
—— (1989) *Justice, Gender, and the Family*, New York: Basic Books.
—— (1994) 'Gender Inequality and Cultural Differences', *Political Theory* 22 (1): 5–24.

SUSAN HEKMAN

ontology

The aim within the discipline of ontology (which owes its name to the medieval philosophers Goclenius and Lohardus, independently, in 1613) is to articulate, very generally, a theory of reality: what entities exist, how is it possible for them to do so, and what are the relations among them? To have an ontology, according to a certain contemporary philosophical way of speaking, is to have undertaken a particular view of what exists, as denizens of the world, as well as a particular organisation of them.

A certain influential twentieth-century doctrine, devised by W.V.O. Quine in *Word and Object* (1960), is that of ontological commitment. This is the doctrine that commitment to a particular set of propositions implies commitment, on the part of someone prepared to embrace that set, to a particular set of entities. As a criterion, Quine proposes the principle that one's theory (which he identifies as the set of assertions one is prepared to make) commits one to all entities that must be counted as 'values of its variables'. Quine, as an empiricist, holds that we find out what there is (the values of variables) by conducting empirical, scientific inquiry. Feminists have generally found Quine's empiricist views liberating, as against traditional classical approaches to metaphysics. They have found that the empiricist approach provides tools for the sort of criticism that promotes the shedding of bias on grounds of race, culture and sexual preference, as well as on grounds of gender.

See also: essentialism; metaphysics; nature/culture; normative v. descriptive; objectivity; positivism; poststructralism/postmodernism

MARIAM THALOS

oppression

Oppression is a broad system of interconnected forces and barriers which (1) organises people into privileged groups and groups which are deprived, exploited, marginalised (e.g., genders, races), and (2) restrains and contains members of the oppressed group by systematically blocking or penalizing their choices and actions. The forces and barriers are of many sorts: laws, implicit rules of conduct, linguistic habits, economic practices, terrorism, social pressure, ideology and values. Membership in an oppressor or an oppressed group does not totally determine one's experience; it shapes experience, interacting with other factors,

like a strong prevailing wind shapes a landscape. Particular events, acts and ideas may be called oppressive, regardless of individual understanding or intention, just insofar as they fit into or express such systemic patterns of social, economic, political and physical forces.

References and further reading

Frye, M. (1983) 'Oppression', in *The Politics of Reality*, Freedom, CA: The Crossing Press.

MARILYN FRYE

oral history

Oral history or the recording of oral testimony is a critical research method for feminist scholarship, a method that has facilitated interdisciplinary dialogue and has provoked substantial debate around feminist epistemology (see **epistemology, feminist**).

Many academic disciplines use oral narratives as a source of research data. As a result, the form oral testimony takes can vary widely, ranging from structured topical interviews to open-ended life histories. When feminist researchers first sought to excavate women's experiences and to recover women's voices the interview techniques of their discipline promised to generate direct evidence of women's lives usually not represented in traditional sources of data. Oral history could, quite literally, break the silence that characterised women's place in academic knowledge production. Giving women 'voice' also challenged the traditional hierarchy of knowledge within western cultures, in which women were assigned as the known rather than the knowers.

In this process, feminist researchers generated a critique of traditional disciplinary research methodology. Feminist anthropologists, for example, demonstrated that androcentric researchers had uncritically accepted the testimony of male community leaders, while interviews with women revealed very different dimensions of the community under study (see **anthropology**). Similarly, when women's historians used oral testimony to illuminate subject matter about which written sources were silent, they also exposed the patri-archal bias inherent in the creation and main-tenance of archival documents and called into question the positivist traditions of conventional historical scholarship (see **patriarchy**; **positi-vism**).

Regardless of disciplinary background, feminist researchers have recognised common patterns that characterise interviews with women. They observe, for instance, that in the telling of their life experiences women tend to position themselves on the margins, not the centre, of events, to understate achievements, and 'disguise statements of personal power' (Gluck and Patai 1991: 48). Such cross-disciplinary insights suggest how hear-ing women narrate their own experiences contains the potential for a distinctive feminist methodology (see **methodology, feminist**).

Researchers using a feminist methodology have critiqued traditional interviewing techniques. So-ciologist Ann **Oakley**'s provocative 1981 essay 'Interviewing Women: A Contradiction in Terms', challenges the social science oral interview proto-col, a challenge that has reverberated through allied disciplines. For instance, the traditional prescription that interviewers should maintain a neutral and objective demeanour might well inhibit the intimacy required to elicit data on highly personal subject matter. More significantly, such a demeanour threatens to recreate an ontological hierarchy wherein the academic inter-viewer (even if a feminist) retains objective knowl-edge and the interviewee's knowledge base is defined as subjective, and therefore less reliable. If, Oakley and others ask, the goal of feminist research is to break down such hierarchies, how can a research methodology that reconstitutes hierarchy be considered feminist? Thus, Susan Geiger differentiates between interviewing women and feminist oral history, the latter of which 'can only become a feminist methodology if its use is systemised in particular feminist ways and if the objectives for collating oral data are feminist' (Geiger 1990: 170).

In the light of this critique, feminist oral historians strive to create collaborative relation-ships, referring to their interviewee not as the subject but as the participant, narrator, interlocu-tor, or interpreter (see **collaboration/colla-borative research**). The researcher asks open-ended questions, answers questions posed by the interviewee, consults the participant on the veracity of the final product, permits participants to edit or revise their 'text', and, in some cases, refuses to edit an oral testimony, but rather publishes it in its entirety. Researchers aim to make the results of their studies accessible to audiences of lay women, including the interview participants themselves. Feminist oral history promises to produce critical knowledge about the lives of women, to make that knowledge central, not subordinate, and, thereby, to contribute to feminist activism.

Whether hierarchies of knowledge and power are so easily dismantled is queried by more sceptical scholars who point to the complications that inevitably arise. Some address the fact that however much the interview is conceived of as a collaborative project, it is usually initiated by the researchers, whose professional interests may con-flict with those of the participant. Ethical issues also arise when a participant discloses personal experi-ences with highly charged social issues, which the researcher may feel politically obliged to make public, but which the participant insists remain private. Does the interviewee feel diminished when, having revealed intimate details of their lives, the researcher moves on to her next project? Most importantly, common gender identity be-tween interviewee and participant may not erase social differences of class, race, age or sexuality which may fundamentally shape the power rela-tions at work in the interview process. Assumptions about shared female experiences may blind researchers to the real social power they continue to wield, even as they hope to bring disempowered women into the fore. For this reason, Susan Geiger concludes that while feminist oral history involves recognising 'existing differences' and forging 'con-ditions of mutual respect', the methodology 'is about intellectual work and its processes, not about the potential for or realisation of a relationship beyond or outside that framework' (Geiger 1990: 175–6).

Debates over interpretation and epistemology have proven equally complex. At one end of the spectrum are researchers who present women's narratives as authentic and accurate reflections of women's experiences. At the other end are poststructuralist analysts who argue that determining the veracity of the story is less important than how the story is structured and what it reveals about power relations (see **poststructuralism/postmodernism**). For them there is no single, knowable truth and researchers must identify the multiple narratives created and deconstruct the discourses produced for contemporary political or personal reasons (see **deconstruction, feminist**). Many feminist researchers place themselves somewhere in the middle of this debate, accepting that, like other research documents, oral accounts provide partial and multiple truths, but that those accounts reveal both discursive structures and material life experiences.

References and further reading

Geiger, S. (1990) 'What's So Feminist About Women's Oral History?' *Journal of Women's History* 2, 1: 169–70.

Gluck, S.B. and Patai, D. (1991) *Women's Words: The Feminist Practice of Oral History*, New York: Routledge.

Oakley, A. (1981) 'Interviewing Women: A Contradiction in Terms', in H. Roberts, (ed.) *Doing Feminist Research*, London: Routledge, Kegan and Paul.

KATHRYN McPHERSON

organisational theory

Organisational theory is the theory of how organisations work, and more broadly, how we think about those assumptions which underlie our analysis of the process of organising. Feminist organisational theory, which coincides with the second wave of feminist analysis beginning in the 1970s, is particularly concerned with the intersection of power and the sexually specific subject, areas that organisational theory generally overlooks in favour of an emphasis on rationality and efficiency.

Early feminist analyses of organisations focused on moving women into organisations, emphasising women's essential sameness to men, or asserting women's essential **difference** to men, reforming organisations by emphasizing in particular women's innate nurturing qualities. In the popular press and in most standard organisational texts, these two views continue to hold sway.

However, with the advent of postmodernism and the deconstruction of all forms of **essentialism**, feminist organisational theorists began to analyse the construction of the categories through which we understand our world, and to call attention to how these constructions are used to exclude and marginalise women. An important work by Calas and Smircich is indicative of this approach. Using Jacques Derrida, they deconstruct the definition of leader to show how it is predicated on a notion of maleness that continually rewrites femaleness as lesser. In so doing, they call into question both the prevailing modernist theories of organisations as well as the organising strategies through which women are to attain success. If women are constantly reconstructed as lesser in our present sexually indifferent symbolic structures of myth, religion, language, stories and ceremonies through which our organising strategies are given expression, what are women to do?

Some feminist organisational theorists are using the work of Luce **Irigaray** and her theorising of sexual difference as the question of the age to evade this relentless repression of women in organisations. Irigaray emphasises that in our present sexually indifferent symbolic structure women are either erased in the guise of sameness to men, or they are consigned to the place of the different as lesser. However, by theorising sexual difference as contiguous, Irigaray creates a place for subject-to-subject positions which provide for new forms of social organisation not based on relations of domination. These contiguous relations form the basis for entrustment, a transformational organising strategy through which the woman who wants is linked to the woman who knows in order to accomplish what neither can separately. This is an organisational move in which women's collective advancement is neither predicated on the erasure of women as the same as men nor on their repression as the lesser, and opens up organising strategies that allow women to shape organisations in a way that suits them.

See also: deconstruction, feminist; post-structuralism/postmodernism

References and further reading

Calas, M. and Smircich, L. (1991) 'Voicing Seduction to Silence Leadership', *Organization Studies* 12, 4: 567–601.

Grazia Campari, M. *et al.* (1991) 'Entrustment Enters the Palace', in P. Bono and S. Kemp (eds) *Italian Feminist Thought, A Reader*, Oxford: Basil Blackwell, pp. 126–9.

Irigaray, L. (1991) 'Women-Amongst-Themselves: Creating a Woman-to-Woman Sociality', in M. Whitford (ed.) *The Irigaray Reader*, Oxford: Basil Blackwell, pp. 190–7.

—— (1993) *An Ethics of Sexual Difference*, Ithaca, NY: Cornell University Press.

Milan Women's Bookstore Collective (1990) *Sexual Difference: A Theory of Social-Symbolic Practice*, Bloomington, IN: Indiana University Press.

Oseen, C. (1997) 'Luce Irigaray, Sexual Difference and Theorizing Leaders and Leadership', *Gender, Work and Organization*, 4, 3: 170–84.

COLLETTE OSEEN

Ortner, Sherry B. (b. 1941)

Ortner, a US anthropologist, made an influential contribution to the emergence of feminist **anthropology** with her 1974 essay 'Is Female to Male as Nature is to Culture?'. She states, influenced by Lévi-Strauss, that '(t)he secondary status of woman in society is one of the true universals, a pan-cultural fact. Yet within that universal fact, the specific cultural conceptions and symbolisations of woman are extraordinarily diverse and even mutually contradictory' (Ortner, 1974: 67).

She attributes this pervasive secondary status of woman to the universal alignment of woman with '"nature", in the most generalised sense' (72), and the fact that all cultures know a difference between nature and culture. Culture is that which works on and transforms nature, and nature is therefore subordinated to it. Man is associated with culture, while woman's reproductive functions make her seem more closely aligned with nature (see **nature/culture**).

Ortner does not argue that the biological functions as such devalue woman, but the system of symbolisation surrounding them. In a more positive interpretation of the situation, and one that allows the system to work for a wide variety of cultures, the difference of woman to man is also her possible source of power. Woman is special as well as secondary. Woman bridges nature and culture. With this essay, Ortner opened up the debate of the relationship between gender and nature.

In 1981, she co-edited with Harriet Whitehead a volume on the cultural construction of gender and sexuality which again acted as a focal point for debate in the 1980s. In it, Ortner writes about Polynesia as a complex hierarchical system of sexuality and gender, where ultimately all female positions are defined by reference to the male.

Her views were criticised together with other structuralist positions which allocated power in binary systems. Specifically, scholars pointed out that nature and culture are themselves constructed polarities which emerge out of a western tradition of thought. To read these positions into gender relations of all cultures reproduces an ethnocentric model. Another criticism focused on the inability of structuralist systems to understand gender relations outside binaries (see **binaries/bipolarity**).

Ortner's later ethnographic work has focused on the negotiations and practices of living in various societies, including studies of the Sherpas in northeast Nepal.

See also: structuralism

Selected writings

Ortner, S. (1974) 'Is Female to Male as Nature is to Culture', in M. Rosaldo and L. Lamphere (eds) *Woman, Culture and Society*, Stanford, CA: Stanford University Press.

—— (1989) *High Religion: A Cultural and Political History of Sherpa Buddhism*, Princeton, NJ: Princeton University Press.

—— (1999) *Life and Death on Mount Everest: Sherpas and Himalayan Mountaineering*, Princeton, NJ: Princeton University Press.

Ortner, S. and Whitehead, H. (1981) *Sexual Mean-*

ings. The Cultural Construction of Gender and Sexuality, Cambridge: Cambridge University Press.

PETRA KUPPERS

Other, the

Simone de **Beauvoir** (1949) originated the concept of woman as the Other in *The Second Sex,* to describe women's oppression, laying the theoretical foundation of **radical feminism**. According to Beauvoir's **existentialism**, we can only justify our lives and achieve individual freedom through transcendence, i.e. concrete projects, in a social world where others may either objectify us as obstacles or means to their own ends, or acknowledge our subjectivity in reciprocity. Women become the Other in an absolute sense when they are prevented by laws and customs from asserting their subjectivity, challenging their objectification by men, and establishing relationships of reciprocity.

Women, under oppression, are forced to deny their freedom and accommodate themselves to a life of immanence as the Other, while men claim subjectivity for themselves alone. Man is the positive, the norm, the universal; while woman is the negative, a deviation, a distortion. Laws, myths, and concepts of woman's nature reflect the projection of men's hopes, fears, and dreams rather than women's subjective experience. Women accept their role as the Other and fail to assert their subjectivity because they lack the concrete means to do so, they desire relationships with men despite the lack of reciprocity, and because they are tempted to flee the anxieties of freedom in bad faith. But gains in legal equality paired with technological advances giving women control over reproduction and lessening the importance of physical strength in production have given women the grounds for waging a separatist political struggle to challenge their objectification as the Other and win their liberation.

Scholars have discovered that Beauvoir's concept of woman as the Other, once assumed to be the application of the Sartrean concept of being-for-others, is formulated much earlier in Beauvoir's work on the philosophical theme of 'the opposition of self and other' in her 1927 diary. Written while Beauvoir studied philosophy at the Sorbonne, two years before she met Sartre, the diary also explores the existential themes of the anquished experience of nothingness and the temptations of bad faith. All three themes are central to Beauvoir's novels and essays from the 1930s and 1940s. Other philosophical influences on Beauvoir's concept of woman as the Other include Hegel's description of the master/slave dialectic, Claude Lévi-Strauss's structuralist analysis of cultural dualism, and Richard Wright's description of the double consciousness of blacks under racism.

See also: dichotomies; 'immanence', woman as; nature/culture; second sex

References and further reading

Le Doeuff, M. (1991) *Hipparchia's Choice,* trans. T. Selous, Cambridge, MA: Basil Blackwell.

Lundgren-Gothlin, E. (1996) *Sex and Existence: Simone de Beauvoir's 'The Second Sex',* trans. L. Schenck. Hanover, NH: Wesleyan University Press.

Simons, M.A. (1999) *Simone de Beauvoir and 'The Second Sex',* Lanham, MD: Rowman and Littlefield.

MARGARET A. SIMONS

P

pagan religion, feminist

The word pagan comes from a Latin root meaning rustic or peasant. Because the early Christians were primarily urban, pagan came to refer to country-dwellers who continued to practise earth-centred pre-Christian religions. Neo-pagans follow a nat-ure-oriented spiritual path and claim ties to pre-Christian religion. The contemporary neo-pagan movement, which overlaps with the **witchcraft** or Wicca movement, can be traced to the work of Margaret Murray and Gerald Gardner in England (see Eller 1993). Murray argues that those persecuted as witches in Europe were practising the pre-Christian religions. Gardner, claiming contact with secret witchcraft traditions, develops his own version of witchcraft which includes worship of the Goddess and the God, secret initiations, celebration of nature's cycles, priestesses and priests, and nudity. While Gardner's recon-struction of witchcraft is influenced by the western occult tradition including alchemy, hermeticism, and masonry, the neo-pagan movement certainly bears some relation to European paganism. With the rebirth of the feminist movement women began seeking the **divine feminine**. Drawing on elements of neo-pagan theology and ritual, espe-cially worship of the **Goddess** and celebration of seasonal rituals, Z. Budapest, a Hungarian refugee living in Los Angeles, claiming ties to European paganism through her mother, in The *Feminist Book of Lights and Shadows* (1975) proposes Dianic witch-craft as a separatist religion for feminists. Starhawk in *The Spiral Dance* offers an alternative feminist interpretation of the 'Old Religion' of Europe, with worship of the Goddess and the Horned God, open to men as well as women. Worship is tied to the movements of the moon and sun, with celebrations on the new or full and moon and on the equinoxes, solstices, and the mid-points in between. Magic is defined by Starhawk as the art of changing consciousness at will. Neo-pagans view all beings as connected in the web of life; many are social and ecological activists. Feminist versions of witchcraft – more female centred, more eclectic, and often less hierarchical than established groups – have provoked considerable controversy in the neo-pagan movement. Budapest and Starhawk crystal-lise the longings of many women for a spirituality rooted in women's experience, affirming the body and nature and the divine feminine. But others are wary. Some have opted to work to transform Christianity and Judaism. Some have resisted the personified Goddess, the High Priestess, secrecy, or following specific ritual forms. The feminist neo-pagan movement is one strand within a larger feminist spirituality movement whose goal is the transformation of patriarchal religion.

See also: Christianity and feminism; Judaism and feminism

References and further reading

Adler, M. (1986) *Drawing Down the Moon*, Boston: Beacon Press.

Eller, C. (1993) *Living in the Lap of the Goddess*, New York: Crossroad.
Starhawk (Miriam Simos) (1979) *The Spiral Dance*, San Francisco: Harper and Row.

CAROL P. CHRIST

paradigms

A paradigm is a network of assumptions that shape the perception of reality shared by a particular community. The notion of paradigms is central to the work of the philosopher of science Thomas Kuhn. He uses the concept to challenge dominant ways of understanding the development of science, specifically the model of rationality that proposes that science always progresses via the discovery of new evidence and the falsification of old theories. Kuhn argues that what counts as falsification is a matter of judgement and interpretation. This represents an attack on the idea of a neutral form of observation and undermines the notion of a determinate set of scientific criteria that can serve as rules for resolving scientific disputes. The very distinction between objectivism and relativism is undermined by the role of judgmental interpretation. On Kuhn's account, paradigms are incommensurable and paradigm shifts cannot be brought about by the force of logic alone (usually emerging from people whose perceptions are not shaped by the dominant paradigm). The notion of paradigms has been highly influential within the social sciences. It is widely argued that a culture can only be understood from within, there being different standards of rationality operating within different cultures.

Many feminists adopt the notion of paradigms to argue that there can be no such thing as value-neutral, objective facts and to convey the idea of there being different male and female rationalities. There is a widespread stress on experience within feminist theory which results in numerous challenges to that concept of objectivity which denies any role for subjectivity. Feminist methodologies are usually characterised by the attempt to ground objectivity in experience, without endorsing the merely subjective. What we perceive as relevant when constructing theories depends in large part on our tacit assumptions, formed by personal (though not idiosyncratic) histories. If women have structurally different experiences to men, it is likely that they will work within a paradigm that is different to the hegemonic masculine one: that assumptions about which questions to ask, which research methods to use, what information is relevant, and which skills to train researchers in, will all differ if women are doing the research. Feminists within numerous distinct disciplines argue that whereas dominant scientific and academic paradigms focus on the discrete and the abstract, women tend to emphasise interconnectedness and particularity. Whether this female paradigm is a better representation of reality, or simply a different one, is a contentious point. Standpoint theorists, such as Nancy Hartsock, have argued the former. Also, the notion of a single female paradigm has generated intense criticism from women who find this claim marginalises their own experiences. The desire to validate the experiences of diverse groups of women, and to recognise the distinct epistemological frameworks generated by such experiences, has tended to undermine the political articulation of a distinctive female paradigm. This, coupled with postmodern challenges to objectivity, has resulted in a widespread celebration of radical relativism. Whether this is compatible with a feminist commitment to the revaluation of women's perception of reality is a controversial question.

See also: empiricism; emotions/rationality; experience; situated knowledges; standpoint theory

References and further reading

Code, L. (1991) *What Can She Know? Feminist Theory and the Construction of Knowledge*, Ithaca, NY: Cornell University Press.
Harding, S. (1986) *The Science Question in Feminism*, Milton Keynes: Open University Press.
Kuhn, T. (1970) *The Structure of Scientific Revolutions*, Chicago, IL: University of Chicago Press.

JUDITH SQUIRES

participant observation

Amongst the research methods of the social sciences, including feminism and anthropology, participant observation has assumed an increasing importance. Rather than using the traditional methods of interview, observation or survey, the participant observer participates in the daily life of the people being studied. Immersion in the culture may bring particular insights not available through other research methods.

Feminist understanding of participant observation highlights the tensions involved. Academic research processes are usually reported in an impersonal, sanitised way denying the role of the personal. Feminists recognise that research is grounded in that no researcher can separate herself from personhood. A feminist studying women's lives, identifying with her subjects, will find it disturbing to participate in a study where, for example, wife-beating is routinely accepted by both men and women.

See also: observational method (in science)

References and further reading

Roberts, H. (ed.) (1981) *Doing Feminist Research*, London, Boston and Henley: Routledge and Kegan Paul.

ALISON ADAM

Pateman, Carole (b. 1940)

Carole Pateman's *The Sexual Contract* (1988) renewed feminist debate on the subjects of consent and obligation in social contract theory and in the institutions and practices of contemporary liberal societies. A feminist political theorist, Pateman focuses on the coercive power dynamics that often underlie apparently consensual relationships. She developed the concept of the sexual contract to reveal the dichotomous character of the fraternal social contract, which signifies freedom for (some) men in the public sphere and subjection for women in the private sphere. Coterminous with, but hidden beneath, the social contract, the sexual contract establishes male sexual access to women's bodies.

In her metaphorical reconstruction of the origins of political society, Pateman suggests the first political act was rape. This primal rape or sexual contract is revived in the heterosexual marriage and **prostitution** contracts, both of which appear to hinge on consent but are actually coercive and serve male sexual desire. Pateman is controversial for her stark representation of sexual relations, as she tends to elide the grey areas between consent and coercion. However, her central point that consent cannot be legitimate unless the parties involved are on equal footing is an important corrective to liberal theory.

Pateman provides an incisive critique of the gendered dichotomy of public and private as it is manifest in **political theory**, law, and contemporary welfare state policies. The dichotomy is legitimated by the belief, best expressed by Rousseau, that women are a source of disorder in politics. According to this view, women are unable to transcend the body and sexuality to fit the model of the masculine individual or citizen. Pateman does not suggest that women are excluded entirely from the public realm, but that women's participation in the public sphere is profoundly affected by their association with reproductive roles. The solution is not to transcend the **body**, according to Pateman, but rather to recognise the political significance of women's bodies and their reproductive capacities, although exactly how that should be achieved remains a difficult question.

See also: citizenship; consensual models of decision making

Selected writings

Pateman, C. (1985) *The Problem of Political Obligation: A Critique of Liberal Theory*, Berkeley, CA: University of California Press.
—— (1988) *The Sexual Contract*, Stanford, CA: Stanford University Press.
—— (1989) *The Disorder of Women: Democracy, Feminism and Political Theory*, Stanford, CA: Stanford University Press.

JOANNE H. WRIGHT

pathologisation

Biomedicine and psychiatry define a broad array of human conditions and social problems as deficiencies of individuals, or disease states, which usually require medical (not political) intervention. Disease categories frequently reflect and reinforce the inferior status attributed to oppressed groups. Some categories function as evidence of the 'natural' inferiority of oppressed groups (as in the case of AIDS), while cultural beliefs about particular groups influence medical understandings of many conditions. Premenstrual changes, childbirth, and menopause – culturally mediated bodily experiences of women – are considered diseases or medical emergencies whether or not they are experienced as such by the individual. Some diagnoses, such as 'dependent personality disorder' attributed to battered women, redefine patriarchal social conditions as the pathologies of individual women. Pathologisation indicates the profoundly mutual influence between the institution of medicine and broader cultural and political values.

See also: AIDS, women and; disability, women and; gynaecology, medical; menopause, PMS, medical; psychology

ABBY WILKERSON

patriarchy

Patriarchal societies enshrine the assumptions that heads of state must be male and male voices rightfully dominate **public/private** spaces. Historically, in the Judaeo-Christian world as under most other world religions, church and state have been paradigmatically patriarchal institutions: late-twentieth-century western debates about the ordination or rabbinical aspirations of women reveal the tenacity of these beliefs.

Although patriarchy has a long history, its introduction into 'second-wave' feminist discourse dates from the 1970 publication of Kate **Millet**'s *Sexual Politics*. The term refers to hierarchical relations between men and women, manifested in familial and social structures alike, in a descending order from an authoritarian – if oftentimes benevolent – male head, to male dominance in personal, political, cultural and social life, and to patriarchal families where the law of the father prevails.

Even where the governing idea is that women and men occupy complementary but equal positions, patriarchal assumptions construct the female position as necessary, but necessarily subordinate, within the pair. A sexual division of labour and consequent social division into public and private spheres acquire justification from patriarchal beliefs that it is right and proper for men to command and women to obey. Yet feminist anthropologists have shown in comparative studies of kinship relations and social organisations that although patriarchal societies are more common, globally, than matriarchal or matrilineal ones, the occurence of matriarchies attests to the 'artefactual' character of patriarchy, to its susceptibility to challenge and modification (see **matriarchy**; **matrifocality**).

In western political theory, 'natural' justifications of patriarchy go back to the Aristotelian assumption that woman's place in man's world derives both from her essential biological, reproductive function (see **biological essentialism**), and the inferiority of her reason to man's. Thus men are to rule over women, in whom the irrational element of the 'soul' overrules the rational. For Aristotle, neither women, children, nor slaves can be citizens. Because only citizens can participate in the political life of the Greek city state, neither women, children nor slaves can realise political **agency**; and because virtue is achievable only in political participation, women, slaves and children cannot achieve true virtue.

Analogous assumptions persist into present-day social-political theory and secular attitudes in areas as disparate as law, education, **childcare** policy, voting behaviour, economic theory, welfare systems, sexual arrangements, and urban planning. Feminists still must counter beliefs that women are incapable (physically, intellectually, or emotionally) of certain kinds of work, or that placing children in day care violates a mother's *natural* duties. The (vanishing) western ideal of the heterosexual nuclear family, with a male wage earner and head of household, and a female sexual partner, housekeeper and child rearer on whose unpaid domestic labour the whole configuration depends, owes its persistence to these patriarchal assumptions.

Almost as prominent as its role in pre-liberal and classical-modern liberal **political theory** is patriarchy's place in Marxist and psychoanalytic theory. Marxists have critiqued patriarchy on issues of private property and the social division of productive and reproductive labour (see **Marxism**), whereas psychoanalytic theorists examine how psychosexual development is governed by the internalised law of the father and the oedipal psychic structure (see **psychoanalysis**).

According to Karl Marx, human nature cannot be understood in abstraction from the social organisation of material productivity. Under capitalism, on which Marx's critique focuses, the two social classes are the working class (the *proletariat*), who do the productive labour, and the ruling class (the *bourgeoisie*), who own the means of production. Not only does the ruling class dominate the mode of production, it also controls the development and circulation of knowledge and values, generating perceptions of human nature and social reality shaped by its own standpoint. This ideology represents the status quo as the 'natural' order of things. Yet because the capitalist social order serves the interests of the ruling class, members of the proletariat who accept it as 'natural' are living in 'false consciousness', which prevents their seeing the world from the standpoint of their own class interests (see **class analysis, UK**; **class analysis, US**).

According to Marx and Frederick Engels, the capitalist division of labour is rooted in the divisions of labour and power within the patriarchal family. The enslavement of a wife and children within this family is the first form of private property: a social evil perpetuated by capitalism. Engels depicts the capitalist nuclear family as a microcosm of the social structure, with the husband occupying the position of the bourgeoisie, and the wife that of the proletariat. Attributing the privatisation and denigration of household labour to the tenacity of this family form, he urges women to reject private domestic labour by entering the public world of productive work. Domestic labour and childcare are to become public, collective responsibilities.

Psychoanalytic theory takes issue with Marxist analyses of patriarchy for reducing psychical reality to the reflection of material and historical circumstances. It focuses on the internalisation of patriarchy within the unconscious, with theorists such as Juliet **Mitchell** claiming that psychoanalysis offers a definitive account of the mechanisms that perpetuate patriarchy, and naming the internalised law of the father as the cornerstone of the late-twentieth-century western social order. Yet if her argument is cogent, it is difficult to see how women, from within a patriarchy that determines even their unconscious, can detach themselves sufficiently to judge whether sexual differences have been instrumental in producing patriarchy or whether patriarchy itself has been the principal influence, generating sexual differences that have served its own self-perpetuation.

Despite patriarchy's heuristic value for theorising hierarchical social structures, for feminists its usefulness is diminished by its essentialism, according to which male dominance of women is an inevitable response to natural differences. Such assumptions sustain ahistorical conceptions of 'woman' and 'man' as universal categories, ignoring racial, class, and other differences. Patriarchy's usefulness as a theoretical concept is contested around these issues.

See also: androcentrism; anthropology; biological essentialism; gender; heterosexism, heteronormativity; liberal feminism

References and further reading

Millet, K. (1970) *Sexual Politics*, New York: Doubleday.

Mitchell, J. (1974) *Psychoanalysis and Feminism*, Harmondsworth: Penguin.

Moore, H. (1988) *Feminism and Anthropology*, Minneapolis, MI: University of Minnesota Press.

Pateman, C. (1988) *The Sexual Contract*, Stanford, CA: Stanford University Press.

Walby, S. (1990) *Theorizing Patriarchy*, Oxford: Basil Blackwell.

LORRAINE CODE

peace

Peace activism is an international social movement which began during the period 1890–1914 when concern developed about modern artillery, including machine guns and heavily armed naval vessels. The interdisciplinary academic fields of peace studies and conflict resolution are associated with this movement. Some see the peace and women's movements as inextricably interconnected. That is, peace is a feminist issue.

Connections between peace and feminism can be drawn in three ways. First, women activists throughout the world have organised to protest war since the early 1900s. Second, feminine culture is seen as embracing values and processes that are more peaceful than those of masculine culture. Third, peace is seen as the absence of both direct **violence** toward women and patriarchal social structures (see **patriarchy**).

In the early 1900s, feminist anti-militarism emerged from within women's suffragist organisations (see **anti-militarism, feminist**). In 1915, with the onset of the First World War, women from 13 countries, including some at war with each other, met at The Hague to discuss alternative solutions to international conflict and established the Women's International League for Peace and Freedom. Emily Green Balch, the first secretary general of WILPF, received the Nobel Peace Prize in 1946.

Despite limited political power and voice, women have mobilised to protest for peace. For example, in 1976, Betty Williams and Mairead Corrigan received the Nobel Peace Prize for their efforts that year to form Irish Women for Peace which articulated a common desire by Catholic and Protestant women in Northern Ireland for an end to political violence there. Beginning in 1977, Argentinean Mothers of Plaza de Mayo demonstrated weekly against a military dictatorship that caused the murder of thousands of citizens. In 1980, Australian-born physician, Helen M. Caldicott established Women's Action for Nuclear Disarmament. Throughout the world, women's grassroots organisations struggle nonviolently for peace and social justice.

Women have worked together – even across political, religious, and racial divides – for common social goals. Women's peace activism demonstrates women's political **agency** and social responsibility. Studies of women's peace movements are an important feminist project because they render women's political experience, practice, and proposals more visible – and potentially more effective.

What would it take for women to prevent war? In her novel-essay *Three Guineas* (1938), Virginia Woolf argues it will take more than women's access to the academy and the public sphere. What will inform women in this process, she predicts, will not be education in the academy so much as women's experience in a subordinated group. To prevent war will ultimately require social change that will transform an education system that reflects and recreates patriarchy, economic inequality, and a militaristic culture.

Why have women mobilised for peace? Feminist peace researchers Birgit Brock-Utne (1985) and Betty Ann Reardon (1993) argue that women's traditional roles have situated them as advocates for peace. For example, as mothers, women may be more nurturing of life and against the death of their children through war. Peace researchers cite Aristophanes's ancient Greek play *Lysistrata* about women who successfully collaborate to stop their men from continual battle by going on a sexual strike. Thus, feminine culture is seen as amenable to peace because it de-emphasises competition and is characterised by caring, consensus-building, and emotional expressiveness. Brock-Utne and Reardon have developed and promoted peace education curricula that embrace nonviolence, interrogate social power relations, and teach for change.

These feminist scholars validate a viewpoint and social processes alternative to dominant and masculine ones. However, by characterising women as more peaceful than men, they may (perhaps unintentionally) attribute too much of the difference between men and women to nature. The attempt to define the feminine inevitably erases differences among women; it essentialises women's identity. Further, this perspective erases women's participation, historically, in armed conflict. Or, military women are explained as having been co-opted by patriarchal culture. This claim may reproduce **sexism** by evaluating women according to predetermined gender norms, denying them the right to define their own experience.

Simone de **Beauvoir** saw it as a liability that women are socialised to be less aggressive than men. Sometimes it is necessary to defend oneself against violence. She believed that both men and women must fight – militantly, if necessary – for peace and justice as human beings (Schwarzer 1984).

Harrriet Hyman Alonso (1993) argues that during the early women's peace movement, women leveraged idealised images of femininity when they had few other sources of **power** or authority. Because of the social regard for **motherhood**, women activists' positioning themselves as mothers was a useful political tool. Alonso points out that many women peace activists, including Emily Green Balch, were never mothers.

Cynthia Enloe (1990) sees both militarism and sexism as having shared roots in **patriarchy**. Military culture and **military metaphors** often associate power with masculinity and weakness with femininity thereby legitimising male dominance over women, including wife battering and rape as a reward of battle. That is, a culture of militarism both produces and is sustained by constructions of feminine and masculine gender.

Increasingly, scholars and activists define peace not only as the absence of direct violence and war ('negative peace'), but also as the absence of all systems of domination ('positive peace'). Thus, patriarchy itself is a form of violence, and peace is the absence of patriarchy. In this view, peace is inextricably interconnected not only with feminism, but with all emancipatory movements. However, peace so broadly defined may lose theoretical precision. For example, Christine Sylvester (1987) argues that subsuming feminism within a broader peace agenda fails to theorise the unique nature of women's oppression and women's resistance to that oppression.

See also: ecofeminism; international relations; political theory

References and further reading

Alonso, H.H. (1993) *Peace as a Women's Issue*, Syracuse, NY: Syracuse University Press.

Brock-Utne, B. (1985) *Educating for Peace*, Elmsford, NY: Pergamon Press.

Enloe, C. (1990) *Bananas, Beaches, and Bases*, Berkeley, CA: University of California Press.

Lorentzen, L.A. and Turpin, J. (eds) *The Women and War Reader*, New York: New York University Press.

Reardon, B.A. (1993) *Women and Peace*, Albany, NY: State University of New York Press.

Schwarzer, A. (1984) *After the Second Sex*, trans. M. Howarth, New York: Pantheon.

Sylvester, C. (1987) 'Some Dangers in Merging Feminist and Peace Projects', in *Alternatives*, XII: 493–509.

Woolf, V. (1938) *Three Guineas*, New York: Harcourt Brace Jovanovich.

JESSICA SENEHI

pedagogy, feminist

Pedagogy is a term often used interchangeably with teaching of any kind, although its origins lie specifically in the education of children. Lusted's (1986) elaboration of pedagogy as 'the process of knowledge production' has been widely embraced by feminists and other 'emancipatory' educators for the attention it draws to the production rather than transmission of knowledge and to the ways in which teaching proceeds. Feminist pedagogy describes teaching situations in which both the substance and the ways of working are based on feminist theory and principles. As such, feminist pedagogy aims to provide students with educational experiences and outcomes that are quite different from mainstream education.

In response to the question, 'What makes pedagogy feminist?' theorists who subscribe to or advocate feminist pedagogy consistently argue that having a feminist teacher or addressing feminist content are insufficient markers of a pedagogy that can be called feminist. From this perspective, feminist pedagogy must attend to how teaching proceeds, not just who is teaching or what is being taught.

The emphasis on process is based on feminist critiques of male-oriented, patriarchal, mainstream education (see **patriarchy**). However, feminist pedagogy is not a simple set of techniques to use in classrooms, but a broad set of principles, commitments and approaches. In particular, feminist pedagogy approaches issues of **power**, knowledge, difference, and language (Ropers-Huilman 1998) in ways that differentiate it from most other forms of pedagogy.

Early work which called itself feminist pedagogy (e.g., Culley and Portuges 1985) emphasised the need for teachers to share classroom power with their students, or at least to use power in nurturing rather than oppressive ways. Feminist pedagogy was to occur in safe, caring environments where power and authority were dissipated. **Conscious-ness-raising**, designed to empower women as students and as feminists, was an approach strongly associated with early forms of feminist pedagogy.

Subsequent scholarship on feminist pedagogy has reclaimed the authority of the teacher, declaring that teachers weaken their capacity to contribute to students' learning if they retreat too far from their institutional and other forms of authority. Indeed, many scholars and teachers now argue that power is to be embraced, not shunned. This position is associated with poststructural theories that offer a complex understanding of power as circulating rather than possessed, productive as well as repressive, and, ultimately, inescapable. From this perspective, feminist educators attempt to acknowledge their power and use it knowingly. Teachers will sometimes be confrontational. Classrooms will sometimes be risky.

In its approach to knowledge, feminist pedagogy proceeds from a view that sees knowledge as incomplete, partial, and produced by participants. All learning is not mediated by the teacher. Instead, students learn from each other as well as from the teacher, and she or he learns from them. Often taking students' life experiences as a starting point, there is an explicit attempt to validate personal knowledge as a legitimate way of knowing. In addition, feminist pedagogy attempts to be inclusive of multiple perspectives and epistemologies, while maintaining a strong political commitment to issues of equality and justice.

Other key issues in feminist pedagogy have centred on speech and silence, raising important questions about the effects of requiring all students to participate actively in class, to engage in activism beyond the class, or to disclose aspects of their personal lives. Questions have also been raised about the important choice of silence made by some students in some contexts (Lewis 1993).

Teachers committed to feminist pedagogy are found in many educational institutions although feminist pedagogy is more commonly, and certainly more systematically, found in higher education institutions (universities and colleges) than in primary and secondary schools. Within universities, feminist pedagogy is most highly developed, both in theory and in practice, in faculties of education, in women's studies programmes, and in other liberal arts and social science disciplines.

The relative scarcity of feminist pedagogy in schools may result from the greater institutional restrictions and imperatives of school systems and from perceptions of the limited space for feminist material in school curricula. Indeed, pedagogical theorists often argue that such institutions, with their focus on assessment and classification of students, place severe limitations on the educational experiences that can occur within them.

Similarly, there are limits to the actual classroom practices that can be enacted in the name of feminist pedagogy. Many of the specific techniques used, such as journals, role play, and peer assessments, are not unique to feminist classrooms. Nonetheless, they are employed more deliberately than in some other teaching contexts, with teachers attempting to be aware of the **hidden curriculum** associated with their practice.

Around all dimensions of feminist pedagogy, there has been acknowledgment of the complexity and contradictions associated with it. Particular classroom practices or approaches are recognised as unlikely to work as intended, and certainly not for all students. Feminist pedagogy's distinctiveness from other forms of pedagogy remains unclear. Its potential for social and or classroom transformation appears highly dependent on various contextual and structural factors. Some critics go so far as to argue that there is nothing methodologically or epistemologically distinct enough to warrant the name. Certainly, there is no simple definition of feminist pedagogy.

Feminist pedagogy is a dynamic enterprise associated with teachers and scholars committed to changing the formal education which has characterised more than a century of mass public education, and committed to social transformation in line with contemporary feminism(s).

See also: education; ethic of care; experience; women's studies (history and development of); women's studies: autonomy v. mainstreaming

References and further reading

Culley, M. and Portuges, C. (1985) *Gendered Subjects: The Dynamics of Feminist Teaching*, London: Routledge and Kegan Paul.

Gore, J.M. (1993) *The Struggle for Pedagogies: Critical and Feminist Discourses as Regimes of Truth*, New York: Routledge.

Lewis, M.G. (1993) *Without a Word: Teaching Beyond Women's Silence*, New York: Routledge.

Luke, C. and Gore, J.M. (1992) *Feminisms and Critical Pedagogy*, New York: Routledge.

Lusted, D. (1986) 'Why Pedagogy?', *Screen* 27, 5: 2–14.

Maher, F.A. and Tetreault. M.K.T. (1994) *The Feminist Classroom*, New York: Basic Books.

Ropers-Huilman, B. (1998) *Feminist Teaching in Theory and Practice: Situating Power and Knowledge in Poststructural Classrooms*, New York: Teachers College Press.

JENNIFER GORE

perspectivism

Perspectivism in theory of knowledge (see **epistemology, feminist**) denies the possibility of a universal, dislocated view of reality, claiming that things and circumstances are known differently according to the perspective (the observational angle or point of view) of the observer(s). Some perspectivists believe that all perspectives will converge into a unified scheme of knowledge; others that perspectives vary so radically from one group of knowers to another that they resist assimilation. Dorothy **Smith**, for example, argues that knowledge derived from the perspective of women's activities differs radically from knowledge available from the lives of affluent, privileged men; Bat-Ami Bar On that knowledge from the point of view of the marginalised differs from that of the occupants of positions of normative privilege (see **normative v. descriptive**). Perspectivism is akin to **standpoint theory**, though it is less explicitly political.

References and further reading

Bat-Ami Bar On (1993) 'Marginality and Episte-
mic Privilege', in L. Alcoff and E. Potter (eds) *Feminist Epistemologies*, New York: Routledge.

LORRAINE CODE

phallic economy

Phallic economy is drawn from feminist readings of structural anthropology. Anthropologist Claude Lévi-Strauss, for instance, argues that the essence of culture lies in relations of exchange: men exchange women to ensure the most elementary of relations between them (**kinship**) and escape the circularity of the natural family (the incest taboo). Gayle Rubin (1975) and Juliet **Mitchell** suggest this describes a 'phallic economy'. Both additionally refer to Jacques Lacan's theory of symbolic castration where biological women come to occupy positions of lack (of the phallus) thereby destined to search for phallus-substitutes in men. But Luce **Irigaray** has posed the question: What if these 'commodities' refused to go to 'market?'

See also: psychoanalysis; transcendental signifier

References and further reading

Rubin, G. (1975) 'The Traffic in Women: Notes on the "Political Economy" of Sex', in R.R. Reiter (ed.) *Toward an Anthropology of Women*, New York: Monthly Review Press.

KWOK WEI LENG

phallogocentrism

The term 'phallogocentrism' is a conflation of the terms 'logocentrism' and 'phallus'. Logocentrism refers to the pervasive assumption that ideas are the origin and organisational centre of all discourse. The term phallus, used most prominently in psychoanalytic theory, denotes that which is symbolically and socially dominant or powerful; though the phallus is not merely the penis, it is heavily dependent upon the visual significance of the penis and is therefore tied to sexual difference between men and women. Phallogocentrism thus refers to the way in which, in patriarchal societies, discourse is organised in reference to the idea of maleness or **masculinity** which tacitly functions as the normative **gender**.

See also: patriarchy

References and further reading

Brennan, T. (ed.) (1989) *Between Feminism and Psychoanalysis*, London and New York: Routledge.

JOAN MASON-GRANT

phenomenological feminism

Phenomenology comprises a range of methodologies, all of which describe concrete experiences of real persons. Descriptions run the gamut from the highly individual to commonalities found across instances, to the seeming invariant for one experience or all similar experiences. This aspect of phenomenology is used by many feminists to analyse experiences specific to women, such as menopause, and specific women's experiences. Louise Levesque-Lopman investigates women's consciousness of gender-identity (*Claiming Reality*, 1994). Sandra Bartky studies the characteristics of gendered consciousness. Maxine Sheets-Johnstone gives analyses of lived **corporeality** in different genders to demonstrate the ways in which gendered embodiment gives rise to concepts within patriarchal consciousness, for example, up/down (*Roots of Power*, 1994).

Another phenomenology, realist, was developed by the Munich phenomenologists, including Max Scheler, and adds reality claims to descriptive efforts. Edith Stein writes about hypermasculinity and hyperfemininity in early-twentieth-century gender ideals, emphasising the need for both women's individual freedom and development of 'feminine' virtues and capacities in women and men alike (*Die Frau*, 1959). Gerda Walther in 1921 criticised the liberalist notion of autonomous individuality and sees human beings as socially constructed, similar to many late twentieth-century feminists (see **autonomy**; **social constructionism**).

A third phenomenology is existentialist, combining the themes of **existentialism** with phenomenological method. This has been a fruitful arena for feminist thinkers (see **existentialist feminism**). The Marxist Frankfurt School's and Sartre's existential Marxisms brought phenomenology's notion of **life-world** into play, leading in part to recent materialist feminist analyses of the concrete circumstances of women's lives: rather than giving grand narratives of the proletariat and its alienation, they detail specifics, for example, of the relation of garment workers to their disabling situations.

A fourth phenomenology, with which the term is often equated, is Husserl's transcendental phenomenology. Because of a widespread and sometimes uncritical rejection of all 'essence' by feminist second- and third-wave discourse (see **essentialism**), few feminists used this method openly until the 1990s, when the first conference with a range of feminist phenomenologists was held in Florida (Fisher and Embree 1999), providing a forum for analysing, from a feminist perspective, the limits and values of several phenomenologies. Linda Martín Alcoff reevaluates the use of experience in feminist theorising and begins a feminist appropriation of Husserl's nonabsolutist elements. Many phenomenologies go beyond description to provide critical elements that feminists are improving upon as they write their own bodies of phenomenological work. Christine Battersby uses a creative phenomenology to establish a 'fleshy' **metaphysics** (*The Phenomenal Woman*, 1998). T. Denean Sharpely-Whiting examines gendered life through Fanon's phenomenology of colonised subjectivity (*Frantz Fanon: Conflicts and Feminism*, 1998).

References and further reading

'Feminism' (1997) *Encyclopedia of Phenomenology*, Boston: Kluwer.
Fisher, L. and Embree, L. (eds) (1999) *Feminist Phenomenology*, Boston: Kluwer.

MARY JEANNE LARRABEE

philosophy

The intersection of feminism and philosophy encompasses many connected projects. First, there is the question of the representation and status of women in philosophy: even with significant gains women are still, at the beginning of the twenty-first century, quite underrepresented in the field. Second, there is the historical project of bringing to light the work of women philosophers which has typically been neglected or misrepresented (Waithe 1987–95). A third area of attention is the sexist – often misogynistic – descriptions of women and 'the feminine' in the western philosophical tradition (Tuana 1992). Among the male philosophers considered important in that tradition only Plato and John Stuart Mill seriously challenge received philosophical notions about women. These exclusions and dismissals have inevitably led to a fourth project which is the basis of what is now called *feminist philosophy*: many feminists argue that the traditional assumption that the male is the norm or ideal of humanness has shaped philosophical concepts, questions, and theories which now need to be critically challenged. Feminist transformations of key philosophical conceptions like human nature, **autonomy**, justice, social order, **human rights**, the **self**, reason, knowledge, freedom, and **objectivity** are thus having an impact in many different areas of philosophy, from ethics, social, political, and legal theory, to **metaphysics**, philosophy of language, epistemology (theory of knowledge), and philosophy of **science**. *Hypatia* (Indiana University Press), first published in 1983, is now internationally recognised as a leading journal in feminist philosophy. Societies for Women in Philosophy in many countries (including Australia, the United Kingdom, Scandanavian countries, Canada, and the USA) provide active forums for debate and progress on feminist issues in philosophy.

Alison **Jaggar**'s 1983 work *Feminist Politics and Human Nature* presented an important discussion of both the possibilities and limitations of traditional political philosophies for feminist liberatory programmes. Jaggar notes that while influential theoretical traditions like liberalism and Marxism provide some insights into the causes and perpetuation of women's oppression, they often overlook the roles of biology, reproduction, and sexual politics in women's lives – these issues have been more directly addressed in **radical feminism**, psychoanalytic feminism, and in socialist feminism which stresses the political significance of social relations in both the **public/private** spheres.

The framework of the debate in feminist philosophy has shifted since the mid-1980s. Many have voiced concern about the general project of determining which overarching theoretical perspective 'wins out' in providing the best explanation of women's situation, especially when any woman's experience is shaped by many interrelated dimensions. More significant, however, is the concern that such theoretical perspectives have often failed to address significant differences among women with respect to **race**, class, **sexuality**, and other social status/power relations (see also **class analysis, UK**; **class analysis, US**). The developments of **black feminism(s)**, **lesbian feminism**, and **identity politics** have provided significant challenges to feminist theories which project general and uniform accounts of women's diverse experiences.

The project of *philosophy* itself, insofar as it seeks general, abstract, and universal accounts of personhood, truth, knowledge, morality, and so on, has also been the object of feminist scrutiny. Some have argued that philosophy has regularly been defined as a distinct and valuable enterprise through a devaluation of, and contrast with, modes of thought and experience that are associated with 'woman' or the symbolic 'feminine'. In Simone de **Beauvoir**'s words, woman has been 'the Other' of the ideal philosopher subject (Le Doeuff 1991). While postmodernist/poststructuralist theories generally critique the notion of a 'master discourse' that is to provide privileged representations of reality, reason, and truth, feminist projects provide crucial insight into the gender-codedness of such discourses, particularly in terms of the way in which they frame the possibilities and expression of thought (see also Luce **Irigaray**; **French feminism**). Many feminist philosophers do not endorse some forms of relativism promoted in postmodernist thought, especially those that question the use of 'gender' as a relatively stable category of analysis and thus undermine efforts to articulate and address systematic injustices in women's experiences. The ongoing debates engendered by these different feminist positions are providing some of the most challenging new thinking that feminism is bringing to philosophy.

Philosophical thinking has relied on conceptual **dichotomies** and dualisms where the masculine-coded term is regularly valued over the feminine-coded term: mind over body, reason over emotion, culture over nature, objectivity over subjectivity, the theoretical over the practical. In response to this, some feminist philosophers have stressed the need to revalue concepts and qualities associated with 'the feminine' – in ethics, for instance, the virtues associated with an **ethic of care**. Others argue that simply revaluing these qualities risks reinforcing these dichotomies which, instead, need to be uprooted. Feminist projects in epistemology and philosophy of science, for example, are showing that philosophical understandings of objectivity are enhanced by taking account of knowing subjectivities and knowledge projects in their situated social, historical, and political contexts (Code 1991; Harding 1991). As a result of feminist work, some stubborn separations between different areas of philosophy (between moral philosophy and philosophy of science, for instance) are being reexamined. In maintaining strong links with feminist theorising in other areas, feminist philosophy is also bringing new dimensions of interdisciplinarity and political awareness to philosophy, a discipline that, in the twentieth century particularly, too often tended toward remoteness and questionable social relevance.

See also: androcentrism; critical theory, feminism and; deconstruction, feminist; emotions/rationality; epistemology, feminist; essentialism; ethics, feminist; existentialism; liberal feminism; logocentrism; Marxism; political science; poststructuralism/postmodernism; science, philosophy of

References and further reading

Code, L. (1991) *What Can She Know? Feminist Theory and the Construction of Knowledge*, Ithaca, NY: Cornell University Press.

Garry, A. and Pearsall, M. (eds) (1996) *Women, Knowledge, and Reality: Explorations in Feminist Philosophy*, London, New York: Routledge, 2nd edn.

Harding, S. (1991) *Whose Science? Whose Knowledge? Thinking from Women's Lives*, Ithaca, NY: Cornell University Press.

Jaggar, A.M. (1983) *Feminist Politics and Human Nature*, Totowa, NJ: Rowman and Allanheld.

Jaggar, A.M. and Young, I.M. (1998) *A Companion to Feminist Philosophy*, Oxford: Blackwell.

Le Doeuff, M. (1991) *Hipparchia's Choice: An Essay Concerning Women, Philosophy, etc.*, trans. T. Selous, Oxford: Basil Blackwell.

Rooney, P. (1994) 'Recent Work in Feminist Discussions of Reason', *American Philosophical Quarterly* 31, 1: 1–21.

Tuana, N. (1992) *Woman and the History of Philosophy*, New York: Paragon.

Vogler, C. (1995) 'Philosophical Feminism, Feminist Philosophy', *Philosophical Topics* 23, 2: 295–319.

Waithe, M.E. (ed.) (1987–95) *A History of Women Philosophers*, vols 1–4, Dordrecht and Boston: Kluwer Academic Publishers.

PHYLLIS ROONEY

political correctness

First invoked literally in the 1793 US Supreme Court decision *Chishold* v. *Georgia*, between the nineteenth century and the 1960s political correctness was used ironically among leftists to characterise extreme interpretations of political doctrine. Later it was deployed in esoteric debates about the 'correct' interpretation of the Marxist corpus, political structures, and alliances.

Its ironic deployment has been strategically elided in the neoconservative **backlash** against new social movements; *politically correct* has become *political correctness* or PC and synonymous with 'McCarthyism of the left' and illiberal education. Dorothy **Smith** and Ellen Messer-Davidow deconstruct how PC functions as an ideological code to discipline feminists. However, Camille Paglia and Christina Hoff Sommers deploy PC against feminists with whom they disagree. According to Catherine **Stimpson**, the reversal in PC's meaning has 'taken hold to such a degree that the label, "'You're P.C.", can now be slapped on like a gag'. It is invoked to censure feminist perspectives on sexual harassment, date rape, sexual minority rights, affirmative action, chilly climate, curriculum review, and *avante garde* perspectives like postmodernism (see **poststructuralism/postmodern-ism**).

See also: backlash; Marxism; postcolonialist feminism; queer theory

References and further reading

Clark, V., Garner Nelson, S., Higonett, M. and Katrak, K.H. (1996) *Anti-Feminism in the Academy*, New York: Routledge.

Messer-Davidow, E. (1996) *Disciplining Feminism: Episodes in the Discursive Production of Social Change*, Durham, NC: Duke University Press.

Stimpson, C. (1993) 'Dirty Minds, Dirty Bodies, Clean Speech', *Michigan Quarterly Review* (Summer).

MALINDA S. SMITH

political economy, feminist

Feminist political economy is an approach to the economy which explores every nook and cranny of women's material lives, entering into areas of everyday life that conventional economics has considered none of its business. Its starting point is the belief that the sexual division of labour is historically produced rather than biologically given. The origins of political economy lie in the practical struggles of women, most notably during the period from the late 1960s. The method and the substance of feminist political economy mark a radical move beyond orthodox economics, dissolving traditional boundaries both between 'the economy' and wider social relationships and between the 'public' and the 'private' (see **public/private**). From this broader scope derives the term 'political economy' rather than simply 'economics'.

Economists conventionally assume that their subject matter is markets, i.e. the exchange of goods and services, and the allocation of scarce resources. They assume these markets – whether they are markets in labour, commodities or capital – can be understood separately from a study of the institutions which frame them and which influence the power of different players within them. The **family** is such an institution. The sexual division

of labour within it; its role in the sexual division of labour throughout the wider economy – this was the initial focus of feminist political economy. 'A woman's work is never done' the saying goes. The young feminists in the 1970s, coming from higher education with expectations of social and occupational equality, uttered this familiar phrase not with a fatalistic sigh but as a statement of a reality that needed analysing in order to change it. They challenged the complacent assumption that housework, women's privatised labour, would disappear with the advance of technology. The search for an explanation about how housework had survived in this gender-based form generated a prolonged debate about how to analyse this distinctive form of labour – unpaid and outside the market. Although there is no single feminist consensus, common to different strands in feminist political economy is an explanation of the division of labour both between waged work and unpaid domestic labour and between the majority of women and men within the paid labour market which understands male domination (some would use the term **patriarchy**) as a distinct and irreducible force. Most feminist economists understand this irreducible gender dimension as combining with class relations and the character of the state to produce historical and structural variations in the ways that women are materially subordinate. Feminist political economy, in tackling the wider economic changes necessary to overcome the material subordination of women, has come to address many fundamental issues: working time; the scope and responsiveness of public services; the planning of cities; the organisation of transport and housing systems to meet the needs of women and children (e.g. with bus routes to childcare facilities or housing estates that include childcare centres).

Feminist political economy is also in the forefront of revealing the previously invisible hold of multinational companies on the lives of poor women in the southern hemisphere, through homeworking, sub-contracting to low paying local companies and through casual employment. Frequently the groundwork of feminist economic analysis is prepared by insights that come from women's movements challenging aspects of the economy that have never before been questioned. This importance of ideas arising from practical experience has always been a characteristic of feminist political economy. Many leading feminist economists, most notably Diane Elson, Nancy Folbre, Swasti Mitter and Jean Gardiner, work closely with either pioneering grassroots organisations of women, for instance Homenet, a British based organisation of homeworkers, or with national or international organisations such as Industrial Restructuring Network of Europe (IRENE) or the UN's UNIFEM, working on their behalf.

One contribution of these feminist economists is to bring to public view the experience of millions of women whose economic position is not recognised by conventional statisticians, legislators and trade unionists because they work outside the regulated, unionised sectors of the economy, in sweatshops or at home. In the process, these feminist economists have moved from analysing women's experience of economic subordination to documenting and theorising their efforts at transforming economic power.

References and further reading

Gardiner, J. (1997) *Gender, Care and Economics*, London: Macmillan Press.

Himmelweit, S. (ed.) (2000) *The Household; from Labour to Care*, London: Macmillan.

Rowbotham, S. and Mitter, S. (eds) (1994) *Dignity and Daily Bread*, London: Routledge.

HILARY WAINWRIGHT

political studies

The study of politics is increasingly overflowing its disciplinary boundaries, due in no small measure to the influence of **feminism** which has insisted on widening definitions of the political. The centrality of **power**, both in defining what is political and in analyses of **gender** inequality, has meant that developments in feminism affect an understanding of politics itself. As a result, many arts and social science departments with an interest in the way language, discourse and culture, or economy and space help constitute and sustain sexual difference might now be identified with political studies in a broad sense. Politics departments have themselves, however, tended to remain on the more traditional terrain of political theory or philosophy on the one hand; of political science and institutions on the other. There has been a general reluctance to expand definitions of the political beyond the realm of the state and the term's meaning is therefore itself a site of political contestation. To some extent the battle lines here coincide with those between the dominant Anglo-American approaches (which focus on formal analyses of public justice in political theory and on more behaviouralist accounts of political activity in political science) and continental philosophy where poststructuralist and psychoanalytical influences have been especially strong (see **poststructuralism/postmodernism**; **psychoanalysis**). In mapping political studies from the perspective of feminism I will begin with a discussion of the discipline's two main components, before concluding with a more general consideration of how feminists have challenged traditional understandings of the meaning and scope of the political.

In **political theory** feminists have reread the history of political ideas, identifying not only what it says about women's role in the polity, but also its foundational assumptions about women's (and men's) natures and functions; the way gender-related **metaphors** render even apparently gender-neutral or emancipatory discourses constitutive of hierarchical sexual difference; the assumptions and inconsistencies that reproduce unequal **citizenship** and legitimise women's exclusion from public life. Recognitions of the **public/private** distinction; the coincidence of norms for **masculinity**, humanity and civic virtue; explicitly discriminatory legal or political structures, and metaphysical edifices identifying women with nature or nonreason, have been important in explaining the profundity with which gender power operates. At the same time such recognitions have inspired feminists to seek more woman-friendly concepts and thus to challenge some of the deepest foundations on which political thought rests.

Political scientists are more interested in empirical than normative questions (see **normative v. descriptive**). Like other scientists, they aim to collect and collate data in an objective, value-free way in order to identify and predict regularities in behaviour (see **objectivity**). Their focus is therefore on the more visible, overt workings of power. Feminist responses to this part of the discipline have been mixed. Some have challenged the epistemological assumptions that underlie it, questioning both the alleged value-neutrality of studies that must make choices regarding their research interests and the theories of knowledge that separate knower from known in a rigid (and, some would argue, a quintessentially masculine) way (see **epistemology, feminist**). Others have criticised the discipline for ignoring women's political activities. In part this reflects political scientists' traditional lack of interest in women, but their association of political behaviour only with the sort of activities conventionally undertaken by men has also contributed to women's invisibility while helping to define the discipline in a male-centred way.

Other feminists have nevertheless insisted on the importance of social scientific methods, while acknowledging their own political commitments. Their success in infiltrating the discipline, coupled with their determination to generate data-bases about women's political activities, has succeeded in making women's political life more visible. Gender has become a significant variable in predicting, for example, voting behaviour, while women's experiences as makers or recipients of legal and policy decisions, as well as their roles in government, political parties and interest groups, have moved up the political science agenda. Indeed the women's movement, with its tactics, goals and successes, has itself become a subject for study.

Feminism has, then, influenced political studies on a number of fronts. It has challenged its basic ideas and methodologies and considerably broadened its research topics. But it has also contested – even thrown into crisis – definitions of the political. Some expansion of the category of the political was always intended by the women's movement, since the earliest feminists insisted on the political implications of, and civil rights within, the domestic sphere. Kate **Millet**'s identification of patriarchy with sexual politics, on the grounds that its often personal and intimate manifestations are supported by public structures of power, has also been widely embraced. Poststructuralists' insistence on the interweaving of power and knowledge and their focus on the politics of the **self** have subsequently rendered power even more ubiquitous, if largely invisible. Their attention to the construction of (diversely) gendered identities and sexed bodies has been immensely influential in redrawing the maps of gender politics, but in ways that have tended to find more enthusiasm outside politics departments themselves.

In conclusion: political studies and feminism are related in a variety of ways. Feminists have been pleased to use the discipline's scientific methods to increase women's political visibility and to research their political activity, while questioning its methodology and dominant perspective as too masculine. They have used its theoretical constructs to understand sexual inequality and difference but have also criticised those constructs as gender-biased. They have politicised an often apolitical discipline while contesting the boundaries of the political and thus the parameters and paradigms of the discipline itself.

See also: Cartesianism, feminist critiques of; citizenship; civil rights; cultural politics; egalitarianism; equality/difference; fact/value distinction; identity politics; language, gender and power; state theory

References and further reading

Butler, J. and Scott, J. (ed.) (1992) *Feminists Theorize the Political*, London and New York: Routledge.

Coole, D. (1988) *Women in Political Theory*, Hemel Hempstead and Boulder, CO: Harvester-Wheatsheaf.

Dean, J. (ed.) (1997) *Feminism and the New Democracy*, London: Sage.

Lovenduski, J. and Norris, P. (eds) (1996) *Women in Politics*, Oxford: Oxford University Press.

Millet, K. (1977) *Sexual Politics*, London: Virago.

Shanley, M.L. and Narayan, U. (1997) *Reconstructing Political Theory*, Cambridge, MA: Polity Press.

Squires, J. (2000) *Gender in Political Theory*, Cambridge, MA: Polity Press.

DIANA COOLE

political theory

Historically, political theory has been an academic field devoted to normative questions related to government and the state. In this tradition, Plato's thought is often contrasted with that of the pre-Socratics in order to make the point that he is the first philosopher in the west to speak about a particular, state and human-centred notion of politics. That is, Plato understands human behaviour not merely as an outcome of the forces of nature, the cosmos or fate, but rather as an outcome of the actions of human beings themselves acting within states. Most political theory since Plato has adopted this basic viewpoint.

Since the 1960s, however, the state has been decentred as the locus of the political. Indeed, feminist and new left slogans such as 'the personal is political' both contribute to and reflect the new multi-centred politics. As a consequence, the field of political theory has been transformed such that one can now speak of a feminist political theory. While feminism was a topic of discussion in early-twentieth-century political theory (most notably in the works on Harriet Taylor, John Stuart Mill, Virginia Woolf and Mary Wollstonecraft), the most significant strides towards the development of a specifically feminist theory have come post-1960s. It was after this time that feminist theory moved significantly away from liberal arguments cast in terms of a woman's right to be equal to the men of her class and race and began to have a theory based on its own political assumptions. Twentieth-century feminist political theory was concerned with a wide range of topics: personal politics, the **public/private** distinction, the care/justice debate, equality/difference, sex and **gender** and production and **reproduction** (see also **production, modes of**). Other issues central to feminist theory in general such as motherhood, sexuality, standpoint epistemology, and the category Woman itself are certainly germane to feminist political theory. The case can be made, in fact, that since a major tenet of feminism is its vastly expanded notion of politics, that all feminist theory is also, by definition, political theory.

Building on the liberal insights of the eighteenth through to the early twentieth centuries, feminists have eschewed theories of human nature that understand women as ahistorical figures associated with reproductive functions and have tended to move toward favouring theories of social construction as foundational. Thus, feminists tend to begin from (though not always accept) the assumption of a sex/gender dichotomy (see **dichotomies**). The former is a biological state of being, while the latter is the social meaning of that condition. Marx and Freud have emerged as major influences on feminist political theory though others like Simone de **Beauvoir** and Gayle **Rubin** adopt the socially constructionist viewpoints of other thinkers like Sartre or Lévi-Strauss. Rubin uses the latter's structuralist theories to argue in the nexus of a 'sex/gender systems' wherein the female body and the social system of gender function together in women's subordination.

Beginning with Beauvoir, many feminists have employed the insight that 'woman' is considered 'other' to, and therefore less than, man in all realms of life. The terms 'Woman' and 'Man' are not merely two terms with opposite though equivalent meanings, but rather the man/woman dualism is a hierarchy with man and the masculine being systematically placed above woman and the feminine. Further, femininity has been conceptualised as a social role where women are essentially taught to be passive. Early feminists split on the question of whether this implies that women need to become less feminine, or whether femininity needs to be re-valued. Critics of the first view claim that the supposedly neutral category 'human' looks suspiciously similar to what is meant by 'man'. On the other side, feminists wonder whether privileging the feminine is not merely valorising a dimension of human behaviour that has been developed under the oppressive conditions of patriarchy. That is, isn't 'femininity' a patriarchal category just as much as 'masculinity' is? This seems to suggest that we need to conceptualise the post-patriarchal human in fundamentally new ways.

Another important strain of feminist political theory has taken the form of a critique of the canon of western political thought. The earliest examples of this kind of work concentrate on the extent to which the body, reproduction, childcare and other overall responsibilities for the family are repeatedly deemed to be the domain of the female. It was usually the case that women were only conceptualised as political actors to the extent that they could transcend this function. Thus, as Susan **Okin** argues, it is no accident that women are allowed to be rulers in Plato's scheme in *The Republic* only insofar as Plato proposes the abolition of the family for the ruling class, and thus inadvertently frees women to be individuals equal in all regards to the men of their class. As this example shows, it is generally the case in western political theory, that politics is considered to be the realm of the public and of freedom. But women tend to live out their lives in the realm of the private where the demands of necessity interfere with the goals of freedom and politics. As such, the private realm is something to be transcended, and this can be accomplished only by men who can rise above the immediate needs of the family and become citizens.

More recent works have made the point that it is not merely woman's subordination in the **family**, but her sexual subordination that interferes with her being conceptualised as fully human either in political theory or in legal systems. These kinds of arguments were particularly central during the so-called 'sexuality debates' of the 1980s. It was then that a connection was made between **pornography** and male domination.

While some have seen **sexuality** as central to women's oppression and feminist theory, others have tended to name 'motherhood' as the more significant and universal female experience. The role given to **motherhood** in female socialisation and experience is so pivotal, such theorists argue, that one could not understand 'woman' without first coming to terms with the impact and function of motherhood in women's lives. Though a psychologist by training, Carol **Gilligan** is perhaps the most significant of these figures from the point of view of political theory. In her *In A Different Voice*, Gilligan makes the now well-known argument that women tend to make moral choices according to an '**ethic of care**' while men tend to do so from the more abstract point of view of an 'ethic of justice'. The subsequent care/justice debate was touched off by the concerns of some feminists that Gilligan's work seemed to imply that female nature is different from male nature.

As feminist theory moved forward in theorising woman's subordination and the conditions under which she might be liberated, theorists began to ponder the nature of 'Woman' itself as a foundational category. Arguments based on assumptions about 'women's experiences' or 'woman's experience' were especially vulnerable to the question, 'which women?' Could Woman be understood as a unified category of people with a shared experience and epistemological point of view? If it could not be so interpreted, was the basis for feminism itself undercut? The ensuing debates about essentialism and poststructuralism consumed the attention of many feminists throughout the 1980s and 1990s. The greatest strides with regard to maintaining the integrity of the category Woman have perhaps come in the form of feminist **standpoint theory** which has argued that there is an epistemological female, and subsequently, a feminist, standpoint of knowledge. Still, the rather relentless criticism from poststructuralist critics and their sympathisers has led to a gradual deconstruction of the category Woman. This was only made worse by the fact that white feminist theorists have never solved the problem of the extreme variations within the category women with regard to race, ethnicity, and culture. Gender, it is now claimed by some, is a performance with no essential, a priori status. Thus, the very subject of feminist politics, women, seems to have disappeared under the scrutiny of theory. Exciting new bodies of thought connected to 'queer theory' have moved forward from the critiques of essentialism to promising discussions of the nature of the gender division itself.

References and further reading

Butler, J. (1989) *Gender Trouble*, New York and London: Routledge.

Coole, D. (1988) *Women in Political Theory*, Hemel Hempstead and Boulder, CO: Harvester-Wheatsheaf.

Di Stephano, C. (1991) *Configurations of Masculinity: A Feminist Perspective on Modern Political Theory*, Ithaca, NY: Cornell University Press.

Hartsock, N. (1999) *The Feminist Standpoint Revisited and Other Essays*, Boulder, CO: Westview Press.

Hekman, S. (1992) *Gender and Knowledge: Elements of a Postmodern Feminism*, Boston: Northeastern University Press.

MacKinnon, C. (1989) *Toward A Feminist Theory of*

the State, Cambridge, MA: Harvard University Press.

Shanley, M. and Pateman, C. (eds) (1991) *Feminist Interpretation and Political Theory*, University Park: Pennsylvania State University Press.

JUDITH GRANT

Pollock, Griselda

Griselda Pollock is a British art historian who draws on contemporary critical theory to analyse the role of art practices and the discourses of art history in sustaining or contesting hierarchies of gender, class, race and sexuality. She began her career in England in the 1970s, when feminists were keenly critical of images of women in popular culture. In 1977, Pollock published an influential essay, 'What's Wrong with Images of Women?', in which she argues that the rubric of 'images of women' should be abandoned, because it treats images as reflections of an already meaningful reality, which could be judged as 'true' or 'false' independent of the system of signs which produce meaning. This realist framework naturalises concepts of gender, whereas the semiotic approach she advocates 'questions the obviousness of Woman' (1977: 28). According to semiotics, the concepts of femininity and masculinity are terms in a language system; each gains its meaning through its difference from the other, and not from its reference to men and women.

In the 1980s, Pollock published two books that intervene in the discourses of art history. In *Old Mistresses* (1981), Pollock and co-author Rozsika Parker argue that it is not by ignoring women artists, but by categorising their art practices as 'inferior' and 'feminine' – which requires acknowledging that women do make art – that art historians produce a masculine discourse that supports the hegemony of male artists. In *Vision and Difference* (1988), she draws on a range of methodologies, including **Marxism**, **psychoanalysis** and Foucault's **discourse analysis**, to challenge traditional disciplinary discourses of art history which perpetuate gendered regimes of knowledge and power. Throughout her career, Pollock has consistently reflected on the practice of

being a feminist intellectual and critic. In her words, 'To write or speak or read as a feminist is to put sexual difference on the line as the topic. To see it as a social, historical and psychic process at work as much in the art historical practices as in the art practices about which art history writes' (1992: 36). Her work has influenced the fields of feminist film criticism and visual culture, as well as art history.

See also: critical theory, feminism and; film theory, feminist; literature, images of women in

Selected writings

Pollock, G. (1977) 'What's Wrong with Images of Women?', *Screen Education*, 24.

—— (1988) *Vision and Difference: Femininity, Feminism, and Histories of Art*, London and New York: Routledge.

Kendall, R. and Pollock, G. (eds) (1992) *Dealing with Degas: Representations of Women and the Politics of Vision*, London: Pandora.

ROSANNE KENNEDY

polysemy

Polysemy is often defined by way of its distinction from homonymy. Whereas homonymy refers to the multiple, unrelated meanings of an ambiguous word (e.g., *bank* designating the side of a river versus *bank* designating a financial instituion), polysemy refers to the meanings of an unambiguous word that are clearly related to one another (the *mouth* of an animal versus the *mouth* of a river). Prescriptive grammarians have often invoked the concept of polysemy in justifying the use of *he/man* terms as referring to both specific males and to human beings more generally (i.e., the generic use of *he/man*). By contrast, advocates of nonsexist language reform have argued that masculine generics do not function generically even though they may be intended to do so. Indeed, psycholinguistic studies have shown that *he/man* generics readily evoke images of men rather than women, and that they have detrimental effects on individuals' beliefs in women's ability to perform certain jobs. Put another way, masculine generics do not seem to be polysemous in the way that traditional grammarians would claim.

See also: discourse analysis; language, gender and power; sexism

SUSAN EHRLICH

pornography

Originally referring to a description of prostitutes or of prostitution, pornography has since the nineteenth century referred to sexually explicit representations, and under the law of obscenity, was prohibited on the basis of its immorality. Since the 1970s, however, the meaning of pornography has become one of the most hotly contested and divisive issues within feminism theory and practice. While some claim that pornography is a major cause of women's subordination, others contend that pornography can be liberating for women.

Dominance or **radical feminism** has argued that pornography harms and subordinates women. Beginning in the 1970s, this feminist theory shifted the harm associated with pornography from sexual explicitness to **sexism**. Some feminists began to identify pornography as a cause of exploitative male sexual practices, and women's subordination – in Robin **Morgan**'s famous phrase 'Pornography is the theory, and rape the practice'. This association of pornography and subordination is developed in the highly influential work of Andrea **Dworkin** and Catharine **MacKinnon**, the leading feminist critics of pornography in the USA, who define pornography as the graphic sexually explicit subordination of women, whether in pictures or in words (Dworkin 1981; MacKinnon 1987). This critique of pornography, closely associated with the radical feminist critique of **sexuality**, identifies it as a primary source of women's subordination. In this view, pornography constructs women as subordinate sexual objects who enjoy pain and humiliation, and who exist for men's sexual pleasure and domination. According to MacKinnon pornography 'is a form of forced sex, a practice of sexual politics, an institution of gender inequality'. (1987: 148) This anti-pornography position often also focuses on the conditions under which pornography is produced, arguing

that women in the sex trade are said to be abused and exploited, often raped and tortured, in the production of pornographic images.

Other feminists have resisted this classification of pornography and sexuality. Beginning with the controversial Barnard Conference entitled 'Toward a Politics of Sexuality' in 1982, feminists who came to be known as 'sex radicals' have questioned the focus on the negative dimensions of pornography and women's sexuality. Carol Vance, among others, argues that anti-pornography feminism focuses too exclusively on the dangerous and negative dimension of sexuality, losing sight of the fact that sexuality is simultaneously a terrain of pleasure, agency and self-definition (1984). The sex radicals are highly critical of the intolerant, anti-sex position that characterises dominance feminism's critique of pornography (Vance 1984; Snitow *et al.* 1983). In striking contrast, they argue that pornography has a subversive quality, in representing and advocating sexual pleasure and agency for women. Some highlight the threat of anti-pornography laws on marginal and subversive sexual representations, such as feminist, gay and lesbian representations (Vance 1984). Many voice concern about the unholy alliance between anti-pornography feminism, and the religious right. Others focus on the liberatory potential of pornography for women's sexual fantasies, desires and practices.

By the 1980s, pornography had emerged as a major issue in feminist theory and practice. Women Against Pornography groups had sprung up across North America, and had become a focal point of much feminist activism. The Barnard Conference, which was picketed by WAP, marks the beginning of the 'sex wars', which continued to be one of the most divisive issues in feminist theory and politics throughout the 1980s and 1990s. The sex wars intensified in the USA, with the legal battle over the Indianapolis Ordinance. The ordinance, based on a model law drafted by Dworkin and MacKinnon, treats the production or distribution of 'pornography' as a violation of women's **civil rights**. The law was challenged by the American Booksellers Association, and was struck down by the US Supreme Court as a violation of the First Amendment of the US Constitution which protects the right to free speech. (The ordinance was ruled unconstitutional by the US Court of Appeals for the Seventh Circuit Court, which the US Supreme Court summarily affirmed.) While anti-pornography feminists defended the Ordinance, FACT – the Feminist Anti-Censorship Taskforce – intervened in the case in support of the constitutional challenge.

In Canada, the sex wars heated up again in the early 1990s and attracted international attention. The Supreme Court of Canada rejected a constitutional challenge to the law of obscenity, and following the arguments of the Women's Legal Education and Action Fund, adopted a radical/dominance feminist understanding of pornography as harm towards women. Shortly thereafter, a gay bookstore was the first to be charged with obscenity under the new law, in relation to a lesbian sex magazine. Many feminists argue that this charge vindicates the sex-radical claims that marginal and subversive representations would always be the most vulnerable (Cossman *et al.* 1997).

The early critique by the early sex radicals was supplemented by a range of feminist perspectives in the 1990s. Feminist theory, drawing on the insights of poststructuralism, argues that pornography has multiple and contradictory meanings (Cossman *et al.* 1997; Gibson and Gibson 1993). Contrary to the continuing claims of dominance feminism (MacKinnon 1993) this strand of feminist theory argues that the meaning of pornographic images is neither uniform nor literal, but shifting, multiple and positional. Some, for example, have explored the subversive potential of pornography, focusing for example, on Annie Sprinkle, a former porn star turned sexual performance artist, or Candida Royal, a former porn star now producing pornography for women. Others have explored the ways in which a range of pornographic images, from S/M to transvestite, disrupt gender roles.

The sex-radical critique of pornography has also given rise to a more general critique of sexuality, closely associated with the development of gay, lesbian and **queer theory**. In the early days of the sex wars, Gayle **Rubin** for example argued that a theory of gender was insufficient to theorise sexuality, and began to develop a theory of sex and sexuality (Rubin 1984). In the 1990s, pro-sex theory and activism continued to be tied with queer theory and practice, from Eve Sedgwick on

gender and sexuality, to the anti-censorship activism of gay and lesbian communities.

See also: cultural theory/cultural studies, feminist; psychoanalysis

References and further reading

Cossman, B., Bell, S., Gotell, L. and Ross, B. (1997) *Bad Attitude/s on Trial: Pornography, Feminism and the Butler Decision*, Toronto: University of Toronto Press.

Dworkin, A. (1981) *Pornography: Men Possessing Women*, New York: Perigee Books.

Gibson, P.C. and Gibson, R. (1993) *Dirty Looks: Women, Pornography, Power*, London, British Film Institute.

MacKinnon, C. (1987) *Only Words*, Cambridge, MA: Harvard University Press, 1993.

Rubin, G. (1984) 'Thinking Sex: Notes for a Radical Theory of the Politics of Sexuality', in Vance (ed.) *Pleasure and Danger: Exploring Female Sexuality*, Boston: Routledge and Kegan Paul.

Snitow, A., Stansell, C. and Thompson, S. (eds) (1983) *Powers of Desire: The Politics of Sexuality*, New York: Monthly Review Press.

Vance, C. (1984) 'Pleasure and Danger: Toward a Feminist Politics of Sexuality', in Vance (ed.) *Pleasure and Danger*, Boston: Routledge and Kegan Paul.

BRENDA COSSMAN

positioning/positionality

Linda Alcoff uses the concept of positionality as a way to avoid essentialising the category Woman while making it possible to take up gender as a political position from which to make change. Positionality includes an understanding both that the concept Woman is in relation to a constantly changing context and that positions in which women find themselves are locations in which to construct, rather than discover, meaning and values. Recognising that women are situated in relation to others in a constantly shifting capillary of relations and that women are subject of and subjected to social construction, positionality both de-universalises and de-essentialises the category

Woman. Rather than posit female gender as essential and universal, positionality makes it possible to account for an interaction between social forces and individual agency in the production of the subject.

References and further reading

Alcoff, L. (1988) 'Cultural Feminism Versus Post-Structuralism: The Identity Crisis in Feminist Theory', in *Signs: Journal of Women in Culture and Society*, 13, 3.

GLORIA FILAX

positivism

Positivism is a form of strict **empiricism** based on the tenet that only those statements directly grounded in experience are meaningful. Originally framed in the mid-nineteenth century by Auguste Comte, it was revised and renamed 'logical positivism' in the early twentieth century when theorists accepted the symbolic logic of Russell and Whitehead's *Principia Mathematica* as its primary tool of analysis. For positivists, only empirical research and logical analysis are a source of knowledge. All statements involving values or any subjective components are deemed meaningless and contaminating to knowledge claims. Positivism is the foundation of 'S knows that p' models of knowledge which assume individualist accounts of generic knowers capable of achieving what Donna **Haraway** labels 'the God-trick' of pure **objectivity** and value-neutrality. The positivist conception of knowledge has been criticised and rejected by many feminist theorists.

See also: epistemology; fact/value distinction; objectivity; science, philosophy of

NANCY TUANA

postcolonial feminism

Postcolonial feminism broadly characterises and addresses feminist preoccupations with race and gender that focus on the formerly colonised societies of Africa, Asia and the Caribbean. These feminist engagements have revolved around crucial issues of cultural identity, language, nationalism and the position of women within the newly-emerging nation states, female self-representation, and critical interrogations of white, bourgeois western feminism. The term postcolonial feminism implies the privileging of a particular moment in the history of feminism, namely, the period of decolonisation. However, Padmini Mongia states that postcolonialism goes beyond mere periodisation to include a methodological revisionism that displaces the centrality of western constructions of knowledge and production. These revisions have provided a common linkage between postcoloniality and feminist theoretical considerations as both discourses revolve around questions of alterity or otherness. If postcolonial discourse examines racialised otherness, postcolonial feminism explores women's racialised and sexualised otherness by locating their marginality and oppression within a three-tiered structure of discrimination maintained by colonial and neo-colonial indigenous patriarchies and the academic and cultural **hegemony** of western feminism. The collusion of nationalist and colonial patriarchies over the woman question has subjected women to a cultural, racial and gendered colonisation that has negated their right to equal **citizenship**. Inderpal Grewal demonstrates how nationalist and imperialist modes of control favour the restriction of women and the confinement of their spheres of influence. Grewal links the idea of patriarchal imposition with the construction of the nation state that is based on a tripartite level of discrimination along race, gender and class lines. While women's participation in nationbuilding is actively solicited, in their capacity as mothers or reproducers of the nation, their commensurate recognition, in the form of equal citizenship and direct participation in national policymaking, has been largely ignored.

In their research on postcolonial Egyptian feminism, Margot Badran and Miriam Cooke have problematised and politicised the dynamics of inner female space by making it a viable ground of resistance and protest, thereby valorising the idea of women's invisible powers of self-affirmation and their capacity to engage in an underground resistance. They question the western feminist assumption that power is located within manifest levels of activism. Badran distinguishes between visible and invisible feminisms using the term discrete feminism to suggest that the association of power with the visible or the concrete is based on a misconception that undermines the integrity of invisible or latent forms of control by women in postcolonial locations.

In her influential essay 'Can the Subaltern Speak?', Gayatri **Spivak** identifies postcolonial Indian women with a racial and economic under-class and shows how the inscription of women in a male-fabricated tradition has dislocated their realm of influence from the political by actively denying them access to law and authority, which remain a male prerogative. Spivak evokes the Hindu wo-man's subaltern position of sexualised otherness in which her inaccessibility to language leaves her in a silenced, aporetic space of abjection.

If the subaltern has a voice, as some feminists would argue, whose language would she use, given the fact that she is silenced within and by the patriarchal economy? Postcolonial feminist inter-rogations of language seek to address the following questions: Does the elaboration of a specific womanspeak, a special language articulated for and by women, provide the necessary space in which women can posit their specificity as sexual, social and political beings? Or is womanspeak in itself based on a pattern of exclusion that under-mines the creation of a common, plurivocal language, accessible to both men and women?

The call for the recognition of a plurality of woman-centred experiences is located within women's interrogations of their respective cultures and traditions and their critical reevaluations of age-old cultural and religious mandates that have lost their present-day applicability. Postcolonial feminisms seek to determine whether women, as the purveyors of culture, can lay claim to their own right of ownership of that culture. For example, feminists from Africa and the African diaspora have embraced the idea of social or othermother-ing, whereby the use of the term mother is not restricted solely to the biological mother and her functions, but extends itself to include a community activist of feminine orientation who works toward the overall benefit of the group. As a result, motherhood has been converted into a mystical

abstraction that has obfuscated the harsh realities of motherhood in several societies. The communal mother, who occupies a privileged place in West African societies, exemplifies Alice Walker's defini-tion of a womanist who is committed to the integrity, survival and wholeness of entire peoples due to her sense of self and her love for her culture.

Several African feminists like Filomena Steady and Chikwenye Ogunyemi are self-identified womanists who have demonstrated how the philosophy and practice of womanism have enabled them to propose a new model of femininity for African women that is independent of patri-archal and western definitions of the feminine. Situating itself at the grassroots level, womanism posits the impracticality and inviability of feminist utopias, by seeking total commitment, as the woman factor is an integral part of the human factor.

The split between womanism and feminism has resulted from the complicity between white western feminism and white patriarchy to further marginalise the experiences of women of colour by representing them as the negative instance of the white, middle class female model. In her ground-breaking essay 'Under Western Eyes' (see Mohanty, Russo, Torres (eds) 1991), Chandra Mohanty has shown how these representations have, for the most part, centred on a sensational or exaggerated sense of the daily reality of indigenous and Third World women who have almost always been defined in terms of their illiteracy, poverty, social and religious victimisation. Mohanty warns against the dangers of such limited representations that tend to freeze women in time, space and history. She deconstructs the notion of a universalised sisterhood by documenting the double alterity experienced by women of colour in different societies who have had to confront a dual system of discrimination, articulated by a white male and female patriarchy.

Postcolonial feminism has also interrogated issues of assimilation in instances of migration and postcolonial sociocultural displacements in which women have had to negotiate the precarious balance between the tenacious forces of integration and the desire to maintain a sense of their cultural identity as a strategy of self-preservation in their country of adoption. Avtar Brah problematises the notion of the diasporic home by asking when a place of residence becomes home and if women's occupation of home space is, in fact, accompanied by the necessary deeds of entitlement.

The field of postcolonialism is vast and is open to regular national, cultural, political and social contestations and interrogations. While the term itself refers to a broad, all-encompassing labelling, individual geographical, historical and cultural specificities must be taken into consideration to avoid the pitfalls of essentialisms, oversimplifications and irresponsible generalisations.

See also: nationalism and gender

References and further reading

Badran, M. and Cooke, M. (eds) (1996) *Opening the Gates*, Bloomington, IN: Indiana University Press.

Boyce-Davies, C. (1994) *Migrations of the Subject*, New York: Routledge.

Brah, A. (1996) *Cartographies of Diaspora*, London: Routledge.

Grewal, I. (1996) *Home and Harem*, Durham: Duke University Press.

James, S. and Busia, A. (eds) (1993) *Theorizing Black Feminisms*, New York: Routledge.

Jayawardena, K. (1986) *Feminism and Nationalism in the Third World*, London: Zed Books.

Mohanty, C., Russso, A. and Torres, L. (eds) (1991) *Third World Women and the Politics of Feminism*, Bloomington, IN: Indiana University Press.

Mongia, P. (ed.) (1996) *Contemporary Postcolonial Theory*, New York: St. Martin's Press.

Ogunyemi, C. (1996) *Africa, Wo/Man, Palava: The Nigerian Novel by Women*, Chicago and London: University of Chicago Press.

Spivak, G. (1988) 'Can the Subaltern Speak?' in C. Nelson and L. Grossberg (eds) *Marxism and the Interpretation of Culture*, Urbana, IL: University of Illinois Press.

Steady, F. (1982) *The Black Woman Culturally*, Cambridge, MA: Schenkman Publishing.

BRINDA J. MEHTA

poststructuralism/ postmodernism

Poststructuralism and postmodernism are two distinct but related terms. Poststructuralism refers to a body of diverse theories (Derrida, Lacan, Foucault, **Kristeva**; see Weedon 1996: 12–131) which take as their initial point of reference the structural linguistics of the Swiss linguist Ferdinand de Saussure. Poststructuralists have transformed the theory of meaning and the assumptions about subjectivity found in structural linguistics. In the process they have challenged some of the fundamental assumptions about knowledge, subjectivity and power in western philosophy. Feminist poststructuralists have developed this critique to identify the absence of woman and the feminine from western thought (Kristeva 1986; **Irigaray** 1985; Braidotti 1991).

The term 'postmodernism' was first used in architecture to describe the ways in which architects were breaking with the conventions of international modernism. It was subsequently taken up in various ways within the humanities and social sciences. In social theory the best known names associated with postmodernism are Jean-François Lyotard and Fredric Jameson. Most often 'postmodernism' and the related term 'postmodernity' are used to describe either the style and form taken by particular cultural phenomena or the present period of global late capitalism. The key aspects of postmodernism, which relate to poststructuralist theory, are cross disciplinary. Like poststructuralism, postmodernism questions some of the fundamental assumptions of the Enlightenment tradition in the west. These include the belief in rational human progress, universal standards and values, and singular truth.

The key issues in poststructuralist theory are meaning, subjectivity and **power**, though not all theorists are concerned with all of these (Weedon 1996). Poststructuralism questions the idea that meaning is a transparent reflection of the world. Following Saussure, poststructuralists insist that language constructs meaning and that it is the effect of a system of differences (see **language, gender and power**). Going beyond Saussure, poststructuralists insist that the meaning of a particular signifier is not fixed in the sign but is plural and changing, governed by the Derridean concept of *différance*. Différance implies that meaning is the effect of a temporary fixing of signifiers within a system of differences in which meaning is always subject to challenge and fixity constantly deferred. This marks a move away from Enlightenment assumptions that it is possible to describe the world accurately. It also opens up meaning to political struggle, making it central to feminist interests.

Poststructuralism further questions the status of the rational subject of western thought. Rational, intentional subjectivity is replaced by a theory in which subjectivity is split (Lacan), discursively produced (Kristeva, Irigaray, Foucault), in process (Kristeva), the effect of unconscious as well as conscious forces (Lacan, Irigaray, Kristeva; see Weedon 1996: 49–70), embodied and an effect of power (Foucault; see Weedon 1996: 104–21).

In Lacanian theory, gendered subjectivity is the precarious effect of the entry of the individual into the symbolic order of language and the Law. It involves the formation of the unconscious as the site of repressed meanings and desires which do not conform to the laws of the patriarchal symbolic order. Feminist rewritings of Lacan have identified the unconscious as the site of the repressed feminine which has its roots in the pre-Oedipal relationship with the mother. In order to enter the symbolic order of language, women must inhabit a patriarchal definition of themselves as lack. The process of assuming subjectivity invests the individual with a temporary sense of control and of sovereignty which evokes a 'metaphysics of presence' (Derrida) in which s/he becomes the source of the meaning s/he speaks, and language appears to be the expression of meaning fixed by the speaking subject. Yet, in poststructuralist theory, the speaker is never the author of the language within which s/he takes up a position. Language pre-exists and produces subjectivity.

Another key concept in poststructuralist theory is discourse. In Foucault, discourses are networks of often conflicting institutionally based discursive practices which constitute discursive fields such as medicine, the law or sexuality. Discourses are material since they inhere not just in language but in the material world and social practices. They constitute subjectivity for the individuals who are their subjects and agents. Drawing on the work of Foucault, feminist theorists have turned their attention to subjectivity as discursively constituted through material practices and as embodied. In the process they have questioned whether there can be any essential foundation to our concepts of gender difference (Butler 1990).

Influenced to different degrees by Foucault, Deleuze, Lacan and Irigaray, recent postmodern feminism has theorised the body and its relation to gendered subjectivity (see Weedon 1999: 99–130). The work of Irigaray has been particularly influential for its theorisation of woman's otherness to men and patriarchal culture. Drawing on poststructuralist theories Gallop (1988) has challenged the binary opposition between culture and the body which has tended to place women outside culture. Like Irigaray, she sees the female body as a site of resistance to **patriarchy**, but one which is refused representation. Grosz (1994) also stresses the materiality of the body, denial of which leads to the dominance of disembodied reason. Butler (1990) draws on Foucault and **psychoanalysis** to theorise the materiality of the sexed body under heterosexism (see **heterosexism, heteronormativity**).

Poststructuralism and postmodernism have questioned the authority of traditional guarantees of meaning, such as religion, **science** and nature, metanarratives which feminists have criticised for their patriarchal **androcentrism**. However, more contentiously poststructuralist and postmodern feminists have also questioned the sovereignty of experience, a category which is fundamental to much feminist epistemology and which underpins the personal as political (see **epistemology, feminist**). The poststructuralist questioning of truth, unified subjectivity and the sovereignty of experience have been fiercely contested by radical and Marxist feminists who see them as necessary to political struggle (see **radical feminism**).

Poststructuralist and postmodern feminists argue, following Foucault, that knowledge and power are integrally related and that knowledge is partial – both incomplete and representing particular interests. It exists in many competing forms which represent conflicting groups and interests. Knowledge should be judged not by reference to truth claims but by its effects in the world. Poststructuralist and modern feminists insist on narratives that are non-universalising, have no foundationalist status and allow for cultural and historical specificity.

References and further reading

Braidotti, R. (1991) *Patterns of Dissonance*, Cambridge, MA: Polity Press.

Butler, J. (1990) *Gender Trouble. Feminism and the Subversion of Identity*, New York and London: Routledge.

Gallop, J. (1988) *Thinking Through the Body*, New York: Columbia University Press.

Grosz, E. (1994) *Volatile Bodies: Towards a Corporeal Feminism*, Bloomington, IN: Indiana University Press.

Irigaray, L. (1985) *This Sex Which is Not One*, trans. C. Porter and C. Burke, Ithaca, NY: Cornell University Press.

Kristeva, J. (1986) *The Kristeva Reader*, ed. T. Moi, Oxford: Blackwell.

Weedon, C. (1996) *Feminist Practice and Poststructuralist Theory*, Oxford: Blackwell.

—— (1999) *Feminism, Theory and the Politics of Difference*, Oxford: Blackwell.

CHRIS WEEDON

power

Questions about power have figured prominently in second-wave feminist theories, although in the early years they were more central to socialist and Marxist feminism than to liberal feminism. Power, in these debates, may refer to power *to* perform certain acts and realise possibilities; or power *over*, that thwarts opportunities, possibilities, activities. The term is central, also, in feminist efforts to promote women's em*power*ment.

For liberal feminists, power tends to figure as someone's possession: in assertions that (certain) men *have* power, whereas women in general *have* less, or none; or in models of 'top-down' sovereign power, in the public realm, where power resides with government, social officials, or multi-national corporations. Emphasising individually-produced situations and autonomous individual solutions, liberals often urge women to claim power, to make it theirs, to develop personal ways of defying the patriarchal power that blocks their road to rights and opportunities equal to men's: to work toward participating equally with men in government and public institutions. For Marxist and many socialist feminists, by contrast, power is systemic, located in the dominance of economic circumstances, or in wider structures of social dominance and subordination. In such analyses, power can rarely be counteracted by individual resistance within a social structure that remains unchallenged at its core. Strategies of resistance come most effectively from collectivities, coalitions with oppositionally articulated, socially transformative agendas that challenge the assumptions of an often-intransigent social order that represents distributions of power and privilege as 'natural': consequent upon women's (or blacks', or the working class') inferior nature.

Feminists have engaged ambivalently, but productively, with the conception of power articulated by Michel Foucault, who draws attention to the 'micro-physics' of power permeating the social order as capilliaries run imperceptibly through human bodies. Power, then, is not the possession of individual agents, but is exercised in myriad practices and loci of power legitimated within localised disciplinary mechanisms of surveillance, regulation, classification. Nor is power merely negative, repressive for Foucault: it is productive of discourse, pleasure, meaning, subversive resistance. Such analyses are useful for understanding the sexual control of women's bodies that often seems to come from nowhere in particular, yet is everywhere felt and enacted. Yet feminists have been critical of Foucault for shifting his focus away from the macro-structures of power whose effects in women's lives – say, in global labour practices – are undeniable; and for failing to provide a viable conception of agency just when women and other Others are renewing their claims to productive subjectivity and agency.

References and further reading

Barrett, M. (1991) *The Politics of Truth: From Marx to Foucault*, Stanford, CA: Stanford University Press.

Hartsock, N. (1990) 'Foucault on Power: A Theory for Women?' in Linda Nicholson (ed.) *Feminism/Postmodernism*, New York: Routledge.

LORRAINE CODE

praxis

Most simply put, praxis is understood as activity or practice, that is the relationship between theory and action. In the Marxist sense, praxis is the creative activity of human beings that shapes their world. Although praxis is seen as the core of Marxist thinking, it also has resonance for feminist scholarship.

Feminists have appropriated praxis in at least two ways. First, feminists invoke praxis to draw our attention to the ways in which theory can be put into action (for example, **consciousness-raising** activities). In this first sense, praxis is not merely the relationship between theory and practice but additionally focuses feminist attention on strategic questions of how to challenge social conditions that oppress women *qua* women. Second, feminists interrogate the moral and ethical implications of social conditions which oppress individuals on the basis of gender. In this second sense, feminist praxis advocates social relationships based upon notions of equality, justice, and an **ethic of care**.

SANDRA REIN

primatology

Primatology is the scientific study of nonhuman primates – apes and monkeys. Because other primates are close to human beings genetically, much primatology is concerned with human origins and evolution. Science historian Donna

Haraway has analysed primatology's development through the twentieth century. In earlier decades, primatologists tended to see conventional **gender roles** or examples of male dominance in primate societies. These were often assumed to be biologically determined, or essentialist. Later primatologists, including feminists such as Sarah Blaffer Hrdy, emphasised instead the central role of women in social organisation of many primate species. This shift in underlying ideas of primatology reflects changing cultural ideas about gender (as well about **race**); or, as Haraway has suggested, 'primatology is politics by other means'.

See also: biological essentialism

References and further reading

Haraway, D. (1989) *Primate Visions: Gender, Race and Nature in the World of Modern Science*, London: Routledge.

LYNDA BIRKE

privilege

Privilege (*priv-us*: private, *lex*: law) is used by feminists to mark a particular class of unearned advantages that are systemically created and culturally nourished (Bailey 1998). Privilege helps members of dominant groups to avoid certain barriers that serve to immobilise members of marginalised groups. This usage differs from traditional philosophical and legal definitions that equate privileges with mere liberties, the absence of duties, benefits and immunities attached to a particular office, or legal benefits that are not rights.

Formally, oppressed groups have had to 'earn' privileges that were granted without question to dominant groups. Suffrage, for example, was automatically granted to white property-owning men; white women, emancipated slaves, and immigrants had to fight for the vote. However, privilege has a less visible informal component that escapes legal analysis. Male privileges include the idea that men almost always benefit from being able to move about freely with little risk of sexual assault, or not having their opinions taken seriously.

Whites, and those who appear to be white, benefit from **white privilege (race privilege)** by being extended the public trust in most instances, and never having their race used as a reason for personal failures. Privilege, however, is not an all or nothing phenomenon; it is mediated by other oppressive factors. For example, outside African American communities, the opinions of black men are rarely taken seriously; and, working-class whites may work harder to gain public trust.

Privilege also has an important epistemic dimension. One of its functions is to structure the world so that mechanisms of privilege are invisible – in the sense that they are unexamined – by those who benefit from them. The structured invisibility of privilege insures that most accomplishments will be recognised more on the basis of individual merit than on group membership.

In response to these claims is a literature on traitorous identities which explores questions of whether privilege can be used subversively.

References and further reading

Bailey, A. (1998) 'Privilege: Expanding on Marilyn Frye's Oppression', *Journal of Social Philosophy*, 29, 3: 104–19.

McIntosh, P. (1988) 'White Privilege and Male Privilege: A Personal Account of Coming to See Correspondences Through Work in Women's Studies', in M.L. Andersen and P.H. Collins (eds) *Race, Class and Gender: An Anthology*, New York: Wadsworth, 1991.

ALISON BAILEY

production, modes of

Modes of production signify the structural form of primary economic production, and by inference, the social forms that accompany it. These are generally categorised as agricultural (subsistence), feudal, or capitalist in form. As conceptualised by malestream theorists from Adam Smith and Karl Marx to the neoclassical economists of the Chicago School, production does not include reproduction, or most of women's unremunerated work.

Economists measure production as activities which produce surplus value, otherwise known as profit. This conceptualisation eliminates women's unpaid labour in the household and community, women's subsistence farming, and women's reproductive labour, a 'fatal flaw' in 'male economics' (Waring 1988: 28). However much destructive activity is measured as productive, as it produces surplus value, while virtually all of women's work is not calculated, as it does not directly attract surplus value (though it often creates the conditions for surplus value). This in turn reinforces women's cultural devaluation and the invisibility of women's productive and reproductive work. The invisibility of women's work has political consequences, as policy-makers are oblivious to women's needs from and contributions to society and the economy (Cohen 1989: 151).

Social and economic processes evolve responsively, as economic processes result in pressure for different social practices, sometimes legislated and supported by government. In the late twentieth century, First World welfare states regulated not only the modes of production, but provided the macroeconomic and social policies designed to ameliorate the most dramatic excesses of the capitalist mode of production, while maintaining the preconditions for continuance of that process (Offe 1984). Globalisation internationally and neoliberalism domestically have eroded this process, which is being transformed by disaggregated production and global regimes of accumulation (see **neoliberalism and neoconservatism** and **economic globalisation**). The mode of production inevitably confronts crises of profitability, initiating transformations by capitalists in search of profit maximisation, and by states in search of economic stability. This motivates a continual search for technologies and commodities to maximise capital accumulation, in what becomes an historical process as well as a relational and adaptive dialectic.

Socialisation, supported by state ideologies and encoded in popular cultures, encourages the support of private familial and communal life for the processes of production so that women's un- and under-paid labour in the home and in pink collar ghettos both sustains male workers at no cost to capitalists, and provides cheap labour ideologically compliant in its own subordination.

State policies, tied to new information and communication technologies, and popular ideology facilitated by mass media, function to both directly and indirectly regulate social behaviour in the interests of the dominant mode of production. Capitalist social relations are grounded in the dominant mode of production, consolidated by political culture, popular ideology, and socialisation around race, class and gender.

References and further reading

Cohen, M. (1989) 'The Problem of Studying "Economic Man"', in A. Miles and G. Finn (eds) *Feminism: From Pressure to Politics*, Montreal: Black Rose Press, pp. 147–59.

Offe, C. (1984) *Contradictions of the Welfare State*, Cambridge, MA: MIT Press.

Waring, M. (1988) *If Women Counted: A New Feminist Economics*, San Francisco: Harper.

JOYCE GREEN

profeminist men's theory

Profeminist men's theory developed out of the profeminist men's movement, which began during the late 1960s when small groups of men, influenced by the women's movement and gay liberation, began questioning masculine norms. By the mid-1970s, these meetings has grown into yearly 'Men and Masculinity' conferences, and a national organisation was formed, now called the National Organization for Men Against Sexism (NOMAS) – a primarily white, middle class, male institution.

During the early years of the profeminist men's movement in the USA, profeminist theory was influenced by two strands of feminism, liberal and radical. Those associated with **liberal feminism** were advocates of men's liberation, and utilised sex role theory to argue that socially scripted behaviours harm men and women. Some men's liberationists went so far as to claim that sexism oppresses both men and women equally. Although sex role theory helped to advance a critique of **essentialism** and the assumption that **masculinity** and femininity are biologically based, more

radical profeminist theorists criticised it for its tendency to depoliticise **oppression** by making it a general condition for everyone. By the late 1970s, sex role theory and men's liberation had begun to lose favour in profeminism.

Central to radical profeminist theory, influenced by **radical feminism**, is the assumption that men oppress women. Radical profeminists believe that masculinity is created and maintained through acts of denigration and violence directed toward women; and that **patriarchy** is the larger social and political order in which masculinity exists. They also assume that **homophobia** is not separate from **misogyny** and plays a role in the creation of manhood. Organising men's task groups to challenge the denigration of women in pornography, and creating activist organisations to end men's violence against women are examples of radical profeminists' devotion to gender justice. Much of the radical profeminist theory appeared in *Changing Men: Issues in Gender, Sex, and Politics*, a profeminist men's movement magazine published by NOMAS from the late 1970s to the early 1990s.

During the mid- to late 1980s profeminist men's theory took a more academic turn with the formation of the Men's Studies Association, a task force group that is an organisational component of NOMAS. Profeminist men's studies theorists, influenced by **social constructionism**, combine the study of how men are institutionally privileged by their gender with an examination of how men are privileged differently. They investigate issues of race, class, gender, and sexual orientation as they are manifested in masculinities – hegemonic and subordinate forms of manhood that are historically and culturally varied. Currently the men's studies and radical contingents of profeminism largely define the movement and its theory.

See also: hegemony; privilege

References and further reading

Clatterbaugh, K. (1996) *Contemporary Perspectives on Masculinity*, Boulder, CO: Westview, 2nd edn.

Messner, M.A. (1997) *Politics of Masculinities*, Thousand Oaks, CA: Sage.

PATRICK McGANN

prostitution

Prostitution is associated with the marketing of sexual labour in capitalist systems of exchange. The labourers in this exchange are typically young, economically disadvantaged, and female, and the consumers are typically mature, economically advantaged, and male. Because of these differences in social rank, and because of the questionable extension of market norms to human sexual behaviour, some feminist theorists regard prostitution as a form of sexual and economic exploitation. Prostitution is the product of **patriarchy** and capitalism, it is not an inevitable phenomenon resulting from a 'natural' male sexual appetite and an inherent female submissiveness. Women must make themselves sexually available to men to obtain things that are denied to them by other means: money, possessions, jobs, social connections, and so on.

Some feminists allege that prostitution would not exist if women had genuine economic alternatives, and a few feminists want governments to enact and enforce laws against trafficking in sexual services. Providing women with alternatives to prostitution involves more than allowing women access to education and employment. It requires disrupting systems of power (especially patriarchal marriage and male dominance in the public sphere) that entitle men to classes of women who cater to their sexual wants (prostitutes, wives, female employees or subordinates).

Feminist sex workers have challenged the accounts offered by feminist academics and activists. Some argue that the extension of market norms to human sexual behaviour is not caused by inequalities of power based on gender or class. The production of sex as a commodity originates from the desire of many people for sexual experiences beyond those they enjoy with romantic or marital partners. On this view, exchanging sex in a capitalist market is a pursuit as worthy as exchanging food or shoes for profit. Furthermore, more sex workers are women because more men are comfortable being the consumers of commercial sex and because of the heterosexual bias in our society. When these factors change, there will be a greater demand for the sexual labour of men. Moreover, the youth of the average sex worker is a result of widespread cultural notions of sexual attractiveness that are admittedly sexist; yet this affects the sex industry no more than other industries such as entertainment, modelling, and so on. Feminist sex workers generally oppose including minors in commercial sex work, on the grounds that children need to develop physically, emotionally, and intellectually before adults exploit their sexual labour. And finally, many feminists argue that the best way to promote non-exploitative labour conditions is to allow sex workers to perform their jobs legally, and to allow them to form worker collectives to defend their rights.

See also: pornography; sexuality; sexual slavery

References and further reading

Nagle, J. (ed.) (1997) *Whores and Other Feminists*, New York: Routledge.

Satz, D. (1995) 'Markets in Women's Sexual Labor', *Ethics* 106,1: 63–85.

Shrage, L. (1994) *Moral Dilemmas of Feminism: Prostitution, Adultery, and Abortion*, New York: Routledge.

LAURIE SHRAGE

psychoanalysis

The influence of psychoanalysis on feminist theory has been substantial, and not only because, like **Marxism**, it has become one of the influential explanations offered of the individual in society. Feminist theory has a specific and theoretical interest in Freud, since his theory explains the establishment of the structure of the self through the operation of sexual difference.

In terms of the political problem feminist theory has set itself – why a woman in virtue of her anatomy experiences systematic subordination and **oppression** – psychoanalytic reflections on the place of the **body**, of **sexuality** and of rationality in the arrangement of a social world have often been regarded as important. Differing emphases on parts of Freudian theory have produced a variety of psychoanalytic approaches to the problem, ranging from object-relations theory to Lacanian poststructuralism (see **poststructuralism/postmodernism**).

Freudian theory

The Freudian account of sexuality is directed at explaining how we come by the desires that we have. Freud sought a consistent theory of the psychical consequences of anatomy, holding that there is no primordial **masculinity** and femininity nor any pre-ordained **heterosexuality**. Everything is formed and tempered in the history of a person's encounter with a social world, which is also a material one.

In describing a psychology, Freud follows the biologist's bias and begins from the body, not the mind, in the notion of the instinct as the basis of their connection. However, the Freudian instinct is far from the notion of a determined behaviour or essential will; and the notion has sometimes been rendered (arguably with more success) in the literature as 'drive'. (See 'Instincts and their Vicissitudes' 1915.)

In the earlier *Three Essays on the Theory of Sexuality* Freud describes the body as being polymorphously perverse in its capacity to experience pleasure attached to any of its sensations, and constitutionally bisexual (the germ of the Oedipus complex). Any bodily need and its process of satisfaction provides a path for erotic development. In the famous oral, anal and genital phases, the acculturation of bodily demands in feeding, toilet training, and the outlawing of auto-eroticism can be observed. In turn, the demands made by a society on the plastic possibilities of the individual create the drama of sexual difference as one organised according to its heterosexual imperative to reproduce itself.

The 'Oedipus complex' is the centrepiece of this account, intended to explain the way the polymorphous child is taken into the social world, in which s/he acquires not only a sexual identity, but a conscience (the 'superego') and the capacity to work (through 'sublimation'). For the little boy, Freud maintains the mechanism of this induction is via the fear of castration; a threat and at the same time an incentive received from his father, as representative of society, to give up his desire for his first love object, his mother, on pain of losing the site of his pleasure.

According to Freud, the boy only credits this threat as real when he sees the woman's body. When he sees she 'lacks' the organ, then he knows it is possible to lack it. As his theory develops, Freud places more emphasis on the 'castration complex', because it has the structural burden of turning the polymorphous pleasures of childhood into organised reproductive sexuality. It cannot be overemphasised that this occurs in relation to the boy's own body and bodily pleasure, on the example of another, different, body – her body underwrites his sexuality and identity.

Nothing underwrites the move to femininity for the girl in quite the same way, for the theory. Freud himself sees, in his later work, that on his account she has no obvious incentive to leave the state of childhood, since the 'castration' has already been effected. This is why he relies on the notion of a 'penis envy' to explain her psychology. But, despite this, the arrival of femininity is never the thunderclap that the oedipal moment presents for the boy.

As he wrote in a letter to Marie Bonaparte: 'The great question that has never been answered and which I have not been able to answer, despite my thirty years of research into the feminine soul is "What does a woman want?"'. The question of femininity became more pressing for psychoanalytic theory as a new generation of analysts (Melanie Klein, Helene Deutsch, Ernest Jones and Karen Horney) took up the issue. Luce **Irigaray** has argued that Freud cannot answer 'the riddle of feminine desire' since for Freud's account there are not two sexes, but only one and its negation. This is signalled, if nowhere else, in his claim that 'libido', or sexual energy, is itself masculine.

The discomfort of Freud's patients with their sexual roles – **hysteria** and obsessional neurosis in both sexes – shows that his idealised formation of sexual **identity** can fail, and this is at least as important in the consequences of Freud's theory as that it can succeed. While Freud's normative prescriptions gave license to a conservative psychiatric establishment that was decidedly not feminist in its diagnosis, the fragility of the process as he describes it gave rise to more positive uses of psychoanalytic insights.

Consequences of Freud

It is possible to find two differing responses to Freud's theory of the psychical formation of **masculinity** and femininity, both of which have been useful in various forms to feminist theorists.

The first, in a re-examination of the maternal role, redefines the nature of the mother/child relation as an active and central site for the formation of subjectivity. 'Object-relations theory', coming out of the work of Klein, D.W. Winnicott and others, has a contemporary feminist voice in the work of Nancy **Chodorow**, who revalues **motherhood** and the role of caring for the infant as an important site of change in **gender** roles and sexual subordination (see also **Flax, Jane**). A difficulty for this position has been its tendency to emphasise heterosexuality to some extent, and to idealise the maternal, thus producing a normative position for women to 'live down'.

The work of Jacques Lacan has been influential in the second response, which focuses on the symbolic place of the father in the social compact. In his notions of 'the phallus' and of the link between the body and the law in the notion of the 'signifier', Lacan draws on structuralist linguistics to produce a view of psychosexual identity as ineluctably symbolic and never securely accomplished. Lacan's **misogyny** has become legendary (in such papers as the 'Encore' seminars) but his positive theoretical resources for feminist theory may lie more with his conceptions of the 'imaginary' and the '**gaze**' as the field of signs and images through which a person's identity is built up. What can be constructed can be 'deconstructed', as the work of Luce **Irigaray** and Julia **Kristeva**, in their different ways, has shown (see also **French feminism**). A problem with this style of psychoanalytic account, however, has been its tendency to exclude women altogether from active subjectivity in the symbolic realm, which has at times been felt to be determinist.

Anglo-American feminists have also taken up the insights of Freud and Lacan, according to this second emphasis – beginning from Juliet Mitchell's 1975 book, *Psychoanalysis and Feminism*. Lacanian feminism, and **psychoanalytic feminist literary theory**, have taken on the diagnosis of a '**phallogocentrism**', often pairing Lacan's theoretical perspective with the corrective of Derridean deconstruction, which analyses Lacan's 'phallus' as a metaphysical concept, being an attempt to name a universal.

The critiques of psychoanalysis made by philosophers Michel Foucault and Gilles Deleuze are now exercising a significant influence on feminist work around '**queer theory**' (for example, the work of Judith **Butler**). They argue against the conservative norms of an analysis which decrees what is sexually, or psychologically, normal. Here the institution of psychoanalysis comes in for analysis itself, and the questions raised for feminism by its practice are arguably distinct from its theoretical questions. The concept of the 'transference', a central concept from the practice rather than the theory of psychoanalysis in which (as Freud described it) the patient falls in love with the doctor, attracts increasing interest as an epistemological mechanism, and plays a part in more creative uses of Freudian theory.

Beyond explicit discussions of the theory of psychoanalysis, the tincture of its intuitions is present in the moves to enunciate both a philosophy of the body, and a philosophy of **difference**, two fields in which feminist theorists have recently shown the way. By employing the methods of unconscious thought, rather than the tenets of theory, these feminist uses have produced both playful and insightful writing.

References and further reading

Ferrell, R. (1996) *Passion In Theory: Conceptions of Freud and Lacan*, London: Routledge.

Freud, S. (1905) 'Three Essays on the Theory of Sexuality', Standard Edition, Hogarth: London, 7:123.

—— (1924) 'The Dissolution of the Oedipus Complex', Standard Edition 19:173.

—— (1933) 'Femininity', Standard Edition, 22:112.

Irigaray, L. (1985) 'The Blind Spot of an Old Dream of Symmetry', in *Speculum of the Other Woman*, trans. G.C. Gill, Ithaca, NY: Cornell University Press.

Klein, M. (1957) *Envy and Gratitude*, London: Tavistock.

Lacan, J. (1977) *Ecrits: A Selection*, trans. Alan Sheridan, London: Tavistock.

Mitchell, J. and. Rose, J. (1982) *Feminine Sexuality: Jacques Lacan and the Ecole Freudienne*, London: Macmillan.

Moi, T. (ed.) (1986) *The Kristeva Reader*, Oxford: Basil Blackwell.

Strouse, J. (1985) *Women and Analysis: Dialogues on Psychoanalytic Views of Femininity*, Boston: G.K. Hall.

ROBYN FERRELL

psychoanalytic feminist literary theory

Psychoanalytic feminist literary theory has developed since the 1980s, in the wake of renewed feminist interest in **psychoanalysis**. Positioned at the intersection of psychoanalytic feminism and feminist literary theory, psychoanalytic feminist literary theorists have been among the main expositors and critics of psychoanalytic texts, and have contributed significantly to exploring and developing the links between feminism and psychoanalysis. In addition to sharing the view of psychoanalytic feminists, that psychoanalysis offers unique insights into the process through which human beings become gendered subjects, psychoanalytic literary feminist theorists explore similarities between psychoanalytic and literary approaches to textuality, focusing on the slippages, ruptures, excesses and silences of the text. They typically either apply psychoanalytic models to literary texts, or use literary strategies to read psychoanalytic texts, as a means of exploring questions of femininity, Woman, sexuality, desire and fantasy. In the 1990s, psychoanalytic feminist literary theory, which traditionally prioritises sexual difference, began to address issues of race and lesbian subjectivity. Dialogues with the fields of black feminist criticism and **queer theory** have opened new avenues of investigation, and revealed the limits of a psychoanalytic paradigm.

Published in 1974, Juliet **Mitchell**'s landmark book, *Psychoanalysis and Feminism*, paved the way for the development of psychoanalytic feminist literary theory. A British marxist-feminist, Mitchell introduced psychoanalysis to feminism as a potential solution to Marxism's ignorance of **sexuality**. Responding to feminists such as Kate **Millet** and Eva Figes, who rejects psychoanalysis as a patriarchal discourse, Mitchell argues that psychoanalysis provides a framework that enables feminists to investigate how **patriarchy** is unconsciously reproduced, and offers 'the way into understanding ideology and sexuality' (Mitchell 1974: xx). In their introduction to French psychoanalyst Jacques Lacan's writings on femininity, Mitchell and co-editor Jacqueline Rose (1982) compellingly argue that psychoanalysis offers feminism a theory of gendered subjectivity, and more importantly, a theory of the subject's resistance to rigid gender identities. Mitchell notes Freud's observation that the little girl will not pass from 'her masculine phase to the feminine one to which she is biologically destined ... without a struggle' (Mitchell and Rose 1982: 24). In *Sexuality in the Field of Vision* (1986), Rose highlights the unstable nature of gender **identity**, arguing that psychoanalysis 'insists, through the concept of the unconscious, that femininity is neither simply achieved nor is it ever complete' (7). She maintains that 'Feminism's affinity with psychoanalysis rests above all ... with this recognition that there is a resistance to identity at the very heart of psychic life' (91).

While British feminists advocate a psychoanalytic feminism grounded in the Lacanian tradition, American feminists turn to object-relations psychology, and particularly to Nancy **Chodorow**'s *The Reproduction of Mothering* (1978). In this sociological analysis of gender identity, Chodorow argues that the mother – the first and primary object in the child's life – plays a major role in reproducing gender identity through the way that she interacts with her children. Many American psychoanalytic feminist literary critics (Hirsch 1981; Garner, Kahane, and Sprengnether 1985) combine Chodorow's insights with those of French feminists, to develop models for interpreting representations of mother/daughter relations in literature.

Although object-relations psychology has had a major impact on feminist criticism in the USA, more important for the development of psycho-analytic literary theory is the work of Franco-American critics such as Shoshana Felman (1981), Naomi Schor (1981) and Jane Gallop (1982). These critics introduced and explicated the difficult and unfamiliar work of French feminists, such as Luce **Irigaray**, Julia **Kristeva** and Hélène **Cixous**, all of whom were trained in the psychoanalytic tradition of Freud and Lacan. Turning her skills of close reading onto the texts of Freud, Lacan, Irigaray and Mitchell, Gallop (1982) teases out the hidden assumptions and blind-spots within psycho-analytic and feminist discourse, in an effort to bring these fields into dialogue and to question their boundaries. Gallop's hermeneutic method, similar to Irigaray's practice, represents one of the main traditions in psychoanalytic feminist literary theory, and differs from the practice of feminists who read psychoanalysis primarily for its content (for in-stance, to extract an account of the process of subjectification). Many feminists (Bernheimer and Kahane 1985) have used a hermeneutic method to interrogate Freud's most contentious case history, *Dora*, an analysis of an eighteen-year-old hysteric.

Although literary critics had been active in exploring the relationship between feminism and psychoanalysis, the field of psychoanalytic feminist literary theory only dates from the early 1980s. Some of the foundational essays are published in a special issue of Yale French Studies, *Feminist Readings: French Texts, American Contexts* (1981). Schor argues that there are few theoretical models for psychoanalytic feminist literary critics, because feminists who articulate links between feminism and psychoanalysis are not primarily interested in literature, and those interested in psychoanalysis and literature are not primarily feminists. Arguing that 'female theorizing is grounded in the body', Schor offers a psychoanalytic feminist hermeneu-tics that focuses on bodily detail in literary texts, which she wittily calls the 'clitoral school of feminist theory' (Schor 1981: 210, 216). Felman re-iterates Freud's famous question – 'what is femininity?' to ask 'what does the question – what is femininity? – *for men*? – mean *for women*?' (Felman 1981: 21). Posing this question in relation to a Balzac story, she examines how sexual difference affects the practice of interpretation.

By the mid-1980s, the situation Schor had lamented – the absence of a psychoanalytic feminist literary theory – had begun to be rectified. In 1985, the first anthology of feminist psycho-analytic criticism, *The (M)other Tongue*, was pub-lished. Concerned to redress the absence of the mother in psychoanalytic theory, the contributors offer readings that examine the relation between femininity and language, and analyse the mother's position, function, and subjectivity in literary texts. In *The Mother–Daughter Plot*, Marianne Hirsch (1989) contributes to the examination of mother/daughter relations in literature, focusing particu-larly on the representation of the mother's subjectivity. Mary Jacobus's 1986 book, *Reading Woman*, uses a hermeneutic method to examine both the function of 'woman' in psychoanalytic texts, and the function of 'theory' in feminist criticism. In 1989, a second anthology of psycho-analytic feminist criticism, *Feminism and Psycho-analysis* (ed. R. Feldstein and J. Roof), attempt to break up the dyadic metaphors of the family romance that critics had used to describe the relationship between feminism and psychoanalysis', by examining a 'third term' that was often present in a text or context. The decade closed with the publication of Rose's dazzling psychoanalytic study, *The Haunting of Sylvia Plath* (1991), which includes interpretation of Plath's writings, and analyses of the cultural effects of her work.

By the 1990s, psychoanalytic feminist literary theory was drawn into debates on difference, which were raging within all fields of feminist theory. Psychoanalytic feminism, which had advanced a psychoanalytic account of the divided subject in response to essentialist theories of gender, was itself attacked for prioritising sexual difference over differences of race, class and sexual orientation. Teresa de **Lauretis**'s call, in *Technologies of Gender* (1987), for a subject conceived of as 'multiple, rather than divided' has been interpreted, by psychoanalytic feminists, as a covert directive for feminists to abandon a psychoanalytic approach grounded in sexual difference, in favour of a Foucauldian approach that examines the construc-tion of subject-positions across multiple discourses. Despite this criticism, Lauretis returns to a renewed engagement with psychoanalysis in *The Practice of Love* (1994). Contributing to the emergent field of queer theory, she draws on Freud's writings to elaborate a model of perverse desire, 'where perverse means not pathological but rather non-heterosexual nor non-normatively heterosexual' (xiii). She then uses this model to examine the representation of lesbian subjectivity in literary and film texts. In *Identification Papers* (1995) literary critic Diana Fuss interrogates the concept of identification through a careful reading of psychoanalytic and cultural texts by Freud, Fanon and others, developing further links between queer theory and psychoanalysis.

In the 1990s, psychoanalytic feminist literary theorists confronted the issue of race: could psychoanalysis be useful in explaining identifications based on **race** as well as sex? Could it explain **black female sexuality** as well as white female sexuality? Prominent white psychoanalytic feminist critics, such as Barbara Johnson (1992) and Judith **Butler** (1993), had used psychoanalytic approaches to read texts by black women writers, and Jane Gallop, in *Around 1981* (1992), had contentiously declared her desire for the approval of black feminist critics. These interventions were debated at a conference that brought together white and black feminist literary critics to discuss psychoanalysis, primarily in relation to **black women's literature**. The anthology that resulted, *Female Subjects in Black and White* (1997), bears witness to the complexity of attempting to bring psychoanalysis, which Freud developed when analysing white middle-class hysterics in late nineteenth-century Vienna, to bear on questions of race and raced sexuality. In her contribution, 'Channeling the Ancestral Muse: Lucille Clifton and Dolores Kendrick', Akasha (Gloria) Hull argues that the psychoanalytic readings of black women's texts performed by white critics often ignore figures rooted in African cosmologies and African American spiritual traditions. Barbara Christian, also contributing, argues in her essay, 'Fixing Methodolgies: *Beloved*', for the need for critics to place black women's texts in historical context. Hortense Spillers adds a different perspective to the anthology; in 'All the Things You Could be by Now, If Sigmund Freud's Wife Was Your Mother', she demonstrates how psychoanalysis could be used to examine the constitution of raced subjectivity. Rather than forge an alliance between psychoanalytic feminism and black feminist criticism, this anthology practices 'complementary theorizing', which has led to new intersections and a new set of questions for psychoanalytic feminist literary theory.

See also: literary theory, feminist; Marxist feminist literature/literary theory

References and further reading

Abel, E., Christian, B., and Moglen, H. (eds) (1997) *Female Subjects in Black and White: Race, Psychoanalysis, Feminism*, Berkeley and Los Angeles: University of California Press.

Bernheimer, C. and Kahane, C. (eds) (1985) *In Dora's Case: Freud – Hysteria – Feminism*, New York: Columbia University Press.

Butler, J. (1993) 'Passing, Queering: Nella Larsen's Psychoanalytic Challenge' in *Bodies that Matter*, New York: Routledge.

Felman, S. (1981) 'Rereading Femininity', *Yale French Studies*, 62: 19–44.

Figes, E. (1970) *Patriarchal Attitudes: Women in Society*, London: Faber.

Gallop, J. (1982) *The Daughter's Seduction: Feminism and Psychoanalysis*, Ithaca, NY: Cornell University Press.

Garner, S., Kahane, C., and Sprengnether, M. (eds) (1985) *The (M)other Tongue: Essays in Psychoanalytic Feminist Interpretation*, Ithaca, NY: Cornell University Press.

Hirsch, M. (1981) 'A Mother's Discourse: Incorporation and Repetition in *La Princesse de Cleves*', *Yale French Studies*, 62: 67–87.

Jacqueline R. (1986) *Sexuality in the Field of Vision*, London: Verso.

Johnson, B. (1992) 'The Quicksands of the Self: Nella Larsen and Heinz Kohut' in J. Smith and H.Smith (eds) *Telling Facts: History and Narration in Psychoanalysis*, Baltimore: Johns Hopkins University Press.

Mitchell, J. (1974) *Psychoanalysis and Feminism*, New York: Pantheon Books.

Mitchell, J. and Rose, J. (eds) (1982) *Feminine Sexuality*, London: Macmillan.

Schor, N. (1981) 'Female Paranoia: The Case for Psychoanalytic Feminist Criticism', *Yale French Studies*, 62: 204–219.

ROSANNE KENNEDY

psychology, feminist

Feminist psychology – psychological theory and practice explicitly informed by the political goals of the feminist movement – developed in opposition to mainstream psychology, a discipline deeply implicated in the patriarchal control of women (see **patriarchy**). Feminist psychology is a social change strategy, aiming to end women's **oppression**.

Feminist psychology has its origins in the work of turn-of-the-century feminists in psychology: for example, Helen Wooley and Leta Hollingworth, who demonstrated the *social* bases of sex differences. Some sixty years later, as second-wave feminism gathered momentum, feminists launched more direct challenges to the discipline. In 1968 Naomi Weisstein asserted that: 'Psychology has nothing to say about what women are really like because psychology does not know' (1993: 197); while in 1970 Phyllis Chesler used a prestigious conference platform to demand one million dollars 'in reparations' for women abused by the mental health professions (1989: xvii).

Mainstream ('scientific') psychology has actively resisted feminist psychology (as 'ideologically-biased') and has used its institutional power to shape and control the field. National psychological organisations have strenuously opposed the formation of internal sub-groups clearly identified as feminist, so that psychologists doing feminist work have sometimes made strategic use of the label 'psychology of women' as a less politically contentious euphemism. The British and American psychological organisations eventually accepted the formation of 'psychology of women' sub-groups.

Feminist psychologists have exposed and challenged the operation of male power in psychology. They have pointed out that psychology's theories often exclude women, or distort women's experience, by assimilating it to male norms or man-made stereotypes; and that psychology ignores diversity, typically considering 'women' as a unitary category, to be understood only in comparison with the unitary category 'men'. Feminist psychologists have also been critical of the harm that psychology (and the popularisation of psychological ideas) has wrought in women's lives, particularly through locating responsibility (and also pathology) *within*

the individual, thereby obscuring the social and structural operation of male power (Wilkinson 1991).

Contemporary feminist psychology is extremely diverse – characterised as much by debate *within* the field as by debate *between* feminist psychology and mainstream psychology. It embraces a rich variety of incompatible – and at times conflicting – theoretical traditions, methodological approaches, and types of activism. Feminist psychologists are unified, however, in challenging psychology's key assumption of women's inferiority. The following five major research traditions all challenge this assumption.

Mismeasure of women

This tradition refutes psychology's assumption that women are inferior by arguing that psychology as presently conducted is *poor science* – it is plagued with methodological errors, and produces biased findings and interpretations. Feminists working in this tradition (the 'mismeasure of women': Tavris 1992) highlight the fact that many of psychology's classic theories are derived from all-male samples, with 'findings' then generalised to both sexes. Women are judged according to how well they 'measure up' to a male norm, and any findings of sex differences are interpreted as female deficits. Feminists in this tradition point to the scientific errors rampant throughout the sex differences literature. They expose empirical studies as riddled with technical flaws. In sum, they say, weak data are used to support sexist prejudices (see **sexism**).

Some feminists argue the main advantage of the 'bad science' allegation is that it challenges the mainstream on its own terms and raises the possibility – by doing 'better science' – of beating the boys at their own game. Others identify its main disadvantage as the failure to challenge the game itself – and argue that, in challenging the scientific objectivity of mainstream psychology, feminist psychologists reinforce the notion that objectivity is potentially attainable, obscuring the extent to which science itself is a socio-political practice.

Internalised oppression

This second feminist tradition *accepts* (to some

extent) psychology's assumption of women's infer-iority – but contends that such 'inferiority' is not intrinsic to women. Rather, it is the *result* of women's oppression. It argues that women are socialised differently from men in ways which encourage the development of personal character-istics detrimental to happiness and achievement. This means that even when external constraints on women's progress are removed, women still oppress themselves. The 'classic' in this tradition is Matina Horner's 1970s research on women's 'fear of success'. Alleged 'fear of success' has subsequently provided a very popular explanation for women's failure to advance in professional life. Other explanations in this tradition include: lack of assertiveness, low self-esteem, poor self-confidence, under-valuation of achievement, and failure to develop an autonomous self (Tavris 1992).

As some feminists point out, a key advantage of this framework is that it is innovative in its focus on women *as women* (i.e. not in relation to, or comparison with, men). It remains the framework of choice for much contemporary feminist psychol-ogy, and underpins the large feminist therapy and self-help industry (see **therapy, feminist**), which is seen as offering 'compensatory socialisation' for women. It is popular because it offers clear prescriptions for creating individual *and* social change. If sufficient individuals are changed (through therapy), they, in turn, will be able to create social change. Feminist critics have seen the disadvantages of this approach as including its victim-blaming implications, and its perpetuation of mainstream psychology's relentless focus on the internal and the individual at the expense of the social and the political.

Listening to women's voices

The third main approach is to agree that women *are* different from men, and to *maximise* and *celebrate* sex differences. Feminists working within this tradition say that psychology has described the world from its own *male* perspective, which it has confused with absolute truth. The task of feminist psychology is to listen to the voices of women and girls who speak in a 'different voice' or who have 'different ways of knowing'. Lyn Mikel Brown and Carol **Gilligan** (1992) have developed a 'voice-

centred relational method' to enable them to listen responsively to the voices of women and girls. A key 'discovery' from listening to women's voices is that women inhabit a more 'relational' world than men: women are more 'connected' with and 'caring' about others.

The importance of this tradition, some feminists say, lies in reversing the frame of reference within which psychology has conceptualised women. However, this approach is criticised by others for unproblematically reproducing the notion of the 'pure' voices of the oppressed – as though women, simply by being women, can utter truths about the world and thereby reveal authentic selves. Other critics emphasise that this concentration on women's 'relational' worlds feeds back into tradi-tional ideas about women, reinforcing the social structures which impose the 'caring' task. Still others say that women are not, as some work within this tradition seems to suggest, a cohesive group who speak in a single voice – they highlight the diversity of women's voices across differences of age, ethnicity, (dis)ability, class, sexual identity and other social divisions.

Displacing sex differences

The fourth tradition argues that women are neither inferior nor superior to men. In fact, these researchers refuse to compare the sexes. They *minimise*, indeed *undermine*, the importance of sex differences, arguing that being male or female is not a central determinant of psychological functioning. Rather, there are elements of mascu-linity and femininity in everyone, and a key aspect of mental health and wellbeing is the ability to deploy these flexibly according to the situation. Such 'psychological **androgyny**' was first pro-posed as a new standard of mental health by Sandra Bem in 1974. This work has had surprising success within mainstream psychologi-cal theory – perhaps because it removes the critical spotlight *both* from psychology *and* from women, and also offers a reframing of the familiar concept of 'sex roles' in the positive context of improving mental health. Detached from its feminist intent, it sits comfortably with psycholo-gy's liberal rhetorics.

At the time it was developed, its proponents suggest, androgyny and the minimising of sex differences offered a powerful corrective to the 'women-as-inferior' position common in mainstream psychology, disrupting traditional ideas about the essential qualities of 'male' and 'female' gender identity. The biggest *dis*advantage of this approach, say its critics, is that it focuses (like traditional psychology) on individuals at the expense of social structure, and it ignores the power differentials which shape 'appropriate' male and female behaviour.

Reconstructing the question of sex differences

Finally – and most recently – feminist psychologists working within the frameworks of **social constructionism** and postmodernism (see **post-structuralism/postmodernism**) have argued that sex/gender should no longer be theorised as 'difference', but reconceptualised as a *principle of social organisation*, structuring power relations between the sexes (e.g. Hare-Mustin and Marecek 1994). This perspective suggests that it is not just the *psychological* attributes of 'masculinity' and 'femininity' which are constructed by society – but the apparently *biological* categories of 'men' and 'women'. Instead of asking questions about the 'real' differences between men and women, feminist psychologists in this tradition ask questions about how they are *constructed* as different sexes. They show how this is accomplished through repeated assertions about what 'men' and 'women' are 'really' like: the effect of these assertions is to *reinforce* the *categories* of 'men' and 'women'. In common with postmodern feminists outside psychology, some social constructionist psychologists propose jettisoning the category of 'woman' altogether. They argue that 'woman' functions only as a marker of otherness and subordination within a social system based on male dominance. To describe 'woman' as a 'natural' category is to give a biologically essentialist underpinning to a historical situation of male dominance and female subordination (see **biological essentialism**).

This perspective is very radical. It moves beyond notions about the sex role stereotypes and socialisation processes supposed to produce 'masculine' men and 'feminine' women, to challenge the very categories 'men' and 'women' – also the categories 'heterosexuality' (Wilkinson and Kitzinger 1993) and 'lesbianism' (Kitzinger 1987). This tradition has gained little recognition in psychology – to most mainstream psychologists it is unrecognisable *as* psychology. Although, as its adherents point out, it provides a fundamental challenge to taken-for-granted ways of thinking, the full implications have rarely been appreciated. Work in this tradition has often been criticised for its unintelligibility – partly due to the difficulty of the concepts, but partly due, too, to the wilful obscurity of much of its writing; and also for the difficulty of translating its theoretical challenge into a clear political programme.

Despite the (sometimes virulent) disagreements among these different traditions, all of them have enabled feminists to make important interventions in psychology – and some of them have also provided a basis for social change. All five traditions have been used to challenge psychology's oppressive practices and to develop a distinctively feminist psychology (c.f. Unger and Crawford 1996; Wilkinson 1996).

References and further reading

Bem, S.L. (1974) 'The Measurement of Psychological Androgyny', *Journal of Consulting and Clinical Psychology* 42: 155–62.

Brown, L.M. and Gilligan, C. (1992) *Meeting at the Crossroads*, Cambridge, MA: Harvard University Press.

Chesler, P. (1989) *Women and Madness*, San Diego, CA: Harcourt Brace Jovanovich, 2nd edn.

Hare-Mustin, R.T. and Marecek, J. (1994) 'Asking the Right Questions', *Feminism and Psychology* 4 (3): 399–403.

Horner, M.S. (1972) 'Toward an Understanding of Achievement-Related Conflicts in Women', *Journal of Social Issues* 28: 157–76.

Kitzinger, C. (1987) *The Social Construction of Lesbianism*, London: Sage Publications.

Tavris, C. (1992) *The Mismeasure of Woman*, New York: Touchstone.

Unger, R. and Crawford, M. (1996) *Women and Gender*, New York: McGraw Hill, 2nd edn.

Weisstein, N. (1993) 'Psychology Constructs the Female', *Feminism and Psychology* 3 (2): 195–210.

Wilkinson, S. (1991) 'Feminism and Psychology', *Feminism and Psychology* 1 (1): 5–18.

Wilkinson, S. (ed.) (1996) *Feminist Social Psychologies*, Buckingham, England and Philadelphia, PA: Open University Press.

Wilkinson, S. and Kitzinger, C. (eds) (1993) *Heterosexuality*, London: Sage Publications.

SUE WILKINSON

public/private

The public/private sphere dualism constructs separate gendered social space for men and women. Particularly in societies which have inherited the philosophical assumptions of the Enlightenment and the theological and social assumptions of Judaeo-Christianity, the private sphere was/is identified with women, and imbued with feminine qualities (intimate, irrational, particularistic, partial and sentimental) that were considered antithetical to the public male (rational, objective, other-regarding, meritocratic and competitive) sphere. Women have been socially constructed (gendered) as naturally suited for private sphere concerns, and unsuited for public sphere activity. Gender roles reflect a social consensus forged by patriarchal elites, and construct a dichotomy in which women are private subjects, not public citizens (see **dichotomies**). This public/private dichotomy, historically inherent in all patriarchies, continues in the classical capitalist and neoliberal (or neoclassical) economics, as these approaches construct rigid and separate categories of the market, public government, family and community. That is, the structure, practice and study of contemporary politics and **economics** are imbued with masculinist assumptions, including the notion of public and private spheres.

Women's disproportionate confinement in the private sphere correlates with women's subordinate status. Until well into the twentieth century, women in most states were restricted from autonomous commercial, political and other public activity, and lacked legal authority in relation to citizenship, contracts and commerce, property ownership, and guardianship of infants. (This continues to be the case for women in some states today, in violation of international law, including the Universal Declaration of Human Rights and the Convention on the Elimination of All Forms of Discrimination Against Women.) Conversely, the concerns that attended women in the private sphere were taken to be beyond the proper purview of political and economic actors and were left to the management of the resident patriarch. Mary **O'Brien** considered the separation of public and private spheres to be 'an *a priori* assumption of patriarchal political praxis' (O'Brien 1989: 338). Liberal ideological **hegemony** further entrenched the notion of the private familial space as properly beyond the purview of the state.

The women's movement has contested the public/private dichotomy, beginning with the slogan 'the personal is political' and organising through the solidarity slogans 'sisterhood is powerful' and 'none of us has made it until all of us have made it'. That is, feminist **praxis** is grounded in the analysis of the power relations inherent in the public/private divide, and strategises for transformation of these power relations in specific ways. This conceptualisation of the shared nature of gender socialisation and subordination foregrounds gendered experiences as politically significant phenomena. Personal problems are not only private idiosyncratic experiences but part of a social phenomenon amenable to political analysis. For example, feminist analysis has pierced the veil of patriarchal privacy in relation to the home and relationships to focus public and political attention on matters such as child and spousal abuse within the hetero-patriarchal family.

References and further reading

O'Brien, M. (1989) 'Feminist Praxis' in A. Miles and G. Finn (eds) *Feminism: From Pressure to Politics*, Montreal: Black Rose Press, pp. 327–44.

JOYCE GREEN

Q

qualitative methodologies

Qualitative research is characterised by subjectivity rather than objectivity, closeness to the subject, uniqueness over universality, self-determination rather than social control, and solidarity and action not impartial advice (Maguire 1987: 17). Qualitative methodologies, then, are 'theor[ies] and analys[es] of how research does or should proceed' (Harding 1987: 3) that seek to achieve these goals. Qualitative methods include participant observation, in-depth interviewing and life histories. For feminist researchers – for whom qualitative methodologies are well suited – feminist methodologies reflect the goal of research by, for and about women. Despite great variation amongst feminists, all share the belief that, historically, knowledge has been skewed by androcentric bias within methodologies and methods and that feminist methodologies should seek to correct this. Often this is achieved through prioritising women's voices and through action-oriented research aimed at improving women's lives. It is these characteristics in addition to a stance as a researcher amongst rather than above or outside the researched that Sandra G. Harding identifies as the characteristics of feminist methodologies (5–9).

References and further reading

Harding, S.G. (ed.) (1987) *Feminism and Methodology: Social Science Issues*, Bloomington, IN: Indiana University Press.
Maguire, P. (1987) *Doing Participatory Research: A Feminist Approach*, Amherst: The Centre for International Education, School of Education, University of Massachusetts.

LISA RUNDLE AND NANCY MANDELL

queer theory

During the early 1990s an interdisciplinary intellectual movement began to take shape, coined (with appropriately camp humour), 'Queer Theory'. Queer theory built upon disciplinary and cultural work that lesbian and gay scholars had been producing, in some instances, since the 1960s, particularly in ethnography, history (including Foucauldian genealogy), sociology, literary criticism, women's studies and cultural studies. The feminist **sex wars** (extended debates around S/M, **pornography**, **prostitution**, **butch/femme**) heightened the need for an analysis of **sexuality** irreducible to **gender**. This, combined with the AIDS crisis, which served to realign and strengthen estranged lesbian and gay ties, created a political, artistic and academic culture receptive to a notion of 'queer'.

Queer theory posits a critical re-thinking or 'querying' of the ideological, psychological, and bodily economies which shape sexual identity, gender and desire. Whereas modern 'homosexuality' had its genesis in an imposed scientific category with its own clear-cut mechanisms of surveillance and control, and 'gay' and 'lesbian' have been self-defined terms with fairly clear political parameters, the most recent reincarnation (reclaiming) of the term 'queer' carries with it considerable ambivalence and uncertainty. How does the abandonment of the category of 'sexual orientation' in favour of the 'sexual pervert' or the 'gender outlaw' help to counter the oppositional and reductionist logic and politic of self-other? As Michael Warner remarks, 'queer gets a critical edge by defining itself against the normal, rather than the heterosexual' (Warner 1992: 18).

In her introduction to a collection of essays drawn from a conference of the same name, Teresa de Lauretis writes that the term 'Queer Theory', was arrived at, in contrast to 'Les/Bi/Gay' or 'Gay and Lesbian', 'in the effort to avoid all of these fine distinctions in our discursive protocols, not to adhere to any one of the given terms, not to assume their ideological liabilities, but instead to both transgress and transcend them – or at the very least problematise them' (Lauretis 1991: v). Lauretis initially took up the term queer with an eye to projects uncovering 'the respective and/or common grounding of current discourses and practices of homosexualities in relation to gender and to race, class, ethnic culture, generational, geographical, and socio-political location'. Hence, the title of her edited collection 'Queer Theory: Lesbian and Gay Sexualities' keeps all the terms in an effort to set up a critical juxtaposition.

The fast-paced discussion of the parameters of 'queer theory', in both popular and academic contexts, attested to its potential and just as quickly produced critiques of its limitations. Critics have asked why Lauretis (and others who embraced the term) are so certain that 'queer' won't prove just as inadequate for the conceptualisation of lesbian as older terms such as 'gay' or 'homosexual'? Could it really represent a vast range of sexualities across gender, race, class, and cultural lines under one rubric? Should it? What's more, the very capaciousness of the term 'queer', its plasticity and inclusivity – at once more inclusive than 'lesbian and gay', and more oppositional – has been the most consistent basis for critiques of queer theory, precisely by those who might be expected to take up the term (bisexuals, transsexuals and transgenders), as well as by earlier generations of lesbian and gay men wary of surrendering the specificity of Lesbian and Gay Studies. **Lauretis** herself soon distanced

herself from the term, disappointed by the vacuousness that its popularity implied.

On the other hand, Judith **Butler**, remarking upon the force, opposition, stability, and variability that accompanies both the interpellative (Althusser) and the performative act of self naming, insists that the value of 'queer' as a rubric is utterly dependent upon the contestability of its meanings:

> If identity is a necessary error, then the assertion of 'queer' will be incontrovertibly necessary .... It is equally necessary ... to let it be vanquished by those who are excluded by the term but who justifiably expect representation by it, to let it take on meanings that cannot now be anticipated.
>
> (Butler 1993: 21)

Butler's earlier book, *Gender Trouble* (1990), was a watershed text for queer theory (even though she was bemused by its adoption by the nascent field). In it Butler argues that the 'naturalness' and originary status of **heterosexuality** and, concomitantly, the ontological category of 'woman' for feminism, need to be undermined by close examination of the gender parodies performed by lesbian and gays. With and against the work of key theorists such as Freud, **Beauvoir**, Newton, **Irigaray**, **Wittig**, **Kristeva**, and Foucault, Butler demonstrates that camp (butch/femme, drag) 'imitations' of gender reveal the 'utterly constructed status of the heterosexual original' (1990: 31).

The indeterminacy of sex and sexuality in 'queerness', in tension with sexual identities built on biological categories (lesbian, gay man), is a cornerstone of 'queer theory'. Diana Fuss's discussion of the choice for the cover of *inside/out: Lesbian Theories, Gay Theories* (1991) is interesting in this respect.

> On the cover of this book is not a face (no attempt was made to select 'representative' gay and lesbian bodies, as if such a thing were possible) but a figure, a knot, a figure-eight knot or four knot to be precise.... The undecidability of this simple topology may be its greatest appeal, for it seems to signify at once an anal, a vaginal, a clitoral, a penile, and a testicular topography.
>
> (Fuss 1991: 17)

This invertible knot could be 'glossed in the context of this book as a figure for (sexual) inversion' but, similarly to Lacan's Borromean Knot of the unconscious, in its 'openings and closures', 'overs and unders', 'ins and outs' it visualises the 'contortions and convolutions of any sexual identity formation'.

Perhaps 'Queer Theory' is a misnomer insofar as *Theory*, at least implicitly, suggests a field of research in which both a discourse and its objects are systematic, coherent, and complete. Michael Warner highlights queer theorists' methodological focus on representational technologies and psychoanalytic models which sidestep liberal minority rights and separatist **identity politics**: 'Almost everything called queer theory is about how texts – literature, mass culture, language – shape sexuality. But representation is inherently unstable, uncontrollable, queer by nature' (Warner 1992: 19). But while some queer theories demonstrate a more marked discursive and psychoanalytic investment than characterised US Lesbian and Gay Studies one cannot reduce queer theory to deconstruction and psychoanalysis for/by queers. Methodologically, queer theory is nomadic in that it participates in a radical project of redrawing the boundaries separating traditional patterns of discourse and knowledge. This 'theory' has not only allowed for an encounter among the various distinct bodies of work to which its interdisciplinary nature can be retraced – feminist criticism, philosophy, history, social and political thought, psychoanalysis, medicine, and literary and cultural studies – it has also provided a site for their mutual contestation and the repudiation of their orthodoxies by taking them in directions so far largely uninvestigated. Queer theory thus involves an insistence on an openness, a continued exchange or 'querying' with the outside which precludes a fixed cannon or methodology.

Whither queer theory? Two scenarios seem plausible: queer theory has already been displaced or (in Butler's words) 'vanquished by those who are excluded by the term but who justifiably expect representation by it' (in Dinshaw and Halperin (eds) 1993: 21); that is, by the non or not exclusively lesbian and gay sexual minorities that Gayle Rubin wrote so eloquently of in 1984. Certainly the growth in scholarship engaging the specificities of bisexual, s/m, transgender and transsexual subjectivities, politics, texts and lives, authored by self-identified and politicised bisexuals, s/m players, transgenders and transsexuals, supports such a reading of the situation. Meanwhile the gathering force of critiques of some strands of queer theory's rhetorical deployment of, and dependence upon, transgressively or transcendently cross-gendered figures uncomfortably recall critiques of early (white, First World) feminist instrumental figurings of the oppressed Third World Woman. These critiques radically undercut claims to queer 'inclusivity'.

And yet, was queer theory ever about inclusivity? Queer theory's radical project envisioned an open-ended and fractured discursive domain disrupting clear cut, restrictive quasi-ontological markers of community membership, be they physical, economic, ethnic, or racial. Many of us working in this field have insisted that queer theory is not merely a theory of the queer designed to generate a credible discourse explaining and defending perverse sexuality, we have in fact argued that queer theory must itself be queered. This, of course, is not meant simply as a reflection of queer theorists' own gender identities or sexual proclivities but rather as a necessary pre-condition for any understanding of the complex web of relays connecting the 'theory' to the 'queer' body. If it is to be defined in oppositional terms at all, queer theory is a function of a resistance not only to the heterosexist norm but also to itself as it encompasses a multitude of differing and discordant communities and political projects.

See also: bisexuality; essentialism; transgender; transsexuality/gender dysphoria

References and further reading

Beemyn, B. and Eliason, M. (eds) (1996) *Queer Studies: A Lesbian, Gay, Bisexual and Transgender Anthology*, New York: New York University Press.
Butler, J. (1990) *Gender Trouble: Feminism and the Subversion of Identity*, New York: Routledge.
—— (1993) *Bodies That Matter: On the Discursive Limits of Sex*, London and New York: Routledge.
Dinshaw, C. and Halperin, D. (eds) (1993) *glq: a Journal of Lesbian and Gay Studies* 1,1.

Fuss, D. (ed.) (1991) *inside/out: Lesbian Theories, Gay Theories*, New York: Routledge.

Gever, M., Greyson, J., and Parmar, P. (eds) (1993) *Queer Looks: Perspectives on Lesbian and Gay Film and Video*, Toronto: Between The Lines.

Lauretis, T. de (1991) 'Queer Theory: Lesbian and Gay Sexualities', *differences: a Journal of Feminist Cultural Studies*, 3,2, pp. iii–xviii.

Schor, N. and Weed, E. (1994) *differences: a Journal of Feminist Cultural Studies*, 6, 2 and 3.

Sedgewick, E. (1990) *Epistemology Of The Closet*, Berkeley, CA: University of California Press.

Stryker, S. (1998) 'The Transgender Issue: An Introduction', *glq: a Journal of Lesbian and Gay Studies* 4, 2: 145–58.

Warner, M. (1992) 'From Queer To Eternity', *Voice Literary Supplement*, June, 18–19.

—— (ed.) (1993) *Fear of a Queer Planet: Queer Politics and Social Theory*, Minneapolis, MI: University of Minnesota Press.

JULIA CREET

R

race

Ethical and political issues raised by racial difference and the formation of racial categories in the USA are important to western feminist theory for several reasons. Race, like **gender**, is largely a product of oppressive social construction (see **social constructionism**) in cultures dominated by white men. Since half of the members of non-white groups are women, white feminists need to understand the distinct problems of these groups. But, non-white women have claimed that western feminists do not address their problems and that they therefore must speak for theselves. This demand may create a need for pluralist feminist theory. However, the complexity and instability of social ideas of race challenge race-based **identity politics**, as well as pluralist feminist theory. Race does not have the biological foundation that is commonly assumed in western society.

Beginning in the eighteenth century, western Europeans and Americans believed that racial difference had a foundation in human biology that in turn determined the psychology and culture of members of different races. The work of Franz Boas and Claude Lévi-Strauss in the first half of the twentieth century resulted in abandonement by mainstream scientists of this idea of cultural racial **essentialism**, or the belief that biological race determines personality and culture. Culture is largely the effect of history and environment, and to the extent that individual psychological differences are hereditary, they are not race-based. Much of the antiracist scholarship and activism since the Second World War has been an attack on cultural racial essentialism. Both the United Nations Charter of 1947 and the American **public/private civil rights** legislation of the 1960s are based on the belief that racial difference does not entail moral, intellectual or any other important form of human difference. Where such differences exist along racial lines, they are presumed to be the result of past discrimination and oppression.

Just as cultural racial essentialism is not supported by scientific evidence, neither is there evidence for biological racial essentialism. Race does not exist biologically because there are no general genetic markers for it. It differs from the way sex has traditionally been viewed, for example. From the presence of XX (female) or XY (male) chromosomes, both primary and secondary sexual characteristics can be reliably predicted. Most of the time, the presence of XX or XY can be said to cause the presence of ovaries and breasts in women or testicles and upper body strength in men. With race, there is nothing general that causes genes for light or dark skin hues, straight or curly hair growth, or any other physical trait associated with black, white, Asian or Native American racial identity. Blacks, Asians and Indians are simply members of historical groups that have had racial identities assigned to them under conditions of oppression. Typical or stereotypical inherited physical racial traits are no different from other inherited physical traits such as height or eye colour and they are far more difficult to demarcate with precision.

In fact, race is no different from ethnicity which

is widely assumed to entail cultural rather than biological difference. (Although, ethnic categories such as Hispanic pose their own problems of false essentialism and social construction.)

Nonetheless, race has a powerful social reality and its social constructions have tended to support and reproduce (false) beliefs in both cultural and biological racial essentialism. In the USA, the difference between black and white has been socially enforced through the one drop rule: a person is black given a black ancestor anywhere in family descent. This 'one drop of black blood' is of course a fiction – differences in the four human blood types do not conform to racial differences and have only a loose statistical connection with world geography.

Besides the lack of general biological racial traits, the different sets of traits associated with each race vary more within races than between races. The lack of a fixed set of traits for each so-called race means that race cannot be inherited as is commonly thought. Rather, the specific physical characteristics variably associated with races in cultural contexts are inherited through family descent, as is the rest of human biology. Race therefore supervenes on human genealogy or family inheritance.

The social definitions of black and white have been set up as contradictories of one another. White equals no black ancestors and black equals at least one black ancestor. Two contradictiory conditions cannot both obtain at the same time, although one of them must. This means, and it has indeed been the case throughout much of American social history, that a person must be black or white, but not both and not neither. Such a stipulation cannot be fulfilled in reality, given the existence of individuals who are both black and white (mixed-race people) or neither black nor white (Asians and Indians). Nevertheless, most current racial debate centres on white racism against blacks.

Non-white women have insisted that they speak for themselves rather than conform to representation by white feminists. Part of their objection to white feminist representation is a belief that they need to be liberated from racial discrimination and oppression before they can address liberation on the grounds of gender. Demands for the recogni-

tion of mixed-race identity present a similar challenge within racial liberation. There are probably as many different ways of forming racial identities as there are different racial identities. To begin with, the identity formation of the four recognised racial groups differs dramatically: white identity is based on a family genealogy of not having non-white ancestors. Black identity is based on the presence of black ancestors – strictly speaking, only one is required. Native American identity is based on the geographical location of ancestors and/or adherence to traditional Native American cultural practices. Asian identity derives from a number of ethnicities and foreign nationalities of kin, all sources of which are somehow subsumed under a category constructed as Asian.

Mixed race identity formation is the most complex of all. It can take any or all of these forms: fractional (half this and one quarter that and one quarter something else); inclusive (this and that); traditional non-white (e.g. black according to the one drop rule); white (if a mixed race person can and does pass for white, or identifies as white based on white ancestry); generic (just mixed or multiracial without specifying in what way); aracial (having no racial affiliation). Some mixed-race individuals consider it their prerogative to change their racial identities as their life experience changes, and quite often, their social contexts create pressures to change.

Besides the complexity of mixed-race identity formation, there is also a complexity of content. From the four primary groups of black, white, Asian and Native American, there are at least fifteen categories: all four groups combined, each of the four groups taken separately – that's five; and the other ten would be black-Asian-Indian, black-white-Asian, black-white-Indian, white-Asian-Indian, black-white, Asian-white, Asian-Indian, Indian-white, black-Asian and black-Indian. Mixed-race identities vary further depending on where in ancestry the 'mixture' occured. All of the possiblities for mixed race identity vary in form and content depending on geographical location in the USA.

These microdiversities of mixed race increase racial ambiguity. Mixed race people are the fastest growing group of Americans. Between 1970 and 1990, the number of children in mixed race families increased from 500,000 to over 2 million. It can no longer be assumed that it is always or even usually possible to tell what race a person is, based on appearance.

The *New York Times* reported on October 29, 1997 that the US Office of Management and Budget had instituted new categories for racial and ethnic makeup on federal forms. As of the year 2000, Americans are allowed to identify themselves as members of more than one race. With this change from the previous 'check one box' policy, the OMB has rejected a general multiracial category that would have applied to all mixed race people. If people can choose to identify according to as many racial components as they want, the common idea of racial purity is officially undermined.

Traditional African American liberatory writers and activists have thus far resisted recognition of mixed race identity on the grounds that it will have a divisive effect on the black community and destabilise socioeconomic gains resulting from affirmative action policies. These critics deem it unfair that mixed black and white Americans should have both the social advantages resulting from their white ancestry and compensatory benefits resulting from their black ancestry. These critics also assume, as do some white advocates, that social justice is best achieved on the basis of traditional non-white racial identities, even if those identities were historically imposed as part of programmes of oppression that were unrelated to race. They reason that since social injustice was based on those identities, they are needed to pick out worthy recipients of social justice programmes. There are, as well, strong traditions of black pride and solidarity based on the one drop rule.

A fully nonessentialist theory of racial liberation would need to take into account the tension between the oppressive history of false racial categories and their liberatory function in resisting oppression. Also, it would need to accommodate international diversity that both resembles and differs from the difficult American case of black and white racial difference. Such a nonessentialist racial theory would be of great importance to feminism because of the connections between sexism, classism and racism in the beliefs and practices of dominant groups.

See also: African feminism; biological essentialism; black feminism(s); Chicana feminism; critical race theory; discrimination and the law; First Nations and women; global feminism; womanist theology

References and further reading

Appiah, K.A. and Gutman, A. (eds) (1996) *Color Conscious: The Political Morality of Race*, Princeton, NJ: Princeton University Press.

Ezorsky, G. (1991) *Racism and Justice*, Ithaca, NY: Cornell University Press.

Hannaford, I. (1996) *Race: The History of an Idea in the West*, Baltimore: Johns Hopkins University Press.

Jaimes, M.A. (ed.) (1992) *The State of Native America*, Boston: South End Press.

Kuper, L. (ed.) (1965) *Race, Science and Society*, New York: Columbia University Press.

Pittman, J.P. (ed.) (1996) *African-American Perspectives and Philosophical Traditions*, New York: Routledge.

Zack, N. (ed.) (1995) *American Mixed Race: The Culture of Microdiversity*, Lanham, MD: Rowman and Littlefield.

—— (1997) *RACE/SEX: Their Sameness, Difference and Interplay*, New York: Routledge.

—— (1998) *Thinking About Race*, Belmont, CA: Wadsworth.

Zack, N., Shrage, L. and Sartwell, C. (eds) (1998) *Race, Class, Gender and Sexuality: The Big Questions*, Malden, MA: Blackwell Publishers.

NAOMI ZACK

radical feminism

Radical feminism is an approach to feminist thinking and action which maintains that the sex/gender system is the fundamental cause of women's oppression. According to Alison **Jaggar** and Paula Rothenberg, this claim may mean that women's oppression is the longest existing, most widespread, deepest, or worst form of human oppression. It can also mean 'that women's oppression ... provides a conceptual model for understanding all other forms of oppression' (Jaggar and Rothenberg 1984: 186). However, just because radical feminists agree about the pernicious nature and functions of sexism does not mean they agree about ways to eliminate it. On the contrary, with the emergence of so-called **essentialism** in feminist thought, radical feminists have divided into two camps: radical-libertarian feminists and radical-cultural feminists.

Radical-libertarian feminists generally espouse the ideas of 1960s and 1970s radical feminists who drew attention to the ways in which the concept of femininity as well as women's reproductive and sexual roles and responsibilities often limit women's development as full human persons. These radical feminists longed for androgyny. For example, Joreen J. wrote: 'What is disturbing about a Bitch is that she is androgynous. She incorporates within herself qualities defined as "masculine" as well as "feminine". A Bitch is blatant, direct, arrogant, at times egoistic. She has no liking for the indirect, subtle, mysterious ways of the "eternal feminine". She disdains the vicarious life deemed natural to women because she wants to live a life of her own' (Koedt *et al.* 1973: 52).

Although this concept of androgyny is flawed due to its 'male' bias, it captured radical feminists' desire to transcend the limits of the sex/gender system by daring to be masculine as well as feminine. Later, some radical feminists questioned whether they wanted to be masculine at all. They believed a 'Bitch' was not a full human person, but a woman who had embraced some of the worst features of masculinity. These radical feminists rejected androgyny as a desirable goal, replacing it with a proposal to embrace women's essential 'femaleness'. Instead of believing liberated women must exhibit both masculine and feminine traits and behaviour, these radical-cultural feminists expressed the view that it is better to be female/feminine than it is to be male/masculine. Thus, women should not try to be like men; they should try to be more like women, emphasising values and virtues culturally associated with women and de-emphasising values and virtues culturally associated with men. Better yet, women should try to discover within themselves the woman Mary **Daly** (1978) terms the 'wild female' who dwells beyond the constructs of femininity and **masculinity** conceived by patriarchal society.

In addition to explaining why some radical feminists idealise androgynous persons and why others celebrate the 'female' female, the libertarian/cultural distinction explains why some radical feminists find sex 'pleasurable' and others find it 'dangerous'. For radical-libertarian feminists, sexuality is a powerful physical force which society aims to control by separating so-called good, normal, legitimate, healthy sexual practices from so-called bad, abnormal, illegitimate, unhealthy sexual practices. Supposedly, married reproductive heterosexuals are society's 'good' girls and boys; deliberately non-reproductive or unmarried heterosexuals, lesbians, gays, and prostitutes, as well as 'those whose eroticism transgresses generational boundaries' are society's 'bad' girls and boys (Rubin 1984: 275). In order to be free from society's attempts to limit 'bad' sex in the name of law and order, radical-libertarian feminists urge women to violate sexual taboos.

Radical-cultural feminists view radical-libertarian feminists as seriously mistaken about their views on heterosexuality. As radical-cultural feminists see it, heterosexual relations as practised within patriarchy are about male domination and female subordination, and they set the stage for pornography, prostitution, sexual harassment, rape, and woman-battering. Thus, radical-cultural feminists conclude the key to women's liberation is to eliminate all patriarchal institutions and sexual practices in which sexual objectifications occur (Ferguson 1984: 108).

Over and beyond expressing different views about the positive and negative effects of sexuality on women's lives, radical-libertarian and radical-cultural feminists also disagree with each other about the ways in which women's reproductive roles affect women. Whereas radical-libertarian feminists believe women should substitute artificial for natural modes of reproduction, radical-cultural feminists believe it is in women's best interests to procreate naturally. Radical-libertarian feminists are convinced that the less women are involved in the reproductive process, the more time and energy they will have to engage in society's productive processes. They advise women to maximise use of the reproduction-controlling technologies of contraception, sterilisation, and abortion. They also advise women to support technologies most likely to result in the development of an artificial placenta or womb so that women do not remain biologically enchained to reproducing the human species.

Radical-cultural feminists find radical-libertarian feminists' ideas about reproduction as misguided as their ideas about sexuality. They believe women's ability to gestate new life is women's ultimate source of power. Radical-cultural feminists insist women's reproductive oppression is caused not by female biology in and of itself, but rather by men's jealousy of women's reproductive abilities and their subsequent desire to seize control of female biology through scientific and technological means. Thus, radical-cultural feminists point out the risks women take when they use certain contraceptives, or work with infertility experts who employ artificial reproduction techniques which may be patriarchy's attempt to make sure women have the number and kind of children men supposedly want and that women's procreative experience is just as alienating as men's.

In sum, the question for *all* radical feminists to ask is what kind of sexual and reproductive practices people would adopt in a society in which all economic, political, and kinship systems were structured to create equality between men and women.

References and further reading

Daly, M. (1978) *Gyn/Ecology*, Boston: Beacon Press.
Dworkin, A. (1974) *Woman Hating: A Radical Look at Sexuality*, New York: E.P. Dutton.
—— (1987) *Intercourse*, New York: The Free Press.
Ferguson, A. (1984) 'Sex Wars: The Debate Between Radical and Liberation Feminists', *Signs* 10,1.
Firestone, S. (1970) *The Dialectic of Sex*, New York: Bantam Books.
Jaggar, A. and Rothenberg, P. (eds) (1984) *Feminist Frameworks*, New York: McGraw-Hill.
Koedt, A., Levine, E., and Rapone, A. (eds) (1973) *Radical Feminism*, New York: Quadrangle.
Rich, A. (1976) *Of Woman Born*, New York: Norton.
Rubin, G. (1984) 'Thinking Sex: Notes for a Radical Theory of The Politics of Sexuality'; in C. Vance (ed.) *Pleasure and Danger*, Boston: Routledge and Kegan Paul.

ROSEMARIE TONG

rape shield laws

Before rape shield laws were enacted, the defence in a rape trial could question the complainant about her prior sexual experience (with the accused or others) and/or call evidence of her sexual experience and reputation. This information was thought to bear on her credibility as a witness and/or on whether she had consented to the sexual acts.

The feminist challenge to the criminal justice system identified the illogical and abusive use of this information. Since the 1970s, many jusrisdictions have enacted rape shield laws to forbid or restrict questions about the complainant's sexual experience or reputation in a rape trial. Though the term 'rape shield' may imply special protective treatment, in reality rape shield laws were enacted to correct wrongs women experience, not to confer a benefit.

However, these laws have not been as successful as hoped in protecting women from unwarranted questioning about prior sexual conduct. Improper questions are not always challenged; exceptions are interpreted widely, favouring the accused; and judges sometimes allow demeaning questions about previous sexual conduct with little or no logical relevance.

See also: feminist legal theory; violence

KATHLEEN M. MACK

reader response theory

Reader response theory, which grew into prominence during the 1960s to 1980s, is part of a longer response to the gradual democratisation of 'literature' in the twentieth century. Conventional **hermeneutics**, working within a narrow social context, often aims for fixed meanings. In contrast, as increasing numbers of people claimed access to cultural power, increasingly varied readings of texts, signalling the diversities of class (see **class analysis, UK**; **class analysis, US**), **gender**, **race** and other positions from which to read, began to claim value if not true interpretation. During the 1930s, both formalist and structuralist theory began to examine the relationship among the writer, reader and the text. More important for feminism was the revival of rhetorical theory which casts the relationship as a contextually bound process. Annette Kolodny, echoing the drive within feminist concerns with reader response, was to argue in 1980 that reading was a learned skill and therefore context bound. Psycholanalytical explanations for reader response, focusing on **identity**, gained ground in the 1950s and 1960s, but the term 'reader response' arose most directly around the aesthetics proposed by Sartre, the phenomenologists R. Ingarden and W. Iser, and later Stanley Fish.

The re-reading and recuperation of women writers in the 1960s and 1970s needed not only new reading strategies, but also a firm sense of reading as a process. Feminist contributions to reader response theory have developed from arguments about what an individual is, and what constitutes aesthetic response. In terms of identity, for some, the reader is subject to ruling ideology and hence only able to take up positions that are represented or permitted by the nation state. These quasi-essentialist approaches can argue that the female reader is necessary to the development of feminist writing, while others point out that women do not necessarily read differently to men. Wai-Chee Dimock (1991) offers a sustained critique of this position in 'Feminism, New Historicism and the Reader'.

John Berger (1972) argues that women 'read' representative images of themselves constructed by men and for men, while Judith Fetterley develops from this insight the idea of the 'resisting reader' (1978): women readers are usually *im*masculated, and have to read from the male point of view; hence the woman reader reading like a feminist (self-conscious of oppression) must read in resistance to representation. Emerging during the 1970s and 1980s, this approach offers a corollary to the type of Lacanian feminism that states that within the symbolic, women are 'lack' or loss or gap or silence because the phalllus is the universal signifier, and so they cannot write like a man. Despite Julia **Kristeva**'s claim that Freudian theory offers women 'desire' as a middle point for interpretation and reading, between fixed meanings and unstable identities (1982), Michèle Barrett points out that feminism has failed to develop a theory of reading or literary value in which women

have a positive individuality (1980). The late 1980s saw several attempts to redress this problem.

Feminist developments in aesthetics have lent weight to reader response theory that was trying to move away from the mainstream idea that response is neutrally conceptual and tied primarily to issues in cognitive psychology. The passive reader envisaged by the phenomenologists, who suggest that the text generates emotion in the reader, is adjusted to analyse the effects of context and of different kinds of knowledge available to the reader on the text. Theory from the 1990s has argued that reading is not only cognitive apprehension but also socially grounded affective involvement, and moves beyond the resistant reader to the legitimation of different emotions as active responses from the reader to the text. This exploration runs alongside a much broader attention to contexts for reading: Janice Radway's *Reading the Romance* (1984) opened up publishing history for women's readings, and other collections have engaged with **history**, cultural studies, gender and race.

A few approaches from the 1980s to 1990s have brought together articulated theories of identity with the developments in aesthetics and knowledge. Mary Jacobus suggests that 'Reading Woman' means reading from within a situated context, that could never be univocal or fully represented (1986), and that an understanding of the position of the reader is vital to the aesthetic legitimation of value. How one might read if one recognised that identity is communal and positioned, and that response is knowledge constructed by conceptual and affective experience, has preoccupied other feminists concerned with witnessing, testimony and **gossip**, **autobiography** and autography. However, reader response theory as a named school of thought has not fully been taken up by feminists. The difficulty of this challenge, as well as the hope it offers, is analysed in detail by Elizabeth Abel (1993) writing on issues of race and reading, who concludes that such reading expands the possibility of dialogue about and across boundaries. Although difficult, the activity is central to the feminist project.

See also: aesthetics, feminist; cultural theory/

cultural studies, feminist; psychoanalytic feminist literary theory

References and further reading

Abel, E. (1993) 'Black Writing, White Reading', *Critical Inquiry*, 19:3, pp. 470–498.

Barrett, M. (1980) *Women's Oppression Today: Problems in Marxist Feminist Analysis*, London: NBL/Verso.

Berger, J. (1972) *Ways of Seeing*, London: Penguin.

Fetterley J. (1978) *The Resisting Reader*, Bloomington, IN: Indiana University Press.

Flynn, E. and Schweickart, P. (1986) *Gender and Reading*, Baltimore: John Hopkins University Press.

Jacobus, M. (1986) *Reading Women: Essays in Feminist Criticism*, London: Methuen.

Kolodny, A. (1980) 'Dancing Through the Minefield', *Feminist Studies*, 6:1, pp. 1–25.

Kristeva, J. (1982) 'Psycholoanalysis and the Polis', *Critical Inquiry*, 9:1, pp. 25–39.

Mills, S. and Pearce, L. (1996) *Feminist Readings/Feminists Reading*, Hemel Hempstead: Harvester-Wheatsheaf.

Radway, J.A. (1984) *Reading the Romance: Women, Patriarchy and Popular LIterature*, Chapel Hill: University of North Carolina Press.

LYNETTE HUNTER

religious studies

Religious studies is the academic, multi-disciplinary study of religion. It investigates and analyses religious behaviours, claims about truth and ultimacy, symbol systems, mythic patterns, ritual actions, worldviews, representations, metaphysical formulations, and the history and development of traditions. Religious studies scholars are divided on the acceptability of confessional approaches within religious studies, that is, approaches where scholars are 'insiders' to the tradition they are analysing.

The modern critical study of religion dates from the seventeenth century, when thinkers like Spinoza analysed the Bible as an historical document rather than as divinely revealed truth. F. Max Muller carried this project further in the nineteenth century by advocating a critical, scientific study of all religions, Christianity included. *Religionswissenschaft*, usually translated as 'science' or 'history of religions', reflects the nineteenth-century concern for 'objective and 'value-free' study, an emphasis which has profoundly marked religious studies' development. The explosion of theories about human nature and culture at this time also contributed to the field's interdisciplinarity, as anthropology, psychology and sociology joined archeology, philology, **philosophy** and history as means to investigate the complex cultural phenomenon of religion.

Academic departments of religious studies first emerged in the middle of the twentieth century as post-secondary institutions shifted from teaching confessional courses in (Christian) Religious Knowledge to more broadly based studies of the human search for meaning. The baby boom generation's demand for courses in eastern traditions and in personal spiritual growth in the 1960s furthered religious studies' expansion. Departments were augmented by representatives of non-Christian traditions who were often expected to bring with them the believer's stance which their Christian/post-Christian colleagues had rejected.

The result of this history is that there are at least three main approaches to the academic study of religion: normative, social-scientific, and comparative. Normative approaches assume that there is an objective referent to religious discourses, that is, that there is an 'ultimate reality' beyond the particularities of human existence, and that we can know what it is. Theology is one form of the normative approach, while the archetypal theory of Carl Jung is another. Social-scientific studies focus not on whether a religion is 'true', but upon religious behaviours in human culture, considering questions such as secularisation, affiliation patterns within 'new religions' or the relation between religious belief and stands on specific social issues. The comparative approach in contrast considers common patterns amongst religions to illuminate what it terms 'the religious dimension' of human culture, a dimension which may or may not be considered of human origin. Comparisons of beliefs or practices amongst religions are a key focus, investigating topics like initiation rituals, notions of the afterlife, and cosmogonic myths. Yet another emerging approach owes much to cultural studies, understanding religion as a 'subject field' which demands interdisciplinary engagement, and taking particular events, histories, or cultural expressions as its topics for analysis. Until recently, most if not all of these approaches have been gender-blind.

Although women are the majority of the world's religious practitioners, they have been underrepresented as religious studies scholars. Proscriptions against female religious leadership in the majority traditions has meant that women were largely absent when departments were originally founded, a pattern of exclusion which continued in future hiring. An emphasis on 'value-free' scholarship raised additional problems. Malestream discourses on religion have tended to operate with essentialist notions of gender, seeing gender identity as determined by nature, either of a physical or metaphysical order (see **malestream thought**; **essentialism**). The result is that male scholars' representations of women and of gender hierarchy within religious traditions have been presented as both true and as discursively neutral, simply 'facts'. Women who challenge dominant notions of their gender construction within religion, either in particular traditions or in theorising about phenomena, are caught. By claiming they are not as either scholars or as the tradition represents them, they speak as 'insiders' whose 'lack of objectivity' undercuts their position. If on the other hand they accept the configuration of women presented in malestream discourses, they accept an 'androcentric judgement' of who they are, as deviant or different from the masculine human norm. The Enlightenment legacy of 'neutral reason' has also obscured the extent to which religious studies is invested in particular forms of heterosexual privilege and Euro-North American cultural normativity, although the latter has been adeptly challenged in David Chidester's *Savage Systems: Colonialism and Comparative Religion in Southern Africa* (1996).

Whether religion is about 'ultimate reality' or not, it is a complex cultural institution which has shaped many human lives. Symbol systems are central to religions and **gender** is central to religious symbol systems. How gender identities are constructed, and to what uses those constructions are put, ought to be an important area of study for those analysing religion. Considerable literature has been generated within religious studies on women's religious lives in various traditions and communities, but less attention has been paid to gender bias in theorising religious phenomena. In addition, much feminist scholarship is dismissive of religion, on the grounds that it is a mistaken belief, and/or has been destructive to women. Given the influence of religion as a determinative cultural factor across the globe, further development of feminist analyses within and about religion is critical, both for religious studies scholars and for women in general.

See also: androcentrism; objectivity; theology, feminist

References and further reading

Chidester, David (1996) *Savage Systems: Colonialism and Comparative Religion in Southern Africa*, Charlottesville: University Press of Virginia.

Cooey, P. *et al.* (1992) *After Patriarchy: Feminist Transformations of the World's Religions*, Maryknoll: Orbis.

Falk, N. and Gross, R.M. (eds) (1989) *Unspoken Worlds: Women's Religious Lives*, Belmont, CA: Wadsworth.

Neumaier-Dargyay, E. and Joy, M. (eds) (1995) *Gender, Genre and Religion: Feminist Reflections*, Waterloo, ON: Wilfrid Laurier University Press.

Warne, R.R. (1995) 'Further Reflections on the "Unacknowledged Quarantine": Feminism and Religious Studies', in S. Burt and L. Code (eds) *Changing Methods: Feminist Transforming Practice*, Peterborough: Broadview.

—— (1998) '(En)gendering Religious Studies', *Studies in Religion/Sciences Religieuses*, 27, (4).

RANDI R. WARNE

reproduction

Reproduction is central to understanding the position of women in society. Feminists have celebrated women's unique biological capacity to bear children as a life-giving capability which makes them compassionate and caring and have bemoaned it as a barrier to their full integration into society. Patriarchal law-makers have used reproduction as an excuse to bar women from voting, attending university, or engaging in many professions. Socialist feminists have analysed reproduction as the basis for women's overwhelming responsibility for **childcare** and housework. Health-care activists have fought to gain female command of reproduction and struggled for adequate birth control, safe abortions, and woman-centred birth practices. They have viewed with trepidation the development of new reproductive technologies which may further wrest control of reproduction from women into the hands of the medical profession.

Some suffragettes argued that women should be given the vote because they would cast their ballots according to their compassionate and maternal natures: against war, for temperance, for social welfare. Women, they believed, would use their franchise more responsibly than men. Feminists like Susan Griffin have made similar claims for a uniquely female caring, healing, ecological consciousness, rooted in a biological capacity for reproduction and nurturing. Such activists attempt to revalue characteristics devalued by **patriarchy** as feminine (see also **ecofeminism**; **cultural feminism**).

The opposite tactic is advocated by Shulamith **Firestone**, who argues that only when reproduction takes place outside women's bodies, using technology, will women be able to take their places as full members of society. Firestone's optimistic view of technology's potential to liberate women seems naive in view of feminist historical analyses of reproductive sciences. Ehrenreich and English describe the advent of modern western medicine as a process for taking dominion over reproduction away from traditional female healers like midwives. As medicine became professionalised, male-dominated medical boards barred women from active roles in health care, restricting them to supportive nursing roles and denying them decision-making control. Practices like supine birthing and forceps deliveries made births slower, more painful, and more dangerous for mothers and children. Martin documents how, even when men permitted women to study and practice medicine, medical textbooks used language which represented women as hysterical, passive, and pathological, in need of constant medical supervision and control. Given this history, few feminists feel sanguine about the development of medical technologies like artificial wombs and cloning and their potential to liberate women.

Socialist feminism has contributed to an analysis of reproduction broadly defined. Engels, in a famous formulation, posited an originary 'tribal' social formation where men secured natural resources for food and tools while women cooked, sewed, and cared for the house. Though differentiated, men and women were equal. With the development of domestic animals, however, men began to control women as a way of securing inheritance of their property. Thus the growth of private property coincided with the subordination of women. Engels's work was revolutionary for its time in taking the status of women as a problem to be analysed and explained. As Harris and Young point out, however, Engels, like many socialist theorists, used reproduction in several senses: the biological bearing of children, the social reproduction of labour through domestic work and socialisation, and the systemic reproduction of a social formation. Subsuming these diverse processes under one term makes it easy to collapse them, as Engels did, and see them as 'naturally' women's domain. By positing that men have always engaged in production, women in biological and social reproduction, Engels naturalised and made inevitable women's domestic work. It is this naturalisation of women's work that socialist feminists have attempted to unmask, by for example advocating wages for housework to make domestic labour recognised and rewarded as productive, not reproductive, work.

Mary **O'Brien** brilliantly turns Engels on his head. She opposes maternity to paternity: a woman's link to her child is obvious and involuntary, while paternity is never certain. In fact the discovery of paternity was a world-historical moment of great import which fundamentally changed men's relations to reproduction. Men mediate their alienation from reproduction by appropriating women and children through the institution of marriage and by peripheralising reproduction as natural, private, and domestic. A second world-historical moment is the development in the late twentieth century of technological contraception, a reproductive revolution which, though driven by a white western desire to limit population growth of non-white and working class 'undesirables', nevertheless gives women the possibility of reconfiguring their relations to reproduction in revolutionary ways. Contraception, if safer, more reliable, and well-distributed, could allow all women the possibility of separating sexuality from reproduction as men have always been able to do.

Most theorists write as if biological reproduction were a natural and inevitable fact of women's lives, to be celebrated or overcome. Donna **Haraway** sees, in the technological and social changes of the late twentieth century, possibilities for sidestepping the **nature/culture** dichotomy and women's grounding in the natural. Her mythical cyborg – part human, part machine – views reproduction with suspicion, and avoids the pitfalls of reproductive technology altogether by replication and regeneration. Haraway reads in recent developments the possibility of a utopian future beyond dichotomies, universalising theory, and domination, a world embracing technology, transcending boundaries, and even, perhaps, overcoming gender.

The struggles feminists wage over the definition and valuation of reproduction are integral to understanding women's positions and charting their future.

References and further reading

Ehrenreich, B. and English, D. (1973) *Complaints and Disorders*, New York: The Feminist Press.

Engels, F. (1972) *The Origin of the Family, Private Property, and the State*, New York: Pathfinder Press, 1984.

Gordon, L. (1976) *Woman's Body, Woman's Right*, New York: Grossman.

Griffin, S. (1978) *Woman and Nature*, New York: Harper Colophon.

Haraway, D.J. (1991) 'A Cyborg Manifesto', in *Simians, Cyborgs, and Women*, New York: Routledge.

Harris, O. and Young, K. (1981) 'Engendered Structures', in Kahn, J.S. and Llobera, J.R. (eds) *The Anthropology of Pre-Capitalist Societies*, London: Macmillan.

Martin, E. (1987) *The Woman in the Body*, Boston: Beacon Press.

O'Brien, M. (1981) *The Politics of Reproduction*, Boston and London: Routledge and Kegan Paul.

NANCY LEWIS

reserve army of labour

A term used by Karl Marx, reserve army of labour describes the pool of unemployed and partially employed workers in capitalist societies. According to Marx, as capital grows, so does the demand for labour. However, as production is mechanised, the demand for labour is reduced. The resulting surplus labour pool prevents workers from negotiating their wages and working conditions when labour demand increases.

Marxist feminists have applied this theory to women, by arguing that women constitute a flexible labour reserve that can be utilised by capital in times of growth when their labour is required, and then sent home during lean times. Married women, especially as part-time workers, can be exploited in this way, since they have household duties to return to during economic recessions.

See also: work, women and

References and further reading

Beechey, V. (1977) 'Some Notes on Female Wage Labour in Capitalist Production', *Capital and Class* 3: 45–66.

NANCY COOK

Rich, Adrienne (b. 1929)

Poet and radical feminist Adrienne Rich emerged alongside her 1950s and 1960s New England contemporaries Sylvia Plath and Anne Sexton. While all three poets examined conflicts between 'femininity', domesticity and female creativity, Rich's work soon demonstrated a more marked personal and political feminism.

From modernist and formalist beginnings, Rich's third poetry collection *Snapshots of a Daughter-in-Law* (1963) anticipates the feminist preoccupations of her ensuing work. The increasingly political *Diving into the Wreck* (1973) evolves into a lesbian-feminist stance, woman-centred relationships, communities and revolutionary language of collections such as *The Dream of A Common Language* (1978), while the later *Your Native Land, Your Life* (1986) denotes Rich's shift to gender, race, class and historical considerations as a Jewish woman.

Principal prose works include *Of Woman Born* (1976) in which Rich distinguishes between the idealising patriarchal constructions of **motherhood** and its lesser discussed emotional frustrations. Against charges of **essentialism**, she posits the union of mind/body schisms through a woman-centred consciousness, to instigate cultural change. Similarly, *Compulsory Heterosexuality and Lesbian Existence* (1980) envisages a woman-identified culture (based on a '**lesbian continuum**') against the 'compulsory **heterosexuality**' perpetuating male-dominated heterosexist power. Subsuming differences between lesbians and heterosexual women through the non-sexual to sexual range of all woman-identified relationships, the 'lesbian continuum' was rejected by many feminists for erasing lesbian individualities. Rich's critique of institutional heterosexuality nonetheless underpins **lesbian feminism**.

In synchronous poetry and prose, Rich's early gynocentric critiques of myth, motherhood, academia, heterosexism and lesbian identity explore personal and political female experientiality in tandem with woman-centred 're-visions' of subjugating patriarchal ideologies. A later formulation of a poetics and politics of location develops Rich's concerns with positionalities of **self** and **identity** as process through globally intersecting perspectives.

Criticised for her earlier universalisms and utopianisms, Rich identifies feminism's need to lose its white solipsistic tendencies as she staunchly opposes phallogocentric western thought (see **phallogocentrism**). Her writings have doubtless fuelled feminist debates yet they acutely echo the evolving process of feminist theory and her own theorisings through her indefatigable revisionings of a dominant culture.

See also: bonding, maternal, feminine; critical

theory, feminism and; language, gender and power; lesbian literature; women's writing

Selected writings

Rich, A. (1976) *Of Woman Born: Motherhood as Experience and Institution*, London: W.W. Norton.
—— (1987) *Blood, Bread and Poetry: Selected Prose 1979–1985*, London: Virago.
—— (1993) *Collected Early Poems, 1950–1970*, London: W.W. Norton.

SATINDER KAUR CHOHAN

romance as genre

The relationship between feminism and romance has been a long and troubled one. Whilst, on the one hand, women writers have been credited with the 'invention' of the romantic novel in the late eighteenth century, the *ideology* of 'romantic love' which accounts for the success of such texts has been regarded by a number of feminist theorists as a key agent in women's continued **oppression**.

The history of women as producers and consumers of romance fiction is synonymous with the history of the novel itself. This history has now been re-written from a feminist perspective by authors like Jane Spencer (*The Rise of the Woman Novelist*, 1986), focusing on the way in which Jane Austen and her 'Gothic' predecessors such as Ann Radcliffe and Mary Shelley established the codes, conventions and narrative templates for all subsequent romance fiction from the 'popular' (Harlequin/Mills and Boon) to the 'classic' (e.g., the Brontës). The 'romance genre' may thus be identified as texts (cinematic as well as literary) which engage a recognisable set of formal conventions regardless of their status as 'high' or 'low' culture.

Theorist Janice Radway (*Reading the Romance*, 1984) has traced the structural origins of the romance back to the fairytale as analysed by Vladimir Propp (*Morphology of the Folk Tale*, 1928). Another way of understanding the persistence and predictablity of romance (in both literature and 'real life') is through the lens of **psychoanalysis**, and writers like Roland Barthes have effectively combined the two – rendering romantic love a structure that is at once cultural *and* psychic, and hence virtually impossible to escape, challenge or transform.

This said, challenges *have* been mounted by a number of feminist writers and critics with respect to both the consumption and re/production of romance texts. There have been a number of critical studies which 'reclaim' the traditional romance (both classic and popular) by arguing that it often contains 'anti-romantic' subtexts (see Joan Forbes in *Romance Revisited*, 1995) or that it offers spaces in which women readers can 're/negotiate' their gendered and sexual identities (see Radway 1984). The twentieth century, meanwhile, saw many attempts to 're-script' romance, particularly with respect to its white, heterosexual superstructure. Lesbian, mixed-race and other 'queer' couplings are now putting the genre under stress like never before, though the extent to which these changes are *really* subversive is likely to remain the site of feminist contention.

References and further reading

Pearce, L. and Stacey, J. (eds) (1995) *Romance Revisited*, London: Lawrence and Wishart.

Radway, J. (1984) *Reading the Romance: Women, Patriarchy and Popular Literature*, Chapel Hill and London: The University of North Carolina Press.

Spencer, J. (1986) *The Rise of the Woman Novelist: From Aphra Behn to Jane Austen*, Oxford: Basil Blackwell.

LYNNE PEARCE

Rose, Hilary (b. 1935)

Hilary Rose is best known for her pioneering work in the radical science movement and in feminist epistemology (see **epistemology, feminist**). Rose studied at the University of London (UK) and completed a Ph.D. in sociology at the University of Bradford (UK). She has published in both social policy and science studies on such issues as housing, **health** and the social movements of the poor and has been especially productive in women's studies. Throughout she has been an advocate for responsible science.

Rose's first work, a collaborative book with Steven Rose entitled *Science and Society* (1969), remains an important contribution to both gender and science studies. In this examination of the history of state support of science in Britain, Rose and Rose dismantle claims of **objectivity** and challenge the 'rationality' of scientific theory and practice.

In disentangling processes of knowledge-making Rose asks what does and does not count as knowledge? She argues that science more than often counts as the *only* acceptable knowledge and suggests that feminists should be critical of the scientific knowledge process. Her interests in epistemology and science are connected through her concern for the position of women in the knowledge-making process. In analysing the various feminist epistemologies, she is critical of postmodern theory for refusing to grant epistemic privilege to the oppressed and of **standpoint theory** for failing to adequately acknowledge **difference**. However, she refuses to polarise the two epistemological stances and uses the best of standpoint theory and situated knowledges to privilege views from below while accounting for differences amongst women.

In her work *Love, Power and Knowledge* (1994) Rose draws together the literature of feminism and science. Some of her concerns are the Human Genome project and feminist resistance against oppressive science. She provides a critical analysis of genes, genetic engineering and reproductive technologies, neither vilifying or idolising science, but instead drawing together feminist critiques of science and recent biological interest in DNA.

In her work she challenges feminists to see the importance of science, and scientists to see the importance of feminism.

See also: poststructuralism/postmodernism

Selected writings

Rose, H. (1983) 'Hand, Brain and Heart: Towards a Feminist Epistemology for the Sciences', *Signs: Journal of Women in Culture and Society*, 9 (3): 73–98.

—— (1994) *Love, Power and Knowledge: Towards a*

Feminist Transformation of the Sciences, Cambridge, MA: Polity Press.

Rose, H. and Rose, S. (1969) *Science and Society*, Harmondsworth: Allen Lane.

MARSHA HENRY

Rosser, Sue V. (b. 1947)

Sue Rosser is well known for her work in both feminist critiques of **biology**, and feminist pedagogy (see **pedagogy, feminist**). She began her career in zoology at the University of Madison, at Wisconsin; from there she went to Mary Baldwin college in Virginia to teach women's studies and biology. After that, she became Director of Women's Studies at the University of South Carolina–Columbia (1986–95), but was seconded for a year to the US National Science Foundation (1994–5) as Senior Program Officer for Women's Programs. She is now Director of the Centre for Women's Studies and Gender Research at the University of Florida-Gainesville.

Rosser is perhaps best known for her extensive work on transforming the curriculum, particularly in the natural sciences. Her first book on this theme was *Teaching Science and Health from a Feminist Perspective: A Practical Guide*, published by Pergamon in 1986. More recently, she has begun to address the much more difficult area of the physical sciences and engineering, looking at the ways in which these curricula could be transformed to attract more women and take their interests into account. Her 1995 collection, *Teaching the Majority* addresses these important (and neglected, within feminism) issues.

Rosser has written extensively about the need to develop forms of 'female-friendly science'. Her introduction to *Teaching the Majority* outlines several of these, such as including women's contributions to scientific discovery, changing experimental procedures to allow more time to develop techniques, developing more interdisciplinary approaches and avoiding gender-bias in language (see **language, gender and power**). But more than simply advocating them, Sue Rosser has herself developed new classroom approaches to science and new curricula which include women's experi-

ences. With Bonnie Kelly, she carried out a project at the University of South Carolina which was aimed at encouraging women to enter into, or stay in, **science**, engineering and mathematics. This project entailed workshops with staff and students, as well as site visits to evaluate progress in recruiting more women. Not only did this project succeed in this quest, but it also seemed to produce greater confidence among students (see *Re-engineering Female Friendly Science*).

Rosser is also well known for her work in feminism and biology. Her 1992 book of that title explores many of the ways in which biology has implications for feminism, including discussion of the (largely neglected) significance of the natural sciences for women's studies. It also looks at ways in which feminist ideas might impact upon biology. This is a theme that she has taken up in several of her published articles – exploring, for instance, the implications of feminist theories for the study of evolution.

See also: Darwin, feminist critique of; women's studies (history and development of); women's studies: autonomy v. mainstreaming

Selected writings

Rosser, S. (1986) *Teaching Science and Health from a Feminist Perspective: A Practical Guide*, New York and Oxford: Pergamon.

—— (1992) *Feminism and Biology*, New York: Twayne/Macmillan.

—— (ed.) (1995) *Teaching the Majority: Science, Mathematics and Engineering Teaching that Attracts Women*, New York: Teachers College Press, Columbia University.

—— *Re-engineering Female Friendly Science* (1997), New York: Teachers Colledge Press.

LYNDA BIRKE

Rubin, Gayle

Gayle Rubin, an American feminist sex radical and activist in queer politics and anti-censorship politics, has made three key contributions to feminist and sexual theory: her concept of the sex/gender system, her concept of radical sexual pluralism and her construction of the prostitute as a sexual/political identity.

In her essay 'The Traffic in Women' (1975), Rubin retheorises the anthropological work of Lévi-Strauss inside a Marxian feminist context locating **gender** as a primary site of female **oppression** (as opposed to work). Rubin, arguing that sex and gender are socially produced and constructed, contends that the subordination of women is the result of the situational relationship by which sex and gender are socially organised and reproduced.

> [W]hat counts as sex … is culturally deter-mined […] Every society … has a sex/gender system – a set of arrangements by which the biological raw material of human sex and pro-creation is shaped by human, social intervention and satisfied in a conventional manner […]
>
> (Rubin 1975: 165)

In 'Thinking Sex' (1984), one of the defining texts in the sex wars/debates, Rubin shows the heterosexual **power** investment in constructing sexuality 'in a conventional manner' (see **hetero-sexuality**). Central to Rubin's theorisation is the development of radical pluralist sexual ethics which contends that non-coercive sexual acts, sexual identity, sexual community or sexual object choice are morally or medically privileged over others as closer to some sexual ideal. Rather, Rubin argues that sexual acts should be assessed by the way partners treat one another, the level of mutual consideration, the presence or absence of coercion, and the quantity and quality of the pleasure they provide (Rubin 1984: 283).

Rubin uses two metaphorical representations, the erotic pyramid and the charmed circle, to depict the stratification of sexual populations and sexual practices according to a hierarchical system of sexual value that structures modern western society. At the apex of the erotic pyramid, inside the charmed circle, is heterosexual, marital, monogamous, reproductive, non-commercial sex; at the bottom of the pyramid, outside the charmed circle, is homosexual, unmarried, promiscuous, non-procreative, commercial sex.

Rubin's work provides a theoretical structure for understanding the hegemonic construction of dissident sexualities as 'deviant' sexual minorities

(see **hegemony**). Situating the prostitute as a sexual minority like the homosexual, and prostitu-tion as a dissident sexuality like homosexuality, Rubin theorises the production of the prostitute as a sexual/political identity, in addition to prostitu-tion being a site of work.

See also: censorship; prostitution; queer theory; sex wars, the

Selected writings

Rubin, G. (1975) 'The Traffic in Women: Notes on the Political Economy of Sex' in R.Reiter, (ed.) *Toward An Anthropology of Women*, New York: Monthly Review.

—— (1984) 'Thinking Sex: Notes for a Radical Theory of the Politics of Sexuality' in C.Vance (ed.) *Pleasure and Danger: Exploring Female Sexuality*, Boston: Routledge.

—— (1993) 'Misguided, Dangerous, and Wrong: An Analysis of Anti-Pornography Politics' in A. Assiter and A. Carol (eds) *Bad Girls and Dirty Pictures: The Challenge to Reclaim Feminism*, London: Pluto.

SHANNON BELL

Ruether, Rosemary Radford (b. 1936)

A Roman Catholic feminist, Rosemary Radford Ruether is the Georgia Harkness Professor of Applied Theology at Garrett-Evangelical Theolo-gical Seminary in Evanston, Illinois. Ruether's perception of the interrelationship of various oppressions including sexism and racism is the basis for her feminist analysis and critique of Christianity. She criticises Christianity for its oppression and exploitation of women. She also searches the tradition for what is liberating and inspiring for women and other oppressed groups. In essence, she uses the church's own teachings to critique its oppressive practices.

Ruether questions church policies on birth control and abortion, sexuality and the exclusion of women from the Roman Catholic priesthood. She links these issues to women's lack of power in a church dominated by clergymen. The use and abuse of authority and power by clergymen are at the root of women's secondary status in the church and its negative attitudes toward sexuality. Ruether's critique of Christianity and Roman Catholicism is similar to Mary **Daly**'s analysis. She also connects sexism to anti-Semitism and racism.

Ruether links sexism in the church and society to ecological issues. She supports the ecofeminist perspective: the domination of women and the domination of the earth are connected. Ruether explores how these dominations are rooted in a Christian dualism. Women and nature are negatively linked opposites of men and the spiritual. Women are associated with nature through menstruation and their child-bearing capacity. Nature and women must be controlled by men to create and maintain the social order believed to be God's will. Ruether sees this twin impulse for control at the root of all hierarchical and militarist as well as patriarchal patterns in society and culture.

While acknowledging that Ruether is the first Christian feminist to attempt to create a feminist christology and ethic with her insight that Jesus sided with the poor and the oppressed, in particular, women, some critics ask how the privileging of an egalitarian Jesus furthers feminism in a time of multiculturalism and a plurality of belief systems? Can a feminist christology further a dialogue with other religious and nonreligious feminists?

See also: Christianity and feminism; earth/Gaia/Mother Earth; ecofeminism; ethics, feminist; theology, feminist

Selected writings

Ruether, R.R. (1974) *Religion and Sexism*, New York: Simon and Schuster.
—— (1975) *New Woman/New Earth*, New York: Crossroad.
—— (1992) *Gaia and God: An Ecofeminist Theology of Earth Healing*, San Francisco: HarperSanFrancisco.

SUSAN A. FARRELL

S

Saadawi, Nawal el (b.1931)

Of all the women writers in the Middle East, Nawal el Saadawi is rightly awarded the title of pioneer. Her personal journey is as remarkable as her professional career in overcoming insurmountable obstacles. El Saadawi considered herself a feminist from childhood although her first career was as a medical practitioner in Egypt. She remains a controversial figure in the Middle East due to her unwavering commitment to engaging a 'double battle'; the fight against colonial and patriarchal domination in the family and society. Her public stance and her explicit writings on the oppression of women in Egypt have led to her imprisonment and a continuing censorship of her work in the Middle East.

The topics and issues encompassed in Saadawi's work are as broad as she is prolific. Her landmark text *The Hidden Face of Eve* outlines her positionality on women's rights in the family, her insistence on women's unity and solidarity, and the necessity for building women's organisations to gain political knowledge, awareness, and power. In her novels, she explores physio-moral topics through her protagonists and the power of corporeal imagery. For Saadawi, whose writing often melds her scientific and aesthetic sensibilities, a consciousness of the body leads to a consciousness of gender, the first means for liberation from oppression. Her characters often take on autobiographical qualities such as in *Memoirs from the Women's Prison*, a text reflecting upon her experiences. Her writings on the physical and social treatment of women have led to much controversy, as does her work to educate those still practising female genital mutilation in Egypt.

Neo-colonialism is taken to task by deconstructing the oppression of women regarding inheritance, land ownership, parenthood, and patriarchal family structures. Additionally, she lays bare the facts of the political, social, economic, sexual, historical and cultural structures that are women's reality in the Middle East. What is unique about Saadawi's approach is her refusal to adopt a pro-western stance to achieve her goals, rather her work remains highly geographically contextualised. Saadawi remains one who lives by her own motto: 'The fight must go on. We must go forward'.

See also: gender roles; Middle Eastern feminism; patriarchy; women's writing

Selected writings

Saadawi, N. el (1980) *The Hidden Face of Eve*, London: Zed Press.
—— (1986) 'Reflections of a Feminist', in *Opening the Gates*, Badran, M. and Cooke, M. (eds) Bloomington, IN: Indiana University Press.

References and further reading

Malti-Douglas, F. (1995) *Men, Women and God(s)*, Berkeley, CA: University of California Press.

LAILAH FARAH

Schutte, Ofelia (b. 1945)

Ofelia Schutte is one of the most prolific feminist philosophers in the USA and one of very few Latinas in philosophy. Schutte's philosophical work has spanned continental philosophy, feminist theory, and Latin American philosophy. The topics she has addressed include **identity**, Marxism, Nietzsche, ethnocentrism, **alterity**, subjectivity, aesthetics, and sexual difference, among others.

Schutte's first work, *Beyond Nihilism: Nietzsche Without Masks*, provides an elucidation and critique of Nietzsche's philosophy. Schutte is sympathetic to Nietzsche's approach in the areas of metaphysics, epistemology, and meta-philosophy, but critical of the political content and implications in his work. She argues that the radical potential of his belief in the ultimately fluid state of the universe is contradicted by his naturalisation of ranking processes. Still, Schutte believes that Nietzsche's critiques of religion and metaphysics can be useful in developing the criteria for a liberatory **philosophy**, in particular toward opposing simplistically dualist accounts of 'oppressor/oppressed' and any belief in a final end to conflict. Against Nietzsche, however, Schutte is also consistently attentive to the internal heterogeneity that must inform any concepts used by liberatory theories such as 'the people,' 'women,' or 'culture'.

Schutte has also worked to introduce Latin American philosophy to Anglophone audiences, to summarise the development of **Latin American feminism**, and to draw out the challenges this body of work poses for the future of feminist theory. In *Cultural Identity and Social Liberation in Latin American Thought* Schutte covers Jose Carlos Mariategui's Indo-Hispanic socialism, the identity debates from Samuel Ramos to Augusto Salazar Bondy, and both the theology and the philosophy of liberation. She emphasises the metaphilosophical differences in Latin American traditions which understand philosophy as formed by culture. Like feminists elsewhere, these traditions have also been suspicious that the Enlightenment paradigm of reason is eurocentric and in the service of colonialism (see **eurocentrism**). She also shows how identity is conceptualised from a position of marginalisation in this tradition, as well as a

dynamic rather than static entity and internally heterogeneous.

Schutte is also writing on Latina identity, cultural alterity, and the need for feminist ethics to become postcolonial (see **ethics, feminist**).

Selected writings

Schutte, O. (1984) *Beyond Nihilism: Nietzsche Without Masks*, Chicago, IL: University of Chicago Press.
—— (1993) *Cultural Identity and Social Liberation in Latin American Thought*, Albany, NY: State University of New York Press.
—— (1994) 'Philosophical Feminism in Latin America and Spain: An Introduction', *Hypatia* 9 (1).

LINDA MARTÍN ALCOFF

science

The feminist critique of science comprises a large and varied scholarship involving theorists from a range of disciplines. Feminist historians have largely viewed the rise of modern western science as a highly gendered process, both in its organisation and techniques. For example, the Baconian view of nature as a feminised domain in need of domination and control by an exclusive fraternity of scientists has been interpreted as a highly sexualised form of knowledge production, reflected in the exclusively male composition of the Royal Society in the UK. The depiction of women's bodies, and in particular their reproductive capacities, as polluting to their mental faculties has also been critiqued as a form of patriarchal dominance built into the origins of modern scientific thought, and reflected in the dualist Cartesian legacy opposing passive feminine nature to the probing **gaze** of the rational masculine intellect (see **Cartesianism, feminist critiques of**).

This legacy is argued to be more than merely linguistic, metaphorical or superficial by feminist scholars engaged in debates about scientific **objectivity** in the contemporary period. The detached stance of the knowing subject, and the relationship of knower to known as one of hierarchy and separation, have been viewed as a kind of patriarchal masquerade of neutrality by many feminist theorists of science. Some feminist scholars, such as Sandra Harding, offer a philosophical alternative to objectivity, based on the principle that all knowledge production occurs within specific social and historical conditions, which must be taken into account in order to produce more truthful accounts of the phenomena they describe. Other scholars have chronicled the lives of women scientists whose ability to pursue research was based on a less hierarchical and distancing relationship to the objects of their research, as is argued by Evelyn Fox Keller for the Nobel prize winning geneticist Barbara McClintock. In turn, critical feminist analyses of the gender dynamics informing the privileging of scientific objectivity have also drawn upon object relations psychology, such as the work of Nancy **Chodorow**, according to which rational detachment is a masculine perspective reinforced within a cyclical structure of gendered social conditioning.

As in feminist literary criticism, a significant amount of attention has been focused upon the lives and careers of women scientists either neglected within, or excluded altogether, from the history of science. Anne Sayre's acute biography of the life and achievements of the mid-twentieth-century radiographer, Rosalind Franklin, whose work was critical to the discovery of the structure of the double-helix but whose contributions are little-known, is a case in point.

The feminist critique of science as a powerful arena of cultural production became increasingly important within feminist theory as the life sciences achieved greater prominence during the twentieth century. From many perspectives, feminists have challenged biological definitions of sex, gender, race, reproduction, evolution and inheritance. The feminist critique of **biology** challenges the extreme importance placed upon gender differences in reproductive behaviour, and the correspondingly reductive tendency to account for male and female activity in terms of maximising their genetic contributions to the next generation. The extent to which models of gender are built into human origin narratives, be they about early sexual divisions of labour, the domestication of animals, or the rise of technology, has been a major focus of critique by feminist anthropologists and theorists

such as Donna **Haraway**, and this is extended in the feminist critique of more recent developments, such as evolutionary psychology. Likewise, the use of animal models to legitimate male dominance as essential to the reproductive success of the species, as is commonly argued from a sociobiological perspective, has been criticised as both inaccurate and ideological.

The continuing exclusion of women from prominent disciplines of science and technology, in particular from physics and engineering, is argued by many feminists to reflect not only gender bias, but deeply ingrained forms of institutionalised male-bonding which render such disciplines particularly inhospitable to young women. Although within some sciences, such as computing and biology, women have become more prominent, the prevalence of male-dominance at the highest levels of scientific research remains conspicuous. It is argued by some feminist historians that the very definition of scientific genius remains an essentially masculine category, much as the institution of literary authorship has retained a strong association with masculine creative power. For other feminists, such criticisms are extreme, and also circular, inhibiting change by perpetuating the very stereotypes which produce gender imbalance to begin with.

While scientific knowledge and practice are seen to reflect a long history of gender inequity, they are also integral to many feminist aims and goals, and it would be inaccurate to describe the majority of feminist science scholars as anti-science. Both in relation to vital health issues, such as breast cancer, and fundamental global concerns, such as agriculture, the effort to reform scientific education and practice remains of singular importance. A significant challenge for the twenty-first century, then, is the creation of new forms of organisation, education, and practice through which scientific knowledge and technique will become more representative and inclusive.

References and further reading

Haraway, D. (1989) *Primate Visions: Gender, Race and Nature in the World of Modern Science*, New York: Routledge.

Harding, S. (1986) *The Science Question in Feminism*, Ithaca, NY: Cornell University Press.

Hubbard, R. (1992) *The Politics of Women's Biology*, New Brunswick, NJ: Rutgers University Press.

Keller, E.F. (1983) *A Feeling for the Organism*, San Francisco: Freeman.

Merchant, C. (1980) *The Death of Nature: Women, Ecology and the Scientific Revolution*, New York: Harper and Row.

Sayre, A. (1975) *Rosalind Franklin and DNA*, New York: Norton.

Vandana S. (1989) *Staying Alive: Women, Ecology and Development*, London: Zed Books.

SARAH FRANKLIN

science fiction, feminist

Mary Shelley's *Frankenstein* (1818) is the foundational text of anglophone science fiction. Yet feminist science fiction (FSF) also cherishes Margaret Cavendish's earlier challenge to the masculine exclusivity of science, *The Description of the New World Called the Blazing World* (1688). Shelley, at only nineteen, took the scientific debate concerning electricity's role in the origins of life, to envisage Frankenstein creating life from inanimate matter. The scientist is revulsed by his creation; denied love the Monster becomes his name.

Despite these proto-feminist SF texts, by the twentieth century the genre was to become both androcentric and authored. There were brilliant exceptions like the pseudonymous 'James Tiptree' and Ursula LeGuin. LeGuin envisages a democratic anarchistic utopia where gender is softened to **androgyny**, and **reproduction** is desexualised. As befits a genre invented by women, SF has a marginal status. But marginality offers chances not least, as the graffiti of 1968 urged, to 'let the imagination take power'.

FSF became central within the torrent of creative imagination unleashed by the women's liberation movement. Two names stand out, both as writers and as articulating the feminisms of the 1970s. The two were the socialist feminist Marge Piercy, and the radical feminist Joanna Russ. Seventies feminists had no truck with fixed blueprints for the future, their worlds were radically indeterminate and always to be fought for. Thus both Piercy (1979) and Russ (1979) depict simultaneous androcentric **dystopias** and feminist utopias in opposition. Piercy's heroine Connie bears the multilayered oppressions of race, class and gender. Influenced by **Firestone** (1971) Piercy asks, can technology be used to socialise pregnancy and motherhood? Piercy's FSF and biomedical actuality met in 1978 in all their ambiguity with the birth of the first IVF baby Louise Brown.

By contrast Russ's pursuit of a post-patriarchal society is centrally preoccupied with **sexuality** and gender, in which race and class get scant attention. Her heroines, from different simultaneous worlds, are the four Js (the multiple fractured self of postmodernist thought). In one world a sexlinked fatal genetic disorder has ironically produced a separatist utopia.

Later new age feminist politics entered with the FSF of Sally Gearhart (1985). Dismissing **science**, she envisages harmony between nature and culture flowing from collectivist separatism (see **nature/culture**). This was unquestionably FSF's golden age, a time when the imagination indeed took power. Its energy, hope and willingness to defend its dreams reach out from every page.

See also: cyborg; heroines; utopias, feminist

References and further reading

Firestone, S. (1971) *The Dialectic of Sex: The Case for Feminist Revolution*, London: Cape.

Gearheart, S. (1985) *The Wanderground: Stories of the Hill Women*, London: The Women's Press.

Piercy, M. (1978) *Woman on the Edge of Time*, London: Zed Press.

Russ J. (1975) *The Female Man*, London: The Women's Press.

Shelley, M. (1918) *Frankenstein: A Modern Prometheus*, Harmondsworth: Penguin.

HILARY ROSE

science, philosophy of

Philosophy of science involves investigation of knowledge formation in the sciences. Although there have been numerous approaches to the philosophy of science, the rise of **positivism** resulted in a focus on logical analyses of the structure of explanation and justification in science, with the aim to identify the components of a universally true scientific method.

By the 1970s, the hegemony of the positivist-inspired conception of science gave way to approaches that emphasise science as an activity that cannot be understood in isolation from the history of its communities. The actual practices of scientists and the social contexts of science became key resources as theorists began to argue for naturalised approaches and/or the relevance of the sociology of scientific knowledge. As feminist science scholarship emerged in the 1970s, it was influenced by both of these approaches and addressed three interrelated topics: 1) the numbers and roles of women within the sciences; 2) the impact of **androcentrism** and **sexism** in the methods, theories, or research projects of various sciences; and 3) critiques of current philosophies of science.

Although feminist science scholarship is not homogeneous, there are a number of common themes. First, many feminists embrace non-individualist epistemologies that address the role of scientific communities in creating standards of evidence and producing knowledge. A second concern is how differences in power or privilege affect justificatory standards. Third, feminists have argued that traditional conceptions of **objectivity** involve a particular ideological stance that values disinterestedness, distrusts emotions, and ignores the role of the body in knowing. This has led to a rejection of the alleged 'value-neutrality' of this conception of objectivity, noting not only its androcentrism, but its particular class and cultural locations. Fourth, such investigations have led feminists to embrace the value of diversity within the scientific community as an epistemic resource. Fifth, many feminists reject the image of science as producing value-neutral knowledge and argue that we must identify and evaluate the values inherent in the methods and practices of particular scientific communities. As a result, feminists have abandoned the ideal of a universal scientific method, arguing that all practices of science are 'indigenous' or 'local' sciences, marked by the social contexts in which they arise. Finally, feminists have investi-

gated the ways in which various practices of science promote or detract from the goal of the development of a just society.

See also: epistemology, feminist; fact/value distinction; naturalistic method/naturalised epistemology; objectivity; observational method (in science); science

References and further reading:

Harding, S. (1991) *Whose Science? Whose Knowledge?*, Ithaca, NY: Cornell University Press.
Longino, H. (1990) *Science as Social Knowledge*, Princeton, NJ: Princeton University Press.
Tuana, N. (ed.) (1989) *Feminism and Science*, Bloomington, IN: Indiana University Press.

NANCY TUANA

Scott, Joan Wallach (b. 1941)

Joan Wallach Scott is Professor of Social Sciences at the Institute for Advanced Study, Princeton, New Jersey. Her appointment in a department of Social Sciences reflects her wide influence and interdisciplinary work as a practitioner and theorist of feminist history. Scott's work has been central to a critical, theoretically informed evaluation of the field's methodology.

Scott trained as a social historian, but by the mid-1970s turned her attention to the emerging field of women's history. Her 1978 book, *Women, Work and Family*, co-authored with Louise Tilly, traces the history of European women's wage work in the nineteenth century and brings to bear the concerns of contemporary feminism on historical writing. The mid-1980s saw Scott engaging once again with contemporary feminism, as theories of difference among women were articulated more vocally. Combining those interests with a critical reading of French poststructuralist theory, Scott writes history that dispenses with preconceived categories, such as men, women, and even difference itself, and instead traces how those categories come to exist.

Categories are configurations of language, and reflect not a pre-given reality, but diffuse power relations. 'Woman' and 'man' are thus not fixed identities; their definition varies across space, time and culture. Gender history is a more useful project than women's history because it allows the historian to conceive of women and men as relational categories continually reconstituted in language through processes of historical change. Scott conceives of historical experience not as a 'pure' set of interactions, but as mediated and understood by subjects through identity and relationships to social structure. This poses a challenge to the foundations of women's history, since the field was initially understood as a project of recovering women's experiences.

Scott's work straddles the boundaries between history and theory. She is often integrative, advancing critiques of methodology within the very structure of her historical argument. She has been criticised for losing sight of the historical realities of women's lives and endangering the philosophical foundations of feminism with her questioning of the category 'woman'. Against this, she has stressed the political importance of her work, often venturing outside the discipline of history to engage with current feminist theories and address their relevance to social change. Scott's historical practice has been crucial to a broad interrogation of the methodological assumptions of women's history.

Selected writings

Scott, J.W. (1988) *Gender and the Politics of History*, New York: Columbia University Press.
—— (1996) *Only Paradoxes to Offer: French Feminists and the Rights of Man*, Cambridge, MA and London: Harvard University Press.
Scott, J.W. and Tilly, L. (1978) *Women, Work and Family*, New York: Holt, Rinehart and Winston.

ILYA PARKINS

second sex

The phrase 'second sex' was made famous by Simone de **Beauvoir** in *The Second Sex* (1949) to indicate women's secondary political, legal, and economic status relative to men, a status evident in myths such as the Biblical tale of creation where God creates Adam first and Eve second, as Adam's companion. According to Beauvoir, male-dominated cultures represent humanity as male and define woman as relative to man. Woman is the **Other**, an object reflective of men's desires and fears. Women, as an oppressed caste, are forced to accommodate themselves to this identity, denying their own freedom. Women must counter these myths with phenomenological descriptions of their own lived experience and challenge their secondary status in a political struggle for women's liberation.

See also: Daly, Mary; discrimination and the law; equality and difference

References and further reading

Beauvoir, S. de (1949) *The Second Sex*, trans. H.M. Parshley, New York: Knopf, 1952.

MARGARET A. SIMONS

self, the

The concept of *the self* is asked to perform numerous philosophical tasks. In ethics and **political theory**, the self is the locus of **agency** and responsibility, and hence is that which comes in for either praise or blame. In epistemology, the self is that which takes responsibility for belief. As the primary subject of investigation in **metaphysics**, the self is that entity – that unity, whatever it is – whose persistence accounts for personal identity over time.

René Descartes (1596–1650) left us two related legacies, the first in the area of epistemology and the second in the area of metaphysics. The first is that inquiry is best conducted from a first-person position, and therefore requires neither the approval nor the summoning of authorities. The second is that the self which conducts inquiry, and which is the self-same entity that moves and takes action among fellow selves, is essentially nonphysical, and therefore not subject to laws governing physical substance. Both Cartesian doctrines flow from the single idea that it is the individual (rather than some other entity or group of entities) which is the proper subject of approbation, but that for one to be subject to criticism, one must be autonomous, the exclusive author of one's actions.

This idea was taken up by Immanuel Kant (1724–1804), who advanced the proposal that autonomy is a property of the rational will alone, and further that it is self-contradictory to say of a nonautonomous will that it heeds reasons, and so is rational, since a nonatonomous will does not direct itself but *takes* direction from another agency (someone or something in authority over it), and so has no use for reasons. But for this proposal to serve the purposes of moral theory, we must be in a position to do two things: (1) make sense of the notion that selves act through the gross physical substance of body (solve the mind/body problem); and (2) reidentify selves, presumably through the evidence of bodies, so that blame and praise can be properly allocated.

While traditional metaphysics takes the two metaphysical problems – the mind/body problem and the problem of personal **identity** (or reidentification) – enormously seriously, feminists have not been troubled by them in the same way. For feminists have not generally perceived the categories of mind and body as mutually exclusive. Physical and mental, as dimensions of human life, have not presented themselves to feminists as opposites, but as two aspects of one and the same reality, which is neither wholly physical nor wholly mental. Many feminists now hold that mental and physical lie on a continuum between purely physical (at one end) and purely mental (at the other). At the purely physical extremum reside features that belong as well to corpses and the inanimate (so that for example being subject to motion is a characteristic humans share with inanimate objects). But all other characteristically psychological dimensions of human life are in reality admixtures of physical and mental, in varying proportions. Drawing on empirical research in psychology and social science, feminists have sought to illuminate the bodily nature of conscious experience, and memory in particular (see in particular Susan Brison, 'Outliving Oneself' in *Feminists Rethink the Self*). In doing so feminists are undermining the value of the traditional distinction between memory-based (thought of as purely mental) accounts of personhood and identity, on the one hand, and bodily accounts, on the other.

And by the same stroke they elevate in importance the philosophical topics of **agency** and responsibility, over that of personal identity and the self. (In this feminist efforts are aligned with the efforts of Derek Parfit, and to a lesser extent also with those of Bernard Williams.)

Defence of the proposition that the **body**, as such, is part of the self (through undermining the distinction between a purely bodily aspect and purely mental aspect), and consequently also of a continuum analysis of mental and physical, is the first of a certain two-pronged feminist agenda. The second prong is to pursue a continuum analysis also of individual and community, and thereby undermine the traditional distinction between autonomy and heteronomy (see especially Annette Baier, 'Second Persons'). The project is to illuminate how the consciousness of an individual is constituted or constructed through normal socialisation processes of interaction with, dependency upon and imitation of other individuals, and thereby to cast doubt on the idea that one could (never mind should) undertake to be autonomous, through being an entity that answers only to its own desires and beliefs, since the individual ownership of those very desires and beliefs is itself in question. This project is much more in contention among feminists than the first.

What is in contention is whether **autonomy**, as traditionally conceived, is in any respect desirable, and whether women in particular ought to achieve autonomy wherever this is possible. There are feminists, for example, who believe that the trouble with autonomy is that women do not enjoy enough of it in real life, others who take a dim view of autonomy on grounds that it is tainted with (unworthy) masculine ideals, and still others who believe that autonomy is all too often confused with (both unrealistic and undesirable) separation from other human beings. What hangs upon how the question of autonomy is decided?

There is a venerated tradition in political philosophy, running from Socrates himself, through seventeenth-century figures Thomas Hobbes and John Locke, to twentieth-century philosophers John Rawls and Robert Nozick, of seeking to found the principles of justice on individual choices made in the interest of self. To this (contractarian) tradition we owe the idea that a legitimate system of governing institutions is one which enjoys the consent of the governed. We are often told, by feminists and others, that this tradition presumes that individuals ought to conduct their lives, and consequently to offer their consent, as wholly autonomous entities. And it is this tradition in social and political thinking which some feminists have undertaken to challenge.

See also: epistemology, feminist; essentialism; ethics, feminist; nature/culture

References and further reading

Baier, A. (1985) *Postures of the Mind*, Minneapolis, MI: University of Minnesota Press.

Christman, J. (ed.) (1989) *The Inner Citadel: Essays on Individual Autonomy*, New York: Oxford University Press.

Hanen, M. and Nielsen, K. (eds) (1987) *Science, Morality and Feminist Theory*, Canadian Journal of Philosophy Supplementary Volume 13.

Meyers, D. (ed.) (1997) *Feminists Rethink the Self*, Boulder, CO: Westview Press.

Parfit, D. (1984) *Reasons and Persons*, Oxford: Clarendon Press.

Williams, B. (1973) *Problems of the Self*, Cambridge: Cambridge University Press.

MARIAM THALOS

separatism

Separatism appears in many forms: black separatism, US-Chinese separatism, Jewish separatism, feminist separatism, lesbian separatism, nationalist separatisms. Separatist resistance emerges when dominant agendas threaten, appropriate, colonise, and/or annihilate other realms of meaning.

Separatism is not segregation. Segregation is enacted by those in power to retain power by marginalising others. Separatism is a form of resistance on the part of those marginalised. Separatism can be seen as segregation only within dominant, mystifying discourse. This essay focuses on feminist and lesbian separatism.

Lesbian separatism emerged as gay men and new Left men persisted in unabated unselfconscious practices of male supremacy, and heterosexual feminists failed to challenge heterosexism (see **heterosexism, heteronormativity**) and **homophobia**.

Separatism is, first, about access. Marilyn **Frye** notes that total power is total access, arguing that male parasitism means men must have access to women:

> Feminist separatism is separation of various sorts or modes from men and from institutions, relationships, roles and activities which are male-defined, male-dominated and operating for the benefit of males and the maintenance of male privilege – this separation being initiated or maintained, at will, *by women*.
>
> (Frye 1983: 96)

Separatism often involves creating distinct spaces where unstated values of the dominant frame do not function automatically. When we engage in a system with oppressive values portrayed as fact, for example white supremacy or male supremacy, we contribute by consensus to its underlying structure even when also challenging the system through reform.

Philosophically, there are at least two ways to challenge a statement: we can argue it false or we can render it nonsense. Rendering it nonsense disrupts its logic, treating it as unintelligible. Arguing it is false may bring satisfaction, but it is nevertheless to agree that the statement is intelligible, indeed possibly true – that it is worth debating. Thus at a deeper level we validate it.

Separatist resistance works at this deeper level: when one continues to respond to the dominant discourse, one continues to reinscribe it. To withdraw from a system or a particular situation is a different kind of challenge. To withdraw or separate (conceptually and/or physically) is to refuse to act according to the system's rules and framework and thereby refuse to validate its underlying values.

Thus separatism is, second, about the creation or affirmation or maintenance of meaning and value distinct from what passes as common sense in a society. Separatism is about moving through different vortexes of meaning with different logics. One's imagination moves in distinct directions. Lesbian separatism is about creating a different ground of meaning, not continually revolving around the hegemonic ideology that women are for men. In a black- or Latino-centred space, the centrality of whiteness dissolves. Zora Neal Hurston's separatism was designed in part to keep black children from absorbing white values.

Critics argue one can never separate from culture, that to think so is to deceive oneself. Economics coerces everyone into relationship with dominant institutions. Separatists strategise existing *in* but not *of* such institutions. In the USA in the 1970s and 1980s, anti-separatists tended to be drawn to socialist logics, and separatists to anarchist logics (see **socialism and feminism**; **anarchist feminism**). Some postmodern theorists suggest we are nothing but creations of language and can operate only within its parameters, resisting a designation, perhaps, but not leaving its logic. Of course, we are never outside language or culture. But it does not follow that we can never move in spaces that do not carry dominant Anglo-European white phallic cultural logic, that there is no sense apart from what makes sense in that discourse.

A more significant criticism is that dominant values make their way into separatist spaces, white gentile lesbians carrying unaddressed racist values, for example, or Christian values. On the one hand, the belief that one can just walk away from what one has learned is naive. But on the other hand, it is colonial arrogance to declare all meaning limited to dominant logic.

Separatism is, third, strategies and tactics for disrupting and resisting hegemony; it is not about safety from men, it is not adhering to rigid rules. It is not refusal to engage, but a different way of engaging.

Separatism is also not purism, or it undermines itself when it tries to be. Connecting purism with monoculturalism, including the effort to construct coalition by erasing differences, María **Lugones** argues:

> When I think of lesbian separation I think of curdle separation.... We contain in our own and in the heterosexist construction of ourselves all sorts of ambiguities and tensions that are threatening to purity, to the construction of women as for use, for exploitation. We are outside the lover of purity's pale, outside his conceptual framework.
>
> (Lugones 1994: 476)

By curdling, we become active subjects, not consumed by the logic of control. For María Lugones, this art is a practice of festive resistance: categorical blurring and confusion, code-switching, caricaturing of the selves, we are in the world of oppressors, emphasising cultural *mestizaje*. When we remain riveted on their categories, we do not succeed in creating new ones.

In other words, separatism is, fourth, about refocusing and creation. Separatism is a no-saying, but also yes-saying. As we choose who we attend, we determine what is significant and what is not. Withdrawal and separation are not perceived as options when the game played appears the only game in town and so is taken for reality. In a sense the game is reality, but its continued existence is not matter of fact so much as a matter of agreement: by what we attend, players agree on what counts as reality. Perhaps the most important aspect of lesbian separatism is its focus on lesbians. Separatism is largely a matter of what Marilyn Frye calls lesbian connectionism. By focusing on ourselves, we create lesbian meaning, and reality.

See also: lesbian feminism

References and further reading

Frye, M. (1983) *The Politics of Reality*, Trumansburg, NY: Crossing Press.

Hoagland, S.L. and Penelope, J. (1988) *For Lesbians Only*, London: Onlywoman Press.

Lugones, M. (1994) 'Purity, Impurity, and Separation' in *Signs*, 19 (2).

SARAH LUCIA HOAGLAND

sex equity v. sexual equality

Since the advent of second-wave feminism, the issue of equality, and what is necessary to achieve it, has been at the centre of many feminist discussions (see **equality and difference**). The debate about sex equity versus sexual equality highlights the importance of defining the meaning of this concept. The specific terminology of sex equity and sexual equality, commonplace in American feminist thought, is paralleled by discussions about formal versus substantive equality in European feminism. Although the terminology is different, both debates arise from the perceived inadequacy of the concept of equality to address women's concerns within either the public or private sphere.

Sexual equality has been identified within feminist literature as strict, formal or legal equality. This position is often associated with **liberal feminism**, founded upon the assumption that equality will result from access to employment, politics, and all those areas of life traditionally dominated by men. This approach, therefore, aims to promote legislation that removes all formal obstacles to women's entry in the public sphere. The elimination of direct and indirect discrimination becomes of utmost importance. Identifying indirect discrimination, however, is often difficult as it thrives upon institutional inequalities, such as gender-based occupational segregation.

This approach, moreover, fails to recognise the impact of structural inequalities in determining women's access to the public sphere. Equality is interpreted as sameness, thus men and women are not only equal, they become the same. This narrow definition of equality not only fails to challenge the **public/private** dichotomy, it also rejects the importance of targeting women's needs. Within this context, pregnancy, for example, is categorised as a disability, because disabling illnesses are the only comparable male experience. Pregnancy, however, is neither a disability, nor an illness, and defining it as such reinforces the masculine norm that defines the public sphere.

The language of sex equity, on the other hand, introduces a new way of discussing women's rights, which critically appraises gender structures and actively promotes substantive equality. This approach is far more women centred, thus acknowledging the impact of socio-economic structures on women's participation in the public sphere. This approach does not force feminist analysis into the position of equality as sameness, rather, it promotes equity as a necessary condition for social justice. Examples of sex equity law can be found in the aims of affirmative action policies in Europe and North America, the EU Parental Leave Directive, and the principle of 'equal pay for work of equal value'.

See also: equality/difference; public/private

References and further reading

Bock, G. and James, S. (eds) (1992) *Beyond Equality and Difference: Citizenship, Feminist Politics and Female Subjectivity*, London: Routledge.

Conaghan, J. (1993) 'Pregnancy and the Workplace: a Question of Strategy?', in A. Bottomley and J. Conaghan (eds) *Feminist Theory and Legal Strategy*, Oxford: Blackwell.

Phillips, A. (ed.) (1987) *Feminism and Equality*, Oxford, Blackwell.

Phillips, A. (1999) *Which Equalities Matter?*, Cambridge, MA: Polity Press.

ROBERTA GUERRINA

sexism

Sexism is a term coined in the late 1960s to refer to social arrangements, policies, language, and practices enacted by men or women that express a systematic, often institutionalised belief that men are superior, women inferior. Its cognitive and political force derived initially from its association with practices that women and men had learned to recognise as 'racist', in a period of increasing awareness of oppressions suffered in affluent western societies by people other than white men. Sexist practices range from the seemingly simple, such as referring to women as 'girls', or treating women as delicate or physically/mentally incapable to the larger and more complex, such as discounting a woman's refusal of sexual activity with assertions that 'no' does not mean 'no', to workplace attitudes and policies that extend oppression into women's working lives by confining them to female-designated jobs on grounds only of their sex, to restricting women's/girls' participation in sport.

See also: heterosexism, heteronormativity

LORRAINE CODE

sexuality

Sexuality is a complex and contested domain. It became central to western understandings of human identity with the birth of scientific sexology just over a hundred years ago, as doctors and policy makers began to usurp the role of the Church in the social regulation of bodily pleasures and reproductive practices. This scientific paradigm remained largely unchallenged until the 1960s, when new perspectives emerged criticising established ideas of **biology** and nature as ideological mechanisms for maintaining men's control over women's bodies (see **nature/culture**). Intervening in what subsequently became known as the '**essentialism** debate', feminists emphasised the cultural acquisition or social construction of sexual conduct (see **social constructionism**). But this debate is more complicated than it might appear. Feminists emphasizing the social construction of sexual practices tended to assume that men and women exhibit stable and abiding patterns of sexual desire and behaviour, in line with culturally imposed, hierarchical gender norms: norms which they set out to change. In contrast, more recently, whether informed by Freud, Foucault or **queer theory**, many feminists have come to question the stability and consistency of sexual behaviour and desire. Here, sexual life and its social codes are seen as forever haunted by conflict, fluidity and contradiction. In addition, recent attention to the racial dimensions of sexual knowledge and regulation, like that of McClintock (1994), has highlighted the historical exploitation and abuse of subordinated ethnic groups, and the discursive investment in non-white bodies as lascivious, bestial and decadent. Today, the one thing we can say for certain is that our sexual lives are never solely a private affair; yet it is just this belief that makes sexuality so central to modernity.

Nineteenth-century sexologists saw male and female sexuality as fundamentally opposed instinctual forces: the one aggressive and forceful, the other passive and responsive. They thereby equated three concepts – *sex*, *gender* and *sexuality* – through a parallel set of oppositions – 'male/female', 'masculine/feminine', 'active/passive'. The early British sexologist and social reformer, Havelock Ellis, upheld the possibility and impor-

tance of female genital sexual pleasure (criticising Victorian doctors who pathologised it as 'unnatural'), yet, as feminists subsequently argued, the naturalism of his day meant that he too saw women as controlled and weakened by their biology. The rigidly gendered sexual polarities of late-nineteenth-century thought contained no space for a notion of women's sexuality independent from that of men. Lesbian sexuality was, by definition here, a type of gender inversion, just as male homosexual activity was seen as 'feminine' in character. Lesbianism was also linked, in contemporary popular thinking with the threatening ideology of feminism. In a way which remains familiar to this day, sexual matters provided the perfect site for the displacement of social fears and panics, conjuring images of sin and disease, self-indulgence and social decay, attached to masturbatory 'self-pollution', and all 'unnatural pleasures' not tied to procreative ends.

However, for all its congruence with patriarchal discourse, the impact of early sexology was contradictory: encouraging some women to affirm their rights to sexual pleasure, even at a time when, as the feminist historian Judith Walkowitz (1992) illustrates, there was little social space, or discursive possibility, for them to live out or imagine alternatives. Then as now, divisions emerged between feminists wanting to question the comprehensively male-centred double standards of their day. Some, like Olive Schreiner and Rebecca West, looked to sexology for enlightenment; others, like Christabel Pankhurst (in her appeal on the eve of the First World War) demanded chastity from men as the price of liberation for women.

Sexologists themselves would soon begin to turn the tables on their founding fathers' most basic assumption: the opposed sexual natures of women and men. First, Alfred Kinsey (1953), in the mid-twentieth century, followed by Masters and Johnson (1966), not only stressed the role of cultural 'conditioning' in creating sexual behaviour, but emphasised the sexual similarities between women and men. This shift of emphasis, once again, was affected by wider social and political shifts, with sexual pleasure now seen as the key to stability in marriage – in the face of rising divorce. The second-wave feminists of the 1960s at first welcomed Masters and Johnson's account of women's multiple orgasmic sexual capacity, said to be greater and more varied than that of men. It encouraged many, like Shere Hite in the 1970s, to set out to uncover what they saw as women's 'authentic sexuality', stressing its clitoral basis and the dispensability of penetrative sex with men for women's orgasmic pleasure. Yet, attentive only to the minutiae of physiological response, Masters and Johnson's behaviouristic perspective remained as biologically reductive as their forebears. As some feminists have later stressed (see Segal 1994), they ignored the psychological dimensions of human sexuality, and the unpredictable centrality of desire in sexual life. They similarly overlooked the cultural context of sexuality, in which men typically have, or at least are expected to have, more power than women, and male sexual performance serves as the imprimatur of that power. This led Leonore Tiefer (1995), a feminist working critically in the field in the USA, to conclude that although sexology has had a significant influence on feminism, and its proponents like to think it is feminist, feminism has had surprisingly little impact on sexology.

One approach which has consistently rejected the biological reductionism of sexology is that of **psychoanalysis**, yet it has proved no less contentious among feminists. Sigmund Freud, its founder, was concerned with 'psychic' or mental life, and the centrality of sexuality in the repressed experiences and desires which live on, unconsciously, within it. His chief purpose was to emphasise that adult sexuality always grows out of and reflects its infantile origins. Freud (1977) argues that adult sexuality is always the result of the repression of the earlier 'polymorphous perversity' of infancy, and only ever comes under the sway of the reproductive or genital function, if it does, in a partial and unstable way.

From early in his career, however, feminists such as Karen Horney criticised Freud's views as essentially phallocentric, especially his account of the girl's pathway to normal 'femininity', via the Oedipus complex. The psychic significance of boys' possession of the penis, Freud suggested, was likely to lead little girls to abandon their early active or 'clitoral' sexuality for a more passive and receptive 'vaginal' orientation (accompanying a shift in erotic desire from the mother to the father). However, other feminists, like Juliet **Mitchell** (1974), have argued that the rejection of Freud's work would be fatal for feminism. Stressing the centrality of the phallus in language and culture, other feminists, like the French philosophers Luce **Irigaray** and Hélène **Cixous**, have also attempted (via the French analyst Jacques Lacan) to explore, and disrupt, what they see as the one-sex or **phallic economy**, with its negative positioning of the 'feminine' within language.

Yet the chief concern of many feminist activists addressing sexuality by the close of the 1970s, especially in the Anglo-American context, was the issue of sexual **violence**. They had begun to analyse the threat of **rape** and men's predatory sexual behaviour as the single, overriding cause of women's subordination and oppression. Andrea **Dworkin** and Catharine **MacKinnon** were the most influential advocates of this postion, initiating popular campaigns against '**pornography**' as incitement to sexual violence. In both Dworkin's and MacKinnon's writing, sexual violence was now understood as an inescapable aspect of genital **heterosexuality**, leading them to dismiss feminists' earlier search for sexual liberation as inimical to women's interests. Their analysis can be seen as congruent with social constructionist positions, stressing the contrasting sexual meanings internalised by women and men, in ways which understand male sexual behaviour as motivated not so much by sexual desire, as by the pursuit of proofs of **masculinity**. A culture which encourages men to prove their masculinity through sexual performance helps to encourage and legitimise male sexual coerciveness. However, the complex ambiguity of sexual feelings and desires (whether of men or women) tends to be downplayed in social constructionist accounts, where sexuality always mirrors normative gender expectations. This encouraged the sexual reductionism evident in the writings of radical feminists like Dworkin and MacKinnon. Such theorising has resulted in the enduring **sex wars** between anti-pornography feminists and feminist sex radicals, most prominent and divisive, as Carole Vance (1984) encapsulates, within North American feminism.

Yet theoretical complexity became the hallmark of those feminists, like Judith **Butler**, influenced by the French poststructuralist, Michel Foucault. For Foucault (1979) 'sexuality' is not a unitary category, but should be understood as an effect of a multiplicity of historically specific discourses, ways of mapping the body's surface, dictating how we describe and hence experience those bodies. It is essentially a form of social regulation: the most powerful form of regulation in modern societies. Foucault's radical anti-essentialism inspired the growth of **queer theory**, especially in recent lesbian and gay scholarship. Rooted in strategies of disruptive resistance, rather than affirmations of sexual identity, it seeks to transcend and erode the key binaries — male/female, heterosexual/homosexual — constructing modern sexualities. This project has led to a rich array of work on sexual diversity, or 'sexualities', subverting the categories of 'normal' sexuality to embrace the fluidities and multiplicities of possible sexual subject positions. Feminists thus continue to battle over strategies for overturning the institutionalised and discursive asymmetries of power which maintain the heterosexual male as the uniquely empowered sexual agent.

See also: AIDS, women and; backlash; black female sexuality; child sexual abuse; courtly love tradition; heterosexism, heteronormativity; lesbian history; monosexuality; transgender; transsexuality/gender dysphoria

References and further reading

Butler, J. (1990) *Gender Trouble*, London, Routledge.

Foucault, M. (1979) *The History of Sexuality, Vol 1: An Introduction*, trans. R. Hurley, London: Allen Lane.

Freud, S. (1977) *Three Essays on Sexuality, The Pelican Freud Library*, (1905) (PFL), vol. 7, Harmondsworth: Penguin.

Horney, K. (1926) 'The Flight from Womanhood' in Strouse (ed.) *Women and Analysis: Dialogue on Psychoanalytic Views on Femininity*, New York: Dell.

Kinsey, A. *et al.* (1953) *Sexual Behavior in the Human Female*, Chicago, IL: Pocket Books.

MacKinnon, C. (1987) *Feminism Unmodified: Discourses on Life and Law*, Cambridge, MA: Harvard University Press.

Masters, W. and Johnson, V. (1966) *Human Sexual Response*, Boston: Little Brown.

McClintock, A. (1994) *Imperial Leather: Race, Gender, and Sexuality in Colonial Contest*, London: Routledge.

Mitchell, J. (1974) *Psychoanalysis and Feminism*, London: Allen Lane.

Segal, L. (1994) *Straight Sex: The Politics of Pleasure*, London: Virago.

Tiefer, L. (1995) *Sex Is Not a Natural Act and Other Essays*, Boulder, CO: Westview Press.

Vance, C. (ed.) (1995) *Pleasure and Danger: Exploring Female Sexuality*, London: Routledge.

Walkowitz, J. (1992) *City of Dreadful Delight: Narratives of Sexual Danger in Late-Victorian London*, London: Virago.

LYNNE SEGAL

sexual slavery

Sexual slavery is an expansion of the nineteenth-century notion of 'white slavery' to include all forced prostitution of women and children within countries (street prostitution) and across international borders (international trafficking). Kathleen Barry's research and writing are pivotal to contemporary feminist theorising on this topic. She documents that women and children are 'purchased, kidnapped, drawn in through syndicates or organised crime, or fraudulently recruited by fronting agencies which offer jobs, positions with dance companies, or marriage contracts that don't exist. Or ... procured through seduction by being promised friendship and love' (1979: 4–5). Barry credits nineteenth-century British feminist Josephine Butler for initiating the domestic and international struggle to combat forced prostitution. Asian feminists have launched the most effective campaigns against sex tours and the traffic in brides.

See also: prostitution; violence

References and further reading

Barry, K. (1979) *Female Sexual Slavery*, New York: New York University, 1984.

O'Toole, L.L. and Schiffman, J.R. (eds) (1997)

Gender Violence: Interdisciplinary Perspectives, New York: New York University.

CHARLENE Y. SENN

sex wars, the

Most feminist scholars examining what have come to be called the 'sex-wars' date their public emergence to the ninth 'Feminist and Scholar' conference held in 1982 at Barnard College in New York on the subject 'Towards a Politics of Sexuality'. Emerging out of this influential conference on female sexuality is the collection of essays *Pleasure and Danger: Exploring Female Sexuality* (Vance 1984), the best representation of the burgeoning feminist sexual libertarian or 'pro-sex' position. This position, which advocates sexual liberation for women through the expression of sexual power and pleasure, defines itself in strict opposition to a radical or cultural feminist construction of sexuality like that articulated by Catharine **MacKinnon** and Andrea **Dworkin**, who argue that in a patriarchal culture, where women are not safe from male violence and pornography, what is sexual is what gives a man an erection. The fierce debates over female **sexuality** that continue to divide feminist and lesbian communities along sexual, political and generational lines have been over the content and expression of female sexual subjectivity and the location of feminist resistance to male domination and heteronormativity.

The pro-sex, sex radical or sexual libertarian position emerged as a defensive response to radical feminist criticism targeted at certain sex practices i.e. SM (sadomasochism), butch/femme, prostitution and inter-generational sex, all perceived to perpetuate and enhance the victimisation of women in patriarchal, sexist society. Called prohibitive, repressive and Victorian, the radical feminist position came under attack for projecting a maternal, heterosexist and essentially conservative victimology onto the lives of its 'daughters': feminist sex-radicals.

The discursive construction of the sex wars as a debate between equal and disparate factions polarises the positions on either 'side' as radically opposed and engaged in a struggle to the theoretical death. Contemporary lesbian and feminist critic Teresa de **Lauretis** resists such reductive analysis, finding the origins of the sex wars in the competing and at times contrary founding principles driving western third-wave feminism. For feminism, de Lauretis argues, is a movement concerned with images of feminism as difference, rebellion, excess, subversion, agency, empowerment, pleasure and danger while concurrently driven toward ideals of community, accountability, entrustment, sisterhood, and bonding. For Foucauldian feminist critic Jana Sawicki, the sex wars bring to light similarities between 'radical feminist' and 'sex radical' politics, namely a shared conception of power as essentially negative, being in the first instance freedom from male violence, and in the second, from repressive sexual norms. Rejecting the morally dogmatic radical feminist position and the sexually libertarian 'anything goes' ethic of the pro-sex feminists, Sawicki joins an increasing number of feminists calling for a third position that questions which desires are liberating, and interrogates the conflation of desire with liberation, and the reduction of sexuality to identity.

See also: butch/femme; cultural feminism; pornography; prostitution; radical feminism; sisterhood

References and further reading

Merck, M. (1993) *Perversions: Deviant Readings*, New York: Routledge.
Sawicki, J. (1991) *Disciplining Foucault: Feminism, Power and the Body*, New York: Routledge.
Vance, C. (ed.) (1984) *Pleasure and Danger: Exploring Female Sexuality*, Boston: Routledge and Kegan Paul.

FIONA MacCOOL

Shiva, Vandana (b. 1952)

Vandana Shiva is a leading contributor to feminist critiques of Third World development, both as a writer and an activist. A physicist by training, she has drawn analogies between the reductionist

nature of western **science** and capitalist development in their combined exploitation of women and
nature, particularly in her country, India. Her
emphasis on women's role in the reproduction both
of human life and ecological biodiversity introduces
a feminist perspective to the critique of genetic
engineering and bio-prospecting.

According to Shiva, western scientific epistemology reduces nature and women to passive
objects for examination and invasion (employing
biotechnology and reproductive technologies
respectively). This reductionist epistemology
permeates capitalist development which, concerned only with efficiency and profits, de-values
the (re)productive capacities of women, non-
western people and nature, rendering them
'deficient', and in need of 'development'.

However, what is currently called development
is essentially maldevelopment, causing ecological
destruction and the impoverishment of Third
World communities, particularly women and
children. These are consequences of 'green revolution' technologies, which introduced the mass
production of agricultural commodities for profit
and displaced women's traditional maintenance
skills. Shiva has supported grassroots, women-
dominated movements resisting massive development in India, such as Chipko, and relates their
work to the recovery of Prakriti – the Indian
cosmology term for the feminine principle, which is
the living force that supports life. The recognition
of the activity, productivity and creativity associated with the feminine principle and the
continuity between society and nature are part of
an ontological shift which Shiva deems necessary in
the western dichotomised **ontology** of male
domination.

The task of redefining development as the
production rather than the destruction of life ties
feminism and ecology in a political project to
promote the indigenous knowledge of women who
through their work as subsistence farmers reproduce and conserve biodiversity. Their traditional
handling of seeds has been challenged by multi-
national biotechnology corporations, which are
introducing genetically engineered products into
local agriculture. Shiva's work with local communities creating seed banks and protecting intellec-

tual property rights is part of her campaign for
maintaining biodiversity.

Vandana Shiva won the Right Livelihood
Award (the 'alternative Nobel Prize') in 1993 for
her work connecting environmentalism and feminism.

See also: ecofeminism; science; sustainable
development

Selected writings

Mies, M. and Shiva, V. (eds) (1993) *Ecofeminism*,
London: Zed Books.
Shiva, V. (1989) *Staying Alive*, London: Zed Books.
Shiva, V. and Moser, I. (eds) (1995) *Biopolitics*,
London: Zed Books.

MEIRA HANSON

Showalter, Elaine (b. 1941)

Elaine Showalter is a founder of second-wave
feminist criticism (see **first-wave/second-wave
feminism**) in America; she is also a journalist,
cultural critic and historian of psychiatry. She is
credited with putting feminist literary criticism on
the map and with having coined the term
'gynocritic' (see **gynocritics**). She emphasises
the importance of studying female writers: bringing
women into the canon, and analysing in terms of
gender roles.

Showalter shows how the representation of
gender in women's English literature has evolved
from the Victorian novel to the present. She
considers the movement in women's literature
(see **women's writing**) in three stages: the
feminine (1840–80) involving the effort to internalise male culture; the feminist (1880–1920)
opposition to the dominant male culture; and the
female (1920 onwards). The latter stage includes
the 1960s phase of self-discovery, rejecting both
imitation and protest, and turning instead to
women's experience as an autonomous art.

She proposes a similar multi-dimensional model
of the growth of feminist criticism. First comes
revision and modification of male critical theory,
next, the discovery of women's own writing, out of
which comes the female aesthetic affirming female

experience. Gynocriticism has developed alongside this aesthetic suggesting that women's literature lies at the centre of feminist critique but rejecting the concept of an essential female **identity**. Showalter argues that theories of women's writing presently employ four models of difference all of which are forms of gynocriticism: biological criticism, focusing on the body as text; linguistic, looking at the use and creation of language; psychoanalytic which focuses on the psyche; and cultural considering social context. These approaches overlap but are roughly sequential and serve to construct a female framework for the analysis of women's literature, rather than adapt male models and theories.

Showalter has written on the history of the feminisation of madness. She argues that the end of the twentieth century was characterised by 'sexual anarchy', as was the previous *fin-de-siècle*. Her work on hysterical epidemics and their manifestations in modern culture has been her most controversial. She is critiqued in this work for suggesting that illnesses such as gulf war syndrome exist only in the realm of the unconscious. Nevertheless she remains an important contributor to a broad area of feminist topics.

See also: hysteria; literary theory, feminist; madness, feminisation of

Selected writings

Showalter, E. (1977) *A Literature of Their Own: British Novelists from Brontë to Lessing*, London: Virago.
—— (1985) *The Female Malady: Women, Madness and English Culture, 1830–1980*, New York: Pantheon Books.

KATE REED

single sex education

Single sex education is a term denoting the organisation of teaching into sex-specific groups rather than mixed sex or 'co-educational' groups. The term can apply to single sex groups within a co-educational classroom or school, or to entire schools or school systems which educate male and female pupils and students separately. Single sex education is supported for various reasons, including religious, cultural, and racial preferences or principles. Its legality has been challenged in some countries. Many feminists have supported single sex education for its potential to enhance girls' academic performance by eliminating boys' disruptive or competitive behaviour and by reducing practices and effects of **sexism**. Although there is some reported evidence that girls perform better academically in such environments, results as to the benefits of single sex schooling remain mixed. Other feminists argue that, irrespective of educational benefits for girls, single sex education does not sufficiently alter social gender relations.

See also: separatism

JENNIFER GORE

single women (spinsters)

Women are defined by their marital status in a way that is not true of men, and the woman who never marries is often the focus of censure. Since the early seventeenth century, 'spinster', once an occupational designation referring to the operator of a spinning wheel, has been used to refer to a never-married woman, usually beyond nubile age. In the western folk model, the spinster was caricatured as virginal and thus childless, ageing, unattractive, gossipy, and dour. The continuing prejudice against the adult woman who never marries is reflected in the extent to which spinsters are the brunt of ageist and sexist jokes and in the popular children's game where the player who draws the 'Old Maid' card becomes an instant loser. There is no equivalent pattern of scornful treatment accorded aged bachelors. In eighteenth- and nineteenth-century Europe, the proportion of spinsters was comparatively high (15 to 20 per cent) with estimates in some jurisdictions ranging up to 40 per cent, prompting concerns about a 'spinster problem'. Impoverished spinsters, particularly, were financially vulnerable and frequently dependent on the good will of others. Nevertheless, single women, without husbands or children of 'their own' often made significant contributions to the domestic lives of others and sometimes to the church and larger community. By the mid-1800s some European spinsters were touting spinsterhood as a conscious choice. Increasingly, social commentators voiced concern that the musings of contented spinsters might lead to disaffection among wives, lowering the birthrate among the advantaged classes who then would fail to reproduce themselves. Criticisms escalated through the late nineteenth and early twentieth century as sexologists, ascribing perversity to celibacy by choice, or to intense or romantic friendships between women (sometimes called 'Boston Marriages'), described spinsters as repressed and frigid. Relatedly, again raising fears of a reproductive short-fall among the advantaged, US elite women's colleges came under criticism as spinster breeding grounds, with too many forever unmarried and childless alumnae.

Research in the 1970s and 1980s suggested that, on average, women who never marry tend to come from more advantaged backgrounds than either married women or never married men. While journalists in the 1990s warned single women of a shortage of 'good men', in fact the supply of 'available' men reflects not only the ratio of men to women in a population but cultural definitions of the appropriate mate. Traditional definitions tend to expand men's choices (e.g., encompassing a broader range of ages), while restricting women's. Today the term single woman often includes not just the never married but also women *currently* unmarried, while the cultural concern has shifted to a focus on single mothers as a 'societal problem'.

References and further reading

Gordon, T. (1994) *Single Women,* New York: New York University Press.

SHARON McIRVIN ABU-LABAN

sisterhood

In the early years of the second-wave feminist/women's movement, affirmations of sisterhood marked women's recognition, in consciousness-raising, of their common oppression under patriarchy. In the name of sisterhood, women declared solidarity across diversity, confident that these affirmations would erase the effects of the differences that had divided women against one another.

A celebratory term in the early 1970s, sisterhood had fallen into disfavour by the early 1980s as it became clear that black women could see no place for themselves in white feminist declarations of sisterhood. Moreover, the inspiring effects of these initial declarations of sisterhood devolved into means of censuring women for behaving like 'bad sisters', as what had been a term of empowerment revealed its coercive, controlling power. Nonetheless, the excitement it generated as an early feminist rallying cry cannot be denied.

See also: patriarchy

References and further reading

Morgan, R. (ed.) (1970) *Sisterhood is Powerful,* New York: Vintage.

LORRAINE CODE

situated knowledges

Donna **Haraway** introduced the term 'situated knowledges' into feminist theory in a 1988 essay which has become a classic of late-twentieth-century feminist theory. Developed to evaluate state-of-the-art feminist theories of knowledge, 'situated knowledges' incorporates the best insights of then-current empiricist, standpoint, and post-modern epistemologies. It forges a position whose central tenet, that all knowledge-making practices are situated in the world, discredits the 'god trick' by which scientists and philosophers of science had claimed to transcend the world: to see 'from nowhere', unimpeded by the specificities of a subjectivity that is always somewhere. Arguing that feminists have a responsibility to learn how to see, and that nature 'talks back', Haraway claims that situation is constitutive of the only responsible form of **objectivity** in knowledge.

See also: empiricism; poststructuralism/postmodernism; standpoint theory

References and further reading

Haraway, D. (1991) 'Situated Knowledges', in D.

Haraway, *Simians, Cyborgs, and Women*, New York: Routledge.

LORRAINE CODE

slavery in the USA

Slavery, the system of forced labour, continues to affect the lives of people of African descent in the diaspora. Historians estimate that between the seventeenth and nineteenth centuries, twenty-eight million Africans were forcibly removed from central and western Africa to become slaves, a transition that forever changed their lives and the world around them. In West African kingdoms, from which many future slaves were taken, the slave trade stimulated expansionism; in the Islamic world, it stimulated commerce. Large American plantations drove capitalist economies.

Branded and chained for the Middle Passage across the Atlantic to the Americas, captive Africans were stacked like books in the hulls of slave ships. Upon arrival, they were auctioned and sold at prices based on their age, physical health, stamina, and in the case of women, their child-bearing potential. On the plantations everyone worked, including children. Women had the added pressure and fear that at any time their master or another white man might rape them.

In *Before the Mayflower: A History of Black America* (1993), Lerone Bennett, Jr. contends that contrary to popular belief, slaves were not docile. Slave women manifested their resistance to bondage in many ways, from slowly poisoning masters and mistresses to fighting back physically when whipped by overseers. After repeated and un-wanted sexual assaults, many slave women report-edly murdered their masters and disposed of the corpses in the fireplaces of their cabins. Some women had babies as a form of self-assertion and resistance.

Those known for fighting and kicking earned reputations for being mule-headed women, but were actually women who took their lives into their own hands and who actively tried to secure their freedom. When Harriet Tubman, a slave in Maryland, decided to run away from her master she encouraged her brothers and husband to accompany her as she fled north. They refused, and in 1849 she left alone, walking by night and hiding by day. Her freedom secured in Philadel-phia, Tubman returned to the south nineteen times over the next eight years to help family and friends escape.

While labour was divided equally among slaves, women had exclusive responsibility for domestic work. Moreover, more women worked in the fields than men and were punished severely if their production was low. Men were selected for more skilled jobs and worked as artisans, overseers, and coachmen. Domestic servitude placed slave women in increased contact with their mistresses, whose cruelty toward them was often prompted by misdirected anger caused by their husbands' sexual liaisons with slave women. This made domestic slave women more vulnerable to whippings.

Under the slavery system, women seemed to fare better than men did if there were opportunities for an urban market culture where produce was bought and sold. In locations such as Charleston, South Carolina and New Orleans, Louisiana, slaveholder patriarchs had to recognise and con-cede, on a limited basis, to the 'laws of the market' that followed the dictates of property and price rather than those of deference and duty. Slaves could assert their own property rights and gain a degree of autonomy and self-control. Slave women were the dominant sellers in these markets that created important social and economic self-em-powerment. Much of the produce they sold had been grown in their gardens, making slave market women an important source of cash and manu-facturers to their country counterparts. This trade made it possible for town and country slaves to form alliances for mutual advantage. The colonial slavery marketplace was a microcosm of complex relationships turned upside-down between slave and master, black and white, women and men, property and authority.

Cities also offered slave women a certain anonymity. In urban households they performed a variety of skilled and unskilled tasks such as cleaning, cooking, sewing and raising children. They also worked in commercial establishments as cooks, laundresses, and housekeepers, and in their off time they rented their services to others. Urban slaves tended to remain within the city's confines, where they passed on their valuable urban 'navigation' skills to their children. Women in this situation could adapt and use traditional African institutions of production and self-reliance.

The price of freedom was higher for men than for women, perhaps because slaveholders felt that women did not pose as much of a physical threat to the white population as black men. For example, after a slave rebellion was thwarted at Pointe Coupee in southern Louisiana, planters executed and imprisoned slaves and free men of colour, but ignored the women who were involved. Some slave women were set free because of the love and care they had shown their owners' families. In most cases, a free relative, husband, or cohabitant freed women. It was also not uncommon for slave women, willingly or unwillingly, to become the concubines of their masters or of other free men, and these relationships often led to freedom for the women and their children. L. Virginia Gould explains that this was especially true in New Orleans. The choices facing slave women were few and difficult, but they had to be made to ensure the futures of their children and the continuance of their descendants.

References and further reading

Bennett, L., Jr. (1993) *Before the Mayflower: A History of Black America*, Chicago, IL: Johnson Publishing.

Giddings, P. (1984) 'Casting of the Die: Morality, Slavery and Resistance', in *When and Where I Enter: The Impact of Black Women on Race and Sex in America*, New York: Morrow.

Gould, L.V. (1996) 'Urban Slavery–Urban Freedom: The Manumission of Jacqueline Lemelle' in D.B. Gaspar and D.C. Hine (eds) *More Than Chattle, Black Women and Slavery in the Americas*, Bloomington and Indianapolis: Indiana University Press.

Robertson, C. (1996) 'African into the Americas? Slavery and Women, the Family, and the Gender Division of Labor' in D.B. Gaspar and D.C. Hine *More Than Chattel, Black Women and Slavery in the Americas*, Bloomington and Indianapolis: Indiana University Press.

LIZZETTA LEFALLE-COLLINS

Smith, Dorothy (b. 1926)

Dorothy E. Smith is a Canadian sociologist who credits feminist **consciousness-raising** for the direction of her challenge to a **sociology** that begins in theory and produces 'theoretical' explanations. Her feminist social organisation of knowledge is her response to noting how women's **experience** was excluded from or had appeared in distorted ways in standard scholarly accounts. Smith believes that social analysis should help people understand the actualities of their lives and has developed, to that end, methods for explicating how things, such as a woman's oppression, actually work as social practices thus, her 1987 analysis of a mother helping with her child's schooling, showing the educational system's reliance on women's work in taken for granted ways.

For Smith, a problematic in the everyday world opens up for empirical study how local experience is coordinated through extra-local relations of ruling, that in twenty-first-century industrialised society are overwhelmingly discursive. Ruling, 'the complex of extra-local relations that provide in contemporary societies a specialisation of organisation, control and initiative' (Smith 1990b: 6) happens to actual people whose experience, knowledge, and standpoint are shaped thereby. **Feminism**, or taking seriously what it means to be a woman, helped Smith to recognise the methodological implications of women's standpoint (see **methodology, feminist**). A woman's knowing, embodied and locally situated, incorporates the social relations of her subordination – what needs to be explored and explicated. Many think that Smith's major achievement is her approach to understanding macro-level social organisation through analysis of the micro-level, as discussed in her 1987 book, *The Everyday World as Problematic*. In this approach that she calls institutional **ethnography**, trustworthy findings about 'how things work' are put in terms of the standpoint that the researcher takes, the experience that is explicated. As a cartography of social relations, she sees that institutional ethnography can illuminate not just women's lives, but the lives of all who are subject to ruling relations.

Two 1990 books, *Texts, Facts and Femininity* and *The Conceptual Practices of Power*, and a 1999 volume,

Writing the Social, set out her thinking about the social organisation of knowledge. Use of these methods opens up discursively organised settings, but keeps the actors present in the analysis as expert knowers, agents of the social practices that are the focus of inquiry (see **agency**). Smith maintains (in the face of postmodern/poststructural views to the contrary) that discourse is a social enactment, and there is truth to be discovered by investigating it as such.

See also: discourse analysis; poststructuralism/postmodernism

References and further reading

Smith, D. (1990a) *The Conceptual Practices of Power: A Feminist Sociology of Knowledge*, Boston: Northeastern University Press.

—— (1990b) *Texts, Facts and Femininity: Exploring the Relations of Ruling*, London: Routledge.

—— (1999) *Writing the Social: Critique, Theory and Investigations*, Toronto: University of Toronto Press.

MARIE L. CAMPBELL

social constructionism

Social constructionist theory is widely used within feminist social science. It is typically contrasted with '**positivism**' or 'existentialism' and has its origins in the classic work of sociologists Berger and Luckmann (1967). It is centrally concerned with understanding how the language we use and the taken-for-granted categories we employ construct our experience in ways which we then reify as 'natural', 'universal' and 'the way things have to be'.

A 'weak' form of social constructionism is widely accepted across sociology and psychology and consists of little more than the claim that individuals cannot be adequately understood without looking at the social, historical and cultural context within which they are embedded. By contrast, the 'strong' form of social constructionism profoundly unsettles both conventional and much feminist social science by proposing that social science categories (such as 'the individual', 'emo-tions', 'sex' and, indeed, 'scientific knowledge' itself) are social rather than natural products.

Weak social constructionism is well represented in feminist social science on gender. Research on 'sex differences', 'sex role stereotypes' and 'gender socialisation' typically distinguish between '**gender**' (masculinity and femininity) and 'sex' (maleness and femaleness), with gender represented as social, and 'sex' as biological. By contrast, feminists using a 'strong' form of social constructionism challenge the taken-for-granted notion of two biological sexes, and depict 'maleness' and 'femaleness' as fundamentally ideological, not biological, categories (e.g. Kessler and McKenna 1978). Feminist social constructionists have posed similar challenges to 'lesbianism' (and 'heterosexuality') as categories (Kitzinger 1987). For many feminists, then, social constructionism offers the possibility of uncovering fundamental processes of patriarchal power in shaping our sense of ourselves and our world.

Some feminist social scientists distrust social constructionism for reasons which, in many ways, parallel the concerns voiced in other disciplines about the implications of postmodernism (see **poststructuralism/postmodernism**). In refusing to treat categories such as 'oppression' or 'patriarchy' as already-existing facts, social constructionism can make it difficult to self-define as an oppressed group: charges of 'essentialism' are sometimes used to dismiss those who make political claims on behalf of a group called 'women'. Moreover, social constructionists' critique of positivism leads to research programmes based upon **qualitative methodologies** (e.g. **discourse analysis**) which emphasise their own constructed nature and so lose the rhetorical impact of 'scientific facts' in the public policy arena. Nonetheless, social constructionism has been important for feminism in exposing and undermining taken-for-granted assumptions in the social sciences which have privileged white ruling-class men.

References and further reading

Berger, P.L. and Luckmann, T. (1967) *The Social Construction of Reality*, Harmondsworth: Penguin.

Kessler, S. and McKenna, W. (1978) *Gender: An Ethnomethodological Approach*, New York: Wiley.

(For a selected reprint from, and contemporary commentaries on, this book see M. Crawford (2000) (ed.) 'A Reappraisal of Gender: An Ethnomethodological Approach', *Feminism and Psychology* 10 (1).)

Kitzinger, C. (1987) *The Social Construction of Lesbianism*, London: Sage.

CELIA KITZINGER

socialism and feminism

Socialism has challenged both inequality and injustice and thus contributed substantially to a distinctive especially European brand of feminist politics.

Socialism predates its sibling Marxism, deriving from the commitment to collectivity of the French thinker Charles Fourier and the British writer and reformer Robert Owen. Followers of both offer a vision of redistribution on egalitarian grounds based on an assessment of both relative production and relative want 'from each according to ability, to each according to need'. Marx and Engels criticise this in the *Anti-Duhring* as what they call Utopian socialism, which relies upon the assumption that everyone would behave in the same way whereas they felt that inequalities of economic power were integral to capitalism however good individual intentions. Feminism too has debated the possibility of change through the effort of will and many critics have argued that male power will not easily be given up just because it should. Socialist feminists historically focused on equality and citizenship, and therefore issues of exclusion from the political order but also a challenge to the morality of social organisation. Owenites in nineteenth-century Britain and North America in particular believed in the possiblity of social transformation through exemplary living arrangements in the form of communities organised on communal lines. Socialism has thus contained a critique of the morality of capitalist society without necessarily emphasising the inevitability of its collapse.

Twentieth-century socialism shared with Marxism an emphasis on distribution and production as constitutive of society but parted from Marxism in its attitude to the state and to social change.

Socialist feminists were prominent in agitation over liberalisation of abortion and divorce laws, birth control provision and questions of access to jobs and to educational opportunity. They saw consciousness-raising as most likely to arise from historical enquiry, trade union organisation or academic work than through women's groups alone; they tended to work with men rather than entirely separately. They are reformists rather than revolutionaries. They have been effective in working in a parliamentary system in introducing substantial changes in inequality between the sexes where most European social democracies have introduced legislation to support equal opportunities and equal pay – but rarely provision of state benefits especially those most specific to one sex.

Socialism has thus provided fertile space for feminism to flourish especially in academic contexts where a formal commitment to equality and radical critique has been most strong. However, socialist feminism itself has been less successful in maintaining the difficult tension between the commitment to equality and the need to represent women's particular needs; or the differences among women which have led to differentiation of political groups on the basis of identity.

Socialist feminists have maintained a cultural politics which challenges consumerism, inequality and exclusion and has been most productive in the emphasis on community initiatives to alter the material conditions of mothering, as in the activities of the women's unit of the Greater London Council in the UK which looked to childcare provision, improved safety on the streets and access to information resources for women's groups as well as the transformation of academic opportunities for women in further and higher education. They have also been active in defending the economic life of cities in campaigns such as Women Against Pit Closures and community mobilisation on housing estates to improve social resources and minimise the impact of unemployment upon social life.

See also: Marxism

References and further reading

Phillips, A. (ed.) (1987) *Feminism and Equality*, Oxford: Basil Blackwell.

Rowbotham, S., Segal, L. and Wainwright, H. (1980) *Beyond the Fragments: Feminism and the Making of Socialism*, London, Merlin Press.

Segal, L. (1997) 'Generations of Feminism', *Radical Philosophy*, 85, May/June: 6–16

DEBORAH THOM

social purity movement, women in

The self-described social purity movements that flourished in English-speaking countries from the 1870s to the First World War were – like the related temperance movements – important sites for the development of both feminine and feminist politics. 'Social purity' was a grand project to morally and physically cleanse the growing urban centres of the USA and Britain of vice, from swearing and smoking to police corruption.

In contrast to the focus of earlier sex regulation campaigners on 'the solitary evil' (masturbation), late-nineteenth-century social purity campaigns focused on what was assumed to be 'the social evil', namely prostitution. Long associated with urbanisation, prostitution became the main focus of the movement partly because of its powerful symbolism. Echoing Biblical texts on 'the whore of Babylon', the discourse of social purity constructed 'the fallen woman' not only as a social problem in her own right but, more powerfully, a synecdoche for fallen cities and degenerate nations.

Particularly in the USA, social purity campaigns served as an important vehicle for a certain type of middle-class feminism. Social purity feminists targeted *masculine* vices, suggesting for instance that the solution to the 'problem' of prostitution was not more severe policing of prostitutes but rather the ideal married monogamy known as 'the white life for two'.

The constant references to 'the white life' and 'white slaves' were not coincidental. The campaign against forced prostitution was overtly racist in both the USA and Canada, with lurid anecdotes about 'white' slaves being drugged and kidnapped by procurers portrayed as Jewish, Italian, French, or black. Throughout North America, in the social purity movement, racist effects converged with the anti-immigrant politics promoted by many suffragists and by nearly all temperance activists (feminists included).

In the United Kingdom, social purity remained a rather marginal cultural phenomenon. In North America, however, although the social purity movement itself did not survive past the First World War, many of its ideals were successfully promoted for some time after the war through the powerful machinery of the WCTU (Women's Christian Temperance Union), an organisation that, although focusing on drinking, included other 'social purity' issues within its mandate. In the 1980s, the spectre of social purity was deployed by both sides in the famous 'sex wars'. The pro-sex activists (which included many historians, especially in the USA) argued that social purity had distorted feminism by allying it with puritanism rather than with sexual liberation; while radical feminists, most notably Sheila Jeffreys, argued that the puritanical 'spinsters' of 1900 should be treated seriously as foremothers, insofar as they developed some feminist tools to critique masculine sexuality. Neither side of the 'sex wars', however, paid serious attention to the 'whiteness' of social purity.

References and further reading

Jeffreys, S. (1985) *The Spinster and Her Enemies: Feminism and Sexuality 1880–1930*, London: Pandora.

MARIANA VALVERDE

social work

Feminism holds an important place in current social work theory and practice. Women's participation in social work takes place at the fulcrum between social control and social care. On one hand, social work developed within ideologies of capitalist **patriarchy**, helping to divert attention from unjust social structures to individual malajustment. On the other hand, social work concentrates on the interdependence of people and environments. Given women's subordination in racist, classist and sexist structures, feminist social work stresses the effects of social disadvantage on women in both the public and private spheres. The relationship between social disadvantage and individual distress is elaborated at multiple levels, including policy analysis and development, advocacy and community development, and direct practice with individual women, or within the context of their family or community relationships.

At macro levels, feminist social workers consider how social policy interacts with the specific circumstances of women. In general, women have either been left out of gender-blind policies, or policies have maintained social control by reproducing the gendered division of labour, particularly through the assumption of women's caring. For example, feminist social workers have called attention to the **feminisation of poverty**. Feminists have also criticised policies which prescribe the gendered division of labour by assuming women's labour as caregivers.

Feminist theorists recognise that differences among women must be acknowledged in social policy development. Policy has different implications for women depending on the interaction of historical categories of **oppression** such as **race**, class, sexual orientation, disability and age.

At a micro level, feminists deal with the effects of social disadvantage at the level of interpersonal distress. Here, feminist practitioners insist that women's distress must be understood within the context of discrimination and inequality. Such distress may be exhibited across a broad range of issues. Effects of women's poverty, for example, may be manifested in child abuse and neglect (see also **child sexual abuse**). Feminist social workers encourage women to reframe personal distress in political terms by connecting distress to the existence of discrimination and oppression.

Feminist social workers take account of the operation of power in women's family and community relationships, as well as within the helping relationship that occurs during social work service. Feminist practice asserts that violence against women, for example, is an effect of male power that must be addressed by political means rather than understood as individual dysfunction. Because of the effects of subordination on women's sense of self, feminist practitioners value an egalitarian helping relationship in which dialogue is privileged over authoritarian professionalism.

Feminist social workers are concerned with the effects of difference on helping relationships. Differences in **power** and **privilege** among women exist as a function of inequalities based on race, class, and other historical exclusions. Consequently, the acknowledgement of practitioners' own socialised selves with respect to power plays a crucial role in practice based on social justice.

See also: age studies and gender; class analysis UK; class analysis US; disability, women and; family, the; sexuality

References and further reading

Afflilia: Journal of Women and Social Work.

Baines, C., Evans, P., and Neysmith, S. (eds) (1991) *Women's Caring: Feminist Perspectives on Social Welfare*, Toronto: McClelland and Stewart.

Bricker-Jenkins, M., Hooyman, N., and Gottlieb, N. (eds) (1991) *Feminist Social Work Practice in Clinical Settings*, Newbury Park, CA: Sage.

AMY ROSSITER

sociology

Twentieth-century feminist sociological theory developed mostly in the USA and England. Like sociology itself, feminist sociology searches for the sources of inequality, injustice, and other social problems, in this case, pertaining to the status of women. Its main contribution to feminism has been to show that men's and women's statuses are the result of social factors and the organisation of society by gender, not individual attributes or behaviour.

The first theories focused around sex roles. Feminist sociologists used the concepts of status as position in a social structure, roles as the behavioural scripts for enactment of the normative prescriptions of the status, and socialisation as the process of learning appropriate role behaviour. Jessie Bernard dissected the roles in the nuclear family to show the conflict of interests between the husband and wife. Her concept of 'his and her marriage' summarises the ways the wife is diminished by the husband's structural dominance in the family.

Examining structure and roles in work organisations, Cynthia Fuchs Epstein and Rosabeth Moss Kanter targeted the contrasting opportunities and constraints for men and women. They argue that women's behaviour as workers is less the result of socialisation than of the pressures put on them as tokens in work situations dominated by men or, in traditional women's jobs, as low-prestige workers with limited opportunities. Moss Kanter theorises that the reason so few women were in positions of authority was the conflation of authoritativeness with masculinity. The well-known 'Kanter hypothesis' bases predictions of change on the numbers of women in male-dominated settings (the tipping point is 15–35 per cent), an objective measure that does not depend on alteration of attitudes. However, later research has shown that women are sometimes more isolated and harassed as their numbers increase, because men colleagues feel threatened.

Marxist and socialist feminist sociologists have done more systemic structural analyses of how capitalism combines with **patriarchy** to show how women's economic dependence on a husband's income is linked to their disadvantaged position in job markets and within the family. Heidi Hartmann, in her influential 1976 article, 'Capitalism, Patriarchy, and Job Segregation by Sex', and later Marxist feminists, such as Sylvia Walby, applied the value theory of capitalism to explain why housework is not considered 'real work', arguing that although women's work in the home contributes important 'use value', what they produce is consumed by their families or is an intangible asset. In contrast, marketplace work produces a profit and so its value is tangible and can be economically rewarded accordingly.

However, in paid work, women are disadvantaged by their primary role as social reproducers of the next generation, whose value to capitalism, like that of their unpaid maintenance of men workers, is grossly underestimated. This theoretical placement of women as workers in the home and workplace has forced a sociological rethinking of the nature of work and the reintegration of the economy and family, which had been analysed as separate spheres, 'public' and 'private' (see **public/private**). Nona Glazer takes that analysis even further, to show how women's caretaking work of ill relatives supplements overworked nurses' work, and helps keep their wages low.

Barbara Katz Rothman brings a socialist feminist analysis to procreation and parenting, locating both in the materialism of capitalism and in the dynamics of the dual-earner family. She also develops the idea of childbirth and parenting as relationships growing out of doing – gestating, birthing, and caring for children – relationships that belong to fathers, nannies, and all caretakers, not only to mothers.

Feminist sociological research on gender segregation and stratification in occupations and professions and on the persistence of job classifications as 'men's work' and 'women's work' has been enormous, as has scholarly analysis of unequal pay scales and the limited-promotion phenomenon known as the **glass ceiling**. However, with the increase in a continuous work history even for married women with small children, the earlier theoretical rationale for gender inequality in the labour force – that women are primarily wives and mothers – has been undercut. As Arlie Hochschild has argued, women who work outside the home work a 'second shift' within it, but there is ample research that shows that women's productivity in their paid job does not suffer because of it.

Other sources of inequality in the work place are the gendered structure of organisations and the continuous recreation of underpaid 'women's work'. Barbara F. Reskin and Patricia A. Roos have shown that occupations do not lose their prestige and high salaries because women enter them in large numbers, but rather that jobs become available to women because they lose their attractiveness for white men. They are deskilled, earnings decline, there is less autonomy, and working conditions deteriorate.

Feminists working in development and the global economy, such as Maria Mies, have combined a class and gender analysis to demonstrate how economies are moving from subsistence agriculture to manufacturing exploit unmarried and married women workers. Laying out the structure of waged work and the marriage market, they have created an integrated theory of the movement of women in and out of the formal and informal economy as their marital status changes. Janet Saltzman Chafetz has developed a similar general theory of women's status, linking it to ability to produce and control economic resources, which in turn is determined by the technology and by family structure and the availability of multiple child-carers.

An analysis of the combined effects of multiple structural and status factors in industrialised societies has been developed by feminist multi-racial/multiethnic theorists. Arguing for the inter-sectionality of race, class, and gender, Patricia Hill **Collins** describes a 'matrix of domination' that stratifies both women and men. Some women are advantaged by education, wealth, job opportu-nities, and white skin colour, and some men are multiply disadvantaged, so that global comparisons of women versus men are inaccurate and mislead-ing methodologically and theoretically. This work challenges conventional sociological concepts of stratification and identity, since race/ethnicity, social class, and gender cross-cut and combine in a variety of ways.

Focusing on **sexuality**, radical feminists, work-ing with Catharine **MacKinnon**'s theory of the patriarchal state, target men's propensity to violence and their control of women's bodies through marital rights, socially sanctioned beatings, rapes, and pornography. They argue that patri-archy is deeply embedded in the institutions and values of western societies, and have collected data on the prevalence of rape, the social dynamics of wife abuse and father/daughter incest, the harmful effects of pornography, and the global sex trade as manifestations of patriarchal institutionalisation of sexual violence against women (see **radical feminism**).

Psychoanalytic theories have been influential for feminist sociology, especially with regard to parent-ing and heterosexual relationships. In the 1970s, Nancy **Chodorow** was at the forefront in devel-oping a sociological analysis of the reproduction of mothering and asymmetrical heterosexual relation-ships using Freudian theory. Most recently, Cho-dorow has promulgated a Freudian theory of multiple masculinities, femininities, and sexualities, and Lynn Chancer has developed a theory of sadomasochism in everyday life as a means of control.

Another important branch of feminist sociology has been the work of Celia Kitzinger, Paula Rust, and Verta Taylor and others on lesbian issues (see **lesbian feminism**). They have used theories of social construction, social movements, and com-munity to examine lesbian identity, politics, families, parenting, work, and harassment and discrimination.

Both women and men feminist sociologists have analysed men and masculinities. R.W. Connell shows how the practices of power are layered and interwoven in western society; stratification in-cludes men's subordination and denigration of other men as well as men's exploitation of women. Important concepts here are hegemonic **mascu-linity** (characteristics of the dominant group – in western societies, economically successful, racially superior, and visibly heterosexual) and multiple masculinities, which differ in work organisations and in sports, and throughout history, as Michael Messner and Michael Kimmel have shown.

An integrative perspective in feminist sociology has been **social constructionism**, which argues that people create their social realities and identities through interactions with families, friends, colleagues. In the 1970s, Suzanne J. Kessler and Wendy McKenna, building on Harold Garfinkel's ethnomethodological analysis of how a transsexual constructs conventional womanhood, argued that everyone constructs their gender. Candace West and Don Zimmerman have devel-oped the widely used idea of 'doing gender' as illustrative of how the social construction of gender builds up masculine dominance and feminine submissiveness. Their article was published in 1987 in the first volume of a new journal, *Gender and Society*.

Using the concept of gender as a social institution, Judith Lorber argues that the socially constructed gendered social order establishes patterns of expectations for individuals, orders the social processes of everyday life, and legitimates political power imbalances. Although individual actions are hemmed in by the general rules of social life, cultural expectations, workplace and occupational norms, and laws and governmental policies, these social restraints are often resisted and rebelled against, and so they are amenable to change.

Methodologically, feminist sociologists have questioned the conventional categories used for comparisons in research designs – especially race, class, gender, and sexuality. Dorothy **Smith** has developed a methodology that integrates women's subordinated status as a devalued class of producers of everyday life and child rearers, with the structural aspects of their situations as members of families, teachers, and service workers. She urges feminist sociologists to combine the experiences and standpoints of insiders with the structural and institutional analysis of the outsider and to unpack the commonly used categories to show how they mask hierarchies, conflicts, and the lines of power – the 'relations of ruling' (see **methodology, feminist**).

Theoretical gaps in feminist sociology that need to be addressed now are rethinking the concept of class to include women's work for the family and in the informal economy, especially in the global economy; developing research methods to analyse gender, race/ethnicity, and class as intersecting positions in a stratified social order; combining data on women's experiences with concepts from organisational and other institutional theories; bringing cultural discourse analyses to bear on political documents; theorising the gendered aspects of **citizenship** and the state, especially with regard to **civil rights** and welfare entitlements; and creating a unified theory of **gender** that encompasses social structure and individual agency.

See also: economic globalisation; Marxism; socialism and feminism; work, women and

References and further reading

Chafetz, J.S. (1984) *Sex and Advantage*, Totowa, NJ: Rowman and Allenheld.

Chancer, L.S. (1992) *Sadomasochism in Everyday Life*, New Brunswick, NJ: Rutgers University of Kentucky Press.

Chodorow, N. (1994) *Femininities, Masculinities, Sexualities*, Lexington, KY: University Press.

Connell, R.W. (1987) *Gender and Power*, Stanford, CA: Stanford University Press.

Glazer, N.Y. (1993) *Women's Paid and Unpaid Labor*, Philadelphia, PA: Temple University Press.

Hochschild, A. (1989) *The Second Shift*, New York: Viking.

Kitzinger, C. (1987) *The Social Construction of Lesbianism*, Newbury Park, CA: Sage.

Lorber, J. (1994) *Paradoxes of Gender*, New Haven, CT: Yale University Press.

Mies, M. (1986) *Patriarchy and Accumulation on a World Scale*, London: Zed Books.

Reskin, B.F. and Roos, P.A. (1990) *Job Queues, Gender Queues*, Philadelphia, PA: Temple University Press.

Rothman, B.K. (1989) *Recreating Motherhood*, New York: Norton.

Walby, S. (1990) *Theorizing Patriarchy*, Oxford: Basil Blackwell.

West, C. and Zimmerman, D. (1987) 'Doing Gender', *Gender and Society* 1: 125–51.

JUDITH LORBER

speech act theory

The basic insight provided by speech act theory, developed by John Austin in *How to Do Things with Words* (1962), concerns the performative nature of linguistic expressions. Austin argues that certain types of verbs (performative verbs such as *promise, bet, name*) do not merely describe or report a state of affairs, but instead have the capacity to perform actions when uttered under appropriate circumstances (e.g., 'I name this ship the *Queen Elizabeth*' as uttered when smashing a bottle against the ship's stern). Using this notion of performativity, Judith **Butler**, in her influential book *Gender Trouble* (1990), proposes that **gender** is performative: it is not a trait that individuals possess, but rather is produced by way of the particular kinds of acts individuals perform.

See also: identity; language, gender and power

References and further reading

Butler, J. (1990) *Gender Trouble: Feminism and the Subversion of Identity*, New York: Routledge.

SUSAN EHRLICH

speech, freedom of

Freedom of speech refers to the right to be free from government restriction in the expression of ideas. The right, associated with liberal democratic theory, is typically seen as promoting three core objectives: (1) the pursuit of truth through the free circulation of a broad range of ideas; (2) democracy and political decision-making through free and open debate; and (3) individual self fulfillment and realisation. Much feminist theory has been highly critical of this liberal right, arguing that the exercise of this liberty often collides with the pursuit of equality (see **equality and difference**). The critique has been the strongest in relation to **pornography**. Dominance or **radical feminism**, for example, argues that pornography harms women and therefore must be restricted (**MacKinnon**). This feminist theory has also been highly critical of the central assumptions of this liberal freedom, arguing that for women and other disadvantaged groups, freedom of speech is a fiction. MacKinnon, for example, argues that the very idea of freedom of speech, as freedom *from* government action, 'tends to presuppose that whole segments of the population are not systematically silenced socially, prior to government action' (1993: 34–5). Women, and other disadvantaged groups do not have equal access to the expression of ideas, to political participation, or to self realisation. Freedom of speech – the right to be free from government restriction of expression – is seen to reinforce existing **power** inequalities, and particularly the subordination of women. Within this framework, freedom of speech is lined up in opposition to equality, and the normative claim to equality is given primacy (see **normative v. descriptive**).

Another strand of feminist theory is highly critical of the claims of dominance feminism, arguing that freedom of speech is important for women (Strossen, McCormack). Liberal feminists, along with a range of other anti-censorship feminists including artists, performers, writers and sex trade workers, have argued that freedom of speech is important for women, and have refused the opposition between equality and liberty. They have argued that freedom of speech has long been a powerful tool for advancing women's equality.

Further, they argue that giving the state the power to censor unpopular speech will, more often than not, be used against women; that is, it will be used to suppress women's sexual and political expression. From the use of the Comstock Law (the first anti-obscenity law enacted in the USA in 1873) which was used to prosecute pioneering feminists and birth control advocates, to the Canada Customs' seizure of feminist books, this position argues that feminist expression has always been a primary target of censorship laws.

More recently, some feminist theory, borrowing from the insights of poststructuralism (see **poststructuralism/postmodernism**), has attempted to critically engage with these claims, arguing that neither radical nor liberal feminism has a sufficiently complex understanding of power, language and subjectivity. Others have similarly interrogated and rejected the distinctions between **public/private**, words/action, subject/object on which the claim to freedom of speech has traditionally rested. But, a revised vision of freedom of speech, and its place within feminist politics, still remains elusive.

See also: liberal feminism

References and further reading:

MacCormack, T. (1991) 'Must We Censor Pornography? Civil Liberties and Feminist Jurisprudence', in D. Schneiderman (ed.) *Freedom of Expression and the Charter*, Toronto: Thomson Professional Publishing.

MacKinnon, C. (1993) *Only Words*, Cambridge, MA: Harvard University Press.

Strossen, N. (1995) *Defending Pornography: Free Speech, Sex and the Fight for Women's Rights*, New York: Scribner.

BRENDA COSSMAN

Spender, Dale (b. 1943)

Spender's first major book *Man Made Language* articulated a radical feminist position (see **radical feminism**) on **language, gender and power** in an accessible language which brought it a wide audience. Women, she argues, have been excluded from the production of cultural forms, of which the most important is language. She describes a process of silencing and appropriation in the use of sexist language (see **sexism**), in asymmetrical male/female interactions, and in the ways early women scholars were rendered invisible to later scholars. She has continued to develop many of these themes in a prolific output of more than thirty books.

Spender's definitions of culture and language are sweeping and occasionally ambiguous and this has sometimes rendered her work controversial. At some moments 'culture' is used to designate high or hegemonic culture (see **hegemony**) and language is used to designate institutional discourse or Foucauldian systems of knowledge, as when she notes women's virtual exclusion from dominant literary and scientific, academic and political institutions. Documenting, redressing and challenging these exclusions has been Spender's goal in compiling anthologies of women writers in Australia and Britain (especially early women writers), in documenting the actions of early feminists, in examining the position of women and girls in schools, and in looking at feminist critiques of and contributions to traditional academic disciplines. In all this work Spender's epistemological goal is to scrutinise the processes by which certain kinds of knowledge are deemed relevant, central and objective (see **epistemology, feminist**; **objectivity**). In this, her work bears some relationship to early **standpoint theory**.

Where Spender's claims have been considered most controversial are when her claims about men's control over language and culture have designated culture in a broader sense as all of human production, and language as everyday interaction. Linguists and anthropologists have offered numerous counterexamples of women's creative and resistant use of language (and even silence), arguing that it is precisely because everyday speech is not easily owned or controlled that it is such a powerful tool for challenging hegemonic groups. Spender's perspectives on gender and power have offered these scholars few theoretical resources for understanding women's **agency** and resistance, the nature of cultural change and the complicated intertwining of sexism with other axes of domination (race, class, age, culture, sexual orientation).

Selected writings

Kramarae, C. and Spender, D. (eds) (1992) *The Knowledge Explosion: Generations of Feminist Scholarship*, New York: Teachers' College Press.

Spender, D. (1980) *Man Made Language*, London: Routledge and Kegan Paul.

—— (ed.) (1981) *Men's Studies Modified: The Impact of Feminism on the Academic Disciplines*, Oxford: Pergamon Press.

—— (1989) *The Writing or the Sex? or Why You Don't Have to Read Women's Writing to Know It's No Good*, New York: Pergamon Press.

BONNIE McELHINNY

spiritual feminism

Feminist spirituality grows within the cracks of a contradiction. The religions privilege the male as subject – as messiahs, mullahs, prophets, disciples, theologians, priests; as Son of God, indeed as God 'Himself'. So the critique of religion has been endemic to the women's movement. According to secularist feminism, emancipation lies in outgrowing the paternalist myths that sanctify dominance and distract us with immaterial hopes. Most forms of academic feminism – liberal, Marxist, existential, psychoanalytic and poststructuralist – repudiate spirituality as mystification. After all, the traditional dualism of spirit versus flesh has sunk women into the status of the more bodily, sensuous partner, whose very salvation depends on discipline by the more 'spiritual' male. Yet women throughout history have found spiritual resources indispensable for their own survival, emancipation from familial and social constraints, and sense of meaning.

Spiritual feminists share the critique of the patriarchal, homophobic, and sex-negative functions of malestream religion (see **malestream thought**): 'if God is male, then the male is God', announced Mary **Daly**, the feminist spiritual philosopher, in 1973. They also often distinguish between spirituality and religion. Feminist spirituality in the 1970s developed a continuum embracing the **divine feminine**, the **Goddess** and the Earth (see **earth/Gaia/Mother Earth**), as mother-*mater*-matter, and interconnectedness with all sentient life, often developed with borrowings from indigenous and Asian spiritualities.

Also in the 1970s, women were increasingly ordained as pastors and rabbis, or teaching feminist theology and biblical studies (see **theology, feminist**; **biblical studies, feminist**). These feminists suspected Goddess feminism of an ahistorical romanticism. But they increasingly absorbed its ecofeminist framework and feminine imagery of the divine (cf. Rosemary Ruether's 'God/ess' and Gaia; Elizabeth Johnson's 'Jesus Sophia'). Thus feminist spirituality began to study its precedents not just in reconstructions of matrilineal traditions, but in mysticism and revolution hidden within our inherited traditions – as for instance the biblical Wisdom/Sophia as the female face of God. Despite backlashes from Christian denominations, womanist and mujerista theology represents a tenacious and growing force within the global church (see **womanist theology**).

Both within and without the 'great religions', spiritual feminism practises an earth-bound, politicising solidarity between women. Even postmodern philosophers like Julia **Kristeva** and Luce **Irigaray** engage in feminist theology. As progressive politics outgrows the modern dualism of religious versus secular, the feminist sense of the sacred intensifies. Increasingly attuned to differences of gender and sexuality, and also race, ethnicity, class, culture, and species, the exploration of postpatriarchal spirituality offers vital resources for building more complex and long-term coalitions among social movements.

References and further reading

Daly, M. (1973) *Beyond God the Father: Toward a Philosophy of Women's Liberation*, Boston: Beacon.

Ruether, R. (1983) *Sexism and God-Talk: Toward a Feminist Theology*, Boston: Beacon.

Spretnak, C. (ed.) (1982) *The Politics of Women's Spirituality: Essays by Founding Mothers of the Movement*, New York: Anchor/Doubleday, 1994.

CATHERINE KELLER

Spivak, Gayatri Chrakravorty (b. 1942)

Gayatri Chrakravorty Spivak is a feminist cultural and literary theorist working in the USA but giving lectures world-wide. As a British-Indian working in the USA, much of her work centres on her unease as a migrant intellectual occupying a space she 'cannot not want to inhabit' but must critique. She attempts to render visible the historical and institutional structures within which she speaks while acknowledging that no one can totally articulate the space she herself inhabits (see her collection of essays *Outside in the Teaching Machine*). She therefore asserts the importance of positionality while refusing to essentialise it. Her work is marked by a particular use of deconstruction, Marxist and feminist theories as well as her commitment to teaching and pedagogy. However, she is frequently referred to as a postcolonial feminist theorist (see **postcolonial feminism**).

In her much cited essay 'Can the Subaltern speak?' Spivak, following Marx's *The Eighteenth Brumaire*, constructs the subaltern as a space of difference. The subaltern is structurally excluded and can only enter existing structures by an identification on her part with those already positioned with the means to represent themselves. In this essay Spivak emphasises two senses of representation; representation as 'speaking for' as in politics – *Vertretung*; and the theatrical sense of representation as re-staging or 'placing there' – *Darstellung*. Representation is also never adequate or complete. Spivak's main concern, then, in relation to the question of, can the subaltern speak?, is with the meaning transaction between speaker and listener. Even when the subaltern makes an effort in death to speak she is not able to be heard. It is speaking *and* hearing that completes the speech act (see **speech act theory**).

Spivak is centrally concerned with the unstable and catechrestical nature of language itself. The idea of catechresis (as a metaphor without an adequate literal referent) is applied to western notions of nation, nationalism, **citizenship** and multiculturalism for which, she suggests, there is no adequate referent in postcolonial contexts. She distances herself from these terms while demonstrating the crimes that are attendant upon them. Her concern is less with producing a legitimating counternarrative than with the deconstructive project of bringing provisional certainties into crisis and examining the shifting limits of knowledge and judgement. Spivak also reflects on the ethics of relationship as she attempts to imaginatively inhabit other people's narratives in such as way as to tell someone else's story as *her* story of feminism, to tell another's story without appropriating it.

Though often accused of being too theoretical and obscure, Spivak suggests that theory provides the necessary reflexivity to fulfil the responsibility of the academic.

See also: cultural imperialism; cultural politics; deconstruction, feminist; essentialism; narrative, feminist uses of; nationalism and gender; pedagogy, feminist

Selected writings

Spivak, G.C. (1987) *In Other Worlds: Essays in Cultural Politics*, New York: Methuen.
—— (1988) 'Can the Subaltern Speak?', in C. Nelson and L. Grossberg (eds) *Marxism and the Interpretation of Culture*, Hampshire and London: Macmillan Education Ltd.
—— (1993) *Outside in the Teaching Machine*, New York: Routledge.
—— (1999) *A Critique of Postcolonial Reason: Toward a History of the Vanishing Present*, Cambridge, MA: Harvard University Press.

BREDA GRAY

split brain theory

Brains have two halves, or hemispheres. 'Split brain theory' is a colloquialism describing the idea that different brain functions are located in different brain areas, or even in different hemispheres. Speech, for instance, is coordinated by part of the left hemisphere.

The brain is thus asymmetrical, or lateralised. Some psychologists claim that there are **gender** differences in lateralisation. Judith Genova has

analysed theories of brain lateralisation, and shown how they have changed as gender roles changed. She argues that earlier ideas of lateralisation supposed that the left hemisphere was more analytic, and dominant in men. This has now been superseded by the idea that the right hemisphere is more holistic and spatial and dominant in men. Both are sexist, Genova suggests; analytic skills were once highly valued, while now holistic skills imply creativity. As one set of skills becomes more valued, so it is likely to be associated with men (see **sexism**).

References and further reading:

Genova, J. (1990) 'Women and the Mismeasure of Thought', in N. Tuana (ed.) *Feminism and Science*, Bloomington, IN: Indiana University Press.

LYNDA BIRKE

standpoint theory

Feminist standpoint theory establishes its starting points and testing grounds in women's experiences. Eschewing epistemological goals of determining necessary and sufficient conditions for 'knowledge in general', standpoint theorists argue that no version of **empiricism** – feminist or otherwise – can offer sufficiently radical analyses of the structural factors that shape women's practices and consciousness in 'the everyday world', where authoritative knowledge derives from the experiences of the dominant (see **epistemology, feminist**).

Standpoint theory locates investigators on the same plane as the investigated, bringing their social, political, racial, economic, and sexual situations – the **power** and **privilege** that naturalise hierarchical arrangements – as much into critical focus as traditional 'objects of knowledge'. Standpoint theorists contest epistemic neutrality, exposing the patterns of dominance and subordination in which knowledge is produced and legitimated. Even allegedly disinterested science is open to scrutiny for the forces that produce both its successes and its failures.

Crafted in the 1980s by Patricia Hill **Collins**, Nancy **Hartsock**, Sandra **Harding**, Hilary **Rose**, and Dorothy **Smith**, standpoint theory has roots in Marxist theory and second-wave feminist **consciousness-raising**. Drawing an analogy between bourgeois/proletarian divisions under capitalism and masculine/feminine divisions under **patriarchy**, standpoint feminists examine how patriarchal ideology represents women's subordination to men as natural, just as capitalist ideology represents proletarian subordination to the bourgeoisie as natural. As Marxist analyses start from the material-historical circumstances of the proletariat, so feminist analyses start from the material-historical circumstances of women to generate the consciousness-raising that enables informed feminist resistance.

A feminist standpoint is neither a 'women's standpoint', theirs by virtue of being women; nor a perspective which anyone could occupy at will. It is a hard-won product of social-political engagement that exposes the falsehoods that sustain social hierarchies, in which the strategic knowledge that enables the oppressed to negotiate the social order becomes a resource for undermining that order.

Poststructuralist critics argue that standpoint theorists have to assume unmediated, 'pure', uncontestable experience and an implausibly unified female identity. But recent standpoint theorists are careful not to aggregate women: they show how women's material, domestic, intellectual, and professional labour constitute knowledgeable, politically effective practices. Their critical exposures of the structures that devalue women's labour, according its practitioners' minimal social-political authority even within the professions, and of the conditions that structure scientific knowledge production to favour certain knowers, while privileging circumscribed areas of research, become the starting points for transformative social action.

See also: Marxism

References and further reading

Haraway, D. (1997) *Modest_Witness@Second_Mille-nium.FemaleMan©_Meets_OncoMouse^{TM}*, New York: Routledge.

Harding, S. (1993) 'Rethinking Standpoint Epistemology', in L. Alcoff and E. Potter (eds) *Feminist Epistemologies*, New York: Routledge.

Smith, D. (1987) *The Everyday World as Problematic*, Toronto: University of Toronto Press.

LORRAINE CODE

state theory

Feminist theorizing about the state has followed several different paths but each version attempts to explain how the state is implicated in the **oppression** of women and whether the state can be modified to advance the goal of **gender** equality. Liberal feminist state theory contends that there is nothing inherently sexist, patriarchal, or phallocentric about the liberal democratic state (see **liberal feminism**). This analysis focuses on the discriminatory practices inscribed in public policies and argues that, once sexist practices are eliminated and barriers torn down through interventions such as **affirmative action**, the state can be instrumental in achieving gender equality. Liberal feminist state theory also emphasises the necessity of women's increased participation and representation in key state institutions such as elected assemblies and the bureaucracy as indicators of gender equality and as means to realising gender equality. Radical and socialist feminist state theorists argue that women's equality cannot be realised through state action alone (see **radical feminism**; **socialism and feminism**). It requires a fundamental restructuring of the **public/ private** spheres, **gender roles** and the gendered division of labour. Both radical and socialist feminists argue that the state is embedded in the more pervasive systems of either patriarchy or capitalism or both. Radical feminist theory stresses the primacy of patriarchal relations and the state's role in perpetuating them by privileging men in law and public policy. Socialist feminist state theory, in contrast, argues that the state enforces both capitalist and patriarchal relations. Most socialist feminists accept what has been termed 'dual systems theory' which effectively argues that the state acts to enforce capitalist relations in the workplace and patriarchal relations in the private sphere. Finally postmodern state theory views it as a combination of discourses and institutions which is instrumental in producing gendered subjects and gendered social relations (see **poststructuralism/postmodernism**). More fundamentally, Judith Allen encourages feminists to abandon efforts to construct a grand theory of the state. She suggests that the state is not an 'indigenous category' for feminists, but, instead, 'a category of abstraction that is too aggregative, too unitary and too unspecific to be of much use' for analysis. Allen's critique reflects a long-standing anti-statist tradition in western feminism. This tradition led many first-wave feminists to view the state and politics as sites of moral corruption and many second-wave feminists to form co-operatives and shelters to avoid state cooptation (see **first-wave/second-wave feminism**).

References and further reading:

Allen, J. (1990) 'Does Feminism Need a Theory of the State?', in S. Watson (ed.) *Playing the State: Australian Feminist Interventions*, London: Verso.

Brodie, J. (1997) 'Meso-Discourses, State Forms and the Gendering of Liberal-Democratic Citizenship', *Citizenship Studies* 1:2.

Brown, W. (1992) 'Finding the Man in the State', *Feminist Studies* 18:1.

Gordon, L (ed.) (1990) *Women, the State and Welfare*, Madison: University of Wisconsin Press.

JANINE BRODIE

Steinem, Gloria (b. 1934)

Gloria Steinem's work as a journalist, founding editor of *Ms.* magazine and activist involved in the 1960s US Women's Liberation, Gay Liberation and **civil rights** radical protest movements have contributed to her influential role as a feminist commentator in the male-dominated media and contemporary women's movement. A crusading liberal feminist campaigning for political, legislative and cultural reforms and equality between women and men, Steinem's second-wave feminism stems from rallying notions of 'sisterhood' and the 'personal as political'. Her later espousal of self-

empowering philosophies traces the potentially revolutionary shifts in women's (and men's) personal lives and individual consciousness.

Steinem's personal and collective feminist activism is documented in *Outrageous Acts and Everyday Rebellions* (1984) and *Moving Beyond Words* (1994). Language, gender and power, reproductive freedom, media, entertainment, masculinisation of wealth, **feminisation of poverty** and fantasised feminist recontextualisations of symptomatic **patriarchy** are confronted to explore female identities and sexualities in public and private arenas. Steinem perceives women's **oppression** as a 'sex-biased caste system' rooted in **race**, class and other divisions (see **class analysis, UK; class analysis, US**). Her understanding of mainstream feminist proclivities retreating into white middle-class exclusivities has sensitised Steinem to variegating experiences of race, class and **sexuality** among women throughout her work.

Later philosophisings promote processes of self-discovery and the ability to assume individual control through the personal revolutions in women's lives. Illuminating her concerns with delimiting ideologies and women's socialised feelings of low self-esteem, Steinem's politicised theorisings developed into the humanist feminism and new age techniques of *Revolution from Within* (1992). Locating low self-esteem in vulnerabilities (or otherwise obsessions with power) and the sex-role stereotyping of childhood, Steinem asserts the necessary release of the self from social conditioning through processes of 'unlearning'. Subsequent self-conditioning processes of 'relearning' incorporate positive thinking, meditation and inspirational philosophies to bolster inner strength and unify dualistic splits of body and mind.

While embracing issues of new age self interest, Steinem has been criticised by some feminists for foregoing social activism and by others for categorising low self-esteem as a largely female problem. Despite this, Steinem's outspoken and anti-intellectual approach renders her work widely accessible, illustrating the conjunction rather than bifurcation of the inner and social change she advocates among all women.

See also: language, gender and power; liberal feminism

Selected writings

Steinem, G. (1984) *Outrageous Acts and Everyday Rebellions*, London: Jonathan Cape.
—— (1992) *Revolution From Within: A Book of Self-Esteem*, London: Simon and Schuster.
—— (1994) *Moving Beyond Words*, London: Simon and Schuster.

SATINDER KAUR CHOHAN

Stimpson, Catharine R. (b. 1936)

Catharine Stimpson, educator, writer, and administrator, has made theoretical contributions to feminism in women's studies, multiculturalism, lesbian studies, and feminist criticism.

As the founding editor of *Signs: Journal of Women In Culture and Society* from 1974–80, Stimpson called for a plurality of approaches, rejecting any essentialist view of 'woman's mind' or 'woman's thought'. This position coincides with the culmination of Stimpson's account of the development of women's studies. She argues that women's studies has consisted of four stages, which are: the repudiation of previous work on women; the study of pernicious differences between men and women (e.g., domestic violence); the study of constructive differences between men and women (e.g., women's institutions); and, finally, the study of multiple differences among women, which leads to a study of differences among individuals and groups.

Building on her theories of the differences among women, Stimpson has further offered a theory of 'cultural democracy', or a way of thinking about multicultural societies. Cultural democracy asks people to act on five principles: access to literacy and education; access to one's own cultural and historical traditions; conversation across cultural borders; respect for cultural and academic freedom; and every society's possession of a unifying principle, such as the Constitution and Bill of Rights in the USA.

In Stimpson's wide-ranging feminist criticism, published in over 150 monographs, essays, and reviews, one of her most important contributions is her argument that Virginia Woolf's *A Room of One's Own* is the wellhead of modern feminist critical theory. In lesbian studies, Stimpson is best known for her article, 'Zero Degree Deviancy', published in her collection of essays, *Where the Meanings Are*, in which she theorises that the lesbian novel in English has two narrative trajectories, that of the damning fall and that of the enabling escape.

Additionally, Stimpson has written extensively on the role of the public intellectual, the humanities, and contemporary education, contributing a regular column to *Change* magazine from 1992–4. In her public service and administrative positions, including Director of the Fellows Programme at the MacArthur Foundation 1994–7, Stimpson is known for her advocacy of theoretical pluralism, as well as of women's studies and feminist criticism.

See also: lesbian feminism; lesbian literature; pedagogy, feminist; women's studies (history and development of); women's studies: autonomy v. mainstreaming

Selected writings

Stimpson, C.R. (1979) *Class Notes*, New York: Times Books.
—— (1988) *Where The Meanings Are*, New York: Methuen.

TASMIN WOLFF

Strathern, Marilyn

Marilyn Strathern is a British sociocultural anthropologist who has written extensively on gender relations in Melanesia, particularly among the Hagen of the New Guinea highlands. She is a critic of universalist theories of culture in general and **gender** in particular, and argues that cultures must be studied in depth, on their own terms, not in relation to western concepts.

Strathern's *The Gender of the Gift* (1988) brings together themes that have dominated her ethnographic work for decades, in particular the too easy application of western ideas to Melanesian society (see **ethnography**). For example, western philosophical traditions take for granted the opposition of individual and society, and conceive of individuals as bounded entities which engage in external relations with each other. By contrast, Melanesian cultures understand people as constructed in and through relationships, with different aspects of the self drawn out in interaction with others. Western feminist thinking assumes that gender differentiation and asymmetry are given and fundamental, and manifested in all cultures. In Melanesia, however, there is no raw material of sex difference; organs can be seen as male or female, depending on what one does with them and the interactions they are deployed in. Gender is not an expression of innate biological difference: people are conceived of as composites of the gendered contributions of both parents, and men and women contain within themselves aspects of each sex. In interpersonal interaction, men sometimes manifest feminine behaviour, just as women sometimes behave in male ways; there is no given correspondence between **biology** and **gender**. Western feminist dichotomies like male activity versus female passivity do not apply to Melanesia: individuals possess equal potential for action, though in particular interactions there may be asymmetry between individuals.

Strathern has characterised the relationship between **feminism** and **anthropology** as awkward: anthropologists strive to achieve a rapport with their 'Other' – non-western cultures – while feminists attempt to reach an understanding of women without recourse to their 'Other' – men. The discordances between these goals are keenly felt by feminist anthropologists like herself.

Strathern has been criticised for difficult and inaccessible writing, sometimes attributed to bad editing. She claims that the complex ideas she works with require complicated language, but many feel that her insightful arguments could be couched in a more approachable style.

Selected writings

Strathern, M. (1972) *Women in Between*, London: Seminar Press.
—— (1987) 'An Awkward Relationship', *Signs* 12, 2: 276–92.
—— (1988) *The Gender of the Gift*, Cambridge: Cambridge University Press.

NANCY LEWIS

structuralism

Structuralism analyses culture as a system of signs. Meaning and value are accorded within the rules of the system. Credited with the origin of the system is the French linguist Ferdinand de Saussure, who posited that words relate to their referent in an arbitrary manner, and that they gain value only in relation to one another, not in themselves. This thought system has influenced feminist theory in anthropology, social sciences and textual analysis. Theorists have analysed the meanings of male and female by locating this binary in relation to other structures such as nature/culture. Social rituals function to keep the two poles apart. Structuralism assumes that the analysed systems are stable, and fully referenced in themselves – these aspects have guided criticisms which have led to a continuation of the debate in poststructuralism.

See also: poststructuralism/postmodernism

References and further reading

Saussure, F. de (1974) *Course in General Linguistics*, London: Fontana.

PETRA KUPPERS

sustainable development

Sustainable development means using local resources to support, nourish, and maintain local economic development. Developing natural resources sustainably requires community members to know and understand their place and purpose in reciprocal relation to the local environment. Sustaining natural resources thus preserves local resources for future generations by understanding relations between human beings and their natural environment. The values that inform practices of sustainable development support local community control of resources that provide community food, shelter, health, labour, and other survival needs. Conversely these practices refuse to participate in subjugating or exploiting peoples or local resources to benefit a global economic system of (inequitable) commodity distribution.

In patriarchal, affluent and militarist countries such as the USA, government-funded organisations protect those corporate enterprises that block sustainable development by using natural resources for corporate (stockholder) capital gain. Global capitalist imperialism harnesses a reign of terror against less industrialised peoples, developing low market and low wage labour especially among women and children. Thus capital accumulation buttresses economic and governmental military destabilisation of nonindustrial, otherwise independently sustainable, communities. Community opposition mobilises itself in Indigenist guerilla warfare and resistance to the theft of resource control and allocation. Sustaining communities under siege necessitates developing local food, shelter, health, and labour resources.

EuroAmerica, the USA, and stockholders world-wide maintain modern economic supremacy quietly, but in complicity with global practices that terrorise Indigenous peoples. The USA claims widespread resource rights on the basis of recent post-genocidal historical inheritance under foreign colonial legal systems; annexation of land and natural resources via specious discovery claims or treaty or 'emergency condition peacekeeping' rights, maintained by military force and supported by corporate interests; harnessing of human labour via child theft, sexual slavery, and shoddy, cheap, and intimidating labour conditions; and manipulation of global capital accumulation and despotic economic market/trade control. Sustainable development, by contrast, envisages an environment that builds upon an interdependent and nurturing community, using native methods to produce food from gardens, decide agricultural techniques, control livestock and fisheries, and accommodate native foods to community needs.

Sustainable development also means that communities define their relationship with surrounding communities by respecting a hallowed process of reciprocal exchanges of goods, services, skills, and knowledge. Building sustainable communities occurs at the grassroots level, and facilitates self-help via innovative, creative local solutions to local needs and issues. Ongoing mobilisation of natural resources, and technical support to develop those

resources, has the potential to revitalise the ecology and culture of sustainable development for indigenous communities.

Yet multinational corporations are claiming patent and intellectual property rights over traditional sustainable knowledge that has been preserved in generations of indigenous farming practices. Many feminists are engaged in struggling against this culture vulture mentality, and some feminists hold that the act of distancing human life from the rest of nature is the product of a binary, dualist epistemology that condones exploitation and the theft of resources.

An epistemology that presupposes the ontological separateness of human beings from their natural habitat is grounded in a binary dualism. Practices based on the assumption of a sharp boundary between human and non-human environments tend to ascribe greater value to the human than to the non-human environment, thus generating a further bifurcation between the controller and the controlled, and justifying control by the 'superior human' over the 'inferior natural environment'. Such postures erase possibilities of conceiving of humanity as continuous and interdependent with nature: an epistemological position that would be required to maintain sustainable development and to preserve the environment. If feminists who advocate this revised epistemological position are right, then not only will a political shift be required for the USA and other affluent societies to value, maintain and assist in preserving sustainable communities, but an epistemological shift will be also necessary to work toward goals of sustainable development. Many feminist epistemologists are questioning this underlying binary dualism, and investigating non-binary epistemological forms.

See also: ecofeminism; economic globalisation; Indigenist feminism

ANNE WATERS

systemic discrimination

Discrimination refers to any act that denies equal treatment or opportunities to individuals and groups on the basis of gender, or membership in other socially defined groups. In the early post-Second World War period, social scientists primarily addressed **race** discrimination, which was understood to result from prejudiced beliefs of individuals. By the early 1970s, drawing on structural-functionalism, the term systemic discrimination (or structural discrimination) seeped into the literature, highlighting the fact that pervasive discrimination can occur even without individual conscious prejudice or intent. With systemic discrimination, society is presented as a social system where the rules, organisation, and procedures have the unintended but real effect of excluding, usually racial minorities. Since the 1970s, systemic discrimination on the basis of gender has garnered more analytical and political attention. The 1981 United Nations Convention on the Elimination of All Forms of Discrimination Against Women views discrimination as an act that intentionally or unintentionally disadvantages women.

YASMEEN ABU-LABAN

T

technology of gender

Teresa de **Lauretis** in *Technologies of Gender* in 1987 develops Foucault's ideas about the 'technology of sex' to theorise gender beyond the limits of sexual difference. She develops theories from poststructuralism which see the subject as multiple, contradictory and divided (see **poststructuralism/ postmodernism**). She also draws attention to the centrality of representations for understanding how identities and subjectivities are produced. To use a theory of technology of **gender** is to see gender as both representation and self-representation, in which all forms of representation are produced by social technologies such as the cinema, institutional discourses, epistemologies and critical practices. De Lauretis also explores how women and men make different investments in **sexuality**. By defining the female-gendered subject as one that is inside and outside gender, attention is drawn to the spatial dimensions of **identity** that see women as constructed across a range of sites which make gender unstable, problematic and open to change.

BEVERLEY SKEGGS

television

One of the most recently established disciplines, television studies draws on both the humanities and the social sciences for its theoretical structures. Though broadcast television began in the UK (1936) it was first established as a mass form in the USA in the immediate post-war period. Its advent in most developed western nations was accompanied by debates focusing first on its economic and political impact, and second on its implications for national cultures. Critical approaches to television coincided with the so-called women's liberation movements of the later 1960s and, as academic television studies gradually emerged in the 1970s, feminist interventions were increasingly utilised to support the cross-disciplinary explorations which television required.

Regarded initially as the source of low-status and largely ephemeral material – with the important exceptions of 'quality' drama and news/current affairs programming – early television is of particular interest for feminists. Routine and, relative to other cultural forms, high-profile representations of women, necessary in order to secure the female audience in the interests of advertisers, co-existed with a pattern of domestic consumption for the establishment of which, again, the female audience was thought to be crucial. Lynn Spigel (1992) explores the impact of television on domestic life in the early 1950s showing how it became the primary locus of wider debates about the family as the foundation of the nation in post-war America.

The wide variety of approaches to this crucial and ubiquitous late-twentieth-century cultural form may be subsumed into four areas. While these overlap, the distinctions between them are useful because it allows attention to the likely interests served in the enquiry as well as pointing to appropriate methodologies. The four areas are *institutional histories*, *industrial structures*, *cultural production*, and *critical concepts*. The first two largely call on the social sciences, including history, and the second two on the humanities, including philosophy.

Institutional histories and industrial structures approaches both assume the unity of television, including all the processes, personnel and productions that constitute it, privileging access to discourses specific to national examples as well as inviting comparative studies across national boundaries. Questions of employment, global economic issues and cultural imperialism will all be raised. Michèle Mattelart's pioneering essays, written between 1971–82, make explicit links between developing feminist insights into the representations of women available in a variety of popular cultural forms amongst which television is, she suggests, the most significant, and the national and trans-national structures – including structures informing academic production – by means of which such representations are produced and disseminated.

Approaches privileging cultural production and critical concepts tend to emphasise questions of representation and reading, and the problematic concept of the television audience may be understood as the bridge between the humanities and the social sciences, both disciplines attempting to theorise the audience and its practices (see Ien Ang 1985, 1991; Brunsdon, D'Acci and Spigel 1997).

It is here that television theory and feminist theory converge in their attention to the relation between representations purveyed via cultural artefacts and the social relations which inform, and are in turn informed by, audience readings of broadcast material. Of particular significance for feminist scholarship is the question of the articulation of the female **body** in popular cultural discourse and the impact of this discourse on material conditions and opportunities for actual women. Most of the leading scholars in the field have addressed this question attempting, by means of specific textual analyses or empirical audience studies, to discover patriarchal hegemonic operations, to account for female readers' pleasure in considering the use-value which certain televisual texts may hold, and/or to articulate negotiated or subversive readings made in the interests of the subordinated feminine. Julie D'Acci's 1994 study of the US series *Cagney and Lacey* demonstrates, by

means of an exemplary analysis of programmes in their twin contexts of production and reception, how the female audience for this innovatory cop show featuring two women as the lead protagonists was able to overcome the powerful network decision to drop the show after the first series. Her study reveals the use-value of the show to its audience as well as the hegemonic struggle among the commissioning network, the producers and the audiences for control of the series, discovering in the process the extraordinarily complex relations at work in such popular cultural productions.

In the course of such studies it has become clear that a crucial interest in the study of television is its special ability to foreground the intersections of the 'public' and the 'private' (see **public/private**). The relation between discourse and access – to power, and to language understood at its broadest to include popular cultural representations – is at its most transparent in television's daily production of public knowledge. This necessarily informs cultural operations – hence power relations – at all levels: the domestic, the local and the national as well as the global. Television can thus be considered as a major site for the construction of **identity** – again the concept operates at both the individual, personal level and at the collective, or national level. In addition to its intrinsic interest, therefore, collaboration between ethnographic and textual studies of television can illuminate the intertwined politics of **race** and **gender**, in the context of mobile postcolonial subjects and their readings of globally disseminated programming.

See also: cultural imperialism; ethnography; hegemony; patriarchy

References and further reading

Ang, I. (1985) *Watching Dallas: Soap Opera and the Melodramatic Imagination*, London: Methuen.
—— (1991) *Desperately Seeking the Audience*, London: Routledge.
Brown, M.E. (1994) *Soap Opera and Women's Talk*, California: Sage.
Brunsdon, C., D'Acci, J. and Spigel, L. (eds) (1997) *Feminist Television Criticism*, Oxford: Oxford University Press.

D'Acci, J. (1994) *Defining Women: Television and the Case of Cagney and Lacey*, Chapel Hill: University of North Carolina Press.

Mattelart, M. (1986) *Women, Media and Crisis: Femininity and Disorder*, London: Comedia.

Spigel, L. (1992) *Make Room for TV: Television and the Family Ideal in Postwar America*, Chicago, IL: University of Chicago Press.

JANET THUMIM

testimonial literature

Feminist critics have tended to conflate testimonial literature with personal writing. Consequently, until the 1990s, testimony received little attention as a distinctive discourse. The feminist slogan that dominated the 1970s – 'the personal is political' – meant, as Nancy Miller observes in *Getting Personal* (1991), that '[f]eminist theory has always built out from the personal: the witnessing 'I' of subjective experience' (14). While correct, Miller's observation that 'feminist teaching ... produced a great deal of personal testimony' (15) exemplifies the tendency of second-wave western feminists to collapse testimony into the 'personal'. Not surprisingly, testimonial literature has suffered from the criticisms that have been levelled at personal writing – that it is confessional, naive, sentimental, individualist and treats language as a transparent medium for representing an already meaningful experience.

In the 1980s, the impetus for re-thinking testimony came from two sources: critics of Holocaust testimony, and critics, including feminists, of Latin American 'testimonio' such as *I, Rigoberta Menchu* (1984). These critics argue that testimony overlaps with but differs significantly from autobiography and documentary. Testimonial literature is motivated by the desire to inform the public about an atrocity. The narrator reveals her personal experience not to express the 'truth' of the self, but to bear witness to a collective injury. Shoshana Felman's definition captures these multiple elements: '[t]o testify is ... not merely to narrate but to commit oneself, and to commit the narrative, to others: to take responsibility – in speech ... for something which ... goes beyond the personal in having general (nonpersonal) validity and consequences' (1992: 204).

Scholarship of the 1990s on trauma and memory furthered interest in testimonial literature, which typically bears witness to a traumatic event or memory – childhood sexual abuse, domestic violence, (war) rape, torture, or witnessing atrocity. Some feminist critics have probably gone too far, however, making trauma an essential component of testimony. Drawing on psychoanalysis, Felman argues that '[b]ecause trauma cannot be simply remembered, it cannot simply be 'confessed': it must be testified to in a struggle shared between a speaker and a listener to recover something the speaking subject is not – and cannot be – in possession of' (Felman 1993: 16). Thus, she contends that '[i]nsofar as any feminine existence is a traumatised existence, feminist autobiography cannot be a confession. It can only be a testimony: to survival' (17). These ideas are developed in Henke's (1988) psychoanalytic study of trauma and testimony in feminist life narratives.

References and further reading

Felman, S. (1993) *What Does a Woman Want? Reading and Sexual Difference*, Baltimore: Johns Hopkins University Press.

Felman, S. and Laub, D. (1992) *Testimony: Crises of Witnessing in Literature, Psychoanalysis and History*, New York and London: Routledge.

Henke, S.A. (1998) *Shattered Subjects: Trauma and Testimony in Women's Life-Writing*, New York: St. Martin's Press.

Miller, N. (1991) *Getting Personal*, New York: Routledge.

ROSANNE KENNEDY

theatre

Theatre, with the larger category of 'performance', has proved an important vehicle for feminists wishing to raise public consciousness, express women's experience, demonstrate and deconstruct the sexist assumptions of dominant culture, and explore alternative modes of cultural production. Feminist scholars, theorists, activists, and artists have found theatre a fertile space for collaboration, a laboratory where feminist theory can be enacted and embodied.

For much of western theatre history, women were excluded from the stage and prevented from using theatre's cultural power. In the fourth century BCE, Aristotle's *Poetics* outlined a set of rules for drama, including the single-climax plot structure and male-centred character values, that have governed most theatre to this day. Female characters in classical theatre were written and performed by men for male audiences, perpetuating myths of female identity. Even when women gained access to the stage their performances were controlled through a patriarchal system of spectatorship. In the twentieth century, pioneering feminists had to begin by challenging Aristotle's patriarchal principles. In her groundbreaking work *Feminism and Theatre (1988)*, Sue-Ellen Case proposed a new poetics that discusses non-linear structures, and posits women as subjects rather than objects of the dramatic narrative.

Other feminist theorists and practitioners continue to work against the oppressions inherent in many theatrical conventions. As Case notes, for example, Stanislavsky's acting 'method' is based on patriarchal assumptions embedded in Freudian psychology. Design choices and staging often underscore women's position as the object of the **gaze**, rather than the speaking subject, and the labour of theatrical production is usually organised according to a strict hierarchy in which performers have little power. Feminist theatre, particularly since the 1960s, has addressed each of these issues, striving to find alternative modes of theatre-making designed to empower the female artist and address the female spectator.

Theatre theorists Jill Dolan and Gayle Austin divide feminist approaches to theatre production into three categories. Liberal feminists work to infiltrate the established theatrical system, while cultural (or radical) feminists use theatre to express a unique 'female aesthetic'. Materialist (or Marxist) feminists concentrate on exposing theatrical illusion as a tool of dominant ideology, and on using theatre to denaturalise gender constructs. Women of colour and lesbians often find that their issues of visibility and representation are not fully addressed by white heterosexual feminist theatre in these categories, and many have created independent theories of performance.

Feminist theatre theorists and artists have made use of feminist film criticism, semiotics, French feminist notions of the **body**, Brechtian techniques, performance art and other experimental avenues to shift the theatrical frame allowing women to take centre stage.

See also: film theory, feminist; liberal feminism; Marxism; narrative, feminist uses of; radical feminism

References and further reading:

Case, S.E. (1988) *Feminism and Theatre*, Basingstoke: Macmillan.
Dolan, J. (1988) *The Feminist Spectator as Critic*, Ann Arbor: University of Michigan Press.

AMY SEHAM

theology, feminist

Theology is the constructive reflection on ultimate reality from within the perspective of a religious tradition. The term is taken from the Greek *theos* (God) and *logos* (word) – that is, theology is discourse about God. Historically, this discourse was considered epistemically neutral. Characteristics like race, social positioning, or gender ostensibly did not shape the theology produced, although the imprint of particular communities might be acknowledged. Feminist theology fundamentally challenges traditional theology by claiming it is androcentric and excludes or is biased against women. It presents itself as a necessary corrective and a creative resource for more adequate thinking about and representation of God/ultimate reality.

Feminist theology takes several forms. Initially, the term was used in relation to the Protestant and Catholic denominations of Christianity, and to Judaism. It first gained currency in the 1960s when the European model of theology was challenged from several quarters. One of the most dramatic developments within Christian theology emerged from the congress of Roman Catholic Bishops of Latin America held at Medellin, Columbia in 1968.

The Bishops unsettled centuries of convention by announcing that the Catholic church was complicit in the oppression of the poor in Latin America. The 'liberation theology' which developed from this new vision asserted that theology must emerge from critical reflection on Christian practice, including political and social action, and that Marxist analysis provided important tools for this project. Black theology emerged at the same time out of racial unrest in the USA. Representatives like James Cone argued for a 'black Christ' who sides with the black community against white racism. While sharing their challenge to dominant theological discourses, feminist theology criticised black and Latin American liberation theologies for their masculine God imagery and often violent rhetoric.

Feminist theology is a related but parallel movement with earlier origins. For example, in 1960 Valerie Saiving Goldstein argued that the Christian view of sin as pride, making too much of oneself, is based on male experience; for women, the impediment to wholeness is self-abnegation. In the 1970s and into the 1980s there was an explosion of material challenging the Christian church. Theological sexism, God language, redefinitions of religious leadership, racism, and sexuality were some of the many topics addressed. Feminist scholars took up the challenge mounted in the nineteenth century by Elizabeth Cady Stanton's *The Woman's Bible* and engaged Christian scripture to determine whether Christianity was irretrievably patriarchal. Elizabeth Schüssler Fiorenza is a particularly influential feminist biblical critic whose work identifies a suppressed tradition within Christianity of female discipleship and apostolic leadership.

Christian and Jewish feminist theology has been criticised by women of colour as the product of white cultural privilege. Black womanist theologians build on a sense of black community and black women's resourcefulness in the face of oppression to articulate a creative and resistant religious experience often expressed in artistic, literary forms. Hispanic feminist theologians, or mujeristas, likewise criticise feminist theology for race and class blindness. For both womanists and mujeristas, religious life is properly grounded in a community of resistance to structures of oppression, reflecting emphases found in earlier black and Latin American liberation theologies. Lesbian feminist theologians like Carter Heyward similarly resist traditional heterosexist configurations of spirituality and embodiment, arguing for new forms of human relationship.

Asian scholars like Kwok Pui-lan challenge the ethnocentrism of feminist Biblical scholarship by developing postcolonial approaches to Biblical interpretation. Like the other contextual theologies, postcolonial Biblical criticism begins with experience. Asian experience typically involves adherence to several religious traditions simultaneously, with a resulting multicanonical approach to scriptures. Working from within this perspective Kwok Pui-lan characterises the Bible not as the single authoritative 'Word of God' but rather as a 'talking book' with which many different conversations might be held.

Feminist theology has also been undertaken in non-Christian traditions. Judith Plaskow's *Standing Again at Sinai* (1990) uses a feminist perspective to rethink key notions of history, community, God language, and sexuality. Although less developed overall, constructive critical engagements with tradition are emerging in Muslim, Hindu, and Buddhist communities. Rita Gross, a **religious studies** scholar known for her methodological work, has made a significant contribution with *Buddhism After Patriarchy* (1993).

A key question for feminist theologians is the extent to which tradition is redeemable from sexism. That is, are there resources available either within or outside tradition, which make it possible for women to exist in wholeness within their religious tradition? While critical of the many ways patriarchal structures and practices have limited and damaged women, most feminist theologians find sufficient affirmation to continue their religious affiliation. Some do not. Mary **Daly** was one of the earliest and most dramatic feminist theologians to leave her religious tradition behind. Arguing that 'no feminist can save God', Naomi Goldenberg offers depth psychology as a feminist religious resource. Another alternative is Goddess religion, which develops a spirituality focused on a divine feminine, as Carol Christ explores in her *Laughter of Aphrodite: Reflections on a Journey to the Goddess* (1987). Wicca, or **witchcraft**, is a related form of neo-paganism emphasizing connection with nature and the spiritual forces residing therein. While both Goddess worship and Wicca have gained in popularity, they have been criticised by some feminists as essentialist.

By doing feminist theology women claim the cultural power of articulating in an authoritative way what they and their communities understand to be the nature of ultimate reality. Feminist theology can thus be an important site of resistance to and transformation of institutionalised structures of oppression. Its analyses of the structures, dynamics, practices, sacred texts, and gender ideology of religions are of value to religious and non-religious feminists alike.

See also: womanist theology

References and further reading

Cannon, K. (1988) *Black Womanist Ethics*, Atlanta: Scholars Press.

Schüssler Fiorenza, E. (ed.) (1993–4) *Searching the Scriptures* 2 vols, New York: Crossroad.

Plaskow, J. and Christ, C. (eds) (1989) *Weaving the Visions: Patterns in Feminist Spirituality*, San Francisco: Harper.

Ruether, R. (ed.) (1974) *Religion and Sexism*, New York: Simon and Schuster.

RANDI R. WARNE

therapy, feminist

Feminist therapy originated in the late 1960s, inspired by the Women's Liberation Movement and other progressive movements such as radical psychiatry, community psychology, and the mental patients' rights movement. Feminist therapists have had a dual focus: to critique the mental health establishment and to develop innovative forms of treatment. They have mobilised against the sexual abuse of clients by therapists and against excessive prescriptions of psychotropic medication to women. Recognizing that psychiatric diagnoses are potent means of social control, they have vigorously opposed psychiatric diagnoses that are sexist, heterosexist, homophobic, or racist, as well as clinical theories that dictate domestic and subservient roles for women, blame mothers, and

legitimise men's sexual entitlement, dominance, and violence.

Some feminist researchers have studied problems prevalent among women such as eating problems, depression, agoraphobia, and physical and sexual abuse. Others have brought attention to groups of women largely ignored in the mental health literature, such as lesbian and bisexual women, HIV-positive women, immigrant and ethnic-minority women, and women living in poverty. Feminists have figured prominently in debates on such charged issues as 'battered woman's syndrome', recovered memories of childhood trauma, the putative psychiatric consequences of abortion, and lesbian child-custody issues.

Feminist therapy is an umbrella term for therapies that have melded successive trends of second-wave feminism with diverse therapeutic theories and techniques. In the 1970s, consciousness-raising was often regarded as a key therapeutic process; psychological androgyny – defined as a balance or integration of masculine and feminine qualities within an individual man or woman – was extolled as the standard of mental health. In the 1980s, with the rise of cultural feminism, prominent feminist therapies focused on fostering women's 'relationality' and 'connectedness'. In the 1990s, feminist innovators, especially those in couples/family therapy, drew on Foucauldian concepts of power and postmodern ideas of constructed realities; others focused on cultural, racial, and ethnic diversity in therapy. Feminist therapies are so heterogeneous as to resist regulation and codification. Yet there are elements common to most, if not all: 1) a commitment to conceptualising clients' difficulties and distress in social and cultural context; 2) sensitivity to the power dynamics of the therapy relationship; 3) a commitment to power-sharing and respect in the therapist/client relationship; and 4) goals of empowering women in their lives outside therapy and promoting social transformation.

See also: consciousness-raising; depression; eating disorders; Miller, Jean Baker; psychology; psychoanalysis

References and further reading:

Brown, L. (1994) *Subversive Dialogues*, New York: Basic Books.

Enns, C.Z. (1997) *Feminist Theories and Feminist Psychotherapies*, New York: Haworth.

Marecek, J. and Hare-Mustin, R. (1991) 'A Short History of the Future: Feminism and Clinical Psychology', *Psychology of Women Quarterly*, 15, 4, 521–36.

JEANNE MARECEK

third-wave feminism

Third-wave feminism is a term for a wide body of both popular and academic works of the 1990s. Bestsellers like Naomi Wolfe's *The Beauty Myth: How Images of Beauty are Used Against Women* (1991) and Susan Faludi's *Backlash: The Undeclared War Against American Women* (1991) set the stage for feminist resistance to the post-feminist decade. Written by young women in their twenties and early thirties, the 'third wave' of feminism represents a generational challenge to second- and first-wave feminism.

Coming of age in the 1990s, third-wave feminists were especially concerned with issues facing adolescent girls and young women. Previous feminist theory had been written about young women, but not authored *by* young women. One important theme, represented by the grassroots Riot Grrrl feminism of the third wave, was the need for more inclusiveness, flexibility, and practicality in feminist theories and definitions of who could be a feminist and how. Battling both anti-feminist charges of **political correctness** and in some cases dismissed as unsophisticated by earlier feminist generations, third wavers nonetheless made their mark by bringing girls' issues and multiple girls' standpoints to the forefront (see **standpoint theory**).

Issues include psychiatric abuse, **sexuality**, harassment in schools, fat activism, and cultural participation. Inspired by several strands of existing feminism, third wavers tried to formulate feminist practices inclusive of race, class, gender, and sexuality. The growth of Women's Studies programmes in the 1990s and the availability of feminist popular literature on adolescent girls produced feminist generations who understand feminism as a process, a continuum, and a pragmatic effort. In academic feminism, *Hypatia*, a feminist journal, dedicated a special issue to third-wave theorizing, and one of the first books appeared: *Third Wave Agenda: Being Feminist, Doing Feminism* (1997).

One feature of third-wave feminism is the centrality of anger, used as a mechanism to provide voice to girls who had been silenced in society and within feminism. Generational debates continue between second wavers, third wavers, and the in-between generation over definitions of feminism, internal feminist politics, and norms of feminist appearance and behaviour. In general, third-wave feminism challenges much of the feminist culture established by previous feminist generations in an ongoing dialogue. As culture has changed, the forms of feminist resistance, symbols of resistance, and strategies of young women have differed from that of their feminist predecessors.

Third-wave feminism is a standpoint feminism in general, concerned with personal aims and with wide social and cultural change accomplished in part by becoming cultural producers.

See also: adolescent girls and feminism; first-wave/second-wave feminism; women's studies: autonomy v. mainstreaming; women's studies (history and development of)

References and further reading

Stanton, E. Cady (1972) *The Woman's Bible*, New York.

Heywood, L. and Drake, J. (eds) (1997). *Third Wave Agenda: Being Feminist, Doing Feminism*, Minneapolis, MI: University of Minnesota Press.

Hypatia, 12 (3) (1997) special issue 'Third Wave Feminisms'.

CHELSEA STARR

transcendental signifier

Transcendental signifier is a term from media theory intended to reveal a central political process in meaning construction. In semiotics, signifiers are the forms (words, images, actions), embedded in socio-cultural texts and contexts, that carry ideas and associations. Transcendent means beyond, 'above' or pure. Transcendental signifiers refer to allegedly real phenomena unbound by history, politics and fallible human perception: states of affairs widely considered natural, universal and unquestionably 'obvious'. **Self**, culture, aesthetics, sex, and race are examples, as is the term 'woman', used as a collective noun to signify essential and timeless 'attributes' of those inhabiting 'female' bodies (see **essentialism**).

Structuralists argue that transcendental signifiers perpetuate repressive (often unconscious) hegemonic notions (see **hegemony**). Poststructuralists dismantle their operations within specific discursive arrangements and cultural imaginaries in the fabrication and performance of 'reality effects' that typify modernist, disciplinary regimes.

See also: discourse analysis; poststructuralism/postmodernism

References and further reading

Kondo, D. (1997) *About Face: Performing Race in Fashion and Theatre*, New York: Routledge.

LYNNE STAR

transgender

The meanings of the term 'transgender' are various, rapidly evolving and highly contested. Commonly transgender functions either as a name employed by individuals whose gender expression is at odds with their physical sex, and/or, as an umbrella term for all those whose **gender** does not follow directly from their apparent sex or the sex to which they were assigned at birth. In this second sense, transgender may include: intersexuals, female-to-male (FTM) transsexuals and male-to-female (MTF) transsexuals, butches, femmes, drag queens and kings, cross dressers, nellies, transgenderists. Some transgender activists argue transgender is a continuum of gender-transgressive behaviour in which all gendered beings participate, to a greater or lesser degree; while some transsexual activists emphasise the predominantly white, middle-class and 'able-bodied' character of the

transgender movement. 'Transgender' derives from 'transgenderist', a term coined to replace the clinical designation, 'transvestite'.

Some scholars also deploy 'transgender' historically, either to refer to all gender variant behaviour across history, or to name individuals' phenomenal, embodied experience of 'being the wrong sex' and the attendant wish to 'change sex' in periods or cultures where the discursive/epistemic and surgically-enabled entity 'transsexuality' does not exist. Modern transgender/transsexual identities are thus linked to nineteenth-century sexology's typology of inversion, and to anthropological accounts of the third sex. Both categories confound psychic hermaphroditism (transgender) with physical hermaphroditism (**intersexuality**).

The contemporary transgender movement is rooted in transvestite and transsexual support networks that have existed from at least the late 1960s, and in activist efforts to secure state and/or insurance coverage for sex reassignment, non-discrimination legislation and so on. Increased transgender visibility since the 1980s has allowed for efforts to create a transgender coalition among gender minorities in much the same way that queer was mobilised as a coalitional term in the early 1990s. This has led to complicated, often controversial, transgender engagement with queer/feminist academic, activist, and arts milieux. There is a significant history of hostility and aggression toward transgender individuals within feminist, and gay and lesbian liberation movements. Ironically transgender critique of queer/feminist transphobia has colluded with a resurgence of butch/femme discourses and considerable involvement of FTM transsexuals with lesbian feminist communities to make transgender queer/feminist discourses perhaps *disproportionately* visible as against other transgender discourses.

See also: butch/femme; gender roles; intersexuality; queer theory; transsexuality/gender dysphoria

References and further reading

Nataf, Z. (1996) *Lesbians Talk Transgender*, London: Scarlet Press.
Stone, S. (1991) '"The Empire Strikes Back": A

Posttransexual Manifesto', in J. Epstein and K. Straub (eds) *BodyGuards: The Cultural Politics of Gender Ambiguity*, New York: Routledge.

Stryker, S. (ed.) (1998) 'The Transgender Issue: An Introduction', in *GLQ: A Journal of Lesbian and Gay Studies*, 4 (2).

TRISH SALAH

transsexuality/gender dysphoria

Transsexuality is an experience of strong conflict between one's sense of self as a gendered and sexed being, and one's anatomical sex. Further, transsexuals desire to bring the body into congruity with the self through a variety of technologies. Transsexual trajectories include female-to-male (FTM) and male-to-female (MTF). 'Non-op' transsexuals do not employ surgical interventions; some describe themselves as **transgender**. Gender dysphoria is a persistent, acute alienation from one's sex and/or the gender normatively attached to that sex. Gender dysphoria and transsexuality appear as gender identity disorder in *The Diagnostic and Statistical Manual of Mental Disorders, Fourth Edition* (DSM IV).

The term transsexual was introduced into sexological literature by David Cauldwell in 1949, and popularised by endocrinologist Harry Benjamin and media attention to the 1952 sex change of Christine Jorgenson. The advent of university-affiliated gender clinics in the 1960s contributed to popular awareness of MTF transsexuality. During this period genital surgery for FTMs was characterised as more difficult and less satisfactory than surgery for MTFs and many individuals who later were self-described as FTM transsexual lived as butch lesbians. Until the early 1990s most gender clinicians maintained that FTM transsexuality was either nonexistent or much rarer than MTF transsexuality.

The 1960s saw the emergence of MTF transsexual networks, support groups, and newsletters, sometimes overlapping those of transvestites. Some transsexuals also participated in women's and gay liberation movements. Cultural feminist and lesbian separatist hostility to MTF transsexuals is usually explained through the gender **essential-**ism of 1970s feminism; the expulsion of transsexual women from women's organisations relied upon a refusal to recognise transsexual women as 'real women'. In the 1990s, exclusion of transsexual women from women's organisations continued while constructivist theories regularly cast transsexuals and transgenders as potential transgressors of the naturalised correlation between gender and sexuality. Though many transgenders embrace this role, most transsexuals remain invested in coherent and intelligible gender presentation as men or women. Henry Rubin suggests constructivists fault transsexuals for 'false consciousness' and 'essentialism' only by eliding the privilege of the coherent legibility of their own gendered and sexed embodiment. Thus many transsexual activists now distance themselves from 'the transgender movement', suggesting that as transgender is increasingly aligned with queer politics the specific interests of transsexuals are sacrificed to the utopian and amorphous project of dismantling, or, at least, troubling gender.

See also: butch/femme; gender; separatism

References and further reading

Namaste, V.K. (2000) *Invisible Lives: The Erasure of Transsexual and Transgendered People in the Cultural and Institutional World*, Chicago, IL: University of Chicago Press.

Prosser, J. (1998) *Second Skins: The Body Narratives of Transsexuality*, New York: Columbia University Press.

Rubin, H. (1998) 'Phenomenology As Method In Trans Studies', *GLQ: A Journal of Lesbian and Gay Studies*, 4,2.

TRISH SALAH

Trinh T. Minh-Ha (b. 1952)

Trinh T. Minh-Ha is a writer and filmmaker from Vietnam whose work examines the intersections of feminism and postcoloniality. As First World feminism began seeking Third World voices to broaden its definition of 'woman', Trinh theorised the role of Third World women in the movement, the potential reductiveness of their identity position, the problematics of 'authenticity', and the power dynamics at play. In *Woman, Native, Other* (1989), Trinh discusses the 'triple bind' women writers of colour find themselves in as they claim their identities and speak from their 'colour-woman condition' but resist having to choose among conflicting and limiting identities. Her text is written in a poetic style that privileges storytelling and lived experience over traditional analytic theorising. Critics have characterised this style as 'low-grade romanticism', (Suleri 1992: 76) but Trinh sees it as an important challenge to western forms of logic and hierarchies of knowledge.

In her second major theoretical text, *When the Moon Waxes Red* (1991), Trinh fuses Chinese mythology and Zen thought with western theory to continue her project of creating a Third World feminist epistemology by 'undermining the west as authoritative subject of knowledge by learning to see into the effects of power and its links with knowledge' (19–20). In this text, Trinh advocates a strategy of displacement, border-crossing and an insistence on **difference** (but not difference based on biological essences) as a means of disturbing clichéd thinking habits, breaking down disciplinary boundaries and avoiding the pitfalls of unitary subject positions and totalising regimes of knowledge. She encourages writers and artists to approach their work with a sense of wonder instead of knowledge and mastery, to avoid linear logical thinking (to take 'delight in detours': 24), to resist the comfort of belonging to a classification, and of producing classifiable works.

In her films, too, Trinh examines the way gender factors into the power relationships between First and Third Worlds. Trinh's first film, *Reassemblage* (1982), shot in Senegal, critiques traditional, western ethnographic films which she feels focus on the exotic and border on the pornographic. Instead she films women of all ages involved in their daily activities, and joins in their 'circle of looks', including herself in the film rather than attempting to remain distant and objective. Also important for feminists is *Surname Viet, Given Name Nam* (1989) which examines Vietnamese women's pivotal relationship to national identity and traces their changing roles throughout history.

See also: film criticism, feminist; postcolonialist feminism; poststructuralism/postmodernism

Selected writings

Trinh T. Minh-Ha (1989) *Woman, Native, Other*, Bloomington, IN: Indiana University Press.
—— (1991) *When the Moon Waxes Red*, London: Routledge.

References for further reading

Suleri, S. (1992) 'Woman Skin Deep' in B. Ashcroft, G. Griffiths and H. Tiffin (eds) *The Post-Colonial Studies Reader*, London: Routledge.

JULIE DENNIS HLAD

two-spirit

'Two-spirit' is a term currently used as a self-descriptor by some lesbian, gay, bisexual and transgendered First Nations, Inuit and Metis people. The term suggests that sexuality, gender and other aspects of identity are not either/or conditions – that is, as two-spirit people, we may be both 'male' and 'female' or 'gay' and 'straight'. The term encompasses the wide variety of social meanings that are attributed to sexuality and gender roles across indigenous North American cultures. Two-spirit people acknowledge that all aspects of personal identity (including ethnicity, sexual orientation and gender) are inseparable from each other, strongly rooted in community and/or place and intimately connected to spirituality. As a self-descriptor, 'two-spirit' is used almost exclusively by indigenous North American people.

The term two-spirit was first commonly used to describe biracial people who were said to possess both a Native and a non-Native spirit. In the 1980s, it was adopted by queer members of the Native community (notably those that attended the International Gathering of Native American/First Nations gays and lesbians in Winnipeg, Manitoba, Canada) as a way to affirm constructions of sexuality and gender which prevailed in their communities before contact with Europeans and to state, with pride, the differences between their identity, experiences and culture and 'mainstream' (European North American) gay identity, experiences and culture. The existence and value of two-spirit people is recognised in most Indigenous North American cultures, oral histories and traditions and in some communities two-spirit people had (have) specific spiritual roles and responsibilities.

See also: First Nations and women

References and further reading

Jacobs, S.-E., Thomas, W. and Lang, S. (eds) (1997) *Two-spirit People: Native American Gender Identity, Sexuality, and Spirituality,* Chicago, IL: University of Illinois Press.

Roscoe, W. (ed.) (1988) *Living the Spirit: A Gay American Indian anthology,* New York: St. Martin's Press.

Wilson, A. (1996) 'How We Find Ourselves: Identity development and two-spirit people', *Harvard Educational Review,* 66 (2), 303–17.

ALEX WILSON

U

urbanisation

Urbanisation refers to the process of becoming urban; it is generally viewed as a process which results in an increase in the proportion of the population living in large, dense, heterogeneous settlements. It is also associated with the development of urbanism as a way of life and with cities becoming the engines of growth of the economy. Although urbanisation is a process that has its origins circa 3,000 BCE, it was with the Industrial Revolution that the pace of urbanisation accelerated, and at the beginning of the twenty-first century approximately 50 per cent of the world's population lives in urban areas.

Feminist concerns focus on both the role played by social relations, especially those of gender, in the production and reproduction of urban form and the extent to which the social position of women has improved with urbanisation. Literatures on First and Third World women have tended to follow separate trajectories and rarely acknowledge each other; although accounts exist of women's lives in Third World towns and cities (see Sheldon 1996), it is in Europe and North America that most analytical work on the role of gender in processes of urbanisation, suburbanisation and counterurbanisation has occurred.

Women's place is in the city (Wekerle 1984); sex ratios in urban areas reveal that women outnumber men, but for centuries there have been various attempts to assign women to the private sphere of the home and even to prevent them from entering public spaces (see **public/private**). Women have thereby been marginalised from the public spheres of society and 'kept in their place'. Hence, the prurient associations of 'women of the street' with deviation and impurity i.e., disorder.

Women have made numerous attempts to create their own urban spaces, from nunneries and women's housing co-operatives to lesbian bars. Probably the most significant in current times are the initiatives that have emerged around women's safety, such as half way houses and refuges for battered women. Indeed the issue of male violence against women provides one of the strongest links between mainstream feminisms and feminist urban issues. But it is not only through engagement in urban politics that women have been transforming city spaces; women have also created imaginary urban places, such as the urban utopia, *Herland* (1915), of Charlotte Perkins Gilman.

Many (white) feminists have argued that urban form, in particular the mid-twentieth-century divide between city centre and suburbs, has served to increase women's subordination by facilitating the removal of job opportunities from women and relegating them to the private sphere of the home. More recently, postmodern feminists, such as Wilson (1991) and others, have emphasised the economic, social and sexual freedoms and opportunities that have arisen from urbanisation. The rise of shopping, for example, gave women a legitimate right to be in public spaces, as did libraries, museums and galleries. Critiques of the double dichotomy of male/public and female/private spaces have also developed from African American feminists who argue that women of colour have a long engagement with waged work. The destabilisation of these heterosexual male and female divides is also evident in the various ways – from the gentrification of neighbourhoods and lesbian and gay pride parades – that lesbians and gays assert their presence in the urban environment.

See also: poststructuralism/postmodernism

References and further reading

Gilman, C.P. (1915) *Herland*, London: Women's Press, 1979.
Sheldon, K. (ed.) (1996) *Courtyards, Markets, City Streets: Urban Women in Africa*, Boulder, CO: Westview Press.
Wekerle, G. (1984) 'A Woman's Place is in the City', *Antipode* 16 (3): 1–16.
Wilson, E. (1991) *The Sphinx in the City: Urban Life, the Control of Disorder and Women*, London: Virago.

LINDA PEAKE

urban planning, women and

Urban planning is preoccupied with the need to control the city and, *inter alia*, women. As much an ideology as a technical practice, with its origins in nineteenth-century scientific rationalism, planning has searched out logical solutions to the allocation of scarce resources in attempts to create 'order out of chaos'.

Many feminist planners consider the interrelationships between land use and transportation to be the most important city-wide factor in determining the degree of ease with which women can live their daily lives. The rigid imposition of zoning, the separation of land uses, and the development of urban sprawl have created arduous time/space activity patterns for women given their responsibilities for childcare and the home. Although regulatory mechanisms are less rigid in many Third World cities, the planning problems experienced by women are exacerbated by non-functioning social and physical infrastructures as well as an increasing inability of national and local governments to manage and regulate urban life (see Moser and Peake 1995).

Since the early 1980s there have arisen vibrant, loosely-knit women and planning movements in both First and Third World countries, such as Women Plan Toronto in Canada. Combining professional and community-based women, these movements have given rise to a sustained feminist critique of urban planning issues such as housing, **childcare**, disability (see **disability, women and**), retailing, safety, sport and leisure, technology and transport. They have illustrated the positive role feminist planners can play in the reproduction of social relations through alternative visions of urban life and the creation of new urban spaces. But little policy change has been evident in the built environment; women-centred planning policies are few and far between. In the 1990s, in many places, the professional (and invariably patriarchal) culture of planning, combined with a scarcity of resources and a feminist backlash further served to marginalise feminist perspectives in planning, as, ironically, did the fashionable tropes of environmental sustainability and human rights. However, there is hope. As Clara Greed asserts, 'The imprint of gender relations on space is not a mechanistic process, and is more likely to be achieved through the spread of ideas, and visions than through enforcement of planning policy' (1994: 18).

References and further reading

Greed, C. (1994) *Women and Planning: Creating Gendered Realities*, London: Routledge.
Hayden, D. (1981) *The Grand Domestic Revolution. A History of Feminist Design for American Homes, Neighbourhoods and Cities*, Chicago, IL: University of Chicago Press.
Moser, C. (1993) *Gender, Planning and Development*, London: Routledge.
Moser, C. and Peake, L. (1995) 'Seeing the Invisible: Women, Gender and Urban Development', in R. Stren and J. Kjellberg Bell (eds) *Urban Research in the Developing World*, vol. 4 *Perspectives on the City*, Toronto: Centre for Urban and Community Studies, University of Toronto, pp.279–348.

LINDA PEAKE

utopias, feminist

Utopia holds a constant appeal for literary feminism and not just because of its intrinsically political nature. Feminism has always gained its transformatory impetus from a belief that the future and the 'not-yet' can become the here-and-now. Toril Moi, for example, identifies the work of Hélène **Cixous** with 'an invigorating utopian evocation of the imaginative powers of women' (Moi 1985: 126), while Angelika Bammer, in her excellent book on 1970s feminism, notes that 'to the extent that feminism was – and is – based on the principle of women's liberation ... it was – and is – not only revolutionary but radically utopian' (Bammer 1991: 2).

Utopia has been an important strand of **women's writing** for centuries. In European terms Bammer identifies Christine de Pizan's *The Book of the City of Ladies* (1405) as the first such publication, although as far as the English literary tradition is concerned, its most famous early practitioner was Margaret Cavendish, who wrote *The Blazing World* in 1668. But it was undoubtedly in the last three decades of the twentieth century that the real explosion of interest in the feminist utopia took place. Three American novels of the 1970s stand at the forefront of contemporary interest in this development: Joanna Russ's *The Female Man* (1975), Marge Piercy's *Woman on the Edge of Time* (1976) and Sally Miller Gearhart's *The Wanderground* (1979), each of which has received substantial critical attention. Collectively these three novels explore, in fiction, many of the central socio-political debates which preoccupied late twentieth-century feminism. In the process each, in their differing ways, refuses to settle into bland escapism (a reductive charge frequently levied at fictional fantasies of all kinds) and engages, instead, with an interrogation of contemporary social 'norms' through defamiliaris(ed/ing) visions of the future.

One problem for the political utopia remains the static nature of the vision it offers. When used as a vehicle for the women's *movement* this proves to be particularly anomalous. This is a problem taken up by Mary Russo in *The Female Grotesque* (1994) which, actively resisting the idealised vision of perfection, calls upon feminism to re-embrace the monstrosity of its turbulent body politic, 'from the "shrieking sisterhood" of the suffragettes to the "bra-burners" and harridans of the second wave' (Russo 1994: 14). Arguing that the utopianism of previous decades of feminism palled, in the 1990s, into a desire to 'appeal' to patriarchy's better nature, Russo's vision of collective monstrosity rethinks utopianism, paradoxically by embracing the grotesque. Her role-models for this are a variety of 'high-fliers' as diverse as the early twentieth-century aviator Amelia Earhart and Angela Carter's fictional protagonist Fevvers in *Nights at the Circus* (1984).

References and further reading

Bammer, A. (1991) *Partial Visions: Feminism and Utopianism in the 1970s*, New York: Routledge.
Moi, T. (1985) *Sexual/Textual Politics: Feminist Literary Theory*, London: Methuen.
Russo, M. (1994) *The Female Grotesque: Risk, Excess and Modernity*, New York: Routledge.

LUCIE ARMITT

V

veil of ignorance

The 'veil of ignorance' enters Anglo-American philosophy from John Rawls's *A Theory of Justice* (1971). It postulates a fictional originary moment to explain how universal, disinterested principles of justice are determined, without fear or favour. 'Men' must deliberate from behind a veil that occludes all 'specific conditions which put [them] at odds and tempt them to exploit social and natural circumstances to their own advantage'. From such absolute neutrality, Rawls believes, impartial principles of justice can be developed. Feminists, however, argue that this exercise requires assuming that there *could be* a level playing field, a perfectly equal starting point for everyone. It requires theorists to imagine away all unequal and oppressive starting points. For feminists, such imaginings permit theorists to overlook the specificities of **oppression**, and thus remove any need to engage seriously with them.

References and further reading

Card, C. (1996) *The Unnatural Lottery: Gender and Moral Luck*, Philadelphia, PA: Temple University Press.

LORRAINE CODE

violence

In traditional discourse, academics have defined violence primarily as physical acts committed by an individual or individuals with the intent to cause harm to objects or persons. Feminists' definitions have encompassed a much wider domain, including physical, sexual, and psychological or emotional abuse committed against persons, harmful cultural practices, and in some contexts, damaging words and images. Feminists view the implications of violence against women and children very broadly to include effects on: quality of life and leisure; psychological and sexual well-being; the general status of women; and physical health. The focus is placed on documenting, understanding, mitigating, and preventing violence perpetrated against women and children by men. Understanding violence committed by women, against themselves and others, is a smaller but similarly important area. While western societies have understood violent behaviour in peace time to be the result of individual pathology, feminist theorists perceive violent behaviour in social context. Radical feminists have been at the forefront of this activism and theorizing since the 1970s (see **radical feminism**).

Perhaps more so than in any other area of feminist theory, both activists and academics have theorised about violence against women. **Consciousness-raising** groups were the sites of the first questions about the commonality of violence, including incest, wife assault, rape and other forms of violence against women. Feminists arranged 'speak outs' for women to 'break the silence' about their experiences. Presses published fictionalised and autobiographical accounts, books exposing professional complicity in keeping silences, research demonstrating the prevalence of various kinds of violence/abuse (e.g., Russell, Wyatt), and theories about the social causes of violence against women. All contributed to awareness among feminists and the wider public. Academic feminist discussions of the topics usually followed grassroots discussions by several years and were influenced heavily by them.

The most creative aspects of feminist theorizing on violence have originated from the broadened definition of violence and the change in focus away from the motives of individual perpetrators. Under these conditions, sexual and physical assault of children and wives by fathers and husbands are inseparable aspects of the economic and social unit known as the patriarchal family; rape is an extension of normal heterosexual arrangements and a form of social control of all women (see Brownmiller's classic text *Against Our Will*); and violent **pornography** is an integral part of the social system of cultural sadism that encourages the actual physical, emotional, and sexual violations that occur against women in the home, on the street, in the workplace, and globally (see Barry's *Female Sexual Slavery*). Theorizing about previously normalised or 'trivial' experiences (e.g., street harassment, obscene phone calls) became possible.

Cultural practices which feminists have implicated as violence against women are: dowry deaths; **bride/widow burning** (**suttee burial**); selective abortion of female children; foot binding; female genital mutilation; forced sterilisation and forced pregnancy; psychiatric labelling and incarceration of women, particularly those who do not fit standard conventions of feminine behaviour; female **sexual slavery**, among others. Cultural practices or norms believed to contribute to the violence are: medicalisation of women's social problems; sexualisation of girl children in the media; nonprosecution of perpetrators; women's economic dependence on men; mainstream pornography; and the commodification of women in advertising, among others.

Feminist contributions to western societies' understanding of violence have been dramatic, with government agencies, politicians, and many non-feminists using feminist ideas, often without the knowledge of where they originated. Some concerns and criticisms have arisen as a result. Catharine **MacKinnon**'s concern about the cooptation of certain aspects of feminist theorising on violence has resonance many years later. She suggests that the political/legal strategy of stressing that rape and other forms of sexual violence were about violence and domination rather than sex would undermine feminist critiques of current sexual arrangements. 'So long as we say that those things are abuses of violence, not sex, we fail to criticise what has been made of *sex*, what has been done to us *through* sex' (1987: 86–7).

Writers have focused predominantly on women's experience, which in most feminist theorizing is a strength. However an emphasis on victims' experiences may have inadvertently led to more victim blaming and an increased focus on the individual survivor rather than on social activism. An industry of books, therapists, and public speakers, has arisen out of this work. With some notable exceptions, this is not an industry dominated by feminists and it is often antithetical to feminist goals.

Early feminist theorists and researchers had to convince the world of the extent of the problem of violence against women by men. Feminist work in the late 1980s and 1990s expanded the frame and asked questions that were not yet satisfactorily answered: Why do some women participate in the genital mutilation of their daughters? Do the dynamics of wife assault apply to abusive lesbian relationships? Is there a downside to the valuing of nonviolence? (White and Kowalski 1994) Is self-harm an example of violence against women?

Feminist writings on violence against women have had a large impact on other areas of feminist theory. Knowledge of the violence women experience when they show independence from men informs Adrienne **Rich**'s (1980) analysis of compulsory heterosexuality. Similarly, recognition of the commonality of violence in women's lives has altered feminist thinking on the family, marriage, women's health and mental health, sexuality, and work, among other topics.

See also: child sexual abuse; female circumcision/female genital mutilation; prostitution

References and further reading

Barry, K. (1979) *Female Sexual Slavery*, New York: New York University Press, 1984.

Brownmiller, S. (1975) *Against Our Will: Men, Women and Rape*, New York: Simon and Schuster.

MacKinnon, C. (1987) 'Sex and Violence: A Perspective (1981)', in *Feminism Unmodified: Discourses on Life and Law*, Cambridge, MA: Harvard University Press.

Rich, A. (1980) 'Compulsory Heterosexuality and Lesbian Existence', *Signs*, 5,4: 631–660.

Russell, D.E.H. (1984) *Sexual Exploitation: Rape, Child Sexual Abuse, and Workplace Harassment*, Beverly Hills: Sage.

White, J.W. and Kowalski, R.M. (1994) 'Deconstructing the Myth of the Non-Aggressive Woman: A Feminist Analysis', *Psychology of Women Quarterly*, 18: 487–508.

Wyatt, G.E. and Riederle, M. (1994) 'Sexual Harassment and Prior Sexual Trauma Among African-American and White American Women', *Violence and Victims*, 9: 233–47.

CHARLENE Y. SENN

Walker, Alice (b. 1944)

Fiction writer, poet and essayist Alice Walker centralises black women's experiences, consciousness and culture from an African American womanist perspective. Focusing on empowered self-determination through regenerative explorations of the self, womanist relationships and community to overcome violent cultural inequities, Walker fearlessly confronts issues from interracial rape and incest to lesbianism and female circumcision in works including *Meridian* (1976), *The Color Purple* (1982) and *Possessing the Secret of Joy* (1992). Walker's pivotal role in an intertextual black women's literary and critical tradition also involves her canonising rediscovery of the writings of Zora Neale Hurston.

Walker derived the term 'womanist' from a black matrilineal folk expression, primarily to describe exponents of a black or coloured feminism. She expatiates on 'womanism' as a universal humanist, non-separatist, creative and spiritual woman culture shaped by **race** and **gender** oppressions, connected to but distinguished apart from a mainstream feminist activism: 'Woman is to feminist as purple is to lavender'.

Dismantling cultural stereotypes, Walker's recurrent metaphors of the black woman as artist and quilt-maker symbolise a creative legacy in the bricolage of both a black female literary tradition and (womanist) community. The conceptual basis and process of quilt-making enacted in both her literary approach and the everyday African American community underscore the vital functionality (rather than fixed artifactuality) of black women's history and heritage. Walker interweaves African ancestral traditions with contemporary black culture, western literary techniques and generic conventions in a polyphonic discourse, invoking recovered and functional African American matrifocal creativities (see **matrifocality**). The daughters fulfil the hampered artistic frustrations of the foremothers, Walker's mother/daughter relationships offering spiritual and creative well-springs of individual and collective (black female) survival.

Walker elicited criticisms for *The Colour Purple*, highlighting the ancestors' denial of responsibility for their involvement in African American slavery. Demonstrated by her unidealised depictions of Africa, however, Walker's writings passionately create a self-critical, self-reflexive space for an evolving black consciousness, aesthetic and feminism, while continuing to offer mainstream feminist theory a transcendent visionary scope in which to extend beyond its white western ethnocentrisms.

See also: African feminism; black female sexuality; black women's history in the USA; black women's literature; oral history; slavery in the USA; womanist theology

Selected writings

Walker, A. (1973) *In Love and Trouble: Stories of Black Women*, London: The Women's Press.
—— (1983) *In Search of Our Mothers' Gardens: Womanist Prose*, London: The Women's Press.
—— (1988) *Living By The Word: Selected Writings 1973–1987*, London: The Women's Press.

SATINDER KAUR CHOHAN

Walkerdine, Valerie (b. 1947)

Valerie Walkerdine is an important contributor to poststructuralist inquiries in pedagogy, schooling and cultural studies (see **pedagogy, feminist; cultural theory/cultural studies, feminist**). Through **psychoanalysis** (Freud/Lacan), she explores the force of fantasy in subject formation. Through Foucault she shows the subject of knowledge as also subjected by that knowledge.

The classic *Democracy in the Kitchen: Regulating Mothers and Socialising Daughters* (1989), co-authored with Helen Lucey, traces the social fantasy of the 'sensitive' and 'nurturing' mother at the heart of liberal educational reforms in Britain in the 1970s and 1980s. Supported by progressive theories of 'natural child development' these reforms increasingly targeted women as key to children's educational success. Subsequent demands for a child-centred approach to mothering regulate women: middle-class women through internalised self-surveillance, working-class women by pathologising their practices as lacking.

Walkerdine's widely received collection of essays, *Schoolgirl Fictions* (1990), refigures how **gender** and relations of **power** have been theorised in the schooling and gender socialisation literature. Gender is theorised as fiction, shot through with fantasy, yet lived as fact, produced and struggled over within the regulatory daily practices of schooling. Like most of Walkerdine's writing, this collection engagingly juxtaposes theory with (auto-) fiction. It also explores Walkerdine's own complex subjectivity, that of a working class girl turned school teacher turned academic.

Daddy's Girl: Young Girls and Popular Culture (1997) studies the pre-teen working class girl in movies, musicals and middle class anxieties. As a figure, the little girl is the site of projective fantasies: in popular culture, 'daddy's girl' frequently functions as a signifier for upward social mobility. Feminist and cultural studies have tended to reduce her to the future revolutionary subject or duped object of consumer ideology. The recent bourgeois panics over the exploitative quality of eroticised images of little girls, for example in advertising, speak to the troubling allure that the little girl holds for adults. Walkerdine suggests that such fantasies and projections ignore the complexities of working class lives and disregard what popular culture has to offer to girls: pleasure and hope for a better life.

By showing the workings of fantasy and the regulatory effects of progressive discourses, Walkerdine sets a refreshing contra-point to many US educationalist discourses and their reliance on individualistic child development theories and ideology critique.

Selected writings

Walkerdine, V. (1990) *Schoolgirl Fictions*, London: Verso.
—— (1997) *Daddy's Girl*, Cambridge, MA: Harvard University Press.
Walkerdine, V. and Lucey, H. (1989) *Democracy in the Kitchen*, London: Virago Press.

SUSANNE LUHMANN

Waring, Marilyn J. (b. 1952)

A writer on political economy/environmental politics, Marilyn Waring's renowned text *Counting for Nothing: What Men Value and What Women Are Worth* deconstructs the assumptions/practices of the national system of accounting developed by western economists – the United Nations System of National Accounts (UNSNA). This public policy instrument, imposed by statisticians, politicians and market regulators on countries around the globe, is claimed to measure economic well-being. Waring challenges the tool's validity, revealing its reliance on reductionist mathematical modelling.

Demystifying the doctrine/methods of economics, she identifies the patriarchal values involved when, in the name of 'value-free empirical science', a rationalist discourse of separation/fragmentation is developed, which reifies men's public activities as 'work', while those performed in the private sphere, by women, are designated as 'non-work'. This formal/informal division (enforced by the national accounts system) ensures that women's productive/reproductive output remains invisible; justified by a biologically determinist portrayal of such labouring as an extension of female physiology.

By compiling figures restricted to *market* 'exchange relations', Waring suggests a moral judgment is instituted/ionalised whereby only monetary interactions are attributed *value* and only those producing surplus value/profit through the instrumentalist fetishised values of 'consumption' and infinite demand for 'growth rates' are validated. In eliminating so much *value* from their 'production' parameters, this mechanistic patriarchal ideology/practice sustains the enslavement of women and imparts ecological damage on the environment.

Waring demonstrates the inadequacy of abstract *quantity* data modelling by documenting the (statistically invisible) productive role performed by women internationally. While proposing that a *monetary* value be attributed to all unpaid work (surpassing the 'wages for house work' campaign), she transmutes economistic categories by nominating that statistical indicators be related to *qualitative* assessments. Adapting the 'masters' tools' to feminist ends, she posits a spiralling framework to facilitate the estimation of life-sustaining *creative* versus *destructive* forms of production/consumption.

As a former politician who brought a government down through adherence to her anti-racist, anti-nuclear values, Waring is no artless assimilationist; rather her informed pragmatics address *what should really count* in society. Her international activist work, researching women's labouring conditions in order to craft empowering developmental programmes, surpasses 'think global act local' strategising by extending notions of location to a heightened level of interaction.

Selected writings

Waring, M.J. (1989) *If Women Counted: The New Feminist Economics*, San Francisco: Harper Collins.

—— (1996) *Three Masquerades: Essays on Equality, Work and Human Rights*, Aukland: Auckland University Press.

NGAIRE LEWIS

welfare

Since the Second World War, social welfare has been seen as one of the primary tasks of democratic governments. The nature of the 'welfare state' varies in different contexts, but generally refers to a situation where the economic and social well-being of a population is secured through public policies and services. Welfare measures range from basic protection against the risks of unemployment, old age, illness and disability, to more substantial support for **childcare** or parental leave. Welfare provisions may take the form of financial payments (such as old age pensions or unemployment benefits) or services (such as public health care or state-run nurseries). The extent and aims of welfare policy have constituted an important domain for feminist arguments; both critical perspectives on existing arrangements and blueprints for reform. Feminists have been concerned with the model of the **family** assumed within welfare policies, and its implications for **gender roles**, women's **autonomy**, and questions of gender equity.

The development of welfare states in different democratic contexts – in North America, western Europe and Australasia – involved a common conception of family structures and gender relations within them. This conception was based on a heterosexual and nuclear family, supported by a male head of household's earnings. The wife and mother, meanwhile, undertook domestic labour and duties of care without pay. Welfare policies in the post-1945 period generally assumed an economic and domestic model based on a male wage that in itself was sufficient to support a family, and the unpaid work of women. This model set a normative standard for welfare provisions, such that unemployment payments, widows' and old age pensions, and disability benefits, were intended to substitute for the male wage. Unequal gender roles were reinforced through welfare arrangements, reproducing a conventional distinction between men's and women's activities within the **public/private** spheres.

Feminists have had a contradictory relation to questions of welfare. On the one hand, welfare structures provided a 'safety net' for women and their children in cases where men could or would not support them, and also made it more viable for women to leave abusive households. Under the extended provisions of welfare states in northern Europe, childcare and maternity leave arrangements supported women's working and domestic roles. On the other hand, it is arguable that welfare structures replaced women's economic

dependency on men with increased state regulation and surveillance of women's private lives. Feminists such as Elizabeth Wilson (1977) in Britain, have analysed welfare policy in terms of the state's organisation of the domestic sphere, in particular its upholding of inequitable family relations. Low benefit levels, meanwhile, contributed to the **feminisation of poverty** in a late capitalist context. Black women in the USA played a central role in welfare rights movements in the 1960s and 1970s, subverting conservative images of passive welfare recipients through their activism within the National Welfare Rights Organization and other campaigns highlighting issues of welfare poverty and the **civil rights** of welfare claimants (see Piven and Cloward 1979).

Conventional models of welfare have also come into serious question on account of changing labour market and household structures. The assumptions underpinning the post-war welfare state had by the 1980s become out of step with many people's experience (see Gordon 1990). Questions of both economic production and social **reproduction** are important here. Processes of **economic restructuring** saw increasing numbers of women active in labour markets, and transformed the nature of work (see **work, women and**). A shift to part-time, temporary and casualised work meant that a single (male) wage was rarely sufficient to support a family. Domestic arrangements changed over the same period, with men and women marrying later and divorcing more frequently together with a growth in lesbian and gay households, in single-person households, and in single-parent (especially female-headed) households.

Feminist theorists have sought to provide alternative models of welfare based on these new structures of gender and work. Nancy Fraser's work has been widely taken up by feminists active in this field. Fraser (1997) contrasts two abstract models for achieving gender equity within welfare provision: one based on equality, the other on **difference** (see also **equality and difference**). A 'universal breadwinner' model – similar to North American arrangements – promotes women's employment activity (for example, through public childcare provision). An alternative 'caregiver parity' model – more European in character – supports women's caring roles (for example, through child and carers'

allowances or maternal leave). Fraser considers both to be problematic: the first requires women to 'act more like men' in the labour market, the second leaves gender roles unchanged.

Fraser's alternative is a 'universal caregiver' model. This is based on the assumption that both women and men will combine paid employment with caring responsibilities – men, that is, should 'act more like women' – and involves a flexible system of parental leave and financial support for carers. In this way Fraser seeks to deconstruct the opposition between 'breadwinning' and 'caregiving', and challenges a conventional gender division of labour. However, this perspective leaves out key questions; for example, regarding the position of lone parents, or same-sex couples with children. While Fraser requires that any system of welfare should accord with principles of anti-poverty, equality of respect, and anti-marginalisation, it remains important for feminist theorists to detail how these issues might be worked out in practice. More generally, the 'universal caregiver' model assumes a generous basis for welfare provision, in a context where many national welfare states have been subject to severe cuts.

See also: citizenship; state theory

References and further reading

Fraser, N. (1989) 'Women, Welfare and the Politics of Need', in *Unruly Practices: Power, Discourse and Gender*, Minneapolis, MI: University of Minnesota Press.

Fraser, N. (1997) 'After the Family Wage: A Postindustrial Thought Experiment', in *Justice Interruptus: Critical Reflections on the 'Postsocialist' Condition*, New York: Routledge.

Gordon, L. (ed.) (1990) *Women, the State and Welfare*, Madison: University of Wisconsin Press.

Piven, F.F. and Cloward, R.A. (1979) *Poor People's Movements: How They Succeed, Why They Fail*, New York: Vintage.

Waring, Marilyn (1988) *Counting for Nothing: What Men Value and What Women Are Worth*, Wellington, New Zealand: Allen and Unwin.

Wilson, E. (1977) *Women and the Welfare State*, London: Tavistock.

FRAN TONKISS

white privilege (race privilege)

White privilege is a particular class of unearned advantages and immunities that is conferred systematically to persons who appear to be, or who 'pass' as, white. Academic efforts (McIntosh 1988; Frankenberg 1993) to examine white privilege began in the late 1980s in response to women of colour's observations that feminist theory engaged racial differences in ways that left privilege uncritically intact.

McIntosh metaphorically describes white privilege as an invisible knapsack of unearned assets that whites can count on cashing in each day, but about which they are meant to remain oblivious. These privileges include: the fact that whites can, if they wish, arrange to be in the company of people of their race most of the time; they can dress any way they want and not have their appearance explained by the perceived tastes of the so-called white race; and, they can be fairly sure that their colour will not count against their financial credibility. The strength of race privilege depends upon the presence of other conditions that might weaken these privileges. Historically, for instance, white privilege was mediated by class oppression, marrying outside the race, having mixed-race children, or by doing civil rights work.

Like racism, white privilege is a product of racial **essentialism**, or the idea that races are biological natural kinds. The view that racial identity is a 'natural' unchangeable fact about a person is central to systems of domination with vested interests in keeping people fastened securely in roles 'appropriate' to their race. Racial segregation, redlining, and discrimination only work if there is some way of racially marking people. However, since 'race-mixing' and immigration continue to challenge existing boundaries, the preservation of race privilege requires that the colour line be well guarded yet intentionally porous.

Feminists and critical race theorists now reject essentialism in favour of the view that races are socially constructed political categories. Since the late 1980s, they have extended the basic observations about race privilege to explore the cultural performative dimensions of the whiteness, how privilege functions in the lives of mixed-race peoples, and whether privilege takes on new dimensions for privilege-cognisant whites who resist the usual assumptions of their race (e.g. race traitors).

See also: privilege

References and further reading

Cuomo, C.J. and Hall, K.Q. (eds) (1999) *Whiteness: Feminist Philosophical Reflections*, Lanham, MD: Rowman and Littlefield Publishers.

Frankenberg, R. (1993) *White Women, Race Matters: The Social Construction of Whiteness*, Minneapolis, MI: University of Minnesota Press.

McIntosh, P. (1988) 'White Privilege and Male Privilege: A Personal Account of Coming to See Correspondences Through Work in Women's Studies', in M.L. Andersen and P.H. Collins (eds) *Race, Class and Gender: An Anthology*, New York: Wadsworth, 1991.

ALISON BAILEY

Whitford, Margaret

Margaret Whitford has always seen her feminist political outlook and her academic writing as intertwined. As she says in the first chapter of her book: *Luce Irigaray, Philosophy in the Feminine*, 'feminist philosophy is political and committed' (p.13). Her inaugural lecture, as Professor of Feminist Thought, which took place at Queen Mary and Westfield College, University of London in 1996 is both an intellectual tour de force, and a political statement on behalf of feminism in the academy. In the lecture, she argues that feminist theorising has both changed the face of the academy and has retained the 'cutting edge' of an outsider discourse.

Because of her strong sense of the interconnections among the academic, the personal and the political, Whitford, when she heard that she was to be honoured with a place in this Encyclopaedia, was at pains to insist that she was 'only' one of a collective. This 'collective', consisting of Margaret Whitford, Alison Assiter, Morwenna Griffiths, Jean Grimshaw, Anne Sellar, and later Kathleen Lennon met together in the early 1980s to convene a seminar on women and philosophy. Out of this seminar the British Society for Women in

Philosophy was born. The initial aims of this society were to widen the network of women interested in or involved in philosophy, through organising meetings, conferences and a newsletter.

It is true that SWIP was formed by a group of women, many of us previously active in feminism for several years before its formation. However, it was the hard work of Margaret Whitford and Morwenna Griffiths who co-produced and edited the *Women's Philosophy Newsletter* (renamed the *Women's Philosophy Review* in 1993, and now edited by Christine Battersby) from 1991–7, without the help of a publisher to produce and distribute it for them, that SWIP has grown in strength. It was indeed the energy and drive of Margaret Whitford and Morwenna Griffiths that enabled the production of the first book of papers to come out of British feminist philosophy, *Feminist Perspectives in Philosophy* (Macmillan), which they co-edited.

But it is for her work on Luce **Irigaray** that Margaret Whitford is particularly known. Her book *Luce Irigaray: Philosophy in the Feminine* came out in 1991. It is difficult to remember, in a climate where Irigaray is accepted as part of the fashionable 'poststructuralist and post modern' orthodoxy or a least as a fashionable and sophisticated feminist thinker, how Irigaray was viewed in the English-speaking world, before Margaret's book came out. Her work was frequently derided and often dismissed as 'essentialist' and 'reductionist' – terms that were often used at the time in a denigratory fashion. Margaret Whitford's work changed all that. In a paper she published in 1989, 'Reclaiming Irigaray', in *Feminism and Psycho-analysis*, ed. T. Brennan, Whitford begins: 'Irigaray's project is to effect change in the symbolic order, and that what she has been interpreted as advocating or positing in fact resembles more closely her diagnosis of what is wrong with the symbolic order' (ch. 6, p. l.106). In other words, it is the 'patriarchal symbolic' which, according to Whitford's reading of Irigaray, constitutes women in the derogatory fashion, and the feminist project therefore is to 'effect change in the symbolic order'. Irigaray was accused of denigrating women. However, what she is doing, Whitford points out, is describing the representation of women in the patriarchal symbolic. The problem Irigaray sets out to address is the non-symbolisation of the relation

to the mother and the mother's body. Whitford's book explains, in rich and subtle ways, how Irigaray does this. Whitford's work has enabled Irigaray's project to be treated with the seriousness it deserved. Whitford has effected a repositioning of Irigaray's work upon the psychical and feminist imagination in the English (as a first language) speaking world.

ALISON ASSITER

Williams, Patricia (b. 1951)

Patricia Joyce Williams combines story-telling with legal analysis to bring attention to the experiences of marginalised groups with the law. Her work has been praised as an outstanding example of feminist narrative method in legal scholarship. She is also acclaimed for her contributions to **critical race theory** and for her powerful re-affirmation of the symbolic value of rights.

In addition to being the author of several books and scholarly articles, Williams contributes regularly to publications with a more general readership, including *The Nation* magazine. She is considered a 'major voice in American letters' and has been described by one reviewer as 'the very best and most useful kind of public intellectual' (Rapping 1996: 5).

Consistent with the narrative method, Williams's writing is characterised by the telling of life experiences, quite frequently her own. Her aim is to tell the stories of those who are typically left out of mainstream legal accounts and to expose the ways in which apparently neutral principles of law operate to reinforce their marginalisation. With her detailed descriptions of how African Americans and other historically oppressed groups experience the law, Williams's work challenges the legal establishment to critically consider the assumptions that underlie their analyses and to identify more closely with the experiences of those who are outsiders to the legal hierarchy. In all of these respects, Williams's work exemplifies the narrative method, which has been associated with both feminist and critical race scholarship.

Williams's emphasis on the experiences of those who are usually excluded from legal analysis – and on the experiences of African Americans in particular – has also enabled her to make important contributions to rights-based theory. While many left-wing scholars have argued that rights-based legal strategies should not be encouraged because they instil false hope in the law as a tool for overcoming oppression, Williams argues that rights assertions play an important symbolic role in social struggles. Williams acknowledges that rights-based legal strategies have, at best, been only marginally effective at achieving social change. Nevertheless, she maintains that the language of rights can play an important role in providing oppressed groups with the discourse they need to articulate resistance, as exemplified in the African American struggle for civil rights.

Williams is criticised by the radical left for her defence of rights-based discourse and by mainstream legal scholars, who view her use of the narrative method as at odds with the academy's commitment to legal analysis that is based on so-called 'neutral principles'.

See also: black feminism(s); epistemology, black feminist; epistemology, feminist; narrative, feminist uses of

Selected writings

Williams, P. (1991) *The Alchemy of Race and Rights*, Cambridge, MA: Harvard University Press.
—— (1995) *The Rooster's Egg*, Cambridge, MA: Harvard University Press.
—— (1998) *Seeing a Color-blind Future*, New York: Noonday Press.

References and further reading

Rapping, E. (1996) 'Putting the World in Perspective', *Women's Review of Books* 13,5: 5–6.

ANNE BLOOM

witchcraft

Witchcraft is a nature-based religion whose practitioners worship Goddess, the immanent life force within and connecting all, manifest in both female and male images of the divine, most especially **Goddess**, and who is monist, henotheist, polytheist and/or panentheistic in concept. To witches, the Earth is alive and all life is sacred and interconnected.

Witchcraft is the largest of many contemporary religions which fit under the broader term pagan in the sense of being Earth-based and distinct from predominant Judaeo-Christian thought. Certain traditions (similar to a denomination) of witchcraft have existed in Europe, North America and Australia, since the early twentieth century, and some claim lineage of hundreds of years and more.

A revival of interest in the Craft occurred in the late 1960s and early 1970s, with the weaving of many threads: interest in western ceremonial magic; exploration of intuitive, non-linear modes of perception; seeking meaning and spirit in a materially oriented culture; awakened respect for folk tradition; honour for our direct experience of Nature and of our bodies; concern for the survival of Earth and the quality of life on the planet; women's sense of oppression, anger, and the profound need to honour their life experiences with ritual. Witchcraft respects both rational, scientific pursuit of knowledge and emotional, intuitive, experiential perceptions. It is practised by women and men in small, intimate, groups commonly called covens, and in larger gatherings, sometimes open to the public. Rituals celebrate the seasons on the solar solstices and equinoxes and agricultural/deity-related cross quarters and lunations. They may honour life passages or be done for healing of an individual or the Earth herself.

Important religious symbols are spirals, pentacles, circles, sun and moon, natural objects, and seasonal vegetation. Use of the term 'Witch' reclaims individual 'power from within', affirms collective power to effect change in the world, and identifies with people of independent spirit, personal power, and special skills who were persecuted and martyred as witches during the fourteenth through sixteenth centuries. Historical roots are perceived in the image of the sacred female in the art and culture of ancient Europe and the Middle East, and in the writings of archeologist Marija Gimbutas, anthropologist Margaret Murray, and the teachings of Gerald B. Gardner. Early theologians include Morgan McFarland, Robin

Morgan, and most significantly, Starhawk (Miriam Simos).

See also: earth/Gaia/Mother Earth; pagan religion, feminist; spiritual feminism; theology, feminist

References and further reading

Adler, M. (1979) *Drawing Down the Moon*, Boston: Beacon Press, 1986.
Starhawk (1979) *The Spiral Dance*, San Francisco: Harper Collins, 1999.

M. MACHA NIGHTMARE

Wittig, Monique (b.1935)

'I am a lesbian', announced Monique Wittig in 1978, 'not a woman'. Always controversial, Wittig has produced some of the most challenging literary and theoretical work of second-wave feminism. It is possible, Wittig claims, 'for a work of literature to operate as a war machine upon its epoch' (1992: 69); not through direct political intervention, but, rather, by 'universalizing' a particular point of view. Wittig's 1964 first novel, *L'Opoponax*, won France's prestigious Prix Médicis by grammatically and figuratively 'universalizing' the world of childhood and nascent lesbian desire.

Wittig's 1971 *Les Guérillères*, is an epic chronicle of warfare in which *elles* are the sovereign conquerors of the world and the word. *Elles* are not 'the women' – an error in David Le Vay's translation – but the universal 'they', a linguistic assault on the masculine collective pronoun *ils*. For Wittig, linguistic **gender** marks social convention, 'cast[ing] sheaves of reality upon the social body, stamping it and violently shaping it' (1992:78).

Wittig's work on language and lesbian subjectivity culminates in her 1973 *Le Corps lesbien*. In the book's title the linguistic difficulty surfaces immediately: the masculine *corps* is lesbian. This text 'lesbianises' familiar figures: Ulyssea returns from her long voyage to the Amazon islands, and Sappho becomes a Goddess. *Le Corps lesbien* is also a cycle of poems in which *j/e* (I) and *tu* (you) violently tear each other to pieces in the process of love. The slashed pronoun *j/e* enacts women's violent entry into language.

Wittig emigrated from France to the USA in 1976. Her 1992 *The Straight Mind* collects theoretical essays written during the 1980s on feminism, language and literature. Here Wittig develops her 'materialist lesbianism', where lesbians represent escapees from the category of 'woman' by refusing both 'woman's role' *and* the 'economic, ideological, and political power of a man'. While these essays are canonical to feminist and queer studies, many scholars consider Wittig's fiction more theoretically productive than her essays: certainly it is more ambivalent. This ambivalence is commonly appealed to in criticism that aligns Wittig's work with that of French post structuralist and psychoanalytic feminisms she, herself, denounces.

See also: French feminism; gender; lesbian literature; Marxism; queer theory

Selected writings

Wittig, M. (1971) *Les Guérillères*, trans. D. Le Vay, New York: Avon Books.
—— (1975) *The Lesbian Body*, trans. D. Le Vay, New York: Avon Books.
—— (1992) *The Straight Mind and Other Essays*, Boston: Beacon Press.

JULIA CREET

womanist theology

Womanist theology, in its original consideration, covered the entire range of issues concerning women of African descent's experiential relationship with God. Its primary development in the USA can be traced to 1983 when Alice **Walker** coined the word womanist. Walker's four-part definition of womanist has played a significant role as an interpretative race/sex/class matrix for raising consciousness among female seminarians regarding the moral agency of African American women. Looking deep into their own social histories, the creators of womanist theology have established twin foci: first, African American women scholars, active members in the American

Academy of Religion and the Society of Biblical Literature, created analytical frameworks that theoretically advance black women's religious discourse about the divine in the dailiness of life, and, second, lay and ordained black church-women, use these critical constructions to protest the domination, exploitation and dehumanisation of women in socio-historical systems and ecclesias-tical-political processes. Hence, during the first decade of womanist development, the scholarly work undertaken by black women theologians in teaching, publications and conferences, challenged inherited religious traditions in their collusion with androcentric patriarchy as well as clarified those aspects of biblical studies, church history, systema-tic theology, social ethics, practical and pastoral ministries that serve as transformative catalysts for the full inclusion of women in all aspects of life.

The current phase of the development of womanist theology has seen the emergence of several contestable issues, all focusing on a different understanding of the conceptual centre-point around which the identity politics in Walker's definition is built. What, precisely, do we mean when we assert that a particular person is or is not a womanist? Or, what affirms 'a black feminist or a feminist of colour' as womanist? Is it vogue, insensitive exploitation to stretch to derivatives that include women of European descent, who possess white-skin privileges, as well as men of all colours? While some women claim Walker's definition exclusively of, by and for black women, others argue that womanist is a self-proclaimed confessional concept, rooted in the central author-ity of advocacy politics for racial justice and gender equality. Another problematic issue in Walker's definition that has yet to be fully addressed is 'a woman who loves other women sexually and/or nonsexually'. Not surprisingly, some theologians reject religious teachings that absolutise hetero-sexuality as the only sexual orientation ordained by God. At the same time there are new initiatives to expand womanist theology to other religious traditions, to bring into balance its growing significance beyond Christianity. Several feminists of colour in the social and biological sciences are beginning to apply and extend womanist structures of signification to their disciplines of study.

References and further reading

Cannon, K. (1995) *Katie's Canon: Womanism and the Soul of the Black Community*, New York: Con-tinuum.

Townes, E. (ed.) (1993) *A Troubling in My Soul: Womanist Perspectives on Evil and Suffering*, Mary-knoll, NY: Orbis.

Walker, A. (1983) *In Search of Our Mothers' Gardens: Womanist Prose*, New York: Harcourt Brace Jovanovich.

KATIE G. CANNON

women's studies (history and development of)

Women's studies is an academic field comprised of feminist-inspired scholarly inquiry, teaching, and outreach to society. It began in the mid-1960s rebirth of **feminism**. Seeking to learn about their predecessors in movements for women's rights to inform their own work, women in cities scattered around the countries of the world began a search through the literature of many peoples, eras, and disciplines, and taught others what they found. The first courses in women's studies appeared as informal, community-based gatherings as well as formal classes in educational institutions. They added to other feminist demands a call for more research and teaching about women in higher education.

By 1970–1 two organised women's studies programmes had been inaugurated in the USA, at San Diego State University and at Cornell University. Multiplying rapidly, by 1975 the number of programmes in the USA reached 150; by 1990 over 600. Undergraduate majors were offered at 187 institutions, graduate work at more than 100. Women's studies appeared in the 1970s in many countries of Europe, Asia, and Latin America, and by the 1990s was taught in at least 58 countries around the globe; 108 countries housed some form of women-oriented institutional orga-nisation, research centre, or publication. The number of women's studies courses was counted in the tens of thousands.

Most women's studies faculty are appointed to

traditional departments, and programmes generally take form through the coordination of coursework drawn from multiple academic units. The existence of separate women's studies courses and specialised academic units is sometimes perceived as establishing 'ghettos' that allow traditional academics to ignore feminist work, and issues of interdisciplinarity and institutional structures remain a matter for debate. Degrees in women's studies are offered at all levels, increasingly including the doctorate. Between 1978 and 1995, over 10,000 doctoral degrees based on dissertations categorised as women's studies were reported. This scholarship is heavily concentrated in literature, history, and the social sciences, but is growing in other areas. A National Women's Studies Association in the USA, founded in 1977, holds annual meetings; regional groups and international conferences abound. One women's studies electronic mail list, WMST-L, counts over 4000 subscribers in more than 40 countries.

Initially spread by manuscripts and manifestos distributed at feminist meetings, the development of women's studies was spurred by the sharing and publication of collections of syllabi and bibliographies. The new scholarship gave rise to feminist journals, presses, and bookstores which by the mid-1970s were joined by university and commercial presses to diffuse a flood of publications. Assistance from private sources in the USA, especially the Ford Foundation, and public agencies helped create a support network of professional associations and research centres.

Women's studies represents a new era in the history of women's demands for higher learning. Unlike earlier feminist claims for admission to equal educational opportunities with men, advocates of women's studies challenge academia to include women as creators of knowledge and as subjects in their epistemologies, sources of evidence, categories of analysis, and interpretations. They aim not only to add new information about neglected female populations, but to create new women-centred fields of knowledge. The goal is courses, curricula, and knowledge itself reconstituted to encompass all human experience.

In pursuing this goal, academic feminists must confront existing academic structures, disciplinary standards, and pressures toward conformity with accepted lines of authority and methods for allocating resources and recognition. Pedagogy provides not only a means for conveying knowledge, but also a way to practise feminist principles. Feminist pedagogy encourages engaging students as active learners, promoting **collaborative learning**, and facilitating connections between the materials studied and students' lives and social concerns. It emphasises critical thinking, questioning answers and authority, and applying theory to practice. This teaching style also reflects the importance women's studies places on empowering women, recognizing individual differences, and imbuing knowledge with purpose (see **pedagogy, feminist**).

Women's studies is dedicated to the feminist goals of serving the interests of all women and of overcoming the subordination and **oppression** that has everywhere, to varying degrees, constituted their experience. While its founders were largely white women, women's studies has broadened its scope by recognizing differences among women and incorporating diversity into classroom materials, courses and curricula, research agendas, conference programmes, organisational structures, and feminist theories.

Questions of **difference** tended to dominate women's studies in the 1990s. The politics of identity, based on an essentialist view of differences as inherent, irreducible qualities of individuals or groups, served to enhance all women's understanding of themselves as products of a specific culture (see **identity politics; essentialism**). It also at times generated accusatory rhetoric and divisiveness that may impede effective challenge to androcentric ideologies and institutions.

While incorporating the work of women of colour in the 1980s and 1990s, feminist theorists, themselves increasingly diverse, also drew on the work of (Continental) European postmodern philosophers as well as postcolonial perspectives to create gender-focused analyses. For many women's studies scholars, the concept of 'relational positionality', which acknowledges the material reality of differences but defines identities situationally, provides both a recognition of diversity and a basis for collaboration. In the quest for theories with greater explanatory and transformational power than the 'Big Three' of the 1970s – liberal, socialist, and radical feminism – many women's studies scholars have come to believe that all academic knowledge, like social experience, is 'constructed', based on politically-grounded perspectives (see **social constructionism**).

An internal debate over the purposes of women's studies that tends to position academic work against political activism has led some feminists both inside and outside the academy to lament women's studies' institutional success. Others find no conflict in the convergence of women's studies' two objectives, finding them inseparable and mutually supportive. For many, the field represents a 'feminist enlightenment' that will ultimately penetrate all academic and public cultures. Embodying a feminist moral claim as well as political stance, women's studies asks for women to be heard wherever knowledge is created, taught, and preserved. Women's studies encourages a countertrend to a long dominant scientism by challenging conventional **dichotomies** such as mind/body, subject/object, theory/practice, personal/professional, and calling for inclusion of the reproductive as well as the productive processes of society as topics of intellectual discourse. With its thrust toward wholistic conceptualisation and 'connected learning', women's studies aims to elicit a reconstruction of higher education.

References and further reading

Boxer, M.J. (1998) *When Women Ask the Questions: Creating Women's Studies in America*, Baltimore: The Johns Hopkins University Press.

Brown, L., Collins, H., Green, P., Humm, M. and Landells, M. (eds) (1993) *W.I.S.H.: The International Handbook of Women's Studies*, New York: Harvester Wheatsheaf.

Luebke, B.F. and Reilly, M.E. (1995) *Women's Studies Graduates: The First Generation*, New York: Teachers College Press.

Musil, C.M. (ed.) (1992) *The Courage to Question: Women's Studies and Student Learning*, Washington, DC: Association of American Colleges and National Women's Studies Association.

O'Barr, J.F. (ed.) (1994) *Feminism in Action: Building Institutions and Community Through Women's Studies*, Chapel Hill: University of North Carolina Press.

Women's Studies Quarterly 22, nos 3 and 4 (1994) special issue 'Women's Studies: A World View'.

Women's Studies Quarterly 25, nos 1 and 2 (1997) special issue 'Looking Back, Moving Forward: 25 Years of Women's Studies History'.

MARILYN J. BOXER

women's studies: autonomy v. mainstreaming

In the early 1980s in the USA – a time of fragility for most Women's Studies (WS) programmes – a discussion ensued on the most efficacious strategies for strengthening these programmes. Some practitioners argued that WS should pursue a path of '**autonomy**', the development of an interdisciplinary discipline in its own right, to be housed in a department, the locus of power in many universities. Other feminist teachers were pursuing an 'integrationist' strategy aimed at bringing the study of women to the existing disciplines.

These ideas were being pursued by individual scholars around the USA but a complex articulation of the differences of approach did not begin until 1982 during meetings of the National Women's Studies Association at Humboldt State University in California. In a talk entitled 'Whatever Happened to Autonomous Women's Studies?', Gloria Bowles and Renate Duelli-Klein questioned the approach of numerous new integrationist programmes, many of them on the East Coast, well funded by private foundations. Their ideas are summarised in the introduction to *Theories of Women's Studies*, ideas in part inspired by Sandra Coyner's vision of 'Women's Studies as an academic discipline' (46–71), also published in *Theories*. Among these questions are: Why are we, at a moment when we have an opportunity to define our own disciplinary future, allowing ourselves to be defined primarily by the existing disciplines? What are we mainstreaming? Does not this new explosion of integrationist projects at this moment in our history endanger any chance we might have to develop autonomous WS programmes?

For their part, some of the integrationists felt

their projects and their feminist faith had been misunderstood and mis-characterised. They argued that 'autonomy' is not feasible within institutions. Another publication ensued in order to expand the dialogue. A special issue of *Women's Studies International Forum* entitled 'Strategies for Women's Studies in the 1980s' includes articles arguing for a 'both/and' position; analyses of effective and ineffective mainstream programmes; a theory of what WS can do that mainstreaming cannot; an exploration of the relationship between 'minority studies' and WS; and a view that with mainstreaming the changers become the changed.

In the ensuing years, feminist teachers, ever practical, have drawn upon these discussions to create WS programmes appropriate to their own institutional structures. For example, faculty seminars to influence curriculum are often successful at small liberal arts colleges while almost impossible to mount at large research universities where teaching is not a priority. A voluminous literature on curriculum transformation is now available; the writing on interdisciplinary Women's Studies is sparser, perhaps awaiting young scholars not as allied to traditional disciplines as its earliest practitioners.

See also: malestream thought

References and further reading

Bowles, G. (ed.) (1984) *Strategies for Women's Studies in the Eighties*, New York: Elsevier.

Bowles, G. and Duelli-Klein, R. (eds) (1983) *Theories of Women's Studies*, London: Routledge.

Friedman, E.G., Kolmar, W.K., Flint, C.B. and Rothenberg, P. (eds) (1996) *Creating an Inclusive College Curriculum*, New York: Teachers College Press.

GLORIA BOWLES

women's writing

Although there have always been women writers, it has only been with modern feminism, and particularly with the emergence of feminist literary criticism, that 'women's writing' has become a distinct literary category, a respectable field of study, and a profitable publishing market (see **literary theory, feminist**). In the early 1970s, the only women's texts included in the literary canon (a list that determines which texts are taught in high schools and universities) were one or two novels by Jane Austen, George Eliot or Virginia Woolf. Since then, feminist critics have been engaged in a massive project of recovering 'lost' women writers; re-reading and re-evaluating their writing; and re-constructing the literary, cultural, economic and political contexts in which they wrote. Feminist presses in the USA, Canada and Britain have aided the recovery project by publishing little-known texts. Today, a bibliographic search on women's writing results in hundreds of books: introductions historical surveys (Shaw 1998) anthologies (Gilbert and Gubar 1985; Franklin 1997), bibliographies, critical editions, casebooks, guides and companions (Davidson and Wagner-Martin 1995; Blain, Clements and Grundy 1990; Baechler and Litz 1991). Yet, 'women's writing' remains a contested category which may be on the verge of redundancy. As women writers continue to attract a wide audience and win prestigious prizes, there may no longer be any practical, political or intellectual reason to treat women's writing separately.

The most important text by a first-wave feminist to address women's writing is Woolf's witty and thoughtful *A Room of One's Own* (1929). Speaking at two Cambridge women's colleges, she analysed the material conditions that are necessary for women to write. Reflecting on what would have happened had Shakespeare had an equally talented sister, she hypothesises that Judith Shakespeare, when faced with the restrictions imposed by her gender, would have gone mad or committed suicide. Woolf insists, however, that no woman with Shakespeare's genius would have emerged during the Renaissance, because genius is the product of an education and life experience that was denied to women. She concludes that 'a woman must have money and a room of her own if she is to write fiction' (4).

While Woolf lamented the lack of women writers of genius, second-wave feminists undertook the daunting but exhilarating task of recovering, historicising, interpreting and evaluating women's writing. Ellen Moers, in *Literary Women* (1976), examines the major women's novels of the nineteenth century. In *A Literature of Their Own*, originally published in 1977, Elaine Showalter argues that women's novels could only properly be understood when they were placed in a literary tradition of their own. Positing a hypothetical chain of influence between writers of successive generations, she views women's writing as a product of a subculture, which evolves in relation to dominant culture (1999: xiii). Showalter later coined the term **gynocritics** to describe the study of women's writing, which she advocated as the core of feminist literary criticism. Sandra Gilbert and Susan Gubar's classic, *The Madwoman in the Attic* (1979), examines the relationship between women's writing and patriarchal culture. Such texts, together with new journals such as the *Women's Review of Books*, *Signs*, and *Tulsa Studies in Women's Literature*, have aided the development of courses on women's writing.

The 1980s and 1990s witnessed both the consolidation of the achievements of the 1970s, and an attack on the homogeneity and essentialism underpinning the category of 'women'. Around 1980, black critics and women of colour criticised white feminists for ignoring writings by women of colour, and ignoring differences of class, race and sexuality that complicate and threaten the category of 'women's writing'. Mixed-genre anthologies of writings by African American, Latina, Native and immigrant women, such as *This Bridge Called My Back* (1981), *Home Girls* (1983), *The Third Woman* (1981), and *Beyond the Echo: Multicultural Women's Writing* (1988), and collections such as *Lesbian Fiction* (1981) and *Nice Jewish Girls* (1982), introduced readers to the diversity of contemporary women's writing. Black critics such as Barbara Christian, Hazel Carby, Deborah McDowell and Claudia Tate wrote social and political histories and critical analysis of black women's writing, aiding the development of curricula.

In addition to feminist critics, women readers have played a significant role in bringing women's writing to the forefront of literary culture. Contemporary women's writing, implicitly or explicitly informed by feminism, has found a ready audience among women in the 1970s and since. Some of the most popular authors include Doris Lessing, Margaret Drabble, Fay Weldon, Angela Carter and Jeanette Winterson in England; Margaret Laurence, Gabrielle Roy, Margaret Atwood, Alice Munro and Ann-Marie MacDonald in Canada; Alice Walker, Toni Morrison, Louise Erdrich, Leslie Marmon Silko and Maxine Hong Kingston in the USA; Christina Stead and Elizabeth Jolley in Australia, and Janet Frame in New Zealand. Poets including Sylvia Plath, Anne Stevenson, Anne Sexton, Adrienne Rich, Audre Lorde and Gloria Anzaldúa; have been claimed as feminist icons, both inside and outside the academy. Women's autobiographies and memoirs, such as Gertrude Stein's *Autobiography of Alice B. Toklas* (1933), Mary McCarthy's *Memoirs of a Catholic Girlhood* (1957), Maya Angelou's *I Know Why the Caged Bird Sings* (1969), Lillian Hellman's *Pentimento* (1973), Carolyn Steedman's *Landscape for a Good Woman* (1986), Sally Morgan's *My Place* (1987), Sylvia Fraser's *My Father's House* (1987), Druscilla Modjeska's *Poppy* (1991) and Mary Karr's *The Liar's Club* (1995) have been widely read over the past thirty years.

Access to women's writing has been greatly increased by feminist presses – Virago (London), The Women's Press (London), and The Feminist Press (New York) – which have published out of print and unfamiliar texts, as well as works by contemporary women. Feminist presses introduced readers to women writers from a range of social and national backgrounds, such as Rebecca West, Radclyffe Hall, Rosamund Lehmann, Olive Schriner, Zora Neale Hurston, Harriet Jacobs, Charlotte Perkins Gilman, Nella Larsen, Kate Chopin, Henry Handel Richardson and Katherine Anne Porter. Publishing diaries, memoirs and journals, feminist presses were instrumental in stimulating interest in marginalised genres. Virago's series on women's travel literature, a genre previously considered to be the exclusive preserve of men, attracted popular and critical interest. Biographies of women writers by women writers, such as Hermione Lee's *Virginia Woolf* (1996), Carol Brightman's *Writing Dangerously: Mary McCarthy and Her World* (1992), and Diane Middlebrook's *Anne Sexton* (1991), as well as edited letters, such as Brightman's *Between Friends: The Correspondence of Mary McCarthy and Hannah Arendt* (1995), have all contributed to expanding public knowledge of the lives and struggles of women writers.

Yet, despite the enormous success of the recovery project, the category of 'women's writing' remains contested, for practical, aesthetic, political and philosophical reasons. From a practical perspective, problems emerge with the constitution of 'women's writing'. Do all texts by women belong to this category simply by virtue of the author's sex? Or does women's writing have to be concerned with 'women's issues', or even more narrowly, be feminist to be included? Aesthetic questions also emerge: does women's writing share metaphors, themes, writing styles, iconographies? If so, can a distinct 'feminine' or 'feminist' aesthetic be identified? Feminist critic Myra Jehlan cautions that by treating women writers separately from dominant culture, feminists risk relegating women's writing to a single-sex ghetto, which could comfortably be ignored by male critics and readers (1997). Many women writers object to the label, on the grounds that it pigeonholes their work. Finally, there have been philosophical disputes. Critics contest the assumption that there is some essential attribute – biological or cultural – that unifies 'women's writing' despite social and political differences of the authors. They contend that this assumption naturalises the category of 'women', when critics should be analysing and challenging its construction. Many of the problems with the category of 'women's writing' have been discussed in reviews of Gilbert and Gubar's *The Norton Anthology of Women's Writers* (1985). Intended as a teaching text, it has been criticised for creating a new female canon that excludes many worthy writers, often women of colour. Although Gilbert and Gubar offer a broader representation of women's writing in the second edition, Lillian Robinson (1997), in a stinging critique, argues that the anthology reinforces the concept of a canon of great books, and leaves unquestioned the politics of canon construction.

It may be that 'women's writing' will be made redundant not because of academic debates, but rather, through the successes of women writers. In the 1990s, several women received the most prestigious literary prizes in the world. Toni Morrison, author of *Beloved* (1987), one of the most important American novels of the century, was awarded the Nobel Prize. England's Booker Prize has been awarded to several women, including the English writers A.S. Byatt (for *Possession*, 1990) and Pat Barker (for *The Ghost Road*, 1995), and the

Indian writer, Arundhati Roy (for *The God of Small Things*, 1997). Women dominate popular genres as well, including not only female enclaves such as romance fiction, but also traditionally male genres such as detective fiction. Some of the most widely-read detective novelists today are American authors Sue Grafton and Patricia Cornwell, both of whom have fashioned female heroines, and British authors Dorothy Sayers, Ruth Rendell and P.D. James. Barker's *Regeneration Trilogy* (of which *The Ghost Road* is the third volume), a rich historical novel of masculinity, sexuality, and trauma in the First World War, exemplifies Showalter's observation that '[w]omen novelists have joined the mainstream as postmodern innovators, politically engaged observers, and limitless storytellers' (323). With such a text setting the standard, we should celebrate the possibility that 'British women's writing at the millennium may ... be coming to the end of its history as a separate "literature of their own"' (Showalter 1999: 320).

See also: literature, images of women in; Showalter, Elaine

References and further reading

Baechler, L. and Litz, A.W. (eds) (1991) *Modern American Women Writers*, New York: Charles Scribner and Sons.

Blain, V., Clements, P. and Grundy, I. (eds) (1990) *The Feminist Companion to Literature in English: Women Writers from the Middle Ages to the Present*, London: B.T. Batsford.

Davidson, C. and Wagner-Martin, L. (eds) (1995) *The Oxford Companion to Women's Writing in the United States*, New York: Oxford University Press.

Franklin, C. (1997) *Writing Women's Communities: the Politics and Poetics of Contemporary Multi-Genre Anthologies*, Madison: University of Wisconsin Press.

Gilbert, S. and Gubar, S. (1985) *The Norton Anthology of Literature By Women: The Tradition in English*, New York: Norton.

Jehlen, M. (1997) 'Archimedes and the Paradox of a Feminist Criticism' (1981) reprinted in R. Warhol and D. Herndl (eds) *Feminisms*, New Brunswick, New Jersey: Rutgers University Press.

Robinson, L. (1997) *In the Canon's Mouth: Dispatches From the Culture Wars,* Bloomington, IN: Indiana University Press.

Shaw, M. (ed.) (1998) *An Introduction to Women's Writing: from the Middle Ages to the Present Day,* London: Prentice Hall.

Showalter, E. (1999) *A Literature of Their Own: British Women Novelists from Brontë to Lessing,* Princeton, NJ: Princeton University Press.

ROSANNE KENNEDY

work, women and

Currently, about 41 per cent of the world's women aged fifteen and over are economically active. In industrialised countries, women's work opportunities were increased after the Second World War as a result of higher educational achievement, a need for the type of labour women could provide, increased control over fertility and heightened social expectations about women's roles. In developing countries, women have not moved into the labour force in the past fifty years as much as they have altered the type of work they perform, combining subsistence farming with informal income generation and/or formal labouring (Bullock 1994; Krahn and Lowe 1993).

Women do not enter into, nor operate within, the formal or informal labour market on the same basis as men (Bullock 1994). *Occupational gender segregation* describes the concentration of women and men into different occupations, jobs and places of work. Two types occur. *Horizontal occupational segregation* refers to the fact that women and men predominate in different kinds of occupation. Most women tend to be concentrated in certain occupations and in a more narrow range of occupations than men, namely catering, cleaning, hairdressing and other personal services; clerical and related occupations; and professional and related occupations in education, welfare and health. *Vertical occupational segregation* refers to the fact that within occupations, women tend to be clustered at the lower levels of skill, responsibility and pay. Occupational hierarchies are thus constructed as gender hierarchies. Men tend to predominate in higher-level occupations such as the middle and upper echelons of managerial and professional forms of work while women tend to be concentrated in lower professional and clerical jobs as well as semi-skilled and unskilled manual jobs.

Even when women occupy professional and managerial positions, few actually reach the top of their fields. A combination of factors explain this 'glass ceiling': lack of education and training, child and kin care responsibilities which interrupt work, part-time work patterns and sexist work environments. Job ghettos increase competition among women and depress their earnings to between 30 – 40 per cent less than those of men. Gender differences in pay – be it in cash or kind, and including allowances, 'perks' and even food for work – is one of the clearest signs of workplace inequality (Bullock 1994). Views of women as secondary earners and unskilled workers reinforce their discrimination.

Gender, class, race, ethnicity and age affect women's experience of waged work. While the movement of married, middle-class western women into the labour force has extended their work lives, working-class, visible minority and women in emerging economies have always worked longer and more continuously. Gains made by white women in higher grade jobs are not equally shared. Ethnic minority women are more likely to be working longer hours for lower pay and are twice as likely as white women to be unemployed (Das Gupta 1996). Fluctuating economies mean working-class women are the last to benefit from job expansion and the first to suffer from job contraction (Phillips and Phillips 1993). Younger women are more likely to possess higher educational qualifications, enabling them to find more secure, continuous full-time employment than older women who are disproportionately placed in newly restructured, lower skilled, part-time and poorly paid jobs (Witz 1997). Increasingly women work part-time, not voluntarily, but as a response to underemployment and unemployment and as a personal strategy for managing their dual responsibilities for domestic and wage labour.

While some women have benefited from recent legislative changes, neither union membership nor state or corporate equity policies have altered significantly women's employment experiences. Other than adding sexual harassment to collective bargaining, union practices, such as protection of seniority and relocation rather than job loss, continue to favour male workers. Employment equity measures, including pay equity ('equal pay for work of equal value') and affirmative action, mostly benefit white women in middle- and lower-income jobs (Phillips and Phillips 1993). The lack of universal, affordable childcare means women frequently switch from full-time to part-time work or choose non-standard jobs, such as contract work or self-employment in order to manage their childrearing responsibilities. Moreover, the emergence of the global economy mitigates national advances. Internationalisation of capital, deregulation of labour markets, the drive towards flexibility by firms, the restructuring of economies away from manufacturing toward service, the introduction of new information technologies and the casualisation of work continue to ensure women's discrimination (Teeple 1995). A lifetime of job interruptions and of stress from juggling family duties with paid employment often impairs women's mental and physical health. Women often enter old age living on insufficient pensions, facing poverty and health problems.

Feminists have broadened the definition of work beyond the economic to include unpaid domestic and caring tasks as gender-specific aspects of women's work, developing such concepts as caring, sexual and emotional work to analyse the gendering of domestic and wage labour. Interconnections between sexuality, power and embodiment at work reveal how gendered power relations are discursively produced, the ways in which sexuality suffuses households and organisations, the 'doing' of gender as women work, and how women's work involves the production of emotional or sexual work (Witz 1997).

See also: economics

References and further reading

Bullock, S. (1994) *Women and Work*, London: Zed Books.

Das Gupta, T. (1996) *Racism and Paid Work*, Toronto: Garamond Press.

Krahn, H. and Lowe, G.S. (1993) *Work, Industry and Canadian Society*, Toronto: Nelson.

Phillips, P. and Phillips, E. (1993) *Women and Work*, Toronto: Lorimer, revised edn.

Teeple, G. (1995) *Globalization and Social Reform*, Toronto: Garamond.

Witz, A. (1997) 'Women and Work', in V. Robinson and D. Richardson (eds) *Introducing Women's Studies*, New York: New York University Press, 2nd edn.

NANCY MANDELL AND JULIANNE MOMIROV

Index

Page numbers in **bold** indicate references to the main entry.